A Digest of
the Law of Libel and Slander

And of actions on the case for words causing damage,
with the evidence, procedure, practice, and precedents of
pleadings, both in civil and criminal cases

William Blake Odgers,

James Bromley Eames

Alpha Editions

This edition published in 2019

ISBN : 9789353895693

Design and Setting By
Alpha Editions
email - alphaedis@gmail.com

A DIGEST

OF THE LAW OF

LIBEL AND SLANDER

&c.

FIFTH EDITION.

1911

TO

ARTHUR CHARLES, Esq., Q.C.,

RECORDER OF BATH,

IN ACKNOWLEDGMENT OF MANY KINDNESSES,

I Dedicate

THIS BOOK.

February, 1881.

PREFACE TO THE FIFTH EDITION.

THE fourth edition of this book, which was published in March, 1905, is now out of print. Since its appearance there have been numerous decisions which have affected the law of Libel and Slander in many respects, particularly in regard to the law of Fair Comment. These have rendered necessary considerable modification of the former edition. One branch of the law of privilege has become of increasing importance— that relating to statements made in or copied from Parliamentary or official papers. We have therefore introduced a new sub-division of Qualified Privilege under this title in Chapter XI. All relevant decisions have been noted down to April, 1911, and the whole book has been thoroughly revised and brought up to date.

W. B. O.
J. B. E.
W. B. O., Junr.

TEMPLE,
May, 1911.

PREFACE

TO THE FIRST EDITION.

———♦———

This book has been called "A Digest of the Law of Libel and Slander," because an attempt has been made to state the law on each point in the form of an abstract proposition, the decided cases being cited in smaller type merely as illustrations of that abstract proposition.

Every reported case decided in England or Ireland during the last fifteen years has been noticed. Every case reported in England during this century has, I believe, been considered and mentioned, unless it has either been distinctly overruled or has become obsolete by a change in the practice of the Courts or by the repeal of some statute on which it depended. The earlier cases have been more sparingly cited, but I think no case of importance since 1558 has been overlooked. The leading American decisions have also been referred to, and whenever the American law differs from our own, the distinction has been pointed out and explained. Canadian and Australian decisions have also been quoted, whenever the English law was doubtful or silent on the point. The cases have been brought down to the early part of January, 1881.

It would be of but little use to place all these decisions before the reader and leave him to draw his own conclusions. A huge collection of reported cases piled one on the top of the other is not a legal treatise, any more than a tumbled pile of bricks is a house. I have throughout attempted to strike a balance, as it were, and state the net result of the authorities. But this is a process requiring the greatest care and much expenditure of time. When I commenced this book in 1876, I did not at all realize the amount of labour which was requisite in order to ascertain the law and state it clearly in an abstract form.

It is often very difficult to determine whether or no a decision has ceased to be a binding authority : our judges in the present day seldom expressly overrule a previous decision ; they comment on it, distinguish it, explain it away, and then leave it with its lustre tarnished, but still apparently a binding authority, should identically the same facts recur. There is no rule which decides how long the process of " blowing upon " a case must continue before it may be considered overruled. Whenever such a case has been cited, I have always referred the reader to the places where it has been criticised, adding, however, my own opinion as to the effect of such criticism on the authority of the case. And in many places it has been necessary to review the cases in a note, showing how they bear one on another, and justifying the view which I have taken of their result. Such notes are printed in a medium type, smaller than that devoted to the abstract propositions of the Digest, larger than the Illustrations which follow them.

My object throughout has been to save the reader trouble. All the references to every decision have always been cited. All considerations of style, &c., have been sacrificed to clearness and convenience. I have abruptly changed from the third to the first or second person, whenever there was any possibility of mistaking the antecedent of any pronoun. It is sometimes difficult to follow A., B., and C., through a long sentence : it is easier to distinguish between " I," " you," and " he." Again, whenever I have been in doubt whether the law on a particular subject should be noticed in one chapter or in another, I have invariably stated it in both. So, too, for the sake of practical convenience, all the cases as to the Innuendo, and the construction to be put on Defamatory Words, have been collected in Chapter V. In Chapter XXI. all the law as to Husband and Wife, Principal and Agent, &c., &c., has been gathered together under the somewhat stilted but convenient title of The Law of Persons. A separate chapter has been devoted to the subject of Costs. In the chapters on Blasphemous and Seditious Words, I have not hesitated to express freely my conviction that many of the early decisions would not be followed in the present day.

One difficulty connected with the subject-matter of the book I have endeavoured to avoid, by restoring the word " malice " to its simple and ordinary meaning. The distinction between " malice in law " and " malice in fact " is of comparatively recent origin.

"Malice in law" is the vaguest possible phrase; it merely denotes "absence of legal excuse." The plaintiff is never called on to prove the existence of "malice in law;" the defendant has to show the existence of some legal excuse. In short, to say that a libel must be published "maliciously" is untrue; absence of malice is no defence, unless the words be published on a privileged occasion. I have therefore abandoned this technical and fictitious use of the word. Throughout this book (to use the words of Brett, L.J., in *Clark* v. *Molyneux,* see p. 343) "'Malice' does not mean 'malice in law,' a term in pleading, but actual malice, that which is popularly called malice."

The second part of the book is devoted to Practice, Procedure, and Evidence. I have fought both a civil action and a criminal trial through from beginning to end, giving practical hints to each side. Indeed, I have taken up the subject at an earlier point than is usual in law books, and have submitted to the plaintiff certain matters which he should carefully consider before he issues his writ (p. 597).

In the Appendix will be found a full collection of Precedents of Pleadings, both in Civil and Criminal cases. Some are drawn from the reports; others are hypothetical cases of my own invention; but the majority are pleadings in actions in which friends of mine, or I myself, have been professionally engaged.

W. BLAKE ODGERS

5, HARE COURT, TEMPLE, E.C.,
February, 1881.

TABLE OF CONTENTS.

PART I.

A DIGEST OF THE LAW OF LIBEL AND SLANDER.

CHAPTER I.

CHAPTER II.

CHAPTER III.

CHAPTER VI.

CHAPTER VII.

CHAPTER VIII.

CHAPTER IX.

CHAPTER XII.

CHAPTER XIII.

O.L.S. *b*

CHAPTER XIV.

CHAPTER XV.

CHAPTER XX.

CHAPTER XXI.

PART II.

PRACTICE, PROCEDURE, AND EVIDENCE IN CIVIL CASES.

CHAPTER XXII.

CHAPTER XXIII.

CHAPTER XXVII.

PART III.

PRACTICE AND EVIDENCE IN CRIMINAL CASES.

CHAPTER XXVIII.

CHAPTER XXIX.

APPENDICES.

TABLE OF CASES.

TABLE OF STATUTES CITED.

TABLE OF RULES AND ORDERS CITED.

PART I.

THE LAW OF LIBEL AND SLANDER.

CHAPTER I.

DEFAMATORY WORDS.

No man may disparage or destroy the reputation of another. Every man has a right to have his good name maintained unimpaired. This right is a *jus in rem*, a right absolute and good against all the world.

Words which produce, in any given case, appreciable injury to the reputation of another are called DEFAMATORY.

Defamatory words, if false, are actionable.

False defamatory words, if written and published, constitute a libel; if spoken, a slander.

Words, which on the face of them must injure the reputation of the person to whom they refer, are clearly defamatory, and, if false, are actionable without proof that any particular damage has followed from their use.

Words, on the other hand, which merely might tend to injure the reputation of another are *primâ facie* not defamatory, and even though false are not actionable, unless as a matter of fact some appreciable injury has followed from their use.

Illustrations.

To say "A. is a coward," or "a liar," or "a rascal," is not defamatory, unless it can be proved that some one seriously believed and acted on the assertion, to the prejudice of A. Such words, though false, are not actionable without some evidence to show that A s reputation has as a matter of fact been actually impaired thereby. *De minimis non curat lex.*

To say of B. :—" He forged his master's signature to a cheque for 100*l*." is clearly defamatory, and, if false, actionable. It must injure B.'s reputation to bring such a specific charge against him.

No general rule can be laid down defining absolutely and once for all what words are defamatory, and what are not. Words, which would seriously injure A.'s reputation, might do no harm to B.'s. Each case must be decided mainly on its own facts. In each case the question will be : Have the defendant's words appreciably injured the plaintiff's reputation ?

Such injury may be either

      (i) presumed from the nature of the words themselves ; or (ii) proved by evidence of their consequences.

(i) It will be presumed from the nature of the words themselves,

      (*a*) if the words, being written and published or printed and published, disparage the plaintiff or tend to bring him into ridicule and contempt.

      (*b*) if the words, being spoken,

            (1) charge the plaintiff with the commission of a crime ;

            (2) impute to the plaintiff a contagious disorder tending to exclude him from society ;

            (3) are spoken of the plaintiff in the way of his profession or trade, or disparage him in an office of public trust, or

            (4) impute unchastity or adultery to any woman or girl.

In all these cases the words are said to be actionable *per se*, because on the face of them they clearly must have injured the plaintiff's reputation.

(ii) But in all other cases of spoken words, the fact that the plaintiff's reputation has been injured thereby, must be proved at the trial by evidence of the consequences that directly resulted from their utterance. Such evidence is called " evidence of special damage," as distinguished from that general damage which the law assumes, without express proof, to follow from the employment of words actionable *per se.*

If in any given case the words employed by the defendant have appreciably injured the plaintiff's reputation, the plaintiff has suffered an injury which is actionable without proof of any other damage. Every man has an absolute right to have his person, his property, and his reputation, preserved inviolate. And just as any invasion of a man's property is actionable without proof of any pecuniary loss, so is any actual disparagement of his good name. "His reputation is his property, and, if possible, more valuable than other property." (Per Malins, V.-C., in *Dixon* v. *Holden,* L. R. 7 Eq. 492; 17 W. R. 482; 20 L. T. 357.) "Indeed, if we reflect on the degree of suffering occasioned by loss of character, and compare it with that occasioned by loss of property, the amount of the former injury far exceeds that of the latter." (Per Best, C.J., in *De Crespigny* v. *Wellesley,* 5 Bing. at p. 406.) Often, too, a man's livelihood depends on his reputation. Whenever, therefore, the words are such that they will necessarily injure the reputation of the plaintiff, they are defamatory on the face of them, and actionable *per se.*

But in many cases of slander it is by no means clear from the words themselves that they must have injured the plaintiff's reputation, *e.g.,* where the words are merely idle abuse or expressions of contempt which injure no man's credit; in such cases, therefore, the Court requires proof of some special damage to show that as a matter of fact the words have in this case impaired the plaintiff's good name. The injury to the plaintiff's reputation is the gist of the action; and where this is not obvious, he must prove to the satisfaction of the jury that he has in fact sustained some appreciable damage for which compensation can be assessed.

Illustrations.

To say of A., " He is a forger and a felon," or " He hath the French pox," to call a physician a quack, or a tradesman a bankrupt, to say of a magistrate that he is a corrupt judge, is in each case actionable without proof of special damage. *A fortiori,* if the words be written, or printed, and published.

To call a man a rogue, a fool, or a blackguard, is not actionable, without proof of special damage, if the words be spoken only; but is actionable *per se,* if the accusation be reduced into writing and published to any third person.

Thus the presumption that words are defamatory arises much more easily in cases of libel than in cases of slander. Many words, which if printed and published would be presumed to have injured the plaintiff's reputation, will not be actionable *per se*, if merely spoken. Two reasons are usually given for this distinction :—

1. A slander may be uttered in the heat of a moment, and under a sudden provocation ; the reduction of the charge into writing and the subsequent publication of a libel show greater deliberation and malice.

2. *Vox emissa volat ; litera scripta manet.* The written or printed matter is permanent, and no one can tell into whose hands it may come. Every one now can read. The circulation of a newspaper is enormous, and many people implicitly believe every word they see in print. And even a private letter may turn up in after years, and reach persons for whom it was never intended, and so do incalculable mischief ; whereas a slander only reaches the immediate bystanders, who can observe the manner and note the tone of the speaker—who have heard the rest of the conversation which may greatly qualify his assertion—who probably are acquainted with the speaker, and know what value is to be attached to any charge made by him ; the mischief is thus much less in extent, and the publicity less durable.

This sharp distinction between slander and libel has been recognised in English law by Hale, C.B., in *King* v. *Lake*, (1678) Hardres, 470 ; by Lord Hardwicke, C.J., in *Bradley* v. *Methwyn*, Selw. N. P. 982 ; by Sir James Mansfield, C.J., in *Thorley* v. *Lord Kerry*, (1812) 4 Taunt. 355 ; 3 Camp. 214, n., and in numerous other cases, and is far too well established to be ever shaken.

The intention or motive with which the words were employed is, as a rule, immaterial. If the defendant has in fact injured the plaintiff's reputation, he is liable, although he did not intend so to do, and had no such purpose in his mind when he wrote or spoke the words. Every man must be presumed to know and to intend the natural and ordinary consequences of his acts : and this presumption cannot be rebutted merely by proof that at the time he published the words the defendant did not attend to or think of their natural or probable consequences, or hoped or expected that these consequences would not follow. Such proof can only go to mitigate the damages.

Sometimes, however, it is a man's duty to speak fully and freely, and without thought or fear of the consequences; and then the above rule does not apply. The words are privileged by reason of the occasion on which they were employed; and no action lies therefor, unless it can be proved that the defendant was actuated by some wicked or indirect motive. But in all other cases (although the pleader invariably alleges that the words were published falsely *and maliciously*) malice in fact need never be proved at the trial; the words are actionable, if false and defamatory, although published accidentally or inadvertently, or with an honest belief in their truth.

"That unfortunate word 'malice' has got into cases of actions for libel. We all know that a man may be the publisher of a libel without a particle of malice or improper motive. Therefore the case is not the same as where actual and real malice is necessary. Take the case where a person may make an untrue statement of a man in writing, not privileged on account of the occasion of its publication; he would be liable although he had not a particle of malice against the man." (Per Lord Bramwell in *Abrath* v. *North Eastern Rail. Co.*, 11 App. Cas. at pp. 253, 254; 55 L. J. Q. B. at p. 460; 55 L. T. at p. 65.)

Illustrations.

The Protestant Electoral Union published a book called "The Confessional Unmasked." Their motive in doing so, "however mistaken, was an honest one," viz.:—to promote the spread of the Protestant religion, by exposing the errors of the Roman Catholic system; but certain passages in the book were obscene. *Held*, that its publication was a misdemeanour. All copies which the defendant had for sale were ordered to be destroyed as obscene books. Neither the law nor the religion of England permits any one to "do evil that good may come."

> *R.* v. *Hicklin*, L. R. 3 Q. B. 360; 37 L. J. M. C. 89; 16 W. R. 801; 18 L. T. 395; 11 Cox, C. C. 19.

> *Steele* v. *Brannan*, L. R. 7 C. P. 261; 41 L. J. M. C. 85; 20 W. R. 607; 26 L. T. 509.

> And see *R.* v. *Bradlaugh and Besant*, 2 Q. B. D. 569; 46 L. J. M. C. 286.

If a man deliver by *mistake* a paper out of his study where he had just written it, he will be liable to an action if the paper prove libellous, although he never intended to publish that paper, but another innocent one.

> Note to *Mayne* v. *Fletcher*, 4 M. & Ry. 312; 9 B. & C. 382; cf. *R.* v. *Paine*, 5 Mod. 167; Carth. 405; Comb. 358.

The plaintiff told a laughable story against himself in company; the defendant published it in the newspaper to amuse his readers, assuming that the plaintiff would not object.   The plaintiff recovered damages 10*l.*

> *Cook* v. *Ward*, 6 Bing. 409 ; 4 M. & P. 99.

For though he told it of himself to his friends, he by no means courted public ridicule.

Where, a clergyman in a sermon recited a story out of Foxe's Martyrology, that one Greenwood, being a perjured person and a great persecutor, had great plagues inflicted upon him and was killed by the hand of God; whereas in truth, he never was so plagued, and was himself actually present at that discourse,—the words being delivered only as a matter of history, and not with any intention to slander, it was adjudged for the defendant.

> *Greenwood* v. *Prick*, cited in Cro. Jac. 91, and 1 Camp. 270 ; and
> also in *R.* v. *Williams*, 13 How. St. Tr. 1387.

But Lord Denman and the Court of Q. B. said most positively in *Hearne* v. *Stowell*, 12 A. & E. 726, that this case is not law.   Mr. Greenwood would therefore in the present day have recovered at least nominal damages.

The proprietor of the *Times* retired to live in the country, leaving the entire management of the paper to his son, with whom he never interfered ; yet he was held *criminally* liable for a libel which appeared in the paper in his absence and without his knowledge.   And though now since Lord Campbell's Act he would probably be acquitted in any criminal proceeding, he would certainly be held liable for damages in a civil action.

> *R.* v. *Walter*, 3 Esp. 21.
>
> *R.* v. *Gutch and others*, Moo. & Mal. 433.
>
> *R.* v. *Dodd*, 2 Sess. Cas. 33.

A corporation is liable for a libel published by its authority, or by its officer, within the scope of his employment.

> *Citizens' Life Assurance Co., Limited* v. *Brown*, [1904] A. C. 423; 73
> L. J. P. C. 102 ; 90 L. T. 739 ; 20 Times L. R. 497.
>
> *Corporation of Glasgow* v. *Riddell*, (H. L.) [1911] W. N. 71.

Even a lunatic is liable to an action for libel or slander unless his insanity is well known to all who hear or read his words.

> *Dickinson* v. *Barber*, 9 Tyng. (Mass.) 225.
>
> *Yeates et ux.* v. *Reed et ux.*, 4 Blackf. (Indiana) 463.

A barrister editing a book on the Law of Attorneys, referred to a case, *Re Blake*, as reported in 30 Law Journal, Q. B. 32, and stated that Mr. Blake was struck off the rolls for misconduct.   He was in fact only suspended for two years, as appeared from the Law Journal report.   The publishers were held liable for this carelessness, although of course neither they nor the writer bore Mr. Blake any malice.   Damages 100*l.*

> *Blake* v. *Stevens and others*, 4 F. & F. 232 ; 11 L. T. 543.

The printers of a newspaper by a mistake in setting up in type the announcements from the *London Gazette*, placed the name of the plaintiff's firm under the heading "First Meetings under the Bankruptcy Act," instead of under "Dissolutions of Partnership."   An ample apology was inserted in the next issue : no damage was proved to have followed to the plaintiff : and there was no suggestion of any malice.   In an action for libel against the proprietor of the paper, the jury awarded the plaintiff 50*l.* damages.   *Held*, that the publication was libellous, and that the damages awarded were not excessive.

> *Shepheard* v. *Whitaker*, L. R. 10 C. P. 502 ; 32 L. T. 402.

The defendants published in their newspaper, in the list of "Births," that the plaintiff, a married lady, had given birth to twins. This was untrue, and the lady had been married only one month. The defendants were not aware of either fact. *Held*, that the defendants were liable, though the advertisement on the face of it was not libellous.

> *Morrison* v. *Ritchie & Co.*, (1902) 4 F. 645 (Ct. of Sess.).

The defendants published in their newspaper an article descriptive of Dieppe during the motor races. The article purported to describe the doings and behaviour of various types of Englishmen abroad, to one of whom the name "Artemus Jones" was given. The plaintiff, whose name was Artemus Jones, brought an action for libel. The evidence showed that neither the writer of the article nor the defendants had any intention of referring to the plaintiff, and that the writer thought he was using a purely fictitious name. *Held*, that this evidence disclosed no defence and that the jury had rightly found a verdict for the plaintiff.

> *Hulton & Co.* v. *Jones*, [1910] A. C. 20; 79 L. J. K. B. 198; 101 L. T. 831 ; 26 Times L. R. 128.

False defamatory words, then, if spoken, constitute a slander : if written and published, a libel. The word "written" includes any printed, painted, or any other permanent representation not transient in its nature as are spoken words. A picture, statue, or effigy may also be a libel, or any other mark or sign exposed to view, if it conveys a defamatory meaning. (5 Rep. 125.)

There is a further important distinction between slander and libel. A libel is a crime ; a slander on a private individual is not. It is only when the words uttered are blasphemous, seditious or obscene that the State is concerned to interfere and punish the speaker.

It is clearly necessary that there should be a criminal as well as a civil remedy for libel, for the following reasons :—

1. The evil done by libels is so extensive, the example set so pernicious, that it is desirable that they should be repressed for the public good. Slanders do less mischief as a rule, are not permanent, and are more easily forgotten ; their evil influence is not so widely diffused.

2. Many libellers are penniless, and a civil action has no terrors for them. The plaintiff will never get his damages. In fact the proprietor of many a low newspaper rather rejoices at the prospect of a civil action for libel being brought against him. He regards it as a gratuitous advertisement for his paper.

3. Another reason often assigned for the interference of the State is, that libels conduce to a breach of the peace; but that reason would possibly apply with equal, if not greater force to slanders.

Lush, J., says, in *R.* v. *Holbrook*, 4 Q. B. D. at p. 46, "Libel on an individual is, and has always been, regarded as both a civil injury and a criminal offence. The person libelled may pursue his remedy for damages or prefer an indictment, or by leave of the Court a criminal information, or he may both sue for damages and indict. It is ranked amongst criminal offences because of its supposed tendency to arouse angry passion, provoke revenge, and thus endanger the public peace, but the libeller is not the less bound to make compensation for the pecuniary or other loss or injury which the libel might have occasioned to the person libelled."

The fact that libel is a crime as well as a tort, produces other consequences in law which it may be well to notice briefly here, though they are not strictly within the scope of the present treatise.

No action can be maintained for the price of libellous pictures (*Fores* v. *Johnes*, 4 Esp. 97), or for their value, if destroyed by the person ridiculed. (*Du Bost* v. *Beresford*, 2 Camp. 511.) A printer cannot recover for printing a libel. (*Poplett* v. *Stockdale*, Ry. & M. 337.) If a printer undertakes to print a book for a certain price, and discovers as the work proceeds that the matter is defamatory, he may decline to continue the work, and can recover for such part of the work printed as is not defamatory in an action for work and labour done and materials provided, the special contract notwithstanding. (*Clay* v. *Yates*, 1 H. & N. 73; 25 L. J. Ex. 237; 4 W. R. 557; 27 L. T. (Old S.) 126.) Nor can an action be maintained for breach of a contract to furnish manuscript of defamatory matter (*Gale* v. *Leckie*, 2 Stark. 107), or of a contract to let rooms to be used for the delivery of blasphemous lectures (*Cowan* v. *Milbourn*, L. R. 2 Ex. 230; 36 L. J. Ex. 124; 15 W. R. 750; 16 L. T. 290), or for pirating a libellous book. (*Stockdale* v. *Onwhyn*, 5 B. & C. 173; 7 D. & R. 625; 2 C. & P. 163.) There is no copyright in any libellous or immoral book, or picture. A Court of Equity will not interfere in one way or another. It will not grant an injunction to restrain a piracy of an illegal book or picture, nor decree an account of the profits made thereby. (Per Lord Eldon, in *Walcot* v. *Walker*, 7 Ves. 1; in *Southey* v. *Sherwood*, 2 Mer. 435, and in *Lawrence* v. *Smith*, Jacob, 471.)

No contract will be implied to indemnify a party against the consequences of an illegal act, such as the publication of a libel. The proprietor of a newspaper, convicted and fined for the publication of a libel which was inserted in his paper without his knowledge or consent by the editor, has no right of action against the editor for the damages sustained through such conviction. (*Colburn.* v. *Patmore*, 1 C. M. & R. 73; 4 Tyr. 677; and see *Merryweather* v. *Nixan*, 2 Sm. L. C. 11th ed. 398; 8 T. R. 186; *Moscati* v. *Lawson*, 7 C. & P. at p. 35.) Even an express promise to indemnify another if he will publish a libel is void (*Shackell* v. *Rosier*, 3 Scott, 59; 2 Bing. N. C. 634; *Arnold* v. *Clifford*, 2 Sumner, 238), as is also a contract to indemnify the printer if matter supplied to him to be printed should prove to be libellous (*Apthorpe* v. *Neville & Co.*, (1907) 23 Times L. R. 575; *W. H. Smith and Son* v. *Clinton and Harris*, (1908) 99 L. T. 840); for it is a promise on an illegal executory consideration, an incitement to do an illegal act. But it has been decided in America that an express promise under seal to indemnify another against the consequences of an illegal act already done is binding. (*Griffiths* v. *Hardenburgh*, 41 N. Y. 469; *Howe* v. *Buffalo and Erie Rail. Co.*, 38 Barbour (N. Y.) 124.)

So, too, a promise to abstain from publishing a libel is no consideration for a contract. (*Brown* v. *Brine*, (1875) 1 Ex. D. 5; 45 L. J. Ex. 129; 24 W. R. 177; 33 L. T. 703.) Whether such a promise could be enforced at all may be doubted. But in the absence of an express promise to that effect, no claim can be maintained by the publishers of a libellous work against any one who informs the persons libelled of the publication, even though such persons bring actions against the publishers and recover damages. (*Saunders* v. *Seyd and Kelly's Credit Index Co., Limited*, (1896) 75 L. T. 193; 12 Times L. R. 546.)

Criminal proceedings for libel may be taken either at common law, or under certain statutes; the ordinary remedy is by indictment, but there is also an extraordinary remedy by information, which is only granted in urgent cases, where the publication of the libel is likely to produce great public mischief, and must therefore be promptly suppressed.

Thus we see that there are two criminal remedies for libel—by criminal information and by indictment—in addition to the civil remedy of action for damages. Lush, J., says, in the passage cited *ante,* p. 8, the person libelled may " both sue for damages and indict ; " and so in strict law he may. But practically he has to elect between his three remedies. He cannot take both civil and criminal proceedings at once ; a judge would stay one or the other. Strictly, if he means to take both, he should take criminal pro ceedings first. But an action for damages after the defendant had been either acquitted or convicted for the same libel would be very hopeless work. And so would a criminal prosecution after an action. After a rule for a criminal *information* has been made absolute, no civil action can be brought. (*R.* v. *Sparrow,* 2 T. R. 198.) If it be refused or discharged, the applicant can indict the defendant, or by leave of the Court he may bring a civil action : see *post,* p. 612.

There is no longer any censorship of the press in this country. Any man is free to speak or to write and publish whatever he chooses of another, subject only to this, that he must take the consequences, should a jury deem his words defamatory. " The liberty of the press," says Lord Mansfield, in *R.* v. *Dean of St. Asaph,* 3 T. R. 431, n., " consists in printing without any previous licence, subject to the consequences of law." Lord Ellenborough says in *R.* v. *Cobbett,* 29 Howell's St. Tr. 49 : " The law of England is a law of liberty, and consistent with this liberty, we have not what is called an *imprimatur ;* there is no such preliminary licence necessary ; but if a man publish a paper, he is exposed to the penal consequences, as he is in every other act, if it be illegal." Lord Kenyon shortly puts it thus in *R.* v. *Cuthell,* 27 Howell's St. Tr. 675 : " A man may publish anything which twelve of his countrymen think is not blamable."

But it was by no means always so in England. It was quickly perceived that the printing-press may be as great a power for evil as for good. And whenever any large proportion of a nation is disaffected towards its Government, a free press becomes a source of danger.

(i) Our English monarchs at first endeavoured to keep all the printing-presses in their own hands, and allow no one to *print* anything except by special Royal licence. All printing-presses were kept under the immediate supervision of the King in Council, and regulated by proclamations and decrees of the Star Chamber, by virtue of the King's prerogative. In 1557 the Stationers' Company. of London was formed, and the exclusive privilege of printing and publishing in the English dominions was given to ninety-seven London stationers and their successors by regular apprenticeship. The Company was also empowered to seize all publications printed by men who were not members of the guild. Later, by a decree of the Star Chamber in 1586, one printing-press was allowed to each University. This exercise of the Royal prerogative continued, in theory, at all events, till 1637.

(ii) Queen Elizabeth, however, was not content with this Government monopoly of the "Art and mysterie of Printing." In 1559 she determined to have all books read over by loyal bishops and privy councillors before they were allowed to go to the official press. In 1586 the Star Chamber enacted that all books should be read over in manuscript, and licensed by either the Archbishop of Canterbury or the Bishop of London, save law books, which were to be read and licensed by the Chief Justice of either Bench or the Lord Chief Baron (a practice which continued down to the middle of the 18th century ; see the prefaces to Burrows' and Douglas' Reports). Subsequently the Master of the Revels usurped the right of revising poems and plays, and the Vice-Chancellors of the Universities were allowed for convenience sake to licence books to be printed at the University presses. It was soon found impossible to restrict the number of printing-presses in the country, and the Government therefore insisted all the more vehemently that no book should be *published* without a previous licence. By the Star Chamber decree dated July 11th, 1637, all printed books were required to be submitted to the licensers and entered upon the registers of the Stationers' Company before they could be published ; if this was not done, the printer was to be fined, and for ever disabled from exercising the art of printing, and his press and all copies of the unlicensed book forfeited to the Crown. The old word "*Imprimatur*" = "let it be *printed*," was still used to denote the consent of the licenser to its *publication*. After the abolition of the Star Chamber, the Long Parliament issued two orders, March 9th, 1642, and June 14th, 1643, very similar in effect to the decree of the Star Chamber last mentioned. Against these orders Milton published his noble but ineffectual protest, the "Areopagitica" (November 24th, 1644). The censorship of the press continued in England till 1695, and then its abolition was rather accidental than otherwise. (See Macaulay's "History of England," c. xix., vol. iii., pp. 399—405 ; 13 & 14 Car. II. c. 33 ; Proclamation of May 17th,

1680; 1 Jac. II. c. 17.) The only vestige remaining of such censorship is the control of the Lord Chamberlain over plays. By the
Theatres Regulation Act, 1843 (6 & 7 Vict. c. 68), s. 14, it is enacted
that it shall be lawful for the Lord Chamberlain for the time being,
whenever he shall be of opinion that it is fitting for the preservation
of good manners, decorum, or of the public peace so to do, to forbid
the acting or presenting any stage play, or any act, scene, or part
thereof, or any prologue or epilogue, or any part thereof, anywhere
in Great Britain, or in such theatres as he shall specify, and either
absolutely or for such time as he shall think fit.

(iii) A third plan is to allow any book to be printed and published
without any supervision or licence : but as soon as the attention of
the Government is called to its harmful tendencies, to seize all the
stock at the publishers and booksellers, and prevent the publisher
from issuing any further copies. The Lord Lieutenant was till the
year 1875 empowered to do this in Ireland, should any work appear
to him seditious. Magistrates in England may deal thus with books
proved to be obscene by virtue of Lord Campbell's Act (20 & 21 Vict.
c. 83). The Court of Chancery and the House of Lords occasionally forbade by injunction the further publication of libels which they
deemed contempts of Court. Every Division of the High Court
now has jurisdiction to restrain a contempt which is an attack upon
itself or one of its judges. (See Chapter XX.) The High Court of
Justice, moreover, by virtue of the powers conferred by s. 25,
sub-s. 8, of the Judicature Act, 1873, may grant an injunction to
restrain the further sale or distribution of any matter clearly
libellous whenever it considers that such a course is just or convenient. (See Chapter XIV., *post*, p. 421.)

(iv) Our present law permits any one to say, write, and publish
what he pleases ; but if he makes a bad use of this liberty, he must
be punished. If he unjustly attack an individual, the person
defamed may sue for damages ; if, on the other hand, the words be
written or printed, or if treason or immorality be thereby inculcated,
the offender can be tried for the misdemeanour either by information or indictment. In order that the criminal might be easily
detected, it was enacted in 1712 that no person, under a penalty of
20*l.*, should sell or expose for sale any pamphlet without the name
and place of abode of some known person by or for whom it was
printed or published, written or printed thereon. (10 Anne, c. 19,
s. 113, repealed in 1871 by the 33 & 34 Vict. c. 99.) A similar
enactment as to newspapers, 6 & 7 Will. IV. c. 76, was also repealed
by the 32 & 33 Vict. c. 24. And now every paper or book which is

meant to be published or dispersed must bear on it the name and address of the printer (2 & 3 Vict. c. 12, s. 2*); and the printer must for six calendar months carefully preserve at least one copy of each paper printed by him, and write thereon the name and address of the person who employed and paid him to print it. (39 Geo. III. c. 79, s. 29.*) While by the Newspaper Libel and Registration Act, 1881 (44 & 45 Vict. c. 60), a register of newspaper proprietors is established at Somerset House, where anyone can ascertain for a shilling who is the person responsible for what has appeared in any newspaper. Newspapers were indeed formerly regarded with great jealousy by the Government, and subjected to heavy duties. Under Charles II. and James II. the *London Gazette* (a small sheet appearing twice a week, every Monday and Thursday) was the only paper permitted to publish political news. Even their size was regulated by statute. The 6 Geo. IV. c. 119, first allowed newspapers to be printed on paper of any size. Moreover, till the 18 Vict. c. 27, they had to be printed on stamped paper. But in spite of all such petty restrictions, our press has been, ever since the passing of Fox's Libel Act, 32 Geo. III. c. 60, the freest in the world.

A man's reputation may also be injured by the deed or action of another without his using any words; and for such an injury he has an action on the case; but such matters are not within the scope of the present treatise.

Illustrations.

A banker having in his hands sufficient funds belonging to his customer dishonours his cheque; the customer may recover substantial damages, without proof of any special damage; for it is clear that such an act must injure the customer's reputation for solvency.

Marzetti v. *Williams,* 1 B. & Ad. 415.

Robinson v. *Marchant,* 7 Q. B. 918; 15 L. J. Q. B. 134; 10 Jur. 156.

Rolin and another v. *Steward, P. O.,* 14 C. B. 595; 23 L. J. C. P. 148; 18 Jur. 576; 2 C. L. R. 759.

As to a returned cheque which was never presented, see

Frost v. *London Joint Stock Bank,* (1906) 22 Times L. R. 760.

The reputation of a manufacturer may be injured if marks resembling his trade marks are placed on inferior goods manufactured and sold by the defendant.

See *Manton and others* v. *Bales,* 1 C. B. 444.

The defendant caused the plaintiff's goods to be seized on an unfounded

---

* Both these sections continue in force, although other portions of the Acts were repealed by 32 & 33 Vict. c. 24; see Second Schedule.

claim for debt; the neighbours consequently deemed the plaintiff insolvent. The plaintiff was held entitled to substantial damages.

> *Brewer* v. *Dew and another*, 11 M. & W. 625.
>
> *Bracegirdle* v. *Orford*, 2 Maule & S. 77.

The defendant set up a lamp on the wall adjoining the plaintiff's dwelling-house and kept it burning in the daytime, thereby inducing the passers-by to believe that the plaintiff's house was a brothel. This was held to be a trespass to the wall and being permanent in its nature, also a libel.

> *Jefferies* v. *Duncombe*, 2 Camp. 3; 11 East, 226.
>
> *Spall* v. *Massey*, 2 Stark. 559.
>
> *Plunket* v. *Gilmore*, Fortescue, 211.

And so as to "riding Skimmington," "rough music," burning in effigy, and other modes of holding a man up to public obloquy without especial *words* of defamation.

> See *Sir William Bolton* v. *Dean*, cited in *Austin* v. *Culpepper*, Skin. 123; 2 Show. 313.
>
> *R.* v. *Roberts and others*, 3 Keble, 578.
>
> *Mason* v. *Jennings*, Sir Thos. Raym. 401.
>
> *Cropp* v. *Tilney*, 3 Salk. 226.
>
> *Eyre* v. *Garlick*, 42 J. P. 68.

So too in actions of false imprisonment and malicious prosecution, the jury may award damages for the injury done to the plaintiff's reputation by the charge made against him, and by his being marched in custody through the public streets; although in the former, the gist of the action is the direct trespass to the *person*, and in the latter the maliciously setting the law in motion without reasonable or probable cause.

So if a trespass be accompanied by violent or insulting words, this fact may be proved in aggravation of damage.

> *Merest* v. *Harvey*, 5 Taunt. 442.

But in actions for wrongful dismissal, no damages can be recovered for the use of injurious or contumelious words, which do not in themselves give a cause of action.

> *Addis* v. *Gramophone Co., Ltd.*, [1909] A. C. 488; 78 L. J. K. B. 1122; 101 L. T. 466.

On the other hand, words may cause a man damage without in any way affecting his reputation; and for such words, if written or spoken without lawful occasion, an action on the case will lie, provided it can be shown that such damage is the natural and necessary consequence of the words, or was the result which the defendant designed and intended.

Illustrations.

It is actionable for A. to assert falsely and maliciously that there is a flaw in B.'s title to certain freehold land, if B. is thereby prevented from selling it, although no imputation is cast on B.'s personal character.

> See Chapter IV., *post*, pp. 79—88.

If A. without lawful occasion publishes a false statement of fact (as distinct from a mere expression of opinion) concerning an article which B. makes or sells, and special damage to B. results therefrom, an action lies.

See Chapter IV., *post*, pp. 88—95.

But an attack on a man's property or on the things he makes or sells may sometimes be also an indirect attack on himself.

See *post*, p. 34.

As a rule A. cannot sue for words defamatory of B., although he may suffer loss or inconvenience therefrom. But if A. can satisfy the jury that the defendant desired and intended to injure A., and thought that his best way to do so was by publishing a libel on B., and the damage to A. was the natural and necessary consequence of that libel on B., it is submitted that an action will lie.

Ashley v. *Harrison*, 1 Esp. 48; Peake, 194.

Brayne v. *Cooper*, 5 M. & W. 249.

If A. and B. are rival shopkeepers, and B. spreads a false and groundless report that A.'s shopman has the scarlet fever, intending thereby to prevent the public from going to A.'s shop, and succeeds in this malicious device, A. can sue B.

Per Kelly, C.B., in *Riding* v. *Smith*, 1 Ex. D. 96; 45 L. J. Ex. 281; 24 W. R. 487; 34 L. T. 500.

Any person, who knowingly publishes or sells without the consent of the artist an altered painting, drawing, or photograph as the unaltered work of the artist, is liable to a penalty under the Fine Arts Copyright Act, 1862 (25 & 26 Vict. c. 68), s. 7, sub-s. 4.

Carlton Illustrators v. *Coleman & Co. Ltd.*, [1911] 1 K. B. 771, 780.

If a man menace my tenants at will, of life and member, *per quod* they depart from their tenures, an action upon the case will lie against him, but the menace without their departure is no cause of action.

Conesby's Case, Year Book, 9 Hen. VII., pp. 7, 8; 1 Roll. Abr. 108.

If the defendant threatens the plaintiff's workmen, so that they do not dare to go on with their work, whereby the plaintiff loses the selling of his goods, an action lies.

Garret v. *Taylor*, (1621) Cro. Jac. 567; 1 Roll. Abr. 108.

Tarleton and others v. *McGawley*, Peake, 270.

And see *Springhead Spinning Co.* v. *Riley*, L. R. 6 Eq. 551; 37 L. J. Ch. 889; 16 W. R. 1138; 19 L. T. 64.

If a man should lie in wait "and fright the boys from going to school, that schoolmaster might have an action for the loss of his scholars."

Per Holt, C.J., in *Keeble* v. *Hickeringill*, 11 East, 576, n.

If a man induces a servant to break his contract with his master and quit his employment, the master has an action *per quod servitium amisit*.

Lumley v. *Gye*, 2 E. & B. 216; 22 L. J. Q. B. 463; 17 Jur. 827.

Bowen v. *Hall and others*, 6 Q. B. D. 333; 50 L. J. Q. B. 305; 29 W. R. 367; 44 L. T. 75; 45 J. P. 373.

CHAPTER II.

LIBEL.

FALSE defamatory words, if written and published, constitute a libel. In cases of libel, any words will be deemed defamatory which appreciably injure the reputation of another, which make men think worse of him. All written words which expose the plaintiff to hatred, contempt, ridicule, or obloquy, which tend to injure him in his profession or trade, or cause him to be shunned or avoided by his neighbours, are libellous.

"Everything, printed or written, which reflects on the character of another, and is published without lawful justification or excuse, is a libel, whatever the intention may have been." (Per Parke, B., in *O'Brien* v. *Clement*, 15 M. & W. 435.) "Libel is a tort which consists in using language which others knowing the circumstances would reasonably think to be defamatory of the person complaining of and injured by it." (Per Lord Loreburn, L.C., in *Hulton & Co.* v. *Jones*, [1910] A. C. at p. 23.) The words need not necessarily impute disgraceful conduct to the plaintiff; it is sufficient if they render him contemptible or ridiculous. (*Cropp* v. *Tilney*, 3 Salk. 226; *Villers* v. *Monsley*, 2 Wils. 403; *Watson* v. *Trask*, 6 Ohio, 531.)

Any printed or written words are defamatory which impute to the plaintiff that he has been guilty of any crime, fraud, dishonesty, immorality, vice, or dishonourable conduct, or has been accused or suspected of any such misconduct; or which suggest that the plaintiff is suffering from any infectious disorder; or which have a tendency to injure him in his office, profession, calling, or trade. And so, too, are all words which hold the plaintiff up to contempt, hatred, scorn, or ridicule, and which, by thus engendering an evil opinion of him in the minds of right-thinking men, tend to deprive him of friendly intercourse and society.

It appears to be impossible to define a libel with any greater precision or lucidity. We proceed at once therefore to give instances.

Illustrations.

It is libellous to write and publish of a man that he is—
" an infernal villain,"
> *Bell* v. *Stone,* 1 B. & P. 331 ;
" an impostor,"
> *Cooke* v. *Hughes,* R. & M. 112 ;
> *Campbell* v. *Spottiswoode,* 3 B. & S. 769 ; 32 L. J. Q. B. 185 ; 9 Jur. N. S. 1069 ; 11 W. R. 569 ; 8 L. T. 201 ;
" a great defaulter,"
> *Warman* v. *Hine,* 1 Jur. 820 ; 1 J. P. 346 ;
> *Bruton* v. *Downes,* 1 F. & F. 668 ;
" a hypocrite,"
> *Thorley* v. *Lord Kerry,* 4 Taunt. 355 ; 3 Camp. 214, n. ;
" a frozen snake,"
> *Hoare* v. *Silverlock,* (No. 1, 1848) 12 Q. B. 624 ; 17 L. J. Q. B. 306 ; 12 Jur. 695 ;
" a rogue and a rascal,"
> Per Gould, J., in *Villiers* v. *Monsley,* 2 Wils. 403 ;
" a dishonest man,"
> Per *cur.* in *Austin* v. *Culpepper,* Skin. 124 ; 2 Show. 314 ;
" a mere man of straw,"
> *Eaton* v. *Johns,* 1 Dowl. N. S. 602 ;
" an itchy old toad,"
> *Villers* v. *Monsley,* 2 Wils. 403 ;
" a desperate adventurer," association with whom " would inevitably cover" gentlemen " with ridicule and disrepute,"
> *Wakley* v. *Healey,* 7 C. B. 591 ; 18 L. J. C. P. 241 ;
that " he grossly insulted two ladies,"
> *Clement* v. *Chivis,* 9 B. & C. 172 ; 4 M. & R. 127 ;
that " he is unfit to be trusted with money,"
> *Cheese* v. *Scales,* 10 M. & W. 488 ; 12 L. J. Ex. 13 ; 6 Jur. 958 ;
that " he is insolvent and cannot pay his debts,"
> *Metropolitan Omnibus Co.* v. *Hawkins,* 4 H. & N. 87 ; 28 L. J. Ex. 201 ; 5 Jur. N. S. 226 ; 7 W. R. 265 ; 32 L. T. (Old S.) 281.
that " he was once in difficulties," though it is stated that such difficulties are now at an end,
> *Cox* v. *Lee,* L. R. 4 Ex. 284 ; 38 L. J. Ex. 219 ; 21 L. T. 178 ;
that the plaintiff " will not sue in a particular county, because he is known there,"
> *Cooper* v. *Greeley,* 1 Denio (N. Y.) 347 ;
that he is " the most artful scoundrel that ever existed," " is in every person's

debt," that " his ruin cannot be long delayed," that " he is not deserving
of the slightest commiseration,"

> *Rutherford* v. *Evans*, 6 Bing. 451 ; 8 L. J. C. P. (Old S.) 86 ;

that he is " at the head of a gang of swindlers," that he is " a common
informer, and has been guilty of deceiving and defrauding divers persons
with whom he had dealings,"

> *I'Anson* v. *Stuart*, 1 T. R. 748 ; 2 Smith's L. C. 6th ed. 57 ;
>
> *R.* v. *Saunders*, Sir Thos. Raym. 201 ;

that the plaintiff sought admission to a club and was black-balled, and bolted
the next morning without paying his debts.

> *O'Brien* v. *Clement*, 16 M. & W. 159 ; 16 L. J. Ex. 76 ; 4 D. & L. 343.

So it is libellous to write and publish of a landlord that he put in a distress in
order to help his insolvent tenant to defraud his creditors.

> *Haire* v. *Wilson*, 9 B. & C. 643 ; 4 M. & R. 605.

It is libellous for a defendant to write a letter charging his sister with having
unnecessarily made him a party to a Chancery suit, and adding, " It is a pleasure
to her to put me to all the expense she can."

> *Fray* v. *Fray*, 17 C. B. N. S. 603 ; 34 L. J. C. P. 45 ; 10 Jur. N. S. 1153.

It is libellous to write of a lady applying for relief from a charitable society,
that her claims are unworthy, and that she spends all the money given her by
the benevolent in printing circulars filled with abuse of the society's secretary.

> *Hoare* v. *Silverlock*, (No. 1, 1848) 12 Q. B. 624 ; 17 L. J. Q. B. 306 ;
> 12 Jur. 695.

It is libellous to charge the plaintiff with having published a libel,

> *Brookes* v. *Tichborne*, 5 Exch. 929 ; 20 L. J. Ex. 69 ; 14 Jur. 1122 ;

Or to write and publish that he has been tried for murder, though it is not
stated that he was convicted or was guilty,

> *Monson* v. *Tussauds, Limited*, [1894] 1 Q. B. at p. 686 ;

Or to state in writing that the plaintiff is insane, or that her mind is affected.

> *Morgan* v. *Lingen*, 8 L. T. 800.

It is libellous for the manager of a private lunatic asylum to write of a lady,
" I have been to her house this morning and seen her. I think it my duty to
inform you it is imperative that immediate steps to secure her should be taken."

> *Weldon* v. *Winslow, Times*, March 14th—19th, 1884.

Ironical praise may be a libel : *e.g.*, calling an attorney " an honest lawyer."

> *Boydell* v. *Jones*, 4 M. & W. 446 ; 7 Dowl. 210 ; 1 H. & H. 408.
>
> *R.* v. *Brown*, 11 Mod. 86 ; Holt, 425.
>
> *Sir Baptist Hicks' Case*, Hob. 215 ; Poph. 139.

A hypothetical instance may be a libel ; *e.g.*, " Supposing I were to tell certain
stories about you to the effect that you, &c."

> *Ritchie & Co.* v. *Sexton*, (H. L.) 64 L. T. 210 ; 55 J. P. 389.

An obituary notice of a living person may be a libel.

> *McBride* v. *Ellis*, 9 Richardson (41 South Carolina) 313.

It is libellous to impute to a Presbyterian " gross intolerance " in not allowing
his hearse to be used at the funeral of his Roman Catholic servant.

> *Teacy* v. *McKenna*, Ir. R. 4 C. L 374.

It is libellous to charge the plaintiff with ingratitude, even though the
facts on which the charge is based be stated, and they do not bear it out.

> *Cox* v. *Lee*, L. R. 4 Ex. 284 ; 38 L. J. Ex. 219 ; 21 L. T. 178.

It is libellous to state in a newspaper of a young nobleman that he drove over a lady and killed her, and yet attended a public ball that very evening (although this only amounts to a charge of unfeeling conduct).

> *Churchill* v. *Hunt*, 1 Chit. 480 ; 2 B. & Ald. 685.

As to a charge of want of delicacy, see

> *A. B.* v. *Blackwood & Sons*, (1903) 5 F. 25 (Ct. of Sess.).

It is libellous to write and publish of a lady of high rank that she has her photograph taken incessantly, morning, noon, and night, and receives a commission on the sale of such photographs.

> *R.* v. *Rosenberg*, *Times*, Oct. 27th, 28th, 1879.

It is a libel to impute or imply that a grand jury have found a true bill against the plaintiff for any crime.

> *Harvey* v. *French*, 1 Cr. & M. 11.

It is libellous to call a manufacturer a "truckmaster," for this implies that he has been guilty of practices in contravention of the Truck Act.

> *Homer* v. *Taunton*, 5 H. & N. 661 ; 29 L. J. Ex. 318 ; 8 W. R. 499 ; 2 L. T. 512.

It is libellous to write and publish that a child is illegitimate.

> *Shelby* v. *Sun Printing Association*, 38 Hun, (45 N. Y. Supr. Ct.) 474.

It is libellous to write and publish of an unmarried woman that she has a daughter,

> *Chattell* v. *Daily Mail Publishing Co., Limited*, (1901) 18 Times L. R. 165 ;

Or of a married woman that she gave birth to twins one month after her marriage.

> *Morrison* v. *Ritchie & Co.*, (1902) 4 F. 645 (Ct. of Sess.).

It is libellous to write and publish of a man that a certain notorious prostitute is "under his patronage or protection,"

> *More* v. *Bennett*, (1872) 48 N. Y. R. (3 Sickels) 472 ;

Or of a married man that his conduct towards his wife is so cruel that she was compelled to summon him before the magistrates.

> *Hakewell* v. *Ingram*, (1854) 2 C. L. Rep. p. 1397.

It is libellous " to paint a man playing at cudgels with his wife."

> Per Lord Holt, C.J., in *Anon.*, 11 Mod. 99.

> See *Du Bost* v. *Beresford*, 2 Camp. 511.

It is a libel on a married lady to assert that her husband is petitioning for a divorce from her.

> *R.* v. *Leng*, 34 J. P. 309.

It is a libel for a husband to publish in writing that A. has committed adultery with his wife.

> Per Kelly, C.B., in *Brown* v. *Brine*, 1 Ex. D. 5 ; 45 L. J. Ex. 129 ; 24 W. R. 177 ; 33 L. T. 703.

It is libellous to charge a man in writing with having cheated at dice or on the turf, although all gambling and horse-racing transactions are illegal or at least void.

> *Greville* v. *Chapman*, 5 Q. B. 731 ; 13 L. J. Q. B. 172 ; 8 Jur. 189 ; D. & M. 553.

> *Yrisarri* v. *Clement*, 3 Bing. 432 ; 11 Moore, 308 ; 2 C. & P. 223.

It is libellous to call a man a "black-leg" or a "black-sheep." But there should be an averment that these words mean a person guilty of habitually cheating and defrauding others.

> *M'Gregor* v. *Gregory*, 11 M. & W. 287; 12 L. J. Ex. 204; 2 Dowl. N. S. 769.
>
> *O'Brien* v. *Clement*, 16 M. & W. 166; 16 L. J. Ex. 77.
>
> *Digby* v. *Thompson and another*, 4 B. & Ad. 821; 1 N. & M. 485.
>
> *Barnett* v. *Allen*, 3 H. & N. 376; 27 L. J. Ex. 412; 4 Jur. N. S. 488; 1 F. & F. 125.

The Court of Exchequer Chamber thought the words "If Mrs. W. chooses to entertain the Duke of Brunswick, she does what very few will do," a libel on the Duke.

> *Gregory* v. *The Queen*, (No. 1) 15 Q. B. 957; 15 Jur. 74; 5 Cox, C. C. 247.

It is libellous to publish in a newspaper a story of the plaintiff calculated to make him ludicrous, though he had previously told the same story of himself.

> *Cook* v. *Ward*, 6 Bing. 409; 4 M. &. P. 99.

It is libellous to publish in a newspaper an after-dinner speech which contained good-humoured chaff of the plaintiff, pardonable in the speaker on the occasion, but not intended by him to be republished to all the world.

> *Dolby* v. *Newnes*, (1887) 3 Times L. R. 393.

But it is not defamatory to write of another that he is "Man Friday."

> *Forbes* v. *King*, 2 L. J. Ex. 109; 1 Dowl. 672.

For, as Lord Denman, C.J., observes in *Hoare* v. *Silverlock*, (No. 1, 1848) 12 Q. B. 626; 17 L. J. Q. B. 308: "That imputed no crime at all. The 'Man Friday,' we all know, was a very respectable man, although a black man, and black men have not been denounced as criminals yet." The law is otherwise in the United States.

> *King* v. *Wood*, 1 Nott & M. (South Car.) 184.

Where the defendants posted up in a public club-room the following notice: "The Rev. J. Robinson and Mr. J. K., inhabitants of this town, not being persons that the proprietors and annual subscribers think it proper to associate with, are excluded this room;" this was held no libel; *sed quære*.

> *Robinson* v. *Jermyn*, 1 Price, 11.

It is not libellous to publish in a newspaper that the plaintiff has sued his mother-in-law in the County Court.

> *Cox* v. *Cooper*, 12 W. R. 75; 9 L. T. 329.

It is not libellous to send a circular to the members of a certain society, stating that the plaintiffs are not proper persons "to be proposed to be balloted for as members thereof."

> *Goldstein* v. *Foss*, 6 B. & C. 154; (in Ex. Ch.) 4 Bing. 489; 2 C. & P. 252; 2 Y. & J. 146; 1 M. & P. 402.

It is not libellous to print and circulate a handbill, "B. Oakley, of Chillington, Game and Rabbit Destroyer, and his wife the seller of the same in country and town," unless it be averred and proved that the words imputed some illegal or improper slaughter or sale of game or rabbits.

> *R.* v. *James Yates*, 12 Cox, C. C. 233.

It is not a libel to write and publish the words:—"We are requested to state that the honorary secretary of the Tichborne Defence Fund is not and never was a captain in the Royal Artillery as he has been erroneously described," for these words do not impute that the plaintiff had so represented himself.

Hunt v. *Goodlake,* 43 L. J. C. P. 54; 29 L. T. 472.

Defendant posted up several placards which ran thus:—"W. Gee, Solicitor, Bishop's Stortford. To be sold by auction, if not previously disposed of by private contract, a debt of the above, amounting to 3,197*l.,* due upon partnership and mortgage transactions." Bramwell, B., left the question to the jury, telling them that "a mere offer to sell an alleged debt did not necessarily imply inability to pay it," and that "it was not libellous to publish of another that he owed money" unless there be words implying that he cannot pay. The jury returned a verdict of Not Guilty.

R. v. *Coghlan,* (1865) 4 F. & F. 316.

McCann v. *Edinburgh Roperie Co.,* 28 L. R. Ir. 24, *post,* p. 135.

It is not defamatory to write and publish of the plaintiff words implying that he endeavoured to suppress dissension and discourage sedition in Ireland; for, though such words might injure him in the minds of criminals and rebels, they would not tend to lower him in the estimation of right-thinking men.

Mawe v. *Pigott,* Ir. R. 4 C. L. 54.

And see *Clay* v. *Roberts,* 9 Jur. N. S. 580; 11 W. R. 649; 8 L. T. 397.

So a notice sent by a landlord to his tenants:—"Messrs. Henty and Sons hereby give notice that they will not receive in payment any cheques drawn on any of the branches of the Capital and Counties Bank," is not defamatory.

Capital and Counties Bank v. *Henty and Sons,* 7 App. Cas. 741; 52 L. J. Q. B. 232; 31 W. R. 157; 47 L. T. 662; 47 J. P. 214.

It is not libellous for the defendants to write and publish of one who had formerly been in their employment that his engagement had ceased, that "his agency has been closed by the directors," or that "his connection with the institute has ceased": for such words without more do not imply that his engagement was terminated in consequence of any misconduct on his part.

Mulligan v. *Cole and others,* L. R. 10 Q. B. 549; 44 L. J. Q. B. 153; 33 L. T. 12; 39 J. P. 805.

O'Hea v. *Guardians of Cork Union,* 32 L. R. Ir. 629, *post,* p. 135.

Nevill v. *Fine Art and General Insurance Co.,* [1897] A. C. 68; 66 L. J. Q. B. 195; 75 L. T. 606; 61 J. P. 500.

A libel is generally "written," a word which includes any printed, painted, or any other permanent representation not transient in its nature as are spoken words. The writing may be on paper, parchment, copper, wood, stone, or any other substance; and may be made with any instrument, pen and ink, blacklead pencil (*Geary* v. *Physic,* (1826) 5 B. & C. 234), or in chalk, &c. But a libel need not necessarily be in writing or printing. A picture, statue, or effigy, or any other mark or sign exposed to view, if it conveys a defamatory meaning, may also be a libel. (5 Rep. 125.)

Illustrations.

A caricature or scandalous painting is a libel.

> *Anon.*, 11 Mod. 99.
>
> *Austin* v. *Culpepper*, 2 Show. 313; Skin. 123.
>
> *Du Bost* v. *Beresford*, 2 Camp. 511.

A statue, wax model, or effigy, may be a libel.

> *Monson* v. *Tussauds, Limited*, [1894] 1 Q. B. 671; 63 L. J. Q. B. 454;
> 70 L. T. 335; 58 J. P. 524; 9 R. 177.

A chalk mark on a wall may be a libel, and as the wall cannot conveniently be brought into Court, secondary evidence may be given of the inscription.

> *Mortimer* v. *M'Callan*, 6 M. & W. 58.
>
> *Tarpley* v. *Blaby*, 7 C. & P. 395.
>
> See *Spall* v. *Massey and others*, 2 Stark. 559.

Burning a man in effigy may be a libel on him; but those who merely stand by looking on are not liable.

> *Eyre* v. *Garlick*, 42 J. P. 68.

Fixing up a gallows or other reproachful or ignominious sign against a man's door may be a libel on him.

> *De famosis libellis*, 5 Rep. 125, b.
>
> Hawkins' Pleas of the Crown, ch. 28, 6, 8th edition, p. 542.
>
> *Jefferies* v. *Duncombe*, (1809) 11 East, 226; 2 Camp. 3, *ante*, p. 14.

Hieroglyphics, a rebus, an anagram, or an allegory may be a libel.

Ironical praise may be a libel.

But in all these cases there must be a definite imputation upon a definite person; and that person must be the plaintiff. A. cannot, as a rule, sue for words defamatory only of B., although he may have suffered loss or inconvenience therefrom. But see *post*, p. 147.

Illustrations.

A brother cannot sue for slander of his sister.

> *Subbaiyar* v. *Kristnaiyar and another*, I. L. R., 1 Madras, 383.

No one can claim damages for libel on a dead man; but such a libel may be the subject of criminal proceedings, if its tendency be clearly to provoke the living to a breach of the peace, in vindication of the honour of the family.

> *R.* v. *Topham*, 4 T. R. 126, *post*, p. 457.
>
> *R.* v. *Ensor*, (1887) 3 Times L. R. 366.
>
> *Broom* v. *Ritchie*, (1905) 6 F. 942 (Ct. of Sess.).

The defendants attended the funeral ceremony of Premji Ludha, the headman of the Karàd caste, and there before a large concourse of people made a violent attack on the moral and religious character of the deceased, declaring that he was " patit," a term of great opprobrium and reproach among Hindoos. Many of those assembled left at once in consequence, and the family of the deceased suffered great pain and annoyance, and also were much lowered in public estimation. The plaintiff sued as the heir and nearest relation of the deceased for damages. *Held*, no action lay.

> *Luckumsey Rowji* v. *Hurbun Nursey and others*, I. L. R., 5 Bom. 580.

But a husband may recover, without joining his wife as a co-plaintiff, for damage caused to himself by words defamatory solely of her.

> *Baldwin* v. *Flower*, 3 Mod. 120.
>
> *Guy* v. *Gregory*, 9 C. & P. 584.
>
> *Dengate* v. *Gardiner*, 4 M. & W. 5 ; 2 Jur. 470.
>
> *Wilson* v. *Goit*, 3 Smith (17 N. Y. R.) 445.

If, however, the plaintiff can satisfy the jury that the defendant desired and intended to injure him, and thought that his best way of doing so was by publishing a libel on B., and the damage to the plaintiff was the natural and necessary consequence of that libel on B., it is submitted that an action would lie.

> *Ashley* v. *Harrison*, 1 Esp. 48 ; Peake, 194.
>
> *Brayne* v. *Cooper*, 5 M. & W. 249.

If the words are not reasonably susceptible of any defamatory meaning, the judge at the trial will stop the case. But if the words are reasonably susceptible of two constructions, the one an innocent, the other a libellous construction, then it is a question for the jury which construction is the proper one (*Jenner and another* v. *A'Beckett*, L. R. 7 Q. B. 11 ; 41 L. J. Q. B. 14 ; 20 W. R. 181 ; 25 L. T. 464 ; *Linotype Co., Limited* v. *British Empire, &c.*, (1899) 81 L. T. 331 : 15 Times L. R. 524) ; and if the judge stops the case, the Court will order a new trial. (*Hart and another* v. *Wall*, 2 C. P. D. 146 ; 46 L. J. C. P. 227 ; 25 W. R. 373 ; *Ritchie & Co.* v. *Sexton*, 64 L. T. 210.)

The jury should always read the alleged libel through before deciding that its effect is injurious. A word at the end may alter the whole meaning. The jury must look at the context. If in one part appears something to the plaintiff's discredit, in another something to his credit, the "bane" and the "antidote" should be taken together. The jury should not dwell on isolated passages, but judge of the publication as a whole. (Per Lord Ellenborough, C.J., in *R.* v. *Lambert and Perry*, 2 Camp. 398 ; 31 How. St. Tr. 340 ; per Lord Kenyon, C.J., in *R.* v. *Reeves*, Peake, Add. Cas. 84 ; per Fitzgerald, J., in *R.* v. *Sullivan*, 11 Cox, C. C. 58.) They must decide first what in their opinion any reasonable man would understand from the alleged libel, and then it will be easy for them to say whether it is a libel or not.

Illustrations.

The report of a trial for libel contained some strong observations against the plaintiff, which were indeed a necessary part of the report, as the defendant had justified. At the end it was stated that the jury found a verdict for the plaintiff for 30*l.* *Held*, that the publication, taken as a whole, was not injurious to the plaintiff.

Chalmers v. *Payne*, 2 C. M. & R. 156; 5 Tyrw. 766 ; 1 Gale, 69.

And see *Hunt* v. *Algar*, 6 C. & P. 245, *post*, p. 115.

The defendants published in a newspaper certain stories about the plaintiff, and then added: " I do not venture to say these stories are true." *Held*, that in spite of this qualification the words were capable of being reasonably understood in a libellous sense, and that the question must go to the jury.

Ritchie & Co. v. *Sexton*, (H. L.) 64 L. T. 210; 55 J. P. 389.

PUBLIC OFFICES, PROFESSIONS AND TRADES.

Apart from words which injure the plaintiff in his private character and reputation, an action will lie for words which injure him in his office, profession, or trade. The law will protect a man from any attack which tends to impair his means of livelihood, or to bring upon him professional or commercial discredit. Hence words may be libellous, if written of one man, who holds a public office or carries on a profession or trade, which would not be actionable if published of another, who held no such office, or did not follow such profession or trade.

Public Offices.

It is libellous to impute to any one holding an office that he has been guilty of improper conduct in that office, or has been actuated by wicked, corrupt, or selfish motives or is incompetent for the post which he holds. And it is not necessary (as it is in cases of slander, *post*, p. 54) that the person libelled should at the time still hold that office : it is actionable to impute past misconduct when in office. (*Parmiter* v. *Coupland*, 6 M. & W. 108 ; *Boydell* v. *Jones*, 4 M. & W. at p. 450 ; *Warman* v. *Hine*, 1 Jur. 820 ; *Goodburne* v. *Bowman*, 9 Bing. 532.)

In cases of slander a distinction is drawn between offices of profit and offices of honour merely, such as that of justice of the peace ; and it has been held that merely to impute incompetency or want of ability (as distinct from a want of integrity or impartiality) to a man whose office is not of profit, is not actionable, see p. 55. There is no authority, however, for supposing that an action of libel would not lie, if such words were printed and published. And see *post*, p. 54.

Illustrations.

It is libellous to write and publish of an ex-mayor and a justice of the peace that during his mayoralty he was guilty of partiality and corruption, and displayed ignorance of his duties ; and this notwithstanding the public nature of the offices he held.

Parmiter v. *Coupland*, 6 M. & W. 105; 9 L. J. Ex. 202; 4 Jur. 701.

Goodburne v. *Bowman*, 9 Bing. 532.

The trustees of a charity can sue jointly for a libellous letter published in a newspaper imputing to them, as a body, improper management of the charity funds.

Booth v. *Briscoe*, 2 Q. B. D. 496; 25 W. R. 838.

It is libellous to charge an overseer of a parish with " oppressive conduct " towards the paupers.

Woodard v. *Dowsing*, 2 M. & Ry. 74.

A placard stating of a certain overseer that when out of office he advocated low rates, when in office he advocated high rates, and that the defendant would not trust him with 5*l*. of his property, is a libel.

Cheese v. *Scales*, 10 M. & W. 488; 12 L. J. Ex. 13.

It is libellous to accuse a vestry clerk of having in any way misapplied the money of the parish.

May v. *Brown*, 3 B. & C. 113.

It is libellous to charge a guardian of the poor with having been during the preceding year " a great defaulter " in his account.

Warman v. *Hine*, 1 Jur. 820; 1 J. P. 346.

It is libellous to charge the clerk to the justices of a borough with corruption.

Blagg v. *Sturt*, 10 Q. B. 899; 16 L. J. Q. B. 39; 11 Jur. 101.

It is libellous to charge the deputy returning officer in charge of a polling station at an election with being a partisan and showing party bias in the discharge of his duties.

Hunt v. *Star Newspaper Company, Ltd.*, [1908] 2 K. B. 309; 77 L. J. K. B. 732; 98 L. T. 629; 24 Times L. R. 452.

Professions.

It is libellous to impute to a member of any profession, that he does not possess the skill or the technical knowledge necessary for the proper practice of such profession, or that he has been guilty of any discreditable conduct in his profession.

Illustrations.

Clergymen and Ministers.

It is libellous to write and publish of a Protestant archbishop that he attempted to convert a Catholic priest by offers of money and of preferment in the Church of England and Ireland.

> *Archbishop of Tuam* v. *Robeson and another,* 5 Bing. 17; 2 M. & P. 32.

It is libellous to write and publish of a clergyman that he came to the performance of divine service in a towering passion, and that his conduct is calculated to make infidels of his congregation.

> *Walker* v. *Brogden,* 19 C. B. N. S. 65; 11 Jur. N. S. 671; 13 W. R. 809; 12 L. T. 495.
>
> *Gathercole* v. *Miall,* 15 M. & W. 319; 15 L. J. Ex. 179; 10 Jur. 337.
>
> But see *Kelly* v. *Tinling,* L. R. 1 Q. B. 699; 35 L. J. Q. B. 231; 12 Jur. N. S. 940; 14 W. R. 51; 13 L. T. 255.

It is libellous to write and publish of a dissenting minister:—"A serious misunderstanding has recently taken place amongst the Independent Dissenters of Great Marlow and their pastor, in consequence of some personal invectives publicly thrown from the pulpit by the latter against a young lady of distinguished merit and spotless reputation. We understand, however, that the matter is to be taken up seriously.—*Bucks Chronicle.*"

> *Edwards* v. *Bell and others,* 1 Bing. 403.

As to a Roman Catholic priest, see

> *Hearne* v. *Stowell,* 12 A. & E. 719; 4 P. & D. 696; 6 Jur. 458.

Medical Men.

To advertise falsely that certain quack medicines were prepared by a physician of eminence is a libel upon such physician.

> *Clark* v. *Freeman,* 11 Beav. 112; 17 L. J. Ch. 142; 12 Jur. 149.
>
> See also *Walter* v. *Ashton,* [1902] 2 Ch. 282; 71 L. J. Ch. 839; 51 W. R. 131; 87 L. T. 196.

It is libellous to describe a medical practitioner in print as "the Harley Street Quack, Physician Extraordinary to several ladies of distinction."

> *Long* v. *Chubb,* 5 C. & P. 55.
>
> *Wells* v. *Webber,* 2 F. & F. 715.
>
> *Hunter* v. *Sharpe,* 4 F. & F. 983; 15 L. T. 421; 30 J. P. 149.

But it is no libel to write and publish of a physician that he has met homœopathists in consultation, although it be averred in the declaration that to do so would be a breach of professional etiquette.

> *Clay* v. *Roberts,* 9 Jur. N. S. 580; 11 W. R. 649; 8 L. T. 397.

Where the name of a doctor had been used without his consent in an advertisement of a patent medicine, the Court declined to interfere.

> *Dockrell* v. *Dougall,* 78 L. T. 840; 80 L. T. 556.

It is libellous to write of a person having professional qualifications, who advertises as an ear specialist, that he is a quack of the rankest species. But if the facts of the case warrant such an inference, the jury may find for the defendant on the ground that such words are fair comment on a matter of public interest.

> *Dakhyl* v. *Labouchere,* [1908] 2 K. B. 325, n.; 77 L. J. K. B. 728; 96 L. T. 399; 23 Times L. R. 364.

Barristers.

To write and publish of a barrister that he is " a quack lawyer and a mountebank " and " an impostor," is actionable.

> *Wakley* v. *Healey*, 7 C. B. 591; 18 L. J. C. P. 241.
> *Sir W. Garrow's Case*, 3 Chit. Crim. L. 884.

Solicitors.

It is libellous to compare the conduct of an attorney in a particular case to that of the celebrated firm of Quirk, Gammon and Snap in " Ten Thousand a Year."

> *Woodgate* v. *Ridout*, 4 F. & F. 202.

It is actionable to write and publish of a solicitor that he had been " severely reprimanded by one of the Masters of the Queen's Bench for what is called sharp practice in his profession."

> *Boydell* v. *Jones*, (1838) 4 M. & W. 446; 7 Dowl. 210.

A correct report in the *Observer* of certain legal proceedings was headed " Shameful conduct of an attorney." *Held*, that the heading was a libel, even though all that followed was protected.

> *Clement* v. *Lewis*, 3 Br. & Bing. 297; 3 B. & Ald. 702; 7 Moore, 200.

An information was granted for these words written to the mayor of Richmond: " I am sure you will not be persuaded from doing justice by any little arts of your town clerk, whose consummate malice and wickedness against me and my family will make him do anything, be it ever so vile "

> *R.* v. *Waite*, (1743) 1 Wils. 22.
> *Cory* v. *Bond*, 2 F. & F. 241.

Words complained of :—" If you will be misled by an attorney, who only considers his own interest, you will have to repent it : you may think, when you have once ordered your attorney to write to Mr. Giles, he would not do any more without your further orders, but if you once set him about it, he will go to any length without further orders." *Held*, a libel on the attorney who had been employed to write to Mr. Giles.

> *Godson* v. *Home*, 1 Br. & Bing. 7; 3 Moore, 223.

The libel complained of was headed—" How Lawyer B. treats his clients," followed by a report of a particular case in which one client of Lawyer B.'s had been badly treated. That particular case was proved to be correctly reported, but this was held insufficient to justify the heading, which implied that Lawyer B. *generally* treated his clients badly.

> *Bishop* v. *Latimer*, 4 L. T. 775.

Libel complained of, that the plaintiff, a proctor, had three times been suspended from practice for extortion. Proof that he had once been so suspended was held insufficient.

> *Clarkson* v. *Lawson*, 6 Bing. 266, 587; 3 M. & P. 605; 4 M. & P. 356.
> *Blake* v. *Stevens and others*, 4 F. & F. 232; 11 L. T. 543.

It is libellous to impute to a solicitor " disgraceful conduct " in having at an election disclosed confidential communications made to him professionally.

> *Moore* v. *Terrell and others*, 4 B. & Ad. 870; 1 N. & M. 559.

But it is not a libel to say of a solicitor that he was admitted in 1879, when he was admitted in 1869.

> *Raven* v. *Stevens and Sons*, (1886) 3 Times L. R. 67.

Singers and Actors.

It is libellous to write and publish of an actress and singer that her performance was " the only touch of vulgarity " in a variety entertainment in which she appeared, and that a song sung by her was " written in gross bad taste," which was not redeemed by her manner of dancing.

Cooney v. *Edeveain,* (1897) 14 Times L. R. 34.

It has been held to be libellous to publish a programme in which the names of the singers at a concert are arranged in such an order that the plaintiff's name does not occupy a position worthy of her professional reputation.

Russell v. *Notcutt,* (1896) 12 Times L. R. 195.

It is a libel to write and publish of an actor that it would be conferring a benefit on the public to induce him to return to " his old profession, that of a waiter," when in fact he never had been a waiter.

Duplany v. *Davis,* (1886) 3 Times L. R. 184.

It is a libel on an actress, in the way of her profession, to print and publish words that imply that she is at least ten years older than she really is.

Chattell v. *Daily Mail Publishing Co., Ld.,* (1901) 18 Times L. R. p. 167.

The plaintiffs were vocalists, who advertised that certain publishers had given them permission " to sing any *morceaux* from their musical publications." The defendant wrote to the proprietors of certain music halls, at which the plaintiffs were engaged to sing, stating that the advertisement was calculated to lead proprietors to incur penalties under the Copyright Act, as he held the power of attorney over the performing rights of certain publications belonging to two of the publishers specified in the advertisement, and that one of these firms had informed him that they had granted no such permission as that claimed by the plaintiffs. *Held,* that the words were capable of a libellous meaning, and that the case was one for a jury.

Hart and another v. *Wall,* (1877) 2 C. P. D. 146 ; 46 L. J. C. P. 227 ; 25 W. R. 373.

As to publishing the name of a professional musician in a " black list," see

Newton v. *Amalgamated Musicians' Union,* (1896) 12 Times L. R. 623, *post,* 432.

Authors.

To write and publish falsely that the plaintiff edited the third edition of a law book is actionable, if the book is proved to be full of inaccuracies which would seriously prejudice the plaintiff's reputation.

Archbold v. *Sweet,* 1 Moo. & Rob. 162 ; 5 C. & P. 219.

Cf. *Manton and others* v. *Bales,* (1845) 1 C. B. 444.

So to represent that the plaintiff is the author of a mutilated edition of a portion of his book may be a libel on him.

Lee v. *Gibbings,* (1892) 67 L. T. 263 ; 8 Times L. R. 773.

Seeley v. *Fisher,* (1841) 11 Sim. 581.

To write and publish falsely that the plaintiff is the author of a play, the plot of which turns on adultery, is a libel on him ; it is not a fair comment on his play.

Merivale and Wife v. *Carson,* 20 Q. B. D. 275 ; 36 W. R. 231 ; 58 L. T. 331 ; 52 J. P. 261.

It is libellous to write and publish of an author that in writing the biography of a dead man he has not made proper use of the material available, has obtruded his own personality to the exclusion of that of the deceased, and that his work is a slight upon the memory of the dead.

> *Thomas* v. *Bradbury, Agnew & Co., Ld.*, [1906] 2 K. B. 627 ; 77 L. J.
> K. B. 726 ; 54 W. R. 608 ; 95 L. T. 23.

Journalists.

It is libellous to impute to the editor and proprietor of a newspaper that in advocating the sacred cause of the dissemination of Christianity among the Chinese, he was an impostor, anxious only to put money into his own pocket by extending the circulation of his paper ; and that he had published a fictitious subscription list with a view to induce people to contribute.

> *Campbell* v. *Spottiswoode*, 3 B. & S. 769 ; 32 L. J. Q. B. 185 ; 9 Jur.
> N. S. 1069 ; 11 W. R. 569 ; 8 L. T. 201.

It is libellous to call the editor of a newspaper " a libellous journalist."

> *Wakley* v. *Cooke and Healey*, 4 Exch. 511 ; 19 L. J. Ex. 91.

It is a libel on the war-correspondent of a newspaper to accuse him of intriguing with private soldiers against their officers in a manner " destructive of all discipline."

> *Williams* v. *Beresford-Hope*, (1886) 3 Times L. R. 20.

The plaintiff was a physician and the editor of a periodical called *The London Medical and Physical Journal*. The defendant published words tending to cast ridicule on the plaintiff as an editor, which, the defendant alleged, referred to the plaintiff only as an author. *Held*, that if the jury thought the words were not a fair comment, the plaintiff was entitled to a verdict.

> *Macleod* v. *Wakley*, 3 C. & P. 311.

Newspaper Proprietors.

It is a libel on the proprietor and publisher of a newspaper to say that its advertisement columns are swollen with advertisements copied from other newspapers without any order for their insertion.

> *Latimer* v. *Western Morning News Co.*, 25 L. T. 44.

It is libellous to write and publish that a newspaper has a separate page devoted to the advertisements of usurers and quack doctors, and that the editor takes respectable advertisements at a cheaper rate if the advertisers will consent to their appearing in that page.

> *Russell and another* v. *Webster*, 23 W. R. 59.

It is not libellous for one newspaper to call another " the most vulgar, ignorant and scurrilous journal ever published in Great Britain ; " but it is libellous to add, " it is the lowest now in circulation ; and we submit the fact to the consideration of advertisers ; " for that affects the sale of the paper and the profits to be made by advertising. (Lord Kenyon, C.J.)

> *Heriot* v. *Stuart*, 1 Esp. 437.

It is not libellous to write and publish of a newspaper that its net sales are 5,000 when in fact they are much greater, though such words may be the foundation of an action on the case for disparagement of goods. (Per Darling, J.)

> *Publishers of the Observer Limited* v. *Advertisers Protection Society
> Limited, Times Newspaper*, Feb. 3, 1910.

The plaintiff and the defendant were the owners of newspapers circulating in the same locality, and the defendant published a statement that the circulation of his newspaper was 20 to 1 of any other weekly paper in the district, and that "where others count by the dozen, we count by the hundred." It was held that the above statements were not a mere puff by the defendant of his own newspaper, but amounted to an untrue disparagement of the plaintiff's newspaper, and were actionable on proof of actual damage; but that as no damage was proved the action failed.

> *Lyne* v. *Nicholls*, (1906) 23 Times L. R. 86.

It is a libel to write of the owner of a newspaper that he endeavours to grind down his workmen by improperly reducing their wages, that his newspaper is almost defunct, and that the greater part of the advertisements in the newspaper are fictitious.

> *Harrison* v. *Pearce*, 32 L. T. (Old S.) 298 ; 1 F. & F. 567.

" No doubt offensive language applied to a newspaper may cast a reflection, and be understood as casting a reflection, upon persons connected with the newspaper. But it clearly cannot be maintained that every imputation upon a newspaper is a personal imputation upon everybody connected with the newspaper. Whether it is an imputation which would attach to any individual, and, if so, to whom, must depend in each case upon the language used and upon the circumstances."

> Per Lord Herschell, L.C., in *Australian Newspaper Co., Limited* v. *Bennett*, [1894] A. C. at p. 288 ; 63 L. J. P. C. 105; 70 L. T. 597; 58 J. P. 604 ; 6 R. 484.

Other Professions.

It is libellous to impute to a certificated master mariner drunkenness when in charge of his ship, or other misconduct or incapacity in the management of his ship, or that he is an habitual drunkard.

> *Harwood* v. *Green*, 3 C & P. 141.
>
> *Coxhead* v. *Richards*, 2 C. B. 569 ; 15 L. J. C. P. 278 ; 10 Jur. 984.

It is a libel on an architect to print and publish of him that his plans are worthless.

> *Henwood* v. *Harrison*, L. R. 7 C. P. 606, 628; 41 L. J. C. P. 206; 20 W. R. 1000; 26 L. T. 938.

Where an architect is engaged to execute certain work, it is a libel upon him in the way of his profession to write to his employers asserting that he has no experience in that particular kind of work, and is therefore unfit to be entrusted with it.

> *Botterill and another* v. *Whytehead*, 41 L. T. 588.

It is libellous to write and publish of a quantity surveyor that there are great errors in the quantities taken out by him.

> *Sadgrove* v. *Hole*, [1901] 2 K. B. 1; 70 L. J. K. B. 455; 49 W. R. 473; 84 L. T. 647; 17 Times L. R. 332.

Where two architects designed certain public buildings, and one of them published pictures of the buildings, saying that they were designed by himself, without any reference to his fellow architect, it was held that the omission of the plaintiff's name did not constitute a libel on him.

> *Green* v. *Archer*, (1891) 7 Times L. R. 542.

Traders.

Any printed or written words are libellous which impeach the credit of any merchant or trader by imputing to him bankruptcy, insolvency, or even embarrassment, either past, present, or future, or which impute to him fraud or dishonesty or any mean or dishonourable conduct in his business, or which impugn his skill or otherwise injure him in the way of his trade or employment.

" The law has always been very tender of the reputation of tradesmen, and therefore words spoken of them in the way of their trade will bear an action that will not be actionable in the case of another person, and if bare words are so, it will be stronger in the case of a libel in a public newspaper which is so diffusive." (*Per curiam* in *Harman* v. *Delany*, 2 Str. 898; 1 Barnard. 289; Fitz. 121.)

Illustrations.

The printers of a newspaper, by a mistake in setting up in type the announcements from the *London Gazette*, placed the name of the plaintiff's firm under the heading " First Meetings under the Bankruptcy Act " instead of under " Dissolutions of Partnership." An ample apology was inserted in the next issue: no damage was proved to have followed to the plaintiff: and there was no suggestion of any malice. In an action for libel against the proprietors of the paper, the jury awarded the plaintiff 50*l.* damages. *Held*, that the publication was libellous, and that the damages awarded were not excessive.

> *Shepheard* v. *Whitaker*, L. R. 10 C. P. 502 ; 32 L. T. 402.

[N.B.—The chief clerk thought 10*l.* sufficient in a very similar case, *Stubbs* v. *Marsh*, 15 L. T. 312.]

It is libellous to write of a bank as " now in liquidation " when no steps have been taken, or are in contemplation, with a view to liquidation.

> *London and Northern Bank, Limited* v. *George Newnes, Limited*, (1899) 16 Times L. R. 76.

It is libellous to advertise that a certain optician is " a licensed hawker " and " a quack in spectacle secrets."

> *Keyzor and another* v. *Newcomb*, 1 F. & F. 559.

It is a libel on a firm of pianoforte makers to publish that they carry on a " pernicious system of sweating " at their works.

> *Collard* v. *Marshall*, [1892] 1 Ch. 571; 61 L. J. Ch. 268 ; 40 W. R. 473.

It is a libel on a colliery proprietor to publish of him that he " locked his men out of their pits for six weeks, until stocks were cleared out and coal had reached a fabulous price ; and then his conscience would not allow him to starve the poor miner any longer."

> *Bayley* v. *Edmunds and others*, (1895) 11 Times L. R. 537.

It is a libel on a firm of merchants to publish of them that they " have deliberately and persistently boycotted five lightermen who were in their employ, because they are members of a trades union."

> *Pink* v. *Federation of Trades Unions*, (1892) 67 L. T. 258.

It is actionable to put a man's name on a "black list," with the object of inducing people not to have business dealings with him, or to bring him into public odium and contempt. "Black lists are real instruments of coercion, as every man whose name is on one soon discovers to his cost." Per Lord Lindley in

> *Quinn* v. *Leathem*, [1901] A. C. 495 ; 70 L. J. P. C. 76 ; 50 W. R. 139 ;
> 85 L. T. 289 ; 65 J. P. 708.

> *Trollope and Sons* v. *London Building Trades Federation*, (1895) 72
> L. T. 342 ; 11 Times L. R. 228, 280, and see *post*, p. 431.

It is a libel to write and publish of a licensed victualler that his licence has been refused, as it suggests that he had committed some breach of the licensing laws.

> *Bignell* v. *Buzzard*, 3 H. & N. 217 ; 27 L. J. Ex. 355.

The plaintiff, who had formerly been a member of the defendant's firm of H. & Sons, was carrying on a similar business by himself under the name of H. & Co. The defendants brought an action against the plaintiff for passing himself off as a member of their firm. The judge at the trial was satisfied that no such representation had been made, and dismissed the action. It appeared that such a representation had on two or three occasions been made by the plaintiff's agent without his knowledge, and the plaintiff gave an undertaking, which was inserted in the judgment, that he would never make such a representation. The defendants issued a circular relating to the litigation, stating that by the judgment the plaintiff had been ordered not to represent that his firm was, or that the defendants' firm was not, the original firm of H. & Sons, and that they had been compelled to issue such circular through finding that serious misrepresentations were in circulation to their prejudice. *Held*, that this was a libel on the plaintiff and that he was entitled to an injunction without proof of special damage.

> *Hayward & Co.* v. *Hayward and Sons*, (1886) 34 Ch. D. 198 ; 56 L. J.
> Ch. 287 ; 35 W. R. 392 ; 55 L. T. 729.

It is libellous to write and publish of the plaintiff that he regularly or purposely supplied bad and unwholesome water to ships, whereby the passengers were made ill.

> *Solomon* v. *Lawson*, 8 Q. B. 823 ; 15 L. J. Q. B. 253 ; 10 Jur. 796.

> *Barnard* v. *Salter*, W. N. 1872, p. 140.

It is libellous to write and publish of a dairyman that the milk supplied by him is "three quarts short" of the proper measure.

> *Beamish* v. *Dairy Supply Co., Limited*, (1897) 13 Times L. R. 484.

It is libellous to write and publish of the plaintiff that he endeavours to sell the articles which he manufactures under a well-known trade name which he has no right to use.

> *Thorley's Cattle Food Co.* v. *Massam*, 14 Ch. D. 763 ; 28 W. R. 295,
> 966 ; 41 L. T. 542 ; 42 L. T. 851.

> *Anderson* v. *Liebig's Extract of Meat Co.*, 45 L. T. 757.

> *Liebig's Extract of Meat Co.* v. *Anderson*, 55 L. T. 206.

> *Hatchard* v. *Mège and others*, 18 Q. B. D. 771 ; 56 L. J. Q. B. 397 ; 35
> W. R. 576 ; 56 L. T. 662, *post*, p. 37.

Partners may sue jointly for a libel defamatory of the partnership.

> *Le Fanu* v. *Malcolmson*, 1 H. L. C. 637 ; 8 Ir. L. R. 418 ; *post*, p. 590.

So a company or corporation can sue even one of their own members for a libel relating to their management of their business.

> *Williams* v. *Beaumont,* 10 Bing. 260 ; 3 Moore & Sc. 705.
>
> *Metropolitan Omnibus Co.* v. *Hawkins,* 4 H. & N. 87 ; 28 L. J. Ex. 201 ; 5 Jur. N. S. 226 ; 7 W. R. 265 ; 32 L. T. (Old S.) 281.
>
> *South Hetton Coal Co., Limited* v. *North Eastern News Association,* [1894] 1 Q. B. 133 ; 63 L. J. Q. B. 293 ; 42 W. R. 322 ; 69 L. T. 844.

A married woman trading under her own name may sue as a trader, without joining her husband, for a libel on her in the way of her trade.

> Per Brett, J., in *Summers* v. *City Bank,* L. R. 9 C. P. 583 ; 43 L. J. C. P. 261.
>
> And see 45 & 46 Vict. c. 75, s. 1, *post,* pp. 568—577.

And see cases collected in Chapter V., *post,* p. 109.

Sometimes also an attack upon a thing may be defamatory of the owner of that thing, or of others immediately connected with it. But this is only so where an attack upon the thing is also an indirect attack upon the individual. If the words do not involve any reflection upon the personal character or the professional or commercial reputation of some person, they are not defamatory, and therefore are not actionable unless they fall within the rules relating to actions on the case (as to which see Chapter IV., *post,* p. 77.) But to impute, for example, that the goods which the plaintiff sells or manufactures are adulterated to his knowledge is a distinct charge against the plaintiff of fraud and dishonesty in his trade.

"While mere criticism upon a manufacture or goods is lawful, an imputation upon a man in the way of his trade is, even without special damage, properly the subject of an action. . . . It is quite possible to make a reflection which, by the mere form of expression, would seem to be only a criticism of goods, but nevertheless would involve a reflection upon the seller or maker. Could it be gravely argued that to say of a fishmonger that he was in the habit of selling decomposed fish would not be a libel on him in the way of his trade? And if so, would it not be a mere juggle with language to alter the form of that allegation and to say that all the fish in A.'s shop is decomposed? Or to say of a baker that such a baker's bread is always unwholesome? In each of these cases you could adopt a form of speech which would seem only to deal with the article sold or manufactured, but in each case it would tend to, and probably would succeed in, destroying the trade of the person thus referred to." (Per Lord Halsbury, L.C., in *Linotype Co., Limited* v. *British Empire Type-setting Machine Co., Limited*, (1899) 81 L. T. 331; 15 Times L. R. 524; and see the observations of Lord Esher, M.R., in *South Hetton Coal Co.* v. *North Eastern News Association*, [1894] 1 Q. B. at p. 139.)

Illustrations.

The defendant published an advertisement in these words :—" Whereas there was an account in the *Craftsman* of John Harman, gunsmith, making guns of two feet six inches to exceed any made by others of a foot longer (with whom it is supposed he is in fee), this is to advise all gentlemen to be cautious, the said gunsmith *not daring to engage with any artist in town*, nor ever did make such an experiment (except out of a leather gun), as any gentleman may be satisfied of at the Cross Guns in Longacre." *Held*, a libel on the plaintiff in the way of his trade. Verdict for the plaintiff. Damages 50*l.*

Harman v. *Delany*, (1731) 2 Stra. 898; 1 Barnard. 289, 438; Fitz. 121.

It is libellous to write and publish of a bookseller that he publishes and sells books of an absurd, immoral, and improper tendency and description for children.

Tabart v. *Tipper*, (1808) 1 Camp. 350.

It is a libel on a shipowner and on him in the way of his trade to write and publish that his ship is unseaworthy. " It is as bad as saying of a wine merchant that his wine is poisoned, or of a tea merchant that his tea is made green by drying it on copper."

Ingram v. *Lawson*, (1840) 6 Bing. N. C. 212; 8 Sc. 471, 479; 4 Jur. 151; 9 C. & P. 326.

A declaration alleged that the plaintiff carried on the trade of an engineer, and was the inventor of, and sold, goods called " self-acting tallow syphons or lubricators," and that the defendant published of the plaintiff in his said trade and as such inventor, as follows :—" This is to caution parties employing steam power from a person, offering what he calls self-acting tallow syphons or lubricators, stating that he is the sole-inventor, manufacturer and patentee, thereby monopolising high prices at the expense of the public. R. Harlow (the defendant) takes this opportunity of saying that such a patent does not exist, and that he has to offer an improved lubricator, which dispenses with the necessity of using more than one to a steam engine, thereby constituting a saving of 50 per cent. over every other kind yet offered to the public. Those who have already adopted the lubricators against which R. H. would caution, will find that the tallow is wasted instead of being effectually employed as professed." No innuendo was put upon the words, and no special damage was alleged. *Held* (on demurrer), no libel on the plaintiff, either generally or in the way of his trade.

Evans v. *Harlow*, (1844) 5 Q. B. 624; 13 L. J. Q. B. 120; 8 Jur. 571; D. & M. 507.

In this case Patteson, J., said (at p. 633) : " This is not, in effect, a caution against the plaintiff as a tradesman in the habit of selling goods which he knows to be bad; if it were, it would be a libel upon him personally : but it is a caution against the goods, suggesting that the articles which the plaintiff sells do not answer their purpose; which is not actionable unless it were shown that the plaintiff, by reason of the publication, was prevented from selling his goods to a particular person."

So where one tradesman wrote and published words disparaging the goods of a rival trader, and no special damage was alleged, and the innuendo did not allege any imputation defamatory of the plaintiff, either generally or in the way of his trade, it was held on demurrer that no action lay.

> *Young and others* v. *Macrae*, (1862) 3 B. & S. 264; 32 L. J. Q. B. 6; 11 W. R. 63; 9 Jur. N. S. 539; 7 L. T. 354.

It is libellous to write and publish that the guano sold by the plaintiff is a mixture of sand, sawdust, and other worthless compounds.

> *Salmon* v. *Isaac*, (1869) 20 L. T. 885.

It is a libel on the proprietor and publisher of a newspaper to say that the advertisement columns of the newspaper are swollen with advertisements copied from other newspapers without any order for their insertion.

> *Latimer* v. *Western Morning News Co.*, (1871) 25 L. T. 44.
> And see *Russell and another* v. *Webster*, (1874) 23 W. R. 59.

The plaintiffs were manufacturers of bags, and had manufactured a bag which they called the "Bag of Bags." The defendant printed and published the following words:—"As we have not seen the Bag of Bags, we cannot say that it is useful, or that it is portable, or that it is elegant. All these it may be, but the only point we can deal with is the title, which we think very silly, very slangy, and very vulgar; and which has been forced upon the notice of the public *ad nauseam*." Mellor and Hannen, JJ., held that these words were capable of being construed as disparaging the plaintiffs in the way of their business, and that the case must therefore go to the jury. Lush, J., dissented, as in his opinion the words were not capable of being a libel upon the plaintiffs either personally or in the way of their trade.

> *Jenner and another* v. *A'Beckett*, (1871) L. R. 7 Q. B. 11; 41 L. J. Q. B. 14; 20 W. R. 181; 25 L. T. 464.

Where the defendant wrote and published of the plaintiffs that they were "seeking to foist upon the public an article which they pretend is the same as that manufactured by the late Joseph Thorley," it was held that this was a libel on the plaintiffs in the way of their trade.

> *Thorley's Cattle Food Co.* v. *Massam*, (1879) 14 Ch. D. 763; 28 W. R. 295, 966; 41 L. T. 542; 42 L. T. 851.

It is a libel to write and publish of a firm which exports needles words that imply that their needles are not an honest and independent make of needles, but are a spurious imitation of those made by another and a well-known firm.

> *Thomas* v. *Williams*, (1880) 14 Ch. D. 864; 49 L. J. Ch. 605; 28 W. R. 983; 43 L. T. 91.

In certain lawsuits the Courts had held that the words "Liebig's Extract of Meat" were only a descriptive title, and that any person in this country may make such extract according to Liebig's receipt and sell it under the above title, or as "Baron Liebig's Extract," and may use a photograph of Baron Liebig. The defendant sold extract of meat with wrappers containing the words: "This is the only genuine brand," and stating that he was the "founder and sole proprietor of Brand Baron Liebig." *Held*, that the plaintiffs were entitled to an injunction as the words "only genuine" misrepresented the result of the preceding litigation, implied that the plaintiffs' goods were not genuine, and were injurious to the plaintiffs in the way of their trade.

> *Liebig's Extract of Meat Co., Limited* v. *Anderson*, (1886) 55 L. T. 206.

The defendants published an advertisement in the following terms: " Caution: Delmonico Champagne. Messrs. D. & Co. finding that wine stated to be Delmonico Champagne is being advertised for sale in Great Britain, hereby give notice that such wine cannot be the wine it is represented to be, as no champagne shipped under that name can be genuine unless it has their names on the labels." They further announced that if such wines were shipped from France they should take legal proceedings. *Held,* that this was a libel on the plaintiff as charging him with being a dishonest man, and a libel on him in the way of his trade as being a dishonest wine merchant.

> *Hatchard* v. *Mège,* (1887) 18 Q. B. D. 771; 56 L. J. Q. B. 397; 35 W. R. 576; 56 L. T. 662.

It is libellous to write and publish of a colliery company that the cottages let by them to their workmen are situate in a highly insanitary village, and are for the most part unfit for human habitation, from absence of proper and decent conveniences, from inadequate accommodation for the occupants, and from want of sufficient water supply.

> *South Hetton Coal Co., Limited* v. *North Eastern News Association, Limited,* [1894] 1 Q. B. 133; 63 L. J. Q. B. 293; 42 W. R. 322; 69 L. T. 844.

The plaintiff was the manager, conductor, and part-proprietor of a newspaper, printed and published in Market Street, Sydney, and known as the *Evening News.* The defendants conducted a rival newspaper. The *Evening News* contained an account of a boat-race, in which it was stated that the race had been won by M., whereas, as appeared from the context, it had been won by K. The defendants thereupon in their newspaper published this paragraph :— " According to the Market Street Ananias, both K. and M. won the boat-race yesterday. Poor little silly Noozy." *Held,* that as the word " Ananias " was used in relation to the newspaper and not to the plaintiff individually, there was no personal imputation on the plaintiff, and that the jury had properly found a verdict for the defendants.

> *Australian Newspaper Co.* v. *Bennett,* [1894] A. C. 284; 63 L. J. P. C. 105; 70 L. T. 597.

The plaintiffs carried on the business of paint manufacturers, and exported a large quantity of zinc to the East. The defendants, who carried on a similar business, published a report, saying that their white zinc was superior to that of the plaintiffs, which was headed :—" Copy of a report of a trial of Bell Brand . Genuine White Zinc in comparison with Hubbuck's Patent White Zinc," which the plaintiffs alleged to mean that the defendants' white zinc was genuine, but the plaintiffs' was not genuine. *Held,* that these words did not amount to a defamatory libel.

> *Hubbuck and Sons* v. *Wilkinson, Heywood and Clark,* [1899] 1 Q. B. 86; 68 L. J. Q. B. 34; 79 L. T. 429.
> But see *Alcott* v. *Millar's Karri and Jarrah Forests, Ltd., and another,* (1904) 91 L. T. 722; 21 Times L. R. 30.

The plaintiffs and defendants were rival manufacturers of type-setting machinery. The defendants sent to a newspaper for publication the following paragraph :—" The Empire Type-setter in America: *The Union Printer and American Craftsman,* the most wideawake and spirited of American trade journals, has recently contained several references to the Empire composing machines, which were installed in the office of the New York *Evening Sun* with such a flourish of trumpets. From these paragraphs we gather that five machines altogether have been employed in this office—the first being introduced some time in the month of February last, and the other four commencing operations on the 9th March last. So short-lived, however, does this installation appear to have been, that we learn the machines were discontinued on Wednesday, the 29th April, and now the Empire Company is in receipt of notice to remove them altogether in the course of a few days. This will be a very serious blow for this machine." The jury found that these words meant to impute that the plaintiffs were knowingly selling worthless machines. Verdict for the plaintiffs for 500*l*. *Held*, by the House of Lords, that as the words imputed that the plaintiffs sold bad and worthless machines. and as such an imputation was capable of being a libel on the plaintiffs in the way of their trade, the question was properly left to the jury, and that their verdict could not be disturbed.

Linotype Co., Limited v. *British Empire Type-setting Machine Co., Limited*, (1899) 81 L. T. 331 ; 15 Times L. R. 524.

The *onus* of proving that the words are defamatory of the plaintiff and not merely a disparagement of his goods lies on the plaintiff.

Griffiths v. *Benn*, (1911) 27 Times L. R. 346.

CHAPTER III.

SLANDER.

WORDS which are clearly defamatory when written and published may not be actionable when merely spoken. The reasons for the distinction have been already discussed, *ante*, pp. 2—4. Spoken defamatory words are actionable whenever special damage has in fact resulted from their use. They are also actionable when the imputation cast by them on the plaintiff is on the face of it so injurious that the Court will presume, without any proof, that his reputation has been thereby impaired. And the Court will so presume in four cases :—

> I. Where the words charge the plaintiff with the commission of a crime; or,

> II. Impute to him a contagious disease tending to exclude him from society; or,

> III. Are spoken of him in the way of his office, profession, or trade; or

> IV. Impute unchastity or adultery to any woman or girl.

In no other case are spoken words actionable, unless they have caused some special damage to the plaintiff.

I. *Where the Words impute a Crime.*

Spoken words which impute that the plaintiff has been guilty of a crime punishable with imprisonment are actionable without proof of special damage. If the offence imputed be only punishable by penalty or fine, the words will not be actionable *per se*. (*Webb* v. *Beavan*, 11 Q. B. D.

609; 52 L. J. Q. B. 544; 49 L. T. 201; 47 J. P. 488.)
And this is so even where there is power to commit to prison
on non-payment of the penalty or fine.

The Courts to-day show no disposition to enlarge the class of
spoken words actionable *per se.* All indictable offences are punishable with imprisonment; but there are many offences which are
not indictable and yet are punishable summarily with imprisonment in the first instance. Words which merely impute an offence
for which a magistrate can inflict imprisonment only in default of
payment of a fine imposed are not actionable *per se.* (*Hellwig* v.
Mitchell, [1910] 1 K. B. 609; 79 L. J. K. B. 270; 102 L. T. 110;
Michael v. *Spiers & Pond*, (1909) 101 L. T. 352; 25 Times L. R.
740). Words imputing to a licensed victualler that he had been
guilty of an offence against the Licensing Acts would be actionable,
as spoken of him in the way of his trade; and so would words
spoken of a dairyman or grocer falsely alleging that he had been
convicted under the Sale of Food and Drugs Act, 1875.

There has been considerable fluctuation of opinion as to the exact
limits of this rule. In Queen Elizabeth's days some judges considered that words were actionable which imputed to the plaintiff
conduct which would be sufficient ground for binding him over to
good behaviour. (See *Sir Edward Bray* v. *Andrews*, (1564) Moore,
63; *Lady Cockaine's Case*, (1586) Cro. Eliz. 49; *Tibbott* v. *Haynes*,
(1590) Cro. Eliz. 191.) In Queen Anne's reign, on the other hand,
Holt, C.J., in *Ogden* v. *Turner*, 6 Mod. 104; Holt, 40; 2 Salk. 696,
laid it down that every charge of treason or felony was actionable,
but not every charge of misdemeanour, only of such as entail a
"scandalous" and "infamous" punishment. We presume, however,
this will include all indictable misdemeanours, except such semi-
civil proceedings as an indictment for the obstruction or non-repair
of a highway.

It is not necessary that the defendant should specify the crime
imputed, if it is clear that the plaintiff is accused of some crime
punishable with imprisonment. An innuendo, "meaning thereby
that the plaintiff had been and was guilty of having committed some
criminal offence or offences," was held sufficient in *Webb* v. *Beavan*,
11 Q. B. D. 609; 52 L. J. Q. B. 544; 49 L. T. 201; 47 J. P. 488

Illustrations.

A general charge of felony is actionable, though it does not specify any particular felony. *E.g.:*

" If you had had your deserts, you would have been hanged before now."

> *Donne's Case,* Cro. Eliz. 62.

" You have committed an act for which I can transport you."

> *Curtis* v. *Curtis,* 10 Bing. 477 ; 3 M. & Scott, 819 ; 4 M. & Scott, 337.

" You have done many things for which you ought to be hanged, and I will have you hanged."

> *Francis* v. *Roose,* 3 M. & W. 191 ; 1 H. & H. 36.

" I have got a warrant for Tempest. I shall transport him for felony."

> *Tempest* v. *Chambers,* 1 Stark. 67.

" I will lock you up in Gloucester gaol next week. I know enough to put you there."

> *Webb* v. *Beavan,* 11 Q. B. D. 609 ; 52 L. J. Q. B. 544 ; 49 L. T. 201 ;
> 47 J. P. 488.

So are all charges of specific felonies. *E.g.:*

Assault with intent to rob :—

> *Lewknor* v.ᵉ *Cruchley and wife,* Cro. Car. 140.

Attempt to murder :—

> *Scot et ux.* v. *Hilliar,* Lane, 98 ; 1 Vin. Abr. 440.
> *Preston* v. *Pinder,* Cro. Eliz. 308.

Bigamy :—

> *Heming et ux.* v. *Power,* 10 M. & W. 564.
> *Delany* v. *Jones,* 4 Esp. 191.

Demanding money with menaces :—

> *Neve* v. *Cross,* Sty. 350.

Embezzlement :—

> *Williams* v. *Stott,* 1 C. & M. 675 ; 3 Tyrw. 688.

Forgery :—

> *Baal* v. *Baggerley,* Cro. Car. 326.
> *Jones* v. *Herne,* 2 Wils. 87.

Housebreaking :—

> *Somers* v. *House,* Holt, 39 ; Skin. 364.

Larceny :—

> *Foster* v. *Browning,* Cro. Jac. 688.
> *Baker* v. *Pierce,* 2 Ld. Raym. 959 ; Holt, 654 ; 6 Mod. 23 ; 2 Salk.
> 695.
> *Slowman* v. *Dutton,* 10 Bing. 402.
> *Tomlinson* v. *Brittlebank,* 4 B. & Ad. 630 ; 1 N. & M. 455.

Manslaughter :—

> *Ford* v. *Primrose,* 5 D. & R. 287.
> *Edsall* v. *Russell,* 4 M. & G. 1090 ; 5 Scott, N. R. 801 ; 2 Dowl. N. S.
> 641 ; 12 L. J. C. P. 4 ; 6 Jur. 996.

Murder :—

> *Peake* v. *Oldham,* Cowp. 275 ; S. C. *sub nom. Oldham* v. *Peake,* 2
> W. Bl. 959.
> *Button* v. *Hayward,* 8 Mod. 24.

Receiving stolen goods, knowing them to have been stolen :—

> *Brigg's Case,* Godb. 157.
> *Clarke's Case de Dorchester,* 2 Rolle's Rep. 136.
> *Alfred* v. *Farlow,* 8 Q. B. 854 ; 15 L. J. Q. B. 258 ; 10 Jur. 714.

Robbery :—

> *Lawrence* v. *Woodward*, Cro. Car. 277 ; 1 Roll. Abr. 74.
>
> *Rowcliffe* v. *Edmonds et ux.*, 7 M. & W. 12 ; 4 Jur. 684.

Treason :—

> *Sir William Waldegrave* v. *Ralph Agas*, Cro. Eliz. 191.
>
> *Stapleton* v. *Frier*, Cro. Eliz. 251.
>
> *Fry* v. *Carne*, 8 Mod. 283.

Unnatural offences :—

> *Thompson* v. *Nye*, 16 Q. B. 175; 20 L. J. Q. B. 85 ; 15 Jur.
> 285.
>
> *Woolnoth* v. *Meadows*, 5 East, 463; 2 Smith, 28.
>
> *Colman* v. *Godwin*, 3 Dougl. 90 ; 2 B. & C. 285, n.

So it is actionable without proof of special damage to charge another with the commission of the following misdemeanours :—

Bribery and corruption :—

> *Bendish* v. *Lindsay*, 11 Mod. 194.

Cheating at cards :—

> *Gordon Cumming* v. *Green and others*, (1891) 7 Times L. R. 408.

Conspiracy :—

> *Tibbott* v. *Haynes*, Cro. Eliz. 191.

Keeping a bawdy-house :—

> *Brayne* v. *Cooper*, 5 M. & W. 249.
>
> *Huckle* v. *Reynolds*, 7 C. B. N. S. 114.

Libel :—

> *Sir William Russell* v. *Ligon*, 1 Roll. Abr. 46 ; 1 Vin. Abr. 423.

Perjury :—

> *Ceely* v. *Hoskins*, Cro. Car. 509.
>
> *Holt* v. *Scholefield*, 6 T. R. 691.
>
> *Roberts* v. *Camden*, 9 East, 93.

Even in an ecclesiastical Court.

> *Shaw* v. *Thompson*, Cro. Eliz. 609.

Soliciting another to commit a crime :—

> *Sir Thomas Cockaine and wife* v. *Witnam*, Cro. Eliz. 49.
>
> *Leversage* v. *Smith*, Cro. Eliz. 710.
>
> *Tibbott* v. *Haynes*, Cro. Eliz. 191.
>
> *Passie* v. *Mondford*, Cro. Eliz. 747.
>
> *Deane* v. *Eton*, 1 Buls. 201.
>
> *Sir Harbert Crofts* v. *Brown*, 3 Buls. 167.

Subornation of perjury : —

> *Guerdon* v. *Winterstud*, Cro. Eliz. 308.
>
> *Harris* v. *Dixon*, Cro. Jac. 158.
>
> *Bridges* v. *Playdel*, Brownl. & Golds. 2.
>
> *Harrison* v. *Thornborough*, 10 Mod. 196 ; Gilbert's Cases in Law &
> Eq. 114.

Where the words impute merely a trespass in pursuit of game, punishable primarily by fine alone, no action lies without proof of special damage, although imprisonment in the pillory may be inflicted in default of payment of the fine (3 Wm. & M. c. 10).

> *Ogden* v. *Turner*, (1705) 6 Mod. 104; 2 Salk. 696 ; Holt, 40.

[Certain *dicta* in this case which appear to go further were disapproved of by De Grey, C.J., in 3 Wils. 186, and must be now considered as bad law.]

Where the words imputed an offence against the Fishery Acts punishable only by fine and forfeiture of the nets and instruments used : *Held*, that no action lay without proof of special damage.

McCabe v. *Foot*, 18 Ir. Jur. (Vol. xi. N. S.) 287 ; 15 L. T. 115.

And even where an offence is punishable with a fine or penalty, and in default of payment thereof with imprisonment, an action will not lie for spoken words imputing the offence, unless the defendant can prove special damage.

> *Hellwig* v. *Mitchell*, [1910] 1 K. B. 609 ; 79 L. J. K. B. 270 ; 102 L. T. 110 ; 26 Times L. R. 244.
>
> *Michael* v. *Spiers and Pond*, (1909) 101 L. T. 352 ; 25 Times L. R. 740.

Defendant charged plaintiff with a breach of the 9th bye-law of the Great Western Railway Company, which is punishable with a penalty of 42*s.* only. Field, J., held that no action lay.

> *Preston* v. *De Windt*, *Times*, July 7th, 1884.

In Maryland adultery is still an offence against the State, but punishable only by fine. Hence to impute adultery to a married woman is not actionable there. (We believe this is the only one of the United States in which the law is so.)

> *Griffin* v. *Moore*, 43 Maryland, 246.
>
> *Shafer* v. *Ahalt*, 48 Maryland, 171 ; 30 Amer. Rep. 456.

Words which merely impute a criminal intention, not yet put into action, are not actionable. Guilty thoughts are not a crime. But as soon as sufficient steps have been taken to carry out such intention, an attempt to commit a crime has been made ; and every attempt to commit an indictable offence is at common law a misdemeanour, and in itself indictable. To impute such an attempt is therefore clearly actionable.

> *Harrison* v. *Stratton*, 4 Esp. 217.

Words imputing a purely military offence are not actionable without proof of special damage.

> *Hollingsworth* v. *Shaw*, 19 Ohio St. 430.

But where the speaker makes no definite charge of crime but uses words which merely disclose a doubt or suspicion that is in his mind, no action lies, without proof of special damage.

Illustrations.

The clerk of the Crown for the Island of Grenada said of the plaintiff, " He lies here under suspicion of having murdered a man named *Emanuel Vancrossen* at the *Spout* some years ago," and also, " Haven't you heard that *Charles Simmons* is suspected of having murdered one *Vancrossen*, his brother-in-law ? A proclamation offering a reward for the apprehension of the murderer is now in my office, and there is only one link wanting to complete the case." *Held*, that this amounted at the most to words of mere suspicion, and that no action lay.

> *Simmons* v. *Mitchell*, 6 App. Cas. 156 ; 50 L. J. P. C. 11 ; 29 W. R. 401 ; 43 L. T. 710 ; 45 J. P. 237.

The following words do not amount to a charge of larceny :—
" You as good as stole the canoe,"

> *Stokes* v. *Arey*, 8 Jones (North Carolina) 66.

Or, " A man that would do that would steal."

> *Stees* v. *Kemble*, 3 Casey (27 Penna. St.) 112.

So, to say, " You will be a thief ere long " is not actionable.

> Per Tirrell, J., in *Annison* v. *Blofeld*, Carter, 214.

The words, " I will take him to Bow Street on a charge of forgery," are not actionable, for they do not necessarily mean that the plaintiff had committed any felony.

> *Harrison* v. *King*, 4 Price, 46 ; 7 Taunt. 431.

The words " I charge him with felony," were held insufficient in three cases.

> *Poland* v. *Mason*, (1620) Hob. 305, 326.
>
> *Wheeler* v. *Poplestone*, (1624) 1 Roll. Abr. 72.
>
> *King* v. *Merrick*, (1626) Popham, 210 ; Latch, 175 ; 1 Roll. Abr. 73.

But, " Bear witness, my masters, I arrest him of felony," was held sufficient in

> *Serle* v. *Maunder*, (1620) 1 Roll. Abr. 72.

The words were, " I have a suspicion that you and Bone have robbed my house, and therefore I take you into custody." At the trial, Pollock, C.B., told the jury that if they found that the defendant meant to impute to the plaintiff an absolute charge of felony, in such case the plaintiff was entitled to the verdict ; but, on the other hand, if they should think that he imputed a mere suspicion of felony, the defendant would be entitled to the verdict. Verdict for defendant. *Held*, that the direction and the verdict were right.

> *Tozer* v. *Mashford*, 6 Exch. 539 ; 20 L. J. Ex. 225.

But the words " I have got a warrant for Tempest. I will advertise a reward for 20 guineas to apprehend him. I shall transport him for felony," were properly found by the jury to amount to a substantive charge of felony.

> *Tempest* v. *Chambers*, 1 Stark. 67.

An action lies for these words : " Many an honester man has been hanged ; and a robbery hath been committed, and I think he was at it ; and I think he is a horse-stealer."

> *Stich* v. *Wisedome*, Cro. Eliz. 348.

And for these : " I think in my conscience if Sir John might have his will, he would kill the king."

> *Sidnam* v. *Mayo*, 1 Roll. Rep. 427 ; Cro. Jac. 407.
>
> *Peake* v. *Oldham*, Cowp. 275 ; 2 Wm. Bl. 959, *post*, p. 140.

The words were : " He is under a charge of a prosecution for perjury. *Griffith Williams* (meaning an attorney of that name) has the Attorney-General's directions to prosecute for perjury." Defendant did not justify. After verdict for the plaintiff it was moved in arrest of judgment that the words were not actionable, as they do not amount to an assertion that the charge is well founded. Lord Ellenborough, C.J., said : " These words fairly and naturally construed, appear to us to have been meant, and to be calculated to convey the imputation

of perjury actually committed by the person of whom they are spoken; " and
the verdict and judgment stood.

> *Roberts* v. *Camden*, 9 East, 93.

It is not necessary that the words should accuse the
plaintiff of some fresh, undiscovered crime, so as to put
him in jeopardy or cause his arrest. Of course, if such
consequences have followed, they may be alleged as special
damage, but where such consequences are impossible, the
words are still actionable. Thus, to call a man a returned
convict, or otherwise to impute falsely that he has been
tried and convicted of a criminal offence, is actionable
without proof of special damage.

It is at least quite as injurious to the plaintiff's reputation, to
say that he has in fact been convicted, as to say that he will be, or
ought to be, convicted. Many think that such statements should be
actionable, even when true, if they are maliciously or unnecessarily
volunteered. See *post*, p. 190.

Illustrations.

It is actionable without proof of special damage to say of the plaintiff that—
He had been in Launceston gaol and was burnt in the hand for coining.

> *Gainford* v. *Tuke*, Cro. Jac. 536.

He "was in Winchester gaol, and tried for his life, and would have been
hanged, had it not been for Leggatt, for breaking open the granary of Farmer A.
and stealing his bacon." [Note here that the speaker appears to admit that the
plaintiff was acquitted, but still asserts that he was in fact guilty.]

> *Carpenter* v. *Tarrant*, Cas. temp. Hardwicke, 339.

" He was a thief and stole my gold." It was argued here that " was " denotes
time past; so that it may have been when he was a child, and therefore no
larceny; or in the time of Queen Elizabeth, since when there had been divers
general pardons; *Sed per cur.*: " It is a great scandal to be once a thief; for
pœna potest redimi, culpa perennis erit."

> *Boston* v. *Tatam*, Cro. Jac. 623.

It is actionable to call a man " thief " or " felon," even though he once committed larceny, if after conviction he was pardoned either under the Great Seal
or by some general statute of pardon.

> *Cuddington* v. *Wilkins*, Hobart, 67, 81 ; 2 Hawk. P. C. c. 37, s. 48.
>
> *Leyman* v. *Latimer and others*, 3 Ex. D. 15, 352 ; 46 L. J. Ex. 765 ;
>   47 L. J. Ex. 470 ; 25 W. R. 751 ; 26 W. R. 305 ; 37 L. T. 360,
>   819.

It is actionable to call a man falsely " a returned convict."

> *Fowler* v. *Dowdney*, 2 M. & Rob. 119.
>
> And see *Bell* v. *Byrne*, 13 East, 554.

In dealing with old cases on this point, care must be taken to remember the state of the criminal law as it existed at the date when the slander was uttered.

Illustrations.

So long as the 18 Eliz. c. 3 was in force, it was actionable to charge a woman with being the mother, a man with being the putative father, of a bastard child chargeable to the parish.

> *Anne Davis's Case*, 4 Rep. 17; 2 Salk. 694; 1 Roll. Abr. 38.
>
> *Salter* v. *Browne*, Cro. Car. 436; 1 Roll. Abr. 37.

So long as the penal statutes against Roman Catholics were in force, it was actionable to say " He goes to mass," or " He harboured his son, knowing him to be a Romish priest."

> *Walden* v. *Mitchell*, 2 Ventr. 265.
>
> *Smith* v. *Flynt*, Cro. Jac. 300.

Secus, before such statutes were passed.

> *Pierepoint's Case*, Cro. Eliz. 308.

So in many old cases such words as " She is a witch " were held actionable, the statute 1 Jac. I. c. 11 being then in force. But that statute is now repealed by the 9 Geo. II. c. 5, s. 3, which also expressly provides that no action shall lie for charging another with witchcraft, sorcery, or any such offence.

> *Rogers* v. *Gravat*, Cro. Eliz. 571.
>
> *Hughs* v. *Farrer*, Cro. Car. 141.
>
> *Dacy* v. *Clinch*, Sid. 53.

It was formerly the custom of the City of London, of the borough of Southwark, and also, it is said, of the City of Bristol, to cart whores. Hence, to call a woman a " whore" or " strumpet " in one of those cities is actionable, if the action be brought in the City Courts, which take notice of their own customs without proof. But no action lay in the Superior Courts at Westminster for such words, because such custom had never been certified by the Recorder, and strict proof of it was very difficult. To accuse a man of adultery or fornication was never ground for an action in the civil Courts. The person accused had a remedy in the spiritual Courts till the 18 & 19 Vict. c. 41; now he has none. See *post*, pp. 69—72.

> *Oxford et ux.* v. *Cross*, (1599) 5 Rep. 18.
>
> *Hassell* v. *Capcot*, (1639) 1 Vin. Abr. 395; 1 Roll. Abr. 36.
>
> *Cook* v. *Wingfield*, 1 Str. 555.
>
> *Roberts* v. *Herbert*, Sid. 97; 1 Keble, 418.
>
> *Stainton et ux.* v. *Jones*, 2 Selw. N. P. 1205 (13th edn.); 1 Dougl. 380, n.
>
> *Theyer* v. *Eastwick*, 4 Burr. 2032.
>
> *Brand and wife* v. *Roberts and wife*, 4 Burr. 2418.
>
> *Vicars* v. *Worth*, 1 Str. 471.

So, in Queen Elizabeth's days, it was held that no action lay for saying, " He keeps a bawdy-house; " " for, by the common law, he is not punishable, but by the custom of London ; and therefore this action ought to have been sued in the spiritual Court" (*dissentiente* Glanvile).

> *Anon.*, (1598) Cro. Eliz. 643; Noy, 73.

But by 1606 the opinion of Glanvile prevailed; and such words were held actionable; "the keeping of a brothel-house is inquirable in the leet, and so a temporal offence."

> *Thorne* v. *Alice Durham*, (1606) Noy, 117.
> And see *Plunket* v. *Gilmore*, (1724) Fortescue, 211.
> *Grove and wife* v. *Hart*, (1752) Sayer, 33 ; Buller's N. P. 7.

It was not apparently clear law till the beginning of the last century (*R.* v. *Higgins*, (1801) 2 East, 5 ; *R.* v. *Philipps*, (1805) 6 East, 464) that it was a misdemeanour to solicit another to commit a crime, although the person solicited did nothing in consequence. Hence, in the following cases words were held not to be actionable, because no overt act was alleged to have followed the solicitation. They would be held actionable now.

> *Sir Edward Bray* v. *Andrews*, (1564) Moore, 63.
> *Eaton* v. *Allen*, (1598) 4 Rep. 16 ; Cro. Eliz. 684.
> *Sir Harbert Crofts* v. *Brown*, (1617) 3 Buls. 167.

It was held in 1602 that no action lay for saying "Master Barham did burn my barn with his own hands ; " for at that date it was not felony to burn a barn unless it were either full of corn or parcel of a mansion-house ; and the defendant had not stated that his barn was either.

> *Barham's Case*, (1602) 4 Rep. 20 ; Yelv. 21.

So it was in 1602 held not actionable to say :—" Thou hast received stolen swine, and thou knowest they were stolen ; " for receiving is not a common law offence, unless it amounts to comforting and assisting the felon as an accessory after the fact. But ever since 3 Wm. & M. c. 9, s. 4, and 4 Geo. I. c. 11, such words would be clearly actionable.

> *Dawes* v. *Bolton* or *Boughton*, Cro. Eliz. 888 ; 1 Roll. Abr. 68.
> *Cox* v. *Humphrey*, Cro. Eliz. 889.

A charge of deer stealing would be actionable now, although in 1705 it was held not actionable, because it was subject only to a penalty of 30*l.*

> *Ogden* v. *Turner*, 2 Salk. 696 ; Holt, 40 ; 6 Mod. 104.

So now it would of course be actionable to accuse a man of secreting a will, though such an accusation was held not actionable in

> *Godfrey* v. *Owen*, Palm. 21 ; 3 Salk. 327.

And is still apparently not actionable in America.

> *O'Hanlon* v. *Myers*, 10 Rich. 128.

Where a vicar of a parish falsely declared that the plaintiff, a parishioner, was excommunicated, it was held an action lay, possibly because the person excommunicated was at that date liable to imprisonment under the writ *de excommunicato capiendo ;* but there seems to have been some allegation of special damage in the declaration.

> *Barnabas* v. *Traunter*, 1 Vin. Abr. 396.

In South Carolina it was formerly actionable to call a white or his wife a mulatto.

> *Eden* v. *Legare*, 1 Bay, 171.
> *Atkinson* v. *Hartley*, 8 McCord, 203.
> *King* v. *Wood*, 1 Nott & M. (South Car.) 184.

The words must clearly impute a crime punishable with imprisonment, although they need not state the charge

with all the precision of an indictment. If merely fraud,
dishonesty, or vice, not amounting to crime, be imputed,
no action lies without proof of special damage. And even
where words of specific import are employed (such as
" thief " or " traitor "), still no action lies if the defendant
can satisfy the jury that they were not intended to impute a
crime, but merely as general terms of abuse, and meant no
more than " rogue " or " scoundrel," and were so understood
by all who heard the conversation. But if the bystanders
reasonably understand the words as definitely charging the
plaintiff with the commission of a crime, an action lies.

Illustrations.

" You forged my name ; " these words are actionable, although it is not stated
to what deed or instrument.

> *Jones* v. *Herne*, 2 Wils. 87.
> Overruling *Anon.*, 3 Leon. 231 ; 1 Roll. Abr. 65.

To say that a man is " forsworn " or " has taken a false oath " is not a sufficiently definite charge of perjury ; for there is no reference to any judicial proceeding. But to say " Thou art forsworn in a Court of record " is a sufficient
charge of perjury ; for this will be taken to mean that he was forsworn while
giving evidence in a Court of record.

> *Stanhope* v. *Blith*, (1585) 4 Rep. 15.
> *Holt* v. *Scholefield*, 6 T. R. 691.
> *Ceely* v. *Hoskins*, Cro. Car. 509.

To say " I have been robbed of three dozen winches ; you bought two, one at
3s., one at 2s. ; you knew well when you bought them that they cost me three
times as much making as you gave for them, and that they could not have been
honestly come by," is a sufficient charge of receiving stolen goods, knowing them
to have been *stolen*. [An indictment which merely alleged that the prisoner
knew the goods were not honestly come by would be bad. *R.* v. *Wilson*, 2
Mood. C. C. 52.]

> *Alfred* v. *Farlow*, 8 Q B. 854 ; 15 L. J. Q. B. 258 ; 10 Jur. 714.

" He is a pickpocket ; he picked my pocket of my money," was once held an
insufficient charge of larceny.

> *Walls* or *Watts* v. *Rymes*, 2 Lev. 51 ; 1 Ventr. 213 ; 3 Salk. 325.

But now this would clearly be held sufficient.

> *Baker* v. *Pierce*, 2 Ld. Raym. 959 ; Holt, 654 ; 6 Mod. 23 ; 2 Salk. 695.
> *Stebbing* v. *Warner*, 11 Mod. 255.

" He has defrauded a mealman of a roan horse " held not to imply a criminal
act of fraud ; as it is not stated that the mealman was induced to part with his
property by means of any false pretence.

> *Richardson* v. *Allen*, 2 Chit. 657.
> *Needham* v. *Dowling*, 15 L. J. C. P. 9.

To say of a barman that he removed from his house owing a month's rent, and that his landlord could not get the money from him, is not actionable without proof of special damage.

> *Speake* v. *Hughes,* [1904] 1 K. B. 138 ; 73 L. J. K. B. 172 ; 89 L. T. 576.

It is not actionable without proof of special damage to say of a man that he has not paid his bets,

> *Smith and another* v. *Willoughby,* (1899) 15 Times L. R. 314 ;

Or to say that he has committed a breach of the peace, which is not indictable,

> *Hellwig* v. *Mitchell,* [1910] 1 K. B. 609 ; 79 L. J. K. B. 270 ; 102 L. T. 110 ; 26 Times L. R. 244 ;

Or to say that he has been disorderly or drunk on licensed premises and been ejected therefrom.

> *Hellwig* v. *Mitchell, suprà.*
>
> *Michael* v. *Spiers & Pond,* (1909) 101 L. T. 352 ; 25 Times L. R. 740.

So none of the following words are actionable without proof of special damage :—

"A cheat" :—

> *Savage* v. *Robery,* 2 Salk. 694 ; 5 Mod. 398.
>
> *Davis* v. *Miller et ux.,* 2 Str. 1169.

"A fraud" :—

> *Agnew* v. *British Legal Life Assurance Co.,* (1906) 8 F. 422 (Ct. of Sess.).

"Swindler" :—

> *Savile* v. *Jardine,* 2 H. Bl. 531.
>
> *Black* v. *Hunt,* 2 L. R. Ir. 10.
>
> *Ward* v. *Weeks,* 7 Bing. 211 ; 4 M. & P. 796.

"Rogue," "rascal," "villain," &c. :—

> *Stanhope* v. *Blith,* 4 Rep. 15.

"Runagate" :—

> *Cockaine* v. *Hopkins,* 2 Lev. 214.

"Cozener" :—

> *Brunkard* v. *Segar,* Cro. Jac. 427 ; Hutt. 13 ; 1 Vin. Abr. 427.

"Common-filcher" :—

> *Goodale* v. *Castle,* Cro. Eliz. 554.

"Welcher" :—

> *Blackman* v. *Bryant,* 27 L. T. 491.

But "welcher" is actionable, if the jury are satisfied the word means "one who takes money from those who make bets with him, intending to keep such money for himself and never to part with it again," for such conduct is criminal.

> *Williams* v. *Magyer, Times,* March 1st, 1883.
>
> *R.* v. *Buckmaster,* 20 Q. B. D. 182 ; 57 L. J. M. C. 25 ; 36 W. R. 701 ; 57 L. T. 720.

The words "gambler," "black-leg," "black-sheep," are not actionable unless it can be shown that the bystanders understood them to mean "a cheating gambler punishable by the criminal law."

> *Barnett* v. *Allen,* 3 H. & N. 376 ; 27 L. J. Ex. 412 ; 1 F. & F. 125 ; 4 Jur. N. S. 488.
>
> *Gordon Cumming* v. *Green and others,* (1891) 7 Times L. R. 408.

But it is actionable to say of A. that he has brought a blackmailing action against B.

> *Marks* v. *Samuel*, [1904] 2 K. B. 287 ; 73 L. J. K. B. 587 ; 53 W. R. 88 ; 90 L. T. 590 ; 20 Times L. R. 430.

If the crime imputed be one of which the plaintiff could not by any possibility be guilty, and all who heard the imputation knew that he could not by any possibility be guilty of it, no action lies, for the plaintiff is never in jeopardy, nor is his reputation in any way impaired. (Buller's N. P. 5.)

In America this doctrine was carried to great lengths. If one joint owner accused his partner of stealing the joint property, no action lay, because a joint owner cannot steal the joint property. But now the more sensible rule prevails, that if the words would convey an imputation of felony to the minds of ordinary hearers unversed in legal technicalities, an action lies, *e.g.*, where an infant is accused of a crime, and nothing is said about special malice. (*Stewart* v. *Howe*, 17 Ill. 71 ; and see *Chambers* v. *White*, 2 Jones, 383, as to physical inability to commit the crime alleged.) The words are actionable if they are calculated to induce the belief that the plaintiff had committed a crime. (*Drummond* v. *Leslie*, 5 Blackf. (Indiana) 453.)

Illustrations.

Words complained of :—" Thou hast killed my wife." Everyone who heard the words knew at the time that defendant's wife was still alive : they could not therefore understand the word " kill " to mean " murder."

> *Snag* v. *Gee*, 4 Rep. 16, as explained by Parke, B. in *Heming* v. *Power*, 10 M. & W. 569.
>
> And see *Web* v. *Poor*, Cro. Eliz. 569.
>
> *Talbot* v. *Case*, Cro. Eliz. 823.
>
> *Dacy* v. *Clinch*, Sid. 53.
>
> *Jacob* v. *Mills*, 1 Ventr. 117 ; Cro. Jac. 343.

It is no slander to say of a churchwarden that he stole the bell-ropes of his parish church; for they are officially his property, and a man cannot steal his own goods. [But such words might be actionable as a charge on him in his office.]

> *Jackson* v. *Adams*, 2 Bing. N. C. 402 ; 2 Scott, 599 ; 1 Hodges, 339.

It is no slander to say of a husband : " He robbed his wife of 75*l.* ; " because at common law no such offence can be committed. It would be a slander, however, if the words imputed that he stole his wife's money while they were living apart, or when he was about to desert her, as then criminal proceedings would be possible under section 12 of the Married Women's Property Act, 1882.

> *Lemon* v. *Simmons*, (1888) 57 L. J. Q. B. 260 ; 36 W. R. 351 ; 4 Times L. R. 306.

But where a married woman said, " You stole my faggots," and it was argued for the defendant that a married woman could not own faggots and therefore no one could steal faggots of hers, the Court construed the words according to common sense and ordinary usage to mean, " You stole my husband's faggots."

> *Stamp and wife* v. *White and wife*, Cro. Jac. 600.
>
> -　*Charnel's Case*, Cro. Eliz. 279.

So it is not actionable for A. to charge a man who is not A.'s clerk or servant with embezzling A.'s money ; for no indictment for embezzlement would lie. [But surely this can only be the case where the bystanders are aware of the exact relationship between A. and the plaintiff.　And now see the Larceny Act, 1901 (1 Edw. VII. c. 10).]

> *Williams* v. *Stott*, (1833) 1 C. & M. 675 ; 3 Tyrw. 688.

II.　*Where the Words impute a Contagious Disease.*

Words imputing to the plaintiff that he has an infectious or contagious disease are actionable without proof of special damage.　For the effect of such an imputation is naturally to exclude the plaintiff from society.　Such disease may be either leprosy, venereal disease, or, it seems, the plague (*Villers* v. *Monsley*, 2 Wils. 403) ; but not the itch, the falling sickness, or the small-pox.　The words must distinctly impute that the plaintiff has the disease at the time of publication : an assertion that he *has had* such a disease would not cause him to be shunned.　(*Carslake* v. *Mapledoram*, 2 T. R. 473 ; *Taylor* v. *Hall*, 2 Str. 1189.)

Any words which the hearers would naturally understand as conveying that the plaintiff then has such a disease are sufficient.　Many distinctions are drawn in old cases about the pox, a word which may imply either the actionable syphilis, or the less objectionable small-pox.　It has been decided that " he has the pox " (*simpliciter*) shall be taken to mean " he has the small-pox ; " but that if any other words be used referring to the effects of the disease, or the way in which it was caught, or even the medicine taken to cure it, these may be referred to as determining which pox was meant.

Illustrations.

To say of a person, " He hath the falling sickness," is not actionable unless it be spoken of him in the way of his profession or trade.

> *Taylor* v. *Perr*, (1607) 1 Rolle's Abr. 44.

To say to the plaintiff in the presence of others, " Thou art a leprous knave," is actionable.

> *Taylor* v. *Perkins*, (1607) Cro. Jac. 144 ; 1 Rolle's Abr. 44.

To say of the plaintiff that " He hath the pox" is actionable, whenever the word " wench " or " whore " occurs in the same sentence.

> *Brook* v. *Wise*, (1601) Cro. Eliz. 878.
> *Pye* v. *Wallis*, (1658) Carter, 55.
> *Grimes* v. *Lovel*, 12 Mod. 242.
> *Whitfield* v. *Powel*, 12 Mod. 248.
> *Clifton* v. *Wells*, 12 Mod. 634.
> *Bloodworth* v. *Gray*, 7 M. & Gr. 334 ; 8 Scott, N. R. 9.
> And see *Clerk* v. *Dyer*, 8 Mod. 290.

III. Public Offices, Professions, and Trades.

Words which disparage the plaintiff in the way of his office, profession, or trade are actionable without proof of any special damage. It must injure the plaintiff's reputation to disparage him in his very means of livelihood. Where the Court sees that the words spoken affect the plaintiff in his office, profession, or trade, and directly tend to prejudice him therein, they ask for no further proof of damage.

Where a special kind of knowledge is essential to the proper conduct of a particular profession, denying that the plaintiff possesses such special knowledge will be actionable, if the plaintiff belongs to that particular profession, but not otherwise. For example, words may be actionable when spoken of a physician or lawyer which would not be actionable of a trader or a clerk.

But it is not the law that any words spoken to the disparagement of an officer, professional man, or trader, will *ipso facto* be actionable *per se*. Words to be actionable on this ground, "must *touch* the plaintiff in his office, profession, or trade : " that is, they must be shown to have been spoken of the plaintiff in relation thereto, and to be such as would prejudice him therein. They must impeach either his skill or knowledge, or attack his conduct therein. His special office or profession need not be expressly named or referred to, if the charge made be such as must necessarily affect him in it. And in determining whether the words used would necessarily so affect the plaintiff, regard must be had to the mental and moral requirements of the office he holds, or the profession or trade he carries on. Where integrity and ability are essential to the due conduct of plaintiff's office or profession, words impugning his integrity or ability are clearly actionable; for they then imply that he is unfit to continue therein. But words which merely charge the plaintiff with some misconduct outside his office, or not connected with his special profession or trade, will not be actionable. " Every authority, which I have been able to find, either shows the want of some general requisite, as honesty, capacity, fidelity, &c., or connects the imputation with the plaintiff's office, trade, or business." (Per Bayley, B., in *Lumby* v. *Allday*, 1 Cr. & J. at pp. 305, 306, cited with approval by Lord Denman, C.J., in *Ayre* v. *Craven*, 2 A. & E. at p. 8, and by Lord Herschell, L.C., in *Alexander* v. *Jenkins*, [1892] 1 Q. B. at p. 800.)

Whether or no the words were spoken of the plaintiff in the way of his office, profession, or business, is a question for the jury to determine at the trial. (Per Cockburn, C.J., in *Ramsdale* v. *Greenacre*, 1 F. & F. 61.) The jury must be satisfied that the words were so spoken, and that the plaintiff held such office, or was actively engaged in such profession or trade, at the time the words were spoken. (*Moore* v. *Synne*, 2 Rolle's Rep. 84; *Collis* v. *Malin*, Cro. Car. 282; *Bellamy* v. *Burch*, 16 M. & W. 590.) If not, proof of special damage will be required. (*Hopwood* v. *Thorn*, 8 C. B. 293; 19 L. J. C. P. 94.) There should always be an averment in the Statement of Claim that the words were so spoken; though, where the words are clearly of such a nature as necessarily to affect the plaintiff in his office, profession, or business, the omission of such an averment will not be fatal. (*Stanton* v. *Smith*, 2 Ld. Raym. 1480; 2 Str. 762; *Jones* v. *Littler*, 7 M. & W. 423; 10 L. J. Ex. 171.)

Offices, Paid and Honorary.

An action of slander will lie without proof of special damage for words imputing dishonesty or malversation in a public office of trust, whether the office be one of profit or not, and whether there is a power of removal from the office for such conduct as is alleged, or not. An action of slander will also lie without proof of special damage, whenever there is a power of removal from the office, and the words complained of impute to the plaintiff conduct which, if true, would be good ground for his dismissal. But where the words merely impute general unfitness for (as distinct from misconduct in) an office, there no action lies if the office be honorary, as in the case of a sheriff, a justice of the peace, an alderman, town councillor, or vestryman; though it will lie, if the office be one of profit.

The office held by the plaintiff need not be one of profit; it may be honorary, as in the case of an M.P. or a justice of the peace. The gist of an action for slander is the injury to the plaintiff's reputation, and not any presumed loss of money. Although there is no emolument attached to his office, so that his removal from it would involve no pecuniary loss, still to be dismissed from such an office would be a most serious injury to his reputation. He can recover damages, therefore, for any words which, if believed, would be ground for his removal. (See *post* pp. 56—60.) A barrister may sue for any slander imputing professional misconduct, although in contemplation of law his fees are mere gratuities; for such words will injure him in his profession, and also will probably cause him pecuniary loss.

The plaintiff must always aver on the pleadings that he was carrying on the profession or trade, or holding the office, at the time the words were spoken. Sometimes this is admitted by the slander itself, and if so, evidence is of course unnecessary in proof of this averment. (*Yrisarri* v. *Clement*, 2 C. & P. 223; 3 Bing. 432.) But in other cases, unless it is admitted on the pleadings, evidence must be given at the trial of the special character in which plaintiff sues. As a rule, it is sufficient for plaintiff to prove that he was acting in the office or actively engaged in the profession or trade without proving any appointment thereto, or producing a diploma or other formal qualification. *Omnia presumuntur rite esse acta.* (*Rutherford* v. *Evans*, 4 C. & P. 79; 6 Bing. 451; *Berryman* v. *Wise*, 4 T. R. 366; *Cannell* v. *Curtis*, 2 Bing. N. C. 228.) That he so acted on one occasion before the one in question is evidence to go to the jury. (*R.* v. *Murphy*, 8 C. & P. 297.) But there is an exception to this rule where the very slander complained of imputes to a medical or legal practitioner that he is a quack or impostor, not legally qualified for practice : here the plaintiff must be prepared to prove his qualification strictly by producing diplomas or certificates duly sealed, signed and stamped. (*Collins* v. *Carnegie*, 3 N. & M. 703; 1 A. & E. 695; *Moises* v. *Thornton*, 8 T. R. 303; *Wakley* v. *Healey and Cooke*, 4 Exch. 53; 18 L. J. Ex. 426.)

"It is quite clear that as regards a man's business, or profession, or office, if it be an office of profit, the mere imputation of want of ability to discharge the duties of that office is sufficient to support an action. It is not necessary that there should be imputation of immoral or disgraceful conduct. It must be either something said of him in his office or business which may damage him in that office or business, or it must relate to some quality which would show that he is a man who, by reason of his want of ability or honesty, is unfit to hold the office. So much with regard to offices of profit ; the reason being that in all those cases the law presumes such a probability of pecuniary loss from such imputation, in that office, or employment, or profession, that it will not require special damage to be shown. But when you come to offices that are not offices of profit, the loss of which, therefore, would not involve necessarily a pecuniary loss, the law has been differently laid down, and it is quite clear that the mere imputation of want of ability or capacity, which would be actionable if made in the case of a person holding an office of profit, is not actionable in the case of a person holding an office which has been called an office of credit or an office of honour. . . . Where the imputation is an imputation, not of misconduct in an office, but of unfitness for an office, and the office for which the person is said to be unfit is not an office of profit, but one merely of what has been called honour or credit, the action will not lie, unless the conduct charged be such as would enable him to be removed from or deprived of that office." (Per Lord Herschell, L.C., in *Alexander* v. *Jenkins*, [1892] 1 Q. B. pp. 800—802.) "Words imputing want of integrity, dishonesty, or malversation to any one holding a public office of confidence, or trust, whether an office of profit or not, are actionable *per se.* On the other hand, when the words merely impute unsuitableness for the office, incompetency, or want of ability, without ascribing any misconduct touching the office, then no action lies, where the office is honorary, without proof of special damage." (Per Lopes, L.J., in *Booth* v. *Arnold*, [1895] 1 Q. B. at p. 576.)

In both cases it is essential that the plaintiff should hold the office at the time the words were spoken. (Per De Grey, C.J., in *Onslow* v. *Horne*, 3 Wilson, 188.)

Illustrations.

The plaintiff was elected town councillor for a borough, and the defendant said of him: " He is never sober, and is not a fit man for the council. On the night of the election he was so drunk that he had to be carried home." *Held*, that without proof of special damage, no action lay.

> *Alexander* v. *Jenkins*, [1892] 1 Q. B. 797; 61 L. J. Q. B. 634;
> 40 W. R. 546; 66 L. T. 391.

Merely to express an opinion that such a candidate is unfit for the post which he seeks, is not actionable ; but whoever makes or publishes any false statement of fact in relation to the personal character or conduct of any candidate at a Parliamentary election for the purpose of affecting his return will be guilty of an illegal practice, and liable also to be restrained by injunction from any repetition of such false statement.

> 58 & 59 Vict. c. 40, ss. 1 and 3, and see *post*, p. 437.

The plaintiff was an alderman of a borough, and chairman of the Town Improvement Committee of the council. He was also managing director and chief shareholder of a company which sold some land to the town council for the purpose of town improvement. The defendant used words which bore the construction that the plaintiff had availed himself of his position on the town council, and as chairman of the Improvement Committee, to obtain an improper advantage for himself and his company in the purchase. *Held*, that an action of slander lay without proof of special damage.

> *Booth* v. *Arnold*, [1895] 1 Q. B. 571; 64 L. J. Q. B. 443; 43 W. R.
> 360; 72 L. T. 310; 11 Times L. R. 246.

It is actionable without proof of special damage :—

To say that a judge gives corrupt sentences.

> *Cæsar* v. *Curseny*, Cro. Eliz. 305.

To accuse a Royal Commissioner of taking bribes.

> *Moor* v. *Foster*, Cro. Jac. 65.
> *Purdy* v. *Stacey*, 5 Burr. 2698.

To say of a justice of the peace, " Mr. Stuckley covereth and hideth felonies, and is not worthy to be a justice of peace; " " for it is against his oath and the office of a justice of peace, and a good cause to put him out of the commission."

> *Stuckley* v. *Bulhead*, 4 Rep. 16.
> And see *Sir John Harper* v. *Beamond*, Cro. Jac. 56.
> *Sir Miles Fleetwood* v. *Curl*, Cro. Jac. 557 ; Hob. 268.

To say of a justice of the peace that " he is a Jacobite and for bringing in the Prince of Wales and Popery; " for this implies that he is disaffected to the established Government and should be removed from office immediately.

> *How* v. *Prin*, (1702) Holt, 652; 7 Mod. 107; 2 Ld. Raym. 812;
> 2 Salk. 694. Affirmed in House of Lords *sub nom. Prinne* v. *Howe*,
> 1 Brown's Parly. Cases, 64.

To insinuate that a justice of the peace takes bribes or " perverts justice to serve his own turn."

> *Cæsar* v. *Curseny*, Cro. Eliz. 305.
>
> *Carn* v. *Osgood*, 1 Lev. 280.
>
> *Alleston* v. *Moor*, Hetl. 167.
>
> *Masham* v. *Bridges*, Cro. Car. 223.
>
> *Isham* v. *York*, Cro. Car. 15.
>
> *Beamond* v. *Hastings*, Cro. Jac. 240.
>
> *Aston* v. *Blagrave*, 1 Str. 617; 8 Mod. 270; 2 Ld. Raym. 1369; Fort. 206.
>
> *Lindsey* v. *Smith*, 7 Johns. 359.

To say of the deputy of Clarencieux, king-at-arms, " He is a scrivener and no herald."

> *Brooke* v. *Clarke*, Cro. Eliz. 328 ; 1 Vin. Abr. 464.

To say to a churchwarden, " Thou art a cheating knave and hast cheated the parish of 40*l.*"

> *Strode* v. *Holmes*, (1651) Style, 338; 1 Roll. Abr. 58.
>
> *Woodruff* v. *Wooley*, 1 Vin. Abr. 463.
>
> *Jackson* v. *Adams*, 2 Bing. N. C. 402; 2 Scott, 599; 1 Hodges, 339.

To call an escheator, attorney, or other officer of a Court of Record, an " extortioner."

> *Stanley* v. *Boswell*, 1 Roll. Abr. 55.

To say of a town clerk that he hath not performed his office according to law.

> *Fowell* v. *Cowe*, Rolle's Abr. 56.
>
> *Wright* v. *Moorhouse*, Cro. Eliz. 358.

Or that he destroyed votes at an election.

> *Dodds* v. *Henry*, 9 Mass. 262

To state that a head-fireman was drunk at a fire is actionable.

> *Guttbehuet* v. *Hubachek*, 36 Wisconsin, 515.

In America it has been held actionable to charge a member of a nominating convention of a political party with having been influenced by a bribe.

> *Hand* v. *Winton*, 38 New Jersey (9 Vroom) 122.
>
> And see *Sanderson* v. *Caldwell*, 45 N. Y. 398.
>
> *Dolloway* v. *Turrell*, 26 Wend. (N. Y.) 383.
>
> *Stone* v. *Cooper*, 2 Denio (N. Y.) 293.

And to charge any public officer falsely with gross ignorance of his duties is actionable *per se* in America.

> *Spiering* v. *Andrae*, 45 Wisconsin, 330.

But it is *not* actionable without proof of special damage :—

To impute insincerity to a Member of Parliament.

> *Onslow* v. *Horne*, 3 Wils. 177 ; 2 W. Bl. 750.

Or weakness of understanding to a candidate for Congress.

> *Mayrant* v. *Richardson*, 1 Nott & M. (South Car.) 347.

Or to call such a candidate " a corrupt old Tory."

> *Hogg* v. *Dorrah*, 2 Post. (Alabama) 212.

To say of a justice of the peace, " He is a fool, an ass, and a beetle-headed justice ; " for these are but general terms of abuse and disclose no ground for removing the plaintiff from office.

> *Bill* v. *Neal*, 1 Lev. 52.
>
> *Sir John Hollis* v. *Briscow et ux.*, Cro. Jac. 58.

To say of a justice of the peace, "He is a logger-headed, a slouch-headed, bursen-bellied hound."

> *R.* v. *Farre*, 1 Keb. 629.

To say of a justice of the peace, "He is a blood-sucker and sucketh blood : " " for it cannot be intended what blood he sucketh."

> *Sir Christopher Hilliard* v. *Constable*, Cro. Eliz. 306 ; Moore, 418.

To say of a superintendent of the police that " he has been guilty of conduct unfit for publication " is not actionable, unless the words were spoken of him with reference to his office.

> *James* v. *Brook*, 9 Q. B. 7 ; 16 L. J. Q. B. 17 ; 10 Jur. 541.

Clergymen and Ministers.

A beneficed clergyman of the Church of England holds an office of profit : hence an action lies without proof of special damage for words which impute to him—

(i) serious misconduct in the discharge of his official duties ;

(ii) any misconduct which, if proved against him, would be ground for degradation or deprivation ; whether such misconduct occur in the course of his official duties or not (*Pemberton* v. *Colls*, 10 Q. B. 461 ; 16 L. J. Q. B. 403) ;

(iii) general unfitness or incapacity for his office.

A clergyman who holds any chaplaincy or paid lectureship or readership from which he can be removed, comes within the same rules as a beneficed clergyman. (*Payne* v. *Beuwmorris*, 1 Lev. 248.) But a clergyman without cure of souls or any other preferment is an honorary officer ; and words which would have been actionable, if spoken of a beneficed clergyman, will not necessarily be actionable, if spoken of him. (*Gallwey* v. *Marshall*, 9 Exch. 294 ; 23 L. J. Ex. 78.)

A dissenting minister is not, in the eye of the law, an officer at all ; he is engaged by his congregation or some other body of persons, to perform certain duties. Any charge made against him which, if true, would justify his summary dismissal from his employment, is actionable *per se.*

Illustrations.

It is actionable without proof of special damage :—

To say of a parson that " he had two wives ; " for though bigamy was not made felony until 1603, still in 1588 it was " cause of deprivation."

> *Nicholson* v. *Lyne*, Cro. Eliz. 94.

To say that "he is a drunkard, a whoremaster, a common swearer, a common liar, and hath preached false doctrine, and deserves to be degraded ; " for " the matters charged are good cause to have him degraded, whereby he should lose his freehold."

> *Dod* v. *Robinson*, (1648) Aleyn, 63.
>
> *Dr. Sibthorpe's Case*, W. Jones, 366 ; 1 Roll. Abr. 76.

To say, " He preacheth lyes in the pulpit : " " *car ceo est bon cause de deprivation*."

> *Drake* v. *Drake*, (1652) 1 Roll. Abr. 58 ; 1 Vin. Abr. 463.

[These cases clearly overrule *Parret* v. *Carpenter*, Noy, 64 ; Cro. Eliz. 502, wherein it was held that an action could lie only in the spiritual Court for saying of a parson :—" Parret is an adulterer, and hath had two children by the wife of J. S., and I will cause him to be deprived for it."   See the remarks of Pollock, C.B., 23 L. J. Ex. 80.]

To say to a parson, " Thou hast made a seditious sermon, and moved the people to sedition to-day."

> *Philips, B.D.* v. *Badby*, (1582) cited in *Brittridge's Case*, 4 Rep. 19.

To say of a parson, " He preaches nothing but lies and malice in the pulpit ; " for the words are clearly spoken of him in the way of his profession.

> *Crauden* v. *Walden*, 3 Lev. 17.
>
> *Bishop of Sarum* v. *Nash*, Buller's N. P. 9 ; Willes, 23.
>
> And see *Pocock* v. *Nash*, Comb. 253.
>
> *Musgrave* v. *Bovey*, 2 Str. 946.

To say to a clergyman, " Thou art a drunkard," is not of itself actionable ; but it is submitted that to impute to a clergyman habitual drunkenness, or drunkenness whilst engaged in the discharge of his official duties, would be actionable.

> *Anon.*, 1 Ohio, 83, n.
>
> *Tighe* v. *Wicks*, 33 Up. Can. Q. B. Rep. 470.
>
> *Brandrick* v. *Johnson*, 1 Vict. L. R. C. L. 306.
>
> *Dod* v. *Robinson*, Aleyn, 63.
>
> *McMillan* v. *Birch*, 1 Binn. 178.

To charge a clergyman with immorality and misappropriation of the sacrament money is clearly actionable.   Damages 750*l.*

> *Highmore* v. *Earl and Countess of Harrington*, 3 C. B. N. S. 142.

And, of course, to charge a clergyman with having indecently assaulted a woman on the highway is actionable.

> *Evans* v. *Gwyn*, 5 Q. B. 844.

To say of a beneficed clergyman that he drugged the wine he gave the speaker, and so fraudulently induced him to sign a bill of exchange for a large amount is actionable without proof of special damage ; but it is not actionable merely to say of a beneficed clergyman, " He pigeoned me."

> *Pemberton* v. *Colls*, 10 Q. B. 461 ; 16 L. J. Q. B. 403 ; 11 Jur. 1011.

To charge a clergyman with incontinence is not actionable, unless he hold some benefice or preferment, or some post of emolument, such as preacher, curate, chaplain, or lecturer, from which he could be dismissed for incontinence.

> *Gallwey* v. *Marshall*, 9 Exch. 294 ; 23 L. J. Ex. 78 ; 2 C. L. R. 399.

To say of one who has been a linendraper, but at time of publication was a dissenting minister, that he had been guilty of fraud and cheating when a linen-draper, is no slander of the plaintiff in his character of dissenting minister; and, therefore, is not actionable without proof of special damage.

　　　Hopwood v. *Thorn*, 8 C. B. 293; 19 L. J. C. P. 94; 14 Jur. 87.

But to charge a dissenting minister with incontinence while a dissenting minister, "insomuch that the persons frequenting the said chapel by reason of the speaking of the said words have wholly refused to permit him to preach at the said chapel," is actionable.

　　　Hartley v. *Herring*, 8 T. R. 130.

Barristers-at-Law.

It is quite clear that barristers may sue for words touching them in their profession, although their fees are honorary.

Illustrations.

The plaintiff was a barrister and gave counsel to divers of the king's subjects. The defendant said to J. S. (the plaintiff's father-in-law), concerning the plaintiff, "He is a dunce, and will get little by the law." J. S. replied, "Others have a better opinion of him." The defendant answered, "He was never but accounted a dunce in the Middle Temple." *Held*, that the words were actionable, though no special damage was alleged. Damages, one hundred marks. [Here it was argued for the defendant that Duns Scotus was "a great learned man;" that though to call a man "a dunce" might, in ordinary parlance, imply that he was dull and heavy of wit, yet it did not deny him a solid judgment; and that to say "he will get little by the law" might only mean that he did not wish to practise.]

　　　Peard v. *Jones*, (1635) Cro. Car. 382.

It is actionable without proof of special damage to say of a barrister :—

"Thou art no lawyer; thou canst not make a lease; thou hast that degree without desert; they are fools who come to thee for law."

　　　Bankes v. *Allen*, 1 Roll. Abr. 54.

"He hath as much law as a Jackanapes." (N.B.—The words are not "*no more* law *than* a Jackanapes.")

　　　　　Palmer v. *Boyer*, Owen, 17; Cro. Eliz. 342, cited with approval in
　　　　　Broke's Case, Moore, 409.
　　　　　[And see *Cawdry* v. *Tetley*, Godb. 441, where it is said that had the
　　　　　words been, "He has no more *wit* than a Jackanapes," no action
　　　　　would have lain; wit not being essential to success at the bar
　　　　　according to F. Pollock, 2 A. & E. p. 4.]

"He has deceived his client, and revealed the secrets of his cause."

　　　Snag v. *Gray*, 1 Roll. Abr. 57; Co. Entr. 22.

"He will give vexatious and ill counsel, and stir up a suit, and milk her purse, and fill his own large pockets."

　　　Anon., 3 Salk. 328.

　　　King v. *Lake*, (1682) 2 Ventr. 28.

　　　And see *Snow* v. *Etty*, 22 Law Journal (newspaper), 292.

Solicitors and Attornies.

It is actionable without proof of special damage :—

To say of an attorney, " He has no more law than Master Cheyny's bull," or " He has no more law than a goose."

>   *Baker* v. *Morfue*, vel *Morphew*, Sid. 327 ; 2 Keble, 202.

[According to the report in Keble, an objection was taken in this case on behalf of the defendant, that it was not averred in the declaration, "that Cheyny had a bull, *sed non allocatur*, for the scandal is the greater, if he had none." And the Court adds a solemn *quære* as to saying " He has no more law than the man in the moon."]

To say of an attorney, " He cannot read a declaration."

>   *Powell* v. *Jones*, 1 Lev. 297.

To say of an attorney, " He is a very base rogue and a cheating knave, and doth maintain himself, his wife and children, by his cheating."

>   *Anon.*, (1638) Cro. Car. 516.

>   See *Jenkins* v. *Smith*, Cro. Jac. 586.

To say of an attorney that " he hath the falling sickness ; " for that disables him in his profession.

>   *Taylor* v. *Perr*, (1607) 1 Roll. Abr. 44.

To say of an attorney, " What, does he pretend to be a lawyer ? He is no more a lawyer than the devil; " or any other words imputing gross ignorance of law.

>   *Day* v. *Buller*, 3 Wils. 59.

To say of an attorney, " He is only an attorney's clerk, and a rogue ; he is no attorney," or any words imputing that he is not a fully qualified practitioner.

>   *Hardwick* v. *Chandler*, 2 Stra. 1138.

To say of an attorney, " He is an *ambidexter*," *i.e.*, one who being retained by one party in a cause, and having learnt all his secrets, goes over to the other side, and acts for the adversary. Such conduct was subject for a *qui tam* action under an old penal statute : see Rastell's Entries, p. 2, Action sur le case vers Attorney, 3.

>   *Annison* v. *Blofield*, Carter, 214 ; 1 Roll. Abr. 55.

>   *Shire* v. *King*, Yelv. 32.

To impute that he will betray his clients' secrets and overthrow their cause.

>   *Martyn* v. *Burlings*, Cro. Eliz. 589.

>   *Garr* v. *Selden*, 6 Barb. (N.Y.) 416 ; 4 Comst. 91.

>   *Foot* v. *Brown*, 8 Johns. 64.

To charge an attorney with barratry, champerty, or maintenance.

>   *Boxe* v. *Barnaby*, 1 Roll. Abr. 55 ; Hob. 117.

>   *Proud* v. *Hawes*, Cro. Eliz. 171 ; Hob. 140.

>   *Taylor* v. *Starkey*, Cro. Car. 192.

To say to a client " Your attorney is a bribing knave, and hath taken twenty pounds of you to cozen me."

>   *Yardley* v. *Ellill*, Hob. 8.

To say of an attorney, " He stirreth up suits, and once promised me, that if he did not recover in a cause for me, he would take no charges of me ; " " because stirring up suits is barratry, and undertaking a suit, no purchase no pay, is maintenance."

Smith v. *Andrews*, 1 Roll. Abr. 54 ; Hob. 117.

To assert that an attorney has been guilty of professional misconduct and ought to be struck off the rolls.

Byrchley's Case, 4 Rep. 16.

Phillips v. *Jansen*, 2 Esp. 624.

Warton v. *Gearing*, 1 Vict. L. R. C. L. 122.

But it is not actionable to say of an attorney, "He has defrauded his creditors and has been horsewhipped off the course at Doncaster ; " for it is no part of his professional duties to attend horse-races, and his creditors are not his clients.

Doyley v. *Roberts*, 3 Bing. N. C. 835 ; 5 Scott, 40 ; 3 Hodges, 154.

Nor to abuse him in general terms, such as "cheat," "rogue," or "knave ; " though to say, "You cheat your clients," would be actionable.

Alleston v. *Moor*, Het. 167.

And see *Bishop* v. *Latimer*, 4 L. T. 775.

And where the defendant said of a solicitor: "He has gone for thousands instead of hundreds this time," and : " It seems to be a worse job than the other was ; he has lost thousands," it was held that the words were not actionable *per se*, as they did not reasonably convey any imputation of impropriety or misconduct on the part of the plaintiff in relation to or in connection with his profession or business, or of unfitness to carry on his profession or business in a proper or satisfactory manner.

Dauncey v. *Holloway*, [1901] 2 K. B. 441 ; 70 L. J. K. B. 695 ; 49 W. R. 546 ; 84 L. T. 649.

But see *A. B.* v. *C. D.*, (1905) 7 F. 22 (Ct. of Sess.).

Physicians, Surgeons, &c.

Any words imputing to a practising medical man misconduct or incapacity in the discharge of his professional duties are actionable *per se*.

Illustrations.

Thus it is actionable without proof of special damage :—

To say of a physician that "he is no scholar," " because no man can be a good physician, unless he be a scholar."

Cawdry v. *Highley al. Tythay*, Cro. Car. 270 ; Godb. 441.

To accuse any physician, surgeon, accoucheur, midwife or apothecary, with having caused the death of any patient through his ignorance or culpable negligence.

Poe v. *Mondford*, Cro. Eliz. 620.

Watson v. *Vanderlash*, Hetl. 71.

Edsall v. *Russell*, 4 M. & Gr. 1090 ; 12 L. J. C. P. 4 ; 5 Scott, N. R. 801 ; 2 Dowl. N. S. 641 ; 6 Jur. 996.

Foster v. *Scripps*, 39 Mich. 376 ; 33 Amer. R. 403.

To call a practising medical man " a quack-salver," or "an empiric," or a " mountebank."

Allen v. *Eaton*, 1 Roll. Abr. 54.

Goddart v. *Haselfoot*, 1 Viner's Abr. (S. a.), pl. 12 ; 1 Roll. Abr. 54.

To say of a surgeon to his patient:—" I wonder you had him to attend you. Do you know him ?   He is not an apothecary; he has not passed any examination; he is a bad character; none of the medical men here will meet him. Several persons have died that he had attended, and there have been inquests held on them," was held actionable in

    Southee v. *Denny*, 1 Exch. 196; 17 L. J. Ex. 151.

The Court, in this case, inclined to think the words, " He is a bad character; none of the medical men here will meet him," were actionable by themselves.

    But see *Clay* v. *Roberts*, 9 Jur. N. S. 580; 11 W. R. 649; 8 L. T. 397.

    Rumadge v. *Ryan*, 9 Bing. 333; 2 M. & Sc. 421.

To charge any medical man or apothecary with either ignorantly or unskilfully administering the wrong medicines, or medicine in excessive doses.

    Collier, M.D. v. *Simpson*, 5 C. & P. 73..

    Tutty v. *Alewin*, 11 Mod. 221.

    Secor v. *Harris*, 18 Barb. 425.

    Carroll v. *White*, 33 Barb. 615; 42 N. Y. 161.

    March v. *Davison*, 9 Paige, 580.

    Edsall v. *Russell*, 4 M. & Gr. 1090; 5 Scott, N. R. 801; 2 Dowl. N. S. 641; 12 L. J. C. P. 4; 6 Jur. 996.

To say of a midwife, " Many have perished for her want of skill."

    Flowers' Case, Cro. Car. 211.

But it is not actionable *per se :*—

To say of a surgeon, " He did poison the wound of his patient; " without some averment that this was improper treatment of the wound; for else " it might be for the cure of it."

    Suegos' Case, Hetl. 175.

To call a person who practises medicine without full legal qualification " a quack," or " an impostor; " for the law only protects *lawful* employments.

    Collins v. *Carnegie*, 1 A. & E. 695; 3 N. & M. 703.

It is for the jury and not the judge to decide what is the meaning of the word " quack."

    Dakhyl v. *Labouchere*, [1908] 2 K. B. 325, n., 329, n. ; 77 L. J. K. B. 728; 96 L. T. 399; 23 Times L. R. 364.

To charge a physician with adultery unconnected with his professional conduct. It would be otherwise if he had been accused of seducing, or committing adultery with, one of his patients.

    Ayre v. *Craven*, 2 A. & E. 2; 4 N. & M. 220.

To charge a physician or surgeon generally with " malpractice; " not stating that he caused his patient's death by malpractice.

    Rodgers v. *Kline*, 56 Miss. 808; 31 Amer. R. 389.

To say of an " accoucheuse," "A lady who has established a medical college at —— has issued a prospectus, in which my name appears as president. I have sanctioned the issue of no prospectus with my name in it. I wish to know what remedy I have," was held no slander on her in the way of her trade.

    Brent v. *Spratt, Times*, Feb. 3rd, 1882.

The plaintiff was a surgeon and accoucheur; the defendant told one of his patients that the plaintiff's female servant had had a child by the plaintiff; and the patient consequently ceased to employ the plaintiff. *Held*, that special damage being proved, the action lay.

    Dixon v. *Smith*, 5 H. & N. 450; 29 L. J. Ex. 125.

Other Professions.

So, to impute incompetency to any one practising an art, as a dentist, a schoolmaster, a land surveyor, or an architect, is actionable *per se.*

Illustrations.

Thus, it is actionable without proof of special damage :—

To say of a schoolmaster, " Put not your son to him, for he will come away as very a dunce as he went."

> *Watson* v. *Vanderlash,* Hetl. 71.

To accuse a schoolmaster of habitual drunkenness.

> *Hume* v. *Marshall,* 42 J. P. 136.
> *Brandrick* v. *Johnson,* 1 Vict. L. R. C. L. 306.

And it was held a slander on a schoolmaster in the way of his profession to say :—" You had one here whom the boys say liked his glass ; they smelt him continually. I saw him so that he could not walk straight."

> *Goslett* v. *Garment,* (1897) 13 Times L. R. 391.

It is actionable without proof of special damage to impute drunkenness to a master mariner in command of a vessel.

> *Irwin* v. *Brandwood,* 2 H. & C. 960 ; 33 L. J. Ex. 257 ; 12 W. R.
> 438 ; 9 L. T. 772 ; 10 Jur. N. S. 370.
> *Hamon* v. *Falle,* 4 App. Cas. 247 ; 48 L. J. P. C. 45.

But to say that a private citizen was drunk once is not.

> *Warren* v. *Norman,* Walk. (Mississippi) 387.
> *Buck* v. *Hersey,* 31 Maine, 558.
> And see *Chaddock* v. *Briggs,* 13 Mass. 248.
> *Hayner* v. *Cowden,* 27 Ohio St. 292.

Nor to say that he was drunk and disorderly on licensed premises.

> *Hellwig* v. *Mitchell,* [1910] 1 K. B. 609 ; 79 L. J. K. B. 270 ; 102 L. T.
> 110 ; 26 Times L. R. 244.

Nor to say of the director of a company that he has been drunk on licensed premises.

> *Michael* v. *Spiers and Pond,* (1909) 101 L. T. 352 ; 25 Times L. R.
> 740.

To charge a woman with being drunk is actionable in Massachusetts.

> *Brown* v. *Nickerson,* 1 Gray, 1.

It is actionable without proof of special damage to say of an auctioneer or appraiser, who had valued goods for the defendant :—" He is a damned rascal, he has cheated me out of 100*l.* on the valuation."

> *Bryant* v. *Loxton,* 11 Moore, 344.
> *Ramsdale* v. *Greenacre,* 1 F. & F. 61.

Or to say of a land surveyor, in the way of his profession :—" Thou art a cozener and a cheating knave, and that I can prove."

> *London* v. *Eastgate,* 2 Rolle's Rep. 72.

Or to say of a governess that she has been guilty of immorality with her employer. (Before the Slander of Women Act.)

> *Quinn* v. *Wilson,* (1850) 13 Ir. L. R. 381.
> And see *Gillett* v. *Bullivant,* 7 L. T. (Old S.) 490 ; *post,* p. 416.

But to say of a dancing mistress :—" She is as much a man as I am ; she is an hermaphrodite," is not actionable of her in the way of her profession, for girls are taught dancing by men as often as by women.

> *Wetherhead* v. *Armitage,* 2 Lev. 233 ; 3 Salk. 328 ; Freem. 277 ;
> 2 Show. 18.
> *Secus,* in America, *Malone* v. *Stewart,* 15 Ohio, 319.

And to say of a land speculator :—" He cheated me of 100 acres of land," was held in Canada not to touch him in his profession and therefore not actionable.

> *Fellowes* v. *Hunter,* 20 Up. Can. Q. B. 382.

It is not actionable to say of a trainer of race-horses that he has not paid his bets, there being no evidence that it is part of his business to make bets.

> *Smith and another* v. *Willoughby,* (1899) 15 Times L. R. 314.

Traders, Artisans, Servants, &c.

So if the plaintiff carry on any trade recognised by the law, or be engaged in any lawful employment, however humble, an action lies for any words which prejudice him in the way of such trade or employment. But the words must relate to his trade or employment, and " touch " him therein.

Illustrations.

Thus, it is actionable without proof of special damage :—
To say of a clerk or servant that he had " cozened his master."

> *Seaman* v. *Bigg,* Cro. Car. 480.
> *Reignald's Case,* (1640) Cro. Car. 563.

To say of a gamekeeper that he trapped three foxes ; for that would be clearly a breach of his duties as gamekeeper.

> *Foulger* v. *Newcomb,* L. R. 2 Ex. 327 ; 36 L. J. Ex. 169 ; 15 W. R.
> 1181 ; 16 L. T. 595.

To say of a servant girl that she had had a miscarriage, and had lost her place in consequence.

> *Connors* v. *Justice,* 13 Ir. C. L. R. 451.

To say to the mistress of a servant girl :—" You are not aware, Mrs. C., what kind of a girl you have in your service ; if you were, you would not keep her, for I can assure you she is often out with our married man." Coltman, J., held that these words were actionable without proof of special damage ; and on a motion for a new trial, Tindal, C.J., said " The words are actionable, inasmuch as they are spoken of the plaintiff in her vocation."

> *Rumsey* v. *Webb et ux.,* 11 L. J. C. P. 129 ; Car. & M. 104.

To say to an innkeeper, "Thy house is infected with the pox, and thy wife was laid of the pox ; " for even if small-pox only was meant, still " it was a discredit to the plaintiff, and guests would not resort " to his house. Damages 50*l.*

> *Levet's Case,* Cro. Eliz. 289.
> And see the remarks of Kelly, C.B., in *Riding* v. *Smith,* 1 Ex. D. 94 ;
> 45 L. J. Ex. 281 ; 24 W. R. 487 ; 34 L. T. 500.

To say of a watchmaker, " he is a bungler, and knows not how to make a good watch."

> *Redman* v. *Pyne*, 1 Mod. 19; 3 Salk. 328.

But it is not actionable *per se* :—

To say of a livery stable keeper, " You are a regular prover under bankruptcies, a regular bankrupt maker; " for it is not a charge against him in the way of his trade.

> *Angle* v. *Alexander*, 7 Bing. 119; 1 Cr. & J. 143; 4 M. & P. 870; 1 Tyrw. 9.

Nor to say to a clerk to a gas company, " You are a fellow, a disgrace to the town, unfit to hold your situation for your conduct with whores."

> *Lumby* v. *Allday*, 1 Cr. & J. 301; 1 Tyrw. 217.
> And see *James* v. *Brook*, 9 Q. B. 7; 16 L. J. Q. B. 17; 10 Jur. 541.

Nor to impute to a staymaker that his trade is maintained by the prostitution of his shopwoman.

> *Brayne* v. *Cooper*, 5 M. & W. 249.

The defendant said of the plaintiff who was a working stone-mason :—" He has ruined the town by bringing about the nine hours' system," and " He has stopped several good jobs from being carried out, by being the ringleader of the system at Llanelly." *Held*, on demurrer, that no action lay, the words not being in themselves defamatory, nor connected by averment or by implication with the plaintiff's trade.

> *Miller* v. *David*, L. R. 9 C. P. 118; 43 L. J. C. P. 84; 22 W. R. 332; 30 L. T. 58.

The law guards most carefully the credit of all merchants and traders; any imputation on their solvency, any suggestion that they are in pecuniary difficulties, or are attempting to evade the operation of any Bankruptcy Act, is therefore actionable *per se*.

Illustrations.

Thus, it is actionable without proof of special damage :—

To impeach the credit of any merchant or tradesman by imputing to him bankruptcy or insolvency, either past, present or future.

> *Johnson* v. *Lemmon*, 2 Rolle's Rep. 144.
> *Thompson* v. *Twenge*, 2 Rolle's Rep. 433.
> *Vivian* v. *Willet*, Sir Thos. Raym. 207; 3 Salk. 326; 2 Keble, 718.
> *Stanton* v. *Smith*, 2 Ld. Raym. 1480; 2 Str. 762.
> *Whittington* v. *Gladwin*, 5 B. & C. 180; 2 C. & P. 146.
> *Robinson* v. *Marchant*, 7 Q. B. 918; 15 L. J. Q. B. 134; 10 Jur. 156.
> *Harrison* v. *Bevington*, 8 C. & P. 708.
> *Gostling* v. *Brooks*, 2 F. & F. 76.
> *Brown* v. *Smith*, 13 C. B. 596; 22 L. J. C. P. 151; 17 Jur. 807; 1 C. L. R. 4.

To say to a tailor, " I heard you were run away," &c. from your creditors.

> *Davis* v. *Lewis*, 7 T. R. 17.
> And see *Dobson* v. *Thornistone*, 3 Mod. 112.
> *Chapman* v. *Lamphire*, 3 Mod. 155.

Arne v. *Johnson*, 10 Mod. 111.

Harrison v. *Thornborough*, 10 Mod. 196; Gilb. Cas. 114.

To say of a brewer that he has been arrested for debt. And this although no express reference to his trade was made at the time of publication, for such words must necessarily affect his credit therein.

Jones v. *Littler*, 7 M. & W. 423; 10 L. J. Ex. 171.

To assert that the plaintiff had once been bankrupt in another place, when carrying on another trade; for that may still affect him here in his present trade.

Leycroft v. *Dunker*, Cro. Car. 317.

Hall v. *Smith*, 1 M. & S. 287.

Figgins v. *Cogswell*, 3 M. & S. 369.

To say of any trader, " He is not able to pay his debts."

Drake v. *Hill*, Sir Thos. Raym. 184; 2 Keble, 549; 1 Lev. 276; Sid. 424.

Hooker v. *Tucker*, Holt, 39; Carth. 330.

Morris v. *Langdale*, 2 Bos. & Pul. 284.

Orpwood v. *Barkes* (vel *Parkes*), 4 Bing. 261; 12 Moore, 492.

To say of a farmer, " He cannot pay his labourers."

Barnes v. *Holloway*, 8 T. R. 150.

To impute insolvency to an innkeeper, even though at that date innkeepers were not subject to the bankruptcy laws.

Whittington v. *Gladwin*, (1825) 5 B. & C. 180; 2 C. & P. 146.

Southam v. *Allen*, Sir Thos. Raym. 231.

But it is not actionable to say merely, "A. owes me money," if no words be added imputing that A. is unable to pay the debt.

Per Bramwell, B., 4 F. & F. 321, 322.

So if the defendant's words impute to the plaintiff dishonesty and fraud in the conduct of his trade, such as knowingly selling inferior articles as superior, or wilfully adulterating his wares, they will be actionable *per se*. If the words merely impugn the value of the goods which the plaintiff sells, they are not actionable unless they fall within the rules relating to " Actions on the Case," *post*, p. 77; for they are but an attack on a thing, not on a person. But often an attack on a commodity may be also an indirect attack upon its vendor; *e.g.*, if it be insinuated that there was fraud or dishonesty in offering it for sale. (See *ante*, p. 34.) In such case, if the words touch a man in his trade, they are actionable *per se*.

Illustrations.

Thus, it is actionable without proof of special damage:—

To say of a trader, " He is a cheating knave, and keeps a false debt-book."

Crawfoot v. *Dale*, 1 Vent. 263; 3 Salk. 327.

Overruling *Todd* v. *Hastings*, 2 Saund. 307.

Or that he uses false weights or measures.

> *Griffiths* v. *Lewis*, 7 Q. B. 61 ; 14 L. J. Q. B. 197 ; 9 Jur. 370 ; 8
> Q. B. 841 ; 15 L. J. Q. B. 249 ; 10 Jur. 711.
>
> *Bray* v. *Ham*, 1 Brownlow & Golds. 4.
>
> *Stober* v. *Green*, *Ib.* 5.
>
> *Prior* v. *Wilson*, 1 C. B. N. S. 95.

To say to a corn factor, " You are a rogue and a swindling rascal, you delivered me 100 bushels of oats, worse by 6*s.* a bushel than I bargained for."

> *Thomas* v. *Jackson*, 3 Bing. 104 ; 10 Moore, 425.

To say of a tradesman that he adulterates the goods he sells.

> *Jesson* v. *Hayes*, (1636) 1 Roll. Abr. 63.

To say of a contractor, " He used the old materials," when his contract was for new, is actionable, with proper innuendoes.

> *Baboneau* v. *Farrell*, 15 C. B. 360 ; 24 L. J. C. P. 9 ; 1 Jur. N. S. 114 ;
> 3 C. L. R. 42.
>
> *Sir R. Greenfield's Case*, Mar. 92 ; 1 Viner's Abr. 465.
>
> See *Smith* v. *Mathews*, 1 Moo. & Rob. 151.

To say of a butcher that he changed the lamb bought of him for a coarse piece of mutton.

> *Crisp* v. *Gill*, 29 L. T. (Old S.) 82.
>
> *Rice* v. *Pidgeon*, Comb. 161.

To say of a keeper of a restaurant, " You are an infernal rogue and swindler," was held not to be actionable without proof of special damage, as not of itself necessarily injurious to a restaurant keeper; for, as the Supreme Court of Victoria remarked, "in fact there might be very successful restaurant keepers, who were both rogues and swindlers."

> *Brady* v. *Youlden*, Kerferd & Box's Digest of Victoria Cases, 709 ;
> *Melbourne Argus* Reports, 6th September, 1867.

But to call a tradesman " a rogue," or " a cheat," or " a cozener," is not actionable, unless it can be shown that the words refer to his trade. To impute distinctly that he cheats or cozens *in his trade* is actionable.

> *Johns* v. *Gittings*, Cro. Eliz. 239.
>
> *Cotes* v. *Ketle*, Cro. Jac. 204.
>
> *Terry* v. *Hooper*, 1 Lev. 115.
>
> *Savage* v. *Robery*, 5 Mod. 398 ; 2 Salk. 694.
>
> *Surman* v. *Shelleto*, 3 Burr. 1688.
>
> *Bromefield* v. *Snoke*, 12 Mod. 307.
>
> *Savile* v. *Jardine*, 2 H. Bl. 531.
>
> *Lancaster* v. *French*, 2 Stra. 797.
>
> *Davis* v. *Miller et ux.*, 2 Stra. 1169.
>
> *Fellowes* v. *Hunter*, 20 Up. Can. Q. B. 382.
>
> *Brady* v. *Youlden*, *Melbourne Argus* Reports, *suprà*.

[N.B.—*Lancaster* v. *French* appears to go a little further than the other cases cited : but if so, it must be taken to be so far overruled by them.]

So to say to a pork butcher, " Who stole Fraser's pigs ? You did, you bloody thief, and I can prove it—you poisoned them with mustard and brimstone," was held not actionable (the jury having found that the words were not intended to impute felony); for there was nothing to show that they were spoken of the plaintiff in relation to his trade.

> *Sibley* v. *Tomlins*, 4 Tyrw. 90.

So to say of a grocer, "His shop is in the market," is not actionable, in the primary sense of the words at all events.

Ruel v. *Tatnell*, 29 W. R. 172 ; 43 L. T. 507.

It must be averred and proved that the plaintiff carried on his trade at the time the words were spoken ; else the words cannot be spoken of him in the way of such trade. (*Bellamy* v. *Burch*, 16 M. & W. 590.) Moreover the trade or employment must be one recognised by the law as a legitimate means of earning one's living.

Illustrations.

A stock-jobber could not sue for words spoken of him in the way of his trade, so long as that trade was illegal within the 7 Geo. II. c. 8, s. 1 (Sir John Barnard's Act; now repealed by 23 & 24 Vict. c. 28).

Morris v. *Langdale*, 2 Bos. & Pul. 284.
Collins v. *Carnegie*, 1 A. & E. 695 ; 3 N. & M. 703.

If the plaintiff avers that he carries on two trades, it will be sufficient to prove that he carries on one, if the words can affect him in that one.

Figgins v. *Cogswell*, 3 M. & S. 369.
Hall v. *Smith*, 1 M. & S. 287.

Where insolvency is imputed to one member of a firm, either he or the firm may sue, for it is a reflection on the credit of both.

Harrison v. *Bevington*, 8 C. & P. 708.
Cook and another v. *Batchellor*, 3 Bos. & Pul. 150.
Forster and others v. *Lawson*, 3 Bing. 452 ; 11 Moore, 360.

A married woman, carrying on a separate trade, may sue without joining her husband for any tort affecting such separate trade or her credit therein.

Summers v. *City Bank*, L. R. 9 C. P. 580 ; 43 L. J. C. P. 261.
And see 45 & 46 Vict. c. 75, ss. 1, 12, *post*, pp. 568—577.

And see cases collected under Chapter V., *post*, p. 109.

IV. *Words which impute Unchastity or Adultery to any Woman or Girl.*

By the Slander of Women Act, 1891 (54 & 55 Vict. c. 51), s. 1, it is enacted that " words spoken and published after the passing of this Act which impute unchastity or adultery to any woman or girl shall not require special damage to render them actionable. Provided always, that in any action for words spoken and made actionable by this Act, a plaintiff shall not recover more costs than damages, unless the judge shall certify that there was reasonable ground for bringing the action."

The Act does not apply to Scotland, as a verbal imputation of unchastity was already actionable there without proof of special damage. And it is submitted that it does not apply to any case in which gross epithets are used merely as general terms of abuse; the words must be such as to convey to the hearers a definite imputation that the plaintiff has in fact been guilty of adultery or unchastity.

Prior to 1891, it was the law in England and Ireland—though it was otherwise in Scotland and America—that words imputing unchastity or adultery to a woman, married or unmarried, however gross and injurious they might be, were not actionable, unless the plaintiff could prove that they had directly caused her special damage, which it was generally impossible for her to do. It was true that up to 1855 she had a nominal remedy in the ecclesiastical Courts, which had jurisdiction over such charges, and could inflict penance on the defendant for the good of his soul, though they could not award damages to the plaintiff. But by the statute 18 & 19 Vict. c. 41, the power of the ecclesiastical Courts " to entertain or adjudicate upon any suit for or cause of defamation " was abolished; and no attempt was made to substitute any remedy in the secular Courts. Again, there was in theory a remedy if such words were spoken in the city of London, or in the borough of Southwark (Sid. 97), or, it was said, in the city of Bristol (*Power* v. *Shaw*, 1 Wils. 62), and an action was brought in the local Courts. For it was formerly the custom in those localities to cart and whip whores, tingling a basin before them. Hence to call a woman " whore " or " strumpet " (*Cook* v. *Wingfield*, 1 Str. 555) or " bawd " (1 Vin. Abr. 396), or her husband a " cuckold " (*Vicars* v. *Worth*, 1 Str. 471), was supposed to be an imputation of a criminal offence to the female plaintiff, and therefore actionable. But such custom has been entirely extinct for more than a century. The plaintiffs in the case of *Stainton et ux.* v. *Jones* (2 Selwyn, N. P. 13th ed. 1205), tried to prove its existence in 1782, and failed. Hence a woman who had been slandered in her most precious possession was practically without remedy. The state of our law on this point was frequently denounced by learned judges. (See the remarks of Willes, C.J., in *Jones* v. *Herne*, 2 Wils. 87; of Lord Campbell, C.J., and Lord Brougham in *Lynch* v. *Knight and wife*, 9 H. L. C.

593, 594 ; and of Cockburn, C.J., Crompton, and Blackburn, JJ., in *Roberts and wife* v. *Roberts,* 5 B. & S. 384; 33 L. J. Q. B. 249.)

Illustrations of the former law.

To say of a young woman that " she had a bastard " was not actionable without proof of special damage; " because it is a spiritual defamation, punishable in the spiritual Court."

Per Holt, C.J., in *Ogden* v. *Turner,* Holt, 40; 6 Mod. 104 ; 2 Salk. 696. But see *ante,* p. 46.

To call a woman " a whore " or " a strumpet " was not actionable, except by special custom, if the action were tried in the cities of London and Bristol. " To maintain actions for such brabling words is against law."

Oxford et ux. v. *Cross,* (1599) 4 Rep. 18.

Hassell v. *Capcot,* (1639) 1 Vin. Abr. 395 ; 1 Roll. Abr. 36.

Roberts v. *Herbert,* (1662) Sid. 97 ; S. C. *Caus* v. *Roberts,* 1 Keble, 418 (Southwark).

Watson v. *Clerke,* (1688) Comberbach, 138.

Gascoigne et ux. v. *Ambler,* (1703) 2 Ld. Raym. 1004.

Vicars v. *Worth,* (1722) 1 Str. 471.

Hodgkins et ux. v. *Corbet et ux.,* (1723) 1 Str. 545.

Cook v. *Wingfield,* (1723) 1 Str. 555.

Power v. *Shaw,* (1744) 1 Wils. 62 (Bristol).

Theyer v. *Eastwick,* (1767) 4 Burr. 2032.

Brand and wife v. *Roberts and wife,* (1769) 4 Burr. 2418.

Stainton et ux. v. *Jones,* (1782) 2 Selw. N. P. 1205 (13th ed.).

It was not actionable to call a woman a " bawd,"

Hollingshead's Case, (1631) Cro. Car. 229 ;

Hixe v. *Hollingshed,* (1632) Cro. Car. 261 ;

unless the words were spoken in the city of London.

Rily v. *Lewis,* (1640) 1 Vin. Abr. 396.

The words " You are living by imposture ; you used to walk St. Paul's Churchyard for a living,"—spoken of a woman with the intention of imputing that she was a swindler and a prostitute,—were not actionable without special damage.

Wilby v. *Elston,* 8 C. B. 142 ; 18 L. J. C. P. 320; 13 Jur. 706; 7 D. & L. 143.

The defendant told a married man that his wife was " a notorious liar " and " an infamous wretch," and had been all but seduced by Dr. C. of Roscommon before her marriage. The husband consequently refused to live with her any longer. *Held,* no action lay.

Lynch v. *Knight and wife,* 9 H. L. C. 577; 8 Jur. N. S. 724; 5 L. T. 291.

Where the defendant asserted that a married woman was guilty of adultery, and she was consequently expelled from the congregation and Bible society of her religious sect, and was thus prevented from obtaining a certificate, without which she could not become a member of any similar society, *held,* no action lay.

Roberts and wife v. *Roberts,* 5 B. & S. 384; 33 L. J. Q. B. 249; 10 Jur. N. S. 1027; 12 W. R. 909; 10 L. T. 602.

Shafer v. *Ahalt*, 48 Maryland, 171 ; 30 Amer. R. 456.

Dwyer v. *Meehan*, 18 L. R. Ir. 138.

The defendant falsely imputed incontinence to a married woman. In consequence of his words she lost the society and friendship of her neighbours, and became seriously ill and unable to attend to her affairs and business, and her husband incurred expense in curing her, and lost the society and assistance of his wife in his domestic affairs. *Held,* that neither husband nor wife had any cause of action.

Allsop and wife v. *Allsop,* 5 H. & N. 534; 29 L. J. Ex. 315; 8 W. R. 449 ; 6 Jur. N. S. 433; 36 L. T. (Old S.) 290.

But see *Davies* v. *Solomon,* L. R. 7 Q. B. 112; 41 L. J. Q. B. 10 ; 20 W. R. 167 ; 25 L. T. 799, *post,* p. 418.

V. *Words actionable only by reason of Special Damage.*

No other words are actionable without proof of special damage. Thus, to accuse a man of fraud, dishonesty, immorality, or any vicious and dishonourable (but not criminal) conduct, is not actionable, unless it has produced as its natural and necessary consequence some pecuniary loss to him. Words imputing adultery, profligacy, immoral conduct, &c., even when spoken of a man holding an office or carrying on a profession or business, will not be actionable, unless they relate to his conduct in that office, profession, or business, or otherwise injure him therein. The imputation must be connected with the professional duties of the plaintiff.

Illustrations.

To say of a man, "He is the reputed father of that bastard child," is not actionable, without proof of some temporal loss, *e.g.,* "that he lost thereby his marriage, or that he by this means should be chargeable for the maintenance of such bastard child."

Salter v. *Browne,* Cro. Car. 436; 1 Roll. Abr. 37.

So to say of a married man that he has "had two bastards and should have kept them," is not actionable, though it is averred that by reason of such words "discord arose between him and his wife, and they were likely to have been divorced."

Barmund's Case, Cro. Jac. 473.

Words imputing adultery to a physician were laid to have been spoken "of him in his profession," but there was nothing in the declaration to connect the imputation with the plaintiff's professional conduct. *Held*, that the words were not actionable without special damage.

> *Ayre* v. *Craven*, 2 A. & E. 2; 4 N. & M. 220.
>
> *Walklin* v. *Johns*, (1891) 7 Times L. R. 292.
>
> *Argent* v. *Donigan*, (1892), 8 Times L. R. 432.

Words imputing immorality to a trader or his clerk are not actionable without proof of special damage.

> *Lumby* v. *Allday*, 1 Cr. & J. 301; 1 Tyrw. 217.

Nor are words imputing to a staymaker that his trade is maintained by the prostitution of his shopwoman.

> *Brayne* v. *Cooper*, 5 M. & W. 249.
>
> But now see *Riding* v. *Smith*, 1 Ex. D. 91; 45 L. J. Ex. 281; 24 W. R. 487; 34 L. T. 500.

The following words are not actionable without proof of special damage:—

"Thou art a scurvey bad fellow."

> *Fisher* v. *Atkinson*, 1 Roll. Abr. 43.

"A villain, or a rogue, or a varlet" (for these, and words of the like kind, are "usual words of passion").

> *Per cur.* in *Stanhope* v. *Blith*, 4 Rep. 15.

"A runagate rogue."

> *Cockaine* v. *Hopkins*, 2 Lev. 214.

"A cozening knave."

> *Brunkard* v. *Segar*, Cro. Jac. 427; Hutt. 13; 1 Vin. Abr. 427.

"A liar."

> *Kimmis* v. *Stiles*, 44 Vermont, 351.

"A cheat."

> *Savage* v. *Robery*, 2 Salk. 694; 5 Mod. 398.

"You are a swindler."

> *Savile* v. *Jardine*, 2 H. Bl. 531.
>
> *Black* v. *Hunt*, 2 L. R. Ir. 10.

"He is a rogue and a swindler; I know enough about him to hang him."

> *Ward* v. *Weeks*, 7 Bing. 211; 4 M. & P. 796.

"He is a rogue, and has cheated his brother-in-law of upwards of 2,000*l.*"

> *Hopwood* v. *Thorn*, 8 C. B. 293; 19 L. J. C. P. 94; 14 Jur. 87.

"Thy credit hath been called in question, and a jury being to pass upon it, thou foistedst in a jury early in the morning; and the lands thou hast are gotten by lewd practices."

> *Nichols* v. *Badger*, Cro. Eliz. 348.

"This gentleman has defrauded us of 22,000*l.*"

> *Needham* v. *Dowling*, 15 L. J. C. P. 9.
>
> *Richardson* v. *Allen*, 2 Chit. 657.

"The conduct of the plaintiffs was so bad at a club in Melbourne, that a round robin was signed urging the committee to expel them; as, however, they were there only for a short time, the committee did not proceed further."

> *Chamberlain and another* v. *Boyd*, 11 Q. B. D. 407; 52 L. J. Q. B. 277; 31 W. R. 572; 48 L. T. 328; 47 J. P. 372.

"I have seen the plaintiff; and from what I have seen and heard, I think it is my duty to urge you" (plaintiff's husband) "to send for one or two doctors to see her; some opinion ought to be taken as to the state of her mind."

> *Weldon* v. *De Bathe*, 33 W. R. 328.

To say, "You cheat everybody, you cheated me, you cheated Mr. Saunders," is not actionable unless it be spoken of the plaintiff in the way of his profession or trade.

> *Davis* v. *Miller et ux.*, 2 Stra. 1169.
>
> *Lucas* v. *Flinn*, 35 Iowa, 9.

To call a man a "blackleg" is not actionable unless it can be shown that word was understood by the bystanders to mean "a cheating gambler liable to be prosecuted as such."

> *Barnett* v. *Allen*, 3 H. & N. 376; 27 L. J. Ex. 412; 4 Jur. N. S. 488;
> 1 F. & F. 125.

In an American case the difficulty caused by absence of special damage was surmounted by suing in trespass:—A man, who, instead of walking along the street, stops on the pavement opposite the plaintiff's freehold shop using insulting and abusive language towards the plaintiff, and persists in such conduct, though requested to move on, is a trespasser, and the jury in an action of trespass may award substantial damages, though no special damages be proved, and although the abusive words be not actionable *per se*. (*Adams* v. *Rivers*, 11 Barbour (New York Reports) 390.) For as one of the public he was only entitled to use the highway for passing and repassing. (*Dovaston* v. *Payne*, 2 Sm. L. Cas. (9th ed.) p. 154.) And evidence of his language while committing a trespass is properly admitted to show in what spirit the act was done. (*Merest* v. *Harvey*, 5 Taunt. 442.) "Where a wrongful act is accompanied by words of contumely and abuse, the jury are warranted in taking that into consideration and giving retributory damages." Per Byles, J., in

> *Bell* v. *Midland Rail. Co.*, 10 C. B. N. S. 287, 308; 30. L. J. C. P.
> 273; 9 W. R. 612; 4 L. T. 293.

By virtue of certain ancient statutes, words which would not be actionable, if spoken of an ordinary subject, were formerly actionable if spoken of a peer of the realm, or of a judge, or of any of the great officers of the Crown, without proof of any special damage. These were called the Statutes of *Scandalum Magnatum* : they were three in number :—3 Edw. I. Stat. Westminster I. c. 34; 2 Rich. II. Stat. 1, c. 5; 12 Rich. II. c. 11. But these statutes had become obsolete; no proceeding had been taken under any of them since 1710; and they were all three repealed by the Statute Law Revision Act, 1887 (50 & 51 Vict. c. 59).

All words, if published falsely and without lawful occasion, are actionable, if they have in fact produced special damage to the plaintiff, such as the law does not deem too remote. "Any words by which a party has a special damage" are actionable. (Comyns' Digest, Action upon the Case for Defamation, D. 30.) "Undoubtedly all words are actionable, if a special damage follows" (per

Heath, J., in *Moore* v. *Meagher*, 1 Taunt. 44), provided they are in their nature defamatory. (*Kelly* v. *Partington*, 5 B. & Ad. 645 ; *Sheahan* v. *Ahearne*, (1875) Ir. R. 9 C. L. 412.)

If the words are not in their nature defamatory, that is, if they have not injured the reputation of any one, no action of libel or slander will lie, however maliciously they were published. But if the defendant maliciously intended to injure the plaintiff by his words and succeeded in his malicious intent, and damage to the plaintiff was the direct result of the defendant's words, an action on the case will lie, whatever the nature of the words, provided they are untrue.

Actions of this kind are discussed in the next chapter.

CHAPTER IV.

ACTIONS ON THE CASE FOR WORDS WHICH CAUSE DAMAGE.

So far we have dealt only with defamatory words : that is, with words which injure the reputation of some person. In all actions for defamatory words the law presumes in favour of the plaintiff that the words are false ; the plaintiff need not prove any actual malice ; and special damage, as we have seen, need only be proved in certain cases.

We pass now to words of an entirely different character— to words, that is, which are not defamatory of any individual, which do not injure the reputation of any one, either personally or in the way of his profession or trade, but which were intended to cause, and which did cause, pecuniary loss to some one. No action of libel or slander will lie for such words. But when a defendant either knows or ought to know that special damage will happen to the plaintiff if he writes or speaks certain words, and he writes or speaks those words, desiring and intending that such damage shall follow, or recklessly indifferent whether such damage follows or not, then, if the words be false, and if such damage does in fact follow directly from their use, an action on the case will lie. And in such an action on the case it is the plaintiff who must prove that the words are false, that they were published by the defendant with some degree of malice, and that actual damage has ensued. He must prove his whole case ; there is no presumption to lighten his burden. The right of action is one that survives to an executor for damage done to the estate of his testator ; whereas a right of action for libel or slander dies with the person. (*Hatchard* v. *Mège*, (1887) 18 Q. B. D. 771.)

" That an action will lie for written or oral falsehoods, not actionable *per se*, nor even defamatory, where they are maliciously published, where they are calculated in the ordinary course of things to produce, and where they do produce, actual damage, is established law. Such an action is not one of libel or of slander, but an action on the case for damage, wilfully and intentionally done without just occasion or excuse, analogous to an action for slander of title. To support it, actual damage must be shown, for it is an action which only lies in respect of such damage as has actually occurred." (*Per cur.* in *Ratcliffe* v. *Evans*, [1892] 2 Q. B. at p. 527; and see the judgment of Day, J., in *Hatchard* v. *Mège*, (1887) 18 Q. B. D. at p. 775.)

" There is a class of cases, of which this is one, the true legal aspect of which, however they may be described technically, is that they are actions for unlawfully causing damage. The damage is the gist of the action." (Per Lord Halsbury, L.C., in *Royal Baking Powder Company* v. *Wright, Crossley & Co.*, (1900) 18 Rep. Pat. Cas. at p. 104.) " This is not an action for libel or defamation of character. I think it can only be maintained as . . . an action on the case for maliciously damaging the plaintiffs in their trade. . . . To support such an action it is necessary for the plaintiffs to prove (1) that the statements complained of were untrue; (2) that they were made maliciously, *i.e.*, without just cause or excuse; (3) that the plaintiffs have suffered special damage thereby. The damage is the gist of the action, and therefore, according to the old rules of pleading, it must be specially alleged and proved." (Per Lord Davey, *Ib.*, p. 99.) " The plaintiff must prove two things: first, that the libel* was maliciously published; and, secondly, that specific money damage has resulted from it. If either of these ingredients be absent the action must fail." (Per Lord James of Hereford, *Ib.*, p. 101.) " Unless the plaintiff has in fact suffered loss which can be and is specified, he has no cause of action. The fact that the defendant has acted maliciously cannot supply the want of special damage." (Per Lord Robertson, *Ib.*, p. 103.) " The gist of the action is the special damage." (Per Swinfen Eady, J., in *Lyne* v. *Nicholls*, (1906) 23 Times L. R. at p. 88.)

This special damage must be some pecuniary loss or some other loss of the kind indicated in Chapter XIII., *post*, p. 371; it must be capable of assessment in monetary value, and it must not be too remote; that is, it must be either the natural and necessary result

---

* See note on p. 79.

of the defendant's words, or a result which the defendant in fact contemplated and desired.

It is clear law, then, that no plaintiff can recover damages in actions of this kind without proof that he sustained special damage before the commencement of the action. Nor can he, it is submitted, obtain an *injunction:* but the latter question will be found discussed in the chapter on Injunctions (*post,* p. 421).

Words which give rise to actions of this kind may be divided into five classes :—

I. Words which disparage a man's title to any property, real or personal (usually called Slander of Title).

II. Words which disparage the goods manufactured or sold by another.*

III. Threats of legal proceedings.*

IV. Other words which injure a man in his profession or trade.*

V. Other words which cause loss.

I. *Words which Disparage a Man's Title to any Property, Real or Personal.*

Such words are usually called " Slander of Title," whether they be written or spoken. " An action for slander of title is not properly an action for words spoken, or for libel written and published, but an action on the case for special damage sustained by reason of the speaking or publication of the slander of the plaintiff's title." (Per Tindal, C.J., in *Malachy* v. *Soper*, 3 Bing. N. C. p. 383 ; 3 Scott, 723.) Where the plaintiff possesses an estate or interest in any real or personal property, an action lies against any one who maliciously comes forward and falsely denies or impugns the plaintiff's title thereto, if any damage be thereby caused

---

* The term Trade Libel is often applied to words which fall within Classes II., III., IV., but the phrase is misleading, as such words are not libellous in the proper sense of the term. Its use has led to confusion between words of this kind and words which are a libel on a trader in the way of his trade (see *ante,* p. 32). We have, therefore, thought it best to discontinue using it.

to the plaintiff. (*Pater* v. *Baker*, 3 C. B. 831 ; 16 L. J. C. P. 124 ; 11 Jur. 370.)

The statement must be *false ;* if there be such a flaw in the plaintiff's title as the defendant asserted, no action lies. And it is for the plaintiff to prove it false, not for the defendant to prove it true. (Per Maule, J., in *Pater* v. *Baker*, 3 C. B. at p. 869.) Next, the statement must be *malicious ;* if it be made in the *bonâ fide* assertion of the defendant's own right, real or supposed, to the property, no action lies. But whenever a man unnecessarily intermeddles with the affairs of others with which he is wholly unconcerned, such officious interference will be deemed malicious and he will be liable, if damage follow. " The jury *may* infer malice from the absence of probable cause ; but they are not *bound* to do so. The want of probable cause does not necessarily lead to an inference of malice ; neither does the existence of probable cause afford any answer to the action." (Per Maule, J., in *Pater* v. *Baker*, 3 C. B. at p. 868. And see *post*, p. 94.) Lastly, *special damage* must be proved, and shown to have arisen from the defendant's words. (*Sir Thomas Gresham* v. *Grinsley*, (1609) Yelv. 88.) And for this, where the special damage alleged is that the plaintiff has lost the sale of his property, it is necessary for the plaintiff to prove that he was in the act of selling his property either by public auction or private treaty, and that the defendant by his words prevented an intending purchaser from bidding or completing. (*Tasburgh* v. *Day*, Cro. Jac. 484 ; *Law* v. *Harwood*, Cro. Car. 140 ; Sir W. Jones, 196.) So proof that plaintiff wished to let his lands and that the defendant prevented an intending tenant from taking a lease will be sufficient. But a mere apprehension that plaintiff's title might be drawn in question, or that the neighbours placed a lower value on plaintiff's lands in their own minds in consequence, the same not being offered for sale, will not be sufficient evidence of damage. " This action lieth not but by reason of the prejudice in the sale." (Per Fenner, J., in *Bold* v. *Bacon*, Cro. Eliz. 346.) The special damage must always be such as naturally or reasonably arises from the use of the words. (*Haddon* v. *Lott*, 15 C. B. 411; 24 L. J. C. P. 49; see *post*, Chapter XIII., p. 371.)

It makes no difference whether the defendant's words be spoken or written or printed; save as affecting the amount of damages, which should be larger where the publication is more permanent or extensive, as by advertisement. (*Malachy* v. *Soper and another*, 3 Bing. N. C. 371; 3 Scott, 723.)

The property may be either real or personal, corporeal or incorporeal; and the plaintiff's interest therein may be either in possession or reversion. It need not be even a vested interest, so long as it is anything that is saleable or that has a market value. The word "property" includes a patent right, copyright, the right to use a trade mark or a trade name.

Illustrations.

The plaintiff was a justice of the peace, seised in fee of the advowson of Sancroft, and intended to sell it towards payment of his debts. The defendant said that the plaintiff had lost the patronage and presentation, by reason of being a simonist and a recusant. *Held*, that no action lay, as the plaintiff had not shown " that there was any communication to sell it to any, nor that any who intended to buy it was thereby hindered in his buying."

Tasburgh v. *Day*, (1618) Cro. Jac. 484.

Lands were settled on D. in tail, remainder to the plaintiff in fee. D. being an old man and childless, plaintiff was about to sell his remainder to A. when the defendant interfered and asserted that D. had issue. A. consequently refused to buy. *Held*, that the action lay.

Bliss v. *Stafford*, (1588) Owen, 37; Moore, 188; Jenk. 247.

The plaintiff's father being tenant in tail of certain lands, which he was about to sell, the purchaser offered the plaintiff a sum of money to join in the assurance so as to estop him from attempting to set aside the deed, should he ever succeed to the estate tail; but the defendant told the purchaser that the plaintiff was a bastard, wherefore he refused to give the plaintiff anything for his signature. *Held*, that the plaintiff had a cause of action, though he was the youngest son of his father, and his chance of succeeding was therefore remote.

Vaughan v. *Ellis*, (1609) Cro. Jac. 213.

Plaintiff succeeded to certain lands as heir-at-law; the defendant asserted that plaintiff was a bastard; plaintiff was in consequence put to great expense to defend his title. Judgment for the plaintiff. Damages 50*l*.

Elborow v. *Allen*, (1623) Cro. Jac. 642.

To call a man a bastard while his father or other ancestor is alive may be actionable on general principles, if special damage ensue, such as the loss of a marriage, or if he be disinherited in consequence of defendant's words; but it is not the subject of an action for slander *of title ;* for, even though heir-apparent, plaintiff has no title ; but only a mere expectancy.

    Nelson v. *Staff,* (1618) Cro. Jac. 422.

    Humphrys v. *Stanfeild,* vel *Stridfield,* (1638) Cro. Car. 469 ; Godb. 451 ; Sir Wm. Jones, 388 ; 1 Roll. Abr. 38.

    Turner v. *Sterling,* (1671) 2 Vent. 26 ; *Anon.,* 1 Roll. Abr. 37.

    Banister v. *Banister,* (1583) cited in 4 Rep. 17.

    Poulett v. *Chatto and Windus,* (1887) 4 Times L. R. 35, 142.

The defendant falsely represented to the bailiff of a manor that a sheep of the plaintiff was an estray, in consequence of which it was wrongfully seized. *Held,* that an action on the case lay against him.

    Newman v. *Zachary,* (1647) Aleyn, 3.

The plaintiff was desirous to sell his lands to any one who would buy them, when the defendant said that the plaintiff had mortgaged all his lands for 100*l.,* and that he had no power to sell or let the same. No special damage being shown, judgment was stayed. It was not proved that any one intending to buy plaintiff's lands heard defendant speak the words.

    Manning v. *Avery,* (1674) 3 Keb. 153 ; 1 Vin. Abr. 553.

The plaintiff was possessed of tithes which he desired to sell ; the defendant falsely and maliciously said "His right and title thereunto is nought, and I have a better title than he." As special damage it was alleged that the plaintiff " was likely to sell, and was injured by the words ; and that by reason of the defendant speaking the words, the plaintiff could not recover his tithes." *Held,* insufficient.

    Cane v. *Golding,* (1649) Style, 169, 176.

    Law v. *Harwood,* (1629) Cro. Car. 140 ; Sir Wm. Jones, 196 ; Palm. 529.

The plaintiff was the assignee of a beneficial lease, which he expected would realise 100*l.* But the defendant, the superior landlord, came to the sale, and stated publicly, " The whole of the covenants of this lease are broken, and I have served notice of ejectment ; the premises will cost 70*l.* to put them in repair." In consequence of this statement the property fetched only 35 guineas. Rolfe, B., left to the jury only one question—Was the defendant's statement true or false ? and they found a verdict for the plaintiff ; damages, 40*l.* But the Court of Exchequer granted a new trial on the ground that two other questions ought to have been left to the jury as well :—Was the statement or any part of it made maliciously ? and, Did the special damage arise from such malicious statement or from such part of it as was malicious ?

    Brook v. *Rawl,* (1849) 4 Exch. 521 ; 19 L. J. Ex. 114.

    And see *Smith* v. *Spooner,* (1810) 3 Taunt. 246.

    Milman v. *Pratt,* (1824) 2 B. & C. 486 ; 3 D. & R. 728.

    Watson v. *Reynolds,* (1826) Moo. & Mal. 1.

An advertisement was sent to the *Wolverhampton Chronicle,* in the ordinary course of business and published once on January 6th, 1868. It was as follows :— "Important notice. Horsehill Estate. The public are respectfully requested not to buy any property formerly belonging to A., B., and C., without ascertaining that the title deeds of the same are correct ; as the heirs are not dead nor abroad, but are still alive." This estate was at that moment advertised for sale in building lots ; but this advertisement revived all previous doubts about plaintiff's title, and rendered the estate practically unsaleable. On January

13th plaintiff wrote and complained of this advertisement, and asked for the name and address of the person who sent it to the paper. This the proprietor of the paper at once furnished; but on January 30th he was served with a writ. On February 10th he inserted an apology. But the jury, under the direction of Keating, J., found for the plaintiff.

Ravenhill v. *Upcott*, (1869) 20 L. T. 233 ; 33 J. P. 299.

The plaintiff held 160 shares in a silver mine in Cornwall, which he said were worth 100,000*l*. Tollervey and Hayward each filed a bill in Chancery against the plaintiff and others claiming certain shares in the mine, and praying for an account and an injunction, and for the appointment of a receiver. To these bills plaintiff demurred. Before the demurrers came on for hearing, a paragraph appeared in the defendant's newspaper to the effect that the demurrers had been overruled, that an injunction had been granted, that a receiver had been duly appointed, and had actually arrived at the mine; all of which was quite untrue. A verdict having been obtained for the plaintiff, damages 5*l*., the Court of Common Pleas arrested judgment on the ground that there was no sufficient allegation of special damage, and this although the declaration contained averments to the effect that " the plaintiff is injured in his rights; and the shares so possessed by him, and in which he is interested, have been, and are, much depreciated and lessened in value ; and divers persons have believed and do believe that he has little or no right to the shares, and that the mine cannot be lawfully worked or used for his benefit; and that he hath been hindered and prevented from selling or disposing of his said shares in the said mine, and from working and using the same in so ample and beneficial a manner as he otherwise would have done."

Malachy v. *Soper and another*, (1836) 3 Bing. N. C. 371 ; 3 Scott, 723 ; 2 Hodges, 217.

Where the steward of a manor had stated in writing to an intending purchaser of the interest of a copyhold tenant that a forfeiture had been declared : *Held*, that the copyholder was entitled, in an action against the lord, to have the cloud on his title dispersed by a declaration that there had been no forfeiture or authority to forfeit, and to be paid the costs of the action.

Pawley v. *Scratton*, (1886) 3 Times L. R. 146.

The defendants, who owned the copyright of a picture by Millais, issued a circular threatening proceedings against all persons who bought copies of the plaintiff's magazine, containing a woolwork pattern, which the defendants wrongly deemed to be an infringement of their copyright. The plaintiff brought an action for an injunction, and also for damages. He failed to prove that he had sustained any damage: wherefore the Court of Appeal refused to grant him any injunction.

Dicks v. *Brooks*, (1880) 15 Ch. D. 22 ; 49 L. J. Ch. 812 ; 29 W. R. 87 ; 43 L. T. 71.

The plaintiff imported and sold in England a brand of champagne known as "Delmonico." Thereupon the defendants circulated the following notice : " Caution. Delmonico Champagne. Messrs. Delbeck & Co., finding that wine, stated to be Delmonico Champagne, is being advertised for sale in Great Britain, hereby give notice that such wine cannot be the wine it is represented to be, as no champagne shipped under that name can be genuine unless it has their names on their labels." They further announced that if such wines were shipped from

France, they should take legal proceedings. After the close of the pleadings, and before trial, the plaintiff died. *Held*, that these words were a libel on the plaintiff personally, and in the way of his trade; and that the cause of action for such personal libel abated at his death. But that the words were also ground for an action of slander of title; for they imputed that the plaintiff had no right to use his trade-mark; and that this cause of action survived to the plaintiff's executor, who was entitled to sue in respect of the loss, if any, sustained by the plaintiff's estate in consequence of these words.

> *Hatchard* v. *Mège and others*, (1887) 18 Q. B. D. 771 ; 56 L. J. Q. B. 397 ; 35 W. R. 576 ; 56 L. T. 662.

The executor accordingly continued the action, but failed; for the jury found that there was no malice on the part of the defendants.

> S. C., (1887) 4 Times L. R. 118.

The defendants issued a circular stating that the plaintiffs were using a label for their goods which it was illegal for them to use, as they, the defendants, had obtained an order expunging the label from the register of trade-marks. They also stated that they intended to take proceedings against any person selling goods so labelled. *Held*, that if the circular had been issued maliciously, and had produced special damage to the plaintiffs, an action would lie.

> *Royal Baking Powder Co.* v. *Wright, Crossley & Co.*, (1900) 18 Rep. Pat. Cas. 95.

It is not actionable for any man to assert his own rights at any time. And even where the defendant fails to prove such right on investigation, still if at the time he spoke he *bonâ fide* supposed such right to exist, no action lies. (*Carr* v. *Duckett*, 5 H. & N. 783; 29 L. J. Ex. 468.) Hence, whenever a man claims a right or title in himself, in possession or in remainder, it is not enough for the plaintiff to prove that he had no such right; he must also give evidence of express malice (*Smith* v. *Spooner*, 3 Taunt. 246); that is, he must also attempt to show that the defendant could not honestly have believed in the existence of the right he claimed, or at least that he had no reasonable or probable cause for so believing. If there appear no reasonable or probable cause for his claim of title, still the jury are not bound to find malice; the defendant may have acted stupidly, yet from an innocent motive. (*Pitt* v. *Donovan*, 1 M. & S. 648; *Steward* v. *Young*, L. R. 5 C. P. 122; 39 L. J. C. P. 85; 18 W. R. 492; 22 L. T. 168; *Clark* v. *Molyneux*, 3 Q. B. D. 237; 47 L. J. Q. B. 230; 26 W. R. 104; 37 L. T. 694.) But in all cases where it appears that the defendant at the time he spoke knew that what he said was false, the jury should certainly find malice ; lies which injure another cannot be told *bonâ fide.*

" If some portions of the statement which a person makes are *bonâ fide*, but others are *malâ fide*, and occasion injury to another, the injured party cannot recover damages unless he can distinctly trace the damage as resulting from that part which is made *malâ fide.*" (Per Parke, B., in *Brook* v. *Rawl*, 4 Exch. 524.) So if part be true and part false. (*Ib.* 523.)

Illustrations.

If the defendant asserts that plaintiff is a bastard, and that he himself is the next heir, no action lies.

> *Banister* v. *Banister*, (1583) cited in 4 Rep. 17.
> *Cane* v. *Golding*, (1649) Style, 169, 176.

Plaintiff had purchased the manor and castle of H. in fee from Lord Audley, and was about to demise them to Ralph Egerton for a term of twenty-two years, when the defendant, a widow, said, " I have a lease of the castle and manor of H. for ninety years; " and she showed Egerton what purported to be a lease from a former Lord Audley to her husband for a term of ninety years. This lease was a forgery ; and the defendant knew it. *Held*, that an action lay for slander of title ; though the defendant had claimed a right to the property herself. It would have been otherwise had she not known that the lease was a forgery.

> *Sir G. Gerard* v. *Dickenson*, (1590) 4 Rep. 18 ; Cro. Eliz. 197.
> And see Fitzh. Nat. Brev. 116 (B. & D.).
> *Lovett* v. *Weller*, 1 Roll. R. 409.

The plaintiff put up for sale by public auction eight unfinished houses in Agar Town. The defendant, a surveyor of roads appointed under the 7 & 8 Vict. c. 84, had previously insisted that these houses were not being built by the plaintiff in conformity with the Act. He now attended the sale and stated publicly, " My object in attending the sale is to inform purchasers, if there are any present, that I shall not allow the houses to be finished until the roads are made good. I have no power to compel the purchasers to complete the roads ; but I have power to prevent them from completing the houses until the roads are made good." In consequence only two of the unfinished houses were sold ; and they realised only 35*l.* each, instead of 65*l.* The jury found a verdict for the plaintiff for 18*l.* 12*s.* But the Court of Common Pleas held that there was no evidence of malice to go to the jury. For malice is not to be inferred from the circumstance of the defendant having acted upon an incorrect view of his duty, founded upon an honest misconstruction of the statute.

> *Pater* v. *Baker*, 3 C. B. 831 ; 16 L. J. C. P. 124 ; 11 Jur. 370.

The plaintiff was the widow and administratrix of her deceased husband, and advertised a sale of some of his property. Defendant, an old friend of the husband, thereupon put an advertisement in the papers offering a reward for the production of the will of the deceased. The defendant subsequently called on the solicitor of the deceased, and was assured by him there was no will ; but, in spite of this, the defendant attended at the sale and made statements which effectually prevented any person present from bidding. After waiting twelve months, the plaintiff again put the same property up for sale, and defendant again stopped the auction. Cockburn, C.J., left it to the jury to say whether, after the interview with the solicitor, defendant could still possess an honest and reasonable belief that the deceased had left a will. The jury found that he had not that belief. Verdict for the plaintiff. Damages 54*l.* 7*s.*

　　　Atkins v. *Perrin*, 3 F. & F. 179.

The defendant wrongfully and maliciously caused certain persons who had agreed to sell goods to the plaintiff to refuse to deliver them, by asserting that he had a lien upon them, and ordering those persons to retain the goods until further orders from him, he well knowing at the time that he had no lien. *Held*, that the action was maintainable, though the persons who had the goods were under no legal obligation to obey the orders of the defendant, and their refusal was their own spontaneous act.

　　　Green v. *Button*, 2 C. M. & R. 707.

　　　Barley v. *Walford*, 9 Q. B. 197 ; 15 L. J. Q. B. 369 ; 10 Jur. 917.

The lessee of an hotel agreed to sell her lease and certain valuable tenant's fixtures to Turner. Defendant, the assignee of the lessor, thereupon gave notice to Turner that he claimed most of the fixtures as landlord's fixtures, and that if Turner bought them, he would have to give them up at the end of the term or pay defendant for them. *Held*, that no action lay; for there was no evidence of malice, although defendant had no present property in the goods.

　　　Baker and others v. *Piper*, (1886) 2 Times L. R. 733.

A. falsely asserts that the plaintiff's patent is invalid. If A. has no interest in the plaintiff's patent or any other patent, the jury will as a rule conclude that he acted maliciously, unless he can show that he had some reasonable or probable cause for such a statement. But if A. holds a prior patent for the manufacture of articles very similar to those manufactured by the plaintiff, the jury will probably infer that A. was acting honestly in defence of his own rights and A. will then be entitled to judgment, even though he has failed to prove that the plaintiff's patent is in fact invalid.

　　　Wren v. *Weild*, L. R. 4 Q. B. 730 ; 10 B. & S. 51 ; 38 L. J. Q. B. 88, 　　　　327 ; 20 L. T. 277.

　　　Halsey v. *Brotherhood*, 19 Ch. D. 386 ; 51 L. J. Ch. 233 ; 30 W. R. 　　　　279 ; 45 L. T. 640.

　　　And see *post*, pp. 94, 95.

An action lies against a defendant who issues a circular stating that the plaintiff's invention " had been proved to be an infringement " of his own, when no proceeding had ever been taken to test its validity. For there was no ground whatever for the positive statement made ; and therefore clearly no reasonable or probable cause for making it.

　　　Crampton v. *Swete and Main*, 58 L. T. 516.

The defendant posted notices on the plaintiff's park walls and elsewhere calling on the plaintiff's tenants to pay their rents to the defendant as " the lawful heir to and owner of the Newburgh estates," which had for many years been in the possession of the plaintiff and his ancestors. The defendant also publicly accused the plaintiff and his relatives of having tampered with registers, and committed other frauds. There was no foundation whatever for these reckless charges; and no reasonable ground for the defendant's claim to the estates. Kekewich, J., granted an injunction to restrain any further slander of the plaintiff's title; and the Court of Appeal upheld his decision.

Leslie v. *Cave*, (1887) 3 Times L. R. 584 ; (1888) 5 Times L. R. 5.

The law is the same where the defendant is an agent or attorney, and claims for his principal or client a title which he honestly believes him to possess. (*Hargrave* v. *Le Breton*, 4 Burr. 2422 ; *Steward* v. *Young*, L. R. 5 C. P. 122 ; 39 L. J. C. P. 85 ; 18 W. R. 492 ; 22 L. T. 168 ; *Dunlop Pneumatic Tyre Co., Limited* v. *Maison Talbot and others*, (1904) 20 Times L. R. 579.) So where a man *bonâ fide* asserts a title in his father or other near relative to whom he or his wife is heir apparent. (*Pitt* v. *Donovan*, 1 M. & S. 639 ; *Gutsole* v. *Mathers*, 1 M. & W. 495 ; 5 Dowl. 69 ; 2 Gale, 64 ; 1 Tyrw. & Gr. 694.) But where the defendant makes no claim at all for himself or any connection of his, but asserts a title in some one who is a stranger to him, here he clearly is meddling in a matter which does not concern him ; and such officious and unnecessary interference will be deemed malicious. (*Pennyman* v. *Rabanks*, Cro. Eliz. 427 ; 1 Vin. Abr. 551 ; *Mildmay et ux.* v. *Standish*, 1 Rep. 177 b ; Moore, 144 ; *Gerard* v. *Dickenson*, Cro. Eliz. 197.)

Illustrations.

Loveday mortgaged his lands to the plaintiff, who subsequently put them up for sale by auction. The defendant who was attorney for Lee, another creditor of Loveday's, came to the auction-room and stated publicly that Loveday was a bankrupt before he made the mortgage to the plaintiff; that there was a docket made out for a bankruptcy commission against him, &c. It was not true that a docket was yet made out, nor had Lee told the defendant to state this. *Held*, that there was no evidence of any malice, expressed or implied; and that therefore no action lay.

Hargrave v. *Le Breton*, 4 Burr. 2422.

Plaintiff held lands on lease from Home, which he put up for sale. Defendant who was Home's attorney, attended and said publicly before the first lot was put up, "There is a suit depending in the Court of Chancery in respect to this property; encroachments have been made; proceedings will be taken against the purchaser; there is no power to sell the premises; a good title cannot be made," &c. Home had asked the defendant to go to the sale and mention the encroachments, but had not desired him to make any other statement. Littledale, J., directed the jury that defendant was not liable, if he *bonâ fide*, though without authority, raised such objections only as Home, if present, might lawfully have raised. Verdict for the plaintiff. Damages, one farthing.

Watson v. *Reynolds*, Moo. & Mal. 1.

A. died possessed of furniture in a beer-shop. His widow, without taking out administration, continued in possession of the beer-shop for three or four years, and then died, having whilst so in possession conveyed all the furniture by bill of sale to her landlords by way of security for a debt she had contracted with them. After the widow's death, the plaintiff took out letters of administration to the estate of A., and informed the defendant, the landlords' agent, that the bill of sale was invalid, as the widow had no title to the furniture. Subsequently the plaintiff was about to sell the furniture by auction, when the defendant interposed to forbid the sale, and said that he claimed the goods for his principals under a bill of sale. On proof of these facts, in an action for slander of title, the plaintiff was nonsuited. *Held,* that the mere fact of the defendant's having been told before the sale that the bill of sale was invalid, was no evidence of malice to be left to the jury, and that the plaintiff was therefore properly nonsuited.

Steward v. *Young,* L. R. 5 C. P. 122; 39 L. J. C. P. 85; 18 W. R. 492; 22 L. T. 168.

A solicitor, acting on behalf of his client, gave written notice to an auctioneer not to part with the proceeds of the sale of certain goods, entrusted to the auctioneer for sale, on the ground that the owner of the goods had committed an act of bankruptcy upon which an order in bankruptcy might be made against him. In an action by the owner of the goods against the solicitor for libel, *held,* that no action lay, as the solicitor was acting in the ordinary and proper course of his duty to his client.

Baker v. *Carrick,* [1894] 1 Q. B. 838; 63 L. J. Q. B. 399; 42 W. R. 338; 70 L. T. 366; 9 R. 283.

II. *Words which Disparage the Goods Manufactured or Sold by Another.*

Not all such words are actionable. A man may always puff his own goods. He may even name his rivals in the trade, compare his goods with theirs, and assert that his own goods are better than theirs, either generally or in some particular respect. The Courts will not enter on an inquiry into the comparative merits of the goods of rival traders. (*White* v. *Mellin,* [1895] A. C. at pp. 164, 165.) No action will lie for such expressions of opinion so long as the defendant asserts no fact about his rivals' goods. But if a man after lauding his own goods and expressing his opinion that they are superior to the goods manufactured by others, goes on to make assertions of fact about his rivals' goods, which he cannot prove to be true, such disparagement will give rise to an action on the case, provided the words be published without just cause or occasion, and special damage ensue.

To give instances. Any trader may say : " My goods are the best in the market ; they are far superior to A.'s." And no action will lie for such words, even though they be written or spoken maliciously and cause special damage to A. But if he asserts without just cause that " A.'s food for infants contains large quantities of starch," or " There is opium in B.'s soothing syrup," when there is no starch or opium in either, and damage follows, both A. and B. have a good cause of action on the case.

Moreover, as we have already seen (*ante*, p. 34), the defendant, while purporting to attack only the plaintiff's goods, may use words which defame the plaintiff personally or in the way of his trade, and so render himself liable to an ordinary action of libel or slander. Thus, if he said of a baker, " He always buys mildewed flour for the bread which he supplies to the workhouse," this would be a slander on the baker, as well as a disparagement of his goods, and for such words an action of slander would lie without proof of any special damage ; if, however, actual damage could be shown, the baker would have in addition an action on the case. The action of slander would die with him: the action on the case would survive to his executors. (*Hatchard* v. *Mège*, (1887) 18 Q. B. D. 771.)

The three preceding paragraphs are an attempt to state the net result of the decisions on this point, which at first sight appear to conflict. The old authorities have been qualified to some extent by recent decisions.

To review briefly the cases in their chronological order : in *Harman* v. *Delany*, (1731) 2 Str. 898, which was an action for a libel on a tradesman in the way of his trade, the Court of King's Bench expressed the opinion that it was not actionable for a man to advertise that he can make as good articles as any other person in the trade. *Evans* v. *Harlow*, (1844) 5 Q. B. 624, was argued on demurrer. The words are set out *ante*, p. 35 ; they related only to the plaintiff's goods. No special damage was alleged,* and the Court held the declaration bad. *Young* v. *Macrae*, (1862) 3 B. & S. 264; 32 L. J. Q. B. 6, was also argued on demurrer. Special damage was alleged, nevertheless the Court held the declaration bad on the ground apparently that the falsity of the words was not alleged with sufficient precision. Cockburn, C.J., said (32 L. J. Q. B. at p. 8): "The defendant is alleged to have falsely and maliciously published a disparaging comparison between the oil manufactured by the plaintiffs and that which he was advertising; . . . it is not averred that the defendant falsely represented that the oil of the plaintiffs had a reddish-brown tinge, was much thicker, and that it had a more disagreeable odour. If that had been falsely represented, and special damage had ensued, an action might have been maintained." In *Western Counties Manure Co.* v. *Lawes Chemical Manure Co.*, (1874) L. R. 9 Ex. 218, which was also argued on demurrer, the words complained of were more than a comparative estimate of the plaintiffs' and the defendants' goods respectively. It was stated as a fact that the plaintiffs' guano "appears to contain a considerable quantity of coprolites, and is altogether an article of low quality." Special damage was alleged, and it was held that the action lay. *White* v. *Mellin*, [1895] A. C. 154, was merely a case of a man puffing his own goods and expressing his opinion that they were better than his rival's. Lord Watson stated the law thus, in *White* v. *Mellin*, [1895] A. C. at p. 167: "Every extravagant phrase used by a tradesman in commendation of his own goods may be an implied disparagement of the goods of all others in the same trade; it may attract customers to him and diminish the business of others who sell as good and even better articles at the same price; but this is a disparagement of which the law takes no cognizance." Similarly, in *Hubbuck* v. *Wilkinson*, [1899] 1 Q. B. 86, the Court was of opinion that the defendants' circular, when attentively read, came to no more than a statement that the defendants' white zinc was equal to and, indeed, somewhat better than the plaintiffs'. "Even if each particular charge of falsehood is established, it will only come to this—that it is untrue that the defendants' paint is better than or equal to that of the plaintiffs', for which no action lies. The particular reasons for making that statement are immaterial if the statement itself is not actionable. . . . For a person

---

* Lindley, M.R., is in error in *Hubbuck* v. *Wilkinson*, [1899] 1 Q. B. at p. 92, in saying that special damage was alleged in this case.

in trade to puff his own wares and to proclaim their superiority over those of his rivals is not actionable. . . . But in *Young* v. *Macrae* it was pointed out that there were different ways of disparaging a man's goods—that some false statements about them might be actionable if special damage could be proved, and *Western Counties Manure Co.* v. *Lawes Chemical Manure Co.* was decided on this ground. But in *Young* v. *Macrae* it was also pointed out that, if the only false statement complained of is that the defendant's goods are better than the plaintiff's, such a statement is not actionable, even if the plaintiff is damnified by it." (Per Lindley, M.R., [1899] 1 Q. B. at pp. 92, 93.)

It is clear, then, that the general rule laid down by Bramwell, B., in *Western Counties Manure Co.* v. *Lawes Chemical Manure Co.*, that "an untrue statement, disparaging a man's goods, published without lawful occasion, and causing him special damage, is actionable," is stated too widely. But it is submitted that the decision on the facts alleged in that case is still good law.

Illustrations.

The defendant published an advertisement cautioning the public that the plaintiff's "self-acting tallow syphons or lubricators" wasted the tallow. No special damage was alleged. *Held*, that the words were not a libel on the plaintiff either generally or in the way of his trade, but were only a reflection upon the goods sold by him, which was not actionable without proof of special damage.

> *Evans* v. *Harlow,* 5 Q. B. 624; 13 L. J. Q. B. 120; Dav. & M. 507; 8 Jur. 571; *ante,* p. 35.

The defendant published a certificate by a Dr. Muspratt, who had compared the plaintiffs' oil with the defendant's, and deemed it inferior to the defendant's. It was alleged that the certificate was false, and that divers customers of the plaintiffs after reading it had ceased to deal with the plaintiffs and gone over to the defendant. *Held*, that the plaintiffs' oil, even if inferior to the defendant's, might still be very good; and that the falsity was alleged too generally, and that therefore no action lay. It was consistent with the declaration that every word said about the plaintiffs' oil should be true, and the only falsehood the assertion that defendant's was superior to it, which would not be actionable.

> *Young and others* v. *Macrae,* 3 B. & S. 264; 32 L. J. Q. B. 6; 11 W. R. 63; 9 Jur. N. S. 539; 7 L. T. 354.

The defendants falsely and without lawful occasion published a detailed analysis of the plaintiffs' artificial manure and of their own, and stated that the plaintiffs' manure appeared to contain a considerable quantity of coprolites, and was altogether an article of low quality. Special damage having resulted, *held*, that the action lay.

> *Western Counties Manure Co.* v. *Lawes Chemical Manure Co.,* L. R. 9 Ex. 218; 43 L. J. Ex. 171; 23 W. R. 5.

The plaintiffs manufactured and sold (to the defendant among others) a "Food for Infants." The defendant affixed to bottles of the plaintiffs' Food a label to the following effect:—"*Notice.* The public are recommended to try Dr. Vance's prepared food for infants and invalids, it being far more nutritious and healthful than any other preparation yet offered. . . . Local agent, Timothy White, chemist, Portsmouth." *Held*, that for such disparagement no action lay.

> *White* v. *Mellin*, [1895] A. C. 154; 64 L. J. Ch. 308; 43 W. R. 353;
> 72 L. T. 334.

The defendants printed and published a circular which purported to contain a copy of a report of a trial of plaintiffs' and defendants' white zinc, which ended with the words: "Judging the finished work, it is quite evident that W. H. & Co.'s zinc has a slight advantage over Hubbucks', but for all practical purposes they can be regarded as being in every respect equal." *Held*, that no action lay; although the plaintiffs alleged actual loss attributable to the defendants' circular.

> *Hubbuck and Sons* v. *Wilkinson*, [1899] 1 Q. B. 86; 68 L. J. Q. B.
> 34; 79 L. T. 429.
> But see *Alcott* v. *Millar's Karri & Jarrah Forests, Ltd., and another*,
> (1904) 91 L. T. 722; 21 Times L. R. 30.

The plaintiff and the defendant were the owners of newspapers circulating in the same locality, and the defendant published a statement that the circulation of his newspaper was 20 to 1 of any other weekly paper in the district, and that " where others count by the dozen, we count by the hundred." It was held that the above statements were not a mere puff by the defendant of his own newspaper, but amounted to an untrue disparagement of the plaintiff's newspaper, and were actionable on proof of actual damage; but that as no damage was proved the action failed.

> *Lyne* v. *Nicholls*, (1906) 23 Times L. R. 86.

A newspaper published a statement that the plaintiff's house was haunted; and the plaintiff thereupon brought an action for disparagement. It was shown that the house had fallen in value owing to its having the reputation of being thus affected, but from the evidence it appeared that such reputation was acquired before the publication by the defendant. *Held*, that the plaintiff had no cause of action.

> *Barrett* v. *Associated Newspapers, Ltd.*, (1907) 23 Times L. R. 666.

The doctrine that a man may puff his own goods, even by publishing words which he knows to be false, has been carried very far in equity.

Only two persons, A. and B., obtained medals for pickles at the International Exhibition of 1862. Nevertheless, a third manufacturer of pickles, C., dishonestly proceeded to sell his goods labelled " Prize Medal, 1862." Yet the Court of Chancery refused to interfere.

> *Batty* v. *Hill*, (1863) 1 H. & M. 264.

The Legislature afterwards came to the relief of the plaintiff in this case, and passed an Act prohibiting any such misrepresentation in the future as to prize medals awarded at the Exhibitions of 1851 and 1862.

> The Exhibition Medals Act, 1863 (26 & 27 Vict. c. 119).

A prize was offered for the best sewing machine. Both plaintiff and defendant competed, and the plaintiff won it. Then the defendant falsely advertised that he had won it. The Supreme Court of Georgia refused to grant an injunction on the following ground : The defendant is "publishing untruths—lies, if you will—calculated and intended to help himself and damage the complainant. To say that he may be enjoined from doing this, is to say that the writ of injunction may issue to restrain a libel or to stop slander " ; which in those days it could not. It is submitted that this would now be held actionable, if plaintiff could show a loss of business in consequence of the defendant's advertisement.

> *Singer Manufacturing Co.* v. *Domestic Sewing Machine Co.,* (1873)
> 49 Georgia Rep. 70 ; 15 Amer. Rep. 674.

A. and B. each invented a system of hot-air treatment. B. issued a pamphlet in which he appropriated to his own system favourable notices which A.'s system had received in the Press, omitting all mention of the plaintiff's name. There was evidence that some of the plaintiff's patients were misled by these extracts, but no evidence of any actual damage. *Held*, by Stirling, J., that in the absence of any attempt by the defendant to pass off his system as the plaintiff's, the Court ought not to interfere by way of interlocutory injunction.

> *Tallerman* v. *Dowsing Radiant Heat Co.,* [1900] 1 Ch. 1 ; 68 L. J.
> Ch. 618 ; 69 L. J. Ch. 46 ; 48 W. R. 146.

Of course, if the words used by the defendant amount to an attempt to "pass off" his goods as the plaintiff's goods, an action will lie.

> *Birmingham Vinegar Brewery Co.* v. *Powell,* [1897] A. C. 710 ;
> 66 L. J. Ch. 763 ; 76 L. T. 792.

Now assuming that the words are reasonably capable of being construed as an actionable disparagement of the plaintiffs' goods, " to support such an action it is necessary for the plaintiffs to prove

(i.) That the statements complained of were untrue ;

(ii.) That they were made maliciously, *i.e.*, without just cause or excuse ;

(iii.) That the plaintiffs have suffered special damage thereby." (Per Lord Davey, in *Royal Baking Powder Co.* v. *Wright, Crossley & Co.,* (1900) 18 Rep. Pat. Cas. at p. 99.)

Whether the words are reasonably capable of being an actionable disparagement, is a question for the judge : all other questions are for the jury. If the words are incapable of being an actionable disparagement the judge should stop the case ; or the Court will, on application under Order XXV. r. 4, strike out the Statement of Claim. (*Hubbuck* v. *Wilkinson,* [1899] 1 Q. B. 86.)

It is somewhat difficult to define the precise degree of malice necessary to sustain the action. In *Western Counties,*

&c. v. *Lawes, &c.*, the Court held that it was sufficient if the words were published without lawful occasion. In *Royal Baking Powder Co.* v. *Wright, Crossley & Co.* (18 Rep. Pat. Cas. 95 at p. 99), Lord Davey treated "maliciously" and "without just cause" as convertible terms in actions for disparagement of goods and as equivalent to "for the purpose of injuring the plaintiff and not for the *bonâ fide* protection of the defendants' rights."* This view was adopted by Collins, M.R., in delivering judgment in *Dunlop Pneumatic Tyre Co.* v. *Maison Talbot and others* ((1904) 20 Times L. R.at p. 580). Of course, clear evidence of any other kind of actual malice will be sufficient. (See *ante*, p. 84.) If the words were published on a privileged occasion, the plaintiff must, of course, prove actual malice. (*Wren* v. *Weild*, (1869) L. R. 4 Q. B. at p. 737 ; *Halsey* v. *Brotherhood*, (1881) 19 Ch. D. at p. 388.)

The mere fact that the plaintiff and the defendant are rivals in the same line of business is by itself no evidence of malice ; indeed, it rather tends to negative malice ; as it renders it probable that the words were published with the object of promoting the defendant's own trade and not of injuring the plaintiff. "It was not malice if the object of the writer was to push his own business, though at the same time it might incidentally injure another person's business. To make the act malicious it must be done with the direct object of injuring that other person's business. Therefore,

---

* In the cases where it has been held that an action lies for wrongfully procuring a person to break his contract, the effect of the decisions is that anything will be evidence of malice which may reasonably lead the jury to infer that the words were published without "justification" or without "just cause or excuse." (*Lumley* v. *Gye*, (1853) 2 E. & B. 216; 22 L. J. Q. B. 463; *Quinn* v. *Leathem*, [1901] A. C. 495 ; *Read* v. *Friendly Society of Operative Stonemasons*, [1902] 2 K. B. 732 ; *Glamorgan Coal Co.* v. *South Wales, &c.*, [1903] 2 K. B. 545 ; [1905] A. C. 239.) But it is doubtful whether the doctrine so laid down can be applied to actions of the kind discussed in this chapter. A notable distinction is that the *onus* of proof is different, as in actions for wrongfully procuring a breach of contract the *onus* is on the defendant to show that he acted with just cause or lawful excuse, whereas in actions on the case of the kind here discussed the *onus* is on the plaintiff to prove that the defendant published the words maliciously.

the mere fact that it would injure another person's business was no evidence of malice." (Per Collins, M.R., in *Dunlop Pneumatic Tyre Co., Limited* v. *Maison Talbot and others,* (1904) 20 Times L. R. at p. 581. And see *White* v. *Mellin,* [1895] A. C. at p. 164.) There is no malice in honestly repeating another person's apparently honest statement. (*Barrett* v. *Associated Newspapers, Ltd.,* (1907) 23 Times L. R. 666.)

III. *Threats of Legal Proceedings.*

The plaintiff's business may also be injured by the defendant issuing circulars or other notices warning the plaintiff's customers, or the public generally, not to buy his goods on the ground that they are infringements of a patent of the defendant's. But when this occurs, it is generally the case that the defendant has a subsisting patent for articles similar to the plaintiff's, and issues the notices in the honest and reasonable defence of his rights thereunder. If so, no action lies. It may be said that the defendant should defend his rights under his patent, not by issuing such notices, but by bringing an action against the plaintiff for infringement. And if the defendant has brought such an action, the fact always tells in his favour : as it is cogent (though not conclusive) proof that he honestly believes that the plaintiff's goods are an infringement of his patent. But the defendant is in no way bound to bring an action ; and his not doing so is no proof of *mala fides ;* the infringer may desist on warning being given, or he may not be worth suing. "A man merely giving notice that his rights are being infringed, believing that they are being infringed, is not to be subjected to an action for giving that notice, even although he does not follow up that notice by bringing an action at law for the infringement." (Per Jessel, M.R., in *Halsey* v. *Brotherhood,* 15 Ch. D. at p. 519.)

But though the fact that the defendant has commenced an action for infringement against the plaintiff will generally prevent the plaintiff's succeeding in an action at common law for damages caused to his business by the defendant's threatening notices, yet the commencement of the infringement action may itself enable the plaintiff to stop the further circulation of such notices. This however depends largely on the language of the notices themselves. If they are merely general warnings against possible future infringements of the defendant's patent, they will be deemed harmless. But if, in the opinion of the Court, they tend to prejudice the fair trial of the action they will be restrained as a contempt of Court. (*Fusee Vesta Co.* v. *Bryant and May*, 56 L. T. 136; 4 R. P. C. 191; *Goulard and another* v. *Lindsay*, 56 L. T. 506; *Coats* v. *Chadwick*, [1894] 1 Ch. 347; 63 L. J. Ch. 328. See however *Dunlop Pneumatic Tyre Co.* v. *Clifton Rubber Co.*, (1902) 19 Rep. Pat. Cas. 527; *Haskell Golf Ball Co.* v. *Hutchinson*, (1904) 20 Times L. R. 606; 21 Rep. Pat. Cas. 497; and *post*, p. 435.)

Illustrations.

The defendant had a subsisting patent for the manufacture of spooling machines; so had the plaintiff. The defendant wrote to certain manufacturers, customers of the plaintiff, warning them against using the plaintiff's machine, on the ground that it was an infringement of the defendant's patent. *Held*, that " the action could not lie unless the plaintiff affirmatively proved that the defendant's claim was not a *bonâ fide* claim in support of a right which, with or without cause, he fancied he had, but a *malâ fide* and malicious attempt to injure the plaintiff by asserting a claim of right against his own knowledge that it was without any foundation." Evidence to show that the defendant's patent, though subsisting, was void for want of novelty, was not admitted, as being irrelevant in this action.

> *Wren* v. *Weild*, L. R. 4 Q. B. 730, 737; 10 B. & S. 51; 38 L. J. Q. B. 88, 327; 20 L. T. 277.

The defendants, who owned the copyright of a picture by Millais, issued a circular threatening proceedings against all persons who bought copies of the plaintiff's magazine, containing a woolwork pattern, which the defendants wrongly deemed to be an infringement of their copyright. The plaintiff brought an action for an injunction, and also for damages. He failed to prove that he had sustained any damage: wherefore the Court of Appeal refused to grant him any injunction.

> *Dicks* v. *Brooks*, 15 Ch. D. 22; 49 L. J. Ch. 812; 29 W. R. 87; 43 L. T. 71.
>
> *Hammersmith Skating Rink Co.* v. *Dublin Skating Rink Co.*, 10 Ir. R. Eq. 235.

But a patentee is not entitled to publish statements that he intends to institute legal proceedings in order to deter persons from purchasing alleged infringements of his patent, unless he does honestly intend to follow up such threats by really taking such proceedings.

> *Rollins* v. *Hinks*, L. R. 13 Eq. 355; 41 L. J. Ch. 358; 20 W. R. 287; 26 L. T. 56.

Axmann v. *Lund*, L. R. 18 Eq. 330; 43 L. J. Ch. 655; 22 W. R. 789.

Watson v. *Trask*, 6 Ohio, 531.

The holder of a patent, the validity of which is not impeached, who issues notices to the trade, alleging that certain articles are infringements of his patent, and threatening legal proceedings against those who purchase them, is not liable to an action for damages by the vendor of those articles for the injury done to the vendor's trade thereby, provided such notices are issued *bonâ fide* in the belief that the articles complained of are infringements of the patent. Nor is he liable to be restrained by injunction from continuing to issue them until it is proved that they are untrue, so that his further issuing them would not be *bonâ fide*.

Halsey v. *Brotherhood*, 19 Ch. D. 386; 51 L. J. Ch. 233; 30 W. R. 279; 45 L. T. 640; affirming the decision of Jessel, M.R., 15 Ch. D. 514; 49 L. J. Ch. 786; 29 W. R. 9; 43 L. T. 366.

The defendant agreed by letter to grant the plaintiff a licence under his patent; and the plaintiff at once commenced to make and sell goods in accordance with the patent. Then disputes arose as to the form in which the licence was to be drawn up; and thereupon the defendant published advertisements and circulars threatening the plaintiff's customers and others with proceedings for infringement of his patent. An injunction was granted to restrain the defendant from thus derogating from his grant.

Clark v. *Adie*, 21 W. R. 456, 764.

The defendant obtained in 1879 a patent for folding window screens. In 1885 (after six years' undisturbed possession of this patent) he issued a circular calling attention to it, and threatening proceedings against all infringers. The plaintiff, who also made folding screens, commenced an action to restrain the issue of this circular to his customers and others. Then the defendant commenced an action against the plaintiff for infringement. In that action he failed; the plaintiff proved the defendant's patent invalid. Still Bacon, V.-C., held that the defendant was perfectly justified in issuing the circular at the time he did so; that there was no evidence of any malice; and he dismissed the action without costs.

Brauer v. *Sharp*, 3 Reports of Patent Cases, 193.

Sugg v. *Bray*, 2 R. P. C. 241; 54 L. J. Ch. 132.

Interim Injunction.

Where a plaintiff applies for an *interim* injunction before the trial of the action to restrain the defendant from continuing to issue circulars or notices asserting that the plaintiff in selling certain goods is infringing the defendant's patent rights, or that the plaintiff has used labels for his goods, which the defendant alone had the right to use, and threatening the plaintiff's customers with legal proceedings, the *onus* lies on the plaintiff throughout to prove malice, falsity, and damage. It is for the plaintiff to prove that the defendant's statements are false, and if no *mala fides* is proved, so that no damages could be recovered, the Court will not grant an injunction. If, however, in a judicial proceeding the defendant's statements are proved to be false in fact, and there is any evidence that he intends to continue issuing them, an injunction will be granted restraining any further publication, which necessarily now would be *malâ fide*.

> *Burnett* v. *Tak*, 45 L. T. 743.
>
> *Anderson* v. *Liebig's Extract of Meat Co.*, 45 L. T. 757.

In fact, a very strong *primâ facie* case must be shown by the plaintiff for the Court to restrain the *bonâ fide* issue of circulars, warning persons that if they buy of the plaintiff they will infringe the defendant's patent and be liable to proceedings.

> *Société Anonyme des Manufactures de Glaces* v. *Tilghman's Patent Sand Blast Co.*, 25 Ch. D. 1; 53 L. J. Ch. 1; 32 W. R. 71; 49 L. T. 451.

The plaintiffs were the makers of "Rainbow Water Raisers or Elevators," and they commenced an action for an injunction to restrain the defendants from issuing a circular cautioning the public against the use of such elevators as being direct infringements of certain patents of the defendants. The plaintiffs subsequently gave notice of a motion to restrain the issue of this circular until the trial of the action. The defendants then commenced a cross action, claiming an injunction to restrain the plaintiffs from infringing their patents. *Held*, by Kay, J., that as there was no evidence of *mala fides* on the part of the defendants, they ought not to be restrained from issuing the circular until their action had been disposed of, but that they must undertake to prosecute their action without delay.

> *Household and another* v. *Fairburn and another*, 51 L. T. 498.

This order was made by Kay, J., on May 8th, 1884. But in spite of this undertaking the defendants did not proceed with their action with due diligence, and on April 30th, 1885, the plaintiffs renewed their motion, and obtained an injunction to restrain the defendants from issuing the circulars complained of.

> S. C. 2 Reports of Patent Cases, 140.

The plaintiff appointed the defendants his sole agents for the sale of his mineral waters in Great Britain. The plaintiff subsequently terminated the defendants' agency. The defendants thereupon issued circulars and advertisements representing that they were the sole agents of the plaintiff, and threatening with legal proceedings any person who should buy, import, or sell, the plaintiff's mineral waters from or through any other persons than the defendants. The plaintiff applied for an *interim* injunction to restrain the issue of such circulars and advertisements. *Held*, that though the defendants had misconceived and misstated their legal rights under the circumstances, still, there was no evidence that they knew this, or that they were acting in bad faith; injunction refused, but without prejudice to any fresh application in the event of any further circulars or advertisements being issued by the defendants.

> *Hirschler* v. *Hertz and Collingwood*, (1895) 11 Times L. R. 466; 99 L. T. Journal, 213.

In this state of the law, a new statutory right of action was created, in the case of a patentee, by section 32 of the Patents, Designs, and Trade Marks Act, 1883 (46 & 47 Vict. c. 57), which is now repealed by the Patents and

Designs Act, 1907 (7 Edw. VII. c. 29), and re-enacted in s. 36 as follows :—

"Where any person claiming to be the patentee of an invention, by circulars, advertisements, or otherwise, threatens any other person with any legal proceedings or liability in respect of any alleged infringement of the patent, any person aggrieved thereby may bring an action against him, and may obtain an injunction against the continuance of such threats, and may recover such damage (if any) as he has sustained thereby, if the alleged infringement to which the threats related was not in fact an infringement of any legal rights of the person making such threats : Provided that this section shall not apply if the person making such threats with due diligence commences and prosecutes an action for infringement of his patent."

It will be observed that the section refers only to " the patentee of an invention." It does not apply to an alleged infringement of a trade-mark, or to cases in which the defendant asserts that the plaintiff is misleading the public by the use of the defendant's trade name. And again, it is expressly provided that the section shall not apply if the defendant " with due diligence commences and prosecutes an action for infringement of his patent." All such cases are outside the section, and the law with regard to them is not affected by the statute.

In an action brought under this section, the plaintiff must prove that the defendant claims to be entitled to a patent; that the defendant has published "threats" within the meaning of the section; and that he, the plaintiff, is a person aggrieved thereby. He need not prove malice or any special damage.

It is not necessary that the defendant should be the legal owner of a patent, or that he should in fact be entitled to any patent; it is enough if he claims to be entitled to it, whether as inventor, or as an assignee of the patentee. As to the nature of the threats employed, the language of the section is very general. They may be printed, written, or spoken. (*Kurtz* v. *Spence*, 57 L. J. Ch. 238; 58 L. T. 438.) They may be addressed to the public generally (*Barney* v. *United Telephone Co.*, 28 Ch. D. 394; 33 W. R. 576;

н 2

52 L. T. 573), or to the customers of the plaintiff (*Johnson* v. *Edge*, [1892] 2 Ch. 1; 61 L. J. Ch. 262) or to the customers of his licensees (*Burt* v. *Morgan*, (1887) 3 Times L. R. 666), or even to the plaintiff himself (*Driffield, &c., Co.* v. *Waterloo, &c., Co.*, 31 Ch. D. 638; 55 L. J. Ch. 391; *Kurtz* v. *Spence, suprà; Combined Co.* v. *Automatic Weighing Machine Co.*, 42 Ch. D. 665; 58 L. J. Ch. 709). They may be published "by circulars, advertisements, *or otherwise*"; and the last two words are not to be limited to documents *ejusdem generis* with circulars or advertisements, but will include a private letter written in answer to a *bonâ fide* enquiry. (*Skinner & Co.* v. *Shew & Co.*, [1893] 1 Ch. 413; 62 L. J. Ch. 196.) If the circular or letter which contained a threat of legal proceedings has never been qualified or withdrawn, the threat will be held to be continued. (Per Bacon, V.-C., in *Driffield Co.* v. *Waterloo Co.*, 31 Ch. D. at p. 643.) A mere general warning giving notice to the public that the issuer holds a patent and intends to enforce his legal rights under it, may not be a "threat" within the meaning of the section so long as it is not pointed, or understood to be pointed, at any particular person or goods. But where the notice is clearly aimed at the plaintiff or at the plaintiff's goods, it will be deemed a "threat." (*Johnson* v. *Edge*, [1892] 2 Ch. 1; 61 L. J. Ch. 262; explaining the judgment of Bowen, L.J., in *Challender* v. *Royle*, 36 Ch. D. at p. 441.) It is not necessary that the threat should expressly or impliedly assert that the defendant's patent had been already infringed; it is sufficient if it asserts or implies that certain goods which the plaintiff is about to make or sell will be infringements of the defendant's patent. (*Ib.*) To assert that those who buy and sell goods of a specified kind are liable to legal proceedings is a sufficient threat. (*Fusee Vesta Co.* v. *Bryant and May*, 56 L. T. 136; 4 Reports of Patent Cases, 191.) It is not necessary that the plaintiff should be named or referred to in the threatening notices; if his trade is injured thereby, he is "a person aggrieved," and can sue. And the threats need not be addressed or sent to the plaintiff himself: "it may be a person other than the person to whom the threat is issued, who is 'aggrieved' by that threat having been issued." (Per Mathew, J., in *Johnson* v. *Edge*, [1892] 2 Ch. at p. 6.)

As soon as the plaintiff has established that the defendant published "threats" within the section, it is for the defendant to prove that the acts of which he complained in such threats were in fact an infringement of his patent. (*Ungar* v. *Sugg*, (1889) 6 Reports of Patent Cases, 337; 5 Times L. R. 372.) That he honestly believed them to be infringements, though they are not, is no defence. His *bona fides* is immaterial in an action under this section, nor can any defence of privilege be raised. (*Skinner & Co.* v. *Shew & Co.,* [1893] 1 Ch. 413 ; 62 L. J. Ch. 196.) The only defence open to a defendant who has not commenced, or who has not prosecuted with due diligence, an action for infringement of his patent, is to show that the statements contained in his threatening notices are true. He must give the plaintiff particulars of the patent which he alleges have been infringed. (*Union Electrical Power Co.* v. *Electrical Power Storage Co.,* 38 Ch. D. 325 ; 36 W. R. 913 ; 59 L. T. 427.) The plaintiff may, if he thinks fit, attack the validity of the defendant's patent, whether he denies or admits that he has infringed it. (*Challender* v. *Royle,* 36 Ch. D. 425 ; 56 L. J. Ch. 995 ; *Kurtz* v. *Spence,* (C. A.) 36 Ch. D. 770 ; 36 W. R. 438 ; 58 L. T. 320.) If he decides to attack it, he must plead that the defendant's patent is invalid either in his Statement of Claim or in his Reply (*Dowson* v. *Drosophore Co., Limited,* 12 Reports of Patent Cases, 95.) He must also give the defendant particulars of objections such as a defendant delivers in an ordinary infringement action under Order LIII. A. rr. 14, 15, and 17—21 ; for the *onus* of proving the invalidity of the defendant's patent lies on the plaintiff. (*Ungar* v. *Sugg, suprà.*)

It is a defence to an action under this section if the defendant can show that he has commenced, and has prosecuted with due diligence, an action for infringement of his patent. (See *Haskell Golf Ball Co.* v. *Hutchinson and another,* (1904) 20 Times L. R. 606 ; 21 R. P. C. 497.) Proof of this takes the case out of the section altogether, although the action for infringement was commenced after the action for threats ; so that the plaintiff had a good cause of action under the section at the date of his writ. (*Combined Co.* v. *Automatic Weighing Machine Co.,* 42 Ch. D. 665 ; 58 L. J. Ch. 709 ; *Colley* v. *Hart,* 44 Ch. D. 179 ; 59 L. J. Ch. 308.) But the defendant will not be entitled to the benefit of the proviso at the end of the section if the plaintiff can establish that the action for infringement is not one in which the validity of the patent could beyond all doubt be tried ; the *onus* of proving this lies on the plaintiff. (*Craig* v. *Dowding,* (1908) 98 L. T. 231 ; 24 Times L. R. 248.) Moreover, it must be the defendant himself who commences the infringement action ; if he is merely an equitable assignee, an action by his assignor, the original patentee, or any third person, will not avail him. (*Kensington Co.* v. *Lane Fox Co.,* [1891] 2 Ch. 573 ; 39 W. R. 650.) The action need not be brought against the plaintiff, provided it is brought against some one who is alleged to have infringed the same patent, and in respect of substantially the same infringement as that referred to in the threats. (*Challender* v. *Royle*, 36 Ch. D. 425 ; 56 L. J. Ch. 995 ; *Barrett* v. *Day, Day* v. *Foster*, 43 Ch. D. 435 ; 59 L. J. Ch. 464.) Nor is it necessary that the defendant should succeed in his action, if it were brought *bonâ fide*. (*Colley* v. *Hart*, 44 Ch. D. 179 ; 59 L. J. Ch. 308.) He need not prosecute it to judgment if he finds that it will fail. But the action must be commenced *bonâ fide* and then prosecuted with due diligence. And for this purpose the Court will have regard to the time of issuing the threats, and not the time when the defendant first became aware of the acts of which he complains. (*Challender* v. *Royle, suprâ.*) He is not bound to apply for an *interim* injunction in his action for infringement. (*Anderson* v. *Liebig, &c., Co.*, 45 L. T. 757.) He may wait three months before commencing such an action ; but a year is too long. (*Herrburger* v. *Squire*, 5 Reports of Patent Cases, 581.) Time spent in honest attempts to negotiate a settlement will not be reckoned. (*Edlin* v. *Pneumatic Tyre Agency*, 10 Reports of Patent Cases, 311.) The defendant may wait to see the Statement of Claim in the threats action, and then counterclaim in that action instead of incurring the expense of a separate action for infringement, if he thinks fit. (*Colley* v. *Hart*, 44 Ch. D. 179 ; 59 L. J. Ch. 308.) Although this may be a proper course, still the defendant is not bound to assert his rights by a counterclaim ; he is entitled to bring a separate action for the alleged infringement of his patent. But in that case arrangements ought to be made to consolidate the two actions or to stay one to abide the result of the other. (*Combined Co.* v. *Automatic Weighing Co.*, 42 Ch. D. 665 ; 58 L. J. Ch. 709.)

The plaintiff in an action under this section may claim both damages and an injunction ; and he may obtain both, as in *Skinner & Co.* v. *Shew & Co.*, [1893] 1 Ch. 413 ; 62 L. J. Ch. 196. But as a rule, when an injunction is granted, nominal damages only will be given, unless there be clear proof of substantial damages, such as the loss of a customer or actual suspension of business in consequence of the defendant's threats. (See *Driffield Co.* v. *Waterloo Co.*, 31 Ch. D. at p. 644 ; 55 L. J. Ch. at p. 394.)

So far we have dealt with the trial of the action. If the plaintiff applies before trial for an *interim* injunction under this section, a different rule prevails. On such an application the *onus* lies on the plaintiff to prove that there has been no infringement on his part. He must at all events establish a *primâ facie* case of non-infringement. (The *dicta* to the contrary in *Walker* v. *Clarke*, 56 L. J. Ch. 239 ; 35 W. R. 245 ; 56 L. T. 111, are no longer followed ; see

36 Ch. D. 436.) It will then be open to the defendant to file affidavits showing that there has in fact been an infringement. If
satisfactory affidavits to that effect be filed, the Court will not
decide the question of infringement on that application, but will
refuse to grant any *interim* injunction, even though the defendant
declines to take legal proceedings in respect of such alleged infringement. (*Barney* v. *United Telephone Co.*, 28 Ch. D. 394; 33 W. R.
576; 52 L. T. 573.) If, however, after reading the affidavits on both
sides, the plaintiff's case is still so far unimpaired that if the evidence remains the same at the hearing, it is probable that he will
obtain a decree, he will be entitled to an *interim* injunction.
(*Challender* v. *Royle*, 36 Ch. D. 425; 56 L. J. Ch. 995.)

Illustrations.

The solicitors to the defendants sent a letter to the plaintiffs alleging an infringement of patents claimed by the defendants, and stating that unless the
plaintiffs forthwith discontinued such infringement legal proceedings would be
taken. The defendants, however, did not follow up the letter by any legal
proceedings, and admitted at the trial that the plaintiffs had not infringed the
patents. *Held*, that the plaintiffs were entitled to a perpetual injunction,
with costs.

> *Driffield, &c., Co.* v. *Waterloo, &c., Co.*, (1886) 31 Ch. D. 638; 55
> L. J. Ch. 391; 34 W. R. 360; 54 L. T. 210; 3 R. P. C. 46.

The plaintiff and the defendant independently invented the same process.
The defendant completed his discovery first, but unfortunately claimed too
much in his specification, which rendered his patent invalid. Before, however,
this invalidity was known to either party, the defendant had threatened the
plaintiff with legal proceedings, both by letter and verbally at an interview.
Kekewich, J., declared the defendant's patent invalid, and granted an injunction restraining all such threats, and ordered the defendant to pay 40*s.* damages
and costs on the higher scale.

> *Kurtz* v. *Spence*, 57 L. J. Ch. 238; 58 L. T. 438; 5 R. P. C. 161.

The plaintiff supplied nine lamps to a draper, who had them erected in front of
his shop. The defendants claimed that these lamps were an infringement of their
patent, but took no legal proceedings. At the trial the lamps were produced,
and proved not to be any infringement. The defendants then set up that the
lamps had been altered since their representative had seen them. The jury found
this issue also in favour of the plaintiff. Damages 500*l.*

> *Ungar* v. *Sugg & Co.*, (1889) 5 Times L. R. 372; 6 R. P. C. 337; 9
> R. P. C. 113.

The defendant issued a circular stating that the plaintiff was infringing his
trade-mark and his patent, and threatening proceedings against all persons who
retailed the goods alleged to be infringements. The plaintiff issued a writ under
s. 32 of the 46 & 47 Vict. c. 57, and applied for an *interim* injunction. He
satisfied the Court, on the balance of evidence, that he was not infringing the
defendant's patent. The defendant had brought no action for infringement.

Chitty, J., granted an injunction restraining the threats, so far as they related to the patent, till trial or further order. No order as to threats relating to the trade-mark.

Colley v. *Hart*, (1888) 6 Reports of Patent Cases, 17.

The defendant held a patent for a " tap union " for connecting loose pipes with taps. The plaintiff subsequently obtained a patent for a similar invention, which he sold to many plumbers, among others to the Manchester Plumbiug Co., who retailed them to their customers. The defendant then issued a notice to the public stating, in general terms, that it had come to his knowledge that certain of his patents were being infringed, and that his solicitor had instructions to take proceedings against all infringers. The plaintiff then commenced this action for threats; and the defendant four days afterwards, but before the writ in this action was served on him, issued a writ against the Manchester Plumbing Co. for infringement. *Held*, that the defendant's action was an answer to an application for an *interim* injunction, and further that, if honestly prosecuted with reasonable diligence, it would take the case out of the section altogether.

Challender v.~*Royle*, 36 Ch. D. 425 ; 56 L. J. Ch. 995 ; 36 W. R. 357 ; 57 L. T. 734 ; 4 R. P. C. 363.

The plaintiff and the defendant were rival manufacturers of "blue." The defendant enclosed in his boxes of " blue " the following circular signed by his solicitors:—" Notice to grocers and others. Information of extensive violation of Mr. William Edge's patent rights has been received. All parties are warned not to infringe these rights." Subsequently, however, the defendant consented to his patent being revoked. *Held*, that the circular was a " threat," and that the plaintiff was " a person aggrieved " thereby. No injunction, the defendant having given an undertaking that the circular should not be issued or used again. Inquiry as to damages, to be assessed by an official referee.

Johnson v. *Edge*, [1892] 2 Cb. 1 ; 61 L. J. Ch. 262 ; 40 W. R. 437 ; 66 L. T. 44 ; 9 R. P. C. 144.

Both Barrett and Day owned patents. Each granted Foster an exclusive licence under his patent. Then Day sued Foster for infringing Day's patent by selling Barrett's goods. Subsequently Barrett sued Day for " threats " under this section. *Held*, that Day's action against Foster was an answer to Barrett's action against Day, and took the case out of the section altogether.

Barrett v. *Day, Day* v. *Foster*, 43 Ch. D. 435 ; 59 L. J. Ch. 464 ; 38 W. R. 362 ; 62 L. T. 597 ; 7 R. P. C. 54.

The plaintiffs and the defendants were rival manufacturers of photographic cameras. The London Stereoscopic Company dealt with both. The plaintiffs offered that company a new portable camera, for which they had just filed a provisional specification. The company thought it right before purchasing this camera to send it to the defendants, and ask whether they " thought that it in any way encroached upon their rights." The defendants replied that it was " undoubtedly in our opinion an infringement," and that they were prepared to stop the sale of it, if it were placed upon the market. It was placed upon the market ; the defendants took no proceedings ; but the company, in consequence of the defendants' letter, refused for two seasons to purchase a single one of the plaintiff's new cameras. *Held*, that the defendants' letter was a " threat; " that in an action under this section no defence can be raised that the defendants had acted *bonâ fide*, or on a privileged occasion ; and that the plaintiffs were entitled to an injunction and to damages, which were subsequently assessed at 700*l.*

> *Skinner & Co.* v. *Shew & Co.*, [1893] 1 Ch. 413; 62 L. J. Ch. 196; 41 W. R. 217; 67 L. T. 696; 2 R. 179; 9 R. P. C. 406; [1894] 2 Ch. 581; 63 L. J. Ch. 826; 71 L. T. 110; 8 R. 455; 10 R. P. C. 1.

IV. *Other Words which Injure a Man in his Profession or Trade.*

There are many other cases in which words produce special damage to the plaintiff in his business without in any way affecting either his personal or his commercial reputation; and for such words, if spoken without lawful occasion, an action on the case will lie, provided the damage be the necessary or probable consequence of the words.

Illustrations.

The *County Herald* printed and published that the plaintiff had ceased to carry on his business of engineer and boiler-maker, and that the firm of Ratcliffe & Sons no longer existed. This statement was untrue, and the plaintiff's business fell off in consequence. The jury found that the words did not reflect upon the plaintiff's character, and were not libellous; that they were not published *bonâ fide;* and that the plaintiff's business suffered injury to the extent of 120*l.* from their publication. Judgment for the plaintiff for 120*l.* damages with costs.

> *Ratcliffe* v. *Evans*, [1892] 2 Q. B. 524; 61 L. J. Q. B. 535; 40 W. R. 578; 66 L. T. 794; 56 J. P. 837.

The efendants published a circular stating that the plaintiff was "retiring from business," and it was proved that such publication was malicious. It was held by Eve, J., that the plaintiff could recover on proving special damage, but that evidence that the circular was calculated to keep away customers and that in the plaintiff's opinion they would not come to him was insufficient.

> *Concaris* v. *Duncan & Co.*, [1909] W. N. 51.

The plaintiff and the defendant were architects, who formerly carried on business in partnership, and as such they joined in, designed, and supervised the construction of many important buildings in London. Immediately after the dissolution of their partnership the defendant circulated photographs of these buildings, with the words below: "Designed by Thomas Archer, F.R.I.B.A." omitting all reference to the plaintiff. *Held*, that no action lay, for the omission of the plaintiff's name was no libel on him; and there was no slander of title and no special damage.

> *Green* v. *Archer*, (1891) 7 Times L. R. 542.

There are two kinds of Australian hardwood, "karri" and "jarrah." The plaintiffs dealt in "jarrah" only; the defendants dealt in both. The defendants advertised that they were "the only importers of both;" and two learned judges held that this advertisement might be taken to mean that the plaintiffs did not deal in either, and that if so, an action might lie. Grantham, J., dissented.

Jarrahdale Timber Co. v. *Temperley & Co.*, (1894) 11 Times L. R. 119.

Procuring a breach of contract of sale by a false claim of lien is an actionable wrong.

Green v. *Button*, 2 C. M. & R. 707.

The plaintiff was making money at Glasgow by printing silk handkerchiefs with an ornamental design; the defendant, hoping to acquire that design for himself, falsely represented to the plaintiff that it was a registered pattern, that the true owner had compelled him to give up the plaintiff's name, and was about to proceed against the plaintiff in Chancery for an injunction; the plaintiff, naturally alarmed, stayed the execution of certain orders in hand for handkerchiefs with that design, and travelled up to London to explain matters to the supposed true owner; the defendant meanwhile went on printing and selling silk handkerchiefs printed with the design. *Held*, that the plaintiff had a good cause of action, it appearing that the defendant had knowingly uttered a falsehood with intent to deprive the plaintiff of a benefit and acquire it to himself, as the damage naturally flowed from the plaintiff's belief in the truth of the defendant's statement.

Barley v. *Walford*, (1846) 9 Q. B. 197 ; 15 L. J. Q. B. 369 ; 10 Jur. 917.

The defendant uttered words imputing adultery to Mrs. Riding, and certain customers ceased to deal with Mr. Riding in consequence. Mr. and Mrs. Riding as co-plaintiffs brought an action of slander, but at that time it was not actionable to impute adultery to a married woman unless the words caused special damage to her. The Court therefore struck out her name as a plaintiff and amended the declaration so that it ran " that the plaintiff carried on business as a grocer and draper, and was assisted in the conduct of his business by his wife, and that the defendant falsely and maliciously published of the plaintiff's wife in relation to the business that she had committed adultery, whereby the plaintiff was injured in his business and sustained special damage." And the Court held that on a declaration so framed an action might be maintained.

Riding v. *Smith*, 1 Ex. D. 91 ; 45 L. J. Ex. 281 ; 24 W. R. 487 ; 34 L. T. 500.

And in the same case (1 Ex. D., p. 94) Kelly, C.B., says : " Here the statement was that the wife of the plaintiff was guilty of adultery, and it is the natural consequence of such a statement that persons should cease to resort to the shop. Supposing the statement made not to be slander, but something else calculated to injure the shopkeeper in the way of his trade, as, for instance, the statement that one of his shopmen was suffering from an infectious disease, such as scarlet fever, this would operate to prevent people coming to the shop; and whether it be slander or some other statement which has the effect I have mentioned, an action can, in my opinion, be maintained on the ground that it is a statement made to the public which would have the effect of preventing their resorting to the shop and buying goods of the owner."

And see *Levet's Case*, Cro. Eliz. 289 ; *ante*, p. 65.

Baldwin v. *Flower*, 3 Mod. 120 ; *post*, p. 573.

The defendants published in their newspaper a report that the plaintiff's house was haunted, honestly believing the same to be true, and reproducing what had been told them in the honest belief that the house was in fact thus affected. The plaintiff proved that the value of the house had fallen, but the evidence showed that it had acquired the reputation of being haunted before the publication by the defendants. *Held,* that the plaintiff had failed to make out a cause of action, and (per Cozens-Hardy, M.R.) that even if he had proved special damage there was no malice.

> *Barrett* v. *Associated Newspapers, Ltd.,* (1907) 23 Times L. R. 666.

It is actionable to put a man's name on a "black list," with the object of inducing people not to have business dealings with him, or with the object of bringing him into public odium and contempt. .

> *Trollope & Sons* v. *London Building Trades Federation,* (1895) 72 L. T. 342; 11 Times L. R. 228, 280.
> *Same* v. *Same,* (1896) 12 Times L. R. 373.
> *Leathem* v. *Craig and others,* [1899] 2 Ir. R. 667.
> *Quinn* v. *Leathem,* [1901] A. C. 495; 70 L. J. P. C. 76; 50 W. R. 139; 85 L. T. 289; 65 J. P. 708.
> *Newton* v. *Amalgamated Musicians' Union,* (1896) 12 Times L. R. 623.
> And see *ante,* p. 33.

The defendant was a retail dealer in pianos. He advertised for sale in a newspaper a new piano of the plaintiffs' manufacture at the price at which the plaintiffs supplied the same to the trade, and thereby caused other dealers to give up dealing with the plaintiffs. He continued the advertisement after he ceased to have in stock any pianos of the plaintiffs' manufacture, and after the plaintiffs had refused to supply him. He expected to be able to acquire pianos of the plaintiffs from other dealers. *Held,* as the defendant honestly intended to sell the pianos at the price named, he had a legal right to issue the advertisement; and that though the advertisement amounted to an implied representation that the defendant had in his possession a piano of the advertised description, which latterly was not the case, this representation was not the cause of the damage to the plaintiffs' trade, and consequently gave no right of action.

> *Ajello* v. *Worsley,* [1898] 1 Ch. 274; 67 L. J. Ch. 172; 46 W. R. 245; 77 L. T. 783.

V. *Other Words which cause Damage.*

Words which injure a man's reputation are defamatory, and give rise to an action of libel or slander. Words which impugn his title to property or injure him in his profession or trade are actionable in the cases indicated in the preceding pages of this chapter: There remain words which do not affect a man's reputation, profession, or trade, but which yet cause him special damage. It is submitted that if such words are written or spoken by the defendant with the malicious intention of injuring the plaintiff, and the contemplated injury follows as the direct result of the defendant's words, an action on the case will lie whatever be the nature of the words which the defendant has employed to carry into effect his malicious design.

A curious point of this kind was raised and discussed in the case of *Kelly* v. *Partington,* 4 B. & Ad. 700 ; 5 B. & Ad. 645, decided in 1833. The Solicitor-General (Sir John Campbell) contended that, if praise produced special damage, praise was actionable, an argument with which the Court appeared much amused. Littledale, J., puts him a case (p. 648), "Suppose a man had a relation of a penurious disposition, and a third person, knowing that it would injure him in the opinion of that relation, tells the latter a generous act which the first had done, by which he induces the relation not to leave him money, would that be actionable ? " And Sir John Campbell answers, "If the words were spoken falsely with intent to injure, they would be actionable." And surely he is right. It might be difficult to prove the intent with which the words were spoken. But if a malicious intent be clear, the damage is not too remote, for the defendant contemplated it; and the speaking of the words was wrongful because done maliciously, falsely, and with intent to injure the plaintiff ; so here is *et damnum et injuria,* and an action lies.

Illustrations.

A solicitor, who was one of the creditors of a bankrupt firm, advertised, for the information of all other creditors, that the plaintiff was a partner in that firm, and was solvent. The plaintiff was solvent, but he was not a partner in the bankrupt firm. Malins, V.-C., granted an injunction.

Dixon v. *Holden,* L. R. 7 Eq. 488 ; 17 W. R. 482; 20 L. T. 357.

An action will lie for persuading, procuring, and enticing a married woman to continue absent and apart from her husband, whereby he loses the comfort and society of his wife, and her aid and assistance in domestic affairs.

Winsmore v. *Greenbank,* (1745) Willes Rep. (Common Pleas) 577.

Lynch v. *Knight and wife,* 9 H. L. C. 577; 8 Jur. N. S. 724; 5 L.T. 291.

Smith v. *Kaye and another,* (1904) 20 Times L. R. 261.

The defendant told the plaintiff, a married woman, that her husband had met with an accident and had broken both his legs. These statements were false to the knowledge of the defendant, but were made as a practical joke by him with the intent that they should be believed. The plaintiff became seriously ill as a result of shock to the nervous system caused by the publication of the words. *Held,* by Wright, J., that an action lay.

Wilkinson v. *Downton,* [1897] 2 Q. B. 57; 66 L. J. Q. B. 493; 45 W. R. 525 ; 76 L. T. 493.

And see *R.* v. *Martin,* 8 Q. B. D. 54; 51 L. J. M. C. 36; 30 W. R. 106 ; 45 L. T. 444; 46 J. P. 228; 14 Cox, C. C. 633.

CHAPTER V.

CONSTRUCTION AND CERTAINTY.

CONSTRUCTION is the correct interpretation of words, the method of ascertaining the sense in which they were understood by those who first heard or read them.

What meaning the speaker intended to convey is immaterial in all actions of defamation. (*Haire* v. *Wilson*, 9 B. & C. 645.) He may have had no intention of injuring the plaintiff's reputation, but if he has in fact done so, he must compensate the plaintiff. He may have meant one thing and said another; if so he is answerable for so inadequately expressing his meaning. If a man in jest conveys a serious imputation, he jests at his peril. (Per Smith, B., in *Donoghue* v. *Hayes*, (1831) Hayes (Irish Exch.) at p. 266.) Or he may have used ambiguous language which to his mind was harmless, but to which the bystanders attributed an injurious meaning; if so, he is liable for the injudicious phrase he selected. What was passing in his own mind is immaterial, save in so far as his hearers could perceive it at the time. Words cannot be construed according to the secret intent of the speaker. (*Hankinson* v. *Bilby*, 16 M. & W. 445; 2 C. & K. 440.) " The slander and the damage consist in the apprehension of the hearers." (*Per cur.* in *Fleetwood* v. *Curley*, (1619) Hobart, 268.)

The question therefore is always: How were the words understood by those to whom they were originally published ? We must assume that they were persons of ordinary intelligence. We must assume, too, that they gave to ordinary English words their ordinary English meaning, to local or technical phrases their local and technical meaning. That being done, what meaning did the whole passage convey to an unbiassed mind ?

This clearly is rather a question for the jury than for the judge. And accordingly by the 32 Geo. III. c. 60 (Fox's Libel Act) it is expressly provided that in all criminal proceedings for libel the jury are to decide the question of libel or no libel subject to the direction of the judge. In civil proceedings for libel, the practice is, and always was, the same (*Baylis* v. *Lawrence*, 11 A. & E. 920 ; 3 Perry & D. 526 ; 4 Jur. 652), save that here, if the judge thinks that the words cannot possibly bear a defamatory meaning, he may shorten the proceedings by stopping the case. "It is only when the judge is satisfied that the publication cannot be a libel, and that, if it is found by the jury to be such, their verdict will be set aside, that he is justified in withdrawing the question from their cognizance." (Per Kelly, C.B., in *Cox* v. *Lee*, L. R. 4 Ex. at p. 288 ; and see *Fray* v. *Fray*, 17 C. B. N. S. 603 ; 34 L. J. C. P. 45 ; 10 Jur. N. S. 1153 ; *Teacy* v. *McKenna*, Ir. R. 4 C. L. 374 ; *Hunt* v. *Goodlake*, 43 L. J. C. P. 54 ; 29 L. T. 472 ; *Hart and another* v. *Wall*, 2 C. P. D. 146 ; 46 L. J. C. P. 227 ; 25 W. R. 373.)

If, however, the judge considers that words are reasonably susceptible of a defamatory meaning as well as an innocent one, it will then be a question for the jury which meaning the words would convey to ordinary Englishmen who heard or read them without any previous knowledge of the circumstances to which they relate. (*Fisher* v. *Clement*, 10 B. & C. 472 ; 5 Man. & Ry. 730 ; *Hankinson* v. *Bilby*, 16 M. & W. 442 ; 2 C. & K. 440.) The judge is in no way bound to state to the jury his own opinion on the point ; it would, in fact, be wrong for him to lay down as a matter of law that the publication complained of was, or was not, a libel. (*Baylis* v. *Lawrence*, 11 A. & E. 920.) The proper course is for the judge to define what is a libel in point of law, and to leave it to the jury to say whether the publication in question falls within that definition. (*Parmiter* v. *Coupland and another*, 6 M. & W. 105 ; 9 L. J. Ex. 202 ; 4 Jur. 701.) And this is a question preeminently for the jury ; whichever way they find, the

Court will rarely, if ever, disturb the verdict, if the question was properly left to them.

So, too, in cases of slander, the judge usually decides whether the words are, or are not, actionable *per se*, and whether the special damage assigned is, or is not, too remote. If the defendant's words cannot reasonably bear the meaning ascribed to them by the innuendo, and the judge is clearly of opinion that the words without that meaning are not actionable, he will stop the case. So, too, if the words even with the alleged meaning are not actionable (though pleaders seldom err on that side). But in all other cases, where there is any reasonable doubt as to the true construction of the words, the judge leaves the question to the jury. All circumstances which were apparent to the bystanders at the time the words were uttered should be put in evidence, so as to place the jury as much as possible in the position of such bystanders; and then it is for the jury to say what meaning such words would fairly have conveyed to their minds. And their finding is practically conclusive on the point; the Court will not set the verdict aside, unless it be such as no reasonable men could have properly found (see *post*, p. 704).

Formerly, however, the practice was very different. After a verdict for the plaintiff, the defendant constantly moved in arrest of judgment on the ground that a defamatory meaning was not shown on the record with sufficient precision, or, as it soon came to be, on the ground that it was just possible in spite of the record to give the words an innocent construction. For it was said to be a maxim that words were to be taken *in mitiori sensu* whenever there were two senses in which they could be taken. And in these early times the Courts thought it their duty to discourage actions of slander. They would, therefore, give an innocent meaning to the words complained of, if by any amount of legal ingenuity such a meaning could be put upon them; and would altogether disregard the plain and obvious signification which must have been conveyed to bystanders ignorant of legal technicalities. Thus where a married woman falsely said, " You have stolen my goods," and the jury found a verdict for the plaintiff, the Court entered judgment for the defendant, on the ground that a married woman could have no goods of her own, and that therefore the words conveyed no charge of felony. (*Anon.*, Pasch. 11 Jac. I.; 1 Roll. Abr. 746; overruled by *Stamp and wife* v. *White and wife*, Cro. Jac. 600.) Again, where the words complained of were, "He hath delivered false evidence and untruths in his answer to a bill in Chancery," it was held that no action lay; for though every answer to a bill in Chancery was on oath, and was a judicial proceeding, still in most Chancery pleadings "some things are not material to what is in dispute between the parties," and "it is no perjury, although such things are not truly answered"! (*Mitchell* v. *Brown*, 3 Inst. 167; 1 Roll. Abr. 70.) For further instances of such refinements, see *Peake* v. *Pollard*, Cro. Eliz. 214; *Cox* v. *Humphrey*, *ib.* 889; *Holland* v. *Stoner*, Cro. Jac. 315; and *Bury* v. *Wright*, (1609) Yelv. 126.

But in the days of Charles II. the Court of Common Pleas decided in a case of *scandalum magnatum* (*Lord Townshend* v. *Dr. Hughes*, (1676) 2 Mod. 159) that "words should not be construed either in a rigid or mild sense, but according to the general and natural meaning, and agreeable to the common understanding of all men." And this decision soon became law. In *Naben* v. *Miecock*, (1683) Skin. 183, Levinz, J., said he was "for taking words in their natural, genuine, and usual sense and common understanding, and not according to the witty construction of lawyers, but according to the apprehension of the bystanders." (And see *Somers* v. *House*, Holt, 39; Skin. 364; and *Burgess* v. *Bracher*, 8 Mod. 238.) In 1722, Fortescue, J., declared in *Button* v. *Hayward et ux.*, 8 Mod. 24, "The maxim for expounding words *in mitiori sensu* has for a great while been exploded, near fifty or sixty years." In *Peake* v. *Oldham*, Cowp. 277, 278, Lord Mansfield commented severely on the constant practice of moving in arrest of judgment after verdict found: "What? After verdict, shall the Court be guessing and inventing a mode in which it might be barely possible for these words to have been spoken by the defendant without meaning to charge the plaintiff with being guilty of murder? Certainly not. Where it is clear that words are defectively laid, a verdict will not cure them. But where, from their general import, they appear to have been spoken with a view to defame a party, the Court ought not to be industrious in putting a construction upon them different from what they bear in the common acceptation and meaning of them." And his Lordship quoted a *dictum* of Parker, C.J., in *Ward* v. *Reynolds*, Pasch. 12 Anne, B. R., to the same effect. So in *Harrison* v. *Thornborough*,

10 Mod. 197, the Court says : " The rule that has now prevailed is that words are to be taken in that sense that is most natural and obvious, and in which those to whom they are spoken will be sure to understand them." (See also the remarks of De Grey, C.J., in *R.* v. *Horne*, 2 Cowp. 682—689 ; Buller, J., in *R.* v. *Watson and others*, 2 T. R. 206 ; and the judgments in *Baker* v. *Pierce*, 2 Ld. Raym. 959 ; Holt, 654 ; and *Woolnoth* v. *Meadows*, 5 East, 463 ; 2 Smith, 28.)

And such is now the law. The Courts no longer strain to find an innocent meaning for words *primâ facie* defamatory, neither will they put a forced construction on words which may fairly be deemed harmless. " Formerly," says Lord Ellenborough in 2 Camp. 403, " it was the practice to say that words were to be taken in the more lenient sense ; but that doctrine is now exploded ; they are not to be taken in the more lenient or more severe sense, but in the sense which fairly belongs to them." And, again, in *Roberts* v. *Camden*, 9 East, 95, the same learned judge says : " The rule which once prevailed, that words are to be understood *in mitiori sensu*, has been long ago superseded ; and words are now to be construed by Courts, as they always ought to have been, in the plain and popular sense in which the rest of the world naturally understand them." Now, therefore, the only question for the judge or the Court is whether the words are *capable* of the defamatory meaning attributed to them ; if they are, then it is for the jury to decide what is in fact the true construction.

So long as the defendant's words are not absolutely unintelligible, a jury will judge of the meaning as well as other readers or hearers. It matters not whether the defamatory words be in English or in any other language that is understood in England, whether they be spelt correctly or incorrectly, whether the phrase be grammatical or not, whether cant or slang terms be employed, or the most refined and elegant diction. (*R.* v. *Edgar*, 2 Sess. Cas. 29 ; 5 Bac. Abr. 199.) The insinuation may be indirect, and the allusion obscure ; it may be put as a question or as an " on dit " ; the language may be ironical, figurative, or allegorical ; still, if there be a meaning in the words at all, the Court will find it out, even though it be disguised in a riddle or in hieroglyphics. In all cases of ambiguity it is purely a question for the jury to decide what meaning the words would convey to persons of ordinary intelligence. (*Grant* v. *Yates*, (1886) 2 Times L. R. 368 ; *Dakhyl* v. *Labouchere*, [1908] 2 K. B. at p. 328, n.) If an article in a newspaper conveys a defamatory meaning to a person who reads it in the manner in which such articles are usually read by an ordinary person, it is immaterial that another meaning might be derived from a critical scrutiny of the words. (*Hunter* v. *Ferguson & Co.*, (1906) 8 F. 574 (Ct. of Sess.).)

And before answering that question the jury should well weigh all the circumstances of the case, the occasion of speaking, the relationship between the parties, &c. Especially they should consider the words as a whole, not dwelling on isolated passages, but giving its proper weight to every part. (Per Tindal, C.J., in *Shipley* v. *Todhunter*, 7 C. & P. at p. 690.) The sting of a libel may sometimes be contained in a word or sentence placed as a heading to it, which will often render the defendant liable where without it he would have had a perfect answer to the action. So, too, a word added at the end may altogether vary the sense of the preceding passage. "It is obvious that an adjective, or even an adverb, may carry with it such a sting as to be a statement of some one particular fact." (Per Pollock, B., in *Borough of Sunderland Election Petition*, (1896) 5 O'M. & H. at p. 62.) The defendant is, therefore, entitled to have the whole of the alleged libel read as part of the plaintiff's case. (*Cooke* v. *Hughes*, R. & M. 112.) And for the purpose of showing that what he wrote is no libel, and will not bear the construction which the plaintiff seeks to put upon it, the defendant may give in evidence any other passages in the same publication which plainly refer to the same matter, or which qualify or explain the passage sued on. (*R.* v. *Lambert and Perry*, 2 Camp. 400; 31 Howell St. Tr. 340; *Darby* v. *Ouseley*, 25 L. J. Ex. 229; 1 H. & N. 1; 2 Jur. N. S. 497; *Bolton* v. *O'Brien*, 16 L. R. Ir. 97.)

So, too, with a slander; very often the words immediately preceding or following may much modify those relied on by the plaintiff. (*Brittridge's Case*, 4 Rep. 19; *Thompson* v. *Bernard*, 1 Camp. 48.) When the language sued on is ambiguous, and some extrinsic evidence is necessary to make the meaning clear, evidence may be given of other libels or slanders published by the defendant of the plaintiff which explain or qualify that sued on. When, however, such evidence is admitted, the jury should always be cautioned not to give any damages in respect of it as a separate cause of action. (Per Tindal, C.J., in *Pearson* v. *Lemaitre*, 5 M. & Gr. 720; 12 L. J. Q. B. 253; 7 Jur. 748; 6 Scott, N. R. 607; *Anderson* v. *Calvert*, (1908) 24 Times L. R. 399.)

Illustrations.

The *Observer* gave a correct account of some proceedings in the Insolvent Debtor's Court, but headed it "Shameful Conduct of an Attorney." The rest of the report was held privileged; but the plaintiff recovered damages for the heading.

> *Clement* v. *Lewis*, 3 Br. & B. 297 ; 7 Moore, 200 ; 3 B. & Ald. 702.
> And see *Mountney* v. *Watton*, 2 B. & Ad. 673.
> *Bishop* v. *Latimer*, 4 L. T. 775.
> *Boydell* v. *Jones*, 4 M. & W. 446 ; 7 Dowl. 210 ; 1 H. & H. 408.
> *Harvey* v. *French*, 1 Cr. & M. 11 ; 2 M. & Scott, 591 ; 2 Tyr. 585.
> *Lewis* v. *Levy*, E. B. & E. 537 ; 27 L. J. Q. B. 282 ; 4 Jur. N. S. 970.
> *Street* v. *Licensed Victuallers' Society*, 22 W. R. 553.
> *Stanley* v. *Webb*, 4 Sandf. (N. Y.) 21.

An action was brought for an alleged libel published in the *True Sun* newspaper :—" Riot at Preston.—From the *Liverpool Courier*.—It appears that Hunt pointed out Counsellor Seager to the mob, and said, ' There is one of the black sheep.' The mob fell upon him and murdered him. In the affray Hunt had his nose cut off. The coroner's inquest have brought in a verdict of wilful murder against Hunt, who is committed to gaol.—Fudge ! " The plaintiff contended that the word " fudge " was merely introduced with reference to the future, in order that the defendants might afterwards, if the paragraph were complained of, be able to refer to it, as showing that they intended to discredit the statement. Lord Lyndhurst, C.B., told the jury that the question was, with what motive the publication was made. It was not disputed that if the paragraph, which was copied from another paper, stood without the word " fudge," it would be a libel. If they were of opinion that the object of the paragraph was to vindicate the plaintiff's character from an unfounded charge, the action could not be maintained ; but if the word " fudge " was only added for the purpose of making an argument, at a future day, then it would not take away the effect of the libel. Verdict for the plaintiff. Damages, one farthing.

> *Hunt* v. *Algar and others*, (1833) 6 C. & P. 245.

Of the Innuendo.

In arriving at the meaning of the defendant's words, the Court and jury are often materially assisted by an averment in the plaintiff's Statement of Claim, called an *innuendo*. This is a statement by the plaintiff of the construction which he puts upon the words himself, and which he will endeavour to induce the jury to adopt at the trial. Where a defamatory meaning is apparent on the face of the words, no innuendo is necessary, though even here the pleader occasionally inserts one to heighten the effect of the words. But where the words *primâ facie* are not actionable, an innuendo is essential to the action. It is necessary to bring out the latent injurious meaning of the defendant's words ; and such innuendo must distinctly aver that the words bear a specific meaning which is actionable. (*Cox* v. *Cooper*, 12 W. R. 75 ; 9 L. T. 329.)

It is the office of an innuendo to define the defamatory meaning which the plaintiff sets on the words; to show how they come to have that defamatory meaning ; and also to show how they relate to the plaintiff, whenever that is not clear on the face of them. But an innuendo may not introduce new matter, or enlarge the natural meaning of words. It must not put upon the defendant's words a construction which they will not bear. It cannot alter or extend the sense of the words, or make that certain which is in fact uncertain. (*James* v. *Rutlech*, 4 Rep. 17.) If the words are incapable of the meaning ascribed to them by the innuendo, and are *primâ facie* not actionable, the judge at the trial will stop the case. If, however, the words are capable of the meaning ascribed to them, however improbable it may appear that such was the meaning conveyed, it must be left to the jury to say whether or no they were in fact so understood. (*Hunt* v. *Goodlake*, 43 L. J. C. P. 54; 29 L. T. 472 ; *Broome* v. *Gosden*, 1 C. B. 728; *Dakhyl* v. *Labouchere*, [1908] 2 K. B. at p. 328, n.) This is so in America. (*Patch* v. *Tribune Association*, 38 Hun (45 N. Y. Supr. Ct.), 368.)

An innuendo no longer requires a prefatory averment to support it.* (Common Law Procedure Act, 1852, s. 61. And see *Hemmings* v. *Gasson*, E. B. & E. 346 ; 27 L. J. Q. B. 252.) The libel or slander sued on must of course be set out *verbatim* in the Statement of Claim ; the innuendo usually follows it immediately. Such a pleading is to be considered as two counts under the old system, one with an innuendo and one without. And if the plaintiff can show a good cause of action, either with or without the alleged meaning, he is entitled to recover. (Per Blackburn, J., in *Watkin* v. *Hall*, L. R. 3 Q. B. 402; 37 L. J. Q. B. 125; 16 W. R. 857; 18 L. T. 561.)

The defendant is in no way embarrassed by the presence of the

---

* Formerly this was necessary   See *Goldstein* v. *Foss*, 6 B. & C. 154 ; *Gompertz* v. *Levy*, 9 A. & E. 282   *Capel and others* v. *Jones*, 4 C. B. 259 ; *Angle* v. *Alexander*, 7 Bing. 119.

innuendo in the Statement of Claim. He can either deny that he ever spoke the words, or he can admit that he spoke them, but deny that they conveyed that meaning. He can also assert that the words are true, either with or without the alleged meaning. It will then be for the jury to say whether the plaintiff's innuendo is borne out. If the jury reject the innuendo, the plaintiff may fall back upon the words themselves, and urge that, taken in their natural and obvious signification, they are actionable *per se* without the alleged meaning, and that therefore his unproved innuendo may be rejected as surplusage. (*Harvey* v. *French*, 1 Cr. & M. 11 ; 2 M. & Scott, 591 ; 2 Tyrw. 585.) But he cannot in the middle of the case discard the innuendo in his pleading, and start a fresh one not on the record ; he must abide by the construction he put on the words in his Statement of Claim, or else rely on their natural and obvious import. (*Simmons* v. *Mitchell*, 6 App. Cas. 156 ; 50 L. J. P. C. 11 ; *Hunter* v. *Sharpe*, 4 F. & F. 983 ; 15 L. T. 421 ; *Ruel* v. *Tatnell*, 29 W. R. 172 ; 43 L. T. 507.) If the jury negative his innuendo, and the words are not actionable in their natural and primary sense, judgment must pass for the defendant. (*Brembridge* v. *Latimer*, 12 W. R. 878 ; 10 L. T. 816 ; *Maguire* v. *Knox*, Ir. R. 5 C. L. 408.)

Illustrations.

" He hath forsworn himself." These words are not in themselves a sufficient imputation of perjury, because he is not said to have sworn falsely while giving evidence in Court. Hence an innuendo " before the justice of assize " is clearly bad : for it is not an explanation of defendant's words, but an addition to them.

Anon., 1 Roll. Abr. 82.

Holt v. *Scholefield*, 6 T. R. 691.

A libel alleged that a gentleman was on a certain night hocussed and robbed of 40*l.* in the plaintiff's public-house. An innuendo " meaning thereby that the said public-house was the resort of, and frequented by, felons, thieves, and depraved and bad characters," after verdict for the defendant was held too wide.

Broome v. *Gosden*, 1 C. B. 728.

Clarke's Case de Dorchester, (1619) 2 Rolle's Rep. 136.

The words " I was speaking to a lady about Mrs. Y.'s case " cannot support an innuendo, meaning thereby that the plaintiff (Mrs. Y.) had been guilty of adultery.

York v. *Johnson*, 116 Mass. 482.

Libel complained of :—" He has become so inflated with self-importance by the few hundreds made in my service—God only knows whether honestly or otherwise—that," &c. Innuendo, " meaning thereby to insinuate that the plaintiff had conducted himself in a dishonest manner in the service of the defendant." The Court refused to disturb a verdict for the plaintiff.

Clegg v. *Laffer*, 3 Moore & Sc. 727 ; 10 Bing. 250.

The defendant said, " Master Barham did burn my barn with his own hands, and none but he." At that date it was not felony to burn a barn unless it were either full of corn or parcel of a mansion-house. An innuendo, "a barn full of corn," was held too wide. ["That is not," says De Grey, C.J., commenting on this case in Cowp. 684, "an *explanation* of what was said before, but an *addition* to it. But if in the introduction it had been averred that the defendant had a barn full of corn, and that in a discourse about the barn the defendant had spoken the words charged in the libel of the plaintiff, an innuendo of its being the barn full of corn would have been good. For by coupling the innuendo in the libel with the introductory averment, 'his barn full of corn,' it would have made it compleat."]

> *Barham's Case,* (1602) 4 Rep. 20; Yelv. 21.
>
> See *Capital and Counties Bank* v. *Henty and Sons,* (C. A.) 5 C. P. D. 514; 49 L. J. C. P. 830; 28 W. R. 851; 43 L. T. 651; (H. L.) 7 App. Cas. 741; 52 L. J. Q. B. 232; 31 W. R. 157; 47 L. T. 662; 47 J. P. 214.

An information was filed against a Nonconformist minister for a libel upon "the bishops" contained in a book, called "A Paraphrase upon the New Testament." An innuendo, "the bishops of *England*," was held to be allowable, if from the nature of the libel this was clearly what was meant.

> *R.* v. *Baxter,* (1685) 3 Mod. 69.

The libel accused a gentleman of saying, "He could see no probability of the war's ending with France, until the little gentleman on the other side of the water was restored to his rights." Innuendo, "the Prince of Wales," allowed to be good; in fact the Court thought the meaning was clear without any innuendo.

> *Anon.,* (1707) 11 Mod. 99.
>
> *R.* v. *Matthews,* (1719) 15 How. St. Tr. 1323.

Libel:—"The mismanagements of the navy have been a greater tax upon the merchants than the duties raised by Government." An innuendo, "the royal navy of this kingdom," *held* not too wide.

> *R.* v. *Tutchin,* (1704) 14 How. St. Tr. 1095; 5 St. Tr. 527; 2 Ld. Raym. 1061; 1 Salk. 50; 6 Mod. 268.
>
> *R.* v. *Horne,* (1777) Cowp. 672; 11 St. Tr. 264; 20 How. St. Tr. 651.

The words: "We have no doubt sufficient information will be obtained for a strong case to lay before the Home Secretary to enable that functionary to cause it to be intimated to the suspected party that his presence here can be dispensed with, as far as it may be attended with danger to himself," were held in the Exchequer Chamber not to support an innuendo, meaning thereby that the prosecutor was suspected of having and had committed some crime which would bring his life into danger from the laws of England.

> *Gregory* v. *The Queen,* (No. 2) 5 Cox, C. C. 252.

The words complained of in their natural sense conveyed only suspicion, and were therefore not actionable; there were innuendoes, but none of them stated that the words imputed felony, though there was a prefatory averment stating that the defendant's motive was to cause it to be believed that the plaintiff had been guilty of felony. *Held,* that this prefatory averment could not be substituted for the innuendoes whereby the plaintiff undertook to give the meaning of the words spoken.

> *Simmons* v. *Mitchell,* 6 App. Cas. 156; 50 L. J. P. C. 11; 29 W. R. 401; 43 L. T. 710; 45 J. P. 237.

Words complained of:—"He is a regular prover under bankruptcies." An innuendo, "the defendant meaning thereby that the plaintiff had proved and was in the habit of proving fictitious debts against the estates of bankrupts, with the knowledge that such debts were fictitious," is now all that is necessary.

C. L. P. Act, 1852, Sched. B., form 33.

Words may be :—

(1) obviously defamatory ;

(2) ambiguous : that is, words which, though *primâ facie* defamatory, are still on the face of them susceptible of an innocent meaning ;

(3) neutral ; *i.e.*, words which are meaningless till some explanation is given ; such are slang expressions, words in a foreign language, words used in some special local, technical, or customary sense.

(4) *primâ facie* innocent, but capable of a defamatory meaning ;

(5) obviously innocent ; words which cannot properly be construed so as to convey any imputation on the plaintiff.

To these different classes of words special rules of pleading, evidence, and construction apply.

1. *Words Obviously Defamatory.*

Here no innuendo is necessary. No parol evidence is admissible at the trial to explain the meaning of the words. The defendant cannot be heard to say that he did not intend to injure the plaintiff's reputation, if he has in fact done so. The question is still of course for the jury ; but the judge will practically direct them that the words are actionable, and that they should find for the plaintiff on that issue. Should the jury perversely refuse to follow the judge's direction a new trial will be granted. (*Levi* v. *Milne*, 4 Bing. 195 ; 12 Moore, 418.)

But the defendant may plead circumstances which made it clear at the time he spoke or wrote that the words were not used in their ordinary signification. He may thus take the words out of this class into class 2, words *primâ facie* defamatory. It will then be a question for the jury in what sense the words were understood. But such question only arises where the words are susceptible of the innocent meaning which the defendant seeks to place on them, and where also the circumstances which are alleged to qualify the injurious words were known at the time to all to whom they were published.

Illustrations.

It is libellous, without any innuendo, to write and publish that a newspaper has a separate page devoted to the advertisements of usurers and quack doctors, and that the editor takes respectable advertisements at a cheaper rate if the advertisers will consent to their appearing in that page. The Court, however, expressed surprise at the absence of some such innuendo as " meaning thereby that the plaintiff's paper was an ill-conducted and low-class journal."

Russell and another v. *Webster*, 23 W. R. 59.

Where a libel called the plaintiff a "truckmaster," and the defendant justified ; but no evidence was given at the trial as to the meaning of the word ; the Court held, after some hesitation, that, though the word was not to be found in any English dictionary, its meaning was sufficiently clear to sustain the action, there being a statute called " The Truck Act."

Homer v. *Taunton*, 5 H. & N. 661 ; 29 L. J. Ex. 318 ; 8 W. R. 499 ; 2 L. T. 512.

To write and publish that a certain woman is a prostitute, and that " she is, I understand, under the patronage or protection of" the plaintiff, was held actionable in the Court of Appeals in New York, although there was no innuendo averring that she was under the plaintiff's protection for immoral purposes.

More v. *Bennett*, (1872) 48 N. Y. R. (3 Sickels) 472 ;
reversing the judgment of the Supreme Court below, reported 33 How. Pr. R. 180 ; 48 Barbour, N. Y. 229.

It is libellous to write and publish these words :—" Threatening letters. The Middlesex grand jury have returned a true bill against a gentleman of some property named French." And no innuendo is necessary to explain the meaning of the words ; for they can only import that the grand jury had found a true bill against French for the misdemeanour of sending threatening letters.

Harvey v. *French*, 1 Cr. & M. 11 ; 2 M. & Scott, 591 ; 2 Tyrw. 585.

Allegorical terms of well-known import are libellous *per se*, without innuendoes to explain their meaning ; *e.g.*, imputing to a person the qualities of the " frozen snake," or calling him " Judas."

Hoare v. *Silverlock*, (No. 1, 1848) 12 Q. B. 624 ; 17 L. J. Q. B. 306 ; 12 Jur. 695.

Words complained of :—" Thou art a thief : " no innuendo at all is necessay, as larceny is clearly imputed.

Blumley v. *Rose*, 1 Roll. Abr. 73.

Slowman v. *Dutton*, 10 Bing. 402.

Words complained of :—" You stole my apples." The defendant cannot be allowed to state that he only meant to say, " You have tortiously removed my apples under an unfounded claim of right." The bystanders could not possibly have understood from the word used that a civil trespass only was imputed.

> *Deverill* v. *Hulbert,* (Jan. 25th, 1878) *unreported.*

Words complained of :—" You robbed me, for I found the thing you have done it with." *Held,* that the words were actionable *per se,* and that no *colloquium* or innuendo was necessary to explain the sense in which they were used.

> *Rowcliffe* v. *Edmonds and wife,* 7 M. & W. 12 ; 4 Jur. 684.

To say, " He robbed John White" is actionable as imputing an offence punishable by law. If the words conveyed any other sense, the defendant must show it.

> *Tomlinson* v. *Brittlebank,* 4 B. & Ad. 630 ; 1 Nev. & Man. 455.
>
> *Hankinson* v. *Bilby,* 16 M. & W. 442 ; 2 C. & K. 440.
>
> *Martin* v. *Loeï,* 2 F. & F. 654, *post,* p. 682.

" Blackmailing " is clear, and requires no innuendo to support it, whether the word be written or spoken.

> *Edsall* v. *Brooks,* 2 Robt. 29 ; 3 Robt. 284 (New York).
>
> *Marks* v. *Samuel,* [1904] 2 K. B. 287; 73 L. J. K. B. 587 ; 53 W. R. 88 ; 90 L. T. 590 ; 20 Times L. R. 430.

So is " pettifogging shyster" when applied to a lawyer. " Courts have no right to be ignorant of the meaning of current phrases which everybody else understands."

> *Bailey* v. *Kalamazoo Publishing Co.,* (1879) 4 Chaney, (40 Michigan) 251.

2. *Words* primâ facie *Defamatory.*

Here, too, no innuendo is necessary, and no parol evidence is admissible at the trial to explain the meaning of the words. The judge will direct the jury that the words are *primâ facie* actionable.

But the defendant may prove circumstances which made it clear at the time that the words were not used by him in their ordinary signification. " People not unfrequently use words, and are understood to use words, not in their natural sense, or as conveying the imputation which in ordinary circumstances and apart from their surroundings they would convey, but extravagantly and in a manner which would be understood by those who hear or read them as not conveying the grave imputation suggested by a mere consideration of the words themselves." (Per Lord Herschell, L.C., in *Australian Newspaper Co., Limited* v. *Bennett,* [1894] A. C. at pp. 287, 288.) Thus the defendant may plead that the words were uttered merely in a joke, and were so understood by all who heard them; or that the words were part of a longer conversation, the rest of which limits and explains the words sued on; or any other facts which tend to show that they were uttered with an innocent meaning, and were so understood by the bystanders. If such a defence be pleaded, parol evidence may be given of the facts alleged; and then it becomes a question for the jury whether the facts as pleaded are substantially proved, and whether they do put on the words a colour different from what they would *primâ facie* bear. It is generally difficult to induce the jury to adopt the defendant's harmless view of his own language. But see *Grant* v. *Yates*, (1886) 2 Times L. R. 368.

The defendant may not plead or give in evidence any facts which were not known to the bystanders at the time the words were uttered. The defendant's secret intent in uttering the words is immaterial. (*Hankinson* v. *Bilby*, 16 M. & W. 445; 2 C. & K. 440.) He must be taken to have intended the natural consequences of his act.

The defendant is allowed thus to give evidence of all " the surrounding circumstances," in order to place the jury so far as possible in the position of bystanders, that they may judge how the words would be understood on the particular occasion. But though evidence of such extrinsic facts is admitted, parol evidence merely to explain away the words used, to show that they did not for once bear their ordinary signification, is inadmissible. A witness cannot be called to say, " *I* should not have understood defendant to make any imputation whatever on the plaintiff." The jury know what ordinary English means, and need no witness to inform them.

The leading case on this point is one cited in the *Lord Cromwell's Case*, (1578) 4 Rep. 13, 14. (At least, it appears to be a decided case, not a mere illustration.) " If a man brings an action on the case for calling the plaintiff murderer, the defendant will say, that he was talking with the plaintiff concerning unlawful hunting, and the plaintiff confessed that he killed several hares with certain engines; to which the defendant answered and said, ' Thou art a murderer ' (innuendo the killing of the said hares). . . . Resolved by the whole Court, that the justification was good. For in case of slander by words, the sense of the words ought to be taken, and the sense of them appears by the cause and occasion of speaking of them; for *sensus verborum ex causâ dicendi accipiendus est et sermones semper accipiendi sunt secundum subjectam.* . . . And it was said, God forbid that a man's words should be by such strict and grammatical construction taken by parcels against the manifest intent of the party upon consideration of all the words, which import the true cause and occasion which manifest the true sense of them; *quia quæ ad unum finem loquuta sunt, non debent ad alium detorqueri:* and, therefore, in the said case of murder, the Court held the justification good; and that the defendant should never be put to the general issue, when he confesses the words and justifies them, or confesses the words, and by special matter shows that they are not actionable." (And see *Shipley* v. *Todhunter,* 7 C. & P. 680.)

Illustrations.

Words complained of :—" Thou hast killed my wife." Defendant's wife was still alive, and the bystanders knew it. *Held,* that plaintiff was not put " in any jeopardy, and so the words vain, and no scandal or damage to the plaintiff."

> *Snag* v. *Gee,* 4 Rep. 16, as explained by Parke, B., in *Heming* v. *Power,* 10 M. & W. 569.

To call a man " Ananias " *primâ facie* imports that he is a wilful and deliberate liar. But to describe a newspaper as " The Evening Ananias " is no reflection on its proprietor when it sufficiently appears from the same publication that the reference was to a mistake accidentally made in his newspaper through an obvious blunder.

> *Australian Newspaper Co., Limited* v. *Bennett,* [1894] A. C. 284; 63 L. J. P. C. 105; 70 L. T. 597; 58 J. P. 604; 6 R. 484.

Where the words complained of are, " Thou art a thief; for thou tookest my beasts by reason of an execution, and I will hang thee," no action lies, for it is clear that the whole sentence taken together imports only a charge of trespass.

> *Wilk's Case,* 1 Roll. Abr. 51.
>
> *Smith* v. *Ward,* Cro. Jac. 674.
>
> *Sibley* v. *Tomlins,* 4 Tyrw. 90.

Where words are used which clearly import a criminal charge (as " You thief," or " You traitor "), it is still open to the defendant to show if he can that he used them merely as vague terms of general abuse, and that the bystanders must have understood him as meaning nothing more than " You rascal " or " You scoundrel." When such words occur in a string of non-actionable epithets, or in a torrent of general vulgar abuse, the jury may reasonably infer that no felony was seriously imputed. They may, however, put the harsher construction on defendant's language; it is a question entirely for them.

> *Minors* v. *Leeford,* Cro. Jac. 114.
>
> *Penfold* v. *Westcote,* 2 Bos. & P. N. R. 335.

Such words as " You are a thief; you robbed Mr. Lake of 30*l.,*" are *primâ* *facie* clearly actionable, for they impute a criminal offence. But it is open to the defendant to show, if he can, that that is not the sense in which the words were understood by bystanders who listened to the whole conversation, though previously unacquainted with the matter to which the words related.

Hankinson v. *Bilby*, 16 M. & W. 442 ; 2 C. & K. 440.

Tomlinson v. *Brittlebank*, 4 B. & Ad. 630 ; 1 Nev. & Man. 455.

The plaintiff was convicted of bird-liming, an offence under a Wild Birds Protection Order. The defendant, in reporting the case in his newspaper, stated : " The mode of operation of the bird-limer is as follows :—The thieves set up decoy birds in cages in a hedge in the vicinity of a house, where the birds on which they have their eye are. The hedge itself is strewn with twigs coated with lime, and the thieves have merely to wait," &c. The plaintiff laid an innuendo that these words charged him with larceny. *Held*, that the words could not reasonably bear this meaning, as it was plain from the context that the word " thieves " was used as designating persons who contrive to get some advantage to which they are not morally entitled but keep within their legal rights.

Campbell v. *Ritchie*, (1907) S. C. 1097 (Ct. of Sess.).

Where the defendant said to the plaintiff in the presence of others, " You are a thief, a rogue, and a swindler," it was held that the defendant could not call a witness to explain the particular transaction which he had in his mind at the time, since he did not in any way expressly refer to it in the presence of his hearers.

Martin v. *Loei*, 2 F. & F. 654.

Read v. *Ambridge*, 6 C. & P. 308.

But where the defendant said, " Thompson is a damned thief ; and so was his father before him, and I can prove it ; " but added, " Thompson received the earnings of his ship, and ought to pay the wages," Lord Ellenborough held that the latter words qualified the former and showed no felony was imputed ; the person to whom the words were spoken being the master of the ship and acquainted with all the circumstances referred to.

Thompson v. *Bernard*, 1 Camp. 48.

Brittridge's Case, 4 Rep. 19.

Cristie v. *Cowell*, Peake, 4.

Day v. *Robinson*, 1 A. & E. 554 ; 4 N. & M. 884.

So the ordinary slang expression of calling a person " a fraud " does not mean that such person has committed a fraud in the legal sense of the term, and to call a man a " liar and fraud " is not actionable ; the expression is merely abusive language.

Agnew v. *British Legal Life Assurance Co.*, (1906) 8 F. 422 (Ct. of Sess.).

Defendant stated publicly that plaintiff had been detected taking dead bodies out of the churchyard and fined, &c. He meant it as a joke ; but there was no evidence that the bystanders so understood it. The Court set aside a verdict for the defendant. Per Joy, C.B., " the principle is clear that a person shall not be allowed to murder another's reputation in jest. But if the words be so spoken that it is obvious to every bystander that only a jest is meant, no injury is done, and consequently no action would lie."

Donoghue v. *Hayes*, (1831) Hayes (Irish Exch.) 265.

3. *Neutral Words.*

Where the defendant has used only ordinary English words, the judge can decide at once whether they are *primâ facie* actionable or not. But where the words are in a foreign language, or are technical or provincial terms, an innuendo is absolutely necessary to disclose an actionable meaning. So, too, an innuendo is essential where ordinary English words are not in the particular instance used in their ordinary English signification, but in some peculiar sense.

Where the words are spoken in a foreign language the original words should be set out in the Statement of Claim, and then an exact translation should be added. (*Zenobio* v. *Axtell*, 6 T. R. 162.) In the case of slander an averment was formerly required to the effect that those who were present understood that language. (*Fleetwood* v. *Curl*, Cro. Jac. 557; Hob. 268; *Gibbs* v. *Davie*, Hutton, p. 8.) And though such an averment is no longer necessary, the fact must still be proved at the trial. For if words be spoken in a tongue altogether unknown to the hearers, no action lies (*Jones* v. *Davers* (vel *Dawkes*), (1597) Cro. Eliz. 496; 1 Roll. Abr. 74); for no injury is done to the plaintiff's reputation. But if a single bystander understood them, that is enough. Where, however, the words are spoken in the vernacular of the place of publication (as Welsh words spoken in Wales), it will be presumed that the bystanders understood them. At the trial the correctness of the translation, if not admitted, must be proved by a sworn interpreter.

So at the trial whenever the words used are not ordinary English, but local, technical, provincial, or obsolete expressions, or slang or cant terms, evidence is admissible to explain their meaning, provided such meaning has been properly alleged in the Statement of Claim. But when the words are well known and perfectly intelligible English, the Court will give them their ordinary English meaning, unless it is in some way shown that that meaning is inapplicable. This may appear from the words themselves ; for in some cases to give them their ordinary English meaning would make nonsense of them. But if in their ordinary English meaning the words would be intelligible, facts must be given in evidence to show that they may have been used in another special meaning on this particular occasion. After that has been done a bystander may be asked, " What did you understand by the expression used ? " But without such a foundation being first laid, the question is not allowable. (*Daines* v. *Hartley*, 3 Exch. 200 ; 18 L. J. Ex. 81 ; 12 Jur. 1093 ; *Gallagher* v. *Murton*, (1888) 4 Times L. R. 304.)

Illustrations.

Words complained of :—" You are a bunter." No innuendo : Willes, J., nonsuited the plaintiff, on the ground that the word had no meaning at all, and could not therefore be defamatory in ordinary acceptation ; and he refused to allow the plaintiff to be asked what the word " bunter " meant. *Aliter*, had there been an innuendo averring a defamatory sense to the word " bunter."

    Rawlings et ux. v. *Norbury*, 1 F. & F. 341.

Words spoken to an attorney :—" Thou art a daffodowndilly." Innuendo, meaning thereby that he is an " ambidexter," *i.e.*, one who takes a fee from both sides, and betrays the secrets of his client. *Held*, that an action lay.

    Anon., (Exch.) 1 Roll. Abr. 55.

    Annison v. *Blofield*, Carter, 214.

It is actionable to say, " Thou art a clipper, and thy neck shall pay for it." " For though ' clipper ' is general, and may be intended a clipper of wool, cloth, &c., yet the following words show it to be intended of clipping for which he shall be hanged."

    Naben v. *Miecock*, Skin. 183.

    Walter v. *Beaver*, 3 Lev. 166.

It is actionable to say of a stockjobber that, " He is a lame duck ; " innuendo, " meaning thereby that the plaintiff had not fulfilled his contracts in respect of the said stocks and funds " (stockjobbing being now legalised by the 23 & 24 Vict. c. 28).

    Morris v. *Langdale*, 2 Bos. & Pul. 284.

It is a libel on L. to write and publish of him that he is one of " a gang who live by cardsharping," there being an innuendo, " meaning thereby that L. is a swindler and a cheat, and lives by cheating or playing at cards, and that he and B. and G. had, previous to the libel, conspired together in cheating divers persons in playing at cards."

    Reg. pros. Lambri v. *Labouchere*, 14 Cox, C. C. 419.

The word " welcher " requires an innuendo to explain its meaning.

    Blackman v. *Bryant*, 27 L. T. 491.

Pollock, C.B., thought the word " truckmaster " required no innuendo to explain its meaning, as it "is composed of two English words intelligible to everybody."

> *Homer* v. *Taunton,* 5 H. & N. 661; 29 L. J. Ex. 318; 8 W. R. 499;
> 2 L. T. 512.

But so are "blackleg" and "blacksheep," and these words do require an innuendo.

> *M'Gregor* v. *Gregory,* 11 M. & W. 287; 12 L. J. Ex. 204; 2 Dowl.
> N. S. 769.
>
> *O'Brien* v. *Clement,* 16 M. & W. 166; 16 L. J. Ex. 77.
>
> *Barnett* v. *Allen,* 1 F. & F. 125; 3 H. & N. 376; 27 L. J. Ex. 412;
> 4 Jur. N. S. 488.

The defendant charged the plaintiff, a pawnbroker and silversmith, with "duffing": an innuendo, "meaning thereby the dishonourable practice of furbishing up damaged goods and pledging them with other pawnbrokers as new," was held good.

> *Hickinbotham* v. *Leach,* 10 M. & W. 361; 2 Dowl. N. S. 270.

The words, "He is a mainsworn," were spoken in one of the northern counties where "mainsworn" is equivalent to "perjured" (forsworn with his *hand* on the book). *Held* actionable.

> *Slater* v. *Franks,* Hob. 126.
>
> And see *Coles* v. *Haveland,* Cro. Eliz. 250; Hob. 12.

A. and B. were partners, and were conversing with the defendant. A. said they held some bills on the plaintiffs' firm; the defendant said:—"You must look out sharp that they are met by them." At the trial B. was called as a witness, and stated these facts. The counsel for the plaintiffs then proposed to ask B.:—"What did you understand by that?" But the question was objected to, and disallowed by the judge (Pollock, C.B.). The jury found a verdict for the defendant; and the Court of Exchequer refused to grant a new trial.

> *Daines and another* v. *Hartley,* 3 Exch. 200; 18 L. J. Ex. 81; 12
> Jur. 1093.
>
> *Gallagher* v. *Murton,* (1888) 4 Times L. R. 304.

Libel complained of:—"There are very few persons in society who do not look upon the whole affair to be got up for a specific occasion, and consider that it has been neither more nor less than a 'plant.' We have heard it roundly asserted that a clerk of Mr. Hamer, the notorious lawyer, was placed under a sofa at his lordship's residence when the Earl of Cardigan called there." The indictment stated, "that the said Thomas Holt used the words 'a plant' for the purpose of expressing and meaning, and the said words used by him were by divers, to wit, all the persons to whom the said libel was published, understood as expressing and meaning, an artful and wicked plan and contrivance made and entered into by the said William Paget, Esq., and other persons by false and unfounded testimony and a wrongful and wicked perversion of facts to make out, support and establish the said charge, and by concert and arrangement falsely to fix upon the said earl the commission of the said trespass and assault for the purpose of obtaining divers of the moneys of the said earl to the use of the said William Paget, Esq.," and concluded with the following innuendo:—"Thereby then and there meaning that the said William Paget, Esq., had with other persons artfully and wickedly planned and contrived to make a false and unfounded charge against the said earl of his having been guilty of the said trespass and assault upon the said wife of the said William Paget, Esq., and to make out, support and establish such charge by the false and unfounded testimony and a wicked and wrongful perversion of facts for the purpose of extorting and obtaining from the said earl divers of his moneys to the use of the said William Paget, Esq." A reporter for one of the London newspapers was called to define a "plant," and his evidence justified the innuendo. The recorder left it to the jury whether they were satisfied that the word "plant" bore the meaning attributed to it by the prosecution; if so, the passage was libellous. Verdict, guilty.

R. v. *Thomas Holt,* 8 J. P. 212.

The defendant, the editor of a newspaper, owed plaintiff money under an award; and wrote and published in his newspaper these words:—"The money will be forthcoming on the last day allowed by the award, but we are not disposed to allow him to put it into Wall Street for shaving purposes before that period." "Shaving" in New York means, (i) discounting bills or notes; (ii) fleecing men of their goods or money by overreaching, extortion, and oppression. The declaration contained no innuendo alleging that the words were used in the second defamatory sense. *Held* no libel, on demurrer.

Stone v. *Cooper,* (1845) 2 Denio, (N. Y.) 293.

The plaintiff, an outside stockbroker, sued a clergyman in the Mayor's Court for differences. The defendants, in commenting on the action, described the plaintiff as a "tout" who had "landed a parson." The jury, after deliberating for an hour and a half, found that these words were not libellous.

Asch v. *"Financial News," Limited, Times,* June 13th, 1893.

4. *Words* primâ facie *Innocent, but capable of a Defamatory Meaning.*

Where the defendant's words, if taken literally in the primary and obvious meaning, are harmless, it is still open to the plaintiff to show from the surrounding circumstances, &c., that on the occasion in question they bore a secondary and defamatory meaning. And it will then be for the jury to decide which meaning the hearers or readers would on the occasion in question have reasonably given to the words. (See *Frost* v. *London Joint Stock Bank,* (1906) 22 Times L. R. 760.) In such a case, however, an innuendo is essential to show the latent injurious meaning. Without an innuendo, there would be no cause of action shown on the record. (*Jacobs* v. *Schmaltz,* 62 L. T. 121.) And such innuendo should be carefully drafted; for on it the plaintiff must take his stand at the trial. He cannot during the course of the case adopt a fresh construction. He may, it is true, fall back on the natural and obvious meaning of the words; but that we assume here not to be actionable. And such innuendo must be specific; it must distinctly aver a definite actionable meaning. A general averment, such as, "using the words in a defamatory sense," or "for the purpose of creating an impression unfavourable to the plaintiff," would be insufficient. (*Cox* v. *Cooper*, 12 W. R. 75; 9 L. T. 329.)

The words, too, must be fairly susceptible of the defamatory meaning put upon them by the innuendo, or the judge at the trial will stop the case. "The judge must decide if the words are reasonably capable of two meanings; if he so decide, the jury must determine which of the two meanings was intended." (Per Sir Montague Smith, 6 App. Cas. at p. 158; *Jenner and another* v. *A'Beckett*, L. R. 7 Q. B. 11; 41 L. J. Q. B. 14; *Grant* v. *Yates*, (1886) 2 Times L. R. 368.) "It is for the Court to determine whether the words used are capable of the meaning alleged in the innuendo, it is for the jury to determine whether that meaning was properly attached to them." (Per Lord Herschell, L.C., in *Australian Newspaper Co., Limited* v. *Bennett*, [1894] A. C. at p. 287; 63 L. J. P. C. 105; 70 L. T. 597.) And the decision of the jury on the point is final and conclusive, unless it be such as no reasonable men could have found. (*Webster* v. *Friedeberg*, 17 Q. B. D. 736; 55 L. J. Q. B. 403; 55 L. T. 49; *post*, p. 704.)

In determining this question the jury will consider the whole of the circumstances of the case, the occasion of publication, the relationship between the parties, &c. (*Churchill* v. *Gedney*, 53 J. P. 471.) A further question of fact may arise: Were there any facts known both to speaker and hearer which would reasonably lead the latter to understand the words in a secondary and a defamatory sense? And this is a question for the jury, provided there be any evidence to go to them of such facts, and provided also it is reasonably conceivable that such facts, if proved, would have induced the hearers so to understand the words.

O.L.S.   K

(*Capital and Counties Bank* v. *Henty and Sons,* (C. A.) 5 C. P. D. 514; 49 L. J. C. P. 830; (H. L.) 7 App. Cas. 741; 52 L. J. Q. B. 232; *Griffiths* v. *Benn,* (1911) 27 Times L. R. 346.) Also whenever the words are ambiguous, or the intention of the writer equivocal, subsequent libels or slanders are admissible in evidence to explain the meaning of the first, or to prove the innuendoes, even although such subsequent publications be after action brought.

Hence, " if the defendant can get *either* the Court or the jury to be in his favour, he succeeds. The prosecutor or plaintiff cannot succeed unless he gets *both* the Court and the jury to decide for him." (Per Lord Blackburn, 7 App. Cas. at p. 776.)

Illustrations.

" He is a healer of felons ; " innuendo, a concealer of felons. *Held* actionable.
  Pridham v. *Tucker,* Yelv. 153; Hob. 126; Cart. 214.

" He has set his own premises on fire." These words are *primâ facie* innocent ; but will become actionable, if it be averred that the house was insured, and that the words were intended to convey to the hearers that the plaintiff had purposely set fire to his own premises with intent to defraud the insurance office. There being no such averment, the Court arrested judgment.
  Sweetapple v. *Jesse,* 5 B. & Ad. 27; 2 N. & M. 36.
  Cutler v. *Cutler,* 10 J. P. 169, *post,* p. 151.
  Jacobs v. *Schmaltz,* (1890) 62 L. T. 121; 6 Times L. R. 155, *post,*
   p. 141.

" She secreted one and sixpence under the till, stating, ' These are not times to be robbed.' " No innuendo. There being nothing to show that the 1*s.* 6*d.* was not her own money, the Court arrested judgment ; for, though special damage was alleged, it was not the necessary and natural consequence of the words, as set out in the declaration.
  Kelly v. *Partington,* 5 B. & Ad. 645; 3 N. & M. 116.

The plaintiff, Mary Griffiths, was a butcher, and had a son, Matthew. Words spoken by defendant :—" Matthew uses two balls to his mother's steelyard ; " innuendo, " meaning that plaintiff by Matthew, her agent and servant, used improper and fraudulent weights in her said trade, and defrauded and cheated in her said trade." After verdict for the plaintiff, held that the words, as stated and explained, were actionable.
  Griffiths v. *Lewis,* 7 Q. B. 61; 8 Q. B. 841; 14 L. J. Q. B. 197; 15
   L. J. Q. B. 249; 9 Jur. 370; 10 Jur. 711.

To say that the plaintiff is " Man Friday " to another is not actionable, without an innuendo averring that the term imputed undue subserviency and self-humiliation.
  Forbes v. *King,* 2 L. J. Ex. 109; 1 Dowl. 672.
  See *Woodgate* v. *Ridout,* 4 F. & F. 202.

Words complained of :—" The old materials have been relaid by you in the asphalte work executed in the front of the Ordnance Office, and I have seen the work done." Innuendo, "that the plaintiff had been guilty of dishonesty in his trade by laying down again the old asphalte which had before been used at the entrance of the Ordnance Office, instead of new asphalte according to his contract ; " and this innuendo was held not too large. Verdict for the plaintiff. Damages, 40s.

> *Baboneau* v. *Farrell*, 15 C. B. 360 ; 24 L. J. C. P. 9 ; 3 C. L. R. 42 ;
> 1 Jur. N. S. 114.

An action was brought for the following libel on the plaintiff in the way of his trade :—"Society of guardians for the protection of trade against swindlers and sharpers. I am directed to inform you that the persons using the firm of Goldstein & Co. are reported to this society as improper to be proposed to be balloted for as members thereof." After verdict for the plaintiff, the Court arrested judgment, because there was no averment that it was the custom of the society to designate swindlers and sharpers by the term "improper persons to be members of this society." [There was an innuendo, "meaning thereby that the plaintiff was a swindler and a sharper," &c., which would be sufficient now ; but before the C. L. P. Act, 1852, s. 61, an innuendo required a prefatory averment to support it.] The words in their natural and obvious meaning were held to be no libel.

> *Goldstein* v. *Foss*, 6 B. & C. 154 ; 1 M. & P. 402 ; 2 Y. & J. 146 ;
> 9 D. & R. 197 ; (in Ex. Ch.) 4 Bing. 489 ; 2 C. & P. 252.
> *Capel and others* v. *Jones*, 4 C. B. 259 ; 11 Jur. 396.

The defendants published in their newspaper an article discussing an appeal for subscriptions to a charity which was being made by A., and asked : "What guarantee is there that the money subscribed does not go to the private pocket of A. ? " *Held*, that these words were capable of the innuendo that A. was capable of appropriating funds collected for charity to his own use and purposes.

> *Boal* v. *Scottish Catholic Printing Co., Ltd.*, (1907) S. C. 1120 (Ct. of
> Sess.).
> But see *Green* v. *Reid*, (1906) 7. F. 891 (Ct. of Sess.).

To say of a merchant, "He hath eaten a spider," Mr. Justice Wild said was "actionable with a proper averment what the meaning is." But the report does not vouchsafe any explanation of the meaning.

> *Franklyn* v. *Butler*, (1636) cited in *Annison* v. *Blofield*, Carter, 214.

The words "'Ware Hawk there ; mind what you are about," will, with proper averments, amount to a charge of insolvency against the plaintiff, a trader ; and so are actionable.

> *Orpwood* v. *Barkes* (vel *Parkes*), 4 Bing. 261 ; 12 Moore, 492.

The plaintiff was a grocer, and had started what is known as a Christmas club, to which he endeavoured to obtain 1,000 subscribers. The defendant, a fellow-tradesman, said "His shop is in the market." Innuendo, "meaning thereby that the plaintiff was going away, and was guilty of fraudulent conduct in his business, inasmuch as he had received subscriptions from members of the club, well knowing that they would be unable to obtain any benefit therefrom." *Held*, that the words not being in themselves defamatory, and there being no evidence to support the innuendo, the defendant was entitled to judgment.

> *Ruel* v. *Tatnell*, 43 L. T. 507 ; 29 W. R. 172.

The defendant said to an upholsterer :—" You are a soldier ; I saw you in your red coat doing duty; your word is not to be taken." These words are *primâ facie* not actionable; but it was explained that there was then a common practice for tradesmen to sham enlisting so as to avoid being arrested for debt. The words were therefore held actionable as damaging the credit of a trader.

Arne v. *Johnson*, 10 Mod. 111.

Gostling v. *Brooks*, 2 F. & F. 76.

The defendant said of the plaintiff:—"Foulger trapped three foxes in Ridler's wood." These words are *primâ facie* not actionable. But the declaration averred that the plaintiff was a gamekeeper, that it is the duty of the gamekeeper not to kill foxes, that the plaintiff was employed expressly on the terms that he would not kill foxes, and that no one who killed foxes would be employed as a gamekeeper. *Held*, on demurrer, a good declaration; for the words so explained, clearly imputed to the plaintiff misconduct in his occupation, and were therefore actionable without proof of special damage.

Foulger v. *Newcomb*, L. R. 2 Ex. 327; 36 L. J. Ex. 169; 15 W. R. 1181; 16 L. T. 595.

But an indictment for publishing a handbill, " B. Oakley, of Chillington, Game and Rabbit Destroyer, and his wife, the seller of the same in country and town," was quashed, there being no innuendo explaining the words or showing that they implied any offence or referred to the trade or calling of the prosecutor.

R. v. *James Yates*, 12 Cox, C. C. 233.

A landlord sent to his tenants a notice:—"Messrs. Henty and Sons hereby give notice that they will not receive in payment any cheques drawn on any of the branches of the Capital and Counties Bank." Innuendo, "meaning thereby that the plaintiffs were not to be relied upon to meet the cheques drawn upon them, and that their position was such that they were not to be trusted to cash the cheques of their customers." *Held*, that the words in their natural and primary sense were not libellous; that the *onus* lay on the plaintiffs to show that they conveyed some secondary libellous meaning; and that as no evidence was offered of facts known to the tenants which could reasonably induce them to understand the words in the defamatory sense ascribed to them by the innuendo, there was no case to go to the jury, and the defendants were entitled to judgment.

Capital and Counties Bank v. *Henty and Sons*, (C. A.) 5 C. P. D. 514; 49 L. J. C. P. 830; 28 W. R. 851; 43 L. T. 651; (H. L.) 7 App. Cas. 741; 52 L. J. Q. B. 232; 31 W. R. 157; 47 L. T. 662; 47 J. P. 214.

The plaintiff drew a cheque in favour of A. on a bank where the plaintiff had a large balance on current account. A. paid it into his bank, which by an error returned it to A. with a slip attached marked "Reason assigned—Not Stated." The plaintiff brought an action of libel, alleging that these words meant that the cheque had been dishonoured through want of assets. *Held*, that the words on the slip, coupled with the return of the cheque, were not in their natural meaning libellous, and that it lay upon the plaintiff to prove facts and circumstances leading to the conclusion that they would naturally be understood by reasonable persons as conveying the libellous imputation alleged; and that the plaintiff not having proved this, there was no case to go to the jury.

Frost v. *London Joint Stock Bank*, (1906) 22 Times L. R. 760.

Defendant posted up several placards which ran thus:—"W. Gee, Solicitor, Bishop's Stortford. To be sold by auction, if not previously disposed of by private contract, a debt of the above, amounting to 3,197*l.* due upon partnership and mortgage transactions." There was no innuendo. Bramwell, B., told the jury that in his opinion this was no libel, " because it was not libellous to publish of another that he owed money ; " and the jury returned a verdict of Not guilty.

> *R.* v. *Coghlan,* (1865) 4 F. & F. 316.

The surrounding circumstances and the time and place of publication may often materially assist the jury in arriving at the true meaning of the words.

Illustrations.

The defendants published what was perfectly true, that judgment had been recovered against the plaintiff in the County Court for 27*l.* 1*s.* 0*d.* But they published it in a trade gazette by the side of " Bankruptcy Notices " and items as to " Bills of Sale ; " and it was held that the jury might properly find that the words so published implied that the plaintiff was unable to satisfy the said judgment or to pay his just debts.

> *Williams* v. *Smith,* (1888) 22 Q. B. D. 134 ; 58 L. J. Q. B. 21 ; 37 W. R. 93 ; 59 L. T. 757.

The result would have been otherwise, had a proper note been prefixed to the extract, as in

> *Searles* v. *Scarlett,* [1892] 2 Q. B. 56 ; 61 L. J. Q. B. 573 ; 40 W. R. 696 ; 66 L. T. 837 ; 56 J. P. 789 ; 8 Times L. R. 562.

So where a wax figure of the plaintiff was placed at the threshold of the " Chamber of Horrors," and in close proximity to images of Mrs. Maybrick, Pigott, and Scott, the Court held that it was open to the jury to find that the defendants intended their visitors to draw from these surroundings an inference injurious to the plaintiff.

> *Monson* v. *Tussauds, Limited,* [1894] 1 Q. B. 671 ; 63 L. J. Q. B. 454 ; 70 L. T. 335 ; 9 R. 177.

The defendants published in their newspaper, in the list of " Births," that Mrs. M. had given birth to twins. Many who read the advertisement knew that Mr. and Mrs. M. had only been married one month. *Held,* that the words amounted to a charge of unchastity, and were therefore actionable.

> *Morrison* v. *Ritchie & Co.,* (1902) 4 F. 645 (Ct. of Sess.).
> But see *Wood* v. *Edinburgh Evening News,* (1910) S. C. 895 (Ct. of Sess.).

The plaintiff may also aver in his Statement of Claim that the words were spoken ironically ; and it will then be a question for the jury whether the words were so spoken.

Illustrations.

Ironical praise may be a libel ; *e.g.,* calling an attorney " an honest lawyer."

> *Boydell* v. *Jones,* 4 M. & W. 446 ; 1 H. & H. 408 ; 7 Dowl. 210.

It is actionable to say ironically, " *You* will not play the Jew or the hypocrite."

> *R.* v. *Garret (Sir Baptist Hicks' Case),* Hob. 215 ; Popham, 139.

Ironical advice to the Lord Keeper by a country parson, " to be as wise as

Lord Somerset, to manage as well as Lord Haversham, to love the Church as well as the Bishop of Salisbury," &c., is actionable.

> *R.* v. *Dr. Brown*, 11 Mod. 86; Holt, 425.

5. *Words incapable of a Defamatory Meaning.*

But where the words can bear but one meaning, and that is obviously not defamatory, then no innuendo or other allegation on the pleadings can make the words defamatory; no action lies; and the judge at the trial should enter judgment for the defendant and not permit the case to go to the jury. No parol evidence is admissible to explain the meaning of ordinary English words, in the absence of any evidence to show that in the case before the Court the words do not bear their usual signification. "It is not right to say that a judge is to affect not to know what everybody else knows—the ordinary use of the English language." (Per Brett, J., 1 C. P. D. 572.) The fact that actual damage has followed from the publication is immaterial in considering what is the true construction of the words. (Per Lord Coleridge, C.J., 2 C. P. D. 150.) Except, perhaps, as showing that one person at all events understood the words in a defamatory sense. "It shall be adjudged *ex effectu dicendi.*" (Per Jones and Croke, JJ., in *Southold* v. *Daunston*, Cro. Car. 269.)

Illustrations.

Words complained of:—"He was the ringleader of the nine hours' system," and "He has ruined the town by bringing about the nine hours' system," &c. The declaration contained no innuendo, and no sufficient averment that the words were spoken of the plaintiff in the way of his trade, and on demurrer was held bad.

> *Miller* v. *David*, L. R. 9 C. P. 118; 43 L. J. C. P. 84; 22 W. R. 332; 30 L. T. 58.

Words complained of:—"We are requested to state that the honorary secretary of the Tichborne Defence Fund is not and never was a captain in the Royal Artillery, as he has been erroneously described." Innuendo that the plaintiff was an impostor, and had falsely and fraudulently represented himself to be a captain in the Royal Artillery. Bovill, C.J., held that the words were not reasonably capable of the defamatory meaning ascribed to them by the innuendo, and nonsuited the plaintiff. *Held*, that the nonsuit was right.

> *Hunt* v. *Goodlake*, 43 L. J. C. P. 54; 29 L. T. 472.

A board of guardians published the following advertisement :—" Cork Union. To Solicitors. The Cork Board of Guardians will, at their next meeting, appoint a solicitor, other than the late solicitors, to do all the legal business of the Union," &c. An action of libel was commenced by the late solicitors of the Board. *Held,* that the words were not libellous *per se,* and that, in the absence of legal evidence of extrinsic facts proper to be submitted to the jury as proof of a libellous tendency, the defendants were entitled to judgment.

> *O'Hea* v. *Guardians of Cork Union,* 32 L. R. Ir. 629.

The plaintiff was a certificated art master, and had been master of the Walsall Science and Art Institute. His engagement there ceased in June, 1874, and he then started, and became master of, another school which was called " The Walsall Government School of Art," and was opened in August. In September the following advertisement appeared in the *Walsall Observer,* signed by the defendants, as chairman, treasurer, and secretary of the institute respectively :— " Walsall Science and Art Institute. The public are informed that Mr. Mulligan's connection with the institute has ceased, and that he is not authorised to receive subscriptions on its behalf." The declaration set out this advertisement with an innuendo, " meaning thereby that the plaintiff falsely assumed and pretended to be authorised to receive subscriptions on behalf of the said institute." At the trial, Quain, J., directed a nonsuit on the ground that the advertisement was not capable of the defamatory meaning attributed by the innuendo. *Held,* that the nonsuit was right; that the advertisement was not capable of any defamatory meaning.

> *Mulligan* v. *Cole and others,* L. R. 10 Q. B. 549 ; 44 L. J. Q. B. 153 ; 33 L. T. 12.

> *Brent* v. *Spratt, Times,* Feb. 3rd, 1882, *ante,* p. 63.

> *Raven* v. *Stevens & Sons,* (1886) 3 Times L. R. 67.

The plaintiff had been employed as a commercial traveller by the defendant. The defendant signed and circulated among his customers cards in unfastened envelopes with these words upon them :—" H. Beswick is no longer in our employ. Please give him no order or pay him any money on our account." In an action of libel the jury found that the words were libellous, and that the defendant acted maliciously in circulating them. *Held,* that the words were not capable of a defamatory meaning, and that the defendant was entitled to judgment.

> *Beswick* v. *Smith,* (1908) 24 Times L. R. 169.

A dispute having arisen between the defendants and their agent, the plaintiff, as to one small item in the plaintiff's accounts, the defendants sent the plaintiff a postcard in the following words :—" Settlement. If you do not remit by return the matter will be handed to our Dublin solicitors." There was no evidence to show that anyone who saw the postcard understood it in a libellous sense. *Held,* that the judge at the trial acted rightly in directing a verdict for the defendants.

> *McCann* v. *Edinburgh Roperie Co.,* 28 L. R. Ir. 24.

The plaintiff resigned his agency for the defendant company. The defendants sent out a circular stating that his agency had " been closed by the directors." Innuendo, " that the plaintiff had been dismissed by the defendants from his employment as their agent for some reason discreditable to him." After a verdict for the plaintiff it was held by the House of Lords that the words were incapable of a libellous meaning.

Nevill v. *Fine Art and General Insurance Co., Limited,* [1897] A. C. 68; 66 L. J. Q. B. 195; 75 L. T. 606; 61 J. P. 500.
Havard v. *Corbett and others,* (1899) 15 Times L. R. 222.
Keogh v. *Incorporated Dental Hospital* (No. 2), [1910] 2 Ir. R. 577.

CERTAINTY.

But even where the meaning of the defendant's words is clear or has been ascertained, the question remains :—Has he said enough ? Was the imputation sufficiently definite to injure the plaintiff's reputation ? Is it clear that it is the plaintiff to whom it referred ? Unless these questions can be answered in the affirmative, no action lies. There must be a specific imputation cast on the person suing.

" In every action on the case for slanderous words, two things are requisite :

1. That the person who is scandalised is certain ;

2. That the scandal is apparent by the words themselves. . . . As an innuendo cannot make the person certain which was incertain before, so an innuendo cannot alter the matter or sense of the words themselves." (*James* v. *Rutlech,* 4 Rep. 17 b.)

This is clearly only a part of the construction of the words ; but it is convenient to collect the cases under a separate head, which may be denoted by the well-known pleading phrase "certainty." Often the only question of construction arising in a case may be one of certainty.

The Court formerly expected to be assisted in dealing with the question by a variety of minute averments in the plaintiff's declaration. Thus it was necessary that there should be a *colloquium,* an averment that the defendant was speaking of the plaintiff, as well as constant innuendoes in the statement of the words themselves, " he (meaning thereby the plaintiff)." So, too, many other allegations were required describing the locality, the relationship between the various persons mentioned, and all the surrounding circumstances necessary to fully understand the defendant's words. And these matters could not properly be proved at the trial unless they were set out on the record; if they were not, and the plaintiff had a verdict, the Court would subsequently arrest judgment on the ground that it did not appear clearly on the face of the record that the words were actionable. And this technicality was carried to an absurd extent. Thus, where the defendant said, " Thou art a murderer, for thou art the fellow that didst kill Mr. Sydnam's man," the Court of Exchequer Chamber, on error brought, arrested judgment, because there was no averment that any man of Mr. Sydnam's had in fact been killed. (*Barrons* v. *Ball*, (1614) Cro. Jac. 331. See *Ratcliff* v. *Michael*, *ib.* ; and *Upton* v. *Pinfold*, Comyns, 267.) Had the words been " *and* thou art," instead of " *for* thou art," the plaintiff would probably have been allowed to recover. (See *Minors* v. *Leeford*, Cro. Jac. 114.) Again, in *Ball* v. *Roane*, (1593) Cro. Eliz. 308, the words were : " There was never a robbery committed within forty miles of Wellingborough but thou hadst thy part in it." After a verdict for the plaintiff, the Court arrested judgment, " because it was not averred there *was* any robbery committed within forty miles, &c., for otherwise it is no slander." So in *Foster* v. *Browning*, (1625) Cro. Jac. 688, where the words were, " Thou art as arrant a thief as any is in England," the Court arrested judgment, because the plaintiff had not averred " that there was any thief in England." (See also *Johnson* v. *Sir John Aylmer*, Cro. Jac. 126 ; *Sir Thomas Holt* v. *Astrigg*, Cro. Jac. 184 ; *Slocomb's Case*, Cro. Car. 442.) But the climax was reached in a case cited in *Dacy* v. *Clinch*, (1661) Sid. 53, where the defendant had said to the plaintiff, " As sure as God governs the world, or King James this kingdom, you are a thief." After verdict for the plaintiff, the defendant moved in arrest of judgment, on the ground that there was no averment on the record that God did govern the world, or King James this kingdom. But here the Court drew the line, and held that, " these things were so apparent" that neither of them need be averred. And even in the last century instances of similar technicality were not wanting, though their absurdity was not so flagrant. Thus, in *Solomon* v. *Lawson*, 8 Q. B. 823 ; 15 L. J. Q. B. 253 ; 10 Jur. 796, the libel consisted of two letters to the *Times* ; the first made a charge generally on " the authorities " at St. Helena ; the second letter brought it home to the plaintiff in particular. Neither letter was thus a complete libel in itself. In the first count of the declaration the first letter was fully set out ; in the second count *both* letters were set out *verbatim*. The first count was held bad, because it set out only half the libel. The second count was also held bad, because the pleader in setting out the first letter for the second time had introduced it with the words " in *substance* as follows." The Court decided that it ought to have been set out *verbatim* : so it was ; but because the pleader *said* he had only set out the substance, judgment was arrested.

Lord Denman would, it seems, have given judgment for the plaintiff had the pleader used the word "*tenour*" instead of "*substance*." So, too, in *Angle* v. *Alexander*, 7 Bing. 119; 1 Cr. & J. 143; 4 M. & P. 870; 1 Tyrw. 9, the words were thus set out with innuendoes in the declaration : " You " (meaning the said plaintiff) " are a regular prover under bankruptcy " (meaning that the said plaintiff was accustomed to prove fictitious debts under commissions of bankruptcy); " you are a regular bankrupt-maker ; if it was not for some of your neighbours your shop would look queer." And the Court arrested judgment because there was no prefatory averment that the defendant had been accustomed to employ the words "prover under bankruptcy" in the meaning set out in the innuendo. (See also *Goldstein* v. *Foss and another*, 6 B. & C. 154; 4 Bing. 489; 9 D. & R. 197; 2 C. & P. 252; 1 M. & P. 402; 2 Y. & J. 146; and other cases cited *ante*, pp. 118, 119.)

But by sect. 61 of the Common Law Procedure Act, 1852, the *colloquium* and all other preliminary averments were rendered unnecessary. And now Order XIX. r. 4 requires that only material facts need be stated in the pleadings. The pleader must judge what facts are material; and he will also insert averments which, though not essential, will help to make the case clear by explaining what is to follow (as in *Foulger* v. *Newcomb*, L. R. 2 Ex. 327; 36 L. J. Ex. 169; 15 W. R. 1181; 16 L. T. 595). But where the plaintiff is suing for words spoken of him in the way of his office, profession, or trade, there it is absolutely necessary to aver that at the time when the words were spoken the plaintiff held such office, or carried on such profession or trade. And there should also be an averment that the words were spoken of the plaintiff in the way of his office, profession, or trade.

1. *Certainty of the Imputation.*

Where spoken words are sought to be made actionable, as charging the plaintiff with the commission of a crime, we have seen that a criminal offence must be specifically imputed. It will not be sufficient to prove words which only amount to an accusation of fraudulent, dishonest, vicious, or immoral, but not criminal, conduct. Still it is not necessary that the alleged crime should be stated with all the technicality or precision of an indictment ; it is enough if the crime be imputed in the ordinary language usually employed to denote it in lay conversation. Again, if criminal conduct be distinctly imputed, it is not necessary to specify the kind of crime imputed. All that is requisite is that the bystanders should clearly understand that the plaintiff is charged with the commission of a crime. " The meaning of the words is to be gathered from the vulgar import, and not from any technical legal sense." (Per Buller, J., in *Colman* v. *Godwin*, 3 Dougl. 91; 2 B. & C. 285, *n.*)

But spoken words which merely impute a criminal intention or design are not actionable, if no criminal act be directly or indirectly alleged. So, too, words of mere suspicion, not amounting to an assertion of guilt, are not actionable; and no innuendo can make them so. (See *ante*, pp. 116, 118.)

Illustrations.

General Criminal Conduct.

The following words have been held sufficient :—

" You have done many things for which you ought to be hanged, and I will have you hanged."

> *Francis* v. *Roose*, 3 M. & W. 191; 7 L. J. Ex. 66; 1 H. & H. 36.
> *Tempest* v. *Chambers*, 1 Stark. 67.
> *Curtis* v. *Curtis*, 10 Bing. 477; 4 M. & Scott, 337.

" I will lock you up in Gloucester gaol next week. I know enough to put you there."

> *Webb* v. *Beavan*, 11 Q. B. D. 609; 52 L. J. Q. B. 544; 49 L. T. 201; 47 J. P. 488.

No innuendo is necessary in such cases, or in any case where the words plainly impute a crime. If any were necessary, an innuendo, " meaning thereby that the plaintiff had been guilty of a criminal offence," is sufficient without specifying what particular crime is meant.

> *Webb* v. *Beavan*, *supra*.
> *Saunders* v. *Edwards*, 1 Sid. 95.
> *Kinnahan* v. *McCullagh*, Ir. R. 11 C. L. 1.
> *Francis* v. *Roose*, *suprà*.

Treason.

The following words have been held sufficiently definite to constitute a charge of treason, or at least of sedition, and therefore actionable :—

" Thy master is no true subject."

> *Waldegrave* v. *Agas*, Cro. Eliz. 191; 1 Roll. Abr. 75.
> *Sed quære, Fowler* v. *Aston*, Cro. Eliz. 268; 1 Roll. Abr. 43.

" Thou hast committed treason beyond the seas;" for there is a violent intendment that he committed treason to the State here, and not to a foreign State.

> *Lewis* v. *Coke*, Cro. Jac. 424,

"He consented to the late rebels in the North."

> *Stapleton* v. *Frier*, Cro. Eliz. 251.

"Thou art a rebel, and all that keep thee company are rebels, and thou art not the Queen's friend."

> *Redston* v. *Eliot*, Cro. Eliz. 638; 1 Roll. Abr. 49.

"Thou art an enemy to the State."

> *Charter* v. *Peter*, Cro. Eliz. 602.

"He doth hold constant correspondency with the Cavilliers."

> *Trevilian* v. *Welman*, (1654) Style, 400.

"He has the Pretender's picture in his room, and I saw him drink his health. And he said he had a right to the crown."

> *Fry* v. *Carne*, (1724) 8 Mod. 283.
>
> *How* v. *Prin*, (1702) Holt, 652; 7 Mod. 107; 2 Ld. Raym. 812; 2 Salk. 694; 1 Brown, Py. C. 64.

"Thou hast made a seditious sermon, and moved the people to sedition this day."

> *Philips (B. D.)* v. *Badby*, (1582) cited 4 Rep. 19.

But to say merely, "Thou art a rebel," was adjudged not actionable.

> *Fountain* v. *Rogers*, (1601) Cro. Eliz. 878.

Murder.

So it is a sufficient charge of murder to say :—

"Thou hast killed thy master's cook."

> *Cooper* v. *Smith*, Cro. Jac. 423; 1 Roll. Abr. 77.

"I am thoroughly convinced that you are guilty of the death of Daniel Dolly, and rather than you should want a hangman I will be your executioner."

> *Peake* v. *Oldham*, Cowp. 275; 2 Wm. Bl. 959.

"Keymer is a base gentleman, and hath had four or five children by Ann, his own maid, and hath either killed them or procured them to be killed."

> *Keymer* v. *Clark*, (1625) Latch, 159; 1 Roll. Abr. 75.

But it is not sufficient to say :—

"Hext seeks my life." "Because he may seek his life lawfully upon just cause."

> *Hext* v. *Yeomans*, 4 Rep. 15.

"He was the cause of the death of Dowland's child," because a man might innocently cause the death of another by accident or misfortune.

> *Miller* v. *Buckdon*, 2 Buls. 10.

"Thou wouldst have killed me," for here a murderous intention only is imputed.

> *Dr. Poe's Case*, 1 Vin. Abr. 440, cited in 2 Buls. 206.

Forgery.

The following words have been held a sufficient charge of forgery :—

"This is a counterfeit warrant made by Mr. Stone."

> *Stone* v. *Smalcombe*, Cro. Jac. 648.

"Thou hast forged a privy seal, and a commission." *Per cur.* "'A commission' shall be intended the king's commission, under the privy seal."

> *Baal* v. *Baggerley*, Cro. Car. 326.

"You forged my name," although it is not stated to what deed or instrument.
> *Jones* v. *Herne*, 2 Wils. 87.
> Overruling *Anon.*, 3 Leon. 231 ; 1 Roll. Abr. 65.

Arson.

"*I* never set *my* premises on fire," was held sufficiently clear in
> *Cutler* v. *Cutler*, 10 J. P. 169.
> But see *Sweetapple* v. *Jesse*, 5 B. & Ad. 27 ; 2 N. & M. 36.
> *Barham's Case*, 4 Rep. 20 ; Yelv. 21.

"Did he have a fire twice ? He is a funny fellow." *Held,* insufficient in the absence of a proper innuendo.
> *Jacobs* v. *Schmaltz*, (1890) 62 L. T. 121 ; 6 Times L. R. 155.

Embezzlement.

"He made a few hundreds in my service—God only knows whether honestly or otherwise," is a sufficient imputation of embezzlement.
> *Clegg* v. *Laffer*, 3 Moore & Sc. 727 ; 10 Bing. 250.

Larceny.

The following words are a sufficient charge of larceny :—

"Baker stole my box-wood, and I will prove it." It was argued that it did not appear from the words that the box-wood was not growing ; and that to cut down and remove growing timber is a trespass only, not a larceny. But the Court gave judgment for the plaintiff, holding that "ex vi termini" stealing "did import felony."
> *Baker* v. *Pierce*, 2 Ld. Raym. 959 ; 6 Mod. 23 ; Holt, 654.
> Overruling *Mason* v. *Thompson*, Hutt. 38.

Gybbons asked May : "Have you brought home the forty pounds you stole ? " *Held,* that an action lay.
> *May* v. *Gybbons*, Cro. Jac. 568.

"Thou hast stolen our bees, and thou art a thief." After verdict it was contended that larceny cannot be committed of bees, unless they be hived ; but the Court held that the subsequent words "thou art a thief" showed that the larceny imputed was of such bees as could be stolen.
> *Tibbs* v. *Smith*, 3 Salk. 325 ; Sir Thos. Raym. 33.
> *Minors* v. *Leeford*, Cro. Jac. 114.

"Thou art a corn-stealer" held sufficient, in spite of the objection "that it might be that the corn was growing, and so no felony."
> *Anon.*, (1597) Cro. Eliz. 563.
> *Smith* v. *Ward*, (1624) Cro. Jac. 674.

So a charge of being "privy and consenting to" a larceny is actionable.
> *Mot et ux.* v. *Butler*, Cro. Car. 236.

"He is a pickpocket ; he picked my pocket of my money," was once held an insufficient charge of larceny.
> *Watts* v. *Rymes*, 2 Lev. 51 ; 1 Ventr. 213 ; 3 Salk. 325.

But now this would clearly be held sufficient.
> *Baker* v. *Pierce, suprà.*
> *Stebbing* v. *Warner*, 11 Mod. 255.

"He was put into the round-house for stealing ducks at Crowland."
> *Beavor* v. *Hides*, 2 Wilson, 300.

" You have been cropped for felony."

> *Wiley* v. *Campbell,* 5 Monroe (19 Kentucky), 396.

But it is not actionable to say—

" You as good as stole the canoe."

> *Stokes* v. *Arey,* 8 Jones (North Carolina), 66.

Or, " A man that would do that would steal."

> *Stees* v. *Kemble,* 27 Penn. St. (3 Casey) 112.

Or, " If you have got money you stole it. I believe you will steal."

> *McKee* v. *Ingalls,* 4 Scam. (Illinois) 30.

Receiving Stolen Goods.

To say, "I have been robbed of three dozen winches; you bought two, one at 3*s.*, one at 2*s.*; you knew well when you bought them that they cost me three times as much making as you gave for them, and that they could not have been honestly come by," is a sufficient charge of receiving stolen goods, knowing them to have been stolen.

[An indictment which merely alleged that the prisoner knew the goods were not honestly come by would be bad. *R.* v. *Wilson,* 2 Moo. C. C. 52.]

> *Alfred* v. *Farlow,* 8 Q. B. 854 ; 15 L. J. Q. B. 258 ; 10 Jur. 714.
>
> *Clarke's Case de Dorchester,* 2 Rolle's Rep. 136.
>
> *King* v. *Bagg,* Cro. Jac. 331.

Bigamy.

Mrs. Heming was sister to Mr. Alleyne. The defendant said :—" It has been ascertained beyond all doubt that Mr. Alleyne and Mrs. Heming are not brother and sister, but man and wife." *Held,* that it was open to the jury to construe this as a charge of bigamy as well as of incest.

> *Heming and wife* v. *Power,* 10 M. & W. 564.

Perjury.

" I will make thee an example, for a perjured knave " is sufficient.

> Comyns' Digest, Defamation E. 1.

" You are forsworn," without more, is insufficient.

> *Stanhope* v. *Blith,* (1585) 4 Rep. 15.
>
> *Holt* v. *Scholefield,* 6 T. R. 691.
>
> *Hall* v. *Weedon,* 8 D. & R. 140.

But to write and publish that they " did not scruple to turn affidavit-men " is sufficient.

> *Roach* v. *Garvan, Re Read and Huggonson,* (1742) 2 Atk. 469 ; 2 Dick, 794.

" Thou art forsworn in a court of record, and that I will prove," was held sufficient, though it was argued after verdict that he might only have been talking in the court-house and so forsworn himself; but the Court held that the words would naturally mean forsworn while giving evidence in some judicial proceeding in a court of record.

> *Ceely* v. *Hoskins,* (1639) Cro. Car. 509, practically overruling
>
> *Brawn* v. *Michael,* (1595) Cro. Eliz. 375.

Plaintiff had recently given evidence in an action against defendant, who thereupon wrote and published of him :—" The man at the sign of the Bible is no slouch at swearing to an old story." *Held*, that if these words did not amount to a charge of actual perjury, they at least imputed that he swore with levity without due regard to the solemnity of an oath, and therefore, being written, were actionable.

> *Steele* v. *Southwick*, 9 Johns. (New York) 214 ; see *post*, p. 153.

Conspiracy.

"He had, in conjunction with his sister, broken open a box belonging to his wife." No innuendo. These words were held not to amount to a charge of a criminal conspiracy.

> *Lemon* v. *Simmons*, (1888) 57 L. J. Q. B. 260 ; 36 W. R. 351 ; 4 Times
> L. R. 306.
> But see *O'Connell* v. *Mansfield*, 9 Ir. L. R. 179.

False Pretences.

The words "He has defrauded a mealman of a roan horse," held not to imply a criminal act of fraud, as it is not stated that the mealman was induced to part with his property by means of any false pretence.

> *Richardson* v. *Allen*, 2 Chit. 657.
> *Needham* v. *Dowling*, 15 L. J. C. P. 9.

Blackmailing.

It is actionable to say of A. that he brought a blackmailing action against B.

> *Marks* v. *Samuel*, [1904] 2 K. B. 287 ; 73 L. J. K. B. 587 ; 53
> W. R. 88 ; 90 L. T. 590 ; 20 Times L. R. 430.

Attempt to Commit a Felony.

The following words were held sufficient :—
"He sought to murder me, and I can prove it."

> *Preston* v. *Pinder*, Cro. Eliz. 308.

"She would have cut her husband's throat, and did attempt it."

> *Scot et ux.* v. *Hilliar*, Lane, 98 ; 1 Vin. Abr. 440.

The following insufficient :—
"Thou wouldst have killed me."

> *Dr. Poe's Case*, cited in *Murrey's Case*, 2 Buls. 206 ; 1 Vin. Abr. 440.

'Sir Harbert Crofts keepeth men to rob me."

> *Sir Harbert Crofts* v. *Brown*, 3 Buls. 167.

"He would have robbed me."

> *Stoner* v. *Audely*, Cro. Eliz. 250.

For here no overt act is charged, and mere intention is not criminal.

> *Eaton* v. *Allen*, 4 Rep. 16 b ; Cro. Eliz. 684.

Other instances of a criminal charge indirectly made will be found in

> *Snell* v. *Webling*, 2 Lev. 150 ; 1 Vent. 276.
> *Woolnoth* v. *Meadows*, 5 East, 463 ; 2 Smith, 28.

Where words clearly refer to the plaintiff's office and his conduct therein, or otherwise clearly touch and injure him therein, it is unnecessary that the defendant should expressly name his office or restrict his words thereto; it shall be intended that he was speaking of him in the way of his office or trade.

To say of a clerk, " He cozened his master," is actionable, though the defendant did not expressly state that the cozening was done in the execution of the clerk's official duties; that will be intended.

Reignald's Case, (1640) Cro. Car. 563.

Reeve v. *Holgate,* (1672) 2 Lev. 62.

To say of a trader, " He has been arrested for debt," is actionable, though no express reference be made to his trade at the time of publication; for such words must necessarily affect his credit in his trade, whatever it was.

Jones v. *Littler,* 7 M. & W. 423; 10 L. J. Ex. 171.

So where the plaintiff was charged with being " a public robber; " it was held in Canada, that it was not necessary for him to aver that he was in any office, trade, or employment in which he could have robbed the public.

Taylor v. *Carr,* 3 Up. Can. Q. B. Rep. 306.

It is not necessary that the imputation on the plaintiff should be stated explicitly in so many words, or expressed in direct and positive language. Frequently the defendant only hints at or insinuates his meaning. He may try to guard himself by prefixing such words as " I think," " I understand," or " I hear so-and-so; " but this will not avail him. If an actionable imputation be in fact conveyed, it does not matter how it was expressed. " The stereotyped formulas of slander ' they say,' ' it is said,' ' it is generally believed,' are about as effectual modes of blasting reputation as distinctly and directly to charge the crime." (*Per cur.* in *Johnson* v. *St. Louis Despatch Co.,* 65 Missouri, at p. 541.)

The following words have been held to convey an imputation with sufficient certainty and precision :—

" Master Halley is infected of the robbery and murder lately committed, and doth smell of the murder."

Halley v. *Sidenham,* (1572) Dyer, 318.

" Kempe will be within these two days a bankrupt."

Kempe's Case, (1553) Dyer, 72.

" I heard a bird sing that you had committed a felony," or " I dreamed so." Per Lord North, C.J., in

Earl of Peterborough v. *Mordant,* (1669) 1 Lev. 277.

" I believe all is not well with Daniel Vivian; there be many merchants who have lately failed, and I expect no otherwise of Daniel Vivian ; " for this is a charge of present pecuniary embarrassment.

Vivian v. *Willet,* 3 Salk. 326 ; Sir Thos. Raym. 207 ; 2 Keble, 718.

" Two dyers are gone off, and for aught I know Harrison will be so too within this twelvemonth."

Harrison v. *Thornborough,* 10 Mod. 196 ; Gilb. Cas. 114.

" He has become so inflated with self-importance by the few hundreds made in my service—God only knows whether honestly or otherwise ; " for the speaker clearly means to insinuate that they were made dishonestly.

Clegg v. *Laffer,* 3 Moore & Sc. 727 ; 10 Bing. 250.

" I think in my conscience if Sir John might have his will, he would kill the king ; " for this is a charge of compassing the king's death.

Sidnam v. *Mayo,* 1 Roll. Rep. 427 ; Cro. Jac. 407.

Peake v. *Oldham,* Cowp. 275 ; 2 Wm. Bl. 959 ; *ante,* p. 140.

It is actionable to say, " I am of opinion that such a Privy Councillor is a traitor," or " I think such a judge is corrupt."   Per Wyndham and Scroggs, JJ., and North, C.J., in

Lord Townshend v. *Dr. Hughes,* 2 Mod. 166.

So where the defendant, on hearing that his barns were burnt down, said, " I cannot imagine who it should be but the Lord Sturton."

Lord Sturton v. *Chaffin,* (1563) Moore, 142.

" I have every reason to believe he burnt the barn " is actionable.

Logan v. *Steele,* 1 Bibb (Kentucky), 593.

" It is the general opinion of the people in Jones's neighbourhood that he burnt C.'s house " is actionable.

Waters v. *Jones,* 3 Port. (Alabama), 442.

To state that criminal proceedings are about to be taken against the plaintiff (*e.g.,* that the Attorney-General had directed a certain attorney to prosecute him for perjury) is actionable, although the speaker does not expressly assert that the plaintiff is guilty of the charge.

Roberts v. *Camden,* 9 East, 93.

Tempest v. *Chambers,* 1 Stark. 67.

But where the defendant said, " I have a suspicion that you and B. have robbed my house, and therefore I take you into custody," the jury found that the words did not amount to a direct charge of felony, but only indicated what was passing in defendant's mind (*ante,* p. 44).

Tozer v. *Mashford,* 6 Exch. 539 ; 20 L. J. Ex. 225.

Harrison v. *King,* 4 Price, 46 ; 7 Taunt. 431 ; 1 B. & Ald. 161.

No action lies for such words as " Thou deservest to be hanged ; " for here no fact is asserted against the plaintiff.

Hake v. *Molton,* Roll. Abr. 43.

Cockaine v. *Hopkins,* 2 Lev. 214.

" If you have got money, you stole it.   I believe you will steal " are not such words as will sustain an action.

McKee v. *Ingalls,* 4 Scam. (Illinois), 30.

A defamatory charge may be insinuated in a question, *e.g.* :

" We should be glad to know how many popish priests enter the nunneries at Scorton and Darlington each week, and also how many infants are born in them every year, and what becomes of them, whether the holy fathers bring them up or not, or whether the innocents are murdered out of hand or not." Alderson, B., directed the jury that if they thought the defendant by asking the question meant to assert the facts insinuated, the passage was a libel.

> *R.* v. *Gathercole*, 2 Lew. C. C. 237, 255.

Though the sentence be in the form of a question, the words may amount to an affirmative charge.

> *Nelson* v. *Staff*, Cro. Jac. 422.
> *May* v. *Gybbons*, Cro. Jac. 568.
> But see *Barnes* v. *Holloway*, 8 T. R. 150.

So a slander may be conveyed in a question and answer, or in a series of questions and answers.

> *Gainford* v. *Tuke*, (1620) Cro. Jac. 536.
> *Haywood* v. *Nayler*, (1636) 1 Roll. Abr. 50.
> *Ward* v. *Reynolds*, (1714) cited Cowp. 278.

A libellous charge may be sufficiently conveyed by a mere adjective. (*Osborn* v. *Poole*, 1 Ld. Raym. 236.)

"Thou art a leprous knave."

> *Taylor* v. *Perkins*, Cro. Jac. 144; 1 Roll. Abr. 44.

"He is a bankrupt knave," spoken of a trader.

> *Squire* v. *Johns*, Cro. Jac. 585.
> *Loyd* v. *Pearse*, Cro. Jac. 424.

"Thou art a broken fellow."

> *Anon.*, Holt, 652.
> *Walkenden* v. *Haycock*, (1654) Style, 425.

"I will make thee an example, for a perjured knave."

> Comyns' Digest, Defamation E. 1.

"Mr. Brittridge is a perjured old knave."

> *Brittridge's Case*, 4 Rep. 19.
> *Croford* v. *Blisse*, 2 Buls. 150.

"A libellous journalist," a phrase which will be taken to mean that the plaintiff *habitually* publishes libels in his paper, not that he *once* published *one* libel merely.

> *Wakley* v. *Cooke and Healey*, 4 Exch. 511; 19 L. J. Ex. 91.

So if the defendant is obviously only repeating gossip, and not asserting the charge as a fact within his own knowledge, still an action lies.

"I heard you had run away" (*sc.* from your creditors).

> *Davis* v. *Lewis*, 7 T. R. 17.

"Thou art a sheep-stealing rogue, and Farmer Parker told me so."

> *Gardiner* v. *Atwater*, Sayer, 265.

"One told me that he heard say that Mistress Meggs had poisoned her first husband."

> *Meggs* v. *Griffith* (vel *Griffin*), Cro. Eliz. 400; Moore, 408.
> *Read's Case*, Cro. Eliz. 645.

"Did you not hear that C. is guilty of treason?"

> *Per cur.* in *Earl of Northampton's Case*, 12 Rep. 134.

So, where the defamatory words incidentally slip into a conversation on another matter, an action lies, *e.g.* :

Where the defendant said, "Mr. Wingfield, you never thought well of me since Graves did steal my lamb," it was held that Graves could sue.
Graves' Case, Cro. Eliz. 289.
Or, "I dealt not so unkindly with you when you stole a sack of my corn."
Cooper v. *Hawkeswell*, 2 Mod. 58.

2. *Certainty as to the Person defamed.*

The defamatory words must refer to some ascertained or ascertainable person, and that person must be the plaintiff.

If the words used really contain no reflection on any particular individual, no averment or innuendo can make them defamatory. " An innuendo cannot make the person certain which was incertain before." (4 Rep. 17 b.) So if the words reflect impartially on either A. or B., or on some one of a certain number or class, and there is nothing to show which one was meant, no one can sue. Where the words reflect on each and every member of a certain number or class, each or all can sue. " Every member of the class who could satisfy the jury that he was a person aimed at and defamed could recover." (Per Farwell, L.J., in *Jones* v. *Hulton & Co.*, [1909] 2 K. B. at p. 481.)

Illustrations.

" Suppose the words to be ' A murder was committed in A.'s house last night ; ' no introduction can warrant the innuendo ' meaning that B. committed the said murder ; ' nor would it be helped by the finding of the jury for the plaintiff. For the Court must see that the words do not and cannot mean it, and would arrest the judgment accordingly. *Id certum est, quod certum reddi potest.*" Per Lord Denman, C.J., in
Solomon v. *Lawson*, 8 Q. B. 837 ; 15 L. J. Q. B. 257 ; 10 Jur. 796.

" If a man wrote that all lawyers were thieves, no particular lawyer could sue him, unless there is something to point to the particular individual." Per Willes, J., in
Eastwood v. *Holmes*, 1 F. & F. at p. 349.

If a man says "My brother " or " My enemy " is perjured, and hath only one brother or one enemy, such brother or enemy can sue ; but if he says, " One of my brothers is perjured," and he hath several brothers, no one of them can sue [without special circumstances to show to which one he referred].
Jones v. *Davers*, Cro. Eliz. 496 ; 1 Roll. Abr. 74.
Wiseman v. *Wiseman*, Cro. Jac. 107.

L 2

So if a man says to the plaintiff's servant, "Thy master Brown hath robbed me," Brown can sue; for it shall not be intended that the person addressed had more than one master of the name of Brown. So if the defendant had said, "Thy master," *simpliciter;* or to a son, "Thy father;" to a wife, "Thy husband."

> Per Haughton, J., in *Lewes* v. *Walter,* (1617) 3 Bulstr. 226.
>
> *Brown* v. *Low,* or *Lane,* Cro. Jac. 443; 1 Roll. Abr. 79.
>
> *Waldegrave* v. *Agas,* Cro. Eliz. 191.

But if the defendant said to a master, "One of thy servants hath robbed me," in the absence of special circumstances no one could sue; for it is not apparent who is the person slandered.

> *James* v. *Rutlech,* 4 Rep. 17.

So where a party in a cause said to three men who had just given evidence against him, "One of you three is perjured," no action lies.

> *Sir John Bourn's Case,* cited Cro. Eliz. 497, and Hob. 268.

If the defendant says "A. or B." committed such a felony, and there is nothing in his tone or manner or in the surrounding circumstances to indicate which he deems to be the real criminal, neither A. nor B. can sue. Both, no doubt, are brought into suspicion. But no action lies for spoken words which imply merely suspicion and not guilt. There are ancient *dicta* to the contrary. In 1666, Bridgman, C.J., said, "J. S. is killed; if one saith A. or B. killed him, A. may bring an action, and so may B., and there must be an averment that neither did it." And in 1714 Parker, C.J., said the same. But in both cases the majority of the Court differed from their Chief Justice.

In the earlier case the words were, "She had a child, and either she or somebody else made it away." Two judges held that an action lay, Erle, J., relying on the charge of incontinency, Bridgman, C.J., on the suggestion of murder. But four judges held no action lay for either imputation.

> *Falkner* v. *Cooper,* (1666) Carter, 55.

In the later case the words were, "You or he hired one Bell to forswear himself." Chief Justice Parker held that for these words an action lay at the suit of either; but the rest of the Court did not share this view.

> *Harrison* v. *Thornborough,* (1714) Gilbert's Cases in Law and Equity, 114.

Words complained of: "He or somebody altered the indorsement on the note from a larger to a less sum." No action lies.

> *Ingalls* v. *Allen,* 1 Breese (Illinois), 300.

The defendant wrote and published that his hat had been stolen by *some* of the members of No. 12 Hose Company. This hose company was a volunteer fire brigade unincorporated, and the members brought a joint action. *Held,* that the action could not be maintained, and that the defendant could not be compelled to declare to which individual member he referred.

> *Girand* v. *Beach,* 3 E. D. Smith (New York City Common Pleas), 337.

But where seventeen men were indicted for conspiracy, and A. said, "These defendants are those that helped to murder Henry Farrer," each one of the defendants can bring a separate action as much as if they each had been specially named.

> *Foxcroft* v. *Lacy,* Hobart, 89; 1 Roll. Abr. 75.

To assert that an acceptance is a forgery is no libel on the drawer, unless it somehow appear that it was he who was charged with forging it.

Stockley v. *Clement*, 4 Bing. 162; 12 Moore, 376.

The defendant in a speech commented severely on the discipline of the Roman Catholic Church, and the degrading punishments imposed on penitents. He read from a paper an account given by three policemen of the severe penance imposed on a poor Irishman. It appeared incidentally from this report that the Irishman had told the policemen that his priest would not administer the Sacrament to him till the penance was performed. The plaintiff averred that he was the Irishman's priest, but it did not appear how enjoining such a penance on an Irishman would affect the character of a Roman Catholic priest. The alleged libel was in no other way connected with the plaintiff. *Held*, no libel, and no slander, of the plaintiff.

Hearne v. *Stowell*, 12 A. & E. 719; 6 Jur. 458; 4 P. & D. 696.

Where an architect employed the plaintiff, a quantity surveyor, to take out the quantities for a proposed building, and the agent of the building owner sent to one of the builders, who had tendered, a postcard containing the words: "The quantities sent you this morning by the architect are all wrong," it was held that there was no publication of a libel on the quantity surveyor except to the builder; for if any other persons read the postcard they would not know by whom the quantities were taken out.

Sadgrove v. *Hole*, [1901] 2 K. B. 1; 70 L. J. K. B. 455; 49 W. R. 473; 84 L. T. 647.

Where the defendant published a facsimile of the handwriting of a drunken man as having been produced in a condition of alcoholic insanity by a person who had since died, and the plaintiff claimed that the writing was his, the Court held that, as the defendant gave no name and there was no evidence to connect the plaintiff with the publication, the jury had rightly found a verdict for the defendant.

Fournet v. *Pearson*, (1897) 14 Times L. R. 82.

Though the words used may at first sight appear only to apply to a class or number of persons, and not to be specially defamatory of any individual, still an action may be maintained by any particular member of that class or number who can satisfy the jury that the words referred solely or especially to himself. The words must be capable of bearing such special application, or the judge should stop the case. And there must be an averment in the Statement of Claim that the words were spoken of the plaintiff. The plaintiff may also aver extraneous facts, if any, showing that he was the person expressly referred to.

"Where a class is described, it may very well be that the slander refers to a particular individual. That is a matter of which evidence is to be laid before a jury, and the jurors are to determine

whether the individual is justified in making such a complaint."
(Per Lord Campbell, C.J., in *Le Fanu and another* v. *Malcolmson*,
1 H. L. C. at p. 668.) If the plaintiffs " are so described that they
are known to all their neighbours as being the parties alluded to,
and if they are able to prove to the satisfaction of a jury that the
party writing the libel did intend to allude to them, it would be
unfortunate to find the law in a state which would prevent their
being protected against such libels." (Per Lord Cottenham, *ib.*, at
p. 664.)

In any case in which a doubt can arise as to the identity of the
person defamed, the plaintiff should insert in his Statement of Claim
an innuendo, " he (meaning the plaintiff)." Such an innuendo
does not extend the meaning of the defamatory matter; it only
points out the particular individual to whom such matter does in
fact apply. The decision of the jury on the point is practically
conclusive. After a verdict for the plaintiff, it is very difficult for
the defendant to argue that it does not sufficiently appear to whom
the words relate. And in support of his innuendo the plaintiff may
give evidence at the trial of the cause and occasion of publication,
and of all the surrounding circumstances affecting the relation
between the parties, and also of any subsequent article referring to
the former one or of any statement or declaration made by the
defendant as to the person referred to. (*Barwell* v. *Adkins*, 1 M. &
Gr. 807; 2 Scott, N. R. 11; *Knapp* v. *Fuller*, 55 Vermont, 311; 45
Amer. R. 618.) And whenever the words spoken or written,
though plain in themselves, apply equally well to more persons
than one, the plaintiff may also call at the trial his friends, or those
acquainted with the circumstances, to state that on reading the libel
they at once concluded that it was aimed at the plaintiff. (*Bourke*
v. *Warren*, 2 C. & P. 307; *Broome* v. *Gosden*, 1 C. B. 728; *Hulton
& Co.* v. *Jones*, (C. A.) [1909] 2 K. B. 444; (H. L.) [1910] A. C. 20.)
For if the application to a particular individual could be thus
perceived, the publication is a libel on him, however general its
language may be. " Whether a man is called by one name, or
whether he is called by another, or whether he is described by a
pretended description of a class to which he is known to belong, if
those who look on know well who is aimed at, the very same
injury is inflicted, the very same thing is in fact done, as would be
done if his name and Christian name were ten times repeated."
(Per Lord Campbell, C.J., in *Le Fanu and another* v. *Malcolmson*,
1 H. L. C. 668.)

Where the libel consists of an effigy, picture, or caricature, care should be taken to show by proper innuendoes and averments the libellous nature of the representation, and its especial reference to the plaintiff. It is often in such cases difficult for the plaintiff to prove that he is the person caricatured.

Illustrations.

Where plaintiff's house has been insured and burnt down, and the insurance company at first demurred to pay, but ultimately did pay, the insurance money, and defendant subsequently, in the course of a quarrel with the plaintiff, said, in the presence of others, "I never set my premises on fire," and "I was never accused of setting my premises on fire," this was held to be a slander on the plaintiff.

> *Cutler* v. *Cutler*, 10 J. P. 169.
> And see *Snell* v. *Webling*, 2 Lev. 150.
> *Clerk* v. *Dyer*, 8 Mod. 290.

Words complained of :—"We would exhort the medical officers to avoid the traps set for them by desperate adventurers (innuendo, thereby meaning the plaintiff among others), who, participating in their efforts, would inevitably cover them with ridicule and disrepute." The jury found that the words were intended to apply to the plaintiff. Judgment accordingly for the plaintiff.

> *Wakley* v. *Healey*, 7 C. B. 591 ; 18 L. J. C. P. 241.

A newspaper article imputed that "in some of the Irish factories" cruelties were practised upon the workpeople. Innuendo, "in the factory of the plaintiffs," who were manufacturers. The jury were satisfied that the newspaper was referring especially to the plaintiffs' factory, and found a verdict for the plaintiffs, and the House of Lords held the declaration good.

> *Le Fanu and another* v. *Malcolmson*, 1 H. L. C. 637 ; 13 L. T. (Old S.) 61 ; 8 Ir. L. R. 418.

A label reflected on all kinds of "Food for Children," except Vance's. The defendant (an agent for Vance) affixed this label to the bottles of the plaintiff's Food for Children, which he sold. *Held*, that he thus sufficiently pointed the general terms of the label to the plaintiff's preparation in particular.

> *White* v. *Mellin*, [1895] A. C. 154 ; 64 L. J. Ch. 308 ; 43 W. R. 353 ; 72 L. T. 334 ; 11 Times L. R. 236.

Words complained of :—"I have no doubt they (*i.e.*, certain letters) were embezzled at the post office at F." The postmaster at F. can sue, if proper averments connecting him with the loss of the letters be pleaded and proved.

> *Taylor* v. *Kneeland*, 1 Douglass (Michigan), 67.

A libel was published on "a certain newspaper of limited circulation, published in a town remote from Guildford." *Held*, that the plaintiff could call evidence to show that the libel was intended to apply, and was understood to apply, to his paper.

> *Latimer* v. *Western Morning News Co.*, 25 L. T. 44.

Plaintiff had been in defendant's employment as a gardener, and was dismissed by him and entered Mr. Pierce's service. Defendant wrote to Mr. Pierce that he had dismissed plaintiff for dishonesty, adding, "I have reason to suppose that many of the flowers of which I have been robbed are growing upon your premises." An innuendo, "thereby meaning that the plaintiff was guilty of larceny, and had stolen defendant's flowers and had disposed of them unlawfully to Mr. Pierce, &c.," was held good.

Williams v. *Gardiner*, 1 M. & W. 245; 1 Tyr. & Gr. 578; 2 C. M. & R. 78.

"There is strong reason for believing that a considerable sum of money was transferred by power of attorney obtained by undue influence;" an innuendo "meaning as a fact that the plaintiff had by undue influence procured the money to be transferred" was held not too wide; for such would be the meaning conveyed to readers by the defendant's insinuation.

Turner v. *Meryweather*, 7 C. B. 251; 18 L. J. C. P. 155; 13 Jur. 683; 19 L. J. C. P. 10.

Some libellous verses were written about "L——y, the Bum;" the Court was satisfied, in spite of the finding of the jury, that the words related to the plaintiff, a sheriff's officer.

Levi v. *Milne*, 4 Bing. 195; 12 Moore, 418.

"All the libellers of the kingdom know now that printing initial letters will not serve the turn, for that objection has been long got over." Per Lord Hardwicke in

Roach v. *Garvan, Re Read and Huggonson*, (1742) 2 Atk. 470; 2 Dick. 794.

Bourke v. *Warren*, 2 C. & P. 307; see *post*, p. 154.

"His name was O'B." (meaning thereby the plaintiff). This was held sufficient in

O'Brien v. *Clement*, 16 M. & W. 159; 16 L. J. Ex. 77.

To say "I have seen women steal yarn before" may amount to a charge of larceny against some particular woman now; provided there be proper averments in the pleadings and sufficient evidence of the surrounding circumstances at the trial.

Hart v. *Coy*, 40 Ind. 553.

To say "I believe that will to be a rank forgery" may be a slander on the solicitor who prepared it and attested the signature.

Seaman v. *Netherclift*, 1 C. P. D. 540; 45 L. J. C. P. 798; 24 W. R. 884; 34 L. T. 878.

The defendant published a libel upon the directors of a certain Bank. The prosecutors proved that they were *de facto* the directors of that Bank, and acted in that capacity in the matters referred to in the libel. *Held*, that it was unnecessary for them to go further and prove that they were *de jure* directors, and properly appointed as such.

R. v. *Boaler*, 67 L. T. 354; 56 J. P. 792; 17 Cox, C. C. 569.

A placard ran as follows:—

"Subscriptions for A. and B., who have been ruined in their business and their living taken away by the animosity of one man." This is a libel on the plaintiff, if he can satisfy the jury that the placard was understood by those who read it to refer to himself.

Hird v. *Wood*, 38 Sol. J. 234.

A. said to B., "One of us two is perjured," B. answered, "It is not I," and A. replied, "I am sure it is not I." B. can sue A. for charging him with perjury.

Coe v. *Chambers*, 1 Roll. Abr. 75; Vin. Abr. o. b. 4.

Where the defendant said to his companion B., " He that goeth before thee is perjured," the plaintiff can sue, if he aver and prove that he was the person who was at that moment walking before B.

> *Aish* v. *Gerish*, (1633) 1 Roll. Abr. 81.

A libel was published on a " diabolical character," who, " like Polyphemus, the man-eater, has but one eye, and is well-known to all persons acquainted with the name of a certain noble circumnavigator." The plaintiff had but one eye, and his name was I'Anson ; so it was clear that he was the person referred to.

> *I'Anson* v. *Stuart*, 1 T. R. 748 ; 2 Smith's L. Cas. (6th ed.), 57 [omitted in 7th and 8th eds.].
> *Fleetwood* v. *Curl*, Cro. Jac. 557 ; Hob. 268.

Defendant wrote and published of plaintiff, a bookseller: "The man at the sign of the Bible is no slouch at swearing to an old story." The sign over plaintiff's shop was a book, lettered " Bible," and he had recently given evidence against defendant in another action. *Held*, that he could recover.

> *Steele* v. *Southwick*, 9 Johns. (New York) 214.

If the defendant's words have in fact injured the plaintiff's reputation, it is no defence to an action that the defendant intended them to refer to some one else. He should have been more explicit ; his secret intention is immaterial. The plaintiff is entitled to recover if he can show that the defamatory words were understood as referring to him by persons who knew him, or if the words are such that the world would apply them to the plaintiff. Again, if a writer intends to portray a real person under an imaginary name, and chooses for that purpose what he supposes to be a fictitious name, he will nevertheless be liable if he happens to choose the name of a real person, though he had no intention whatever of doing so. If, however, the defendant's words obviously relate to a fictitious or historical character, no action will lie, even though some one may have misunderstood them as referring to the plaintiff. (*Hulton & Co.* v. *Jones*, (C. A.) [1909] 2 K. B. 444 ; (H. L.) [1910] A. C. 20.) At the same time a narrative apparently fictitious may be in fact a libel upon living persons.

"Libel is a tortious act. What does the tort consist in ? It consists in using language which others knowing the circumstances would reasonably think to be defamatory of the person complaining of and injured by it. A person charged with libel cannot defend himself by showing that he intended in his own breast not to defame, or that he intended not to defame the plaintiff, if in fact he did both. He has none the less imputed something disgraceful, and has none the less injured the plaintiff. . . . Just as the defendant could not excuse himself from malice by proving that he wrote it in the most benevolent spirit, so he cannot show that the libel was not of and concerning the plaintiff by proving that he never heard of the plaintiff. His intention in both respects equally is inferred from what he did. His remedy is to abstain from defamatory words." (Per Lord Loreburn, L.C., *ib.*, [1910] A. C. at pp. 23, 24.) "In the publication of matter which would be libellous if applying to an actual person, the responsibility is as follows: In the first place there is responsibility for the words used being taken to signify that which readers would reasonably understand by them; in the second place there is responsibility also for the names used being taken to signify those whom the readers would reasonably understand by those names; and in the third place the same principle is applicable to persons unnamed but sufficiently indicated by designation or description." (Per Lord Shaw, *ib.*, [1910] A. C. at p. 26.)

Illustrations.

If asterisks be put instead of the name of the party libelled, it is sufficient that those who know the plaintiff should be able to gather from the libel that he is the person meant. "It is not necessary that all the world should understand the libel; it is sufficient if those who know the plaintiff can make out that he is the person meant."

> *Bourke* v. *Warren*, 2 C. & P. 307.
> And see the remarks of Lord Coleridge, C.J., in *Gibson* v. *Evans*, 23 Q. B. D. at p. 386.

There appeared in *Mist's Weekly Journal* an account professedly of certain intrigues, &c., at the Persian Court, really, at the English. King George I. was described under the name of "Merewits," George II. appeared as "Esreff," the Queen as "Sultana," while a most engaging portrait was drawn of the Pretender under the name of "Sophi." It was objected on behalf of the prisoner that there was no evidence that the author intended his seemingly harmless tale to be thus interpreted and applied; but the Court held that they must give it the same meaning as the generality of readers would undoubtedly put upon it.

> *R.* v. *Clerk*, (1728) 1 Barnard. 304.

But "if the character had been purely imaginary, a creature of fancy, then, although it turns out that the plaintiff bears the name of the fictitious character, it would not be a libel at all." No person can say that a character in a novel bearing his name applies to himself. Per Lush, J., in

> *Harrison* v. *Smith and others*, 20 L. T. at p. 715.

The plaintiff was a barrister in practice, who at one time had been on the staff of the defendant's paper and had contributed to it articles signed in his own name, and was therefore known to the readers of that paper by that name. There subsequently appeared in the defendant's paper an article defamatory of a person who was called by the plaintiff's name. At the trial friends of the plaintiff gave evidence that they had read the libel and believed that it referred to the plaintiff. The writer of the article and the editor of the paper both swore that they did not know of the plaintiff's existence, and this was accepted as true by the plaintiff's counsel. The jury found a verdict for the plaintiff for £1750 damages, and a judgment was entered for him, which was affirmed both in the Court of Appeal and in the House of Lords.

> *Hulton & Co.* v. *Jones,* (C. A.) [1909] 2 K. B. 444; 78 L. J. K. B. 937; 101 L. T. 330; (H. L.) [1910] A. C. 20; 79 L. J. K. B. 198; 101 L. T. 831.

Words defamatory of A. may in some cases be also indirectly defamatory of B.

Illustrations.

Where a married man was called " cuckold " in the City of London, his wife could sue ; for it was tantamount to calling her " whore."

> *Vicars* v. *Worth,* 1 Stra. 471.

> *Hodgkins et ux.* v. *Corbet et ux.,* 1 Stra. 545.

To say that a child is a bastard may, with proper averments, amount to a charge of adultery or unchastity against its mother.

> *Maxwell and wife* v. *Allison,* 11 S. & R. (Pennsylvania Sup. Ct.) 343.

Where a new firm has taken over a business, statements made by a rival firm which would have been true enough, if clearly limited to the old firm, may be actionable, if the statements are in such terms as will lead the public to apply them to the new firm.

> *Coulson* v. *Coulson,* (1887) 3 Times L. R. 846.

So where there are two companies with very similar names, one solvent and the other insolvent, an advertisement which would have been perfectly legitimate if properly worded, will be a libel on the solvent company, if persons reading it would understand it to refer to the solvent company and to impute that it is insolvent.

> *Briton Life Association, Limited* v. *Roberts,* (1886) 2 Times L. R. 319.

Slander addressed to plaintiff's wife :—" You are a nuisance to live beside of. You are a bawd ; and your house is no better than a bawdy-house." *Held,* that the plaintiff could maintain the action without joining his wife, and without proving special damage ; because if in fact his wife did keep a bawdy-house, the plaintiff could be indicted for it.

> *Huckle* v. *Reynolds,* (1859) 7 C. B. N. S. 114.

Where the words *primâ facie* apply only to a thing, and not to a person, still if the owner of the thing can show that the words substantially reflect upon him, he may sue without giving proof of special damage and without proving malice.

Illustration.

To write and publish that plaintiff's ship is unseaworthy and has been sold to the Jews to carry convicts, is a libel upon the plaintiff in the way of his business, as well as upon his ship.

> *Ingram* v. *Lawson*, (1840) 6 Bing. N. C. 212 ; 4 Jur. 151 ; 9 C. & P. 326 ; 8 Scott, 471.
>
> *Solomon* v. *Lawson*, (1846) 8 Q. B. 823 ; 15 L. J. Q. B. 253 ; 10 Jur. 796.
>
> And see *ante,* pp. 34, 38.

CHAPTER VI.

PUBLICATION.

PUBLICATION is the communication of the defamatory words to some person or persons other than the person defamed. It is essential to the plaintiff's case that the defendant's words should be expressed; the law permits us to think as badly as we please of our neighbours, so long as we keep our uncharitable thoughts to ourselves. Merely composing a libel is not actionable unless it be published. And in a civil proceeding it is no publication if the words are only communicated to the person defamed; for that cannot injure his reputation. A man's reputation is the estimate in which others hold him; not the good opinion which he has of himself. The communication, whether it be in words, or by signs, gestures, or caricature, must be intelligible to and understood by some third person.* If the words used be in the vernacular of the place of publication, it will be presumed that such third person understood them, until the contrary be proved. And it will be presumed that he understood them in the sense which such words properly bear in their ordinary signification, unless some reason appear for assigning them a different meaning.

The publication of a slander involves only one act by the defendant; he must speak the words, so that some third person hears and understands them. But the publication of a libel is a more composite act. First, the defendant must compose and write the libel; next, he must hand

---

* In Scotland no publication to a third person is necessary. Defamatory statements, either oral or written, concerning the person to whom they are addressed, will found an action for damages at his instance although no third person has heard or read them.

Mackay v. *M'Cankie*, (1883) 10 R. 537 (Ct. of Sess. Cases, 4th Series).

what he has written, or cause it to be delivered, to some
third person ; then that third person must read and understand its contents ; or, it may be that, after composing and
writing it, the defendant reads it aloud to some third person,
who listens to the words and understands them : in this case
the same act may be both the uttering of a slander and the
publication of a libel. And even when the defendant is
not himself the author, writer, or printer of a libel, or in
any way connected with or responsible for its being composed or written or printed, still he may be liable as its
publisher. But to make him so liable, three things must
concur : first, the defendant must receive the libel and read
it for himself, or in some other way become aware that it is,
or probably may be, a libel ; next, he must deliver it to some
third person ; and then that third person must read it or hear
and understand its contents. For in this case, if the defendant can prove that he was wholly ignorant of the contents
of the document, and had no reason to suppose that it was
likely to contain libellous matter, he will escape liability,
because he has not consciously published a libel. And
again, if the person to whom he delivers it never reads it or
hears it read, the reputation of the plaintiff is in no way
injured by any act of this defendant.

Every publication of a libel is a distinct and separate
act, and a distinct and separate cause of action. For the
defendant always has it in his power to restrict the number
of persons to whom he will publish a libel—he may show it
or hand it to as many or as few as he pleases ; and each time
that he chooses to publish it he commits a fresh tort. But
the uttering of a slander is one act and one cause of action,
whether one person or one hundred persons heard the
words. The words are published at once to all who happen
to be within earshot, though the defendant may not know
how many such there be. If, therefore, the plaintiff has
recovered damages for that slander on the footing that, say,
three bystanders, A., B., and C., alone heard it, and subsequently he discover that D., E., and F. also heard the same

words, he cannot bring a second action for the publication to D., E., and F., for it is the same tort. But if a libel be published first to A. and then to B., two separate actions lie, although the two publications may be part of one transaction; and judgment in an action brought for the publication to A. would be no bar to a second action claiming damages for the publication to B. So, too, if the publication of the libel to A. were privileged, this would afford no defence in the second action, which is based on the publication to B. Whereas, in the case of slander, if it was the defendant's duty to speak when and where he did, his utterance is privileged, however many persons heard his words. (*Pittard* v. *Oliver*, [1891] 1 Q. B. 474; 60 L. J. Q. B. 219.)

The *onus* lies on the plaintiff to prove publication; he must prove a publication by the defendant; and such publication must, of course, be prior to the date of the writ.

Although husband and wife are generally to be considered one person in actions of tort as well as of contract (*Phillips* v. *Barnet*, 1 Q. B. D. 436), still the plaintiff's wife is sufficiently a third person to make a communication to her of words defamatory of her husband a publication in law. (*Wenman* v. *Ash*, 13 C. B. 836; 22 L. J. C. P. 190; 1 C. L. R. 592; 17 Jur. 579; *Jones* v. *Williams*, (1885) 1 Times L. R. 572.) And it is submitted that similarly a communication to the husband of a charge against his wife is a sufficient publication. The doubt suggested by Jervis, C.J., in *Wenman* v. *Ash* must mean that he considered a communication to the husband of a report prejudicial to his wife was *primâ facie* privileged as being a friendly act; not that it was no publication. To communicate to a wife a charge or complaint against her husband is not a friendly act, and is not privileged. (*Jones* v. *Williams*, *supra*.)

In the converse case of the defendant and his wife a different rule prevails. Communications between husband and wife are "held sacred." (Per Manisty, J., 20 Q. B. D. at p. 639.) They are clearly privileged. In cases apart from the Married Women's Property Acts, there is in law no publication where the words merely pass between husband and wife. (*Wennhak* v. *Morgan*, 20 Q. B. D. 635; 57 L. J. Q. B. 241; 36 W. R. 697; 59 L. T. 28; 52 J. P. 470; citing with approval an American case of *Trumbull* v.

Gibbons, 3 City Hall Recorder, 97.) Moreover, the fact that defendant's wife was present on a privileged occasion, and heard what her husband said, will not take away the privilege, so long as her presence, though not necessary, was not improper. (*Jones* v. *Thomas,* 34 W. R. 104; 53 L. T. 678; 50 J. P. 149; *Collins* v. *Cooper,* (1902) 19 Times L. R. 118.) And see *post,* p. 298.

Illustrations.

To shout defamatory words on a desert moor where no one can hear you, is not a publication; but if any one chances to hear you, it is a publication, although you thought no one was by.

To utter defamatory words in a foreign language is not a publication, if no one present understands their meaning; but if defamatory words be written in a foreign language, there will be a publication as soon as ever the writing comes into the hands of anyone who does understand that language, or who gets them explained or translated to him.

If defamatory words be spoken in English when the only person present besides the plaintiff is a German who does not understand English, this is no publication.

> *Hurtert* v. *Weines,* 27 Iowa, 134.

Sending a letter through the post to the plaintiff, properly addressed to him, and fastened in the usual way, is no publication, and the defendant is not answerable for anything the plaintiff may choose to do with the letter after it has once safely reached his hands.

> *Barrow* v. *Lewellin,* Hob. 62.

In an American case the plaintiff, after so receiving a libellous letter from the defendant, sent for a friend of his and also for the defendant; he then repeated the contents of the letter in their presence, and asked the defendant if he wrote that letter; the defendant, in the presence of the plaintiff's friend, admitted that he had written it. *Held,* no publication *by the defendant* to the plaintiff's friend.

> *Fonville* v. *Nease,* Dudley, S. C. 303 (American).

It is otherwise if a message be sent to the plaintiff by telegraph; the contents of the telegram are necessarily communicated to all the clerks through whose hands it passes.

> *Whitfield and others* v. *S. E. Ry. Co.,* E. B. & E. 115; 27 L. J. Q. B. 229; 4 Jur. N. S. 688.
>
> *Williamson* v. *Freer,* L. R. 9 C. P. 393; 43 L. J. C. P. 161; 22 W. R. 878; 30 L. T. 332.
>
> *Smith* v. *Crocker,* (1889) 5 Times L. R. 441.
>
> *Robinson* v. *Robinson,* (1897) 13 Times L. R. 564.

But even in this case the publication is not necessarily actionable.

> *Edmondson* v. *Birch & Co., Ltd.,* [1907] 1 K. B. at p. 381.

If the defendant writes libellous words on a postcard and posts it, publication to a third person will be presumed. It will be for the defendant to show that in fact no one but the plaintiff read it.

> *Robinson* v. *Jones,* 4 L. R. Ir. 391.
>
> *Chattell* v. *Turner,* (1896) 12 Times L. R. 360.
>
> *Beamish* v. *Dairy Supply Co., Limited,* (1897) 13 Times L. R. 484.
>
> *Sadgrove* v. *Hole,* [1901] 2 K. B. 1; 70 L. J. K. B. 455; 49 W. R. 473; 84 L. T. 647

Merely to be in possession of a copy of a libel is no crime, unless some publication thereof ensue.

> *R.* v. *Beere,* Carth. 409 ; 12 Mod. 219 ; Holt, 422 ; 2 Salk. 417, 646 ; 1 Ld. Raym. 414.
>
> And see 11 Hargrave's St. Tr. 322, sub. *Entick* v. *Carrington,* and *John Lamb's Case,* 9 Rep. 60, *post,* p. 165.

But the delivery of a manuscript to a printer to be printed is a sufficient publication if any copies be printed ; even though the author repent and suppress all the copies printed. For the compositor must read it or hear it read.

> *Baldwin* v. *Elphinston,* 2 W. Bl. 1037.

[This may be considered a somewhat harsh decision, as the compositor does not attend to the substance of the manuscript, but sets it up in type mechanically ; it has, however, been acted on in America.

> *Trumbull* v. *Gibbons,* 3 City Hall Recorder, 97.
>
> And see *Watts* v. *Fraser and another,* 7 A. & E. 223 ; 6 L. J. K. B. 226 ; 7 C. & P. 369 ; 1 M. & Rob. 449 ; 2 N. & P. 157 ; 1 Jur. 671 ; W. W. & D. 451.]

Sending a libellous letter or speaking defamatory words to the plaintiff's agent or solicitor is a sufficient publication to a third person.

> *Tuson* v. *Evans,* 12 A. & E. 733.
>
> *Huntley* v. *Ward,* 1 F. & F. 552 ; 6 C. B. N. S. 514 ; 6 Jur. N. S. 18.
>
> *Hancock* v. *Case,* 2 F. & F. 711.
>
> *Stevens* v. *Kitchener,* (1887) 4 Times L. R. 159.

Where the defendant wrote a letter to the plaintiff himself, but read it to a friend before posting it, this was held a publication to the friend.

> *Snyder* v. *Andrews,* 6 Barbour (New York), 43.
>
> *McCombs* v. *Tuttle,* 5 Blackford (Indiana), 431.

So where the defendant, before posting the letter to the plaintiff, had it copied. *Held,* a publication by the defendant to his own clerk who copied it.

> *Keene* v. *Ruff,* 1 Clarke (Iowa), 482.

The managing director of the defendant company dictated a letter, containing words defamatory of the plaintiffs, to a shorthand clerk, who transcribed it by a type-writing machine. This type-written letter was then signed by the managing director, and having been press-copied by the office boy, was sent direct to the plaintiff's office. This was held by the Court of Appeal to be a publication both to the type-writer and the office boy.

> *Pullman and another* v. *Hill & Co.,* [1891] 1 Q. B. 524 ; 60 L. J. Q. B. 299 ; 39 W. R. 263 ; 64 L. T. 691.

It is doubtful whether the facts as proved at the trial in *Pullman and another* v. *Hill & Co.* support the decision of the Court of Appeal on the issue of publication. Dictating to a shorthand clerk words which that shorthand clerk takes down in writing is not publishing a libel to the shorthand clerk. No libel is yet in existence. Such dictation may be an actionable slander—indeed, in *Pullman and another* v. *Hill & Co.* it was so, but the fact that spoken words are intended to be written down after they are uttered does not make their utterance the publication of a libel. Then,

O.L.S. M

again, after the spoken words were taken down in shorthand, and copied out in type-writing, the manager signed the type-written document and handed it to the office boy to be press copied. Is this a publication? Apparently the attention of the Court was not called to the fact that press-copying is a purely mechanical process. The office boy would not read a word of the letter. Surely there was no publication by the manager to the office boy, unless the latter made himself acquainted with the contents of the document which was handed to him.

The plaintiff must prove a publication by the defendant *in fact.* A libel is deemed to be published as soon as the manuscript has passed out of defendant's possession (per Holroyd, J., in *R.* v. *Burdett,* 4 B. & Ald. 143), unless it comes directly and unread into the possession and control of the plaintiff. That some third person had the opportunity of reading it in the interval is not sufficient, if the jury are satisfied that he did not in fact avail himself of it; even though it is clear that the defendant desired and intended publication to such third person.

Illustrations.

A letter is published as soon as posted, and in the place where it is posted, if it is ever opened anywhere by any person other than the person to whom it is addressed.

> *Ward* v. *Smith,* 6 Bing. 749; 4 M. & P. 595; 4 C. & P. 302.
> *Clegg* v. *Laffer,* 3 Moore & Scott, 727; 10 Bing. 250.
> *Warren* v. *Warren,* 4 Tyr. 850; 1 C. M. & R. 250.
> *Shipley* v. *Todhunter,* 7 C. & P. 680.

The defendant wrote a letter and gave it to B. to deliver to the plaintiff. It was folded, but not sealed. B. did not read it; but conveyed it direct to the plaintiff. *Held,* no publication.

> *Clutterbuck* v. *Chaffers,* 1 Stark. 471.
> *Day* v. *Bream,* 2 Moo. & Rob. 54.

The defendant threw a sealed letter addressed to the plaintiff, "or C.," into M.'s enclosure. M. picked it up and delivered it unopened to the plaintiff himself, who alone was libelled. No publication.

> *Fonville* v. *Nease,* Dudley, S. C. 303 (American).

The defendant resolved to murder A. and then shoot himself: he wrote a libellous paper stating his reasons for committing the crime, which he hoped would be found on his dead body and published to all the world. He shot at A. and wounded him; but was arrested before he could shoot himself. He was taken to the police-station and searched, and the paper found on him by a sergeant of police, who subsequently read it aloud at the trial, to prove that the crime was committed deliberately. It was copied into many newspapers. Mathew, J., expressed the opinion that there was no publication by the defendant; the sergeant was not his agent.

> *Jacobs* v. *Lindus*, June 27th, 1894 (*unreported*).

Posting up a libellous placard and taking it down again before anyone could read it, is no publication; but if it was exhibited long enough for anyone to read it, then defendant must satisfy the jury that no one actually did read it.

> 2 Starkie on Libel, p. 16, note *n*.

So it is no defence that the third person was not intended to overhear the slander or to read the libel, if in fact he has done so. An accidental or inadvertent communication is a sufficient publication, if it be occasioned by any act or default of the speaker or writer. It is otherwise if it be occasioned by the wrongful act of some third person.

Illustrations.

I slander the plaintiff, believing I am alone in the room with him. But I speak so loudly that his clerk in the outer office hears what I say. This is a publication by me to the plaintiff's clerk. It is my fault that I spoke so loud.

I write libellous words on a postcard and address it to the plaintiff. They are read by the postman and by the plaintiff's servant. This is a publication by me to them. I should not have used a postcard.

I write a libel and fasten it up in an envelope; I direct it to the plaintiff, and send it to him by hand. My messenger wrongfully breaks the envelope open and reads the libel. This is no publication by me.

I write a libel and leave it about on the top of the desk in my study, so that it will catch the eye of any chance visitor. A visitor is shown into the room in my absence; he sees the libel there and reads it. This, it is submitted, is a publication of the libel by me to that visitor. I am to blame for leaving it about.

"If the writer of a letter locks it up in his own desk, and a thief comes and breaks open the desk and takes away the letter and makes its contents known, I should say that would not be a publication." Per Lord Esher, M.R., in

> *Pullman and another* v. *Hill & Co.*, [1891] 1 Q. B. at p. 527.
>
> And see *Weir* v. *Hoss*, 6 Alabama, 881.

The printers of a newspaper made a mistake in setting up the type; they placed the name of the plaintiff's firm last among the "Bankruptcies" instead of first among the "Dissolutions of Partnership;" and the proprietors had to pay 50*l*. damages.

> *Shepheard* v. *Whitaker*, L. R. 10 C. P. 502; 32 L. T. 402.
>
> *Stubbs* v. *Marsh*, 15 L. T. 312.

Where the defendant knew that the plaintiff's letters were always opened by his clerk in the morning, and yet sent a libellous letter addressed to the plaintiff, which was opened and read by the plaintiff's clerk lawfully and in the usual course of business, *held*, a publication by the defendant to the plaintiff's clerk.

> *Delacroix* v. *Thevenot*, 2 Stark, 63,

So where the jury found that the defendant knew the letter would probably be so opened.

> *Gomersall* v. *Davies*, (1898) 14 Times L. R. 430.

The defendant sent a libellous letter to the plaintiff, who was a solicitor, and addressed it to him at his office as that was the only address of the plaintiff known to him. The letter was delivered at the plaintiff's office in his absence, and opened in the ordinary course of business and read by the plaintiff's partner. The jury found that it was usual for letters addressed to the plaintiff at his office to be opened in his absence by his partner, but that the defendant did not know that this was possible. *Held*, no publication.

> *Sharp* v. *Skues*, (1909) 25 Times L. R. 336 (C. A.).
> *Keogh* v. *Incorporated Dental Hospital* (No. 2), [1910] 2 Ir. R. 577.

There were five partners in the firm of Pullman & Co.; two of them owned some land as their private property. The defendant had a dispute with these two about a hoarding on the land. The firm had nothing to do with the land, and no concern with the dispute. The defendant addressed a letter to "Messrs. Pullman & Co.," at their business address; and it was opened there in the ordinary course of business by a clerk who had authority to open letters addressed to the firm. The defendant believed the two Messrs. Pullman, whom he knew, to be sole partners in the firm. He did not, therefore, address the letter to them personally, or mark it "Private." *Held*, a publication by the defendant to the clerk of the firm.

> *Pullman and another* v. *Hill & Co.*, [1891] 1 Q. B. 524; 60 L. J. Q. B.
>   299; 39 W. R. 263; 64 L. T. 691.
> *Boxsius* v. *Goblet Frères and others*, [1894] 1 Q. B. 842; 63 L. J. Q. B.
>   401; 42 W. R. 392; 70 L. T. 368; 58 J. P. 670.
> But see *Edmondson* v. *Birch & Co., Ltd.*, [1907] 1 K. B. 371; 76
>   L. J. K. B. 346; 96 L. T. 415; 23 Times L. R. 234.

The defendant by mistake directed and posted a libellous letter to the plaintiff's employer instead of to the plaintiff himself. The employer opened and read it. *Held*, a publication.

> *Fox* v. *Broderick*, 14 Ir. C. L. Rep. 453.

The defendant by mistake placed a letter he had written to A. in an envelope addressed to B., who received and read it. *Held*, a publication by the defendant to B.

> *Tompson* v. *Dashwood*, 11 Q. B. D. 43; 52 L. J. Q. B. 425; 48 L. T.
>   943; 48 J. P. 55.

Rev. Samuel Paine sent his servant to his study for a certain paper which he wished to show to Brereton; the servant by mistake brought a libellous epitaph on Queen Mary, which Paine inadvertently handed to Brereton, supposing it to be the paper for which he sent; and Brereton read it aloud to Dr. Hoyle. This would probably be deemed a publication by Paine to Brereton in a civil case (Note to *Mayne* v. *Fletcher*, 4 Man. & Ry. 312); but would not be sufficient in a criminal case.

> *R.* v. *Paine*, (1695) 5 Mod. 167; Carth. 405; Comb. 358.

But "where the *fact* of publication is ambiguous (as where it may be a doubt whether the party pulled the paper out of his pocket by accident or on purpose, or whether he gave one paper instead of another, or any such supposable case), there the maxim holds that '*actus non facit reum, nisi mens sit rea.*'" Per Ashurst, J., in

> *R.* v. *Shipley*, (1784) 4 Douglas, at p. 177.

For in a criminal case it is essential that there should be a guilty intention.

R. v. *Lord Abingdon*, 1 Esp. 228.

See also *Brett* v. *Watson*, 20 W. R. 723.

Blake v. *Stevens*, 4 F. & F. 232; 11 L. T. 543.

R. v. *Munslow*, [1895] 1 Q. B. 758; 64 L. J. M. C. 138; 43 W. R. 495; 72 L. T. 301; 15 R. 192.

Next take the case where the defendant is neither the author nor the writer of the libel. Although merely composing a libel without publishing it is not actionable, merely publishing it, not having composed it, is actionable, whenever the publisher knows or ought to know that it is a libel. "The mere delivery of a libel to a third person by one conscious of its contents amounts to a publication, and is an indictable offence." (Per Wood, B., in *Maloney* v. *Bartley*, 3 Camp. 213.) "If one reads a libel, that is no publication of it; or if he hears it read, it is no publication of it; for before he reads or hears it, he cannot know it to be a libel; or if he hears or reads it, and laughs at it, it is no publication of it; or if he writes a copy of it, and does not publish it to others, it is no publication of the libel; but if after he has read or heard it, he repeats it, or any part of it, in the hearing of others, or after that he knows it to be a libel, he reads it to others, that is an unlawful publication of it." (Per Lord Coke in *John Lamb's Case*, 9 Rep. 60.)

Illustrations.

The plaintiff and defendant were both members of a Druid's Lodge, and were both present at a meeting, when an anonymous letter came by post addressed to the defendant. It was brought to the defendant in the meeting; he read it to himself. He then asked leave of the chairman to read it aloud. This being granted, he read it aloud to the meeting. It did not refer to the plaintiff by name. But after reading it aloud, the defendant said he thought it must refer to the plaintiff, and handed it to him. The defendant had not written the letter or procured it to be written. Still, it was held that he had published it.

Forrester v. *Tyrrell*, (1893) 9 Times L. R. 257; 57 J. P. 532.

A man may thus be guilty both of libel and slander at the same moment and by the same act, as by reading aloud a defamatory paper written by another. (See Precedent No. 4, App. A.).

Hearne v. *Stowell*, 12 A. & E. 719; 6 Jur. 458; 4 P. & D. 696.

A libellous placard having been erected by the roadside, the defendant sat by it, saying nothing, but constantly pointing to the placard so as to attract to it the attention of the passers-by. *Held*, that there was evidence of publication by the defendant which ought to have been left to the jury.

> *Hird* v. *Wood*, 38 Sol. J. 234.
>
> *Spall* v. *Massey and others*, 2 Stark. 559.

"Printing a libel may be an innocent act; but, unless qualified by circumstances, shall, *primâ facie*, be understood to be a publication. It must be delivered to the compositor, and the other subordinate workmen." *Per cur.* in

> *Baldwin* v. *Elphinston*, 2 Wm. Bl. 1038.

But where a man, who has just received a newspaper, lends it to a friend without having read it, and without knowing that it contains a libel, this is no publication.

> *McLeod* v. *St. Aubyn*, [1899] A. C. 549 ; 68 L. J. P. C. 137 ; 48 W. R. 173 ; 81 L. T. 158.

But the writer or publisher of a libellous book has no cause of action against a man who shows the book to the persons libelled therein, who in consequence bring actions of libel, unless there is an express contract that the book shall not be so used.

> *Saunders* v. *Seyd and Kelly, &c. Co.*, (1896) 75 L. T. 193 ; 12 Times L. R. 546.

So, again, every sale or delivery of a written or printed copy of a libel is a fresh publication. It makes no difference in law (though it may affect the amount of damages) whether such copy is sold to the public or merely shown confidentially to a friend. Either act is equally a publication. Every person who sells or gives away a written or printed copy of a libel is liable in damages, unless he can satisfy the jury that he was ignorant of its contents, and had no reason to suspect they were libellous. The *onus* of proving this lies on the defendant; and where he has made a large profit by selling a great many copies of a libel, it will be very difficult to persuade the jury that he was not aware of its libellous nature. (*Chubb* v. *Flannagan*, 6 C. & P. 431.) But if the paper was sold in the ordinary way of business by a news-vendor who neither wrote nor printed the libel, and who neither knew nor ought to have known that the paper he was so selling did contain or was likely to contain any libellous matter, he will not be deemed to have published the libel which he thus innocently disseminated. (*Emmens* v. *Pottle*, 16 Q. B. D. 354 ; 55 L. J. Q. B. 51.) The *onus* of establishing this defence lies upon the defendant. (*Vizetelly* v. *Mudie's Select Library, Limited*, [1900] 2 Q. B. 170.) Such defence is not open to the author, printer, or the original publisher of the libel. (*Morrison* v. *Ritchie & Co.*, (1902) 4 F. 645 (Ct. of Sess.).)

Illustrations.

The plaintiff's agent, with a view to the action, called at the office of the defendant's newspaper, and made them find for him a copy of the paper that had appeared seventeen years previously, and bought it. *Held*, that this was a fresh publication by the defendant, and that the action lay in spite of the Statute of Limitations.

> *Duke of Brunswick* v. *Harmer*, 14 Q. B. 185; 19 L. J. Q. B. 20; 14 Jur. 110; 3 C. & K. 10.

A porter who, in the course of business, delivers parcels containing libellous handbills, is not liable in an action for libel, if shown to be ignorant of the contents of the parcel, for he is but doing his duty in the ordinary way.

> *Day* v. *Bream*, 2 M. & Rob. 54.

A servant carries for his master a letter addressed to C., containing a libel on D. It is his duty not to read it. If he does read it, and then delivers it to C., this is a publication by the servant to C., and D. can sue either the master, or ✓ the servant or both. If the servant never reads it, but simply delivers it as he was bidden, then he is not liable to any action, unless he either knew or ought to have known that he was being employed illegally. If he either knew or ought to have known that, then it is no defence for him to plead, " I was only obeying orders."

The defendant kept a pamphlet shop; she was sick and upstairs in bed; a libel was brought into the shop without her knowledge, and subsequently sold by her servant on her account. She was held criminally liable for the act of her servant on the ground that " the law presumes that the master is acquainted with what his servant does in the course of his business."

> *R.* v. *Dodd*, 2 Sess. Cas. 33.
> *Nutt's Case*, Fitzg. 47; 1 Barnard. 306.

But later judges would not be so strict; the sickness upstairs, if properly proved by the defendant, would now be held an excuse, at all events in a criminal case.

> *R.* v. *Almon*, 5 Burr. 2686.
> *R.* v. *Gutch, Fisher and Alexander*, Moo. & Mal. 433.
> And see 6 & 7 Vict. c. 96, s. 7, *post*, p. 587.

A rule was granted calling on Wiatt to show cause why he should not be attached for selling a book containing a libel on the Court of King's Bench. The book was in Latin. On filing an affidavit that he did not understand Latin, and on disclosing the name of the author and the name of the printer from whom he obtained it, the rule was discharged.

> *R.* v. *Wiatt*, (1722) 8 Mod. 123.

The defendants were newsvendors, on a large scale at the Royal Exchange. In the ordinary course of their business they sold several copies of a newspaper called " Money," which contained a libel on the plaintiff. The jury found that the defendants did not, nor did either of them, know that the newspapers at the time they sold them contained libels on the plaintiff; that it was not by negligence on the defendants' part that they did not know there was any libel in the newspapers ; and that the defendants did not know that the newspaper was of such a character that it was likely to contain libellous matter, nor ought they to have known so. *Held*, that defendants had not published the libel, but had only innocently disseminated it.

> *Emmens* v. *Pottle and Son*, 16 Q. B. D. 354 ; 55 L. J. Q. B. 51 ;
> 34 W. R. 116 ; 53 L. T. 808 ; 50 J. P. 228.
> *Ridgway* v. *W. H. Smith and Son*, (1890) 6 Times L. R. 275.
> *Mallon* v. *W. H. Smith and Son*, (1893) 9 Times L. R. 621.

But where the libellous book had been called in by the publisher, and notices calling it in had been received by the defendant, though not read by him, the Court of Appeal held that the jury had rightly found that the defendant was guilty of negligence, and therefore the defence failed.

> *Vizetelly* v. *Mudie's Select Library, Limited*, [1900] 2 Q. B. 170 ;
> 69 L. J. Q. B. 645 ; 16 Times L. R. 352.

The defendants were the Trustees and the Librarian of the British Museum. They purchased two pamphlets relating to the litigation between the Rev. Henry Ward Beecher and Mr. Tilton, which they catalogued for reference. In the course of years some four or five readers consulted these pamphlets, which were now proved to contain libels on the female plaintiff. None of the defendants or their servants knew that these pamphlets contained libels on the plaintiff or libels at all. The findings of the jury were construed to mean that there was no negligence on the part of the defendants. *Held*, no publication.

> *Martin and wife* v. *Trustees of the British Museum and Thompson*,
> (1894) 10 Times L. R. 338.

Every one who requests or procures another to write, print, or publish a libel, is answerable as though he wrote, printed, or published it himself. And such request need not be express. Thus, it may be inferred from the defendant's conduct in sending his manuscript to the editor of a magazine, or making a statement to the reporter of a newspaper, with the knowledge that they will be sure to publish it, and without any effort to restrain their so doing. And it is not necessary that the defendant's communication be inserted *verbatim*, so long as the sense and substance of it appear in print.

This rule is of great value in cases where the words employed are not actionable when spoken; but are so if written. Here, though the proprietor of the newspaper is of course liable for printing them, still it is more satisfactory, if possible, to make the author of the scandal defendant. An action of slander will not lie; but if he spoke the words under such circumstances as would ensure their being printed, or if in any other way he requested or contrived their publication in the paper, he is liable in an action of libel as the actual publisher. *Qui facit per alium facit per se.*

Illustrations.

Hudson brought the manuscript of a libellous song to Morgan to have 1,000 copies printed; Morgan printed 1,000 and sent 300 to Hudson's shop. Hudson gave several copies to a witness, who sang it about the streets. It did not appear in whose handwriting the manuscript was, but probably it was not in Hudson's. *Held*, that both Hudson and Morgan had published the libel.

> *Johnson* v. *Hudson and Morgan*, 7 A. & E. 233, n.; 1 H. & W. 680.

If a manuscript in the handwriting of the defendant be sent to the printer or publisher of a magazine, who prints and publishes it, the defendant will be liable for the full damages caused by such publication, although there is no proof offered that he expressly directed the printing and publishing of such manuscript.

> *Bond* v. *Douglas*, 7 C. & P. 626.
>
> *R.* v. *Lovett*, 9 C. & P. 462.
>
> *Burdett* v. *Abbot*, 5 Dow, H. L. 201; 14 East, 1.

And this is so, although the editor has cut the article up, omitting the most libellous passages and only publishing the remainder.

> *Tarpley* v. *Blabey*, 2 Bing. N. C. 437; 2 Scott, 642; 1 Hodges, 414;
> 7 C. & P. 395.
>
> *Pierce* v. *Ellis*, 6 Ir. C. L. R. 55.
>
> *Strader* v. *Stryder*, 67 Ill. 404.

If I compose a libel and leave it inside my desk among my papers, and my clerk surreptitiously takes a copy and sends it to the newspapers, he is liable, but I am not, for the damage caused thereby. For although he could not have taken a copy had I not first written the libel, still its subsequent publication in print is caused entirely by my clerk's own independent and wrongful act, for the consequences of which he alone is liable. *Secus*, if I in any way encouraged or contrived his taking a copy, knowing that he would be sure to publish it in the newspapers.

A newspaper reporter told defendant he should send defendant's statements to the paper for publication. Defendant replied, "Let them go." *Held*, that defendant had published them in the paper.

> *Clay* v. *People*, 86 Ill. 147.

So where Cooper told the editor several good stories against the Rev. J. K., and asked him to "show Mr. K. up;" and subsequently the editor published the substance of them in the newspaper, and Cooper read it and expressed his approval; this was held a publication by Cooper, although the editor knew of the facts from other quarters as well.

> *R.* v. *Cooper*, 15 L. J. Q. B. 206; 8 Q. B. 533.
>
> And see *Adams* v. *Kelly*, Ry. & Moo. 157; and the judgments of
> Byles and Mellor, JJ., in the next case, L. R. 4 Ex. 181—186.

At the meeting of a board of guardians, at which reporters were present, it was stated that the plaintiff had turned his daughter out of doors, and that she consequently had been admitted into the workhouse and had become chargeable to the parish. Ellis, one of the guardians, said, "I hope the local press will take notice of this very scandalous case," and requested the chairman, Prescott, to give an outline of it. This Prescott did, remarking, "I am glad gentlemen of the press are in the room, and I hope they will give publicity to the matter." Ellis added, "And so do I." From the notes taken in the room the reporters prepared a condensed account, which appeared in the local newspapers, and which, though partly in the reporter's own language, was substantially a correct report of what took place at the meeting. *Held*, by the majority of the Court of Exchequer Chamber (Montague Smith, Keating, and Hannen, JJ., Byles and Mellor, JJ., dissenting), that Martin, B., was wrong in directing the jury that there was no evidence to go to the jury that Prescott and Ellis had directed the publication of the account which appeared in the papers. [N.B.—Of the six judges concerned, three were of one opinion, three of the other.]

> *Parkes* v. *Prescott and Ellis*, L. R. 4 Ex. 169; 38 L. J. Ex. 105; 17 W. R. 773; 20 L. T. 537.

The defendants were the trustees of a trade union, called the General Railway Workers' Union. They entered into a written agreement with the proprietors and publishers of a newspaper called *The Railway Workmen's Times*. The agreement provided that the proprietors of the paper should print and publish for the Union every week a special edition of *The Workmen's Times* under the style and title of "*The Railway Workmen's Times*, the organ of the General Railway Workers' Union;" and that the secretary of the Union should furnish to the proprietors of *The Workmen's Times* matter to fill up one page of the said special edition each week. The editor was to have full and free liberty to reject wholly or partially any matter supplied by the secretary, or to vary it as he might think best, and with a view to fulfilling the provisions of the Newspaper Libel Act. This agreement, though the defendants were therein described in their representative capacity of trustees for the Union, was signed by them personally without any limitation. *Held*, that the defendants were personally liable for the publication of a libel supplied by the secretary of the Union and published in the special weekly edition of *The Workmen's Times*.

> *Rapkins* v. *Hall and others*, (1894) 10 Times L. R. 466.

It is on this principle that the proprietor of a newspaper is always liable for whatever appears in its columns : for he has given general orders to his men to print whatever the editor passes and sends into the printing department. The editor is on the same principle responsible for all matter which he sends to press. It is of no avail for either proprietor or editor to plead that he never read the libellous words ; for they have both in fact ordered the compositors to set them up in type, and their other employés to print and circulate them. So a master-printer is liable for all that his men print.

Illustrations.

The proprietor of a newspaper is always liable for whatever appears in its columns; although the publication may have been made without his knowledge and in his absence.

    R. v. *Walter,* 3 Esp. 21.

    Storey v. *Wallace,* 11 Ill. 51.

    Scripps v. *Reilly,* 38 Mich. 10.

    Morrison v. *Ritchie & Co.,* (1902) 4 F. 645 (Ct. of Sess.).

"Surely a person who derives profit from, and who furnishes means for, carrying on the concern, and intrusts the conduct of the publication to one whom he selects, and in whom he confides, may be said to cause to be published what actually appears, and ought to be answerable, although you cannot show that he was individually concerned in the particular publication." Per Lord Tenterden, C.J., in

    R. v. *Gutch and others,* Moo. & Mal. 433.

But now in criminal cases, see 6 & 7 Vict. c. 96, s. 7, *post,* p. 587.

    R. v. *Holbrook and others,* 3 Q. B. D. 60; 4 Q. B. D. 42; 47 L. J.
        Q. B. 35; 48 L. J. Q. B. 113; 26 W. R. 144; 27 W. R. 313; 37
        L. T. 530; 39 L. T. 536.

The printer is also liable, even though he has no knowledge of the contents.

    R. v. *Dover,* 6 How. St. Tr. 547; and see 2 Atkyns, at p. 472.

So, in England, the acting editor is always held liable.

    Watts v. *Fraser and another,* 7 C. & P. 369; 7 A. & E. 223; 1 M. &
        Rob. 449; 2 N. & P. 157; 1 Jur. 671; W. W. & D. 451.

In America, however, though the proprietor and printer of a paper are always held liable, the editor is, it would seem, allowed to plead as a defence that the libel was inserted without his orders and against his will.

    The Commonwealth v. *Kneeland,* Thacher's C. C. 346.

Or without any knowledge on his part that the article was a libel on any particular individual.

    Smith v. *Ashley,* (1846) 52 Mass. (11 Met.) 367.

The proprietor of a newspaper is liable even for an advertisement inserted and paid for in the ordinary course of business; although the plaintiff is bringing another action against the advertiser at the same time.

    Harrison v. *Pearce,* 1 F. & F. 567; 32 L. T. (Old S.) 298.

"If you look upon the editor as a person who has published a libellous advertisement incautiously, of course, he is liable." Per Pollock, C.B., in

    Keyzor and another v. *Newcomb,* 1 F. & F. 559.

Every one who writes, prints, or publishes a libel, or is in any way responsible for its being written, printed, or published, may be sued by the person defamed. And to such an action it is no defence that another wrote it, or that it was printed or published by the desire or procurement of another, whether that other be made a defendant to the action or not. All concerned in publishing the libel or in procuring it to be published are equally responsible for all damages which flow from the joint publication, whether the author be sued or not. If the libel appear in a newspaper, the proprietor, the editor, the printer, and the publisher are all liable to be sued, either separately or together; and each defendant is liable for all the ensuing damage, for there is no contribution between tort-feasors. So that the proprietor of a paper sued jointly with his careless editor or with the actual composer of the libel cannot compel either of his co-defendants to recoup him the damages, which he has been compelled to pay the plaintiff. (*Colburn* v. *Patmore*, 1 C. M. & R. 73; 4 Tyr. 677.) But if there be two distinct and separate publications of the same libel, a defendant who was concerned in the first publication, but wholly unconnected with the second, would not be liable for any damages which he could prove to have been the consequence of the second publication and in no way due to the first.

Illustrations.

"If a man receives a letter with authority from the author to publish it, the person receiving it will not be justified, if it contains libellous matter, in inserting it in the newspapers. No authority from a third person will defend a man against an action brought by a person who has suffered from an unlawful act." Per Best, C.J., in

De Crespigny v. *Wellesley*, 5 Bing. at p. 402.

If a country newspaper reproduces a libellous article from a London newspaper, the country paper makes the article its own, and is liable for all damages resulting from its publication in the country. The fact that it had previously appeared in the London paper is no defence; and, strictly, it should not even tend to mitigate the damages, though it probably will have that effect.

Talbutt v. *Clark*, 2 M. & Rob. 312.

Saunders v. *Mills*, 3 M. & P. 520; 6 Bing. 213.

Evidence that the plaintiff had in a previous action recovered damages against the London paper for the same article was formerly held inadmissible; as in that action damages were given only for the publication of the libel in London.

Creevy v. *Carr*, 7 C. & P. 64.

And see *Hunt* v. *Algar and others*, 6 C. & P. 245.

But now such evidence has been made admissible in an action against a newspaper by the Law of Libel Amendment Act, 1888 (51 & 52 Vict. c. 64, s. 6).

Every repetition of a slander is a wilful publication of it, rendering the speaker liable to an action. "Tale-

bearers are as bad as tale-makers." *   It is no defence that
the speaker did not originate the scandal, but heard it from
another, even though it was a current rumour and he *bonâ
fide* believed it to be true. (*Watkin* v. *Hall*, L. R. 3 Q. B.
396 ; 37 L. J. Q. B. 125 ; 16 W. R. 857 ; 18 L. T. 561.)
It is no defence that the speaker at the time named the
person from whom he heard the scandal. (*M'Pherson* v.
Daniels, 10 B. & C. at p. 270 ; 5 M. & R. 251.)

This proposition, it is submitted, correctly states the existing law
on the point; but it would certainly not have been accepted as clear
law in the 18th century.   Great difficulty was presented by the
fourth resolution in *Lord Northampton's Case* (in the Star Chamber,
1613), 12 Rep. 134, which runs as follows :—"In a private action
for slander of a common person, if J. S. publish that he hath heard
J. N. say that J. G. was a traitor or thief ; in an action of the case,
if the truth be such he may justify.   But if J. S. publish that he
hath heard generally without a certain author, that J. G. was a
traitor or thief, there an action *sur le case* lieth against J. S. for
this, that he hath not given to the party grieved any cause of action
against any but against himself who published the words, although
that in truth he might hear them ; for otherwise this might tend
to a great slander of an innocent ; for if one who hath *læsam
phantasiam*, or who is a drunkard, or of no estimation, speak
scandalous words, if it should be lawful for a man of credit to
report them generally that he had heard scandalous words, without
mentioning of his author, that would give greater colour and
probability that the words were true in respect of the credit of the
reporter, than if the author himself should be mentioned."
Now, in the first place, the reason here assigned for the distinction
applies only to cases in which the originator of the scandal is of less
credit than the retailer of it, and is known to be so by those to whom
it is retailed.   If those who hear the tale repeated know nothing of
the person cited as the authority for it, it is to them precisely as if
the name were omitted altogether, and it had been told as an *on dit*.

---

* MRS. CAN.   "But surely you would not be quite so severe on those who
only repeat what they hear?"
   SIR PET.   "Yes, Madam, I would have law merchant for them too ; and in
all cases of slander currency whenever the drawer of the lie was not to be found,
the injured parties should have a right to come on any of the indorsers."—*The
School for Scandal*.

If, on the other hand, the person named as the author of the assertion is of greater credit and respectability than the reporter, vouching his authority clearly does the plaintiff's reputation a greater injury than if no name had been given at all. And even in the case where the author of the story is well known to be a person of no credit, how does that excuse the defendant's act in repeating and circulating it? It appears to us to make it all the worse; he cannot even plead :—"I had it on good authority, and reasonably believed it true." By the mere repetition of it the defendant endorses and gives credit to the tale, although he states that he heard it from A. B.; and those who hear it from him will repeat it everywhere, and cite as their authority, not A. B., but the defendant, whom we presume to be of greater respectability and credit.

Again, on general principles, how can a slander by A. be any justification for a subsequent slander by B.? "Because one man does an unlawful act to any person, another is not to be permitted to do a similar act to the same person. Wrong is not to be justified, or even excused, by wrong." (Per Best, C.J., in *De Crespigny* v. *Wellesley*, 5 Bing. 404.)

Moreover, the twelfth volume of Reports is a book of questionable authority; it was issued after Lord Coke's death, compiled by some-one else from papers which Lord Coke had neither digested nor intended for the press. (See the remarks of Mr. Hargrave, 11 St. Tr. 301; of Holroyd, J., in *Lewis* v. *Walter*, 4 B. & Ald. 614; and of Parke, J., in *M'Pherson* v. *Daniels*, 10 B. & C. 275; 5 M. & R. 251.) The fourth resolution, as reported, appears inconsistent with the preceding resolution, the third; and also with the many decisions in the case. And even if it be correctly reported, it is but an *obiter dictum*, for the Star Chamber had no jurisdiction over private slander, and the case before them was one of *scandalum magnatum*, a branch of the law which was governed by special statutes of its own, now at last repealed. (See *ante*, p. 74.) And, moreover, the defendant in that case had not in fact named his authority at the time, but only confessed it subsequently.

Still, so great was the weight justly given to every word of Lord Coke, that this resolution was assumed to be law in *Crawford* v. *Middleton*, (1662) 1 Lev. 82; *Davis* v. *Lewis*, (1796) 7 T. R. 17; and *Woolnoth* v. *Meadows*, (1804) 5 East, 463; 2 Smith, 28. The last two cases decided that at all events it is too late to name the author of the report for the first time in the plea of justification; he must be named at time of publication to raise any ground of defence under this resolution.

In *Maitland* v. *Goldney*, (1802) 2 East, 426, Lord Ellenborough intimated that the doctrine did not apply where the reporter knew that his informant, whom he named, had retracted the charge since making it, or where for any other reason the reporter at the time of repeating the tale knew it was false, and unfounded. Next, in *Lewis* v. *Walter*, (1821) 4 B. & Ald. 615, Holroyd and Best, JJ. expressed an opinion that the rule had been laid down too largely in the *Earl of Northampton's Case*, and ought to be qualified by confining it to cases where there is a fair and just reason for the repetition of the slander (that is, we presume, to cases where the repetition is privileged). Then, in February, 1829, the Court of Common Pleas decided that in actions of *libel* there was no such rule. (*De Crespigny* v. *Wellesley*, 5 Bing. 392, in which case Best, C.J., says:—"Of what use is it to send the name of the author with a libel that is to pass into a country where he is entirely unknown : the name of the author of a statement will not inform those who do not know his character, whether he is a person entitled to credit for veracity or not; whether his statement was made in earnest or by way of joke ; whether it contains a charge made by a man of sound mind or the delusion of a lunatic.") And lastly, in *M'Pherson* v. *Daniels*, 10 B. & C. 263; 5 M. & R. 251 (Michaelmas, 1829), the rule in *Lord Northampton's Case* was directly challenged and expressly overruled; and it was held that for a defendant to prove that he said at the time that he heard the tale from A., and that A. did in fact tell it to the defendant, was no justification. It must be proved that the defendant repeated the story on a justifiable occasion, and in the *bonâ fide* belief in its truth [and that is a defence of privilege, see *Bromage* v. *Prosser*, 4 B. & C. 247; 6 D. & R. 296; 1 C. & P. 475, *post*, p. 256]. This decision has been approved of and followed in *Ward* v. *Weeks*, 7 Bing. 211; 4 M. & P. 796; and in *Watkin* v. *Hall*, L. R. 3 Q. B. 396; 37 L. J. Q. B. 125; 16 W. R. 857; 18 L. T. 561; and see *Bennett* v. *Bennett*, 6 C. & P. 588.

And in America the law appears to be the same. (*Jarnigan* v. *Fleming*, 43 Miss. 711; *Treat* v. *Browning*, 4 Connecticut, 408; *Runkle* v. *Meyers*, 3 Yeates (Pennsylvania), 518; *Dole* v. *Lyon*, 10 Johns. (New York), 447; *Inman* v. *Foster*, 8 Wend. 602.)

Illustrations.

Woor told Daniels that M'Pherson's horses had been seized from the coach on the road, that he had been arrested, and that the bailiffs were in his house. Daniels went about telling everyone, "Woor says that M'Pherson's horses have been seized from the coach on the road, that he himself has been arrested, and that the bailiffs are in his house." *Held,* that Daniels was liable to an action by M'Pherson for the slander, although he named Woor at the time as the person from whom he had heard it; that it was no justification to prove that Woor did in fact say so: the defendant must go further and prove that what Woor said was true.

> *M'Pherson* v. *Daniels,* 10 B. & C. 263; 5 M. & R. 251.

The defendant said to the plaintiff in the presence of others:—"Thou art a sheep-stealing rogue, and Farmer Parker told me so." *Held,* that an action lay. It was urged that the plaintiff ought not to have judgment, because it was not averred that Farmer Parker did not tell the defendant so; but the Court was of opinion that such an averment was unnecessary, it being quite immaterial whether Farmer Parker did or did not tell the defendant so.

> *Gardiner* v. *Atwater,* (1756) Sayer, 265.
>
> *Lewes* v. *Walter,* (1617) 3 Bulstr. 225; Cro. Jac. 406, 413; Rolle's Rep. 444.
>
> *Meggs* v. *Griffith,* Cro. Eliz. 400; Moore, 408; *ante,* p. 146.
>
> *Read's Case,* Cro. Eliz. 645.

The defendant said to the plaintiff, a tailor, in the presence of others:—"I heard you were run away," *scilicet,* from your creditors. *Held,* that an action lay.

> *Davis* v. *Lewis,* 7 T. R. 17.

A rumour was current on the Stock Exchange that the chairman of the S. E. Ry. Co. had failed; and the shares in the company consequently fell; thereupon the defendant said, "You have heard what has caused the fall—I mean, the rumour about the South-Eastern chairman having failed?" *Held,* that a plea that there was in fact such a rumour was no answer to the action.

> *Watkin* v. *Hall,* L. R. 3 Q. B. 396; 37 L. J. Q. B. 125; 16 W. R. 857; 18 L. T. 561.
>
> See *Richards* v. *Richards,* 2 Moo. & Rob. 557.

So the prior publication of a libel is no justification for its being copied and republished. If the first publication be privileged, that will not render the second publication privileged.

Illustrations.

Mr. and Mrs. Davies wrote a libellous letter to the Directors of the London Missionary Society, and sent a copy to the defendant, who published extracts from it in a pamphlet. The defendant stated that the letter was written by Mr. and Mrs. Davies, and at the time he wrote the pamphlet he believed all the statements made in the letter to be true. *Held,* no justification for his publishing it.

> *Tidman* v. *Ainslie,* (1854) 10 Exch. 63.
>
> And see *Mills and wife* v. *Spencer and wife,* (1817) Holt, N. P. 533.
>
> *M'Gregor* v. *Thwaites,* (1824) 3 B. & C. 24; 4 D. & R. 695.

No privilege attaches to the publication of an incorrect extract from a public document, even though the extract was officially supplied.

> *Reis* v. *Perry*, (1895) 64 L. J. Q. B. 566; 43 W. R. 648; 11 Times L. R. 373, as explained by Phillimore, J., in *Mangena* v. *Wright*, [1909] 2 K. B. at p. 977.

And here note a distinction between libel and slander. The actual publisher of a libel may be an innocent porter or messenger, a mere hand, unconscious of the nature of his act; and for which, therefore, his employers shall be held liable, and not he. Whereas in every case of the republication of a slander, the publisher acts consciously and voluntarily; the repetition is his own act. Therefore, if I am in any way concerned in the making or publishing of a libel, I am liable for all the damage that ensues to the plaintiff from its publication. But if I slander A., I am only liable for such damages as result directly from that one utterance by my own lips. If B. hears me and chooses to repeat the tale, that is B.'s own act; and B. alone is answerable, should damage to A. ensue. In an action against me such special damage would be too remote. For each publication of a slander is a distinct and separate tort, and every person repeating it becomes an independent slanderer, and he alone is answerable for the consequences of his own unlawful act.

Thus by the law of England, as it at present stands, the person who invents a lie and maliciously sets it in circulation may sometimes escape punishment altogether, while a person who is merely injudicious may be liable to an action through repeating a story which he believed to be the truth, as he heard it told frequently in good society. For if I originate a slander against you of such a nature that the words are not actionable *per se*, the utterance of them is no ground of action, unless special damage follows. If I myself tell the story to your employer, who thereupon dismisses you, you have an action against me: but if I only tell it to your friends and relations and no pecuniary damage ensues from my own communication of it to any one, then no action lies against me; although the story is sure to get round to your master sooner or later. The unfortunate man whose lips actually utter the slander to your master, is the only person that can be made defendant; for it is his publication alone which is actionable as causing special damage. The law is the same in America. (*Gough* v. *Goldsmith*, 44 Wis. 262; 28 Amer. R. 579; *Shurtleff* v. *Parker*, 130 Mass. 293; 39 Amer. R. 454.) But this apparent hardship only arises where the words are not actionable without proof of special damage. Where the words are actionable *per se*, the jury find the damages *generally*, and will judge from the circumstances which of the defendants is most to blame.

There are two apparent exceptions to this rule:

I. Where by communicating a slander to A., the defendant puts A. under a moral obligation to repeat it to some other person immediately concerned; here, if the defendant knew the relation in which A. stood to this other person, he will be taken to have contemplated this result when he spoke to A. In fact, here A.'s repetition is the natural and necessary consequence of the defendant's communication to A. (See the judgment of Lopes, L.J., in *Speight* v. *Gosnay*, 60 L. J. Q. B. 231; 55 J. P. 501.)

II. *Where there is evidence that the defendant, though he spoke only to A., intended and desired that A. should repeat his words, or expressly requested him to do so; here the defendant is liable for all the consequences of A.'s repetition of the slander; for A. thus becomes the agent of the defendant.* (As to Principal and Agent, see Law of Persons, c. XXI., *post*, p. 567.)

Illustrations.

Weeks was speaking to Bryce of the plaintiff, and said, "He is a rogue and a swindler; I know enough about him to hang him." Bryce repeated this to Bryer as Weeks' statement. Bryer consequently refused to trust the plaintiff, who thereupon sued Weeks. *Held*, that the judge was right in nonsuiting the plaintiff: for the words were not actionable *per se*; and the damage was too remote.

Ward v. *Weeks*, (1830) 7 Bing. 211; 4 M. & P. 796.

The defendant's wife charged Mrs. Parkins with adultery. She indignantly told her husband, her natural protector; he was unreasonable enough to insist

---

* This passage was cited with approval by the Court in *Whitney and others* v. *Moignard*, 24 Q. B. D. at p. 631.

upon a separation in consequence. *Held*, that for the separation the defendant was not liable.

> *Parkins et ux.* v. *Scott et ux.*, (1862) 1 H. & C. 153; 31 L. J. Ex. 331;
> 8 Jur. N. S. 593; 10 W. R. 562; 6 L. T. 394.
> See *Dixon* v. *Smith*, (1860) 5 H. & N. 450; 29 L. J. Ex. 125.

H. told Mr. Watkins that the plaintiff, his wife's dressmaker, was a woman of immoral character; Mr. Watkins naturally informed his wife of this charge, and she ceased to employ the plaintiff. *Held*, that the plaintiff's loss of Mrs. Watkins' custom was the natural and necessary consequence of the defendant's communication to Mr. Watkins.

> *Derry* v. *Handley*, (1867) 16 L. T. 263.
> See *Gillett* v. *Bullivant*, (1846) 7 L. T. (Old S.) 490.
> *Kendillon* v. *Maltby*, (1842) Car. & Marsh. 402.

The defendant uttered a slander consisting of a false imputation upon the chastity of the plaintiff, an unmarried woman, in the presence of her mother. The mother repeated it to the plaintiff, who repeated it to the man to whom she was engaged to be married, and he broke off the engagement. There was no evidence that the defendant authorised or intended the repetition of the slander, or that he knew of the plaintiff's engagement. *Held*, that an action of slander could not be maintained against him. [N.B. This was prior to the Slander of Women Act, 1891.]

> *Speight* v. *Gosnay*, (1891) 60 L. J. Q. B. 231 ; 55 J. P. 501; 7 Times
> L. R. 239.
> *Ecklin* v. *Little*, (1890) 6 Times L. R. 366.

The defendants' servant, when in charge of a public bar on licensed premises, charged the plaintiff with being drunk and had him ejected. The plaintiff, fearing the occurrence would be reported to his father, informed him of the fact. The father, who was the chairman of the board of a company, of which the plaintiff was a director, threatened him with the loss of his directorship if he did not clear his character. *Held*, that even if such a threat amounted to special damage, it was not due to the act of defendants' servant.

> *Michael* v. *Spiers and Pond*, (1909) 25 Times L. R. 740.

It has sometimes been held, on the principle of *Volenti non fit injuria*, that if the only publication proved at the trial be one brought about by the plaintiff's own contrivance, the action must fail. Thus, in *King* v. *Waring et ux.*, 5 Esp. 15, Lord Alvanley decided that if a servant, knowing the character which his master will give him, procures a letter to be written, not with a fair view of inquiring the character, but to procure an answer upon which to ground an action for a libel, no such action can be maintained. So in *Smith* v. *Wood*, 3 Camp. 323, where the plaintiff, hearing that defendant had in his possession a copy of a libellous caricature of the plaintiff, sent an agent who asked to see the picture, and the defendant showed it him at his request, Lord Ellenborough ruled that this was no sufficient evidence of publication, and nonsuited the plaintiff.

But these cases, so far as the question of *publication* merely is concerned, must be taken to be overruled by the *Duke of Brunswick* v. *Harmer*, 14 Q. B. 185 ; 19 L. J. Q. B. 20 ; 14 Jur. 110 ; 3 C. & K. 10.   Whether or no the plaintiff's conduct in himself provoking or inviting the publication on which he afterwards bases his action may amount to a ground of privilege as excusing the publication made, is a different question, which will be discussed *post*, pp. 294—298.   And indeed in many of the older cases the judges say, " there is no sufficient publication to support the action," when they mean in modern parlance that the publication was privileged by reason of the occasion.   (See the judgment of Best, J., in *Fairman* v. *Ives*, 5 B. & Ald. 646 ; 1 D. & R. 252 ; 1 Chit. 85, and *Robinson* v. *May*, 2 Smith, 3.)   And note that a publication induced by the prosecutor is sufficient in a criminal case.   (*R.* v. *Carlile*, 1 Cox, C. C. 229.)

CHAPTER VII.

JUSTIFICATION.

The truth of any defamatory words is, if pleaded, a complete defence to any action of libel or slander (though alone it is not a defence in a criminal trial). The *onus*, however, of proving that the words are true, lies on the defendant. The falsehood of all defamatory words is presumed in the plaintiff's favour, and he need give no evidence to show they are false; but the defendant can rebut this presumption by giving evidence in support of his plea. If the jury are satisfied that the words are true in substance and in fact, they must find for the defendant, though they feel sure that he spoke the words spitefully and maliciously. On the other hand, if the words are false, and there be no other defence, the jury must find for the plaintiff, although they are satisfied that the defendant *bonâ fide* and reasonably believed the words to be true at the time he uttered them.

But the whole libel must be proved true; it will be no defence to the action to prove that a part merely is true. The defence must be pleaded to the words set out in the Statement of Claim, and not to some other words of the defendant's own. (*Rassam* v. *Budge*, [1893] 1 Q. B. 571; 62 L. J. Q. B. 312.) The justification must be as broad as the charge, and must justify the precise charge. If any material part be not proved true, the plaintiff is entitled to damages in respect of such part. (*Weaver* v. *Lloyd*, 1 C. & P. 295; 2 B. & C. 678; *Ingram* v. *Lawson*, 5 Bing. N. C. 66; 6 Scott, 775; 6 Bing. N. C. 212; 8 Scott, 471.) Thus, where a libellous paragraph in a newspaper is introduced by a libellous heading, it is not enough to prove the truth of the facts stated in the paragraph; the defendant must also prove the truth of the heading. (*Mountney* v.

Watton, 2 B. & Ad. 673 ; *Chalmers* v. *Shackell,* 6 C. & P. 475 ; *Mangena* v. *Edward Lloyd, Ltd.,* (1908) 99 L. T. 824 ; 25 Times L. R. 26.)

But where the gist of the libel consists of one specific charge which is proved to be true, the defendant need not justify every expression which he has used in commenting on the plaintiff's conduct. Nor, if the substantial imputation be proved true, will a slight inaccuracy in one of its details prevent defendant's succeeding, provided such inaccuracy in no way alters the complexion of the affair, and would have no different effect on the reader than that which the literal truth would produce. (*Alexander* v. *N. E. Rail. Co.,* 34 L. J. Q. B. 152 ; 11 Jur. N. S. 619 ; 13 W. R. 651 ; 6 B. & S. 340 ; cf. *Stockdale* v. *Tarte,* 4 A. & E. 1016 ; *Blake* v. *Stevens,* 4 F. & F. 239 ; 11 L. T. 544.) If epithets or terms of general abuse be used which do not add to the sting of the charge, they need not be justified (*Edwards* v. *Bell,* 1 Bing. 403 ; *Morrison* v. *Harmer,* 3 Bing. N. C. 767 ; 4 Scott, 533 ; 3 Hodges, 108) ; but if they insinuate some further charge in addition to the main imputation, or imply some circumstance substantially aggravating such main imputation, then they must be justified as well as the rest. (Per Maule, J., in *Helsham* v. *Blackwood,* 11 C. B. 129 ; 20 L. J. C. P. 192 ; 15 Jur. 861.)

In such a case it will be a question for the jury whether the substance of the libellous statement has been proved true to their satisfaction. (*Warman* v. *Hine,* 1 Jur. 820 ; *Weaver* v. *Lloyd,* 2 B. & C. 678 ; 4 D. & R. 230 ; 1 C. & P. 295 ; *Behrens* v. *Allen,* 8 Jur. N. S. 118 ; 3 F. & F. 135.) "It would be extravagant," says Lord Denman, C.J. (in *Cooper* v. *Lawson,* 8 A. & E. 753 ; 1 P. & D. 15 ; 1 W. W. & H. 601 ; 2 Jur. 919), "to say that in cases of libel every comment upon facts requires a justification. A comment may introduce independent facts, a justification of which is necessary, or it may be the mere shadow of the previous imputation." And see *Lefroy* v. *Burnside,* (No. 2) 4 L. R. Ir. 556.

So in criminal cases, if the whole of the plea of justification be not proved, the Crown will be entitled to a verdict. (*R.* v. *Newman*, 1 E. & B. 268, 558; 22 L. J. Q. B. 156; Dears. C. C. 85; 17 Jur. 617; 3 C. & K. 252.)

In actions on the case for words causing damage the plaintiff has to prove that the words are false; it does not lie on the defendant to prove them true. (See Chap. IV., *ante*, p. 77.)

Illustrations.

"Upon a charge of murder, it would be no plea to allege that manslaughter had been committed, because such a plea would not confess what was imputed or any part of it." Per Tindal, C.J., in

> *Clarkson* v. *Lawson*, 6 Bing. at p. 593.

A defendant cannot set out his own version of the defamatory words which differs materially from those set out in the Statement of Claim, and then plead that his own words are true in substance and in fact. "It is like pleading to a Statement of Claim, alleging that the defendant had said the plaintiff stole a pair of boots, that what the defendant said was that the plaintiff's footman stole the boots, and that was true."

> *Rassam* v. *Budge*, [1893] 1 Q. B. 571, 578; 62 L. J. Q. B. 312; 41 W. R. 377; 68 L. T. 717; 5 R. 336.
>
> And see *Fleming* v. *Dollar*, 23 Q. B. D. 388; 58 L. J. Q. B. 548; 37 W. R. 684; 61 L. T. 230.

The editor of one newspaper called the editor of another "a felon editor." Justification, that the plaintiff had been convicted of felony, and sentenced to twelve months' imprisonment. The Court of Appeal held the plea bad, for not averring that the plaintiff was still enduring the punishment when the words were uttered; for that by the 9 Geo. IV. c. 32, s. 3, a person who has been convicted of felony, and who has undergone the full punishment, is in law no longer a felon. [A strong decision; for ordinary readers unacquainted with that statute would surely understand "felon editor" to mean a man who had been convicted of felony, but was now out of prison, editing a paper. The felon when in prison is usually called a "convict."]

> *Leyman* v. *Latimer*, 3 Ex. D. 15, 352; 47 L. J. Ex. 470; 25 W. R. 751; 26 W. R. 305; 37 L. T. 360, 819; 14 Cox, C. C. 51.

Words complained of, that the plaintiff was a "libellous journalist." Proof that he had libelled one man, who had recovered from him damages £100, held insufficient.

> *Wakley* v. *Cooke and Healey*, 4 Exch. 511; 19 L. J. Ex. 91.

Libel complained of:—That no boys had for the last seven years received instruction in the Free Grammar School at Lichfield, of which plaintiff was head master, and that the decay of the school seemed mainly attributable to the plaintiff's violent conduct. Plea of justification, that no boys had in fact received instruction in the school for the last seven years, and that the plaintiff had been guilty of violent conduct towards several of his scholars, was held bad on special demurrer, because it wholly omitted to connect the decay of the school with the alleged violence, and, therefore, left the second part of the libel unjustified.

> *Smith* v. *Parker*, 13 M. & W. 459; 14 L. J. Ex. 52; 2 D. & L. 394.

Libel complained of:—"I see that the restoration of Skirlaugh Church has fallen into the hands of an architect who is a Wesleyan, and can have no experience in church work. Can you not do something to avert the irreparable loss which must be caused if any of the masonry of this ancient gem of art be ignorantly tampered with?" Justification: "The facts contained in the letter are true, and the opinions expressed in it, whether right or wrong, were honestly held and expressed by the defendant." Particulars under this plea: "The plaintiff cannot show experience in church work, *i.e.*, of the kind which in the opinion of the defendant was requisite." *Held,* that this was no justification at all, because the letter obviously meant that the plaintiff could show no experience in the work which he had been employed to execute. Verdict for the plaintiff, damages 50*l.*

> *Botterill and another* v. *Whytehead*, 41 L. T. 588.

Libel complained of:—That the plaintiff had "*bolted*," leaving some of the tradesmen of the town to lament the fashionable character of his entertainments. Proof that he had *quitted* the town leaving some of his bills unpaid, held insufficient.

> *O'Brien* v. *Bryant*, 16 M. & W. 168; 16 L. J. Ex. 77; 4 D. & L. 341.

Libel complained of:—That the plaintiff, having challenged his opponent to a duel, spent the whole of the night preceding in practising with his pistol, and killed his opponent, and was therefore guilty of murder. Proof that the plaintiff had killed his opponent, and had been tried for murder, held insufficient. For the charge of pistol practising was considered a separate and substantial charge, and it was not justified.

> *Helsham* v. *Blackwood*, 11 C. B. 128; 20 L. J. C. P. 187; 15 Jur. 861.

The libel complained of was headed—"How Lawyer B. treats his Clients," followed by a report of a particular case in which *one* client of Lawyer B. had been badly treated. That particular case was proved to be correctly reported, but this was held insufficient to justify the heading, which implied that Lawyer B. *generally* treated his clients badly.

> *Bishop* v. *Latimer*, 4 L. T. 775.
>
> See also *Mountney* v. *Watton*, 2 B. & Ad. 673.
>
> *Chalmers* v. *Shackell*, 6 C. & P. 475.
>
> *Clement* v. *Lewis and others*, 3 Brod. & Bing. 297; 7 Moore, 200;
>   3 B. & Ald. 702.

Libel complained of:—That the plaintiff, a proctor, had three times been suspended from practice for extortion. Proof that he had *once* been so suspended was held insufficient.

> *Clarkson* v. *Lawson*, 6 Bing. 266; 3 M. & P. 605; 6 Bing. 587;
>   4 M. & P. 356:
>
> See also *Johns* v. *Gittings*, Cro. Eliz. 239.
>
> *Goodburne* v. *Bowman and others*, 9 Bing. 532.
>
> *Clarke* v. *Taylor*, 2 Bing. N. C. 654; 3 Scott, 95; 2 Hodges, 65.
>
> *Blake* v. *Stevens and others*, 4 F. & F. 232; 11 L. T. 543.

But when the libel complained of exposed the "homicidal tricks of those impudent and ignorant scamps who had the audacity to pretend to cure all diseases with one kind of pill," asserted that " several of the rotgut rascals had been convicted of manslaughter, and fined and imprisoned for killing people with enormous doses of their universal vegetable boluses," and characterised the plaintiffs' system as " one of wholesale poisoning "; and it was proved at the trial " that the plaintiffs' pills, when taken in large doses, as recommended by the plaintiffs, were highly dangerous, deadly, and poisonous," and " that two persons had died in consequence of taking large quantities of them "; and that the people who administered these pills were tried, convicted, and imprisoned for the manslaughter of these two persons "; this was held a sufficient justification, although the expressions, " scamps," " rascals," and " wholesale poisoning," had not been fully substantiated : the main charge and gist of the libel being amply sustained.

Morrison v. *Harmer*, 3 Bing. N. C. 767 ; 4 Scott, 533 ; 3 Hodges, 108.

Edsall v. *Russell*, 4 M. & Gr. 1090; 5 Scott, N. R. 801; 2 Dowl. N. S. 641 ; 12 L. J. C. P. 4 ; 6 Jur. 996.

Sharp v. *Stephenson*, 12 Ired. 348.

But where the defendant called the plaintiffs " thieves and swindlers," particulars delivered under a plea of justification, showing conduct which did not amount to *criminal* dishonesty, were held insufficient and struck out.

Wernher, Beit and Co. v. *Markham*, (1901) 18 Times L. R. 143 ; (1902) *ib.* 763.

Libel complained of :—" L., B., and G. are a gang who live by card-sharping." Pleas: Not guilty, and a justification giving several specific instances in which persons named had been cheated by the trio at cards. *Held*, by Cockburn, C.J., when two specific instances had been proved, that the plea had been proved in substance, and that it was not necessary to prove the other instances alleged.

R. pros. Lambri v. *Labouchere*, 14 Cox, C. C. 419.

And see *Willmett* v. *Harmer and another*, 8 C. & P. 695.

The libel complained of was a notice published by a railway company to the effect that the plaintiff had been convicted of riding in a train for which his ticket was not available, and was sentenced to be fined 1*l.*, or to three weeks' imprisonment in default of payment. Proof that he had been so convicted and fined 1*l.* and sentenced to a fortnight's imprisonment in default of payment, held sufficient; as the error could not have made any difference in the effect which the notice would produce on the mind of the public.

Alexander v. *N. E. Ry. Co.*, 34 L. J. Q. B. 152 ; 11 Jur. N. S. 619 ; 13 W. R. 651 ; 6 B. & S. 340.

But where a placard stated that the plaintiff (giving his full name and address) had been convicted of a breach of the by-laws, and sentenced to a fine of one shilling, or in default to imprisonment for three days WITH HARD LABOUR, the last three words being printed on a separate line in large capital letters, whereas no hard labour had been imposed by the sentence, the jury found a verdict for the plaintiff for 250*l.* damages.

Gwynn v. *S. E. Ry. Co.*, 18 L. T. 738.

Biggs v. *G. E. Ry. Co.*, 16 W. R. 908 ; 18 L. T. 482.

See also *Lay* v. *Lawson*, 4 A. & E. 795.

Edwards v. *Bell and others*, 1 Bing. 403.

Tighe v. *Cooper*, 7 E. & B. 639 ; 26 L. J. Q. B. 215 ; 3 Jur. N. S. 716.

This rule, that the whole of the libel must be justified to enable the defendant to succeed, applies to all cases of reported speeches or repetitions of slander. Thus, if the libel complained of be, " A. said that the plaintiff had been guilty of fraud, &c.," it is of no avail to plead that A. did in fact make that statement on the occasion specified. Each repetition is a fresh defamation, and the defendant by repeating A.'s words has made them his own, and is legally as liable as if he had invented the story himself. To succeed in the action, the defendant must not merely show that A. did in fact say so, but must go on to prove that every statement which A. is reported to have made is true in substance and in fact. A previous publication by another of the same defamatory words is no justification for their repetition. (See *ante,* Chap. VI., pp. 172—179.) Still less is it any evidence of their truth. (*R.* v. *Newman,* 1 E. & B. 268, 558; 3 C. & K. 252; Dears. C. C. 85; 22 L. J. Q. B. 156; 17 Jur. 617.) Particulars will be ordered of any plea which leaves it doubtful whether the defendant intends at the trial to say that A.'s words are true, or merely to prove that A. said so—evidence of which might tend to mitigate the damages, though it would be no answer to the action. (*Hennessy* v. *Wright,* 57 L. J. Q. B. 594; 36 W. R. 878; 59 L. T. 795; 4 Times L. R. 548, 651.)

The opposite doctrine was laid down in the fourth resolution in the *Earl of Northampton's Case,* 12 Rep. 134, but that case never professed to apply to actions of libel, but to actions for slander only; and even in actions of slander it is no longer law. (See *ante,* pp. 172—176; *De Crespigny* v. *Wellesley,* 5 Bing. 392; 2 M. & P. 695; *M'Pherson* v. *Daniels,* 10 B. & C. 270; 5 M. & R. 251; *Watkin* v. *Hall,* L. R. 3 Q. B. 396; 37 L. J. Q. B. 125; 16 W. R. 857; 18 L. T. 561.)

It was considered that this rule pressed too severely upon newspaper proprietors and editors, who had in the ordinary course of their business presented to the public a full, true, and impartial account of what really took place at a public meeting, considering no doubt that thereby they were merely doing their duty, whereas the law held them guilty of libel. And so the second section of the

Newspaper Libel and Registration Act was passed in 1881 for their protection ; and as that proved insufficient, a wider privilege was conferred on them by section 4 of the Law of Libel Amendment Act, 1888. (See *post*, pp. 328—336.) Fair and accurate reports of judicial and parliamentary proceedings were already privileged (*post*, pp. 307—328).

Illustrations.

Woor told Daniels that M'Pherson was insolvent; Daniels went about telling his friends, " Woor says M'Pherson is insolvent." Proof that Woor had in fact said so was held no answer to the action. Daniels was liable in damages unless he could also prove the truth of Woor's assertion.

> *M'Pherson* v. *Daniels*, 10 B. & C. 263 ; 5 M. & R. 251.

A rumour was current on the Stock Exchange that the chairman of the S. E. Ry. Co. had failed; and the shares of the company consequently fell; thereupon the defendant said, " You have heard what has caused the fall—I mean, the rumour about the South-Eastern chairman having failed ?" *Held*, that a plea that there was in fact such a rumour was no answer to the action.

> *Watkin* v. *Hull*, L. R. 3 Q. B. 396; 37 L. J. Q. B. 125 ; 16 W. R. 857; 18 L. T. 561.
>
> *Richards* v. *Richards*, 2 Moo. & Rob. 557.

At a meeting of the West Hartlepool Improvement Commissioners, one of the commissioners made some defamatory remarks as to the conduct of the former secretary of the Bishop of Durham in procuring from the Bishop a licence for the chaplain of the West Hartlepool cemetery. These remarks were reported in the local newspaper ; and the secretary brought an action against the owner of the newspaper for libel. A plea of justification alleging that such remarks were in fact made at a public meeting of the commissioners, and that the alleged libel was an impartial and accurate report of what took place at such meeting, was held bad on demurrer.

> *Davison* v. *Duncan*, 7 E. & B. 229; 26 L. J. Q. B. 104; 3 Jur. N. S. 613; 5 W. R. 253; 28 L. T. (Old S.) 265.

So also a newspaper proprietor was held liable for publishing a report made to the vestry by their medical officer of health, even although the vestry was required by Act of Parliament sooner or later to publish such report themselves.

> *Popham* v. *Pickburn*, 7 H. & N. 891; 31 L. J. Ex. 133; 8 Jur. N. S. 179; 10 W. R. 324 ; 5 L. T. 846.
>
> See also *Charlton* v. *Watton*, 6 C. & P. 385.

So even in reports of judicial proceedings, which if fair and accurate, are privileged, if the reporter merely sets out the facts as stated by counsel for one party, and does not give the evidence, or merely says that all that counsel stated was proved, a justification that counsel did in fact say so, and that all he stated was in fact proved, is insufficient; the facts stated by counsel must also be justified and proved.

> *Lewis* v. *Walter*, 4 B. & Ald. 605.
>
> *Saunders* v. *Mills*, 3 M. & P. 520 ; 6 Bing. 213.
>
> See also *Flint* v. *Pike*, 4 B. & C. 473; 6 D. & R. 528; and the remarks of Lord Campbell in
>
> *Lewis* v. *Levy*, E. B. & E. 544 ; 27 L. J. Q. B. 282 ; 4 Jur. N. S. 970.

It is libellous to publish a highly-coloured account of judicial proceedings, mixed with the reporter's own observations and conclusions upon what passed in Court, containing an insinuation that the plaintiff had committed perjury; and it is no justification to pick out such parts of the libel as contain an account of the trial, and to plead that such parts are true and accurate, leaving the extraneous matter altogether unjustified.

> *Stiles* v. *Nokes*, 7 East, 493 ; same case *sub nomine Carr* v. *Jones*, 3 Smith, 491.
>
> *Roberts* v. *Brown*, 10 Bing. 519 ; 4 M. & Scott, 407.

Justifying Part of the Words.

A plea of justification will not be a bar to the action, unless it justifies the whole of the words set out in the Statement of Claim. Still, the defendant may, in mitigation of damages, justify part only of the words, provided such part contains a distinct imputation which can be separated from the rest. (Per Tindal, C.J., in *Clarke* v. *Taylor*, 2 Bing. N. C. 664 ; 3 Scott, 95 ; 2 Hodges, 65.) Thus he may sometimes justify one portion of the libel and plead privilege, or pay money into Court for another portion, or he may deny that he ever spoke or published the rest of the words. But in all these cases the portion justified must be fairly severable from the remainder so as to be intelligible by itself, and must also convey a distinct and separate imputation against the plaintiff. (*M'Gregor* v. *Gregory*, 11 M. & W. 287 ; 12 L. J. Ex. 204 ; 2 Dowl. N. S. 769 ; *Churchill* v. *Hunt*, 2 B. & Ald. 685 ; 1 Chit. 480 ; *Roberts* v. *Brown*, 10 Bing. 519 ; 4 M. & Scott, 407 ; *Biddulph* v. *Chamberlayne*, 17 Q. B. 351 ; *Davis* v. *Billing*, (1891) 8 Times L. R. 58.) And the plaintiff must not be left in doubt how much the defendant justifies, and how much he does not. (*Fleming* v. *Dollar*, 23 Q. B. D. 388 ; 58 L. J. Q. B. 548 ; 37 W. R. 684 ; 61 L. T. 230.)

Justifying the Innuendo.

Again, the plaintiff often attempts by the aid of an innuendo in his Statement of Claim to give the words a secondary meaning different from that which they would naturally bear. In such a case, the defendant may justify the words either with or without the meaning alleged in such innuendo; or he may do both.* (*Watkin* v. *Hall*, L. R. 3 Q. B. 396; 37 L. J. Q. B. 125; 16 W. R. 857; 18 L. T. 561.) He may deny that the plaintiff puts the true construction on his words, and assert that, if taken in their natural and ordinary meaning, his words will be found to be true; such a plea involves the justification of every injurious imputation which a jury may think is to be found in the alleged libel. (*Digby* v. *Financial News, Ltd.*, [1907] 1 K. B. at p. 507.) Or he may boldly allege that the words are true even in the worst signification that can be put upon them. But a defendant may not put a meaning of his own on the words, and say that in that sense they are true; for if he deny that the meaning assigned to his words in the Statement of Claim is the correct one, he must be content to leave it to the jury at the trial to determine what meaning the words naturally bear. (*Brembridge* v. *Latimer*, 12 W. R. 878; 10 L. T. 816.) Nor may he plead: "I did not publish precisely the words stated in the claim; but something similar, and that something similar is true in substance and in fact." (*Rassam* v. *Budge*, [1893] 1 Q. B. 571; 62 L. J. Q. B. 312.) If the defendant pleads simply that the words are true without any reference to the innuendo, he must be prepared at the trial to prove the words true in whatever sense the jury may think it right to put upon them. (*Ford* v. *Bray*, (1894) 11 Times L. R. 32.) But if he pleads in the more qualified form that "the words without the said meaning" are true; he will not be allowed at the trial, should the jury deem the said meaning the true one, to turn round and give evidence that the words in that sense are true.

---

* In Ireland the defendant must justify the innuendo as well as the words; he cannot justify the words without the meaning which the plaintiff has thought fit to put upon them. (*Hort* v. *Reade*, Ir. R. 7 C. L. 551.)

Illustration.

The defendants published what was perfectly true, that judgment had been recovered against the plaintiff in the County Court for 27*l.* 1*s.* 0*d.* But they published it in a trade gazette by the side of " Bankruptcy Notices " and items as to " Bills of Sale," and it was held that the jury might properly find that the words so published implied that the plaintiff was unable to satisfy the said judgment or pay his just debts. And the defendants could not possibly justify their words in this sense, because the plaintiff had paid off the judgment before the date of the defendants' publication. Verdict for the plaintiff for 25*l.* damages.

Williams v. *Smith and another*, 22 Q. B. D. 134; 58 L. J. Q. B. 21; 37 W. R. 93; 59 L. T. 757.

Plea of Justification.

A justification must always be specially pleaded, and with sufficient particularity to enable the plaintiff to know precisely what is the charge he will have to meet. Where the words complained of are precise and convey a specific charge in full detail, it is sufficient to plead that they are " true in substance and in fact," and no particulars are necessary. (*Gordon Cumming* v. *Green and others*, (1891) 7 Times L. R. 408.) But where a vague general charge is made, as, for instance, that the plaintiff is a swindler, it is not sufficient to plead that he is a swindler; the defendant must set forth the specific facts which he means to prove in order to show that the plaintiff is a swindler. (*I'Anson* v. *Stuart*, 1 T. R. 748; *Zierenberg and wife* v. *Labouchere*, [1893] 2 Q. B. 183; 63 L. J. Q. B. 89; 41 W. R. 675; 69 L. T. 172; *Arnold & Butler* v. *Bottomley*, [1908] 2 K. B. 151; 77 L. J. K. B. 584; 98 L. T. 777.) And the particulars delivered must justify the precise charge, and not some similar charge which falls short of the one in fact made. (*Wernher, Beit & Co.* v. *Markham*, (1901) 18 Times L. R. 143; (1902) *ib.* 763.) A plea of justification is always construed strictly against the party pleading it. (*Leyman* v. *Latimer*, 3 Ex. D. 15, 352.) " The plea ought to state the charge with the same precision as in an indictment." (Per Alderson, B., in *Hickinbotham* v. *Leach*, 10 M. & W. 363; 2 Dowl. N. S. 270.)

And at the trial it must be proved as strictly as an indictment for the offence which it imputes. (Per Tindal, C.J., in *Chalmers* v. *Shackell*, 6 C. & P. at p. 478. Per Lord Denman, C.J., in *Willmett* v. *Harmer*, 8 C. & P. at p. 697.) Indeed, it is said that if the words amount to a charge of felony, and the defendant justifies, and the jury find the plea proved, the plaintiff may at once be put upon his trial before a petty jury, without the necessity of any bill being found by a grand jury. (Per Lord Kenyon in *Cook* v. *Field*, 3 Esp. 134. See the note to *Prosser* v. *Rowe*, 2 C. & P. 422 ; *Johnson* v. *Browning*, 6 Mod. 217.)

Placing a justification on the record is not by itself evidence of malice on the part of the defendant : but it will certainly tend to aggravate the damages, if the defendant either abandons the plea at the trial or fails to prove it. (*Warwick* v. *Foulkes*, 12 M. & W. 508 ; *Wilson* v. *Robinson*, 7 Q. B. 68 ; 14 L. J. Q. B. 196 ; 9 Jur. 726 ; *Simpson* v. *Robinson*, 12 Q. B. 511 ; 18 L. J. Q. B. 73 ; 13 Jur. 187 ; *Caulfield* v. *Whitworth*, 16 W. R. 936 ; 18 L. T. 527.)

In a criminal case it is not sufficient to prove the truth of the libel ; the defendant must also prove that it was for the public benefit that the matters charged should be published (6 & 7 Vict. c. 96, s. 6, *post*, p. 473). And, indeed, before 1843 the truth of the libel was no defence at all to an indictment ; the maxim prevailed, " the greater the truth, the greater the libel." Yet it was always otherwise with a civil action ; there the truth was always a complete defence. For in a civil action the benefit or detriment to the public is not in issue ; the plaintiff is seeking to put in his own pocket damages for an alleged injury to a character, to which, if the words be true, he had no right. It has been urged that an action ought to lie, where the plaintiff's antecedents have been maliciously raked up and wantonly published to the world, without any benefit to society. Yet it is difficult to see how any change can be made in the law in this respect. It is part of the punishment of a wrongdoer that he can never escape from his misdeeds. And as a rule the strictness with which a defendant is made to prove his plea of justification is a sufficient protection against malevolence : for if a man is really malicious in making a statement, he is almost sure to go beyond the truth, and say too much.

In Rome the truth of the libel was a defence both to criminal and to civil proceedings. "Eum qui nocentem infamavit non esse bonum æquum ob eam rem condemnari."—Pauli Sent. V. 4.

CHAPTER VIII.

COMMENTS ON MATTERS OF PUBLIC INTEREST.

Every one has a right to comment, both by word of mouth and in writing, on matters of public interest and general concern, provided he does so fairly and with an honest purpose. Such comments are not actionable, however severe in their terms, so long as the writer or speaker truly states his real opinion of the matter on which he comments. Every citizen has full freedom of speech on such subjects; but he must not abuse it.

This branch of the law is of modern growth. Cockburn, C.J., says in *Wason* v. *Walter*, L. R. 4 Q. B. 93, 94: " Our law of libel has, in many respects, only gradually developed itself into anything like a satisfactory and settled form. The full liberty of public writers to comment on the conduct and motives of public men has only in very recent times been recognised. Comments on governments, on ministers and officers of state, on members of both houses of Parliament, on judges and other public functionaries, are now made every day, which half a century ago would have been the subject of actions or *ex officio* informations, and would have brought down fine and imprisonment on publishers and authors. Yet who can doubt that the public are gainers by the change, and that, though injustice may often be done, and though public men may often have to smart under the keen sense of wrong inflicted by hostile criticisms, the nation profits by public opinion being thus freely brought to bear on the discharge of public duties ? "

The right to comment upon the public acts of public men is the right of every citizen. " The liberty of the press is no greater and no less than the liberty of every subject of the Queen." (*Per cur.* in *R.* v. *Gray*, [1900] 2 Q. B. at p. 40.) But newspaper writers, though in strict law they stand in no better position than any other person, are generally allowed greater latitude by juries. It is regarded as in some measure the duty of the press to watch narrowly the conduct of all government officials, and the working of all public institutions, to comment freely on all matters which concern the nation, and fearlessly to expose abuses should any be found to exist.

It has often been said by learned judges that fair and honest criticism on matters of public concern is *privileged*. See especially the judgments in *Henwood* v. *Harrison*, L. R. 7 C. P. 606 ; 41 L. J. C. P. 206 ; 20 W. R. 1000 ; 26 L. T. 938. This does not mean that the words have been published on what is technically known as a " privileged occasion." There is, it is true, a close analogy between the two defences of " fair comment " and " privilege " ; yet they are not identical. As Lord Esher, M.R., says in the case of *Merivale* v. *Carson*, 20 Q. B. D. at p. 280 : " A privileged occasion is one on which the privileged person is entitled to do something which no one who is not within the privilege is entitled to do on that occasion. A person in such a position may say or write about another person things which no other person in the kingdom can be allowed to say or write. But in the case of a criticism upon a published work, every person in the kingdom is entitled to do, and is forbidden to do, exactly the same things, and therefore the occasion is not privileged."

In some cases it has been laid down that a fair comment on a matter of public interest is no libel or slander. This, however, does not mean that the words are not defamatory, *i.e.*, not injurious to the reputation. If they were not defamatory, of course no action would lie. It is only when the words do tend to injure the reputation of the person to whom they refer that the question arises : Can they be excused as being a fair comment on a matter of public interest ? Thus a fair criticism on a literary work may be injurious to the reputation of the author, and therefore defamatory. Nevertheless, the critic would not be liable in damages, but will be protected if he has simply discharged his duty to the public. The words may be in themselves libellous, but as soon as they are shown to be a fair and *bonâ fide* comment on a matter of public interest they cease to be actionable. It is only in this sense that they can be said to be no libel. It is submitted that those judges who have laid down that fair comment is no libel have used the words " no libel " in this latter sense, and not in the sense that the words were not defamatory. See the discussion in *Thomas* v. *Bradbury, Agnew & Co., Limited*, [1906] 2 K. B. 627. " It is precisely where the criticism would otherwise be actionable as a libel that the defence of fair comment comes in." (Per Lord Loreburn, L.C., in *Dakhyl* v. *Labouchere,* [1908] 2 K. B. at p. 327.)

Criticism.

The following are the essential characteristics of fair criticism :—

1. Criticism deals only with such things as invite public attention, or call for public comment. It does not follow a public man into his private life, or pry into his domestic concerns.

2. Criticism does not attack the individual but only his *work.* Such work may be either the policy of a government, the speech or action of a member of Parliament, a public entertainment, a book published, or a picture exhibited. In every case the attack is on a man's *acts*, or on some *thing*, and not upon the man in his private capacity. A true critic never indulges in personalities, or recklessly imputes dishonourable motives, but confines himself to the merits of the subject-matter before him.

3. The critic never takes advantage of the occasion to gratify private malice, or to attain any other object beyond the fair discussion of matters of public interest, and the judicious guidance of the public taste. He will carefully examine the production before him, and then honestly and fearlessly state his true opinion of it.

Every one has a right to publish such fair and candid criticism. "One writer in exposing the follies and errors of another, may make use of ridicule, however poignant. Ridicule is often the fittest weapon that can be employed for such a purpose . . . . We really must not cramp observations upon authors and their works. They should be liable to criticism, to exposure, and even to ridicule, if their compositions be ridiculous . . . . Reflection upon personal character is another thing. Show me an attack upon the moral character of the plaintiff, or any attack upon his character unconnected with his authorship, and I should be as ready as any judge who ever sat here to protect him. But I cannot hear of malice on account of turning his works into ridicule . . . . Every man who publishes a book commits himself to the judgment of the public, and any one may comment upon his performance. If the commentator does not step aside from the work, or introduce fiction for the purpose of condemnation, he exercises a fair and legitimate right." (Per Lord Ellenborough in the celebrated case of *Sir John Carr* v *Hood,* 1 Camp. at pp. 357, 358, n.) So in *Tabart* v. *Tipper,* 1 Camp. 351, the same learned judge says: "Liberty of criticism must be allowed, or we should neither have purity of taste nor of morals. Fair discussion is essentially necessary to the truth of history and the advancement of science. That publication, therefore, I shall never consider as a libel, which has for its object, not to injure the reputation of any individual, but to correct the misrepresentations of fact, to refute sophistical reasoning, to expose a vicious taste in literature, or to censure what is hostile to morality." "A critic must confine himself to criticism, and not make it the veil for personal censure, nor allow himself to run into reckless and unfair attacks merely from the love of exercising his power of denunciation." (Per Huddleston, B., in *Whistler* v. *Ruskin, Times,* Nov. 27th, 1878.)

It is then a defence to an action of libel or slander that the words complained of are a fair comment on a matter of public interest. But this defence will fail, unless the words complained of are :—

    (i) A comment and not the assertion of some alleged matter of fact ;

    (ii) A comment on some matter of public interest ;

    (iii) A fair comment, and

    (iv.) A comment published without malice.

Whether the matter commented on is or is not a matter of public interest is a question for the judge. (See *post,* p. 206.) All other questions are for the jury. "The *onus* of proving that his words are a comment and that they are a comment on a matter of public interest lies on the defendant." (Per Vaughan Williams, L.J., in *Peter Walker & Son, Ltd.* v. *Hodgson,* [1909] 1 K. B. at p. 249.) If the judge thinks that there is no evidence on which a rational verdict could be found to the effect that the comment is unfair, he should stop the case. (Per Willes, J., in *Henwood* v. *Harrison,*

L. R. 7 C. P. p. 628, and Collins, M.R., in *McQuire* v. *Western Morning News Co.*, [1903] 2 K. B. pp. 112, 113). If he thinks that there is any such evidence fit to go to the jury it will be for the jury to say whether the words do or do not exceed the limits of a fair comment. No witness should be asked whether in his opinion the comment is unfair, for that is the very issue which the jury is asked to decide. It is of course for the defendant to prove the existence of any facts on which he alleges that his comment was based. Lastly, it is for the plaintiff, if need arises, to prove that the words were published maliciously.

The plaintiff will fail " unless the criticism exceeded the bounds of fair comment. . . . It is always for the judge to say whether the document is capable in law of being a libel. It is, however, for the plaintiff, who rests his claim upon a document which on his own statement purports to be a criticism of a matter of public interest, to show that it is a libel, *i.e.*, that it travels beyond the limit of fair criticism; and therefore it must be for the judge to say whether it is reasonably capable of being so interpreted. If it is not, there is no question for the jury, and it would be competent for him to give judgment for the defendant. . . . In my opinion, there is in this case, in the language of Willes, J., above cited, no evidence on which a rational verdict for the plaintiff can be founded, and the defendants are therefore entitled to have judgment entered for them." (Per Collins, M.R., *ib.* pp. 108, 111, 112.) But if the words are reasonably capable of being construed as unfair it is for the jury to determine whether they were or were not a fair comment. (*Cooney* v. *Edeveain*, (1897) 14 Times L. R. 34.)

(i.) *Comment, not Allegation of Fact.*

A comment as we have already stated, is the expression of the judgment passed upon certain alleged facts by one who has applied his mind to them; and who while so commenting, assumes that such allegations of fact are true. The assertion of a fact is not a comment at all. If the words complained of contain allegations of fact which are denied by the plaintiff, and which the defendant cannot prove to be true, there must be a verdict for the plaintiff. It is of no avail for the defendant to urge that he honestly believed them to be true. (*Campbell* v. *Spottiswoode*, 3 B. & S. 769 ; 32 L. J. Q. B. 185.)

Comment on well-known or admitted facts is a very different thing from the assertion of unsubstantiated facts for comment. " There is no doubt that the public acts of a public man may lawfully be made the subject of fair comment or criticism not only by the press, but by all members of the public. But the distinction cannot be too clearly borne in mind between comment or criticism and allegations of fact, such as that disgraceful acts have been committed, or discreditable language used. It is one thing to comment upon or criticise, even with severity, the acknowledged or proved acts of a public man, and quite another to assert that he has been guilty of particular acts of misconduct." (*Per cur.* in *Davis and Sons* v. *Shepstone*, 11 App. Cas. at p. 190 ; 55 L. J. P. C. 51.)

" It was contended, that this libel might be justified as a matter of public discussion on a subject of public interest. The answer is :—This is not a discussion or comment. It is the statement of a fact. To charge a man incorrectly with a disgraceful act, is very different from commenting on a fact relating to him truly stated,—there, the writer may by his opinion, libel himself rather than the subject of his remarks." (Per Wilde, B., in *Popham* v. *Pickburn*, 7 H. & N. at p. 898.) " That a fair and *bonâ fide* comment on a matter of public interest is an excuse of what would otherwise be a defamatory publication is admitted. The very statement, however, of this rule assumes the matters of fact commented upon to be somehow or other ascertained. It does not mean that a man may invent facts, and comment on the facts so invented in what would be a fair and *bonâ fide* manner on the supposition that the facts were true. . . . If the facts as a comment upon which the publication is sought to be excused do not exist, the foundation of the plea fails." (*Lefroy* v. *Burnside* (No. 2), 4 L. R. Ir. at pp. 565, 566 ; *Blair* v. *Cox*, 37 Sol. J. 130.)

It is not enough that the writer honestly believed the facts to be as he alleged. (*Campbell* v. *Spottiswoode*, 3 B. & S. 769; 32 L. J. Q. B. 185; *Peters* v. *Bradlaugh*, (1888) 4 Times L. R. 467.) Immaterial errors as to details will be excused. " It is not to be expected that a public journalist will always be infallible." (Per Cockburn, C.J., 4 F. & F. 217.) But a libellous statement of fact is not a comment or criticism on anything. (Per Field, J., in *R.* v. *Flowers*, 44 J. P. 377.) The facts on which the comments are founded, if not admitted, must be proved substantially as stated by the writer. " A comment cannot be fair which is built upon facts which are not truly stated." (Per Kennedy, J., in *Joynt* v. *Cycle Trade Publishing Co.*, [1904] 2 K. B. at p. 294.)

Illustrations.

If a writer goes out of his way to make a personal attack on the character of the author of the work which he is criticising, he is " going beyond the limits of criticism altogether, and therefore beyond the limits of fair criticism."

> Per Bowen, L.J., in *Merivale and wife* v. *Carson*, 20 Q. B. D. at p. 284.

Again, " the writer would be travelling out of the region of fair criticism if he imputes to the author that he has written something which in fact he has not written. That would be a misdescription of the work."

> Per Bowen, L.J., *ib.*

" Criticism cannot be used as a cloak for mere invective, nor for personal imputations not arising out of the subject-matter or not based on fact."

> Per Collins, M.R., in *McQuire* v. *Western Morning News Co.*, [1903] 2 K. B. at p. 109.

If definite charges of misconduct be made against any public officer on an unprivileged occasion, the only defence to an action is for the defendant to prove his charges true; even though the truth of such charges be a matter of public interest, for such charges are not comments at all.

> *Purcell* v. *Sowler*, 2 C. P. D. 215; 46 L. J. C. P. 308; 36 L. T. 416.

The medical officer of health made a report to the vestry in pursuance of the Metropolis Local Management Act, in which he asserted that the plaintiff, a chemist and druggist, had given false medical certificates, and advised that he should be prosecuted for forgery. The defendant published the whole report in his paper without any comments. *Held*, that there was no privilege, and that the Act afforded the defendant no protection.

> *Popham* v. *Pickburn*, 7 H. & N. 891; 31 L. J. Ex. 133.

A newspaper may comment upon the hearing of a charge of felony and the evidence produced thereat, and discuss the conduct of the magistrates in dismissing the charge without hearing the whole of the evidence ; but it may not proceed to disclose " evidence which might have been adduced " and thus argue from facts not in evidence before the magistrates that the accused was really guilty of the felony. Verdict for the plaintiff. Damages 25*l.*

> *Hibbins* v. *Lee,* 4 F. & F. 243 ; 11 L. T. 541.
>
> And see *Helsham* v. *Blackwood,* 11 C. B. 111, 113 ; 20 L. J. C. P. 187 ; 15 Jur. 861.
>
> *R.* v. *White and another,* 1 Camp. 359, n.

A writer in a newspaper may comment on the fact that corrupt practices extensively prevailed at a parliamentary election ; but may not give the names of individuals as guilty of bribery, unless he can prove the truth of the charge to the letter.

> *Wilson* v. *Reed and others,* 2 F. & F. 149.
>
> *Dickeson* v. *Hilliard and another,* L. R. 9 Ex. 79 ; 43 L. J. Ex. 37 ; 22 W. R. 372 ; 30 L. T. 196.

A newspaper reported that the mother of a lady, who was dead and buried, had applied to the coroner on affidavits for an order that the body might be exhumed, and then proceeded to give a long sensational narrative of shocking acts of cruelty to the deceased committed by her husband, imputing that he had caused her death. This narrative commenced with the words : " From inquiries made by our reporter it appears that the deceased," &c. As a matter of fact the reporter had made no inquiries ; he had merely read the affidavits and accepted the *ex parte* statements contained in them as truth ; they were in fact wholly false. He was convicted and fined 50*l.*

> *R.* v. *Andrew Gray,* 26 J. P. 663.

The defendant published a book entitled " Letters from a Staff Officer in the Crimea," in which he observed that, at the charge of the Light Brigade at Balaclava, Lord Cardigan was not present when most needed, owing to his horse taking fright, swerving, and galloping to the rear. In a note the defendant added : " The author has relied on statements furnished by officers actually engaged in the charge, but as the excellence of Lord Cardigan's horsemanship is unquestionable, the idea that his horse ran away with him is no doubt erroneous." The Court of Queen's Bench held that this was a libel.

> *R.* v. *Calthorpe,* 27 J. P. 581.

A Dublin newspaper asserted that the plaintiff, who was the manager of the Queen's Printing Office in Ireland, had corruptly supplied *Freeman's Journal* with official information and surreptitious copies of official documents. A plea of fair comment, stating that *Freeman's Journal* did somehow get official information earlier than other papers, and that defendant *bonâ fide* believed that such information could only have been obtained from the Queen's Printing Office, was held bad on demurrer.

> *Lefroy* v. *Burnside,* (No. 2) 4 L. R. Ir. 557.

Defendant wrote " A History of New Zealand," and therein stated that the plaintiff, a lieutenant in the Kai Jwi cavalry, had charged at some women and young children who were harmlessly hunting pigs, " and cut them down gleefully and with ease " ; that he had dismissed from the service a subordinate officer who had protested against this cruelty, and that he was ever afterwards known among the Maoris by the nickname " Kohuru " (the murderer). Defendant admitted that these facts did not appear in the official reports, or in any other history of New Zealand ; but he said he had heard rumours to the effect, and he called a witness who had made a statement to the Governor of New Zealand on hearsay evidence, containing substantially the same charge, a copy of which statement the Governor had forwarded to the defendant. Huddleston, B., directed the jury that it was no defence whatever that the charges were made in the *bonâ fide* belief that they were true, and without any malice towards the plaintiff. Verdict for the plaintiff. Damages 5,000*l*.

> *Bryce* v. *Rusden,* (1886) 2 Times L. R. 435.
> *Brenon* v. *Ridgway,* (1887) 3 Times L. R. 592.

The appellants were the owners of a daily newspaper called the *Natal Witness,* in which they constantly attacked the official conduct of the respondent, the British Resident Commissioner in Zululand, asserting that he had himself violently assaulted a Zulu chief, that he had set on his native police to assault and abuse others, &c. They vouched for the truth of these stories, declaring that though some doubt had been thrown on them, they would prove to be true on investigation. They then proceeded, on the assumption that the charges were true, to comment on the respondent's conduct in most offensive and injurious language. At the trial in Natal, on September 4th, 1883, it was proved that the charges against the respondent were absolutely without foundation ; the appellant made no attempt to support them by evidence. Verdict for the plaintiff. Damages 500*l*. Motion for a new trial refused by the Supreme Court of Natal. *Held,* on appeal to the Judicial Committee of the Privy Council, that the distinction must be closely drawn between comment or criticism and allegations of fact ; that such a publication was in no way privileged, and that the damages were not excessive.

> *Davis and Sons* v. *Shepstone,* 11 App. Cas. 187 ; 55 L. J. P. C.
>   51 ; 34 W. R. 722 ; 55 L. T. 1 ; 50 J. P. 709.
> *Walker* v. *Brogden,* 19 C. B. N. S. 65 ; 11 Jur. N. S. 671 ; 13
>   W. R. 809 ; 12 L. T. 495.

A politician asserted that the Marquis of Salisbury had given the plaintiff a cheque to be used " in connexion with the so-called fair-trade meeting of the unemployed, which preceded the riotous meetings in Trafalgar Square." Huddleston, B., held that there was no defence for this statement except an absolute justification.

> *Peters* v. *Bradlaugh,* (1888) 4 Times L. R. 467.
> *Duplany* v. *Davis,* (1886) 3 Times L. R. 184, *ante,* p. 29.

The plaintiff, who was not a qualified medical practitioner but had taken the degree of M.D. at a foreign university, described himself as " a specialist for the treatment of deafness, ear, nose, and throat diseases." The defendant in his newspaper, in discussing the plaintiff's pretensions, said : " Possibly this gentleman may possess all the talents which his alleged foreign degrees denote, but, of course, he is not a qualified medical practitioner, and he happens to be the 'late' physician to the notorious Drouet Institution for the Deaf. In other words he is a quack of the rankest species." *Held,* that these words were capable of being fair comment if warranted by the facts.

> *Dakhyl* v. *Labouchere,* [1908] 2 K. B. 329, n. ; 77 L. J. K. B. 728 ; 96 L. T. 399 ; 23 Times L. R. 364.

The defendants published an account of the conduct of the plaintiff as deputy returning officer at an election, and described it as "an assertion of political bias" and as unfair treatment towards the candidates of one party. *Held,* that the judge should have directed the jury that this language was capable of being a comment and not a statement of fact.

> *Hunt* v. *Star Newspaper Co., Limited,* [1908] 2 K. B. 309 ; 77 L. J. K. B. 732 ; 98 L. T. 629 ; 24 Times L. R. 452.

If, then, in the same article allegations of fact are mixed up with comment, and both are *primâ facie* libellous and are included in the Statement of Claim, the defendant must establish two things :—

(a) That so much of the article as alleges facts is true, or is privileged, and

(b) That so much of the article as expresses the defendant's opinion on the facts stated relates to a matter of public interest, and is a fair and *bonâ fide* comment thereon.

The defence of fair comment is now usually pleaded in the form which received the sanction of the Divisional Court in *Penrhyn* v. *The Licensed Victuallers' Mirror,* (1890) 7 Times L. R. 1 (see *post,* p. 634), which runs as follows :—

"In so far as they consist of allegations of fact, the said words are true in substance and in fact, and in so far as they consist of expressions of opinion they are fair comments made in good faith and without malice upon the said facts, which are matters of public interest." It will be observed that this is a distinct and different plea from the plea that the words are no libel and also from the plea that the words are true in substance and in fact. It is a plea of justification only so far as the allegations of fact contained in the libel are concerned ; it is not necessary to justify the comments. Nor is it necessary in every case for the defendant to justify the allegations of fact ; it is enough if those statements are privileged. They may be privileged as being a fair and accurate report of a trial or of the proceedings at a public meeting or an extract from a Parliamentary or other official paper. (*Cox* v. *Feeney,* 4 F. & F. 13, *post,* p. 212 ; and see *Cooper* v. *Lawson,* 8 A. & E. at pp. 753, 754 ; *Mangena* v. *Wright,* [1909] 2 K. B. at p. 977.)

Where a writer is commenting on a speech made at a public

meeting, or the evidence given at a certain trial, so long as he makes it clear that he is only repeating what was said on those privileged occasions, he will not be compelled to justify his report. But if, in repeating the statements of the speaker or witness, the writer expressly or impliedly warrants the accuracy of such statements, and asserts that they are true, then he makes them his own statements, and he must justify them. He is no longer commenting on the speech or the evidence; he is asserting facts. Again, if the defendant was criticising statements of fact made by the plaintiff, he need not aver or prove the truth of such statements; for where a critic accepts the plaintiff's statements and makes them the basis of his comment, the truth of those statements is not in issue. (*Digby* v. *Financial News, Ltd.*, [1907] 1 K. B. 502; 76 L. J. K. B. 321; 96 L. T. 172.)

Sometimes, however, it is difficult to distinguish an allegation of fact from an expression of opinion. It often depends on what is stated in the rest of the article. If the defendant accurately states what some public man has really done, and then asserts that " such conduct is disgraceful," this is merely the expression of his opinion, his comment on the plaintiff's conduct. So, if without setting it out, he identifies the conduct on which he comments by a clear reference. In either case, the defendant enables his readers to judge for themselves how far his opinion is well founded; and, therefore, what would otherwise have been an allegation of fact becomes merely a comment. But if he asserts that the plaintiff has been guilty of disgraceful conduct, and does not state what that conduct was, this is an allegation of fact for which there is no defence but privilege or truth.

The same considerations apply where a defendant has drawn from certain facts an inference derogatory to the plaintiff. If he states the bare inference without the facts on which it is based, such inference will be treated as an allegation of fact. But if he sets out the facts correctly, and then gives his inference, stating it as his inference from those facts, such inference will, as a rule, be deemed a comment. But even in this case the writer must be careful to state the inference as an inference, and not to assert it as a new and independent fact ; otherwise, his inference will become something more than a comment, and he may be driven to justify it as an allegation of fact.

A statement of one fact may be a fair comment upon another fact. But "when a matter of fact is to be excused as comment upon another fact, the fact alleged and sought to be excused must be a reasonable inference from the fact alleged, and upon which it is a comment." (Per Palles, C.B., in *Lefroy* v. *Burnside*, (No. 2) 4 L. R. Ir. 556 ; *O'Brien* v. *Marquis of Salisbury*, (1889) 6 Times L. R. 133, 137.) Whether it can be reasonably inferred is a question of law for the judge. If it can, it is for the jury to determine in any particular case whether it ought to be inferred. (Per Lord Atkinson in *Dakhyl* v. *Labouchere*, [1908] 2 K. B. at p. 329.)

"Real comment is merely the expression of opinion. Misdescription is matter of fact. If the misdescription is such an unfaithful representation of a person's conduct as to induce people to think that he has done something dishonourable, disgraceful, and contemptible, it is clearly libellous. To state accurately what a man has done, and then to say that in your opinion such conduct is dishonourable or disgraceful, is comment which may do no harm, as every one can judge for himself, whether the opinion expressed is well founded or not. Misdescription of conduct, on the other hand, only leads to the one conclusion detrimental to the person whose conduct is misdescribed, and leaves the reader no opportunity of judging for himself of the character of the conduct condemned, nothing but a false picture being presented for judgment." (Per Windeyer, J., in *Christie* v. *Robertson*, 10 New South Wales Law Reports, at p. 161.)

Illustrations.

If a man put himself forward as a public man holding a public office, every one has a right to comment on his fitness for the office which he held ; and so long as the critic confines himself to comments on the man's fitness or unfitness for the office, the comments are not actionable. Per Martin, B., in

Harle v. *Catherall and others,* 14 L. T. at p. 801.

Two sureties were proposed for the Berwick election petition, neither of whom had any connection with the borough. Affidavits were put in to show that one of them (the plaintiff) was an insufficient surety, being embarrassed in his affairs. The *Times* set out these affidavits and added the remarks, "But why, it may be asked, does this cockney tailor take all this trouble, and subject himself to all this exposure of his difficulties and embarrassments ? He has nothing to do with the borough of Berwick-upon-Tweed or its members. How comes it then that he should take so much interest in the job ? There can be but one answer to these very natural and reasonable queries : *he is hired for the occasion.* The affair in fact is a foul job throughout, and it is only by such aid that it can possibly be supported." In an action brought on the whole article, the defendant pleaded that the publication was a correct report of certain legal proceedings, " together with a fair and *bonâ fide* commentary thereon." But the jury thought the comment was not fair, and gave the plaintiff damages, 100*l.*

> *Cooper* v. *Lawson,* 8 A. & E. 746 ; 1 P. & D. 15 ; 1 W. W. & H. 601 ; 2 Jur. 919.

The plaintiff in this case relied mainly on the words " he is hired for the occasion." As to this allegation, Lord Denman, C.J., in his judgment, said :—" It would be extravagant to say that, in cases of libel, every comment upon facts requires a justification. But a comment may introduce independent facts, a justification of which is necessary. The plea is perfectly good, justifying the libel, partly as the report of proceedings before a Court, partly as stating that which is in itself true, and partly as giving a fair and *bonâ fide* commentary on the proceedings stated. Now a comment may be the mere shadow of the previous imputation ; but, if it infers a new fact, the defendant must abide by that inference of fact, and the fairness of the comment must be decided upon by a jury. The defendant here cannot say that if the plaintiff became bail under the circumstances stated, it followed as a necessary inference that he was hired."

> *Ib.,* 8 A. & E. pp. 753, 754.

The secretary of a company in liquidation was examined before the official receiver, and in his answers made statements derogatory to one of the directors who was not present or represented at the examination. A local newspaper commented on the statements made by the witness in a spirit hostile to the absent director, and then proceeded :—" How Mr. S. could have been a party to such proceedings passes our comprehension. As a matter of fact, however, he was not merely a party to the affair, but one of the principals," &c. *Held,* by Lawrance, J., that none of the observations that followed the words " As a matter of fact, however," could claim protection as comment. Damages 100*l.*

> *Strauss* v. *Heard and Son,* (Bodmin Summer Assizes, 1894) *unreported.*

If a man puts himself forward as qualified to treat diseases anybody may discuss his pretensions, and if the facts warrant such an inference, he may be described as " a quack of the rankest species."

> *Dakhyl* v. *Labouchere,* [1908] 2 K. B. 325, n. ; 77 L. J. K. B. 728 ; 96 L. T. 399 ; 23 Times L. R. 364.

(ii.) *The Comment must be on a Matter of Public Interest.*

What are matters of public interest ?

The public conduct of every public man is a matter of

public concern. So is the management of every public institution; and the conduct of every public body, imperial, local, or municipal.

"A clergyman with his flock, an admiral with his fleet, a general with his army, and a judge with his jury, are all subjects of public discussion. Whoever fills a public position renders himself open thereto. He must accept an attack as a necessary, though unpleasant, appendage to his office." (Per Bramwell, B., in *Kelly* v. *Sherlock*, L. R. 1 Q. B. 689; 35 L. J. Q. B. 209; 12 Jur. N. S. 937.)

Matters of public interest may be conveniently grouped under the following heads :—

1. Affairs of State ;
2. The administration of justice ;
3. Public institutions and local authorities ;
4. Ecclesiastical matters ;
5. Books, pictures, and architecture ;
6. Theatres, concerts, and other public entertainments ;
7. Other appeals to the public.

Lord Coleridge, C.J., decided in *Weldon* v. *Johnson, Times,* May 27th, 1884, that it was a question for the judge and not for the jury, whether a particular topic was or was not a matter of public interest. And in *South Hetton Coal Co., Ltd.* v. *North Eastern News Association,* [1894] 1 Q. B., at p. 141, Lopes, L.J., says : "The Court decides whether the matter commented on is one of public interest." The Court of Appeal expressed the same opinion in *Dakhyl* v. *Labouchere, Times,* July 29th, 1904.

1. *Affairs of State.*

The conduct of all public servants, the policy of the Government, our relations with foreign countries, all suggestions of reforms in the existing laws, all bills before Parliament, the adjustment and collection of taxes, and all other matters which touch the public welfare, are clearly matters of public interest, which come within the preceding rule. "Every subject has a right to comment on those acts of public men which concern him as a subject of the realm, if he do not make his commentary a cloak for malice and slander." (Per Parke, B., in *Parmiter* v. *Coupland*, 6 M. & W. 108.) Those who fill " a public position must not be too thin-skinned in reference to comments made upon them. It would often happen that observations would be made upon public men which they knew from the bottom of their hearts were undeserved and unjust; yet they must bear with them, and submit to be misunderstood for a time, because all knew that the criticism of the press was the best security for the proper discharge of public duties." (Per Cockburn, C.J., in *Seymour* v. *Butterworth*, 3 F. & F. 376, 377; and see the *dicta* of the judges in *R.* v. *Sir R. Carden*, 5 Q. B. D. 1; 49 L. J. M. C. 1; 28 W. R. 133; 41 L. T. 504.)

Illustrations.

The presentation of a petition to Parliament impugning the character of one of His Majesty's judges, and praying for an inquiry, and for his removal from office should the charge prove true, is a matter of high public concern, on which all newspapers may comment, and in severe terms. So is a debate in the House on the subject of such petition.

> *Wason* v. *Walter,* L. R. 4 Q. B. 73; 8 B. & S. 730; 38 L. J.
> Q. B. 34; 17 W. R. 169; 19 L. T. 409.

The presentation of a petition to Parliament against quack doctors is matter for public comment.

> *Dunne* v. *Anderson,* 3 Bing. 88; Ry. & Moo. 287; 10 Moore,
> 407.

Evidence given before a Royal Commission is matter *publici juris,* and every one has a perfect right to criticise it. Per Wickens, V.-C., in

> *Mulkern* v. *Ward,* L. R. 13 Eq. 622; 41 L. J. Ch. 464; 26
> L. T. 831.

So is evidence taken before a Parliamentary Committee on a local gas bill.

> *Hedley* v. *Barlow,* 4 F. & F. 224.

A report of the Board of Admiralty upon the plans of a naval architect, submitted to the Lords of the Admiralty for their consideration, is a matter of national interest.

> *Henwood* v. *Harrison,* L. R. 7 C. P. 606; 41 L. J. C. P. 206;
> 20 W. R. 1000; 26 L. T. 938.

The appointment of a Roman Catholic to be Calendarer of State Papers is a matter of public concern.

> *Turnbull* v. *Bird,* 2 F. & F. 508.
> *Lefroy* v. *Burnside,* (No. 2) 4 L. R. Ir. 556.

All appointments by the Government to any office are matters of public concern.

> *Seymour* v. *Butterworth,* 3 F. & F. 372.

The conduct of the officials in charge of a polling booth at an election is a matter of public interest.

> *Hunt* v. *Star Newspaper Co., Limited,* [1908] 2 K. B. 309 ; 77
> L. J. K. B. 732 ; 98 L. T. 629 ; 24 Times L. R. 452.

A newspaper is entitled to comment on the fact (if it be one) that corrupt practices extensively prevailed at a recent Parliamentary election, so long as it does not make charges against individuals.

> *Wilson* v. *Reed and others,* 2 F. & F. 149.

A meeting assembled to hear a political address by a candidate at a Parliamentary election, and the conduct thereat of all persons who take any part in such meeting, are fair subjects for *bonâ fide* discussion by a writer in a public newspaper.

> *Davis* v. *Duncan,* L. R. 9 C. P. 396 ; 43 L. J. C. P. 185 ; 22
> W. R. 575 ; 30 L. T. 464.

The public career of any member of Parliament, or of any candidate for Parliament, is of course a matter of public interest in the constituency, but not his private life and history. "However large the privilege of electors may be," said Lord Denman, C.J., "it is extravagant to suppose that it can justify the publication to all the world of facts injurious to a person who happens to stand in the situation of a candidate."

> *Duncombe* v. *Daniell,* 8 C. & P. 222 ; 2 Jur. 32 ; 1 W. W. &
> H. 101.

It is submitted, however, that the electors are entitled to investigate all matters in the past private life of a candidate which, if true, would prove him morally or intellectually unfit to represent them in Parliament ; but not to state as facts what they only know as rumours.

> *Harwood* v. *Sir J. Ashley,* 1 B. & P. N. R. 47.
> *Wisdom* v. *Brown,* (1885) 1 Times L. R. 412.
> *Pankhurst* v. *Hamilton,* (1887) 3 Times L. R. 500.

"Any person who before, or during any Parliamentary election, shall, for the purpose of affecting the return of any candidate at such election, make or publish any false statement of fact in relation to the personal character or conduct of such candidate, shall be guilty of an illegal practice," and shall also be liable to be restrained by an injunction from any repetition of such false statement.

> 58 & 59 Vict. c. 40, ss. 1, 2, and 3 ; see *post,* 437, 438.

In America the law on this point varies greatly in the different States.

In New York no attack is allowed even on the public character of any public officer ; and that the defendant honestly believed in the truth of the charge is no defence. No distinction is made between a public man and a private citizen.

> *Hamilton* v. *Eno,* 81 N. Y. 116.
> *Lewis* v. *Few,* 5 Johns. 1.
> *Root* v. *King,* 7 Cowen, 613 ; 4 Wend. 113.

So in West Virginia.

> *Sweeney* v. *Baker,* 13 West Virginia R. 158.

And in Massachusetts.

Commonwealth v. *Clap,* 4 Mass. 103.

Curtis v. *Mussey,* 6 Gray (72 Mass.), 261.

In Michigan, the Supreme Court decided that " the public are interested in knowing the character of candidates for Congress, and while no one can lawfully destroy the reputation of a candidate by falsehood, yet, if an honest mistake is made in an honest attempt to enlighten the public, it must reduce the damages to a minimum if the fault itself is not serious."

Bailey v. *Kalamazoo Publishing Co.,* 40 Mich. (4 Chaney) 251.

Scripps v. *Foster,* 39 Mich. 376 ; 41 Mich. 742.

In New Hampshire, a newspaper may state in good faith and on reasonable grounds that any public officer has been guilty of official misconduct.

Palmer v. *Concord,* 48 N. H. 211.

And in Iowa charges affecting the *moral* character of any public man are protected if made in good faith and on reasonable grounds.

Mott v. *Dawson,* 46 Iowa, 533.

2. *Administration of Justice.*

The administration of the law, the verdicts of juries, the conduct of suitors and their witnesses, are all matters of lawful comment as soon as the trial is over. But no observations on the case are permitted during its progress. Any comment pending action is a contempt of Court, by whomsoever made ; it is especially so where the comment is supplied by one of the litigants or his solicitor or counsel. (*Daw* v. *Eley,* L. R. 7 Eq. 49 ; 38 L. J. Ch. 113 ; 17 W. R. 245.) And see Chap. XX., *post,* p. 535.

As soon as the case is over, every one has "a right to discuss fairly and *bonâ fide* the administration of justice as evidenced at this trial. It is open to him to show that error was committed on the part of the judge or jury ; nay, further, for myself I will say that the judges invite discussion of their acts in the administration of the law, and it is a relief to them to see error pointed out, if it is committed ; yet, whilst they invite the freest discussion, it is not open to a journalist to impute corruption." (Per Fitzgerald, J., in *R.* v. *Sullivan,* 11 Cox, C. C. 57.) " That the administration of justice should be made a subject for the exercise of public discussion is a matter of the most essential importance. But, on the other hand, it behoves those who pass judgment, and call upon the public to pass judgment, on those who are suitors to, or witnesses in courts of justice, not to give reckless vent to harsh and uncharitable views of the conduct of others; but to remember that they are bound to exercise a fair and honest, and an impartial judgment upon those whom they hold up to public obloquy." (Per Cockburn, C.J., in *Woodgate v. Ridout,* 4 F. & F. 223, 224.) "Writers in public papers are of great utility, and do great benefit to the public interests by watching the proceedings of courts of justice, and fairly commenting on them if there is anything that calls for observation; but they should be careful, in discharging that function, that they do not wantonly assail the character of others, or impute criminality to them, and if they do so, and do not bring to the performance of the duty they discharge that due regard for the interests of others which the assumption of so important a censorship necessarily requires, they must take the consequences." (Per Cockburn, C.J., in *R. v. Tanfield,* 42 J. P. at p. 424.)

Illustrations.

It is lawful with decency and candour to discuss the propriety of the verdict of a jury, or the decisions of a judge; but if the words complained of contain no reasoning or discussion, but only declamation and invective, and were written not with a view to elucidate the truth, but to injure the character of individuals and to bring into contempt and hatred the administration of justice, they cannot be considered fair comment on a matter of public interest.

> *R. v. White and another,* (1808) 1 Camp. 359, n.

It is not a fair comment on a criminal trial to suggest that the prisoner, though acquitted, was really guilty.

> *Risk Allah Bey v. Whitehurst and others,* 18 L. T. 615.
>
> *Lewis v. Walter,* 4 B. & Ald. 605.

It is not a fair comment on any legal proceeding to insinuate that a particular witness committed perjury in the course of it.

> *Roberts v. Brown,* 10 Bing. 519; 4 Moo. & S. 407.
>
> *Stiles v. Nokes,* S. C. *Carr v. Jones,* 7 East, 493; 3 Smith, 491.
>
> *Littler v. Thomson,* 2 Beav. 129.
>
> *Felkin v. Herbert,* 33 L. J. Ch. 294; 10 Jur. N. S. 62; 12 W. R. 241, 332; 9 L. T. 635.

The plaintiff was a dissenting minister. His maidservant gave birth to an illegitimate child and accused him of being its father. She took out an affiliation summons against him, which was dismissed for want of corroboration. The defendants inserted articles and letters in their paper, which insisted that the girl's story was true, and alluded to the plaintiff as "a gay deceiver," &c. Damages 2,000l. The Divisional Court refused to set aside the verdict or to reduce the amount of damages.

> *Roberts v. Owen and others,* (1888) 5 Times L. R. 11; 53 J. P. 502.

A newspaper may comment on the evidence given by any particular witness in any inquiry on a matter of public interest; but may not go the length of declaring such evidence to be "maliciously or recklessly false." Verdict for the plaintiff ; damages 250*l.*

> *Hedley* v. *Barlow,* 4 F. & F. 224.

A newspaper may comment on the conduct of magistrates in dismissing a case without hearing the whole of the evidence, or in committing the prisoner for trial on insufficient evidence ; but it must not impute that in so doing the magistrates acted deliberately and consciously from political motives.

> *Hibbins* v. *Lee,* 4 F. &. F. 243 ; 11 L. T. 541.

No comment is admissible on any facts or documents which were not put in evidence at the trial.

> *Helsham* v. *Blackwood,* 11 C. B. 111 ; 20 L. J. C. P. 187 ; 15 Jur. 861.
>
> *R.* v. *Andrew Gray,* 26 J. P. 663.

The details of a long protracted squabble between a professional singer and a great composer do not become matters of public interest, merely because the former ultimately applies to a police magistrate for a summons against the latter.

> *Weldon* v. *Johnson, Times,* May 27th, 1884.

The *Morning Post* published an article on a trial which had greatly excited public attention, giving a highly-coloured account of the conduct of the attorneys on one side, concluding with the sweeping condemnation : —"Messrs. Quirk, Gammon, and Snap, were fairly equalled, if not outdone," alluding to the notorious firm of pettifoggers in "Ten Thousand a Year." This account of plaintiff's conduct was taken almost *verbatim* from the speech of counsel on the other side, and no allusion was made to the evidence subsequently produced to rebut his statements. Verdict for the plaintiff ; damages 1,000*l.*

> *Woodgate* v. *Ridout,* 4 F. & F. 202.

3. *Public Institutions and Local Authorities.*

The working of all public institutions, such as colleges, hospitals, asylums, homes, is a matter of public interest, especially where such institutions appeal to the public for subscriptions, or are supported by the rates, or are, like our Universities, national property. The management of local affairs by the various local authorities, *e.g.,* county councils, district councils, town councils, boards of guardians, vestries, &c., is a matter of public, though it may not be of universal, concern.

"Whatever is matter of public concern when administered in one of the Government departments, is matter of public concern when administered by the subordinate authorities of a particular district. It is one of the characteristic features of the government of this country that, instead of being centralised, many important branches of it are committed to the conduct of local authorities. Thus, the business of counties, and that of cities and boroughs, is, to a great extent, conducted by local and municipal government. It is not, therefore, because the matter under consideration is one which in its immediate consequence affects only a particular neighbourhood that it is not a matter of public concern. The management of the poor and the administration of the poor-law in each local district are matters of public interest. In this management the medical attendance on the poor is a matter of infinite moment, and consequently the conduct of a medical officer of the district may be of the greatest importance in that particular district, and so may concern the public in general." (Per Cockburn, C.J., in *Purcell* v. *Sowler*, 2 C. P. D. at p. 218 ; and see the remarks of the same learned judge in *Cox* v. *Feeney*, 4 F. & F. at p. 20.)

Illustrations.

The sanitary condition of a large number of cottages let by the proprietors of a colliery to their workmen, and in which over 2,000 persons resided, is a matter of public interest.

> *South Hetton Coal Co., Limited* v. *North Eastern News Association,* [1894] 1 Q. B. 133 ; 63 L. J. Q. B. 293 ; 42 W. R. 322 ; 69 L. T. 844 ; 58 J. P. 196 ; 9 R. 240.

The official conduct of a way-warden may be freely criticised in the local press.

> *Harle* v. *Catherall,* (1866) 14 L. T. 801.

The manner in which a coroner's officer treats the poor relatives of the deceased when serving them with a summons for an inquest, and the behaviour of such officer in Court, are matters of public concern.

> Per Bowen, J., in *Sheppard* v. *Lloyd, Daily Chronicle,* March 11th, 1882.

The Charity Commissioners sent an inspector to inquire into the working of a medical college at Birmingham. He made a report containing passages defamatory of the plaintiff, one of the professors. The mismanagement of the college continued and increased. The warden at last filed a bill to administer the funds in Chancery. Thereupon the defendant, the proprietor of a local paper, procured an official copy of the report of the inspector, and published it *verbatim* in his paper. This was nearly three years after the report had been written. The plaintiff contended that this was a wanton revival of stale matter which could not be required for public information ; but Cockburn, C.J., left it to the jury to say whether public interest in the matter had not rather increased than declined in the interval. Verdict for the defendant.

> *Cox* v. *Feeney,* (1836) 4 F. & F. 13.

But the conduct of the trustee of a private corporation, as such trustee, is not a matter of public interest.

Wilson v. *Fitch,* 41 Cal. 363.

The conduct of a returning officer at a county council election is a matter of public interest.

Hunt v. *Star Newspaper Co., Limited,* [1908] 2 K. B. 309 ; 77 L. J. K. B. 732 ; 98 L. T. 629 ; 24 Times L. R. 452.

4. *Ecclesiastical Affairs.*

A bishop's government of his diocese, a rector's management of his parish, or of the parochial school, are matters of public interest. So is the manner in which public worship is celebrated in the Established Church.

Illustrations.

The press may comment on the fact that the incumbent of a parish has, contrary to the wishes of the churchwarden, allowed books to be sold in the church during service, and cooked a chop in the vestry after the service was over.

Kelly v. *Tinling,* L. R. 1 Q. B. 699 ; 35 L. J. Q. B. 231 ; 14 W. R. 51 ; 13 L. T. 255 ; 12 Jur. N. S. 940.

But where a vicar started a clothing society in his parish, expressly excluding all Dissenters from its benefits, it was held that this was essentially a private society, the members of which might manage it as they pleased, without being called to account by any one outside : and that therefore a Dissenting organ was not justified in commenting on the limits which the vicar had imposed on the desire of his parishioners to clothe the poor.

Gathercole v. *Miall,* 15 M. & W. 319 ; 15 L. J. Ex. 179 ; 10 Jur. 337.

And see *Walker* v. *Brogden,* 19 C. B. N. S. 65 ; 11 Jur. N. S. 671 ; 13 W. R. 809 ; 12 L. T. 495.

Booth v. *Briscoe,* 2 Q. B. D. 496 ; 25 W. R. 838.

The Court in *Gathercole* v. *Miall* were equally divided on the question whether sermons preached in open church, but not printed and published, were matter for public comment. If the sermon itself dealt with matters of public interest, it is submitted it would be.

5. *Books, Pictures, &c.*

"A man who publishes a book challenges criticism." (Per Cockburn, C.J., in *Strauss* v. *Francis,* 4 F. & F. 1114 ; 15 L. T. 675.) Therefore all fair and honest criticism on any published book is not libellous. But the critic must not go out of his way to attack the private character of the author. (*Fraser* v. *Berkeley,* 7 C. & P. 621.) So, too, it is not libellous fairly and honestly to criticise a painting publicly exhibited, or the architecture of any public building, however strong the terms of censure used may be. (*Thompson* v. *Shackell*, Moo. & Mal. 187.)

Illustrations.

The *Athenæum* published a critique on a novel written by the plaintiff, describing it as " the very worst attempt at a novel that has ever been perpetrated," and commenting severely on " its insanity, self-complacency, and vulgarity, its profanity, its indelicacy (to use no stronger word), its display of bad Latin, bad French, bad German, and bad English," and its abuse of persons living and dead. After Erle, C.J., had summed up the case, the plaintiff withdrew a juror.

> *Strauss* v. *Francis* (No. 1), 4 F. & F. 939.
> See *Sir John Carr* v. *Hood,* 1 Camp. 355, n.

The *Athenæum* thereupon published another article stating their reason for consenting to the withdrawal of a juror, which was in fact that they considered the plaintiff would have been unable to have paid them their costs, had they gained a verdict. The plaintiff thereupon brought another action which was tried before Cockburn, C.J., and the jury found a verdict for the defendants.

> *Strauss* v. *Francis* (No. 2), 4 F. & F. 1107 ; 15 L. T. 674.

To accuse a dramatic author falsely of having written an immoral play is a libel on him, not fair comment on his play.

> *Merivale and wife* v. *Carson,* 20 Q. B. D. 275 ; 36 W. R. 231 ;
> 58 L. T. 331 ; 52 J. P. 261.

A charge of plagiarism is not a fair comment.

> Per Vaughan Williams, L.J., in *Joynt* v. *Cycle Trade Publishing Co.,* [1904] 2 K. B. at p. 297.

It is doubtful how far a book printed for private circulation only may be criticised.

> Per Pollock, C.B., in *Gathercole* v. *Miall,* 15 M. & W. 334 ; 15 L. J. Ex. 179 ; 10 Jur. 337.

A comic picture of the author of a book, *as author,* bowing beneath the weight of his volume, may be fair criticism ; though a personal caricature of him as he appeared in private life would not be.

> *Sir John Carr* v. *Hood,* 1 Camp. 355, n.

The articles which appear in a newspaper and its general tone and style may be the subject of adverse criticism, as well as any other literary production ; but no attack should be made on the private character of any writer on its staff.

> *Heriot* v. *Stuart,* 1 Esp. 437.
> *Stuart* v. *Lovell,* 2 Stark. 93.
> *Campbell* v. *Spottiswoode,* 3 F. & F. 421 ; 32 L. J. Q. B. 185 ;
> 3 B. & S. 769 ; 9 Jur. N. S. 1069 ; 11 W. R. 569 ; 8 L. T. 201.

The greatest art critic of the day wrote and published in *Fors Clavigera* an article on the pictures in the Grosvenor Gallery, in which the following passage occurred : " Lastly, the mannerisms and errors of these pictures [alluding to the pictures of Mr. Burne Jones], whatever may be their extent, are never affected or indolent. The work is natural to the painter, however strange to us, and is wrought with the utmost conscience of care, however far to his own or our desire the result may yet be incomplete. Scarcely as much can be said for any other pictures of the modern school ; their eccentricities are almost always in some degree forced, and their imperfections gratuitously, if not impertinently, indulged. For Mr. Whistler's own sake, no less than for the protection of the purchaser, Sir Coutts Lindsay ought not to have admitted works into the gallery in which the ill-educated conceit of the artist so nearly approached the aspect of wilful imposture. I have seen and heard much of cockney impudence before now, but never expected to hear a coxcomb ask 200 guineas for flinging a pot of paint in the public's face." The jury considered the words " wilful imposture " as just overstepping the line of fair criticism, and found a verdict for the plaintiff ; damages one farthing. Each party had to pay his own costs.

Whistler v. *Ruskin, Times,* Nov. 26th and 27th, 1878.

Thompson v. *Shackell,* Moo. & Mal. 187.

The plaintiff was a professor of architecture in the Royal Academy. The defendant published an account of a new order of architecture called " the Bœotian," said to be invented by the plaintiff, whom he termed " the Bœotian professor." He set forth several absurd principles as the rules of this new order, illustrating them by examples of buildings all of which were the works of the plaintiff. The jury, under the direction of Lord Tenterden, C.J., found a verdict for the defendant.

Soane v. *Knight,* Moo. & Mal. 74.

And see *Gott* v. *Pulsifer,* 122 Mass. 235.

Cooper v. *Stone,* 24 Wend. 434.

The plaintiff, having published a biography of a deceased editor of the *Daily News* named Robinson, which was reviewed in *Punch,* brought an action for libel against the printers and publishers and the reviewer. The article, which was headed " Mangled Remains," implied that the plaintiff was lacking in skill and capacity, and charged him with having relegated the subject of the biography to the background in order to obtrude his own personality on the reader. The reviewer spoke of the plaintiff " brushing off the bloom " from the anecdotes, mutilating the extracts from Robinson's MS., and being unjust to Robinson and unfair to the public, and characterised the work generally as a " slight " on the deceased. Evidence of personal *animus* in the reviewer was given. *Held,* that the jury had rightly found for the plaintiff.

Thomas v. *Bradbury, Agnew & Co., Limited,* [1906] 2 K. B. 627 ; 77 L. J. K. B. 726 ; 54 W. R. 608 ; 95 L. T. 23 ; 22 Times L. R. 656.

6. *Theatres, Concerts, and Public Entertainments.*

All theatrical and musical performances, flower shows, concerts, public balls, &c., may be freely criticised, provided that the comments be not malevolent, and no misstatement of fact be made.

Illustrations.

The prosecutor, who was wholly unconnected with the stage, got up what he called " a Dramatic Ball." The company was disorderly and far from select. No actor or actress of any reputation was present at the ball, or took any share in the arrangements. The *Era,* the special organ of the theatrical profession, published an indignant article, commenting severely on the conduct of the prosecutor in starting such a ball for his own profit, and particularly in calling such an assembly " a Dramatic Ball." See the article, 44 J. P. 377. Criminal proceedings were taken against the editor of the *Era,* but the jury found him Not guilty.

> *R.* v. *Ledger, Times,* Jan. 14th, 1880.
> And see *Dibdin* v. *Swan and Bostock,* (1793) 1 Esp. 28.
> *Cooney* v. *Edeveain,* (1897) 14 Times L. R. 34.

The defendant wrote an article in a newspaper advising an actor to return to " his old profession, that of a waiter." This actor had never been a waiter. Damages 100*l.*

> *Duplany* v. *Davis,* (1886) 3 Times L. R. 184.

A newspaper, commenting on a flower show, denounced one exhibitor by name as " a beggarly soul," " famous in all sorts of dirty work," and spoke of " the tricks by which he and a few like him used to secure prizes" as being now " broken in upon by some judges more honest than usual." Such remarks are clearly *not* fair criticism on the flower show.

> *Green* v. *Chapman,* (1837) 4 Bing. N. C. 92 ; 5 Scott, 340.

The plaintiff, the proprietor of Zadkiel's Almanac, had a ball of crystal by means of which he pretended to tell what was going on in the other world. The *Daily Telegraph* published a letter which stated that the plaintiff had " gulled " many of the nobility with this crystal ball, that he took money for " these profane acts, and made a good thing of it." Cockburn, C.J., directed the jury that a newspaper might expose what it deemed an imposition on the public ; but that this letter amounted to a charge that the plaintiff had made money by wilful and fraudulent misrepresentations, a charge which should not be made without fair grounds. Verdict for the plaintiff. Damages one farthing.

> *Morrison* v. *Belcher,* (1863) 3 F. & F. 614.

7. *Other Appeals to the Public.*

A man may by his conduct bring himself, or his inventions, or the goods in which he deals, within the rule relating to matters of public interest. This is so when a vendor advertises some new invention, or distributes handbills or circulars recommending the public to purchase his wares.

Again, where a man appeals to the public by writing

letters to the newspaper, either to expose what he deems abuses, or to call attention to his own particular grievances, he cannot complain if the editor inserts other letters in answer to his own, refuting his charges, and denying his facts. A man who has commenced a newspaper warfare cannot complain if he gets the worst of it. But if such answer goes further, and touches on fresh matter in no way connected with the plaintiff's original letter, or unnecessarily assails the plaintiff's private character, then it ceases to be an answer; it becomes a counter-charge, and if defamatory will be actionable. (See *post*, p. 292.)

And generally when a man puts himself prominently forward in any way, and acquires for a time a *quasi*-public position, he cannot escape the necessary consequence—the free expression of public opinion. Whoever seeks notoriety, or invites public attention, is said to challenge public criticism; and he cannot resort to the law Courts if that criticism be less favourable than he anticipated.

Illustrations.

A medical man who had obtained a diploma and the degree of M.D. from America advertised most extensively a new and infallible cure for consumption. The *Pall Mall Gazette* published a leading article on the subject of such advertisements, in which they called the advertiser a quack and an impostor, and compared him to "scoundrels who pass bad coin." The jury gave the plaintiff one farthing damages.

> *Hunter* v. *Sharpe*, 4 F. & F. 983; 15 L. T. 421.
>
> And see *Morrison and another* v. *Harmer and another*, 3 Bing. N. C. 759; 4 Scott, 524; 3 Hodges, 108.
>
> *Dakhyl* v. *Labouchere*, [1908] 2 K. B. 325, n.; 77 L. J. K. B. 728; 96 L. T. 399; 23 Times L. R. 364.

Any advertisement issued by a trader puffing his wares or inviting the public to do business with him is a matter of public concern.

> *Paris* v. *Levy*, 9 C. B. N. S. 342; 30 L. J. C. P. 11; 9 W. R. 71; 3 L. T. 324; 7 Jur. N. S. 289; *post*, p. 221.
>
> And see *Eastwood* v. *Holmes*, 1 F. & F. 347.
>
> *Jenner and another* v. *A'Beckett*, L. R. 7 Q. B. 11; 41 L. J. Q. B. 14; 20 W. R. 181; 25 L. T. 464; *ante*, p. 36.

Two clergymen were engaged in a controversy; one, the plaintiff, wrote a pamphlet; subsequently he published a "collection of opinions of the press" on his own pamphlet, including an inaccurate or garbled extract from an article which had appeared in the defendant's newspaper. The defendant thereupon felt it his duty, in justice to the other clergyman, to publish an article in his newspaper exposing the inaccuracy of the extract as given by the plaintiff, and accusing him of purposely adding some passages and suppressing others, so as to entirely alter the sense. Erle, C.J., pointed out to the jury that the defendant was maintaining the truth, and that although he was led into exaggerated language, the plaintiff had also used exaggerated language himself. Verdict for the defendant.

> *Hibbs* v. *Wilkinson*, 1 F. & F. 608.

But where the editor of the *Lancet* attacked the editor of a rival paper, the *London Medical and Physical Journal*, by rancorous aspersions on his private character, the plaintiff recovered a verdict ; damages 5*l.*

> *Macleod* v. *Wakley*, 3 C. & P. 311.

So wherever a man calls public attention to his own grievances or those of his class, whether by letters in a newspaper, by speeches at public meetings, or by the publication of pamphlets, he must expect to have his assertions challenged, the existence of his grievances denied, and himself ridiculed and assailed.

> *Odger* v. *Mortimer*, 28 L. T. 472.
> *Kœnig* v. *Ritchie*, 3 F. & F. 413.
> *R.* v. *Veley*, 4 F. & F. 1117.
> *O'Donoghue* v. *Hussey*, Ir. R. 5 C. L. 124.
> *Dwyer* v. *Esmonde*, 2 L. R. Ir. 243.

But where the defendant in answering a letter which the plaintiff has sent to the paper, does not confine himself to rebutting the plaintiff's assertions, but retorts upon the plaintiff by inquiring into his antecedents, and indulging in other uncalled-for personalities, the defendant will be held liable ; for such imputations are neither a proper answer to, nor a fair comment on, the plaintiff's speech or letter.

> *Murphy* v. *Halpin*, Ir. R. 8 C. L. 127.

Three clergymen of the Church of England, residing near Swansea, being Conservatives, chose to attend a meeting of the supporters of the Liberal candidate for Swansea ; they behaved in an excited manner, hissed and interrupted the speakers, and had eventually to be removed from the room by two policemen. *Held*, that such conduct might fairly be commented on in the local newspapers ; and that even a remark that "appearances were certainly consistent with the belief that they had imbibed rather freely of the cup that inebriates" was not, under the circumstances, a libel.

> *Davis* v. *Duncan*, L. R. 9 C. P. 396 ; 43 L. J. C. P. 185 ; 22 W. R.
> 575 ; 30 L. T. 464.

But *semble*, the conduct of the solicitor for certain shareholders in a public company who are opposing the directors is not a matter of public interest.

> Per Vaughan Williams, L.J., in *Joynt* v. *Cycle Trade Publishing Co.*,
> [1904] 2 K. B. at p. 297.
> And see *Ponsford* v. *Financial Times, Limited*, (1900) 16 Times
> L. R. 248.

(iii.) *The Comment must be Fair.*

Whether a comment is or is not technically "fair" depends upon the language in which it is expressed. This is a question for the jury, unless the comment is so clearly fair and legitimate that there can be no question about it on the admitted facts, in which event the judge may stop the case. (*McQuire* v. *Western Morning News Co.*, [1903] 2 K. B. 100.) The limits of fair comment have been laid down from time to time in the Courts, and it is for the jury to say whether those limits have been exceeded. The limits are perhaps best stated in the following passage :—

"What is the meaning of a 'fair comment'? I think the meaning is this: Is the article, in the opinion of the jury, beyond that which any fair man, however prejudiced, or however strong his opinion may be, would say of the work in question? Every latitude must be given to opinion and to prejudice, and then an ordinary set of men with ordinary judgment must say whether any fair man would have made such a comment on the work. It is very easy to say what would be clearly beyond that limit; if, for instance, the writer attacked the private character of the author. But it is much more difficult to say what is within the limit. That must depend upon the circumstances of the particular case. . . . Mere exaggeration, or even gross exaggeration, would not make the comment unfair. However wrong the opinion expressed may be in point of truth, or however prejudiced the writer, it may still be within the prescribed limit. The question which the jury must consider is this: Would any fair man, however exaggerated or obstinate his views, have said that which this criticism has said?" (Per Lord Esher, M.R., in *Merivale and wife* v. *Carson*, 20 Q. B. D. at pp. 280, 281.) "The criticism is to be 'fair,' that is, the expression of it is to be fair. The only limitation is upon the mode of expression. In this country a man has a right to hold any opinion he pleases, and to express his opinion, provided that he does not go beyond the limits which the law calls 'fair,' and although we cannot find in any decided case an exact and rigid definition of the word 'fair,' this is because the judges have always preferred to leave the question what is 'fair' to the jury. . . . It must be assumed that a man is entitled to entertain any opinion he pleases, however wrong, exaggerated, or violent it may be, and it must be left to the jury to say whether the mode of expression exceeds the reasonable limits of fair criticism." (Per Bowen, L.J., in the same case, 20 Q. B. D. at pp. 283, 284.)

In *Wason* v. *Walter*, L. R. 4 Q. B. at p. 96 ; 8 B. & S. 730 ; 38 L. J. Q. B. 34, the Court held that the following direction to the jury was "perfectly correct." "The jury were told that they must be satisfied that the article was an honest and fair comment on the facts ; in other words, that in the first place, they must be satisfied that the comments had been made with an honest belief in their justice ; but that this was not enough, inasmuch as such belief might originate in the blindness of party zeal, or in personal or political aversion ; that a person taking upon himself publicly to criticise and to condemn the conduct or motives of another, must bring to the task not only an honest sense of justice, but also a reasonable degree of judgment and moderation, so that the result may be what a jury shall deem, under the circumstances of the case, a fair and legitimate criticism on the conduct and motives of the party who is the object of censure."

The following summing-up of Kennedy, J., in *Joynt* v. *Cycle Trade Publishing Co.*, [1904] 2 K. B. at p. 294, was approved by the Court of Appeal : "The comment must be such that a fair mind would use under the circumstances, and it must not misstate facts, because a comment cannot be fair which is built upon facts which are not truly stated, and further, it must not convey imputations of an evil sort, except so far as the facts truly stated warrant the imputation."

Illustrations.

The plaintiff McQuire was a theatrical manager who with his travelling company performed a play at Plymouth called "The Major." The defendant newspaper inserted the following criticism of the performance :—" A three-act musical absurdity, entitled ' The Major,' written and composed by Mr. McQuire, was presented last evening before a full house by the author's company. It cannot be said that many left the building with the satisfaction of having seen anything like the standard of play which is generally to be witnessed at the Theatre Royal. Although it may be described as a play, ' The Major ' is composed of nothing but nonsense of a not very humorous character, whilst the music is far from attractive. This comedy would be very much improved had it a substantial plot, and were a good deal of the sorry stuff taken out of it which lowers both the play and the players. No doubt the actors and actresses are well suited to the piece, which gives excellent scope for music-hall artistes to display their talent. Among Mr. McQuire's company there is not one good actor or actress, and, with the exception of Mr. Ernest Braine, not one of them can be said to have a good voice for singing. The introduction of common, not to say vulgar, songs does not tend to improve the character of the performance, and the dancing, which forms a prominent feature, is carried out with very little gracefulness." The jury held that this was not fair comment, and awarded the plaintiff 100*l.* damages. *Held*, by the Court of Appeal, that there was no evidence on which a rational verdict for the plaintiff could be founded, and that the words complained of were fair comment.

McQuire v. *Western Morning News Co.*, [1903] 2 K. B. 100 ; 72 L. J. K. B. 612 ; 51 W. R. 689 ; 88 L. T. 757.

The plaintiff, a retail rag merchant, published an advertisement in the form of a handbill offering unusually high prices for kitchen stuff, rags, dripping, old metals, old bottles, left-off clothes, &c. The defendant in his newspaper published the following comment :—" Guildhall. Encouraging servants to rob their masters. Alderman Humphery at the close of the public business drew our reporter's attention to the following extraordinary handbill, which he said had been extensively circulated in the neighbourhood of Clapham—a system which he stigmatised as most pernicious in its effects, as offering great inducements to servants to rob their masters and mistresses. He mentioned the matter in order that the publicity of such an insidious proceeding might put the masters on their guard against such practices. The handbill contains such a number of unheard-of perquisites that we give it *in extenso*." The handbill was then set out in full. *Held*, that this did not exceed the limits of fair comment and that the jury had properly found a verdict for the defendant.

Paris v. *Levy*, 9 C. B. N. S. 342 ; 30 L. J. C. P. 11 ; 7 Jur. N. S. 289 ; 9 W. R. 71 ; 3 L. T. 324.

The plaintiff published, in addition to two other works describing his travels, one in quarto, entitled, " The Stranger in Ireland." The defendant published a parody of this which he styled : " My Pocket Book, or Hints for a Ryghte Merrie and Conceited Tour, in quarto, to be called *The Stranger in Ireland*, 1805." To this there was a " frontispiece " entitled " The Knight leaving Ireland with regret," which showed a ludicrous picture of a man, bending under the weight of three heavy books, and holding a handkerchief tied by the corners and labelled " Wardrobe." Lord Campbell told the jury that this did not exceed the limits of fair comment, and a verdict was found for the defendant.

Sir John Carr v. *Hood*, (1808) 1 Camp. 355, n.

Imputation of Bad Motives.

It is too much the practice for writers in newspapers to assign wicked or corrupt motives for the conduct of their opponents. When no grounds are assigned for such an inference, or when the writer vouches for the existence of such motives as a fact within his knowledge, and not as a mere inference, then his only defence is a strict justification. But where the facts from which the writer deduces this imputation are well known and clearly referred to, or are expressly set out in the article, there the imputation, as we have seen, becomes a comment.

But can it ever be " a fair comment " within the technical meaning of that phrase to impute dishonourable motives to the person whose conduct is criticised ?

At first, the Courts held that such an inference could not possibly be a legitimate criticism on a public man. In *Parmiter* v. *Coupland*, (1840) 6 M. & W. 105 ; 9 L. J. Ex. 202, the Court of Exchequer held that, though some words which are clearly libellous of a private person may not amount to a libel when written of a person in a public capacity, still any imputation of unjust or corrupt motives is equally libellous in either case. So in *Cooper* v. *Lawson*, (1838) 8 A. & E. at p. 752, Patteson, J., lays it down in general terms that " where the comment raises an imputation of motives, which may, or may not be, a just inference from the preceding statement, it is a distinct libel."

Now, however, greater liberty prevails. It appears to be conceded that so long as a writer confines himself to discussing matters of public interest, the mere fact that improper motives have been unjustly assigned for the plaintiff's conduct is not of itself sufficient to destroy the defence of fair comment, though of course it will tell strongly in favour of the plaintiff. As Cockburn, C.J., says in *Wason* v. *Walter*, L. R. 4 Q. B. at p. 93 : " The full liberty of public writers to comment on the conduct *and motives* of public men has only in very recent times being recognised." " A line must be drawn," says the same great judge in *Campbell* v. *Spottiswoode*, 3 B. & S. 776, 777 ; 32 L. J. Q. B. 199, " between criticism upon public conduct and the imputation of motives by which that conduct may be supposed to be actuated ; one man has no right to impute to another, whose conduct may be open to ridicule or disapprobation, base, sordid, and wicked motives, unless there is so much ground for the imputation that a jury shall find, not only that he had an honest belief in the truth of his statements, but that his belief was not without foundation. . . . I think the fair position in which the law may be settled is this : That where the public conduct of a public man is open to animadversion, and the writer who is commenting upon it makes imputations on his motives, which arise fairly and legitimately out of his conduct, so that a jury shall say that the criticism was not only honest but also well founded, an action is not maintainable. But it is not because a public writer fancies that the conduct of a public man is open to the suspicion of dishonesty, he is therefore justified in assailing his character as dishonest." " In my opinion it is clear law, that, when a criticism, whether of a literary production, or of a trade advertisement, or of a public man, includes such an imputation (*i.e.*, of sordid motives), there being no facts to warrant it, it is open to the jury to find, not only that the publication complained of is libellous, but also that the defence of 'fair comment' has no application. The truth is that in such a case that which is called a 'criticism' ceases to be a criticism, and becomes a defamatory libel." (Per Vaughan Williams, L.J., in *Joynt* v. *Cycle Trade Publishing Co.*, [1904] 2 K. B. at p. 298.)

"A personal attack may form part of a fair comment upon given facts truly stated, if it be warranted by those facts; in other words, in my view, if it be a reasonable inference from those facts." (Per Lord Atkinson in *Dakhyl* v. *Labouchere*, [1908] 2 K. B. 325, n.; quoted with approval by Cozens-Hardy, M.R., and Fletcher Moulton, L.J., in *Hunt* v. *Star Newspaper Co., Ltd.*, [1908] 2 K. B. 309.)

Illustrations.

An article in the *Saturday Review* imputed to the plaintiff, the editor and part proprietor of the *British Ensign*, that, in advocating the propagation of Christianity among the Chinese, his purpose was to merely increase the circulation of his own paper, and so put money into his own pocket; that he was an impostor, and that he put forth a list of fictitious subscribers in order to delude others into subscribing. The jury found that the writer honestly believed the imputations contained in the article to be well founded, but the Court held that the limits of fair criticism had been undoubtedly exceeded.

> *Campbell* v. *Spottiswoode*, 3 F. & F. 421; 32 L. J. Q. B. 185; 3 B. & S. 769; 9 Jur. N. S. 1069; 11 W. R. 569; 8 L. T. 201.

The plaintiff, who was a Q.C. and a Member of Parliament, was appointed Recorder of Newcastle. The defendant's paper, the *Law Magazine and Review*, thereupon discussed the desirability of giving such an appointment to a member of the House of Commons, and declared that it was a reward for his having steadily voted for his party. Cockburn, C.J., directed the jury that a public writer was fairly entitled to comment on the distribution of Government patronage, but that he was not entitled to assert that there had been a corrupt promise or understanding that the plaintiff would be thus rewarded, if he always voted according to order. Verdict for the plaintiff; damages, 40*s.*

> *Seymour* v. *Butterworth*, 3 F. & F. 372.

The plaintiff was ex-mayor of Winchester. The *Hampshire Advertiser* imputed to him partiality and corruption and ignorance of his duties as mayor and justice of the peace for the borough. *Held*, that "every subject has a right to comment on those acts of public men which concern him as a subject of the realm, if he do not make his commentary a cloak for malice and slander; but any imputation of wicked or corrupt motives is unquestionably libellous." Per Parke, B., in

> *Parmiter* v. *Coupland*, 6 M. & W. 105; 9 L. J. Ex. 202; 4 Jur. 701.

The plaintiff extensively advertised a new cure for consumption. The *Pall Mall Gazette* denounced him as an impostor and a quack. Cockburn, C.J., directed the jury that if the defendant really believed that the plaintiff's system of treatment was a delusion, "then he had a right to maintain that it was so; and that, even if, in drawing inferences of imposture and bad intention, he fell into error, yet if he wrote honestly, and with the intention of exercising his vocation as a public writer fairly and with reasonable moderation and judgment, he is entitled to the verdict."

> *Hunter* v. *Sharp*, 4 F. & F. 983; 15 L. T. 421.

(iv.) *The Comment must not be Published Maliciously.*

In order that the defence of fair comment may avail, it must have been made *bonâ fide* and not from any malicious motive. A critic must always state his true opinion of the work before him; if he thinks well of the work and yet condemns it, he is acting dishonestly and will fail in his defence, even though the language used does not exceed the limits of a fair comment. "The comment would not then really be a criticism of the work. The mind of the writer would not be that of a critic, but he would be actuated by an intention to injure the author." (Per Lord Esher, M.R., in *Merivale and wife* v. *Carson*, 20 Q. B. D. at p. 281.) "The view expressed must be honest." (Per Collins, M.R., in *McQuire* v. *Western Morning News Co.*, [1903] 2 K. B. at p. 110.) "Comment distorted by malice cannot be fair on the part of the person who makes it." (Per Collins, M.R., in *Thomas* v. *Bradbury, Agnew & Co., Ltd.*, [1906] 2 K. B. at p. 642.) "Proof of malice may take a criticism *primâ facie* fair outside the right of fair comment, just as it takes a communication *primâ facie* privileged outside the privilege." (*Ib.* at p. 640.)

On the other hand, honesty of purpose will not avail if the words do exceed the limits of a fair comment. The fact that the writer, at the time he wrote, honestly believed in the truth of the charges he was making, will be no defence to an action if such charges be made recklessly, unreasonably, and without any foundation in fact. (*Campbell* v. *Spottiswoode*, 3 F. & F. 421; 3 B. & S. 769; 32 L. J. Q. B. 185; 8 L. T. 201.)

For a long time it was doubtful whether malice was in issue when a plea of fair comment was set up. It was argued that as every citizen has a right to publish a fair comment on a matter of public interest, the fact that he published it maliciously would not make it actionable. (*Cf. Mayor, &c., of Bradford* v. *Pickles*, [1895] A. C. 587; *Allen* v. *Flood and another*, [1898] A. C. 1.) " An allegation that the statement was made maliciously is not enough to convert what is *primâ facie* a lawful into a *primâ facie* unlawful statement." (Per Lindley, M.R., in *Hubbuck and Sons* v. *Wilkinson*, [1899] 1 Q. B. at p. 91.) But it has now been clearly laid down in *Thomas* v. *Bradbury, Agnew & Co., Ltd.*, ([1906] 2 K. B. 627; 77 L. J. K. B. 726; 95 L. T. 23), that a plea of fair comment will not avail a defendant who is proved to have acted maliciously. The *onus* of proving malice is on the plaintiff, and any facts that would go to show malice, were the defence one of ordinary privilege, may be proved to rebut a defence of fair comment (*Plymouth Mutual Co-operative and Industrial Society, Ltd.* v. *Traders' Publishing Association, Ltd.*, [1906] 1 K. B. 403; 75 L. J. K. B. 259; 94 L. T. 258), or it may " be inferred from the terms of the article itself." (Per Collins, M.R., in *Thomas* v. *Bradbury, Agnew & Co., Ltd.*, *suprà*, at p. 637.) These cases have established the view which had been less clearly indicated in *McQuire* v. *Western Morning News Co.* ([1903] 2 K. B. 100; 72 L. J. K. B. 612; 51 W. R. 689; 88 L. T. 757) and *Caryll* v. *Daily Mail Publishing Co.* ((1904) 90 L. T. 307). If the right to publish a fair comment on a matter of public interest is misused to gratify any indirect motive, the malice thus shown destroys the defence.

CHAPTER IX.

PRIVILEGE—ABSOLUTE PRIVILEGE.

IT is a defence to an action of libel or slander to prove that the circumstances under which the defamatory words were written or spoken were such as to make it right that the defendant should plainly state what he honestly believed to be the plaintiff's character, and speak his mind fully and freely concerning him. In such a case, the occasion is said to be *privileged*, and though the statement may at the trial be proved or admitted to be erroneous, still its publication on such privileged occasion is excused for the sake of common convenience, and in the interests of society at large.

Privileged occasions are of two kinds :—
    (i.) Those absolutely privileged.
    (ii.) Those in which the privilege is but qualified.

In the first class of cases it is so much to the public interest that the defendant should speak out his mind fully and fearlessly, that all actions in respect of words spoken thereon are absolutely forbidden, even though it be alleged that the words were spoken falsely, knowingly, and with express malice. This is confined to cases where the public service, or the due administration of justice, requires complete immunity, *e.g.*, words spoken in Parliament; everything said by a judge on the bench, or a witness in the box; reports of military officers on military matters to their military superiors. In all such cases the privilege afforded by the occasion is an *absolute* bar to any action.

In less important matters, however, the interests of the public do not demand that the speaker should be freed from *all* responsibility, but merely require that he should be protected so far as he is speaking honestly for the common good ; in these cases the privilege is said not to be *absolute* but *qualified* only.   In such cases the plaintiff will recover damages in spite of the privilege, if he can prove that the defendant in using the defamatory words was not acting in good faith, but was actuated by some improper motive. Such improper motive is called "malice."

Illustrations.

Anyone who is called as a witness, and is sworn to speak the truth, the whole truth, and nothing but the truth, may do so without fear of any legal liability, even though he be thus compelled to defame his neighbour.

This is so even where a witness in the box volunteers a defamatory remark, quite irrelevant to the cause in which he is sworn, with a view of gratifying his own vanity, and of injuring the professional reputation of another ; the words are still absolutely privileged ; for they were spoken in the box.

> *Seaman* v. *Netherclift*, 1 C. P. D. 540 ; 45 L. J. C. P. 798 ; 24 W. R. 884 ; 34 L. T. 878 ; 2 C. P. D. 53 ; 46 L. J. C. P. 128 ; 25 W. R. 159 ; 35 L. T. 784.

Anyone who is asked as to the character of a former servant by one to whom the servant has applied for a situation, may state in reply all he knows about the servant without being liable to an action, provided he does so truthfully and honestly to the best of his ability.

But if he maliciously gives a good servant a bad character in order to prevent her "bettering herself," and so to compel her to return to his own service, the case is thereby taken out of the privilege, and the servant will recover damages.

> *Jackson* v. *Hopperton*, 16 C. B. N. S. 829 ; 12 W. R. 913 ; 10 L. T. 529.

In Roman law an intention to injure the plaintiff was essential to the action for *injuria.* (D. 47. 10. 3, 3 & 4.)   Hence, they never presumed malice ; the plaintiff had to prove that the defendant expressly intended to impair his good name.   Thus, if an astrologer or soothsayer, in the *bonâ fide* practice of his art, denounces A. as a thief when he is an honest man, A. has no action ; for the astrologer only committed an honest mistake.   But it would be otherwise if the soothsayer did not really believe in his art, but from motives of private enmity pretended, after some jugglery, to arrive at A.'s name. (D. 47. 10. 15. 13.)   That being so, it was unnecessary for the Romans to have any law as to *qualified* privilege ; unless there was some evidence of malice the plaintiff failed in every case. But neither did they allow any *absolute* privilege ; on express malice proved the plaintiff recovered.   Even the fact that the libel was contained in a petition sent to the Emperor was no protection. (D. 47. 10. 15. 29.) If a prefect or other official in the course of his duty charged a man with crime, he was not liable to an action if he did so in the belief that the charge was true, and without any malicious intention of publicly defaming the man; but if, in a sudden quarrel, he made the charge in the heat of the moment, and without any ground for the accusation, then he would be liable to an action when his term of office had expired, unless the Statute of Limitations would help him. (Rescript to Victorinus, A.D. 290; Krueger's Codex, ed. 1877, p. 855.) Two adversaries in litigation were of course allowed great latitude; a certain amount of mutual defamation being essential to the conduct of the case, and so not malicious: but even here moderation had to be observed. (Pauli Sent. V. iv. 15.) The Roman plan had at least the merit of simplicity.

Whether the communication is, or is not, privileged by reason of the occasion, is a question for the judge alone, where there is no dispute as to the circumstances under which it was made. (*Stace* v. *Griffith*, L. R. 2 P. C. 420; 6 Moore, P. C. C. N. S. 18; 20 L. T. 197.) If there be any doubt as to these circumstances, the jury must find what the circumstances in fact were, or appeared to the defendant to be; and on their findings the judge will decide whether the occasion is privileged or not. (*Hebditch* v. *MacIlwaine and others*, [1894] 2 Q. B. at p. 58; *Hope* v. *I'Anson and Weatherby*, (1901) 18 Times L. R. 201.) If the occasion is not privileged, and no other defence is raised, the jury must find a verdict for the plaintiff. If the occasion is absolutely privileged, judgment will at once be given for the defendant. If, however, the judge decides that the occasion is one of qualified privilege only, the plaintiff must then, if he can, satisfy the judge that there is evidence of malice on the part of the defendant to go to the jury. If the plaintiff has given no such evidence, it is the duty of the judge to direct a verdict for the defendant. If he has given any evidence of malice sufficient to go to the jury, then it is a question for the jury whether the defendant was or was not actuated by malicious motives in writing or speaking the defamatory words. (See Chapter XII., Malice, *post*, p. 341.)

ABSOLUTE PRIVILEGE.

There are occasions when it is for the public interest that persons should not in any way be fettered in their statements, but should speak out freely and fearlessly. In these cases the privilege is absolute, and no action lies for words spoken on such an occasion ; the plaintiff cannot be heard to say that the defendant did not intend honestly to discharge a duty, but maliciously availed himself of the privileged occasion to injure the plaintiff's reputation. The immunity is complete. Consequently a Statement of Claim which alleges publication on an occasion which is absolutely privileged may be struck out (*Law* v. *Llewellyn*, [1906] 1 K. B. 487), and the action dismissed as frivolous and vexatious. (*Burr* v. *Smith*, [1909] 2 K. B. 306.)

There are not many such cases, nor is it desirable that there should be many. The Courts refuse to extend their number. (*Stevens* v. *Sampson*, 5 Ex. D. 53 ; 49 L. J. Q. B. 120 ; 28 W. R. 87 ; 41 L. T. 782 ; *Royal Aquarium* v. *Parkinson*, [1892] 1 Q. B. at p. 451.) They may be grouped under three heads :—

> (i.) Parliamentary proceedings.
> (ii.) Judicial proceedings.
> (iii.) Naval and military affairs, &c.

" Privilege or immunity in respect of defamation is of two kinds —absolute privilege, which is conceded to members of the Houses of Parliament, judges, &c. ; and qualified privilege, to which every subject of the Queen is entitled, provided the occasion on which the defamatory matter is written or spoken is privileged, and there is an absence of express malice. The first seems rather to attach to the person or character of the person writing or speaking the defamatory matter ; the second, to the occasion when the defamatory matter is written or spoken. The authorities establish beyond all question this : that neither party, witness, counsel, jury, nor judge, can be put to answer civilly or criminally for words spoken in office ; that no action of libel or slander lies, whether against judges, counsel, witnesses, or parties, for words written or spoken in the course of any proceeding before any Court recognised by law, and this though the words written or spoken were written or spoken maliciously, without any justification or excuse, and from personal ill-will and anger against the person defamed. This 'absolute privilege' has been conceded on the grounds of public policy to ensure freedom of speech where it is essential that freedom of speech should exist, and with the knowledge that Courts of justice are presided over by those who, from their high character, are not likely to abuse the privilege, and who have the power, and ought to have the will, to check any abuse of it by those who appear before them. It is, however, a privilege which ought not to be extended." (Per Lopes, L.J., in *Royal Aquarium* v. *Parkinson*, [1892] 1 Q. B. at pp. 450, 451.)

(i.) *Parliamentary Proceedings.*

No member of either House of Parliament is in any way responsible in a Court of justice for anything said in the House. (*Dillon* v. *Balfour*, 20 L. R. Ir. 600.) "The freedom of speech, and debates or proceedings in Parliament, ought not to be impeached or questioned in any Court or place out of Parliament." (Bill of Rights, 1 Will. & Mary, sess. 2, c. 2.) This statutory provision merely declares the common law on the subject. (*Fielding* v. *Thomas*, [1896] A. C. at p. 612.) And no indictment will lie for an alleged conspiracy by members of either House to make speeches defamatory of the plaintiff. (*Ex parte Wason*, L. R. 4 Q. B. 573; 38 L. J. Q. B. 302; 40 L. J. M. C. 168; 17 W. R. 881.)

But this privilege does not extend outside the walls of the House.

Hence, at common law, even if the whole House ordered the publication of parliamentary reports and papers, no privilege attached. (*R.* v. *Williams*, (1686) 2 Shower, 471; Comb. 18 (see, however, the comments on this case in *R.* v. *Wright*, (1799) 8 T. R. 293); *Stockdale* v. *Hansard*, (1837) 2 Moo. & Rob. 9; 7 C. & P. 731; (1839) 9 A. & E. 1—243; 2 P. & D. 1; 3 Jur. 905; 8 Dowl. 148, 522.) But by stat. 3 & 4 Vict. c. 9, all reports, papers, votes, and proceedings ordered to be published by either House of Parliament were made absolutely privileged, and all proceedings at law, civil or criminal, will be stayed at once on the production of a certificate that they were published by order of either House.   By s. 3, however, of the same Act, if an extract from or abstract of any such Parliamentary paper be published not by the authority of Parliament, such publication has only a qualified privilege, and the plaintiff can recover on proof of actual malice.*

A petition to Parliament is absolutely privileged, although it contain false and defamatory statements.   (*Lake* v. *King,* 1 Saund. 131; 1 Lev. 240; 1 Mod. 58; Sid. 414.)   So is a petition to a committee of either House.   (See *Kane* v. *Mulvany,* Ir. R. 2 C. L. 402.)   But a publication of such a petition to others not members of the House is not privileged.

Illustrations.

Words spoken by a member of Parliament in Parliament are absolutely privileged: the Court has no jurisdiction to entertain an action in respect of them, and will upon motion set aside the writ of summons and the statement of claim in such action.

> *Dillon* v. *Balfour,* 20 L. R. Ir. 600.

But if a member of either House of Parliament publishes to the world the speech he delivered in his place in the House, he will be liable to an action as any private individual would be, who reported such speech.

> *R.* v. *Lord Abingdon,* 1 Esp. 226.
>
> *R.* v. *Creevey,* 1 M. & S. 273.

A report of a speech made in either House is conditionally privileged; *i.e.,* the plaintiff cannot recover, unless he can prove malice.

> Per Lord Campbell in *Davison* v. *Duncan,* 7 E. & B. 233 ; 26 L. J. Q. B. 107.
>
> Per Cockburn, C.J., in *Wason* v. *Walter,* L. R. 4 Q. B. 95 ; 8 B. & S. 730 ; 38 L. J. Q. B. 42 ; 17 W. R. 169 ; 19 L. T. 416.
>
> Per Palles, C.B., in *Dillon* v. *Balfour,* 20 L. R. Ir. 600.
>
> And see *post*, pp. 323—328.

Evidence given before a Select Committee of the House of Commons is absolutely privileged.

> *Goffin* v. *Donnelly,* 6 Q. B. D. 307 ; 50 L. J. Q. B. 303 ; 29 W. R. 440 ; 44 L. T. 141 ; 45 J. P. 439.

But a letter written to the Privy Council, touching the conduct of one of their officers, is not absolutely privileged ; it is open to the plaintiff to prove express malice if he can.

> *Proctor* v. *Webster,* 16 Q. B. D. 112 ; 55 L. J. Q. B. 150 ; 53 L. T. 765.

---

* The Act is set out in full in Appendix C., *post*, pp. 826—828, and is further discussed at *post*, pp. 337, 338.

(ii.) *Judicial Proceedings.*

No action will lie for defamatory statements made or sworn in the course of a judicial proceeding before any Court of competent jurisdiction. Everything said by a judge on the bench, a witness in the box, the parties or their advocates in the conduct of the case, is absolutely privileged, so long as it is in any way connected with the inquiry. So are all statements contained in documents necessary to the proceedings, such as writs, pleadings, and affidavits. This immunity rests on obvious grounds of public policy and convenience. It attaches to all proceedings taken before any person who lawfully exercises judicial functions, whether he be technically a judge or not, provided he is acting in his *judicial* capacity and not merely in the discharge of some *administrative* duty. (*Royal Aquarium* v. *Parkinson*, [1892] 1 Q. B. 431; 61 L. J. Q. B. 409; *Barratt* v. *Kearns*, [1905] 1 K. B. 504; 74 L. J. K. B. 318; 92 L. T. 255.)

"Public policy requires that a judge, in dealing with the matter before him, a party in preferring or resisting a legal proceeding, and a witness in giving evidence, oral or written, in a Court of justice, shall do so with his mind uninfluenced by the fear of an action for defamation or a prosecution for libel." (Per Pigott, C.B., in *Kennedy* v. *Hilliard*, 10 Ir. C. L. R. at p. 209, cited with approval by Brett, M.R., in *Munster* v. *Lamb*, 11 Q. B. D. at pp. 604, 605.) "Neither party, witness, counsel, jury, nor judge can be put to answer, civilly or criminally, for *words spoken in office*" (per Lord Mansfield, in *R.* v. *Skinner*, Lofft, at p. 56), or for any act done or proceeding taken "in the course of justice." (*Kennedy* v. *Hilliard*, 10 Ir. C. L. R. 195; 1 L. T. 78; *M'Laughlin* v. *Doey*, 32 L. R. Ir. at p. 530.)

Judges.

A judge of a superior Court has an absolute immunity, and no action can be maintained against him, even though it be alleged that he spoke maliciously, knowing his words to be false, and also that his words were irrelevant to the matter in issue before him, and wholly unwarranted by the evidence. It is essential to the highest interests of public policy to secure the free and fearless discharge of high judicial functions. (*Floyd* v. *Barker*, 12 Rep. 24.) "The public are deeply interested in this rule, which, indeed, exists for their benefit, and was established to secure the independence of the judges, and prevent their being harassed by vexatious actions." (Per Crompton, J., in *Fray* v. *Blackburn*, 3 B. & S. at p. 578.)

The judge of an inferior Court of record enjoys the same immunity in this respect as the judge of a superior Court, so long as he has jurisdiction over the matter before him. For any act done in any proceeding in which he either knows, or ought to know, that he is without jurisdiction, he is liable as an ordinary subject. (*Houlden* v. *Smith*, 14 Q. B. 841; *Calder* v. *Halket*, 3 Moo. P. C. C. 28.) And so he would be for words spoken after the business of the Court is over. (*Paris* v. *Levy*, 9 C. B. N. S. 342; 30 L. J. C. P. 12; 7 Jur. N. S. 289; 9 W. R. 71; 3 L. T. 324.) A justice of the peace enjoys the same privilege. No action will lie against him for defamatory words, even though spoken maliciously and without reasonable or probable cause, if they arise out of any matter properly before him. (See *Kirby* v. *Simpson*, 10 Exch. 358; *Gelen* v. *Hall*, 2 H. & N. 379; *Law* v. *Llewellyn*, [1906] 1 K. B. 487; 75 L. J. K. B. 320; 54 W. R. 368; 94 L. T. 359.)

"No action lies for acts done or words spoken by a judge in the exercise of his judicial office, although his motive is malicious, and the acts or words are not done or spoken in the honest exercise of his office. If a judge goes beyond his jurisdiction a different set of considerations arise. The only difference between judges of the superior Courts and other judges consists in the extent of their respective jurisdiction." (Per Lord Esher, M.R., in *Anderson* v. *Gorrie*, [1895] 1 Q. B. at p. 671.)

The law is the same in Scotland. (*Primrose* v. *Waterston*, (1902) 4 F. 783 (Ct. of Sess.).)

Illustrations.

No action will lie against a judge of one of the superior Courts for any judicial act, though it be alleged to have been done maliciously and corruptly.

> *Fray* v. *Blackburn*, 3 B. & S. 576.
>
> See *Floyd* v. *Barker*, 12 Rep. 24.
>
> *Groenvelt* v. *Burwell*, 1 Ld. Raym. 454, 468 ; 12 Mod. 388.
>
> *Anderson* v. *Gorrie and others*, [1895] 1 Q. B. 668 ; 71 L. T. 382 ; 14 R. 79.

This is so whether he is sitting in open Court or at chambers :

> *Taaffe* v. *Downes*, 3 Moo. P. C. C. 36, n.

Or in bankruptcy.

> *Dicas* v. *Lord Brougham*, 6 C. & P. 249 ; 1 M. & R. 309.

Colonial judges have the same privilege ;

> *Anderson* v. *Gorrie and others, suprà.*

So has the vice-chancellor of a university when sitting as a judge in the university court ;

> *Kemp* v. *Neville*, 10 C. B. N. S. 523 ; 31 L. J. C. P. 158 ; 4 L. T. 640.

So with the Recorder of London.

> *Hamond* v. *Howell*, 2 Mod. 218.

Scott was an accountant and scrivener. A County Court judge, while sitting in Court and trying an action in which Scott was defendant, said to him : " You are a harpy, preying on the vitals of the poor." *Held*, that no action lay for words so spoken by the County Court judge, although they were alleged to have been spoken falsely and maliciously, and without any reasonable or probable cause or any foundation whatever, and to have been wholly irrelevant to the case before him.

> *Scott* v. *Stansfield*, L. R. 3 Ex. 220 ; 37 L. J. Ex. 155 ; 16 W. R. 911 ; 18 L. T. 572.

So if the County Court judge be sitting in Bankruptcy.

> *Myers* v. *Defries*, *Times*, July 23rd, 1877.
>
> *Ryalls* v. *Leader and others*, L. R. 1 Ex. 296 ; 4 H. & C. 555 ; 35 L. J. Ex. 185 ; 12 Jur. N. S. 503 ; 14 W. R. 838 ; 14 L. T. 563.

An arbitration before a County Court judge under the Workmen's Compensation Act is a judicial proceeding.

> *R.* v. *Crossley*, [1909] 1 K. B. 411 ; 78 L. J. K. B. 299 ; 100 L. T. 463 ; 73 J. P. 119 ; 25 Times L. R. 225.

Proceedings before a Master of the Supreme Court are absolutely privileged.

> *Pedley and May* v. *Morris*, 61 L. J. Q. B. 21 ; 40 W. R. 42 ; 65 L. T. 526.

No action will lie against the chief clerk of a judge of the Chancery Division of the High Court for anything contained in a report made by him to the judge.

> Per Farwell, L.J., in *Burr* v. *Smith*, [1909] 2 K. B. at p. 316.

No action lies against a judge for unjustly censuring and denouncing a counsel then engaged in the cause before him, even although it be alleged that it was done from motives of private malice.

> *Miller* v. *Hope*, 2 Shaw, Sc. App. Cas. 125.

No action lies against a coroner for anything he says in his address to the jury impannelled before him, however defamatory, false, or malicious it may be ; unless the plaintiff can prove that the statement was wholly irrelevant to the inquisition, and not warranted by the occasion, the coroner's Court being " a Court of record of very high authority."

> *Thomas* v. *Churton,* 2 B. & S. 475 ; 31 L. J. Q. B. 139 ; 8 Jur. N. S. 795.
>
> See also *Yates* v. *Lansing,* 5 Johns. 283 ; 9 Johns. 395 (American).
>
> *Garnett* v. *Ferrand,* 6 B. & C. 611 ; 9 D. & R. 657.

A chairman of quarter sessions may denounce the grand jury as " a seditious, scandalous, corrupt, and perjured jury."

> *R.* v. *Skinner,* Lofft, 55.

The proceedings of a court-martial are absolutely privileged, though it is not a Court of record.

> *Jekyll* v. *Sir John Moore,* 2 B. & P. N. R. 341 ; 6 Esp. 63.
>
> *Home* v. *Bentinck,* 2 B. & B. 130 ; 4 Moore, 563.
>
> *Oliver* v. *Bentinck,* 3 Taunt. 456.

" A Court of inquiry, though not a Court of record, nor a Court of law, nor coming within the ordinary definition of a Court of justice, is, nevertheless, a Court duly and legally constituted, and recognised in the articles of war and many Acts of Parliament."

> *Per cur.* in *Dawkins* v. *Lord Rokely,* (1873) L. R. 8 Q. B. at p. 266.

A magistrate commented severely on the conduct of a policeman which came under his judicial notice, and in consequence the policeman was dismissed from the force. *Held,* that no action lay.

> *Kendillon* v. *Maltby,* 2 M. & Rob. 438 ; Car. & Mar. 402.

[The *dicta* in this case, implying that an action would lie against a magistrate for words uttered in the course of his duty, on proof both of malice and of the absence of all reasonable and probable cause, are expressly overruled by the Court of Appeal in *Munster* v. *Lamb,* 11 Q. B. D. 608 ; 52 L. J. Q. B. 726 ; 32 W. R. 243 ; 49 L. T. 252.]

No action will lie against a police magistrate for defamatory words, spoken by him when performing his duties as a magistrate, if they arise out of any matter properly before him.

> *Law* v. *Llewellyn,* [1906] 1 K. B. 487 ; 75 L. J. K. B. 320 ; 54 W. R. 368 ; 94 L. T. 359 ; 70 J. P. 220.

So in Scotland.

> *Primrose* v. *Waterston,* (1902) 4 F. 783 (Ct. of Sess.), explaining
>
> *Allardice* v. *Robertson,* 1 Dow, N. S. 514 ; 1 Dow & Clark, 495 ; 6 Shaw & Dun. 242 ; 7 Shaw & Dun. 691 ; 4 Wils. & Shaw, App. Cas. 102, which is expressly disapproved in *Law* v. *Llewellyn, suprá.*

And in America.

> *Pratt* v. *Gardner,* 2 Cushing (Massachusetts), 63.

The proceedings on an application to a justice of the peace under the Lunacy Act, 1890, are absolutely privileged.

> *Hodson* v. *Pare,* [1899] 1 Q. B. 455 ; 68 L. J. Q. B. 309 ; 47 W. R. 241 ; 80 L. T. 13.

The presentation to the Court of a report made by the Official Receiver under s. 8 (2) of the Companies (Winding-up) Act, 1890, is absolutely privileged. So is the presentation to the Board of Trade of a report made under s. 29 of the same Act.

> *Bottomley* v. *Brougham*, [1908] 1 K. B. 584; 77 L. J. K. B. 311; 99 L. T. 111; 24 Times L. R. 262.
>
> *Burr* v. *Smith*, [1909] 2 K. B. 306; 78 L. J. K. B. 889; 101 L. T. 194; 25 Times L. R. 542.

But a magistrate's clerk has no right to make any observation on the conduct of the parties before the Court; and no such observation will be privileged.

> *Delegal* v. *Highley*, 3 Bing. N. C. 950; 5 Scott, 154; 3 Hodges, 158; 8 C. & P. 444.

An absolute privilege also attaches to all proceedings of, and to all evidence given before, any tribunal which by law, though not expressly a Court, exercises judicial functions—that is to say has power to determine the legal rights and to affect the status of the parties who appear before it. All preliminary steps which are in accordance with the recognised and reasonable procedure of such a tribunal are also absolutely privileged. It is not necessary that the tribunal should have all the powers of an ordinary Court; *e.g.*, the proceedings will still be absolutely privileged although the tribunal cannot compel the attendance of witnesses, or has no power to administer an oath, provided it can discharge its judicial duties without such powers. (Per Lord Holt, C.J., in *Dr. Groenvelt* v. *Dr. Burwell and others, Censors of the College of Physicians*, (1700) 1 Ld. Raym. at p. 472; and per Cozens-Hardy, L.J., in *Barratt* v. *Kearns*, [1905] 1 K. B. at p. 511.) Whenever a statute or a charter creating a corporation invests certain of its members with judicial authority in certain matters, no action will lie against those members for anything done by them in the exercise of such authority in those matters.

Illustrations.

The General Medical Council when holding an inquiry under the Medical Act, 1858 (and also, it is submitted, when holding a similar inquiry under the Dentists Act, 1878), is a tribunal which is acting judicially, and therefore all proceedings before it are absolutely privileged. So are the original complaint, all statutory declarations made in support and in answer to the complaint, and all proper proceedings subsequent thereto, whether the Penal Cases Committee decide to institute an inquiry or not.

> *Groenvelt* v. *Burwell and the Censors of the Royal College of Physicians*, (1700) 1 Ld. Raym. 454 ; 12 Mod. 388.
>
> *Allbutt* v. *General Medical Council*, (1889) 23 Q. B. D. 400 ; 58 L. J. Q. B. 606 ; 37 W. R. 771 ; 61 L. T. 585.
>
> *Leeson* v. *General Medical Council*, (1889) 43 Ch. D. 366 ; 59 L. J. Ch. 233 ; 38 W. R. 303 ; 61 L. T. 849.
>
> *Allinson* v. *General Medical Council*, (1892) 8 Times L. R. 727, 784.

The hearing of an application complaining of the conduct of a solicitor, made to the Committee of the Law Society under ss. 12 and 13 of the Solicitors Act, 1888, is absolutely privileged.

> *Lilley* v. *Roney*, (1892) 61 L. J. Q. B. 727 ; 8 Times L. R. 642.

Proceedings before a private ecclesiastical commission appointed by the Bishop of a diocese under s. 77 of the Pluralities Act, 1838, as amended by the Pluralities Acts Amendment Act, 1885, s. 3, are absolutely privileged.

> *Barratt* v. *Kearns*, [1905] 1 K. B. 504 ; 74 L. J. K. B. 318 ; 53 W. R. 356 ; 92 L. T. 255 ; 21 Times L. R. 212.

But the members of a county council when transacting licensing business are not exercising judicial functions, and the proceedings before them have only a qualified privilege.

> *Royal Aquarium* v. *Parkinson*, [1892] 1 Q. B. 431 ; 61 L. J. Q. B. 409 ; 40 W. R. 450 ; 66 L. T. 513.
>
> *R.* v. *London County Council ; In re Empire Theatre*, (1894) 71 L. T. 638 ; 15 R. 66.

The same is true of licensing justices.

> *Boulter* v. *Kent JJ.*, [1897] A. C. at p. 561 ; 66 L. J. Q. B. 787 ; 46 W. R. 114 ; 77 L. T. 288 ; 61 J. P. 532.
>
> *R.* v. *Sharman*, [1898] 1 Q. B. 578 ; 67 L. J. Q. B. 460 ; 46 W. R. 367 ; 78 L. T. 320 ; 62 J. P. 296.
>
> *R.* v. *Howard*, [1902] 2 K. B. 363 ; 71 L. J. K. B. 754 ; 51 W. R. 21 ; 86 L. T. 839 ; 66 J. P. 579.
>
> *R.* v. *Russell*, (1905) 93 L. T. 407 ; 69 J. P. 450 ; 21 Times L. R. 749.

But the confirming authority, whose confirmation is, under the provisions of the Licensing Acts, necessary to the validity of certain classes of new licences is—for some purposes at all events—a Court exercising judicial functions.

> *R.* v. *Manchester JJ.*, [1899] 1 Q. B. 571 ; 68 L. J. Q. B. 358 ; 47 W. R. 410 ; 80 L. T. 531 ; 63 J. P. 360.
>
> *R.* v. *Sunderland JJ.*, [1901] 2 K. B. 357 ; 70 L. J. K. B. 946 ; 85 L. T. 183 ; 65 J. P. 599.

The hearing of a dispute by the Jockey Club, or by the local stewards of a race-meeting, is not a judicial proceeding.

> *Hope* v. *I'Anson and Weatherby*, (1901) 18 Times L. R. 201.

Parties and Advocates.

No action will lie against a barrister for defamatory words spoken as counsel in the course of any judicial proceeding with reference thereto, even though they were unnecessary to support the case of his client, and were uttered without any justification or excuse, and from personal ill-will or anger towards the plaintiff arising from some previously existing cause, and are irrelevant to every question of fact which is in issue before the tribunal. (*Munster* v. *Lamb*, 11 Q. B. D. 588 ; 52 L. J. Q. B. 726 ; 32 W. R. 243 ; 49 L. T. 252 ; 47 J. P. 805.)

This decision gives to an advocate the same absolute immunity as is enjoyed by a judge of a superior Court. The previous cases had not gone so far. In *Brook* v. *Sir Henry Montague*, (1606) Cro. Jac. 90, the Court decided that " counsel in law retained hath a privilege to enforce anything which is informed him by his client, and to give it in evidence, being pertinent to the matter in question, and not to examine whether it be true or false ; but it is at the peril of him who informs him." And the Court assumed in favour of counsel that his client had instructed him to say what he did. Thus, in *Wood* v. *Gunston*, Style, 462, Glyn, C.J., says : " It is the duty of a counsellor to speak for his client, and it shall be intended to be spoken according to his client's instructions." In *Flint* v. *Pike*, 4 B. & C. 473, Bayley, J., says : " The law presumes that he acts in discharge of his duty, and in pursuance of his instructions." In *Butt, Q.C.* v. *Jackson*, 10 Ir. L. R. 120, the Court expressly decided that instructions to counsel are not the test by which to try whether or not the line of duty has been passed. Hence, the words are still absolutely privileged, although counsel may have exceeded his instructions. (See also *Hodgson* v. *Scarlett*, 1 B. & Ald. 232 ; Holt, N. P. 621 ; *Needham* v. *Dowling*, 15 L. J. C. P. 9 ; *R. pros. Armstrong, Q.C.* v. *Kiernan*, 7 Cox, C. C. 6 ; 5 Ir. C. L. R. 171 ; and *Taylor* v. *Swinton*, (1824) 2 Shaw's Scotch App. Cas. 245.) But the decision of the Court of Appeal in *Munster* v. *Lamb* removes all limitations whatever on the absolute privilege of an advocate for all words uttered in the course of his duty. The rule is made so wide (as Brett, M.R., points out, 11 Q. B. D. 604) not to protect counsel who deliberately and maliciously slander others, but in order that innocent counsel who act *bonâ fide* may not be " unrighteously harassed with suits."

An attorney acting as an advocate in a County Court or a police Court enjoys the same immunity as counsel.

(*Mackay* v. *Ford*, 5 H. & N. 792 ; 29 L. J. Ex. 404 ; 6 Jur. N. S. 587 ; 8 W. R. 586 ; *Munster* v. *Lamb, suprà.*) So with a proctor in an ecclesiastical Court. (*Higginson* v. *Flaherty*, 4 Ir. C. L. R. 125.) The party himself, because of his ignorance of the proper mode of conducting a case, is allowed even greater latitude. (Per Holroyd, J., in *Hodgson* v. *Scarlett*, 1 B. & Ald. 244.) Any observation made by one of the jury during the trial is equally privileged, provided it is pertinent to the inquiry. (*R.* v. *Skinner*, Lofft, 55.) And so is any presentment by a grand jury. (*Little* v. *Pomeroy*, Ir. R. 7 C. L. 50.)

Illustrations.

A woman was charged before a Court of petty sessions with administering drugs to the inmates of the plaintiff's house in order to facilitate the commission of a burglary there. The plaintiff was the prosecutor, and the defendant, who was a solicitor, appeared for the defence of the woman. It was admitted that she had been at the plaintiff's house on the evening before the burglary ; and there was some evidence, though very slight, that a narcotic drug had been administered to the inmates of the plaintiff's house on that evening. During the proceedings before the magistrates the defendant, acting as advocate for the woman, suggested that the plaintiff might be keeping drugs at his house for immoral or criminal purposes. There was no evidence called or tendered that the plaintiff kept any drugs in his house at all. *Held*, that no action would lie against the defendant for these words, as the occasion was absolutely privileged.

    Munster v. *Lamb*, 11 Q. B. D. 588 ; 52 L. J. Q. B. 726 ; 32 W. R. 243 ; 49 L. T. 252 ; 47 J. P. 805.

A servant summoned his master before a Court of conscience for a week's wages. The master said : " He has been transported before, and ought to be transported again. He has been robbing me of nine quartern loaves a week." Lord Ellenborough held the remark absolutely privileged, if the master spoke them in opening his defence to the Court ; but otherwise if he spoke them while waiting about the room and not for the purpose of his defence.

    Trotman v. *Dunn*, 4 Camp. 211. [N.B.—The latter part of the headnote to the report of this case is misleading.]

Plaintiff made an affidavit in an action he had brought against defendant in the King's Bench. Defendant (apparently conducting his own case) said in Court, in answer to this affidavit : "It is a false affidavit, and forty witnesses will swear to the contrary." *Held*, that no action lay for these words.

    Boulton v. *Chapman*, (1640) Sir W. Jones, 431 ; March, 20, pl. 45.

A charge of felony made by the defendant when applying in due course to a justice of the peace for a warrant to apprehend the plaintiff on that charge is absolutely privileged.

> *Ram* v. *Lamley*, Hutt. 113.
> See *Johnson* v. *Evans*, 3 Esp. 32.
> *Weston* v. *Dobniet*, Cro. Jac. 432.
> *Dancaster* v. *Hewson*, 2 Man. & R. 176.

Witnesses.

A witness in the box is absolutely privileged in answering all the questions asked him by the counsel on either side; and even if he volunteers an observation (a practice much to be discouraged), still, if it has reference to the matter in issue, or fairly arises out of any question asked him by counsel, though only going to his credit, such observation will also be privileged. (*Seaman* v. *Netherclift*, 1 C. P. D. 540; 2 C. P. D. 53; 46 L. J. C. P. 128.) The privilege extends to statements made to a solicitor when preparing the witness's proof. (*Watson* v. *M'Ewan*, [1905] A. C. 480; 74 L. J. P. C. 151; 93 L. T. 489.) But a remark made by a witness in the box, wholly irrelevant to the matter of inquiry, uncalled for by any question of counsel, and introduced by the witness maliciously for his own purposes, would not be privileged, and would also probably be a contempt of Court. So, of course, an observation made by a witness while waiting about the Court, before or after he has given his evidence, is not privileged. (*Trotman* v. *Dunn*, 4 Camp. 211; *Lynam* v. *Gowing*, 6 L. R. Ir. 259.) But if a remark be made for the information of the Court by the witness after he has left the box but while he is still under the sanction of the oath it would be privileged. (*Hope* v. *Leng*, (1907) 23 Times L. R. 243.)

Illustrations.

Defendant, an expert in handwriting, gave evidence in the Probate Court in the trial of *Davies* v. *May*, that, in his opinion, the signature to the will in question was a forgery. The jury found in favour of the will, and the presiding judge made some very disparaging remarks on defendant's evidence. Soon afterwards defendant was called as a witness in favour of the genuineness of another document, on a charge of forgery before a magistrate. In cross-examination he was asked whether he had given evidence in the suit of *Davies* v. *May*, and whether he had read the judge's remarks on his evidence. He answered, "Yes."

Counsel asked no more questions, and defendant insisted on adding, though told by the magistrate not to make any further statement as to *Davies* v. *May* :. " I believe that will to be a rank forgery, and shall believe so to the day of my death." One of the attesting witnesses to the will brought an action of slander for these words. *Held*, that the words were spoken by defendant as a witness, and had reference to the inquiry before the magistrate, as they tended to justify the defendant, whose credit as a witness had been impugned; and the defendant was therefore absolutely privileged.

> *Seaman* v. *Netherclift*, 1 C. P. D. 540; 45 L. J. C. P. 798; 24 W. R. 884; 34 L. T. 878; (C. A.) 2 C. P. D. 53; 46 L. J. C. P. 128; 25 W. R. 159; 35 L. T. 784.

Defamatory communications made by witnesses or officials to a court-martial, or to a court of inquiry instituted under articles of war, are absolutely privileged.

> *Keighley* v. *Bell*, 4 F. & F. 763.
>
> *Dawkins* v. *Lord Rokeby*, L. R. 8 Q. B. 255; 42 L. J. Q. B. 63; 21 W. R. 544; 4 F. & F. 806; 28 L. T. 134; L. R. 7 H. L. 744; 45 L. J. Q. B. 8; 23 W. R. 931; 33 L. T. 196.

Similarly with regard to statements made before a private ecclesiastical commission appointed under the Pluralities Acts.

> *Barratt* v. *Kearns*, [1905] 1 K. B. 504; 74 L. J. K. B. 318; 53 W. R. 356; 92 L. T. 255 ; 21 Times L. R. 212.

A letter written privately to the judge to influence his decision, whether by a party, or a witness, or anyone else, is not privileged. It is indeed a contempt of Court.

> *Gould* v. *Hulme*, 3 C. & P. 625.

Documents used in Judicial Proceedings.

All documents necessary to or properly used in a judicial proceeding are absolutely privileged ; *e.g.*, all pleadings delivered or affidavits sworn in the course of a judicial proceeding before a Court of competent jurisdiction. (*Revis* v. *Smith*, 18 C. B. 126; 25 L. J. C. P. 195 ; *Henderson* v. *Broomhead*, 4 H. & N. 569; 28 L. J. Ex. 360; 5 Jur. N. S. 1175.) The proof of a witness is a privileged document. (*Watson* v. *M'Ewan*, [1905] A. C. 480.) So is any indorsement on a writ. (*Lord Beauchamps* v. *Sir R. Croft*, Dyer, 285, *a*.) So is the official record of any judicial proceeding even though inaccurately or improperly entered. (*MacCabe* v. *Joynt*, [1901] 2 Ir. R. 115.) But the charge sheet at a police station is not part of the record of a Court. (*Furniss* v. *Cambridge Daily News, Ltd.*, (1907) 23 Times L. R. 705.) A report of a judicial proceeding is not a document in the case and the privilege attaching to it is only qualified. (See *post*, Chap. XI.)

The only exception is where an affidavit is sworn before a Court that has no jurisdiction in the matter, and no power to entertain the proceeding. (*Buckley* v. *Wood*, 4 Rep. 14, *a*; Cro. Eliz. 230; *R.* v. *Salisbury*, 1 Ld. Raym. 341; *Maloney* v. *Bartley*, 3 Camp. at p. 212; *Lewis* v. *Levy*, E. B. & E. 554; 27 L. J. Q. B. 282; 4 Jur. N. S. 970.) In all other cases the plaintiff's only remedy is to indict the deponent for perjury. (*Doyle* v. *O'Doherty*, Car. & M. 418; *Astley* v. *Younge*, 2 Burr. 807.) The Court will, however, sometimes order scandalous matter in such an affidavit to be expunged. (*Christie* v. *Christie*, L. R. 8 Ch. 499; 42 L. J. Ch. 544; 21 W. R. 493; 28 L. T. 607.) But, even for matter thus expunged, no action can be brought. (*Kennedy* v. *Hilliard*, 10 Ir. C. L. R. 195; 1 L. T. 78.)

Illustrations.

No action of libel can be maintained against a plaintiff for signing judgment in an action, even though such judgment be subsequently set aside, as being irregular or contrary to good faith. "The procuring by the plaintiff of the entry of the judgment upon the rolls of the Court cannot amount to an actionable publication of a libel." Nor can the subsequent docketing and registration of such judgment in the official books of any statutory Registry.

> *M'Laughlin* v. *Doey*, 32 L. R. Ir. 518, 528.
>
> *MacCabe* v. *Joynt*, [1901] 2 Ir. R. 115.

No action lay for defamatory expressions contained in a bill in Chancery;

> *Hare* v. *Mellers*, 3 Leon. 138, 163 : as explained by Pollock, B., 16 Q. B. D. at p. 113;

or in any pleading or proceeding in an ecclesiastical court;

> *Weston* v. *Dobniet*, Cro. Jac. 432;

or in articles of the peace.

> *Cutler* v. *Dixon*, 4 Rep. 14, *a*.

Statements contained in the judgment of a court-martial, or in the report of a military court of inquiry, are absolutely privileged, as it is the duty of the court-martial to forward such report to the Secretary of State.

> *Jekyll* v. *Sir John Moore*, 2 B. & P. N. R. 341; 6 Esp. 63.
>
> *Home* v. *Bentinck*, 2 B. & B. 130; 4 Moore, 563.
>
> *Oliver* v. *Bentinck*, 3 Taunt. 456.

So also are statements contained in a written declaration handed in by a witness who gives evidence before a court-martial.

> *Dawkins* v. *Lord Rokeby*, L. R. 7 H. L. 744; 45 L. J. Q. B. 8; 23 W. R. 931; 33 L. T. 196.

Statements made in a report to the Court by an Official Receiver under s. 148 of the Companies (Consolidation) Act, 1908, or to the Board of Trade under s. 235 of the same Act are absolutely privileged.

> *Bottomley* v. *Brougham*, [1908] 1 K. B. 584; 77 L. J. K. B. 311; 99 L. T. 111; 24 Times L. R. 262.
>
> *Burr* v. *Smith*, [1909] 2 K. B. 306; 78 L. J. K. B. 889; 101 L. T. 194; 25 Times L. R. 542.

No action will lie for defamatory expressions against a third party contained in an affidavit made and used in the proceedings in a cause, though such statements be false, to the knowledge of the party making them, and introduced out of malice.

> *Henderson* v. *Broomhead*, 28 L. J. Ex. 360; 4 H. & N. 569; 5 Jur.
> N. S. 1175.
> *Astley* v. *Younge*, 2 Burr. 807; 2 Ld. Kenyon, 536.
> *Revis* v. *Smith*, 18 C. B. 126; 25 L. J. C. P. 195; 2 Jur. N. S. 614.
> *Gompas* v. *White*, (1889) 6 Times L. R. 20; 54 J. P. 22.
> *Hartsock* v. *Reddick*, 6 Blackf. (Indiana) 255.

Nor for defamatory statements contained in a witness's proof taken with a view to a trial.

> *Watson* v. *M'Ewan*, [1905] A. C. 480; 74 L. J. P. C. 151; 93 L. T.
> 489.

The defendant exhibited a bill in the Star Chamber charging the plaintiff, *inter alia*, with procuring murders and piracies, and for maintaining murderers and pirates, charges over which the Star Chamber had no jurisdiction. *Held*, that for so much of the bill as contained matter which was "not examinable in the said Court, an action on the case lies; for that cannot be in a course of justice."

> *Buckley* v. *Wood*, 4 Rep. 14, a; Cro. Eliz. 230.
> *Thorn* v. *Blanchard*, 5 Johns. (Amer.) 508.

Statements contained in objections carried in against a solicitor's bill of costs, in proceedings before a Master of the Supreme Court under Order LXV. r. 27 (39) are absolutely privileged.

> *Pedley and May* v. *Morris*, 61 L. J. Q. B. 21; 40 W. R. 42; 65 L. T.
> 526.

So are statements made under s. 4, sub-s. 2, of the Lunacy Act, 1890, in the particulars given in the form required by the Act, upon an application to a justice of the peace, or other judicial authority, for a detention order.

> *Hodson* v. *Pare*, [1899] 1 Q. B. 455; 68 L. J. Q. B. 309; 47 W. R.
> 241; 80 L. T. 13.

A letter of complaint against a solicitor in respect of his professional conduct, with affidavit of alleged charges attached, forwarded to the Registrar of the Law Society in accordance with Form 1 in the Schedule of the Rules under the Solicitors Act, 1888, is a step in a judicial proceeding, and the statements contained in such letter and affidavit are absolutely privileged.

> *Lilley* v. *Roney*, (1892) 61 L. J. Q. B. 727; 8 Times L. R. 642.

But the proceeding must be in its nature judicial—that is, it must be either the adjudication and determination by a competent tribunal of the legal rights of the parties before it, or some necessary step preliminary thereto.

Illustrations.

The London County Council is not a Court: no judicial business was transferred to it (see s. 78, sub-s. 2, of the Local Government Act, 1888). When it is discussing the advisability of granting a music and dancing licence, it is dealing with the administrative business of the county: it is not acting judicially.

Hence, the remarks made by a county councillor during such a discussion are not absolutely privileged.

> *Royal Aquarium* v. *Parkinson*, [1892] 1 Q. B. 431; 61 L. J. Q. B. 409; 40 W. R. 450; 66 L. T. 513; 56 J. P. 404.

When a grand jury is dealing with the fiscal business of the county, a statement made by one of their number, impugning the solvency of a proposed road-contractor, is privileged, but not absolutely privileged.

> *Little* v. *Pomeroy*, Ir. R. 7 C. L. 50.

The service on a debtor of a notice under the Canadian Insolvent Act of 1869, demanding payment of a debt, though an important piece of evidence, should bankruptcy proceedings follow, is not in itself a judicial proceeding; and the delivery of such a notice to a lawyer's clerk for service is a privileged, but not an absolutely privileged, publication.

> *Bank of British North America* v. *Strong*, 1 App. Cas. 307; 34 L. T. 627.

It is submitted that a case laid before counsel for his opinion is not absolutely privileged; at all events, if no writ be yet issued.

> *Minter* v. *Brockman*, May 23rd, 1895 (not reported).
> But see *Watson* v. *M'Ewan*, [1905] A. C. 480; 74 L. J. P. C. 151.

An affidavit made voluntarily when no cause is pending, or made *coram non judice*, is not privileged as a judicial proceeding.

> *Maloney* v. *Bartley*, 3 Camp. 210.

An attorney's bill of costs is in no sense a judicial proceeding, though delivered under a judge's order, and no privilege can be claimed for it.

> *Bruton* v. *Downes*, 1 F. & F. 668.

(iii) *Acts of State.*

A similar immunity, resting also on obvious grounds of public policy, is accorded to all reports made by a military officer to his military superiors in the course of his duty, and to evidence given by any military man to a court-martial or other military court of inquiry; it being essential to the welfare and safety of the State that military discipline should be maintained without any interference by civil tribunals. In short, " all acts done in the honest exercise of military authority are privileged." The law is the same as to the navy. Naval and military matters are for naval and military tribunals to determine, and not the ordinary civil courts. (*Hart* v. *Gumpach*, L. R. 4 P. C. 439; 9 Moore, P. C. C. (N. S.) 241; 42 L. J. P. C. 25; 21 W. R. 365; *Dawkins* v. *Lord Paulet*, L. R. 5 Q. B. 94; 39 L. J. Q. B. 53; 18 W. R. 336; 21 L. T. 584; *Dawkins* v. *Lord Rokeby*, L. R. 7 H. L. 744; 45 L. J. Q. B.

8; 23 W. R. 931; 33 L. T. 196; 4 F. & F. 806; *Att.-Gen. of the Cape of Good Hope* v. *Van Reenen*, [1904] A. C. 114; 73 L. J. P. C. 13; 89 L. T. 591.)   A similarly absolute privilege extends to all acts of State, and to the official notification thereof in the *London Gazette*, to all State papers, and to all advice given to the Crown by its ministers.

Illustrations.

A military court of inquiry may not be strictly a judicial tribunal, but where such court has been assembled under the orders of the General Commanding-in-Chief in conformity with the King's Regulations for the government of the army, a witness who gives evidence thereat stands in the same situation as a witness giving evidence before a judicial tribunal, and all statements made by him thereat, whether orally or in writing, having reference to the subject of the inquiry, are absolutely privileged.

> *Dawkins* v. *Lord Rokeby*, L. R. 7 H. L. 744; 45 L. J. Q. B. 8; 23
> W. R. 931; 33 L. T. 196; in the Exch. Ch. L. R. 8 Q. B. 255.
> And see *Keighley* v. *Bell*, 4 F. & F. 763.

So also are statements contained in the report made by the presiding officer of such a court to the Commander-in-Chief.

> *Home* v. *Bentinck*, 2 B. & B. 130; 4 Moore, 563.

The defendant being the plaintiff's superior officer, in the course of his military duty forwarded to the Adjutant-General certain letters written by the plaintiff, and at the same time, also in accordance with his military duty, reported to the Commander-in-Chief on the contents of such letters, using words defamatory of the plaintiff.   It was alleged that the defendant did so maliciously, and without any reasonable, probable, or justifiable cause, and not in the *bonâ fide* discharge of his duty as the plaintiff's superior officer. *Held*, on demurrer, by the majority of the Court of Q. B. (Mellor and Lush, JJ.), that such reports being made in the course of military duty were absolutely privileged, and that the civil courts had no jurisdiction over such purely military matters.   Cockburn, C.J., dissented, on the grounds that it never could be the duty of a military officer falsely, maliciously, and without reasonable and probable cause to libel his fellow-officer; that the courts of common law have jurisdiction over all wilful and unjust abuse of military authority; and that it would not in any way be destructive of military discipline or of the efficiency of the army to submit questions of malicious oppression to the opinion of a jury.

> *Dawkins* v. *Lord Paulet*, L. R. 5 Q. B. 94; 39 L. J. Q. B. 53; 18
> W. R. 336; 21 L. T. 584.

[N.B.—There was no appeal in this case.   The arguments of Cockburn, C.J., deserve the most careful attention.   In *Dawkins* v. *Lord Rokeby*, *suprâ*, the decision of the House of Lords turned entirely on the fact that the defendant was a witness in a proceeding of a judicial nature.   Neither Kelly, C.B., nor any of the Law Lords (except perhaps Lord Penzance), rest their judgment on the incompetency of a court of common law to inquire into purely military matters. The Court of Exchequer Chamber no doubt express an opinion that " questions of military discipline and military duty alone are cognisable only by a military

court, and not by a court of law." (L. R. 8 Q. B. 271.) But after referring to
"the eloquent and powerful reasoning of Cockburn, C.J., in *Dawkins* v. *Lord
F. Paulet*," the Court goes on to express its satisfaction that the question "is
yet open to final consideration before a court of the last resort." However, in a
court of first instance, at all events, it must now be taken to be the law that
the civil courts of common law can take no cognisance of *purely* military or
purely naval matters (*Sutton* v. *Johnstone*, (1785) 1 T. R. 493; *Grant* v. *Gould*,
(1792) 2 Hen. Bl. 69; *Barwis* v. *Keppel*, (1766) 2 Wils. 314); but wherever the
civil rights of a person in the military or naval service are affected by any
alleged oppression or injustice at the hands of his superior officers, or any illegal
action on the part of a military or naval tribunal, there the civil courts may
interfere. (*In re Mansergh*, 1 B. & S. 400; 30 L. J. Q. B. 296; *Warden* v. *Bailey*,
4 Taunt. 67.)]

But *private letters* written by the commanding officer of the regiment to his
immediate superior on military matters, as distinct from his official reports, are
not absolutely privileged; the question of malice should be left to the jury.

> *Dickson* v. *Earl of Wilton*, 1 F. & F. 419.
> *Dickson* v. *Combermere*, 3 F. & F. 527.

[N.B.—If this be not the distinction, these cases must be taken to be overruled
by the cases cited above. See L. R. 8 Q. B. 272, 273.]

By a general order it was declared that all unemployed Indian officers ineligible
for public employment by reason of misconduct or physical or mental inefficiency
should be removed to the pension list. Under this order the plaintiff was
removed to the pension list and a notification of such removal was published in
the *Indian Gazette. Held*, on demurrer, that no action lay either for the removal
of the plaintiff, or for the official publication of the fact: although special damage
was alleged.

> *Grant* v. *Secretary of State for India*, 2 C. P. D. 445; 25 W. R. 848;
> 37 L. T. 188.

> See *Doss* v. *Secretary of State for India in Council*, L. R. 19 Eq. 509;
> 23 W. R. 773; 32 L. T. 294.

> And *Oliver* v. *Lord Wm. Bentinck*, 3 Taunt. 456.

A petition to the King is absolutely privileged.

> *Hare* v. *Mellers*, 3 Leon. 138, 163.

Any communication relating to State matters made by one officer of State to
another in the course of his official duty is absolutely privileged and cannot be
made the subject of an action for libel.

> *Chatterton* v. *Secretary of State for India in Council*, [1895] 2 Q. B.
> 189; 64 L. J. Q. B. 676; 72 L. T. 858; 59 J. P. 596.

CHAPTER X.

QUALIFIED PRIVILEGE.

WE now pass to the consideration of those occasions which afford the defendant a qualified privilege only, *i.e.*, to cases in which it is open to the plaintiff to destroy the *primâ facie* privilege arising out of the occasion by showing that the defendant acted from an improper motive.

Occasions of qualified privilege may be grouped under five heads:

    I. Where it is the duty of the defendant to make a communication to another person who has an interest in the subject-matter of the communication, or some duty in connection with it.

    II. Where the defendant has an interest in the subject-matter of the communication, and the person to whom the communication is made has a corresponding interest, or some duty in connection with the matter.

    III. Communications made in self-defence, &c.

    IV. Fair and accurate reports of the proceedings of any Court of Justice, or of Parliament, or of a public meeting.

    V. Statements made in or copied from Parliamentary or Official Papers.

The last two heads of qualified privilege are discussed in the next chapter. This chapter is confined to occasions on which a qualified privilege arises from duty or common interest, or self-defence. Fair comments on matters of public interest, which are sometimes treated as a sixth class of privileged communications, have been already dealt with in Chapter VIII., *ante*, pp. 193—225.

"The reason for holding any occasion privileged is common convenience and welfare of society, and it is obvious that no definite line can be so drawn as to mark off with precision those occasions which are privileged, and separate them from those which are not." (Per Lindley, L.J., in *Stuart v. Bell*, [1891] 2 Q. B. at p. 346.) But the canon or guiding principle is clear. It is thus stated by Lord Campbell, C.J., in *Harrison* v. *Bush*, 5 E. & B. at p. 348 ; 25 L. J. Q. B. at p. 29 :—

"A communication made *bonâ fide* upon any subject-matter in which the party communicating has an *interest*, or in reference to which he has a *duty*, is privileged, if made to a person having a corresponding *interest* or *duty*, although it contain criminatory matter, which, without this privilege, would be slanderous and actionable."

But the duty or interest on which the privilege is founded must exist. It is not enough for the defendant honestly to believe that a duty or interest exists. It is true that the judge on a question of privilege always looks at the surrounding circumstances as they appeared to the defendant at the date of the publication, and not at the actual facts as proved at the trial. "The true mode of judging upon the question is to put oneself as much as possible in the position of the defendant." (Per Kay, L.J., [1891] 2 Q. B. at p. 359.) But if the judge holds that the surrounding circumstances, as they then appeared, did not make it the duty of the defendant to act as he did, then the fact that the defendant honestly believed that he was discharging a moral or social duty is immaterial. (See *Stuart* v. *Bell*, [1891] 2 Q. B. at pp. 349, 356, 358.) So, again, it is immaterial that the defendant, reasonably or unreasonably, believed that the person to whom he made the communication had some duty or interest with regard to its subject-matter ; if such person had in fact no such duty or interest, the defence of privilege fails. (*Hebditch* v. *MacIlwaine and others*, [1894] 2 Q. B. 54; 63 L. J. Q. B. 587.) In short, the defendant's *bona fides* is never an element in the question whether a particular occasion is or is not privileged. No distinction can be drawn between one class of privileged communications and another in this respect. (*Jenoure* v. *Delmege*, [1891] A. C. 73; 60 L. J. P. C. 11.) As soon as the judge rules that the occasion is privileged, then, but not till then, it becomes material to inquire into the motives of the defendant, and to ask whether he honestly believed in the truth of what he stated. "That the defendant acted under a sense of duty, though important on the question of malice, is not, I think, relevant to the question whether the occasion was or was not privileged. That question does not depend on the defendant's belief, but on whether he was right or mistaken in that belief." (Per Lindley, L.J., in *Stuart* v. *Bell*, [1891] 2 Q. B. at p. 349, cited with approval by Lord Esher, M.R., in *Hebditch* v. *MacIlwaine and others*, [1894] 2 Q. B. at pp. 60, 61.)

"It is for the defendant to prove that the occasion was privileged. If the defendant does so, the burden of showing actual malice is cast upon the plaintiff; but, unless the defendant does so, the plaintiff is not called upon to prove actual malice. The question whether the occasion is privileged, if the facts are not in dispute, is a question of law only, for the judge, not for the jury. If there are questions of fact in dispute upon which this question depends, they must be left to the jury; but when the jury have found the facts, it is for the judge to say whether they constitute a privileged occasion." (Per Lord Esher, M.R., in *Hebditch* v. *MacIlwaine and others*, [1894] 2 Q. B. at p. 58.)

The defence of privilege is open to a defendant in actions on the case for words causing damage as in actions for defamation (*Wren* v. *Weild*, (1869) L. R. 4 Q. B. at p. 737; *Halsey* v. *Brotherhood*, (1881) 19 Ch. D. at p. 388); except in an action for threats by a patentee under s. 36 of the Patents and Designs Act, 1907. (*Skinner & Co.* v. *Shew & Co.*, [1893] 1 Ch. 413; 62 L. J. Ch. 196; 41 W. R. 217; 67 L. T. 696.)

I. WHERE IT IS THE DUTY OF THE DEFENDANT TO MAKE A COMMUNICATION TO ANOTHER PERSON WHO HAS AN INTEREST IN THE SUBJECT-MATTER OF THE COMMUNICATION, OR SOME DUTY IN CONNECTION WITH IT.

The word "duty" in this connection "cannot be confined to legal duties, which may be enforced by indictment, action, or *mandamus*, but must include moral and social duties of imperfect obligation." (Per Lord Campbell, C.J., in *Harrison* v. *Bush*, 5 E. & B. at p. 349; 25 L. J. Q. B. at p. 29.) It is for the judge to decide whether such a duty exists or not. A legal duty is one which is imposed by the common law or created by statute. "The question of moral or social duty being for the judge, each judge must decide it as best he can for himself. I take moral or social duty to mean a duty recognised by English people of ordinary intelligence and moral principle, but at the same time not a duty enforceable by legal proceedings, whether civil or criminal." (Per Lindley, L.J., in *Stuart* v. *Bell*, [1891] 2 Q. B. at p. 350.) "The underlying principle is 'the common convenience and welfare of society'—not the convenience of individuals or the convenience of a class, but, to use the words of Erle, C.J., in *Whiteley* v. *Adams* (15 C. B. N. S. at p. 418), 'the general interest of society.'" (*Per cur.* in *Macintosh* v. *Dun*, [1908] A. C. at p. 399.)

In deciding whether such a duty exists or not, the most important question to be considered is this : Did the defendant make the communication in answer to an inquiry or was it volunteered ? Hence cases under this head of privilege naturally fall into two classes :—

A. Statements made in answer to inquiry.

B. Statements not in answer to a previous inquiry.

A. STATEMENTS MADE IN ANSWER TO INQUIRY.

Characters of Servants.

The instance that occurs most frequently in ordinary life of a privileged communication made in pursuance of a social duty is where the defendant is asked as to the character of his former servant, by one to whom the servant has applied for a situation. A duty is thereby cast upon the former master to state fully and honestly all that he knows either for or against the servant; and any communication, made in the performance of this duty, is clearly privileged for the sake of the common convenience of society, even though it should turn out that the former master was mistaken in some of his statements. (*Edmondson* v. *Stephenson et ux.*, (1766) Buller's N. P. 8.)

No one is bound to give a character to his servant when asked for it. (*Carrol* v. *Bird*, 3 Esp. 201.) The old statute 5 Eliz. c. 4, which required a master in certain cases to satisfy two justices of the peace that he had reasonable and sufficient cause for putting away his servant had long been obsolete, and now is wholly repealed by the 38 & 39 Vict. c. 86, s. 17. But if any character is given, it must be such as the master honestly believes to be true. Of course, the mere fact that at the trial the master does not attempt to prove that his words were literally true is immaterial; that is no evidence of malice. (See *post*, p. 361.) But if out of anger, or any ill-feeling against the servant, or from a desire to retain her in his own service, he gives her a bad character when he knows that she deserves a good one, he is acting maliciously, and all privilege is lost. So if from any wrong motive, he makes statements about her character or her work which he does not know to be true, careless whether they are true or false, such recklessness is tantamount to malice, and takes the case out of the privilege.

Other Answers to Inquiries.

The rule which applies to characters of servants governs all other answers to confidential inquiries. " There is no reason why any greater protection should be given to a communication made in answer to an inquiry with reference to a servant's character, than to any other communication made from a sense of duty, legal, moral, or social." (Per Lord Macnaghten, in *Jenoure* v. *Delmege*, [1891] A. C. at p. 78.)

" If a person who is thinking of dealing with another in any matter of business asks a question about his character from some one who has means of knowledge, it is for the interests of society that the question should be answered; and if answered *bonâ fide* and without malice, the answer is a privileged communication." (Per Brett, L.J., in *Waller* v. *Loch*, 7 Q. B. D. 622; 51 L. J. Q. B. 274; 30 W. R. 18; 45 L. T. 242.) "Every one owes it as a duty to his fellow men to state what he knows about a person when inquiry is made." (Per Grove, J., in *Robshaw* v. *Smith*, 38 L. T. at p. 424.) But the inquiry must be made by a person who has a legitimate interest in the matter, and, therefore, a right to the information for which he applies. Idle gossip has no privilege. And the mere fact that one person has contracted with another to supply information does not create such a duty or common interest that communications made in pursuance of the contract are privileged. (*Macintosh* v. *Dun*, [1908] A. C. 390; 77 L. J. P. C. 113; 99 L. T. 64.)

So, too, it is a duty every one owes to society to assist in the discovery of any crime, dishonesty, or misconduct, and to afford all information which will lead to the detection of the culprit. "It is a perfectly privileged communication if a party who is interested in discovering a wrong-doer comes and makes inquiries, and a person in answer makes a discovery or a *bonâ fide* communication which he knows or believes to be true, although it may possibly affect the character of a third person." (Per Parke, B., in *Kine* v. *Sewell*, 3 M. & W. 302.)

When once such a confidential inquiry is set on foot, all subsequent interviews between the parties will be privileged, so long as what takes place thereat is still relevant to the original inquiry. And it is a question for the jury whether any further communication, though apparently casual and voluntary, did not take place under the confidential relation already established. (*Beatson* v. *Skene*, 5 H. & N. 838; 29 L. J. Ex. 430; *Hopwood* v. *Thorn*, 8 C. B. 293; 19 L. J. C. P. 94; *Wallace* v. *Carroll*, 11 Ir. C. L. R. 485.)

But the defendant's answer must always be pertinent to the inquiry. He must not wander off into matters wholly unconnected with the question. If he is asked the plaintiff's name or address, he must not commence to disparage the plaintiff's credit, conduct, family, or wares. The reply must be an answer to the question, or reasonably induced thereby, and not irrelevant information gratuitously volunteered. (*Southam* v. *Allen*, Sir Thos. Raym. 231 ; *Huntley* v. *Ward*, 6 C. B. N. S. 514.)

Illustrations.

Statements made by a servant in answer to inquiries made by her mistress with reference to the conduct and character of another servant, are privileged.

Mead v. *Hughes and wife*, (1891) 7 Times L. R. 291.

If A. is about to have dealings with B., but first comes to C. and confidentially asks him his opinion of B., C.'s answer is privileged. "Everyone is quite at liberty to state his opinion *bonâ fide* of the respectability of a party thus inquired about." Per Lord Denman in

Storey v. *Challands*, 8 C. & P. 234.

So if the owner of a vacant farm ask me as to the character of a person who is applying to become his tenant, it is my duty to tell him what I know about that person.

If a friend of mine comes down into the country to live near me, and asks me which of the local doctors or tradesmen he should employ, the advice which I give him in answer to his question is privileged.

A husband asked a medical man to see his wife and ascertain her mental condition. He reported to the husband that she was insane. *Held*, a privileged communication.

Weldon v. *Winslow*, *Times*, March 14th to 19th, 1884.

Both the Marquis of Anglesey and his agent told the defendant, the tenant of Haywood Park Farm, to inform them if he saw or heard anything wrong respecting the game. The defendant heard that the gamekeeper was selling the game, and believing the fact to be so, wrote and informed the Marquis. *Held*, that the letter was privileged ; but Parke, J., intimated that if the defendant had not been previously directed to communicate anything he thought going wrong, the letter would have been unauthorised and libellous.

Cockayne v. *Hodgkisson*, 5 C. & P. 543.

See *King* v. *Watts*, 8 C. & P. 615.

Barton, a friend of the defendant, employed a builder, the plaintiff's master, to build a house for him : the defendant informed Barton that the plaintiff while at work on his house had removed some quarterings. Barton complained to the master builder, who came down to the defendant's and said, "I am told you say that you saw my man Kine take away some of the quarterings from Mr. Barton's premises." A repetition of the charge made then to the plaintiff's master without malice was held privileged, and as the plaintiff had not called Barton to prove the original remark, the jury found for the defendant, and a new trial was refused. Parke, B., said, "Is a man's mouth to be closed when I ask him if he has seen another man take away my timber?"

Kine v. *Sewell*, 3 M. & W. 297.

Where a father employed the defendant to make inquiries about the position and antecedents of his daughter's husband, a report by the defendant to the father of the result of his inquiries is privileged.

> *Atwill* v. *Mackintosh,* 6 Lathrop (120 Mass.), 177.

So where an attorney employed defendant to translate some German into English, no action lies for the publication of such translation to the attorney.

> *Luckerman* v. *Sonnenschein,* 32 Freeman (62 Illinois), 115.
> And see *Kerr* v. *Shedden,* 4 C. & P. 528.
> *Du Barré* v. *Livette,* Peake, 76.

Watkins met the defendant in Brecon, and addressing him said: "I hear that you say the bank of Bromage and Snead at Monmouth has stopped. Is it true?" Defendant answered, "Yes, it is. I was told so. It was so reported at Cricklewell, and nobody would take their bills, and I came to town in consequence of it myself." *Held,* that if the defendant understood Watkins to be asking for information by which to regulate his conduct, and spoke the words merely by way of advice, they were privileged.

> *Bromage* v. *Prosser,* 4 B. & C. 247; 1 C. & P. 475; 6 D. & R. 296.

The defendant was asked to sign a memorial, the object of which was to retain the plaintiff as trustee of a charity from which office he was about to be removed. The defendant refused to sign, and on being pressed for his reasons, stated them explicitly. *Held,* a privileged communication.

> *Cowles* v. *Potts,* 34 L. J. Q. B. 247; 11 Jur. N. S. 946; 13 W. R. 858.

Whenever a transfer of shares is presented at the office of a railway company, the secretary of the company writes to the transferor to know if the transfer is in order and duly authorised. Any relevant reply to such an inquiry is privileged.

> *Hesketh* v. *Brindle,* (1888) 4 Times L. R. 199.

The plaintiff had been a Major-General commanding a corps of irregular troops during the war in the Crimea. Complaint having been made of the insubordination of the troops, the corps commanded by the plaintiff was placed under the superior command of General Vivian. The plaintiff then resigned his command. General Vivian directed General Shirley to inquire and report on the state of the corps, and particularly referred him for information on the matter to the defendant, who was General Vivian's private secretary and civil commissioner, to whom he also wrote that he should give General Shirley every aid in his power. The defendant thereupon communicated to General Shirley information which the plaintiff alleged was slanderous. *Held,* that the occasion was privileged.

> *Beatson* v. *Skene,* 5 H. & N. 838; 29 L. J. Ex. 430; 6 Jur. N. S. 780;
> 2 L. T. 378.
> *Hopwood* v. *Thorn,* 8 C. B. 293; 19 L. J. C. P. 94; 14 Jur. 87.

The plaintiff was a London merchant who had had business relations with the London and Yorkshire Bank (Limited). The defendant, the manager of that bank, on being applied to by one Hudson for information about the plaintiff, showed Hudson an anonymous letter which the bank had received about the plaintiff, and which contained the libel in question. *Held,* that handing Hudson the letter in confidence was a privileged communication. Grove, J., in refusing a rule for a new trial, made the following remarks:—"The defendant did not act as a volunteer, but was applied to for information. When applied to he did give such information as he possessed. He might have refused to give that information. He had no legal duty cast upon him to give any opinion. But he was entitled to give his opinion when asked, and *à fortiori*, as it seems to me, to show any letters he had received bearing upon the subject. If one man shows another a letter, he leaves him to estimate what value attaches to it; whereas any opinion he gives might be based on very insufficient grounds. It is better to state facts than to give an opinion. Every one owes it as a duty to his fellow-men to state what he knows about a person, when inquiry is made; otherwise no one would be able to discern honest men from dishonest men. It is highly desirable, therefore, that a privilege of this sort should be maintained. An anonymous letter is usually a very despicable thing. But anonymous letters may be very important, not by reason of what they say, but because they lead to inquiry, which may substantiate what they have said. It seems to me, therefore, that he was fully entitled to show this anonymous letter for what it was worth."

Robshaw v. *Smith*, (1878) 38 L. T. 423.

B. Statements not in answer to a previous inquiry.

In the cases just quoted the defendant did not volunteer the information, but was expressly applied to for it. This is always no doubt a very material fact in the defendant's favour; but it is never alone decisive. "It is not necessary in all cases that the information should be given in answer to an inquiry." (Per Jessel, M.R., in *Waller* v. *Loch*, 7 Q. B. D. 621; 51 L. J. Q. B. 274; 45 L. T. 242.) "Communications injurious to the character of another may be made in answer to inquiry or may be volunteered. If the communication be made in the legitimate defence of a person's own interest, or plainly under a sense of duty such as would be 'recognised by English people of ordinary intelligence and moral principle' (*Stuart* v. *Bell*, [1891] 2 Q. B. at p. 350), to borrow again the language of Lindley, L.J., it cannot matter whether it is volunteered or brought out in answer to an inquiry. But in cases which are near the line, and in cases which may give rise to a difference of opinion, the circumstance that the information is volunteered is an element for consideration certainly not without some importance." (*Per cur.* in *Macintosh* v. *Dun*, [1908] A. C. at p. 399.) The test in every case is this:—Assume in the defendant's favour that the circumstances really were such as they appeared to him to be; then in those circumstances was it the duty of an honest man to act as the defendant did in this case? And the circumstances may be such as to make it clearly the duty of a good citizen to go at once to the person most concerned and tell him everything, without waiting for him to come and inquire. The defendant may honestly believe that a crime is about to be committed, or that his neighbour's life, or property, is in serious danger. And it may well be that his neighbour has no suspicions, and never would inquire into the matter, unless warned. If, however, the facts as they appeared to the defendant did not, in the opinion of the learned judge at the trial, impose on him any duty to speak or write to the person concerned then there is no privilege, although the defendant may have honestly believed that it was his duty to act as he did.

Hence, in cases where neither life nor property is in imminent and obvious peril, there the circumstance that the defendant was applied to for the information, and did not volunteer it, will materially affect the issue. Where the matter is not of great or immediate importance, interference on the defendant's part may be considered officious and meddlesome; although, had he been applied to, it would clearly have been his duty to give all the information in his power. An answer to a confidential inquiry may be privileged where the same information, if volunteered, would be actionable.

Illustrations.

If an intending customer comes to me and inquires as to the respectability or credit of a tradesman, it is my duty to tell him all I know. But I am not justified in standing at the door of a tradesman's shop and voluntarily defaming his character to his intending customers.

> *Southam* v. *Allen*, Sir Thos. Raym. 231.
> And see *Picton* v. *Jackman*, 4 C. & P. 257.
> *Storey* v. *Challands*, 8 C. & P. 234.
> And other cases cited *post*, p. 265.

Nash selected plaintiff to be his attorney in an action. Defendant, apparently a total stranger, wrote to Nash to deprecate his so employing the plaintiff. This was held to be clearly not a privileged communication. Damages 1*s.*

> *Godson* v. *Home*, 1 B. & B. 7 ; 3 Moore, 223.

The defendant wrote two letters and addressed two envelopes, one to A. and the other to B.   He then inadvertently placed the letter intended for A. in the envelope addressed to B.   The letter intended for A. contained a libel on the plaintiff, but would have been privileged if sent direct to A.   B., however, had no interest in the matter, and no duty to perform in connection with it.   It was held at first that the publication to B. was privileged, because the defendant had intended the letter for A.

> *Tompson* v. *Dashwood*, 11 Q. B. D. 43 ; 52 L. J. Q. B. 425 ; 48 L. T. 943 ; 48 J. P. 55.

But this decision was expressly overruled in a subsequent case, in which the Court of Appeal held that it does not matter to whom the defendant may have *intended* to make the communication.   There is no privilege unless the person to whom he does in fact publish the defamatory words has some duty or some interest in the matter.

> *Hebditch* v. *MacIlwaine and others*, [1894] 2 Q. B. 54 ; 63 L. J. Q. B. 587 ; 42 W. R. 422 ; 70 L. T. 826 ; 58 J. P. 620.

The defendant, the tenant of a farm, required some repairs to be done at his house ; the landlord's agent sent up two workmen, one of whom was the plaintiff.   They made a bad job of it ; the plaintiff undoubtedly got drunk while on the premises ; and the defendant was convinced from what he heard that the plaintiff had broken open his cellar door and drunk his cider.   Two days afterwards the defendant met the plaintiff and a man called Taylor, and charged the plaintiff with breaking open his cellar door, getting drunk, and spoiling the job.   He repeated this charge later in the same day to Taylor alone in the absence of the plaintiff, and also to the landlord's agent.   *Held*, that the communication to the landlord's agent was clearly privileged, as both were interested in the repairs being properly done ; that the statement made to the plaintiff in Taylor's presence was also privileged ; but that the repetition of the statement to Taylor in the absence of the plaintiff was unnecessary and officious, and therefore not protected, although made in the belief of its truth.

> *Toogood* v. *Spyring*, 1 C. M. & R. 181 ; 4 Tyrw. 582.

Communications made in discharge of a Duty arising from a Confidential Relationship existing between the parties.

In what cases then will a defendant be privileged in going of his own accord to the person concerned, and giving him information for which he has not asked ? This is often a difficult question to answer.   But in one class of cases it is clear that it is not only excusable, but that it is imperative on the defendant so to do ; and that is where there exists between the defendant and the person to whom he makes the communication such a confidential relation as to throw on the defendant the duty of protecting the interests of the person concerned.

s 2

Such a confidential relationship exists between husband and wife, father and son, brother and sister, guardian and ward, master and servant, principal and agent, solicitor and client, partners, or even intimate friends : in short, wherever any trust or confidence is reposed by the one in the other. In other words it will be the duty of A. to volunteer information to B., whenever B. could justly reproach A. for his silence if he did not volunteer such information.

Merely labelling a letter " *Private and confidential,*" or merely stating "*I speak in confidence,*" will not make a communication confidential in the legal sense of that term, if there is in fact no relationship between the parties which the law deems confidential. (*Picton* v. *Jackman,* 4 C. & P. 257; *Kitcat* v. *Sharp,* 52 L. J. Ch. 134; 48 L. T. 64.)

Thus it is clearly the duty of my steward, bailiff, foreman, or housekeeper to whom I have entrusted the management of my lands, business, or house, to come and tell me if they think anything is going wrong, and not to wait till my own suspicions are aroused, and I myself begin asking questions. So my family solicitor may voluntarily write and inform me of anything which he thinks it is to my advantage to know, without waiting for me to come down to his office and inquire. But it would be dangerous for another solicitor, whom I have never employed, to volunteer the same information; for there is no confidential relation existing between us. So a father, guardian, or an intimate friend may warn a young man against associating with a particular individual; or may warn a lady not to marry a particular suitor; though in the same circumstances it might be considered officious and meddlesome, if a mere stranger gave such a warning. So if the defendant is in the army or navy or in a government office, it would be his duty to inform his official superiors of any serious misconduct on the part of his subordinates; for the defendant is in some degree answerable for the faults of those immediately under his control. But it does not follow that, if A. and B. are officers, clerks, or servants of equal rank and standing, it is the duty of A. to tell tales of B., except in self-defence; for A.'s superiors expect him to do his own work merely, and have not

invested him with any authority or control over B. (See *Bell* v.
Parke, 10 Ir. C. L. R. 284; 11 Ir. C. L. R. 418.)

Illustrations.

Communications between husband and wife are " held sacred." There is in
such a case no publication in law.

> *Wennhak* v. *Morgan*, 20 Q. B. D. 635; 57 L. J. Q. B. 241; 36 W. R.
> 697; 59 L. T. 28; 52 J. P. 470.

My regular solicitor may unasked give me any information concerning third
persons of which he thinks it to my interest that I should be informed, even
although he is not at the moment conducting any legal proceedings for me; for
I have a right to expect that he will give me all information material to my
interest which comes to his knowledge.

> *Davis* v. *Reeves*, (1855) 5 Ir. C. L. R. 79.

A solicitor who is conducting a case for a minor may inform his next friend
of the minor's misconduct.

> *Wright* v. *Woodgate*, 2 C. M. & R. 573; 1 Tyr. & G. 12; 1 Gale, 329
> (approved in L. R. 4 P. C. 495).

If a solicitor reasonably believes that his services may be required by a
possible client who does afterwards retain him to appear before a magistrate
and to apply for a summons, all communications passing between the solicitor
and the client leading up to the retainer and relevant to it, and having that and
nothing else in view are privileged.

> *Browne* v. *Dunn*, (H. L.) (1893) 6 R. 67.

A report by the Comptroller of the Navy to the Board of Admiralty upon the
plans and proposals of a naval architect, is clearly privileged. Per Grove, J., in

> *Henwood* v. *Harrison*, L. R. 7 C. P. 606; 41 L. J. C. P. 206; 20
> W. R. 1000; 26 L. T. 938.

A timekeeper employed on public works, on behalf of a public department,
wrote a letter to the secretary of the department, imputing fraud to the contractor. Blackburn, J., directed the jury that if they thought the letter was
written in good faith and for the information of his employers, it was privileged.

> *Scarll* v. *Dixon*, 4 F. & F. 250.

A relation or intimate friend may confidentially advise a lady not to marry
a particular suitor, and assign reasons; and the statements he makes will be
privileged.

> *Todd* v. *Hawkins*, 2 M. & Rob. 20; 8 C. & P. 88.
> And see per Erskine, *amicum curiæ*, 2 Smith, p. 4.
> *Adams* v. *Coleridge*, (1884) 1 Times L. R. 84.

The defendant and Tinmouth were joint owners of *The Robinson*, and engaged
the plaintiff as master; in April, 1843, defendant purchased Tinmouth's share;
in August, 1843, defendant wrote a business letter to Tinmouth, claiming a
return of 150*l.*, and incidentally libelled the plaintiff with respect to his conduct
while in their joint employ. *Held*, a privileged communication, as a confidential
relationship still existed between the defendant and Tinmouth.

> *Wilson* v. *Robinson*, 7 Q. B. 68; 14 L. J. Q. B. 196; 9 Jur. 726.

A., B., and C. are brother officers in the same regiment. A. meets B. and
says, " I have learnt that C. has been guilty of an atrocious offence: I wish to

consult you whether I should divulge it—whether I should speak of it to the commanding officer." Such remark and the discussion that ensued are both privileged. Per Pigot, C.B., in

> *Bell* v. *Parke*, 10 Ir. C. L. R. 284. [The decision in the case turned on the language of the plea.]

But a complaint of a man's conduct is not privileged, if addressed by the employer to the man's wife.

> *Jones* v. *Williams*, (1885) 1 Times L. R. 572.

The officers and men of the garrison of St. Helena gave an entertainment at the theatre, at which considerable noise and disturbance took place. The commanding officer was informed that this was caused by the plaintiff, who was said to have been drunk. The plaintiff was an assistant master in the Government School. The commanding officer reported the circumstances to the colonial secretary of the island, and the plaintiff was in consequence suspended from his appointment. Verdict for the plaintiff disapproved and set aside, and judgment arrested.

> *Stace* v. *Griffith*, L. R. 2 P. C. 420 ; 6 Moore, P. C. C. N. S. 18 ; 20 L. T. 197.

A statement made by the clerk to a board of guardians to the relieving officer as to an alleged neglect of duty by the medical officer is privileged.

> *Sutton* v. *Plumridge*, 16 L. T. 741.

It is the duty of the second master in a school to inform the headmaster and the governors of the school that reports have been for some time in circulation imputing habits of drunkenness to an assistant master.

> *Hume* v. *Marshall* (Cockburn, C.J.), (1877) 42 J. P. 136.
> *Keith* v. *Lauder*, (1906) 8 F. 356 (Ct. of Sess.).

So a statement made to a chief constable regarding the official conduct of a police sergeant is privileged.

> *Cassidy* v. *Connochie*, (1907) S. C. 1112 (Ct. of Sess.).
> *A.* v. *B.*, (1907) S. C. 1154 (Ct. of Sess.).

But no privilege attaches to a statement made to a headmaster that a person, who had formerly been a second master at the school and had now left, had been seen drunk in the street on a Sunday while he was a master at the school.

> *Goslett* v. *Garment*, (1897) 13 Times L. R. 391.

Where, after an election, the agent of the defeated candidate wrote a letter to the agent of the successful candidate, asserting that the plaintiff and another (both members of the successful candidate's committee) had bribed a particular voter, the letter was held not to be privileged, as there was no confidential relation existing between the two agents.

> *Dickeson* v. *Hilliard and another*, L. R. 9 Ex. 79 ; 43 L. J. Ex. 37 ; 22 W. R. 372 ; 30 L. T. 196.

The defendants carried on, under the name of "The Mercantile Agency," the business of obtaining information with reference to the commercial standing and position of persons in New South Wales and elsewhere, and of communicating such information confidentially to subscribers to the agency in response to specific and confidential inquiries on their part. The defendants in reply to such an inquiry supplied information to a customer defamatory of the plaintiff. It was held by the Judicial Committee of the Privy Council, that there was no privilege as such information was supplied, not in the general interests of society or from a sense of duty, but from motives of self-interest, and as part of the defendants' business, which consisted in trading for profit in the characters of other persons.

> *Macintosh* v. *Dun,* [1908] A. C. 390; 77 L. J. P. C. 113; 99 L. T. 64; 24 Times L. R. 705.

> But see *Clover* v. *Royden,* L. R. 17 Eq. 190; 43 L. J. Ch. 665; 22 W. R. 254; 29 L. T. 639.

The law is otherwise in America. It appears to be generally accepted there that when a merchant inquires from Messrs. Stubbs or Perry, or any other mercantile agency, as to the solvency of a person with whom he is about to deal, the answer to such inquiry is privileged. But where a mercantile agency or trade protection society issues a weekly circular or notification sheet and sends it to all its subscribers, some of whom will be interested in one item, others in another item, but none in all the items of information contained in it, the judges of the Court of Errors and Appeals in New Jersey were divided in opinion; the majority (9 to 5) holding that such a communication was not privileged.

> *King* v. *Patterson,* (1887) 20 Vroom (49 New Jersey), 417; 83 Law Times Journal, 408.

> *Newbold* v. *Bradstreet and Son,* 57 Maryland, 38; 10 Amer. Rep. 426.

> And see *Andrews* v. *Nott Bower,* [1895] 1 Q. B. 888; *post,* p. 303.

Information volunteered when there is no Confidential Relationship existing between the parties.

Where the defendant does not stand in any confidential relation to the person interested, it is difficult to define what circumstances will be sufficient to impose on him the duty of volunteering the information. The rule of law applicable to such cases cannot be better expressed than in the following passage :—" Where a person is so situated that it becomes right in the interests of society that he should tell to a third person certain facts, then if he *bonâ fide* and without malice does tell them, it is a privileged communication " (per Blackburn, J., in *Davies* v. *Snead,* L. R. 5 Q. B. 611; 39 L. J. Q. B. 202; 23 L. T. 609)—a passage cited with approval by Jessel, M.R., and Brett, L.J., in *Waller* v. *Loch,* 7 Q. B. D. 621, 622; 51 L. J. Q. B. 274; 30 W. R. 18; 45 L. T. 242; 46 J. P. 484. But the difficulty is in any given case to determine whether it had or had not become right in the interests of society that the defendant should act as he did. And this is a question rather of social morality than of law.

For instance, if I learn that one of my tradesmen is about to supply goods on credit to a man whom I know to be practically insolvent, may I warn him not to do so? Is it right, in the interests of society, that I should tell him what I know, or am I to stand by and see him lose his money? In the days of Elizabeth, it was considered clear law that no action would lie for such a caution given as " good counsel." (*Vanspike* v. *Cleyson*, Cro. Eliz. 541; 1 Roll. Abr. 67.) So it was in the days of George III. (*Herver* v. *Dowson*, Bull. N. P. 8.) But in 1838 Lord Abinger, C.B., held that no such communication should be *volunteered*: the defendant must wait till the tradesman applies to him for advice. " If the defendant had been asked by Mr. Butler as to the plaintiff, and had said what he did without malice, no action would have been maintainable; but as he made the communication without being asked in any way to do so, he is liable in this action, if the words reflect on the character of the plaintiff as a tradesman." (*King* v. *Watts*, 8 C. & P. at p. 615.) And in *Bennett* v. *Deacon*, (1846) 2 C. B. 628; 15 L. J. C. P. 289, the Court of Common Pleas was equally divided on this question. The judgments of Tindal, C.J., and Erle, J., would probably be followed in the present day rather than those of Coltman and Cresswell, JJ.

In *Coxhead* v. *Richards*, (1846) 2 C. B. 569; 15 L. J. C. P. 278; 10 Jur. 984, the same Court was equally divided on a very similar question, whether a man may inform the owner of a ship that his captain has been guilty of gross misconduct at sea. Here again, probably, the view taken by Tindal, C.J., and Erle, J., would prevail in the present day. Willes, J., said in *Amann* v. *Damm*, (1860) 8 C. B. N. S. at p. 602; 29 L. J. C. P. at p. 314, that he was prepared " to go the whole length " with them. Lindley, L.J., expresses the same opinion in *Stuart* v. *Bell*, [1891] 2 Q. B. at p. 347. It was admitted on all hands in *Clark* v. *Molyneux*, 3 Q. B. D. 237; 47 L. J. Q. B. 230; 26 W. R. 104; 36 L. T. 466; 37 L. T. 694; 14 Cox, C. C. 10, that a letter sent to an absent vicar, informing him of the misconduct of the curate whom he had left in charge of the parish, was privileged. And generally, am I justified in informing a master or employer of any misconduct on the part of his servant or workman which has come to my knowledge, and not to his? It is submitted that such a communication is privileged. In *Stuart* v. *Bell*, [1891] 2 Q. B. 341; 60 L. J. Q. B. 577; 39 W. R. 612; 64 L. T. 633, the Court of Appeal was divided on a question of this kind; Lindley and Kay, L.JJ., holding that such a communication was privileged, Lopes, L.J., agreeing with the judge below (Wills, J.) that it was not. The decision of the majority of the Court of Appeal is, of course, binding.

" If a neighbour makes inquiry of another respecting his own servants, that other may state what he believes to be true; but the case is different when the statement is a voluntary act; yet, even in this case, the jury is to consider whether the words were dictated by a sense of the duty which one neighbour owes to another." (Per Coltman, J., in *Rumsey* v. *Webb et ux.*, (1842) Car. & M. at p. 105; and this direction was approved by the Court, 11 L. J. C. P. 129.)

But in every case the test would appear to be, Did the defendant act under a sense of duty, or from any motive of self-interest? In the former case, whenever a moral or legal duty exists, he is protected: in the latter he is not. (*Macintosh* v. *Dun*, [1908] A. C. 390; 77 L. J. P. C. 113; 99 L. T. 64.)

It appears to be clear that if the defendant reasonably supposes that human life would be seriously imperilled by his remaining silent, he may volunteer information to those thus endangered, or to their master, though he be not himself personally concerned (see per Cresswell, J., 2 C. B. 605). So, if the money or goods of the person to whom he speaks would be in great and obvious danger of being stolen or destroyed. So, too, it appears, that the defendant may, without being applied to for the information, acquaint a master with the misconduct of his servants, if instances have come under the special notice of the defendant which have been concealed from the master's eye. (*Stuart* v. *Bell*, *suprà*.) But in most cases other than those with which we have dealt, the defendant runs a great risk in volunteering statements which afterwards turn out to be inaccurate, unless indeed he is himself personally interested in the matter, or compelled to interfere by the fiduciary relationship in which he stands to some person concerned.

Illustrations.

The defendant said to one Dudley, " Doth Vanspike (the plaintiff, a merchant) owe you any money?" Dudley replied that he did. Defendant then said, " You had best call for it; take heed how you trust him." And it was adjudged for the defendant; for it is not any slander to the plaintiff, but good counsel to Dudley.

Vanspike v. *Cleyson*, (1597) Cro. Eliz. 541; 1 Roll. Abr. 67.

The plaintiff kept livery stables and an inn at the Belsavage; and the defendant had other stables for the same purpose, in the same yard. A stranger comes with a waggon into the yard, and demands of the defendant, "Which is Belsavage Inn?" The defendant replied, "This is Belsavage Inn; deal not with Southam; for he is broke, and there is neither entertainment for man or horse." Verdict for plaintiff, with "great damages."

Southam v. *Allen*, (1674) Sir Thos. Raym. 231.

So where defendant said of the plaintiff, who was a tradesman, "He cannot stand it long, he will be a bankrupt soon;" and it was laid as special damage in the declaration, that one Lane had, in consequence, refused to trust the plaintiff for a horse. Lane was the only witness called for the plaintiff; and it appearing on his evidence, that the words were not spoken maliciously, but in confidence and friendship to Lane, and by way of warning to him, and that in consequence of that advice he did not trust the plaintiff with the horse: Pratt, C.J., directed the jury, that though the words were otherwise actionable, yet if they should be of opinion that the words were not spoken out of malice, but in the manner before mentioned, they ought to find the defendant not guilty; and they did so accordingly.

Herver v. *Dowson*, (1765) Buller's N. P. 8.

Plaintiff had been tenant to the defendant; a wine-broker went to defendant to ask him plaintiff's present address. Defendant commenced to abuse the plaintiff. The broker said: "I don't come to inquire about his character, but only for his address: I have done business with him before." But the defendant continued to denounce the plaintiff as a swindler, adding, however, "I speak in confidence." The broker thanked defendant for his remarks, and declined in future to trust the plaintiff. *Held*, that it was rightly left to the jury to say if defendant spoke *bonâ fide* or maliciously.

Picton v. *Jackman*, 4 C. & P. 257.

Horsford was about to deal with the plaintiff, when he met the defendant, who said at once, without his opinion being asked at all, "If you have anything to do with Storey, you will live to repent it; he is a most unprincipled man," &c. Lord Denman directed a verdict for the plaintiff, because the defendant began by making the statement, without waiting to be asked.

Storey v. *Challands*, 8 C. & P. 234.

The plaintiff was a maltster, and had bought a quantity of barley of Butler. The defendant said to Butler, "Don't trust that damned rogue, he will never pay you a farthing. Have you sold King some barley? You mind and have the money for it before it goes out of the waggon, or you will never have it." Butler, in consequence, refused to deliver the barley till he was paid for it. Lord Abinger, C.B., directed the jury that the defendant's words were unprivileged, because they were volunteered. Verdict for the plaintiff accordingly. Damages one farthing.

King v. *Watts*, 8 C. & P. 614.

Defendant met Clark in the road, and asked him if he had sold his timber yet. Clark replied that Bennett (plaintiff) was going to have it. Defendant asked if he was going to pay ready money for it, and being answered in the negative, said, "Then you'll lose your timber; for Bennett owes me about 25*l*., and I am going to arrest him next week for my money, and your timber will help to pay my debt." Clark subsequently declined to sell the timber to the plaintiff. Plaintiff really did owe defendant about 23*l*. Coltman, J., directed the jury that the caution was altogether unprivileged because volunteered: and they therefore found a verdict for the plaintiff, damages 40*s*. The Court of C.P. was equally divided on the question whether the judge was right in his direction, and therefore the verdict for the plaintiff stood.

> *Bennett* v. *Deacon*, 2 C. B. 628 ; 15 L. J. C. P. 289.

A. and B. are tenants to the same landlord with similar clauses in their respective leases. A. has reason to believe that B. is breaking his covenants, committing waste, violating the rotation of crops, &c. The landlord is away abroad. It is submitted on the authority of *Cockayne* v. *Hodgkisson*, 5 C. & P. 543, *ante*, p. 255, that it is not the duty of A. to write and inform the landlord of his suspicions, and that therefore such a letter would not be privileged ; unless the landlord had in some way set A. in authority over B.

A housemaid thinks the cook is robbing their master. It is not her duty to speak at once on bare suspicion merely ; but as soon as she sees something which reasonably appears to her inconsistent with the cook's innocence, she will be justified, it is submitted, in telling her master all she knows.

" If a man write to a father scandalous matter concerning his children, of which he gives notice to the father, and adviseth the father to have better regard to his children ; this is only reformatory, without any respect of profit to him which wrote it ; it shall not be intended to be a libel."

> *Peacock* v. *Reynal*, (1612) 2 Brownlow & Goldesborough, 151.
>
> Approved by Erle, C.J., 15 C. B. N. S. 418 ; 33 L. J. C. P. 95.

Communications confidentially made to a master as to the conduct of his servants, by one who has had an opportunity of noticing certain malpractices on their part, are privileged.

> *Cleaver* v. *Sarraude*, 1 Camp. 268.
>
> *Kine* v. *Sewell*, 3 M. & W. 297.
>
> *Amann* v. *Damm*, 8 C. B. N. S. 597 ; 29 L. J. C. P. 313 ; 7 Jur. N. S. 47 ; 8 W. R. 470.
>
> *Musters* v. *Burgess*, (1886) 3 Times L. R. 96.

The plaintiff was Mr. Stanley's valet, and stayed with his master at the house of the defendant, the Mayor of Newcastle. During the visit, the chief constable showed the defendant a letter which he had received from the chief constable of Edinburgh to the effect that the plaintiff was suspected of stealing a watch in Edinburgh. The defendant did nothing at the time, but just before Mr. Stanley left Newcastle, the defendant told him what was in the letter. Mr. Stanley in consequence dismissed the plaintiff from his service. *Held*, by the majority of the Court of Appeal, a privileged occasion.

> *Stuart* v. *Bell*, [1891] 2 Q. B. 341 ; 60 L. J. Q. B. 577 ; 39 W. R. 612 ; 64 L. T. 633.

A letter written to a Board of Guardians by their clerk complaining that one of the under-clerks in the office neglected his duty and behaved in an offensive and insubordinate manner, is privileged.

> *Keight* v. *Hill*, (1879) 43 J. P. 176.

The occupier of a house may complain to the landlord of the workmen he has sent to repair the house.

> *Toogood* v. *Spyring*, 1 C. M. & R. 181 ; 4 Tyrw. 582.

A landlord may, it seems, complain to his tenant of the conduct of her lodgers.

> *Knight* v. *Gibbs*, 1 A. & E. 43 ; 3 N. & M. 467.

If a report be current in a parish as to the disgraceful conduct of the incumbent, bringing scandal on the church, a good churchman may inform the bishop of the diocese thereof, although he does not reside in the district and is not personally interested.

> *James* v. *Boston*, 2 C. & K. 4.

A letter written by a private individual to the chief secretary of the Postmaster-General complaining of the misconduct of an official under the authority of the Postmaster-General, is privileged, even though some of the charges made in the letter may not be true, and though the defendant stood in no relation, past or present, either to the plaintiff or to the Post Office authorities.

> *Blake* v. *Pilfold*, 1 Moo. & Rob. 198.
> *Woodward* v. *Lander*, 6 C. & P. 548, *post*, p. 278.

The first mate of a merchant ship wrote a letter to the defendant, an old and intimate friend, stating that he was placed in a very awkward position owing to the drunken habits, &c., of the captain, and saying :—"How shall I act ? It is my duty to write to Mr. Ward (the owner of the ship), but my doing so would ruin " the captain and his wife and family. The defendant, after much deliberation and consultation with other nautical friends, thought it his duty to show the letter to Ward, who thereupon dismissed the captain. The defendant knew nothing of the matter except from the mate's letter. Tindal, C.J., told the jury that the publication was privileged ; and they negatived malice. The Court of C.P. was equally divided on the question whether so showing the letter was privileged ; and therefore the verdict for the defendant stood.

> *Coxhead* v. *Richards*, 2 C. B. 569 ; 15 L. J. C. P. 278 ; 10 Jur. 984.
> *Keith* v. *Lauder*, (1906) 8 F. 356 (Ct. of Sess.).

A former friend of the plaintiff, who knew all about plaintiff's past wild life, hearing plaintiff was about to be married, wrote, after consulting the clergyman of his parish, to the lady, to whom he was apparently a stranger, disclosing plaintiff's antecedents. Hill, J., held that the occasion was *primâ facie* privileged.

> *Ex relatione* Coleridge, Q.C., 15 C. B. N. S. 410, 411.

It is apparently clear law in America, that though any near relative may write such a letter warning a lady not to marry the plaintiff, no mere friend, not related to her, may volunteer such advice. Though the friendship may be most intimate and of long standing, there is no privilege unless the lady has consulted her friend on the matter.

> *Krebs* v. *Oliver*, 12 Gray (78 Mass.), 239.
> *Count Joannes* v. *Bennett*, 5 Allen (87 Mass.), 169.
> *Byam* v. *Collins*, (1886) 39 Hun (46 N. Y. Supr. Ct.), 204.

The plaintiff had been a candidate for the post of engineer to the Wear Commissioners, but failed to obtain the appointment. Shortly after this, the defendant wrote a letter to one L. informing him that the plaintiff had formerly been guilty of misconduct when he was secretary to a railway company, in which company the defendant and L. were both shareholders. L. was a Wear Commissioner, but the defendant did not know this. *Held*; no privilege.

> *Brooks* v. *Blanshard*, 1 Cr. & M. 779 ; 3 Tyrw. 844.

The defendant was a director of two companies ; of one of which the plaintiff was secretary, of the other auditor. The plaintiff was dismissed from his post as secretary of the first company for alleged misconduct. Thereupon the defendant, at the next meeting of the board of the second company, informed his co-directors of this fact, and proposed that he should also be dismissed from his post of auditor of the second company. *Held*, a privileged communication.

Harris v. *Thompson*, 13 C. B. 333.

Dawes told the defendant that he intended to employ the plaintiff as surgeon and accoucheur at his wife's approaching confinement; the defendant thereupon advised him not to do so, on account of the plaintiff's alleged immorality. Martin, B., thought this was a privileged communication, though it was volunteered.

Dixon v. *Smith*, 29 L. J. Ex. at p. 126.

The defendant, a parishioner, mentioned to her rector a report, widely current in the parish, that the rector and his solicitor were grossly mismanaging a trust estate, and defrauding the widow and orphans, &c. The solicitor brought an action for the slander. The jury found that she did so in the honest belief that it was a benefit to the rector to inform him of the report in order that he might clear his character. The Court held that the statement was clearly privileged so far as the rector was concerned, and that as the statement was not divisible it must also be privileged with regard to the plaintiff.

Davies v. *Snead*, L. R. 5 Q. B. 611; 39 L. J. Q. B. 202; 23 L. T. 609.

Information given to a vicar absent on the continent as to rumours affecting the moral character of the curate he has left in charge, is privileged; so is similar information given verbally to the absent vicar's solicitor, with a view to his informing the vicar, should he think it right to do so; so is similar information given to a neighbouring vicar who has asked the curate in charge to preach for him.

Clark v. *Molyneux*, 3 Q. B. D. 237; 47 L. J. Q. B. 230; 26 W. R. 104; 36 L. T. 466; 37 L. T. 694; 14 Cox, C. C. 10.

The plaintiff, an architect, had been employed by a certain committee to superintend and carry out the restoration of Skirlaugh Church; thereupon the defendant, who was a clergyman residing in the county, but who had no manner of interest in the question of the employment of the plaintiff to execute the work, wrote a letter to a member of the committee saying, "I see that the restoration of Skirlaugh Church has fallen into the hands of an architect who is a Wesleyan, and can have no experience in church work. Can you not do something to avert the irreparable loss which must be caused if any of the masonry of this ancient gem of art be ignorantly tampered with?" The letter was clearly a libel on the plaintiff in the way of his profession or calling. Bramwell, L.J., thought it was privileged, because the restoration was a matter of public interest, and one in which a neighbouring clergyman would be especially interested; but a special jury found that there was evidence of malice in the unfair expressions employed, and gave the plaintiff 50*l.* damages. But Kelly, C.B., on a motion for a new trial, declared that he was at a loss to see what privilege the defendant possessed, under the circumstances of the case, to interfere between the committee and the plaintiff in respect of the contract between them; the defendant being neither the patron, nor the minister of the church, nor a member of the committee appointed to effect its restoration, nor even a parishioner.

[It did not appear that the defendant was even a subscriber to the restoration fund.]

Botterill and another v. *Whytehead*, 41 L. T. 588

It is the duty of a building owner, who has discovered an error in the quantities, to inform a builder who has tendered for the work that the quantities are incorrect.

> *Sadgrove* v. *Hole*, [1901] 2 K. B. 1; 70 L. J. K. B. 455; 49 W. R. 473; 84 L. T. 647; 17 Times L. R. 332.

Two ladies, A. and B., were interested in the plaintiff, a lady who "had seen better days." A. applied to the Charity Organisation Society for information concerning the plaintiff. Defendant, the secretary of that society, drew up and sent A. a report unfavourable to the plaintiff, and gave A. permission to show it to B. *Held*, that the publication of this report both to A. and to B. was privileged, although B. had made no inquiries of the defendant, and was not a member of the society or in any way connected with it.

> *Waller* v. *Loch*, 7 Q. B. D. 619; 51 L. J. Q. B. 274; 30 W. R. 18; 45 L. T. 242; 46 J. P. 484.
>
> *Clover* v. *Royden*, L. R. 17 Eq. 190; 43 L. J. Ch. 665, *post*, p. 288.

Characters of Servants.

There are other cases in which the duty to make communication may exist, although there is no confidential relation between the parties. Thus, reverting to a class of cases already discussed (*ante*, p. 252), it is not always necessary for a master to wait till inquiries are made of him as to the character of a former servant. If he hears that the servant is seeking employment with a neighbour of his, he may write to that neighbour and warn him not to take that servant into his employment. "I do not mean to say that in order to make libellous matter written by a master privileged, it is essential that the party who makes the communication should be put into action in consequence of a third party's putting questions to him. I am of opinion he may (when he thinks that another is about to take into his service one whom he knows ought not to be taken) set himself in motion, and do some act to induce that other to seek information from and put questions to him. The answer to such questions, given *bonâ fide* with the intention of communicating such facts as the other party ought to know, will, although they contain slanderous matter, come within the scope of a privilged communication." (Per Bayley, J., in *Pattison* v. *Jones*, 8 B. & C. at p. 584.)

If, after a favourable character has been given, facts come to the knowledge of the former master which induce him to alter his opinion, it is his duty to inform the person to whom he gave the character of his altered opinion. Hence, a letter written to retract a favourable character previously given will also be privileged. (*Gardner* v. *Slade*, 13 Q. B. 796; 18 L. J. Q. B. 334; 13 Jur. 826; *Child* v. *Affleck and wife*, 9 B. & C. 403; 4 M. & R. 338.)

So, again, if a servant comes with a good character given her by B., and her master is sadly disappointed in her, he may write and inform B. that she does not deserve the character he gave her, so that he may refrain from recommending her to others; and such a letter would be privileged. (*Dixon* v. *Parsons*, 1 F. & F. 24. But see the *dicta* in *Fryer* v. *Kinnersley*, 15 C. B. N. S. 429; 33 L. J. C. P. 96.)

When a master discharges a servant, it is his duty to tell her why she is dismissed; he may also tell her parents or guardians; and the privilege will not be lost, if his wife or a friend be present at the interview. (*Taylor* v. *Hawkins*, 16 Q. B. 308; 20 L. J. Q. B. 313.) A master may also warn his present servants against associating with a former servant whom he has discharged, and state his reasons for dismissing her. (*Somerville* v. *Hawkins*, 10 C. B. 590; 20 L. J. C. P. 131.)

Illustrations.

After a mercantile firm has given to one of its clerks a general recommendation by means of which he obtains a situation, if a partner subsequently discovers facts which alter his opinion of that clerk's character, it is his duty to communicate the new facts and his change of opinion to the new employer of that clerk, in order to guard against his being mislead by the previous recommendation of the firm.

Fowles v. *Bowen*, 3 Tiffany (30 N. Y. R.), 20.

If I happen to hear that a discharged servant of mine is about to enter the service of B., it may be my duty to write off at once and inform B. of the servant's misconduct. It is certainly safer to wait till B. applies to me for the servant's character. Eagerness to prevent a former servant obtaining another place has the appearance of malice, and if it were found that I wrote systematically to every one to whom the plaintiff applied for work, the jury would probably give damages against me. On the other hand, if B. was an intimate friend or a relation of mine, and there was no other evidence of malice, except that I *volunteered* the information, the occasion would still be privileged. In short, when a master " volunteers to give the character, stronger evidence will be required that he acted *bonâ fide*, than in the case where he has given the character after being required so to do." Per Littledale, J., in

> *Pattison* v. *Jones*, 8 B. & C. 578, 586 ; 3 C. & P. 387.

The defendant, a linendraper, dismissed his apprentice without sufficient legal excuse : he wrote a letter to her parents, informing them that the girl would be sent home, and giving his reasons for her dismissal. Cockburn, C.J., held this letter privileged.

> *James* v. *Jolly*, Bristol Summer Assizes, 1879.
> See *Fowler and wife* v. *Homer*, 3 Camp. 294.

So, of course, a letter to the girl herself, stating in detail the faults which her late employer found with her, is privileged.

> *R.* v. *Perry*, 15 Cox, C. C. 169.

So where a lady, who had dismissed her maid-servant, wrote a similar letter to the aunt of the plaintiff, who was in the position of a mother to her.

> *Aberdein* v. *Macleay*, (1893) 9 Times L. R. 539.

If a master about to dismiss his servant for dishonesty, calls in a friend to hear what passes, the presence of such third person does not take away privilege from words which the master then uses, imputing dishonesty.

> *Taylor* v. *Hawkins*, 16 Q. B. 308 ; 20 L. J. Q. B. 313 ; 15 Jur. 746.
> *Jones* v. *Thomas*, 34 W. R. 104 ; 53 L. T. 678 ; 50 J. P. 149.

Where a master discharged his footman and cook, and they asked him his reason for doing so, and he told the footman, in the absence of the cook, that " he and the cook had been robbing him ; " and told the cook, in the absence of the footman, that he had discharged her " because she and the footman had been robbing him : " *held*, that these were privileged communications as respected the absent parties, as well as those to whom they were respectively made.

> *Manby* v. *Witt*,   } 18 C. B. 544 ; 25 L. J. C. P. 294 ; 2 Jur. N. S.
> *Eastmead* v. *Witt*, }   1004.

The plaintiff was a guard in the service of the defendants, a railway company. The defendants dismissed him on the ground that he had been guilty of gross neglect of duty, and published his name in a printed monthly circular addressed to their servants, stating that he had been dismissed and the ground of his dismissal. The plaintiff brought an action for libel against the defendants. *Held*, affirming the decision of Stephen, J., that the statement was made on a privileged occasion, and that the defendants were not liable.

> *Hunt* v. *Great Northern Railway Co.*, [1891] 2 Q. B. 189 ; 60 L. J. Q. B. 498 ; 55 J. P. 234, 648 ; 7 Times L. R. 113, 493.

Information as to Crime or Misconduct of others.

Again, it is a duty which every one owes to society and to the State to assist in the investigation of any alleged misconduct, and to promote the detection of any crime.

All information given *bonâ fide* in response to any inquiries made with this object is clearly privileged (*ante*, p. 254). But this duty does not arise merely when confidential inquiries are made. If facts come to my knowledge which lead me reasonably to conclude that a crime has been, or is about to be, committed, it is my duty at once to give information to the police or to the persons interested.

" When it comes to the knowledge of any one that a crime has been committed, a duty is laid on that person, as a citizen of the country, to state to the authorities what he knows respecting the commission of the crime ; and if he states only what he knows and honestly believes, he cannot be subjected to an action of damages merely because it turns out that the person as to whom he has given the information is, after all, not guilty of the crime." (Per Inglis, Lord President, in *Lightbody* v. *Gordon*, 9 Scotch Sessions Cases, 4th Series, 937, 938.)

*So all material statements made by the persons interested in the detection of a crime, during their investigations and relevant thereto, are privileged. " For the sake of public justice, charges and communications which would otherwise be slanderous, are protected if *bonâ fide* made in the prosecution of an inquiry into a suspected crime." (Per Coleridge, J., in *Padmore* v. *Lawrence*, 11 A. & E. 382.)* See also the remarks of Lord Eldon, C.J., in *Johnson* v. *Evans*, 3 Esp. 33, and of Lord Ellenborough, in *Fowler et ux.* v. *Homer*, 3 Camp. at p. 295.

Illustrations.

Defendant discharged his servant, the plaintiff, and sent for a constable, intending to give her in charge. All that he said to the constable in the course of his charge and complaint against the plaintiff is privileged, although ultimately he did not give her into charge.

Johnson v. *Evans, Clerk,* 3 Esp. 32.

Defendant was a haberdasher. On a Saturday evening, while he was absent, Mrs. Fowler came into his shop and bought some goods. Soon after she was gone his shopman missed a roll of riband, and mistakenly supposed that she had stolen it, but did not then pursue her. On the

---

* This passage was cited with approval by Collins, M.R., in *Collins* v. *Coope* (1902), 19 Times L. R. at p. 119.

following Monday, as she was again passing the shop, the shopman pointed her out to the defendant as the person who had stolen the riband. The defendant brought her into the shop and accused her of the robbery, which she positively denied. He then took her into an adjoining room and sent for her father, to whom he repeated the accusation. After a good deal of altercation she was allowed to go home, and there the matter rested. Lord Ellenborough decided that no action lay.

Fowler et ux. v. *Homer,* 3 Camp. 294.

Mensel sent his servant, the plaintiff, to the defendant's shop on business ; while there, the plaintiff had occasion to go into an inner room. Shortly after he left, a box was missed from that inner room. No one else had been in the room except the plaintiff. The defendant thereupon went round to Mr. Mensel's, and calling him aside into a private room, told him what had happened, adding that the plaintiff must have taken the box. Later on, the plaintiff came to the defendant's house, and the defendant repeated the accusation to him ; but, an English girl being present, defendant was careful to speak in German. Both communications were held privileged.

Amann v. *Damm,* 8 C. B. N. S. 597 ; 29 L. J. C. P. 313 ;
7 Jur. N. S. 47 ; 8 W. R. 470.

Hurtert v. *Weines,* 27 Iowa, 134.

Dale v. *Harris,* 13 Browne, (109 Mass.) 193.

Defendant charged the plaintiff, his porter, with stealing his bed-ticks, and with plaintiff's permission subsequently searched his house, but found no stolen property. The jury found that defendant *bonâ fide* believed that a robbery had been committed by the plaintiff, and made the charge with a view to investigation, but added, "The defendant ought not to have said what he could not prove." *Held,* that this finding was immaterial, that the occasion was privileged, and that there was no evidence of malice. Judgment for the defendant.

Howe v. *Jones,* (1884) 1 Times L. R. 19 ; (1885) *ib.* 461.

Fowler et ux. v. *Homer,* 3 Camp. 294.

Farquharson forged the name " J. Smith " on a cheque and sent a boy to present it and get the money. The defendant was cashier of the bank. He looked hard at the boy, and satisfied himself as he thought that it was Smith's boy, the plaintiff, and so gave him the money. When inquiries were made, defendant told Smith it was his boy who presented the cheque, and described him accurately. He told the detective so too. Plaintiff was accordingly tried along with Farquharson, who pleaded guilty. The Sheriff found the charge not proven against the plaintiff. Then plaintiff sued defendant and recovered damages 50*l.*, by a verdict of eight jurymen to four. The Court set the verdict aside on the ground that there was no evidence whatever of malice.

Lightbody v. *Gordon,* 9 Scotch Sessions Cases, 4th Series, 934.

Barton, a friend of the defendant, employed a builder, the plaintiff's master, to build a house for him : the defendant informed Barton that the plaintiff while at work on his house had removed some quarterings. Barton complained to the master builder, who came down to the defendant's and said, " I am told you say that you saw my man Kine take away some of the quarterings from Mr. Barton's premises." A repetition of the charge made then to the plaintiff's master without malice was held privileged, and as the plaintiff had not called Barton to prove the original remark, the jury found for the defendant, and a new trial was refused. Parke, B., said, "Is a man's mouth to be closed when I ask him if he has seen another man take away my timber?"

Kine v. *Sewell*, 3 M. & W. 297.

Certain merchants in New York, believing on reasonable grounds that they had been defrauded by plaintiff and others, drew up an agreement reciting that they had "been robbed and swindled" by plaintiff and others named, whom they were determined to prosecute, and promising that each person signing would pay his fair share towards the expenses of the prosecution, &c. This agreement was left with A.'s manager in order that he might procure A.'s signature thereto. *Held*, a privileged publication.

Klinck v. *Colby, and others*, 1 Sickels (46 N. Y.), 427.

Defendant accused the plaintiff, in the presence of a third person, of stealing his wife's brooch; plaintiff wished to be searched; defendant repeated the accusation to two women, who searched the plaintiff and found nothing. Subsequently it was discovered that defendant's wife had left the brooch at a friend's house. *Held*, that the mere publication to the two women did not destroy the privilege attaching to charges, if made *bonâ fide*; but that all the circumstances should have been left to the jury, who should determine whether or no the charge was made recklessly and unwarrantably, and repeated before more persons than necessary.

Padmore v. *Lawrence*, 11 A. & E. 380; 4 Jur. 458; 3 P. & D. 209.

Jones v. *Thomas*, (1885) 34 W. R. 104; 53 L. T. 678; 2 Times L. R. 95.

A discharged servant of the defendant's charged plaintiff, her former manager, with embezzlement. Defendant went to plaintiff's house, and, finding him out, said to his wife, "He has robbed me." This was held not to be privileged; though the jury found that defendant spoke in the performance, as she believed, of a duty and in the *bonâ fide* belief that what she said was true, and without malice. Judgment for the plaintiff. Damages 5*l*.

Jones v. *Williams*, (1885) 1 Times L. R. 572.

Plaintiff assaulted the defendant on the highway; defendant, meeting a constable, requested him to take charge of the plaintiff, and the constable refusing to arrest the plaintiff unless the defendant would charge him with felony, the defendant did so. *Held*, on demurrer to the defendant's plea, that the charge of felony made in these circumstances was not privileged.

Smith v. *Hodgeskins*, Cro. Car. 276.

But where the defendant's shop had undoubtedly been robbed, and he went with a policeman to the house of a discharged servant whom he suspected, and the servant's mother in her presence asked him what he wanted, the defendant's answer was held privileged in

Brow v. *Hathaway*, (1866) 13 Allen (95 Mass.), 239; 19 L. T. 105.

T 2

Plaintiff and defendant were neighbours and both drapers. Defendant, from facts which came to his knowledge, and which were sufficient to arouse suspicion, concluded that he was being robbed by one of his assistants with the collusion of the plaintiff. He went to A., in whose employ plaintiff had formerly been, and inquired as to plaintiff's honesty. A. asked, "What do you want to know for?" Defendant replied, "Oh, the man has robbed me; I mean to get him imprisoned." Defendant then made inquiries of B., one of his own assistants, who said she knew nothing at all of the matter, whereupon defendant repeated what he had said to A. Damages 5*l*. Lindley, J., on further consideration, held both statements unprivileged, as neither A. nor B. was concerned in or connected with the matter.

　　　　Harrison v. Fraser, 29 W. R. 652.

The defendant, in the presence of his wife, accused the plaintiff, "a ladies' wardrobe dealer," of having received certain goods stolen from his house. The plaintiff denied receiving them. The defendant then said, "Would it surprise you if I could bring five people to say you had taken the things away from here?" The plaintiff said it would surprise her. Four boys and a maidservant were then sent into the room, and the defendant said to them, "Is this the person who came and took the things away?" They replied, "Yes." The Court of Appeal held the whole conversation privileged.

　　　　Collins v. *Cooper,* (1902) 19 Times L. R. 118.

"The publication at the request of any Government office or department, officer of State, Commissioner of Police, or Chief Constable, of any notice or report issued by them for the information of the public, shall be privileged, unless it shall be proved that such report or publication was published or made maliciously."

　　　　51 & 52 Vict. c. 64, s. 4.

[N.B.—The portion of this section quoted above is not limited to publication in a newspaper.]

Charges against Public Officials.

So, too, it is the duty of all who witness any misconduct on the part of a magistrate or any public officer to bring such misconduct to the notice of those whose duty it is to inquire into and punish it; and, therefore, all petitions and memorials complaining of such misconduct, if forwarded to the proper authority, are privileged. And it is not necessary that the informant or memorialist should be in any way personally aggrieved or injured: for all persons have an interest in the pure administration of justice and the efficiency of our public offices in all departments of the State. So with ecclesiastical matters: all good churchmen are concerned to prevent any scandal attaching to the Church. If, however, the informant be the person immediately affected by the misconduct complained of, he can claim privilege also on the ground that he is acting in self-defence. (See the cases cited, *post*, p. 292.) Every communication made with a view to obtain redress for some injury received, or to prevent some public abuse, is privileged, if it be published only to persons who have jurisdiction to entertain the complaint, or power to redress the grievance, or some duty or interest in connection with it. Statements made to a stranger who has nothing to do with the matter cannot be privileged.

"To protect those who are not able to protect themselves is a duty which every one owes to society." (Per Lord Macnaghten in *Jenoure v. Delmege*, [1891] A. C. at p. 77; 60 L. J. P. C. at p. 13.) "In this land of law and liberty all who are aggrieved may seek redress; and the alleged misconduct of any who are clothed with public authority may be brought to the notice of those who have the power and the duty to inquire into it, and to take steps which may prevent the repetition of it." (Per Lord Campbell, C.J., in *Harrison v. Bush*, 5 E. & B. at p. 349; 25 L. J. Q. B. at p. 29.) "If, without express malice, I make a defamatory charge which I *bonâ fide* believe to be true, against one whose conduct in the respect defamed has caused me injury, to one whose duty it is . . . to inquire into and redress such injury, the occasion is privileged; because I have an interest in the subject-matter of my charge, and the person to whom I make the communication has on hearing the communication a duty to discharge in respect of it." (Per Fitzgerald, B., in *Waring v. M'Caldin*, (1873) 7 Ir. Rep. C. L. at p. 288.)

Illustrations.

A petition to the House of Commons charging the plaintiff with oppression and extortion in his office of Vicar-General to the Bishop of Lincoln is privileged, although the petition was printed, and copies distributed amongst the members.

> *Lake v. King,* 1 Lev. 240; 1 Saund. 131; Sid. 414; 1 Mod. 58.

The defendant deemed it his duty as a churchman to write to the Bishop of London informing him that a report was current in the parish of Bethnal Green that a stand-up fight had occurred in the school-room of St. James-the-Great between the plaintiff, the incumbent, and the schoolmaster, during school hours. The letter was held privileged under the Church Discipline Act, 3 & 4 Vict. c. 86, s. 3, although the defendant did not live in the district of which the plaintiff was incumbent, but in an adjoining district of the same parish.

James v. *Boston,* 2 C. & K. 4.

A letter sent to the Postmaster-General, or to the Secretary to the General Post Office, complaining of misconduct in a postmaster, is privileged, if it was written as a *bonâ fide* complaint, to obtain redress for a grievance that the party really believed he had suffered ; and particular expressions are not to be too strictly scrutinised, if the intention of the defendant was good.

Woodward v. *Lander,* 6 C. & P. 548.
Bannister v. *Kelty,* 59 J. P. 793.

The defendant drafted a memorial to the Home Secretary on a matter within his jurisdiction, and read it to M. in the presence of M.'s wife, and asked M. to sign it. M. signed it, and the defendant then sent it to the Home Secretary. Grove, J., held that both the petition and the conversation with M. were privileged.

Spackman v. *Gibney,* Bristol Spring Assizes, 1878.

The plaintiff was a sanitary inspector under the statute 41 & 42 Vict. c. 74, s. 42, appointed by the local authority, but removable by the Privy Council ; the defendant addressed a letter to the Privy Council, charging the plaintiff with corruption and misconduct in his office. *Held,* that no action lay without proof of malice.

Proctor v. *Webster,* 16 Q. B. D. 112 ; 55 L. J. Q. B. 150 ;
53 L. T. 765.
Wieman v. *Mabee,* 45 Mich. 484 ; 40 Amer. R. 477.

An elector of Frome petitioned the Home Secretary, stating that the plaintiff, a magistrate of the borough, had made speeches inciting to a breach of the peace, and praying for an inquiry, and that the Home Secretary should advise her Majesty to remove the plaintiff from the commission of the peace. Such petition was held to be privileged, although it should more properly have been addressed to the Lord Chancellor.

Harrison v. *Bush,* 5 E. & B. 344 ; 25 L. J. Q. B. 25 ; 1 Jur.
N. S. 846 ; 2 Jur. N. S. 90.

A timekeeper employed on public works, on behalf of the Board of Works, wrote a letter to the secretary of the Board, imputing fraud to the contractor. Blackburn, J., directed the jury that if they thought the letter was written in good faith for the information of his employers, it was privileged, although such a complaint should have been addressed to the resident engineer, in the first instance.

Scarll v. *Dixon,* 4 F. & F. 250.

The defendant wrote to the inspector of constabulary, saying that he had been informed that the plaintiff, a Government medical officer, had refused to attend a poor woman, who died in consequence. *Held,* that the occasion was privileged, although such a complaint should more properly have been submitted to the superintending medical officer.

Jenoure v. *Delmege,* [1891] A. C. 73 ; 60 L. J. P. C. 11 ; 39
W. R. 388 ; 63 L. T. 814 ; 55 J. P. 500.

The plaintiff was about to be sworn in as a paid constable, by the justices, when the defendant, a parishioner, made a statement against the plaintiff's character in the hearing of several by-standers. *Held*, that even if such statement ought rather to have been made to the vestry, who drew up the list of constables whom the justices were to swear in, still it was privileged, as the justices had a discretion to select from that list the persons who were to be sworn in as paid constables.

> *Kershaw* v. *Bailey*, 1 Exch. 743; 17 L. J. Ex. 129.

A letter to the Secretary at War, with the intent to prevail on him to exert his authority to compel the plaintiff (an officer in the army) to pay a debt due from him to defendant, was held privileged, although the Secretary at War had no direct power or authority to order the plaintiff to pay his debt.

> *Fairman* v. *Ives*, 5 B. & Ald. 642; 1 Chit. 85; 1 D. & R. 252.

The plaintiff was a teacher in a district school; the inhabitants of the district prepared a memorial charging the plaintiff with drunkenness and immorality, which they sent to the local superintendent of schools. It ought strictly to have been sent to the trustees of that particular school in the first instance, and such trustees would then, if they thought fit, in due course forward it to the local superintendent for him to take action upon it. *Held*, that the publication was nevertheless privileged, as the ultimate decision lay with the local superintendent.

> *McIntyre* v. *McBean*, 13 Up. Canada Q. B. Rep. 534.

But where the defendant wrote a letter to the Home Secretary complaining of the conduct of the plaintiff, a solicitor, as clerk to the borough magistrates, this was held not to be privileged, because the Home Secretary had no power or jurisdiction whatever over the plaintiff.

> *Blagg* v. *Sturt*, 10 Q. B. 899; 16 L. J. Q. B. 39; 8 L. T. (Old S.) 135; 11 Jur. 101.

A lieutenant in the navy was appointed by the Government agent or superintendent on board a transport ship, *The Jupiter*. He wrote a letter to the secretary of Lloyd's Coffee-house imputing misconduct and incapacity to the plaintiff, the master of *The Jupiter*. This was held altogether unprivileged; the information should have been given to the Government alone, by whom the defendant was employed.

> *Harwood* v. *Green*, 3 C. & P. 141.

Where the defeated candidates at an election of guardians of the poor wrote and signed a memorial, accusing a successful candidate of bribery and treating, and sent it to the new board of guardians, who had no jurisdiction in the matter and no duty or interest in connection with it, this was held not to be a privileged communication.

> *Hebditch* v. *MacIlwaine, and others*, [1894] 2 Q. B. 54; 63 L. J. Q. B. 587; 42 W. R. 422; 70 L. T. 826; 58 J. P. 620.

An Irish coroner sent to the Chief Secretary of Ireland a report of an inquest which he had held on the body of an out-door pauper, and at which the plaintiff, who was the relieving officer, had given evidence. He mentioned in this report that the parish priest, who happened to be in Court, stated publicly at the conclusion of plaintiff's evidence, " This is nothing short of perjury." *Held,* that this portion of the report at all events was not privileged, as the Chief Secretary could have no interest in hearing Father Callary's opinion of the plaintiff's evidence.

Lynam v. *Gowing,* 6 L. R. Ir. 259.

II. WHERE THE DEFENDANT HAS AN INTEREST IN THE SUBJECT-MATTER OF THE COMMUNICATION, AND THE PERSON TO WHOM THE COMMUNICATION IS MADE HAS A CORRESPONDING INTEREST OR SOME DUTY IN CONNECTION WITH THE MATTER.

Every communication made in such circumstances is privileged by reason of the occasion. (Per Lopes, L.J., in *Hunt* v. *Great Northern Ry. Co.,* [1891] 2 Q. B. at p. 192.) In the same case Lord Esher, M.R., said (p. 191) :—" The occasion had arisen if the communication was of such a nature that it could be fairly said that those who made it had an interest in making such a communication, and those to whom it was made had a corresponding interest in having it made to them. When those two things co-exist, the occasion is a privileged one, and the question whether it was or was not misused, is an entirely different one."

Such common interest is generally a *pecuniary* one ; as that of two customers of the same bank, two directors of the same company, two creditors of the same debtor. But it may also be *professional,* as in the case of two officers in the same corps, or masters in the same school, anxious to preserve the dignity and reputation of the body to which they both belong. In short, it may be any interest arising from the joint exercise of any legal right or privilege, or from the joint performance of any duty imposed or recognised by the law. Thus, two executors of the same will, two trustees of the same settlement, have a common interest, though not a pecuniary one, in the management of the trust estate. So the ratepayers of a parish have a common interest in the selection of fit and proper officers to serve in the parish, their salary being paid out of the rates. So relations by blood or marriage have a common interest in their family concerns.

The " common interest " must be one which the law recognises and appreciates. No privilege attaches to gossip, however interesting it may be to both speaker and hearer. (*Rumsey* v. *Webb et ux.,* Car. & M. 104; 11 L. J. C. P. 129.) The law never sanctions mere vulgar curiosity or officious intermeddling in the concerns of others. To be within the privilege, the statement must be such as the occasion warrants, and must tend to protect the private interests both of the speaker and of the person addressed. If, in fact, the defendant had no other interest in the matter beyond that which any other educated person would naturally feel, interference on his part would be officious and unprivileged. (*Botterill and another* v. *Whytehead,* 41 L. T. 588.) Again, the mere fact that one party has contracted to supply the other with information does not create such a common interest that communications made in pursuance of the contract will be therefore privileged. (*Macintosh* v. *Dun,* [1908] A. C. 390; 77 L. J. P. C. 113; 99 L. T. 64.)

Illustrations.

The defendant and Messrs. Wright & Co., his bankers, were both interested in a concern, the management of which the bankers had entrusted to the plaintiff, their solicitor. A confidential letter written by the defendant to Messrs. Wright & Co., charging the plaintiff with professional misconduct in the management of such concern, was held privileged by Lord Ellenborough.

 M'Dougall v. *Claridge,* 1 Camp. 267.

A creditor of the plaintiff may comment on the plaintiff's mode of conducting his business to the man who is surety to that creditor for the plaintiff's trade debts.

 Dunman v. *Bigg,* 1 Camp. 269, n.

Where A. and B. have a joint interest in a matter, a letter, written by A. to induce B. to become a party to a suit relating thereto, is privileged, though it may refer to the plaintiff in angry terms.

 Shipley v. *Todhunter,* 7 C. & P. 680.

 Klinck v. *Colby and others,* 1 Sickels (46 N. Y.), 427, *ante,*
  p. 275.

A creditor was appointed trustee in liquidation of the debtor's estate, the debtor continuing to manage his former business for the benefit of the estate. A letter written by the trustee to another creditor, commenting in very severe terms on the debtor's conduct, is privileged.

> *Spill* v. *Maule,* L. R. 4 Ex. 232 ; 38 L. J. Ex. 138 ; 17 W. R. 805 ; 20 L. T. 675.

A person interested in the proceeds of a sale may give notice to the auctioneer not to part with them to the plaintiff, who ordered the sale, on the ground that he has committed an act of bankruptcy.

> *Blackham* v. *Pugh,* 2 C. B. 611 ; 15 L. J. C. P. 290.

> *Baker* v. *Carrick,* [1894] 1 Q. B. 838 ; 63 L. J. Q. B. 399 ; 42 W. R. 338 ; 70 L. T. 366 ; 58 J. P. 669 ; 9 R. 283.

A bishop's charge to his clergy is *primâ facie* privileged, although it contain defamatory matter.

> *Laughton* v. *Bishop of Sodor and Man,* L. R. 4 P. C. 495 ; 42 L. J. P. C. 11 ; 21 W. R. 204 ; 28 L. T. 377 ; 9 Moore, P. C. C. N. S. 318.

A communication made by one director to another, as to the misconduct of the company's auditor when acting as secretary of another company, is privileged.

> *Harris* v. *Thompson,* (1853) 13 C. B. 333.

The reports of the directors and auditors of a company printed and circulated among the shareholders are privileged.

> *Lawless* v. *Anglo-Egyptian Cotton Co.,* L. R. 4 Q. B. 262 ; 10 B. & S. 226 ; 38 L. J. Q. B. 129 ; 17 W. R. 498.

A solicitor, acting for some shareholders in a company, printed and sent to the shareholders, but to no one else, a circular reflecting on the promoters and directors of the company, and inviting the shareholders to meet and discuss their position and take measures to protect their common interests. *Held,* that such publication was privileged.

> *Quartz Hill Gold Mining Co.* v. *Beall,* 20 Ch. D. 501 ; 51 L. J. Ch. 874 ; 30 W. R. 583 ; 46 L. T. 746.

The chairman of a society at a meeting of its members was asked questions as to the conduct of the manager of a local branch ; he stated in reply what he had himself observed. *Held,* that the occasion was privileged. There was no evidence of malice. Nonsuit.

> *Stott* v. *Evans,* (1887) 3 Times L. R. 693.

The defendant was chairman of the Board of Guardians of the Union in which was included a parish for which the plaintiff was collector of rates. At a meeting of the Board the defendant used words defamatory of the plaintiff in his office of collector. *Held,* that in view of s. 62 of the Poor Law Amendment Act, 1844, the Board had an interest in the proper collection of rates within their Union and that the occasion was privileged.

> *Mapey* v. *Baker,* (1909) 73 J. P. 289 ; 7 L. G. R. 636.

A caution sent by the committee of a charity to all the subscribers, warning them not to pay their subscriptions in future to the plaintiff, the former collector, who " was found unworthy of confidence, and dismissed," is privileged.

> *Gassett* v. *Gilbert and others,* 6 Gray (72 Mass.), 94.

The plaintiff was agent for an insurance company ; he resigned that

post, and the secretary of the company then sent a circular to all policy-
holders who had insured through the plaintiff, asking them in future to pay
their premiums to another agent, as the plaintiff's agency " has been closed
by the directors." *Held,* a privileged communication.

> *Nevill* v. *Fine Art and General Insurance Co.,* (C. A.) [1895]
> 2 Q. B. 156 ; 64 L. J. Q. B. 681 ; 72 L. T. 525 ; (H. L.)
> [1897] A. C. 68 ; 66 L. J. Q. B. 195 ; 75 L. T. 606.
> *Smith* v. *Crocker,* (1889) 5 Times L. R. 441.
> *Gallagher* v. *Murton,* (1888) 4 Times L. R. 304.

A communication from a firm of brewers to the tenants of their public-
houses, refusing to accept any longer in payment cheques drawn on a
particular bank, is privileged.

> *Capital and Counties Bank* v. *Henty and Sons,* (C. A.) 5 C. P. D.
> 514 ; 49 L. J. C. P. 830 ; 28 W. R. 851 ; 43 L. T. 651 ;
> (H. L.) 7 App. Cas. 741 ; 52 L. J. Q. B. 232 ; 31 W. R. 157 ;
> 47 L. T. 662.

Defendant was a life governor of a public school to which the plaintiff
supplied butcher's meat ; defendant told the steward of the school, whose
duty it was to examine the meat, that plaintiff had been known to sell
bad meat. *Held,* a privileged communication.

> *Humphreys* v. *Stilwell,* 2 F. & F. 590.
> And see *Crisp* v. *Gill,* 29 L. T. (Old S.) 82.

Several fictitious orders for goods had been sent in the defendant's
name to a tradesman, who thereupon delivered the goods to the defendant.
The defendant returned the goods, and being shown the letters ordering
them, wrote to the tradesman that in his opinion the letters were in the
plaintiff's handwriting. *Held,* that this expression of opinion was privileged, as both defendant and the tradesman were interested in discovering
the culprit.

> *Croft* v. *Stevens,* 7 H. & N. 570 ; 31 L. J. Ex. 143 ; 10 W. R.
> 272 ; 5 L. T. 683.

It has recently been held in the Privy Council that where a mercantile
agency or trade protection society supplies information to its customers
as a matter of business, and in pursuance of a contract to supply such
information, though in response to a confidential inquiry, there is no
privilege.

> *Macintosh* v. *Dun,* [1908] A. C. 390 ; 77 L. J. P. C. 113 ;
> 99 L. T. 64 ; 24 Times L. R. 705.

A prominent member of the church of St. Barnabas, Pimlico, went to
stay in the vacation at Stockcross, in Berkshire, and so conducted himself
there as to gravely offend the parishioners. Letters passing between the
curate of St. Barnabas and the incumbent of Stockcross relative to the
charges of misconduct brought against the plaintiff were held privileged,
as both were interested in getting at the truth of the matter.

> *Whiteley* v. *Adams,* 15 C. B. N. S. 392 ; 33 L. J. C. P. 89 ;
> 10 Jur. N. S. 470 ; 12 W. R. 153 ; 9 L. T. 483.

The defendant had a dispute with the Newry Mineral Water Company,
which they agreed to refer to " some respectable printer who should be
indifferent between the parties," as arbitrator. The manager of the com-

pany nominated the plaintiff, a printer's commercial traveller. The defendant declined to accept him as arbitrator, and, when pressed for his reason, wrote a letter to the manager stating that the plaintiff had formerly been in the defendant's employment, and had been dismissed for drunkenness. The plaintiff thereupon brought an action on the letter as a libel on him in the way of his trade. *Held,* that the letter was privileged, as both parties were interested in the selection of a proper arbitrator.

        Hobbs v. *Bryers,* 2 L. R. Ir. 496.

If a parish officer seeks re-election, charges as to his previous conduct in the office made against him at the parish meeting for the nomination of officers are privileged.

        George v. *Goddard,* 2 F. & F. 689.
        Kershaw v. *Bailey,* 1 Exch. 743 ; 17 L. J. Ex. 129.
        See *Senior* v. *Medland,* 4 Jur. N. S. 1039.
        Pierce v. *Ellis,* 6 Ir. C. L. R. 55.
        Bennett v. *Barry,* 8 L. T. 857.
        Harle v. *Catherall,* 14 L. T. 801.

So are such charges made to a voter, or even to the wife of a voter.

        Wisdom v. *Brown,* (1885) 1 Times L. R. 412.

Where the officers of any town claim to be reimbursed moneys expended by them, any statements made at a town meeting by a ratepayer which tend to show that the expenses were not properly incurred, and ought not to be charged on the rates, are privileged.

        Smith v. *Higgins,* 16 Gray (82 Mass.), 251.

A parish meeting was called to investigate the accounts of the parish constable ; one ratepayer was unable to attend, so he wrote a letter to be read to the meeting concerning the constable and his accounts. This letter was held privileged. For had he attended the meeting and made the same charge orally, such speech would have been privileged.

        Spencer v. *Amerton,* 1 Moo. & Rob. 470.

But a personal attack on the private character of a candidate at a parliamentary election is not privileged (*ante,* p. 208).

        Duncombe v. *Daniell,* 8 C. & P. 222 ; 2 Jur. 32 ; 1 W. W. & H. 101.
        Sir Thomas Clarges v. *Rowe,* 3 Lev. 30.
        How v. *Prin,* Holt, 652 ; 7 Mod. 107 ; 2 Salk. 694 ; 2 Ld. Raym. 812 ; 1 Brown's Parly. Cas. 64.
        Onslow v. *Horne,* 3 Wils. 177 ; 2 W. Bl. 750.
        Harwood v. *Sir J. Astley,* 1 B. & P. N. R. 47.
        Pankhurst v. *Hamilton,* (1887) 3 Times L. R. 500.
        And see the Corrupt and Illegal Practices Prevention Act, 1895 (58 & 59 Vict. c. 40), *post,* pp. 437, 461.

A member of Parliament gave notice that he would ask in the House of Commons why the plaintiff, a colonel in the army, had been dismissed ; thereupon the defendant, the plaintiff's superior officer, who had been instrumental in procuring his discharge, called on the member, whom he knew well, to explain the true facts of the case. Lord Campbell, C.J., held the occasion privileged ; but the jury found it was done maliciously, and awarded the plaintiff 200*l.* damages.

        Dickson v. *Earl of Wilton,* 1 F. & F. 419.

A *bonâ fide* communication between a member of Parliament and his constituents on a matter of political or local interest is privileged ; such as a report of any speech of his circulated privately among his constituents for their information. Per Lord Campbell, C.J., and Crompton, J., in

> *Davison* v. *Duncan,* 7 E. & B. 233 ; 26 L. J. Q. B. 107.

And Cockburn, C.J., in

> *Wason* v. *Walter,* L. R. 4 Q. B. 95 ; 8 B. & S. 730 ; 38 L. J. Q. B. 42 ; 17 W. R. 169 ; 19 L. T. 416.

But a judge of the Bankruptcy Court and an opposing creditor have no such common interest in the case of an insolvent debtor as to render privileged a letter written by the creditor to the judge previously to the hearing of the case. Writing such a letter is indeed a contempt of Court.

> *Gould* v. *Hulme,* 3 C. & P. 625.

So the agents of the rival candidates at an election have no common interest, at all events after the election is over.

> *Dickeson* v. *Hilliard and another,* L. R. 9 Ex. 79 ; 43 L. J. Ex. 37 ; 22 W. R. 372 ; 30 L. T. 196.

A confidential consultation between a vicar and his curate as to the course which the vicar ought to adopt in an ecclesiastical matter was held privileged in

> *Clark* v. *Molyneux,* 3 Q. B. D. 237 ; 47 L. J. Q. B. 230 ; 26 W. R. 104 ; 36 L. T. 466 ; 37 L. T. 694 ; 14 Cox, C. C. 10.
>
> And see *Bell* v. *Parke,* 10 Ir. C. L. R. 279 ; *ante,* p. 262.

But where a rector sent to his parishioners a circular letter warning them not to send their children to a school which plaintiff had opened in the parish against the rector's wishes, and in opposition to the rector's parish school, it was held that no privilege attached.

> *Gilpin* v. *Fowler,* 9 Exch. 615 ; 23 L. J. Ex. 152 ; 18 Jur. 293.

If a clergyman or parish priest, in the course of a sermon, "make an example" of a member of his flock, by commenting on his misconduct, and either naming him or alluding to him in unmistakable terms, his words will not be privileged, although they were uttered *bonâ fide* in the honest desire to reform the culprit, and to warn the rest of his hearers, and although the congregation would probably be more interested in this part of the discourse than in any other. If the words be actionable, the clergyman must justify.

> *Magrath* v. *Finn,* Ir. R. 11 C. L. 152.
>
> *Kinnahan* v. *McCullagh, ib.* 1.
>
> *R.* v. *Knight,* (1736) Bacon's Abr. A. 2 (Libel).
>
> And see *Greenwood* v. *Prick,* cited in Cro. Jac. 91, as overruled by Lord Denman, 12 A. & E. 726 ; *ante,* p. 6.

But where a large number of persons have an interest more or less remote in the matter, defendant will not be privileged in informing them all by circular or otherwise, unless there is no other way of effecting his object. Thus, in the case of most societies there is a council, or a managing committee, or a manager, or a body of trustees, or directors; and communications made confidentially to them will be privileged which would not be privileged if addressed in the first instance to the whole body of subscribers or shareholders. "Such a communication as the present (a charge against the medical officer of a poor law union) ought to be confined in the first instance to those whose duty it is to investigate the charges." (Per Mellish, L.J., in *Purcell* v. *Sowler*, 2 C. P. D. at p. 221.)

If a subscriber to a charity has any complaint against the medical man employed by that charity, he should not address his complaint in the first instance to the whole body of subscribers. "There may be a thousand subscribers to a charity," observed Lord Denman, C.J., in *Martin* v. *Strong*, (1836) 5 A. & E. p. 538. "Such a claim of privilege is too large." But any representation made to the managing committee would be privileged. And if the subscriber deems it necessary in the interests of the charity, he may, after due notice given to the medical man, appeal from the decision of the committee to the general body of subscribers. (*Martin* v. *Strong*, 5 A. & E. 535, as explained in *Kine* v. *Sewell*, 3 M. & W. 297.) But if a subscriber has a charge to bring against the committee or the directors, he is entitled to address himself to the whole body of subscribers or shareholders in the first instance. (*Quartz Hill Gold Mining Co.* v. *Beall*, 20 Ch. D. 501; 51 L. J. Ch. 874; 30 W. R. 583; 46 L. T. 746.)

Illustrations.

A letter written by a subscriber to a charity to the committee of management of the charity concerning the conduct of their secretary in the management of the funds of the charity is privileged.

> *Maitland* v. *Bramwell*, 2 F. & F. 623.
> See also *Hartwell* v. *Vesey*, 3 L. T. 275.

Any statement made by a director of a company to his fellow-directors, as to the conduct and character of their auditor, is privileged, though it relates to his conduct with reference to another company, of which he was secretary and not auditor.

> *Harris* v. *Thompson*, (1853) 13 C. B. 333.

But a statement made by one private shareholder in a company to another about a man who was formerly engineer to the company and sadly mismanaged its affairs is not privileged.

> *Brooks* v. *Blanshard*, 1 Cr. & M. 779; 3 Tyrw. 844.

Defendant, who was a sergeant in a volunteer corps, of which plaintiff also was a member, represented to the committee by whom the general business of the corps was conducted, that plaintiff was an unfit person to be permitted to continue a member of the corps; that he was the executioner of the French king, &c. Lord Ellenborough held the communication privileged.

> *Barbaud* v. *Hookham,* 5 Esp. 109.
> See *Bell* v. *Parke,* 10 Ir. C. L. R. 279; 11 Ir. C. L. R. 413.

But for one member of a charitable institution to send round to all the subscribers a circular calling on them "to reject the unworthy claims of Miss Hoare," and stating that "she squandered away the money which she did obtain from the benevolent in printing circulars abusive of Commander Dickson," the secretary of the institution, is libellous, and not privileged.

> *Hoare* v. *Silverlock,* (No. 1; 1848) 12 Q. B. 624; 17 L. J. Q. B. 306; 12 Jur. 695.

There is in many professions and trades a council or committee, which acts as a kind of domestic tribunal; it settles disputes between members, and sometimes disputes between a member and an outsider who chooses to apply to it; it regulates other matters which concern the members of that profession or trade as a whole. So, in many religious sects there is a synod, or assembly, or other organisation, which often exercises similar functions; its jurisdiction depending solely on the consent of the members. All communications or complaints properly made to such a body, all evidence laid before it, and its discussion of such evidence, are privileged; and so is the announcement of its final decision to the members of the sect, profession, or trade. Such privilege is based on the fact that all concerned have a common interest in the reputation of their sect, the honour of their profession, or the prosperity of their trade, and have created this body to represent them, and clothed it with certain powers to protect their interests. A confidential relationship is thus established, which is in itself a ground of privilege: see *ante,* p. 259.

The Benchers of each Inn of Court have similar powers over barristers: the Committee of the Stock Exchange has jurisdiction over brokers or jobbers who are members of the House. All communications properly addressed to either body are privileged. And it is submitted that either body may safely declare its decision to the members of its society—the Benchers may screen the name of a man whom they have disbarred: the Committee of the Stock Exchange may post the name of a man whom they have declared a defaulter. We know of no decision on the point, but the case is analogous to *Hunt* v. *Great Northern Railway Co.*, [1891] 2 Q. B. 189; 60 L. J. Q. B. 498; 55 J. P. 234, 648.

Illustrations.

The defendants were the chairman and committee of an association formed in 1862 by underwriters at Liverpool, similar to the London "Lloyd's," and called "The Underwriters' Registry." The plaintiffs were members of the association and owners of an iron steamship. The defendants had originally classed the plaintiffs' ship as "A 1"; but subsequently, in consequence of some alterations which the plaintiffs made in their vessel, and to which the defendants' surveyors objected, they published its name in their list with the words "Class suspended, 1871" against it. This list was published by the defendants only to subscribers to the association. *Held*, that the defendants had a right to suspend the class until the plaintiffs altered the ship according to their requirements, and also to publish to their subscribers the fact that the ship's class had so been suspended.

> *Clover* v. *Royden*, L. R. 17 Eq. 190 ; 43 L. J. Ch. 665 ; 22 W. R. 254 ; 29 L. T. 639.

Complaints having constantly arisen among manufacturers of aërated and mineral waters that the bottles marked with the name of one manufacturer were filled with waters made by another, a Mineral Water Bottle Exchange and Trade Protection Society was formed to put a stop to this practice. The rules of the society provided that the council of the society should have power to refer to arbitration any claims or demands against the society or its members : that every member should be required to forward the objects of the society, and to report to the secretary of the society all such information respecting the proceedings of any member in possession of, or otherwise dealing improperly with, the bottles or boxes of any member, or doing any act or acts calculated to injure the trade. The plaintiffs and defendants were both large mineral and aërated water manufacturers, and both were members of the society. The defendants wrote to the secretary of the society complaining that the plaintiffs systematically and habitually filled other people's bottles, especially the defendants', with liquids of their own manufacture. Henn Collins, J., held the letter privileged, on the ground that the defendants had a right to put forward their complaint in the way they did, as the society was the tribunal which both plaintiffs and defendants had chosen to create for that very purpose.

> *White and others* v. *Batey & Co.*, (1892) 8 Times L. R. 698.

Where the committee of a lodge of Freemasons expelled the plaintiff from the lodge, and plaintiff appealed to the Grand Lodge, the committee were held justified in printing and circulating, among the members of the Grand Lodge, a pamphlet justifying their conduct, it being usual for them to report the transactions of their lodge to the Grand Lodge in that form.

Kirkpatrick v. *Eagle Lodge,* 26 Kansas, 384 ; 40 Amer. R. 316.

Words spoken at a church meeting in the regular course of church discipline, when the question before the meeting is whether the plaintiff is or is not fit to be a member of the church, are held privileged in America.

Jarvis v. *Hatheway,* 3 Johns. (N. Y. Sup. Court) 178.
Remington v. *Congdon and others,* 2 Pick. (19 Mass.) 310.
York v. *Pease,* 2 Gray (68 Mass.), 282.

Unless such words are also defamatory of some third person who is not a member of the church, when such outsider may sue.

Coombs v. *Rose,* 8 Blackford (Indiana), 155.
See in England, *R.* v. *Hart,* 1 Wm. Bl. 386.

The owner of a racehorse does not, by referring a dispute to the stewards of the race meeting, authorise the publication of the stewards' decision in the Racing Calendar. And no privilege attaches to such a report.

Hope v. *I'Anson and Weatherby,* (1901) 18 Times L. R. 201.

So where the plaintiff was a member of a provincial assembly of congregational ministers, a resolution proposed at a meeting of that assembly, severely censuring the plaintiff, and all speeches made thereon, are privileged ; so is the publication of the resolution in the denominational papers. But a letter written to the assembly by a person not a member of it is not privileged.

Shurtleff v. *Stevens,* 51 Vermont, 501 ; 31 Amer. R. 698.
Shurtleff v. *Parker,* 130 Mass. 293 ; 39 Amer. R. 454.
And see *Oliver* v. *Bentinck,* 3 Taunt. 456.

Statements necessary to protect Defendant's private Interests.

It is not, however, necessary that there should always be a common or corresponding interest in the defendant and the person to whom he makes the communication. It is sufficient if the defendant has an interest and the other person a duty in the matter. The defendant is entitled to defend his interests ; and any communication is privileged which a due regard to his own interest renders necessary. But such a communication must be addressed to persons who have either some interest in the matter, or some duty to perform in connection with it. And even then it must clearly appear not merely that some such communication was necessary, but that he was compelled to make a communication which was defamatory. If he could have done all that his duty or interest demanded, without libelling or slandering the plaintiff, the words are not privileged. Thus, it is sometimes, though very seldom, necessary for a man in self-defence to advertise his private concerns in the public press: it may be the only way of effecting his object; and, if such object is a lawful one, the publication in such a case is privileged. But if it was not necessary to advertise at all, or if the defendant's object could have been equally well effected by an advertisement which did not contain any words defamatory of the plaintiff, there is no privilege. (*Brown* v. *Croome*, 2 Stark. 297; and *Lay* v. *Lawson*, 4 A. & E. 795, overruling or explaining *Delany* v. *Jones*, 4 Esp. 191; *Stockley* v. *Clement*, 4 Bing. 162; *Head* v. *Briscoe et ux.*, 5 C. & P. 485.)

Illustrations.

The plaintiff, a trader, employed an auctioneer to sell off his goods, and otherwise conducted himself in such a way that his creditors reasonably concluded that he had committed an act of bankruptcy. One of them, the defendant, thereupon sent the auctioneer a notice not to pay over the proceeds of the sale to the plaintiff, "he having committed an act of bankruptcy." *Held* by the majority of the Court of C. P. that this notice was privileged, as being made in the honest defence of defendant's own interests.

> *Blackham* v. *Pugh*, 2 C. B. 611; 25 L. J. C. P. 290.

So where an agent in temperate language claims a right for his principal or a solicitor for his client, the occasion is privileged.

> *Hargrave* v. *Le Breton*, 4 Burr. 2422.
> *Steward* v. *Young*, L. R. 5 C. P. 122; 39 L. J. C. P. 85;
>   18 W. R. 492; 22 L. T. 168.
> *Baker* v. *Carrick*, [1894] 1 Q. B. 838; 63 L. J. Q. B. 399;
>   42 W. R. 338; 70 L. T. 366; 58 J. P. 669; 9 R. 283.

Even if the agent has no express authority.

> *Watson* v. *Reynolds*, Moo. & Mal. 1.

Delivery to a third person for service on the plaintiff of a statutory notice under the Insolvent Act of 1869 (Nova Scotia) is *primâ facie* privileged, if it be made *bonâ fide* with the object of protecting the defendant's rights.

> *Bank of British North America* v. *Strong*, 1 App. Cas. 307;
>   34 L. T. 627.

The defendant had dismissed the plaintiff from his service on suspicion of theft, and upon the plaintiff coming to his counting-house for his wages, called in two other of his servants, and addressing them in the presence of the plaintiff, said, "I have dismissed that man for robbing me : do not speak to him any more, in public or in private, or I shall think you as bad as him." *Held,* a privileged communication, on the ground that it was the duty, and also the interest of the defendant to prevent his servants from associating with such a person.

Somerville v. *Hawkins,* 10 C. B. 583 ; 20 L. J. C. P. 131 ; 16 L. T. (Old S.) 283 ; 15 Jur. 450.

And see *Manby* v. *Witt,* } 18 C. B. 544; 25 L. J. C. P. 294; 2 Jur.
Eastmead v. *Witt,* } N. S. 1004, *ante,* p. 272.

The occupier of a house may complain to the landlord or his agent of the workmen he has sent to repair the house.

Toogood v. *Spyring,* 1 C. M. & R. 181 ; 4 Tyrw. 582.

Kine v. *Sewell,* 3 M. & W. 297.

A customer may call and complain to a tradesman of the goods he supplies and the manner in which he conducts his business : but he should be careful to make the complaint in the hearing of as few persons as possible, and in moderate language.

Oddy v. *Ld. Geo. Paulet,* 4 F. & F. 1009.

Crisp v. *Gill,* 29 L. T. (Old S.) 82.

An insurance company may inform a shipowner that they must refuse to insure his vessel any longer if he put a particular master in command of her.

Hamon v. *Falle,* 4 App. Cas. 247 ; 48 L. J. P. C. 45.

The directors of a charity were informed that the plaintiff, their former collector, continued to solicit and receive subscriptions on behalf of the charity, although dismissed as untrustworthy. They therefore printed at the end of their annual report a "Caution to the Public," warning them against such imposture. *Held,* that such a caution was privileged, if published with the honest desire of protecting the interests of the charity, and guarding the public against imposture, and not with any malicious desire of defaming the plaintiff, with whom they had quarrelled ; and that it was for the jury to decide with which intent it was in fact published.

Gassett v. *Gilbert and others,* 6 Gray (72 Mass.), 94.

Defendant having lost certain bills of exchange, published a handbill, offering a reward for their recovery, and adding that he believed they had been embezzled by his clerk. His clerk at that time still attended regularly at his office. *Held,* that the concluding words of the handbill were quite unnecessary to defendant's object, and were a gratuitous libel on the clerk. Damages, 200*l.*

Finden v. *Westlake,* Moo. & Mal. 461.

III.—COMMUNICATIONS MADE IN SELF-DEFENCE, &c.

In addition to the cases in which the privilege arises owing to the existence of a duty or of a common interest, there is a class of cases which may be grouped under the head of legitimate self-defence. Where an attack has been made on the defendant he is entitled to answer it and to communicate his answer to all who- heard the attack. Every man has a right to defend his character against false aspersion; communications made in fair self-defence are therefore privileged. If the charge was made only in the hearing of two or three persons the reply thereto should as far as possible be limited to those persons. But where the attack has been made on a public occasion or in the press the defendant is entitled to give equal publicity to his reply. He is privileged in addressing his defence through the same channel which has conveyed the attack. (*Per cur.* in *Laughton* v. *Sodor and Man,* L. R. 4 P. C. at p. 504.)

A man who has been attacked may, in rebutting the charges, at the same time retort upon his adversary where such a retort is a necessary part of his defence or fairly arises out of the charges made against him. (*O'Donoghue* v. *Hussey,* Ir. R. 5 C. L. 124.) A man who himself commenced a newspaper war, cannot subsequently come to the Court as plaintiff, to complain that he has had the worst of the fray. But even in rebutting an accusation, the defendant must not intrude unnecessarily into the private life of his assailant, or make counter-charges against his character, unconnected with his original charge against the defendant. The privilege extends only to such retorts as are fairly an answer to the plaintiff's attacks. (See *post,* p. 366.) Such previous attacks may also be matter for a counterclaim. (*Quin* v. *Hession,* 40 L. T. 70; 4 L. R. (Ir.) 35.)

Illustrations.

The plaintiff, a barrister, attacked the Bishop of Sodor and Man before the House of Keys in an argument against a private bill, imputing to the bishop improper motives in his exercise of church patronage. The bishop wrote a charge to his clergy refuting these insinuations, and sent it to the newspapers for publication. *Held,* that under the circumstances the bishop was justified in sending the charge to the newspapers, for an attack made in public required a public answer.

    Laughton v. *Bishop of Sodor and Man,* L. R. 4 P. C. 495; 42 L. J. P. C. 11; 9 Moore, P. C. C. N. S. 318; 21 W. R. 204; 28 L. T. 377.

    See *Hibbs* v. *Wilkinson,* 1 F. & F. 608.

The plaintiff and defendant had a quarrel. The plaintiff's son then wrote a letter to the Rye *Chronicle* referring to the quarrel and attacking the defendant ; the defendant wrote a letter to the Rye *Chronicle* in reply, in which he libelled the plaintiff. *Held*, that this reply was *primâ facie* privileged.

> *Hemmings* v. *Gasson*, E. B. & E. 346 ; 27 L. J. Q. B. 252 ; 4 Jur. N. S. 834.

The defendant was a candidate for the county of Waterford. Shortly before the election the Kilkenny Tenant Farmers' Association published in *Freeman's Journal* an address to the constituency, describing the defendant as "a true type of a bad Irish landlord—the scourge of the country," and charging him with various acts of tyranny and oppression towards his tenants, and especially towards the plaintiff, one of his former tenants. The defendant thereupon published, also in *Freeman's Journal,* an address to the constituency, answering the charges thus brought against him, and, in so doing, necessarily libelled the plaintiff. *Held*, that such an address, being an answer to an attack, was privileged.

> *Dwyer* v. *Esmonde*, 2 L. R. (Ir.) 243, reversing the decision of the Court below ; Ir. R. 11 C. L. 542.
> See also *O'Donoghue* v. *Hussey*, Ir. R. 5 C. L. 124.

The plaintiff was a policy-holder in an insurance company, and published a pamphlet accusing the directors of that company of fraud. The directors published a pamphlet in reply, declaring the charges contained in the plaintiff's pamphlet to be false and calumnious, and also asserting that in a suit he had instituted he had sworn in support of those charges in opposition to his own handwriting. Cockburn, C.J., held the directors' pamphlet privileged, and directed the jury in the following words : "If you are of opinion that it was published *bonâ fide* for the purpose of the defence of the company, and in order to prevent these charges from operating to their prejudice, and with a view to vindicate the character of the directors, and not with a view to injure or lower the character of the plaintiff—if you are of that opinion, and think that the publication did not go beyond the occasion, then you ought to find for the defendants on the general issue." Verdict for the defendants.

> *Kœnig* v. *Ritchie*, 3 F. & F. 413.
> *R.* v. *Veley*, 4 F. & F. 1117.

Whenever money is demanded from the defendant by the plaintiff or his solicitor, the defendant is entitled to reply, and in his reply to state his reasons for refusing to pay the sum demanded. Such reply is privileged so long as it is confined to the matter in hand, although it may contain charges of fraud or misconduct against the plaintiff. Such charges are at most but evidence of malice, which may take the case out of the privilege. See *post*, p. 352.

> *Tuson* v. *Evans*, 12 A. & E. 733, as explained or overruled by
> *Cooke* v. *Wildes*, 5 E. & B. 328 ; 24 L. J. Q. B. 367 ; 1 Jur. N. S. 610 ; 3 C. L. R. 1090.
> *Robertson* v. *M'Dougall*, 4 Bing. 670 ; 3 C. & P. 259.
> *Huntley* v. *Ward*, 1 F. & F. 552 ; 6 C. B. N. S. 514 ; 6 Jur. N. S. 18.
> *Hancock* v. *Case*, 2 F. & F. 711.

Stevens v. *Kitchener,* (1887) 4 Times L. R. 159.

Jacob v. *Lawrence,* 4 L. R. Ir. 579 ; 14 Cox, C. C. 321.

Campbell v. *Cochrane,* (1906) 8 F. 205 (Ct. of Sess.).

The defendant, the manager of a private lunatic asylum, unsuccessfully attempted to seize and carry off a lady, the plaintiff, whom he *bonâ fide* believed to be insane. He did so at the request of her husband, proper certificates having been obtained and all requirements of the Lunacy Act complied with. The plaintiff, who was perfectly sane, constantly afterwards attacked him in the newspapers, challenging him to justify his conduct. Defendant at last wrote a letter in answer to these attacks and sent it to the *British Medical Journal.* Huddleston, B., held this letter privileged.

Weldon v. *Winslow, Times,* March 14th—19th, 1884.

Coward v. *Wellington,* 7 C. & P. 531.

At a vestry meeting called to elect fresh overseers, the plaintiff accused the defendant, one of the outgoing overseers, of neglecting the interests of the vestry, and not collecting the rates ; the defendant retorted that the plaintiff had been bribed by a railway company. *Held,* that the retort was a mere *tu quoque,* in no way connected with the charge made against him by the plaintiff, and was therefore not privileged ; for it was not made in self-defence, but in counter-attack.

Senior v. *Medland,* 4 Jur. N. S. 1039.

And see *Huntley* v. *Ward,* 6 C. B. N. S. 514 ; 6 Jur. N. S. 18 ; 1 F. & F. 552.

Murphy v. *Halpin,* Ir. R. 8 C. L. 127.

Statements invited by the Plaintiff.

Closely akin to retorts provoked by the plaintiff's attack, are communications procured by the plaintiff's contrivance or request. If the only publication that can be proved is one made by the defendant in answer to an application from the plaintiff, or some agent of the plaintiff, demanding explanation, such answer, if fair and relevant, will be held privileged ; for the plaintiff brought it on himself. But this rule does not apply where there has been a previous unprivileged publication by the defendant of the same libel or slander, which causes the plaintiff's inquiry; for in that case it is the defendant who brings it on himself.

A plaintiff is not to be allowed to entrap people into making statements to him on which he can take proceedings. And, again, if rumours are afloat prejudicial to the plaintiff which he is anxious to sift and trace to their source, all statements made *bonâ fide* to him or any agent of his in the course of the investigation are rightly protected. But it makes a great difference if the rumours originated with the defendant, so that what he has himself previously said produces the plaintiff's inquiry. (Per Lord Lyndhurst in *Smith* v. *Mathews*, 1 Moo. & Rob. 151.) If in answer to such an inquiry the defendant does no more than acknowledge having uttered the words, no action can be brought for the acknowledgment: the party injured must sue for the words previously spoken, and use the acknowledgment as proof that those words had been spoken. But if besides saying " Yes " to the question asked, he repeats the words in the presence of a third person, asserting his belief in the accusation and that he can prove it ; such a statement is slanderous and is not privileged, although elicited by the plaintiff's question. See *Griffiths* v. *Lewis*, 7 Q. B. 61 ; 14 L. J. Q. B. 199, in which case Lord Denman remarks : " Injurious words having been uttered by the defendant respecting the plaintiff, the plaintiff was bound to make inquiry on the subject. When she did so, instead of any satisfaction from the defendant, she gets only a repetition of the slander. The real question comes to this, does the utterance of slander once give the privilege to the slanderer to utter it again whenever he is asked for an explanation ? It is the constant course, when a person hears that he has been calumniated, to go, with a witness, to the party who, he is informed, has uttered the injurious words, and to say, ' Do you mean in the presence of witnesses to persist in the charge you have made ? ' And it is never wise to bring an action for slander unless some such course has been taken. But it never has been supposed, that the persisting in and repeating the calumny, in answer to such a question, which is an aggravation of the slander, can be a privileged communication ; and in none of the cases cited has it ever been so decided." And see *Richards* v. *Richards*, 2 Moo. & Rob. 557 ; *Force* v. *Warren*, 15 C. B. N. S. 806. If, however, the second occasion on which the words were spoken is clearly privileged and justifiable, the mere fact that defendant had previously spoken them will not of itself destroy the privilege ; the plaintiff must rely on the first utterance : that may be privileged as well or may be barred by the statute.

This rule is sometimes cited as an instance of the maxim " *Volenti non fit injuria*," and is then not classed as a ground of privilege, but would rather be stated thus :—If the only publication proved at the trial be one brought about by the plaintiff's own contrivance, this is no sufficient evidence of publication ; it is as though the only publication were to the plaintiff himself, which would give him no right of action. Such was the ruling of Lord Ellenborough in

Smith v. *Wood*, 3 Camp. 323 ; but this is inconsistent with *Duke of Brunswick* v. *Harmer*, 14 Q. B. 185 ; and in *Warr* v. *Jolly*, 6 C. & P. 497, it was expressly held that a communication purposely procured by the plaintiff was *privileged*.

Illustrations.

" If a servant, knowing the character which his master will give him, procures a letter to be written, not with a fair view of inquiring the character, but to procure an answer upon which to ground an action for a libel, no action can be maintained." Per Lord Alvanley in

> *King* v. *Waring et ux.*, 5 Esp. 15.
> And see *Fonville* v. *Nease*, Dudley, S. C. 303, *ante*, p. 160.

The defendant discharged the plaintiff, his servant, and when applied to by another gentleman, gave him a bad character. The plaintiff's brother-in-law, Collier, thereupon repeatedly called on the defendant to inquire why he had dismissed the plaintiff ; and at last the defendant wrote to Collier stating his reasons specifically. The plaintiff issued a writ the same day the letter was written. *Held*, by Lord Mansfield, C.J., and Buller, J., that no action lay on such letter, as the defendant was evidently entrapped into writing it.

> *Weatherston* v. *Hawkins*, 1 T. R. 110.
> See also *Taylor* v. *Hawkins*, 16 Q. B. 308 ; 20 L. J. Q. B. 313.
> *R.* v. *Hart*, 1 Wm. Black. 386 ; and the remarks of Lord Alvanley, C.J., in
> *Rogers* v. *Clifton*, 3 B. & P. 592.

A builder employed two men, the plaintiff and Fosdyke, to repair Barton's house. Defendant on a privileged occasion had stated to the builder, " I saw the man employed by you take from Mr. Barton's house and carry away two long pieces of quartering. I hallooed to the man." Plaintiff thereupon brought Fosdyke to the defendant and said, " Is this the man ? " Defendant replied, " No, you are the man." *Held*, no action lay.

> *Kine* v. *Sewell*, 3 M. & W. 297.
> *Amann* v. *Damm*, 8 C. B. N. S. 597 ; 29 L. J. C. P. 313 ; 7 Jur. N. S. 47 ; 8 W. R. 470.

The defendant was asked by a friend of the plaintiff's to sign a memorial in favour of the plaintiff. He declined. The plaintiff's friend pressed him to sign and asked his reasons for declining. Thereupon defendant stated his reasons ; and this statement was held a privileged communication.

> *Cowles* v. *Potts*, 34 L. J. Q. B. 247 ; 11 Jur. N. S. 946 ; 13 W. R. 858.
> *Murdoch* v. *Funduklian*, (1885) 2 Times L. R. 215 ; (1886) *ib.* 614.

A School Board gave the plaintiff, one of their masters, notice to quit their service. He asked them to specify their reasons for dismissing him. The Board passed and recorded a resolution stating their reasons. This was held privileged.

> *Reid* v. *Blisland School Board*, (1901) 17 Times L. R. 626.

A friend of the plaintiff's asked defendant to act as arbitrator between the plaintiff and A. in a dispute about a horse. Defendant declined. The friend wrote again strongly urging defendant to use his influence with A. not to bring the case into court. Defendant again declined, and stated his reasons ; and on this letter plaintiff brought an action. Subsequently another friend of the plaintiff's, with his knowledge and consent, wrote to defendant that she was confident he was misinformed about the plaintiff. Defendant replied that he believed A. and his servant, and not the plaintiff. On this plaintiff brought a second action of libel. *Held,* that both letters were privileged.

> *Whiteley* v. *Adams,* 15 C. B. N. S. 392 ; 33 L. J. C. P. 89 ; 10 Jur. N. S. 470 ; 12 W. R. 153 ; 9 L. T. 483.

Note that the headnote in this case " goes too far, and further than the judgments themselves warrant." Per Lindley, L. J., in

> *Stuart* v. *Bell,* [1891] 2 Q. B. at p. 349.

A witness (whom we must presume to have been an agent of the plaintiff's, though it is not so stated in the report) heard that the defendant had a copy of a libellous print, went to defendant's house, and asked to see it ; the defendant thereupon produced it, and pointed out the figure of the plaintiff and the other persons caricatured. Lord Ellenborough nonsuited the plaintiff, as there was no other publication proved.

> *Smith* v. *Wood,* 3 Camp. 323.

The plaintiff had been in partnership with his brother-in-law, Pinhorn, as a linendraper at Southampton ; but gave up business and became a dissenting minister. Rumours reached his congregation that he had cheated his brother-in-law in the settlement of the accounts on his retirement from the partnership. The plaintiff challenged inquiry, and invited the malcontents in the congregation to appoint someone to thoroughly sift the matter. The malcontents appointed the defendant, and the plaintiff appointed the Rev. Robert Ainslie. *Held,* that all communications between the defendant and Ainslie relative to the matter were privileged, as being made with the sanction and concurrence of the plaintiff.

> *Hopwood* v. *Thorn,* 8 C. B. 293 ; 19 L. J. C. P. 94 ; 14 Jur. 87.
>
> And see *Sayer* v. *Begg,* 15 Ir. C. L. R. 458.
>
> *Remington* v. *Congdon and others,* 2 Pick. (19 Mass.) 310.
>
> *Kirkpatrick* v. *Eagle Lodge,* 26 Kansas, 384 ; 40 Amer. R. 316.

In answer to plaintiff's inquiry as to a rumour against himself, defendant told him, in the presence of a third party, what someone had said to his (defendant's) wife. There was no proof that the defendant had ever uttered a word on the subject till he was applied to by the plaintiff. *Held,* that the answer was privileged.

> *Warr* v. *Jolly,* 6 C. & P. 497, as explained by Lord Denman in
>
> *Griffiths* v. *Lewis,* 7 Q. B. 67 ; 14 L. J. Q. B. 199 ; 9 Jur. 370.
>
> And see *Richards* v. *Richards,* 2 Moo. & Rob. 557.

The plaintiff called at the " Trevor Arms," and asked the landlord, in the presence of witnesses, " What do you mean by saying that I have taken sovereigns over your counter from your barmaid ? " Day, J., held defendant's answer privileged.

> *Palmer* v. *Hummerston,* (1883) Cababé & Ellis, 36.

The plaintiff was a builder, and contracted to build certain school-rooms at Bermondsey. The defendant started a false report, that in the building the plaintiff had used inferior timber ; the report reached the plaintiff, who thereupon suspended the work and demanded an inquiry ; and the committee of the school employed defendant to survey the work and report. He reported falsely that inferior timber was used. Lord Lyndhurst directed the jury, that if they believed that the reports that produced the inquiry originated with the defendant, the defendant's report to the committee was not privileged. Verdict for the plaintiff.

> *Smith* v. *Mathews,* 1 Moo. & Rob. 151.

The *Weekly Dispatch* libelled the Duke of Brunswick in 1830. In 1848 the Duke sent to the office of that newspaper for a copy of the number containing the old libel, and obtained one. *Held,* that he could sue on this publication to his own agent, though all proceedings on the former publication were barred by the Statute of Limitations.

> *Duke of Brunswick* v. *Harmer,* 14 Q. B. 185 ; 19 L. J. Q. B.
> 20 ; 14 Jur. 110 ; 3 C. & K. 10.

Publication to Persons outside the Privilege.

We have now discussed the various classes of privileged occasions, which are based on duty, interest, or self-defence. But in all these cases only those words are protected which are published to persons having a duty or an interest in connection with the matter ; any publication to others will be outside the privilege. Thus, it is very seldom that any privilege attaches to an indiscriminate publication in the public newspapers ; unless, indeed, there was no other way in which the defendant could efficiently protect his interest, or adequately discharge the duty which he owed to society.

Illustrations.

The manager and the directors of a joint stock company have a common interest in discussing the affairs of the company ; but that does not justify the manager in making personal charges of fraud against the directors in a public news-room.

> *Waring* v. *M'Caldin,* 7 Ir. R. C. L. 282.
>
> *Sewall* v. *Catlin,* 3 Wendall (New York), 292.

Where libellous matter, which would have been privileged if sent in a sealed letter, is transmitted unnecessarily by telegraph, the privilege is thereby lost.

> *Williamson* v. *Freer,* L. R. 9 C. P. 393 ; 43 L. J. C. P. 161 ;
> 22 W. R. 878 ; 30 L. T. 332.

Unless the telegram be sent in code so that its meaning is hidden from ordinary readers.

> *Edmondson* v. *Birch & Co., Ltd.,* [1907] 1 K. B. 371 ; 76 L. J. K. B. 346 ; 96 L. T. 415 ; 23 Times L. R. 234.
>
> *Evans and Sons* v. *Stein,* (1905) 7 F. 65 (Ct. of Sess.).

The Court will take judicial notice of the nature of a post-card, and will presume that others besides the person to whom it is addressed will read what is written thereon. It will be for the defendant to show that in fact no one but the plaintiff read it.

> *Robinson* v. *Jones,* 4 L. R. Ir. 391.
>
> *Chattell* v. *Turner,* (1896) 12 Times L. R. 360.
>
> *Beamish* v. *Dairy Supply Co., Limited,* (1897) 13 Times L. R. 484.
>
> *Sadgrove* v. *Hole,* [1901] 2 K. B. 1 ; 70 L. J. K. B. 455 ; 49 W. R. 473 ; 84 L. T. 647.

Defendant having lost certain bills of exchange, published a handbill, offering a reward for their recovery, and adding that he believed they had been embezzled by his clerk. His clerk at that time still attended regularly at his office. *Held,* that the concluding words of the handbill were quite unnecessary to defendant's object, and were a gratuitous libel on the clerk. Damages, 200*l.*

> *Finden* v. *Westlake,* Moo. & Mal. 461.

A personal attack on the private life and character of a candidate at a parliamentary election, published by a voter in the newspapers, is not privileged. " However large the privilege of electors may be," said Lord Denman, C.J., " it is extravagant to suppose that it can justify the publication to all the world of facts injurious to a person who happens to stand in the situation of a candidate."

> *Duncombe* v. *Daniell,* 8 C. & P. 222 ; 2 Jur. 32 ; 1 W. W. & H. 101.

Defendant made a speech at a public meeting called to petition Parliament, and subsequently handed a copy of what he had said to the reporters for publication in the newspapers ; such publication was held to be in excess of the privilege.

> *Pierce* v. *Ellis,* 6 Ir. C. L. R. 55.

A letter sent to a newspaper by members of the town council and published therein, charging certain contractors for the erection of the borough gaol with " scamping " their work, is not privileged ; although preferring the same charge at a meeting of the town council would have been.

> *Simpson* v. *Downs,* 16 L. T. 391.
>
> *Harle* v. *Catherall,* 14 L. T. 801.

But two exceptions to this rule are recognised—

(i.) In cases of slander where the words are addressed by the speaker to persons having a duty or an interest in the matter, but others hear them.

(ii.) Where the main publication, which is privileged,

reasonably involves certain minor and ancillary publications which are necessary or usual in the circumstances, but which do not strictly come within the rule.

(i.) *Extent of Privilege in Slander.*

Every repetition of a slander is of course a separate cause of action, to which the defendant must find a separate defence. But where the words are only uttered once, there is only one tort, and only one occasion. (See *ante*, p. 157.) If that occasion be privileged it is immaterial how many persons heard the words; the privilege attaching to the occasion is a defence to the whole action. But of course the number of persons present on any occasion is a most material factor in deciding the question, Was the occasion privileged? As a rule, the defendant should not speak while persons unconcerned are by. But there are many cases where the matter is urgent, where, if he does not speak at once, the order will be given, or the resolution will be carried, or some other thing will happen which it is his duty, or his interest, to prevent. On such occasions, the accidental presence of an uninterested bystander will not take the case out of the privilege. And there are other cases in which it is only prudent, and is, therefore, permissible, to make the privileged communication in the presence of witnesses.

Illustrations.

The plaintiff had been clerk to a board of guardians, and claimed that money was due to him from the board. After much negotiation and dispute, it was proposed at a meeting of the board, that the plaintiff be paid 89*l*. 16*s*. 8*d*. in settlement of his claim. The defendant, a member of the board, moved an amendment that the plaintiff be paid only 39*l*. 16*s*. 8*d*. ; and in his speech he referred to "the defalcations of an unfaithful servant." Reporters were present in accordance with the regular custom of the board, and also some other persons not guardians but possibly ratepayers. *Held,* that this was a privileged occasion, in spite of the presence of the reporters and the others, whether ratepayers or not ; for it was the duty of the defendant to speak then and there, or the resolution would have been carried and the money voted.

> *Pittard* v. *Oliver,* [1891] 1 Q. B. 474 ; 60 L. J. Q. B. 219 ;
> 39 W. R. 311 ; 63 L. T. 247 ; 64 L. T. 758 ; 55 J. P. 100.
> *Mapey* v. *Baker,* (1909) 73 J. P. 289 ; 7 L. G. R. 636 ; *ante,*
> p. 282.

It was held otherwise where a shareholder in a railway company summoned a meeting of shareholders and himself invited persons not shareholders, and especially reporters for the public press, to be present, and then at the meeting made defamatory comments on the conduct of the plaintiff, who was one of the directors.

> *Parsons* v. *Surgey,* (1864) 4 F. & F. 247.

The landlord of a farm sent some men there to do repairs ; one of them, the plaintiff, got drunk while on the premises, and the farmer was told that the plaintiff had broken open his cellar-door and got drunk on his cider. Two days afterwards he met the plaintiff walking with a man named Taylor, and at once taxed him with his misconduct. *Held,* that the presence of Taylor did not prevent this from being a privileged occasion.

> *Toogood* v. *Spyring,* 1 C. M. & R. 181 ; 4 Tyrw. 582.

The justices were about to swear in the plaintiff as a paid constable when defendant, a parishioner, came forward and stated that the plaintiff was an improper person to be a constable. *Held,* that the fact that several other persons besides the justices were present, as usual, did not destroy the privilege attaching to such *bonâ fide* remark.

> *Kershaw* v. *Bailey,* 1 Exch. 743 ; 17 L. J. Ex. 129.

The fact that defendant's wife was present on a privileged occasion, and heard what her husband said, will not take away the privilege, so long as her presence, though not necessary, was not improper.

> *Jones* v. *Thomas,* 34 W. R. 104 ; 53 L. T. 678 ; 50 J. P. 149.

Where a master about to dismiss his servant for dishonesty calls in a friend to hear what passes, the presence of such third party will not destroy the privilege.

> *Taylor* v. *Hawkins,* 16 Q. B. 308 ; 20 L. J. Q. B. 313 ; 15
> Jur. 746.

Defendant accused the plaintiff, in the presence of a third person, of stealing his wife's brooch ; plaintiff wished to be searched ; defendant repeated the accusation to two women, who searched the plaintiff and found nothing. Subsequently it was discovered that defendant's wife had left the brooch at a friend's house. *Held,* that the mere publication to the two women did not destroy the privilege attaching to charges, if made *bonâ fide;* but that all the circumstances should have been left to the jury, who should determine whether or no the charge was made recklessly and unwarrantably, and repeated before more persons than necessary.

> *Padmore* v. *Lawrence,* 11 A. & E. 380 ; 4 Jur. 458 ; 3 P.
> & D. 209.

The defendant, in the presence of his wife, accused the plaintiff, " a ladies' wardrobe-dealer," of having received certain goods stolen from his house. The plaintiff denied receiving them. The defendant then said,

"Would it surprise you if I could bring five people to say you had taken the things away from here?" The plaintiff said it would surprise her. Four boys and a maidservant were then sent into the room, and the defendant said to them, "Is this the person who came and took the things away?" They replied "Yes." The Court of Appeal held the whole conversation privileged.

Collins v. Cooper, (1902) 19 Times L. R. 118.

(ii.) Subsidiary Publications.

A man is entitled to act on a privileged occasion in whatever way is "reasonably necessary and usual" in such circumstances. And if, in so acting, he reasonably employs methods which, in the ordinary course of business, involve a minor and technical publication of the defamatory matter ancillary to the main publication which is privileged, such minor publication is also privileged. (See the judgments of the Court of Appeal in Boxsius v. Goblet Frères, [1894] 1 Q. B. 842; and in Edmondson v. Birch & Co., Ltd., [1907] 1 K. B. at p. 380.) "If fairly warranted by a reasonable occasion or exigency, and honestly made, such communications are protected for the common convenience and welfare of society, and the law has not restricted the right to make them within any narrow limits." (Per Parke, B., in Toogood v. Spyring, 1 C. M. & R. at p. 193.)

Illustrations.

The defendant in a petition to the House of Commons charged the plaintiff with extortion and oppression in his office of vicar-general to the Bishop of Lincoln. Copies of the petition were printed and delivered to the members of the committee appointed by the House to hear and examine grievances, in accordance with the usual order of proceeding in the House. No copy was delivered to any one not a member of Parliament. Held, that the petition was privileged, although the matter contained in it was false and scandalous; and so were all the printed copies; for, though the printing was a publication to the printers and compositors, still it was the usual course of proceeding in Parliament; and it was not so great a publication as to have so many copies transcribed by several clerks.

Lake v. King, 1 Lev. 240; 1 Saund. 131; Sid. 414; 1 Mod. 58.
See Lawless v. Anglo-Egyptian Cotton and Oil Co., Limited, L. R. 4 Q. B. 262; 10 B. & S. 226; 38 L. J. Q. B. 129; 17 W. R. 498; ante, p. 282.

The watch committee of the Liverpool City Council ordered the chief constable to report to them as to the licensed houses in the city, &c. The chief constable presented his report, to which was appended a schedule giving details as to each licensed house and the grounds of objection alleged against those houses the renewal of whose licence was opposed. This report with its schedule the magistrates ordered to be printed for their own use, and also for the use of "any person who might require and apply for the same in order to facilitate his business" at the approaching licensing sessions. Thirty-six copies of the report were in accordance with this order sold to persons, all of whom had business at the licensing sessions, and required the list to facilitate such business. But each of these thirty-six persons was only interested in a portion of the report—that dealing with his own premises. *Held*, nevertheless, that it was the duty of the chief constable to obey the orders of the magistrates and print the whole report, and that the sale of the whole document so printed to those who required it was privileged.

> *Andrews* v. *Nott Bower*, [1895] 1 Q. B. 888 ; 64 L. J. Q. B. 536 ; 43 W. R. 582 ; 72 L. T. 530 ; 59 J. P. 420 ; 14 R. 404.
>
> And see *King* v. *Patterson*, (1887) 20 Vroom (49 New Jersey), 417 ; 83 Law Times Journal, 408, *ante*, p. 263.

The defendants published in their newspaper a copy of certain notices of receiverships registered at Somerset House under the Companies Act, 1907, and open to the inspection of the public. The original publication at Somerset House being made under statutory authority was privileged. *Held*, that the publication by the defendants was privileged as assisting the Legislature in carrying out its object of making public the appointment of such receivers.

> *John Jones & Sons, Ltd.* v. *Financial Times, Ltd.*, (1909) 25 Times L. R. 677.

A solicitor wrote a letter to the plaintiff on behalf of his clients, containing defamatory statements. The contents of the letter were dictated by the solicitor to a clerk, who took them down in shorthand and transcribed them. The solicitor signed the letter, and it was then handed to another clerk in the office, who copied it into the letter-book. *Held*, that all these minor publications were privileged, because they were made in the ordinary course of a solicitor's business, and were "reasonably necessary and usual" in the discharge of the solicitor's duty to his client.

> *Boxsius* v. *Goblet Frères and others*, [1894] 1 Q. B. 842 ; 63 L. J. Q. B. 401 ; 42 W. R. 392 ; 70 L. T. 368.

In the previous case of *Pullman and another* v. *Hill & Co.*, [1891] 2 Q. B. 524, the Court of Appeal had decided that where a libellous letter was similarly dictated by a merchant and copied by his clerks, the publication to his clerks was not privileged. But note that in that case the main publication—that to Messrs. Pullman & Co.—was not privileged at all. It was addressed to the firm who had no interest in its subject-matter ; it related to the private concerns of two of the five partners in the firm, and should have been addressed to those two partners personally.

> See *ante*, p. 161.

H. was the managing director of the defendant company, and in response to an inquiry from the company's correspondents in Japan dispatched a telegram in code, the real meaning of which was defamatory of the plaintiff. H. dictated the telegram to a clerk, and the telegram was copied into a cable book, in accordance with the usual course of business. The plaintiff alleged publication to the company's clerks and to the telegraph clerks. *Held,* that the publications were privileged.

> *Edmondson* v. *Birch & Co., Ltd., and Horner,* [1907] 1 K. B. 371 ; 76 L. J. K. B. 346 ; 96 L. T. 415 ; 23 Times L. R. 234.

Similarly, it is submitted that where it is the duty of a solicitor to prepare a case for the opinion of counsel, it is reasonable and usual for him to send the case to a law stationer to be fair-copied : and that the publication to the law stationer, being merely auxiliary to the publication to counsel, is also privileged.

So, if a solicitor for the purposes of an action laid libellous letters before an expert in handwriting that he might say who wrote them ; or caused a foreign correspondence to be translated into English ; the publication by the solicitor to the expert and the translator would, it is submitted, be privileged : and also the publications to the solicitor of the expert's report, and of the translation into English.

> *Luckerman* v. *Sonnenschein,* 32 Freeman (62 Illinois), 115.

Privileged Communications.

Not every communication made on a privileged occasion is privileged. The defendant may, in answer to an inquiry, launch out into matters which have no bearing on the question ; or in writing to a person who has a joint interest with himself in one undertaking, he may wander off into other matters with which his correspondent is not concerned. The presence of such irrelevant matter does not of course affect the judge's ruling that the *occasion* was privileged ; as a rule, it will be merely evidence of malice to take the case out of the privilege. But there appear to be some cases, where the communication is so wholly irrelevant and improper, that the judge, while ruling that the occasion was one which would have afforded protection to a proper letter, may yet declare that no privilege at all can attach to the letter which the defendant in fact wrote on that occasion. (*Huntley* v. *Ward,* 6 C. B. N. S. 514 ; *Simmonds.* v. *Dunne,* Ir. R. 5 C. L. 358.) Again, if the communication sued on contain two or more distinct and severable charges, the judge may rule such portion of it as contains relevant charges privileged, and the other portions unprivileged.

(*Warren* v. *Warren*, 1 C. M. & R. 251; *Jacob* v. *Lawrence*,
4 L. R. Ir. 579.) So if, in replying to a question about A.,
irrelevant matter is dragged in defamatory of B., it is submitted, that in an action by B., it would be no defence
that the communication was privileged as against A. (Per
Lord Esher, M.R., [1895] 2 Q. B. at p. 170.) But in other
cases, if the matter impugned as irrelevant can possibly
have any bearing on the question, or throw any light on the
matter, or be of any assistance to the person to whom it
is sent, the judge should not rule that there is no privilege,
but submit the whole communication to the jury on the
issue of malice, if there be evidence to go to them on that
issue (as to which, see *post*, p. 345).

Baron Dowse states the point very clearly (but we think too
strongly) in 6 L. R. Ir. at p. 269: "It is not enough to have an interest
or a duty in making *a* communication; the interest or duty must be
shown to exist in making *the* communication complained of."

So O'Brien, J., says in *O'Hea* v. *Guardians of Cork Union*, 32
L. R. Ir. at p. 642: "Privilege depends on more than time and
place. . . . There must exist a proper motive and need for the
communication; and it would be going a long way to say that any
document could be excused upon the ground of privilege, if it
referred to matters to which there was no necessity to refer at
all." But these Irish *dicta* certainly go further than any English
decision.

Illustrations.

If a friend tells me he wants a good solicitor to act for him, and asks my
opinion of Smith, I am justified in telling him all I know for or against Smith.
But if a stranger asked me in the train: "Is not that gentleman a solicitor?"
I should not, it is submitted, be privileged in replying: "Yes, but he ought to
have been struck off the rolls long ago."

The defendant owed the plaintiff 6*l.* 10*s.*; the plaintiff told his attorney to
write and demand the money and threaten proceedings if it were not paid. The
defendant in reply wrote to the attorney a letter containing very gross aspersions
on the character of the plaintiff, wholly unconnected with the demand made
upon him. The jury expressly negatived malice. *Held*, that though the
occasion was privileged, this letter was not.

Huntley v. *Ward*, 6 C. B. N. S. 514; 6 Jur. N. S. 18.

The plaintiff and defendant were jointly interested in property in Scotland, to
the manager of which the defendant wrote a letter principally about the property and the conduct of the plaintiff with reference thereto, but also containing

a charge against the plaintiff with reference to his conduct to his mother and aunt. *Held*, that though the part of the letter about the defendant's conduct as to the property might be confidential and privileged, such privilege could not extend to the part of the letter about the plaintiff's conduct to his mother and aunt.

> *Warren* v. *Warren*, 1 C. M. & R. 250; 4 Tyr. 850.
>
> *Simmonds* v. *Dunne*, Ir. R. 5 C. L. 358.

The defendant was clerk of the peace of the county of Kent, and as such it was his duty to have the register of county voters printed, the expense of such printing being allowed by the justices in quarter sessions. In 1854 the defendant employed a new printer, who charged less for the job; the defendant wrote a letter to the Finance Committee of the justices stating his reasons for the change, and added that to continue to pay the charges made by his former printer, the plaintiff, would be "to submit to what appears to have been an attempt to extort money by misrepresentation." *Held*, that the occasion was privileged, as it was proper and necessary for the defendant to explain to the Finance Committee what he had done; but it was for the jury to determine whether the words imputing improper motives to the plaintiff were or were not maliciously inserted. Damages 50*l*.

> *Cooke and another* v. *Wildes*, 5 E. & B. 328; 24 L. J. Q. B. 367; 1 Jur. N. S. 610; 3 C. L. R. 1090, overruling.
>
> *Tuson* v. *Evans*, 12 A. & E. 733.
>
> And see *Hancock* v. *Case*, 2 F. & F. 711.
>
> *Robertson* v. *M'Dougall*, 4 Bing. 670; 3 C. & P. 259.
>
> *Stevens* v. *Kitchener*, (1887) 4 Times L. R. 159.

The defendant sent out a notice on a privileged occasion, and unnecessarily inserted in it words which were defamatory of the plaintiff but which had reference to the matters which rendered the occasion privileged. The jury found that these words were not true, and that the defendant by inserting them had exceeded the privileged occasion which entitled him to give the notice, but could not agree on any answer to the question whether the words were inserted maliciously. The Court of Appeal held that the excess was at most but evidence of malice; and that, as the jury had declined to say that the defendant had acted maliciously, judgment must be entered for the defendant. The House of Lords also held that there was no evidence of malice.

> *Nevill* v. *Fine Art and General Insurance Co.*, (C. A.) [1895] 2 Q. B. 156; 64 L. J. Q. B. 681; 72 L. T. 525; (H. L.) [1897] A. C. 68; 66 L. J. Q. B. 195; 75 L. T. 606.

CHAPTER XI.

QUALIFIED PRIVILEGE—*Continued.*

In this chapter we proceed to deal with the two remaining heads of qualified privilege, viz :—

Fair and accurate reports of the proceedings of any Court of justice, or of Parliament, or of a public meeting.

Statements made in or copied from Parliamentary or Official Papers.

IV. PRIVILEGED REPORTS.

Fair and accurate reports of certain proceedings are privileged, because it is a benefit to the public to be accurately informed as to such proceedings. They may be grouped into three classes :—

    (i) Reports of judicial proceedings.
    (ii) Reports of parliamentary proceedings.
    (iii) Reports of public meetings.

The first two classes of reports were privileged at common law ; the third class only acquired privilege by virtue of two Acts of Parliament: the Newspaper Libel and Registration Act, 1881, and the Law of Libel Amendment Act, 1888. The history of this legislation, and the causes which lead to it, are briefly sketched in Appendix B., *post*, p. 811. In all three cases, the privilege is qualified only : it is lost, if the plaintiff can show that the defendant acted maliciously in making and publishing the report.

Privileged reports (of all three classes) differ from those cases in which privilege is founded upon duty, interest or self defence in one important respect. They do not depend upon any private right or special duty enjoyed by or imposed on the defendant, or upon his particular relation towards some third person. Any one may publish such reports to any one, so long as they are fair and accurate. Hence, the right to publish such reports is not a *privilege* in the strictest sense of the word. But it is convenient to treat of these reports in connection with other communications which enjoy a qualified privilege.

(i) *Reports of Judicial Proceedings.*

Every impartial and accurate report of any proceeding in a Court of law is privileged, unless the Court has itself prohibited the publication, or the subject-matter of the trial be unfit for publication.

This rule applies to all proceedings in any Court of justice, superior or inferior, of record or not of record. "For this purpose no distinction can be made between a Court of *piepoudre* and the House of Lords sitting as a Court of justice." (Per Lord Campbell, in *Lewis* v. *Levy*, E. B. & E. 537 27 L. J. Q. B. 287.) It is immaterial whether the proceeding be *ex parte* or not, whether the matter be one over which the Court has jurisdiction or not, and whether it disposes of the case finally or sends it for trial to a higher tribunal. (*Usill* v. *Hales*, 3 C. P. D. 319; 47 L. J. C. P. 323; 26 W. R. 371; 38 L. T. 65; *Kimber* v. *The Press Association*, [1893] 1 Q. B. 65; 62 L. J. Q. B. 152; 41 W. R. 17; 67 L. T. 515.)

The reason for this privilege is thus stated by Lawrence, J., in *R.* v. *Wright*, 8 T. R. 298: "The general advantage to the country in having these proceedings made public more than counterbalances the inconvenience to private persons whose conduct may be the subject of such proceedings." Cockburn, C.J., uses language almost identical in *Wason* v. *Walter*, L. R. 4 Q. B. 87; 8 B. & S. 730. Whenever a Court is engaged in the adjudication of the legal rights of the parties before it, the proceeding is in its nature judicial, and the public is entitled to be present, so long as there is room in the building, unless an order has been properly made for their exclusion. And it is an advantage to the public that fair and accurate reports should be published, which place those who were not present in Court in the same position as those who were. (Per Lord Esher, M.R., in *MacDougall* v. *Knight & Son*, 17 Q. B. D. at p. 638.)

It is only since 1878 that the law has extended so wide an immunity to reports of proceedings before police magistrates or justices of the peace. Thus, while *Lewis* v. *Levy* decided that a report of a preliminary investigation before a magistrate was privileged if the result was that the summons was dismissed and the person accused discharged, still it was expressly held in *Duncan* v. *Thwaites*, 3 B. & C. 556; 5 D. & R. 447, that such a report was unprivileged, if the accused was ultimately sent to take his trial before a jury. The reason for the distinction was that in the one case the decision is final, and the investigation at an end; in the latter the examination is preliminary merely, and the minds of the future jury may possibly be influenced by the publication.

Again, there is an obvious distinction between an *ex parte* application where the accused has no opportunity of defending himself, and a full trial where both parties address the Court by their counsel or solicitors, and call what witnesses they please. There are *dicta* of eminent judges which would seem to deny any privilege to fair and accurate reports of *ex parte* proceedings, even in the superior Courts. (Per Maule, J., in *Hoare* v. *Silverlock* (No. 2, 1850), 9 C. B. 23; 19 L. J. C. P. 215; and Abbott, C.J., in *Duncan* v. *Thwaites*, 3 B. & C. 556.) But *Curry* v. *Walter*, 1 Bos. & P. 525; 1 Esp. 456, is an express decision that such reports are privileged: a case which was at one time doubted, but is now clear law. Cockburn, C.J., in *Wason* v. *Walter*, L. R. 4 Q. B. 93, expressed his clear opinion that a fair and accurate report of an *ex parte* application would be privileged (see *post*, pp. 327, 328). And the decision in *Usill* v. *Hales*, *post*, p. 311, settles the law, and extends immunity to all *bonâ fide* and correct reports of all proceedings in a magistrate's Court, whether *ex parte* or otherwise; and such cases as *R.* v. *Lee*, 5 Esp. 123, must be considered to be overruled, in so far at all events as they lay down any general rule to the effect that it is unlawful to publish any report of *ex parte* proceedings.

A third distinction was as to matters *coram non judice*. It might well be contended that where a magistrate listens to a slanderous complaint and gives some advice as to a matter wholly outside his jurisdiction, he is not discharging any magisterial function nor acting in any judicial capacity. It is as though the conversation took place in his private drawing-room. And to this effect was the decision in *M'Gregor* v. *Thwaites*, 3 B. & C. 24; 4 D. & R. 695. But this decision is practically overruled by *Usill* v. *Hales*, in which case a report of an application made *ex parte* to a magistrate was held privileged, although the magistrate eventually decided that he had no jurisdiction in the matter. Lord Coleridge, C.J., it is true, drew a distinction (3 C. P. D. 324) between " inherent want of jurisdiction on account of the nature of the complaint " and " what may be called resulting want of jurisdiction because the facts do not make out the charge." But Lopes, J., in his judgment, does not rely on any such distinction. It is surely the duty of the magistrate to listen to an applicant until it becomes clear from what he says that the magistrate has no jurisdiction over the subject-matter of the complaint. Hence, we think, since the decision in *Usill* v. *Hales*, newspapers may safely report any application made to a magistrate in open Court, even though the magistrate should prove to have no jurisdiction.

There is nothing, however, in the case of *Usill* v. *Hales*, which expressly overrules the first distinction—that taken in *Duncan* v. *Thwaites*, 3 B. & C. 556,—that a fair report of a magistrate's decision is privileged when it finally disposes of the matter of the application, but is not privileged where the inquiry is but a preliminary one, and the prisoner is committed to take his trial at the Assizes or the Central Criminal Court. In *Usill* v. *Hales*, the matter was finally disposed of by the magistrate; it was unnecessary therefore for the Court to decide the point. But the whole spirit of the decision is against this time-honoured distinction. Lord Coleridge frankly admits (p. 325): —" I do not doubt for my own part that if this argument had been addressed to a Court some sixty or seventy years ago, it might have met with a different result from that which it is about to meet with to-day." And then, after referring to *R.* v. *Fleet*, 1 B. & Ald. 379, and *Duncan* v. *Thwaites*, the learned judge continues :—" But we are not now living, so to say, within the shadow of those cases." And Lopes, J., also doubted how far the old authorities were binding in the present day (3 C. P. D. 329). In Ireland the question was practically settled by the decision of the majority of the judges in *R.* v. *Gray*, 10 Cox, C. C. 184. And now in England it is practically laid to rest by the judgments of the Court of Appeal in *Kimber* v. *The Press Association*, [1893] 1 Q. B. 65. There a fair and accurate report of an *ex parte* application made to justices in open Court for the issue of a summons for perjury was held privileged, although the justices granted the summons, so that the matter was not finally disposed of on that day, but came on for hearing a week later, and was then dismissed. The Court of Appeal held that it was enough if there was a final decision " at one stage or other of the proceedings," and that the reporters need not wait till that stage had been reached, but might report the proceedings at each stage. Now every law suit must come to an end sooner or later ; hence, every step in every law suit taken in open Court may be reported. In other words, a newspaper reporter may now report everything that occurs publicly in open Court without fear of any action, provided only that his reports are fair and accurate, and not interspersed with comments of his own. " The law upon such subjects must bend to the approved usages of society, though still resting upon the same principle, that what is hurtful and indicates malice should be punished, and that what is beneficial and *bonâ fide* should be protected." (Per Lord Campbell, C.J., in *Lewis* v. *Levy*, E. B. & E. at pp. 560, 561 ; 27 L. J. Q. B. at p. 290 ; 4 Jur. N. S. 970.)

Illustrations.

The following passage appeared in the *Daily News*, the *Standard*, and the *Morning Advertiser*, on the same morning :—" Three gentlemen, civil engineers, were among the applicants to the magistrate yesterday, and they applied for criminal process against Mr. Usill, a civil engineer, of Great Queen Street, Westminster. The spokesman stated that they had been engaged in the survey of an Irish railway by Mr. Usill, and had not been paid what they had earned in their various capacities, although from time to time they had received small sums on account ; and, as the person complained of had been paid, they considered that he had been guilty of a criminal offence in withholding their money. Mr. Woolrych said it was a matter of contract between the parties ; and although, on the face of the application they had been badly treated, he must refer them to the County Court." Mr. Usill thereupon brought an action against the proprietor of each newspaper. The three actions were tried together before Cockburn, C.J., at Westminster, on November 15th, 1877. The learned judge told the jury that the only question for their consideration was whether or not the publication complained of was a fair and impartial report of what took place before the magistrate ; and that, if they found that it was so, the publication was privileged. The jury found that it was a fair report of what occurred, and accordingly returned a verdict for the defendant in each case. *Held*, that the report was privileged, although the proceedings were *ex parte*, and although the magistrate decided that he had no jurisdiction over the matter.

Usill v. *Hales,* } 3 C. P. D. 319 ; 47 L. J. C. P. 323 ; 26 W. R. 371 ;
Usill v. *Brearley,* } 38 L. T. 65 ; 41 J. P. 743.
Usill v. *Clarke,* }

See *M'Gregor* v. *Thwaites*, 3 B. & C. 24.

A fair and accurate report in a newspaper of proceedings before a magistrate on a preliminary investigation of a charge of treason-felony is privileged, although the prisoners were ultimately committed for trial, and are awaiting trial at the moment of publication. So held in Ireland by Lefroy, C.J., and Fitzgerald and O'Brien, JJ.; *dissentiente*, Hayes, J.

> *R.* v. *Gray*, 10 Cox, C. C. 184; overruling *Duncan* v. *Thwaites*, 3 B. & C. 556; 5 D. & R. 447.

A fair and accurate report in a newspaper of an *ex parte* application made to justices in open Court for the issue of a summons for perjury, was held privileged by the Court of Appeal in

> *Kimber* v. *The Press Association*, [1893] 1 Q. B. 65; 62 L. J. Q. B. 152; 41 W. R. 17; 67 L. T. 515; 4 R. 95.

A report of proceedings before a judge at chambers on an application under 5 & 6 Vict. c. 122, s. 42, to discharge a bankrupt out of custody, is privileged.

> *Smith* v. *Scott*, 2 C. & K. 580.

The defendants presented a petition in the Croydon County Court to adjudicate the plaintiff a bankrupt; and to set aside a bill of sale which they alleged to be fraudulent. The County Court judge did not hear the case in open Court, but in his own room; the public, however, could walk in and out of the room at their pleasure during the hearing. *Held*, by Cockburn, C.J., at Nisi Prius, that a fair report of what took place before the County Court judge in his room was *primâ facie* privileged.

> *Myers* v. *Defries*, Times, July 23rd, 1877.

Proceedings held in gaol before a registrar in bankruptcy, under the Bankruptcy Act, 1861, ss. 101, 102, upon the examination of a debtor in custody, are judicial and in a public Court. A fair report, therefore, of those proceedings is protected.

> *Ryalls* v. *Leader and others*, L. R. 1 Ex. 296; 4 H. & C. 555; 35 L. J. Ex. 185; 12 Jur. N. S. 503; 14 W. R. 838; 14 L. T. 563.

A fair report of proceedings before the General Medical Council, acting within its statutory powers, is privileged.

> *Allbutt* v. *General Medical Council*, 23 Q. B. D. 400; 58 L. J. Q. B. 606; 37 W. R. 771; 61 L. T. 585.

A fair and accurate report of proceedings before the examiners appointed under 9 Geo. IV., c. 22, s. 7, to inquire into the sufficiency of the sureties offered on the trial of an election petition, was held privileged.

> *Cooper* v. *Lawson*, 8 A. & E. 746; 1 W. W. & H. 601; 2 Jur. 919; 1 P. & D. 15.

But Patteson, J., held that a report of what had occurred at the town-hall at Ludlow on the occasion of one of his Majesty's commissioners of inquiry going to Ludlow to inquire into the state of that corporation, was not privileged.

> *Charlton* v. *Watton*, 6 C. & P. 385.

A conversation took place between a coroner, his officer, and the widow of the deceased in the room in which the inquest was about to be held, after reporters and the coroner had entered and taken their seats there, but before the jury had been sworn. The officer complained that the body had been improperly removed from the hospital; the widow complained of the manner in which she had been served with the summons to the inquest. *Held*, by Bowen, J., that a fair report of such conversation was privileged.

> *Sheppard* v. *Lloyd*, Daily Chronicle, March 11th, 1882.

But no privilege attaches to the report of unsworn statements made by a mere bystander at an inquest.

> *Lynam* v. *Gowing*, 6 L. R. Ir. 259.

An accurate transcript of the records of a Court relating to any judicial proceeding is also privileged.

Illustrations.

A calendar of prisoners at assizes or quarter sessions or a cause list is privileged. Per Rigby, L.J., in

> *Andrews* v. *Nott Bower*, [1895] 1 Q. B. at p. 896.

In Scotland there exists a public register of protested bills of exchange, established by statute, and the registration of such protests has by statute the effect of a " decreet," or final judgment of the Court of Session. The contents of this register being public property, the defendant published an accurate transcript thereof for the benefit of merchants. This was held privileged, as being but a list of judgments of the Court.

> *Fleming* v. *Newton*, 1 H. L. C. 363.

And so long as the words published by the defendant are a correct copy of the record of the Court, it is immaterial that the record is itself inaccurate, so long as the defendant is not aware of such inaccuracy.

> *Annaly* v. *Trade Auxiliary Co.*, 26 L. R. Ir. 11, 394.
> *MacCabe* v. *Joynt*, [1901] 2 Ir. R. 115.

The charge-sheet at a police Court is not a part of the record of the Court, and where the defendants published words taken from the charge-sheet but not essential to the charge preferred at the proceedings reported by them, it was held that that portion of their report was not privileged.

> *Furniss* v. *Cambridge Daily News, Ltd.*, (1907) 23 Times L. R. 705.

But the words, though correctly copied from the register, may yet be published by the defendant at such a time and in such a manner as to convey a false and defamatory meaning to his readers : *e.g.*, where the publisher of such a " Black List " left in it, as a still existing liability, a judgment which had been annulled and satisfied by payment, the Irish Court of Queen's Bench held that this inaccuracy destroyed all privilege.

> *McNally* v. *Oldham*, 16 Ir. C. L. R. 298 ; 8 L. T. 604.

And see *Jones* v. *McGovern*, Ir. R. 1 C. L. 681.

> *Cosgrave* v. *Trade Auxiliary Trade Co.*, Ir. R. 8 C. L. 349.

So in England :

> *Williams* v. *Smith*, 22 Q. B. D. 134 ; 58 L. J. Q. B. 21 ; 37 W. R. 93 ; 59 L. T. 757 ; 52 J. P. 823.

But this difficulty may be overcome by prefixing or appending a note as was done in England in

> *Searles* v. *Scarlett*, [1892] 2 Q. B. 56 ; 61 L. J. Q. B. 573 ; 40 W. R. 696 ; 66 L. T. 837 ; 56 J. P. 789.

And in Ireland in

> *Cosgrave* v. *Trade Auxiliary Co.*, Ir. R. 8 C. L. 349.

The defendants published an incorrect copy of an entry in the register of Deeds of Arrangement kept under s. 7 of the Deeds of Arrangement Act, 1887. *Held,* that there was no privilege, though the register was open to the inspection of the public.

> *Reis* v. *Perry*, (1895) 64 L. J. Q. B. 566; 43 W. R. 648; 59 J. P. 308; 15 R. 427; 11 Times L. R. 373.
>
> See also *Mangena* v. *Wright*, [1909] 2 K. B. at p. 977.
>
> *John Jones & Sons, Ltd.* v. *Financial Times, Ltd.*, (1909) 25 Times L. R. 677, *post*, p. 339.

There are, however, two cases in which reports of judicial proceedings, although fair and accurate, are not privileged, and are indeed illegal.

(i) The first is where the Court has itself prohibited the publication, as it frequently did in former days. "Every Court has the power of preventing the publication of its proceedings pending litigation." (Per Turner, L.J., in *Brook* v. *Evans*, 29 L. J. Ch. 616; 6 Jur. N. S. 1025; 8 W. R. 688.) But such a prohibition now is rare. (And see *Lewis* v. *Levy*, E. B. & E. at p. 560; 27 L. J. Q. B. at p. 290.)

(ii) The second is where the subject-matter of the trial is an obscene or blasphemous libel, or where for any other reason the proceedings are unfit for publication. It is not justifiable to publish even a fair and accurate report of such proceedings; such a report will be indictable as a criminal libel. (See *In re Evening News*, (1886) 3 Times L. R. 255.)

Illustrations.

On the trial of Thistlewood and others for treason, in 1820, Abbott, C.J., announced in open Court that he prohibited the publication of any of the proceedings until the trial of all the prisoners should be concluded. In spite of this prohibition the *Observer* published a report of the trial of the first two prisoners tried. The proprietor of the *Observer* was summoned for the contempt, and failing to appear, was fined 500*l.*

> *R.* v. *Clement*, 4 B. & Ald. 218; 11 Price, 68.

Richard Carlile on his trial read over to the jury the whole of Payne's "Age of Reason," for selling which he was indicted. After his conviction, his wife published a full, true, and accurate account of his trial, entitled, "The Mock Trial of Mr. Carlile," and in so doing republished the whole of the "Age of Reason" as a part of the proceedings at the trial. *Held*, that the privilege usually attaching to fair reports of judicial proceedings did not extend to such a colourable reproduction of the book which the jury had found to be a blasphemous libel; and that it is unlawful to publish even a correct account of the proceedings in a Court of justice, if such an account contains matter of a scandalous, blasphemous, or indecent nature.

> *R.* v. *Mary Carlile*, (1819) 3 B. & Ald. 167. See also the remarks of Bayley, J., in
> *R.* v. *Creevey*, (1813) 1 M. & S. 281.

The Protestant Electoral Union published a book, called "The Confessional Unmasked," intended to show the pernicious influence exercised by the Roman Catholic priests in the confessional over the minds and consciences of the laity. This was condemned as obscene in *R.* v. *Hicklin*, L. R. 3 Q. B. 360; 37 L. J. M. C. 89; 16 W. R. 801; 18 L. T. 395; 11 Cox, C. C. 19. The Union thereupon issued an expurgated edition, for selling which one George Mackey was tried at the Winchester Quarter Sessions on October 19th, 1870, when the jury, being unable to agree as to the obscenity of the book, were discharged without giving any verdict. The Union thereupon published "A Report of the Trial of George Mackey," in which they set out the full text of the second edition of "The Confessional Unmasked," although it had not been read in open Court, but only taken as read, and certain passages in it referred to. A police magistrate thereupon ordered all copies of this "Report of the Trial of George Mackey" to be seized and destroyed as obscene books. *Held*, that this decision was correct.

> *Steele* v. *Brannan*, L. R. 7 C. P. 261; 41 L. J. M. C. 85; 20 W. R. 607; 26 L. T. 509.

The report must be an impartial and accurate account of what really occurred at the trial; else no privilege will attach. The accuracy of the report must not be judged by the same standard as would be applied in criticising a law report made by a professional law reporter, or by a trained lawyer. It must be regarded from the standpoint of persons whose function it is to give the public a fair account of what has taken place in Court. (*Hope* v. *Leng*, (1907) 23 Times L. R. 243.) Hence, if irrelevant evidence be allowed by the judge to be given in Court and appear in the report, this is not the fault of the reporter. (*Ryalls* v. *Leader*, L. R. 1 Ex. 300; 35 L. J. Ex. 185; 14 W. R. 838; 12 Jur. N. S. 503; 14 L. T. 563.) The sworn evidence of the witnesses should be relied on, rather than the speeches of advocates. Counsel are frequently instructed to open to the jury facts which they fail to prove in evidence. If such an unsubstantiated statement be reported at all, the reporter should add, " but this the plaintiff failed to prove : " but it would be better to avoid all allusion to the matter. Especial care should be taken to report accurately the summing-up of the learned judge, especially if the case be of more than transitory interest. In many cases a report has escaped the charge of partiality on the ground that it contained an accurate report of the judge's summing-up of the case to the jury. (*Milissich* v. *Lloyds*, 46 L. J. C. P. 404; 36 L. T. 423; *Chalmers* v. *Payne*, 2 C. M. & R. 156 ; 5 Tyrw. 766 ; 1 Gale, 69.)

The report need not be *verbatim ;* it may be abridged or condensed ; but it must not be partial or garbled. It need not state all that occurred *in extenso ;* but if it omit any fact which would have told in the plaintiff's favour, it will be a question for the jury whether the omission is material. Thus, the entire suppression of the evidence of one witness may render the report unfair. (*Duncan* v. *Thwaites*, 3 B. & C. 580; *Rumney* v. *Walter*, (1892) 8 Times L. R. 256.) But a report will be privileged if it is " *substantially* a fair account of what took place " in Court. (Per Lord Campbell, C.J., in *Andrews* v. *Chapman*, 3 C. & K. 289 ; and see *Leon* v. *Edinburgh Evening News*, (1909) S. C. 1014 (Ct. of Sess.).) " It is sufficient to publish a fair abstract." (Per Mellish, L.J., in *Milissich* v. *Lloyds*, 46 L. J. C. P. 406 ; per Byles, J., in *Turner* v. *Sullivan and others*, 6 L. T. 130.)

The privilege is not confined to reports in a newspaper or law magazine. It attaches equally to fair and accurate reports issued for any lawful reason in pamphlet form or in any other fashion. Though, of course, if there be any other evidence of malice, the mode and extent of publication will be taken into consideration with such other evidence on that issue. (*Milissich* v. *Lloyds*, 46 L. J. C. P. 404; *Salmon* v. *Isaac*, 20 L. T. 885 ; *Riddell* v. *Clydesdale Horse Society*, 12 Ct. of Session Cases, 4th Series, 976.)

Nor does it matter by whom the report is published ; the privilege is the same, as a matter of law, for a private individual as for a newspaper. (Per Brett, L.J., 46 L. J. C. P. 407.) " I do not think the public press has any peculiar privilege." (Per Bramwell, L.J., 5 Ex. D. 56.) " A newspaper has no greater privilege in such a matter than any ordinary person — any person is privileged in publishing such a report if he does so merely to inform the public." (Per Hannen, J., in *Salmon* v. *Isaac,* 20 L. T. at p. 886; and see (1886) 3 Times L. R. 245.)

Illustrations.

In a former action for libel brought by the plaintiff, the then defendant had justified. The report of this trial set out the libel in full, and gave the evidence for the defendant on the justification, concluding, however, by stating that the plaintiff had a verdict for 30*l.* The jury, under the direction of Lord Abinger, took the " bane " and the " antidote " together, and found a verdict for the defendant, on the ground that the report when taken altogether was not injurious to the plaintiff. And the Court refused a rule for a new trial.

> *Chalmers* v. *Payne,* 5 Tyrw. 766; 1 Gale, 69; 2 C. M. & R. 156.
>
> *Dicas* v. *Lawson,* cited in 5 Tyrw. at p. 769; 2 C. M. & R. at p. 159.

The plaintiff and M. were convicted of a conspiracy to extort money from B.; the report of the trial stated that the plaintiff had written a particular letter, which the plaintiff contended had not in fact been written by him, but by his fellow-conspirator, M. *Held,* that as the jury had convicted them of a common purpose, and the letter was written in furtherance of that common purpose and set out in the indictment as an overt act of the conspiracy, it made no difference which of the two wrote it; and that the error, if error it were, was immaterial.

> *Stockdale* v. *Tarte and others,* 4 A. & E. 1016.
>
> *Alexander* v. *N. E. Ry. Co.,* 6 B. & S. 340; 34 L. J. Q. B. 152; 13 W. R. 651; 11 Jur. N. S. 619.

A barrister, editing a book on the Law of Attorneys, referred to a case, *Re Blake,* as reported in 30 L. J. Q. B. 32, and stated that Mr. Blake was struck off the rolls for misconduct. He was in fact only suspended for two years, as appeared from the *Law Journal* report. The publishers were held liable for this careless misstatement. Damages 100*l.*

> *Blake* v. *Stevens and others,* 4 F. & F. 232; 11 L. T. 543.
>
> *Gwynn* v. *S. E. Ry. Co.,* 18 L. T. 738.
>
> *R.* v. *Lofeild,* 2 Barnard. 128.

A report is not privileged if it does not give the evidence, but merely sets out the circumstances " as stated by the counsel " for one party.

> *Saunders* v. *Mills,* 6 Bing. 213; 3 M. & P. 520.
>
> *Woodgate* v. *Ridout,* 4 F. & F. 202.

Still less will it be privileged, if after so stating the case the only account given of the evidence is that the witnesses " proved all that had been stated by the counsel for the prosecution."

> *Lewis* v. *Walter,* 4 B. & Ald. 605.
>
> *Flint* v. *Pike,* 4 B. & C. 473; 6 D. & R. 528.
>
> *Kane* v. *Mulvany,* Ir. R. 2 C. L. 402.

It is doubtful, however, whether the mere omission to state the result of divorce proceedings taken against the plaintiff will render unprivileged a report otherwise fair and accurate of those proceedings.

> *Pope* v. *Outram,* (1909) S. C. 230 (Ct. of Sess.).

The *Morning Post,* in reporting proceedings taken against the plaintiff in the Westminster Police Court, stated that certain matters " appeared from the evidence." No evidence had in fact been given of these matters; but they had been stated in the opening of the solicitor for the prosecution. Lord Coleridge, C.J., directed the jury to find for the defendant. But the Divisional Court granted a new trial, on the ground that there was a substantial discrepancy between the report and what really occurred, and that the question should therefore have been left to the jury whether the report was a fair one; and this decision was affirmed on appeal.

Ashmore v. *Borthwick*, (1885) 49 J. P. 792; 2 Times L. R. 113, 209.

Where a report in the *Times* of a preliminary investigation before a magistrate set out at length the opening of the counsel for the prosecution, but entirely omitted the examination and cross-examination of the prosecutor, the only witness, merely saying that " his testimony supported the statement of his counsel," the jury found a verdict for the plaintiff." Damages 10*l.*

Pinero v. *Goodlake*, 15 L. T. 676.

[N.B.—The headnote to this case is strangely misleading: the proceedings were not *ex parte;* the defendant, himself a solicitor, was present and cross-examined the witnesses. The important monosyllable "no" appears to be omitted in the report of the argument of Coleridge, Q.C., p. 677.]

The mother of a lady, who was dead and buried, applied to the coroner on affidavits for an order that the body might be exhumed; the affidavits imputed that she had been murdered by her husband. Thereupon the coroner issued his warrant for exhumation. A newspaper reported this fact, and proceeded to state the contents of these affidavits in a sensational paragraph, commencing " From inquiries made by our reporter it appears that the deceased," &c. The reporter had made no inquiries; he had merely copied the affidavits. He was convicted and fined 50*l.*

R. v. *Andrew Gray*, 26 J. P. 663.

Where the report of a criminal trial gave the speech for the prosecution, a brief *résumé* of the speech of the prisoner's counsel, who called no witness, and the whole of the Lord Chief Baron's summing-up *in extenso*, but did not give the evidence except in so far as it was detailed in the judge's summing-up; Lord Coleridge, C.J., held the report necessarily unfair because incomplete, and refused to leave the question of fairness to the jury. But the Court of Appeal held that he was wrong in so doing; that it is sufficient to publish a fair abstract of the trial, and that the judge's summing-up was presumably such an abstract; that the question of fairness must be left to the jury, and that therefore there must be a new trial.

Milissich v. *Lloyds*, 46 L. J. C. P. 404; 36 L. T. 423; 13 Cox, C. C. 575.

During the course of a judicial proceeding one of the parties, who appeared in person, after having given his evidence on oath, made from the well of the Court an observation commenting on the evidence of another witness who was then under examination, which observation was defamatory of the plaintiff. A reporter included it in his report of the proceedings. *Held*, that the report was nevertheless privileged.

Hope v. *Leng*, (1907) 23 Times L. R. 243.

A newspaper published a report that the plaintiff had been prosecuted and convicted before magistrates of having issued an invoice as to the quality of manure " which he knew to be false." These words, though appearing in the charge-sheet, which was identical with that subsequently signed by the Chairman of the bench, were no part of the charge and were not essential to the offence for which the plaintiff was being prosecuted. *Held*, that the report was not privileged.

> *Furniss* v. *Cambridge Daily News, Ltd.*, (1907) 23 Times L. R. 705.

An accurate report of a portion of a judicial proceeding will still be privileged, if it does not purport to be a report of the whole. Thus, where a trial lasts more than one day, reports published in the newspapers each morning are protected. (*Lewis* v. *Levy*, E. B. & E. 537; 27 L. J. Q. B. 282.) Each stage of the proceeding may be reported separately. (*Kimber* v. *The Press Association*, [1893] 1 Q. B. 65; 62 L. J. Q. B. 152; 41 W. R. 17; 67 L. T. 515.) Where a man publishes a portion only, when it is in his power to publish the whole, this fragmentary publication will be evidence of malice, if the part selected and published tell more against the plaintiff than a report of the whole trial would have done, *e.g.*, if the opening speech of one counsel or the evidence on one side only were published after the trial was over. But the judgment or summing-up of the learned judge may always be separately published; for it is a distinct part of the proceedings, not affected by any other, complete in itself and fairly severable from the rest; it is also presumably a fair summary of the whole proceedings. (*Milissich* v. *Lloyds*, 46 L. J. C. P. 404; 36 L. T. 423; 13 Cox, C. C. 575.)

Illustrations.

Where judicial proceedings last more than one day, and their publication is not expressly forbidden by the Court, a report published in a newspaper every morning of the proceedings of the preceding day, is privileged, if fair and accurate; but all comment on the case must be suspended till the proceedings terminate.

> *Lewis* v. *Levy*, E. B. & E. 537; 27 L. J. Q. B. 282; 4 Jur. N. S. 970.

The sentence of a court martial may be read at the head of every regiment. Per Heath, J., in

> *Oliver* v. *Bentinck*, 3 Taunt. at p. 459.

The plaintiff had sued defendants in the Chancery Division, and the action was dismissed with costs. Defendants thereupon published, in the form of a pamphlet, a verbatim report of the whole judgment, taken from the shorthand writer's notes, but omitting all the evidence and speeches on either side. The jury having negatived malice, the Court of Appeal held the pamphlet privileged

> *MacDougall* v. *Knight & Son,* 17 Q. B. D. 636; 55 L. J. Q. B. 464; 34 W. R. 727; 55 L. T. 274.
>
> But see the report of this case in the House of Lords: 14 App. Cas. 194; 58 L. J. Q. B. 537; 38 W. R. 44; 60 L. T. 762; 53 J. P. 691.

A weekly paper stated, on December 21st, 1884, that plaintiff had been brought up at the Nottingham Police Court on the preceding Monday (15th) and charged with obtaining money on false pretences, and that " a number of other charges will be brought against him." It omitted all mention of the fact that plaintiff had been brought up again on remand on the 18th (the Thursday preceding the publication) and triumphantly discharged. The jury awarded the plaintiff 45*l.* in addition to the 5*l.* which defendant had paid into Court under Lord Campbell's Act.

> *Grimwade* v. *Dicks and others,* (1886) 2 Times L. R. 627.

The reporter must add nothing of his own. He must not state his opinion of the conduct of the parties, or impute motives therefor: above all, he must not insinuate that a particular witness committed perjury. This is not a report of what occurred; it is the comment of the writer on what occurred, and to this no privilege attaches. Often no doubt comments may be justified on another ground: that they are fair and *bonâ fide* criticism on a matter of public interest and, therefore, are not actionable. (See *ante,* c. VIII.) But such observations, to which quite different considerations apply, should not be mixed up with the report of the case. "If any comments are made, they should not be made as part of the report. The report should be confined to what takes place in Court, and the two things, report and comment, should be kept separate." (Per Lord Campbell, C.J., in *Andrews* v. *Chapman,* 3 C. & K. 288; and see the observations of Fletcher Moulton, L.J., in *Hunt* v. *Star Newspaper Co., Ltd.,* [1908] 2 K. B. at p. 319.) All sensational headings to reports should be avoided.

Illustrations.

The captain of a vessel was charged before a magistrate with an indecent assault upon a lady on board his own ship. The defendants' newspaper published a report of the case, interspersed with comments which assumed the guilt of the captain, commended the conduct of the lady, and generally tended to inflame the minds of the public violently against the accused. *Held*, that no privilege attached to such comments and that the report was neither fair nor dispassionate.

> *R.* v. *Fisher and others*, 2 Camp. 563.
> And see *R.* v. *Lee*, 5 Esp. 123.
> *R.* v. *Fleet*, 1 B. & Ald. 379.

It is libellous to publish a highly-coloured account of criminal proceedings, mixed with the reporter's own observations and conclusions upon what passed in Court, headed " Judicial Delinquency," and containing an insinuation that the plaintiff (" our hero ") had committed perjury : and it is no justification to pick out such parts of the libel as contain an account of the trial, and to plead that such parts are true and accurate, leaving the extraneous matter altogether unjustified.

> *Stiles* v. *Nokes*, 7 East, 493; same case *sub nomine Carr* v. *Jones,* '3 Smith, 491.

The report of a trial set out the speech of the counsel for the prosecution, and then added :—" The first witness was R. P., who proved all that had been stated by the counsel for the prosecution : " but owing to the absence of a piece of formal evidence in no way bearing on the merits of the case, " the jury, under the direction of the learned judge, were obliged to give a verdict of acquittal, to the great regret of a crowded Court, on whom the statement and the evidence, so far as it went, made a strong impression of their guilt." *Held*, that no privilege applied.

> *Lewis* v. *Walter*, 4 B. & Ald. 605.
> *Roberts* v. *Brown*, 10 Bing. 519; 4 Moo. & Sc. 407.

On an examination into the sufficiency of sureties on an election petition, under 9 Geo. IV. c. 22, s. 7, affidavits were put in to show that one of them (the plaintiff) was embarrassed in his affairs, and an insufficient surety. A newspaper report of the examination proceeded to ask why the plaintiff, being wholly unconnected with the borough, should take so much trouble about the matter. " There can be but one answer to these very natural and reasonable queries, *he is hired* for the occasion." *Held*, that this question and answer formed no part of the report; and therefore enjoyed no privilege; and that it was properly left to the jury to say whether they were a fair and *bonâ fide* comment on a matter of public interest in that borough. Verdict for the plaintiff. Damages 100*l.*

> *Cooper* v. *Lawson*, 8 A. & E. 746; 1 W. W. & H. 601; 2 Jur. 919; 1 P. & D. 15.

The *Observer* gave a true and faithful account of some proceedings in the Insolvent Debtors Court, but headed it with the words " Shameful conduct of an attorney." *Held*, that for those words, as they were not justified, the plaintiff was entitled to recover.

> *Clement* v. *Lewis*, (Exch. Ch.) 3 Br. & B. 297; 3 B. & Ald. 702; 7 Moore, 200.
> *Bishop* v. *Latimer*, 4 L. T. 775.
> *Boydell* v. *Jones*, 4 M. & W. 446; 1 H. & H. 408; 7 Dowl. 210.
> *Flint* v. *Pike*, 4 B. & C. 473; 6 D. & R. 528.

A report of the hearing of a charge of perjury before a magistrate was headed " Wilful and Corrupt Perjury," and stated that the " evidence before the

magistrate entirely negatived the story of the " plaintiff. The jury found a
verdict for the defendant, on the ground that it was a fair and correct report of
what occurred at the hearing. But the Court set aside the verdict on this count,
and entered a verdict for the plaintiff with nominal damages.

> *Lewis* v. *Levy,* E. B. & E. 537; 27 L. J. Q. B. 282; 4 Jur. N. S.
> 970.

And see *Mangena* v. *Edward Lloyd, Ltd.,* (1908) 99 L. T. 824;
> 25 Times L. R. 26.

The law is the same in America.

> *Thomas* v. *Croswell,* 7 Johns. (N. Y. Supr. Court) 264.
> *Commonwealth* v. *Blanding,* 3 Pick. (20 Mass.) 304.

The privilege attaching to fair and accurate reports may
be rebutted by proof of actual malice. No report of a
judicial proceeding, by whomsoever published, is absolutely
privileged. (*Stevens* v. *Sampson,* 5 Ex. D. 53; 49 L. J.
Q. B. 120.) But it is of course very difficult to prove that
an ordinary newspaper reporter has been actuated by
malice; whereas, if one of the parties to a cause, or his
solicitor, wrote the report and sent it to the newspapers
the jury would probably start with a presumption that the
report was biassed and unfair. (See the remarks of Wood,
V.-C., in *Coleman* v. *West Hartlepool Harbour and Railway Co.,*
2 L. T. 766; 8 W. R. 734.) Mere negligence in a reporter
is not malice. (*Furniss* v. *Cambridge Daily News, Ltd.,* (1907)
23 Times L. R. 705.)

Illustrations.

A churchwarden obtained a writ of prohibition against the Bishop of
Chichester on an affidavit which falsely stated the facts. He immediately
had the writ translated into English, and dispersed 2,000 copies of such
translation all over the kingdom, with a title-page alleging that by such
writ " the illegality of oaths is declared," which was not the case. *Held,*
" a most seditious libel."

> *Waterfield* v. *Bishop of Chichester,* 2 Mod. 118.

Defendant published, in the form of a circular, headed " Take Notice.
Important to Farmers," a fairly accurate report of two actions brought
by the plaintiff in the Ashford County Court to recover the price of
manures which he had sold. These circulars were extensively distributed
on market days in the home and adjoining counties, and plaintiff's business consequently fell off. The jury considered that the defendant
published it with a view of injuring the plaintiff. Damages 287*l.*

> *Salmon* v. *Isaac,* 20 L. T. 885.

In a County Court action, *Nettlefold* v. *Fulcher,* the defendant, a solicitor, appeared for Nettlefold, and commented severely on the conduct of the plaintiff, who was Fulcher's agent and debt collector. The defendant sent to the local newspapers a report of the case, which the jury found " was in substance a fair report," but they also found that " it was sent with a certain amount of malice." Verdict for the plaintiff. Damages 40s. On appeal it was argued that the defendant was entitled to judgment on the first finding of the jury, and that the motive which the defendant had in sending the report was immaterial. But the Court of Appeal held that Cockburn, C.J., was right in directing judgment to be entered for the plaintiff.

> *Stevens* v. *Sampson,* 5 Ex. D. 53 ; 49 L. J. Q. B. 120 ; 28 W. R. 87 ; 41 L. T. 782.

Plaintiff brought an action against defendant, and applied for an injunction. Defendant applied at the same time for a receiver, which was refused. Thereupon defendant said that he would " make it d——d hot for Dodson," and inserted in a newspaper he owned a report of the application, setting out all his own counsel had said against the plaintiff's solvency, &c., at full length, but omitting all mention of plaintiff's affidavit. *Held,* ample evidence of malice. Damages 250l.

> *Dodson* v. *Owen,* (1885) 2 Times L. R. 111.

The defendants presented a petition in the Croydon County Court to adjudicate the plaintiff a bankrupt, and to set aside a bill of sale which they alleged to be fraudulent. The County Court judge heard the case in his own room, where no reporters were present, and decided that the bill of sale was fraudulent. After the case was over, the defendants sent for a reporter to the Greyhound Hotel, and gave him an account of the proceedings before the County Court judge, from which he drew up a report, which appeared in several papers. The jury found that the report was " fair as far as it went ; " but it did not state the fact that the plaintiff had announced his intention to appeal. *Held,* that neither this omission, nor the fact that the report was furnished by one of the parties, instead of being taken by the reporter in the usual way, was, by itself, sufficient to destroy the privilege attaching to all fair reports of legal proceedings. (Per Cockburn, C.J., at Nisi Prius, *Myers* v. *Defries, Times,* July 23rd, 1877.) But the jury being satisfied from the whole circumstances that the defendants furnished the report with the express intention of injuring the plaintiff, gave the plaintiff 250l. damages on the first trial, and one farthing damages on the second.

> *Myers* v. *Defries,* 4 Ex. D. 176 ; 5 Ex. D. 15, 180 ; 48 L. J. Ex. 446 ; 28 W. R. 406 ; 40 L. T. 795 ; 41 L. T. 659.
>
> And see *Saxby* v. *Easterbrook,* 3 C. P. D. 339 ; 27 W. R. 188.

Hence in these cases there may be two distinct questions for the jury :—(i) Is the report fair and accurate ? If so, it is *primâ facie* privileged ; if not, verdict for the plaintiff. (ii) Was the report though fair and accurate, published maliciously ? The second question only arises when the first has been already answered in the affirmative. The *onus* of proving the accuracy of the report lies on the defendant. (Per Lord Esher, M.R., in *Kimber* v. *The Press Association*, [1893] 1 Q. B. at p. 71.) The *onus* of proving malice lies on the plaintiff.

And, of course, there is in each case the previous question for the judge, "Is there any evidence to go to the jury of inaccuracy or of malice?" Where there is no suggestion of malice and no evidence on which a reasonable man could find that the report is not absolutely fair, the judge should stop the case and direct a verdict for the defendant: *e.g.*, where the report is *verbatim* or nearly so; or corresponds in all material particulars with a report taken by an impartial shorthand writer. (Per Brett, L.J., in *Milissich* v. *Lloyds*, 46 L. J. C. P. 407.) But if anything be omitted in the report which could make any appreciable difference in the plaintiff's favour, or anything erroneously inserted which could conceivably tell against him, then it is a question for the jury whether such deviation from absolute accuracy makes the report unfair; and the judge at Nisi Prius should not direct a verdict for either party. (*Risk Allah Bey* v. *Whitehurst and others*, 18 L. T. 615; *Street* v. *Licensed Victuallers' Society*, 22 W. R. 553; *Ashmore* v. *Borthwick*, (1885) 49 J. P. 792; 2 Times L. R. 113, 209; *ante*, p. 318.)

The jury in considering the question should not dwell too much on isolated passages: they should consider the report as a whole. They should ask themselves what impression would be made on the mind of an unprejudiced reader who reads the report straight through, knowing nothing about the case beforehand. Slight errors may easily occur; and if such errors do not substantially alter the impression of the matter which the ordinary reader would receive, the jury should find for the defendant. (*Stockdale* v. *Tarte and others*, 4 A. & E. 1016; *ante*, p. 317.) If, however, there is a substantial misstatement of any material fact, and such misstatement is prejudicial to the reputation of the plaintiff, then the report is unfair and inaccurate, and the jury should find for the plaintiff.

The common law on this subject being thus clear and satisfactory, the Legislature has thought fit to include in the Law of Libel Amendment Act, 1888, the following provision (51 & 52 Vict. c. 64, s. 3):—"A fair and accurate report in any newspaper of proceedings publicly heard before any Court exercising judicial authority shall, if published contemporaneously with such proceedings, be privileged: provided that nothing in this section shall authorise the publication of any blasphemous or indecent matter."

This section was, no doubt, introduced into the bill with the intention of giving to reports which appear in newspapers, a higher and better position than those prepared by the rest of the public. But this object has not been attained. Fair and accurate reports of judicial proceedings, whether published in a newspaper or not, were already privileged at common law; and we cannot believe that this section creates any *absolute* privilege; a privilege, that is, which is not destroyed by clear proof of express malice. There is no public interest which requires that such an absolute immunity should be extended to newspaper reports. Nor will such an immunity be inferred from the mere absence of the words which are to be found in the next section: " unless it shall be proved that such report was published maliciously." Moreover, in the bill, as originally introduced, this section ran as follows :—" A fair and accurate report published in any newspaper of proceedings of and in any Court exercising judicial authority shall be absolutely privileged." But the section was so modified in Committee as to defeat the whole object of the clause; the words " publicly heard" and " if published contemporaneously with such proceedings " were introduced, and the word " absolutely " omitted, with the full consent and approval of the member in charge of the bill.   .

The clause was thus rendered obscure, if not meaningless. It will be for learned judges hereafter to define its precise meaning and effect. But we venture to suggest that, while it creates no new privilege, it certainly does not destroy or restrict any pre-existing privilege. The section cannot mean that only reports in newspapers are privileged. Any report which would have been privileged before is surely privileged still. It would require clearer and stronger words to restrict a right which every citizen possesses at common law. We are thus driven to the conclusion that the section as it now stands in no way alters the common law—that it is merely an attempt to declare the law as it existed before the Act was passed. If so, it is not a successful attempt. It does not adequately state the privilege already attaching to newspaper reports of judicial proceedings. The words " publicly heard " should not have been inserted; so long as the Court is acting judicially, its proceedings may be published, although none of the general public were actually present in the room. It is enough if the public had a right to be present. (*Smith* v. *Scott*, 2 C. & K. 580.) Again, the words " if published contemporaneously with such proceedings" are embarrassing : as a report of a celebrated trial published, without malice, many months after the proceedings, *e.g.*, in the Annual Register, would be privileged. The omission of the word "seditious" in the concluding proviso is also unfortunate, if the section was in any way intended to express the whole law on the subject. In short, this section is, in our opinion, a blemish on an otherwise useful Act. And see the *dictum* of Kekewich, J., in *Re The Pall Mall Gazette*, (1894) 11 Times L. R. at p. 123.

(ii) *Reports of Parliamentary Proceedings.*

Every fair and accurate report of any proceeding in either House of Parliament, or in any committee thereof, is privileged, even though it contain matter defamatory of an individual.

The analogy between such reports and those of legal proceedings is complete. Whatever would deprive a report of a trial of immunity, will equally deprive a report of parliamentary proceedings of all privilege.

There was for a long time great doubt on this subject, but the law is now clearly and most satisfactorily settled by the decision in *Wason* v. *Walter*, L. R. 4 Q. B. 73 ; 38 L. J. Q. B. 34 ; 17 W. R. 169 ; 19 L. T. 409. Such doubt was caused by the fact that there were Standing Orders, of both Houses of Parliament prohibiting such publications ; and it was argued with some force that no privilege could attach to any report which was published in contravention of such Standing Orders, and was therefore in itself a contempt of the House. We have seen (*ante*, p. 314) that when a learned judge expressly prohibits the publication of the proceedings before him, any report of them is a contempt and wholly unprivileged. (*R.* v. *Clement*, 4 B. & Ald. 218.) And the earliest reports of parliamentary proceedings were only published in fear and trembling as "Debates in the Senate of Lilliput," with the names of the speakers disguised. And even for such reports Cave, the editor of the *Gentleman's Magazine*, was cited before the House of Lords for breach of privilege (April, 1747) ; and Johnson's pen ceased to indite ponderous speeches for "Whig dogs." But in 1749, Cave began again, and his reports now took the form of letters from an M.P. to a friend in the country. After 1752 they were avowedly printed as reports; but still only the initials of the speakers were given. As late as 1801 the printer and publisher of the *Morning Herald* were committed to the custody of Black Rod, for publishing an account of a debate in the House of Lords; but then such account was expressly declared to be "a scandalous misrepresentation" of what had really occurred. And now such Standing Orders are quite obsolete.

A speech made by a member of Parliament in the House is of course absolutely privileged. If he subsequently causes his speech to be printed, and circulates it privately among his constituents, *bonâ fide* for their information on any matter of general or local interest, a qualified privilege would attach to such report: [although such publication is expressly forbidden by an obsolete order of the House of Commons, passed in 1641, and still a Standing Order of the House; 2 Commons' Journal, 209]. (Per Lord Campbell, C.J., and Crompton, J., in *Davison* v. *Duncan*, 7 E. & B. 233; 26 L. J. Q. B. 107; and Cockburn, C.J., in *Wason* v. *Walter*, L. R. 4 Q. B. 95; 38 L. J. Q. B. 42; 19 L. T. 416.) But if a member of Parliament publishes his speech to all the world, and it is defamatory of the plaintiff, he will be liable both civilly and criminally. (*R.* v. *Lord Abingdon*, 1 Esp. 226; *R.* v. *Creevey*, 1 M. & S. 273.)

Illustrations.

The defendant published the report of the select committee of the House of Commons, which contained a paragraph charging an individual with holding views hostile to the Government. But the Court refused to grant a criminal information, on the express ground that the publication was a true copy of a proceeding in Parliament.

R. v. *Wright*, (1799) 8 T. R. 293.

The plaintiff induced Earl Russell to present a petition to the House of Lords, charging a high judicial officer with having suppressed evidence before an election committee some thirty years previously. The charge was shown to be wholly unfounded, and the conduct of the plaintiff in presenting such a petition was severely commented on by the Earl of Derby and others in the debate which followed. The plaintiff sued the proprietor of the *Times* for reporting this debate. Cockburn, C.J., directed the jury, that if they were satisfied that the report was faithful and correct, it was in point of law a privileged communication; and the Court of Queen's Bench subsequently discharged a rule *nisi* which had been obtained for a new trial on the ground of misdirection.

> *Wason* v. *Walter,* L. R. 4 Q. B. 73 ; 8 B. & S. 671 ; 38 L. J. Q. B. 34 ; 17 W. R. 169 ; 19 L. T. 409.

The proceedings of any committee of the House of Lords may be reported and commented on.

> *Kane* v. *Mulvany,* Ir. R. 2 C. L. 402.

As to publication of parliamentary papers or extracts therefrom, see *post,* p. 336.

(iii) *Reports of Public Meetings.*

By the Law of Libel Amendment Act, 1888 (51 & 52 Vict. c. 64), s. 4, "A fair and accurate report published in any newspaper of the proceedings of a public meeting, or (except where neither the public nor any newspaper reporter is admitted) of any meeting of a vestry, town council, school board, board of guardians, board or local authority formed or constituted under the provisions of any Act of Parliament, or of any committee appointed by any of the above-mentioned bodies, or of any meeting of any commissioners authorised to act by letters patent, Act of Parliament, warrant under the Royal Sign Manual, or other lawful warrant or authority, select committees of either House of Parliament, justices of the peace in quarter sessions assembled for administrative or deliberative purposes, and * the publication at the request of any Government Office or department, officer of state, commissioner of police, or chief constable, of any notice or report issued by them for the information of the public, shall be privileged, unless it shall be proved that such report or publication was published or made maliciously : Provided that nothing in this section shall authorise the publication of any blasphemous or indecent matter : Provided also, that the protection intended to be afforded by this section shall not be available as a defence in any proceedings if it shall be proved that the defendant has been requested to insert in the newspaper in which the report or other publication complained of appeared a reasonable letter or statement by way of contradiction or

---

* As to this clause, see *post,* p. 339.

explanation of such report or other publication, and has refused or neglected to insert the same : Provided further, that nothing in this section contained shall be deemed or construed to limit or abridge any privilege now by law existing, or to protect the publication of any matter not of public concern, and the publication of which is not for the public benefit.   ·

"For the purposes of this section 'public meeting' shall mean any meeting *bonâ fide* and lawfully held for a lawful purpose, and for the furtherance or discussion of any matter of public concern, whether the admission thereto be general or restricted."

At Common Law, reports of judicial and parliamentary proceedings were alone privileged.   Hence, if the proceedings at any public meeting or at the meeting of a vestry or board of guardians were fully and accurately reported in a newspaper, the proprietor and editor of that paper were liable in damages if any speaker at that meeting had uttered a slander and they had reproduced it.   (*Davison* v. *Duncan*, 7 E. & B. 229 ; 26 L. J. Q. B. 104 ; 5 W. R. 253 ; 28 L. T. (Old S.) 265 ; *Popham* v. *Pickburn*, 7 H. & N. 891 ; 31 L. J. Ex. 133 ; 10 W. R. 324 ; 5 L. T. 846 ; *Purcell* v. *Sowler*, 1 C. P. D. 781 ; 2 C. P. D. 215 ; 46 L. J. C. P. 308 ; 25 W. R. 362 ; 36 L. T. 416.) And yet the public considered that it was the duty of newspaper editors and proprietors to present to the readers a full, true and impartial account of what had actually occurred at such meetings ; and, indeed, it is often for the public benefit that such proceedings should be fully reported, and the speakers shown in their true colours.   It was felt, therefore, that the severity of the Common Law must be modified.

An effort was made in this direction by sect. 2 of the Newspaper Libel and Registration Act, 1881 (44 & 45 Vict. c. 60), set out on page 837, *post ;* but the privilege conferred by it was so cautiously guarded that it was of little assistance to the newspapers.   The section was therefore repealed by sect. 2 of the Act of 1888, and the above provision substituted.   For a further history of these two important measures, see Appendix B., *post*, p. 811.

The new provision undoubtedly affords more ample protection to the press.   It greatly enlarges the number of meetings whose proceedings may be reported; it permits the publication of police notices and other official announcements. But it still leaves it the duty of the editor of every newspaper to edit all reports of public meetings, and excise all defamatory matter that is "not of public concern, and the publication of which is not for the public benefit."

And surely this is right. For unless there be some advantage to the public countervailing the injury done to the individual libelled, there can be no reason for depriving the latter of his right of action against the newspaper. The original slander may not be actionable *per se*, or the occasion may be privileged, so that no action lies against the speaker. But whether that be so or not, it is the republication in the newspaper which does real and permanent injury to the reputation of the plaintiff. The consequences of reproducing in the papers calumnies uttered at a public meeting are most serious. The meeting may have been thinly attended, or the audience may have known that the speaker was not worthy of credit. But it would be a terrible thing for the person defamed if such words could be printed and published to all the world, merely because they were uttered under such circumstances at such a meeting. Charges recklessly made in the excitement of the moment will thus be diffused throughout the country, and will remain recorded in a permanent form against a perfectly innocent person. No one can tell into whose hands a copy of that newspaper may come. Moreover, additional importance and weight is given to such a calumny by its republication in the columns of a respectable paper. Many people will believe it merely because it is in print. There is in fact an immense difference between the injury done by such a slander, and that caused by its extended circulation by the press. See the remarks of Lord Campbell in *Davison* v. *Duncan*, 7 E. & B. 231; 26 L. J. Q. B. 106; 3 Jur. N. S. 613; 5 W. R. 253; 28 L. T. (Old S.) 265; and of Best, C.J., in *De Crespigny* v. *Wellesley*, 5 Bing. 402—406, cited *post*, p. 375. Where, however, the matter is one of public concern, and the publication of the libellous words is for the public benefit, there the interests of the individual must yield to those of the public.

We proceed to examine the provisions of this section in detail. The word "newspaper" is expressly defined in section 1 of the Act of 1881, see *post*, p. 836.

(a) *Public Meeting.*

A " public meeting " is expressly defined for the purposes of this section as " any meeting *bonâ fide*, and lawfully held for a lawful purpose, and for the furtherance or discussion of any matter of public concern, whether the admission thereto be general or restricted." It seems, at first sight, a contradiction in terms to speak of a public meeting to which admission is restricted. But we think the Legislature intended to include meetings of any specific class or portion of the public ; *e.g.*, of the electors of a certain borough, or the ratepayers of a specified ward or parish ; and also, perhaps, any meeting which was open to the public on payment of a small charge for admission.

Illustrations.

It was held by Wills, J., at Bristol Spring Assizes, 1894, that the ordinary Sunday service at a congregational chapel was not a public meeting within this section, although the chapel was necessarily open to the public.

Chaloner v. *Lansdown & Sons*, (1894) 10 Times L. R. 290.

It is submitted that meetings of the creditors of a bankrupt, or of the shareholders in a company or of the subscribers to a particular charity, are not "public meetings," and that the proceedings thereat cannot be reported without risk.

But see *Ponsford* v. *Financial Times, Limited*, (1900) 16 Times L. R. 248.

It is submitted that a meeting to which admission is by ticket only, is not "a public meeting," unless a ticket can be procured without difficulty by any one who applies for it, and who is willing to pay the price, if any, charged for it.

(b) *Held for a Lawful Purpose.*

Next, the defendant must show that the meeting " was *bonâ fide* and lawfully held for a lawful purpose." Seditious or illegal meetings must not be reported, apparently. The place fixed for the meeting may render it illegal, *e.g.*, where a meeting is advertised to take place in Trafalgar Square in defiance of the authorities, or at Westminster in violation of the Acts against tumultuously petitioning Parliament. (13 Car. II. c. 5 ; 1 Will. & M. sess. 2, c. 2 ; and 57 Geo. III. c. 19, s. 23.) Again, the manner of holding the meeting may render it an unlawful meeting. Thus, any assembly is unlawful which meets under circumstances likely to endanger the peace of the neighbourhood ; and, in order to decide whether an assembly is or is not unlawful, the jury may take into consideration the tumultuous way in which the meeting assembled, the hour at which it met, the excitement which prevailed at it, the inscriptions and devices on banners and flags displayed, the language used by the persons assembled, and by those who addressed them, and even what the chairman of this meeting said and did at a previous meeting, convened for a purpose avowedly similar. (*R.* v. *Hunt and others*, 3 B. & Ald. 566.) But the circumstances must be such as would alarm, not foolish or timid persons only, but also persons of reasonable firmness and courage. (*R.* v. *Vincent*, 9 C. & P. 91, 109.)

Illustrations.

Meetings which are convened for the *bonâ fide* purpose of reforming our laws by petitioning parliament, or by other lawful means, are not seditious ; but whenever persons assemble to bring the constitution into contempt, and to excite discontent and disaffection against the king's government, it is an illegal meeting.

> *Redford* v. *Birley,* 3 Stark. at p. 103.
> *R.* v. *Sullivan,* 11 Cox, C. C. 44.
> *R.* v. *Burns and others,* 16 Cox, C. C. 355.

So, if persons meet for a purpose which, if executed, would make them rioters, but separate without carrying their purpose into effect, this is an unlawful assembly, though they have done nothing.

> *R.* v. *Birt and others,* 5 C. & P. 154.

A meeting called " to adopt preparatory measures for holding a national convention " was held an illegal meeting in

> *R.* v. *Fursey,* 6 C. & P. 81.

A procession with banners is not necessarily unlawful, even though it result in a breach of the peace ; and, where the promoters of a meeting assemble with a lawful purpose, and with no intention of carrying out such purpose in any unlawful manner, the fact that they know that their meeting will be opposed, and have good reason to suppose that a breach of the peace will be committed by their opponents, does not make their meeting unlawful.

> *Beatty and others* v. *Gillbanks,* 9 Q. B. D. 308 ; 51 L. J. M. C.
> 117 ; 31 W. R. 275 ; 47 L. T. 194 ; 46 J. P. 789 ; 15 Cox,
> C. C. 138.
> *R.* v. *Clarkson,* 66 L. T. 297 ; 56 J. P. 375 ; 17 Cox, C. C. 483.
> But see *O'Kelly* v. *Harvey,* 15 Cox, C. C. 435.

By section 7 of the 50 & 51 Vict. o. 20, it was made a criminal offence for any one to publish any notice of the calling together of a meeting of certain prohibited associations or any notice of the proceedings at such meeting.

See *R.* v. *Sullivan,* (1887) 20 L. R. Ir. 550 ; 16 Cox, C. C. 347.

(c) *The Report must be Fair and Accurate.*

This the defendant must prove. It is not necessary that the report should be *verbatim ;* nor is absolute accuracy essential so long as the report is substantially correct. A few slight accidental errors will not destroy the privilege, provided the whole report, as published, produces materially the same effect on the mind of the reader as an absolutely correct report would have done. "It is not to be expected that in discharging this duty of a public journalist he will always be infallible," says Cockburn, C.J., in *Woodgate* v. *Ridout,* 4 F. & F. at p. 217.

(d) *And not Published or made Maliciously.*

The privilege created by this section is only qualified, not absolute. It will be for the plaintiff to prove that the report or publication was published or made maliciously.

(e) *A Reasonable Letter must be Inserted.*

If the defendant is requested to insert in his paper a reasonable letter or statement of explanation or contradiction, and refuses to do so, the privilege is lost. The Legislature, we presume, regarded such a refusal as cogent evidence of malice. If so, this clause was perhaps not strictly necessary, as the section has already provided that the report must not be "published or made maliciously." The presence of this express proviso, however, settles the matter beyond doubt. If there be such a refusal, the case is outside the section, and no question can be left to the jury as to malice or no malice.

Otherwise it is but a poor satisfaction to a plaintiff to

allow him to write "a reasonable letter of contradiction." Many who read the report will not read the plaintiff's letter, and those who do probably will not believe it; they will say: "Oh, of course, he denies it." It will often be difficult, too, for the defendant to decide what is and what is not "a *reasonable* letter." By inserting what the plaintiff has written, he may expose himself to proceedings by some one else.

(f) *The Matter complained of must be of Public Concern, and its Publication for the Public Benefit.*

This is a most important safeguard. Not all the proceedings at a public meeting can be reported without risk. It is not enough for the defendant to show that the meeting was such that *some* report of it was for the public benefit; he must establish a privilege for the very words complained of by the plaintiff. The section does not protect the publication of any matter which is not of public concern, and the publication of which is not for the public benefit.

It will be noticed that a new phrase is introduced by this section into the law of libel—"a matter of public concern." The time-honoured expression "a matter of public interest" has a clear and well-defined meaning: but what is a matter of public "concern"? The change was made deliberately; the word "interest" was struck out, and "concern" substituted in the House of Lords. The two terms are not identical; for there are many matters which concern the public in which they take no interest, while they take great interest in many other matters with which they have no concern. we presume, however, that the Courts will hold that everything which was "a matter of public interest" within the decisions (which will be found *ante*, pp. 205—218) is also "a matter of public concern" within this section.

Next comes the question: Is the publication of such matter necessarily "for the public benefit"? Is it in every case a benefit for the public to learn what concerns it? As a rule, no doubt, this would be so. The question is for the jury, not the judge (*Pankhurst* v. *Sowler, infra*); and whenever the subject-matter is of public concern, the jury would naturally be inclined to find that its publication was for the public benefit. But this must to some extent depend on when and how, and to whom the publication was made. A case might occur in which the premature announcement, say, of an impending prosecution, might be most injurious to the public service, although the matter would be of public concern.

When this case occurs, and not till then, it will become necessary to determine whether the word "and" in the final proviso of this section means "and" or "or." The Legislature, no doubt, intended to restrict the privilege afforded by this section to cases which satisfy *both* requirements, *i.e.*, where the matter is of public concern, and also where its publication is for the public benefit, though it may be doubted whether this construction is strictly in accordance with the letter of the Act.

Illustrations.

After the passing of the Newspaper Libel and Registration Act, 1881, a speaker at a public election meeting at Manchester thought fit to make a personal attack on a gentleman who was a candidate for another constituency 200 miles off. The whole speech was reported in the *Manchester Courier*. The judge at the trial directed the jury in terms which might be understood as meaning that the only question for the jury was this : Is it for the public benefit that reports of election meetings should be published in newspapers? His lordship did not make it clear to the jury that the Act only protected the newspaper when it was for the public benefit that the actual libel complained of should be published broadcast. The jury found for the defendant. But the Divisional Court granted a new trial, which resulted in a verdict for the plaintiff.

  Pankhurst v. *Sowler,* (1886) 3 Times L. R. 193.

The *North Middlesex Chronicle* published in April, 1888, a full and accurate report of the proceedings at a vestry meeting which was open to the whole parish, including a speech made by a ratepayer imputing professional misconduct to the surveyors usually employed by the vestry. It was admitted that the imputation was wholly unfounded, but the defendant relied on s. 2 of the Act of 1881. Mr. Justice Denman directed the jury that the *onus* lay on the defendant to make out affirmatively that the case came within the section ; that it did not destroy the privilege afforded by the section that the matter complained of was now admitted to be untrue ; that there must be some relevancy between the matter published and the objects and intentions of the meeting ; that for the purpose of determining whether it was for the public benefit that the matter complained of should be published they must look at the whole occasion, the position of the parties, the objects of the meeting, in short, at all the facts. The jury found that the publication of the matter complained of was for the public benefit. Judgment for the defendant.

  Venables v. *Fitt,* (1888) 5 Times L. R. 83.

In April, 1889, the plaintiff endeavoured to address a meeting of dock labourers, called to discuss the Sugar Bounties; but he was prevented by a torrent of abusive interruptions from some men who had known him years before at Bristol, and who attended the meeting for the purpose of annoying him and preventing him from speaking. These interruptions were accurately reproduced in the report of the meeting published in the *Star* newspaper, although they had nothing whatever to do with the Sugar Bounties, but related to matters that had occurred at Bristol ten or twelve years previously. Mr. Baron Huddleston left to the jury the question whether such matters were of public concern, and their publication for the public benefit, with a strong intimation of his own opinion that they were neither, in which view the jury concurred.

Kelly v. *O'Malley and others*, (1889) 6 Times L. R. 62.

At a meeting of the shareholders of a company, the chairman made a speech in which he accounted for the losses of the company by imputing fraud and conspiracy to the chief cashier and the secretary. The defendants published in good faith a fair and accurate report of the whole of the proceedings at the meeting including these unfounded charges. Mathew, J., held that these charges were not matters of public concern, and that the publication of them in the report of the meeting was not for the public benefit, and therefore not privileged.

Ponsford v. *Financial Times, Limited*, (1900) 16 Times L. R. 248.

No privilege attaches to any report of a meeting which does not come within this section. If any one publishes a report of a private meeting, or if he publishes a report of a public meeting, but not in a newspaper (say, in the form of a pamphlet), and such report contains expressions defamatory of the plaintiff, the fact that it is a fair and accurate account of what actually occurred, will not avail as a defence, though it may be urged in mitigation of damages. By printing and publishing the statements of the various speakers, he has made them his own; and must either justify and prove them strictly true, or rely upon their being fair and *bonâ fide* comments on a matter of public interest, if they be comments merely and not allegations of fact.

V. Statements made in or copied from Parliamentary or Official Papers.

At common law no privilege attached to the publication of official papers of any kind, excepting such as were absolutely privileged on the ground that they were used in or prepared with a view to judicial proceedings. These have already been discussed (*ante*, p. 242). Statements made in Parliamentary reports or papers, even though published by order of the whole House, were not protected. (*R.* v. *Williams*, (1686) 2 Show. 471; Comb. 18. See, however, the comments on this case in *R.* v. *Wright*, (1799) 8 T. R. 293.) The law on this point was clearly laid down in *Stockdale* v. *Hansard*, (1837) 2 Moo. & Rob. 9; 7 C. & P. 731; (1839) 9 A. & E. 1—243; 2 P. & D. 1; 3 Jur. 905; 8 Dowl. 148, 522. In consequence of this decision the statute known as the Parliamentary Papers Act (3 & 4 Vict. c. 9) was passed in 1840 to protect persons (*a*) employed in the publication of Parliamentary papers and proceedings, or (*b*) who have printed any extract from or abstract of such papers or proceedings. The protection conferred by this statute is different in the two cases. In the former case it takes the form of a stay of proceedings; in the latter, a statutory privilege may be pleaded, to rebut which express malice must be proved. The Act is set out in full in the Appendix, at pp. 826—828.

(*a*) If any person be sued civilly or prosecuted criminally for or on account of or in respect of the publication of any report, paper, vote, or proceeding of either House of Parliament, which such House may deem fit or necessary to be published, whether the publication be by the person himself or his servant or servants, then if such publication be by or under the authority of either House of Parliament, the person so proceeded against may obtain a stay of proceedings, which will put an end to the action. (S. 1.) A person desirous of applying for such a stay must give twenty-four hours' notice of his intention to the plaintiff or prosecutor. He must bring before the Court in which the proceeding has been commenced, or before any judge of the High Court of Justice, a certificate under the hand of the Lord Chancellor, the Lord Keeper, the Speaker of the House of Commons, or the Clerk of the House, stating that the publication was by order or under the authority of the House of Lords or the House of Commons, as the case may be, which certificate must be verified by affidavit. Upon the production of this certificate and affidavit, the judge to whom the application is made will order a stay of all proceedings.*

If the publication in respect of which proceedings have been taken is not of the original but of a copy of such report, paper, votes or proceedings, a stay may be obtained on laying before the Court or judge the original together with an affidavit verifying the original and the correctness of the copy. (S. 2.)

(b) If any person be sued civilly or prosecuted criminally for printing any extract from or abstract of any such report, paper, vote or proceeding, he may plead that such extract or abstract was published *bonâ fide* and without malice; and if the jury shall find in his favour on that issue, a verdict shall be entered for the defendant. The statute provided that evidence in support of such defence may be given under the general plea of Not Guilty, but in civil proceedings, under the rules of procedure now in force in the High Court, such defence must be specially pleaded like any other ground of privilege. (See the discussion in *Mangena* v. *Wright*, [1909] 2 K. B. 958; 78 L. J. K. B. 879; 100 L. T. 960.) The privilege thus conferred does not extend to a headline which is not part of the report or paper from which the extract is taken. (*Mangena* v. *Edward Lloyd, Ltd.*, (1908) 99 L. T. 824; 25 Times L. R. 26.) If the words complained of be an extract from or abstract of such a report or paper together with a comment thereon, the defendant will be completely protected if the comment is fair and relates to a matter of public interest, and the publication was made without malice. (*Mangena* v. *Wright, suprà.*)

By s. 4 of the Law of Libel Amendment Act, 1888 (51 & 52 Vict. c. 64), a similar privilege was extended to

---

* For a form of certificate and of the order of the Court, see *Stockdale* v. *Hansard*, (1840) 11 A. & E. 297.

" the publication at the request of any government office or department, officer of state, commissioner of police, or chief constable of any notice or report issued by them, for the information of the public." This provision was enacted in consequence of the decision in *Murray* v. *Wright*, (1886) 3 Times L. R. 15; it does not extend to the publication of indecent or blasphemous matter, or of any matter not of public concern and the publication of which is not for the public benefit. The defence which it creates can be rebutted by proof of express malice; and also, if the words were published in a newspaper, by proof that the defendant has been requested to insert in his newspaper a reasonable letter or statement by way of contradiction or explanation of such report or other publication, and has refused or neglected to do so. The privilege created by the clause under discussion is not, like the earlier part of the section, limited to publication in a newspaper; the clause starts afresh with the words " and the publication at the request," etc. There is, moreover, no logical ground why the protection should be restricted to newspapers; it ought on grounds of public policy to apply to every defendant.

A like privilege arises where a newspaper publishes copies of notices, of which the Legislature has decided that an open record should be kept in the public interest. The ground of such privilege is that the newspaper is thereby assisting the Legislature. But such copy in order to be privileged must be accurate.

Illustrations.

The defendants in their newspaper published a copy of certain notices of receiverships registered at Somerset House under the Companies Act, 1907. One of these notices was "John Jones & Sons, Ltd. [Engineers, Loughborough]." The words in brackets were added by the defendants in place of the number under which the papers were filed, as there was more than one company registered as John Jones & Sons, Ltd. *Held,* that defendants were entitled to judgment on the ground of privilege.

  John Jones & Sons, Ltd. v. *Financial Times, Ltd.*, (1909) 25 Times L. R. 677.

The Agent-General for Natal wrote to the *Times* a letter containing an extract from a Parliamentary paper, which described the plaintiff as having been guilty of misconduct in Natal for which he was sentenced to imprisonment. The plaintiff had made application to the authorities in Natal and to the Privy Council in respect of the sentence. The defendant pleaded that he published the said letter under a sense of duty and in the interests of the Legislature and the people of Natal and of this country. *Held*, that the plea of privilege was good.

> *Mangena* v. *Wright*, [1909] 2 K. B. at p. 977.

But where the defendants published an incorrect copy of an entry in the register kept under the Deeds of Arrangement Act, 1887, it was held there was no privilege.

> *Reis* v. *Perry*, (1895) 64 L. J. Q. B. 566 ; 43 W. R. 648 ;
> 59 J. P. 308 ; 15 R. 427 ; 11 Times L. R. 373. See the
> remarks of Phillimore, J., in *Mangena* v. *Wright*, [1909] 2
> K. B. at p. 977.

CHAPTER XII.

MALICE.

" In an ordinary action for a libel or for words, though evidence of malice may be given to increase the damages, it never is considered as essential, nor is there any instance of a verdict for the defendant on the ground of a want of malice." (Per Bayley, J., in *Bromage* v. *Prosser*, 4 B. & C. at p. 257; 6 Dowl. & R. 296; and per Mansfield, C.J., in *Hargrave* v. *Le Breton*, 4 Burr. 2425.) As we have seen, an accidental or inadvertent publication of defamatory words may be ground for an action; *ante*, pp. 4—6, 163. The law looks at the tendency and the consequences of the publication, not at the intention of the publisher. (*Haire* v. *Wilson*, 9 B. & C. 643; 4 Man. & Ry. 605; *Fisher* v. *Clement*, 10 B. & C. 472; 5 Man. & Ry. 730; *Hulton & Co.* v. *Jones*, [1910] A. C. 20; 79 L. J. K. B. 198; 101 L. T. 831.) The fact that the jury have expressly found in the defendant's favour that he had no malicious intent, will not avail him (per Maule, J., in *Wenman* v. *Ash*, 13 C. B. 845; 22 L. J. C. P. 190; 17 Jur. 579; *Huntley* v. *Ward*, 6 C. B. N. S. 514; 6 Jur. N. S. 18; 1 F. & F. 552; *Blackburn* v. *Blackburn*, 4 Bing. 395; 1 M. & P. 33, 63; 3 C. & P. 146); for if he has published words which have in fact injured the plaintiff's reputation he must be taken to have intended the consequences naturally resulting from his act.

In former days this rule was not so strictly enforced in actions of slander as of libel; the Courts in those days evincing a strong desire to discourage actions of slander. Thus, where the defendant was sued for saying that he had heard that the plaintiff had been hanged for stealing a horse, and on the evidence it appeared that defendant spoke the words in genuine grief and sorrow at the news, Hobart, J., nonsuited the plaintiff, on the express ground that the words were

not spoken maliciously. (*Crawford* v. *Middleton*, 1 Lev. 82. And
see *Greenwood* v. *Prick*, cited Cro. Jac. 91; *ante*, p. 6.) Now,
however, absence of malice can only be given in evidence in mitigation of damages; and the question whether the defendant acted
maliciously or not, should never be left to the jury, unless the
defence of privilege or fair comment be set up. (*Haire* v. *Wilson*,
9 B. & C. 643; 4 Man. & Ry. 605. Per Lord Denman in *Baylis* v.
Lawrence, 11 A. & E. 924; 3 P. & D. 529; 4 Jur. 652. Per
Parke, B., in *O'Brien* v. *Clement*, 15 M. & W. 437.) The defendant's
intention or motive in using the words is immaterial, if he has in
fact wrongfully injured the plaintiff's reputation. (*Hooper* v.
Truscott, 2 Scott, 672; 2 Bing. N. C. 457; *Godson* v. *Home*, 1 Br.
& B. 7; 3 Moore, 223; *Morrison* v. *Ritchie & Co.*, (1902) 4 F. 645
(Ct. of Sess.), *ante*, p. 7.)

It is true that the word "malicious" is usually inserted in every
definition of libel or slander, that the pleader invariably introduces
it into every Statement of Claim, and that the older cases contain
many *dicta* to the effect that "malice is the gist" of an action of
libel or slander. But in all these cases the word "malice" is used
in a special and technical sense; it denotes merely *the absence of
lawful excuse;* in fact, to say that defamatory words are malicious
in that sense means simply that they are unprivileged, not employed
under circumstances which excuse them. But we have thought it
best to drop this technical and fictitious use of the word altogether
—a use which has been termed "unfortunate" by more than one
learned judge. (Per Lord Bramwell, 11 App. Cas. 253; 55 L. J.
Q. B. 460; 55 L. T. 65; per Stephen, J., 41 L. T. 590.) In this
book the word "malice" is always used in the popular and ordinary
sense of the word; *i.c.*, to denote some spite or ill-feeling against
the plaintiff, or some indirect and improper motive. This is called
"*express* malice" or "*actual* malice" in our older books. Using the
word in this sense, malice is not in issue in an action of defamation,
unless the defendant pleads privilege or fair comment. In the first
case, as soon as the judge rules that the occasion is privileged, the
plaintiff has to prove malice, but not before; in the second case,
evidence of malice will destroy the defence that the alleged libel is a
fair comment on a matter of public interest.

In the words of Lord Justice Brett: "When there has been a
writing or a speaking of defamatory matter, and the judge has held
—and it is for him to decide the question—that although the matter
is defamatory the occasion on which it is either written or spoken is
privileged, it is necessary to consider how, although the occasion is

privileged, yet the defendant is not permitted to take advantage of the privilege. If the occasion is privileged it is so for some reason, and the defendant is only entitled to the protection of the privilege if he uses the occasion for that reason. He is not entitled to the protection if he uses the occasion for some indirect and wrong motive. If he uses the occasion to gratify his anger or his malice, he uses the occasion not for the reason which makes the occasion privileged, but for an indirect and wrong motive. If the indirect and wrong motive suggested to take the defamatory matter out of the privileged is malice, then there are certain tests of malice. Malice does not mean malice in law, a term in pleading, but actual malice, that which is popularly called malice. If a man is proved to have stated that which he knew to be false, no one need inquire further. Everybody assumes thenceforth that he was malicious, that he did do a wrong thing for some wrong motive. So if it be proved that out of anger, or for some other wrong motive, the defendant has stated as true that which he does not know to be true, and he has stated it whether it is true or not, recklessly, by reason of his anger or other motive, the jury may infer that he used the occasion, not for the reason which justifies it, but for the gratification of his anger or other indirect motive. . . . The judgment of Bayley, J., in *Bromage* v. *Prosser,* 4 B. & C. at p. 255, treats of malice in law; and no doubt where the word 'maliciously' is used in a pleading, it means intentionally, wilfully. It has been decided that if the word 'maliciously' is omitted in a declaration for libel, and the words 'wrongfully' or 'falsely' substituted, it is sufficient, the reason being that the word 'maliciously,' as used in a pleading, has only a technical meaning; but here we are dealing with malice in fact, and malice then means a wrong feeling in a man's mind." (*Clark* v. *Molyneux,* 3 Q. B. D. 246, 247; 47 L. J. Q. B. 230; 26 W. R. 104; 37 L. T. 696, 697.)

Malice cannot be exhaustively defined. (Per Lord Esher, M.R., and Lopes, L.J., [1895] 2 Q. B. at pp. 38, 40.) But it may be described as any improper motive which induces the defendant to defame the plaintiff. "Any indirect motive, other than a sense of duty, is what the law calls 'malice.'" (Per Lord Campbell, C.J., in *Dickson* v. *Earl of Wilton,* 1 F. & F. at p. 427.) "Malice means any corrupt motive, any wrong motive, or any departure from duty." (Per Erle, C.J., 2 F. & F. at p. 524.) "Acting maliciously means acting from a bad motive." (Per Parke, B., in *Brook* v. *Rawl*, 19 L. J. Ex. at p. 115.) "Malice means making use of the occasion for some indirect purpose." (Per Lord Herschell in *Browne* v. *Dunn*, (1893) 6 R. at p. 72.) If malice be proved, the privilege attaching to the occasion, unless it be absolute, is lost.

The *onus* of proving malice lies on the plaintiff; the defendant cannot be called on to prove that he did not act maliciously, till some evidence of malice, more than a mere *scintilla*, has been adduced by the plaintiff. (*Taylor* v. *Hawkins*, 16 Q. B. 308; 20 L. J. Q. B. 313; *Cooke and another* v. *Wildes*, 5 E. & B. 340; 24 L. J. Q. B. 367; *Laughton* v. *Bishop of Sodor & Man*, L. R. 4 P. C. 495; 42 L. J. P. C. 11; *Clark* v. *Molyneux*, 3 Q. B. D. 237; 47 L. J. Q. B. 230.) And such evidence must always go to prove that the defendant himself was actuated by malice against the plaintiff. "What must be shown is, that the defendant was malicious, and to show that his informants were malicious, is not evidence that he was malicious." (Per Lord Esher, M.R., in *Hennessey* v. *Wright*, 24 Q. B. D. at p. 447, *n.*) Thus, in an action against the publisher of a magazine, evidence that the editor or the author of any article, not being the defendant, had a spite against the plaintiff, is inadmissible. (*Robertson* v. *Wylde*, 2 Moo. & Rob. 101; *Clark* v. *Newsam*, 1 Exch. 131, 139; *Carmichael* v. *Waterford Railway Co.*, 13 Ir. L. R. 313. So in America, *York* v. *Pease*, 2 Gray (68 Mass.), 282.) Malice in an agent, however, may be malice in the principal. Thus a corporation may be rendered liable for words published on a privileged occasion, by proof of malice in its servant who published them, provided the servant was acting within the scope of his employment. (*Citizens' Life Assurance Co., Ltd.* v. *Brown*, [1904] A. C. 423; 73 L. J. P. C. 102; 90 L. T. 739; *Finburgh* v. *Moss' Empires, Ltd.*, (1908) S. C. 928 (Ct. of Sess.); *Fitzsimons* v. *Duncan*, [1908] 2 Ir. R. 483.)

On the other hand it is not necessary that the defendant should be actuated by any special feeling against the plaintiff in particular. He need not be even personally acquainted with him. If the defendant desires to injure A., and thinks that the safest method by which to attain that end is by defaming the plaintiff on a privileged occasion, that in law is malice against the plaintiff; the defendant defames the plaintiff from an indirect motive, and thus abuses the privileged occasion. So if, from anger or gross and unreasoning prejudice with regard to a particular subject-matter, or against a particular trade or class, the defendant states what he does not know to be true, reckless whether it is true or false, this is malice which will destroy the privilege, although the defendant has no ill-will against the plaintiff as an individual. (*Royal Aquarium, &c., Society, Ltd.* v. *Parkinson,* [1892] 1 Q. B. 431; 61 L. J. Q. B. 409; 40 W. R. 450; 66 L. T. 513; 56 J. P. 404.)

Evidence of malice may either be *extrinsic*—as of previous ill-feeling or personal hostility between plaintiff and defendant, threats, rivalry, squabbles, other actions, former libels or slanders, &c., or *intrinsic*—the violence of defendant's language, the mode and extent of its publication, &c. But in either case, if the evidence adduced is equally consistent with either the existence or non-existence of malice, the judge should stop the case; for there is nothing to rebut the presumption which has arisen in favour of the defendant from the privileged occasion. (*Somerville* v. *Hawkins,* 10 C. B. 590; 20 L. J. C. P. 131; 15 Jur. 450; *Harris* v. *Thompson,* 13 C. B. 333; *Taylor* v. *Hawkins,* 16 Q. B. 308; 20 L. J. Q. B. 313; 15 Jur. 746.) Mere inadvertence or forgetfulness, or careless blundering, is no evidence of malice. (*Brett* v. *Watson,* 20 W. R. 723; *Kershaw* v. *Bailey,* 1 Exch. 743; 17 L. J. Ex. 129; *Pater* v. *Baker,* 3 C. B. 831; 16 L. J. C. P. 124.) Nor is negligence or want of sound judgment (*Hesketh* v. *Brindle,* (1888) 4 Times L. R. 199), or honest indignation (*Shipley* v. *Todhunter,* 7 C. & P. 690). That the words are strong is no evidence of malice, if on defendant's view of the facts strong words were justified. (*Spill* v. *Maule,* L. R. 4 Ex. 232; 38 L. J. Ex. 138; 17 W. R. 805; 20

L. T. 675.) That the statement was volunteered, if it was defendant's duty to volunteer it, is no evidence of malice. (*Gardner* v. *Slade et ux.*, 13 Q. B. 796 ; 18 L. J. Q. B. 336.) That the statement is now admitted or proved to be untrue is no evidence that it was made maliciously (*Caulfield* v. *Whitworth*, 16 W. R. 936 ; 18 L. T. 527); though proof that defendant *knew* it was untrue when he made it would be conclusive evidence of malice. (*Fountain* v. *Boodle*, 3 Q. B. 5 ; *Clark* v. *Molyneux*, 3 Q. B. D. 237 ; 47 L. J. Q. B. 230.) "If you want to show that a statement was malicious, it is not sufficient to show that it was not true." (Per North, J., in *Hayward & Co.* v. *Hayward & Sons*, 34 Ch. D., at p. 206; and see the observations of Williams, J., in *Harris* v. *Thompson*, 13 C. B. at p. 352.) If the defendant is in a position to prove the truth of his statement, "he has no need of privilege : the only use of privilege is in cases where the truth of the statement cannot be proved." (Per Lord Coleridge, C.J., in *Howe* v. *Jones*, (1885) 1 Times L. R. at p. 462. This is so also in America; see *Lewis and Herrick* v. *Chapman* (Selden, J.), 2 Smith (16 N. Y. R.), 369 ; *Vanderzee* v. *McGregor*, 12 Wend. 546; *Fowles* v. *Bowen*, 3 Tiffany (30 N. Y. R.), 20.)

The question of malice or no malice is for the jury. But there is always the prior question : "Is there any evidence of malice to go to the jury ?" and this is for the judge. The presumption in favour of the defendant arising from the privileged occasion remains till it is rebutted by evidence of malice ; and evidence merely equivocal, that is, equally consistent with malice or *bona fides*, will do nothing towards rebutting the presumption ; if, therefore, only such evidence be offered, the judge should direct judgment to be entered for the defendant. So, too, the judge should stop the case if there be no more than a *scintilla* of evidence of malice to go to the jury. But it is difficult to say beforehand what will be deemed a mere *scintilla*, what more than a *scintilla*, in any given case. "It is matter of law for the judge to determine whether the occasion of writing or speaking criminatory language, which would otherwise be actionable, repels the inference of malice ; constituting what is called a *privileged communication* ; and if, at the close of the plaintiff's case, there is no intrinsic or extrinsic evidence of malice, that it is the duty of the judge to direct a nonsuit or a verdict for the defendant, without leaving the question of malice to the jury. . . . Wherever there is evidence of malice, either extrinsic or intrinsic, in answer to the immunity claimed by reason of the occasion, a question arises which the jury, and the jury alone, ought to determine." (Per Lord Campbell, C.J., in *Cooke and another* v. *Wildes,* 5 E. & B. at pp. 340, 341 ; 24 L. J. Q. B. at pp. 372, 373.)

Illustrations.

The defendant on a privileged occasion used language stronger than necessary ; but the jury found "that the words were spoken honestly in the discharge of a public duty, without malice, but carelessly." Judgment for the defendant upheld.

> *Pittard* v. *Oliver,* [1891] 1 Q. B. 474 ; 60 L. J. Q. B. 219 ;
> 39 W. R. 311 ; 63 L. T. 247 ; 64 L. T. 758 ; 55 J. P. 100.

Defendant charged the plaintiff, his porter, with stealing his bed-ticks, and with plaintiff's permission subsequently searched his house, but found no stolen property. The jury found that defendant *bonâ fide* believed that a robbery had been committed by the plaintiff, and made the charge with a view to investigation ; but added, "the defendant ought not to have said what he could not prove." *Held,* that this finding was immaterial, that the occasion was privileged, and that there was no evidence of malice. Judgment for the defendant.

> *Howe* v. *Jones,* (1884) 1 Times L. R. 19 ; (1885) *ib.* 461.
> *Fowler and wife* v. *Homer,* 3 Camp. 294.

A young lady, the daughter of a clergyman, wrote a letter about her investments at her father's dictation ; the letter was a libel on the plaintiff, but the occasion was privileged. She stated in the box that she believed what she wrote to be true, because her father told her to write it : she was ready to sign or write what her father told her ; and she believed he would not tell her what was wrong. It was contended that belief must not be merely passive and irrational ; that the young lady could have no real and honest belief in the truth of what she was writing, if she chose to believe whatever her father told her without any inquiry. The jury found that "the young lady had been like wax in the hands of her father." Verdict for a farthing damages. The Divisional Court set the verdict aside on the ground that there was no evidence whatever of malice.

> *Hesketh* v. *Brindle,* (1888) 4 Times L. R. 199.

A lady wrote a libellous letter on a privileged occasion. It was admitted, on the one hand, that she had therein truthfully stated what she had heard from others, and, on the other hand, that what others so stated to her was untrue. Cave, J., withdrew the case from the jury, and directed a verdict for the defendant.

> *Aberdein* v. *Macleay,* (1893) 9 Times L. R. 539.

The defendant on a privileged occasion, asserted that the plaintiff had written to his agent a letter which showed that a claim which the plaintiff had made was fraudulent. At a subsequent interview with the plaintiff, he said : "You *did* write such a letter. I have seen the letter and I have a copy of it." When challenged to produce his copy, however, he said he had mislaid it. There was no such letter. Cockburn, C.J., left the question of malice to the jury, and they found a verdict for the plaintiff for 40*s.* damages.

Hancock v. *Case,* 2 F. & F. 711.

When a tradesman or manufacturer publishes advertisements vaunting the excellence of his own goods and stating that they are better than those of his rivals, such action is not malicious if it be done solely in order to promote the sale of his own goods, unless, indeed, it can be shown that he knew that his statements were false. That they now prove to be exaggerated is no evidence of malice.

White v. *Mellin,* [1895] A. C. 154 ; 64 L. J. Ch. 308 ; 43 W. R. 353 ; 72 L. T. 334 ; 59 J. P. 628.

Mogul Steamship Co. v. *McGregor, Gow & Co.,* 15 Q. B. D. 476 ; 21 Q. B. D. 544 ; 23 Q. B. D. 598 ; [1892] A. C. 25.

I. *Extrinsic Evidence of Malice.*

Malice may be proved by extrinsic evidence showing that the defendant bore a long-standing grudge against the plaintiff, that there were former disputes between them, that defendant had formerly been in the plaintiff's employ, and was dismissed for misconduct. Any previous quarrel, rivalry, or ill-feeling between plaintiff and defendant,—in short, almost anything defendant has ever said or done with reference to the plaintiff—may be urged as evidence of malice. The plaintiff has to show what was in the defendant's mind at the time of publication, and of that no doubt the defendant's acts and words on that occasion are the best evidence. But if plaintiff can prove that at any other time, before or after, defendant had any ill-feeling against him, that is some evidence that the ill-feeling existed also at the date of publication; therefore, all defendant's acts and deeds that point to the existence of such ill-feeling at any date, are evidence admissible for what they are worth. (*Cooper* v. *Blackmore and others,* (1886) 2 Times L. R. 746.) In fact, whenever the state of a person's mind on a particular occasion is in issue, everything that can throw any light on the state of his mind then, is admissible, although it happened on some other occasion. (See *R.* v. *Francis*, L. R. 2 C. C. R. 128; and *Blake* v. *Albion Assurance Society*, 4 C. P. D. 94; 48 L. J. C. P. 169; 27 W. R. 321; 40 L. T. 211.)

Thus any other words written or spoken by the defendant of the plaintiff, either before or after those sued on, or even after the commencement of the action, are admissible to show the *animus* of the defendant; and for this purpose it makes no difference whether the words tendered in evidence be themselves actionable or not, or whether they be addressed to the same party as the words sued on or to some one else. (*Pearson* v. *Lemaitre*, 5 M. & Gr. 700; 12 L. J. Q. B. 253; 7 Jur. 748; 6 Scott, N. R. 607; *Mead* v. *Daubigny*, Peake, 168; *Anderson* v. *Calvert*, (1908) 24 Times L. R. 399.) Such other words need not be connected with or refer to the libel or slander sued on; provided they in any way tend to show malice in defendant's mind at the time of publication. (*Barrett* v. *Long*, 3 H. L. C. 395; 7 Ir. L. R. 439; 8 Ir. L. R. 331; *Bolton* v. *O'Brien*, 16 L. R. Ir. 97, 483.) And not only are such other words admissible in evidence, but also all circumstances attending their publication, the mode and extent of their repetition, &c.; the more the evidence approaches proof of a systematic practice of libelling or slandering the plaintiff, the more convincing it will be. (*Bond* v. *Douglas*, 7 C. & P. 626; *Barrett* v. *Long*, 3 H. L. C. p. 414.) The jury, however, should be told, whenever the other words so tendered in evidence are in themselves actionable, that they must not give damages in respect of such other words, as though they were being sued on (*Pearson* v. *Lemaitre*, *suprà*); but the omission by the judge to give such a caution will not amount to a misdirection, and will therefore be no ground for a new trial. (*Darby* v. *Ouseley*, 1 H. & N. 1; 25 L. J. Ex. 227; 2 Jur. N. S. 497; *Anderson* v. *Calvert*, *suprà*.) The defendant is always at liberty to prove the truth of such other words so given in evidence; for he could not plead a justification as to them, as they were not set out on the record. (*Stuart* v. *Lovell*, 2 Stark. 93 ; *Warne* v. *Chadwell*, 2 Stark. 457.)

So if the defendant reasserts the libel in numbers of his periodical appearing after commencement of the action (*Chubb* v. *Westley*, 6 C. & P. 436) ; or in private letters written after action (*Pearson* v. *Lemaitre, supra*) ; (unless such letters be themselves privileged, as in *Whiteley* v. *Adams*, 15 C. B. N. S. 392 ; 33 L. J. C. P. 89 ; 10 Jur. N. S. 470 ; 12 W. R. 153 ; 9 L. T. 483) ; or if the defendant continues to sell copies of the libel at his shop up to two days before the trial (*Plunkett* v. *Cobbett*, 5 Esp. 136 ; *Barwell* v. *Adkins*, 2 Scott, N. R. 11 ; 1 M. & Gr. 807) ; these facts are admissible as evidence of deliberate malice, though no damages can be given in respect of them. A plea of justification may be such a reassertion of the libel or slander. Where the words are privileged, the mere fact that a plea of justification was put on the record is not of itself evidence of malice sufficient to go to the jury ; it is rather proof that the defendant still honestly believes in the truth of his assertion. (*Wilson* v. *Robinson*, 7 Q. B. 68 ; *Caulfield* v. *Whitworth*, 16 W. R. 936 ; 18 L. T. 527 ; *Brooke* v. *Avrillon*, 42 L. J. C. P. 126.) But if there be other circumstances suggesting malice, the plaintiff's counsel may also comment on the justification pleaded ; and, indeed, in special circumstances, as where the defendant at the trial will neither abandon the plea, nor give any evidence in support of it, thus obstinately persisting in the charge to the very last without any sufficient reason, this alone may be sufficient evidence of malice. (*Warwick* v. *Foulkes*, 12 M. & W. 508 ; *Simpson* v. *Robinson*, 12 Q. B. 511 ; 18 L. J. Q. B. 73.)

Illustrations.

The defendant wrote a letter to be published in the newspaper. The careful editor struck out all the more outrageous passages, and published the remainder. The defendant's manuscript was admitted in evidence, and the obliterated passages read to the jury, to show the *animus* of the defendant.

Tarpley v. *Blaby*, 2 Scott, 642 ; 2 Bing. N. C. 437 ; 1 Hodges, 414 ; 7 C. & P. 395.

A long practice by the defendant of libelling the plaintiff is cogent evidence of malice ; therefore other libels of various dates, some more than six years old, some published shortly before that sued on, are all admissible to show that the publication of the culminating libel sued on was malicious and not inadvertent.

> *Barrett* v. *Long*, 3 H. L. C. 395 ; 7 Ir. L. R. 439 ; 8 Ir. L. R. 331.

A libel having appeared in a newspaper, subsequent articles in later numbers of the same newspaper, alluding to the action and affirming the truth of the prior libel, are admissible as evidence of malice.

> *Chubb* v. *Westley*, 6 C. & P. 436.
>
> *Barwell* v. *Adkins*, 1 M. & Gr. 807 ; 2 Scott, N. R. 11.
>
> *Mead* v. *Daubigny*, Peake, 168.

So, if there be subsequent insertions of substantially the same libel in other newspapers.

> *Delegal* v. *Highley*, 8 C. & P. 444 ; 5 Scott, 154 ; 3 Bing. N. C. 950 ; 3 Hodges, 158.

Where the defendant has made charges of crime or fraud on a privileged occasion, which have subsequently been clearly disproved in a legal proceeding, it will be deemed malicious for him to repeat these charges or re-assert his belief in their truth.

> *Glendinning* v. *Emanuel*, (1886) 3 Times L. R. 110.
>
> *Seaman* v. *Netherclift*, (1876) 1 C. P. D. 540 ; 45 L. J. C. P. 798 ; 24 W. R. 884 ; 34 L. T. 878 ; 41 J. P. 389.

So, if the defendant persists in repeating the slander or disseminating the libel pending action. In *Pearson* v. *Lemaitre*, 5 M. & Gr. 700 ; 6 Scott, N. R. 607 ; 12 L. J. Q. B. 253 ; 7 Jur. 748, a letter was admitted which had been written subsequently to the commencement of the action, and fourteen months after the libel complained of. In *Macleod* v. *Wakley*, 3 C. & P. 311, Lord Tenterden admitted a paragraph published only two days before the trial. And see *Anderson* v. *Calvert*, (1908) 24 Times L. R. 399.

Defendant was director of a company of which plaintiff was auditor. Defendant made a charge against plaintiff in his absence at a meeting of the Board. At the next meeting of the Board plaintiff attended with his solicitor, having in the meantime written to defendant threatening an action. Defendant in consequence refused to make any charge or produce any evidence against the plaintiff in the presence of his solicitor. *Held*, no evidence of malice.

> *Harris* v. *Thompson*, 13 C. B. 333.

Where the defendant verbally accused plaintiff of perjury, evidence that subsequently to the slander defendant preferred an indictment against the plaintiff for perjury, which was ignored by the grand jury, was received as evidence that the slander was deliberate and malicious, although it was a fit subject for an action for malicious prosecution.

> *Tate* v. *Humphrey*, 2 Camp. 73, n.
>
> And see *Finden* v. *Westlake*, Moo. & Mal. 461.

In an action for slander and libel published on privileged occasions, the only evidence of malice was some vague abuse of the plaintiff, uttered by the defendant in a public-house at Rye shortly before the trial.   Such abuse had no reference to the slander or the libel or to the action. *Held,* that this evidence was admissible ; but that the judge should have called the attention of the jury to the vagueness of the defendant's remarks in the public-house, to the fact that they were uttered many months after the alleged slander and libel, and that therefore they were but very faint evidence that the defendant bore the plaintiff malice at the time of the publication of the alleged slander and libel.   A new trial was ordered.   Costs to abide the event.

> *Hemmings* v. *Gasson,* E. B. & E. 346 ; 27 L. J. Q. B. 252 ; 4 Jur. N. S. 834.

There had been a dispute between plaintiff and defendant prior to the slander about a sum of 20*l.* which the plaintiff claimed from the defendant.   At the trial, also, the plaintiff offered to accept an apology and a verdict for nominal damages if defendant would withdraw his plea of justification.   The defendant refused to withdraw the plea, yet did not attempt to prove it.   *Held,* ample evidence of malice.   Damages 40*l.*

> *Simpson* v. *Robinson,* 12 Q. B. 511 ; 18 L. J. Q. B. 73 ; 13 Jur. 187.

II. *Evidence of Malice derived from the terms employed, the mode and extent of Publication, &c.*

The plaintiff is not restricted to extrinsic evidence of malice (*Wright* v. *Woodgate,* 2 C. M. & R. 573 ; 1 Tyr. & G. 12 ; 1 Gale, 329) ; he may rely on the words of the libel itself and the circumstances attending its publication ; or in the case of slander upon the exaggerated language used, on the fact that third persons were present who were not concerned in the matter, &c.

The fact that the defendant was mistaken in the information he gave is, as we have seen, no evidence of malice : *ante,* p. 345.   The jury must look at the circumstances as they presented themselves to the mind of the defendant at the time of publication — not at what are proved at the trial to have been the true facts of the case—and then ask themselves : Did the defendant act honestly and under a sense of duty ? Did he *bonâ fide* believe that the statement he made was true ?

" For, to entitle matter, otherwise libellous, to the protection which attaches to communications made in the fulfilment of a duty, *bona fides,* or, to use our own equivalent, honesty of purpose, is essential ; and to this again, two things are necessary—1, that the communication be made not merely in the course of duty, that is, on an occasion which would justify the making it, but also from a sense of duty; 2, that it be made with a belief of its truth." (Per Cockburn, C.J., in *Dawkins* v. *Lord Paulet*, L. R. 5 Q. B. at p. 102.).

That other men would not have so acted is immaterial. That shrewder men would have seen through the tangled web of facts, and have discovered that things were not as they seemed, is absolutely immaterial. The question is, Did the actual defendant honestly believe what he said? not whether a reasonable man so placed would have believed it. (Per Brett, L.J., 3 Q. B. D. 248.) The defendant will not lose the privilege afforded by the occasion merely because his reasoning powers were defective. (Per Cotton, L.J., *ib.* 249; and see *Collins* v. *Cooper*, (1902) 19 Times L. R. 118.) "People believe unreasonable things *bonâ fide*," says O'Hagan, J., in *Fitzgerald* v. *Campbell*, 15 L. T. 75.

Similarly, the fact that he relied upon hearsay evidence without seeking primary evidence is no evidence of malice. (Per Lord Westbury, in *Lister* v. *Perryman*, L. R. 4 H. L. at p. 538; overruling (Exch. Ch.) L. R. 3 Ex. 197.) Men of business habitually act upon hearsay evidence in matters of the greatest importance. But it is otherwise where the defendant wilfully shuts his eyes to any source of information. If there be means at hand for ascertaining the truth, of which the defendant purposely neglects to avail himself, and chooses rather to remain in ignorance when he might have obtained full information, this will be evidence of such wilful blindness as may amount to malice. (See *Elliott* v. *Garrett*, [1902] 1 K. B. 870; 71 L. J. K. B. 415; 50 W. R. 504; 86 L. T. 441.) So also may the fact that the defendant knew, or might easily have ascertained, that his informant was a person unworthy of credit. (*White & Co.* v. *Credit Reform Association*, [1905] 1 K. B. 653; *Plymouth Mutual Co-operative and Industrial Society, Ltd.* v. *Traders'*

Publishing Association, Ltd., [1906] 1 K. B. 403; and see *post*, p. 364.)

But if defendant at the time of publication knew that what he said was false, this is clear evidence of malice. A man who knowingly makes a false charge against his neighbour cannot claim privilege. It can never be his duty to circulate lies. And if the statement was made wantonly, without the defendant's knowing or caring whether it was true or false, such recklessness is considered as malicious as deliberate falsehood. (*Clark* v. *Molyneux*, 3 Q. B. D. 237; 47 L. J. Q. B. 230; 26 W. R. 104; 37 L. T. 694.)

And even though it is clear that the defendant believed in the truth of the communication he made, and was acting under a sense of duty on a privileged occasion, the plaintiff may still rely upon the words employed, and the manner and mode of publication, as evidence of malice. An angry man may often be led away into exaggerated or unwarrantable expressions; or he may forget where and in whose presence he is speaking, or how and to whom his writing may be published. Clearly this is often but faint evidence of malice; the jury will generally pardon a slight excess of righteous zeal. In some cases, however (which we will proceed to examine) such excess has secured the plaintiff the verdict. But if the jury find there was no malice in the defendant, such excess becomes immaterial. (*Nevill* v. *Fine Arts and General Insurance Co.*, [1895] 2 Q. B. 156.)

(i.) *Where the Expressions employed are exaggerated and unwarrantable; but there is no other Evidence of Malice.*

" It is sometimes difficult to determine when defamatory words in a letter may be considered as *by themselves* affording evidence of malice." (Per Bramwell, L.J., 3 Q. B. D. 245.) But the test appears to be this. Take the facts as they appeared to the defendant's mind at the time of publication; are the terms used such as the defendant might have honestly and *bonâ fide* employed under the

circumstances ?   If so, the judge should stop the case.
For if the defendant honestly believed the plaintiff's
conduct to be such as he described it, the mere fact that
he used strong words in so describing it is no evidence of
malice to go to the jury.   (*Spill* v. *Maule*, L. R. 4 Ex. 232;
38 L. J. Ex. 138; 17 W. R. 805; 20 L. T. 675.)

But where the language used, though taken in connection with what was in defendant's mind at the time, is
" much too violent for the occasion and circumstances to
which it is applied," or " utterly beyond and dispropor-
tionate to the facts," or where improper motives are unnecessarily imputed, there is evidence of malice to go to
the jury.   (*Fryer* v. *Kinnersley*, 15 C. B. N. S. 422; 33
L. J. C. P. 96; 12 W. R. 155; 9 L. T. 415; *Gilpin* v.
Fowler, 9 Exch. 615; 23 L. J. Ex. 152; 18 Jur. 293.)

An inference of an improper motive will be readily drawn
in cases where a rumour prejudicial to the plaintiff has
reached the defendant, which he feels it his duty to report
to those concerned, if in reporting it he does not state the
rumour as it reached him, but gives an exaggerated or
highly coloured version of it.   Merely adding adjectives or
epithets will not matter; but if the defendant in repeating
such a rumour adds new facts or multiplies offences, this is
evidence of malice, or of that culpable recklessness, which
is tantamount to malice.   " *Inimici famam non ita, ut nata
est, ferunt.*"   (Plaut. Persa, II. i. 23.)   So if in writing or
speaking on a privileged occasion, the defendant breaks out
into irrelevant charges against the plaintiff unconnected
with the occasion whence the privilege is derived, the
defamatory matter thus unnecessarily introduced is evidence
of malice.   (*Picton* v. *Jackman*, 4 C. & P. 257; *Senior* v.
Medland, 4 Jur. N. S. 1039; and see *ante*, p. 304.)   But in
other cases the tendency of the Courts is not to submit the
language of privileged communications to too strict a
scrutiny.   " To hold all excess beyond the absolute
exigency of the occasion to be evidence of malice would in
effect greatly limit, if not altogether defeat, that protection

which the law throws over privileged communications."
(Per Sir Robert Collier, L. R. 4 P. C. 508.) "The particular
expressions ought not to be too strictly scrutinized, provided
the intention of the defendant was good." (Per Alderson, B.,
in *Woodward* v. *Lander*, 6 C. & P. 550. And see *Taylor* v.
Hawkins, 16 Q. B. 308 ; *Ruckley* v. *Kiernan*, 7 Ir. C. L. R. 75 ;
R. v. *Perry*, 15 Cox, C. C. 169.) That the expressions are
angry is not enough ; the jury must go further, and see that
they are malicious. (Per Tindal, C.J., in *Shipley* v. *Todhunter*,
7 C. & P. 690.) "A man may use excessive language, and
yet have no malice in his mind." (Per Lord Esher, M.R.,
[1895] 2 Q. B. at p. 170.)

Illustrations.

The defendant tendered to Brown at Crickhowell two 1*l*. notes on the
plaintiffs' bank, which Brown returned to him, saying there was a run
upon that bank, and he would rather have gold. The defendant, the
very next day, went into Brecon, and told two or three people confidentially that the plaintiffs' bank had *stopped*, and that *nobody* would take
their bills. *Held*, that this exaggeration was *some* evidence of malice to
go to the jury. Verdict for the defendant.

> *Bromage* v. *Prosser*, 4 B. & C. 247 ; 6 D. & R. 296 ; 1
>   C. & P. 475.
> And see *Senior* v. *Medland*, 4 Jur. N. S. 1039.

A gentleman told the second master of a school that he had seen one
of the under-masters of the school on *one* occasion coming home at night
"under the influence of drink," and desired him to acquaint the authorities with the fact. The second master subsequently stated to the governors
that it was *notorious* that the under-master came home "almost *habitually*
in a state of intoxication." There was no other evidence of malice.
Held, that Cockburn, C.J., was right in not withdrawing the case from
the jury.

> *Hume* v. *Marshall, Times,* November 26th, 1877 ; 42 J. P. 136.

Defendant changed his printer, and on a privileged occasion stated in
writing, as his reason for so doing, that to continue to pay the charges
made by his former printer, the plaintiff, would be "to submit to what
appears to have been an attempt to extort money by misrepresentation."
Held, that these words, imputing improper motives to the plaintiff, were
evidence of malice to go to the jury. Damages 50*l*.

> *Cooke* v. *Wildes*, 5 E. & B. 328 ; 24 L. J. Q. B. 367 ; over-
>   ruling
> *Tuson* v. *Evans*, 12 A. & E. 733.
> And see *O'Donoghue* v. *Hussey*, Ir. R. 5 C. L. 124.
> *Stevens* v. *Kitchener*, (1887) 4 Times L. R. 159.

Plaintiff sued defendant on a bond ; defendant in public, but on a privileged occasion, denounced the plaintiff for attempting to extort money from him. *Held,* that the words were in excess of the occasion.

> *Robertson* v. *M'Dougall,* 4 Bing. 670 ; 1 M. & P. 692 ; 3 C. & P. 259.
>
> *Hancock* v. *Case,* 2 F. & F. 711.
>
> *Jacob* v. *Lawrence,* 4 L. R. Ir. 579 ; 14 Cox, C. C. 321.

While the defendant was engaged in winding up the affairs of the plaintiff's firm, of which defendant was also a creditor, the plaintiff took from the cash-box a parcel of bills to the amount of 1,264*l.* Thereupon the defendant wrote to another creditor of the firm that the conduct of the plaintiff "has been most disgraceful and dishonest ; and the result has been to diminish materially the available assets of the estate." *Held,* that the occasion was privileged, and that though the words were strong, they were, when taken in connection with the facts, such as might have been used honestly and *bonâ fide* by the defendant ; for the plaintiff's conduct was equivocal, and might well be supposed by the defendant to be such as he described it ; and that the judge was right in directing a verdict to be entered for the defendant, there being no other evidence of malice.

> *Spill* v. *Maule,* L. R. 4 Ex. 232 ; 38 L. J. Ex. 138 ; 17 W. R. 805 ; 20 L. T. 675.

The defendant on a privileged occasion said that the plaintiff was "as drunk as a sow." It would have been quite enough for all purposes if the defendant had said the plaintiff "was not sober." *Held,* that these words were no evidence of malice. Nonsuit.

> *Sutton* v. *Plumridge,* 16 L. T. 741.

The rector dismissed the parish schoolmaster for refusing to teach in the Sunday School. The schoolmaster opened another school on his own account in the parish. The rector published a pastoral letter warning all parishioners not to support "a schismatical school," and not to be partakers with the plaintiff "in his evil deeds," which tended "to produce disunion and schism," and "a spirit of opposition to authority." *Held,* that there was some evidence to go to the jury that the rector cherished anger and malice against the schoolmaster.

> *Gilpin* v. *Fowler,* 9 Exch. 615 ; 23 L. J. Ex. 152 ; 18 Jur. 293.
>
> *Botterill and another* v. *Whytehead,* 41 L. T. 588.

It was the duty of the defendant on a privileged occasion to send out a notice referring to the plaintiff. The defendant unnecessarily introduced into the notice words relating to the plaintiff, but which yet were not wholly irrelevant to the occasion. *Held,* that the presence of these words did not prevent the privilege arising ; that they were at most evidence of malice, and as the jury had not found malice, judgment was entered for the defendant.

> *Nevill* v. *Fine Art and General Insurance Co.,* (C. A.) [1895] 2 Q. B. 156 ; 64 L. J. Q. B. 681 ; 72 L. T. 525 ; (H. L.) [1897] A. C. 68 ; 66 L. J. Q. B. 195 ; 75 L. T. 606.

(ii.) *Mode and Extent of Publication.*

As a rule, this also is but faint evidence of malice, it is matter rather to be urged at an earlier stage, when the judge is deciding the question whether each publication proved is privileged, or at a later stage when the jury are considering the amount of damages to be awarded. If all the publications proved are included in the pleadings or particulars, they must be held either privileged or unprivileged: if unprivileged, there is no issue as to malice; if privileged, then one privileged publication cannot possibly be evidence to render another publication unprivileged. But where some of the publications proved at the trial are not included in the Statement of Claim or in the particulars, but have only recently been discovered, they may afford valuable evidence of malice.

In any case, moreover, if it can be shown that the mode and extent of publication on a privileged occasion was purposely and deliberately made more injurious to the plaintiff than necessary, this is evidence of malice in the publisher. The defendant should do all in his power to secure that his words reach only those who are concerned to hear them. Words of admonition or of confidential advice should be given privately; not shouted across the street for all the world to hear. (*Wilson* v. *Collins*, 5 C. & P. 373.) Defamatory remarks, if written at all, should be sent in a private letter properly sealed and fastened up—not written on a post-card, or sent by telegraph; for two strangers at least read every telegram, many more most post-cards. (*Williamson* v. *Freer*, L. R. 9 C. P. 393; 43 L. J. C. P. 161; *Whitfield* v. *S. E. Ry. Co.*, E. B. & E. 115; *Robinson* v. *Jones*, 4 L. R. Ir. 391; *Sadgrove* v. *Hole*, [1901] 2 K. B. 1; 70 L. J. K. B. 455.) But if the telegram or post-card be in cypher or code form so as to be unintelligible to a casual reader, the mode of publication is no evidence of malice. (*Edmondson* v. *Birch & Co., Ltd.*, [1907] 1 K. B. at p. 381.) Letters as to the plaintiff's private affairs should not be published in the

newspaper, however meritorious the writer's purpose may
be : unless, indeed, there is no other way in which the
writer can efficiently effect his purpose and discharge the
duty which the law has cast upon him. But where it is
usual and obviously convenient to print such a communication as that complained of, before circulating it amongst
the persons concerned, the privilege will not be lost
merely because of the necessary publication to the compositors and journeymen printers employed in printing
it. (*Lawless* v. *Anglo-Egyptian Cotton and Oil Co.*, L. R.
4 Q. B. 262 ; and see *ante*, p. 302.) So with an advertisement inserted in a newspaper defamatory of the plaintiff ;
if such advertisement be necessary to protect the defendant's interests, or if advertising was the only way of
effecting the defendant's object, and such object is a legal
one, then the circumstances excuse the extensive publication. But if it was not necessary to advertise at all, or
if the defendant's object could have been equally well
attained by an advertisement which did not contain the
words defamatory of the plaintiff, then the extent given
to the announcement is evidence of malice to go to the
jury. (*Brown* v. *Croome*, 2 Stark. 297 ; *Lay* v. *Lawson*,
4 A. & E. 795.)

So with a privileged oral communication, it is important
to observe who is present at the time it is made. A desire
should be shown to avoid all unnecessary publicity. It is
true that the accidental presence of an uninterested bystander will not alone take the case out of the privilege,
and there are some communications which it is wise
to make in the presence of witnesses. There are occasions too, on which a man must speak at once, whoever
may be present, or the mischief which he desires to prevent
will be done. But if it can be proved that the defendant
purposely chose a time for making the communication
when others were by, whom he knew to be most likely
to act upon it to the prejudice of the plaintiff, this is
evidence of malice.

Illustrations.

To give unnecessary publicity to defamatory matter by publishing it to persons unconcerned is evidence of malice : as where the defendant posted up libellous placards.

Cheese v. *Scales*, 10 M. & W. 488 ; 12 L. J. Ex. 13.

Or had a defamatory notice cried by the town-crier.

Woodard v. *Dowsing*, 2 Man. & Ry. 74.

The use of a postcard is *primâ facie* evidence of malice, but if the postcard be so worded that no stranger could understand to whom it referred, it is no evidence of malice.

Sadgrove v. *Hole*, [1901] 2 K. B. 1 ; 70 L. J. K. B. 455 ;
49 W. R. 473 ; 84 L. T. 647.

The defendant was a customer at the plaintiff's shop, and had occasion to complain of what he considered fraud and dishonesty in the plaintiff's conduct of his business ; but instead of remonstrating quietly with him, the defendant stood outside the shop-door, and spoke so loud as to be heard by everyone passing down the street. The language he employed also was stronger than the occasion warranted. *Held*, that there was evidence of malice to go to the jury. Damages 40s.

Oddy v. *Lord George Paulet*, 4 F. & F. 1009.

And see *Wilson* v. *Collins*, 5 C. & P. 373.

That defendant caused the libel to be industriously circulated is evidence of malice.

Gathercole v. *Miall*, 15 M. & W. 319 ; 15 L. J. Ex. 179 ;
10 Jur. 337.

A shareholder in a railway company himself invited reporters for the press to attend a meeting of the shareholders which he had summoned, and at which he made an attack upon one of the directors. *Held*, that the privilege was lost thereby.

Parsons v. *Surgey*, 4 F. & F. 247.

Davis v. *Cutbush and others*, 1 F. & F. 487.

The fact that the defendant's wife was present on a privileged occasion, and heard what her husband said, is no evidence of malice in the defendant.

Jones v. *Thomas*, 34 W. R. 104 ; 53 L. T. 678 ; 50 J. P.
149.

Defendant accused the plaintiff, in the presence of a third person, of stealing his wife's brooch ; plaintiff wished to be searched ; defendant repeated the accusation to two women, who searched the plaintiff and found nothing. Subsequently, it was discovered that defendant's wife had left the brooch at a friend's house. *Held*, that the mere publication to the two women did not destroy the privilege attaching to charges, if made *bonâ fide;* but that all the circumstances should have been left to the jury.

Padmore v. *Lawrence*, 11 A. & E. 380 ; 4 Jur. 458 ; 3 P. & D.
209.

And see *Amann* v. *Damm*, 8 C. B. N. S. 597 ; 29 L. J. C. P.
313 ; 7 Jur. N. S. 47 ; 8 W. R. 470.

The defendant, the tenant of a farm, required some repairs to be done at his house ; the landlord's agent sent up two workmen, one of whom was the plaintiff. They made a bad job of it ; the plaintiff undoubtedly got drunk while on the premises ; and the defendant was convinced from what he heard that the plaintiff had broken open his cellar-door, and drunk his cider. Two days afterwards the defendant met the plaintiff and a mason called Taylor, and charged the plaintiff with breaking open the cellar door, getting drunk, and spoiling the job. He repeated this charge later in the same day to Taylor alone in the absence of the plaintiff, and also to the landlord's agent. *Held*, that the communication to the landlord's agent was clearly privileged, as he was the plaintiff's employer ; that the statement made to the plaintiff in Taylor's presence was also privileged, if made honestly and *bonâ fide;* and that the circumstance of its being made in the presence of a third person did not *of itself* make it unauthorised ; and that it was a question to be left to the jury to determine from the circumstances, including the style and character of the language used, whether the defendant acted *bonâ fide*, or was influenced by malicious motives. But that the statement to Taylor, in the absence of the plaintiff, was unnecessary and officious, and therefore not protected, although made in the belief of its truth, if it were in point of fact false. The defendant had, in fact, repeated the charge once too often.

Toogood v. *Spyring*, 1 Cr. M. & R. 181 ; 4 Tyr. 582.

The foregoing observations may now be applied in detail to the various classes of qualified privilege mentioned in the preceding chapters.

1. *Characters of Servants.*

If a master, out of anger or any ill-feeling against a servant, or from a desire to retain her in his own employ, gives her a bad character when he knows that she deserves a good one, he is acting maliciously, and all privilege is lost. So if from any wrong motive he states about her that which he does not know to be true, careless whether it be true or false, such recklessness is tantamount to malice, and "takes the case out of the privilege." The mere fact that the words are now proved or admitted to be false is no evidence of malice, unless evidence be also given by the plaintiff to show that the defendant knew they were false at the time of publication. (*Fountain* v. *Boodle*, 3 Q. B. 5 ; *Caulfield* v. *Whitworth*, 16 W. R. 936 ; 18 L. T. 527 ; *Clark* v. *Molyneux*, 3 Q. B. D. 237 ; 47 L. J. Q. B. 230.) But where master and servant have been living under one roof for years, it is hardly possible for the master not to know of his own knowledge whether the servant is or is not clean, civil, and truthful. If under such circumstances the master gave her a bad character, declaring that she was slovenly, disrespectful, and untruthful, proof that she was clean, civil, and truthful, would not

merely be proof that the words were untrue; it would also be
evidence that the defendant knew they were untrue, which is strong
evidence of malice. Such evidence, therefore, is admissible under
such circumstances as part of the plaintiff's case, although no
justification is pleaded.

Illustrations.

Where a master has given a servant a bad character, the circumstances
under which they parted, any expression of ill-will uttered by the master
then or subsequently, the fact that the master never complained of the
plaintiff's misconduct whilst she was in his service, or when dismissing
her would not specify the reason for her dismissal, and give her an opportunity of defending herself, together with the circumstances under which
the character was given, and its exaggerated language, are each and all
evidence of malice.

> *Kelly* v. *Partington*, 4 B. & Ad. 700 ; 2 N. & M. 460.

And in such a case the plaintiff is permitted to give general evidence
of her good character, in order to show that the defendant must have
known she did not deserve the bad character which he was writing.

> *Fountain* v. *Boodle*, 3 Q. B. 5 ; 2 G. & D. 455.
> *Rogers* v. *Sir Gervas Clifton*, 3 B. & P. 587.

It is usual for a former master to give the character of a servant *on
application*, and not before. Hence if a master hears a discharged servant
is applying for a place at M.'s house, and writes at once to M. to give
the servant a bad character, the fact that the communication was uncalled
for will be apt to tell against the master. M. would almost certainly
have applied to the defendant for the information sooner or later ; and
the eagerness displayed in thus imparting it unasked will be commented
on as a proof of malice, and if there be any other evidence of malice,
however slight, may materially influence the verdict. But if there be
no other evidence of malice, the communication is still privileged.

> *Pattison* v. *Jones*, 8 B. & C. 578 ; 3 M. & R. 101.
> *Fowles* v. *Bowen*, 3 Tiffany (30 N. Y. R.), 20 ; *ante*, p. 271.

The defendant on being applied to for the character of the plaintiff,
who had been his saleswoman, charged her with theft. He had never
made such a charge against her 'till then ; he told her that he would
say nothing about it, if she resumed her employment at his house ; subsequently, he said that if she would acknowledge the theft he would give
her a character. *Held*, that there was abundant evidence that the charge
of theft was made *malâ fide* with the intention of compelling plaintiff to
return to defendant's service. Damages 60*l.*

> *Jackson* v. *Hopperton*, 16 C. B. N. S. 829 ; 12 W. R. 913 ;
> 10 L. T. 529.

The defendant made a charge of felony against his former shopman to
his relatives during his absence in London, with a view of inducing them
to compound the alleged felony, and not for the purpose of prosecution
or investigation. He actually received 50*l.* from plaintiff's brother as
hush-money. *Held*, that the charge of felony was altogether unprivileged.

> *Hooper* v. *Truscott*, 2 Bing. N. C. 457 ; 2 Scott, 672.

A letter written by an employer dismissing a shopwoman, and stating the reasons why in very forcible language, is a privileged communication, and the Court will not closely scrutinise the language to find evidence of malice.

R. v. *Perry,* 15 Cox, C. C. 169.

Sir Gervas Clifton never made any complaint of his butler's conduct while he was with him; but he suddenly dismissed him without notice and without a month's wages. The butler (naturally, but illegally) refused to leave the house without a month's wages, a violent altercation took place, and eventually a policeman was sent for who forcibly ejected the butler. Sir Gervas subsequently gave the butler a very bad character, in too strong terms, and making some charges against him which were wholly unfounded. Verdict for the plaintiff. Damages 20*l.* New trial refused.

Rogers v. *Sir Gervas Clifton,* 3 B. & P. 587.
Murdoch v. *Funduklian,* (1885) 2 Times L. R. 215 ; (1886) *ib.* 614.

2. *Answers to Inquiries.*

Every answer given by the defendant to any one who has an interest in the matter, and, therefore, a right to ask for the information is privileged. But, of course, the defendant must honestly believe in the truth of the charge he makes at the time he makes it. And this implies that he must have *some* ground for the assertion : it need not be a conclusive or convincing ground : but no charge should ever be made recklessly and wantonly, even in confidence.

The inquirer should be put in possession of all the defendant knows, and of his means of knowledge ; if his only means of knowledge is hearsay, he should tell him so : he should not state a rumour as a fact ; and, in repeating a rumour, he must be careful not to heighten its colour, or exaggerate its extent. If the only information he possesses is contained in a letter, it is best to produce the letter, and leave the inquirer to draw his own conclusions. (*Coxhead* v. *Richards,* 2 C. B. 569 ; 15 L. J. C. P. 278 ; 10 Jur. 984 ; *Robshaw* v. *Smith,* 38 L. T. 423.) A man should not speak with the air of knowing of his own knowledge that what he says is a fact when he is merely repeating gossip. It will tend to negative malice if the defendant, so far as time allowed and means were at hand, made some attempt to sift the charge before spreading it.

3. *Information Volunteered.*

Here the defendant must be especially circumspect ; as the mere fact that the communication is volunteered, that the defendant did not wait for the person concerned to come to him and make inquiries, will raise at least a suspicion of malice in the mind of most jurymen. Of course, the jury must be satisfied in the first place that at the time the defendant made the statement he sincerely believed in its truth. But this alone will afford him no defence. (*Botterill* v. *Whytehead,* 41 L. T. 588.)

In deciding the question of malice or no malice the jury must not ask themselves merely, " Should we have acted as the defendant has done in such circumstances ? " for different people act differently in similar perplexities. Moreover the matter has been thoroughly investigated by the time it comes before the jury, and what to the defendant at the time seemed matter of serious suspicion has all been explained away in Court. The jury must place themselves in the position of the defendant at the time these suspicious circumstances were brought to his knowledge, when first the question arose in his mind, " Ought I not to inform A. ? " It may well be that another man would have said, " It is no concern of mine," and would have done nothing (which is always the safer course). But that does not prove that defendant was wrong in acting as he did. The jury should find for the defendant if they are satisfied that he honestly felt that he could not conscientiously allow A. to continue in secure ignorance, but that he must communicate to him that which he wss so much concerned to know.

It is not necessary that before making such statement the defendant should himself have thoroughly investigated the reports which had reached him. The fact that he acted on hearsay, is no evidence of malice. (*Maitland* v. *Bramwell,* 2 F. & F. 623; *Coxhead* v. *Richards,* 2 C. B. 569; 15 L. J. C. P. 278; *Lister* v. *Perryman,* L. R. 4 H. L. 521; 39 L. J. Ex. 177; 23 L. T. 269.) But the total absence of all inquiry may be *some* evidence of malice. (*Elliott* v. *Garrett,* [1902] 1 K. B. 870; 71 L. J. K. B. 415; 50 W. R. 504; 86 L. T. 441.) " And it is obvious that, if the information upon which he acted was procured from a person or persons who could not possibly know anything about the matters in question, and he nevertheless published the statements complained of as if they were based on sufficient information, that might be cogent evidence of malice." (Per Collins, M.R., in *White & Co.* v. *Credit Reform Association, &c., Ld.,* [1905] 1 K. B. at p. 658.)

Illustrations.

Defendant wrote to his wife's uncle telling him that his son and heir was leading a fast wild life, and was longing for his father's death, and that all his inheritance would not be sufficient to satisfy his debts. The

Court of Star Chamber was satisfied that this letter was written with
the intention of alienating the father from the son, and inducing the
father to leave his lands and money to the defendant or his wife, and not
from an honest desire that the son should reform his life ; and they fined
defendant 200*l.*

Peacock v. *Reynal,* (1612) 2 Brownlow & Goldesborough, 151.

A colonel was dismissed from his command in consequence of charges
made by the defendant. A member of Parliament gave notice that he
would ask a question in the House of Commons relative to this dismissal.
Defendant thereupon called on the member, whom he knew, to explain
matters. The conversation that ensued was held to be *primâ facie* privileged ; but the jury found that the charges were made, not from a sense
of duty, but from personal resentment on account of other matters, and
that the object of the conversation was to prejudice the plaintiff by reason
of such personal resentment. *Held,* ample evidence of malice, taking
away the privilege.

Dickson v. *The Earl of Wilton,* 1 F. & F. 419.

4. *Communications imputing Crime or Misconduct to others.*

Such accusations must always be made in the honest desire to
promote the ends of justice, and not with any spiteful or malicious
feeling against the person accused, nor with the purpose of obtaining any indirect advantage to the accuser. Nor should serious
accusations be made recklessly or wantonly ; they must always be
warranted by some circumstances reasonably arousing suspicion.
And they should not be made unnecessarily to persons unconcerned,
nor before more persons, nor in stronger language, than necessary.
(*Roberts* v. *Richards,* 3 F. & F. 507 ; *Padmore* v. *Lawrence,* 11 A. &
E. 380.)

Illustrations.

Plaintiff assaulted the defendant on the highway ; the defendant met
a constable and asked him to arrest the plaintiff. The constable refused
to arrest the plaintiff unless he was charged with a felony. The defendant
knowing full well that the plaintiff had committed a misdemeanour only,
viz., the assault, charged him with felony, in order to get him locked up
for the night. *Held,* that the charge of felony was malicious, as being
made from an indirect and improper motive.

Smith v. *Hodgeskins,* (1633) Cro. Car. 276.

Plaintiff was defendant's shopman in Plymouth till Nov. 5th, 1834,
when he left and went to London, receiving from the defendant a good
character for steadiness, honesty, and industry. Early in December defendant found one of his female servants in possession of some of his
goods. When charged with stealing them, she said that the plaintiff gave
them to her. Thereupon the defendant, though he knew the girl was of
bad character, went to the plaintiff's relations in Plymouth and charged
him with felony, and eventually induced them to give him fifty pounds

to say no more about the matter. *Held,* that the charge of felony was not made *bonâ fide* with any intention to promote investigation or prosecution, but with the object of compounding the felony and thus putting money into the defendant's own pocket ; that it was therefore altogether unprivileged ; and that no question as to malice in fact should have been left to the jury.

Hooper v. *Truscott,* 2 Bing. N. C. 457 ; 2 Scott, 672.

5. *Charges against Public Officials.*

Every communication made *bonâ fide* with a view to obtain redress for some injury received, or to prevent or punish some public abuse, is privileged, if it be addressed to some person who has a duty or an interest in the matter. "This privilege, however, must not be abused ; for if such communication be made maliciously and without probable cause, the pretence under which it is made, instead of furnishing a defence, will aggravate the case of the defendant." (Per Best, J., in *Fairman* v. *Ives,* 5 B. & Ald. 647, 648.) And a defendant will be taken to have acted maliciously, if he eagerly seizes on some slight and frivolous matter, and without any inquiry into the merits, without even satisfying himself that the account of the matter that has reached him is correct, hastily concludes that a great public scandal has been brought to light which calls for the immediate intervention of the Crown. (*Robinson* v. *May,* 2 Smith, 3.) Moreover, in seeking redress, the defendant must be careful to apply to some person who has jurisdiction to entertain the complaint, or power to redress the grievance, or some duty or interest in connection with it. If he recklessly makes statements to some one altogether unconcerned with the matter, there is no privilege. (Hawk. Pl. Cr. I. 544.) And where the informant is himself the person aggrieved, he should be very careful not to be led away by his indignation into misstating facts, or employing language too violent for the occasion.

6. *Statements necessary to protect the Defendant's private Interests.*

In the first place, the defendant must honestly believe that he possesses the right which he claims. And this involves that he must have some ground for making such a claim. "The jury may infer malice from the absence of probable cause; but they are not bound to do so. The want of probable cause does not necessarily lead to an inference of malice." (Per Maule, J., in *Pater* v. *Baker,* 3 C. B. at p. 868.)

Next, in claiming a right for himself or in resisting a claim made by another, the defendant must be careful to use temperate language, and to restrict himself to matters relevant to the claim. It is seldom necessary in self-defence to impute evil motives to others, or to charge your adversary with dishonesty or fraud. If, therefore, in writing or speaking on a privileged occasion the defendant breaks out into irrelevant charges against the plaintiff, such excess will be evidence of malice, making the relevant matter actionable. Or, indeed, if such charges be wholly irrelevant and entirely unconnected with the occasion whence the privilege is derived, they will be wholly unprivileged; so that no question of actual malice will arise as to them; unless defendant proves them true, the verdict will go against him. (*Huntley* v. *Ward*, 6 C. B. N. S. 514; 6 Jur. N. S. 18; *Warren* v. *Warren*, 1 C. M. & R. 251; 4 Tyr. 850; and see *ante*, p. 304.)

Lastly, in cases where some such communication is necessary and proper in the protection of the defendant's interests, the privilege may be lost if the extent of its publication be excessive. The defendant is not entitled to write to the *Times* because some one has cast a slur on him at a private gathering of friends; in fact by so doing he takes the surest method of disseminating the charge against himself.

Illustrations.

Defendant claimed a leasehold interest in the manor and castle of Hely, and produced a lease which she knew to be a forgery. Judgment for the plaintiff.

> *Gerard* v. *Dickenson*, (1590) 4 Rep. 18; Cro. Eliz. 197 (*ante*, p. 85).
>
> *Leslie* v. *Cave*, (1887) 3 Times L. R. 584; (1888) 5 Times L. R. 5.

Defendant claimed rent of plaintiff; plaintiff's agent told defendant that plaintiff denied his liability; defendant thereupon wrote to the agent, alleging facts in support of his claim, and adding, "This attempt to defraud me of the produce of the land is as mean as it 'is dishonest." *Held*, that the publication, in these terms, was malicious, for one can claim a debt without imputing fraud, and that the judge was justified in directing the jury that it was a libel.

> *Tuson* v. *Evans*, 12 A. & E. 733.

Lord Denman, in delivering the judgment of the Court, said, "Some remark from the defendant on the refusal to pay the rent was perfectly justifiable, because his entire silence might have been construed into an acquiescence in that refusal, and so might have prejudiced his case upon any future claim; and the defendant would, therefore, have been privileged in denying the truth of the plaintiff's statement. But, upon consideration, we are of opinion that the learned judge was quite right in considering the language actually used as not justified by the occasion.

Any one, in the transaction of business with another, has a right to use language *bonâ fide*, which is relevant to that business and which a due regard to his own interest makes necessary, even if it should directly or by its consequence, be injurious or painful to another; and this is the principle on which privileged communication rests. But it was enough for the defendant's interest, in the present case, to deny the truth of the plaintiff's assertion: to characterise that assertion as an attempt to defraud, and as mean and dishonest, was wholly unnecessary."

And see *Robertson* v. *M'Dougall*, 4 Bing. 670; 1 M. & P. 692; 3 C. & P. 259.

"When a man makes a pecuniary claim on another, the other has no right to traduce his character in order to get him to lower his demand." Per Cockburn, C.J., in

Hancock v. *Case*, 2 F. & F. at p. 714.

Jacob v. *Lawrence*, 4 L. R. Ir. 579; 14 Cox, C. C. 321.

The defendant owed the plaintiff 6*l*. 10*s*.; the plaintiff told his attorney to write and demand the money, and threaten proceedings. The defendant in reply wrote to the attorney denouncing the proceedings as a "miserable attempt at imposition," and proceeded to discuss the plaintiff's "transactions in business matters generally," asserting that "his disgusting tricks are looked upon by all respectable men with scorn." Damages one farthing; the jury expressly found that there was no malice; but the judge certified for costs on the express ground that there was.

Huntley v. *Ward*, 1 F. & F. 552; 6 C. B. N. S. 514; 6 Jur. N. S. 18.

Cooke v. *Wildes*, 5 E. & B. 328; 24 L. J. Q. B. 367; 1 Jur. N. S. 610; 3 C. L. R. 1090.

So where the defendant inserts in a newspaper an advertisement defamatory of the plaintiff; if such advertisement be necessary to protect the defendant's interest, or if advertising was the only way of effecting the defendant's object, and such object is a legal one, then the circumstances excuse the extensive publication. But if it was not necessary to advertise at all, or if the defendant's object could have been equally well effected by an advertisement which did not contain the words defamatory of the plaintiff, then the extent given to the announcement is evidence of malice to go to the jury.

Brown v. *Croome*, 2 Stark. 297.

Lay v. *Lawson*, 4 A. & E. 795; overruling

Delany v. *Jones*, 4 Esp. 191.

Gassett v. *Gilbert and others*, 6 Gray (72 Mass.), 94, *ante*, p. 291.

The plaintiff left the defendant's employ and set up business on his own account in premises adjoining the defendant's. Thereupon the defendant sent to certain customers whom the plaintiff had introduced to him, a postcard to the following effect: "I beg to inform you that *in consequence of the unsatisfactory manner in which the late drayman, Smith, performed his duties,* he is no longer in my employ, neither has he any authority to receive money on my behalf." Held, that the postcard would have been equally efficacious to protect the interests of the defendant without the words in italics ; that the insertion of these libellous words was unnecessary and malicious. Verdict for the plaintiff for 10*l.* damages.

> *Smith* v. *Crocker,* (1889) 5 Times L. R. 441.
> *Gallagher* v. *Murton,* (1888) 4 Times L. R. 304.

7. *Privileged Reports.*

In all these cases, whether under the Law of Libel Amendment Act, 1888, or at common law, the privilege can be destroyed by proof of malice in the defendant. It is not enough, if the proprietor of the paper be sued, to prove malice in the editor or the reporter ; malice must be shown in the defendant himself. (*Robertson* v. *Wylde,* 2 Moo. & Rob. 101 ; *Clark* v. *Newsam,* 1 Exch. 131, 139.) And, indeed, whenever the report has been written by the ordinary reporter on the staff of the newspaper it is difficult to prove any malice. If, however, the report was written by a successful litigant or his solicitor, or by the speaker at a meeting, the jury will be more ready to conclude that the act was malicious. Though it must always be remembered that " a newspaper has no greater privilege in such a matter than any ordinary person ; any person is privileged in publishing such a report, if he does so merely to inform the public." (Per Hannen, J., in *Salmon* v. *Isaac,* 20 L. T. at p. 886 ; and see 5 Ex. D. 56 ; and (1886) 3 Times L. R. 245.)

In *Stevens* v. *Sampson,* Bramwell, B., said (5 Ex. D. at p. 56): " Suppose a reporter for the press bore malice towards a person, a party to an action, and published a fair report of the proceedings injurious to him, I incline to think that, as he would be performing a kind of duty, it ought to be taken that he is acting under privilege. However, I only throw this out as a suggestion, and it is unnecessary to decide the point." Surely, however, if the action were brought against the reporter himself, he would be liable, because he acted maliciously. In an action against the editor or the proprietor, the malice of the reporter would be immaterial ; the plaintiff would have to prove malice in the actual defendant. See *ante,* p. 344.

Illustrations.

Even though a report of judicial proceedings be correct and accurate, still if it be published from a malicious motive, whether by a newspaper reporter or any one else, the privilege is lost.

> *Stevens* v. *Sampson,* 5 Ex. D. 53 ; 49 L. J. Q. B. 120 ; 28 W. R. 87 ; 41 L. T. 782.

Plaintiff brought an action against defendant, and applied for an injunction. Defendant applied at the same time for a receiver, which was refused.

O.L.8   B B

Thereupon the defendant said that he would "make it d——d hot for Dodson," and inserted in a newspaper he owned a report of the application, setting out all his own counsel had said against plaintiff's solvency, &c., at full length, but omitting all mention of plaintiff's affidavit. *Held,* ample evidence of malice. Damages 250*l.*

> *Dodson* v. *Owen,* (1885) 2 Times L. R. 111.

A speech made by a member of Parliament in the House is absolutely privileged ; but if he subsequently causes his speech to be printed, and published, with the malicious intention of injuring the plaintiff, he will be liable both civilly and criminally.

> *R.* v. *Lord Abingdon,* (1794) 1 Esp. 226.
> *R.* v. *Creevey,* (1813) 1 M. & S. 273.

8. *Fair Comment.*

The defence that the words are fair comment on a matter of public interest may be rebutted by proof of malice in the defendant. (See *ante,* pp. 224, 225.) Anything that is evidence of malice to rebut a defence of qualified privilege is admissible to show that a comment on a matter of public interest was published maliciously and is therefore " outside the right of fair comment." (*Plymouth Mutual Co-operative and Industrial Society, Ltd.* v. *Traders' Publishing Association, Ltd.,* [1906] 1 K. B. 403 ; *Thomas* v. *Bradbury, Agnew & Co., Ltd., and another,* [1906] 2 K. B. 627, 640.)

As to malice in actions on the case for untrue words causing damage, see *ante,* pp. 77, 93.

CHAPTER XIII.

DAMAGES are of two kinds :—

> (i) General.
> (ii) Special.

General Damages are such as the law will presume to be the natural or probable consequences of the defendant's words ; they need not therefore be proved by evidence.

Special Damages are such as the law will not infer from the nature of the words themselves ; they must therefore be specially claimed on the pleadings, and evidence of them must be given at the trial.   Such damages depend upon the special circumstances of the case, upon the defendant's position, upon the conduct of third persons, &c.

In some cases special damage is a necessary element in the cause of action.   When on the face of them the words used by the defendant clearly must have injured the plaintiff's reputation, they are said to be actionable *per se ;* and the plaintiff may recover a verdict for a substantial amount, without giving any evidence of actual pecuniary loss.   But where the words are not on the face of them such as the Courts will presume to be necessarily prejudicial to the plaintiff's reputation, there evidence must be given to show that in fact some appreciable injury has in this case followed from their use ; if no such evidence be forthcoming the judge will stop the case.   The injury to the plaintiff's reputation is the gist of the action ; he has to show that his character has suffered through the defendant's false assertions : and where there is no presumption in the plaintiff's favour, he can only show this by giving evidence of some special damage.

B B 2

It will be convenient to divide this chapter into the following heads:—

  I.—General Damages.

  II.—Special Damage, where the words are not actionable *per se.*

  III.—Special Damage, where the words are actionable *per se.*

  IV.—Evidence for the plaintiff in aggravation of damages.

  V.—Evidence for the defendant in mitigation of damages:

    (i) Evidence falling short of a justification.

    (ii) Previous publication by others.

    (iii) Liability of others.

    (iv) Absence of malice.

    (v) Plaintiff's bad character.

    (vi) Absence of special damage.

    (vii) Apology and amends.

  VI.—Remoteness of damages.

I.—General Damages.

General Damages are such as the law will presume to be the natural or probable consequence of the defendant's conduct. They arise by inference of law, and need not therefore be proved by evidence. Such damages may be recovered wherever the immediate tendency of the words is to impair the plaintiff's reputation, although no actual pecuniary loss has in fact resulted. (*Watt* v. *Watt*, [1905] A. C. 115; 74 L. J. K. B. 438; 92 L. T. 480.)

Such general damages will only be presumed where the words are actionable *per se.* If any special damage has also been suffered, it should be set out on the pleadings; but, should the plaintiff fail in proving it at the trial, he may still recover general damages. (*Cook* v. *Field*, 3 Esp. 133; *Smith* v. *Thomas*, 2 Bing. N. C. 372, 380; 2 Scott, 546; 4 Dowl. 333; 1 Hodges, 353; *Brown* v. *Smith*, 13 C. B. 596; 22 L. J. C. P. 151; 17 Jur. 807; 1 C. L. R. 4.)

The jury should carefully consider the whole of the words complained of, and give the plaintiff such damages as in their opinion will fairly compensate him for the injury done to his reputation thereby. The amount of damages is " peculiarly the province of the jury." (*Davis & Sons* v. *Shepstone*, 11 App. Cas. at p. 191; 55 L. T. at p. 2.) The Court of Appeal will not disturb the verdict, unless it be such as reasonable men could not have properly found. (*Webster* v. *Friedeberg*, 17 Q. B. D. 736 ; 55 L. J. Q. B. 403; *Metropolitan Railway Co.* v. *Wright*, 11 App. Cas. 152, 154, 156 ; *Praed* v. *Graham*, 24 Q. B. D. 53; 59 L. J. Q. B. 230 ; 38 W. R. 103.) The jury will of course be influenced by the circumstances attending the publication, by the character of the defamatory words, by their falseness, by the malice displayed by the defendant, or the provocation given by the plaintiff. They may also fairly take into their consideration the rank and position in society of the parties, the mode of publication selected, the extent and long continuance of the circulation given to the defamatory words, the tardiness, or inadequacy, or entire absence, of any apology, the fact that the defendant could have easily ascertained that the charge he made was false, &c. Where the words affect a trader in the way of his trade, figures may be laid before the jury, showing that his business has fallen off in consequence. (*Harrison* v. *Pearce*, 1 F. & F. 569 ; *Evans* v. *Harries*, 1 H. & N. 251 ; 26 L. J. Ex. 31; *Ingram* v. *Lawson*, 9 C. & P. 326 ; 6 Bing. N. C. 212.) Even if no evidence be offered by the plaintiff as to damages, the jury are in no way bound to give *nominal* damages only ; they may read the libel and give such substantial damages as will compensate the plaintiff for such defamation. (*Tripp* v. *Thomas*, 3 B. & C. 427.)

The damages which the jury award a plaintiff may be either,—

      (i) contemptuous,
      (ii) nominal,
      (iii) substantial, or
      (iv) vindictive.

(i) *Contemptuous* damages are awarded when the jury consider that the action should never have been brought. The defendant may have just overstepped the line, but the plaintiff is also somewhat to blame in the matter, or has rushed into litigation unnecessarily; so he only recovers a farthing or a shilling. There is no necessary inconsistency in a jury finding that a libel was written maliciously and yet awarding only a farthing damages. (*Cooke* v. *Brogden & Co.*, (1885) 1 Times L. R. 497.)

(ii) *Nominal* damages are awarded where the action was a proper one to bring, but the plaintiff has not suffered any special damage and does not desire to put money into his pocket; he has cleared his character, and is content to accept forty shillings and his costs.

(iii) *Substantial* damages are awarded where the jury honestly endeavour, as men of business, to arrive at a figure which will fairly compensate the plaintiff for the injury which he has in fact sustained.

(iv) *Vindictive* or *retributory* or *exemplary* damages are awarded where the jury desire to mark their sense of the defendant's conduct, by fining him to a certain extent; they, therefore, punish the defendant by awarding the plaintiff damages in excess of the amount which would be adequate compensation for the injury inflicted on his reputation. Thus, where a letter was sent privately to one person only, on whom it made no impression, the jury yet awarded 3,000*l.* damages, on the ground that "there must have been some vindictiveness." (*Adams* v. *Coleridge*, (1884) 1 Times L. R. at p. 87.) It is clearly competent to the jury in a proper case to find vindictive damages in an action of libel or slander. (*Lord Townshend* v. *Hughes*, 2 Mod. 150; *Emblen* v. *Myers*, 6 H. & N. 54; 30 L. J. Ex. 71; *Bell* v. *Midland Ry. Co.*, 10 C. B. N. S. 287; 30 L. J. C. P. 273; 9 W. R. 612; 4 L. T. 293; *Anderson* v. *Calvert*, (1908) 24 Times L. R. 399.) "The damages in such an action are not limited to the amount of pecuniary loss which the plaintiff is able to prove." (*Davis & Sons* v. *Shepstone*, 11 App. Cas. at p. 191; 55 L. J. P. C. 51; 34 W. R. 722; 55 L. T. at p. 2.)

Naturally heavier damages will be awarded for a libel than for a slander, especially if the libel has been published in a newspaper. As Best, C.J., said in *De Crespigny* v. *Wellesley*, 5 Bing. pp. 402—406 : Publication in a newspaper may " circulate the calumny through every region of the globe. The effect of this is very different from that of the repetition of oral slander. In the latter case, what has been said is known only to a few persons, and if the statement be untrue, the imputation cast upon any one may be got rid of ; the report is not heard of beyond the circle in which all' the parties are known, and the veracity of the accuser, and the previous character of the accused, will be properly estimated. But if .the report is to be spread over the world by means of the press, the malignant falsehoods of the vilest of mankind, which would not receive the least credit where the author is known, would make an impression which it would require much time and trouble to erase, and which it might be difficult, if not impossible, ever completely to remove. . . . Before he gave it general notoriety by circulating it in print, he should have been prepared to prove its truth to the letter; for he had no more right to .take away the character of the plaintiff, without being able to prove the truth of the charge that he had made against him, than to take his property without being able to justify the act by which he possessed himself of it. Indeed, if we reflect on the degree of suffering occasioned by loss of character, and compare it with that occasioned by loss of property, the amount of the former injury far exceeds that of the latter." (See *ante*, p. 330, and the summing-up of Huddleston, B., in *Kelly* v. *O'Malley and others*, (1889) 6 Times L. R. at p. 64.)

Again, as Lord Denman, C.J., points out in 9 A. & E. at p. 149, the jury, when considering the mode and extent of publication, should remember that the indiscriminate public sale of a libel inflicts an irretrievable injury on the plaintiff's reputation. The defendant cannot afterwards efficiently recall his statements, should he desire to do so; nor will a contradiction by either party, however widely circulated, reach all those who have read the libel.

The jury must assess the damages once for all (*Gregory and another* v. *Williams*, 1 C. & K. 568) ; no fresh action can be brought for any subsequent damage. (*Fitter* v. *Veal*, 12 Mod.

542 ; Buller's N. P. 7 ; 1 Ld. Raym. 339, 692 ; S. C. 1 Salk. 11.)* They should, therefore, take into their consideration not only the damage that has accrued, but also such damage, if any, as will arise in the future from the defendant's defamatory words. (*Lord Townshend* v. *Hughes,* 2 Mod. 150 ; *Ingram* v. *Lawson,* 6 Bing. N. C. 212 ; 9 C. & P. 326.) They should compensate the plaintiff for every loss which would naturally result from the words employed ; but not for merely problematical damages that may possibly happen but probably will not. (Per De Grey, C.J., in *Onslow* v. *Horne,* 3 Wils. 188 ; 2 W. Bl. 753, and Bayley, B., in *Lumby* v. *Allday,* 1 C. & J. 305 ; 1 Tyr. 217 ; and see *Doyley* v. *Roberts,* 3 Bing. N. C. 835 ; 5 Scott, 40 ; *Darley Main Colliery Co.* v. *Mitchell,* 11 App. Cas. 127 ; 55 L. J. Q. B. 529 ; 54 L. T. 882.)

Where the Statute of Limitations is relied on as a defence, but proof is given that one copy was sold by the defendant shortly before the writ was issued, the judge is not bound, it is said, to direct the jury to limit the damages to the injury which the plaintiff may be supposed to have incurred from that single publication, but they may take all the circumstances into their consideration. (*Duke of Brunswick* v. *Harmer,* 14 Q. B. 185 ; 19 L. J. Q. B. 20 ; 14 Jur. 110 ; 3 C. & K. 10.)

The jury in assessing damages ought not to take into consideration the question of costs. That is a matter entirely for the judge (*post,* p. 439). Unless he interferes, a farthing will carry costs as much as 1,000*l.* † It is for the jury, if they find for the plaintiff, to say to what extent he has been damaged, irrespective of the effect, if any, which their verdict may have on the subsequent action of the judge. (Per Bramwell, B., L. R. 1 Q. B. 691, 692. And see *Best* v. *Osborne, Garrett & Co.,* (1896) 12 Times L. R. 419.)

---

* The rule is somewhat different where the words are not actionable *per se.* See *post,* p. 611.

† See, however, the Slander of Women Act, 1891, *post,* p. 847.

II.—Special Damage where the words are not
actionable *per se*.

Special damage is such a loss as the law will not *presume* to have followed from the defendant's words, but is the actual and temporal loss in fact suffered by the plaintiff. This depends, in part at least, on the special circumstances of the case. It must, therefore, always be explicitly claimed on the pleadings, and proved by evidence at the trial.

In most cases of defamation proof of special damage is not essential to the right of action. Thus it is not necessary to prove special damage—

(i) In any action of libel.

(ii) Whenever words spoken impute to the plaintiff the commission of any indictable offence.

(iii) Or a contagious disease.

(iv) Or disparage him in his office, profession or trade.

(v) Or impute unchastity or adultery to any woman or girl.

Such words, from their natural and immediate tendency to produce injury, the law adjudges to be defamatory, although no special loss or damage is, or can be, proved. Though even in these cases, if any special damage has in fact occurred, the plaintiff may of course plead and prove it, so that it may be superadded to the general damage which the law implies.

But in all cases of slander not included in any of the above classes, and in all actions on the case, proof of special damage is essential to the cause of action. "The actual damage done is the very gist of the action," and "must be proved specially and with certainty." (*Per cur.* in *Ratcliffe* v. *Evans*, [1892] 2 Q. B. at p. 531.) The words do not, upon the face of them, import such defamation as will of course be injurious; it is necessary, therefore, that the plaintiff should aver and prove that some particular damage has in fact resulted from their use. Such damage must have accrued before action brought. A mere apprehension of future loss cannot constitute special damage. "I know of no case where ever an action for words was grounded upon eventual damages which may possibly happen to a man in a future situation," says De Grey, C.J., in *Onslow* v. *Horne,* 3 Wils. 188 ; 2 W. Bl. 753. It must also be the natural, immediate, and legal consequence of the words which the defendant uttered. (See *Remoteness of Damages, post,* pp. 406—419.)

The special damage necessary to support an action for defamation, where the words are not actionable in themselves must be the loss of money, or of some other material temporal advantage capable of being assessed in monetary value. (*Chamberlain* v. *Boyd,* 11 Q. B. D. 407 ; 52 L. J. Q. B. 277 ; 48 L. T. 328.) The loss of a marriage, of employment, of income, of custom, of profits, and even of gratuitous entertainment and hospitality, will be special damage if the plaintiff can show that it was caused by the defendant's words ; but not mere annoyance or loss of peace of mind, nor even physical illness occasioned by the defamatory charge. Such loss may be either the loss of some right or position already acquired, or the loss of some future benefit or advantage the acquisition of which is prevented. Thus, if the defendant causes a servant to lose his situation, or prevents his getting one—if he induces a stranger to abstain from going to the plaintiff's shop, or prevents an old customer from continuing to deal there— in each case that will be sufficient special damage.

Illustrations.

Anthony Elcock, citizen and mercer of London, of the substance and value of 3,000*l.*, sought Anne Davis in marriage ; but the defendant *præmissorum haud ignarus,* accused her of incontinency, wherefore the said Anthony wholly refused to marry the said Anne. *Held,* sufficient special damage. Verdict for the plaintiff for 200 marks.

> *Davis* v. *Gardiner,* 4 Rep. 16 ; 2 Salk. 694 ; 1 Roll. Abr. 38.
> *Holwood* v. *Hopkins,* Cro. Eliz. 787 ; *post,* p. 415.

So, if a man lose a marriage.

> *Matthew* v. *Crass,* Cro. Jac. 323.
> *Nelson* v. *Staff,* Cro. Jac. 422.

A declaration alleged that in consequence of the defendant slandering the plaintiff, a dissenting minister, his congregation diminished ; but this was held insufficient, as it did not appear that the plaintiff lost any emolument thereby.

> *Hopwood* v. *Thorn*, 8 C. B. 293 ; 19 L. J. C. P. 94 ; 14 Jur. 87.
> But see *Hartley* v. *Herring*, 8 T. R. 130, *post*, p. 389.

"If a divine is to be presented to a benefice, and one, to defeat him of it, says to the patron, 'that he is a heretic, or a bastard, or that he is excommunicated,' by which the patron refuses to present him (as he well might if the imputations were true). and he loses his preferment, he shall have his action on the case for those slanders tending to such end."

> *Davis* v. *Gardiner*, 4 Rep. 17.

Loss of a situation will constitute special damage.

> *Martin* v. *Strong*, 5 A. & E. 535 ; 1 N. & P. 29 ; 2 H. & W. 336.
> *Rumsey* v. *Webb et ux.*, 11 L. J. C. P. 129 ; Car. & M. 104.

Or of a chaplaincy.

> *Payne* v. *Beuwmorris*, 1 Lev. 248.

If, however, the dismissal from service be colourable only, the master intending to take the plaintiff back again, as soon as the action is over, and having dismissed him solely in order that he might show special damage at the trial ; this is no evidence that the plaintiff's reputation has been impaired, but rather the contrary. If, therefore, no other special damage can be proved, the plaintiff must fail in his action.

> *Coward* v. *Wellington*, 7 C. & P. 531.

If a man be refused employment through the defendant's slander, this is sufficient special damage.

> *Sterry* v. *Foreman*, 2 C. & P. 592.

So, if a person who formerly had dealt with the plaintiff on credit refuses, in consequence of the defendant's words, to deliver to the plaintiff certain goods he had ordered until the plaintiff has paid for them.

> *Brown* v. *Smith*, 13 C. B. 596 ; 22 L. J. C. P. 151 ; 17 Jur. 807 ; 1 C. L. R. 4.
> *King* v. *Watts*, 8 C. & P. 614.

So, if the agent of a certain firm going to deal with the plaintiff be stopped and dissuaded by the defendant, and this, although such firm subsequently became bankrupt, and paid but 12*s.* 6*d.* in the £, so that had the plaintiff obtained the order he would have lost money by it.

> *Storey* v. *Challands*, 8 C. & P. 234.

The loss of the hospitality of friends gratuitously afforded is sufficient special damage.

> *Moore* v. *Meagher*, 1 Taunt. 39 ; 3 Smith, 135.
> *Davies and wife* v. *Solomon*, L. R. 7 Q. B. 112 ; 41 L. J. Q. B. 10 ; 20 W. R. 167 ; 25 L. T. 799.

So is the loss of any gratuity or present, if it be clear that the slander alone prevented its receipt.

> *Bracebridge* v. *Watson*, Lilly, Entr. 61.
> *Hartley* v. *Herring*, 8 T. R. 130.

In consequence of the defendant's words, a friend who had previously voluntarily promised to give the plaintiff, a married woman, money to enable her to join her husband in Australia, whither he had emigrated three years before, refused to do so. *Held,* sufficient special damage.

> *Corcoran and wife* v. *Corcoran,* 7 Ir. C. L. R. 272.

The defendant said of a married man that he had had two bastards : "by reason of which words discord arose between him and his wife, and they were likely to have been divorced." *Held,* that this constituted no special damage.

> *Barmund's Case,* Cro. Jac. 473.

The plaintiff was a candidate for membership of the Reform Club, but upon a ballot of the members was not elected ; subsequently a meeting of the members was called to consider an alteration of the rules regarding the election of members ; before the day fixed for the meeting, the defendant spoke certain words concerning the plaintiff which, "induced or contributed to inducing a majority of the members of the club to retain the regulations under which the plaintiff had been rejected, and thereby prevented the plaintiff from again seeking to be elected to the club." *Held,* that the damage alleged was not pecuniary or capable of being estimated in money, and was not the natural and probable consequence of the defendant's words.

> *Chamberlain* v. *Boyd,* 11 Q. B. D. 407 ; 52 L. J. Q. B. 277 ;
> Q. B. 493 ; 45 W. R. 525 ; 76 L. T. 493 ; *ante,* p. 108.

So where the words are not actionable *per se,* and no pecuniary damage has followed, no compensation can be given for outraged feelings, nor for sickness induced by such mental distress, even though followed by a doctor's bill.

> *Allsop* v. *Allsop,* 5 H. & N. 534 ; 29 L. J. Ex. 315 ; 6 Jur.
> N. S. 433 ; 8 W. R. 449 ; 36 L. T. (Old S.) 290.
>
> *Lynch* v. *Knight and wife,* 9 H. L. C. 577 ; 8 Jur. N. S.
> 724 ; 5 L. T. 291.
>
> *Victorian Railways Commissioners* v. *Coultas,* 13 App. Cas. 222 ;
> 57 L. J. P. C. 69 ; 37 W. R. 129 ; 58 L. T. 390 ; 52
> J. P. 500.
>
> But see *Wilkinson* v. *Downton,* [1897] 2 Q. B. 57 ; 66 L. J.
> Q. B. 493 ; 45 W. R. 525 ; 76 L. T. 493 ; *ante,* p. 108.
>
> *Dulieu* v. *White & Sons,* [1901] 2 K. B. 669 ; 70 L. J. K. B.
> 837 ; 50 W. R. 76 ; 85 L. T. 126.

Loss of the *consortium* of a husband or of a wife is special damage. Per Lords Campbell and Cranworth in

> *Lynch* v. *Knight and wife,* 9 H. L. C. at p. 589.
>
> *Winsmore* v. *Greenbank,* (1745) Willes' Rep. (Common Pleas)
> 577.
>
> *Smith* v. *Kaye and another,* (1904) 20 Times L. R. 261.

But not merely of the society of friends and neighbours.

> *Medhurst* v. *Balam,* cited in 1 Siderfin, 397.
>
> *Barnes* v. *Prudlin or Bruddel,* 1 Lev. 261 ; 1 Sid. 396 ; 1
> Ventr. 4 ; 2 Keb. 451.

Hence, even the fact that the plaintiff has been expelled from a religious society of which she was a member, will not constitute special damage.

> *Roberts et ux.* v. *Roberts,* 5 B. & S. 384 ; 33 L. J. Q. B.
> 249 ; 10 Jur. N. S. 1027 ; 12 W. R. 909 ; 10 L. T. 602.

Though there is an old case in which a vicar in open church falsely declared that the plaintiff, one of his parishioners, was excommunicated, and refused to celebrate divine service till the plaintiff departed out of the church, whereby the plaintiff was compelled to quit the church, and was scandalised, and was hindered of hearing divine service for a long time ; and it was held that an action lay.

Barnabas v. *Traunter,* (1641) 1 Vin. Abr. 396.

This case was not cited to the Court in *Roberts* v. *Roberts.*

The plaintiff alleged that in consequence of the defendant's words " she had suffered considerable annoyance, trouble, disgrace, loss of friends, credit, and reputation." *Held,* that this was no special damage.

Weldon v. *De Bathe,* 33 W. R. 328 ; 14 Q. B. D. 339 ; 54 L. J. Q. B. 113 ; 53 L. T. 520.

So in Ireland.

The plaintiff alleged that she had been a novice in a convent, and left in order to nurse a sick relative ; that defendant said she had left because she was pregnant ; whereby the plaintiff alleged she was prevented from returning to the convent and becoming a nun, when she would have been maintained and supported by the society ; and had also been brought into disgrace among her neighbours and friends, and had been deprived of and ceased to receive their hospitality. *Held,* that no action lay, as the plaintiff was neither a nun nor a novice at the time the words were spoken, and there was no evidence of special damage sufficient in law to maintain the action.

Dwyer v. *Meehan,* 18 L. R. Ir. 138.

The law is the same in America.

The refusal of civil entertainment at a public-house was held sufficient special damage.

Olmsted v. *Miller,* 1 Wend. 506.

So was the fact that the plaintiff was turned away from the house of her uncle, where she had previously been a welcome visitor, and charged not to return till she had cleared her character.

Williams v. *Hill,* 19 Wend. 305.

So was the circumstance that persons who had been in the habit of so doing refused any longer to provide food and clothing for the plaintiff.

Beach v. *Ranney,* 2 Hill (N. Y.), 309.

The defendant told Neiper that the plaintiff committed adultery with Mrs. Fuller. Neiper had married Mrs. Fuller's sister, and was an intimate friend of the plaintiff's. Neiper thought it his duty to tell the plaintiff what people were saying of him. The plaintiff, who was hoeing at the time, turned pale, felt bad, flung down his hoe, and left the field ; lost his appetite, turned melancholy, could not work as he used to, and had to hire more help. *Held,* that such mental distress and physical illness were not sufficient to constitute special damage ; for they did not result from any injury to the plaintiff's reputation, which had affected the conduct of others towards him. The Court said, in giving judgment, " It would be highly impolitic to hold all language, wounding the feelings and affecting unfavourably the health and ability to labour, of another, a ground of action : for that would be to make the right of action depend often upon whether the sensibilities of a person spoken of are easily excited or otherwise, his strength of mind to disregard abusive insulting remarks concerning him, and his physical strength and ability to bear them. Words which would make hardly an impression on most persons, and would be thought by them, and should be by all, un-deserving of notice, might be exceedingly painful to some, occasioning sickness and an interruption of ability to attend to their ordinary avocations."

> *Terwilliger* v. *Wands*, 3 Smith (17 N. Y. R.), 54, overruling *Bradt* v. *Towsley*, 13 Wend. 253, and *Fuller* v. *Fenner*, 16 Barb. 333.

So, too, a husband cannot maintain an action for the loss of his wife's services caused by illness or mental depression resulting from defamatory words not actionable *per se* being spoken of her by the defendant. For the wife, if *sole*, could have maintained no action. "The facility with which a right to damages could be established by pretended illness where none exists, constitutes a serious objection to such an action as this."

Per Denio, J., in

> *Wilson* v. *Goit*, (1858) 3 Smith (17 N. Y. R.), 445.

But it is not sufficient for the plaintiff merely to prove the existence of such a loss; he must go further and show clearly that the loss is the direct result of the defendant's words, and not the consequence of some independent act, some spontaneous resolve, of a third person. (See *post*, p. 406.) As a rule, where the words are not actionable *per se*, he can only do this by calling as his witnesses at the trial the persons who ceased to employ him, or who were prevented by the defendant from dealing with him; and they must state in the box their reason for not employing or not dealing with the plaintiff. Else it will not be clear that they did so in consequence of the defendant's words; their conduct might well be due to some other cause. (Per Lord Kenyon, C.J., in *Ashley* v. *Harrison*, 1 Esp. at p. 50; per Best, C.J., in *Tilk* v. *Parsons*, 2 C. & P. 201.) But it is not always necessary for the plaintiff to call as his witnesses those who have ceased to deal with him. He may be able to show by his account-books or otherwise, a general diminution of business as distinct from the loss of particular known customers or promised orders. He has still to connect that diminution of business with the defendant's words.

Such a connection may sometimes be established by the nature of the words themselves. Where the defendant has published a statement about the plaintiff's business, which is intended or reasonably calculated to produce, and in the ordinary course of things does produce, a general loss of business, evidence of such loss of business is admissible, and sufficient special damage to support the action, although the words are not actionable *per se*, and although no specific evidence is given at the trial of the loss of any particular customer or order by reason of such publication. (*Ratcliffe* v. *Evans*, [1892] 2 Q. B. 524; 61 L. J. Q. B. 535; 40 W. R. 578; 66 L. T. 794.)

Note the distinction between the loss of individual customers and a general diminution in annual profits. Loss of custom must be specifically alleged; the customers' names must be stated on the pleadings, or in the particulars; and they must be called at the trial to state why they ceased to deal with the plaintiff. A general loss of business, on the other hand, is proved by the plaintiff himself; he produces his books, and shows that fewer orders have been received, and less profit made, since the words were published than before. This is not necessary where the words are actionable *per se;* for the law presumes that such words must injure the plaintiff in his business; and there is no need, therefore, for him to call such evidence. And it has been decided that where the words in their very nature are "intended or reasonably likely to produce, and which in the ordinary course of things do produce, a general loss of business," no further evidence is necessary to connect the decline in the plaintiff's business with the defendant's words. (See *Ratcliffe* v. *Evans, suprà*.) But in all other cases of words not actionable *per se*, some evidence must be given to connect the plaintiff's loss of business with the defendant's words.

Special damage must always be explicitly claimed and particulars given on the pleadings. It must be alleged with certainty and precision. If the plaintiff relies on the loss of particular customers, he must set out their names in the Statement of Claim. If he relies on a diminution in the profits of his business, he must state on his pleading the fact that he has lost profits, shewing by figures how much he alleges he has lost. *See* Precedents, Nos. 12, 16, 17.

" The character of the acts themselves which produce the damage, and the circumstances under which these acts are done, must regulate the degree of certainty and particularity with which the damage done ought to be stated and proved. As much certainty and particularity must be insisted on, both in pleading and proof of damage, as is reasonable, having regard to the circumstances and to the nature of the acts themselves by which the damage is done. To insist upon less would be to relax old and intelligible principles. To insist upon more would be the vainest pedantry." (*Per cur.* in *Ratcliffe* v. *Evans*, [1892] 2 Q. B. at pp. 532, 533.)

Illustrations.

The plaintiff alleged that in consequence of the defendant's slander, she had "lost several suitors." This was held too general an allegation ; for the names of the suitors, if there were any, could hardly have escaped the plaintiff's memory.

> *Barnes* v. *Prudlin, vel Bruddel,* 1 Sid. 396 ; 1 Ventr. 4 ; 1 Lev. 261 ; 2 Keb. 451.
>
> See also, *Hunt* v. *Jones,* Cro. Jac. 499.
>
> *Davies and wife* v. *Solomon,* L. R. 7 Q. B. 112 ; 41 L. J. Q. B. 10 ; 20 W. R. 167 ; 25 L. T. 799.

The defendant spoke words not slanderous *per se* of a dissenting minister, who averred that his congregation diminished in consequence. *Held,* too general an averment to constitute special damage, the names of the absentees not being given.

> *Hopwood* v. *Thorn,* 8 C. B. 293 ; 19 L. J. C. P. 94 ; 14 Jur. 87.

Such an averment would have been sufficient, had the words been spoken of the plaintiff in the way of his office, and so actionable *per se.*

> *Hartley* v. *Herring,* 8 T. R. 130.

" Suppose a biscuit baker in Regent Street is slandered by a man saying his biscuits are poisoned, and in consequence no one enters his shop. He cannot complain of the loss of any particular customers, for he does not know them, and how hard and unjust it would be if he could not prove the fact of the loss under a general allegation of loss of custom." Per Martin, B., in

> *Evans* v. *Harries,* 26 L. J. Ex. 32.
>
> And see *Weiss* v. *Whittemore,* 38 Michigan, 366.

The defendant printed and published in his newspaper that the plaintiff had given up business, and that his firm had ceased to exist. These words were not actionable *per se ;* but they were clearly calculated to injure, and had in fact injured, the plaintiff's business, and the defendant must have known that in all reasonable probability they would injure the plaintiff's business. The plaintiff proved that his business had fallen off, and that his profits had diminished since the publication of the words ; but gave no specific evidence of the loss of any particular customer or order. *Held*, that such evidence was in the special circumstances of the case sufficient to sustain the action.

> *Ratcliffe* v. *Evans*, [1892] 2 Q. B. 524 ; 61 L. J. Q. B. 535 ;
> 40 W. R. 578 ; 66 L. T. 794 ; 56 J. P. 837.

In an action of slander of the plaintiff's title to an advowson, it was alleged that by reason of the defendant's words the plaintiff "was hindered in the sale of his advowson." It was not alleged that any one was in actual treaty to purchase it, or that any one who intended to buy it was in communication with the plaintiff. *Held*, that no action lay, for want of special damage.

> *Tasburgh* v. *Day*, (1618) Cro. Jac. 484.

But where the defendant slandered the plaintiff's title in the auction-room while the sale was proceeding, and thereupon "the bidding immediately ceased, divers persons who would have purchased left the room, and the estate remained unsold," the objection that the names of the persons who would have purchased should have been specified, was "easily answered" thus : "that in the nature of this transaction it was impossible to specify names. The injury complained of is that the bidding was thereby prevented and stopt. No one can tell who would have bid, and who would not. The auction ceased ; and everybody went away. It could not be known who would have been bidders or purchasers, if it had not been thus put an end to."

> *Hargrave* v. *Le Breton*, (1769) 4 Burr. at p. 2424.

The law is the same in America.

The plaintiff alleged that the defendant's words had "injured her in her good name, and caused her relatives and friends to slight and shun her." This was held to disclose no special damage.

> *Bassell* v. *Elmore*, 48 N. Y. R. 563 ; 65 Barb. 627.
> *Geisler* v. *Brown*, 6 Neb. 254.

So where the allegation was merely that by reason of the defendant's words "the plaintiff had been slighted, neglected, and misused by the neighbours and her former associates, and turned out of doors."

> *Pettibone* v. *Simpson*, 66 Barb. 492.

A general allegation that by reason of the defendant's acts, the plaintiff had been compelled to pay a large sum of money, without showing how, was held insufficient.

> *Cook* v. *Cook*, 100 Mass. 194.
> *Pollard* v. *Lyon*, 1 Otto (91 U. S.), 225.

So in Australia.

To say to the keeper of a restaurant, "You are an infernal rogue and swindler," was held, in the Supreme Court of Victoria, not actionable without proof of special damage, as not affecting plaintiff in his trade. But the plaintiff having alleged that, by reason of the words, people who used to frequent his restaurant ceased to deal with him, it was held the special damage made the words actionable, and that the special damage was sufficiently alleged, that the cases of frequenters of theatres, members of congregations, and travellers using an inn, were exceptions to the rule requiring the names of the customers lost to be set forth.

Brady v. *Youlden,* Kerferd & Box's Digest of Victoria Cases, 709 ; *Melbourne Argus* Reports, 6 Sept. 1867, *sed quære.*

Special damage must be strictly proved at the trial. Where the words are not actionable *per se*, the plaintiff will be confined to the special damage laid; he must prove that, or fail: as there are no general damages to which he can have recourse. And when special damage is proved, the jury should strictly find a verdict for the amount of such special damage merely. They ought not to compensate the plaintiff for pain, mental anxiety, or a general loss of reputation, but should confine their assessment to the actual pecuniary loss that has been alleged and proved. (*Dixon* v. *Smith*, 5 H. & N. 450; 29 L. J. Ex. 125.) This rule, however, is frequently neglected in practice; and as soon as *any* special damage is proved, the words are treated as though they were actionable *per se*. It has now been decided that a second action will lie for fresh special damage, in cases where special damage is part of the cause of action. (Cf. *Crumbie* v. *Wallsend Local Board*, [1891] 1 Q. B. 503; 60 L. J. Q. B. 392; 64 L. T. 490; and *West Leigh Colliery Co., Ltd.* v. *Tunnicliffe and Hampson, Ltd.*, [1908] A. C. 27; 77 L. J. Ch. 102; 98 L. T. 4; and see *post*, p. 611.)

Illustrations.

Dawes intended to employ the plaintiff, a surgeon and accoucheur, at his wife's approaching confinement, but the defendant told Dawes that the plaintiff's female servant had had a child by the plaintiff: Dawes consequently decided not to employ the plaintiff: Dawes told his mother and his wife's sister what the defendant had said, and consequently the plaintiff's practice fell off considerably among Dawes' friends and acquaintances and others. The fee for one confinement was a guinea. *Held*, that the plaintiff was entitled to more than the one guinea; the jury should give him such a sum as they considered Dawes' custom was worth to him; but that the plaintiff clearly could not recover anything for the general decline of his business, which was caused by the gossip of Dawes' mother and sister-in-law.

Dixon v. *Smith*, 5 H. & N. 450; 29 L. J. Ex. 125.

The plaintiff invented a new portable camera, and offered it to A., who was willing to sell it to the public; but the defendant falsely stated to A. that it was an infringement of his patent. A.'s negotiations with the plaintiff were consequently broken off. *Held,* that the plaintiff was entitled to recover; that the proper measure of damages was the profits which the plaintiff would have derived from the proposed contract, if it had been carried out, during such period as the defendant's threats still operated to deter A. from dealing with the plaintiff; but that the plaintiff could not claim in respect of any profits which might have been earned under the contract after the litigation was over, and when all apprehension of interference by the defendant was removed.

Skinner & Co. v. *Shew & Co.* or *Perry,* [1894] 2 Ch. 581; 63 L. J. Ch. 826; 71 L. T. 110; 8 R. 455.

III.—SPECIAL DAMAGE WHERE THE WORDS ARE ACTIONABLE *PER SE.*

Where special damage is not essential to the action, it may still of course be proved at the trial to increase the amount of the damages, if it has been properly pleaded. The same particularity is required whether the words be actionable *per se* or not. So, too, the plaintiff must still prove that the special damage alleged is the direct result of the defendant's words, and not of any repetition of them by others. (*Tunnicliffe* v. *Moss,* 3 C. & K. 83; *Hirst* v. *Goodwin,* 3 F. & F. 257.) But in other respects the law is not quite so strict as to what constitutes special damage in the first case as in the second.

Thus, where the words are *not* actionable *per se,* we have seen that mental distress, illness, expulsion from a religious society, &c., do not constitute special damage. But where the words are actionable *per se,* the jury may, take such matters into their consideration in awarding damages. "Mental pain or anxiety the law cannot value, and does not pretend to redress, when the unlawful act complained of causes *that alone;* though where a material damage occurs, and is connected with it, it is impossible a jury, in estimating it, should altogether overlook the feelings of the party interested." (Per Lord Wensleydale, in *Lynch* v. *Knight and wife,* 9 H. L. C. 598. See also

c c 2

Haythorn v. *Lawson*, 3 C. & P. 196 ; *Le Fanu* v. *Malcolmson*, 8 Ir. L. R. 418.)

Again, where words are spoken of the plaintiff in the way of his profession or trade, so as to be actionable *per se*, the plaintiff may allege and prove a general diminution of profits or decline of trade, without naming particular customers or proving why they have ceased to deal with him. (*Ingram* v. *Lawson*, 6 Bing. N. C. 212 ; 8 Scott, 471 ; 4 Jur. 151 ; 9 C. & P. 326 ; *Harrison* v. *Pearce*, 1 F. & F. 569 ; 32 L. T. (Old S.) 298 ; and per Cresswell, J., in *Rose* v. *Groves*, 5 M. & Gr. 618, 619.) If, however, the plaintiff wishes to rely on the loss of particular customers, he must plead such loss specially (either in addition to, or without, the allegation of a general loss of business) ; and in that case he must call the customers named as witnesses at the trial. Still, if the customers are not called at the trial, or if for any other reason the proof of the special damage fails, the plaintiff may still recover on the general damage. (*Cook* v. *Field*, 3 Esp. 133 ; *Evans* v. *Harries*, 1 H. & N. 251 ; 26 L. J. Ex. 31.) The law already presumes that the plaintiff is injured in his business by the defendant's words ; evidence as to the nature of the plaintiff's business before and after publication is admissible to show the extent of such injury.

Lastly, where it is clear that the action lies without proof of any special damage, any loss or injury which the plaintiff has sustained in consequence of the defendant's words, even after action brought, may be proved to support the legal presumption, and to show from what has actually occurred how injurious and mischievous those words were.

Illustrations.

Where the defendant advertised in *Hue and Cry* that the plaintiff had been guilty of fraud, and offered a reward for his apprehension, and the plaintiff immediately sued on the libel, and after action brought was twice arrested in consequence of it : he was allowed to give evidence of these two arrests at the trial, not indeed as special damage, for they happened after action brought, but in order to show the injurious nature of the libel, and that the plaintiff was at time of action brought in serious danger of being arrested.

> *Goslin* v. *Corry,* 7 M. & Gr. 342 ; 8 Scott, N. R. 21.
> *MacLoughlin* v. *Welsh,* 10 Ir. L. R. 19.

Where the defendant published in a newspaper that a certain ship of the plaintiff's was unseaworthy, and had been purchased by the Jews to carry convicts, evidence as to the average profits of a voyage was admitted, and also evidence that upon the first voyage after the libel appeared the profits were nearly 1,500*l.* below the average, and this although the action was brought immediately after the libel appeared, and before the last-mentioned voyage was commenced. The jury, however, awarded the plaintiff only 900*l.* damages.

> *Ingram* v. *Lawson,* 6 Bing. N. C. 212 ; 8 Scott, 471.

Where a declaration alleged that the defendant spoke words of the plaintiff, a dissenting minister, in the way of his office and profession, and his congregation rapidly diminished, and he was compelled for a time to give up preaching altogether, and lost profits thereby ; it was held that this was a sufficient allegation of special damage, although the members of his congregation were not named.

> *Hartley* v. *Herring,* 8 T. R. 130.
> *Hopwood* v. *Thorn,* 8 C. B. 293 ; 19 L. J. C. P. 94 ; 14 Jur. 87.

In an action of libel, the plaintiff in his Statement of Claim alleged that he had been injured in his credit and business. He was allowed under this allegation to give general evidence of a decline of business, presumably due to the publication of the libel. He also tendered evidence of the loss of particular customers. But this had not been pleaded. *Held,* that the judge rightly rejected such evidence at the trial.

> *Bluck* v. *Lovering,* (1885) 1 Times L. R. 497.

Where words actionable *per se* are spoken of an innkeeper in the way of his trade, openly in his inn in the presence of his customers, evidence may be given of a general loss of custom and decline in his business.

> *Evans* v. *Harries,* 1 H. & N. 251 ; 26 L. J. Ex. 31.

But where the defendant charged the plaintiff with larceny in the hearing of H., and the words were repeated by H. to C., who in consequence refused to employ the plaintiff, evidence of such special damage was rejected.

> *Tunnicliffe* v. *Moss,* 3 C. & K. 83.
> *Rutherford* v. *Evans,* 4 C. & P. 74.
> *Hirst* v. *Goodwin,* 3 F. & F. 257.
> *Bateman and wife* v. *Lyall and wife,* 7 C. B. N. S. 638.
> *Clarke* v. *Morgan,* 38 L. T. 354.

IV.—EVIDENCE FOR THE PLAINTIFF IN AGGRAVATION OF DAMAGES.

The violence of the defendant's language, the nature of the imputation conveyed, and the fact that the defamation was deliberate and malicious, will of course enhance the damages. All the circumstances attending the publication may, therefore, be given in evidence, and any previous transactions between the plaintiff and the defendant which have any direct bearing on the subject-matter of the action, or are a necessary part of the history of the case. The jury will also consider the rank or position in society of the parties, the fact that the attack was entirely unprovoked, that the defendant could easily have ascertained that the charge he made was false, &c. Evidence may be given to show that the defendant was culpably reckless or grossly negligent in the matter. The attention of the jury should also be directed to the mode, the extent, and the long continuance of publication. Such evidence is admissible with a view to damages, although the publication has been admitted on the pleadings. (*Vines* v. *Serell*, 7 C. & P. 163.) So, the defendant's subsequent conduct may aggravate the damages; *e.g.*, if he has refused to listen to any explanation, or to retract the charge he made, or has only tardily published an inadequate apology. Lord Esher, M.R., in *Praed* v. *Graham*, 24 Q. B. D. at p. 55; 59 L. J. Q. B. 230; 38 W. R. 103; laid down the rule, that "the jury in assessing damages are entitled to look at the whole conduct of the defendant from the time the libel was published down to the time they give their verdict."

Evidence may be given of antecedent or subsequent libels or slanders to show *quo animo* the words were published. Thus such evidence is admissible to show that a communication *primâ facie* privileged was made maliciously (c. XII., p. 349); when evidence is necessary to explain the meaning of language which without it appears ambiguous (c. V., p. 112); and whenever a subsequent libel has reference to the one sued on, it will be admitted as a necessary part of the *res gestæ*. (*Finnerty* v. *Tipper*, 2 Camp. 72; *May* v. *Brown*, 3 B. & C. 113; 4 D. & R. 670.) It was at one time held that such evidence was not admissible where the occasion was not privileged, and the words of the libel were clear. (*Stuart* v. *Lovell*, 2 Stark. 93; *Pearce* v. *Ornsby*, 1 Moo. & Rob. 455; *Symmons* v. *Blake, ib.* 477; 2 C. M. & R. 416; 4 Dowl. 263; 1 Gale, 182.) But in *Pearson* v. *Lemaitre*, where the occasion was held to be not privileged, the Court laid down the following rule: "Either party may, with a view to the damages, give evidence to prove or disprove the existence of a malicious motive in the mind of the publisher of defamatory matter; but, if the evidence given for that purpose establishes another cause of action, the jury should be cautioned against giving any damages in respect of it. And, if such evidence is offered merely for the purpose of obtaining damages for such subsequent injury, it will be properly rejected." (5 M. & Gr. pp. 719, 720; 12 L. J. Q. B. 253; 6 Scott, N. R. 607; 7 Jur. 748; 7 J. P. 336.) And this has been followed by the Court of Appeal in *Anderson* v. *Calvert*, (1908) 24 Times L. R. 399.

The plaintiff cannot give evidence of general good character in aggravation of damages merely, unless such character is put in issue on the pleadings; or has been attacked by the cross-examination of the plaintiff's witnesses; for till then the plaintiff's character is presumed good. (*Cornwall* v. *Richardson*, Ry. & M. 305; *Guy* v. *Gregory*, 9 C. & P. 584, 587; *Brine* v. *Bazalgette*, 3 Exch. 692; 18 L. J. Ex. 348.) But such evidence is admissible when it goes to show that the defendant knew that the libel was false when he wrote it. (*Fountain* v. *Boodle*, 3 Q. B. 5; 2 G. & D. 455, *ante*, p. 362.)

In all these cases the malice proved must be that of the defendant. If two persons be sued, the motives of one must not be allowed to aggravate the damages against the other. (*Clark* v. *Newsam*, 1 Exch. 131, 139.) Nor should the improper motive of an agent be matter of aggravation against his principal. (*Robertson* v. *Wylde*, 2 Moo. & Rob. 101; but see *Citizens' Life Assurance Co., Ltd.* v. *Brown*, [1904] A. C. 423; 73 L. J. P. C. 102; 90 L. T. 739; 20 Times L. R. 497; and *ante*, p. 344.) So in America.

(*Scripps* v. *Reilly*, 38 Mich. 10 ; *Detroit* v. *McArthur*, 16 Mich. 447.)

Illustrations.

If the libel has appeared in a newspaper, proof that the particular number containing the libel was gratuitously circulated in the plaintiff's neighbourhood, or that its sale was in any way especially pushed, will enhance the damages.

> *Gathercole* v. *Miall,* 15 M. & W. 319 ; 15 L. J. Ex. 179 ;
> 10 Jur. 337.

If the libel was sold to the public indiscriminately, heavy damages should be given, for the defendant has put it out of his power to recall or contradict his statements, should he desire to do so.

> Per Lord Denman, 9 A. & E. at p. 149.
> Per Best, C.J., 5 Bing. at p. 402, *ante,* p. 375.

The number of copies of the libel circulated by the defendant may in some cases tend to aggravate the damages.

> *Parnell* v. *Walter and another,* 24 Q. B. D. 441 ; 59 L. J.
> Q. B. 125 ; 38 W. R. 270 ; 62 L. T. 75 ; 54 J. P. 311 ;
> 6 Times L. R. 138.
> *James* v. *Carr and others,* (1890) 7 Times L. R. 4.
> *Rumney* v. *Walter and another,* (1891) 61 L. J. Q. B. 149 ;
> 40 W. R. 174 ; 65 L. T. 757 ; 8 Times L. R. 96.
> *Whittaker* v. *Scarborough Post,* [1896] 2 Q. B. 148 ; 65 L. J.
> Q. B. 564 ; 44 W. R. 657 ; 74 L. T. 753 ; 12 Times L. R.
> 488.

The defendant printed a libel in the London edition of the *New York Herald,* knowing that it would be, as in fact it was, repeated and published in other editions of that paper published in France and other countries. Evidence of these facts would be admissible at the trial.

> *Whitney and others* v. *Moignard,* 24 Q. B. D. 630 ; 59 L. J.
> Q. B. 324 ; 6 Times L. R. 274.

And where there is no malice, gross negligence on the part of the proprietor of a newspaper in allowing the libel to appear in its columns, may be proved to enhance the damages.

> *Smith* v. *Harrison,* 1 F. & F. 565.

If other words, injurious and abusive, though not actionable *per se,* were uttered on the same occasion as the words complained of, these other words may be given in evidence as an aggravation of the actionable words. "Where a wrongful act is accompanied by words of contumely and abuse, the jury are warranted in taking that into consideration, and giving retributory damages."

> Per Byles, J., in *Bell* v. *Midland Rail. Co.,* 10 C. B. N. S.
> at p. 308.
> And see *Dodson* v. *Owen,* (1885) 2 Times L. R. 111, *ante,*
> p. 323.
> *Blagg* v. *Sturt,* 10 Q. B. 899 ; 16 L. J. Q. B. 39 ; 11 Jur.
> 101 ; 8 L. T. (Old S.) 135.
> *Merest* v. *Harvey,* 5 Taunt. 442, *ante,* p. 74.

The defendant's conduct of his case, even the language used by his counsel at the trial, may aggravate the damages.

> Per Pollock, C.B., *Darby* v. *Ouseley,* 25 L. J. Ex. 230, 233.
>
> *Blake* v. *Stevens and others,* 4 F. & F. 232 ; 11 L. T. 543.
>
> *Risk 'Allah Bey* v. *Whitehurst,* 18 L. T. 615.

So a plea of justification, if persisted in, but not proved, will enhance the damages.

> *Warwick* v. *Foulkes,* 12 M. & W. 508.
>
> *Wilson* v. *Robinson,* 7 Q. B. 68 ; 14 L. J. Q. B. 196 ; 9 Jur. 726.
>
> *Simpson* v. *Robinson,* 12 Q. B. 511 ; 18 L. J. Q. B. 73 ; 13 Jur. 187.

V.—EVIDENCE FOR THE DEFENDANT IN MITIGATION OF DAMAGES.

(i) *Evidence falling short of a Justification.*

The defendant may also urge upon the jury any material circumstance which he thinks will tend to mitigate the damages against him.

But this is of course subject to the general rule that circumstances, which, if pleaded, would have been a bar to the action, cannot be given in evidence in mitigation of damages. (*Speck* v. *Phillips,* 5 M. & W. 279 ; 8 L. J. Ex. 277 ; 7 Dowl. 470.) Evidence of the truth of the slander or libel is therefore inadmissible, unless a justification is pleaded. (*Underwood* v. *Parks,* 2 Strange, 1200 ; *Smith* v. *Richardson,* Willes, 20.) " Even in mitigation of damages it is well settled you cannot go into evidence which, if proved, would constitute a justification. Nor does it appear to me that it makes any difference that the evidence is offered in cross-examination." (Per Lord Halsbury, L.C., in *Watt* v. *Watt,* [1905] A. C. at p. 118.) And where the words are capable of two meanings, one innocent, the other harmful, evidence cannot be given, even in mitigation of damages, that in the innocent sense the words are literally true, without an express plea to that effect. (*Rumsey* v. *Webb et ux.,* Car. & M. 104 ; 11 L. J. C. P. 129.) *À fortiori,* evidence that there was a widespread report or rumour to the same effect as the words complained of is inadmissible ; for it clearly falls short of a justification, and is moreover objectionable as hearsay. (*Scott* v. *Sampson*, 8 Q. B. D. 491; 51 L. J. Q. B. 380; 30 W. R. 541; 46 L. T. 412.)   But a defendant may, if he place a proper plea on the record, give evidence in mitigation of damages that a certain specified portion of the defamatory words is true, provided such portion conveys a distinct imputation on the plaintiff and is divisible from the rest and yet intelligible by itself. (*M'Gregor* v. *Gregory*, 11 M. & W. 287; 12 L. J. Ex. 204; 2 Dowl. N. S. 769; *Lord Churchill* v. *Hunt*, 2 B. & Ald. 685; 1 Chit. 480; *Clarke* v. *Taylor and another*, 2 Bing. N. C. 654; 3 Scott, 95; *Davis* v. *Billing*, (1891) 8 Times L. R. 58.)   But the plea must clearly specify the precise portions justified. (*Stiles* v. *Nokes*, 7 East, 493.)   And without a special plea, evidence that part of the libel is true cannot be received. (*Vessey* v. *Pike*, 3 C. & P. 512.)

(ii) *Previous Publications by others.*

Evidence of previous publications by others is, as a rule, inadmissible even in mitigation of damages; that others besides the defendant have defamed the plaintiff is an irrelevant fact. (*Tucker* v. *Lawson*, (1886) 2 Times L. R. 593.) And so is the fact that on such former occasions the plaintiff did not sue the publisher or take any steps to contradict the charges made against him. (*R.* v. *Newman*, 1 E. & B. 268, 558; 22 L. J. Q. B. 156; 3 C. & K. 252; *R.* v. *Holt*, 5 T. R. 436; *Ingram* v. *Lawson*, 9 C. & P. 333; *Pankhurst* v. *Hamilton*, (1886) 2 Times L. R. 682.) And even when the falsehood thus unchallenged grows to a persistent rumour or general report, which the defendant hears, believes, and repeats; this is not regarded in law as a mitigating circumstance.   Evidence of any such rumour is inadmissible. (*Scott* v. *Sampson*, 8 Q. B. D. 491; 51 L. J. Q. B. 380; 30 W. R. 541; 46 L. T. 412.)

There is, however, one exception.   If the defendant in repeating the story as it reached him gives it as hearsay, and states the source of his information, then, but only then, is the fact that he did not originate the falsehood, but innocently repeated it, allowed to tell in his favour, as proving that he bore the plaintiff no malice. Thus, where it appears on the face of a libel that it is founded on a statement in a certain newspaper, the defendant is entitled to show that he did in fact read such statement in that newspaper, and wrote the libel believing such statement to be true. (*R.* v. *Burdett*, 4 B. & Ald. 95 ; *Mullett* v. *Hulton*, 4 Esp. 248 ; *Hunt* v. *Algar*, 6 C. & P. 245.) So, if in the libel the defendant has named A. as his informant, he may prove in mitigation that he did in fact receive such information from A., though of course this is no defence to the action. (*Tidman* v. *Ainslie*, 10 Exch. 63 ; *Bennett* v. *Bennett*, 6 C. & P. 588; *Mills and wife* v. *Spencer and wife*, Holt, N. P. 533 ; *East* v. *Chapman*, M. & M. 46 ; 2 C. & P. 570 ; *Duncombe* v. *Daniell*, 2 Jur. 32 ; 8 C. & P. 222 ; cited 7 Dowl. 472 ; *Davis* v. *Cutbush and others*, 1 F. & F. 487.) But where the libel does not, on the face of it, purport to be derived from any one, but is stated as of the writer's own knowledge, there evidence is wholly inadmissible to show that it was copied from a newspaper or communicated by a correspondent. (*Talbutt* v. *Clark and another*, 2 Moo. & Rob. 312.) Nevertheless, if the defendant can show that in copying the libel from another newspaper he was careful to omit certain passages which reflected strongly on the plaintiff, his conduct in making such omissions is admissible as showing the absence of *animus* against the plaintiff, and this necessarily involves the admissibility of the original libel copied. (*Creevy* v. *Carr*, 7 C. & P. 64 ; *Creighton* v. *Finlay*, Arm. Mac. & Ogle (Ir.), 385 ; and see *De Bensaude* v. *Conservative Newspaper Co.*, (1887) 3 Times L. R. 538.)

Illustrations.

Mrs. Evans told Mrs. Spencer that she was going to Mrs. Mills' house to learn dress making ; Mrs. Spencer thereupon told Mrs. Evans a few things about Mrs. Mills, which she said Mrs. Lewis and Mrs. Sayer had told her. Gibbs, C.J., would have admitted evidence apparently that these ladies had, in fact, told Mrs. Spencer what she told Mrs. Evans :

but it turned out it was somebody else who had said so, and not the two ladies whom she named as her authorities. Evidence of what was said by these third persons, who were not named by Mrs. Spencer when she uttered the words complained of, was excluded.

> *Mills and wife* v. *Spencer and wife,* (1817) Holt, N. P. 533.

On the day of the nomination of candidates for the representation of the borough of Finsbury, the defendant published in the *Morning Post* certain facts discreditable to one of the candidates, the plaintiff, which he alleged he had heard from one Wilkinson at a meeting of the electors. *Held,* that Wilkinson was an admissible witness to prove, in mitigation of damages, that he did, in fact, make the statement which the defendant had published at the time and place alleged.

> *Duncombe* v. *Daniell,* 2 Jur. 32 ; 8 C. & P. 222 ; 1 W. W. & H. 101.

The *Observer* published an inaccurate report of the trial of an action brought against the plaintiff. The defendant copied this report *verbatim* into his paper. *Held,* that evidence that many other papers besides the defendant's had also copied the statement from the *Observer* was inadmissible.

> *Saunders* v. *Mills,* 6 Bing. 213 ; 3 M. & P. 520.
>
> *Tucker* v. *Lawson,* (1886) 2 Times L. R. 593.

Evidence that the defendant had copied it from the *Observer* into his own paper had been admitted apparently without question at the trial ; but in allowing that evidence, Tindal, C.J., says (6 Bing. 220) : "It appeared to me I had gone the full length." In *Talbutt* v. *Clark* (2 Moo. & Rob. 312), Lord Denman says, referring, no doubt, to *Saunders* v. *Mills,* "I know that in a case in the Common Pleas it has been held that a previous statement in another newspaper is admissible ; but even that decision had been very much questioned."

One officer charged another with stealing a watch ; a third officer in the same regiment was called to state that he had previously heard rumours that the plaintiff had stolen that watch, but his evidence was rejected ; and the Court held that such rejection was right (Pigot, C.B., dissenting).

> *Bell* v. *Parke,* (1860) 11 Ir. C. L. R. 413.

Kelly, C.B., is reported to have given a similar ruling in

> *Dobede* v. *Fisher, Times,* July 29th, 1880.

It is now clearly settled that evidence of such rumours is inadmissible.

> *Scott* v. *Sampson,* 8 Q. B. D. 491 ; 51 L. J. Q. B. 380 ; 30 W. R. 541 ; 46 L. T. 412 ; 46 J. P. 408.
>
> *Wilson* v. *Fitch,* 41 Cal. 363.

But where a libel on the plaintiff, who was Surveyor-General of Upper Canada, was contained in a pamphlet which was not generally circulated, copies being sent only to the principal civil officers of the province, one of whom was called as a witness by the plaintiff, Gibbs, C.J., allowed the defendant's counsel to ask the witness whether he did not read the substance of the libel in a public newspaper before he received the pamphlet. And this, although the pamphlet did not profess to be founded on the newspaper. Such cross-examination is permissible in mitigation of damages, as showing that it was the former publication in the newspaper, and not the subsequent publication of the pamphlet which injured the plaintiff's reputation.

Wyatt v. *Gore,* (1816) Holt, N. P. 299, 304.

(iii) *Liability of others.*

At common law, if the present defendant is liable, the fact that some one else is also liable is immaterial. It will not diminish the amount recoverable from the present defendant, to show that the plaintiff has recovered, or might recover, other damages from others; for each defendant in his turn pays damages for the injury which he himself has occasioned, not for the injury done by others.

But now by s. 6 of the Law of Libel Amendment Act, 1888 (51 & 52 Vict. c. 64), "at the trial of an action for a libel contained in any newspaper, the defendant shall be at liberty to give in evidence in mitigation of damages that the plaintiff has already recovered (or has brought actions for) damages, or has received, or agreed to receive, compensation in respect of a libel or libels to the same purport or effect as the libel for which such action has been brought."

Thus, in cases of slander, the defendant is only liable for such damages as result directly from his own utterance. If he chooses to repeat what another has said, that is his own conscious and voluntary act, for the results of which he alone is responsible. If, on the other hand, others choose to repeat his words, the defendant is not liable for the consequences of such repetition. (See *post*, p. 413.) So in cases of libel, if two newspapers have made each a distinct charge against the plaintiff, and subsequently the plaintiff finds his business falling off, whichever paper he sues may endeavour to show that the loss of trade is due, or partly due, to the charge made against the plaintiff by the other paper. And if there are two distinct and separate publications of the same libel, a defendant who was concerned in the first publication, but wholly unconnected with the second, will not be liable for any damages which he can prove to have been the consequence of the second publication and in no way due to the first.

Further than this the common law did not go. The defendant

could not give any evidence to show that the plaintiff had already sued those who were liable for other publications of the same or a similar libel, and recovered damages, although he might be cross-examined on the matter, if he went into the box. (*Creevy* v. *Carr*, 7 C. & P. 64; *Frescoe* v. *May*, 2 F. & F. 123.) Evidence that other actions were pending against other persons for other publications of the same libel was also inadmissible. (*Harrison* v. *Pearce*, 1 F. & F. 567; 32 L. T. (Old S.) 298.) But in these days, when any sensational paragraph which appears in one newspaper is invariably copied into many others, it was deemed advisable to alter the law on this point, and the above section was accordingly passed: see *post*, p. 696.

(iv) *Absence of Malice.*

As a rule, unless the occasion be privileged, the motive or intention of the speaker or writer is immaterial to the right of action: the court looks only at the words employed and their effect on the plaintiff's reputation. But in all cases, the absence of malice, though it may not be a bar to the action, may yet have a material effect in reducing the damages. The plaintiff is still entitled to reasonable compensation for the injury which he has sustained; but if the injury was unintentional, or was committed under a sense of duty, or through some honest mistake, clearly no vindictive damages should be given. In every case, therefore, the defendant may, in mitigation of damages, give evidence to show that he acted in good faith and with honesty of purpose, and not maliciously. (*Pearson* v. *Lemaitre*, 5 M. & Gr. 700; 12 L. J. Q. B. 253; 6 Scott, N. R. 607; 7 Jur. 748; 7 J. P. 336.) He may show that the remainder of the article not set out on the record modifies the words sued on; or that other passages in the same publication qualify them. But he may not put in passages contained in a subsequent and distinct publication, unless the words sued on are equivocal or ambiguous. (*Cooke* v. *Hughes*, R. & M. 112; *Darby* v. *Ouseley*, 1 H. & N. 1; 25 L. J. Ex. 227; 2 Jur. N. S. 497.) The fact that the defendant did not originate the calumny, but innocently repeated it, is admissible if he gave it as hearsay, and named his authority when he repeated it, but not otherwise, as we have seen, *ante*, p. 394. The defendant may also urge that the plaintiff's conduct was such as would naturally lead the defendant to put the worst construction on his acts; or that in some other way the plaintiff had, by his conduct, brought the libel on himself. So, the defendant's subsequent conduct may mitigate the damages, *e.g.*, if he showed himself open to argument, listened to the explanations that were offered him, stopped the sale of the libel as soon as complaint reached him, &c.

In some cases, as we have seen, the plaintiff's conduct towards the defendant may be a bar to the action; as where the plaintiff, by attacking the defendant, has provoked a reply which is made honestly in self-defence. (See *ante*, p. 291.) But where the facts do not amount to such a defence, they may still tend to mitigate the damages. "There can be no set-off of one libel or misconduct against another; but in estimating the compensation for the plaintiff's injured feelings, the jury might fairly consider the plaintiff's conduct, and the degree of respect he has shown for the feelings of others." (Per Blackburn, J., in *Kelly* v. *Sherlock*, L. R. 1 Q. B. 698; 35 L. J. Q. B. 213; 12 Jur. N. S. 937.) Thus, evidence is admissible in mitigation of damages to show that the plaintiff had previously himself libelled or slandered the defendant, provided it be also shown that this had come to the defendant's knowledge and occasioned his attack on the plaintiff. (*Finnerty* v. *Tipper*, 2 Camp. 76; *Anthony Pasquin's Case*, cited 1 Camp. 351; *Tarpley* v. *Blabey*, 2 Bing. N. C. 437; 2 Scott, 642; 7 C. & P. 395; *Watts* v. *Fraser*, 7 A. & E. 223; 7 C. & P. 369; 1 M. & Rob. 449; 2 N. & P. 157; *Wakley* v. *Johnson*, Ry. & M. 422.) But not, if such previous libels refer to other matters and did not provoke that sued on. (*May* v. *Brown*, 3 B. & C. 113; 4 D. & R. 670; *Sheffill* v. *Van Deusen*, 15 Gray, 485.) The defendant may not branch out into irrelevant matters in his evidence; he may cross-examine the plaintiff thereon; but if he does, he must take the plaintiff's answer; he cannot call evidence to contradict it.

Where no justification is pleaded, the defendant will not be entitled on the trial to give evidence in chief, with a view to mitigation of damages, as to the circumstances under which the libel or slander was published, without the leave of the judge, unless he has seven days at least before the trial furnished particulars to the plaintiff of the matters as to which he intends to give evidence. (Order XXXVI. r. 37.) See *post*, p. 402.

The previous libels and slanders may be made the matter of a counterclaim, even though not immediately connected with the words on which the plaintiff is suing; and the defendant may thus not only reduce the amount of damages due to the plaintiff, but even overtop the plaintiff's claim, and recover judgment for the balance. (*Quin* v. *Hession*, 40 L. T. 70; 4 L. R. Ir. 35.) And where there is no counterclaim, the previous conduct of the plaintiff may be ground for applying to the judge to deprive him of costs. (*Harnett* v. *Vise and Wife*, 5 Ex. D. 307; 29 W. R. 7.)

Illustrations.

The defendant published an inaccurate report of proceedings in a court of justice, reflecting on the character of the plaintiff; any evidence to show that the defendant honestly intended to present a fair account of what took place, and had blundered through inadvertence solely, was held admissible by Coleridge, J., in

> *Smith* v. *Scott,* 2 Car. & Kir. 580.

And, therefore, evidence of what really did take place at the trial is admissible; though no evidence can be given of the truth or falsehood of the statements there made.

> *East* v. *Chapman,* M. & M. 46; 2 C. & P. 570.
>
> *Vessey* v. *Pike,* 3 C. & P. 512.
>
> *Charlton* v. *Watton,* 6 C. & P. 385.

Where a newspaper republished the report of a company containing reflections on the plaintiff, their manager, Wightman, J., directed the jury that if they were satisfied such publication was made innocently, and with no desire to injure the plaintiff, they might give nominal damages only.

> *Davis* v. *Cutbush and others,* 1 F. & F. 487.

Where an editor refused to disclose the name of his correspondent who wrote the libel, but offered to open his columns to the plaintiff, and the plaintiff accepted this offer and wrote several letters which the defendants published, replying to the charges made against him and explaining them away, Martin, B., directed the jury to take these circumstances into their consideration in favour of the defendants.

> *Harle* v. *Catherall and others,* 14 L. T. 801.

A libel by A. on B. is no justification for an assault by B. on A., though if A. sue for the assault, B. may give the libel in evidence to show provocation, and thus reduce the damages.

> *Fraser* v. *Berkeley,* 7 C. & P. 621 ; 2 M. & R. 3.
> *Keiser* v. *Smith,* 46 Amer. Rep. 342.

(v) *Evidence of the Plaintiff's Bad Character.*

One way, but a very dangerous one, of minimising the damages, is to show that the plaintiff's previous character was so notoriously bad that it could not be impaired by any fresh accusation, even though undeserved. The gist of the action is the injury done to the plaintiff's reputation ; and if the plaintiff had no reputation to be injured, he cannot be entitled to more than nominal damages. Hence the fact that the plaintiff had a general bad character before the date of the libel or slander may, after due notice, be given in evidence in mitigation of damages. But the defendant may not go into particular instances ; still less may he prove the existence of a general report that the plaintiff had actually committed the particular offence of which the defendant accused him or any similar offence. (*Scott* v. *Sampson,* 8 Q. B. D. 491 ; 51 L. J. Q. B. 380 ; 30 W. R. 541 ; 46 L. T. 412 ; and see *Wood* v. *Earl of Durham,* 21 Q. B. D. 501 ; 57 L. J. Q. B. 547 ; 37 W. R. 222 ; 59 L. T. 142 ; and *Wood* v. *Cox,* (1888) 4 Times L. R. at p. 655.)

If, however, the plaintiff goes into the box, he can of course be cross-examined "to credit" on details of his previous life which affect his credit ; but, unless such details are material to the issue, the defendant must take the plaintiff's answer, and cannot call evidence ot contradict it.

Evidence as to the plaintiff's general bad character will not, however, be admissible unless it be shown that his character was such previously to the alleged libel or slander ; for otherwise his evil reputation may have been occasioned by the defendant's own publication, which would rather aggravate than diminish the damages. (*Thompson* v. *Nye,* 16 Q. B. 175 ; 20 L. J. Q. B. 85 ; 15 Jur. 285.) And now

O.L.S. D D

by Order XXXVI. r. 37, a defendant who has not justified
will not be entitled on the trial to give evidence in chief,
with a view to mitigation of damages, as to the character
of the plaintiff, without the leave of the judge, unless he
has seven days at least before the trial furnished particulars
to the plaintiff of the matters as to which he intends to give
evidence.

There had been a conflict of opinion as to the admissibility of
evidence of the plaintiff's general bad character, and of rumours
prejudicial to his reputation; but the law on the point was settled
by the decision in *Scott* v. *Sampson, suprà.* It is, therefore, no longer
necessary to refer in detail to the numerous scantily reported and
conflicting rulings on the point at Nisi Prius, which are dealt with
in that exhaustive judgment. The following cases, which are not
referred to, bear out the decision: *Woolmer* v. *Latimer*, 1 Jur. 119;
Mills and wife v. *Spencer and wife*, Holt, N. P. 533; *Rodriguez* v.
T'admire, 2 Esp. 721. The Irish case *Bell* v. *Parke*, 11 Ir. C. L. R.
413, is consistent with *Scott* v. *Sampson*, except in one point: the
Irish judges admitted evidence that the plaintiff had certain
vicious habits which would lead him to commit such acts as
that ascribed to him in the slander. This ruling will not be
followed in England.

But the decision in *Scott* v. *Sampson* does not in any way
restrict the defendant's liberty of cross-examination. Lord
Coleridge did not exclude any question put by the defendant's
counsel to any witness called by the plaintiff. Hence we apprehend
that *Wyatt* v. *Gore*, Holt, N. P. 299; and *Snowdon* v. *Smith*, 1 M.
& S. 286, n., which were not cited in *Scott* v. *Sampson*, as well as
Newsam v. *Carr*, 2 Stark. 69, which is referred to, are still good law.
We do not think they are to be considered as overruled by *Bracegirdle*
v. *Bailey*, 1 F. & F. 536, as in that case the plaintiff had given
no evidence in chief, so that questions merely to credit were
inadmissible, and, moreover, the questions rejected tended to show
that the libel was true, and no justification had been pleaded. (See
ante, p. 393.)

And note that Order XXXVI. r. 37, in no way restricts the right
of cross-examination; the following rule of the same order attempts
to do that; rule 37 does not. It is confined to evidence tendered by
the defendant in chief. And further it in no way alters the substantive rules of evidence, but only the procedure relative thereto. It

merely defines the proper method of getting admissible facts in evidence; it makes no matter admissible in evidence which was not admissible before. (*Mangena* v. *Wright,* [1909] 2 K. B. 958; 78 L. J. K. B. 879; 100 L. T. 960.) Thus evidence of rumours and of particular facts and circumstances, tending to show misconduct on the part of the plaintiff, will not be admitted in reduction of damages, but only evidence of his general bad character. (*Scott* v. *Sampson, suprà; Mangena* v. *Wright, suprà.*) But the Court held further that, assuming such evidence to be in other respects admissible, the particular facts and circumstances must be stated or referred to in the Defence, deeming this to be necessary under Order XIX r. 4. It is to this latter ruling that Order XXXVI. r. 37 is addressed. The pleading is not the proper place for such allegations, which are not material to any issue, but only affect the amount of damages. (See *Wood* v. *Earl of Durham, suprà,* and *post,* p. 644.) Yet it is only fair to the plaintiff that he should have some notice before the trial that this peculiarly offensive line will be taken by the defendant. Hence the Rule Committee required particulars of such evidence as is otherwise admissible in mitigation of damages to be stated, no longer in the Defence, but in a special notice to be delivered seven days at least before the trial.

Illustrations.

In an action for words imputing adultery to a widow, Holroyd, J., held that it was competent to the defendant to go into general evidence to impeach the plaintiff's character for chastity.

Ellershaw v. *Robinson et ux.,* (1824) 2 Starkie on Libel, 2nd ed. p. 90.

And Lord Tenterden is said to have admitted similar evidence, although a justification was pleaded.

Mawby v. *Barber,* (1826) 2 Starkie on Evidence, p. 470.

And see *Maynard* v. *Beardsley,* 7 Wend. 560.

When such general evidence has been given, the plaintiff's counsel may go into particular instances to rebut it.

Rodriguez v. *Tadmire,* 2 Esp. 721.

(vi) *Absence of Special Damage.*

When any special damage is alleged, the *onus* of proving it lies of course on the plaintiff. The defendant may call evidence to rebut the plaintiff's proof, though he generally prefers to rely upon the cross-examination of the plaintiff's witnesses. He may either dispute that the special damage has occurred at all, or he may argue as a matter of law that it is too remote (see *post*, p. 406); or he may call evidence to show that it was not the consequence of the defendant's words, but of some other cause. A plaintiff may not recover the same damages for the same injury twice from two different defendants; but he may recover from two different defendants damages proportioned to the injury which each has occasioned. (*Harrison* v. *Pearce*, 1 F. & F. 567; 32 L. T. (Old S.) 298; *Wyatt* v. *Gore*, Holt, N. P. 299, *ante*, p. 397.)

(vii) *Apology and Amends.*

By Lord Campbell's Act (6 & 7 Vict. c. 96), s. 1, it is enacted, that "in any action for defamation it shall be lawful for the defendant (after notice in writing of his intention so to do, duly given to the plaintiff at the time of filing or delivering the plea in such action) to give in evidence, in mitigation of damages, that he made or offered an apology to the plaintiff for such defamation before the commencement of the action, or as soon afterwards as he had an opportunity of doing so, in case the action shall have been commenced before there was an opportunity of making or offering such apology."

And by s. 2, that "in an action for a libel contained in any public newspaper or other periodical publication, it shall be competent to the defendant to plead that such libel was inserted in such newspaper or other periodical publication without actual malice, and without gross negligence, and that, before the commencement of the action, or at the earliest opportunity afterwards, he inserted in such newspaper or other periodical publication a full apology for the said libel, or if the newspaper or periodical publication in which the said libel appeared should be ordinarily published at intervals exceeding one week, had offered to publish the said apology in any newspaper or periodical publication to be selected by the plaintiff in such action; . . . and that to such plea to such action it shall be competent to the plaintiff to reply generally, denying the whole of such plea." (See *Chadwick* v. *Herapath*, 3 C. B. 885; 16 L. J. C. P. 104; 4 D. & L. 653.) Money must be paid into Court by way of amends at the time any plea under s. 2 is delivered, or it will be treated as a nullity (8 & 9 Vict. c. 75, s. 2). Hence no other defence denying liability can now be joined with such a plea. (Order XXII. r. 1; and see *O'Brien* v. *Clement*, 3 D. & L. 676; 15 M. & W. 435; 15 L. J. Ex. 285; 10 Jur. 395; and *Barry* v. *M'Grath*, Ir. R. 3 C. L. 576.) But the fact that such a payment has been made must not be mentioned to the jury. (Order XXII. r. 22.)

There is a difference between the language of the two sections as to the date at which the apology must appear; but they both mean the same thing. It will not be sufficient for the defendant under s. 2 to plead that the apology was inserted "at the earliest opportunity after" the commencement of the action, if there was an opportunity before. (Per Keating, J., in *Ravenhill* v. *Upcott*, 20 L. T. 233; 33 J. P. 299; and see *Evening News* v. *Tryon*, 36 Amer. R. 450.)

There appears to be no English decision reported as to what is, and what is not, "gross negligence" in the conduct of a newspaper. But in America it has been decided that the jury may take into consideration the hurry necessarily incident to the preparation and publication of a daily newspaper, as where an article is brought in at the last moment before going to press (*Scripps* v. *Reilly*, 38 Mich. 10); but that the excitement of an election is no excuse for negligence. (*Rearick* v. *Wilcox*, 81 Ill. 77.)

But wholly apart from these sections, a defendant may give evidence of any apology or other amends in mitigation of damages; even though such apology was not made "at the earliest opportunity after the commencement of the action." (*Smith* v. *Harrison*, 1 F. & F. 565.) Still a tardy or reluctant apology will not avail the defendant much. A retractation should be made as publicly as the charge, and as far as possible to the same persons; and the defendant should do his utmost to stop the further sale of the libel.

The sufficiency or insufficiency of an apology is peculiarly a question for the jury. (*Risk Allah Bey* v. *Johnstone*, 18 L. T. 620.) But a statement cannot be called an apology, unless it both unreservedly withdraws all imputation and expresses regret for having made it. The defendant must not try to exculpate himself or justify his conduct. (See *post*, p. 614.) The fact that other persons who were similarly slandered on the same occasion have accepted an apology from the defendant and not brought actions, is not admissible in evidence in an action brought by the plaintiff, especially if no apology was offered to the plaintiff. (*Tait* v. *Beggs*, [1905] 2 Ir. R. 525.)

The apology should be full, though it need not be abject; the defendant is not bound to insert an apology dictated by the plaintiff; but it must be such as an impartial person would consider reasonably satisfactory under all the circumstances of the case. (*Risk Allah Bey* v. *Johnstone*, 18 L. T. 620.) The apology should be printed in as conspicuous a place and manner as the libel was. It should be printed in type of ordinary size, and in a part of the paper where it will be seen; not hidden away among the advertisements or notices to correspondents. (*Lafone* v. *Smith*, 3 H. & N. 735; 28 L. J. Ex. 33; 4 Jur. N. S. 1064.)

So, too, a defendant may now, with or without any apology, pay money into court by way of satisfaction or amends, at any time between service of the writ and delivering his Defence, or by leave of a master at chambers at any later time. But if such payment into court be made, no defence denying liability can be pleaded. (Order XXII. r. 1; and see *post*, p. 640.)

VI.—Remoteness of Damages.

The special damage alleged must be the natural and probable result of the defendant's wrongful conduct. "Remoteness as a legal ground for the exclusion of damage in an action of tort means, not severance in point of time, but the absence of direct and natural causal sequence."

(Per Kennedy, J., in *Dulieu* v. *White & Sons*, [1901] 2 K. B. at p. 678.)   In some cases it can be shown that the defendant contemplated and desired such result at the time of publication : in other cases the result is so clearly the natural and necessary consequence of the libel or slander that it may fairly be said the defendant ought to have contemplated it, whether in fact he did so or not.   But where the damage sustained by the plaintiff is neither the necessary and reasonable result of the defendant's conduct, nor such as can be shown to have been in the defendant's contemplation at the time, there the damage will be held too remote.   Evidence cannot be given at the trial of any special damage which would not flow from the defendant's words in the ordinary course of things, unless there are special circumstances in the case which show that the defendant intended and desired that result.   It is not enough that his words have in fact produced such damage, unless it can reasonably be presumed that the defendant, when he uttered the words, either intended that such damage should ensue, or ought to have known that it would.

Illustrations.

The defendant insinuated that the plaintiff had been guilty of the murder of one Daniel Dolly ;   the plaintiff thereupon demanded that an inquest should be taken on Dolly's body, and incurred expense thereby. *Held,* that such expense was recoverable as special damage ;   though it was not *compulsory* on the plaintiff to have an inquest held.

> *Peake* v. *Oldham,* Cowp. 275 ;   2 W. Bl. 960.

"Suppose that during the war of 1870, an Englishman had been pointed out to a Parisian mob as a German spy, and thrown by them into the Seine, it could not be contended that one act was not the natural and necessary consequence of the other."

> Mayne on Damages, 8th ed. p. 569.
> *R.* v. *Burns and others,* 16 Cox, C. C. 355.

The defendant said to Mr. Knight of his wife Mrs. Knight, "Jane is a notorious liar . . . she was all but seduced by a Dr. C., of Roscommon, and I advise you, if C. comes to Dublin, not to permit him to enter your place. . . . She is an infamous wretch, and I am sorry that you had the misfortune to marry her, and if you 'had asked my advice on the subject, I would have advised you not to marry her."   Knight thereupon turned his wife out of the house, and sent her home to her father, and

refused to live with her any longer. *Held,* that loss of *consortium* of
the husband can constitute special damage ; but that in this case the
husband's conduct was not the natural or reasonable consequence of the
defendant's slander. *Secus,* had the words imputed actual adultery since
the marriage.

> *Lynch* v. *Knight and wife,* 9 H. L. C. 577 ; 8 Jur. N. S. 724.
> *Parkins et ux.* v. *Scott et ux.,* 1 H. & C. 153 ; 31 L. J.
>   Ex. 331 ; 8 Jur. N. S. 593 ; 10 W. R. 562 ; 6 L. T. 394 ;
>   *post,* p. 412.

Where the libel attacked the character of both husband and wife and
the declaration alleged that the wife fell ill and died in consequence of
it, evidence of such damage was excluded in an action brought by the
surviving husband.

> *Guy* v. *Gregory,* 9 C. & P. 584.

A declaration alleged that the defendant falsely and maliciously spoke
of the plaintiff, a working stonemason, "He was the ringleader of the
nine hours system," and "He has ruined the town by bringing about the
nine hours system," and "He has stopped several good jobs from being
carried out, by being the ringleader of the system at Llanelly," whereby
the plaintiff was prevented from obtaining employment in his trade at
Llanelly. *Held,* on demurrer, that the alleged damage was not the natural
or reasonable consequence of the speaking of such words, and that the
action could not be sustained.

> *Miller* v. *David,* L. R. 9 C. P. 118 ; 43 L. J. C. P. 84 ; 22
>   W. R. 332 ; 30 L. T. 58.

The plaintiff was a barman. The defendant said to the plaintiff's employers : "You have a barman in your employ who has removed from
his landlord's house, leaving 2*l.* owing for a month's rent, and I cannot
get the money from him." The plaintiff was thereupon dismissed from
his employment. *Held,* that the loss of employment could not reasonably be looked upon as a consequence of the words complained of.

> *Speake* v. *Hughes,* [1904] 1 K. B. 138 ; 73 L. J. K. B. 172 ;
>   89 L. T. 576.

The plaintiff was ejected from the defendants' licensed premises by
their servant who said he was drunk. The plaintiff, fearing that this
would be reported to his father, himself informed his father of the occurrence, who thereupon told the plaintiff he would have to resign his
directorship of a company, of which the father held the control, unless
he cleared his character. The plaintiff to clear his character sued the
defendants for slander. *Held,* that even assuming the plaintiff had suffered
damage, it was not caused by the act of the defendants or their servant,
and could not be pleaded.

> *Michael* v. *Spiers and Pond, Ltd.,* (1909) 101 L. T. 352 ; 25
>   Times L. R. 740.

The plaintiff was the owner of a house which was reported to be
haunted. The defendants gave publicity to this report in their newspaper, and were sued by the plaintiff for disparagement of his property.
It was proved that the value of the house had diminished owing to it
having the reputation of being haunted, but such reputation had been

acquired before the publication by the defendants. *Held,* that the action failed for want of proof of special damage.

> *Barrett* v. *Associated Newspapers, Ltd.,* (1907) 23 Times L. R. 666.

The special damage must be the direct result of the defendant's words. The jury may not take into their consideration any damage which is produced, not so much by the defendant's words as by some other fact or circumstance unconnected with the defendant, such as the spontaneous act of a third person. The defendant's words must at all events be the *predominating* cause of the damage assigned.

Illustrations.

The defendant slandered the plaintiff to his master B. Subsequently B. discovered from another source that the plaintiff's former master had dismissed him for misconduct. Thereupon B. discharged the plaintiff in the middle of the term for which he had engaged his services. *Held,* that no action lay against the defendant; for his words alone had not caused B. to dismiss the plaintiff.

> *Vicars* v. *Wilcocks,* 8 East, 1; 2 Sm. L. C. 553 (8th ed.).
> As explained in *Lynch* v. *Knight and wife,* 9 H. L. C. 590, 600.
> *Michael* v. *Spiers and Pond, Ltd.,* (1909) 101 L. T. 352; 25 Times L. R. 740.

Bingham caused a libel on the plaintiff, the proprietor of a newspaper, to be printed by Hinchcliffe as a placard, and distributed 5,000 such placards. He also put the same libel into a rival newspaper, the defendant's, as an advertisement. The plaintiff sued both Bingham and Hinchcliffe as well as the defendant, alleging that the circulation of his paper had greatly declined. The action against the defendant came on first, and his counsel having failed to prove the justification pleaded, contended that the decline of circulation must principally be ascribed to the 5,000 placards, not to the advertisement. Martin, B., while admitting that the defendant was not liable for damage caused by the placards, ruled that it lay on the defendant to prove that the damage sustained by the plaintiff was in fact due to the placard, and not to the advertisement. Verdict for the plaintiff, 500*l.* In the action against Bingham and Hinchcliffe the plaintiff recovered only 40*s.* The 500*l.* was probably due to the justification pleaded and not proved.

> *Harrison* v. *Pearce,* 1 F. & F. 567; 32 L. T. (Old S.) 298.
> *Wyatt* v. *Gore,* Holt, N. P. 299, *ante,* p. 397.

The plaintiff alleged that certain persons would have recommended him to X., Y., and Z., had not the defendant spoken certain defamatory words of him on the Royal Exchange, and that X., Y., and Z. would, on the recommendation of those persons, have taken the plaintiff into their employment. The plaintiff claimed damages for the loss of the employment. Such damage was *held* too remote, for it was caused by the non-recommendation, not by the defendant's words.

> *Sterry* v. *Foreman,* 2 C. & P. 592.
>
> And see *Hoey* v. *Felton,* 11 C. B. N. S. 142 ; 31 L. J.,
> C. P. 105.

The plaintiff was a candidate for membership of the Reform Club, but upon a ballot of the members was not elected. Subsequently a meeting of the members was called to consider an alteration of the rules regarding the election of members. Before the day fixed for the meeting the defendant spoke certain words concerning the plaintiff, which "induced or contributed to inducing a majority of the members of the club to retain the regulations under which the plaintiff had been rejected, and thereby prevented the plaintiff from again seeking to be elected to the club." *Held,* that the damage alleged was not pecuniary or capable of being estimated in money, and was not the natural and probable consequence of the defendant's words.

> *Chamberlain* v. *Boyd,* 11 Q. B. D. 407 ; 52 L. J. Q. B. 277 ;
> 31 W. R. 572 ; 48 L. T. 328 ; 47 J. P. 372.

In an action of slander of title to a patent, the plaintiff alleged as special damage that in consequence of the defendant's opposition, the Solicitor-General refused to allow the letters-patent to be granted with an amended title, as the plaintiff desired. *Held,* that this damage was too remote, being the act of the Solicitor-General and not of the defendant.

> *Haddon* v. *Lott,* 15 C. B. 411 ; 24 L. J. C. P. 49.
>
> *Kerr* v. *Shedden,* 4 C. & P. 528.

Special damage alleged, that in consequence of the defendant's words, Butler would not deliver some barley which the plaintiff had bought of him, except for cash on delivery. Butler, being called, admitted in cross-examination that he should have insisted on cash on delivery anyhow, even if the defendant had never said anything at all, and that that was his understanding of the contract between himself and the plaintiff, *Held,* no special damage.

> *King* v. *Watts,* 8 C. & P. 614.

The act of a third party, if directly caused by the defendant's language, is not too remote, provided the defendant either did contemplate or ought to have contemplated such a result. The defendant cannot be held liable for any eccentric or foolish conduct on the part of the person he addressed; but only for the ordinary and reasonable consequences of his words. The fact that such act is in itself a ground of action by the plaintiff against such third party is immaterial.

Formerly this was much doubted. It was held in *Vicars* v. *Wilcocks*, 8 East, 1; 2 Sm. L. C. 521 (11th edition), that where the plaintiff's master was induced by the slander to dismiss the plaintiff from his employ before the end of the term for which they had contracted, such dismissal was too remote to be special damage, because it was a mere wrongful act of the master, for which the plaintiff could sue him. The same doctrine was laid down in *Morris* v. *Langdale*, 2 B. & P. 284; and *Kelly* v. *Partington*, 5 B. & Ad. 645; 3 N. & M. 116. But this is clearly contrary to *Davis* v. *Gardiner*, 4 Rep. 16; *ante*, p. 378, and the numerous other cases in which loss of a marriage was held to constitute special damage, although the plaintiff there had an action for breach of promise of marriage. Doubts were thrown on *Vicars* v. *Wilcocks* in *Knight* v. *Gibbs*, 1 A. & E. 43; 3 N. & M. 467; and in *Green* v. *Button*, 2 C. M. & R. 707; and it must now be taken to have been overruled by the *dicta* of the law lords in *Lynch* v. *Knight and wife*, 9 H. L. C. 577, and by the decision in *Lumley* v. *Gye*, 2 E. & B. 216; 22 L. J. Q. B. 463; 17 Jur. 827. It is now, undoubtedly the law that the defendant is liable for any act which it was his obvious intention, or the natural result of his words, to induce another to commit. "To make the words actionable by reason of special damage, the consequence must be such as, taking human nature as it is with its infirmities, and having regard to the relationship of the parties concerned, might fairly and reasonably have been anticipated and feared would follow from the speaking of the words." (Per Lord Wensleydale in *Lynch* v. *Knight and wife*, 9 H. L. C. p. 600.) "If the experience of mankind must lead any one to expect the result, the defendant will be answerable for it." (Per Littledale, J., in *R.* v. *Moore*, 3 B. & Ad. 188. And see *Société Française des Asphaltes* v. *Farrell*, (1885) Cababé & Ellis, 563; *Whitney* v. *Moignard*, (1890) 24 Q. B. D. 630; 59 L. J. Q. B. 324.)

Illustrations.

A man may not recover the same damages for the same injury twice from two different defendants; but he may recover from two different defendants damages proportioned to the injury each has occasioned, and clearly where words are spoken by a defendant *with the intent* to make a third person break his contract with the plaintiff, the fact that such person did break his contract with the plaintiff in consequence of what the defendant said, may be proved as special damage against that defendant.

Carrol v. *Falkiner*, Kerford & Box's Digest of Victoria Cases, 216.

If I tell a master falsely that his servant has robbed him and thereupon he instantly dismisses him, I must be taken to have contemplated this as a natural and probable consequence of my act. But if the master horsewhips his servant instead of dismissing him, this is not the natural result of my accusation ; I could not be held liable for the assault as special damage. See per Williams, J., in

> *Haddon* v. *Lott*, 15 C. B. 411 ; 24 L. J. C. P. 50.

Mrs. Scott charged Mrs. Parkins with adultery. She indignantly told her husband, and he was unreasonable enough to insist upon a separation in consequence. *Held,* that no action lay.

> *Parkins et ux.* v. *Scott et ux.*, 1 H. & C. 153 ; 31 L. J. Ex.
> 331 ; 8 Jur. N. S. 593 ; 10 W. R. 562 ; 6 L. T. 394 ; 2
> F. & F. 799.
> *Lynch* v. *Knight and wife*, 9 H. L. C. 577 ; 5 L. T. 291,
> *ante*, p. 408.

The plaintiff engaged Mdlle. Mara to sing at his concerts ; the defendant libelled Mdlle. Mara, who consequently refused to sing lest she should be hissed and ill-treated ; the result was that the concerts were more thinly attended than they otherwise would have been, whereby the plaintiff lost money. *Held,* that the damage to the plaintiff was too remote a consequence of defendant's words to sustain an action by the plaintiff. It was, in short, not so much the result of defendant's words as of Mdlle. Mara's timidity or caprice.

> *Ashley* v. *Harrison*, 1 Esp. 48 ; Peake, 256.

The defendant is not answerable " if, in consequence of his words, other persons have afterwards assembled and seized the plaintiff and thrown him into a horse-pond by way of punishment for his supposed transgression."

> Per Lord Ellenborough, C.J., in *Vicars* v. *Wilcocks*, 8 East, 3.

It is not essential that the third person, whose act constitutes the special damage, should believe the words spoken by the defendant, if it is shown that the words spoken did directly induce the act. The law is otherwise in America.

Illustrations.

The plaintiff and another young woman worked for Mrs. Enoch, a straw bonnet-maker, and lived in her house. The defendant, Mrs. Enoch's landlord, who lived two doors off, came to Mrs. Enoch and complained that the plaintiff and her fellow lodger had made a great noise and been guilty of openly outrageous conduct, adding, " No moral person would like to have such people in his house." Mrs. Enoch thereupon turned them out of her house, and dismissed them from her employ, not because she believed the charge made, but because she was afraid it would offend her landlord if they remained. *Held,* that the special damage was the direct consequence of the defendant's words.

> *Knight* v. *Gibbs*, 1 A. & E. 43 ; 3 N. & M. 467.
> And see *Gillett* v. *Bullivant*, 7 L. T. (Old S.) 490 ; *post*, p. 416.

But where the plaintiff was under twenty-one and lived at home with her father, and the defendant foully slandered her to her father, in consequence of which he refused to give her a silk dress and a course of music lessons on the piano which he had promised her, although he entirely disbelieved the defendant's story, this was *held* in America *not to* be such special damage as will sustain the action, on the ground that such treatment by a parent of his child is not the natural result of a falsehood told him against her. Per Grover, J. : " I do not think special damage can be predicated upon the act of any one who wholly disbelieves the truth of the story. It is inducing acts injurious to the plaintiff, caused by a belief of the truth of the charge made by the defendant, that constitutes the damage which the law redresses."

Anon., 60 N. Y. 262.

And see *Wilson* v. *Goit,* 3 Smith (17 N. Y. R.), 445.

The special damage must be the direct result of the defendant's words, not of some one else's. If A. chooses of his own accord to republish the defendant's words, this is A.'s own act, for the consequences of which he alone is liable. (See *ante,* pp. 177—180.)

But if a republication by A. be the natural or necessary consequence of the defendant's publication to A., or if the defendant intended or desired A. to repeat his words, the defendant is liable for all the consequences of A.'s republication, for he directly caused it. A republication by A. to B. is not, however, considered in England a necessary consequence of the defendant's publication, unless the original communication made to A. places A. under a legal or moral obligation to repeat the slander to B. And, indeed, if the defendant knew the relation in which A. stood to B., he will be taken to have maliciously contemplated and desired this result when he spoke to A. (*Speight* v. *Gosnay,* 60 L. J. Q. B. 231 ; 55 J. P. 501 ; *Whitney* v. *Moignard* (1890) 24 Q. B. D. 630 ; 59 L. J. Q. B. 324. See *ante,* p. 178.)

Thus, it may happen that a person who invents a lie, and maliciously sets it in circulation, may sometimes escape punishment altogether. For if I originate a slander against you of such a nature that the words are not actionable *per se,* the utterance of them is no ground of action, unless special damage follows. If I myself tell the story to your employer, who thereupon dismisses you, you have an action against me; but if I only tell it to your friends and relations, and no pecuniary damage ensues from my own communication of it to any one, then no action lies against me, although the story is sure to get round to your master sooner or later. The unfortunate man whose lips actually utter the slander to your master is the only person that can be made defendant; for it is his publication alone which is actionable as causing special damage.

It is clear law that when the repetition of a slander is spontaneous and unauthorised, when it is the voluntary act of a free agent, the originator of the slander is not answerable for any mischief caused by its repetition. (*Holwood* v. *Hopkins*, Cro. Eliz. 787. And see *Ward* v. *Weeks*, 7 Bing. 211; 4 M. & P. 796; *Rutherford* v. *Evans*, 4 C. & P. 74; *Tunnicliffe* v. *Moss*, 3 C. & K. 83; *Parkins et ux.* v. *Scott et ux.*, 1 H. & C. 153; 31 L. J. Ex. 331; 8 Jur. N. S. 593; *Dixon* v. *Smith*, 5 H. & N. 450; 29 L. J. Ex. 125; *Bateman* v. *Lyall*, 7 C. B. N. S. 638.) In *Riding* v. *Smith*, 1 Ex. D. 94; 45 L. J. Ex. 281; 24 W. R. 487; 34 L. T. 500, it is true, Kelly, C.B., expressed a "hope that the day will come when the principle of *Ward* v. *Weeks*, and that class of cases, shall be brought under the consideration of the Court of last resort;" but Pollock and Huddleston, BB., upheld that decision. And in *Clarke* v. *Morgan*, 38 L. T. 354, Lindley, J., expressly states his opinion that the decisions in *Ward* v. *Weeks* and *Parkins* v. *Scott* have been in no way overruled by *Riding* v. *Smith* and *Evans* v. *Harries*, 1 H. & N. 251; 26 L. J. Ex. 31.

It is only in cases where the words are not actionable *per se* that the rule as to the remoteness of damages inflicts this apparent hardship upon the plaintiff when he sues the originator of the slander; for where the words are actionable *per se*, and in all cases of libel, the jury find the damages *generally*, and will punish the author of the falsehood with due severity; although, of course, the judge will still direct them not to take into their consideration any damage which ensued from a repetition by a stranger. (*Rutherford* v. *Evans*, 4 C. & P. 74; *Tunnicliffe* v. *Moss*, 3 C. & K. 83.)

When, however, the first publisher either expressly or impliedly requests or procures the republication, he directly causes all damage that flows from the republication; the second publisher is really his agent, for whose act he is liable. So, wherever the original publication to A. places A. under a legal or moral obligation to repeat the defendant's words, such repetition is clearly the natural consequence of the defendant's communication to A.

In America the judges in one or two cases appear to carry this doctrine further, and seem to lay down the rule that wherever the repetition is *innocent* (that is, we presume, not malicious, and on a privileged occasion), the originator must be liable for all consequential damage caused by the repetition; for else, it is said, the person injured would be without a remedy. He cannot sue the person repeating the slander, as the repetition is privileged; therefore he *must* be able to sue the first publisher for the damage caused by his own publication, and by the innocent repetition as well. "Where slanderous words are repeated *innocently,* and without an intent to defame, as under some circumstances they may be, I do not see why the author of the slander should not be held liable for injuries resulting from it as thus repeated, as he would be if these injuries had arisen directly from the words as spoken by himself." (Per Beardsley, J., in *Keenholts* v. *Becker,* 3 Denio, N. Y. 352; and see *Terwilliger* v. *Wands,* 17 N. Y. R. 58.) But it is strange to make the liability of one man depend on the absence of malice in another. Such, at all events, is not the law of England; it by no means follows with us that because the repetition is privileged or innocent it is therefore the natural and necessary consequence of the prior publication. In *Parkins* v. *Scott* (*ante,* p. 412), the repetition was clearly innocent, yet no action lay against the original defamer. Mrs. Parkins was in fact held to have no remedy. (See *Clark* v. *Chambers,* 3 Q. B. D. 327; 47 L. J. Q. B. 427; 26 W. R. 613; 38 L. T. 454; *Bassell* v. *Elmore,* 48 N. Y. R. 561, 567; *Titus* v. *Sumner,* 44 N. Y. R. 266.)

Illustrations.

The plaintiff "was in communication of marriage with J. S., who was seised in fee of land worth 200*l.* per annum." The defendant spoke words to the plaintiff's servant imputing unchastity to the plaintiff "and by reason of these words she lost her marriage." *Held,* that no action lay, because the words were not spoken to J. S.

Holwood v. *Hopkins,* (1600) Cro. Eliz. 787.

Weeks was speaking to Bryce of the plaintiff, and said, "He is a rogue and a swindler; I know enough about him to hang him." Bryce repeated this to Bryer as Weeks' statement. Bryer consequently refused to trust the plaintiff. *Held,* that the judge was right in nonsuiting the plaintiff: for the words were not actionable *per se,* and the damage was too remote.

Ward v. *Weeks,* 7 Bing. 211; 4 M. & P. 796.

A groom in a passion called a lady's-maid "a whore." A lady, hearing the groom had said so, refused to afford the lady's-maid her customary hospitality. *Held,* that no action lay, for the groom had never spoken to the lady.

> *Clarke* v. *Morgan,* (1877) 38 L. T. 354.
>
> *Dixon* v. *Smith,* 5 H. & N. 450 ; 29 L. J. Ex. 125 ; *ante,* p. 386.

G. proposed the plaintiff as a member of a club. The defendant, a member, on the day of election told G. that the plaintiff was leading an immoral life. G. nevertheless voted for the plaintiff. There was no evidence that the defendant spoke to any other member, yet the plaintiff was blackballed. Judgment for the defendant, as the special damage was not the result of the words proved to have been spoken by the defendant.

> *Walklin* v. *Johns,* (1891) 7 Times L. R. 292.
>
> *Argent* v. *Donigan,* (1892) 8 Times L. R. 432.

The defendant said of the plaintiff, a veterinary surgeon, in the White Lion public-house at Barnet, "He does not know his business." No one then in the public-house ceased to employ the plaintiff in consequence ; but some others did, to whom the circumstance was reported. *Held,* that the defendant was not liable for the loss of their custom.

> *Hirst* v. *Goodwin,* 3 F. & F. 257.
>
> *Rutherford* v. *Evans,* 4 C. & P. 74.
>
> *Tunnicliffe* v. *Moss,* 3 C. & K. 83.

The plaintiff was governess to Mr. L.'s children ; the defendant told her father that she had had a child by Mr. L. : the father went straight to Mr. L. and told him what the defendant had said. Mr. L. thereupon said that the plaintiff had better not return to her duties, for although he knew that the charge was perfectly false, still for her to continue to attend to his children would be injurious to her character and unpleasant to them both. *Held,* that the repetition by the father to Mr. L., and his dismissal of the plaintiff, were both the natural consequences of the defendant's publication to the father.

> *Gillett* v. *Bullivant,* (1846) 7 L. T. (Old S.) 490.
>
> *Fowles* v. *Bowen,* (1864) 3 Tiff. (30 N. Y. R.) 20.

H. told Mr. Watkins, that the plaintiff, his wife's dressmaker, was a woman of immoral character. Mr. Watkins naturally informed his wife of this charge, and she ceased to employ the plaintiff. *Held,* that the plaintiff's loss of Mrs. Watkins' custom was the natural and necessary consequence of the defendant's communication to Mr. Watkins.

> *Derry* v. *Handley,* (1867) 16 L. T. 263.

The defendant uttered a slander consisting of a false imputation upon the chastity of the plaintiff (an unmarried woman) in the presence of her mother. The mother repeated it to the plaintiff, who repeated it to the man to whom she was engaged to be married, and he broke off the engagement in consequence. There was no evidence that the defendant authorised or intended the repetition of the slander, or that he knew of the plaintiff's engagement. *Held,* that the special damage was too remote, and that therefore no action lay. (This decision was prior to the Slander of Women Act, 1891.)

> *Speight* v. *Gosnay,* (1891) 60 L. J. Q. B. 231 ; 55 J. P. 501 ; 7 Times L. R. 239.
>
> *Ecklin* v. *Little,* (1890) 6 Times L. R. 366.

The defendant printed a libel in the London edition of the *New York Herald,* knowing that it would be, as in fact it was, repeated and published in other editions of that paper, published in France and other countries. *Held,* that such publication was properly pleaded and could be proved at the trial.

> *Whitney and others* v. *Moignard,* (1890) 24 Q. B. D. 630 ; 59 L. J. Q. B. 324 ; 6 Times L. R. 274.

A police magistrate dismissed a trumped-up charge brought by the plaintiff, a policeman, and added : " I am bound to say, in reference to this charge and a similar one brought from the same spot a few days ago, that I cannot believe William Kendillon on his oath." This observation was duly reported to the Commissioners of Police, who in consequence dismissed the plaintiff from the force. Lord Denman held that the dismissal was special damage for which the defendant would have been liable, if the action had lain at all : for he must have known that such a remark would certainly be reported to the commissioners, and would most probably cause them to dismiss the plaintiff. Nonsuit on the ground of privilege.

> *Kendillon* v. *Maltby,* Car. & Marsh. 402.

The defendant, a passenger on board a steam-packet, complained to the captain that the plaintiff, the third officer, had been guilty of misconduct towards one of the lady passengers. On the arrival of the vessel at Jamaica, the captain reported this charge to the marine superintendent of the company there, who reported it to the directors at the chief office of the company in London, who dismissed the plaintiff from the service of the company. The plaintiff sought leave to issue a writ to be served on the defendant, who resided in Jamaica. None of the above cases were cited to the Court. Leave was refused, on the ground that the case did not come within the words of the repealed rule, Order XI. r. 1 ; but Bramwell, L.J., intimated that in his opinion the alleged special damage was too remote, differing from Denman, J., in the Court below.

> *Bree* v. *Marescaux,* 7 Q. B. D. 434 ; 50 L. J. Q. B. 676 ; 29 W. R. 858 ; 44 L. T. 644, 765.

If I make an oral statement to the reporter of a newspaper, intending and desiring him to insert the substance of it in the paper, I am liable for all the consequences of its appearing in print, although I never expressly requested the reporter to publish it.

> *Bond* v. *Douglas,* 7 C. & P. 626.
>
> *R.* v. *Lovett,* 9 C. & P. 462.
>
> *Adams* v. *Kelly,* Ry. & Moo. 157.
>
> *R.* v. *Cooper,* 8 Q. B. 533 ; 15 L. J. Q. B. 206.

But if I write you a private letter containing a libel on A., and you make a copy of it which you send to a newspaper to be published to all the world, without my leave, and in a way which I could not have anticipated, then this republication is your own unlawful act, for the consequences of which you alone are liable. I must pay damages only for the publication to you.

> Per Best, C.J., 5 Bing. 402, 405.

The damage must of course have accrued to the plaintiff and not to some one else. A loss which has resulted to A. in consequence of the defendant's having defamed B., is too remote to constitute special damage in any action brought by B. Whether A., who has himself suffered the damage, can sue, depends upon the closeness of the relationship between A. and B. If A. is B.'s master, A. may perhaps have an action on the case *per quod servitium amisit*. If A. is B.'s husband, then it is clear law that the husband may sue for any special damage which has accrued to him through the defamation of his wife. (*Post*, p. 567.) But a wife cannot recover for any special damage which words spoken of her have inflicted on her husband. (*Harwood et ux.* v. *Hardwick et ux.*, (1668) 2 Keble, 387.)

This rule pressed very harshly upon married women; for before the Married Women's Property Act there was hardly any special damage which they could suffer. Their earnings were their husbands'; so was their time. Lord Wensleydale, in *Lynch* v. *Knight and wife*, 9 H. L. C. 597, even doubted if loss of *consortium* of her husband was such special damage as would sustain an action of slander by a wife. Loss of the society of her friends and neighbours clearly is not. The only special damage, in fact, which a married woman living with her husband could set up was loss of hospitality. And, even in conceding her this, the judges seem to be straining the law, for her husband was bound to maintain her: so that such gratuitous entertainment was really a saving to the husband's pocket. But in *Davies* v. *Solomon*, L. R. 7 Q. B. 112; 41 L. J. Q. B. 10; 20 W. R. 167; 25 L. T. 799, the judges declined to scrutinise too nicely into such matters; and no doubt the loss is really the wife's. Her friends would supply her with better and other food than that which the law compels her husband to afford her. The operation of the Married Women's Property Acts, and the Slander of Women Act, 1891, has lessened the hardship. In some cases the difficulty might perhaps have been obviated, had the husband sued alone. (See *Coleman et ux.* v. *Harcourt*, 1 Lev. 140; *post*, p. 572.)

Illustrations.

A brother cannot sue for slander of his sister.
        Subbaiyar v. *Kristnaiyar and another*, I. L. R., 1 Madras, 383.

Nor a son for slander of his deceased father.

> *Luckumsey Rowji* v. *Hurbun Nursey and others,* I. L. R., 5
> Bom. 580.

If one partner be libelled, he cannot recover for any special damage
which has occurred to the firm.

> *Solomons and others* v. *Medex,* 1 Stark. 191.
>
> *Robinson* v. *Marchant,* 7 Q. B. 918; 15 L. J. Q. B. 134;
> 10 Jur. 156.

Similarly, if the firm be libelled as a body, they cannot jointly recover
for any private injury to a single partner; though that partner may
now recover his individual damages in the same action.

> *Haythorn* v. *Lawson,* 3 C. & P. 196.
>
> *Le Fanu* v. *Malcolmson,* 1 H. L. C. 637; 8 Ir. L. R. 418;
> 13 L. T. (Old S.) 61.

Where words actionable *per se* were spoken of a married woman, she
was allowed to recover only 20s. damages; all the special damage which
she proved at the trial was held to have accrued to her husband, and not
to her: he ought, as the law then stood, to have sued for it in a separate
action.

> *Dengate and wife* v. *Gardiner,* 4 M. & W. 5; 2 Jur. 470.
>
> *Saville et ux.* v. *Sweeny,* 4 B. & Ad. 514; 1 N. & M. 254.
>
> And other cases, *post,* p. 572.

A declaration by husband and wife alleged that the defendant falsely
and maliciously spoke certain words of the wife imputing incontinence
to her, whereby she lost the society of her neighbours, and became ill
and unable to attend to her necessary affairs and business, and her husband incurred expense in curing her, and lost the society and assistance
of his wife in his domestic affairs. *Held,* that the declaration disclosed
no cause of action.

> *Allsop and wife* v. *Allsop,* (1860) 5 H. & N. 534; 29 L. J.
> Ex. 315; 6 Jur. N. S. 433; 8 W. R. 449; 36 L. T.
> (Old S.) 290.
>
> Approved in *Lynch* v. *Knight and wife,* 9 H. L. C. 577.

CHAPTER XIV.

INJUNCTIONS.

INJUNCTIONS granted in actions of defamation may be divided into two classes :—

    I. Injunctions granted after verdict, or at the final hearing.

    II. Injunctions granted on an interlocutory application before or without any verdict.

I. *Injunctions granted after Verdict or at the Final Hearing.*

After a verdict in his favour, the plaintiff often applies to the judge at the trial to grant an injunction to restrain any further publication of what a jury has found to be an actionable libel or slander. He is entitled to claim protection in the future as well as damages for the injury done him in the past. And if the judge sees reason to apprehend any repetition of the publication which would be injurious to the plaintiff, he will grant the injunction. So, if the action be tried by a judge without a jury, and the judge decides in favour of the plaintiff, he will on the same principle grant an injunction in addition to or in lieu of, damages.

Illustrations.

The plaintiff and the defendant were rival railway signal manufacturers. They both invented practically the same improvement ; but the defendant was the first to patent it. The plaintiff subsequently petitioned for a patent, but was refused as being too late. Thereupon the defendant published an advertisement announcing that "Saxby's application was cancelled by the Crown on the ground of piracy from Easterbrook." The plaintiff claimed damages 1,000*l.*, and an injunction to restrain the defendant from publishing libels against the plaintiff of the like nature and description. The jury awarded forty shillings damages, and Lord Coleridge, C.J., granted a perpetual injunction. The Divisional Court decided that he had full power so to do.

> *Saxby* v. *Easterbrook*, (1878) 3 C. P. D. 339 ; 27 W. R. 188.

Joseph and Josiah Thorley were each entitled to manufacture "Thorley's Food for Cattle," both possessed the secret of its composition, and manufactured the same article. Yet the executors of Joseph advertised that they "alone possessed the secret for compounding that famous condiment," and that Josiah and the company whose manager he was, were "seeking to foist upon the public an article which they pretend is the same as that manufactured by the late Joseph Thorley." Malins, V.-C., refused to grant an injunction on an interlocutory application ; but granted it at the final hearing, and his decision was upheld by the Court of Appeal.

> *Thorley's Cattle Food Co.* v. *Massam* (interlocutory), 6 Ch. D.
> 582 ; 46 L. J. Ch. 713.
> (Before Malins, V.-C.) 14 Ch. D. 763 ; 28 W. R. 295 ; 41
> L. T. 542.
> (C. A.) 14 Ch. D. 781 ; 28 W. R. 966 ; 42 L. T. 851.
> And see *James* v. *James*, L. R. 13 Eq. 421 ; 41 L. J. Ch.
> 253 ; 26 L. T. 568.

Mr. Gandy owned two patents for manufacturing cotton belting ; the plaintiffs were formerly his agents. An injunction was granted by Pearson, J., in 1883, to restrain the plaintiffs from selling the belting of other manufacturers as that of Gandy. Subsequently Gandy inserted an advertisement in the *British Trade Journal*, complaining that unprincipled persons were imitating his belting, and misleading the public, stating that the above injunction had been granted, and that he had reason to believe that the plaintiffs still continued to sell a large quantity of other belting as his. North, J., granted an injunction with costs against both Gandy and the publisher of the *British Trade Journal*, and also ordered Gandy to pay 500*l*. damages.

> *Kerr* v. *Gandy*, (1886) 3 Times L. R. 75.

Where the plaintiff in a trade-mark case failed on all points but one, and afterwards published a "caution" to the trade, which stated the effect of the judgment so far as it was in his favour, but omitted all allusion to the parts of the judgment in the defendant's favour, North, J., held the report unfair, and granted an injunction restraining its circulation, with 5*l*. damages and costs.

> *Hayward & Co.* v. *Hayward & Sons*, 34 Ch. D. 198 ; 56 L. J.
> Ch. 287 ; 35 W. R. 392 ; 55 L. T. 729.

The defendants issued a circular to the secretaries of all co-operative societies, urging them not to purchase goods from the plaintiffs and to do all they could to discourage others from dealing with them. *Held*, that this was actionable, and should be restrained by injunction.

> *Pink* v. *Federation of Trades Unions*, (1892) 67 L. T. 258.
> *Jenkinson* v. *Neild*, (1892) 8 Times L. R. 540.
> *Trollope & Sons* v. *London Building Trades Federation*, (1895)
> 72 L. T. 342 ; 11 Times L. R. 228, 280.

Same v. *Same,* (1896) 12 Times L. R. 373.

Leathem v. *Craig and others,* [1899] 2 Ir. R. 667.

An injunction will in some cases be granted to restrain the unauthorised use of a man's name.

Routh v. *Webster,* (1847) 10 Beav. 561.

Walter v. *Ashton,* [1902] 2 Ch. 282 ; 71 L. J. Ch. 839 ; 51
W. R. 131 ; 87 L. T. 196.

Lloyd's Bank, Ltd. v. *Royal British Bank, Ltd.,* (1903) 19
Times L. R. 548, 604.

But see *Dockrell* v. *Dougall,* (1898) 78 L. T. 840 ; (1899)
80 L. T. 556.

Where, however, the words are not actionable *per se*, it is
submitted that the plaintiff will not be entitled to any
injunction until he has established a complete cause of
action. "Damages and injunction are merely two different
forms of remedy against the same wrong ; and the facts
which must be proved in order to entitle a plaintiff to the
first of these remedies are equally necessary in the case of
the second." (Per Lord Watson, in *White* v. *Mellin,* [1895]
A. C. at p. 167.) Hence, whenever special damage is an
essential part of the cause of action, special damage must
be proved before the plaintiff can obtain either damages or
an injunction.

In some cases of slander and in all actions on the case for
slander of title, words disparaging goods, &c., special damage in
the strictest sense of the term (*i.e.*, as defined in the last chapter,
ante, p. 337) is a necessary part of the cause of action. Until such
special damage has arisen the defendant has committed no tort
and the plaintiff has no cause of action. A mere apprehension of
future damage will not suffice ; the plaintiff can recover no damages
unless special damage has actually accrued.

Can the plaintiff, however, in any such case obtain an injunction
to prevent damage accruing? Although at first sight this might
appear desirable, it is difficult to see how the plaintiff can be
entitled to any remedy when his cause of action is still incomplete.
In actions for personal defamation whenever the words are actionable *per se*, the plaintiff need show no special damage; he has a
good cause of action without it ; and in such actions, therefore, an
injunction will be readily granted, if the Court can see that the
repetition of the words will clearly injure the plaintiff in the way

of his profession or trade. But where special damage is essential to the cause of action different considerations apply.

Take for instance the case of *White v. Mellin*, [1895] A. C. 154; 64 L. J. Ch. 308; 43 W. R. 353; 72 L. T. 334. There the plaintiff alleged that the defendant's words had disparaged the goods which he manufactured; and special damage therefore was a necessary part of the cause of action. No special damage had in fact occurred; yet the plaintiff contended that though it was necessary to allege and prove special damage in an action of this kind in order to recover damages, it was not necessary to do either in order to entitle the plaintiff to an injunction,—that it was enough if the words were proved to be false and published without just occasion or excuse, and were calculated to injure the plaintiff's business if their further publication was not restrained. But the House of Lords decided the contrary, holding that "if special damage was necessary to the maintenance of the action, and special damage was not shown, a tort in the eye of the law would not be disclosed, and no injunction would be granted." (Per Lord Herschell, L.C., at p. 163.) "In order to constitute disparagement which is, in the sense of the law, injurious, it must be shown that the defendant's representations were made of and concerning the plaintiff's goods; that they were in disparagement of his goods and untrue; and that they have occasioned special damage to the plaintiff. Unless each and all of these three things be established, it must be held that the defendant has acted within his rights and that the plaintiff has not suffered any legal *injuria*." (Per Lord Watson, at p. 167.)

The only conclusion to be drawn from these and other observations in the judgments in *White* v. *Mellin*, is that in all cases of slander where the words are not actionable *per se*, and in all actions on the case for words causing damage, whether spoken or written, special damage must be proved before the plaintiff can obtain either damages or an injunction. There is, however, one passage in Lord Watson's judgment which leans the other way:—"The *onus* resting upon a plaintiff who asks an injunction, and does not say that he has as yet suffered any special damage, is if anything the heavier, because it is incumbent upon him to satisfy the Court that such damage will necessarily be occasioned to him in the future" (p. 167). This is the passage which Collins, M.R., subsequently described in *Dunlop Pneumatic Tyre Co., Ltd.* v. *Maison Talbot and others*, (1904) 20 Times L. R. at p. 581, as "the high water mark in favour of the plaintiffs upon this point"; and if taken alone it certainly favours the contention that in some cases a Court may grant an injunction before special damage has actually accrued.

The next decision on the subject was also in the House of Lords (*Royal Baking Powder Co.* v. *Wright, Crossley & Co.*, (1900) 18 R. P. C. 95; *ante*, p. 84); and the observations of the Lords are equally strong and clear. Here again the defendants' words had caused the plaintiffs no special damage which the law could recognise, and the Court refused to grant an injunction. "To support such an action it is necessary for the plaintiffs to prove . . . that they have suffered special damage thereby. The damage is the gist of the action, and therefore, according to the old rules of pleading, it must be specially alleged and proved." (Per Lord Davey, at p. 99.) "The plaintiff must prove two things: first, that the libel was maliciously published; and, secondly, that specific money damage has resulted from it. If either of these ingredients be absent the action must fail." (Per Lord James of Hereford, at p. 101.) "The action, then, being one of trade libel, it must, in order to succeed, comply with the conditions stated in *White* v. *Mellin* ([1895] A. C. 154). As I read that decision, the essential ground, the gist, of the action in a trade libel case is special damage, done maliciously. Unless the plaintiff has in fact suffered loss which can be and is specified, he has no cause of action. The fact that the defendant has acted maliciously cannot supply the want of special damage, nor can a superfluity of malice eke out a case wanting in special damage." (Per Lord Robertson, at pp. 102, 103.) "There is a class of cases, of which this is one, the true legal aspect of which, however they may be described technically, is that they are actions for unlawfully causing damage. The damage is the gist of the action, and, however much the thing complained of may be the subject of animadversion, it gives no right to an action in a court of law unless damage is proved." (Per Lord Halsbury, L.C., at p. 104.)

This question was also much discussed both in the Commercial Court and the Court of Appeal in *Dunlop Pneumatic Tyre Co., Ltd.* v. *Maison Talbot and others*, (1903) 20 Times L. R. 88; (1904) *Ib.* 579. In that case the defendants' manager had written in reply to an inquiry from a customer that neither the plaintiffs nor any other company except the defendants could supply anyone with a particular kind of tyre, as the defendants alone had the right to import such tyres into England. No special damage resulted from this statement, as the customer in spite of it ordered and obtained the tyres in question from the plaintiffs. The plaintiffs applied for an injunction, which Walton, J., granted in spite of the observations in *White* v. *Mellin, suprà* (the case of *Royal Baking Powder Co.* v. *Wright, Crossley & Co., suprà*, was not cited to his Lordship). The learned judge "thought that where, as in the present case, damage would be the natural and direct result likely to follow, and so highly probable that it might be properly described as imminent, an injunction would lie " (at p. 90), although no damage had as yet occurred. On appeal the Court expressed no opinion as to the point under discussion but dissolved the injunction, and directed judgment to be entered for the defendants, on the ground that there was no malice on their part.

Illustration.

The defendant, who owned the copyright of a picture by Millais, issued a circular threatening proceedings against all persons who bought copies of the plaintiff's magazine, containing a woolwork pattern, which the defendant wrongly deemed to be an infringement of his copyright. The plaintiff brought an action for an injunction and also for damages. He failed to prove that he had sustained any appreciable damage ; therefore the Court of Appeal refused to grant him any injunction.

　　　　Dicks v. *Brooks,* (1880) 15 Ch. D. 22 ; 49 L. J. Ch. 812 ; 29 W. R. 87 ; 43 L. T. 71.

II. *Injunctions granted on an Interlocutory Application before or without any Verdict.*

The Court has also power to grant an *interim* injunction in cases of libel and slander. (*Bonnard* v. *Perryman,* [1891] 2 Ch. 269 ; 60 L. J. Ch. 617 ; 39 W. R. 435 ; 65 L. T. 506 ; *Hermann Loog* v. *Bean,* 26 Ch. D. 306 ; 53 L. J. Ch. 1128 ; 32 W. R. 994 ; 51 L. T. 442.) And this jurisdiction is not confined to words affecting a trade or business. (*Monson* v. *Tussauds, Limited,* [1894] 1 Q. B. 671 ; 63 L. J. Q. B. 454 ; 70 L. T. 335.) But this jurisdiction is "of a delicate nature ; it ought only to be exercised in the clearest cases." (Per Lord Esher, M.R., in *Coulson* v. *Coulson,* (1887) 3 Times L. R. 846 ; approved by Lopes and Davey, L.JJ., in *Monson* v. *Tussauds, Limited, suprà.*) Thus, the Court ought not to interfere by way of injunction on an interlocutory application :

(i) Unless the words are so clearly libellous, that if a

jury found them not to be libellous, the Court of Appeal would set the verdict aside as unreasonable. (*Coulson v. Coulson, supra; Bonnard v. Perryman, suprà; Newton v. Amalgamated Musicians' Union*, (1896) 12 Times L. R. 623; *Lloyd's Bank, Limited v. Royal British Bank, Limited*, (1903) 19 Times L. R. 548.)

(ii) If the words are such that a jury might properly find them to be a fair comment on a matter of public interest. (*Armstrong and others v. Armit and others*, (1886) 2 Times L. R. 887.)

(iii) If the words are such that a jury might properly find them to be a fair and accurate report of a judicial proceeding. (*Champion & Co., Limited v. Birmingham Vinegar Brewery Co., Limited*, (1893) 10 Times L. R. 164.)

(iv) If the occasion of publication be privileged; the Court will not (except, perhaps, in the plainest cases) try the issue of malice or no malice on affidavit. (*Quartz Hill Gold Mining Co. v. Beall*, 20 Ch. D. 501; 51 L. J. Ch. 874; 30 W. R. 583; 46 L. T. 746.)

(v) Where the defendant has pleaded or intends to plead a justification, unless the Court is satisfied that there is no reasonable prospect that the defendant will succeed at the trial in proving his words true. (*Bonnard v. Perryman, suprà.*)

(vi) Unless there is some evidence that the defendant intends to continue the circulation of the words complained of. (Per Jessel, M.R., in 20 Ch. D. at pp. 508, 509; and see *Stannard v. Vestry of St. Giles, Camberwell*, 20 Ch. D. at p. 195; 51 L. J. Ch. 629; 30 W. R. 693; 46 L. T. 243.)

(vii) Unless it be established that irreparable or very serious injury will in all probability result to the plaintiff, if the circulation of the libellous statements be allowed to continue. (*Mogul Steamship Co. v. M'Gregor, Gow & Co.*, 15 Q. B. D. 476; 54 L. J. Q. B. 450; *Salomons v. Knight*, [1891] 2 Ch. 294; 60 L. J. Ch. 743; 39 W. R. 506; 64 L. T. 589.) "If the injury done to the plaintiff can be fully compensated for in damages, the Court ought not to interfere by an *interim* injunction to restrain the publication of the libel until the trial of the action." (Per Mathew, J., in *Monson* v. *Tussauds, Limited*, [1894] 1 Q. B. at p. 677.)

(viii) Where the plaintiff has by delaying the proceeding or by other conduct disentitled himself to such relief. (*Monson* v. *Tussauds, Limited*, [1894] 1 Q. B. 671.) An *interim* injunction must always be applied for promptly.

The law is the same in Ireland. (*Punch* v. *Boyd and others*, 16 L. R. Ir. 476. The decision in *Hammersmith Skating Rink Co.* v. *Dublin Skating Rink Co.*, 10 Ir. R. Eq. 235, is no longer followed.)

" Prior to the Common Law Procedure Act, 1854, no Court could grant any injunction in a case of libel. The Court of Chancery could grant no injunction in such a case, because it could not try a libel. Neither could Courts of Common Law until the Common Law Procedure Act of 1854, because they had no power to grant injunctions. Whether they had power to grant an interlocutory injunction after 1854 I think doubtful. As a matter of practice they never did. The Judicature Act of 1873, s. 25, sub-s. 8, confers a larger jurisdiction to grant injunctions than existed before. It says, ' A mandamus or an injunction may be granted, or a receiver appointed by an interlocutory order of the Court in all cases in which it shall appear to the Court to be just or convenient that such order should be made.' " (Per Lopes, L.J., in *Monson* v. *Tussauds, Limited, suprà*.) It is under this section that orders now are made, sections 79 and 82 of the Common Law Procedure Act, 1854, being repealed by the Statute Law Revision Act, 1883 (46 & 47 Vict. c. 49).

Illustrations.

Where a circular was sent by one shareholder to his brother-share-holders, containing statements as to the financial position of the company which were not positively proved to be untrue, and inviting all the share-holders to take some joint action with reference to the company, it was held that though the Court had jurisdiction to grant an interlocutory injunction restraining the publication, yet it would not do so when the circular was, as here, *primâ facie* a privileged communication.

Quartz Hill Gold Mining Co. v. *Beall*, 20 Ch. D. 501 ; 51 L. J. Ch. 874 ; 30 W. R. 583 ; 46 L. T. 746.

A member of a friendly society issued to persons not members of the society circulars containing inaccurate statements as to the financial condition of the society. Kay, J., on motion, granted an injunction to restrain

" the further issuing of this circular, *or any other circular or letter containing false or inaccurate representations as to the credit or financial condition of the said society.*"

> *Hill* v. *Hart Davies,* 21 Ch. D. 798 ; 51 L. J. Ch. 845 ; 31 W. R. 22.

In a subsequent case, Cotton, L. J., questioned the power of the learned judge to insert in his order the words printed above in italics.

> *Liverpool Household Stores* v. *Smith,* 37 Ch. D. at p. 182.

The plaintiff dismissed one of his managers, the defendant, from his employ, who thereupon went about among the plaintiff's customers, making oral statements reflecting on the solvency of the plaintiff, and advised some of them not to pay the plaintiff for machines which had been supplied through himself. The plaintiff brought an action to re-restrain the defendant from making statements to the customers or any other person or persons that the plaintiff was about to stop payment, or was in difficulties or insolvent, and from in any manner slandering the plaintiff or injuring his reputation or business. No special damage was proved ; but it was held both by Pearson, J., and the Court of Appeal, that the Court has jurisdiction to restrain a person from making slanderous statements calculated to injure the business of another person, and that this jurisdiction extends to oral as well as written statements, though it requires to be exercised with great caution as regards oral statements, and that in the present case an injunction ought to be granted.

> *Hermann Loog* v. *Bean,* 26 Ch. D. 306 ; 53 L. J. Ch. 1128 ; 32 W. R. 994 ; 51 L. T. 442 ; 48 J. P. 708.

The coopers of Cork and Limerick, who made butter-firkins by hand, were much annoyed at the plaintiff's starting a manufactory near Limerick for making similar firkins by machinery ; and they induced the butter merchants of Limerick to print and widely distribute a "Notice to Farmers" stating that they would not purchase any butter packed in machine-made firkins, as they found them "to be most injurious to the keeping qualities of butter," to the great injury of the plaintiff's business. The Queen's Bench Division in Ireland granted an injunction to restrain the publication of this notice.

> *Punch* v. *Boyd and others,* 16 L. R. Ir. 476.

A newspaper article, commenting on alleged irregularities in the Ordnance Department of the War Office, whereby defective guns, &c. had been supplied to the nation and accepted without sufficient trial, asserted that the plaintiffs, a gun-manufacturing company, had obtained contracts from Government officials by corrupt means. The plaintiffs brought an action for damages, and also applied for an injunction to restrain the editor and printer of the paper from further publishing libellous matter of the plaintiffs pending the action. The Court (Lord Coleridge, C.J., and Denman, J.) refused the application, as the subject-matter of the article was clearly one of great public interest, and the comments thereon were not proved to be *malâ fide.*

> *Armstrong and others* v. *Armit and others,* (1886) 2 Times L. R. 887.

The firm of William Coulson & Sons became bankrupt, and the plaintiff purchased their business, goodwill, and the right to use the name of the firm. Three months afterwards the defendants (another firm with a similar name) issued a circular in these terms: "James Coulson & Co. beg to state that their establishment is not in any way connected with the firm of William Coulson & Sons, now in bankruptcy." The Court of Appeal dissolved an *interim* injunction which had been granted by the Divisional Court. [The judgment of the Master of the Rolls in this case is especially valuable.]

   Coulson v. *Coulson,* (1887) 3 Times L. R. 846.

The defendant having published a document containing charges of fraud, perjury, and conspiracy against the plaintiff, the plaintiff brought an action for libel, and recovered judgment for 1,000*l.* damages, of no part of which could he obtain payment. The defendant continued to publish documents repeating the same charges, and the plaintiff brought a second action claiming an injunction and damages. *Held,* by North, J., and by the Court of Appeal, that though the Court had jurisdiction to grant an interlocutory injunction to restrain further publication of the libel, there was in this case no reason to apprehend any such danger of injury to the plaintiff in person or property as to make it right to grant one.

   Salomons v. *Knight,* [1891] 2 Ch. 294; 60 L. J. Ch. 743;
    39 W. R. 506; 64 L. T. 589.

Subsequently no proper defence being pleaded the plaintiff obtained a final judgment for an injunction, with costs.

   S. C., (1892) 8 Times L. R. 472.

The General Medical Council, under s. 29 of the Medical Act of 1858 ordered the name of Allinson to be erased from the register of recognised medical practitioners, and published the fact in their proceedings. Allinson applied unsuccessfully for an order to restrain such publication.

   Allinson v. *General Medical Council,* (1892) 8 Times L. R. 727,
    784.

The plaintiffs were manufacturers of pianofortes. The secretary of a trades union circulated amongst french-polishers, and amongst the plaintiffs' customers, the statement that the plaintiffs carried on a "pernicious system of sweating," &c. On motion for an injunction, the defendant did not suggest that he could produce any further evidence at the trial than that set out in his affidavit; and was willing to treat the motion as the trial of the action; but the plaintiffs would not consent to this course. The Court, being satisfied that the statement was false, granted an injunction to restrain its further circulation until the trial.

   Collard v. *Marshall,* [1892] 1 Ch. 571; 61 L. J. Ch. 268; 40
    W. R. 473; 66 L. T. 248; 8 Times L. R. 265.

A newspaper published reports and correspondence containing unfavourable statements as to the position and solvency of a joint stock company, which applied for an injunction to restrain the publication of any future articles reflecting unfavourably upon it. Kekewich, J., and the Court of Appeal refused the application, on the ground that it was very difficult to grant an injunction which would not include matters that might turn out not to be libellous; and because if the injunction was granted in terms to restrain what was libellous, the question of libel or no libel would have to be tried on affidavit on the motion to commit, which would be a most inconvenient course.

> *Liverpool Household Stores Association* v. *Smith,* 37 Ch. D. 170 ; 57 L. J. Ch. 85 ; 36 W. R. 485 ; 58 L. T. 204 ; 4 Times L. R. 28, 93.

The defendant published in his paper, the *Financial Observer,* a gross libel on the plaintiff, who applied for an *interim* injunction to restrain the circulation of the paper. The defendant in his affidavit in answer swore that the statements were true, and that he would be able to prove them true at the trial by calling witnesses and by cross-examination of the plaintiff. *Per cur. :* " We cannot feel sure that the defence of justification is one which, on the facts which may be before them, the jury may find to be wholly unfounded." Injunction refused.

> *Bonnard* v. *Perryman,* [1891] 2 Ch. 269 ; 60 L. J. Ch. 617 ; 39 W. R. 435 ; 65 L. T. 506.

A retail trader was summoned for selling adulterated vinegar ; he stated it was manufactured by the plaintiffs ; the case was adjourned for the plaintiffs to appear and defend their vinegar, if they thought fit ; they did not appear at the adjournment, and the retailer was convicted. A fair and accurate report of these proceedings appeared in the *Grocers' Journal.* The defendants (rival manufacturers of vinegar) had this report reprinted on loose slips, which their travellers distributed among grocers, many of whom were customers of the plaintiffs. The Divisional Court (Lord Coleridge, C.J., and Henn Collins, J.) dissolved an *interim* injunction which had been obtained at chambers. At the trial the plaintiffs recovered 20*l.* damages.

> *Champion & Co., Limited* v. *Birmingham Vinegar Brewery Co., Limited,* (1893) 10 Times L. R. 164.

The defendants placed a wax figure of the plaintiff at the threshold of the "Chamber of Horrors," and in close proximity to images of Mrs. Maybrick, Pigott, and Scott. Lord Halsbury would have granted an *interim* injunction to restrain this exhibition, but for the fact that the defendants' affidavits showed some ground for their assertion that the plaintiff at one time had through a friend consented to the exhibition. Lopes and Davey, L.JJ., refused the injunction on the ground that the case came within the rule in *Bonnard* v. *Perryman.*

> *Monson* v. *Tussauds, Limited,* [1894] 1 Q. B. 671 ; 63 L. J. Q. B. 454 ; 70 L. T. 335 ; 9 R. 177.

The defendants printed and circulated a large poster with a black border, headed " Trollope's Black List," containing the names of all the non-union men employed by the plaintiffs, and of all union men who had disobeyed the defendants' order calling them out. Kekewich, J., granted an injunction to restrain any further circulation of this " Black List," on the ground that its publication was a purely malicious act, unnecessary for the protection of the defendants or the men whom they represented, actuated by ill-will, and intended to injure the plaintiffs and the men who still remained in their employ. The Court of Appeal with some hesitation affirmed the decision of Kekewich, J.

> *Trollope & Sons* v. *London Building Trades Federation,* (1895) 72 L. T. 342 ; 11 Times L. R. 228, 280.

Same v. *Same,* (1896) 12 Times L. R. 373.

Pink v. *Federation of Trades Unions,* (1892) 67 L. T. 258.

Leathem v. *Craig and others,* [1899] 2 Ir. R. 667.

In two very similar cases Jeune, J., refused to grant an *interim* injunction.

Peto v. *Apperley,* 91 L. T. Journal, 386.

Haile v. *Lillingstone, ib.* 387.

Where the defendants placed the plaintiff's name on a black list, headed : "The following musicians have been expelled for assisting the theatrical manager therein named in his endeavour to crush the union. Please make a mark against their names, so that if you meet them you will remember the reason of their expulsion," but the list was marked strictly private, and for the use of members only, and published only to members of the union to which the plaintiff had belonged. Chitty, J., refused to grant an *interim* injunction.

Newton v. *Amalgamated Musicians' Union,* (1896) 12 Times L. R. 623.

A paragraph appeared in the *Money Maker* stating that the London and Northern Bank was "now in liquidation." This statement was wholly unfounded. North, J., granted an *interim* injunction on an *ex parte* application.

London and Northern Bank, Limited v. *George Newnes, Limited,* (1899) 16 Times L. R. 76.

The defendants published, without the consent of the plaintiff, picture postcards on which were depicted incidents in plaintiff's life, and a portrait of herself. The plaintiff applied for an *interim* injunction on the ground that the postcards were a libel on her, but the Court held that no sufficient case had been made out.

Corelli v. *Wall,* (1906) 22 Times L. R. 532.

Rival Manufacturers.

Where a plaintiff applies for an *interim* injunction before the trial of the action to restrain the defendant from continuing to issue circulars or advertisements, asserting that the plaintiff's goods are not genuine, or are an infringement of the defendant's patent, copyright, or trade mark, or that the plaintiff is passing his goods off as the defendant's, and threatening the plaintiff or his customers with legal proceedings, the *onus* lies on the plaintiff throughout to prove malice, falsity, and damage. See *ante,* p. 77. It is for the plaintiff to prove that the defendant's statements are false, and if no *mala fides* is proved, so that no damages can be recovered, the Court will not grant an injunction. If, however, in a judicial proceeding the defendant's statements are proved or admitted to be false in fact, and there is any evidence that he intends to continue issuing them, an injunction may be granted restraining any further publication, which then would necessarily be *malâ fide.* (*Burnett* v. *Tak,* 45 L. T. 743 ; *Anderson* v. *Liebig's Extract of Meat Co.,* 45 L. T. 757.)

Illustrations.

A patent, so long as it subsists, is *primâ facie* good ; but a patentee is not entitled to issue circulars stating his intention to institute legal proceedings, in order to deter persons from purchasing alleged infringements of his patent, if he has no *bonâ fide* intention to follow up his threats by taking such proceedings, and the Court will in such case restrain him from any further issue of such circulars.

> *Rollins* v. *Hinks,* L. R. 13 Eq. 355 ; 41 L. J. Ch. 358 ; 20 W. R. 287 ; 26 L. T. 56.
>
> *Axmann* v. *Lund,* L. R. 18 Eq. 330 ; 43 L. J. Ch. 655 ; 22 W. R. 789.
>
> *Watson* v. *Trask,* 6 Ohio, 531.

The defendant, who owned the copyright of a picture by Millais, issued a circular threatening proceedings against all persons who bought copies of the plaintiff's magazine, containing a woolwork pattern, which the defendant wrongly deemed to be an infringement of his copyright. The plaintiff brought an action for an injunction and also for damages. He failed to prove that he had sustained any damage ; therefore the Court of Appeal refused to grant him any injunction.

> *Dicks* v. *Brooks,* (1880) 15 Ch. D. 22 ; 49 L. J. Ch. 812 ; 29 W. R. 87 ; 43 L. T. 71.

The holder of a patent, the validity of which is not impeached, will not be restrained by injunction from issuing notices warning the public against purchasing certain articles, on the ground that they are infringements of his patent, and threatening legal proceedings against those who purchase them, until it is proved that his statements are untrue ; but as soon as that is proved he will be restrained, as any further issue of them cannot be *bonâ fide.*

> *Halsey* v. *Brotherhood,* 19 Ch. D. 386 ; 51 L. J. Ch. 233 ; 30 W. R. 279 ; 45 L. T. 640 ; affirming the decision of Jessel, M.R., 15 Ch. D. 514 ; 49 L. J. Ch. 786 ; 29 W. R. 9 ; 43 L. T. 366.

The defendant company had issued circulars, declaring that the plaintiff was wrongfully using the defendants' labels upon his jars of extract of meat, and threatening the plaintiff's customers with legal proceedings for buying and reselling his jars bearing those labels ; the plaintiff applied for an injunction to restrain the defendant from issuing such circulars ; but the Court refused to grant it, because it was not satisfied that the statements complained of were untrue. (Chitty, J.)

> *Anderson* v. *Liebig's Extract of Meat Co.,* (1881) 45 L. T. 757.

Subsequently Anderson issued new wrappers for his meat jars, with a photograph of Baron Liebig and the words, "This is the only Genuine Brand." The meat company, whose brand was at least as genuine as Anderson's, thereupon applied for and obtained an injunction restraining him from using such wrappers, although the company had themselves issued misleading advertisements. (Chitty, J.)

Liebig's Extract of Meat Co., Limited v. *Anderson,* (1886) 55 L. T. 206.

The Court will not grant an injunction to restrain the *bona fide* issue of circulars, warning persons that if they buy of the plaintiff they will infringe tho defendant's patent and be liable to proceedings, unless a very strong *primâ facie* case be made out, *e.g.,* by showing that such publication is in violation of an express contract between the parties; however much the balance of convenience may be in favour of granting it.

Société Anonyme des Manufactures de Glaces v. *Tilghman's Patent Sand Blast Co.,* (1883) 25 Ch. D. 1; 53 L. J. Ch. 1; 32 W. R. 71; 49 L. T. 451.

The plaintiffs were the makers of "Rainbow Water Raisers or Elevators," and they commenced an action for an injunction to restrain the defendants from issuing a circular cautioning the public against the use of such elevators as being direct infringements of certain patents of the defendants. The plaintiffs subsequently gave notice of a motion to restrain the issue of this circular until the trial of the action. The defendants then commenced a cross action, claiming an injunction to restrain the plaintiffs from infringing their patents. *Held,* by Kay, J., that as there was no evidence of *mala fides* on the part of the defendants, they ought not to bo restrained from issuing the circular until their action had been disposed of, but that they must undertake to prosecute their action without delay.

Household and another v. *Fairburn and another,* (1884) 51 L. T. 498.

This order was made by Kay, J., on May 8th, 1884. But in spite of this undertaking, the defendants did not proceed with their action with due diligence, and on April 30th, 1885, the plaintiffs renewed their motion, and obtained an injunction to restrain the defendants from issuing the circular complained of.

S. C., (1885) 2 Reports of Patent Cases, 140.

The defendant obtained, in 1879, a patent for folding window screens. In 1885 (after six years' undisturbed possession of this patent) he issued a circular calling attention to it, and threatening proceedings against all infringers. The plaintiff, who also made folding screens, commenced an action to restrain the issue of this circular to his customers and others. Then the defendant commenced an action against the plaintiff for infringement. In that action he failed. The plaintiff proved the defendant's patent invalid. Still Bacon, V.-C., held that the defendant was perfectly justified in issuing the circular at the time he did so; that there was no evidence of any malice; and he dismissed the action without costs.

Brauer v. *Sharp,* 3 Reports of Patent Cases, 193.
Sugg v. *Bray,* 2 R. P. C. 241; 54 L. J. Ch. 132.

The plaintiff appointed the defendants his sole agents for the sale of his mineral waters in Great Britain. The plaintiff subsequently terminated the defendants' agency. The defendants thereupon issued circulars and advertisements representing that they were the sole agents of the plaintiff, and threatening with legal proceedings any persons who should buy the plaintiff's mineral waters from or through any other persons than the defendants. The plaintiff applied for an *interim* injunction to restrain the issue of such circulars and advertisements. *Held,* that though the defendants had misconceived and misstated their legal rights under the circumstances, still there was no evidence that they knew this or were acting in bad faith. Injunction refused, but without prejudice to any fresh application in the event of any further advertisements being issued by the defendants.

Hirschler v. *Hertz and Collingwood,* (1895) 11 Times L. R. 466 ; 99 L. T. Journal, 213.

Threats by a Patentee.

In an action to restrain threats of legal proceedings under s. 36 of the Patents and Designs Act, 1907 (7 Edw. VII. c. 29), no defence can be based upon the ground that what the defendant did was done *bonâ fide,* or that it was done on a privileged occasion. (*Skinner & Co.* v. *Shew & Co.,* [1893] 1 Ch. 413 ; 62 L. J. Ch. 196 ; 41 W. R. 217 ; 67 L. T. 696.) Hence, in order to obtain an *interim* injunction, the plaintiff is under no obligation to prove malice in the defendant; but he must prove that the defendant's statements are false : he must establish at all events a *primâ facie* case of non-infringement. It will then be open to the defendant to file affidavits showing that there has in fact been an infringement. If satisfactory affidavits to that effect be filed, the Court will not decide the question of infringement on that application; but will refuse to grant any *interim* injunction, even though the defendant declines to take legal proceedings in respect of such alleged infringement. (*Barney* v. *United Telephone Co.,* 28 Ch. D. 394 ; 33 W. R. 576 ; 52 L. T. 573.) If, however, after reading the affidavits on both sides, the plaintiff's case is still so far unimpaired that if the evidence remains the same at the hearing, it is probable that he will obtain a decree, he will be entitled to an *interim* injunction. (*Challender* v. *Royle,* 36 Ch. D. 425 ; 56 L. J. Ch. 995.)

Where the plaintiff complains that the defendant is issuing notices to his customers threatening them with proceedings if they deal in plaintiff's goods, and the defendant thereupon carries out his threat, and sues the plaintiff or his customers for infringing the defendant's patent, this infringement action, if prosecuted with due diligence, is an answer to any proceeding under s. 36; for it takes the case altogether out of the section. It also probably affords a defence to any action on the case for damages, as it is strong proof of *bonâ fides.* But it does not follow that the plaintiff must submit to a continuance of these threatening notices till the trial of the action. If they are more than mere general warnings against infringement, if they contain assertions that the plaintiff has in fact infringed the defendant's patent, they may be restrained as a contempt of Court (see *post*, p. 539); for they tend to prejudice the fair trial of the infringement action. (*Coats* v. *Chadwick*, [1894] 1 Ch. 347; 63 L. J. Ch. 328; 42 W. R. 328; 70 L. T. 228; 8 R. 159; *Goulard and another* v. *Lindsay*, 56 L. T. 506; 4 R. P. C. 189; *Fusee Vesta Co.* v. *Bryant and May*, 56 L. T. 136; 4 R. P. C. 191; *In re New Gold Coast Exploration Co.*, [1901] 1 Ch. 860; 70 L. J. Ch. 355; 8 Manson, 296.) And if such an injunction be granted, the applicant will not be required to give any undertaking as to damages. (*Fenner* v. *Wilson*, [1893] 2 Ch. 656; 62 L. J. Ch. 984; 42 W. R. 57; 68 L. T. 748; 3 R. 629.)

Illustrations.

A threat by a private letter is within the section; therefore, where a threat has been so made, but the defendants now admit that the plaintiffs have not infringed their patent, they will be perpetually restrained from making or continuing threats of legal proceedings.

>   *Driffield and East Riding Cake Co.* v. *Waterloo, &c., Cake Co.*,
>   31 Ch. D. 638; 55 L. J. Ch. 391; 34 W. R. 360; 54 L. T. 210.

The defendant issued a circular stating that the plaintiff was infringing his trade-mark and his patent, and threatening proceedings against all persons who retailed the goods alleged to be infringements. The plaintiff issued a writ under s. 32 of the 46 & 47 Vict. c. 57 (now s. 36 of the 7 Edw. VII. c. 29), and applied for an *interim* injunction. He satisfied the Court, on the balance of evidence, that he was not infringing the defendant's patent. The defendant had brought no action for infringement. Chitty, J., granted an injunction restraining the threats, so far as they related to the patent, till trial or further order. No order as to threats relating to the trade-mark.

>   *Colley* v. *Hart;* (1888) 6 Reports of Patent Cases, 17.

The defendant issued a notice to the public stating in general terms that it had come to his knowledge that certain of his patents were being infringed, and that his solicitor had instructions to take proceedings against all infringers. The plaintiff, who held a patent for goods similar to those in which the defendant dealt, then commenced an action for threats. The defendant, four days afterwards, but before the writ in this action was served on him, brought an action for infringement, not against the plaintiff, but against a Plumbing Company who retailed the plaintiff's goods. *Held,* that the defendant's action was an answer to an application for an *interim* injunction, and further that, if honestly prosecuted with reasonable diligence, it would take the case out of the section altogether.

> *Challender* v. *Royle,* 36 Ch. D. 425 ; 56 L. J. Ch. 995 ; 36 W. R. 357 ; 57 L. T. 734 ; 4 R. P. C. 363.
> And see *ante,* pp. 98—105.

Parliamentary Candidates.

By ss. 1 and 3 of the Corrupt and Illegal Practices Prevention Act, 1895 (58 & 59 Vict. c. 40), it is enacted that " any person, who, or the directors of any body or association corporate which, before or during any parliamentary election, shall for the purpose of effecting the return of any candidate at such election, make or publish any false statement of fact in relation to the personal character or conduct of such candidate " . . . . " may be restrained by *interim* or perpetual injunction by the High Court of Justice from any repetition of such false statement or any false statement of a similar character in relation to such candidate ; and, for the purpose of granting an *interim* injunction, *primâ facie* proof of the falsity of the statement shall be sufficient."

Note that s. 2 of this Act, which excuses the defendant " if he can show that he had reasonable grounds for believing, and did believe, the statement made by him to be true," applies only to criminal or *quasi*-criminal proceedings for " such illegal practice ; " it does not apply to an application for an injunction under section 3.

As to what is and what is not a " statement of fact " within section 1, see the careful judgment of Baron Pollock in the case of the *Borough of Sunderland Election Petition,* (1896) 5 O'M. & H. pp. 62—64. He there lays down the rule " that a mere argumentative statement of the conduct of a public man, although it may be in respect of his private life, is not always, and in many cases certainly would not be, a false statement of fact." This passage was approved by Buckley, J., in *Ellis* v. *National Union,*

&c., Associations and others, (1900) 109 L. T. Journal, 493, who added : "The Act was meant to deal with statements of fact as opposed to statements of opinion." And see *Monmouth Election Petition,* (1901) 5 O'M. & H. at p. 174.

Illustrations.

A paragraph appeared in a local newspaper during an election to the effect that the Liberal candidate, who was a colliery proprietor, had locked his men out of their pits for six weeks till stocks were cleared out, and coal had reached a fabulous price. " Then the late member for Chester-field found his 'conscience' would not allow him to starve the 'poor miner' any longer." The defendants reprinted this paragraph in the form of a leaflet, and distributed it among the electors. The Court of Appeal held that this statement was derogatory to the plaintiff's personal character and therefore within the Act ; that it was published for the purpose of injuring the plaintiff in the election ; and, as no attempt was made to prove the charge true, an injunction was granted to restrain the further publication of the leaflet " until the trial of the action, or the election, whichever happened first."

Bayley v. *Edmunds and others,* (1895) 11 Times L. R. 537.

A Parliamentary candidate caused to be printed and circulated in the borough a leaflet headed " Election Facts and Fictions " in which he accused his opponent, who was an employer of labour, of paying his men " wretched wages," commented on " the remarkable differences between his practice in dealing with men in his own employ and his precepts when preaching to the employés of other people," and asserted that he " meanly took advantage of a slander against his opponent," " sheltered himself under a Radical shuffle," that such conduct was " hitting below the belt," &c. Pollock, B., held that these statements were not " statements of fact " in the sense in which these words were intended by the Act.

Borough of Sunderland Election Petition, (1896) 5 O'M. & H. 53.

During the Parliamentary Election of 1900 a candidate published a poster in which he alleged falsely that his opponent was one of a band of " Radical Traitors," " who are always found on the side of Britain's enemies," and who were during the summer of 1899 in correspondence with the Boers. Buckley, J., held that these were not statements of fact within the meaning of the Act.

Ellis v. *National Union, &c., Associations and others,* (1900) 109 L. T. Journal, 493 ; *Times,* October 3rd, 1900.

As to injunctions to restrain the publication of words which are a contempt of Court, see *post,* Chapter XX., p. 535.

CHAPTER XV.

IF an action of libel or slander be tried by a jury, the costs will follow the event, unless the judge before whom such action is tried or the Court " shall for good cause otherwise order." (Order LXV. r. 1.) If by any chance such an action be tried by a judge alone, the costs are wholly in his discretion. Section 116 of the County Courts Act, 1888 (51 & 52 Vict. c. 43), does not apply to actions of libel or slander; for no such action can be brought in the County Court, except by consent (ss. 56, 64).

There is one exception to the above general rule. By section 1 of the Slander of Women Act, 1891, in any action for words spoken and made actionable by that Act, "a plaintiff shall not recover more costs than damages, unless the judge shall certify that there was reasonable ground for bringing the action."

Section 5 of the County Courts Act, 1867, applied to all actions, whether they could be brought in the County Court or not; the words of the Act being wider than the Legislature intended. Formerly also the provisions of Lord Denman's Act (3 & 4 Vict. c. 24), s. 2, applied to actions of libel and slander, and therefore a plaintiff who recovered less than 40s. damages could not recover any costs whatever from the defendant, unless the judge immediately certified on the record that the libel or slander was wilful and malicious. And even if the judge certified both that the action was one fit to be tried in the Superior Court and also that the slander was wilful and malicious, so as to take the case out of both the County Courts Act and Lord Denman's Act, still no certificate could enable a plaintiff to get more costs than damages, if he sued for a slander actionable *per se*, and recovered less than 40s. For the statute 21 Jac. I. c. 16, contained no proviso enabling a judge to make any exemption from the imperative rule that a plaintiff suing on the case for slanderous words, and recovering less than 40*s.*, shall have " only so much costs as the damages so given or assessed amount unto " (s. 6). This statute was held to apply only to words actionable *per se*, and not to actions of libel, of slander of title, of *scandalum magnatum*, or where the words are actionable only by reason of special damage alleged. But now the 21 Jac. I. c. 16, s. 6, and the 3 & 4 Vict. c. 24, s. 2, and the County Courts Act, 1867, are all repealed. (See s. 33 of the Judicature Act, 1875; *Parsons* v. *Tinling*, 2 C. P. D. 119; 46 L. J. C. P. 230; 25 W. R. 255; 35 L. T. 851; *Garnett* v. *Bradley*, 3 App. Cas. 944; 48 L. J. Ex. 186; 26 W. R. 698; 39 L. T. 261; *Ex parte Mercers' Co.*, 10 Ch. D. 481; 48 L. J. Ch. 384; 27 W. R. 424.)

A rule similar to Order LXV. r. 1 prevails in the Salford Hundred Court of Record (*Turner* v. *Heyland*, 4 C. P. D. 432; 48 L. J. C. P. 535; 41 L. T. 556); in the Liverpool Court of Passage (*King* v. *Hawkesworth*, 4 Q. B. D. 371; 48 L. J. Q. B. 484; 27 W. R. 660; 41 L. T. 411); in most Borough Courts; and also in Ireland. (*Cassidy* v. *O'Loghlen*, 4 L. R. Ir. 1, 731.) But in the Mayor's Court, London, the judge has an unfettered jurisdiction over costs. (*Hall* v. *Launspach*, [1898] 1 Q. B. 513; 67 L. J. Q. B. 372; 78 L. T. 243.)

The power given to the judge by s. 5 of the Law of Libel Amendment Act, 1888, to make an order apportioning the costs, when two or more actions of libel have been consolidated under that section, in no way interferes with or affects the general rule that where a case is tried by a jury, the costs shall follow the event, unless the judge shall for good cause otherwise order. (Per Charles, J., in *Hopley* v. *Williams*, 53 J. P. 822.) The provisions of the Public Authorities Protection Act, 1893, which entitle the defendants in certain events to costs as between solicitor and client, do not restrict the power of the judge for good cause to deprive the successful party of his costs. (*Bostock* v. *Ramsey U. D. C.*, [1900] 2 Q. B. 616; 69 L. J. Q. B. 945; 48 W. R. 254; 83 L. T. 358.)

Hence, now, if a plaintiff recovers nominal damages for words which were actionable at common law, he will get his costs, unless the judge or a Court otherwise orders. As soon therefore as the verdict is given, the defendant's counsel must at once apply to the judge to make an order depriving the plaintiff of his costs. As a rule, such an order will only be made where " contemptuous " damages, such as a farthing or a shilling, have been given, and not always then. There must be some " good cause," beside the smallness of the damages, to give the judge jurisdiction to make such an order; something either in the conduct of the parties or in the facts of the case which, in spite of the finding of the jury, makes it more just that the costs should not follow the event.

If the judge thinks fit to make an order, that order is not necessarily that each party should pay his own costs. He may for *very* good cause order that the successful plaintiff shall pay the defendant's costs as well as his own (per Bramwell, L.J., 15 Ch. D. at p. 41 ; and see *Myers* v. *The Financial News*, (1888) 5 Times L. R. 42); and where there has been a new trial the judge who tries the case the second time may, in the absence of any special order by the Court of Appeal, direct that the successful plaintiff shall pay the whole costs of both trials. (*Harris* v. *Petherick*, 4 Q. B. D. 611 ; 48 L. J. Q. B. 521 ; 28 W. R. 11 ; 41 L. T. 146.) But of course such an order would only be made in an extreme case, and where the plaintiff has grossly misconducted himself. (See *Norman* v. *Johnson*, 29 Beav. 77.) A successful defendant may also be deprived of his costs (*Sutcliffe* v. *Smith*, (1886) 2 Times L. R. 881 ; *Bostock* v. *Ramsey U. D. C.*, [1900] 2 Q. B. 616 ; 69 L. J. Q. B. 945 ; 48 W. R. 254 ; 83 L. T. 358), if there be good cause (*Granville & Co.* v. *Firth*, (1903) 72 L. J. K. B. 152 ; 88 L. T. 9). But he cannot be made to pay the whole costs of the action under any circumstances. (*Dicks* v. *Yates*, 18 Ch. D. 76, 85 ; 50 L. J. Ch. 809 ; 44 L. T. 660 ; *Re Foster* v. *Great Western Ry. Co.*, 8 Q. B. D. at pp. 521, 522 ; 30 W. R. 398 ; *Andrew* v. *Grove*, [1902] 1 K. B. 625 ; 71 L. J. K. B. 439 ; 50 W. R. 524 ; 86 L. T. 720.)

What is " good cause " for making an order that costs shall not follow the event ? " No nearer and no closer definition can be

given than that there will be good cause, whenever it is fair and
just as between the parties that" such an order should be made.
(*Per cur.* in *Forster* v. *Farquhar,* [1893] 1 Q. B. at p. 567.) "The
facts must show the existence of something, having regard either to
the conduct of the parties or to the facts of the case, which makes
it more just that an exceptional order should be made than that
the case should be left to the ordinary course of taxation." (Per
Brett, M.R., in *Jones* v. *Curling,* 13 Q. B. D. at p. 268.) "The
mere fact of a plaintiff, in an action for libel or slander, recovering
only a farthing or a shilling damages is not of itself good cause for
depriving him of costs. 'Good cause' must be something more
than the mere smallness of damages. The smallness of the
damages, however, is an important element to be considered, if
there are any other circumstances which can be taken into account."
(Per A. L. Smith, L.J., in *O'Connor* v. *The Star Newspaper Co., Ltd.,*
68 L. T. at p. 148.) "Where a plaintiff comes to enforce a legal
right, and there has been no misconduct on his part—no omission
or neglect which would induce the Court to deprive him of his
costs—the Court has no discretion, and cannot take away the
plaintiff's right to costs. There may be misconduct of many sorts;
for instance, there may be misconduct in commencing the proceedings, or some miscarriage in the procedure, or an oppressive
or vexatious mode of conducting the proceedings, or other misconduct which will induce the Court to refuse costs; but where
there is nothing of the kind the rule is plain and well settled, and
is as I have stated it." (Per Jessel, M.R., in *Cooper* v. *Whittingham,*
15 Ch. D. at p. 504; cited with approval by Brett, M.R., in *Jones*
v. *Curling,* 13 Q. B. D. at pp. 265, 268, and again in *O'Connor* v.
The Star, 68 L. T. at p. 147, as " a good working rule, though not
an exhaustive one." Cf. *Tipping* v. *Jepson,* (1906) 22 Times L. R.
748.) " 'Good cause' really seems to me to mean that there
must exist facts which might reasonably lead the judge to
think that the rule of costs following the event would not
produce justice as complete as the exceptional order which he
himself could make. Now, to ascertain the existence of such facts,
the judge should look in the first place at the result of the action
itself, namely, the verdict of the jury, and he should look also at
the conduct of the parties to see whether either of them had in any
way involved the other unnecessarily in the expense of litigation,
and beyond that he should consider all the facts of the case so far
as no particular fact was concluded by the finding of the jury."
(Per Bowen, L.J., in *Jones* v. *Curling,* 13 Q. B. D. at p. 272.)

"Everything which increases the litigation and the costs, and which places upon the defendant a burden which he ought not to bear in the course of that litigation, is perfectly good cause for depriving the plaintiff of his costs." (Per Lord Halsbury, L.C., in *Huxley* v. *West London Extension Ry. Co.*, 14 App. Cas. at p. 32.) The words " good cause " embrace " everything for which the party is responsible connected with the institution or conduct of the suit, and calculated to occasion unnecessary litigation and expense." (Per Lord Watson, *ib.*, at p. 33.) " The judge is not confined to the consideration of the defendants' conduct in the actual litigation itself, but may also take into consideration matters which led up to and were the occasion of that litigation." (Per A. L. Smith, L.J., in *Bostock* v. *Ramsey U. D. C.*, [1900] 2 Q. B. at p. 622.) " First, in determining whether good cause exists, the judge must accept the verdict as conclusive upon all matters of fact necessarily involved in it, however much he may personally dissent from the finding of the jury. So long, however, as the judge does not base his decision upon matter inconsistent with the verdict, all other matters outside the verdict are open for his consideration—everything which led to the action, every circumstance tending to show that the plaintiff was blamable in bringing it, everything reflecting upon the conduct of the parties in the course of the litigation itself. (*Harnett* v. *Vise*, 5 Ex. D. 307, see per James, L.J., pp. 310, 312.) The judge is under no obligation to give effect to any special reasons or views the jury may have entertained or expressed in giving their verdict—such, for instance, as a hope or recommendation that it may or may not carry costs, unless such views accord with his own ; nor is the amount of damages awarded to be taken as a conclusive test upon the question of ' good cause,' though it properly forms an element for consideration. . . . Should the jury, in an action for an assault or libel, award the plaintiff an ignominious compensation, it would not follow that as of course the judge ought to deprive him of his costs, although he might treat it as an indication of the opinion of the jury, in which he coincided, that the character of the plaintiff was worthless, and that the action never ought to have been brought, and was therefore oppressive." (Per Hawkins, J., in *Roberts* v. *Jones* and *Willey* v. *Great Northern Ry. Co.*, [1891] 2 Q. B. at pp. 197, 198.) See also *Nicolas* v. *Atkinson,* (1909) 25 Times L. R. 568 ; *Red Man's Syndicate* v. *Associated Newspapers, Ltd.,* (1910) 26 Times L. R. 394 ; *Kinnell* v. *Walker,* (1910) 27 Times L. R. 67 ; *Macalister* v. *Steedman,* (1911) *Ib.* 217.

Illustrations.

Where an action of libel was brought on a private letter written by a lady to an intimate friend, and shown only to the plaintiff and two others, and the plaintiff's own conduct had given rise to the suspicions entertained by the writer, and the jury gave a verdict for 10*l*. damages : Huddleston, B., made an order depriving him of costs, and this exercise of his discretion was approved both in the Divisional Court and in the Court of Appeal.

Harnett v. *Vise and wife*, 5 Ex. D. 307 ; 29 W. R. 7.

Whenever a defendant by his misstatements, made under circumstances which impose an obligation upon him to be truthful, brings litigation on himself and renders an action against him reasonable, there is " good cause " to deprive him of costs.

Sutcliffe v. *Smith*, (1886) 2 Times L. R. 881.

If the action is unfairly or oppressively brought, or is unfairly or oppressively persisted in, good cause will exist for depriving the plaintiff of the ordinary costs. Per Lord Esher, M.R., in

Barnes v. *Maltby*, (1889) 5 Times L. R. 207.

But bringing an action to recover money which is, in fact, due to the plaintiff cannot be said to be oppressive. Per Lord Esher, M.R., in

The Wilts, &c., Dairy Association v. *Hammond*, (1889) 5 Times L. R. 196.

The mere fact that a plaintiff in an action for unliquidated damages claimed 600*l*. and only recovered 50*l*. is no ground for depriving him of costs. Per Lord Esher, M.R., in

Pearman v. *Baroness Burdett-Coutts*, (1887) 3 Times L. R. at p. 720.

But where a plaintiff preferred an extravagant and an extortionate claim, supported it by fraudulent statements and dishonest acts, and endeavoured to substantiate it before the jury, by evidence which they very properly disbelieved, the judge at the trial, the Court of Appeal, and the House of Lords all agreed that there was perfectly good cause for depriving him of his costs, although he had recovered 50*l*. damages.

Huxley v. *West London Extension Ry. Co.*, 17 Q. B. D. 373 ; 55 L. J. Q. B. 506 ; 14 App. Cas. 26 ; 58 L. J. Q. B. 305 ; 37 W. R. 625 ; 60 L. T. 642.

Where the jury was apparently satisfied that, though the plaintiff had not been guilty of any misconduct on the two occasions mentioned in the libel, he had been guilty of misconduct of the kind alleged on many other occasions, and bore an evil reputation in consequence, and *therefore* awarded him only a farthing damages, it was held that there was good cause for depriving the plaintiff of costs.

Wood v. *Cox*, (1889) 5 Times L. R. 272.

Where a plaintiff allowed her name to be used by A. for the purpose of raising a political controversy and injuring A.'s political opponents, and signed a letter written by A., the publication of which produced a newspaper warfare, in the course of which the plaintiff was libelled, and the jury awarded her one shilling damages, it was held by the Court of

Appeal that there was good cause for which the judge at the trial might, in the exercise of his discretion, deprive the plaintiff of costs.

> *O'Connor* v. *The Star Newspaper Co., Ltd.*, (1893) 68 L. T. 146 ;
> 9 Times L. R. 233.

[Note, that in this case Bowen, L.J., expressed his private opinion that "when one farthing only is given as damages for a libel, there is *primâ facie* reasonable ground for saying that there was no good cause for bringing the action." But the other members of the Court did not share this view.]

Letters or conversations written or declared to be "without prejudice" cannot be taken into consideration in determining whether there is good cause for depriving a successful litigant of costs.

> *Walker* v. *Wilsher*, 23 Q. B. D. 335 ; 58 L. J. Q. B. 501 ; 37
> W. R. 723.

The unsuccessful defendant will, in ordinary course of taxation, be credited with the costs which he has incurred on any issue which he won. (See *post*, p. 447). Hence, where a taxation on that principle will meet the justice of the case, there is no necessity, and therefore no good cause, for the judge at the trial to make any special order.

> *Jones* v. *Curling and another*, 13 Q. B. D. 262 ; 53 L. J. Q. B.
> 373 ; 32 W. R. 651 ; 50 L. T. 349.

If the judge makes an order under Order LXV. r. 1, he is not bound to deal with the whole costs of the action. He may, for good cause, deprive a successful party of a portion of his costs, leaving the rest of the costs to follow the event.

Illustrations.

The judge may order a successful plaintiff to pay the costs occasioned by a claim for special damage which he has failed to substantiate.

> *Forster* v. *Farquhar*, [1893] 1 Q. B. 564 ; 62 L. J. Q. B. 296 ;
> 41 W. R. 425 ; 68 L. T. 308 ; 4 R. 346.

Or any costs unnecessarily inflicted on the defendant by the successful plaintiff's conduct of the action.

> *Roberts* v. *Jones*, [1891] 2 Q. B. 194 ; 64 L. J. Q. B. 441.
>
> *Hill* v. *Morris*, (1891) 8 Times L. R. 55.

So, too, the judge "has power to order a successful defendant to pay such part of the plaintiff's costs as has been caused by the defendant's misconduct in the action." Per Channell, J., in

> *Andrew* v. *Grove*, [1902] 1 K. B. at p. 628.

E.g., where the costs have been increased by the defendants improperly severing in their defences.

> *In re Isaac*, [1897] 1 Ch. 251 ; 66 L. J. Ch. 160 ; 45 W. R.
> 262 ; 75 L. T. 638.
>
> *Bagshaw* v. *Pimm*, [1900] P. 148 ; 69 L. J. P. 45 ; 48 W. R.
> 422 ; 82 L. T. 175.

If the judge at the trial declines to make an order depriving the plaintiff of his costs, there is no appeal from his decision. (*Moore* v. *Gill*, (1888) 4 Times L. R. 738.) But if he decides to make an order as to costs, then there is an appeal to the Court of Appeal on the question whether any " good cause" existed upon which the judge could exercise his discretion. If there was no " good cause," the judge had no jurisdiction to make any order as to costs, and the Court of Appeal will set the order aside, and no leave is necessary for an appeal on this ground. (*Civil Service Co-operative Society* v. *General Steam Navigation Co.*, [1903] 2 K. B. 756; 72 L. J. K. B. 933; 89 L. T. 429; *King* v. *Gillard*, [1905] 2 Ch. 7; 74 L. J. Ch. 421; 53 W. R. 598; 92 L. T. 605.) If there was anything which could amount to " good cause," then the Court of Appeal will not interfere with the judge's discretion, even though they do not approve of the way in which he has exercised it. (*Jones* v. *Curling and another*, 13 Q. B. D. 262; 53 L. J. Q. B. 373; 32 W. R. 651; 50 L. T. 349; *Huxley* v. *West London Extension Ry. Co.*, 14 App. Cas. 26; 58 L. J. Q. B. 305; 37 W. R. 625; 60 L. T. 642.)

If there are any facts before the judge or the Court which may properly be considered as affording a reason for disallowing costs, " the sufficiency or insufficiency of these considerations are matters of which they are constituted sole arbiters; they are acting within their jurisdiction, and their decisions are final and conclusive. On the other hand, if they give effect to considerations which do not constitute ' good cause' within the meaning of the rule, they exceed the limits of their jurisdiction; and on that ground their decisions are not protected from review." (Per Lord Watson in *Huxley* v. *West London Extension Ry. Co.*, 14 App. Cas. at pp. 33, 34.) " The judge has no jurisdiction to interfere with the costs, unless there is good cause for his interference. The question whether there was good cause is a matter of appeal; but when there is an appeal the only question for this Court to consider is, whether this Court thinks that there was ' good cause' for depriving the plaintiff of his costs upon which the judge might exercise his discretion." (Per Lord Esher, M.R., in *O'Connor* v. *The Star Newspaper Co., Ltd.*, 68 L. T. at p. 147.) " Whether or not there was ' good cause' is subject to appeal, but the Court of Appeal cannot bring the same knowledge to bear on the case as the judge who heard all the witnesses, and therefore the Court will be slow to say there was not ' good cause.' " (Per Bowen, L.J., in *Sutcliffe* v. *Smith*, (1886) 2 Times L. R. at p. 882.)   On such an application the Court of Appeal will assume that the verdict is right, and was obtained by right and lawful means, and will not go into the question whether evidence was rightly or wrongly received, or whether the direction to the jury was right or wrong. (Per Lord Esher, M.R., in *Wood* v. *Cox*, (1889) 5 Times L. R. at p. 273.)

Special Costs.

Application for any special costs, such as those of a special jury, of a commission abroad, of photographic copies of the libel, or any costs reserved to be dealt with by the judge at the trial (*British Provident Association* v. *Bywater*, [1897] 2 Ch. 531 ; 66 L. J. Ch. 787 ; 46 W. R. 28 ; 77 L. T. 22), should be made when judgment is delivered.   No order will be made as to such costs after the judgment has been drawn up ; they must be borne by the party who has incurred them. (*Ashworth* v. *Outram*, 9 Ch. D. 483 ; 27 W. R. 98 ; 39 L. T. 441 ; *Executors of Sir Rowland Hill* v. *Metropolitan District Asylum*, 49 L. J. Q. B. 668 ; 43 L. T. 462 ; W. N. 1880, p. 98 ; *Davey* v. *Pemberton*, 11 C. B. N. S. 629 ; *In re St. Nazaire Co.*, 12 Ch. D. 88 ; 27 W. R. 854 ; 41 L. T. 110.)

Costs of Separate Issues.

The costs of separate issues, unless otherwise ordered, do not necessarily follow the event of the whole action.   Such costs follow the event each of its own issue.   The party in whose favour final judgment is entered is entitled to the general costs of the action but the other party will be entitled to the costs of any issues found for him, and the judgment must be drawn up so as to give him those costs. (*Hubback* v. *British North Borneo Co.*, [1904] 2 K. B. 473 ; 73 L. J. K. B. 654 ; 53 W. R. 70 ; 91 L. T. 672 ; *Hoyes* v *Tate*, [1907] 1 K. B. 656 ; 76 L. J. K. B. 408 ; 96 L. T. 419.)   This is what is meant by the rule that the word " event " must be " read distributively."   The general costs of the action will, however, be found, as a rule, to exceed the costs of any number of issues.   If the judge makes an order giving a party costs, " except so far as they have been occasioned or incurred by or relate to some particular issue," that party will be entitled to all the general costs of the action, *minus* only the amount by which the costs have been increased by such issue.   Or the judge may direct taxation of the whole costs of the action *en bloc*, and award to one party half or

a third or some other proportion of the total amount.   (Order
LXV. r. 2.)

Illustrations.

If a plaintiff sues for several libels, or several slanders, or for libel,
slander, and assault, or any other cause of action, and succeeds on one
cause of action but fails on others, each party is entitled to judgment with
costs on the cause of action which he has won, without any special order
under Order LXV. r. 1.

> *Myers* v. *Defries,* 5 Ex. D. 15, 180 ; 49 L. J. Ex. 266 ; 28
> W. R. 258, 406 ; 41 L. T. 659 ; 42 L. T. 137.
> *Todd and others* v. *N. E. Ry. Co.,* (1903) 88 L. T. 112.

But if there be only one cause of action, and several issues raised concerning it, then if the plaintiff recovers damages on any issue, he will be
entitled to judgment, and such judgment will, in the absence of any special
order, carry with it the general costs of the action, leaving the defendant
the right only to deduct the costs of any issue which he has won.

> *Jones* v. *Curling,* 13 Q. B. D. 262 ; 53 L. J. Q. B. 373 ; 32
> W. R. 651 ; 50 L. T. 349.

So, if a defendant in an action of defamation both justifies and pleads
privilege, and fails on the first plea and wins on the second, he will be
entitled to the general costs of the action, *minus* such costs as the plaintiff can prove to have been occasioned by the plea of justification, and
by that exclusively.

> *Skinner* v. *Shoppee,* 6 Bing. N. C. 131 ; 8 Scott, 275.
> *Harrison* v. *Bush,* 5 E. & B. 344 ; 25 L. J. Q. B. 99 ; 2
> Jur. N. S. 90.
> *Sparrow* v. *Hill,* 8 Q. B. D. 479 ; 50 L. J. Q. B. 675 ; 29
> W. R. 705 ; 44 L. T. 917.
> *Brown* v. *Houston,* [1901] 2 K. B. 855 ; 70 L. J. K. B. 902 ;
> 85 L. T. 160 ; 17 Times L. R. 683.
> *In re Wright, Crossley & Co.,* 86 L. T. 280 ; W. N. [1902] 54.

The same rule was followed where the jury found that the words were
false but that the defendant had never published them, and that they were
no libel.

> *Empson* v. *Fairfax & Weaver,* 8 A. & E. 296 ; 3 N. & P. 385.

Where a libel consists of two severable portions, each making a separate
charge against the plaintiff, the defendant may justify the one without
the other ; and if he raise the issue by a proper plea and succeed on it,
he will be entitled to the costs of proving the one charge true, though he
has to pay damages for the other.   But if the defendant in such a case
foolishly pleads that the whole libel is true, and fails to prove more
than half of it true, the plaintiff will be entitled to a general verdict in
his favour, and the defendant will be entitled to no costs without a special
order, because no issue has been found for him.

> *Biddulph* v. *Chamberlayne,* 17 Q. B. 351 ; as explained in
> *Reynolds* v. *Harris,* 3 C. B. N. S. 267 ; 28 L. J. C. P. 26 ;
> 5 Jur. N. S. 365.

So where the defendant pleads and proves that one half of the libel does not refer to the plaintiff, he will be entitled to any costs occasioned by that half of the libel having been included in the action.

Prudhomme v. *Fraser*, 2 A. & E. 645.

Where immaterial issues are found in favour of one party, and judgment is afterwards entered for the other, neither party is entitled to the costs of the immaterial issues.

Goodburne v. *Bowman*, 9 Bing. 667.

Items of damage are not separate issues : so the judge must be asked to make a special order as to these.

Forster v. *Farquhar*, [1893] 1 Q. B. 564 ; 62 L. J. Q. B. 296 ; 41 W. R. 425 ; 68 L. T. 308.

Costs of Introductory Averments, &c.

A successful plaintiff is entitled to his costs of proving all "matters of inducement" which were reasonably necessary to explain the meaning of the words complained of, or to show the extent of the damage caused thereby. "We ought not to be too nice in cutting down the plaintiff's proof to the exact amount at which, under bare poles, he may conduct his vessel into port." (Per Tindal, C.J., in *Andrews* v. *Thornton*, 8 Bing. at p. 434.)

Payment into Court.

Money cannot be paid into Court in any action of libel or slander without admitting the plaintiff's cause of action ; no defence denying liability can be pleaded at the same time. (Order XXII. r. 1.) As to payment into Court under Lord Campbell's Act, see *post* p. 642. If the plaintiff accepts the sum paid into Court in satisfaction of his claim, he must give the defendant notice to that effect, and may then proceed to tax his costs, unless the Court or a judge otherwise orders, and in case of non-payment he may sign judgment for his costs. (Order XXII. r. 7.) This is the rule, even where the defendant pays sixpence into Court, and the plaintiff accepts that sum in satisfaction of his claim. (*McSheffrey* v. *Lanagan*, 20 L. R. Ir. 528.) But a judge at chambers will deprive the plaintiff of his costs if the whole action was useless or malicious. (*Broadhurst* v. *Willey*, W. N. 1876, p. 21 ; *Nichols* v. *Evens*, 22 Ch. D. 611 ; 52 L. J. Ch. 383 ; 31 W. R. 412 ; 48 L. T. 66.) If the plaintiff does not accept the sum paid into Court, but continues his action for damages *ultra*, he will recover the whole of his costs of the action should the jury find a verdict for an amount larger than the sum paid into Court. If, on the other hand, the verdict be for an amount not greater than the sum in Court, the defendant will strictly be entitled to the whole costs of the action. (*Langridge* v. *Campbell*, 2 Ex. D. 281 ; 46 L. J. Ex. 277 ; 25 W. R. 351 ; 36 L. T.

64; *Goutard* v. *Carr*, 13 Q. B. D. 598, n.; 53 L. J. Q. B. 55, 467, n.; 32 W. R. 242.) But the judge in such a case generally thinks fit to make an order that the plaintiff shall have his costs of the action up to the time when the money was paid into Court, and the defendant shall have only his costs incurred after that time. (*Buckton* v. *Higgs*, 4 Ex. D. 174; 27 W. R. 803; 40 L. T. 755; *The William Symington*, 10 P. D. 1; 51 L. T. 461; *Best* v. *Osborne, Garrett & Co.*, (1896) 12 Times L. R. 419; *Wagstaffe* v. *Bentley*, [1902] 1 K. B. 124; 71 L. J. K. B. 55; 85 L. T. 744; *Smith* v. *Northleach R. D. C.*, [1902] 1 Ch. 197; 71 L. J. Ch. 8; 50 W. R. 104; 85 L. T. 449.)

Counterclaim.

It is seldom that there is a counterclaim in an action of libel or slander; but whenever there is, its presence complicates the question of costs. In an action of libel or slander there can be no set-off, as the damages claimed are unliquidated; in other words, the counterclaim is not a defence to the plaintiff's action, but practically a cross-action brought by the defendant against the plaintiff. Section 116 of the County Courts Act, 1888, does not apply to actions of libel or slander, or to counterclaims of any kind. (*Blake* v. *Appleyard*, 3 Ex. D. 195; 47 L. J. Ex. 407; 26 W. R. 592; *Amon* v. *Bobbett*, 22 Q. B. D. 543; 58 L. J. Q. B. 219; 37 W. R. 329; 60 L. T. 912.) Hence, if the plaintiff's claim is either for libel or slander, and the defendant sets up any counterclaim, and both recover, and no special order is made as to costs, the taxation should proceed thus: The costs of the plaintiff's claim should first be taxed as if it were a separate action with no counterclaim. Then the costs incurred by the counterclaim must be taxed, as though they were part of the costs of a separate action. Any costs which have been incurred partly in support of or in opposition to the defence, and partly in support of or in opposition to the counterclaim, the taxing-master must apportion as best he can, and fix the amount applicable to the defence and the amount applicable to the counterclaim. Then whichever be the smaller amount—the costs of the claim or the costs of the counterclaim—must be deducted from the larger; and the successful party will have judgment for the balance. (*Atlas Metal Co.* v. *Miller*, [1898] 2 Q. B. 500; 67 L. J. Q. B. 815; 46 W. R. 657; 79 L. T. 5; explaining *Baines* v. *Bromley*, 6 Q. B. D. 691; 50 L. J. Q. B. 465; 29 W. R. 706; 44 L. T. 915.) If the plaintiff recover any sum at all, even a farthing, and the defendant nothing on his counterclaim, then the plaintiff, in the absence of any special order to the contrary, is entitled to the whole costs of the action. (*Potter* v. *Chambers*, 4 C. P. D. 457; 48 L. J. C. P. 274; 27 W. R. 414.) If neither plaintiff nor defendant recover anything on either claim or counter-claim, the proper order as to the taxation of costs is that made by Warrington, J., in *James* v. *Jackson*, ([1910] 2 Ch. 92; 79 L. J. Ch. 418; 102 L. T. 804), namely, to direct the defendant's costs of the action, and the plaintiff's costs of the counterclaim, to be separately taxed, to direct that there should be a set-off, and to order the balance, after such set-off, to be paid to the party to whom the taxing master certifies that it is due. If, however, the action be not of libel or slander, but be such that it could have been brought in the County Court, then the plaintiff's right to costs will be subject to s. 116 of the County Courts Act, 1888; while the defendant will be entitled to recover all the costs of his counterclaim, if he recover only a farthing thereunder, unless a special order be made to the contrary. (*Staples* v. *Young*, 2 Ex. D. 324; 25 W. R. 304; *Chat-field* v. *Sedgwick*, 4 C. P. D. 459; 27 W. R. 790; 41 L. T. 438; *Rutherford* v. *Wilkie*, 41 L. T. 435; *Ahrbecker & Son* v. *Frost*, 17 Q. B. D. 606; 55 L. T. 264.)

Costs of a Remitted Action.

If an action of libel or slander be commenced in the High Court, and subsequently remitted to a County Court, under s. 66 of the County Courts Act, 1888, "the action and all proceedings therein shall be tried and taken in such Court as if the action had originally been commenced therein." It follows that the High Court has no jurisdiction to make any order as to the costs of such an action (*Moody* v. *Steward*, L. R. 6 Ex. 35; 40 L. J. Ex. 25; 19 W. R. 161; 23 L. T. 465; *Harris & Sons* v. *Judge*, [1892] 2 Q. B. 565; 61 L. J. Q. B. 577; 41 W. R. 9; 67 L. T. 19); and that the power of the County Court judge over costs is regulated by s. 113 of the County Courts Act, 1888, and not by the Rules of the Supreme Court. That is to say, the judge has absolute discretion over the costs of the action, whether it be tried by a jury or not. Such discretion must, of course, be exercised judicially; but is not restricted by any provision as to "good cause." In the absence of any special direction, the costs will follow the event; the costs of the proceedings in the High Court will be allowed according to the scale in use in the High Court; the costs incurred since the order to remit according to the County Court scale.

Costs of Former Trial.

The costs of the first trial abide the event of the second, unless any special order be made when the new trial is granted, or at the second trial. (*Creen* v. *Wright*, 2 C. P. D. 354; 46 L. J. C. P. 427; 25 W. R. 502; 36 L. T. 355; *Field* v. *Great Northern Ry. Co.*, 3 Ex. D. 261; 26 W. R. 817; 39 L. T. 80; *Harris* v. *Petherick*, 4 Q. B. D. 611; 48 L. J. Q. B. 521; 28 W. R. 11; 41 L. T. 146; *Jones* v. *Richards*, (1899) 15 Times L. R. 398; *Dunn* v. *S. E. & C. Ry. Co.*, [1903] 1 K. B. 358; 72 L. J. K. B. 127; 51 W. R. 427; 88 L. T. 60.) And by "the event" of the second trial is meant the result of that trial as to costs. (*Brotherton* v. *Metropolitan District Ry. Joint Committee*, [1894] 1 Q. B. 666; 42 W. R. 273; 70 L. T. 218; 9 R. 154; and see *post*, p. 709.) If on the new trial the defendants ask leave to amend their Defence and pay money into Court under Order XXII. r. 1, this is an "event" in favour of the plaintiffs. (*Farquhar, North & Co.* v. *Edward Lloyd, Ltd.*, (1901) 17 Times L. R. 568.)

Inquiry as to Damages.

It has been decided by the Court of Appeal that the assessment of damages by a jury before an under-sheriff, upon a writ of inquiry issuing out of the High Court, is the trial of a cause, matter, or issue in the High Court. (*William Radam's Microbe Killer Co., Ltd.* v. *Leather*, [1892] 1 Q. B. 85; 61 L. J. Q. B. 38.) Under the County Courts Act, 1867 (30 & 31 Vict. c. 142), it was decided that an under-sheriff executing such a writ was a "judge," and had power to certify for costs as required by that Act (*Craven* v. *Smith*, L. R. 4 Ex. 146; 38 L. J. Ex. 90; 17 W. R. 710; 20 L. T. 400); although, of course, he is not "a judge of the High Court" within s. 116 of the County Courts Act, 1888. (*Cox* v. *Hill*, 67 L. T. 26.) But as no action of libel or slander can be commenced in a County Court, s. 116 does not apply. Hence, it would seem to follow that the under-sheriff presiding over such an assessment of damages by a jury is "the judge by whom such action, cause, matter, or issue is tried" within the meaning of Order LXV. r. 1, and has, therefore, power for good cause to deprive the plaintiff of his costs. If so, the decision of Field, J., at Chambers in *Gath* v. *Howarth*, W. N. 1884, p. 99, is no longer law. The certificate of the under-sheriff under the Slander of Women Act, 1891, is a sufficient authority for giving costs on the High Court scale. (*Boote* v. *Chirnside*, (1895) not reported; see A. P. 1911, Vol. II., p. 837.)

Husband and Wife.

If a married woman having general separate estate fail in an action of libel or slander, she may be condemned in costs, although her husband was joined with her as a co-plaintiff or a co-defendant. (*Newton and wife* v. *Boodle and others*, 4 C. B. 359; 18 L. J. C. P. 73; *Morris* v. *Freeman and wife*, 3 P. D. 65; 47 L. J. P. D. & A. 79; 27 W. R. 62; 39 L. T. 125; and see the remarks of Jessel, M.R., in *Besant* v. *Wood*, 12 Ch. D. 630; 40 L. T. 453; and ss. 1 and 13 of the Married Women's Property Act, 1882, *post*, pp. 568, 574.) Whenever a married woman institutes proceedings and fails, she may be ordered to pay the costs out of separate property which is subject to a restraint on anticipation. (Sect. 2 of the Married Women's Property Act, 1893.) No such order can be made in any action in which she is a defendant, unless she counterclaims. (*Hood-Barrs* v. *Cathcart* (1), [1894] 3 Ch. 376; 63 L. J. Ch. 793; 71 L. T. 11; *Hood-Barrs* v. *Cathcart* (2), [1895] 1 Q. B. 873; 64 L. J. Q. B. 520; 43 W. R. 560; 72 L. T. 427; *Hood-Barrs* v. *Heriot*, [1897] A. C. 177; 66 L. J. Q. B. 356; 45 W. R. 507; 76 L. T. 299.)

Public Bodies.

As a rule if the officers of any corporation, local board, company, or other public body be libelled or slandered, and take either civil or criminal proceedings to clear themselves, the costs must not be paid out of the corporate funds, which were contributed for other purposes. But if the action be brought against the defendant in respect of anything done as agent of a corporation or a public body and within the scope of his authority, the corporation may apply its funds to indemnify the agent in defending the action. (*Breay* v. *Royal British Nurses' Association*, [1897] 2 Ch. 272; 66 L. J. Ch. 587; 46 W. R. 86; 76 L. T. 735.) And if it be the company itself that is libelled or slandered, the directors may, of course, employ the company's funds in its own defence.

Illustrations.

The house surgeon of the Marylebone workhouse was dismissed by the guardians in consequence of differences which had arisen between him and the honorary physician of the parish infirmary. The house surgeon thereupon brought actions of libel and slander against the honorary physician, and also against the assistant surgeon of the workhouse. He failed in both, became bankrupt, and disappeared. The guardians thereupon paid the costs incurred by their officers out of the poor's rates; and the poor law auditors allowed the payment. But Knight-Bruce, V.-C., held such payment a breach of trust, and ordered those guardians who had authorised it to refund the amount out of their own pockets.

> *Attorney-General* v. *Compton*, 1 Younge & Collyer, Eq. 417.

A Turkish railway company was managed by English directors. Ellissen wrote a letter to Lord Stanley (then Secretary for Foreign Affairs), charging the directors with mismanaging the affairs of the company and misappropriating its funds. At a general meeting of the shareholders a resolution was passed requesting the directors "to adopt the strongest possible measures to put an end to such mischievous action." The directors accordingly prosecuted Ellissen for libel. Wickens, V.-C., held that the costs of such prosecution could not be paid out of the assets of the company.

> *Pickering* v. *Stephenson*, L. R. 14 Eq. 322 ; 41 L. J. Ch. 493 ;
> 20 W. R. 654 ; 26 L. T. 608.

And the directors would now, in such a case, be ordered to repay to the company any costs thus improperly paid out of its funds.

> *Cullerne* v. *London, &c., Building Society*, 25 Q. B. D. 485,
> 490 ; 59 L. J. Q. B. 525 ; 39 W. R. 88 ; 63 L. T. 511.
> *In re Sharpe*, [1892] 1 Ch. 154, 165 ; 61 L. J. Ch. 193 ; 40
> W. R. 241 ; 65 L. T. 806.

A former employé of the Army and Navy Stores took to walking up and down in front of their door, carrying sandwich boards placarded with violent attacks upon the society, denouncing it as "a swindle, and counterfeit," and also upon the directors. *Held*, that as these libels were clearly calculated to injure the credit of the society, and to diminish its business, the costs of a prosecution might rightly be paid out of the funds of the society.

> *Studdert* v. *Grosvenor*, 33 Ch. D. 528 ; 55 L. J. Ch. 689 ; 34
> W. R. 754 ; 55 L. T. 171 ; 50 J. P. 710.

A nursing association incorporated by royal charter were the proprietors and publishers of a newspaper on nursing, and employed one of the members of the association as honorary editor. An action for libel was brought against the editor alone in respect of an article inserted in the newspaper under the express instructions of the association. It was held that the funds of the association could be lawfully applied in undertaking the defence of the action.

> *Breay* v. *Royal British Nurses' Association*, [1897] 2 Ch. 272 ;
> 66 L. J. Ch. 587 ; 46 W. R. 86 ; 76 L. T. 735.

As to costs in criminal proceedings, see, as to indictments, *post*, p. 737; as to criminal informations, *post*, p. 742.

CHAPTER XVI.

CRIMINAL LAW.

IT is a misdemeanour at common law, punishable on indictment or information with fine and imprisonment, to speak any blasphemous, obscene, or seditious words in the hearing of others. *A fortiori*, it is a misdemeanour to write and publish blasphemous, obscene, or seditious words.

It is a misdemeanour at common law, punishable on indictment or information with fine and imprisonment, to write and publish defamatory words of any living private person, or exhibit any picture or effigy defamatory of him. The law presumes that the publication of such words, or the exhibition of such picture or effigy, is calculated to cause a breach of the peace. Where, however, the libel is in fact not of a kind calculated to provoke a breach of the peace, criminal proceedings should not be taken; the person defamed should be content with his civil remedy. It is not a crime merely to speak words defamatory of a private person, however malicious the utterance may be.

When no action would lie without proof of special damage, no indictment or information can be preferred, whether the words be written or spoken.

Not every publication which would be held a libel in a civil case can be made the foundation of criminal proceedings. Hawkins in a passage cited apparently with approval by the Court in *R.* v. *Labouchere*, (1884) 12 Q. B. D. at p. 322, "puts the whole criminality of libels on private persons, as distinguished from the civil liability of those who publish them, on their tendency to disturb the public peace." He says (1 Hawk. P. C., c. 28, s. 3): "The Court will not grant this extraordinary remedy (a criminal information), nor should a grand jury find an indictment, unless the offence be of such signal enormity that it may reasonably be construed to have a tendency to disturb the peace and harmony of the community. In such a case the public are justly placed in the character of an offended prosecutor to vindicate the common right of all, though violated only in the person of an individual." And in a subsequent case Lord Coleridge, L.C.J., told the jury that "the principles on which such prosecutions should be allowed had been laid down by himself, as the mouthpiece of a strong Court, in a recent case (*The Queen* v. *Labouchere*), in which he had cited the opinions of great judges to this effect:—'A criminal prosecution ought not to be instituted unless the offence be such as can be reasonably construed as calculated to disturb the peace of the community. In such a case the public prosecutor has to protect the community in the person of an individual. But private character should be vindicated in an action for libel, and an indictment for libel is only justified when it affects the public, as an attempt to disturb the public peace.'" (*Wood* v. *Cox*, (1888) 4 Times L. R. at p. 654.)

It is a misdemeanour at common law, punishable on indictment with fine and imprisonment, to write and publish defamatory words of any deceased person, provided it be alleged and proved that this was done with intent to bring contempt and scandal on his family and relations, and so provoke them to a breach of the peace. (5 Rep. 125*a*; Hawkins P. C. i. 542 ; *R.* v. *Topham*, 4 T. R. 126.)

It is also a misdemeanour to libel any sect, company, or class of men, without mentioning any person in particular ; provided it be alleged and proved that such libel tends to excite the hatred of the people against all belonging to such sect or class, and conduces to a breach of the peace. (*R.* v. *Gathercole*, (1838) 2 Lewin, C. C. 237.)

Such intention may sufficiently appear from the words of the libel itself, or it may be proved by the consequences, if any, of its publication.

The criminal remedy for libel, as it is the earlier, so it is in some respects the more extensive remedy; a libel may be indictable, though it be not actionable. Thus, in neither of the above cases would an action lie for want of a proper plaintiff. (And see *R.* v. *Darby*, 3 Mod. 139.)

In *R. pros. Vallombrosa* v. *Labouchere,* 12 Q. B. D. 320 ; 53 L. J. Q. B. 362 ; 32 W. R. 861 ; 50 L. T. 177 ; 15 Cox, C. C. 415 ; 48 J. P. 165, the Court expressed some doubt as to whether it was a crime to libel a dead man, but abstained from expressing any decided opinion on the point. This doubt certainly operated as one reason among others for refusing the extreme remedy of a criminal information in that case ; and it will thus be very difficult to obtain a criminal information in any subsequent case of libel on a person deceased. But these *dicta* do not affect the remedy by way of indictment, and we think the law remains as stated above. See, however, the judgment of Stephen, J., in *R.* v. *Ensor,* (1887) 3 Times L. R. 366.

It is not necessary to prove that the libeller in fact desired that a breach of the peace should follow on his publication ; that is probably the last thing he wished for ; still less is it necessary to prove that an actual assault ensued, though, if it did, evidence of such assault is admissible. (*R.* v. *Osborn,* Kel. 230 ; 2 Barnard. 138, 166.) It is sufficient if the necessary or natural effect of the words is to vilify the memory of the deceased, and to injure his posterity to such an extent as to render a breach of the peace imminent or probable.

Illustrations.

Libel complained of : " On Saturday evening died of the small-pox, at his house in Grosvenor Square, Sir Charles Gaunter Nicoll, Knight of the Most Honourable Order of the Bath, and representative in Parliament for the town of Peterborough. . . . He could not be called a friend to his country, for he changed his opinions for a red ribbon, and voted for that pernicious object, the excise." It was alleged that this passage was published with intent to vilify, blacken, and defame the memory of the said Sir Charles, and to stir up the hatred and evil will of the people against the family and posterity of the said Sir Charles. An information was granted.

R. v. *Critchley,* (1734) 4 T. R. 129, n.

But an indictment which alleged that a libel on the late Earl Cowper had been published with intent to disgrace and vilify his memory, reputation, and character, but did not go on to aver any intent to create ill blood or throw scandal on the children and family of Earl Cowper, or to provoke them to a breach of the peace, was held bad, after a verdict of guilty, and judgment arrested.

R. v. *Topham,* (1791) 4 T. R. 126.

R. v. *Ensor,* (1887) 3 Times L. R. 366.

If the words only injure the character of the deceased, and do not tend to injure or bring contempt on his family, the defendant must be acquitted.

And, *à fortiori,* to discuss the characters of deceased statesmen and noblemen as a matter of history is no crime.

Per Lord Kenyon, C.J., 4 T. R. at p. 129.

An attack upon the character and policy of William III. and George I. was held a seditious libel in the reign of George II., and the writer was put in the pillory, and imprisoned for three years.

> R. v. Dr. Shebbeare, (1758) Holt on Libel, p. 82, cited in R. v. Dean of St. Asaph, 3 T. R. 430, n.

The defendant published a sensational account of a cruel murder committed by certain Jews said to have lately arrived from Portugal, and then living near Broad Street. They were said to have burnt a woman and a new-born baby, because its father was a Christian. Certain Jews who had arrived from Portugal, and who then lived in Broad Street, were attacked by the mob, barbarously treated, and their lives endangered. A criminal information was granted, although it was objected that it did not appear precisely who were the persons accused of the murder.

> R. v. Osborn, Kel. 230 ; 2 Barnard. 138, 166.

It is a crime to write of a Roman Catholic nunnery that it is a "brothel of prostitution ; " for this is an aspersion on the characters of the nuns in general, though none are singled out by name.

> R. v. Gathercole, (1838) 2 Lew. C. C. 237.
> R. v. J. A. Williams, (1822) 2 B. & Ald. 595 ; 2 Townsend's Modern State Trials, 231.

A pamphlet reflecting on the Government, and asserting that its officers are corrupt, ignorant, and incapable, will be a libel, and punishable as a crime ; although no particular member of the Government, and no individual officer, is mentioned or referred to.

> R. v. Tutchin, 14 Howell's St. Tr. 1095 ; 5 St. Tr. 527 ; Holt, 424 ; 2 Ld. Raym. 1061 ; 1 Salk. 50 ; 6 Mod. 268.

A notice was posted in church calling attention to certain abuses permitted by "the trustees" of Lambeth workhouse ; an information was granted on behalf of the whole body of trustees [although the trustees could not before the Judicature Act have jointly sued for the libel ; post, p. 581].

> R. v. Griffin, 1 Sess. Cas. 257.

An information was granted for a libel commencing :—"Whereas an East India director has raised the price of green tea to an extravagant rate," although there was nothing to show which particular director was intended.

> R. v. Jenour, 7 Mod. 400.

But an indictment for a libel on "persons to the jurors unknown," is bad, even after verdict.

> R. v. Orme (vel Alme) and Nutt, 1 Ld. Raym. 486 ; 3 Salk. 224.

It is a misdemeanour at common law to utter words which amount to a direct challenge to fight a duel, or to utter insulting words with the intention of provoking another to send a challenge. (R. v. Philipps, 6 East, 464, and note on p. 476.) À fortiori, it is a misdemeanour to write a challenge or consciously to deliver a written challenge.

And indeed all words which amount to a solicitation to commit a crime, whether spoken or written, are indictable, whether the person solicited commit the crime or not. (*R.* v. *Higgins*, 2 East, 5; *R.* v. *Gregory*, L. R. 1 C. C. R. 77.)

It is also said to be a misdemeanour to fabricate and publish false news in writing (Dig. L. L. 23), or to endeavour, by spreading false rumours, to raise or lower the price of food or merchandise. (See *R.* v. *Waddington*, (1800) 1 East, 143). According to Scroggs, J., it is a misdemeanour to publish any news at all, though true and harmless. (See 11 Hargrave's St. Tr. 322.) Where eight persons combined to raise the price of Government stocks on Feb. 21st. 1814, by spreading a false rumour of the death of Napoleon Buonaparte, they were indicted and convicted of a conspiracy, for their common purpose was illegal. (*R.* v. *De Berenger*, 3 M. & S. 67.) But this is scarcely an authority for holding that the merely spreading a false rumour is in itself indictable. The statutes of *Scandalum Magnatum*, 3 Edw. I. c. 34; 2 Rich. II. st. 1, c. 5; and 12 Rich. II. c. 11, which had long been practically obsolete, were repealed by the Statute Law Revision Act, 1887 (50 & 51 Vict. c. 59).

In all the above cases of misdemeanour at common law, the defendant may be fined or imprisoned, or both; but he cannot be sentenced to hard labour. He may also be required to find sureties to keep the peace and to be of good behaviour for any length of time. A married woman could not, before the Married Women's Property Act, 1870, be fined, but she could be required to find sureties, though she could not enter into recognizances herself.

None of the above offences can be tried at quarter sessions, except an indictment for obscene words; *post*, p. 505.

Certain statutes have been passed in aid of the common law:—

By section 3 of Lord Campbell's Act (6 & 7 Vict. c. 96), it is a misdemeanour to publish, or threaten to publish, any libel upon any other person, or to threaten to print or publish, or propose to abstain from printing or publishing, or to offer to prevent the printing or publishing of, any matter or thing touching another, with intent to extort money or gain, or to procure for anyone any appointment or office of profit. The offender may be sentenced to imprisonment for any term not exceeding three years, either with or without hard labour.

Except under the first clause of the section, the matter or thing threatened to be published need not be libellous; the intent to extort money is the gist of the offence; and to demand money which the defendant honestly believes to be due and owing to him is no evidence of such an intent. (*R.* v. *Coghlan,* 4 F. & F. 316.) Whether the words amount to a threat must be determined by the language itself. (*R.* v. *Plaisted,* (1910) 22 Cox, C. C. 5.) Threatening to commence, or offering to prevent, legal proceedings of any kind is not an offence within the section. (*R.* v. *Yates and another,* 6 Cox, C. C. 441.) A corporation is not a "person" within the meaning of this section. (*R.* v. *M'Laughlin,* 14 J. P. 291.)

By section 4 of the same Act, it is a misdemeanour to publish maliciously any defamatory libel knowing the same to be false; the punishment may be fine or imprisonment, or both, such imprisonment not to exceed two years.

By section 5 of the same Act, it is a misdemeanour to maliciously publish any defamatory libel; the punishment may be fine or imprisonment, or both, such imprisonment not to exceed one year. This section does not create any new offence, or attempt to define any existing offence; it merely fixes the punishment to be awarded for the existing common law misdemeanour of maliciously publishing a libel. (*R.* v. *Munslow,* [1895] 1 Q. B. 758; 64 L. J. M. C. 138; 43 W. R. 495; 72 L. T. 301.)

See the whole statute in Appendix C., *post,* pp. 828—831.

By section 44 of the Larceny Act, 1861 (24 & 25 Vict. c. 96), it is a felony for anyone knowing the contents thereof, to send, deliver, or utter, or cause to be received, any letter or writing, demanding of any person with menaces and without any reasonable or probable cause, any property or money. Such menace need not necessarily be either a threat of injury to the person or property of the prosecutor, or a threat to accuse him of a crime; a threat to accuse him of immorality or misconduct may be sufficient. (*R.* v. *Tomlinson*, [1895] 1 Q. B. 706; 64 L. J. M. C. 97; 43 W. R. 544; 72 L. T. 155.)

By sections 46 and 47 of the same Act it is a felony to accuse or threaten to accuse another of any infamous crime, whether by letter or otherwise, with intent to extort money or gain. The offender may be sentenced to penal servitude for life, or for any term not less than three years [now *five* years, 27 & 28 Vict. c. 47, s. 2], or to imprisonment, with or without hard labour, for any term not exceeding two years. (See *R.* v. *Redman*, L. R. 1 C. C. R. 12; 39 L. J. M. C. 89; *R.* v. *Ward*, 10 Cox, C. C. 42.)

By section 1 of the Corrupt and Illegal Practices Prevention Act, 1895, "any person who, or the directors of any body or association corporate which, before or during any parliamentary election, shall, for the purpose of affecting the return of any candidate at such election, make or publish any false statement of fact in relation to the personal character or conduct of such candidate shall be guilty of an illegal practice within the meaning of the provisions of the Corrupt and Illegal Practices Prevention Act, 1883 (46 & 47 Vict. c. 51), and shall be subject to all the penalties for and consequences of committing an illegal practice in the said Act mentioned;" that is to say, he is on summary conviction liable to a fine not exceeding 100*l.*, and will be incapable of voting at any election in the same constituency for five years. Such conduct may also render the election void (see section 4). The form of petition is given in Precedent No. 87, *post*, p. 810. But by section 2, "no person shall be deemed to be guilty of such illegal practice if he can show that he had reasonable grounds for believing, and did believe, the statement made by him to be true." (See *ante*, pp. 437, 438.) It had already been provided by section 9, sub-section (2) of the Act of 1883, that "any person who, before or during an election, knowingly publishes a false statement of the withdrawal of a candidate at such election for the purpose of promoting or procuring the election of another candidate, shall be guilty of an illegal practice."

Criminal Informations.

In some cases of indictable words, the prosecutor may also, if he prefer, proceed by way of criminal information. Criminal informations are of two kinds :—

(i.) Those filed by the Attorney-General himself, usually called *ex officio* informations.

(ii.) Those filed by the King's coroner and attorney by the direction of the King's Bench Division at the instance of some private individual, who is called the "relator."

(i.) The first class is, as a rule, confined to libels of so dangerous a nature as to call for immediate suppression by the officers of the State ; especially blasphemous, obscene, or seditious libels, or such as are likely to cause immediate outrage and public riot and disturbance. In these cases, therefore, the Attorney-General himself takes the initiative. There had been no *ex officio* information for libel filed in England since 1887 until the case of *R.* v. *Mylius* in 1911.

(ii.) In the second class of informations the relator is generally some private individual who has been defamed. But still the words complained of must be such as call for the prompt and immediate interference of the Court. It must be shown that the ordinary remedies by action or indictment are insufficient in the particular case. The Court, moreover, always looks at all the circumstances which occasioned or provoked the libel. Thus, no information will be granted if the relator has himself libelled the defendant (*R.* v. *Nottingham Journal*, 9 Dowl. 1042), or in any way invited the publication of the libel of which he now complains (*R.* v. *Larrieu*, 7 A. & E. 277), or had an opportunity of expressing his disapproval of its terms, of which he did not avail himself (*R.* v. *Lawson*, 1 Q. B. 486 ; 1 Gale & D. 15), or has demanded and received explanations from the defendant (*Ex parte Doveton*, 7 Cox, C. C. 16 ;

26 L. T. (Old S.) 73 ; 19 J. P. 741 ; *Ex parte Haviland,* 41 J. P. 789), or has demanded an apology and threatened an action for damages (*Ex parte Pollard,* (1901) 17 Times L. R 773), or has himself written to the papers or published a pamphlet provoking the libel (*R.* v. *Hall,* 1 Cox, C. C. 344), or replying to it (*Ex parte Rowe,* 20 L. T. (Old S.) 115 ; 17 J. P. 25). And generally, if the relator has been guilty of any misconduct in relation to the matter, a rule will be refused, except in cases where the public have a direct and independent interest in the prompt suppression of such libels. (*R.* v. *Casey,* 13 Cox, C. C. 310 ; following *R.* v. *Norris,* 2 Lord Kenyon, 300.)

It is not necessary that the libel should charge a criminal offence to induce the Court to grant a criminal information. It is enough that the libel, though on a private individual, is one requiring prompt suppression. So, if there be general reflections on a body or class, no particular individual being especially attacked ; still, if the words are likely to cause outrage and violence, the Court will grant an information : as where the libel was on the Jews, and certain Jews in consequence had been ill-used by the mob (*Anon.,* 2 Barnard. 138 ; *R.* v. *Osborn, ib.* 166 ; *ante,* p. 458) ; so where the general body of clergymen in a particular diocese were libelled (*R.* v. *Williams,* 5 B. & Ald. 595) ; or a public body, such as the directors of the East India Company (*R.* v. *Jenour,* 7 Mod. 400).

The rank and dignity of the person libelled was formerly taken into consideration ; and informations have been granted for imputing that the children of a marquis were bastards (*R.* v. *Gregory,* 8 A. & E. 907 ; 1 P. & D. 110) ; that a peer had married an actress (*R.* v. *Kinnersley,* 1 Wm. Bl. 294) ; that a naval captain was a coward, a bishop a bankrupt, a peer a perjurer, &c. But now it is settled that rank confers no superior claim to the summary interference of the Court. A peer is no more entitled to a criminal information when his *private* character is attacked than the humblest subject of the King. (*R. pros.*

Vallombrosa v. *Labouchere*, 12 Q. B. D. 320; 53 L. J. Q. B. 362; 32 W. R. 861; 50 L. T. 177; 15 Cox, C. C. 415; 48 J. P. 165.) A grocer obtained a criminal information for a libel in *R.* v. *Benfield*, (1760) 2 Burr. 980; a housekeeper in *R.* v. *Tanfield*, (1878) 42 J. P. 423.

But latterly the Court has been much more chary of granting criminal informations; and in future they will, as a rule, be only granted where the applicant holds some public office or position in England and has been attacked in his official character (*R.* v. *Labouchere, suprà; R.* v. *Russell*, (1905) 93 L. T. 407; 21 Times L. R. 749); or where the libel tends to obstruct the course of justice, or to prejudice the fair trial of any accused person. (*R.* v. *Watson and others*, 2 T. R. 199; *post*, p. 529; *R.* v. *Jolliffe*, 4 T. R. 285; *R.* v. *White*, 1 Camp. 359, n.; *Ex parte Duke of Marlborough*, 5 Q. B. 955; 13 L. J. M. C. 105; 1 Dav. & Mer. 720; *R.* v. *Gray*, 10 Cox, C. C. 184.) And the mere fact that the applicant is employed by the State is not sufficient. There must be some special circumstances to entitle him to the extraordinary remedy of a criminal information. (*Ex parte The Postmistress of Littleton*, (1888) 52 J. P. 264.)

No information will be granted for a libel contained in a private letter never made public (*Ex parte Dale*, 2 C. L. R. 870); nor for any matter of mere trade dispute, even though fraud be imputed; nor in any case where no malicious intention appears (*Ex parte Doveton*, 7 Cox, C. C. 16; 19 J. P. 741; 26 L. T. (Old S.) 73); nor where the remedy by action or indictment is sufficient (*R.* v. *Mead*, 4 Jur. 1014; *In re Evening News*, (1886) 3 Times L. R. 255).

À fortiori, no information will be granted where the words are privileged by reason of the occasion on which they were published (*R.* v. *Bailie*, (1790) Holt, N. P. 312, n.; *Ex parte Hoare*, 23 L. T. 83); or where they appear to be true (*R.* v. *Draper*, 3 Smith, 390).

In every case the application for a criminal information must be made promptly; any delay in making the application after knowledge of the libel has reached the prosecutor will be ground for refusing an information, unless such delay can be satisfactorily explained. No information will be granted where the libel can no longer " exercise any prejudicial influence." (*Ex parte Wm. Smith*, (1869) 21 L. T. 294.) The prosecutor, too, must come to the Court in the first instance, and must not have attempted to obtain redress in other ways before applying for a criminal information. (*R.* v. *Calthorpe*, 27 J. P. 581; *Ex parte Pollard*, (1901) 17 Times L. R. 773.)

Illustrations.

An information was refused where the alleged libel was proved to be a true copy of a report of a Committee of the House of Commons, though it did reflect on the individual prosecutor, and though its publication was not authorised by the House.

> *R.* v. *Wright,* (1799) 8 T. R. 293.

A French gentleman, D'Eon de Beaumont, published a libel on the Count de Guerchy, then French Ambassador in England. The libel chiefly referred to private disputes between D'Eon and the Count, alleging that the Count had supplanted D'Eon at the Court of Versailles by trickery; but it also reflected on the public conduct of the ambassador, and insinuated that he was not fit for his post. An information was filed and D'Eon convicted. (Lord Mansfield.)

> *R.* v. *D'Eon,* (1764) 3 Burr. 1514; 1 W. Bl. 501; Dig.
> L. L. 88.
> And see *R.* v. *Peltier,* (1803) 28 Howell's St. Tr. 617; *post,*
> p. 583.

Lord George Gordon was tried in 1787 and convicted upon an information charging him with libelling Marie Antoinette, Queen of France, and " her tool " the French Ambassador in London. He was fined 500*l.* and sentenced to two years' imprisonment, and at the expiration of that time to find sureties for his good behaviour. This he could not do, so he remained in prison till he died on November 1st, 1793. (Ashurst, J.)

> *R.* v. *Lord George Gordon*, 22 Howell's St. Tr. 177.

The *Courier* published the following passage :—" The Emperor of Russia is rendering himself obnoxious to his subjects by various acts of tyranny, and ridiculous in the eyes of Europe by his inconsistency. He has now passed an edict prohibiting the exportation of timber, deals, and other naval stores. In consequence of this ill-timed law, upwards of 100 sail of vessels are likely to return to this country without freights." This was deemed a libel upon the Emperor Paul I. An information was granted, and the proprietor of the *Courier* was fined 100*l.*, sentenced to six months' imprisonment, and to find sureties for good behaviour for five years from the expiration of that term. The printer and publisher were also sentenced to one month's imprisonment. (Lord Kenyon, C.J.)

> *R.* v. *Vint,* (1799) 27 Howell's St. Tr. 627.

O.L.S. H H

The publication and circulation in London of a newspaper article written in German exulting over the murder of the Emperor Nicholas of Russia and commending it as an example to revolutionists throughout the world is an incitement to murder under s. 4 of the 24 & 25 Vict. c. 100, although not addressed to any person in particular ; and is also a criminal libel.

> *R.* v. *Most,* (1881) 7 Q. B. D. 244 ; 50 L. J. M. C. 113 ; 29 W. R. 758 ; 44 L. T. 823 ; 14 Cox, C. C. 583.

The Prince Regent obtained an information against the editor and printer of the *Examiner.*

> *R.* v. *Leigh and John Hunt,* 3 Chit. Cr. L. 881.

So did a bishop, "dishonourable and degrading conduct" being imputed to him *quâ* bishop.

> *R.* v. *Clouter,* Cole on Cr. Inf. p. 22.

Certain justices of Leicestershire obtained a rule for a criminal information for a libel imputing that, in convicting a particular prisoner they had deliberately acted from motives of political partisanship.

> *Ex parte Hoskyns,* (1869) 33 J. P. 68.
> *Ex parte Earl of Radnor,* (1869) 33 J. P. 740.
> *Ex parte Umfreville,* (1889) 5 Times L. R. 600.
> *R.* v. *Masters,* (1889) 6 Times L. R. 44.

The mayor of a borough obtained a criminal information for a libel imputing to him gross misconduct in his office.

> *Ex parte the Mayor of Great Yarmouth,* 1 Cox, C. C. 122.

Magistrates of a borough have also obtained a criminal information for a libel which imputed that they had neglected or refused to do their duty.

> *R.* v. *Brigstock,* Cole on Cr. Inf. p. 23 ; 6 C. & P. 184.

So on two occasions did a stipendiary magistrate.

> *Ex parte Travis,* (1868) 32 J. P. 772.
> *R.* v. *John Rea,* 17 Ir. C. L. R. 584 ; 9 Cox, C. C. 401.

And two town-clerks.

> *R.* v. *Waite,* (1743) 1 Wils. 22 ; *ante,* p. 28.
> *R.* v. *Hatfield,* (1830) 4 C. & P. 244.

But where a magistrate demanded an apology and threatened an action for damages, before making his application for an information, a rule was refused.

> *Ex parte Pollard,* (1901) 17 Times L. R. 773.

So a clerk to justices who was accused of embezzling moneys paid to him for fines was left to his ordinary remedies.

> *Ex parte Freer,* (1870) 34 J. P. 68.

A chief constable obtained a rule nisi for a libel imputing misconduct in his office.

> *Ex parte Parry,* (1877) 41 J. P. 85.

But a rule was refused to a superintendent of police.

> *Ex parte Little,* (1865) 29 J. P. 742.

A Queen's counsel obtained a criminal information for libellous verses and for a caricature imputing to him professional misconduct in the conduct of a case.

> *Sir W. Garrow's Case,* 3 Chit. Cr. Law, 884.

But it was held that the musical critic of the *Times* was not entitled to a criminal information for a libel charging him with corruption, on the ground that his was not a public office.

> *Ex parte Davison,* 42 J. P. 727 ; cited 12 Q. B. D. 328.

Nor a foreign duke, whose deceased father was libelled.

> *R. pros.* !*Vallombrosa* v. *Labouchere,* 12 Q. B. D. 320 ; 53 L. J. Q. B. 362 ; 32 W. R. 861 ; 50 L. T. 177 ; 15 Cox, C. C. 415 ; 48 J. P. 165.

The solicitors to a railway company were refused a rule for a criminal information for a libel on them by the directors, imputing extortion and fraud. They were left to bring an action.

> *Ex parte Baxter,* 28 J. P. 326.

A County Court judge illegally refused to hear a barrister who appeared before him. The barrister memorialised the Lord Chancellor. Obtaining no redress, he applied to the Court of Queen's Bench for a criminal information. This would have been granted him, had he not previously applied to the Lord Chancellor.

> *R.* v. *Marshall,* 4 E. & B. 475.

An Irish Q.C., in addressing the jury as counsel in a cause, made a fierce attack on the plaintiff, who was an attorney. This attack was pertinent to the issue and not malicious ; at the same time, the observations were unusually harsh and irritating. The plaintiff won the action, and then wrote to the Q.C., calling on him to retract the charges he had made. The Q.C. refused ; thereupon the plaintiff wrote the Q.C. a letter, couched in the most offensive language, and obviously intended to provoke a duel. The Court made the rule for a criminal information absolute ; but ordered that the information should not issue without further order.

> *R. pros. Armstrong, Q.C.* v. *Kiernan,* 7 Cox, C. C. 6 ; 5 Ir. C. L. R. 171.
>
> *R. pros. Butt, Q.C.* v. *Jackson,* 10 Ir. L. R. 120.

Publication.

The prosecutor must prove that the defendant published the defamatory words. In civil cases it is necessary to show a publication to some third person other than the person defamed. In criminal cases this is not absolutely necessary; it is sufficient to prove a publication to the prosecutor himself, provided the obvious tendency of the words be to provoke the prosecutor and excite him to break the peace. (*Hicks' Case,* Hob. 215 ; Poph. 139 ; cited 6 East, 476 ; *Clutterbuck* v. *Chaffers,* 1 Stark. 471 ; *R.* v. *Wegener,* 2 Stark. 245 ; *Phillips* v. *Jansen,* 2 Esp. 624 ; *R.* v. *Hornbrook,* Selwyn's Nisi Prius, 12th ed. at p. 1065; 13th ed. at p. 1000 ; *R.* v. *Brooke,* 7 Cox, C. C. 251. See *post,* p. 722.) Nor is it essential for the prosecutor to show that his reputation has in fact been injured : as he is not claiming damages for himself, but only seeking to protect the interests of the public.

Illustrations.

The defendant wrote a letter to a young lady of virtuous and modest character, soliciting her chastity. He enclosed it in an envelope properly fastened and addressed to the young lady herself. *Held,* that he had published a libel, for which he could be convicted at common law, for it might reasonably tend to provoke a breach of the peace.

> *R.* v. *Adams,* 22 Q. B. D. 66 ; 58 L. J. M. C. 1 ; 59 L. T. 903 ; 53 J. P. 377 ; 16 Cox, C. C. 544.

By the 38 Geo. III. c. 71, s. 17 (now repealed), the proprietor of every newspaper was required to send a copy of every issue to the Stamp Office for Revenue purposes. *Held,* that proof of the delivery of a newspaper to the officer at the Stamp Office was sufficient evidence of the publication of a libel contained in it to render the proprietor liable ; " as the officer of the Stamp Office would at all events have an opportunity of reading the libel himself." It was not necessary for the prosecution to prove that the officer had in fact read it.

> *R.* v. *Amphlit,* 4 B. & C. 35 ; 6 D. & R. 125.
> *Mayne* v. *Fletcher,* 9 B. & C. 382 ; 4 Man. & Ry. 312.

Merely to be in possession of a copy of a libel is no crime.

> *R.* v. *Beere,* Carth. 409 ; 12 Mod. 219 ; Holt, 422 ; 2 Salk. 417 ; 1 Lord Raym. 414.
> *John Lamb's Case,* 9 Rep. 60 ; *ante,* p. 165.
> Overruling *R.* v. *Algernon Sidney,* 9 Howell's St. Tr. 817, 867 ; 3 Hargrave's St. Tr. 807 ; 4 St. Tr. 197.
> *McLeod* v. *St. Aubyn,* [1899] A. C. 549 ; 68 L. J. P. C. 137 ; 48 W. R. 173 ; 81 L. T. 158 ; 15 Times L. R. 487.

As soon as the manuscript of a libel has passed out of the defendant's possession and control, it is deemed to be published, so far as the defendant is concerned.

> Per Holroyd, J., in *R.* v. *Burdett,* 4 B. & Ald. 143.

A libel was printed and published ; the printer produced the manuscript from which he had printed it, and this manuscript was proved to be in the handwriting of the prisoner ; there was no evidence to show that he authorised or directed the printing or publishing. This is evidence of publication sufficient to go to the jury, though the prisoner may give evidence to rebut it.

> *R.* v. *Lovett,* 9 C. & P. 462.

Cooper told the editor of a newspaper several good stories against the Rev. J. K., and asked him to "show Mr. K. up ; " subsequently the editor published the substance of them in the newspaper ; this was held to be a publication of a libel by Cooper, although the editor knew of the facts from other quarters as well.

> *R.* v. *Cooper,* 8 Q. B. 533 ; 15 L. J. Q. B. 206.

In all other respects the law as to publication is practically identical in civil and criminal cases.

Thus, the author, printer, and publisher are each and all liable to be prosecuted for a libel contained in any book or newspaper. In the latter case the proprietor of the newspaper will also be liable. Every fresh publication of a libel is a fresh crime. The sale of every separate copy of a libel is a distinct offence. (*R.* v. *Carlisle,* 1 Chitty, 453.) " Not only the party who originally prints, but every party who sells, who gives, or who lends a copy of an offensive publication will be liable to be prosecuted as a publisher." (Per Bayley, J., in *R.* v. *Mary Carlile,* 3 B. & Ald. 169.) " The mere delivery of a libel to a third person by one conscious of its contents amounts to a publication, and is an indictable offence." (Per Wood, B., in *Maloney* v. *Bartley,* 3 Camp. 213; and see *McLeod* v. *St. Aubyn,* [1899] A. C. 549; 68 L. J. P. C. 137; 48 W. R. 173; 81 L. T. 158.)

In the last extract, the learned Baron is careful to insert the words " by one conscious of its contents." For although any delivery to a third person will amount to a *primâ facie* publication, it is open to the defendant to prove, both in civil and criminal cases, that he delivered the libel without any knowledge of the libellous nature of its contents: *e.g.,* where a postman or messenger carries a sealed letter (per Lord Kenyon, C.J., in *R.* v. *Topham,* 4 T. R. 129), or a parcel in which libellous handbills were wrapped up (*Day* v. *Bream,* 2 Moo. & Rob. 55), or where the defendant cannot read (per Lord Kenyon, in *R.* v. *Holt,* 5 T. R. 444). And see *Emmens* v. *Pottle,* 16 Q. B. D. 354; 55 L. J. Q. B. 51; 34 W. R. 116; 53 L. T. 808; *ante,* p. 168. Even if the defendant had read the libel, yet if the words were innocent on the face of them, and only derived a defamatory meaning from certain extrinsic facts and circumstances wholly unknown to him, then he would still be unconscious that what he published was a libel, and such a publication would be no crime: *e.g.,* where the libel was contained in an allegory or a riddle, to which the defendant had no clue. Again, where the defendant was in possession of a paper which he knew to be libellous, and handed it inadvertently to a third person in mistake for some other paper, he was held not to be criminally liable for such an accident, though he would probably be liable in a civil case. " The delivering it by mistake is no publication." (*R.* v. *Paine,* (1695) 5 Mod. at p. 167; Carth. 405; Comb. 358: and see the *dicta* of Lord Kenyon in *R.* v. *Topham,* 4 T. R. 129; and in *R.* v. *Lord Abingdon,* 1 Esp. 228; and the ruling of Abbott, C.J., in *R.* v. *Harvey,* 2 B. & C. 257.)

A master will be liable criminally for the acts of his servant done in the ordinary course of his employment in pursuance of his master's orders, general or express. The criminal liability of a defendant for such constructive publication is now defined by the 7th section of Lord Campbell's Act (6 & 7 Vict. c. 96), which, however, rather declared than altered the existing law :—" Whensoever, upon the trial of any indictment or information for the publication of a libel, under the plea of not guilty, evidence shall have been given which shall establish a presumptive case of publication against the defendant by the act of any other person by his authority, it shall be competent to such defendant to prove that such publication was made without his authority, consent, or knowledge, and that the said publication did not arise from want of due care or caution on his part."

The section only says that evidence may be given of such facts; but it has always been construed to mean that such facts, if proved, shall be an answer to the indictment; for such evidence was always admissible at common law in mitigation of punishment (if not in defence). The word " authority," in the above section, means something more than the general authority given by the proprietor of a newspaper to the editor to insert in the paper whatever he thinks fit. (*R.* v. *Holbrook and others,* 3 Q. B. D. 60; 47 L. J. Q. B. 35; 26 W. R. 144; 37 L. T. 530; 4 Q. B. D. 42; 48 L. J. Q. B. 113; 27 W. R. 313; 39 L. T. 536; *post,* p. 589. And see *Ex parte Parry,* 41 J. P. 85.)

The section applies to all cases of criminal libel, blasphemous, seditious, and otherwise. (*R.* v. *Bradlaugh and others,* 15 Cox, C. C. 218.)

Illustrations.

The defendant was the proprietor of *The Times,* but resided in the country, leaving the management of the paper entirely to his son, with whom he never interfered. A libel on the late Lord Cowper having appeared therein, the defendant was held criminally liable, and convicted.

R. v. *Walter,* (1799) 3 Esp. 21.

And see *R.* v. *Gutch, Fisher, and Alexander,* Moo. & Mal. 433.

A rule was granted calling on Wiatt to show cause why he should not be attached for selling a book containing a libel on the Court of King's Bench. The book was in Latin. On his filing an affidavit stating that he did not understand Latin, and giving up the name of the printer from whom he obtained it and the name of the author, the rule was discharged.

R. v. *Wiatt,* (1722) 8 Mod. 123.

The defendant was a bookseller, who published a seditious libel written by the Rev. Gilbert Wakefield ; he was convicted, but filed an affidavit in mitigation of punishment that he had no knowledge whatever of the nature of the book or its contents ; he was accordingly discharged on payment of a fine of thirty marks. The Rev. Gilbert Wakefield was sentenced to two years' imprisonment.

R. v. *Cuthell,* (1799) 27 Howell's St. Tr. 642.

There appeared in *Mist's Weekly Journal* an account professedly of certain intrigues, &c., at the Persian Court ; but, any reader of ordinary intelligence could see that it was the English Court that the author really meant, that the Sultan " Esreff " was intended for George II., his father the late Sultan " Merewits " for George I., " Sophi " for the Pretender, &c., &c. The two compositors who set it up divided the work between them, one taking one column, the other the next. It was almost impossible that thus they could gain any notion of the general sense of what they were printing. Yet one of them was convicted of publishing a seditious libel ; and so was the servant whose business " was only to clap down the press."

R. v. *Knell,* (1728) 1 Barnard. 305.

R. v. *Clerk, ib.* 304.

In Massachusetts it has been held that the publisher of a newspaper is not liable for publishing an article which he reasonably and *bonâ fide* believes to be a fancy sketch or a fictitious narrative, in no way applicable to any living person ; although the writer intended it to be libellous of the plaintiff. [Probably this would be a defence in England in a criminal case, if not in a civil action. See Precedent No. 31, p. 771.]

Smith v. *Ashley,* (1846) 52 Mass. (11 Met.) 367.

Harrison v. *Smith,* (1869) 20 L. T. at p. 717.

Dexter v. *Spear,* 4 Mason, 115.

See *Chubb* v. *Flannagan,* 6 C. & P. 431.

Rev. Samuel Paine sent his servant to his study for a certain paper which he wished to show Brereton ; the servant by mistake brought a libellous epitaph on Queen Mary which Paine inadvertently handed to Brereton. This would probably be deemed a sufficient publication in a civil case (note to *Mayne* v. *Fletcher*, 4 Man. & Ry. 312), but it was held insufficient in a criminal case.

> *R.* v. *Paine*, (1695) 5 Mod. 167 ; Carth. 405 ; Comb. 358.
>
> See the remarks of Lord Kenyon in *R.* v. *Lord Abingdon*, 1 Esp. 228 ; and of Wills, J., in *R.* v. *Munslow*, [1895] 1 Q. B. at p. 765.

A libel appeared in the *Man of the World* of May 11th, 1878. On May 25th the defendant was appointed publisher of the paper and the back-stock was sent to his office. On December 13th the relator's agent applied at the defendant's office for a copy of the number for May 11th, and the defendant told his assistant to look it up and deliver it, which was done. The defendant swore that he had not examined the back numbers at all and knew nothing of the libel. Cockburn, L.C.J., intimated that in those circumstances no jury would ever find the defendant guilty of criminally publishing the libel.

> *R.* v. *Barnard, Ex parte Lord Ronald Gower*, 43 J. P. 127.

The defendant and Mrs. Besant carried on business as publishers at 22, Stonecutter Street, the defendant being rated as the occupier of those premises. Ramsey was their manager. They at first published two papers, the *National Reformer* and the *Freethinker ;* but in 1881 they arranged with Ramsey that, in addition to managing their business, he might also carry on a publishing business of his own on their premises, and Ramsey's salary was reduced in consequence of this arrangement. In November, 1881, the defendant was registered as proprietor of the *National Reformer* and Ramsey as proprietor of the *Freethinker*. In 1882 copies of the *Freethinker*, containing blasphemous libels, were purchased at 22, Stonecutter Street, from a shopman in the employ of the defendant and Mrs Besant. The defendant knew that the *Freethinker* was still being published and sold on his premises, but did not know anything as to the contents of the numbers in question. *Held*, by Lord Coleridge, C.J., that the defendant was *primâ facie* liable, but that on the above facts the jury might acquit him under s. 7 of Lord Campbell's Act. Verdict, not guilty.

> *R.* v. *Bradlaugh and others*, 15 Cox, C. C. 217.
>
> And see *R.* v. *Ramsey and Foote*, 15 Cox, C. C. 231 ; 48 L. T. 734 ; 1 C. & E. 132.

The directors of a printing company are not criminally liable for a libel contained in a paper printed by the servants of the company, unless they knew of or saw the libel before its publication, or gave express instructions for its appearance.

> *R.* v. *Allison, Judd, and others*, 37 W. R. 143 ; 59 L. T. 933 ; 53 J. P. 215 ; 16 Cox, C. C. 559.

Privilege.

A defendant on the trial of any information or indictment may give evidence to show that the alleged libel was privileged by reason of the occasion ; and, unless such privilege be absolute, the prosecutor may rebut this defence by evidence of malice, precisely as in civil cases.

Except in such cases of privilege it is quite unnecessary to prove malice in a criminal proceeding for a defamatory libel; it is enough that the defendant intended to publish that which the jury have found to be a libel. After conviction, however, the defendant is allowed to file affidavits in mitigation of punishment, showing that he honestly believed in the truth of what he wrote, and published it without malice. (*R.* v. *Sir F. Burdett,* 4 B. & Ald. 95.)

The law is otherwise in Scotland; there malice must be proved in all criminal proceedings, though it never need be in civil. (1 Hume, 342; Borthwick, 190, 195.)

Justification.

But it is in the matter of justification that the main difference lies between civil and criminal proceedings. In a civil trial, as we have seen, *ante,* p. 181, the truth of the matters charged in a libel is and always was a perfect answer to the action; the plaintiff was never allowed to recover damages for an injury done to a reputation to which he had no right. But in all criminal proceedings the truth of the libel by the common law constituted no defence. The maxim used to be " the greater the truth, the greater the libel; " meaning that the injudicious publication of the truth about A. would be more likely to provoke him to a breach of the peace than if some falsehood were invented about him, which he could easily and completely refute. Accordingly, on a criminal trial, whether of an indictment or an information, no evidence could be received of the truth of the matters charged, not even in mitigation of punishment. But now, by the 6th section of Lord Campbell's Act (6 & 7 Vict. c. 96), "On the trial of any indictment or information for a defamatory libel, the defendant having pleaded such plea as hereinafter mentioned, the truth of the matters charged may be inquired into, but shall not amount to a defence, unless it was for the public benefit that the said matters charged should be published. To entitle the defendant to give evidence of the truth of such matters charged as a defence to such indictment or information, it shall be necessary for the defendant, in pleading to the said indictment or information, to allege the truth of the said matters charged in the manner now required in pleading a justification to an action for defamation, and further to allege that it was for the public benefit that the said matters charged should be published, and the particular fact or facts by reason whereof it was for the public benefit that the said matters charged should be published ; to which plea the prosecutor shall be at liberty to reply generally, denying the whole thereof. If after such plea the defendant shall be convicted on such indictment or information, it shall be competent to the Court, in pronouncing sentence, to consider whether the guilt of the defendant is aggravated or mitigated by the said plea and by the evidence given to prove or disprove the same : Provided always, that the truth of the matters charged in the alleged libel complained of by such indictment or information shall in no case be inquired into without such plea of justification : Provided also, that in addition to such plea, it shall be competent to the defendant to plead a plea of not guilty : Provided also, that nothing in this Act contained shall take away or prejudice any defence under the plea of not guilty which it is now competent to the defendant to make under such plea to any action or indictment, or information for defamatory words or libel."

Hence there is still a most important distinction between civil and criminal cases on this point. The mere truth is an answer to a civil action, however maliciously and unnecessarily the words were published. But in a criminal case, the defendant has to prove, not only that his assertions are true, but also that it was for the public benefit that they should be published. Moreover, the statute does not apply in cases of blasphemous, obscene, or seditious words. (*R.* v. *Duffy*, 9 Ir. L. R. 329 ; 2 Cox, C. C. 45 ;

Ex parte O'Brien, 12 L. R. Ir. 29 ; 15 Cox, C. C. 180 ; *R.* v. *M'Hugh*, [1901] 2 Ir. R. 569.) It does not apply, by its express terms, unless there be a special plea of justification. In short, the truth of the matter complained of " can only become a defence under the statute, and then only when the statutory conditions are complied with." Wherever Lord Campbell's Act does not apply, the law remains still as it was settled prior to that Act. Hence a magistrate at the preliminary investigation of a charge of libel, whether under s. 5 of the 6 & 7 Vict. c. 96, or at common law, has no power to receive and perpetuate any evidence of the truth of the matters charged (*R.* v. *Townsend*, 4 F. & F. 1089; 10 Cox, C. C. 356; *R.* v. *Sir Robert Carden*, 5 Q. B. D. 1 ; 49 L. J. M. C. 1 ; 28 W. R. 133 ; 41 L. T. 504; 14 Cox, C. C. 359) ; unless the libel appeared in a newspaper, as to which see s. 4 of the Newspaper Libel Act, 1881, *post*, p. 837.

CHAPTER XVII.

BLASPHEMOUS WORDS.

IT is a misdemeanour, punishable by indictment and by criminal information, to speak, or write and publish any profane words vilifying or ridiculing God, Jesus Christ, the Holy Ghost, the Old or New Testament, or Christianity in general, with intent to shock and insult believers, or to pervert or mislead the ignorant and unwary. This is the crime of blasphemy, and on conviction thereof the blasphemer may be sentenced to fine or imprisonment to any extent, in the discretion of the Court. Formerly he was frequently also sentenced to the pillory or to banishment.* He may also be required to give security for his good behaviour for any reasonable time after he comes out of prison; and can be detained in prison till such sureties be found. [Thomas Emlyn, in 1703, and Richard Carlile, in 1820, were condemned to find sureties for their good behaviour throughout the remainder of their lives.] Also under the 60 Geo. III. & 1 Geo. IV. c. 8, s. 1, the Court may, after conviction, make an order for the seizure of copies of the blasphemous libel in the possession of the

---

* In Scotland up till the year 1813 blasphemy was in certain circumstances a capital offence. The only person executed for blasphemy appears to have been Thomas Aikenhead, a young student just twenty years of age, and the son of a surgeon in Edinburgh; he seems to have been very harshly, if not illegally, treated; no counsel appeared for him: his crime consisted in loose talk about Ezra and Mahomet and in crude anticipations of Materialism. He was hanged on January 8th, 1697, buried beneath the gallows, and all his moveables forfeited to the Crown. (See Macaulay's History of England, vol. IV., pp. 781-784; Maclaurin's Crim. Cases, 12; 3 Mer. 382, n.) Two other persons were prosecuted—Kinninmouth and Borthwick—but neither was convicted; in the first case the prosecution dropped, while Borthwick fled the country. (Hume on Crimes, II. 518.)

prisoner, or in the possession of any person to his use. The defendant cannot plead a justification: nor can he be permitted at the trial to argue that his blasphemous words are true. (Per Abbott, L.C.J., in *Cooke* v. *Hughes,* R. & M. 115.)

The intent to shock and insult believers, or to pervert or mislead the ignorant and unwary, is an essential element in the crime. *Actus non facit reum, nisi mens sit rea.* The existence of such an intent is a question of fact for the jury, and the *onus* of proving it lies on the prosecution. The best evidence of such an intention is usually to be found in the work itself. If it is full of scurrilous and opprobrious language, if sacred subjects are treated with offensive levity, if indiscriminate abuse is employed instead of argument, then a malicious design to wound the religious feelings of others may be readily inferred. If, however, the author abstains from ribaldry and licentious reproach, a similar design may still perhaps be inferred if it be found that he has deliberately had resort to sophistical arguments, that he has wilfully misrepresented facts within his knowledge, or has indulged in sneers and sarcasms against all that is good and noble; for this would tend to show that he did not write from conscientious conviction, but desired to pervert and mislead the ignorant; or at all events that he was criminally indifferent to the distinctions between right and wrong. But where the work is free from all offensive levity, abuse and sophistry, and is in fact the honest and temperate expression of religious opinions conscientiously held and avowed, the author is entitled to be acquitted; for his work is not a blasphemous libel.

"It is indeed, still blasphemy," says Mr. Justice Erskine in *Shore* v. *Wilson,* 9 Clark & Fin. at pp. 524, 525, "punishable at common law, scoffingly or irreverently to ridicule or impugn the doctrines of the Christian faith; yet any man may, without subjecting himself to any penal consequences, soberly and reverently examine and question the truth of those doctrines which have been assumed as essential to it." Mr. Justice Coleridge said, in the same case, 9 Clark & Fin. at p. 539, "I apprehend that there is nothing unlawful at common law in reverently denying doctrines parcel of Christianity, however fundamental. It would be difficult to draw a line in such matters according to perfect orthodoxy, or to define how far one might depart from it in believing or teaching without offending the law. The only safe and, as it seems to me, practical rule, is that which I have pointed at, and which depends on the sobriety, and reverence, and seriousness with which the teaching or believing, however erroneous, are maintained."

And mere vehemence or even virulence of argument must not be taken as evidence of this intent to injure. Sarcasm and ridicule are fair weapons even in heterodox hands, so long as they do not degenerate into profane scoffing or irreverent levity. "If the decencies of controversy are observed, even the fundamentals of religion may be attacked without a person being guilty of blasphemous libel." (Per Lord Coleridge, C.J., in *R.* v. *Ramsey and Foote*, 48 L. T. 739; 15 Cox, C. C. 231; 1 C. & E. 146; *R.* v. *Boulter*, (1908) 72 J. P. 188.)

It is not blasphemy, then, seriously and reverently to propound any opinions, however heretical, which are conscientiously entertained by the accused. Honest error is no crime in this country, so long as its advocacy is rational and dispassionate, and does not degenerate into fanatical abuse, or into scurrilous attacks upon individuals. Heresy and blasphemy are entirely distinct and different things. "The law visits not the honest errors, but the malice of mankind." ("Starkie on Libel," 2nd edition, p. 147.) "Every man may fearlessly advance any new doctrines, provided he does so with proper respect to the religion and government of the country." (Per Best, J., in *R.* v. *Burdett*, (1820) 4 B. & Ald. 132.)

Or, to quote the words of Lord Mansfield in the great case of *Evans* v. *The Chamberlain of London* (1767): " The common law of England, which is only common reason or usage, knows of no prosecution for mere opinions." (16 Parl. History, (1813) p. 325 ; 2 Burn, Eccl. Law, 218.)

Illustrations.

Taylor was convicted of uttering disgusting and scurrilous language about Jesus Christ in the market-place at Guildford (see *post*, p. 490).

> R. v. *Taylor*, (1676) 1 Ventris, 293 ; 3 Keble, 607 ; Tremayne's Entries, 226.

It is blasphemy to write and publish that Jesus Christ is an impostor, the Christian religion a mere fable, and those who believe in it infidels to God.

> R. v. *Eaton*, (1812) 31 Howell's St. Tr. 927.

It is blasphemy to write and publish that Jesus Christ was an impostor, a murderer in principle, and a fanatic. The jury found as a fact that the intention of the prisoner was malicious ; and the Court on motion refused to arrest the judgment.

> R. v. *Waddington*, (1822) 1 B. & C. 26 ; 1 St. Tr. (N. S.) 1339.

A publication which denies the divinity of Jesus Christ is not a blasphemous libel, if written in a reverent and temperate tone, and expressing the conscientious convictions of the author.

> *Shore and others* v. *Wilson and others*, (1842) 9 Clark & F. 355.

Edward Elwall was indicted before Mr. Justice Denton for a book alleged to be blasphemous, entitled " A True Testimony for God and for His Sacred Law ; being a plain, honest defence of the First Commandment of God against all Trinitarians under Heaven, Thou shalt have no other gods but me." He was acquitted, though he admitted publication.

> R. v. *Elwall*, Gloucester Summer Assizes, 1726.

To write and publish that the Christian miracles were not to be taken in a literal but in an allegorical sense was held blasphemous in 1729 ; but there the Court clearly considered that to attack the miracles was to attack Christianity in general, and could not be included amongst " disputes between learned men upon particular controverted points." " I would have it taken notice of," says Lord Raymond, C.J., " that we do not meddle with any differences of opinion, and that we interpose only where the very root of Christianity is struck at."

> R. v. *Woolston*, (1729) 2 Str. 834 ; Fitz. 66 ; 1 Barnard. 162.

To deliver a lecture publicly maintaining that the character of Christ is defective, and his teaching misleading, and that the Bible is no more inspired than any other book, was held blasphemy by the Court of Exchequer in a civil case without any regard to the style of the lecture, or the religious convictions of the lecturer.

> *Cowan* v. *Milbourn*, (1867) L. R. 2 Ex. 230 ; 36 L. J. Ex. 124 ; 15 W. R. 750 ; 16 L. T. 290.

It was held blasphemy to publish or sell Paine's " Age of Reason."

> R. v. *Williams*, (1797) 26 Howell's St. Tr. 656.
>
> R. v. *Richard Carlile*, (1819) 3 B. & Ald. 161.

Richard Carlile on his trial read over to the jury the whole of Paine's "Age of Reason," for selling which he was indicted. After his conviction, his wife published a full, true, and accurate account of his trial, entitled "The Mock Trial of Mr. Carlile," and in so doing republished the whole of the "Age of Reason" as a part of the proceedings at the trial. *Held,* that the privilege usually attaching to fair reports of judicial proceedings did not extend to such a colourable reproduction of a book adjudged to be blasphemous ; and that it is unlawful to publish even a correct account of the proceedings in a Court of justice, if such an account contain matter of a scandalous, blasphemous, or indecent nature.

   R. v. *Mary Carlile,* (1819) 3 B. & Ald. 167.

   See also *Steele* v. *Brannan,* (1872) L. R. 7 C. P. 261 ; 41 L. J. M. C. 85 ; 20 W. R. 607 ; 26 L. T. 509 ; *post,* p. 509.

Richard Carlile was sentenced to pay a fine of 1,500*l.*, to be imprisoned for three years, and to find sureties for his good behaviour for the term of his life. He was still in Dorchester Gaol in 1825. In the meantime the sale of heterodox books continued at his shop, and his shopmen were sentenced to various terms of imprisonment. In June, 1824, William Campion, John Clarke, William Maley, and Thomas Perry were sentenced to imprisonment in Newgate for three years, Richard Hassell for two years, and Thomas Jeffryes for a year and a half, for selling blasphemous publications.

An information was filed against Jacob Ilive for publishing a profane and blasphemous libel, tending to vilify and subvert the Christian religion, and to blaspheme our Saviour Jesus Christ, to cause His Divinity to be denied, to represent Him as an impostor ; to scandalise, ridicule, and bring into contempt His most holy life and doctrine ; and to cause the truth of the Christian religion to be disbelieved and totally rejected, by representing the same as spurious and chimerical, and a piece of forgery and priestcraft.

   R. v. *Ilive,* (1756) Dig. L. L. 83.

An information was exhibited against Peter Annet for a certain malignant, profane, and blasphemous libel, entitled "The Free Inquirer," tending to blaspheme Almighty God, and to ridicule, traduce, and discredit His Holy Scriptures, particularly the Pentateuch, and to represent, and to cause it to be believed, that the prophet Moses was an impostor, and that the sacred truths and miracles recorded and set forth in the Pentateuch were impositions and false inventions ; and thereby to diffuse and propagate irreligious and diabolical opinions in the minds of his Majesty's subjects, and to shake the foundations of the Christian religion, and of the civil and ecclesiastical government established in this kingdom. To this information he pleaded guilty. "In consideration of which, and of his poverty, of his having confessed his errors in an affidavit, and of his being seventy years old, and some symptoms of wildness that appeared on his inspection in Court, the Court declared they had mitigated their intended sentence to the following, viz. to be imprisoned in Newgate for a month ; to stand twice in the pillory, with a paper on his forehead, inscribed *blasphemy ;* to be sent to the house of correction to hard labour for a year ; to pay a fine of 6*s.* 8*d.*, and to find security, him-

self in 100*l.* and two sureties for 50*l.* each, for his good behaviour during
life."

> *R.* v. *Peter Annet,* (1763) 1 Wm. Bl. 395 ; 3 Burn, Eccl. Law,
> 9th ed. 386.

An information was exhibited against John Wilkes for publishing an
obscene and impious libel, tending to vitiate and corrupt the minds and
manners of his Majesty's subjects ; to introduce a total contempt of
religion, modesty, and virtue ; to blaspheme Almighty God ; and to
ridicule our Saviour and the Christian religion.

> *R.* v. *Wilkes,* (1768) 4 Burr. 2527 ; 2 Wils. 151.

In 1817 Mr. Wright, of Liverpool, was prosecuted at common law for
denying the existence of a future life ; but the prosecution was abandoned.

> *R.* v. *Wright,* (1817) 3 Mer. 386, n.

In the same year William Hone was tried on three successive days,
December 18th, 19th, and 20th, 1817, for publishing three parodies on
the Catechism, the Litany, and the Athanasian Creed, before Abbott, J.,
on the first day, and Lord Ellenborough, C.J., on the other two. He was
on each occasion acquitted, the libels being political attacks on the Government, and not written with any intent of ridiculing the compositions
parodied.

> "The Three Trials of William Hone," London, 1818.

Reflections on the Old Testament may amount to blasphemy.

> *R.* v. *Hetherington,* (1841) 5 Jur. 529.

Queen Mab was found by a jury in 1841 to be a blasphemous libel.

> *R.* v. *Moxon,* (1841) 2 Townsend's Mod. St. Tr. 356.

But this prosecution was a purely vindictive one by Hetherington, and
no sentence was ever passed. Blackburn, J., expresses his disapproval of
this finding in

> *R.* v. *Hicklin,* (1868) L. R. 3 Q. B. 374 ; 37 L. J. M. C. 89 ;
> 16 W. R. 803 ; 18 L. T. 395 ; 11 Cox, C. C. 19.

Southwell was convicted of blasphemy in January, 1842, for publishing
the "Oracle of Reason."

Later in the same year Adams was tried before Mr. Justice Erskine at
Gloucester Assizes for selling No. 25 of the said "Oracle of Reason," and
convicted.

At the same Assizes George Jacob Holyoake was tried before Mr.
Justice Erskine for oral blasphemy. It appeared that he had been lec-
turing on emigration and the poor laws, and at the close a man, said
to have been sent on purpose to entrap him, rose and said : "The lecturer
has been speaking of our duty to man ; he has nothing to tell us as to
our duty to God ?" Holyoake, being thus challenged, replied, "I do not
believe there is such a thing as a God. . . . I would have the Deity
served as they serve the subalterns—place him on half-pay." But Holyoake was known to be a friend of Southwell's, and a writer in the
"Oracle of Reason," and he was convicted and sentenced to six months'
imprisonment.

> See *Trial of Holyoake,* London, 1842.

Father Vladimir Petcherini, a monk, was indicted in Ireland in 1855
for having contemptuously, irreverently, and blasphemously burnt a Bible

in public with intent to bring the same into disregard, hatred, and contempt, and in other counts with intent to bring religion into discredit, and in other counts with having caused and procured it to be burnt with such intents. There was some evidence that a Bible had been burnt in the defendant's presence among a heap of other books and papers, but very little that he knew it or sanctioned it. Greene, B., directed the jury, that if he sanctioned it, it would follow "as of course that the intention of the act could only be to bring into contempt the authorised version of the Holy Scriptures." The defendant was acquitted.

R. v. *Petcherini,* (1855) 7 Cox, C. C. 79.

A man called Pooley was indicted at the Bodmin Summer Assizes, July, 1857, before Coleridge, J., his son, afterwards Lord Coleridge, C.J., being counsel for the prosecution. The prisoner had scribbled on a gate some disgusting language concerning Jesus Christ, and was convicted of a blasphemous libel, but was subsequently discovered to be insane.

R. v. *Pooley,* (1857) Digest of Criminal Law, 97.

In November, 1868, John Thompson was committed for trial by the Southampton magistrates on the prosecution of the Rev. Arthur Bradley, the incumbent of a church there, for publishing the following blasphemous libel :—"I believe Jesus of Nazareth to be the Messiah at his first coming, as an antitypical Paschal Lamb who died for sins in allegory ; and I believe John Cochran of Glasgow to be the Messiah at his second coming, and the antitypical High Priest who has taken away sin in reality." In March, 1869, the grand jury ignored the bill.

Foote, Ramsey, and Kemp were indicted for blasphemous libels and pictures contained in the Christmas number of the *Freethinker,* Foote being the editor, Ramsey the registered proprietor, and Kemp the printer and publisher of that paper. On the first trial, March 1st, 1883, the jury could not agree, and were discharged. The prisoners were tried again on Monday, March 5th, 1883, and convicted and sentenced to twelve, nine, and three months' imprisonment respectively. North, J., directed the jury that any publication containing "contumelious reproach or profane scoffing against Holy Scripture and the Christian religion" was a blasphemous libel.

R. v. *Foote, Ramsey, and Kemp, Times,* March 2nd and 6th, 1883.

In the same year Ramsey and Foote were indicted for articles which had appeared in other numbers of the *Freethinker,* which were alleged to be blasphemous. The late Mr. Bradlaugh, M.P., was at first included also in this indictment, but the case against him was tried separately, and he was acquitted on the ground that he was in no way responsible for the publication. See 15 Cox, C. C. 217 ; *ante,* p. 472. Ramsey and Foote were tried before Lord Coleridge, C.J., on April 24th, 1883 ; the jury could not agree upon a verdict ; and on Tuesday, May 1st, the Attorney-General issued his *fiat* for a *nolle prosequi.*

R. v. *Ramsey and Foote,* (1883) 48 L. T. 733 ; 15 Cox, C. C. 231 ; 1 C. & E. 126.

For other cases of blasphemy at common law, see

Traske's Case, (1618) Hobart, 236 ; *post,* p. 490.

R. v. *Atwood*, (1618) Cro. Jac. 421 ; 2 Roll. Abr. 78 ; *post,*
    p. 490.
The Commonwealth v. *Tydford, Kearby and others,* (1651).
R. v. *Clendon*, (1712) cited 2 Str. 789.
R. v. *Hall,* (1721) 1 Str. 416.
Paterson's Case, (1843) 1 Brown (Scotch), 629.
Robinson's Case, (1843) *ib.* 643.

In aid of the common law, many statutes have at different times been passed to punish particular species of
blasphemy. Of these the following are still unrepealed :—

"Whatsoever person or persons shall deprave, despise
or contemn the most blessed Sacrament in contempt thereof
by any contemptuous words or by any words of depraving,
despising, or reviling, or what person or persons shall
advisedly in any other wise contemn, despise, or revile the
said most blessed Sacrament, shall suffer imprisonment of
his or their bodies and make fine and ransom at the king's
will and pleasure." (1 Edw. VI. c. 1, s. 1.)

"Any vicar or other minister whatsoever that shall
preach, declare, or speak anything in the derogation or
depraving of the Book of Common Prayer, or anything
therein contained, or of any part thereof," shall on conviction for the first offence suffer forfeiture of one year's
profit of benefices and six months' imprisonment, and for
the second offence, one year's imprisonment and deprivation, and for the third offence, deprivation and imprisonment for life : or, if not beneficed, for the first offence
imprisonment for one year, and for the second offence,
imprisonment for life. (2 & 3 Edw. VI. c. 1, s. 2 ; 1 Eliz.
c. 2, s. 2.)

Any person whatsoever, lay or clerical, who "shall in
any interludes, plays, songs, rhymes, or by other open words,
declare or speak anything in the derogation, depraving, or
despising of the same book, or of anything therein contained, or any part thereof," shall for the first offence
forfeit one hundred marks, for the second offence four
hundred marks, and for the third offence shall forfeit all
his goods and chattels to the king and be imprisoned

for life. (2 & 3 Edw. VI. c. 1, s. 3; and 1 Eliz. c. 2, s. 3.)

These provisions are applied to our present Book of Common Prayer by the 14 Car. II. c. 4, s. 1.

Every person ecclesiastical, who shall persist in maintaining or affirming any doctrine directly contrary or repugnant to any of the articles agreed on in the Convocation holden at London in 1562, shall be deprived of his living. (13 Eliz. c. 12, s. 2.)

The statute 3 Jac. I. c. 21, against profanity in stageplays, was repealed in 1843 by the 6 & 7 Vict. c. 68, s. 1.

" If any person, having been educated in, or at any time having made profession of, the Christian religion within this realm, shall by writing, printing, teaching, or advised speaking, assert or maintain that there are more Gods than one, or shall deny the Christian religion to be true, or the Holy Scriptures of the Old and New Testament to be of divine authority," he shall, on conviction by the oath of two or more credible witnesses, be deprived of all offices, civil, ecclesiastical, and military, unless he renounce his errors within four months from the date of his conviction; and for a second offence he shall be declared unable to sue in any Court of law or equity, to be a guardian, an executor or administrator, to take any legacy, or to hold any office, and shall also suffer imprisonment for three years. But information must be given on oath to a magistrate within four days after such words are spoken, and the prosecution must be commenced within three months after such information. (9 & 10 Will. III. c. 35 [c. 32 in the Statutes at Large], as amended by 53 Geo. III. c. 160.)

But this statute does not affect or alter the common law (*R.* v. *Richard Carlile*, 3 B. & Ald. 161; *R.* v. *Williams*, 26 Howell's St. Tr. 656); nor would its repeal. (*R.* v. *Waddington*, 1 B. & C. 26; 1 St. Tr., (N. S.) 1339; *Att.-Gen.* v. *Pearson*, 3 Mer. at pp. 399, 405, 407.) It appears to be directed rather against apostasy than blasphemy. So far as we are aware, there never has been a prosecution under it), possibly because the punishment for the first offence is so slight. "Advised speaking" probably means words spoken deliberately, as opposed to "a casual expression dropped inadvertently." (See *Heath* v. *Burder*, 15 Moore, P. C. C. 80; Brodrick & Fremantle, at p. 284.)

By the Burial Laws Amendment Act, 1880 (43 & 44 Vict. c. 41, s. 7), any person who shall at any burial under the Act, "under colour of any religious service or otherwise, in any churchyard or graveyard, wilfully endeavour to bring into contempt or obloquy the Christian religion, or the belief or worship of any church or denomination of Christians, or the members or any minister of any such church or denomination, or any other person, shall be guilty of a misdemeanour."

Heresy and Blasphemy.

HERESY and BLASPHEMY are entirely distinct and different things, both in their essence and in their legal aspect. Originally, both were ecclesiastical offences not cognizable in the secular Courts. Then statutes were passed under which both became *crimes* punishable in the ordinary law Courts. Now heresy is once more a purely ecclesiastical offence, punishable only in the clergy; while blasphemy is the technical name for a particular offence against the State.

Heresy ($ \alpha \H{\iota} \rho \epsilon \sigma \iota s $, from $ \alpha \iota \rho \epsilon \omega \mu \alpha \iota $, I choose for myself) is the deliberate selection and adoption of a particular set of views or opinions, which the majority consider erroneous. To persist in the tenet of your choice after its error and its injurious tendency have been pointed out to you was regarded as a sin, and the obstinate heretic who refused to recant was bidden to do penance for the good of his soul. Blasphemy, on the other hand, is a crime against the peace and good order of society; it is an outrage on men's religious feelings, tending to a breach of the peace. The word necessarily involves an intent to do harm or to wound the feelings of others, for it is derived from $ \beta \lambda \alpha \pi \tau \omega $, I hurt, and $ \phi \eta \mu \acute{\iota} $, I speak, and denotes, therefore, "speaking so as to hurt."

Heresy.

At common law heresy was no crime. The secular Courts took no cognizance of any man's religious opinions; and indeed before the days of Wiclif heretics were scarce. Towards the end of the fourteenth century, however, heresy came to be regarded as a crime punishable with death, and Acts were passed in the reigns of Henry IV. and Henry V., which condemned all heretics to be burnt alive, and gave the clergy the power of defining heresy just as they pleased. This state of things lasted till the reign of Henry VIII., when the law was rendered in some particulars less severe. Under Edward VI. there were but two executions for heresy. Mary restored the old system for a short period, during which about 300 persons were burnt.

But by the 1 Eliz. c. 1, s. 6, all statutes relating to heresy were repealed, though somehow two men were burnt in her reign, and two under James I. "At this day," says Sir Edward Coke, "no person can be indicted or impeached for heresy before any temporal judge, or other that hath temporal jurisdiction." (12 Rep. 57.) By the 29 Car. II. c. 9, s. 1, the writ *de hæretico comburendo* was abolished; but s. 2 of the same Act expressly provides "that nothing in this Act shall extend, or be construed to take away or abridge the jurisdiction of Protestant archbishops or bishops, or any other judges of any Ecclesiastical Courts, in cases of atheism, blasphemy, heresy, or schism, and other damnable doctrines and opinions, but that they may proceed to punish the same according to his Majesty's ecclesiastical laws, by excommunication, deprivation, degradation, and other ecclesiastical censures, not extending to death, in such sort, and no other, as they might have done before the making of this Act, anything in this law contained to the contrary in anywise notwithstanding." By the 53 Geo. III. c. 127, s. 3, it is enacted that "no person who shall be pronounced or declared excommunicate shall incur any civil penalty or incapacity whatever, in consequence of such excommunication, save such imprisonment, not exceeding six months, as the Court pronouncing or declaring such person excommunicate shall direct."

These enactments are obsolete; but they were better repealed. No case is reported of any layman having been prosecuted for heresy since 1640. And indeed there is considerable authority for holding that at the present day the Ecclesiastical Courts no longer possess any criminal jurisdiction over laymen. In *Burder* v. ———, 3 Curteis, 827, May 31st, 1844, Sir H. Jenner Fust says: "As against laymen, whatever may be the nature of the charge, undoubtedly the Court has no jurisdiction to entertain a criminal suit." And though four years earlier a criminal suit was commenced against a layman for an incestuous marriage, Dr. Lushington contented himself with pronouncing the marriage null and void, which was clearly within his power, and did not impose any punishment or penance on the defendant. (*Woods* v. *Woods*, 2 Curt. 516, July 18th, 1840.) And in *Phillimore* v. *Machon*, 1 P. D. 481, Lord Penzance says : " Speaking generally, and setting aside for the moment all questions as to the clergy, it cannot, I think, be doubted that a recurrence to the punishment of the laity for the good of their souls by Ecclesiastical Courts, would not be in harmony with modern ideas, or the position which ecclesiastical authority now occupies in the country. Nor do I think that the enforcement of such powers, where they still exist, *if they do exist*, is likely to benefit the community."

This much is quite clear at all events—that no Ecclesiastical Court can any longer proceed against a layman for mere *nonconformity*. By the 4th section of the Toleration Act (1 William & Mary, c. 18), no Dissenter shall be prosecuted in any Ecclesiastical Court for or by reason of his nonconformity to the Church of England. And although by s. 17 it was provided that the benefits of the Act should not extend to Unitarians, this exception was repealed in 1813 by the statute 53 Geo. III. c. 160. With respect to dissenting ministers, however, one relic of the past still lingers. By s. 5 of 52 Geo. III. c. 155, any justice of the peace may call on the minister of " any place of religious worship certified " under that Act to make a declaration to the following effect :—" I am a Christian and a Protestant, and as such I believe that the Scriptures of the Old and New Testament contain the revealed will of God, and I receive the same as the rule of my doctrine and practice." It is improbable that any justice of the peace is aware at the present moment that he possesses this power ; still less probable is it that he would ever exercise it. The section applies only to ministers of chapels certified under the 52 Geo. III. c. 155, and very few, if any, dissenting chapels are now certified under that Act : they are all, we believe, " registered " under the subsequent and more comprehensive Act, 18 & 19 Vict. c. 81, an Act which applies to Jews, Roman Catholics, and every other denomination and which requires no declaration of any kind. Still, it is wrong that a justice of the peace should have the power to impose such a test on anyone, and the section should be repealed forthwith.

Even over clergymen of the Established Church the power of the Ecclesiastical Courts on questions of heresy is very limited. The judgment of the Privy Council (including the then Archbishop of Canterbury), in the case of the Rev. Rowland Williams, February 8, 1864, decided that it is not an ecclesiastical offence, even for the clergy, to dispute the dates and authorship of the several Books of the Old and New Testaments, to deny that the whole of the Holy Scriptures was written under the inspiration of the Holy Spirit, to reject parts of Scripture upon their own opinion that the narrative is inherently incredible, to disregard precepts in Holy Writ because they think them evidently wrong, so long as they do not contradict any doctrine laid down in the Articles or Formularies of the Church of England. (*Williams* v. *Bishop of Salisbury, Wilson* v. *Fendall,* (1864) 2 Moore, P. C. C. (N. S.) 375 ; Brodrick & Fremantle, 247 ; *Gorham* v. *Bishop of Exeter,* (1850) *ib.* 64.)

It must, moreover, be pointed out, before leaving the Ecclesiastical Courts, that no blasphemous publication, which is punishable in the secular Courts, can be taken cognizance of in the ecclesiastical. For "where the common or statute law giveth remedy *in foro seculari* (whether the matter be temporal or spiritual) the conusance of that cause belongeth to the King's temporal Courts only." (Coke upon Littleton, 96 b., and see *Phillimore* v. *Machon,* 1 P. D. 481.) Hence it is only over blasphemous libels not punishable by the common law or under any statute that the Ecclesiastical Courts can have any jurisdiction at all. (*Curl's Case,* 2 Str. 789 ; 1 Barnard. 29.) The canon law, speaking generally, is not binding, at all events on laymen. "The canon law forms no part of the law of England, unless it has been brought into use and acted upon in this country : the burden of proving which rests on those who affirm the adoption of any portion of it in England." (Per Lord Denman, C.J., in *The Queen* v. *The Archbishop of Canterbury,* 11 Q. B. 649 ; 17 L. J. Q. B. 268 ; *Middleton* v. *Croft,* (1734 and 1736) Cases temp. Hardwicke, 57, 326. See Year Book, 34 Hen. VI. fo. 38 (1459) ; Prisot, c. 5 ; Fitzh. Abr. quare imp. 89 ; Bro. Abr. qu. imp. 12.) Hence the Ecclesiastical Courts have no concurrent criminal jurisdiction over libels ; and their jurisdiction, by way of civil proceeding for defamation, was expressly taken away by the 18 & 19 Vict. c. 41, s. 1.

Blasphemy.

I.

So much for the ecclesiastical offence of HERESY. We come now to the law relating to BLASPHEMY. How are the secular Courts concerned in such a matter at all ?

The answer in former days was clear and obvious. The secular Courts interfered to punish blasphemous libels for the same reason as they did in the case of any other libel, viz., in order to prevent a disturbance of the peace. Blasphemous preaching and writing led to dangerous outbreaks of fanaticism, and the State had, therefore, a direct interest in their suppression.

This was the point decided in the Star Chamber, in *Traske's Case* (1618), the earliest reported decision on the subject. The defendant, John Traske, was, in the words of the report, " a minister that held opinion that the Jewish Sabbath ought to be observed, and not ours, and that we ought to abstain from all manner of swine's flesh. Being examined upon these things, he confessed that he had divulged these opinions, and had laboured to bring as many to his opinion as he could. And had also written a letter to the king, wherein he did seem to tax his Majesty of hypocrisy, and did expressly inveigh against the Bishops High Commissioners, as bloody and cruel in their proceedings against him and a Papal Clergy. Now he, being called *ore tenus*, was sentenced to fine and imprisonment, not for holding those opinions (for those were examinable in the Ecclesiastical Courts and not here), but for making of conventicles and factions by that means, which may tend to sedition and commotion, and for scandalising the king, the bishops, and the clergy." (Hobart's Reports, 236.)

In the same year (1618) there was a similar decision in the King's Bench, in *Atwood's Case*, Cro. Jac. 421 ; 2 Roll. Abr. 78. The language complained of in that case sounds to us now very harmless ; it was aimed chiefly at the prevailing mode of worship :—" The religion now professed is but fifty years old : preaching is but prating, prayer once a day is more edifying." The Court at first (in Easter Term) doubted if they had jurisdiction, as the words did not clearly tend to a breach of the peace. The Attorney-General, Sir Henry Yelverton, thought the case ought to go before the Ecclesiastical Court of High Commission. (Croke, Jac. 421.) But the King's Bench in Michaelmas Term decided that the indictment lay ; " for these words are seditious words against the State of our Church and against the peace of the Realm, and although they are spiritual words, still they draw after them a temporal consequence—viz., the disturbance of the peace." (2 Rolle's Abridgment, 78.)

The next decision that we have on the subject is *R.* v. *Taylor*, (1676) 1 Ventr. 293 ; 3 Keble, 607, 621 ; Tremayne's Entries, p. 226. This case contains the celebrated *dictum* of Sir Matthew Hale, that " Christianity is parcel of the laws of England," a phrase that is very often quoted, and has, we think, been misunderstood. Let us first look at the facts of the case which was before him, for it is most unfair to learned judges to seize on one line of a judgment, force it from its context, and treat it as a general proposition of abstract law to be pushed to all extremes.

Taylor was proved to have preached aloud and persistently in the market-place at Guildford words of which the following are a sample :—" Religion is a Cheat, and Profession is a Cloak, and they are both cheats. . . . All the Earth is mine, and I am a King's Son; my Father sent me hither, and made me a Fisherman to take Vipers, and I neither fear God, Devil nor Man; I am a Younger Brother to Christ, an Angel of God. . . . No Man fears God but an Hypocrite. . . . Christ is a Bastard. . . . God damn and confound all your Gods," &c. The information, which is set out in full in Tremayne's Entries, p. 226, alleged, among other things, that these words tended to destroy Christian government and society. It was no doubt argued on behalf of Taylor, as it was in the earlier case of Atwood, that the offence was punishable only in the spiritual Court. But " Hale said that such kind of wicked, blasphemous words were not only an offence to God and religion, but a crime against the laws, state, and government, and therefore punishable in this Court ; for to say Religion is a cheat is to dissolve all those obligations whereby the civil societies are preserved; and Christianity is parcel of the laws of England, and therefore to reproach the Christian religion is to speak in subversion of the law." (1 Ventris, 293.) Or, as the judgment is more briefly given in the report in 3 Keble, at p. 607 :— " Hale, C.J. These words, though of ecclesiastical cognizance, yet that ' Religion is a cheat,' tends to dissolution of all government, and therefore punishable here, and so of contumelious reproaches of God or the Religion established."

When we consider the date at which this judgment was delivered (1676), and remember how mighty a part religious fanaticism had played in the social disturbances of the earlier part of the century, it cannot, we think, be said that the decision in *Taylor's Case* was wrong either in fact or in law. The concluding sentence, as reported in Ventris, is undoubtedly too wide. It should have been limited (and probably was by the Chief Justice) to " *such* kind of blasphemous words " as the prisoner was charged with uttering. The earlier part of the judgment is expressly so limited.

Yet the *dictum* at the end of the judgment of Hale, C.J., in Ventris' Report, has constantly been misconstrued into a general and abstract proposition of law, as though the Chief Justice had said, in syllogistic form,—

" To disparage any part of the law of England is a crime.

"Christianity is a part of the law of England.

"Therefore to disparage Christianity is a crime."

But Hale, C.J., would himself have been the first to deny the major premiss. "For," as the Commissioners on Criminal Law remarked in their Sixth Report (May 3rd, 1841, p. 83) : "It is not criminal to speak or write either against the common law of England generally, or against particular portions of it, provided it be not done in such a manner as to endanger the public peace by exciting forcible resistance." See also Jefferson's Letter to Major Cartwright, published in Cartwright's Life and Correspondence. It is a fact, no doubt, that Christianity is the religion of the church which is by law established in this land ; but it does not follow that to attack Christianity in peaceable and temperate language is or ever was a crime. What the Court intended to decide in *Taylor's Case* was simply this :—" These words are not only a sin ; they are also a crime. They are punishable in a temporal Court : for they tend to subvert the established order of things, of which Christianity is a part, and are therefore dangerous to the State. They are in fact seditious." And as though to make the grounds of their decision clear beyond all doubt the Court condemned Taylor, as part of his punishment, to stand in the pillory, both at Westminster Palace-yard and also at Guildford, where he spoke the words, with a paper fixed to his head with these words written on it in large letters :— "For Blasphemous Words tending to the Subversion of all Government." (Tremayne, 226 ; 3 Keble, 621.)

This, then, is the first stage in the development of our law of libel. The State steps in to suppress harangues which endanger the peace and good order of society. The substance or matter of the harangue is comparatively immaterial ; the "secular arm" is only concerned with its political consequences.

To one charge, therefore, which has been brought against our law as to blasphemy, it is not amenable, at all events in this its earliest form. It does not "take the Deity under its protection." It does not attempt to "avenge the insult done to God." The offender is punished for his offence against his fellow-men, not for his offence against God. No judge and jury ever tried a man for a *sin* that was not also a *crime*. As Erskine, J., said, in sentencing Holyoake in 1842: "The arm of the law is not stretched out to protect the character of the Almighty ; we do not assume to be the protectors of our God, but to protect the people from such indecent language." Very similar words were spoken by Mr. Justice Ashurst in passing sentence upon Williams, who was tried in 1797 for publishing Paine's "Age of Reason": "Although the Almighty does not stand in need of the feeble aid of mortals to vindicate His honour and law, it is, nevertheless, fit that Courts of judicature should show their abhorrence and detestation of people capable of sending into the world such infamous and wicked books. Indeed, all offences of this kind are not only offences to God, but crimes against the law of the land, and are punishable as such, inasmuch as they tend to destroy those obligations whereby civil society is bound together. And it is upon this ground that the Christian religion constitutes part of the law of England." (26 Howell's State Trials, p. 714.)

So, in 1838, Alderson, B., told the jury, in *Gathercole's Case*, 2 Lewin C. C. at p. 254, that "a person may, without being liable to prosecution for it, attack any sect of the Christian religion, save the established religion of the country; and the only reason why the latter is in a different situation from the others, is because it is the form established by law, and is therefore a part of the constitution of the country. In like manner and for the same reason any general attack upon Christianity is the subject of criminal prosecution, because Christianity is the established religion of the country." And he directed the jury to acquit the prisoner if they thought the libel "was merely an attack upon the Roman Catholic Church" (see *ante*, p. 458). This ruling, while it clearly states the grounds on which the law against blasphemy was supported, shows with equal clearness how one-sided was its operation.

II.

But with the eighteenth century comes a new development in this branch of the law. In the case of *R.* v. *Woolston*, (1729) Fitzg. 64; 1 Barnard. 162, 266; 2 Str. 832, the Court of King's Bench, while professing to follow *R.* v. *Taylor*, greatly extended the principle of that decision, making criminal liability depend on the heretical character of the opinions expressed. Woolston was a Fellow of Sidney College, Cambridge, who had published six "Discourses on the Miracles of our Saviour," urging that they were not to be taken literally, but allegorically or mystically. His arguments, which were conveyed in most forcible language, gave great offence to the bishops, and Woolston was prosecuted and found guilty. The indictment against him contained an express allegation that these discourses were published "with an intent to vilify and subvert the Christian religion" (see the report in Fitzgibbon);

hence the verdict of the jury amounted to a finding (probably erroneous) that such was Woolston's intent. His counsel, Dr. Worley, moved in arrest of judgment that these discourses did not amount to a libel upon Christianity, since the Scriptures were not denied; that the offence was of ecclesiastical cognizance: that the defendant should have been proceeded against upon the stat. 9 & 10 Will. III. c. 32; and he was prepared to go further and argue that even though the book was a libel upon Christianity, yet the common law had not cognizance of such an offence, when he was stopped by the Court, Raymond, C.J., declaring on the authority of *Taylor's Case* (1 Ventris, 293; 3 Keble, 607), that "Christianity in general is parcel of the common law of England, and, therefore, to be protected by it. Now whatever strikes at the very root of Christianity tends manifestly to a dissolution of the civil government. So that to say an attempt to subvert the established religion is not punishable by those laws upon which it is established is an absurdity. I would have it taken notice of that we do not meddle with any differences in opinion, and that we interpose only where the very root of Christianity itself is struck at, as it plainly is by this allegorical scheme, the New Testament, and the whole relation of the life and miracles of Christ being denied; and who can find this allegory?"

Similarly, in 1708, when a man called Read was indicted for publishing an obscene libel, Chief Justice Holt expressed a strong opinion that such a publication was a purely ecclesiastical offence, not punishable in the temporal Courts. (Fortescue, 98; 11 Mod. 142.) But afterwards in *Curl's Case* (1727: 1 Barnard. 29; 2 Str. 788), the judgment of Hale, C.J., in *Taylor's Case* was cited, and the Court of King's Bench decided that an obscene libel was "punishable at common law, as an offence against the peace, intending to weaken the bonds of civil society, virtue, or morality;" the Chief Justice giving his judgment somewhat guardedly: "If it reflects on religion, virtue, or morality, if it tends to disturb the civil order of society, I think it is a temporal offence" (2 Str. 790).

The same law was laid down in 1716 by Hawkins, in his "Pleas of the Crown," Book I. c. 5:—"Offences of this nature, because they tend to subvert all religion and morality, which are the foundation of government, are punishable by the temporal judges with fine and imprisonment." So in summing up to the jury in the Irish case of *R.* v. *Father Petcherini*, (1855) (7 Cox, C. C. at p. 84), Greene, B., told them that there could be no doubt that the act complained of—burning a Bible in public—was "one of grave and serious nature, and amounts by the law of the land to a criminal offence. It has been truly stated to you that the Christian religion is part and parcel of the law of this land. Any publication or any conduct tending to bring Christianity or the Christian religion into disrespect, or expose it to hatred or contempt, is not only committing an offence against the majesty of God, but is in violation of the common law of the land. Among the ways in which that offence may be committed is by exposing the Word of God, or any part of it, to obloquy or hatred. The highest authorities have laid down the law in that way, both ancient and modern."

And the decision in *R. v. Woolston* was followed again in the nineteenth century in a civil case, *Cowan* v. *Milbourn,* (1867) L. R. 2 Ex. 230; 36 L. J. Ex. 124; 15 W. R. 750; 16 L. T. 290, in which the Court of Exchequer decided that the defendant was justified in refusing to carry out a contract to let certain rooms, because the plaintiff proposed to deliver in them lectures, the titles of two of which were advertised as follows:—" The Character and Teachings of Christ; the former defective, the latter misleading;" "The Bible shown to be no more inspired than any other book." The action was tried in the Passage Court at Liverpool, and the Recorder directed the verdict to be entered for the defendant, but gave the plaintiff leave to move the Court of Exchequer to enter the verdict for him, the damages being contingently assessed at 10*l.* on each count. The plaintiff accordingly moved *ex parte* for a rule *nisi* in pursuance of the above leave. The lectures never were delivered, and the propositions intended to be maintained in them could hardly have been expressed on the placards in less offensive language. Yet Kelly, C.B., held that it was clear from the advertisements that the lecturer was going to attack Christianity in general, and that to do this publicly was clearly blasphemy at common law. Baron Bramwell, on the other hand, relied on the statute 9 & 10 Will. III. c. 32, s. 1, the Recorder having elicited from the plaintiff at the trial, as appears from the report in the Law Times, that he had been educated in the Christian religion. But at the end of his judgment the learned Baron seems to abandon this ground and to admit that possibly the intended lectures were not positively criminal, in the sense of being indictable, while maintaining that they were still unlawful as being *contra bonos mores.* This, no doubt, is a solid distinction in many cases; but with all respect we venture to doubt if there can be such a distinction in the case of alleged blasphemy. Either the words are criminal or they are innocent. The right of free speech applies the instant the veto of the law is removed : there can be no *tertium quid,* no debatable ground of language not criminal, yet reprobated by the law.

The learned Baron also remarked during the argument (16 L. T. 291), " I have heard it said by a learned judge that blasphemy is more in the manner and spirit of treating the subject than in the actual matter itself." And Baron Martin's judgment was as follows :—" I am quite of the same opinion. I protest against the notion that this is any punishment of the persons advocating these opinions. It is merely the case of the owner of property exercising his rights over its use." Hence it cannot be said that either of these learned Barons concurred in the law laid down by the Lord Chief Baron. And the case is in other respects unsatisfactory as an authority on a point of criminal law, being a somewhat hurried decision, refusing an application for a rule *nisi* in a civil case in which only 20*l.* was in dispute.

Still, these cases, if they stood alone, would undoubtedly establish this proposition, that " whatever strikes at the very root of Christianity tends manifestly to a dissolution of the civil government," and is therefore punishable as a crime, although the language and temper of the writer be irreproachable. This proposition appears to us to be inconsistent with the law laid down in the earlier cases ; it is in fact punishing a man for his opinions, which, as was held in *Traske's Case* (*ante,* p. 490), were examinable only in the Ecclesiastical Courts.

What reason, then, is alleged for this extension of the former law ? It is based on the maxim that " every man must be taken to have intended the natural and necessary consequences of his act." This is the argument, as we understand it :—Though the writer may honestly desire to arrive at the truth, and though he may have expressed his objectionable arguments with no more profanity than their statement necessarily involved, still it will be the duty of both judge and jury to consider the effect of a general dissemination of those opinions. If the doctrines maintained are such that their direct tendency is to subvert religion, to destroy morality, and " to dissolve all the bonds and obligations of civil society," then the maxim applies, and the judge must direct a conviction, for the necessary malice is presumed.

Now everyone would naturally be reluctant to construe into a crime the fair and temperate expression of opinions sincerely entertained, merely in obedience to a legal presumption. And it will be observed that the whole of the above argument rests on the assumption that the natural and necessary consequence of publishing heretical opinions is to destroy religion and morality, and to subvert the civil government.

Such an assumption is unfounded. No doubt where a man intentionally shocks or insults the religious feelings of others he is weakening that sentiment of reverence for holy things which is a safeguard of morality: and his conduct also may conduce to a breach of the peace. But where a man honestly states in calm and temperate language and without any sophistical argument the views which he conscientiously entertains, and at which he has arrived by careful and reverent study of the question, the avowal of his convictions, however heretical they may be, does not tend to subvert religion, or to destroy morality, or to dissolve any of the bonds and obligations of civil society.

"For, if we be sure we are in the right," says Milton, in his *Areopagitica* (p. 65, Arber's Reprint), "and do not hold the truth guiltily, which becomes not, . . . what can be more fair than when a man judicious, learned, and of a conscience for aught we know as good as theirs that taught us what we know, shall . . . openly by writing publish to the world what his opinion is, what his reasons, and wherefore that which is now thought cannot be sound."

We know now that such a book as Woolston's does not in fact produce the consequences which Lord Raymond held it would. It was perhaps natural that in those days the Chief Justice should anticipate and dread such a result. But it has been found by practical experience that it is to the public interest that heretical opinions should be freely advanced and fairly answered, so long as this is done without unnecessary irreverence.

There is one argument frequently adduced in the earlier cases in favour of prosecutions for blasphemy—that all attacks upon the established religion tend to destroy the solemnity of an oath " on which the due administration of justice depends," and thus " the law will be stripped of one of its principal sanctions—the dread of future punishment." But the strength of this argument is now destroyed by the Acts, which permit atheists and persons who do not believe in a future life to give evidence in our law courts. (See 1 & 2 Vict. c. 105, s. 1; 32 & 33 Vict. c. 68, s. 4; 33 & 34 Vict. c. 49, s. 1.)

III.

In the nineteenth century the law against blasphemy reaches a third stage. There is no longer any danger to the State from a frank avowal of heretical convictions. Nor does our law any longer interfere with men's religious opinions; no Secular Court in England will now take cognizance of such matters. It is the malicious intent to insult the religious feelings of others by profanely scoffing at all they hold sacred, which deserves and receives punishment.

This view of our law against blasphemy was strongly advocated by that eminent lawyer, the late Mr. Starkie, the first edition of whose Treatise on the Law of Slander and Libel was published in 1812, the second in 1830. (See especially Vol. II. (2nd ed.), pp. 143—147.) This is the view adopted by the judges in the House of Lords in *Shore* v. *Wilson*, 9 Cl. & Fin. 355. This is the view expressed in the admirable address of the late Lord Chief Justice Coleridge to the jury in the case of *R.* v. *Ramsey and Foote*, 48 L. T. 733; 15 Cox, C. C. 231; 1 C. & E. 126. Lord Coleridge in that address stated in the most clear and convincing language the principles that are truly to be deduced from the early authorities on the subject: "If the law, as I have laid it down to you, is correct—and I believe it has always been so—if the decencies of controversy are observed, even the fundamentals of religion may be attacked without a person being guilty of blasphemous libel. There are many great and grave writers who have attacked the foundations of Christianity. Mr. Mill undoubtedly did so; some great writers now alive have done so too; but no one can read their writings without seeing a difference between them and the incriminated publications, which I am obliged to say is a difference, not of degree, but of kind. There is a grave, an earnest, a reverent, I am almost tempted to say a religious, tone in the very attacks on Christianity itself, which shows that what is aimed at is not insult to the opinions of the majority of Christians, but a real, quiet, honest pursuit of truth. If the truth at which these writers have arrived is not the truth we have been taught, and which, if we had not been taught it, we might have discovered, yet because these conclusions differ from ours, they are not to be exposed to a criminal indictment. With regard to these persons, therefore, I should say they are within the protection of the law, as I understand it."

This is no new law. Precisely the same view was held by the father of the late Lord Chief Justice, Mr. Justice Coleridge, and stated by him to the jury in the case of *R.* v. *Pooley*, tried at Bodmin Summer Assizes in 1857. (See Sir James Stephen's Digest of the Criminal Law, p. 97, n.) Mr. Justice Erskine, in sentencing

Adams at Gloucester in 1842, for selling No. 25 of the *Oracle of Reason*, said:—" By the law of this country, every man has a right to express his sentiments in decent language." And in summing up the case of *R.* v. *Holyoake*, the same learned judge told the jury:—"If you are convinced that he uttered the words with levity, for the purpose of treating with contempt the majesty of the Almighty God, he is guilty of the offence. If you think he made use of these words in the heat of argument without any such intent, you will give him the benefit of the doubt." Mr. Justice Best gave a similar direction to the jury in the case of *R.* v. *Mary Ann Carlile* (1821); see 1 State Trials (New Series), at pp. 1046, 1047. Lord Denman, C.J., in *Moxon's Case* (2 Townsend's Modern State Trials, at p. 388), expressly directed the attention of the jury to the fact that " the purpose of the passage cited from ' Queen Mab ' was, he thought, to cast reproach and insult upon what, in Christian minds, were the peculiar objects of veneration," and left to the jury these questions:—" Were the lines indicated calculated to shock the feelings of any Christian reader ? Were their points of offence explained, or was their virus neutralized by any remarks in the margin, by any note of explanation or apology ? If not, they were libels on God, and indictable." (June 23rd, 1841.)

And there is a long string of decisions in Chancery, bearing on the subject, which strongly support the opinion expressed by Lord Coleridge. In equity, no trust will be enforced, no legacy will be held valid, the object of which is to promote an illegal or immoral act. Hence, if the doctrines advocated by a particular sect were blasphemous, a legacy or trust in favour of that sect would be set aside. It follows that where we find a legacy or trust for the dissemination of any particular doctrines upheld after argument in the Court of Chancery, those doctrines cannot be illegal or immoral and certainly are not blasphemous. It would be absurd to contend that one Division of the High Court of Justice will punish as a crime teaching which another branch of the same Court wil encourage and enforce. Or, to quote the words of Lord Mansfield in *Evans' Case*, already cited : " Nothing can be plainer than that the law protects nothing in that very respect, in which it is at the same time in the eye of the law a crime." (16 Parliamentary History, p. 320; *ante*, p. 479.)

Now, Lord Raymond would certainly have held that to deny the Deity of Christ was " to strike at the very roots of Christianity." Yet bequests and trusts in favour of Unitarianism are always enforced in Chancery. So much of the Toleration Act as excepted persons denying the Trinity from its benefits, and so much of the Blasphemy Act of William III. as related to persons who " deny any one of the Three Persons in the Holy Trinity to be God," were repealed in 1818 by 53 Geo. III. c. 160. Lord Eldon, in 1817, pointed out that this repeal only left the common law exactly as it was before the 9 & 10 Will. III. c. 32, was passed, and deliberately abstained from expressing any opinion as to whether the publication of Unitarian opinions was or was not an offence at common law. (*Att.-Gen.* v. *Pearson*, (1817) 3 Mer. 405, 407.) At the same time, the Lord Chancellor expressly laid down the principle at p. 399:—"It is quite certain that I ought not to execute a trust, the object of which is illegal." But all doubt has since been set at rest. In the case of *Lady Hewley's Charities* (*Shore* v. *Wilson*, 9 Clark & Fin. 355) in the House of Lords in 1842, the question was put to the judges whether ministers and preachers of Unitarian belief and doctrine were, in the then state of the law, incapable of partaking of religious charities (p. 499); and they all (Mr. Justice Maule, Mr. Justice Erskine, Mr. Justice Coleridge, Mr. Justice Williams, Baron Gurney, Baron Parke, and Lord Chief Justice Tindal) answered this question in the negative. Mr. Justice Maule said (p. 509):—"There is no statute now in force prohibiting the profession or preaching of Unitarian doctrines, and I have not found any authority to show that it is prohibited at common law." Mr. Justice Erskine said (p. 524):—"Although the repeal by the statute 53 Geo. III. c. 160, of the incapacities and penalties imposed by the earlier statutes has not made any difference as to the truth or error of their tenets, and cannot, in my opinion, reflect back any light upon Lady Hewley's intentions in 1704, it has removed the only obstacle that could have intercepted her bounty if they had been originally objects of it. It is indeed still blasphemy punishable at common law scoffingly or irreverently to ridicule or impugn the doctrines of the Christian faith, and no one would be allowed to give or claim any pecuniary encouragement for such a purpose; yet any man may, without subjecting himself to any penal consequences, soberly and reverently examine and question the truth of those doctrines which have been assumed as essential to it. And I am not aware of any impediment to the application of any charitable fund for the encouragement of such enquiries." Mr. Justice Coleridge said (p. 539), that (in order to arrive at the same conclusion), it was " not necessary to break in upon any of those *dicta* by which Christianity has been declared parcel of the common law, nor to extend the operation of the different Toleration Acts beyond the literal meaning of their language. But Unitarians profess to be Christians as much, and we doubt not as sincerely, as Trinitarians; and I apprehend that there is nothing unlawful at common law in reverently denying doctrines parcel of Christianity, however fundamental. It would be difficult to draw a line in such matters according to perfect orthodoxy, or to define how far one might depart from it in believing or teaching without offending the law. The only safe, and, as it seems to me, practical rule, is that which I have pointed at, and which depends on the sobriety and reverence and seriousness with which the teaching or believing, however erroneous, are maintained." Baron Parke (at p. 565) agreed "that the preaching of doctrines called Unitarian is not on that account illegal at common law, and all the statutory penalties have been repealed." Chief Justice Tindal said (at p. 578) :—"I consider that since the statute 53 Geo. III. c. 160, all distinction between Unitarians and other Protestant Dissenters as to this purpose is by law taken away."

These opinions are, of course, of the highest authority, and have been treated as settling the law in all subsequent cases in which they have been cited. Thus in 1846 in *Shrewsbury* v. *Hornby* (5 Hare's Reports, 406), a bequest to the treasurer of the Unitarian Association to assist Unitarian congregations and maintain a Unitarian missionary, was upheld. In *Re Barnett* (29 L. J. Ch. 871), a legacy to the minister of Cross Street Chapel, Manchester, to be applied "towards the support of the Unitarians," was also upheld. In Scotland, Lord Jeffrey, in an eloquent judgment, gave a similar decision. (*General Assembly of General Baptist Churches* v. *Taylor*, 3 Dunlop & Bell, 2nd Series, Cases in the Court of Session, p. 1030.) It was in accordance with these judgments that it was held in February, 1874, in a Scotch Court that the Rev. Page Hopps's Life of Jesus, a Unitarian book written in a reverent spirit, could not be pirated with impunity by an orthodox missionary, who sought to justify his piracy by the plea that it was a blasphemous publication and therefore incapable of copyright. (See Copinger on Copyright, 3rd edition, p. 94.) It cannot therefore be maintained that Unitarianism is, or ever was, blasphemous at common law, and it follows that the *dicta* in *Woolston's Case* are unreliable, and cannot be regarded in the present day as good law without considerable qualification. And see the recital in the Dissenters' Chapels' Act, 7 & 8 Vict. c. 45.

Again, trusts and legacies to promote the spread of the Jewish religion clearly "strike at the very root of Christianity;" yet they are always enforced in our law courts. Formerly, no doubt, it was different. In 1754 Lord Hardwicke, in the case of *Da Costa* v. *De Pas* (Ambler, 228 ; 2 Swanston, 487, n.), decided, on the express authority of *R.* v. *Taylor* and *R.* v. *Woolston,* that a bequest contained in a Jewish will of 1,200*l.* to found a " Jesuba or assembly for reading the law and instructing people in our holy religion," was void, as being "in contradiction to the Christian religion, which is part of the law of the land." But this is not law now. By the statute 9 & 10 Vict. c. 59, Jews were placed on the same footing as Protestant Dissenters, and all bequests to promote the propagation of Judaism are now valid. And, indeed, trusts and legacies in favour of Jewish synagogues were valid before this statute, a distinction being taken between an act of worship and the inculcation of anti-Christian doctrine. (Per Abbott, J., in *Lazarus* v. *Simmonds,* (1818) 3 Mer. 393, n.)

There is only one modern equity case in which either the letter or the spirit of *Woolston's Case* has been followed, and that is *Briggs* v. *Hartley,* (1850) 19 L. J. Ch. 416. There a testator left a legacy for the "best essay on the subject of natural theology, treating it as a science, and demonstrating the truth, harmony, and infallibility of the evidence on which it is founded, and the perfect accordance of such evidence with reason; also demonstrating the adequacy and sufficiency of natural theology when so treated and taught as a science to constitute a true, perfect, and philosophical system of universal religion (analogous to other universal systems of science, such as astronomy, &c.), founded on immutable facts and the works of creation, and beautifully addressed to man's reason and nature, and tending, as other sciences do, but in a higher degree, to improve and elevate his nature, and to render him a wise, happy, and exalted being." And this was the judgment of Vice-Chancellor Shadwell :—" I cannot conceive that the bequest in the testator's will is at all consistent with Christianity, and therefore it must fail." The editors of Jarman on Wills, 6th edition, p. 216, note (*p*), say "this case would probably not be followed ;" no cases were cited in the argument. This decision stands alone. In *Thornton* v. *Howe,* (1862) 31 Beav. 14, a trust for "printing, publishing, and propagating the sacred writings of the late Joanna Southcote," was held good by Romilly, M.R. ; and in *Pare* v. *Clegg,* (1861) 29 Beav. 589, the same learned judge held that there was nothing illegal or immoral in a society whose chief object was to propagate the visionary doctrines of the late Robert Owen.

It must, of course, be admitted that the law laid down by Lord

Coleridge in *R.* v. *Ramsey and Foote* cannot be reconciled with every one of the earlier decisions. It is not to our mind inconsistent with *R.* v. *Taylor*, but it is certainly opposed to the *dicta*, if not to the decision, in *R.* v. *Woolston*. But Lord Coleridge was not bound to follow these *dicta*. It is in no way the duty of a judge to accept all the *dicta* of his predecessors without regard to the circumstances in which they were uttered and apply them literally in a different age and in other circumstances. Still less is this the duty of a judge when those *dicta* are avowedly based on considerations of public policy which are now admitted to be erroneous. Again, it must be admitted that Lord Coleridge's view of the law is entirely opposed to both the *dicta* and the decision in the civil case, *Cowan* v. *Milbourn, ante,* p. 495. And since the summing-up was delivered his view has not been universally accepted by the Bench. Huddleston, B., was certainly disposed to dissent from it in *Pankhurst* v. *Thompson*, (1886) 3 Times L. R. 199; but the case was settled, so that it was unnecessary to deliver any judgment. See also *Pankhurst* v. *Hamilton*, (1887) 3 Times L. R. 500. And Mr. Justice Stephen, in his " History of the Criminal Law of England " (vol. ii. p. 474, first edition, 1883), undoubtedly inclines to the view that "the true legal doctrine upon the subject is that blasphemy consists in the character of the matter published, and not in the manner in which it is stated;" though he admits that " there is no doubt some authority in favour of a different view of the law." But in a former work, "The Digest of Criminal Law " (in the first edition (1877) at p. 97; in the latest edition (1904) at p. 125), Mr. Justice Stephen placed his present definition of the law and that given by Lord Coleridge in parallel columns as equally good law, adding in a note, " There is authority for each of these views; most of the cases are old, and I do not think that, in fact, any one has been convicted of blasphemy in modern times for a mere decent expression of disbelief in Christianity." And it is now, we think, generally conceded that the law laid down in *Shore* v. *Wilson* and *R* v. *Ramsey and Foote* is " the better opinion " in point of law, and we have therefore stated it at the beginning of this chapter as the existing law of blasphemy.

We feel sure, moreover, that it is the only law on the subject which it is possible to enforce in the present day—the only law which is at all consonant with our modern ideas of universal toleration and religious equality. It does not place any barrier in the way of the freest inquiry or of the largest intellectual or spiritual progress. It permits the frankest avowal and the warmest advocacy of all opinions, however heretical, which the writer or speaker sincerely entertains. It only interferes where our religious feelings are insulted and outraged by wanton and unnecessary profanity: and there surely it is right that some provision should exist to prevent such an offence to the highest and noblest instincts of our nature.

CHAPTER XVIII.

OBSCENE WORDS.

IT is a misdemeanour punishable on indictment or information to publish obscene and immoral books and pictures: for such an act is destructive of the public morality and welfare, though it may not reflect on any particular person, and as such it is punishable at common law. (*R*. v. *Curl*, (1727) 2 Str. 788 ; 1 Barnard. 29, *ante*, p. 494.)

The test of obscenity is this :—" Whether the tendency of the matter charged as obscenity is to deprave and corrupt those whose minds are open to such immoral influences, and into whose hands a publication of this sort may fall." (Per Cockburn, C.J., in *R*. v. *Hicklin*, (1868) L. R. 3 Q. B. 371 ; 37 L. J. M. C. 89 ; 16 W. R. 801 ; 18 L. T. 395 ; 11 Cox, C. C. 19 ; cited with approval by Lord Alverstone, C.J., in *R*. v. *Barraclough*, [1906] 1 K. B. at p. 211.)

Similarly it is a crime to speak vicious and immoral words; provided they be uttered publicly in the hearing of many persons, for else there is no detriment to the general public.

Obscene words and libels are within the jurisdiction of Courts of Quarter Sessions; not being excepted by the 5 & 6 Vict. c. 38.

The punishment may be either fine or imprisonment for a term of any length, and either with or without hard labour. (14 & 15 Vict. c. 100, s. 29.)

It is no longer necessary to set out in the indictment the obscene passages in full. It is " sufficient to deposit the book, newspaper, or other documents containing the alleged libel with the indictment, or other judicial proceeding, together with particulars showing precisely, by reference to pages, columns, and lines, in what part of the book, newspaper, or other document, the alleged libel is to be found, and such particulars shall be deemed to form part of the record." (Law of Libel Amendment Act, 1888, s. 7.) It is not necessary that the book or document alleged to be obscene should be handed in with the indictment, if it is already in the custody of the clerk of assize as an exhibit attached to the depositions. (*R.* v. *Barraclough*, [1906] 1 K. B. 201; 75 L. J. K. B. 77; 94 L. T. 111.)

Illustrations.

Wilkes was fined 500*l.* and imprisoned for a year for printing and publishing " An Essay on Woman."

    R. v. *John Wilkes*, (1768) 4 Burr. 2527; 2 Wils. 151; Dig.
        L. L. 69.

Actors have been prosecuted for performing obscene plays.

    Tremayne's Entries, 209, 213, 214, 215; (1727) 2 Str. 790.

An information was granted against the printer of a newspaper called " The Daily Advertiser, Oracle and True Briton," for publishing an advertisement by a young married woman offering to become anybody's mistress on certain pecuniary terms.

    R. v. *Stuart,* 3 Chit. Crim. L. 887.

Where an officer of the Society for the Suppression of Vice purposely went to the prisoner's shop and asked to see some indecent prints, and was shown several by the prisoner in a back room, of which he bought two in order to found a prosecution thereon, this was held a sufficient publication to sustain the charge.

    R. v. *Carlile,* (1845) 1 Cox, C. C. 229.

The identical print or picture sold or exhibited by the defendant must be produced at the trial: it is not enough for a witness to swear that the one produced is similar to the one exhibited to him by the defendant.

    R. v. *Rosenstein,* (1826) 2 C. & P. 414.

" Obtaining and procuring" obscene works for the purpose of uttering and selling them is a misdemeanour indictable at common law; for it is an overt act done in pursuance of an unlawful intention. But merely " preserving and keeping them in one's possession " for the same purpose is not indictable; for " there is no act shown to be done which can be considered as the first step in the prosecution of a misdemeanour." (Per Lord Campbell, C.J., in *Dugdale* v. *Reg.*, (1853) Dears, C. C. 64; 1 E. & B,

425; 22 L. J. M. C. 50; 17 Jur. 546; and per Park, J., in *R. v. Rosenstein*, (1826) 2 C. & P. 414.)

By the 20 & 21 Vict. c. 83, if any one reasonably believes that any obscene books, or pictures, are kept in any place for the purpose of being sold or exhibited for gain, he may make a complaint on oath before the police magistrate, stipendiary magistrate, or any two justices, having jurisdiction over such place. The magistrate or justices must be satisfied :—

(i.) That such belief was well founded: and for that purpose the complaint must also state on oath that at least one such book or picture has in fact been sold or exhibited for gain in such place.

(ii.) That such book or picture is so obscene that its publication would be a misdemeanour.

(iii.) That such publication would be a misdemeanour proper to be prosecuted as such.

Thereupon the magistrate or justices issue a special warrant authorizing their officer to search for and seize all such books and pictures, and bring them into Court; and then a summons is issued calling upon the occupier of the place to appear and show cause why such books and pictures should not be destroyed. Either the owner, or any other person claiming to be the owner, of such books and pictures may appear: but if no one appears, or if in spite of appearance the justices are still satisfied that the books and pictures, or any of them, are of such a character that their publication would be a misdemeanour proper to be prosecuted, they must order them to be destroyed; if not so satisfied, they must order them to be restored to the occupier of the place in which they were seized. The order for the destruction of such books must state, not only that the magistrate is satisfied that the books are obscene, but also that he is satisfied that the publication of them would be a misdemeanour, and proper to be prosecuted as such : else such order will be bad on the face of it, as not showing that the magistrate had jurisdiction

to make it, and a *certiorari* will be granted to bring it
up and quash it. (*Ex parte Bradlaugh*, (1878) 3 Q. B. D.
509 ; 47 L. J. M. C. 105 ; 26 W. R. 758 ; 38 L. T. 680.)

Any person aggrieved by the determination of the justices may appeal to Quarter Sessions by giving notice in
writing of such appeal, and of the grounds thereof, and
entering into a recognizance, within seven days after such
determination. Hence the books and pictures ordered to
be destroyed will be impounded only for such seven days ;
on the eighth day, if no notice of appeal has been given,
they will be destroyed. If the appeal be dismissed, or not
prosecuted, the Court of Quarter Sessions may order the books
and pictures to be destroyed. (See the Act *in extenso* in
Appendix C., *post*, p. 833.) The death of the complainant
after the issuing of the summons will not cause the proceedings to lapse. (*R.* v. *Truelove*, (1880) 5 Q. B. D. 336 ; 49
L. J. M. C. 57 ; 28 W. R. 413 ; 42 L. T. 250 ; 14 Cox, C. C. 408.)

If the work be in itself obscene, its publication is an
indictable misdemeanour, and the work may be seized
under this Act, however innocent may be the motive of the
publisher. (*R.* v. *Hicklin*, (1868) L. R. 3 Q. B. 371 ; 37 L. J.
M. C. 89 ; 16 W. R. 801 ; 18 L. T. 398 ; 11 Cox, C. C. 19.)

If any point of law arises under this Act, the magistrates
or justices may state a case for the opinion of a superior
Court, under the 20 & 21 Vict. c. 43, or the 43 & 44 Vict.
c. 49, irrespective of the power of appeal given by section 4.
That the libel is an accurate report of a judicial proceeding
is no defence, if it contain matter of an obscene and
demoralizing character. (*Steele* v. *Brannan*, (1872) L. R. 7
C. P. 261 ; 41 L. J. M. C. 85 ; 20 W. R. 607 ; 26 L. T. 509.)

Illustrations.

The Protestant Electoral Union published a book, called "The Confessional Unmasked," intended to expose the abuses of the Roman Catholic
discipline, and to promote the spread of the Protestant religion. But however praiseworthy such a motive may be thought, many passages in the
book were obscene, and it was seized and condemned as an obscene libel.

R. v. *Hicklin,* (1868) L. R. 3 Q. B. 360 ; 37 L. J. M. C. 89 ;
16 W. R. 801 ; 18 L. T. 395 ; 11 Cox, C. C. 19.

The Protestant Electoral Union thereupon issued an expurgated edition of "The Confessional Unmasked," with some new matter. For selling this George Mackey was tried at the Winchester Quarter Sessions on October 19th, 1870, when the jury, being unable to agree as to the obscenity of the book, were discharged without giving any verdict. The Union thereupon published "A report of the Trial of George Mackey," in which they set out the full text of the second edition of "The Confessional Unmasked;" although it had not been read in open Court, but only taken as read, and certain passages in it referred to. A police magistrate thereupon ordered all copies of this "Report of the Trial of George Mackey" to be seized and destroyed as obscene books. *Held,* that this decision was correct.

Steele v. *Brannan,* (1872) L. R. 7 C. P. 261 ; 47 L. J. M. C. 85 ; 20 W. R. 607 ; 26 L. T. 509.

Any one who openly exposes or exhibits any indecent exhibition or obscene prints or pictures in any street, road, public place or highway, or in any window or other part of any house situate in any street, road, public place or highway, shall be deemed a rogue and vagabond, and punished on summary conviction. (5 Geo. IV. c. 83, s. 4, as explained by the 1 & 2 Vict. c. 38, s. 2.)

By the 33 & 34 Vict. c. 79, s. 20, the Postmaster-General may prevent the delivery by post of any obscene or indecent prints, photographs, or books. And by s. 4 of the Post Office (Protection) Act, 1884 (47 & 48 Vict. c. 76), it is provided that a person who sends or attempts to send a postal packet which encloses any indecent or obscene print, painting, photograph, engraving, book, or card, or any indecent or obscene article, or which has on it or on the cover any words, marks, or designs of an indecent, obscene, or grossly offensive character, shall be guilty of a misdemeanour. It does not matter that the offender did not know the actual contents of the books or the details of the photographs sent through the post, if he knew that they were of an indecent character.

Illustration.

The defendant inserted in his newspaper advertisements which, though not obscene in themselves, related, as he knew, to the sale of obscene books and photographs, and informed the readers where such books and photographs could be obtained abroad. A police officer wrote to the addresses given in the advertisements, and received in return from the advertisers obscene books and photographs. The defendant was tried and convicted on an indictment under the last mentioned section. *Held*, that the conviction was right, although he did not know what precise books or photographs would be forwarded by the foreign advertisers to each applicant.

R. v. de Marny, [1907] 1 K. B. 388; 76 L. J. K. B. 210; 96 L. T. 159; 71 J. P. 14; 23 Times L. R. 221.

And by section 3 of the Indecent Advertisements Act, 1889 (52 & 53 Vict. c. 18), "Whoever affixes to or inscribes on any house, building, wall, hoarding, gate, fence, pillar, post, board, tree, or any other thing whatsoever so as to be visible to a person being in or passing along any street, public highway, or footpath, and whoever affixes to or inscribes on any public urinal, or delivers or attempts to deliver, or exhibits, to any inhabitant or to any person being in or passing along any street, public highway, or footpath, or throws down the area of any house, or exhibits to public view in the window of any house or shop, any picture or printed or written matter which is of an indecent or obscene nature, shall, on summary conviction, in manner provided by the Summary Jurisdiction Acts, be liable to a penalty not exceeding forty shillings, or, in the discretion of the Court, to imprisonment for any term not exceeding one month, with or without hard labour."

By section 4, "Whoever gives or delivers to any other person any such pictures, or printed or written matter mentioned in section 3 of this Act with the intent that the same, or some one or more thereof, should be affixed, inscribed, delivered, or exhibited as therein mentioned, shall, on conviction in manner provided by the Summary Jurisdiction Acts, be liable to a penalty not exceeding five pounds, or, in the discretion of the Court, to imprisonment for any term not exceeding three months, with or without hard labour."

Section 5 enacts that any advertisement relating to any complaint or infirmity arising from or relating to sexual intercourse, shall be deemed to be printed or written matter of an indecent nature within the meaning of the above sections; while section 6 provides that "any constable or other peace officer may arrest without warrant any person whom he shall find committing any offence against this Act."

CHAPTER XIX.

SEDITIOUS WORDS.

SEDITIOUS words may be defined generally in the language of section 1 of the statute 60 Geo. III. & 1 Geo. IV. c. 8, as any words which tend "to bring into hatred or contempt the person of his Majesty, his heirs or successors, or the Regent, or the government and constitution of the United Kingdom as by law established, or either House of Parliament, or to excite his Majesty's subjects to attempt the alteration of any matter in Church or State as by law established, otherwise than by lawful means." Whoever by language, written or spoken, incites or encourages others to use physical force or violence in some public matter connected with the State, is guilty of publishing a seditious libel. The test whether the statement is a seditious libel is not either the truth of the language or the innocence of the motive with which the statement is published, but is this: Is the language used calculated to promote public disorder or physical force or violence in a matter of State? (Per Lord Coleridge, J., in *R.* v. *Aldred*, (1909) 74 J. P. 55.)

Seditious words may in some special cases amount to Treason or to Treason-felony. This chapter will, therefore. be divided into

I.—*Treasonable Words.*

(i) Words merely spoken.
(ii) Words written or printed but not published.
(iii) Words written or printed and published.

II.—*Seditious Words.*

(i) Words defamatory of the Sovereign himself.
(ii) Words defamatory of the King's Ministers and Government.

(iii) Words defamatory of the Constitution and of our Laws generally.

(iv) Words defamatory of either House of Parliament, or of the members thereof.

(v) Words defamatory of Courts of Justice, and of the Judges thereof.

  (*a*) Superior Courts.

  (*b*) Inferior Courts.

I.—Treason and Treason-Felony.

(i) Words *merely spoken* against the King or his ministers cannot amount to treason. It was resolved in *Hugh Pine's Case*, Cro. Car. 117 (overruling several arbitrary decisions of earlier date), "that, unless it were by some particular statute, no words will be treason."* There is no such statute; but by section 3 of the 11 & 12 Vict. c. 12, to express, utter, and declare, *by open and advised speaking*, certain traitorous compassings, imaginations, inventions, devices, or intentions, is made treason-felony. The words in italics were not in the earlier statutes to the same effect, and are now repealed by the Statute Law Revision Act, 1891 (54 & 55 Vict. c. 67).

But words accompanying any act may always be given in evidence to explain the intention with which such act is done.

(ii) Words written or printed, but not published, cannot be treason at common law: and they do not constitute an overt act of treason within the meaning of the 25 Edw. III. c. 2. The decisions to the contrary in *R.* v. *Peacham*, (1615) Cro. Car. 125, 2 Cobbett's St. Tr. 870, and *R.* v.

---

* The story so frequently repeated that in the reign of Edward IV. Thomas Burdett was convicted of high treason for saying that he wished the horns of his stag were in the belly of him who had advised the King to shoot it (though it is still to be found in Blackstone, vol. iv. c. 6), has been proved by Hallam to be mythical. The charge against Burdett was of a much more serious nature; and these idle words of his are not anywhere alluded to in the indictment against him. ("Middle Ages," c. viii. *ad fin.*)

Algernon Sidney, (1683) 9 St. Tr. 889, 893, were reversed by a private Act of Parliament in 1689. (See Hallam's Const. Hist. i. 467.) But by the 6 Anne, c. 7 (al. 41), s. 1, (passed in 1707, probably in consequence of a libel called " Mercurius Politicus : " see *R.* v. *Brown*, Holt, 425 ; 11 Mod. 86 ; *post*, p. 524), " maliciously, advisedly, and directly, *by writing or printing*, to maintain and affirm," that Queen Anne was not the rightful Queen, that the Pretender or any one else, except the descendants of the Electress Sophia, had any right or title to the Crown, or that an Act of Parliament could not bind the Crown, and limit the descent thereof, was made high treason ; and it does not appear that any publication is requisite to complete the offence created by this statute.

(iii) But to publish a writing which imports a compassing the King's death within the meaning of 25 Edw. III. c. 2, is an overt act of treason.

Illustration.

Williams, a barrister of the Middle Temple, wrote two books, " Balaam's Ass " and the " Speculum Regale," in which he predicted that King James I. would die in the year 1621. He was indicted for high treason, convicted, and executed.

R. v. *Williams*, (1620) 2 Rolle, R. 88.

By the 36 Geo. III. c. 7, made perpetual by the 57 Geo. III. c. 6, to compass, devise, or intend death or wounding, imprisonment, or bodily harm to the person of the Sovereign, and such compassing, device, or intention to express, utter, or declare, *by publishing any printing or writing*, or by any overt act or deed, is made high treason, punishable with death.

And by the 11 & 12 Vict. c. 12, s. 3, to compass, devise, and intend to depose the King, or to levy war against him in order by force or constraint to compel him to change his counsels, or to intimidate either House of Parliament, or to stir up any foreigner or stranger with force to invade any of his dominions ; and such compassings, devices, or

intentions, or any of them, to express, utter, or declare, *by
publishing any printing, or writing or by open and advised
speaking*, or by any overt act or deed, is made treason-felony,
punishable with transportation (now penal servitude) for
life.

II.—SEDITION.

It is a misdemeanour, punishable by indictment or by
information, to libel or to slander the Sovereign, or his
administration, or the constitution of the realm, or either
House of Parliament, or its members, or any judge or
magistrate.   It is also a high misprision or contempt; and
therefore the defendant may be fined to any amount, or
sentenced to a term of imprisonment of any length, or both,
at the discretion of the judge, as in *præmunire*.   Formerly,
banishment and pillory could also be inflicted; but these
punishments are now abolished.   (60 Geo. III. & 1 Geo. IV.
c. 8, ss. 1, 2, 3, 4 ; 11 Geo. IV. & 1 Will. IV. c. 73, s. 1;
7 Will. IV. & 1 Vict. c. 23).   In cases not calling for severer
punishment, the offender may be required to find sureties
for his good behaviour.   (*Ex parte Seymour* v. *Michael Davitt*,
12 L. R. Ir. 46 ; 15 Cox, C. C. 242.)

The offence cannot be tried at Quarter Sessions.

(i) *Words defamatory of the Sovereign himself.*

It is sedition to speak or publish of the King any words
which would be libellous and actionable *per se*, if printed
and published of any other public character.

Thus, any words will be deemed seditious, which strike
at the King's private life and conduct, which impute to him
any corrupt or partial views, or assign bad motives for his
policy, which insinuate that he is a tyrant, careless of the
welfare of his subjects, or which charge him with deliberately
favouring or oppressing any individual or class of men in
distinction to the rest of his subjects.   (*R.* v. *Dr. Shebbeare*,
(1758) Holt on Libel, p. 82 ; *R.* v. *Mylius*, (1911).)   *À fortiori,*

any words are seditious which strike at his title to the Crown, call his legitimacy in question, or are otherwise treasonable. (*R.* v.*Clerk*, (1728) 1 Barnardiston, 304, *ante*, p. 154.)

But to assert that the King is misled by his ministers, or that he takes an erroneous view of some great question of policy, is not seditious, if it be done with decency and moderation.

Illustrations.

The following words appeared in the *Morning Chronicle* for October 2nd, 1809 :—"What a crowd of blessings rush upon one's mind that might be bestowed upon the country in the event of a total change of system ! Of all monarchs, indeed, since the Revolution, the successor of George the Third will have the finest opportunity of becoming nobly popular." On the trial of a criminal information against the proprietor and printer of the paper for libel, Lord Ellenborough told the jury that if they considered that the words meant that the King's death would be a blessing to the nation, and that the sooner it happened the better, then they should find the prisoners guilty ; but that if they thought the passage could fairly be construed as an expression of regret that an erroneous view had been taken of public affairs, and of a wish for some change in the policy and system of administration under his Majesty, they might acquit them. The jury found the prisoners, Not Guilty.

> *R.* v. *Lambert and Perry*, (1810) 2 Camp. 398 ; 31 How. St. Tr. 340.

To print and publish falsely of the King that he is insane is a criminal libel, as it would be of any other person.

> *R.* v. *Harvey and Chapman*, (1823) 2 B. & C. 257.

So is charging the King with a breach of his coronation oath.

> *Oliver St. John's Case*, (1615) Noy, 105.

To insinuate that the King is a liar and a deceiver, and to assert that he has treacherously betrayed the interests of his subjects and allies, and prostituted the honour of his crown (*The North Briton*, No. 45), is a seditious libel.

> *R.* v. *John Wilkes*, (1768) 4 Burr. 2527 ; 19 How. St. Tr. 1075.
>
> *R.* v. *Kearsley*, } Dig. L. L. 69.
> *R.* v. *John Williams*, }

As to certain of the letters of Junius, see

> *R.* v. *Woodfall*, (1770) 5 Burr. 2661.
> *R.* v. *Almon*, (1770) *ib.* 2686.

Many *dicta* in the old text-books represent the law as stricter on this point than is stated above. According to Hawkins' "Pleas of the Crown," i. c. 6 (8th ed. by Curwood, p. 66), and 4 Blackstone,

123, c. ix. ii. 3, it is a high misprision and contempt merely to speak contemptuously of the King, or curse him or wish him ill, to assert that he lacks wisdom, valour or steadiness, or, in short, to say anything "which may lessen him in the esteem of his subjects, weaken his government, or raise jealousies between him and his people." But we can find no decision reported which supports so wide a proposition: and we venture to doubt if in the present day it would be deemed a crime to call the King a coward or a fool. Mere words of vulgar abuse can hardly amount to sedition. In fact, the only distinctions that the law makes between words defamatory of the King, and of any other leading public character appear to be:—

(i) That the former may be criminal when only *spoken*; whereas the latter must be written or printed and published;

(ii) That in the case of the former it cannot be pleaded as a defence that the words are true. (*R.* v. *Francklin*, (1731) 9 St. Tr. 255; 17 Howell's St. Tr. 626; *Ex parte O'Brien*, 12 L. R. Ir. 29; 15 Cox, C. C. 180.)

(ii) *Words defamatory of the King's Ministers and Government.*

It is sedition to speak or publish of individual members of the Government words which would be libellous and actionable *per se*, if written and published of any other public character.

It is also sedition to speak or publish words defamatory of the Government collectively, or of their general administration, with intent to subvert the law, to produce public disorder, or to foment or promote rebellion.

"There is no sedition in censuring the servants of the Crown, or in just criticism on the administration of the law, or in seeking redress of grievances, or in the fair discussion of all party questions." (Per Fitzgerald, J., in *R.* v. *Sullivan*, 11 Cox, C. C. 50.)

Where corrupt or malignant motives are attributed to the ministry as a whole, and no particular person is libelled, the jury must be satisfied that the author or publisher maliciously and designedly intended to subvert our laws and constitution, and to excite rebellion or disorder. There must be a criminal intent. But such an intent will be presumed, if the natural and necessary consequence of the words employed be "to excite a contempt of her Majesty's Government, to bring the administration of its laws into disrepute, and thus impair their operation, to create disaffection, or to disturb the public peace and tranquillity of the realm." (*R.* v. *Collins*, (1839) 9 C. & P. 456; *R.* v. *Lovett, ib.* 462.)

In determining whether such is a natural and necessary consequence of the words employed, the jury should consider the state of the country and of the public mind at the date of the publication: passages which in tranquil times might be comparatively innocent may be most pernicious in a time of insurrection. (Per Fitzgerald, J., 11 Cox, C. C. 50, 59.) On the other hand, the circumstances which provoked the attack may tell in the prisoner's favour. If a man be smarting under a grievance, or honestly indignant at some act of a Government official, he cannot be expected to speak or write as calmly and deliberately as if he were discussing matters in which he felt no special interest. (Per Littledale, J., in *R.* v. *Collins*, 9 C. & P. 460.) The jury should, in every case, consider the book or newspaper article as a whole, and in a fair, free, and liberal spirit: not dwelling too much upon isolated passages, or upon a strong word here or there, which may be qualified by the context, but endeavouring to gather the general effect which the whole composition would have on the minds of the public. Considerable latitude must be given to political writers. (Per Lord Kenyon, C.J., in *R.* v. *Reeves*, Peake, Add. Ca. 84; 26 How. St. Tr. 530.)

A document published in this country calculated to bring into hatred and contempt the Government of a foreign country is not a seditious libel. (*R.* v. *Antonelli*, (1906) 70 J. P. 4.)

The Statutes of *Scandalum Magnatum* (3 Edw. I. c. 34; 2 Rich. II. st. 1, c. 5; and 12 Rich. II. c. 11), which made it a crime to tell or publish false news or tales of the great officers of the realm, are now all repealed by the 50 & 51 Vict. c. 59.

Illustrations.

To attribute "the sad state of the country to the influence of French gold on those who have the conduct of affairs," is a seditious libel, though no particular minister is singled out ; but to complain of "the mismanagement of the navy through the ignorance and incapacity of those who have the management of it," would (it is submitted) not be held a libel in the present day.

> *R.* v. *Tutchin,* (1704) 5 St. Tr. 527 ; 14 Howell's St. Tr. 1095 ;
> Holt, 424 ; 2 Lord Raym. 1061 ; 1 Salk. 50 ; 6 Mod. 268.

An announcement that a collection had been made for "the relief of the widows, orphans, and aged parents of our beloved American fellow-subjects, who, faithful to the character of Englishmen, preferring death to slavery, were for that reason only inhumanly murdered by the King's troops at or near Lexington and Concord in the province of Massachusetts on the 19th of April last," was held a seditious libel on his Majesty's Government and their employment of his troops, tending to foment discord and to promote rebellion.

> *R.* v. *John Horne* (afterwards *John Horne Tooke*), (1777) 11
> St. Tr. 264 ; 20 Howell's St. Tr. 651 ; Cowp. 672.

An article in the *Examiner* declaring that an improper and cruel method of punishment was practised in the King's army, and that his soldiers were punished with excessive severity thereby, was declared by the jury, in spite of the summing up of Lord Ellenborough, not to be a seditious libel on the Government and the military service of the King tending to excite disaffection in the army and to deter others from becoming recruits.

> *R.* v. *John Hunt & John Leigh Hunt,* (1811) 31 Howell's St. Tr.
> 408 ; 2 Camp. 583.

Sir Francis Burdett, M.P. for Westminster, wrote and published an address to his constituents, severely commenting on the conduct of the military who had dispersed the meeting assembled at St. Peter's Field, near Manchester, on August 16th, 1819. He was found guilty of publishing a seditious libel, sentenced to three months' imprisonment, and fined 1,000*l.*

> *R.* v. *Burdett,* (1820) 4 B. & Ald. 95, 115, 314.
>
> See also *R.* v. *Pym vel Prim,* (1664) Sid. 219 ; 1 Keble, 773.
>
> *R.* v. *Beere,* (1698) 12 Mod. 219 ; Holt, 422 ; Carth. 409 ;
> 2 Salk. 417 ; 1 Ld. Raym. 414.
>
> *R.* v. *Laurence,* (1699) 12 Mod. 311 ; Dig. L. L. 121.
>
> *R.* v. *Bedford,* (1714) cited in 2 Str. 789 ; Dig. L. L. 19, 121.
>
> *R.* v. *Bliss,* (1719) Dig. L. L. 122.
>
> *R.* v. *Francklin,* (1731) 9 St. Tr. 255 ; 17 Howell's St. Tr. 626.
>
> *R.* v. *Owen,* (1752) 18 Howell's St. Tr. 1203 ; Dig. L. L. 67.
>
> *R.* v. *Cobbett,* (1804) 29 Howell's St. Tr. 1.
>
> *R.* v. *Johnson,* (1805) 29 Howell's St. Tr. 103 ; 7 East, 65 ;
> 3 Smith, 94.
>
> *R.* v. *Collins,* (1839) 9 C. & P. 456.
>
> *R.* v. *Lovett,* (1839) 9 C. & P. 462.
>
> *R.* v. *John Mitchell,* (1848) 11 L. T. (Old S.) 112; 3 Cox, C. C. 94.
>
> *Re Crowe,* (1848) 3 Cox, C. C. 123.
>
> *R.* v. *Fussell,* (1848) 3 Cox, C. C. 291.

There are old cases which appear to go further, and to decide that any publication tending to beget an ill opinion of the Government is a criminal libel. " If persons should not be called to account for possessing the people with an ill opinion of the Government, no Government can subsist : for it is very necessary for all Governments that the people should have a good opinion of it " (*sic*). (Per Lord Holt, C.J., in *R.* v. *Tutchin*, (1704) 5 St. Tr. 532 ; 14 Howell's St. Tr. 1127.) And Lord Ellenborough, C.J., expressly following this decision, told the jury in *R.* v. *Cobbett*, (1804) 29 Howell's St. Tr. 49 :—" It is no new doctrine that if a publication be calculated to alienate the affections of the people, by bringing the Government into disesteem, whether the expedient be by ridicule or obloquy, . . . it is a crime." If this is to be taken literally, all Opposition newspapers commit such crime every day. Such a doctrine, if strictly enforced, would destroy all liberty of the press, and is, moreover, in conflict with more recent *dicta* :—" The people have a right to discuss any grievances that they may have to complain of." (Per Little-dale, J., in *R.* v. *Collins*, 9 C. & P. 461.) " A journalist may canvass and censure the acts of the Government and their public policy—and indeed it is his duty. . . . It might be the province of the press to call attention to the weakness or imbecility of a Government when it was done for the public good." (Per Fitzgerald, J., 11 Cox, C. C. 54, 57.) It is clearly legitimate and constitutional to endeavour, by means of arguments addressed to the people, to replace one set of ministers by another. And the precise object of such arguments is to bring the ministers now in office into disesteem, and to alienate from them the affections of the people. Sir Francis Burdett could not possibly be convicted in the present day for such an electoral address as he issued on August 22nd, 1819. (See 4 B. & Ald. 116, 117, n.)

But Lord Holt's words must not be taken strictly in their modern signification ; we must construe them with reference to the times in which he spoke. He clearly was not referring to a quiet change of ministry which in no way shakes the throne, or loosens the reins of order and government. In 1704 the present system of party-government was not in vogue : it was barely conceived by William III., and was certainly not generally understood under Queen Anne. And even in Lord Ellenborough's time the ministry were still appointed by the King, and not by the people. By " the Government " both judges meant, not so much a particular set of ministers, as the political system settled by the Constitution, the general order and discipline of the realm. " To subvert the

Government " is the phrase employed in the earlier case of *R.* v. *Beere*, 12 Mod. 221 ; Holt, 422 ; and to Lord Holt's mind "subverting the Government " meant bringing in the Pretender ; to Lord Ellenborough's, the introduction of Jacobinism and Red Republicanism from France : not the substitution of one statesman for another as First Lord of the Treasury.

(iii) *Words defamatory of the Constitution and of our laws generally.*

All malicious endeavours by word, deed or writing, to promote public disorder or to induce riot, rebellion or civil war, are clearly seditious, and may be overt acts of treason. But where no such conscious endeavour is proved, still, if the natural and necessary consequence of any word, deed, or writing, be to subvert our laws and constitution and to excite or promote discontent and disorder amongst the people, a criminal intent will be presumed : and the author is guilty of sedition. (*R.* v. *Burdett*, (1820) 4 B. & Ald. 95 ; *R.* v. *Collins*, (1839) 9 C. & P. 456 ; *R.* v. *Grant*, 7 St. Tr. (N. S.) 507 ; *R.* v. *Tibbits and Windust*, [1902] 1 K. B. at p. 88.) Thus all publications, the direct tendency of which is to bring the constitution of the realm into hatred and contempt, and to induce the people to disobey the laws and to defy legally constituted authority, are seditious libels, for which the author is criminally liable. (*R.* v. *Sullivan*, 11 Cox, C. C. 44.)

But mere theoretical discussions of abstract questions of political science, comparisons of various forms and systems of government, and controversies as to the details of our own constitutional law, are clearly permissible. And so is any *bonâ fide* effort to repeal or alter the law by constitutional methods. The prosecution must satisfy the jury that the publication is calculated to disturb the tranquillity of the State and to lead ignorant persons to endeavour to subvert the Government and to break the laws of the realm. (*R.* v. *Burns and others*, 16 Cox, C. C. 355.) Without satisfactory proof of such tendency, there is no evidence of that criminal intention which is essential to constitute the offence.

The old cases *R.* v. *Brewster,* (1663) Dig. L. L. 76 ; *R.* v. *Harrison,* (1677) 3 Keb. 841 ; Ventr. 324, and *R.* v. *Bedford,* (1714) cited in 2 Str. 789, so far as they run counter to this proposition, must be considered as overruled. It seems that Harrison would not have been convicted but for the statute 13 Car. II. c. 1, which remains still in part unrepealed. See *post,* p. 525.

The jury must find, first, that the defendant in fact spoke or published the words complained of : secondly, that the words are seditious and were spoken or published with the intent alleged in the indictment. The latter as well as the former is entirely a question for the jury. The fact that the House of Commons has resolved that the same publication is " a malicious, scandalous and seditious libel, tending to create jealousies and divisions amongst the liege subjects of her Majesty, and to alienate the affections of the people of this country from the Constitution," ought not to have the least weight with the jury. The defendant is not to " be crushed by the name of his prosecutor." (Per Lord Kenyon, C.J., in *R.* v. *Reeves,* Peake, Add. Ca. 84.)

"In a free country like ours," says Lord Kenyon, C.J., in the same case, p. 86, "the productions of a political author should not be too hardly dealt with." The jury should "recollect that they are dealing with a class of articles which, if written in a fair spirit and *bonâ fide,* might be productive of great public good, and were often necessary for public protection " ; and they should therefore " deal with them in a broad spirit, allowing a fair and wide margin, looking upon the whole, not on isolated words." And they should also take into their consideration the state of the country and of the public mind at the date of the publication. (Per Fitzgerald, J., in *R.* v. *Sullivan,* 11 Cox, C. C. 50, 59.)

Illustrations.

To assert that a Parliament would be justified in making war against any king who broke the Social Compact was naturally deemed seditious in the days of Charles II., as tending to a renewal of the Civil War.

R. v. *Brewster,* (1663) Dig. L. L. 76.

R. v. *Harrison,* (1677) 3 Keble, 841 ; Ventr. 324 ; Dig. L. L. 66.

To assert that "the late revolution was the destruction of the laws of England," or an unjustifiable and unconstitutional proceeding, and that the Act of Settlement was "illegal and unwarrantable," and "had been attended with fatal and pernicious consequences to the subjects of this realm," was deemed seditious in the days of Queen Anne and of George II., as tending to favour the cause of the Pretender.

> *R.* v. *Dr. Brown,* (1707) 11 Mod. 86 ; Holt, 425.
>
> *R.* v. *Richard Nutt,* (1754) Dig. L. L. 68.
>
> And see *R.* v. *Thomas Paine,* (1792) 22 Howell's St. Tr. 358.

The Reverend William Winterbotham was convicted for preaching a sermon on November 18th, 1792, containing the following words, which were deemed seditious :—"Darkness has long cast her veil over the land. Persecution and tyranny have carried universal sway. Magisterial powers have long been a scourge to the liberties and rights of the people." He was fined 100*l.* and sentenced to two years' imprisonment.

> *R.* v. *Winterbotham,* 22 Howell's St. Tr. 823, 875.
>
> *R.* v. *Richard Carlile,* 4 C. & P. 415.

To habitually republish in Ireland during a time of political excitement and threatened insurrection extracts from American papers expressing sympathy with the Fenians, and inciting all Irishmen to rebel, without one word of editorial comment or disapproval, is an act of sedition.

> *R.* v. *Pigott,* (1868) 11 Cox, C. C. 44.
>
> See Irish St. Tr. 1848, 1865, 1867, 1868.

It is a misdemeanour for a Roman Catholic priest to address a meeting of his parishioners and to urge them not to pay any rent till a certain evicted tenant is reinstated in his holding ; such advice coming from a person in his position being an incitement to the parishioners to conspire not to pay their just debts.

> *R.* v. *JJ. of Queen's County,* 10 L. R. Ir. 294 ; 15 Cox, C. C. 149.
>
> *R.* v. *JJ. of Cork,* 10 L. R. Ir. 1 ; 15 Cox, C. C. 78.
>
> *Ex parte Seymour* v. *Michael Davitt,* 12 L. R. Ir. 46 ; 15 Cox, C. C. 242.

An intention to excite ill-will between different classes of his Majesty's subjects may be a seditious intention ; whether or not it is so in any particular case, must be decided by the jury after taking into consideration all the circumstances of the case. And where in a prosecution for uttering seditious words with intent to incite to riot, it is proved that previously to the happening of a riot seditious words were spoken, it is a question for the jury whether or not such rioting was directly or indirectly attributable to the seditious words proved to have been spoken.

> *R.* v. *Burns and others,* (1886) 16 Cox, C. C. 355.

(iv) *Words defamatory of either House of Parliament or of the Members thereof.*

It is a misdemeanour to speak or publish of individual members of either House of Parliament, in their capacity as such, words which would be libellous and actionable *per se*, if written and published of any other public man.

It is also a misdemeanour to speak or publish words defamatory of either House collectively, with intent to obstruct or invalidate their proceedings, to violate their rights and privileges, to diminish their authority and dignity, or to bring them into public odium or contempt.

In both cases, all such words are also a contempt and breach of privilege, punishable summarily by the House itself, with fine and imprisonment.

By an entirely obsolete, but still unrepealed provision of the statute 13 Car. II. (stat. I. c. 1, s. 3), any person who shall maliciously and advisedly declare and publish by writing, printing, preaching, or other speaking that the Parliament begun at Westminster on November 3rd, 1640 (the Long Parliament), is not yet dissolved, or that it still ought to be in being, or hath yet any continuance or existence, or that both Houses of Parliament or either House of Parliament have or hath a legislative power without the King, or any other words to the same effect, incurs the penalties of a *præmunire*. See also 6 Anne, c. 7 (al. 41), s. 2.

Illustration.

Rainer printed a scandalous libel, reflecting both on the House of Lords and on the House of Commons, called "Robin's Game, or Seven's the Main"; he was tried in the Court of King's Bench, fined 50*l.*, and sentenced to be imprisoned for two years and until he should pay such fine.
R. v. *Rainer,* (1733) 2 Barnard. 293; Dig. L. L. 125.

On three occasions the House of Commons has voted a particular publication a scandalous and seditious libel, and a breach of privilege, &c., and petitioned the Crown to direct the Attorney-General to prosecute the author, printers and publishers thereof. But on each occasion the prosecution was unsuccessful; the jury in each of the three cases acquitted the prisoner. (*R.* v. *Owen,* (1752) 18 Howell's St. Tr. 1203, 1228; *R.* v. *Stockdale,* (1789) 22 Howell's St. Tr. 238; *R.* v. *Reeves,* (1796) Peake, Add. Ca. 84; 26 Howell's St. Tr. 530.) The House of Commons now invariably deals with offenders itself.

The House of Lords can inflict fine and imprisonment for any length of time. In former days the pillory was sometimes added; *e.g.*, in the case of Thomas Morley, in

1623, and of William Carr in 1667, who were sentenced to stand in the pillory for libelling individual peers.

The House of Commons can inflict fine and imprisonment, and, in the case of a member, expulsion. One unfortunate member, Arthur Hall, suffered all three penalties in 1581 for publishing a book disparaging the authority of the House of Commons, and reflecting upon certain individual members—see Hallam, Const. Hist. vol. i. c. v.—the first instance of a libel being punished by the House. But in the case of a commitment by the House of Commons, the imprisonment can only last to the close of the existing session. The prisoner must be liberated on prorogation. (*Stockdale* v. *Hansard,* 9 A. & E. 114; *Grissell's Case,* Aug. 1879.) It is otherwise with the House of Lords.

The Speaker's warrant is a perfect answer to any writ of *habeas corpus,* and fully justifies the Serjeant-at-arms and his officers in arresting the offender, and protects them from any action of assault or false imprisonment. (*Howard* v. *Gosset,* 10 Q. B. 359; *Burdett* v. *Colman,* 14 East, 163.) It will not be scanned too strictly by the courts of law, nor set aside for any defect of form. (*R.* v. *Paty,* 2 Ld. Raym. 1108; *R.* v. *Hobhouse,* (1819) 2 Chit. 210.) Thus, the libel for which the prisoner was committed need not be set out in such warrant. (*Burdett* v. *Abbot,* 14 East, 1; see 1 Moore, P. C. C. 80.) Still less will any court of common law inquire into the propriety of the commitment and hear it argued that the act complained of did not amount to a contempt, or that the privilege of the House alleged to have been broken does not exist. (*Stockdale* v. *Hansard,* 9 A. & E. 165, 195.) The King's Bench Division cannot admit to bail a prisoner committed for a contempt of the House of Commons. (*Hon. Alex. Murray's Case,* 1 Wilson, 299.)

The House is the best judge of its own privileges, and of what is a contempt of them. But if on the face of a warrant it plainly and expressly appears that the House is exceeding its jurisdiction, it will be the duty of the High Court to order the release of the prisoner. (9 A. & E. 169; Hawkins, 3 Pl. Cr. II. 15, 73, p. 219; *R.* v. *Evans and another,* 8 Dowl. 451.)

The House may commit for any contempt of one of its committees, or of the members of any such committee; instances of such committals occurred in 1832, 1858, and 1879.

So in America the House of Representatives has a general power of committing for contempt, whether the offender be a member or a stranger. (*Anderson* v. *Dunn*, 6 Wheat. 204.) But, as with the English House of Commons, the imprisonment terminates at the adjournment or dissolution of Congress.

But with subordinate legislative bodies it is different. No power of committing for contempt is inherent in them. (*Kielley* v. *Carson*, 4 Moore, P. C. C. 63; *Fenton* v. *Hampton*, 11 Moore, P. C. C. 347, overruling *dicta* of Lord Denman, C.J., in *Stockdale* v. *Hansard*, 9 A. & E. 114, and of Parke, B., in *Beaumont* v. *Barrett*, 1 Moore, P. C. C. 76.) But they have, of course, power to preserve order during their deliberations, which involves a power to remove from the Chamber any person obstructing their proceedings, or otherwise guilty of disorderly conduct in the presence of the House itself, and, if the offender be a member, to exclude him for a time, or even to expel him altogether. Such latter power is necessary for self-preservation; and is quite distinct from the judicial power of sentencing the obstructive to a term of imprisonment as a punishment for his misconduct. (*Doyle* v. *Falconer*, L. R. 1 P. C. 328; 36 L. J. P. C. 33; 15 W. R. 366; *Attorney-General of New South Wales* v. *Macpherson*, L. R. 3 P. C. 268; 7 Moore, P. C. C. (N. S.) 49; 39 L. J. P. C. 59; *Barton* v. *Taylor*, 11 App. Cas. 197; 55 L. J. P. C. 1; 55 L. T. 158.) Thus the House of Assembly of Newfoundland (*Kielley* v. *Carson*, 4 Moore, P. C. C. 63); the Legislative Council of Van Diemen's Land (*Fenton* v. *Hampton*, 11 Moore, P. C. C. 347); the House of Keys in the Isle of Man (*Ex parte Brown*, 5 B. & S. 280; 33 L. J. Q. B. 193; 12 W. R. 821; 10 L. T. 453); and the Legislative Assembly of the Island of Dominica (*Doyle* v. *Falconer*, L. R. 1 P. C. 328; 36 L. J. P. C. 33; 15 W. R. 366), possess no inherent powers to commit for contempt.

But though such a power is not inherent in any inferior legislature, it may be expressly granted by statute; thus the Legislative Assembly of Victoria possesses this privilege by virtue of the 18 & 19 Vict. c. 55, s. 35, and the

Colonial Act, 20 Vict. No. 1. (*Dill* v. *Murphy*, 1 Moore, P. C. C. (N. S.) 487; *Speaker of the Legislative Assembly of Victoria* v. *Glass*, L. R. 3 P. C. 560; 40 L. J. P. C. 17; 24 L. T. 317.) Also, it is said that such a power may be acquired by prescription, acquiescence and usage. (Per Lord Ellenborough, C.J., in *Burdett* v. *Abbot*, 14 East, 137, and Cockburn, C.J., in *Ex parte Brown*, 5 B. & S. 293.) And it is by virtue of such acquiescence and usage that the Jamaica House of Assembly has the power of committing a libeller, if indeed it has such power at all. (*Beaumont* v. *Barrett*, 1 Moore, P. C. C. 80, as explained by Parke, B., in 4 Moore, P. C. C. 89.)

(v) *Words defamatory of Courts of Justice and of Individual Judges.*

(a) Superior Courts.

It is a misdemeanour to speak or publish of any judge of a Superior Court words which would be libellous and actionable *per se*, if written and published of any other person holding a public office.

It is also a misdemeanour to speak or publish words defamatory of any court of justice or of the administration of the law therein, with intent to obstruct or invalidate its proceedings, to annoy its officers, to diminish its authority and dignity, and to lower it in public esteem.

Such words, whether spoken or written, are punishable on indictment or information, with fine or imprisonment or both. They are also in every such case a contempt of court punishable summarily by the Court itself with fine or commitment, as to which see *post*, Chap. XX.

It is immaterial whether the words be uttered in the presence of the Court or at a time when the Court is not sitting, and at a distance from it (*Crawford's Case*, 13 Q. B. 613; 18 L. J. Q. B. 225; 13 Jur. 955); nor need they necessarily refer to the judges in their official capacity.

But "there is no sedition in just criticism on the administration of the law. . . . A writer may freely criticise the proceedings of courts of justice and of individual judges — nay, he is invited to do so, and to do so in a free, and fair, and liberal spirit. But it must be without malignity, and not imputing corrupt or malicious motives." (Per Fitzgerald, J., in *R.* v. *Sullivan*, 11 Cox, C. C. 50.) " It certainly is lawful, with decency and candour, to discuss the propriety of the verdict of a jury, or the decisions of a judge, . . . but if the extracts set out in the information contain no reasoning or discussion, but only declamation and invective, and were written, not with a view to elucidate the truth, but to injure the characters of individuals, and to bring into hatred and contempt the administration of justice in the country," then the defendants have transgressed the law, and ought to be convicted. (Per Grose, J., in *R.* v. *White and another*, 1 Camp. 359, n.)

Illustrations.

To assert that a judge had been bribed, or that in any particular case he had endeavoured to serve his own interest, or those of his friends or of his party, or wished to curry favour at Court, or was influenced by fear of the Government or of any great man, or by any motive other than a simple desire to arrive at the truth and to mete out justice impartially, is seditious.

See *R.* v. *Lord George Gordon,* 22 Howell's St. Tr. 177.

To call the Lord Chief Justice " a traitor and a perjured judge," and to allege that a recent judgment delivered by him was treason, is a misdemeanour.

R. v. *Jeff,* (1630) 15 Vin. Abr. 89.

Hutton, J. v. *Harrison,* Hutton, 131.

To say that the Lord Chief Justice disgraces his high station and prevents justice being done, is a misdemeanour.

R. v. *Hart and White,* (1808) 30 How. St. Tr. 1168, 1345 ; 10 East, 94.

R. v. *Wrennum,* (1619) Popham, 135.

Butt v. *Conant,* 1 Brod. & Bing. 548 ; 4 Moore, 195 ; Gow, 84.

Hurry sued Watson for a malicious prosecution, and recovered damages 3,000*l.* : the corporation of which Watson was a member thereupon resolved " that Mr. Watson had been actuated by motives of public justice in prosecuting Hurry," and voted him 2,300*l.* towards payment of his damages. The Court of King's Bench granted an information against the members of the corporation.

R. v. *Watson and others,* (1788) 2 T. R. 199.

[That the vote of money was an improper employment of the corporate funds is very probable ; but it is doubtful whether an information would be granted for such words in these days.]

The term "Superior Court" includes the House of Lords, the Judicial Committee of the Privy Council, the Court of Appeal, the Court of Criminal Appeal, the High Court of Justice, and any Divisional Court thereof, and any judge of any Division sitting in Court alone (Jud. Act, 1873, s. 39). Also the Central Criminal Court, and all Courts held under any Commission of Oyer and Terminer, Assize, Gaol Delivery, or Nisi Prius. (*Ex parte Fernandez*, 6 H. & N. 717 ; 10 C. B. N. S. 3 ; 30 L. J. C. P. 321 ; 7 Jur. N. S. 529, 571 ; 9 W. R. 832 ; 4 L. T. 296, 324 ; *In re McAleece*, Ir. R. 7 C. L. 146.) And the Superior Courts of Law and Equity in Dublin, and the Court of Session in Scotland. Colonial Courts of Record are also Superior Courts. (*Crawford's Case*, 13 Q. B. 613 ; 18 L. J. Q. B. 225 ; 13 Jur. 955 ; *In re McDermott*, L. R. 1 P. C. 260 ; L. R. 2 P. C. 341 ; 38 L. J. P. C. 1 ; 20 L. T. 47 ; *Hughes* v. *Porral and others*, 4 Moore, P. C. C. 41.)

(b) Inferior Courts.

The judge of an Inferior Court is in no better position than any other public officer, so far as words written and published are concerned. It is a misdemeanour to write and publish concerning him in the execution of his office any words which would be libellous and actionable *per se*.

It is not indictable to speak disrespectful and abusive words of the judge of an Inferior Court behind his back, or even to his face, provided he be out of court.

But it is indictable to speak aloud in open court, when the judge is present in the discharge of his duty, words reflecting upon him in his official capacity.

Hence words which would be indictable if published with respect to a Superior Court may not be indictable if they refer merely to an Inferior Court.

Illustrations.

It is indictable—
to give the lie to the steward of a manor holding a court leet,
   Earl of Lincoln v. *Fisher,* Cro. Eliz. 581 ; Owen, 113 ; Moore, 470 ;

to put on your hat in the presence of the lord of a court leet and refuse to take it off, saying, "I care not what you can do,"

    Bathurst v. *Coxe,* 1 Keb. 451, 465 ; Sir Thos. Raym. 68 ;

to rise up in court and say, to the justices in session, "Though I cannot have justice here, I will have it elsewhere,"

    R. v. *Mayo,* 1 Keb. 508 ; 1 Sid. 144 (although Twisden, J., mercifully endeavoured to construe the words to mean merely, "I propose to appeal from your decision ") ;

to say to a justice of the peace in the execution of his office, "You are a rogue and a liar,"

    R. v. *Revel,* 1 Str. 420 ;

to call the Mayor of Yarmouth in his court, in the hearing of the suitors, a puppy and a fool,

    Ex parte The Mayor of Yarmouth, 1 Cox, C. C. 122.

But it is not indictable—

to call a justice of the peace "a logger-headed, a slouch-headed, bursen-bellied hound,"

    R. v. *Farre,* 1 Keb. 629 ;

nor to say that a justice is a fool, or an ass, or a coxcomb, or a blockhead, or a bufflehead. Per Holt, C.J., in

    R. v. *Wrightson,* 2 Salk. 698 ; 11 Mod. 166 ; 2 Roll. Rep. 78 ; 4 Inst. 181 ;

nor to say of an alderman of Hull, that "Whenever he comes to put on his gown, Satan enters into him,"

    R. v. *Baker,* 1 Mod. 35 ;

nor to say of a justice of the peace in his absence that he is a scoundrel and a liar. Per Lord Ellenborough in

    R. v. *Weltje,* 2 Camp. 142 ;

nor to accuse a justice of partiality or corruption, unless the words were uttered at a time when the magistrate was in the actual execution of his office,

    Ex parte The Duke of Marlborough, 5 Q. B. 955 ; 1 Dav. & Mer. 720 ;

nor to tell a borough magistrate, out of court but to his face, that he is a liar, and unfit to be a magistrate, and that he will hear the same every time he comes into town ; unless, indeed, the words can be construed as tending to provoke a breach of the peace.

    Ex parte Chapman, 4 A. & E. 773.

    See also *Anon.,* (1650) Style, 251.

    Simmons v. *Sweete,* Cro. Eliz. 78.

    Bagg's Case, 11 Rep. 93, 95 ; 1 Roll. Rep. 79, 173, 224.

    R. v. *Burford,* 1 Ventris, 16.

    R. v. *Leafe,* Andrews, 226.

    R. v. *Penny,* 1 Ld. Raym. 153.

    R. v. *Langley,* 2 Ld. Raym. 1029 ; 2 Salk. 697 ; 6 Mod. 125 ; Holt, 654.

    R. v. *Rogers,* 2 Ld. Raym. 777 ; 7 Mod. 28.

    R. v. *Nun,* 10 Mod. 186.

    R. v. *Granfield,* 12 Mod. 98.

R. v. *Pocock,* 2 Str. 1157.

R. v. *Burn,* 7 A. & E. 190.

These cases overrule *R.* v. *Darby,* 3 Mod. 139 ; Comb. 65 ; Carth. 14.

Some Inferior Courts are Courts of Record, others are not. Thus the Mayor's Court, London ; the City of London Court, the Tolzey Court of Bristol, the Salford Hundred Court, the Court of Passage, Liverpool, all County Courts and Courts of Quarter Sessions, and Coroners' Courts are Inferior Courts of Record ; while Courts of Petty Sessions and of Revising Barristers are Inferior Courts not of record.

An Inferior Court of Record has in some cases power to commit for contempt. These cases are dealt with in the next chapter (*post,* p. 560).

An Inferior Court not of record has no power to fine or commit for contempt, unless such power be conferred by statute. (*McDermott* v. *Judges of British Guiana,* L. R. 2 P. C. 341 ; 20 L. T. 47.) But it has another remedy : the offender may be required to find sureties for his good behaviour,

(i) If he use any disrespectful or unmannerly expressions in the face of the Court. (1 Lev. 107 ; 1 Keb. 558.)

(ii) If, out of court, he uses words disparaging the judge or magistrate in relation to his office.

(iii) If, out of court, he obstruct or insult an officer of the court in the execution of his duty. (Hawk. P. C. c. 61, ss. 2, 3.)

(iv) And generally, if he use any words which directly tend to a breach of the peace.

But not for contemptuous and uncivil words spoken of the judge in his private capacity.

Such binding over should be done as soon as possible after the contempt is committed ; and in the case of petty sessions, it should be done, not by the justice specially attacked, but by one of his brethren. (*R.* v. *Lee,* 12 Mod. 514.) The person accused may call evidence to disprove the matters charged against him (which he could not do in a case of " articles to keep the peace "), and he may now give evidence himself. (42 & 43 Vict. c. 49, s. 25.) In default of sureties being provided, the justices may commit either to the common gaol or to the House of Correction (6 Geo. I. c. 19, s. 2) ; but it should appear clearly upon the face of their warrant that the committal is for want of sureties, and not merely for contempt. (*Dean's Case*, Cro. Eliz. 689.) And the committal should be for a time certain, not " until he shall find such sureties," else a poor and friendless man might be imprisoned for life. (*Prickett* v. *Gratrex*, 8 Q. B. 1020.)

CHAPTER XX.

WORDS WHICH ARE A CONTEMPT OF COURT.

IT is a contempt of court to publish words which tend to bring the administration of justice into contempt, to prejudice the fair trial of any cause or matter which is the subject of civil or criminal proceedings, or in any way to obstruct the course of justice. Thus it is a contempt of court to insult the judge, jury or witnesses, to obstruct any officer of the court, to calumniate the parties or prejudice the minds of the judge, jury or general public against them, or in any way to taint the source of justice or to divert or interrupt its ordinary course.

"There are three different sorts of contempt.

"One kind of contempt is, scandalising the Court itself.

"There may be likewise a contempt of this Court, in abusing parties who are concerned in causes here.

"There may be also a contempt of this Court, in prejudicing mankind against persons, before the cause is heard.

"There cannot be anything of greater consequence, than to keep the streams of justice clear and pure, that parties may proceed with safety both to themselves and their characters." (Per Lord Hardwicke, L.C., in *Roach* v. *Garvan, Re Read and Huggonson*, (1742) 2 Atk. p. 471.)

"Nothing is more incumbent upon Courts of justice than to preserve their proceedings from being misrepresented; nor is there anything of more pernicious consequence, than to prejudice the minds of the public against persons concerned as parties in causes, before the cause is finally heard." (*Ib.* p. 469.)

"Any act done or writing published calculated to bring a court or a judge of the court into contempt, or to lower his authority, is a contempt of court. That is one class of contempt. Further, any act done or writing published calculated to obstruct or interfere with the due course of justice or the lawful process of the courts is a contempt of court. The former class belongs to the category which Lord Hardwicke, L.C., characterised as ' scandalising a Court or a judge.' That description of that class of contempt is to be taken subject to one and an important qualification. Judges and Courts are alike open to criticism, and if reasonable argument or expostulation is offered against any judicial act as contrary to law or the public good, no Court could or would treat that as contempt of court." (Per Lord Russell, C.J., in *R.* v. *Gray,* [1900] 2 Q. B. at p. 40.)

"The reason why the publication of articles like those with which we have to deal is treated as a contempt of Court is because their tendency and sometimes their object is to deprive the Court of the power of doing that which is the end for which it exists—namely, to administer justice duly, impartially, and with reference solely to the facts judicially brought before it. Their tendency is to reduce the Court which has to try the case to impotence, so far as the effectual elimination of prejudice and prepossession is concerned." (*Per cur.* in *R.* v. *Davies,* [1906] 1 K. B. at p. 36.)

For words, which are a contempt of court, the law has provided three remedies :—

I. Such words are punishable as a misdemeanour on information or indictment.

II. The publication of such words may be restrained by injunction.

III. The Court, of which the words are a contempt, may also take the law into its own hands and punish the offender with fine or imprisonment.

I.—INFORMATION OR INDICTMENT.

We have already dealt with such contemptuous words as are defamatory of the Courts of Law, or of individual judges, or of the administration of justice as a whole ; such words are seditious and punishable as such (see *ante,* p. 528). But there are other words which, although they make no attack on the Courts or any judge thereof, are yet indictable because they tend to prejudice the fair trial of some action or criminal case.

It is a misdemeanour, punishable on information or indictment by fine or imprisonment, to speak or publish words which are calculated to prejudice the fair trial of any pending action or criminal proceeding ; or to perform any play, or to exhibit any picture or effigy which would have the same effect. " The essence of the offence is conduct calculated to produce, so to speak, an atmosphere of prejudice in the midst of which the proceedings must go on." (Per Lord Alverstone, C.J., in *R.* v. *Tibbits and Windust,* [1902] 1 K. B. at p. 88.)

" It is the pride of the constitution of this country that all causes should be decided by jurors, who are chosen in a manner which excludes all possibility of bias, and who are chosen by ballot, in order to prevent any possibility of their being tampered with. But, if an individual can break down any of those safeguards which the constitution has so wisely and so cautiously erected, by poisoning the minds of the jury at a time when they are called upon to decide, he will stab the administration of justice in its most vital parts. And, therefore, I cannot forbear saying, that, if the publication be brought home to the defendant, he has been guilty of a crime of the greatest enormity." (Per Lord Kenyon, C.J., in *R.* v. *Jolliffe,* 4 T. R. at p. 289 ; cited with approval by Lord Alverstone, C.J., in *R.* v. *Tibbits and Windust,* [1902] 1 K. B. at p. 86.)

Illustrations.

Where a prisoner, awaiting trial on an information, circulated in the assize town and sent to the solicitor for the prosecutor a written statement vindicating his conduct in the matter with which he was charged, the Court granted an information for a misdemeanour.

R. v. *Jolliffe,* (1791) 4 T. R. 285.

The defendants were the printers and publishers of a newspaper called the *Sussex Journal,* in which they published an account of the shooting of an excise officer named Bignold by a smuggler who had been committed to Lewes Gaol to take his trial on a charge of having murdered Bignold. The account consisted of a statement of the facts set out in the depositions taken before the committing magistrate, with expressions and representations prejudicial to the character of Bignold. On an information filed by the Attorney-General the defendants were found guilty of a misdemeanour.

R. v. *Lee,* (1804) 5 Esp. 123.

A charge was preferred before the Lord Mayor of London by Mrs. P. against the captain of a ship for indecent assault when she was on board his vessel, with the result that the captain was committed for trial. The defendant published a highly sensational account of the hearing of the charge, in which all the allegations of the prosecutrix were set out as facts, and the guilt of the captain assumed. It was further stated that the captain had " employed a barrister, a shorthand-writer and a phalanx of friends, if possible, to intimidate his accuser by the publicity of her exposure," and made comments unfavourable to the fair trial. The defendant was found guilty on an indictment for publishing a scandalous and malicious libel.

  R. v. *Fisher and others,* (1811) 2 Camp. 563.

A riot took place at Brighton, to suppress which the high constable thought it necessary to call out the military and to order them to charge. In the charge an assistant of the high constable was killed by one of the soldiers, who mistook him for a rioter. A coroner's jury brought in a verdict of murder against the high constable, one of his assistants, and the soldier. The defendant, before the coroner's jury had found their verdict, published in his newspaper a statement of the evidence that had been given, and made comments to the effect that the action of the high constable was imprudent and unnecessary. The Court granted an information on the ground that the words were calculated to prejudice a fair trial.

  R. v. *Fleet,* (1818) 1 B. & Ald. 379.

John Thurtell and others had been committed to the gaol at Hertford to take their trial for the murder of a gambler named Weare. A true bill had been found against Thomas Thurtell, his brother, for conspiracy to defraud an insurance company by setting on fire the cottage in which the brothers Thurtell lived. The defendant Williams was the proprietor of the Surrey Theatre, at which was performed, while the brothers Thurtell were awaiting trial, a play in which all the incidents of the alleged murder and burning of the cottage were dramatically represented. An information was granted against Williams for a misdemeanour by endeavouring to obstruct the course of public justice.

  R. v. *Williams and Romney,* (1823) 2 L. J. K. B. (Old S.) 30.

Tibbits was the editor of a London newspaper, which circulated in Bristol. Windust was a reporter on the staff of the newspaper, and described himself as " Crime Investigator." A. and C. were charged before the magistrates on various days from January 1st to February 8th, 1901, with felony and misdemeanour, and were committed to take their trial at the ensuing Bristol Assizes : they were tried and convicted, the trial lasting from March 1st to March 5th. Articles appeared in the newspaper at various dates from January 13th to March 3rd, purporting to be written by the " Special Crime Investigator," which contained statements making grave imputations against A. and C., evidence of which would have been inadmissible at the trial. At the next Bristol Assizes Tibbits and Windust were convicted on an indictment for a misdemeanour in attempting to obstruct and pervert the course of law and justice. The Court of Crown Cases Reserved held that it is unnecessary to prove that the defendants intended to pervert the course of justice, if the words used are in the opinion of the jury calculated to produce that result.

> *R.* v. *Tibbits and Windust,* [1902] 1 K. B. 77 ; 71 L. J. K. B. 4 ; 50 W. R. 125 ; 85 L. T. 521 ; 66 J. P. 5 ; 20 Cox, C. C. 70.

H. was arrested on a charge of abandoning her child at Swansea, where she was brought before the justices on September 5th, and remanded from time to time till October 11th, when she was committed for trial at the Swansea Assizes on a charge of attempting to murder the child, which charge had been preferred in the meantime. Davies was the editor, printer and publisher of a newspaper, which had a wide circulation in Glamorgan, and in which, before the charge of attempted murder was preferred, were published certain paragraphs headed "Traffic in Babies" and "Baby Farming Sensation," reflecting upon the character and antecedents of H. and asserting that she passed under a false name and had been previously convicted at Bristol. *Held,* that this was a contempt of Court, and a rule absolute for a writ of attachment issued.

> *R.* v. *Davies,* [1906] 1 K. B. 32 ; 75 L. J. K. B. 104 ; 54 W. R. 107 ; 93 L. T. 772 ; 22 Times L. R. 97.

II.—MOTION FOR AN INJUNCTION.

Recourse is had to an injunction in cases where the words either tend to prejudice the fair trial of some legal proceeding, or are published in defiance of some lawful order of a court. If the result of the publication is obviously to affect the administration of justice, it is immaterial whether the writer intended that result or no. (Per Lord Romilly, M.R., in *Daw* v. *Eley,* L. R. 7 Eq. 49 ; 38 L. J. Ch. 113.) Such an injunction must be applied for promptly ; and it will not be granted if the applicant has himself entered into a controversy on the matter in the public Press. The motion for an injunction may or may not be accompanied by a motion to commit the offender.

Illustrations.

While the evidence in a Chancery suit was being taken before the examiner, the plaintiff caused the following advertisement to be inserted in the *Times* :—" To the share and debenture holders of the West Hartlepool Harbour and Railway Company :—I have just published a reply to the proceedings of a meeting of proprietors, held at West Hartlepool on the 28th June last, which may be had of King, Parliament Street, and all booksellers. B. Coleman, —— Street, London." The pamphlet was full of abuse of the chairman of the defendant company, and also gave a digest of the plaintiff's evidence before the examiner, &c. Vice-Chancellor Wood granted an injunction "to restrain the plaintiff, his solicitors, servants, agents, and workmen from publishing so much of the pamphlet (stating the objectionable passages), and from publishing or offering for sale, during the progress of this suit, any book or pamphlet containing statements of the proceedings in this suit ; and also from making public any of such proceedings otherwise than in the due course of the prosecution of this suit until the hearing of this cause, or until the further order of this Court."

> *Coleman* v. *West Hartlepool Harbour and Rail. Co.,* (1860) 8 W. R. 734 ; 2 L. T. 766.

One of the defendants in an action, who was a Nonconformist minister, circulated a handbill through the town in the following words :—

> "Chancery Suit.
>
> "Congregational Church, Herne Bay.

"On Sunday morning, June 25th, the Rev. Thomas Blandford will preach a sermon with special reference to the trial in which the town is so deeply interested, and which is fixed for the 27th and following days.

> "Divine service to commence at 11 o'clock."

About forty inhabitants of Herne Bay were to be examined as witnesses at the trial. Bacon, V.-C., on Saturday, the 24th, granted an injunction to restrain Blandford from preaching any sermon or delivering any address with special or other reference to the trial, and from issuing these handbills, or being in any way instrumental in the publication or distribution of these or any other like handbills or notices, and from otherwise prejudicing or interfering with the trial of the action or the persons to be examined as witnesses therein.

> *Mackett* v. *Commissioners of Herne Bay,* (1876) 24 W. R. 845.

The defendant, on receiving a Statement of Claim charging him with fraud, wrote an angry letter to the plaintiff, a clergyman, threatening to have a few thousand copies printed, with the defendant's own remarks thereon, and copies of the defendant's letters, and distributed amongst all the clergy, "addressed from the Clergy List." Fry, J., granted an injunction to restrain the threatened publication, as being both a libel on the plaintiff as plaintiff, and also as tending to prejudice the fair trial of the action.

> *Kitcat* v. *Sharp,* (1882) 52 L. J. Ch. 134 ; 31 W. R. 227 ; 48 L. T. 64.
>
> *Chesshire* v. *Strauss,* (1896) 12 Times L. R. 291.

The plaintiffs and the defendant were ship brokers ; the plaintiffs delivered a Statement of Claim charging the defendant with unfair and improper conduct in his business, and before any Defence was delivered circulated copies among the business connections of both parties. Malins, V.-C., held that the plaintiffs had committed a contempt of Court, and must pay the costs of a motion to commit them ; he also granted an injunction to restrain the plaintiffs from publishing or circulating copies of the Statement of Claim in the action.

> *Bowden and another* v. *Russell,* (1877) 46 L. J. Ch. 414 ; 36 L. T. 177.

And see cases on pp. 548—554.

Closely akin to the power of restraining contempts of court, is the power which all Superior Courts undoubtedly possess of forbidding for a time reports of or comments on their own proceedings, whenever the presiding judge considers that such publication will prejudice future proceedings.

Illustrations.

On the trial of Thistlewood and others for treason, in 1820, Abbott, C.J., announced in open court that he prohibited the publication of any of the proceedings until the trial of all the prisoners should be concluded. In spite of this prohibition, the *Observer* published a report of the trial of the first two prisoners tried. The proprietor of the *Observer* was summoned for the contempt, and, failing to appear, was fined 500*l.*.

> *R.* v. *Clement,* (1821) 4 B. & Ald. 218 ; 11 Price, 68.
>
> *R.* v. *Gray,* [1900] 2 Q. B. 36 ; 69 L. J. Q. B. 502 ; 48 W. R. 474 ; 82 L. T. 534 ; 64 J. P. 484.

Where one of two prisoners charged with murder confessed before his trial, and by his confession seriously implicated the other, the Court of Session prohibited the *Edinburgh Evening Courant* from publishing the confession, lest it should prejudice the fair trial of the other prisoner.

> *Bell's Notes,* 165.
>
> See also *Emond's Case* (Dec. 7th, 1829), Shaw, 229.
>
> *Fleming and others* v. *Newton,* 1 H. L. C. 363 ; 6 Bell's App. 175.
>
> *Riddell* v. *Clydesdale Horse Society,* 12 Court of Session Cases (4th Series), 976.

Where several prisoners were to be tried at one session for similar acts of sedition, and on the trial of the first one the jury disagreed, and the *Dublin Evening Post* severely attacked the jury for not convicting him, the Dublin Assize Court made an order prohibiting all comments in any newspaper upon the proceedings of the session till all the prisoners had been tried, considering that such comments were calculated to excite feelings of hostility towards the prisoners about to be tried.

> *R.* v. *O'Dogherty,* 5 Cox, C. C. 348.

The House of Lords, when sitting as a Court of Law, claimed for many years the right to appoint one printer to publish their proceedings, and to order that no other person should presume to publish the same, even after the case was at an end. So, in the case of an impeachment, Lord Erskine, L.C., held, after great hesitation, that such an order must be enforced by injunction. [Such a decision would not be upheld in the present day.]

> *Gurney* v. *Longman,* (1807) 13 Ves. 493.
>
> And see *Millar* v. *Taylor,* (1769) 4 Burr. 2303—2417.
>
> *Manby* v. *Owen,* (1755) cited in 4 Burr. 2329, 2404.
>
> *Roper* v. *Streater,* Skin. 234 ; 1 Mod. 217.
>
> *The Stationers* v. *Patentees of Rolle's Abridgment,* Carter, 89.
>
> *Butterworth* v. *Robinson,* (1801) 5 Ves. 709.

III.—Motion to Commit.

(1) *Superior Courts.*

We have already dealt with those kinds of contemptuous words, which can be made the subject of an indictment or information, or an application for an injunction. In all such cases a Superior Court has in addition power to interfere summarily and to fine the offender or commit him to prison. This power also exists in some cases in which an indictment would not lie. (Per Lord Holt, C.J., in *R.* v. *Rogers*, 7 Mod. 29.) It may be exercised either on the application of any person aggrieved, or by the Court of its own motion. It is necessary that the Court should have power thus promptly to protect itself, and the litigants before it.

"The power summarily to commit for contempt of court is considered necessary for the proper administration of justice. It is not to be used for the vindication of the judge as a person. He must resort to action for libel or criminal information. Committal for contempt of court is a weapon to be used sparingly, and always with reference to the interests of the administration of justice. . . . It is a summary process, and should be used only from a sense of duty and under the pressure of public necessity, for there can be no landmarks pointing out the boundaries in all cases." (*Per cur.* in *McLeod* v. *St. Aubyn*, [1899] A. C. at p. 561.)

"This is not a new-fangled jurisdiction; it is a jurisdiction as old as the common law itself, of which it forms part. It is a jurisdiction, the history, purpose, and extent of which are admirably treated in the opinion of Wilmot, C.J., then Wilmot, J., in his Opinions and Judgments. (*R.* v. *Almon*, (1765) Wilmot's Opinions, 243.) It is a jurisdiction, however, to be exercised with scrupulous care, to be exercised only when the case is clear and beyond reasonable doubt; because, if it is not a case beyond reasonable doubt, the Courts will and ought to leave the Attorney-General to proceed by criminal information." (Per Lord Russell, C.J., in *R.* v. *Gray*, [1900] 2 Q. B. at pp. 40, 41.)

"The reason why the publication of articles like those with which we have to deal is treated as a contempt of court is because their tendency and sometimes their object is to deprive the Court of the power of doing that which is the end for which it exists—namely, to administer justice duly, impartially, and with reference solely to the facts judicially brought before it. Their tendency is to reduce the Court which has to try the case to impotence, so far as the effectual elimination of prejudice and prepossession is concerned. It is difficult to conceive an apter description of such conduct than is conveyed by the expression 'contempt of court.' " (*Per cur.* in *R.* v. *Parke*, [1903] 2 K. B. at p. 436.)

" Every libel on a person about to be tried is not necessarily a contempt of court; but the applicant must show that something has been published which either is clearly intended, or at least is calculated, to prejudice a trial which is pending." (Per Lord Russell, C.J., in *R.* v. *Payne*, [1896] 1 Q. B. at p. 580.)

An application to commit for contempt must be made promptly. The applicant should not, before coming to the court, invite or take part in a discussion of the matter in the public Press. Motions for committal, which are made out of anger or ill-feeling, or with a view to obtaining costs, where there is no real ground for committing any one to prison, will be severely discouraged, although the conduct complained of may be technically a contempt. (*Plating Co.* v. *Farquharson*, 17 Ch. D. 49 ; 50 L. J. Ch. 406 ; 29 W. R. 510 ; 44 L. T. 389 ; *Hunt* v. *Clarke*, 58 L. J. Q. B. 490 ; 37 W. R. 724 ; 61 L. T. 343 ; *In re Martindale*, [1894] 3 Ch. at p. 202 ; 64 L. J. Ch. 9 ; 43 W. R. 53 ; 71 L. T. 468 ; 8 R. 729 ; *R.* v. *Parke*, [1903] 2 K. B. 432 ; 72 L. J. K. B. 839 ; 89 L. T. 439 ; 19 Times L. R. 627.) No attempt must be made to compromise such an application. (*R.* v. *Newton*, (1903) 67 J. P. 453 ; 19 Times L. R. 627.)

Acts without words may amount to a contempt of court; *e.g.*, where the defendant assaults an officer of the Court when serving its process or carrying out its orders ; or destroys the records of the Court; or destroys documentary evidence which should be brought before it. Again, wilful disobedience to any lawful order of a Court or a judge is a contempt. But all these cases, in which the acts and not the words of the accused are impugned, are beyond the scope of this book.

Illustrations.

SPOKEN WORDS.

Using abusive and violent language towards any officer serving the process of any Court, is a contempt, punishable by committal.

> *Price* v. *Hutchison,* (1869) L. R. 9 Eq. 534 ; 18 W. R. 204.
>
> *R.* v. *Jones,* (1719) 1 Stra. 185.

So if a party on being served with a lawful order of any Court expresses in defiant and contemptuous language his intention to disregard or disobey such order.

> *Anon.,* (1711) 1 Salk. 84.
>
> *Mr. Long Wellesley's Case,* (1831) 2 Russ. & Mylne, 639.

It is a contempt of court for one committed for trial, or for any of his partisans, to address public meetings, alleging that there is a conspiracy against him, and that he will not have a fair trial.

> *Castro, Onslow and Whalley's Case,* (1873) L. R. 9 Q. B. 219 ; 12 Cox, C. C. 358.
>
> *Skipworth's Case,* (1873) L. R. 9 Q. B. 230 ; 12 Cox, C. C. 371.

Threats and insults addressed either to a party or a witness pending a suit, whether by word or letter, are a contempt of court.

> *Smith* v. *Lakeman,* (1856) 26 L. J. Ch. 305 ; 2 Jur. N. S. 1202 ; 28 L. T. (Old S.) 98.
>
> *Shaw* v. *Shaw,* (1861) 31 L. J. Pr. & Matr. 35 ; 6 L. T. 477 ; 2 Sw. & Tr. 515.
>
> *In re Mulock,* (1864) 33 L. J. Pr. & Matr. 205 ; 10 Jur. N. S. 1188 ; 13 W. R. 278.

So are insulting words addressed to counsel engaged in the cause, or to the opponent's solicitor while actually engaged in any duty devolving on him as solicitor in the proceedings.

> *Lessee Sturgeon* v. *Douglass,* 10 Ir. L. R. 128, n.
>
> *In re Johnson,* (1887) 20 Q. B. D. 68 ; 57 L. J. Q. B. 1 ; 36 W. R. 51 ; 58 L. T. 160.
>
> *In re Clements,* (1877) 46 L. J. Ch. 375 ; 36 L. T. 332.

À fortiori, if addressed to the judge or a master.

> *Lechmere Charlton's Case,* (1836) 2 Myl. & Cr. 316.

Even the prisoner in the dock, who is always allowed great latitude, if he be defending himself, may be fined for contempt of court, if he persist in using blasphemous language and in applying offensive epithets to the presiding judge in the course of his speech to the jury.

> *R.* v. *Davison,* (1821) 4 B. & Ald. 329.

It is a contempt of court for the brother of a prisoner just convicted to visit the foreman of the jury at his residence, accuse him of having bullied the jury into finding his brother guilty, and challenge him to mortal combat.

> *R.* v. *James Martin,* 5 Cox, C. C. 356.

So, too, a barrister may be guilty of contempt of court if he unnecessarily insults one of the jury in the course of his address to them.

> *In re Pater,* (1864) 5 B. & S. 299 ; 33 L. J. M. C. 142 ; 10 Jur. N. S. 972 ; 12 W. R. 823 ; 10 L. T. 376.

The most innocent words, if uttered in a peculiar manner and tone, may be a contempt of court. For an insult may be conveyed either by language or by manner.

> *Carus Wilson's Case,* (1845) 7 Q. B. 984, 1015.

If a high sheriff proceeds to address the grand jury in open Court at the close of the judge's charge, and persists in so doing, though ordered by the judge to sit down and be quiet, he may be fined 500*l.* for contempt.

> *In re The Sheriff of Surrey,* (1860) 2 F. & F. 234, 237.

WRITTEN OR PRINTED WORDS.

It is a contempt of court and a libel, punishable by attachment, to publish a pamphlet asserting that judges have no power to issue an attachment for libels upon themselves, and denying that reflections upon individual judges are contempts of court at all. [Note that at the date when this pamphlet appeared the action which gave occasion for it was still pending.]

> *R. v. Almon,* (1765) Wilmot's Notes of Opinions and Judgments, p. 253.

Any attempt to bribe a judge, or to influence his probable decision on a matter before him by any private communication, is a contempt of court.

> *Martin's Case,* (1747) 2 Russ. & Mylne, 674, n.
>
> *Macgill's Case,* 2 Fowl. Ex. Pr. 404.

But not every silly or impudent letter addressed to a judge about a matter which he has already decided will be treated as a contempt ;

> *R. v. Faulkner,* (1835) 2 Mont. & Ayr. 321, 322 ; 2 C. M. & R. 525 ; 1 Gale, 210.

Nor every inaccurate report of judicial proceedings which either party may think fit to publish.

> *Matthews* v. *Smith,* 3 Hare, 331.
>
> *Brook* v. *Evans,* (1860) 29 L. J. Ch. 616 ; 6 Jur. N. S. 1025 ; 8 W. R. 688.
>
> *Buenos Ayres Gas Co.* v. *Wilde,* (1880) 29 W. R. 43 ; 42 L. T. 657.

It is a contempt of court to seek " by flattering the judge to taint the source of justice."

> *Ex parte Jones,* (1806) 13 Ves. 237.

To preach a sermon with special reference to a pending trial is a contempt of court.

> *Mackett* v. *Herne Bay Commissioners,* (1876) 24 W. R. 845 ; *ante,* p. 540.

As to exhibiting models of the person murdered and the alleged murderer in the assize town during the assizes, see

> *R.* v. *Gilham,* 1 Moo. & Mal. 165.

It is a contempt for a party to a suit to publish before the case has come on for hearing a copy of his brief, or even an abstract of his petition or Statement of Claim, or of the affidavits filed on either side, or any other *ex parte* statement tending to prepossess the minds of the public in his favour, or to calumniate his adversary.

> *Captain Perry's Case,* cited (1742) 2 Atk. 469, 472 ; 2 Dick. 794.

> *Mrs. Farley's Case, Cann v. Cann,* (1754) 2 Ves. senr. 520 ; 3
> Hare, 333, n.
> *Coleman v. West Hartlepool Harbour and Railway Co.,* (1860)
> 8 W. R. 734 ; 2 L. T. 766, *ante,* p. 540.
> *Chesshire v. Strauss,* (1896) 12 Times L. R. 291.

The plaintiffs in an action delivered a Statement of Claim, charging the
defendant with unfair and over-reaching conduct in his business. They
subsequently, before the hearing of the action, circulated copies of this
pleading amongst some of their and his business correspondents. It was
held that the plaintiffs had committed a contempt of court ; they were
ordered to pay the costs of the motion to commit ; and an injunction was
granted to restrain all further circulation of the Statement of Claim.

> *Bowden v. Russell,* (1877) 46 L. J. Ch. 414 ; 36 L. T. 177.

A local board of health sued the defendant for breach of their bye-laws.
Pending the action, an election for members of the board came on. The
defendant stood as a candidate, and in that capacity issued an address to
all the ratepayers, attacking the former board, and referring to their
"spiteful proceedings" against himself. The circular also contained a
false statement as to what the judge had said on an interlocutory application. The excitement of the election was urged as an excuse ; but the
defendant was committed to prison for ten days, and ordered to pay the
costs of the motion.

> *Ilkley Local Board v. Lister,* (1895) 11 Times L. R. 176.

But where, pending a shareholders' petition, a committee of shareholders
issued to their brother shareholders, for the purpose of bringing to their
attention the facts on which they relied, a printed letter containing their
accusations against the directors, and some extracts from the evidence,
it was held that this did not amount to contempt of court.

> *In re The London Flour Co.,* (1868) 16 W. R. 474 ; 17 L. T.
> 636.
> But see *In re Sir John Moore Gold Mining Co.,* (1877) 37 L. T.
> 242.

Merely to announce, "I have brought an action against A. for damages
for," &c., is not a contempt of court, if such be the fact. Per Pollock,
B., and Day, J., in

> *Collins v. Primrose Club,* July 30th, 1894 (not reported).

Pending an action for infringing a trade mark the plaintiffs are at
liberty to warn the trade by circular that they regard such an article as
an infringement. But to discuss the merits of the case in any manner
calculated to prejudice the fair trial of the action is a contempt.

> *Coats v. Chadwick,* [1894] 1 Ch. 347 ; 63 L. J. Ch. 328 ; 42
> W. R. 328 ; 70 L. T. 228 ; 8 R. 159, *ante,* p. 436.
> *R. v. Payne,* [1896] 1 Q. B. 577 ; 65 L. J. Q. B. 426 ; 44
> W. R. 605 ; 74 L. T. 351.

Statements are not the less a contempt because they are libellous, or
because the party making them is prepared to justify the libel.

> *In re New Gold Coast Exploration Co.,* [1901] 1 Ch. 860 ; 70
> L. J. Ch. 355 ; 8 Manson, 296.

While an action for infringement of a patent was pending, the plaintiff made an unsuccessful motion for an injunction. The defendants sent an unfair and inaccurate report of this proceeding to certain newspapers for publication, and also published this report in the form of a circular, with the statement of their own counsel printed in heavily-leaded type. Chitty, J., held this a contempt of court. The defendants gave an undertaking to abstain from all such publication in future, and were ordered to pay the costs of the motion in any event.

> *Edlin* v. *Pneumatic Tyre Agency* (2), 10 Reports of Patent
> Cases, 317.

An injunction having been granted to restrain the defendants from infringing a patent for nickel-plating, they gave notice of appeal, and published in a newspaper an advertisement inviting the trade to subscribe towards the expenses of the appeal, and also an advertisement offering a reward of 100*l*. to anyone who could produce documentary evidence that nickel-plating was done before 1869. It was held that neither advertisement was a contempt of court.

> *Plating Co.* v. *Farquharson,* (1881) 17 Ch. D. 49; 50 L. J.
> Ch. 406; 29 W. R. 510; 44 L. T. 389; 45 J. P. 568;
> overruling *Pool* v. *Sacheverel,* (1720) 1 P. Wms. 675.

But where a co-respondent in a suit for divorce, immediately after the service of the citation, caused advertisements to be published denying the charges made in the petition, and offering a reward for information which would lead to the discovery and conviction of the authors of them, it was held that these advertisements constituted a contempt of court.

> *Brodribb* v. *Brodribb and Wall,* (1886) 11 P. D. 66; 55 L. J.
> P. 47; 34 W. R. 580; 56 L. T. 672; 50 J. P. 407.

So an advertisement offering a reward for certain specific evidence in a divorce suit, published *malâ fide* and not solely in order to obtain evidence, is a contempt of court.

> *Butler* v. *Butler,* (1888) 13 P. D. 73; 57 L. J. P. 42; 58
> L. T. 563.

It is a contempt of court for the solicitor to a plaintiff to write letters to probable witnesses with the object of prejudicing them against the defendant, and of preventing their giving evidence for the defendant.

> *Welby* v. *Still,* (1892) 66 L. T. 523.

So it is a contempt of court for the solicitor to a defendant to publish in a newspaper anonymous letters full of arguments in the defendant's favour, and denying the facts on which the plaintiff would rely at the trial.

> *Daw* v. *Eley,* (1868) L. R. 7 Eq. 49; 38 L. J. Ch. 113; 17
> W. R. 245.

The committee of a lunatic published a pamphlet, written by his wife, reflecting upon persons who were managing the lunatic's estate under the orders of the Court of Chancery, with an address, by way of dedication, to the Lord Chancellor, " flattering the judge to taint the source of justice." Lord Erskine, L.C., committed him to prison for contempt, and the printer as well.

> *Ex parte Jones,* (1806) 13 Ves. 237.

A libel on the business carried on by a receiver and manager appointed by the Court is a contempt of court, and may be punished by committal of the offender.

> *Helmore* v. *Smith* (2), (1886) 35 Ch. D. 449 ; 56 L. J. Ch. 145 ; 35 W. R. 157 ; 56 L. T. 72.

If a person innocently lends to another a newspaper containing a libel which is a contempt of court, in ignorance that any such libel is contained in the newspaper, he cannot be held guilty of a contempt of court.

> *McLeod* v. *St. Aubyn,* [1899] A. C. 549 ; 68 L. J. P. C. 137 ; 48 W. R. 173 ; 81 L. T. 158 ; 15 Times L. R. 487.

Contempt of Court by Newspapers.

The publication in any newspaper of words calculated to prejudice the fair trial of an action is especially objectionable, as the mischief done is so widespread. No doubt all judicial proceedings, the official acts of every judge and jury, of all litigants and witnesses, are matters of lawful comment as soon as the proceedings are terminated. But no observations on the case are permitted during its progress. Any comment pending action is a contempt of court, by whomsoever made; it is especially so where the publisher knows that the comment is supplied by one of the litigants or his solicitor. So, too, an unfair and inaccurate report of any interlocutory proceeding in the action, published in a newspaper, may amount to a contempt of court, if it tends to prejudice the fair trial of the action. The editor cannot escape liability by alleging that he did not know that the contemptuous words had been inserted in his newspaper. (*Chesshire* v. *Strauss,* (1896) 12 Times L. R. 291 ; *R.* v. *Parke,* [1903] 2 K. B. 432 ; 72 L. J. K. B. 839 ; 89 L. T. 439.) Nor can the printer. (*Ex parte Jones,* (1806) 13 Ves. 237; *R.* v. *Davies,* [1906] 1 K. B. 32 ; 75 L. J. K. B. 104 ; 93 L. T. 772.)

Illustrations.

Any article in a newspaper commenting on a case still before the Court is a contempt, if it in any way tends to pervert the course of justice, though written temperately and respectfully, and in all other respects such an article as might properly and legitimately be written and published after the trial is ended.

> *Roach* v. *Garvan, Re Read and Huggonson,* (1742) 2 Atk. 469 ; 2 Dick. 794.

Littler v. *Thomson*, (1839) 2 Beav. 129.

Tichborne v. *Mostyn*, (1867) per Wood, V.-C., L. R. 7 Eq. 57, n. ; 15 W. R. 1074 ; 17 L. T. 7.

Tichborne v. *Tichborne*, (1870) 39 L. J. Ch. 398 ; 18 W. R. 621 ; 22 L. T. 55.

Vernon v. *Vernon*, (1870) 40 L. J. Ch. 118 ; 19 W. R. 404 ; 23 L. T. 697.

Buenos Ayres Gas Co. v. *Wilde*, (1880) 29 W. R. 43 ; 42 L. T. 657.

The publication in a newspaper of a correct report of proceedings before a police magistrate which terminated in the committal of the prisoners is not a contempt of court, though it may tend to prejudice the mind of the public against the prisoners. But the publication in a newspaper of comments on such proceedings, and on the conduct of the prisoners, is a contempt of court if it tends in any way to 'prejudice the public mind' against them before the trial.

R. v. *Gray*, (1865) 10 Cox, C. C. 184.

R. v. *O'Dogherty*, (1848) 5 Cox, C. C. 348.

The publication of articles with sensational headings and making statements prejudicial to a person against whom proceedings are pending before the magistrates is a contempt.

R. v. *Davies*, [1906] 1 K. B. 32 ; 75 L. J. K. B. 104 ; 54 W. R. 107 ; 93 L. T. 772 ; 22 Times L. R. 97 ; *ante*, p. 539.

The editor of a newspaper was fined 100*l.* and costs for publishing an article commenting on a criminal case then pending in the High Court, and intimating that the prisoner would certainly be convicted.

R. v. *Balfour, In re Stead*, (1895) 11 Times L. R. 492.

There may, however, be comments on pending proceedings which do not tend to prejudice either party, or to interfere with the fair trial of the cause. Such comments are not a contempt of court.

In re Martindale, [1894] 3 Ch. at p. 202 ; 64 L. J. Ch. 9 ; 43 W. R. 53 ; 71 L. T. 468 ; 8 R. 729.

In re Gates and others, (1895) 11 Times L. R. 204.

And though observations be published in a newspaper which are technically a contempt, yet where the offence is of a slight and trifling nature and not likely to cause any substantial prejudice to the party in the conduct of the action, or to the due administration of justice, no application to commit ought to be made.

Hunt v. *Clarke, In re O'Malley*, (1889) 58 L. J. Q. B. 490 ; 37 W. R. 724 ; 61 L. T. 343.

Dallas v. *Ledger*, (1888) 52 J. P. 328 ; 4 Times L. R. 432.

Metropolitan Music Hall Co., Ltd. v. *Lake*, (1889) 58 L. J. Ch. 513 ; 60 L. T. 749.

"Every case must depend on its own circumstances." Per Lord Alverstone, C.J., in

In re Labouchere, (1901) 18 Times L. R. at p. 209.

But if any such comment tends to excite prejudice against either party to the proceedings in the mind of the judge, or of possible witnesses or jurymen, or of the public generally, or if in any other way it tends to interfere substantially with the fair trial of the action, it is a contempt of court.

> *Russell* v. *Russell*, (1894) 11 Times L. R. 38.
> *In re The Pall Mall Gazette, ib.* 122.
> *In re Yorkshire Provident Assurance Co., &c., ib.* 143, 167.
> *In re Robinson,* (1895) *ib.* 345.
> *In re Johnson and Mitchell, ib.* 376.
> *Fielden* v. *Sweeting, ib.* 534.

Especially if, in addition to such comments, the article contain a misstatement of a material fact.

> *Ilkley Local Board* v. *Lister,* (1895) 11 Times L. R. 176.
> *Spurrell* v. *De Rechberg, ib.* 313.

The publisher of a newspaper was committed for printing an article which attacked the persons who had made affidavits in a suit in Chancery not yet concluded, imputing to them ignorance of facts and interested motives.

> *Felkin* v. *Herbert,* (1864) 33 L. J. Ch. 294 ; 12 W. R. 241, 332 ; 9 L. T. 635 ; 10 Jur. N. S. 62.
> See also *Littler* v. *Thomson,* (1839) 2 Beav. 129.
> *In re William Watson,* Shaw's Cases (Scotch), No. 6.

A petition for winding up a company, containing charges of fraud against the directors, was published *in extenso* in a newspaper before the hearing of the petition. This was held a contempt of court, and the publishers of the paper were ordered to pay the costs of a motion to commit them.

> *In re The Cheltenham and Swansea Wagon Co.,* (1869) L. R. 8 Eq. 580 ; 38 L. J. Ch. 330 ; 17 W. R. 463 ; 20 L. T. 169.
> *Tichborne* v. *Mostyn,* (1867) L. R. 7 Eq. 55, n. ; 15 W. R. 1072 ; 17 L. T. 5.
> *Kitcat* v. *Sharp,* (1882) 52 L. J. Ch. 134 ; 31 W. R. 227 ; 48 L. T. 64.
> *Bowden* v. *Russell,* (1877) 46 L. J. Ch. 414 ; 36 L. T. 177.

It is a contempt of court for a newspaper to publish the Statement of Claim in a pending action.

> *Chesshire* v. *Strauss,* (1896) 12 Times L. R. 291.

W. brought an action against a company. At a subsequent meeting of the shareholders, one of the directors (M.) referred to the action in his speech, and this led the shareholders to ask questions about the action, which M. answered. A full report of the proceedings at this meeting, including M.'s remarks, subsequently appeared in a newspaper of which M. was the proprietor. *Held,* that though M.'s remarks were privileged when uttered at the meeting, their republication in the newspaper was not privileged, and was a contempt of court.

> *Watt* v. *Maxim-Weston Electric Co.,* (1888) 5 Times L. R. 170.

A shareholder presented a petition to wind up a banking company, and proposed to cross-examine the directors in the liquidation. A newspaper thereupon published an article referring to the approaching cross-examination of these directors, and saying, "If they are compelled to make a full statement of the affairs of the bank, we shall have some interesting revelations." The Court found that the article had been instigated by the petitioning shareholder ; and the publisher of the newspaper was ordered to pay a fine of 50*l.* and costs.

In re Crown Bank, In re O'Malley, (1890) 44 Ch. D. 649 ; 59 L. J. Ch. 767 ; 39 W. R. 45 ; 63 L. T. 304.

Not every letter that is published in a newspaper and is a libel on a judge, is a contempt of court. It must be one calculated to obstruct or interfere with the course of justice or the due administration of the law.

In re Moseley, [1893] A. C. 138 ; 62 L. J. P. C. 79 ; 68 L. T. 105.

À fortiori, an inaccurate report of an interlocutory proceeding published in a newspaper is not a contempt of court unless it tends to prejudice the approaching trial.

Duncan v. Sparling, (1894) 10 Times L. R. 353.

But section 3 of the Law of Libel Amendment Act, 1888, affords no protection to any report which is a contempt of court.

In re The Pall Mall Gazette, (1894) 11 Times L. R. 122.

Where an action has been brought against a newspaper for libel, merely repeating the charge made in the libel and asserting that the defendant will be ready to prove it true before the jury, is not necessarily a contempt of court.

Robertson v. Labouchere, 42 J. P. 710.

So where the defendants, who were being sued in respect of some libellous paragraphs which had appeared in their newspaper, republished substantially the same charges in their newspaper after action brought, an application by the plaintiff to commit the defendants for contempt of court was refused.

Cronmire v. The " Daily Bourse," Limited, (1892) 9 Times L. R. 101.

But where the editor of a newspaper who was being sued for libel, after issue joined, published an article attacking the witnesses whom he knew the plaintiff intended to call at the trial, he was ordered to pay the costs of the motion as between solicitor and client, and to give an undertaking to abstain from all such comments till after the trial.

Birmingham Vinegar Brewery Co. v. Henry, (1894) 10 Times L. R. 586.

A person whose name appeared on a newspaper as a printer and publisher of it was held liable for an article contained in it which was a contempt of court, although he was only a salaried foreman printer, whose duties did not require that he should read the matter printed, and who had no knowledge of the contents of the article complained of.

The American Exchange Co., Ltd. v. Gillig, (1889) 58 L. J. Ch. 706 ; 61 L. T. 502.

The Press Association, which is a limited company, disseminated among many newspapers, paragraphs amounting to contempt of court. The Court held the manager of the Association responsible, and ordered him personally to pay the costs of the motion as between solicitor and client.

Ex parte Green and others, (1891) 7 Times L. R. 411.

The appellant was the manager of the London Office of the *Freeman's*

Journal, and as such had published in this country copies of that journal containing an article written and printed in Ireland, which was a contempt of court. The appellant was held personally responsible, and an order was made that a writ of attachment should issue against him unless he should within a fortnight pay a fine of 100*l.* He was also ordered to pay all costs as between solicitor and client.

> *O'Shea* v. *O'Shea and Parnell,* (1890) 15 P. D. 59 ; 59 L. J. P.
> 47 ; 38 W. R. 374 ; 62 L. T. 713 ; 17 Cox, C. C. 107.

As a rule no report of or comment on a legal proceeding can be a contempt of court if that legal proceeding is at an end before the words are published. "When a trial has taken place and the case is over, the judge or the jury are given over to criticism." (*Per cur.* in *McLeod* v. *St. Aubyn,* [1899] A. C. at p. 561.) "It is possible very effectually to poison the fountain of justice before it begins to flow. It is not possible to do so when the stream has ceased." (*Per cur.* in *R.* v. *Parke,* [1903] 2 K. B. at p. 438.)

If the writer, however, is not aware that an action is pending, or honestly believes the proceedings are at an end when they are not, his comments, though still strictly a contempt, may be excused; provided they are such as would have been legitimate had the case been at an end. But if the writer knew the proceedings were still pending, then the fact that he did not desire or intend to prejudice the case is immaterial (except as to the extent of his punishment), if the Court be satisfied that such was the obvious and necessary result of his words. (*Daw* v. *Eley,* L. R. 7 Eq. at p. 59 ; *In re Martindale,* [1894] 3 Ch. at p. 200 ; *In re Marquis of Townshend,* (1906) 22 Times L. R. 341.)

Illustrations.

In an action of libel, the plaintiff obtained an *interim* injunction at chambers. The defendant appealed to a Divisional Court, and the injunction was dissolved. The editor of a newspaper read a report of this application, took it to be the trial of the action, and honestly believing that the action was at an end, he proceeded to comment on the conduct of the parties and the decision of the Court, in a manner calculated to prejudice the approaching trial. On a motion to commit the editor, the Court, being satisfied of his *bona fides,* made no order except that each party should pay his own costs of the motion. (Mathew and Henn Collins, JJ.)

> *In re Food and Sanitation Journal,* (Feb. 1st, 1894) (not reported).

But see *In re Robinson,* (1895) 11 Times L. R. 345.

So, where the defendant did not know any action had been commenced and the words complained of were but a continuation of previous attacks.

> *In re Labouchere,* (1901) 18 Times L. R. 208.
> *Phillips* v. *Hess,* (1902) 18 Times L. R. 400.

If a person innocently lends to another a newspaper containing words which are a contempt of court, not knowing that the newspaper contains such words, he is not guilty of a contempt.

> *McLeod* v. *St. Aubyn,* [1899] A. C. 549 ; 68 L. J. P. C. 137 ;
> 48 W. R. 173 ; 81 L. T. 158 ; 15 Times L. R. 487.

The liquidator of a company issued a circular to the shareholders with reference to the affairs of the company, stating *inter alia* that he had obtained leave to bring an action against L., the promoter of the company. The respondent published this circular in his newspaper, not knowing that any action had been actually commenced. A motion to commit the respondent for contempt was refused with costs.

> *Metropolitan Music Hall Co., Ltd.* v. *Lake,* (1889) 58 L. J.
> Ch. 513 ; 60 L. T. 749 ; 5 Times L. R. 329.

In an action for libel against the proprietor of the *Era,* the jury found a verdict for 40*s.* damages, and judgment was entered for the plaintiff for that amount. The defendant gave notice of motion for a new trial ; and then published in his paper an article commenting on the verdict in a manner which would admittedly have been legitimate if the action had been at an end. *Held,* that the mere fact that a notice of a motion for a new trial had been given did not make the article a contempt of court.

> *Dallas* v. *Ledger,* (1888) 52 J. P. 328 ; 4 Times L. R. 432.

But where on the trial of a criminal charge the jury disagree, it is a contempt to publish words calculated to prejudice the future trial, unless it has been formally stated that a fresh jury will not be empannelled.

> *R.* v. *Freeman's Journal,* [1902] 2 Ir. R. 82.

On March 9th, 1895, the plaintiffs sent out amongst the defendants' customers circulars commenting on the pending action. On March 22nd, 1895, the action was settled on terms arranged between the parties. On May 10th, 1895, the defendants moved to commit the plaintiffs for the contempt which they had committed while the action was still pending. Chitty, J., dismissed the motion with costs, as there was no longer anything to be tried.

> *Kelly & Co.* v. *Pole and others,* (1895) 11 Times L. R. 405.

But the rule that, on a motion to commit, the applicant must show that a proceeding is still pending, does not apply in three cases :—

(i) Where the words amount to a scandalising of the Court itself;

(ii) Where the words are a report of, or comment on, proceedings purposely taken by a judge *in camera.*

(iii) Where the words are a report of proceedings, of which the Court has forbidden that any report should be published.

Illustrations.

Mr. Justice North heard an application relating to a ward of Court in his private room. A report of what transpired there was published in several newspapers. *Held,* that such publication was a contempt of court.

> *In re Martindale,* [1894] 3 Ch. 193; 64 L. J. Ch. 9; 43 W. R. 53; 71 L. T. 468; 8 R. 729.

It would have been otherwise if merely the result of the proceedings—the decision of the judge—had been reported.

> *Lawrence v. Ambery,* 91 L. T. Journal, 230.

It is a contempt of court to publish prematurely, and without the consent of a liquidator, a report of the examination of a witness taken privately under section 115 of the Companies Act, 1862.

> *The American Exchange Co., Ltd. v. Gillig,* (1889) 58 L. J. Ch. 706; 61 L. T. 502.

As to comments on proceedings taken in chambers in the King's Bench Division, see

> *Peters v. Bradlaugh,* (1888) 4 Times L. R. 414.

A Court of general gaol delivery has undoubtedly the power to make an order prohibiting the publication of its proceedings pending a trial which is likely to last for several successive days, and to punish those who disobey such order by fine. Abbott, C.J., made such an order on the trial of Thistlewood and others for treason in 1820. He announced in open Court that he prohibited the publication of any of the proceedings until the trial of all the prisoners should be concluded. In spite of this prohibition, the *Observer* published a report of the trial of the first two prisoners tried. The proprietor of the *Observer* was summoned for the contempt, and, failing to appear, was fined 500*l.* in his absence.

> *R. v. Clement,* (1821) 4 B. & Ald. 218; 11 Price, 68.

At the Birmingham Assizes one W. was about to be tried for publishing an obscene libel. Darling, J., before the trial commenced, stated that it was inexpedient that a full or detailed account of the proceedings should be published, and that if his advice were disregarded he should make it his business to see that the law in that respect was enforced. After the trial was concluded, the *Birmingham Daily Argus* published a violent attack on the learned judge, abusing him for having supposed that it was necessary to warn the Birmingham Press not to publish obscene matter, and containing also scurrilous remarks about the judge personally. The Court held this a contempt and fined the writer of the article, who had apologized and admitted his offence, 100*l.* and 25*l.* for costs.

> *R. v. Gray,* [1900] 2 Q. B. 36; 69 L. J. Q. B. 502; 48 W. R. 474; 82 L. T. 534; 64 J. P. 484.

When the words which are alleged to be a contempt of court relate to a pending legal proceeding, it was formerly held that the motion to commit must be made to the Court in which the proceeding is pending. "The Court can only punish for contempt of itself." (Per Hawkins, J., in *Ex parte Burns,* (1886) 2 Times L. R. at p. 352.) But now it has been decided that the King's Bench Division has power to punish by attachment contempts of inferior Courts which have no power to deal with contempt of themselves. (*R.* v. *Davies,* [1906] 1 K. B. 32.)

Illustrations.

Where proceedings are pending before a police magistrate, the High Court will commit for a contempt of the police court.

> *R.* v. *Davies,* [1906] 1 K. B. 32 ; 75 L. J. K. B. 104 ; 54 W. R. 107 ; 93 L. T. 772 ; 22 Times L. R. 97 ; overruling *Ex parte Burns,* (1886) 2 Times L. R. 351.

Proceedings are pending as soon as a warrant has been issued by the court for the arrest of the offender.

> *R.* v. *Clarke, Ex parte Crippen,* (1910) 103 L. T. 636 ; 27 Times L. R. 32.

If a prisoner is charged before a Court of Petty Sessions with a crime which can only be tried at the Assizes, the High Court has power to commit for a contempt consisting of words tending to prejudice the fair trial of the prisoner at the Assizes.

> *R.* v. *Parke,* [1903] 2 K. B. 432 ; 72 L. J. K. B. 839 ; 52 W. R. 215 ; 89 L. T. 439 ; 67 J. P. 421.

The King's Bench Division of the High Court will not commit for a contempt of the Probate Division.

> *Cook* v. *Cook,* (1885) 2 Times L. R. 10.

Nor has it jurisdiction to commit for contempt of a Master in Lunacy.

> *In re B——,* [1892] 1 Ch. at p. 462 ; 61 L. J. Ch. 446 ; 40 W. R. 369 ; 66 L. T. 38.

If the contempt is committed in open court and in presence of the judge, he may commit the offender *instanter,* and without any prior notice. (*Watt* v. *Ligertwood,* L. R. 2 H. L. Sc. 361.) A written warrant is not essential to such a committal, though it is usual. (Per Wightman, J., in *Carus Wilson's Case,* 7 Q. B. 1017.) But when the offender is not present, and the contempt is committed by words spoken or published out of court, the Court still has power, on clear and satisfactory evidence, to grant an attachment in the first instance, and issue its warrant, so that the offender shall answer for his contempt in custody. (*Anon.,* (1711) 1 Salk. 84; *R.* v. *Jones,* (1719) 1 Stra. 185.) But such power would only be exercised in very flagrant cases. The usual course is for the applicant to serve the person alleged to have been guilty of a contempt of court with a notice of motion, similar in form to that set out in Precedent No. 66. The applicant usually files affidavits in support of his motion, though in special cases the Court may proceed on its own knowledge, without any suggestion. (*In re The Sheriff of Surrey,* 2 F. & F. 236; *Skipworth's and Castro's Cases,* L. R. 9 Q. B.

230; 12 Cox, C. C. 358.) If the offender fails to appear and show cause, a warrant may issue for his apprehension (*Lechmere Charlton's Case*, 2 Myl. & Cr. 316); or he may be fined in his absence (*R. v. Clement*, 4 B. & Ald. 218). If he appears, he in his turn usually files affidavits, either disputing the facts alleged against him or endeavouring to purge his contempt. If the Court is not satisfied, it may commit him to prison for a time certain, or may impose a fine, or may do both; and in every case the Court may further order the offender to pay the costs of the proceedings. (*Martin's Case*, 2 Russ. & Myl. 674, n.) Where the contempt is slight or unintentional and the offender submits himself to the Court, and has done all in his power to clear his contempt, the Court often makes no other order except that he pay the costs of the motion. (See L. R. 7 Eq. 58, n.) The costs are of course in the discretion of the Court; and none will be granted where the proceedings are clearly vexatious, and the party instituting them is himself to blame. (*Vernon v. Vernon*, 40 L. J. Ch. 118; 19 W. R. 404; 23 L. T. 697.)

The commitment must be for a time certain. (*R. v. James*, 5 B. & Ald. 894; *Green v. Elgie and another*, 5 Q. B. 99; *In re Maria Annie Davies*, 21 Q. B. D. 236; 37 W. R. 57.) But the warrant may be in general terms; no special grounds need be stated; nor need the facts which are the cause of the arrest be specified; it is sufficient to state that the offender is committed for contempt of court. (*Howard v. Gosset*, 10 Q. B. 411; *Ex parte Fernandez*, 6 H. & N. 717; 10 C. B. N. S. 3.) "A rule of Court of two lines" is sufficient (*R. v. Paty*, 2 Ld. Raym. 1108), and will justify the officer of the Court in arresting the offender, and protect him from any action of false imprisonment. It will be presumed that the Court was acting regularly and rightly, unless, indeed, the contrary appears expressly on the face of the writ. (*R. v. Evans and another*, 8 Dowl. 451.) And the decision of the judge committing cannot be reviewed by any other Court. (*Burdett v. Abbot*, 14 East, 1; *Stockdale v. Hansard*, per Littledale, J., 9 A. & E. 169; *Carus Wilson's Case*, per Lord Denman, C.J., 7 Q. B. 1008.) If a fine is imposed, it is usual to add a sentence of imprisonment till the fine be paid, in addition to any other term of imprisonment that may have been inflicted. (L. R. 9 Q. B. 228, 229, 240.) If a plaintiff be guilty of contempt, he is liable, in addition to fine or imprisonment, to have all proceedings in his action stayed, or even the whole action dismissed, and money paid into court returned to the defendant. (*Republic of Liberia v. Roye*, 1 App. Cas. 139; 45 L. J. Ch. 297; 24 W. R. 967; 34 L. T. 145.)

Where the period for which the offender is committed is expressed in the margin of the writ, or may be gathered from it by necessary inference, the gaoler should discharge the prisoner at the end of that period. (*Moone* v. *Rose*, L. R. 4 Q. B. 486; 38 L. J. Q. B. 236.) But if the warrant does not state the period for which he is to be kept in custody, nor refer to the nature of the contempt committed, the gaoler should not release him without an order of the Court. (*Greaves* v. *Keene*, 4 Ex. D. 73; 27 W. R. 416; 40 L. T. 216; *McCombe* v. *Gray*, 4 L. R. (Ir.) 432.) When the period assigned comes to an end, the offender may not be detained in custody merely for the costs of the application to the Court to commit. (*Jackson* v. *Mawby*, 1 Ch. D. 86; 45 L. J. Ch. 53; 24 W. R. 92; *Hudson* v. *Tooth*, 2 P. D. 125; 35 L. T. 820.) *A fortiori*, where condemnation in costs is the only punishment inflicted, the Court has no power subsequently to commit to prison for default in payment. (*Mickelthwaite* v. *Fletcher*, 27 W. R. 793; *Weldon* v. *Weldon*, 10 P. D. 72; 54 L. J. P. & D. 26, 60; 33 W. R. 370, 427; 52 L. T. 233; 49 J. P. 517.)

Formerly there was a sharp distinction between committal and attachment. Committal was the proper punishment for doing a prohibited act, and attachment for neglecting to do some act ordered to be done. But now for most purposes the distinction is of no importance. (Per Chitty, J., in *Harvey* v. *Harvey*, 26 Ch. D. at p. 654. See, however, the valuable report of Mr. Registrar Lavie, in the notes to [1893] 1 Ch. pp. 259—264.) A writ of attachment still issues to the sheriff, while an order for committal is placed in the hands of the tipstaff of the Court. "A person committed by the Court is unable to be bailed out, whereas under a writ of attachment the sheriff may accept bail." (Per Jessel, M.R., in *Buist* v. *Bridge*, 43 L. T. 432; 29 W. R. 117.) Neither attachment nor committal can now be obtained by a litigant without notice of motion, which should as a rule be personally served, though this is not indispensable. (*Browning* v. *Sabin*, 5 Ch. D. 511; 46 L. J. Ch. 728; *Howarth* v. *Howarth*, 11 P. D. 95; 55 L. J. P. 49; *In re Morris*, 44 Ch. D. 151; 59 L. J. Ch. 407; *In re Evans*, [1893] 1 Ch. 252; 62 L. J. Ch. 413.) And if such notice of motion ask for a writ of attachment where committal is the proper remedy, the judge will amend it. (*Callow* v. *Young*, 56 L. T. 147—Chitty, J.)

The officer charged with the execution of a writ of attachment may break open the outer door of the defendant's house in order to arrest him (*Harvey* v. *Harvey*, 26 Ch. D. 644; 32 W. R. 76; 51 L. T. 508; 48 J. P. 468)—an attachment for such contempt of court as is dealt with in this chapter being a criminal and not a civil process.

(*In re Freston*, 11 Q. B. D. 545; 52 L. J. Q. B. 545; 31 W. R. 581, 804; 49 L. T. 290; *In re Dudley*, 12 Q. B. D. 44; 53 L. J. Q. B. 16; 32 W. R. 264; 49 L. T. 737; *In re Strong*, 32 Ch. D. 342; 55 L. J. Ch. 553; 34 W. R. 614; 55 L. T. 3.) A motion to commit for contempt of court any person who has published comments calculated to prejudice the fair trial of an action is a " criminal cause or matter," and no appeal from an order made on such a motion can be brought to the Court of Appeal. (*O'Shea* v. *O'Shea and Parnell*, 15 P. D. 59; 59 L. J. P. 47; 38 W. R. 374; 62 L. T. 713; 17 Cox, C. C. 107; *Attorney-General* v. *Kissane*, 32 L. R. Ir. 220; *Ex parte Fernandez*, 10 C. B. N. S. 3; 6 H. & N. 717.)

The term " Superior Court " includes the House of Lords, the Judicial Committee of the Privy Council, the Court of Appeal, the Court of Criminal Appeal, the High Court of Justice, and any Divisional Court thereof, and any judge of any Division sitting in Court alone. Also the Central Criminal Court, and all Courts held under any Commission of Oyer and Terminer, Assize, Gaol Delivery, or Nisi Prius. (*Ex parte Fernandez*, 6 H. & N. 717; 10 C. B. N. S. 3; 30 L. J. C. P. 321; 7 Jur. N. S. 529, 571; 9 W. R. 832; 4 L. T. 296, 324; *In re McAleece*, Ir. R. 7 C. L. 146.) And the Superior Courts of Law and Equity in Dublin, and the Court of Session in Scotland. The Court in Lunacy has power to commit for contempt. (*Ex parte Jones*, (1806) 13 Ves. 237; *In re B——*, [1892] 1 Ch. 459; 61 L. J. Ch. 446; 40 W. R. 369; 66 L. T. 38.)

But whether a judge sitting at chambers is a " Superior Court," and has such power to commit for contempt, may well be doubted. Wilmot, C.J., was clearly of opinion that a judge at chambers had such a power, as appears by the very learned judgment which he intended to deliver in *R.* v. *Almon* (Wilmot's Opinions and Judgments, 253), but it was not delivered in fact, the case having dropped on the resignation of the then Attorney-General, Sir Fletcher Norton. But there is no instance reported of a judge at chambers himself inflicting fine or imprisonment. He invariably reports any insult offered to him at chambers to the full Court, and leaves it to the Court to punish the offender. And in *R.* v. *Faulkner* (2 Mont. & Ayr. 338; 2 C. M. & R. 533; 1 Gale, 215), Lord Abinger, C.B., states most distinctly that a judge at chambers has *no* power to commit for contempt. Sect. 39 of the Jud. Act, 1873, seems in no way to enlarge the powers of a judge at chambers; and its concluding sentence certainly implies that a judge at chambers is not "a Court," and in so far confirms Lord Abinger's opinion. In the analogous case of the Court of Review, it was decided that a single judge had no power to commit for contempt, except when sitting as the Court. (*Ex parte Van Sandau*, 1 Phillips, 445; *Van Sandau* v. *Turner*, 6 Q. B. 773; compare, also, *In re Ramsay*, L. R. 3 P. C. 427; 7 Moo. P. C. C. (N. S.) 263; *Rainy* v. *Justices of Sierra Leone*, 8 Moo. P. C. C. 47; *Macartney* v. *Corry*, 7 Ir. R. C. L. 242.) Hence, the better opinion appears to be that a judge at chambers cannot safely commit summarily for a contempt of himself; although, of course, he con-stantly issues at chambers writs of attachment after notice to the party in default under Order XLIV. (See *Salm-Kyrburg* v. *Pos-nanski*, 13 Q. B. D. 218; 53 L. J. Q. B. 428; 32 W. R. 752; *Amstell* v. *Lesser*, 16 Q. B. D. 187; 55 L. J. Q. B. 114; 34 W. R. 230; 53 L. T. 759; *In re Johnson*, 20 Q. B. D. 68; 57 L. J. Q. B. 1; 36 W. R. 51; 58 L. T. 160; *Davis* v. *Galmoye*, 39 Ch. D. 322; 58 L. J. Ch. 120; 37 W. R. 227; S. C. (North, J.) 40 Ch. D. 355; 58 L. J. Ch. 338; 37 W. R. 399; 60 L. T. 130.)

No official or special referee and no arbitrator can commit for contempt. (Order XXXVI. r. 51.) A master in lunacy has power to order a writ of attachment to issue against an alleged lunatic in order to compel him to attend an inquisition which is being held as to his sanity; but in ordinary cases the better course is for the master to refer the application to the Court in Lunacy. (*In re B——*, [1892] 1 Ch. 459; 61 L. J. Ch. 446; 40 W. R. 369; 66 L. T. 38.)

The Colonial Courts of Record are also Superior Courts and possess the power of committing for contempt in all the above cases. (*Crawford's Case*, 13 Q. B. 613; 18 L. J. Q. B. 225; 13 Jur. 955; *In re McDermott*, L. R. 1 P. C. 260; L. R. 2 P. C. 341; 38 L. J. P. C. 1; 20 L. T. 47; *Hughes* v. *Porral and others*, 4 Moore, P. C. C. 41.) But if it appear on the face of the writ that the Court has exceeded its jurisdiction (*In re Ramsay*, L. R. 3 P. C. 427; 7 Moore, P. C. C. (N. S.) 263; *Rainy* v. *The Justices of Sierra Leone*, 8 Moore, P. C. C. 47), or if the offender had no opportunity given him of defending or explaining his conduct (*In re Pollard*, L. R. 2 P. C. 106;

5 Moore, P. C. C. (N. S.) 111), or if it is clear that no contempt was in fact committed (*McLeod* v. *St. Aubyn*, [1899] A. C. 549; 68 L. J. P. C. 137; 48 W. R. 173; 81 L. T. 158), or if the punishment awarded for the contempt was not appropriate to the offence (*In re Wallace*, L. R. 1 P. C. 283; 36 L. J. P. C. 9; 15 W. R. 533; 14 L. T. 286; *In re Downie and Arrindell*, 3 Moore, P. C. C. 414), an appeal will lie to the Judicial Committee of the Privy Council, which has power to set aside the order of commitment and to order the fine to be remitted.   But if it sufficiently appears that the prisoner was punished for contempt, and that the Court had power to commit for such a contempt, and if there was any ground for holding that such a contempt had in fact been committed, the offender cannot be heard to say that no such contempt had in fact been committed. "Every Court in such a case has to form its own judgment." (Per Lord Denman, C.J., in *Carus Wilson's Case*, 7 Q. B. 1015.)   But the governor of the colony, as representing the King, has power to remit the sentence and pardon the offender. (*In re Moseley*, [1893] A. C. 138; 62 L. J. P. C. 79; 68 L. T. 105; 57 J. P. 277.)

When a competent Court, acting clearly within its jurisdiction, states certain matters of *fact*, affidavits are not admissible to contradict such findings.   So if the Colonial Court administers a different system of law from ours, affidavits cannot be received in England to show that the Colonial Court was acting contrary to its own law.   The English Courts must "give full credit to that Court for knowing and administering their own law."   (Per Lord Denman, C.J., in *Carus Wilson's Case*, 7 Q. B. 1014.)

(2.) *Inferior Courts.*

The power of an Inferior Court to deal itself with contempts is more restricted than that of a Superior Court. For, as we have seen, a Superior Court can commit to prison in cases where the offence is not indictable; while an Inferior Court cannot commit in every case which is indictable, and certainly in none which is not. (*R.* v. *Revel*, 1 Str. 420.) The King's Bench Division of the High Court of Justice as *custos morum* can commit for a libel which is a contempt of an Inferior Court that has no such power of protecting itself. (*R.* v. *Davies*, [1906] 1 K. B. 32; 75 L. J. K. B. 104; 93 L. T. 772; and see *R.* v. *Parke*, [1903] 2 K. B. 432; 72 L. J. K. B. 839; 89 L. T. 439.)

(a) Inferior Courts of Record.

A distinction must be drawn between Inferior Courts of record and Inferior Courts not of record. (See *ante*, p. 532.)

An Inferior Court of Record can only commit for contempts committed in open court, *in facie curiæ*. (*R.* v. *Lefroy*, L. R. 8 Q. B. 134; 42 L. J. Q. B. 121; 21 W. R. 332; 28 L. T. 132.) The judge* must at the moment be actually discharging his duty; and the words employed or act done must either be pointedly and personally disrespectful to the judge himself, or else amount to a serious obstruction of the course of justice. The power to punish for such a contempt is an inherent part of the jurisdiction of every court of record. But the High Court has authority to intervene and prevent any usurpation of jurisdiction by an Inferior Court, and will protect the person punished when there is no reasonable ground for treating his conduct as a contempt. (*In re Pater*, 5 B. & S. 299; 33 L. J. M. C. 142; 10 Jur. N. S. 972; 12 W. R. 823; 10 L. T. 376.)

Before actually committing, the judge should always give the offender an opportunity of explaining his conduct and showing cause why he should not be committed. If the judge does commit, he must—in the absence of any special custom or defined practice to the contrary—issue a warrant in writing and duly signed; he may not commit by word of mouth, as a judge of a Superior Court may

---

* The word "judge" is here used to include a coroner, or other officer that presides over an Inferior Court of Record.

sometimes do. (*Mayhew* v. *Locke*, 7 Taunt. 63.) Such a warrant will justify any officer of the Inferior Court in arresting the offender, and protect him from any action of assault or false imprisonment. (*Levy* v. *Moylan*, 10 C. B. 189; 19 L. J. C. P. 308; 1 L. M. & P. 307.) It must state clearly the cause for which the prisoner was committed and all facts necessary to give jurisdiction to commit. Affidavits are inadmissible to contradict any statement of fact contained in the warrant (*In re John Rea* (2), 4 L. R. Ir. 345; 14 Cox, C. C. 256); though they are admissible to show want of jurisdiction (*R.* v. *Bolton*, 1 Q. B. 73). But where it sufficiently appears that the prisoner was committed for a contempt, and the Court had power to commit for such a contempt, and on the facts stated by it there was ground for holding that such a contempt had in fact been committed, its decision cannot be reviewed by any other Court. (*Carus Wilson's Case*, 7 Q. B. 984, 1014; *Garnett* v. *Ferrand*, 6 B. & C. 625; *R.* v. *Bolton*, 1 Q. B. 73.) The Court alone can judge of the insult offered to it.

Illustrations.

If a coroner for any reason (and the sufficiency of such reason is a matter entirely for the coroner in the exercise of his discretion) order a particular person to quit the room where he is about to hold an inquest, and such person wholly refuse to go, and defiantly continue in the room to the hindrance of the inquest, the coroner may lawfully order him to be expelled.

Garnett v. *Ferrand*, (1827) 6 B. & C. 611.

The solicitor for a plaintiff in a County Court wrote a letter to the local newspaper, accusing the judge of the County Court of " arbitrary and tyrannical abuse of power," and calling one statement he had made a " monstrosity " and " an untruth." *Held*, that the judge had no power to proceed against the solicitor for contempt of court; although the action was still pending.

R. v. *Lefroy, Ex parte Jolliffe*, (1873) L. R. 8 Q. B. 134; 42 L. J. Q. B. 121; 21 W. R. 332; 28 L. T. 132.

A County Court judge has no jurisdiction to commit for contempt a person who has acted as a solicitor in an action in the County Court without being qualified.

R. v. *Judge of Brompton County Court*, [1893] 2 Q. B. 195; 62 L. J. Q. B. 604; 41 W. R. 648; 68 L. T. 829; 5 R. 462.

Charles Carus Wilson, an English attorney, went to reside in Jersey, and there brought an action against Peter Le Sieur in the Royal Court of Jersey, which was composed of a bailiff and two jurats, or lieutenant-bailiffs. On September 23rd, 1844, the Court was about to deliver an interlocutory judgment in the cause against Wilson, when he interposed, and, in an unbecoming manner, protested against the competency of the Court, his own counsel being present and silent. Wilson had previously been repeatedly warned that his conduct was disrespectful. The Court thereupon, after giving Wilson full opportunity to explain or apologise for his conduct, sentenced him to pay a fine of 10*l.* and apologise to the Court, and in default to be imprisoned till obedience. This sentence was duly recorded in the judgment book, and read aloud to Wilson and his counsel then and there ; but Wilson wholly refused either to pay or to apologise, and was accordingly at once arrested by the viscount of the island, whose duty it was to carry into effect the sentences of the Royal Court, and lodged in Her Majesty's gaol. A writ of *habeas corpus* was obtained, on the ground that there was no written warrant for his arrest or detainer. The return to the writ set out all the facts, and also stated that by the law and practice of the Island of Jersey no written warrant was necessary or usual, but that the sentence duly recorded was of itself a sufficient authority, justifying and compelling the viscount to arrest, and the gaoler to detain, the offender. *Held,* by Lord Denman, C.J., Patteson, Williams, and Wightman, JJ., that affidavits could not be received on behalf of Wilson to show that such was not the law or practice of Jersey, or that in other respects the Royal Court had acted inconsistently with its own law ; that no written warrant was necessary ; that the contempt was a matter which the Royal Court had to decide for itself ; that its decision, being the decision of a competent Court, could not be reviewed by the Queen's Bench ; and Wilson was accordingly, on April 22nd, 1845, remanded to Her Majesty's prison in Jersey.

Carus Wilson's Case, (1845) 7 Q. B. 984.

As to some Inferior Courts special statutes have been passed. Thus, by sections 162 and 163 of the County Courts Act, 1888 (51 & 52 Vict. c. 43), a limited power of committal is given to the judge of any county court in case he, or any juror or witness, or any of the officers of the court be wilfully insulted, or the proceedings of the court wilfully interrupted. (See *Levy* v. *Moylan,* 10 C. B. 189 ; 19 L. J. C. P. 308 ; 1 L. M. & P. 307 ; *R.* v. *Jordan,* 57 L. J. Q. B. 483 ; 36 W. R. 797.) The judge of a County Court has a wider power when sitting in bankruptcy (Bankruptcy Act, 1883, s. 100 ; *R.* v. *Judge of County Court of Surrey,* 13 Q. B. D. 963 ; 53 L. J. Q. B. 545 ; 51 L. T. 102 ; *Skinner* v. *Northallerton County Court Judge,* [1899] A. C. 439 ; 68 L. J. Q. B. 896 ; 80 L. T. 814), and when exercising the powers conferred on him by the Companies (Consolidation) Act, 1908, s. 131, sub-s. 3 (*In re New Par Consols, Ltd.,* (No. 2), [1898] 1 Q. B. 669 ; 67 L. J. Q. B. 598 ; 46 W. R. 369 ; 78 L. T. 312). A County Court judge has no power to commit in any case not within these sections. (*R.* v. *Lefroy, Ex parte Jolliffe,* L. R. 8 Q. B. 134; 42 L. J. Q. B. 121; 21 W. R. 332; 28 L. T. 132; *R.* v. *Judge of Brompton County Court,* [1893] 2 Q. B. 195; 62 L. J. Q. B. 604; 41 W. R. 648; 68 L. T. 829.) Except, of course, for breach of injunction, and in other cases of ordinary civil procedure coming within Rules 57 and 59 of Order XXV. of the County Court Rules, 1903. (*Martin* v. *Bannister,* 4 Q. B. D. 212, 491; 48 L. J. Ex. 300; 27 W. R. 431; and see section 48 of the County Courts Act, 1888; *Lewis* v. *Owen,* [1894] 1 Q. B. 102; 63 L. J. Q. B. 233; and *R.* v. *Judge of County Court of Surrey,* 13 Q. B. D. 963.)

Illustrations.

A solicitor called Turner applied to Judge Jordan to grant a new trial in a County Court case. His Honour refused the application, and in the course of his judgment made certain remarks which Turner considered to be reflections on his personal character. Turner therefore interrupted the judge by calling out, "That is a most unjust remark." The judge at once committed him for contempt; and the Court of Appeal upheld the committal.

R. v. *Jordan,* (1888) 57 L. J. Q. B. 483; 36 W. R. 797.

Many acts may come within the provisions of section 162 of the County Courts Act, 1888, which it would be impossible adequately to describe in the warrant; hence it is unnecessary for the judge to say more in the warrant than that he has been wilfully insulted or interrupted (using the words of the section).

Levy v. *Moylan,* (1850) 10 C. B. 211; 19 L. J. C. P. 308; 1 L. M. & P. 307.

(b) Inferior Courts not of Record.

An Inferior Court not of Record has at common law no power to commit for contempt; in some few cases such a power has been expressly conferred by statute. (*McDermott* v. *Judges of British Guiana,* (1868) L. R. 2 P. C. 341; 38 L. J. P. C. 1; 20 L. T. 47.) It has, however, power to require an offender to find sureties for his good behaviour, as to which see *ante,* p. 532. It may also enforce order by ejecting any offender whose misconduct obstructs the business of the court.

By the County Voters Registration Act, 1865 (28 Vict. c. 36), s. 16, power is given to every revising barrister " to order any person to be removed from his court who shall interrupt the business of the court, or refuse to obey his lawful orders in respect of the same."

By the Petty Sessions (Ireland) Act, 1851 (14 & 15 Vict. c. 93), s. 9, it is enacted that "if any person shall wilfully insult any justice or justices . . . sitting in any . . . court or place, or shall commit any contempt of any such court it shall be lawful for such justice or justices by any verbal order, either to direct such person to be removed from such court or place, or to be taken into custody, and at any time before the rising of such court, by warrant, to commit such person to gaol for any period not exceeding seven days, or to fine such person in any sum not exceeding forty shillings."

Illustrations.

Langley said to the Mayor of Salisbury whilst in the execution of his office, " Mr. Mayor, I do not care for you ; you are a rogue and a rascal." *Held,* that the words were not indictable ; but that the mayor might have bound him over then and there to be of good behaviour, and ought to have done so instantly.

> *R. v. Langley,* (1703) 2 Ld. Raym. 1029 ; 6 Mod. 125 ; 2 Salk. 697 ; Holt, 654.

Rogers spoke unmannerly words to Sir Robert Jeffryes, an Alderman of the City of London, while he was holding a wardmote in a church. Holt, C.J., said "No information or indictment will lie for these words. For the common law has provided a proper method for punishment of scandalous words, viz., binding to the good behaviour ; such words being a breach of the peace."

> *R. v. Rogers,* (1702) 2 Ld. Raym. 777 ; 7 Mod. 28.

A material witness against a prisoner committed for trial on a charge of felony refused to be bound over to appear at the quarter sessions to give evidence against him, saying that she would not go to Maidstone, and nobody should make her. After fully explaining the matter, and expending nearly an hour in the attempt to persuade her to go, the committing magistrate issued a warrant by virtue of which she was taken to Maidstone, and gave her evidence, and the prisoner was convicted ; without her evidence he could not have been convicted. *Held,* that the arrest was lawful, by necessary implication from 1 & 2 Ph. & M. c. 13.

> *Bennet and wife v. Watson and another,* (1814) 3 M. & S. 1.

To persist, in spite of repeated remonstrance, in interrupting and insulting a Court of petty sessions in Ireland by shouting at the bench in the most violent and unseemly manner, so that none of the justices could speak a word, is a contempt for which the Court may commit to prison even a solicitor practising before them.

In re John Rea, (1878) 2 L. R. Ir. 429 ; 14 Cox, C. C. 139.

Where, at petty sessions in Ireland, a contempt committed in court is brought to the notice of the justices there sitting, and while the offender is still in court, the justices can order that he be attached to answer there and then for such alleged contempt ; the mere fact that the order so made is carried out after the offender, in order to evade arrest, has left the court, is not sufficient to render his arrest illegal.

Mitchell v. *Smyth* (1), [1894] 2 Ir. R. 351.

In 1874 Thomas Willis claimed to vote as a freeholder ; but the revising barrister on the meagre evidence before him held that the property in respect of which he claimed was copyhold and disallowed the vote. His cousin, William Willis, who was present in court as agent for the opposite political party, knew perfectly well that it was really freehold, but held his tongue. In 1875 Thomas Willis accordingly claimed as a copyholder. Then William came forward and produced the family title-deeds and proved clearly that the land was freehold. The revising barrister was compelled again to disallow Thomas's vote ; but ordered William to be turned out of the room for not having produced this evidence in 1874. *Held,* that such expulsion was wrongful, as William's conduct in 1874, though possibly deserving of moral reprobation, was certainly no "interruption" of the proceedings of the court then being held in 1875.

Willis v. *Maclachlan,* (1876) 1 Ex. D. 376 ; 45 L. J. Ex. 689 ; 35 L. T. 218.

The Ecclesiastical Courts have no power to commit for contempt at all. All that such Courts can do is to signify such contempt to the Lord Chancellor, who thereupon, under 2 & 3 Will. IV. c. 93, issues a writ *de contumace capiendo* for taking the offender into custody. (*Adlam* v. *Colthurst,* L. R. 2 Adm. & Ecc. 30; 36 L. J. Ec. Cas. 14; *Ex parte Dale,* 43 L. T. 534.) But such writ will not issue if the alleged offender be a peer, a lord of Parliament, or a member of the House of Commons (sect. 2). Note, that both Mr. Long Wellesley and Mr. Lechmere Charlton were members of Parliament, and yet both were committed to the Fleet for contempt of the Court of Chancery. (2 Russ. & Mylne, 639; 2 Mylne & Cr. 316.) And see the remarks of Cockburn, C.J., in *Onslow's* and *Whalley's Cases,* L. R. 9 Q. B. 228, 229 ; 12 Cox, C. C. 369.

CHAPTER XXI.

THE LAW OF PERSONS IN BOTH CIVIL AND CRIMINAL CASES.

We have hitherto dealt with the plaintiff and defendant as individuals under no disability, who sue and are sued singly and in their own right. We propose in this chapter to show how rights and liabilities are affected by personal disability or special personal relations with others, both in civil and criminal cases.

It will be convenient to divide this chapter into the following heads :—

    1. Husband and Wife.
    2. Infants.
    3. Lunatics.
    4. Bankrupts.
    5. Receivers.
    6. Executors and Administrators.
    7. Trustees.
    8. Aliens.
    9. Master and Servant ; Principal and Agent.
    10. Partners.
    11. Corporations and Companies.
    12. Trade Unions.

1. *Husband and Wife.*

When words actionable *per se* are spoken of a married woman, she may either sue alone, or she may join her husband as co-plaintiff; in the latter case, he will be entitled to recover in the same action for any special damage that may have occurred to him. When the words are not actionable *per se*, she may sue, provided she can show that some special damage has followed from the words to *her.* That special damage has accrued to her husband in consequence of such words will not avail her ; he alone can sue for such damage, although it is *her* reputation that has been assailed.

Hence, if words not actionable *per se* be spoken of a married woman and damage ensue to the husband, none to her, she cannot sue, but he can. The damage to him is in fact the sole cause of action.

This right of the husband to sue for words defamatory of his wife is somewhat anomalous, for *his* reputation is in no way assailed. Generally speaking, if words defamatory of A., but not actionable in themselves, produce damage only to B., neither A. nor B. can sue. But the reputation of a husband is so intimately connected with that of his wife, that he has always been allowed to sue whenever he has received damage, just as though the words had been spoken of himself.

That this is law, is clearly laid down in Siderfin, 346, under the year 1667 : "Nota, si parols queux de eux m̄ ne sont Actionable mes solement in respect del collateral dam̄s. sont p̄te. (parlés) del feme covert, Le Baron sole port L'action, et si le feme soit joyn ove luy le Judgment serra pur ceo arrest, coment soit apres verdict." (And see *Coleman et ux.* v. *Harcourt,* (1664) 1 Levinz, 140 ; *Harwood et ux.* v. *Hardwick et ux.,* (1668) 2 Keble, 387 ; *Grove et ux.* v. *Hart,* (1752) Sayer, 33 ; Buller's N. P. 7.) In the case of *Riding* v. *Smith,* 1 Ex. D. 91 ; 45 L. J. Ex. 281 ; 24 W. R. 487 ; 34 L. T. 500, the wife's name was struck off the record by the judge at the trial, and the husband recovered for the damage to his business caused by words not actionable *per se,* spoken of his wife ; though there it is true the Court bases its judgment on the fact that Mrs. Riding helped her husband in the shop, and was therefore his servant or assistant as well as his wife.

By the Married Women's Property Act, 1882 (45 & 46 Vict. c. 75), s. 1, sub-s. (2), a married woman is now capable " of suing and being sued, either in contract or in tort, or otherwise, in all respects as if she were a *feme sole,* and her husband need not be joined with her as plaintiff or defendant, or be made a party to any action or other legal proceeding brought by or taken against her ; and any damages or costs recovered by her in any such action or proceeding shall be her separate property ; and any damages or costs recovered against her in any such action or proceeding shall be payable out of her separate property, and not otherwise." A married woman, therefore, may now sue for libel or slander without her husband or any next friend ; and she cannot be ordered to give security for the costs of the action, even although she have at the time of action no separate estate, and there be nothing upon which, if she fails, the defendant can issue available execution. (*In re Isaac, Jacob* v. *Isaac*, 30 Ch. D. 418 ; 54 L. J. Ch. 1136 ; 33 W. R. 845 ; 53 L. T. 478 ; *Threlfall* v. *Wilson*, 8 P. D. 18 ; 48 L. T. 238 ; *Severance* v. *Civil Service Supply Association*, 48 L. T. 485.)

Formerly a married woman was always bound to join her husband as co-plaintiff, otherwise the defendant might plead in abatement. But the action was still regarded as solely hers. If she died, it abated ; if he died, the action survived to her and she continued it as sole plaintiff. No damages could be recovered in such an action for any pecuniary loss suffered by the husband ; if the words were not actionable *per se*, and the female plaintiff could show no damage to herself, they were non-suited.

The husband was formerly obliged to bring a separate action for any damage he had sustained. But by the Common Law Procedure Act, 1852, s. 40, he was allowed to add claims in his own right whenever he was necessarily made a co-plaintiff in any action brought for an injury done to his wife ; and it was provided that on the death of either party the action should not abate so far as the causes of action belonging to the survivor were concerned. And now, by Order XVIII. r. 4, " Claims by or against husband and wife may be joined with claims by or against either of them separately."

Married women still frequently adopt the old common law method and join their husband as co-plaintiff. And there is this practical convenience in so doing, that thus all damages sustained by either can be recovered in one action. And there is also a twofold chance of proving special damage. In all cases of the class of *Allsop* v. *Allsop*, 5 H. & N. 534 ; 29 L. J. Ex. 315, *ante*, p. 419, it will clearly be prudent for the pleader to make a separate claim for damages for the husband. For we apprehend that it is clear law that a wife suing alone under the Act of 1882, cannot recover for any special damage which would have been excluded in an action brought at common law by herself and her husband. The damages recovered in such an action are to be her separate property; she cannot, therefore, recover for any loss which her husband has suffered. "The Act does not destroy the husband's right, but only relieves the woman from incapacity." (Per Bowen, L.J., in *Weldon* v. *Winslow*, 13 Q. B. D. 788; 53 L. J. Q. B. 528; 33 W. R. 219; 51 L. T. 643.)

By sect. 12 of the same Act, "Every woman, whether married before or after this Act, shall have in her own name against all persons whomsoever, including her husband, the same civil remedies, and also (subject, as regards her husband, to the proviso hereinafter contained) the same remedies and redress by way of criminal proceedings, for the protection and security of her own separate property, as if such property belonged to her as a *feme sole*, but, except as aforesaid, no husband or wife shall be entitled to sue the other for a tort." This section does not enable a married woman to take criminal proceedings against her husband for a personal libel upon herself. (*The Queen* v. *Lord Mayor of London and Vance*, 16 Q. B. D. 772; 55 L. J. M. C. 118; 34 W. R. 544; 54 L. T. 761; 50 J. P. 614; 16 Cox, C. C. 81.)

Illustrations.

A husband cannot sue his wife for slander, nor a wife her husband.
> *Young* v. *Young*, (1903) 5 F. 330 (Ct. of Sess.).

Even after they are divorced neither spouse can sue the other for defamatory words published during coverture.
> *Phillips* v. *Barnet*, 1 Q. B. D. 436; 46 L. J. Q. B. 277; 24 W. R. 345; 34 L. T. 177.

But a wife, living apart from her husband under a separation order obtained by virtue of the Summary Jurisdiction (Married Women) Act, 1895, can maintain an action of libel against him.
> *Robinson* v. *Robinson*, (1897) 13 Times L. R. 564.
> And see s. 26 of the Matrimonial Causes Act, 1857, as interpreted in *Cuenod* v. *Leslie*, [1909] 1 K. B. 880; 78 L. J. K. B. 695; 100 L. T. 675; 25 Times L. R. 374.

And it is submitted that if in England a married woman carried on a separate trade or profession, and her husband libelled or slandered her in the way of such trade or profession, she could sue him under sect. 12; such an action was held by Brett, J., to be "a remedy for the protection and security" of her separate property within sect. 11 of the Act of 1870, and in the present sect. 12 the same words are used.
> *Summers* v. *City Bank*, L. R. 9 C. P. 580; 43 L. J. C. P. 261.

In New York and Pennsylvania a married woman has for many years been enabled by special statute to sue for libel or slander without joining her husband; but even in those States she cannot sue her husband for defaming her.

> *Freethy* v. *Freethy,* 42 Barb. (N. Y.) 641.
> *Tibbs* v. *Brown,* 2 Grant's Cas. (Penns.) 39.

If the words be spoken of the woman before marriage, the husband's name may still be joined on the writ; if she marry pending action, the husband may be made a party under Order XVII. r. 4, though this is not necessary (r. 1). The right of action survives to the wife on her husband's death, whether he was a party to the action or not; the widow continues sole plaintiff and the action does not abate. If, however, the wife dies before final judgment, the action must cease; it cannot be continued by her husband either *jure mariti,* or as her administrator.

If a married woman fail in an action of libel or slander she may be condemned in costs, although her husband was joined as a co-plaintiff. (*Newton and wife* v. *Boodle and others,* 4 C. B. 359; 18 L. J. C. P. 73.) And by sect. 2 of the Married Women's Property Act, 1893 (56 & 57 Vict. c. 63), "In any action or proceeding now or hereafter instituted by a woman or by a next friend on her behalf, the Court before which such action or proceeding is pending shall have jurisdiction by judgment or order from time to time to order payment of the costs of the opposite party out of property which is subject to a restraint on anticipation, and may enforce such payment by the appointment of a receiver and the sale of the property or otherwise, as may be just." An order may be made under this section as to the costs of a counterclaim raised unsuccessfully by a married woman defendant. (*Hood-Barrs* v. *Cathcart* (2), [1895] 1 Q. B. 873.) Otherwise the section only applies to cases where a married woman is plaintiff; no such order can be made as to the costs of any motion or appeal made by a married woman in an action in which she is a defendant. (*Hood-Barrs* v. *Cathcart* (1), [1894] 3 Ch. 376; 63 L. J. Ch. 793.)

Illustrations.

Where words actionable *per se* were spoken of a married woman, she was allowed to recover only 20*s.* damages; all the special damage which she proved at the trial was held to have accrued to her husband, and not to her : he ought, therefore, to have sued for it in a separate action. He could now claim such damage in his wife's action, if joined as a co-plaintiff.

Dengate and wife v. *Gardiner,* (1838) 4 M. & W. 5 ; 2 Jur. 470.

Where a married woman lived in service apart from her husband, maintaining herself, and was dismissed in consequence of a libellous letter sent to her master, it was held that the husband could sue ; for his was the special damage.

Coward v. *Wellington,* (1836) 7 C. & P. 531.

In such a case, had the cause of her dismissal been slanderous words not actionable *per se,* the wife could not (before the Married Women's Property Act, 1870, at all events) have sued. She would have been held to have suffered no damage at all, her personal property belonging entirely to her husband. Per Lord Campbell in

Lynch v. *Knight and wife,* (1861) 9 H. L. C. 589 ; 8 Jur. N. S. 724 ; 5 L. T. 291.

Action by husband and wife, who kept a victualling-house, against the defendant for saying to the wife, "Thou art a bawd to thine own daughter," whereby J. S. that used to come to the house forbore, &c., to the damage of *both.* After verdict for the plaintiffs, judgment was stayed "because the words are not actionable, except in respect of the special loss, which is the husband's only."

Coleman and wife v. *Harcourt,* (1664) 1 Lev. 140.

The female plaintiff lived separate from her husband and kept a boarding-house. The defendant spoke words imputing to her insolvency, adultery, and prostitution ; some of her boarders left her in consequence, and certain tradesmen refused her credit. After verdict for the plaintiffs, judgment was arrested, on the ground that the husband should have sued alone, for the words were actionable only by reason of the damage to the business, and such damage was solely his.

Saville et ux. v. *Sweeny,* (1833) 4 B. & Ad. 514 ; 1 N. & M. 254.

And so in America where a married woman was living apart from her husband under articles of separation, wherein the husband had covenanted that she might use his name in suing for any injury to her person or character, and the wife brought an action for slander in the joint names of her husband and herself : the defendant induced the husband to execute a deed releasing the cause of action, and pleaded the release in bar of the wife's action, and the Court was compelled to hold this deed a good answer to the action.

Beach et ux. v. *Beach,* (1842) 2 Hill (N. Y.), 260.

Where the libel imputed that the plaintiff, a married man, kept a gaming-house, and that his wife was a woman of notoriously bad character, and the wife fell ill and died in consequence, evidence of such damage was excluded in an action brought by the surviving husband.

Guy v. *Gregory,* (1840) 9 C. & P. 584.

And see *Wilson* v. *Goit,* (1858) 3 Smith (17 N. Y. R.), 445, *ante,* p. 382.

Words directly defamatory of the wife may also be defamatory of the husband, who may therefore sue alone. Thus, where the defendant said to the plaintiff's wife : "You are a nuisance to live beside of. You are a bawd ; and your house is no better than a bawdy-house," it was held unnecessary to make the wife a party to the action, although the husband proved no special damage. For had the charge been true, the plaintiff might have been indicted as well as his wife.

> *Huckle* v. *Reynolds,* (1859) 7 C. B. N. S. 114.
>
> And see *Bash* v. *Somner,* (1852) 20 Pennsylvania St. R. 159.

Where the defendant said to the plaintiff, an innkeeper, "Thy house is infected with the pox, and thy wife was laid of the pox," it was held that the husband could sue ; for even if small-pox only was meant, the words were still actionable, "for it is a discredit to the plaintiff, and guests would not resort hither." Damages 50*l.*

> *Levet's Case,* (1592) Cro. Eliz. 289.

"If an innkeeper's wife be called '*a cheat*' and the house lose the trade, the husband has an injury by the words spoken of his wife." Per Wythens, J., in

> *Baldwin* v. *Flower,* (1688) 3 Mod. 120.
>
> *Grove et ux.* v. *Hart,* (1752) Buller's N. P. 7 ; Sayer, 33.

A husband is liable for all libels published or slanders uttered by his wife during coverture. "They are the torts of her husband, and therefore she creates as against her husband a liability." (Per Jessel, M.R., in *Wainford* v. *Heyl,* L. R. 20 Eq. at p. 325 ; 44 L. J. Ch. 567 ; 23 W. R. 848 ; 33 L. T. 155.) And there is nothing in any of the Married Women's Property Acts removing or affecting this liability. (*Hancocks & Co.* v. *Demeric-Lablache,* 3 C. P. D. 197 ; 47 L. J. C. P. 514 ; 26 W. R. 402 ; 38 L. T. 753 ; *Seroka and wife* v. *Kattenburg and wife,* 17 Q. B. D. 177 ; 55 L. J. Q. B. 375 ; 34 W. R. 542 ; 54 L. T. 649 ; *Earle* v. *Kingscote,* [1900] 2 Ch. 585 ; 69 L. J. Ch. 725 ; 49 W. R. 3 ; 83 L. T. 377.) Lord Justice Moulton, however, expressed a contrary opinion in *Cuenod* v. *Leslie,* [1909] 1 K. B. at pp. 888, 889. But if a decree for judicial separation be obtained before judgment the husband is entitled to be discharged from the action. (*Cuenod* v. *Leslie,* [1909] 1 K. B. 880 ; 78 L. J. K. B. 695 ; 100 L. T. 675.)

Hence, although a plaintiff may now sue the wife alone, if he wishes, for any libel or slander published by her (*ante,* p. 568), it will generally be advisable for him to sue the husband as well. For if he sue the wife alone, he can only obtain execution against her separate estate in the form settled by the Court of Appeal in *Scott* v. *Morley,* 20 Q. B. D. at p 132 57 L. J. Q. B. 43 ; 36 W. R. 67 ;

57 L. T. 919. Moreover, the judgment against the wife, if sued alone, will release the husband from all liability for the same tort ; the plaintiff cannot proceed against him in case the separate property prove insufficient ; whereas if he join both husband and wife as defendants on his writ, he can obtain judgment against the wife's separate estate, and also against the husband for the residue of damages and costs not recovered out of her separate estate.

When husband and wife are both made defendants, they must both be served, unless the Court or a judge shall otherwise order. (Order IX. r. 3.) But " there can only be one Defence and one judgment." (Per Romer, L.J., in *Beaumont* v. *Kaye and wife*, [1904] 1 K. B. at p. 294.) Hence, if either husband or wife pay money into court, the other cannot plead any defence denying liability. (*Ib.* ; Order XXII. r. 1.) And although in the case of a wife's ante-nuptial tort there is an express provision that, as between her and her husband, her separate estate shall be deemed to be primarily liable for damages and costs recovered in such an action, there is no such provision in the case of a post-nuptial tort. Hence, presumably, the ordinary rule applies ; and a husband who has had to pay damages out of his own pocket for his wife's words will have no remedy over against her separate estate. But the plaintiff may, of course, if he will, enforce his joint judgment against the separate property of the wife, and not against the husband. (*Ferguson* v. *Clayworth and wife*, 6 Q. B. 269 ; 13 L. J. Q. B. 329 ; *Ivens* v. *Butler and wife*, 7 E. & B. 159 ; 26 L. J. Q. B. 145 ; *Morris* v. *Freeman and wife*, 3 P. D. 65 ; 47 L. J. P. D. & A. 79 ; 27 W. R. 62 ; 39 L. T. 125.) It is not necessary for this purpose that the trustees of her marriage settlement should be made parties to the action. (*Davies* v. *Jenkins*, 6 Ch. D. 728 ; 46 L. J. Ch. 761 ; 26 W. R. 260.) An inquiry will be directed to ascertain of what her separate estate consists, and in whom it is vested, as in *Collett* v. *Dickenson*, 11 Ch. D. 687 ; 40 L. T. 394 ; and on such inquiry the solicitor to the trustees will be bound to state their names and to produce the deed of settlement. (*Bursill* v. *Tanner*, 16 Q. B. D. 1 ; 55 L. J. Q. B. 53 ; 53 L. T. 445.)

For all libels published, or slanders uttered, by the wife before coverture, her husband was at common law liable to the full extent. But now his liability is restricted in this respect. By the Married Women's Property Act, 1882 (45 & 46 Vict. c. 75), s. 13, " A woman, after her marriage, shall continue to be liable in respect and to the extent of her separate property for all wrongs committed by her before her marriage, and she may be sued for any liability in damages or otherwise in respect of any such wrong, and all sums recovered against her in respect thereof, or for any costs relating thereto, shall be payable out of her separate property; and as between her and her husband, unless there be any contract between them to the contrary, her separate property shall be deemed to be primarily liable for all such wrongs, and for all damages or costs recovered in respect thereof : Provided always, that nothing in this Act shall operate to increase or diminish the liability of any woman married before the commencement of this Act for any such wrong, except as to any separate property to which she may become entitled by virtue of this Act, and to which she would not have been entitled for her separate use under the Acts hereby repealed or otherwise, if this Act had not passed."

By sect. 14, "A husband shall be liable for all wrongs committed by his wife, before marriage, to the extent of all property whatsoever belonging to her which he shall have acquired or become entitled to from or through his wife, after deducting therefrom any payments made by him, and any sums for which judgment may have been *bonâ fide* recovered against him in any proceeding at law, in respect of any debts, contracts or wrongs for or in respect of which his wife was liable before her marriage as aforesaid, but he shall not be liable for the same any further or otherwise ; and any court in which a husband shall be sued for any such debt (*sic*) shall have power to direct any inquiry or proceedings which it may think proper for the purpose of ascertaining the nature, amount, or value of such property. Provided always, that nothing in this Act contained shall operate to increase or diminish the liability of any husband married before the commencement of this Act for or in respect of any such liability of his wife as aforesaid."

By sect. 15, "A husband and wife may be jointly sued in respect of any liability incurred by the wife before marriage as aforesaid, if the plaintiff in the action shall seek to establish his claim, either wholly or in part, against both of them ; and if in any such action, or in any action brought in respect of any such liability against the husband alone, it is not found that the husband is liable in respect of any property of the wife so acquired by him, or to which he shall have become so entitled as aforesaid, he shall have judgment for his costs of defence, whatever may be the result of the action against the wife if jointly sued with him ; and in any such action against husband and wife jointly, if it appears that the husband is liable for the damages recovered, or any part thereof, the judgment to the extent of the amount for which the husband is liable shall be a joint judgment against the husband personally and against the wife as to her separate property ; and as to the residue, if any, of such damages, the judgment shall be a separate judgment against the wife as to her separate property only."

If the husband dies before judgment the action continues against the widow ; if, however, the wife dies in the lifetime of her husband before judgment, the action immediately abates, whether it was for a post-nuptial or an ante-nuptial tort (*Bell and another* v. *Stocker*, 10 Q. B. D. 129 ; 52 L. J. Q. B. 49 ; 47 L. T. 624), unless he himself joined in or authorised it. If they be divorced, the wife must be sued alone ; the husband is released from all liability, even though the words complained of were published before the divorce. (*Capel* v. *Powell and another*, 17 C. B. N. S. 743 ; 34 L. J. C. P. 168 ; 10 Jur. N. S. 1255 ; 13 W. R. 159 ; 11 L. T. 421.) So, if the wife has before action obtained a judicial separation (20 & 21 Vict. c. 85, ss. 25, 26), or a protection order still in force (sect. 21). But if the husband and wife voluntarily live apart under a separation deed, the common law rule prevails ; the husband is liable for her misconduct and may be joined as a defendant. (*Head* v. *Briscoe et ux.*, 5 C. & P. 485 ; 2 L. J. C. P. 101 ; *Utley* v. *The Mitre Publishing Company and others*, (1901) 17 Times L. R. 720.)

A married woman will be held criminally liable for a libel which she has published. (*R.* v. *Mary Carlile,* 3 B. & Ald. 167.) Her coverture will, it seems, be no defence to an indictment for a misdemeanour. (*R.* v. *Ingram,* 1 Salk. 384; *R.* v. *Cruse and Mary his wife,* 2 Moo. C. C. 53; 8 C. & P. 541.)

Illustrations.

The plaintiff sued Orchard and his wife for slanderous words ; the jury found that Orchard had spoken the words, but not Mrs. Orchard. Judgment against the husband. It was moved in arrest of judgment that the speaking of the words could not be a joint act, and that if the husband alone uttered them, the wife ought never to have been made a party to the action. But it was held that this defect was cured by the verdict, and that the plaintiff was entitled to retain his judgment.

    Burcher v. *Orchard et ux.,* (1652) Style, 349.

    But see *Swithin et ux.* v. *Vincent et ux.,* (1764) 2 Wils. 227.

Mrs. Harwood slandered Mrs. White ; wherefore White and wife sued Harwood and wife. Pending action, Harwood died, and his widow remarried. The Court was very much puzzled, and gave no judgment, apparently, though inclining to think that the writ abated. [We think it would now depend on whether the widow had any property at the date of her second marriage ; if so, the second husband could be added as a co-defendant, or the action might proceed against her alone ; if not, it would certainly be of but little use continuing it.]

    White et ux. v. *Harwood et ux.,* (1648) Style, 138 ; Vin. Abr. "Baron and Feme," A.a.

Mrs. Clayworth slandered the plaintiff, who recovered 40s. damages and costs against her and her husband, and took her in execution under a *ca. sa.* The Court refused to discharge her out of the custody of the sheriff without the clearest proof that she had no separate property.

    Ferguson v. *Clayworth and wife,* 6 Q. B. 269 ; 13 L. J. Q. B. 329 ; 8 Jur. 709 ; 2 D. & L. 165.

    But now see *Draycott* v. *Harrison,* 17 Q. B. D. 147 ; 34 W. R. 546.

2. *Infants.*

An infant may bring an action of libel or slander. He may trade and may therefore have an action of slander for words which would damage him in his trade. (*Wild* v. *Tomkinson,* (1827) 5 L. J. K. B. (Old S.) 265.) As to a charge of crime, see *ante,* p. 50. An infant sues by his next friend, who is personally liable for the costs of the suit (*Caley* v. *Caley,* 25 W. R. 528); but security for costs will not be required from him, lest the infant should lose his rights altogether. (*Fellows* v. *Barrett*, 1 Keen, 119.) Any money recovered in the action shall not be paid to the infant or his next friend, unless the Court or a judge shall so direct, but shall be paid to the Public Trustee and held by him in trust for the infant, subject to the control of the Court. (Order XXII. r. 15.) An infant defends by a guardian *ad litem.* (See Order XVI. rr. 18, 19, 21; Order XIII. r. 1; and Order LV. r. 27.) A guardian *ad litem* will not be ordered to pay costs, unless he has been guilty of gross misconduct. (*Morgan* v. *Morgan*, 12 L. T. 199; 11 Jur. N. S. 233.)

The infancy of the defendant is no defence to an action of libel or slander. In *Defries* v. *Davies*, 3 Dowl. 629, the defendant, a lad of fifteen, was imprisoned for default in payment of damages and costs for a slander.

An infant will also be criminally liable for any libel, if he be above the age of fourteen. If he be under fourteen, but above seven, he might possibly be found guilty of a libel, if evidence were given of a disposition prematurely wicked. But more than the proof of malice ordinarily given in cases of privilege would probably be required.

That an infant has been defamed gives his parents no right of action, unless in some very exceptional case it deprives the parent of services which the infant formerly rendered, in which case an action on the case may lie for the special damage thus wrongfully inflicted, provided it be the natural and probable consequence of the defendant's words. (See *post*, Master and Servant, p. 583.) A child will be held to be the servant of its parents, provided it is old enough to be capable of rendering them any act of service. (*Dixon* v. *Bell*, 5 Maule & S. 198; *Hall* v. *Hollander*, 4 B. & C. 660; 7 D. & R. 133; *Evans* v. *Walton*, L. R. 2 C. P. 615; 15 W. R. 1062.)

3. *Lunatics.*

It is almost inconceivable that an admitted lunatic should bring an action of libel or slander. But, should such an event happen, he ought to sue by his next friend, if he has not yet been found of unsound mind by inquisition; if he has been, then by his committee, who before commencing the action must obtain the sanction of the Master and of the Judge in Lunacy in the proper way.

Any damages or money recovered in an action by a person of unsound mind, not so found by inquisition, will be paid to the Public Trustee, as in the case of an infant. (Order XXII. r. 15.) Lunatics defend an action by their committee, if one be appointed, and if he has no adverse interest; in other cases by a guardian *ad litem.* Lunacy is in England, it is said, no defence to an action for slander or libel. (Per Kelly, C.B., in *Mordaunt* v. *Mordaunt,* 39 L. J. Prob. & Matr. 59.) In America, however, insanity at the time of speaking the words is considered a defence, "where the derangement is great and notorious, so that the speaking the words could produce no effect on the hearers," because then "it is manifest no damage would be incurred." But where the degree of insanity is slight, or not uniform, there evidence of it is only admissible in mitigation of damages. (*Dickinson* v. *Barber,* 9 Tyng. (Mass.) 218; *Yeates et ux.* v. *Reed et ux.,* 4 Blackford (Indiana), 463; *Horner* v. *Marshall's Administratrix,* 5 Munford (Virginia), 466; *Gates* v. *Meredith,* 7 Ind. 440.)

A lunatic cannot be held criminally liable for a libel published under the influence of mental derangement; but the *onus* of proving this defence lies on the accused.

4. *Bankrupts.*

An undischarged bankrupt may sue for and recover damages for a personal wrong, such as libel or slander, whether committed before or during his bankruptcy; and such damages will not pass to his trustee. (*Dowling* v. *Browne,* (1854) 4 Ir. C. L. R. 265; *Ex parte Graham, In re Job,* (1870) 21 L. T. 802; *Ex parte Vine, In re Wilson,* (1878) 8 Ch. D. 364; 26 W. R. 582; 38 L. T. 730; and see *Beckham* v. *Drake,* (1849) 2 H. L. C. p. 639; 13 Jur. 921.) The right of action is not assignable (*Benson* v. *Flower,*

Sir Wm. Jones, 215); and the trustee cannot interfere. "Assignees can maintain no action for libel, although the injury occasioned thereby to the man's reputation may have been the sole cause of his bankruptcy." (Per Alderson, B., in *Howard* v. *Crowther*, 8 M. & W. at p. 604.) The defendant is not entitled to security for costs. (*Rhodes* v. *Dawson*, 16 Q. B. D. 548; 55 L. J. Q. B. 134; 34 W. R. 240; *Cook* v. *Whellock*, 24 Q. B. D. 658; 59 L. J. Q. B. 329; 38 W. R. 534; 62 L. T. 675.) Neither the bankruptcy of the plaintiff nor that of the defendant is any defence to the action. If a plaintiff likes to sue an insolvent defendant for unliquidated damages, he may do so.

5. *Receivers.*

If receivers, appointed by the Court in an administration suit to carry on a gazette, publish a libel therein, they are of course personally liable for damages and costs. The damages, it would seem, may be paid out of the estate, but not the costs; those the receivers must pay out of their own pocket. (*Stubbs* v. *Marsh*, 15 L. T. 312.) So in America. (*Marten* v. *Van Schaick*, 4 Paige, 479.) Leave to sue a receiver must be obtained from the Court before action.

6. *Executors and Administrators.*

The maxim *actio personalis cum personâ moritur* applies to all actions of libel and slander. If, therefore, either party die before verdict, the action is at an end. "There shall be no abatement by reason of the death of either party between the verdict or finding of the issues of fact and the judgment, but judgment may in such case be entered, notwithstanding the death." (Order XVII. r. 1; *Palmer* v. *Cohen*, 2 B. & Ad. 966.) But if interlocutory judgment be signed and a writ of inquiry issue, and then plaintiff die, final judgment cannot be entered. (8 & 9 Will. III. c. 11, s. 6; *Ireland* v. *Champneys*, 4 Taunt. 884; and see *Bowker* v. *Evans*, 15 Q. B. D. 565; 54 L. J. Q. B.

421; 33 W. R. 695; 53 L. T. 801.) If, however, verdict and final judgment has once been entered in the plaintiff's favour, and then plaintiff dies and defendant appeals, the action will not abate; but the executors or administrators of the late plaintiff may appear as respondents to the appeal. (*Twycross* v. *Grant and others*, 4 C. P. D. 40; 47 L. J. Q. B. 676; 27 W. R. 87; 39 L. T. 618.) So in America. (*Sandford* v. *Bennett*, 24 N. Y. 20.) So if either party die after final judgment, execution can issue under Order XLII. r. 23. If the plaintiff die before trial his executor may obtain an order for payment out of money paid into Court by defendant. (*Maxwell* v. *Viscount Wolseley*, [1907] 1 K. B. 274; 76 L. J. K. B. 163; 96 L. T. 4.)

An action on the case for words causing special damage, such as an action for slander of title, survives to the plaintiff's executor if and so far as damage can be shown to the plaintiff's estate. (*Hatchard* v. *Mège and others*, 18 Q. B. D. 771; 56 L. J. Q. B. 397; 35 W. R. 576; 56 L. T. 662.)

7. *Trustees.*

Actions for libel or slander may be brought by or against trustees as such. Thus the trustees of a charity may sue jointly for a libel charging them with not properly administering the funds of the charity. (*Booth* v. *Briscoe*, 2 Q. B. D. 496; 25 W. R. 838.) So, too, they may as a body take criminal proceedings. (*R.* v. *Griffin*, 1 Sess. Cas. 257.) An action may be brought against trustees for publishing a libel in the performance of their duties as trustees. (*Martin and wife* v. *Trustees of British Museum and another*, (1894) 10 Times L. R. 338.) And if a newspaper vested in trustees contain a libel, the trustees are personally liable in damages (*Rapkins* v. *Hall and others*, (1894) 10 Times L. R. 466, *ante*, p. 170), though they may claim an indemnity from their *cestuis que trustent*. (*Linaker* v. *Pilcher and others*, (1901) 70 L. J. K. B. 396; 49 W. R. 413; 84 L. T. 421; 17 Times L. R. 256.)

Illustrations.

A charity near Wisbeach was managed by a body of trustees, eight in number. A libellous letter was published in the *Wisbeach Chronicle*, imputing to the trustees misconduct in the management of the funds of the charity. The eight trustees sued the proprietor of the paper in one joint action for the libel. *Held,* that they were empowered so to do by Order XVI. r. 1 ; although before the Judicature Act it would never have been allowed. The jury having returned a single verdict for the plaintiffs, damages 40s., the Court of Appeal refused, on the motion of the defendant, to disturb the verdict.

> *Booth and others* v. *Briscoe,* (1877) 2 Q. B. D. 496 ; 25 W. R. 838.

A newspaper, which was carried on to protect the interests of the members of a trade union, was registered in the names of the trustees of the trade union as the proprietors. A libel upon the plaintiff was published in the newspaper, and he brought an action against the trustees. It was held that though the trustees had not authorised the publication of the libel, yet, as the property of the newspaper was vested in them, they were liable ; and that they were entitled to be indemnified out of the funds of the union, as the carrying on of the newspaper was not *ultra vires.*

> *Linaker* v. *Pilcher and others,* (1901) 70 L. J. K. B. 396; 49 W. R. 413 ; 84 L. T. 421 ; 17 Times L. R. 256.
>
> *Rapkins* v. *Hall and others,* (1894) 10 Times L. R. 466, *ante,* p. 170.

8. *Aliens.*

An alien friend residing abroad may sue in England for a libel or slander published of him in England. (*Pisani* v. *Lawson,* 6 Bing. N. C. 90 ; 5 Scott, 418.) The domicil of the plaintiff or the defendant is not the test of jurisdiction. (See *post,* p. 606.) But any plaintiff whose ordinary place of residence is not in the British Isles, will, as a rule, be ordered to give security for costs, unless he either has real property within jurisdiction available in execution, or is co-plaintiff with others resident in England. (Order LXV. r. 6, a ; 31 & 32 Vict. c. 54, s. 5.)

Any one who at date of writ was an alien enemy or any one who adheres to the King's enemies, whether an alien or a British subject, cannot bring an action in the Courts of this country. (*Netherlands South African Ry. Co., Ltd.* v. *Fisher,* (1901) 18 Times L. R. 116.)

Every foreigner within jurisdiction, for however short a time, owes the King allegiance during his stay and is subject to our laws. He will be liable, therefore, both civilly and criminally, for every libel published within the jurisdiction of the English Courts; he will also be civilly liable for every slander uttered within jurisdiction. If, however, he has left England before the writ is issued, the plaintiff will have great difficulty in obtaining leave, under Order XI., to serve notice of a writ abroad. He will also be liable civilly for words published abroad, whether spoken or written, if the publication of such words is either a tort or a crime by the law of the place where they were published, provided he is now within jurisdiction and can be served with a writ. (*Machado* v. *Fontes*, [1897] 2 Q. B. 231; 66 L. J. Q. B. 542; 45 W. R. 565; 76 L. T. 588.) And see *post*, p. 606.

Illustrations.

A French refugee in England wrote a stilted poem about the apotheosis of Napoleon Buonaparte, then first consul of the French Republic, suggesting that it would be an heroic deed to assassinate him. He was held amenable to the English criminal law, although the libel was purely political, affected no one in the British Isles, and attacked the man who was England's greatest enemy at the time. The jury found him guilty; but war broke out again between England and France soon afterwards, and no sentence was ever passed.

> *R.* v. *Jean Peltier*, 28 Howell's St. Tr. 617.

The defendant out of jurisdiction made a statement in the nature of slander of title to the plaintiff's ship. The Court refused to allow the writ to be served, although the ship was at the time within jurisdiction.

> *Casey* v. *Arnott*, 2 C. P. D. 24; 46 L. J. C. P. 3; 25 W. R. 46; 35 L. T. 424.

Where words spoken out of the jurisdiction indirectly caused special damage to the plaintiff within the jurisdiction, the Court refused leave to issue a writ to be served out of jurisdiction, on the ground that such special damage was not an "act done" within jurisdiction, within the meaning of the former Order XI. r. 1.

> *Bree* v. *Marescaux*, 7 Q. B. D. 434; 50 L. J. Q. B. 676; 29 W. R. 858; 44 L. T. 644, 765.

> But see *Tozier and wife* v. *Hawkins*, 15 Q. B. D. 650, 680; 55 L. J. Q. B. 152; 34 W. R. 223; and other cases cited, *post*, pp. 607, 608.

9. *Master and Servant—Principal and Agent.*

If a servant or apprentice be libelled or slandered, he can of course sue in his own right. In some cases his master also can sue in an action on the case, if the words have directly caused him pecuniary loss ; *e.g.*, if the servant has been arrested and the master deprived of his services in consequence of the defendant's words ; or if in any other way the natural consequence of the words has been to injure the master in the way of his profession or trade. And this appears to be the law whether the words be actionable *per se* or not. (See *Riding* v. *Smith, ante,* p. 106.)

If any agent or servant be in any way concerned in writing, printing, publishing, or selling a libel, he will be both civilly and criminally liable. If a clerk or servant copy a libel and deliver the copy he has made to a third person, he will be liable as a publisher. That his master or employer ordered him to do so, will be no defence. (Per Wood, B., in *Maloney* v. *Bartley*, 3 Camp. 210.) "For the warrant of no man, not even of the King himself, can excuse the doing of an illegal act ; for although the commanders are trespassers, so are also the persons who did the fact." (*Per cur.* in *Sands, qui tam, &c.* v. *Child and others*, (1693) 3 Lev. 352.) The agent or servant cannot recover any contribution from his employer (*Merryweather* v. *Nixan*, 2 Sm. L. Cases (11th edn.), 398 ; 8 T. R. 186) ; and any previous promise to indemnify him against the consequences of the publication, or against the costs of an action brought for the libel, will be void. (See cases cited *ante*, p. 8.)

But it will be a defence if the agent or servant can satisfy the jury that he never read the paper he delivered, and was wholly unaware that it was a libel; *e.g.*, where a postman or messenger carries a sealed letter, of the contents of which he is ignorant.

So, too, a servant will be liable for any slander uttered on his master's behalf and by his master's orders : but here he cannot set up as a defence that he did not know his master's orders were illegal; for he must be conscious of what he himself is saying.

Illustrations.

A compositor was once held criminally liable for setting up the type of a libel; so was a man whose business it was merely "to clap down the press."

> *R. v. Knell,* (1728) 1 Barnard. 305.
> *R. v. Clerk,* (1728) 1 Barnard. 304.

A porter who, in the course of business, delivers parcels containing libellous handbills, is not liable in an action of libel if shown to be ignorant of the contents of the parcel.

> *Day v. Bream,* (1837) 2 M. & Rob. 54.

A master or principal will be liable to an action, if false defamatory words be spoken or published by his servant or agent with his authority and consent. The mere fact that the actual publisher was the servant or agent of the defendant is not alone sufficient; for authority to commit an unlawful act will not in general be presumed. It must be further proved that the servant or agent had instructions from the defendant to speak or publish the words complained of, or else that in so doing he was acting within the general scope of his employment. In *Citizens' Life Assurance Co., Ltd. v. Brown,* [1904] A. C. 423; 73 L. J. P. C. 102; 90 L. T. 739; 20 Times L. R. 497, the Judicial Committee of the Privy Council held that the scope of a servant's authority is the same thing as the scope of his employment.

The instructions may be either express or implied. The proprietor of a newspaper is both civilly and criminally responsible for whatever appears in its columns, although the publication may have been made without his knowledge and in his absence. For he must be taken to have ordered his servants to print and publish whatever the editor might send them for that purpose. The proprietor trusts to the discretion of the editor to exclude all that is libellous; if the editor fails in his duty, still the paper and all its contents will be printed and published by the proprietor's servants by virtue of his general orders. So, if a master-printer has contracted to print a magazine, he will be liable for any libel that may appear in any number printed at his office. So, every bookseller must be taken to have told his shopmen to sell whatever books or pamphlets are in his shop for sale; if any one contain libellous matter, the bookseller is (*primâ facie* at all events) liable for its publication by his servant by reason of such general instructions. But where a master employs a clerk or manager to conduct his general business correspondence, and he thinks it is to the interest of his master to insert libellous words in his master's letters, the master will be liable. (*Citizens' Life Assurance Co., Ltd.* v. *Brown,* [1904] A. C. 423; 73 L. J. P. C. 102; 90 L. T. 739; 20 Times L. R. 497.)

Although the master has not authorised the act of the servant, still if it was done for his benefit and on his behalf, he may subsequently ratify it. *Omnis ratihabitio priori mandato œquiparatur.* But "in order that there may be a valid ratification, there must be both a knowledge of the fact to be ratified and an intention to ratify it." (Per Keating, J., in *Edwards* v. *London & N. W. Ry. Co.,* L. R. 5 C. P. 449.) The master must do something more than merely stand by and let the servant act. Non-intervention is not ratification. (*Moon* v. *Towers,* (1860) 8 C. B. N. S. 611; *Weston* v. *Beeman and another,* (1857) 27 L. J. Ex. 57.)

Illustrations.

At a meeting of a board of guardians, at which reporters were present, the chairman made a statement reflecting on the plaintiff, and added, "I am glad gentlemen of the Press are in the room and I hope they will take notice of it; publicity should be given to the matter." A report accordingly appeared in two local papers. *Held,* by the majority of the Exchequer Chamber (three judges against two) that there was some evidence to go to the jury that the defendant had expressly authorised the publication of the alleged libel in the newspapers.

> *Parkes* v. *Prescott and another,* L. R. 4 Ex. 169; 38 L. J. Ex. 105; 17 W. R. 773; 20 L. T. 537.
> See also *Clay* v. *People,* 86 Ill. 147.
> *Tarpley* v. *Blabey,* 2 Bing. N. C. 437; 2 Scott, 642; 1 Hodges, 414; 7 C. & P. 395.

The defendant's daughter, a minor, was authorised to make out his bills and write his general business letters; she chose to insert libellous matter in one letter. The father was held not liable for the wrongful act of his daughter, in the absence of any direct instructions.

> *Harding* v. *Greening,* (1817) 8 Taunt. 42; 1 Moore, 477; Holt, N. P. 531.

Corporation of Glasgow v. *Riddell,* (H. L.) [1911] W. N. 71.

But see *Citizens' Life Assurance Co., Ltd.* v. *Brown,* [1904] A. C.
    423 ; 73 L. J. P. C. 102 ; 90 L. T. 739 ; 20 Times L. R. 497.

Moyes regularly printed *Fraser's Magazine ;* but had nothing to do with
preparing the illustrations. One number contained a libellous lithographic
picture. Moyes was held liable for this picture (though he had never
seen it) because it was referred to in a part of the accompanying letter-
press, which had been printed by his servants. The editor was of course
liable also.

Watts v. *Fraser and Moyes,* 7 C. & P. 369 ; 7 A. & E. 223 ;
    1 Jur. 671 ; 1 M. & Rob. 449 ; 2 N. & P. 157 ; W. W. & D.
    451.

The proprietor of a newspaper will be held liable for an accidental slip
made by his printer's man in setting up the type.

Shepheard v. *Whitaker,* L. R. 10 C. P. 502 ; 32 L. T. 402.

And for a libellous advertisement inserted by the editor without his
knowledge.

Harrison v. *Pearce,* 1 F. & F. 567 ; 32 L. T. (Old S.) 298.

Morrison v. *Ritchie & Co.,* (1902) 4 F. 645 (Ct. of Sess.),
    ante, p. 7.

The proprietor of a newspaper in America on going away for a holiday
expressly instructed his acting editor to publish nothing exceptional, personal or abusive, and warned him especially to scan very particularly any
article brought in by B., who was known to be a "smart" writer. The
editor permitted an article of B.'s to appear which contained libellous
matter. The proprietor was held liable, though the publication was made
in his absence and without his knowledge.

Dunn v. *Hall,* 1 Carter (Indiana), 345 ; 1 Smith, 288.

Huff v. *Bennett,* 4 Sand. (New York) 120.

Curtis v. *Mussey,* 6 Gray ('72 Mass.), 261.

Andres v. *Wells,* 7 Johns. (New York) 260.

A master or principal is criminally liable for any libel
published by his servant or agent with his authority or
consent. At common law he was criminally liable for such
libel, even although he had no knowledge of it, if his servant was acting in pursuance of general orders. Whenever
an employer was civilly liable for a libel published by his
servants, he was, before Lord Campbell's Act, criminally
liable also. But now by sect. 7 of that Act (6 & 7 Vict.
c. 96), it is enacted "that whensoever, upon the trial of
any indictment or information for the publication of a libel,
under the plea of 'Not Guilty,' evidence shall have been
given which shall establish a presumptive case of publication

against the defendant by the act of any other person by
his authority, it shall be competent to such defendant to
prove that such publication was made without his authority,
consent, or knowledge, and that the said publication did not
arise from want of due care or caution on his part." Hence
the proprietor of a newspaper is no longer criminally liable
for a libel which has appeared in it without his knowledge
or consent, merely because he has given the editor a
general authority to insert what he thinks fit therein. (*R.
v. Holbrook and others*, 3 Q. B. D. 60; 47 L. J. Q. B. 35;
4 Q. B. D. 42; 48 L. J. Q. B. 113.)

Illustrations.

The defendant kept a pamphlet shop; she was sick and upstairs in
bed; a libel was brought into the shop without her knowledge, and subsequently sold by her servant on her account. She was held criminally
liable for the act of her servant, on the ground that "the law presumes
that the master is acquainted with what his servant does in the course
of his business."

> *R. v. Dodd*, 2 Sess. Cas. 33.
> *Nutt's Case*, Fitzg. 47; 1 Barnard. K. B. 306.

[But it is doubtful if later judges would have been so strict: the sickness upstairs would surely have been held an excuse, even before the
6 & 7 Vict. c. 96, s. 7, became law. See

> *R. v. Almon*, 5 Burr. 2686.]

A libel was published in a London newspaper, *The Morning Journal*.
At the time of publication, Mr. Gutch, one of the proprietors, was away
ill in Worcestershire, in no way interfering with the conduct of the paper,
which was managed entirely by Alexander. Lord Tenterden directed the
jury to find Gutch guilty, on the ground that it was with his capital that
the paper was carried on, that he derived profit from its sale, and that he
had selected the editor who had actually inserted the libel. Lord Tenterden
the next day admitted (at p. 438) that some possible case might occur in
which the proprietor of a newspaper might be held not criminally answerable for a libel which had appeared in it. Gutch was convicted, but subsequently discharged on his own recognizances.

> *R. v. Gutch, Fisher, and Alexander*, Moo. & Mal. 433.
> *R. v. Walter*, 3 Esp. 21.

And see *Attorney-General v. Siddon*, 1 Cr. & J. 220.

The defendant told the editor of a newspaper several good stories against
the Rev. J. K., and asked him to "show Mr. K. up;" and the editor
subsequently published the substance of them in the paper, and the defendant read it and expressed his approval; this was held a publication by
the defendant, although the editor knew of the facts from other quarters
as well.

> *R. v. Cooper*, 8 Q. B. 533; 15 L. J. Q. B. 206.

The defendants were the proprietors of the *Portsmouth Times and Naval Gazette :* each of them managed a different department of the newspaper, but the duty of editing what was called the literary department was left by them entirely to an editor whom they had appointed, named Green. A libel was inserted in the paper by Green without the express authority, consent, or knowledge of the defendants. At the trial of a criminal information the judge directed a verdict of guilty against the defendants. *Held,* by Cockburn, C.J., and Lush, J., that there must be a new trial ; for upon the true construction of 6 & 7 Vict. c. 96, s. 7, the libel was published without the defendants' authority, consent, or knowledge, and it was a question for the jury whether the publication arose from any want of due care and caution on their part : by Mellor, J., dissenting, that the defendants, having for their own benefit employed an editor to manage a particular department of the newspaper, and given him full discretion as to the articles to be inserted in it, must be taken to have consented to the publication of the libel by him ; that 6 & 7 Vict. c. 96, s. 7, had no application to the facts proved, and that the case was properly withdrawn from the jury.

> *R.* v. *Holbrook and others,* 3 Q. B. D. 60 ; 47 L. J. Q. B. 35 ; 26 W. R. 144 ; 37 L. T. 530 ; 13 Cox, C. C. 650.

On the new trial Green was called as a witness, and stated that he had general authority to conduct the paper, that the defendants left it entirely to his discretion to insert what he pleased, and that he had allowed the letter complained of to appear in the paper without the knowledge or express authority of the defendants, one of whom was absent from Portsmouth at the time. The jury found all the defendants guilty. On a motion for a new trial, on the ground that the verdict was against evidence, and of misdirection, *held* (by Cockburn, C.J., and Lush, J., Mellor, J., still dissenting), that the general authority given to the editor was not *per se* evidence that the defendants had authorised or consented to the publication of the libel, within the meaning of 6 & 7 Vict. c. 96, s. 7, and that as the learned judge at the trial had summed up in terms which might have led the jury to suppose that it was, and the jury had apparently given their verdict on that footing, there must be another new trial.

> *R.* v. *Holbrook and others,* 4 Q. B. D. 42 ; 48 L. J. Q. B. 113 ; 27 W. R. 313 ; 39 L. T. 536 ; 14 Cox, C. C. 185.

The prosecutor, Mr. John Howard, Clerk of the Peace for the borough of Portsmouth, died shortly afterwards, so the proceedings dropped, and no third trial ever took place.

> And see *R.* v. *Bradlaugh and others,* 15 Cox, C. C. 217, *ante,* p. 472.
>
> *R.* v. *Ramsey and Foote,* 15 Cox, C. C. 231.

The liability of a candidate at a parliamentary election for false statements made and published by his agents in relation to the personal character or conduct of his opponent is very clearly defined by

> Sect. 4 of the 58 & 59 Vict. c. 40.
>
> See *Borough of Sunderland Election Petition,* (1896) 5 O'M. & H. 53 ; *ante,* p. 438.

10. *Partners.*

Partners could always jointly sue for a libel defamatory of the firm. (*Ward and another* v. *Smith*, 6 Bing. 749; 4 C. & P. 302; *Le Fanu* v. *Malcolmson*, 1 H. L. C. 637.) But in such an action no damages could formerly have been given for any private injury thereby caused to any individual partner; nor for the injury to the feelings of each member of the firm. Only joint damages could be recovered in the joint action; for the basis of such action was the injury to their joint trade. (*Haythorn* v. *Lawson*, 3 C. & P. 196; *Robinson* v. *Marchant*, 7 Q. B. 918; 15 L. J. Q. B. 134.) But now, by virtue of Order XVIII. r. 6, " claims by plaintiffs jointly may be joined with claims by them or any of them separately against the same defendant." (And see Order XVI. r. 1.) Hence it is no longer necessary to bring two actions for the same words. Each individual partner who is named on the writ can recover separate damages for any special injury done to himself, the firm at the same time recovering their joint damages.

If a partner in conducting the business of a firm causes a libel to be published, the firm will be liable as well as the individual partner. So, if any agent or servant of the firm defames anyone by the express direction of the firm, or in accordance with the general orders given by the firm for the conduct of their business; *ante*, p. 584. But if there be any doubt as to the liability of the firm, it is always safer to join the individual partner or agent or servant as a co-defendant with the firm. (See Order XVI. rr. 4, 7.)

Illustrations.

If one partner be libelled in his private capacity he cannot recover for any special damage which has resulted to the business of the firm. All the partners should sue for that jointly. They may now do so in the same action.

Solomons and others v. *Medex*, 1 Stark. 191.

Robinson v. *Marchant*, 7 Q. B. 918; 15 L. J. Q. B. 134; 10 Jur. 156.

Cook and another v. *Batchellor,* 3 Bos. & Pul. 150.

Maitland and others v. *Goldney, and another,* 2 East, 426.

Similarly, if the firm be libelled as a body, they cannot jointly recover for any private injury to a single partner ; though that partner may now recover his individual damages in the same action.

Haythorn v. *Lawson,* 3 C. & P. 196.

Le Fanu v. *Malcolmson,* 1 H. L. C. 637 ; 13 L. T. (Old S.) 61 ; 8 Ir. L. R. 418.

But if insolvency be imputed to one member of the firm, this is a reflection on the credit of the firm as well : therefore either he, or the firm, or both may sue, each for their own damages.

Harrison v. *Bevington,* 8 C. & P. 708.

Forster and others v. *Lawson,* 3 Bing. 452 ; 11 Moore, 360.

But if one partner be defamed as to his private life, the conduct of the firm not being attacked directly or indirectly, nor any special damage resulting to them from the defendant's words, then the individual partner must sue alone.

11. *Corporations and Companies.*

A corporation or company may sue for any words which affect its property, or injure its trade or business (*South Hetton Coal Co., Ltd.* v. *North-Eastern News Association, Ltd.,* [1894] 1 Q. B. 133 ; 63 L. J. Q. B. 293 ; 42 W. R. 322 ; 69 L. T. 844 ; 9 R. 240.) Whether it can sue for words which merely affect its honour or dignity is not clear ; it has been doubted whether a corporation has a reputation apart from its property or trade. (*Mayor, &c., of Manchester* v. *Williams,* [1891] 1 Q. B. 94 ; 60 L. J. Q. B. 23 ; 39 W. R. 302 ; 63 L. T. 805. But see *South Hetton Coal Co., Ltd.* v. *North Eastern News Association, Ltd., suprà.*) But it clearly cannot sue for any words which are a libel or slander, not on it, but on its members individually (unless special damage has thereby been caused to it, *ante,* p. 584). Nor can it bring an action in respect of any words which impute to it conduct of which a corporation physically cannot be guilty. A corporation " could not sue in respect of an imputation of murder, or incest, or adultery, because it could not commit those crimes. Nor could it sue in respect of a charge of corruption ; for a corporation cannot be guilty of corruption, although the individuals composing it may be." (Per Pollock, C.B., 4 H. & N. 90 ; and Lopes, L.J., [1894] 1 Q. B. at p. 141.)

The law is the same with regard to unincorporated trading companies, which may sue for libel in the manner directed by the special Act creating them, or any statute applicable to them. (*Williams* v. *Beaumont,* 10 Bing. 260; 3 M. & Scott, 705.)

Corporations and companies may maintain actions for slander of their title, whether the slander be uttered by one of their own members or by a stranger. (*Metropolitan Omnibus Co.* v. *Hawkins,* 4 H. & N. 87; 28 L. J. Ex. 201; 5 Jur. N. S. 226; 7 W. R. 265; 32 L. T. (Old S.) 281; *Trenton Insurance Co.* v. *Perrine,* 3 Zab. (New Jersey) 402.)

A corporation will be liable to an action for a libel published by its servants or agents, whenever such publication comes within the scope of the general duties of such servants or agents, or whenever the corporation has expressly authorised or directed such publication. (See *ante, Master and Servant,* p. 586 ; *Yarborough* v. *Bank of England,* 16 East, 6; *R.* v. *City of London,* E. B. & E. 122, n; *Latimer* v. *Western Morning News, Co.,* 25 L. T. 44; *Abrath* v. *North-Eastern Ry. Co.,* 11 App. Cas. 253, 254; 55 L. J. Q. B. 460; 55 L. T. 65, 66. And in America, *Aldrich* v. *Press Printing Co.,* 9 Min. 133; *Johnson* v. *St. Louis Dispatch Co.,* 65 Missouri, 539; 2 M. App. R. 565; 27 Amer. R. 293.)

It has now been decided that a corporation may be rendered liable for words published on a privileged occasion, by proving malice in its servant who published them, provided the servant was acting within the scope of his employment. (*Citizens' Life Assurance Co., Ltd.* v. *Brown,* [1904] A. C. 423; 73 L. J. P. C. 102; 90 L. T. 739; 20 Times L. R. 497.) This was formerly much doubted (see the remarks of Lord Campbell, C.J., in E. B. & E. at p. 121; 27 L. J. Q. B. at p. 231, and of Lord Bramwell in *Abrath* v. *North-Eastern Ry. Co.,* 11 App. Cas. 253, 254).

A corporation can be indicted for libel and fined. (Per Lord Blackburn in *Pharmaceutical Society* v. *London and Provincial Supply Association,* 5 App. Cas. 869, 870; 49 L. J. Q. B. 742; 28 W. R. 960; 43 L. T. 389; dissenting from the remarks of Bramwell, L.J., in the Court below, 5 Q. B. D. 313 ; 49 L. J. Q. B. 338 ; 28 W. R. 608 ; 42 L. T. 569.)

Illustrations.

A joint-stock company, incorporated under the 19 & 20 Vict. c. 47, may. sue in its own corporate name for words imputing to it insolvency, dishonesty, and mismanagement of its affairs, and this although the defendant bo ono of its own shareholders.

> *Metropolitan Omnibus Co.* v. *Hawkins,* (1859) 4 H. & N. 87 ; 28 L. J. Ex. 201 ; 5 Jur. N. S. 226 ; 7 W. R. 265 ; 32 L. T. (Old S.) 281.

Where, before the 19 & 20 Vict. c. 47, a joint-stock insurance company, though not incorporated, was authorised by statute to sue in the name of its chairman, it was held that the chairman might bring an action for a libel which attacked the mode in which the company carried on its business.

> *Williams* v. *Beaumont,* (1833) 10 Bing. 260 ; 3 M. & Scott, 705.

An action of libel will lie at the suit of an incorporated trading company. in respect of a libel calculated to injure its reputation in the way of its business without proof of special damage. Hence, where the defendants published a sensational article, headed "The Homes of the Pitmen," giving an exaggerated description of the insanitary condition of a large number of cottages let by an incorporated colliery to their workmen, it was held that the colliery could sue.

> *South Hetton Coal Co., Ltd.* v. *North-Eastern News Association, Ltd.,* [1894] 1 Q. B. 133 ; 63 L. J. Q. B. 293 ; 42 W. R. 322 ; 69 L. T. 844 ; 9 R. 240.

But where the defendant published in a newspaper a letter asserting that bribery and corruption existed in "two, if not three departments of our Manchester City Council," a Divisional Court held that these words were only a libel on the individual members or officials of the council, and that therefore the corporation itself could not sue.

> *Mayor, &c., of Manchester* v. *Williams,* [1891] 1 Q. B. 94 ; 60 L. J. Q. B. 23 ; 39 W. R. 302 ; 63 L. T. 805 ; 54 J. P. 712.

A railway company was held liable for transmitting a telegram to the effect that the plaintiffs' bank had stopped payment.

> *Whitfield and others* v. *South Eastern Railway Co.,* (1858) E. B. & E. 115 ; 27 L. J. Q. B. 229 ; 4 Jur. N. S. 688.

Fitzpatrick was the superintendent of a life assurance company. He sent to several persons insured in the company a circular libelling the plaintiff, who had formerly been in its employ, but who was now canvassing for a rival company. Fitzpatrick wrote this circular in the interests of his company and in answer to attacks made upon it by the plaintiff ; but it contained statements which he knew to be untrue. The jury found that "Fitzpatrick was acting in publishing the libel within the scope of his employment and in the course of his employment." Verdict for the plaintiff for 650*l.* damages. On appeal, the Judicial Committee of the Privy Council held that although the occasion was privileged, and although Fitzpatrick had no actual authority, express or implied, to write the libel, still the company was liable if in so doing he was acting in the course of his employment.

> *Citizens' Life Assurance Co., Ltd.* v. *Brown,* [1904] A. C. 423 ;
> 73 L. J. P. C. 102 ; 90 L. T. 739 ; 20 Times L. R. 497.
> *Corporation of Glasgow* v. *Riddell,* (H. L.) [1911] W. N. 71.

12. *Trade Unions.*

Formerly the law was that a trade union, though not a corporation, might be sued whether it was registered or unregistered. (*Taff Vale Ry. Co.* v. *Amalgamated Society of Railway Servants,* [1901] A. C. 426; 70 L. J. K. B. 905; 50 W. R. 44; 85 L. T. 147.) An action might even have been brought against it by one of its own members. (*Yorkshire Miners' Association* v. *Howden,* [1905] A. C. 256 ; 74 L. J. K. B. 511 ; 53 W. R. 667 ; 92 L. T. 701.) If a trade union published a libel, its funds were available to compensate the person defamed. (*Linaker* v. *Pilcher and others,* (1901) 70 L. J. K. B. 396 ; 49 W. R. 413 ; 84 L. T. 421 ; 17 Times L. R. 256, *ante,* p. 582.) If it published a black list it might be restrained by injunction. (*Trollope & Sons* v. *London Building Trades Federation,* (1895) 72 L. T. 342; 11 Times L. R. 228, 280 ; *Same* v. *Same,* (1896) 12 Times L. R. 373 ; *Newton* v. *Amalgamated Musicians' Union,* (1896) 12 Times L. R. 623.)

If the funds of a trade union were vested in trustees, and an action for libel or slander were brought against the trade union, the trustees might be joined as defendants, so that the funds might be made liable for damages. (*Taff Vale Ry. Co.* v. *Amalgamated Society of Railway Servants, suprà; South Wales Miners' Federation* v. *Glamorgan Coal Co.,* [1905] A. C. 239 ; 74 L. J. K. B. 525 ; 53 W. R. 593 ; 92 L. T. 710.)

The law has been changed by the Trade Disputes Act, 1906 (6 Edw. VII. c. 47), section 4 of which provides that an action against a trade union, or against any officials or members thereof on behalf of themselves and all other members of the trade union in respect of any tortious act alleged to have been committed by or on behalf of the trade union, shall not be entertained by any court. But by sub-section 2 of section 4, it is provided that the trustees of a trade union may still be sued in the events provided for by section 9 of the Trade Union Act, 1871, except in respect of a tortious act committed by or on behalf of the union in contemplation or in furtherance of a trade dispute. (*Rickards* v. *Bartram and others*, (1908) 25 Times L. R. 181.) As to what is a trade dispute, see section 5, sub-section 3 of the Act and *Conway* v. *Wade*, [1909] A. C. 506 ; 78 L. J. K. B. 1025 ; 101 L. T. 248. Hence, if a libel be published by a trade union not in contemplation or in furtherance of a trade dispute, an action may be maintained against the trustees. Trustees of a trade union still remain personally liable for a libel published in a trade union paper. (*Rapkins* v. *Hall*, (1894) 10 Times L. R. 466; *Linaker* v. *Pilcher and others*, (1901) 84 L. T. 421.) Neither section 3 nor section 4 of the Trade Disputes Act, 1906, affords any protection to trustees or to officials of a trade union so far as their personal liability for a tortious act is concerned. (*Bussy* v. *Amalgamated Society of Railway Servants*, (1908) 24 Times L. R. 437 ; *United County Theatres, Ltd.* v. *Durrant and others, Times,* July 6th, 1909.)

PART II.

PRACTICE, PROCEDURE, AND EVIDENCE IN CIVIL CASES.

CHAPTER XXII.

LAUNCHING THE ACTION.

AN action of libel or slander should not be lightly undertaken; it is a dangerous experiment; many a plaintiff, even though nominally successful, has bitterly regretted that he ever issued his writ. Every one who proposes to bring an action of defamation should remember that he is about to stake his reputation on the event of a lawsuit, and to invite the public to be spectators of the issue. No step, therefore, should be taken in hot haste. There are many matters which require careful consideration before an action is commenced.

Considerations before Writ.

First, is it clear that the plaintiff is the person defamed? Libels are often couched in guarded language, so that none but the initiated can tell to whom they refer. Thus, if the libel be on " a certain vicar," no individual vicar should sue, unless by other passages in the libel he is unmistakably identified; otherwise he will be " putting the cap on his own head." It is not enough that one or two of the plaintiff's dearest friends feel convinced that he is the person aimed at; he should not sue unless his acquaintances generally have reasonably arrived at the same conclusion.

Next, is the charge, or any part of it, true? If so, the plaintiff, by bringing an action, takes the surest method of advertising his own disgrace. When once the action is brought and a justification pleaded, no honourable compromise can be effected; the matter must be fought out to the bitter end; and every detail will become matter of " town talk." It would be better, therefore, for such a plaintiff to affect an indifference which he does not feel, and treat the libel as " beneath contempt."

And even if the charge itself be false, still, if the plaintiff has been at all to blame in the matter, he will be wise not to bring an action. He should consider whether he has not by his own conduct brought the libel or slander on himself. Sometimes it is a defence to an action that the plaintiff challenged or invited the defendant's attack (*ante*, p. 294) ; and in every case the defendant may show in mitigation of damages the provocation given by the plaintiff (*ante*, p. 399). A man who has commenced a newspaper controversy comes with a very bad grace to the law courts for assistance against too powerful an adversary. If both parties are to blame, the result of the trial is generally :—Damages, one farthing ; each party to pay his own costs. Whenever the plaintiff's conduct, though not morally reprehensible, has yet been indiscreet or unbecoming, or such as would naturally lead people to make unkind remarks, it will be better for him not to sue (see *Davis* v. *Duncan*, L. R. 9 C. P. 396 ; *ante*, p. 218 ; and *Harnett* v. *Vise and wife*, 5 Ex. D. 307 ; *ante*, p. 444). He will have to be cross-examined in open court, and every admission wrung from him will be published in all the county papers ; the blackest motives will be imputed to him, and the worst possible construction be put upon his conduct. And although the verdict be ultimately in the plaintiff's favour, many of his acquaintances to their dying day will remember with pleasure what a sorry figure he cut in the box.

And wholly apart from the above considerations, Is it worth while to bring an action? Is the matter sufficiently serious? A man does not advance either his dignity or his reputation by showing himself too sensitive to calumny. People will think that he is eager for litigation, because he knows that his character cannot stand the least wear and tear. This remark applies especially to actions of slander. It is not wise to inquire too curiously what others say of us behind our backs. The slander is only heard by few; it will soon be forgotten ; whereas if you bring an action, it will be disseminated throughout the country, and recorded in a permanent shape.

Still, it may be a man's duty to take proceedings, if the charge made against him be really serious. But even in cases of libel, it is better to exhaust every other method first. If the libel has appeared in a newspaper, the person defamed should write to the editor a calm and dignified letter, avoiding all " smart writing," and indulging in no *tu quoque*. This will probably bring an apology from the writer of the libel. And a prompt apology and retractation of the charge is always worth more to a plaintiff than any amount of damages. If, however, no apology comes, but another libel worse than the first, the plaintiff's position is improved thereby ; for the defendant's persistence in the charge after the explanation afforded is evidence of malice, entitling the plaintiff to heavier damages.

Next, before issuing a writ, the plaintiff should make sure what were the defendant's exact words. He should obtain possession of the original libel, if he possibly can ; if he cannot he should get an accurate copy, and serve the person who holds the original with a notice to preserve it carefully till the trial. With slanders there is often more difficulty. What has reached the plaintiff's ears may be a highly-exaggerated version of what the defendant actually said. The plaintiff is usually the last person who hears the charge against him ; and it has probably grown on each repetition ; words not actionable *per se* are frequently converted into actionable words in the intermediate process. The person slandered should, therefore, take a friend with him (who will make a good witness) and go and ask the alleged slanderer :—" Is it true that you have been saying this of me ? " If he denies that he ever said so, as is very possible, appear at all events to believe him, and bring no action ; if he confesses that he did say so, but has since discovered he was mistaken, get him to write you a letter acknowledging his error, to show anyone if necessary, and then forgive him. If, however, he admits that he said so and reiterates the charge, then you are provided by anticipation with the best possible evidence of publication—an admission by the defendant. See the remarks of Lord Denman in *Griffiths* v. *Lewis*, 7 Q. B. 61 ; 14 L. J. Q. B. 199 ; 9 Jur. 370 (*ante*, p. 295).

As soon as it is clear what is the precise charge made by the defendant, the next question will be :—Are the words actionable ? On this point the plaintiff should take legal advice ; see Chapters II., III., and IV., *ante*, pp. 17—108. If the words are not actionable without special damage, the plaintiff must wait for some damage to accrue before commencing his action.

Parties.

Next the plaintiff must consider who are the proper parties to be named as plaintiffs or defendants on the writ. There may be parties who must be joined ; there may be others whom he may join or not at his pleasure. He must also consider whether any of the proposed parties is incapable of suing or being sued in an action for defamation. This subject is dealt with under the "Law of Persons" (see Chapter XXI., *ante*, p. 567). A Master may at any stage of the proceedings before the trial order that the names of any parties improperly joined, whether as plaintiffs or defendants, be struck out, and that the names of any parties who ought to have been joined be added (Order XVI., r. 11). But any amendment of this kind always involves trouble, expense, and delay.

Several Plaintiffs.

As a rule there is only one plaintiff in an action for defamation. If two or more persons are libelled or slandered, each of them must bring a separate action, unless their causes of action arise out of the same transaction or series of transactions, *and* involve some common question of law or fact. A plaintiff cannot, as a rule, join in one action a claim by himself and a claim brought by him in a representative capacity (Order XVIII. rr. 3, 5; and see *Stroud* v. *Lawson*, [1898] 2 Q. B. 44; 67 L. J. Q. B. 718; 46 W. R. 626; 78 L. T. 729); and it is submitted that, in spite of r. 9 of the same Order, a plaintiff cannot bring an action of defamation on behalf of himself and other members of a class.

Order XVI. r. 1, runs as follows: "All persons may be joined in one action as plaintiffs, in whom any right to relief in respect of or arising out of the same transaction or series of transactions is alleged to exist, whether jointly, severally, or in the alternative, where if such persons brought separate actions any common question of law or fact would arise; provided that, if upon the application of any defendant it shall appear that such joinder may embarrass or delay the trial of the action, the Court or a judge may order separate trials, or make such other order as may be expedient, and judgment may be given for such one or more of the plaintiffs as may be found to be entitled to relief, for such relief as he or they may be entitled to, without any amendment. But the defendant, though unsuccessful, shall be entitled to his costs occasioned by so joining any person who shall not be found entitled to relief, unless the Court or a judge in disposing of the costs shall otherwise direct."

There is a little difficulty in applying the language of this rule, as it now stands, to actions of libel and slander. In such actions the right to relief arises out of a publication by the defendant. It is submitted, therefore, that the words "the same transaction" mean "the same publication," and not that the words complained of refer to the same transaction or series of transactions.

Hence, if two or more persons who occupy some position of joint responsibility known to the law (*e.g.*, partners in a firm, co-owners of property, executors of the same will, trustees of the same settlement, members of the same corporation) be charged collectively with some joint misconduct or neglect of duty, this is a joint imputation on them all as a body, and all can join as co-plaintiffs in one action if they wish. And generally, if A. and B. be both defamed by the same libel or slander and if some common question of law or fact would arise in each action, should they sue separately, A. and B. can join as co-plaintiffs on one writ. But if the same defendant defames A. on one occasion and B. on another, A. and B. cannot join as co-plaintiffs, although the charges made against them may be " historically connected "; for their respective rights to relief do not arise out of the same publication. Unless the case falls within the precise words of Order XVI. r. 1, the old rule of law applies that no action can be maintained jointly by two plaintiffs where the wrong done to one is no wrong to the other (*Barratt and Hodsoll* v. *Collins*, (1825) 10 Moore, 446), and each plaintiff must issue a separate writ.

Illustrations.

Where trustees were libelled as a body in respect of an act done by them collectively in the performance of their duties, it was held that they might all join in one action.

> *Booth and others* v. *Briscoe,* (1877) 2 Q. B. D. 496 ; 25 W. R. 838.

Partners may sue jointly for a libel on them in the way of their partnership business.

> *Le Fanu* v. *Malcolmson,* (1848) 1 H. L. C. 637 ; 8 Ir. L. R. 418 ; 13 L. T. (Old S.) 61.
> And see the notes to *Coryton* v. *Lithebye,* in 2 Wms. Saunders, 5th ed. 117 a ; Ed. 1871, p. 383.

So two co-proprietors of a newspaper may sue jointly for a libel on them in the management of their paper.

> *Russell and another* v. *Webster,* (1874) 23 W. R. 59.

But where the female defendant uttered several separate and distinct slanders, of which some imputed that Mrs. Sandes had been guilty of larceny, while the others imputed larceny to her daughter, it was held that the mother and daughter must bring separate actions.

> *Sandes and another* v. *Wildsmith and another,* [1893] 1 Q. B. 771 ; 62 L. J. Q. B. 404 ; 69 L. T. 387.

Several Defendants.

As a rule there can be only one defendant in an action of slander, viz. the person whose lips uttered the words complained of. If, however, the plaintiff can show that A. instructed B. to utter the slander sued on, the slander becomes a joint tort, and A. and B. can be made defendants in the same action.

Where special damage is essential to the cause of action, the plaintiff should be careful to sue only that person whose utterance of the slander actually caused him special damage. He should not sue the originator of the falsehood, if his utterance of it has produced no direct injury to the plaintiff, unless he can prove that the originator desired and intended the publication which has produced the damage. (*Whitney* v. *Moignard,* 24 Q. B. D. 630 ; 59 L. J. Q. B. 824 ; 6 Times L. R. 274.)

With a libel, however, the case is different. Whenever more persons than one are concerned in the same publication, the plaintiff may sue all or any of them in the same action. Thus, where the libel has appeared in a newspaper, he can always join as defendants in the same action the proprietor, the editor, the printer, and the publisher, or so many of them as he thinks fit. But where there are two distinct and separate publications, even of the same libel, one by A. and the other by B., separate actions must, as a rule, be brought. (*Sadler* v. *Gt. W. Ry. Co.,* [1896] A. C. 450; 65 L. J. Q. B. 462; 45 W. R. 51; 74 L. T. 561; but see *Compania Sansinena, &c.* v. *Houlder Brothers & Co., Ltd.,* [1910] 2 K. B. 354, *post,* p. 605). The plaintiff is not now, and never was, obliged to join as a defendant every person who is liable. He may, if he prefer, sue only one or two ; and the liability of the others will be no defence for those sued, and will not mitigate the damages recoverable. (*Ante,* p. 397.) But the judgment against these is a bar to any subsequent action on the same publication against anyone else who was jointly liable with them ; for all persons engaged in a common wrongful act are liable jointly and severally for the consequent damage. (Co. Lit. 232 a ; 1 Wms. Saund. 291 f ; *Sutton* v. *Clarke,* 6 Taunt. 29.) The non-joinder of a defendant in an action of tort never was any ground of objection ; the present defendant could not plead either in abatement or in bar that another joint wrong-doer had not been made a co-defendant. (*Mitchell* v. *Tarbutt and others,* 5 T. R. 649 ; *Ansell* v. *Waterhouse,* 6 M. & S. 385.) So, too, the misjoinder of one defendant will not avail the others ; it will only entitle the defendant misjoined to a verdict in his favour. (*Morrow* v. *Belcher and others,* 4 B. & C. 704 ; *Govett* v. *Radnidge and others,* 3 East, 62 ; *Bretherton and others* v. *Wood,* 3 B. & B. 54.) But the plaintiff will have to pay the costs of the defendant who is proved to be not liable, unless such defendant has colluded with the other defendant found to be liable, or has otherwise been guilty of misconduct. (See *Bullock* v. *L. G. O. Co.*, [1907] 1 K. B. 264; 76 L. J. K. B. 127; 96 L. T. 905.)

The plaintiff can only bring one action in respect of the same publication; he cannot recover twice over from different defendants the same damages for the same injury. He may sue one or more or all of the joint publishers in his one action, at his election; but as soon as he recovers judgment in the first action, everyone else who was jointly liable is released. No second action can be brought on that publication against anyone who might have been sued in the first action, but was not (*Brown* v. *Wootton*, Cro. Jac. 73; Yelv. 67; Moo. 762; *Duke of Brunswick* v. *Pepper*, 2 C. & K. 683; *Brinsmead* v. *Harrison*, L. R. 7 C. P. 547; 41 L. J. C. P. 190; 20 W. R. 784; 27 L. T. 99); even though the plaintiff was not then aware that such other person was liable. (*Munster* v. *Cox*, 10 App. Cas. 680; 55 L. J. Q. B. 108; 34 W. R. 461; 53 L. T. 474.)

In cases where a libel has been written or printed by one man at the direction of another, it is often wise to sue the person who actually wrote or printed the libel, as well as his master or employer. For, if this be done, although the plaintiff may fail to prove agency at the trial, he will yet be entitled to judgment against the writer or printer.

Where a libel has appeared in a newspaper, the person defamed can, as we have seen, sue the proprietor, the editor, the printer, and the publisher, or any one or more of them. If the action be originally brought against the publisher only, a Master at chambers will subsequently, on proper terms, join the proprietor as a co-defendant. (*Edward* v. *Lowther*, 45 L. J. C. P. 417; 24 W. R. 434; 34 L. T. 255.) The plaintiff, however, generally and naturally prefers to sue the author. Hence his solicitor frequently writes to the editor of the paper before issuing the writ, demanding the writer's name and address. This information the editor will, as a rule, refuse to give. Editors generally regard it as a point of honour not to disclose the name of any contributor. In *Hibbins* v. *Lee*, 11 L. T. 541, Cockburn, C.J., expressed his opinion that an editor ought always to give up the name of the writer where the libel is not confined to public matters, but reflects on the private character of the plaintiff. " At all events, if he does not choose to do so, he must be content to stand in the shoes of the writer, and to take the consequences." On the other hand, in *Harle* v. *Catherall and others*, 14 L. T. 802, Martin, B., said, " When a man went to an editor to ask for the name of an anonymous correspondent, no blame attached to the editor for refusing to give the name. Indeed, an editor would almost be mad to do so. He should blame no editor for so refusing." If the plaintiff be met with such a refusal, he must be content to sue the proprietor of the paper, who generally obtains an indemnity from the writer. And the plaintiff cannot, in such action, compel the proprietor to produce the original manuscript so that he may recognise the handwriting. (*British and Foreign Contract Co.* v. *Wright,* 32 W. R. 413 ; *Hope* v. *Brash,* [1897] 2 Q. B. 188 ; 66 L. J. Q. B. 653 ; 45 W. R. 659 ; 76 L. T. 823, *post,* p. 654.) Nor can he, in the absence of special circumstances, interrogate the proprietor or editor as to the name of the author. (*Hennessy* v. *Wright* (No. 2), 24 Q. B. D. 445, n. ; 36 W. R. 879 ; *Gibson* v. *Evans,* 23 Q. B. D. 384 ; 58 L. J. Q. B. 612 ; 61 L. T. 388 ; *Edmondson* v. *Birch & Co., Ltd.,* [1905] 2 K. B. 523 ; 74 L. J. K. B. 777 ; 54 W. R. 52 ; 93 L. T. 462.) The printer of a libel, on the other hand, will generally disclose the name of his employer ; there is no reason why he should not ; and see the statute 39 Geo. III. c. 79, s. 29, which provides that the printer must for six calendar months carefully preserve at least one copy of each paper printed by him, and write thereon the name and address of the person who employed and paid him to print it. (See *ante,* p. 12.) As to election placards, see 46 & 47 Vict. c. 51, s. 18.

Joinder of Causes of Action.

The Judicature Act permits a plaintiff to join on one writ any number of causes of action, provided they be all between the same parties. But as a rule, in cases of libel and slander, the plaintiff should not avail himself of this power. Defamation is a matter *sui generis,* and it would be imprudent to complicate the issue by joining irrelevant claims. Any number of libels or slanders published by the same defendant of the same plaintiff may be and ought to be included in the same action. So may a claim for malicious prosecution, or wrongful dismissal, or even assault, between the same parties ; but such joinder would only be advisable if all such causes of action arose out of the same circumstances, and would be substantiated by the same witnesses as the claim for libel or slander.

A claim by a plaintiff A. cannot be joined with a separate claim by a plaintiff B. even against the same defendant, unless the case falls within Order XVI. r. 1, as to which see *ante,* p. 600. It was till recently clear law that a claim for libel or slander by a plaintiff against one defendant X. could never be joined with a separate claim by the same plaintiff against another defendant Y. (*Sadler* v. *Gt. W. Ry. Co.*, [1896] A. C. 450 ; 65 L. J. Q. B. 462 ; 45 W. R. 51 ; 74 L. T. 561 ; *Thompson* v. *London County Council*, [1899] 1 Q. B. 840 ; 68 L. J. Q. B. 625 ; 47 W. R. 433 ; 80 L. T. 512.) But it has now been held by the Court of Appeal that there is power under Order XVI. r. 4, to join several defendants in the same action for the purpose of claiming relief against them severally or in the alternative, and that this power is not confined to cases in which the causes of action alleged against the several defendants are identical, but extends to all cases in which the subject-matter of complaint against the several defendants is substantially the same, although the respective causes of action against them are different in form, and their respective liabilities are to some extent based on different grounds. (*Bullock* v. *L. G. O. Co.*, [1907] 1 K. B. 264 ; 76 L. J. K. B. 127 ; 96 L. T. 905 ; *Compania Sansinena de Carnes Congeladas* v. *Houlder Brothers & Co., Ltd.*, [1910] 2 K. B. 354.) It was thought apparently that the alteration made in 1896 in the wording of Order XVI. r. 1, which only applies to plaintiffs, had in some way rendered incorrect the construction placed by the House of Lords in *Sadler's Case* upon r. 4 of the same Order, which applies only to defendants, and which remains unaltered. Nevertheless, the decision in *Gower* v. *Couldridge*, [1898] 1 Q. B. 348 ; 67 L. J. Q. B. 251 ; 46 W. R. 214 ; 77 L. T. 707, appears to be overruled, and probably also that in *Pope* v. *Hawtrey*, (1901) 85 L. T. 263 ; 17 Times L. R. 717.

Special provision has been made for cases of husband and wife, and for persons jointly interested. Before the Common Law Procedure Act, 1852, if a wife was libelled or slandered and the husband sustained special damage in consequence, two actions had to be brought, one by the husband and wife jointly for the injury to her reputation, and a second by the husband alone to recover the special damage which he had personally sustained. (See *ante*, p. 569.) But now by Order XVIII. r. 4, claims by or against husband and wife may be joined with claims by or against either of them separately. Again, before the Judicature Act if a firm was libelled and one partner suffered separate special damage he had to bring a separate action for this special damage ; he could not recover it in an action brought by the firm, although in that action he was a necessary plaintiff. (See *ante*, p. 590.) But now by Order XVIII. r. 6, " claims by plaintiffs jointly may be joined with claims by them, or any of them, separately against the same defendant." It will be observed, however, that this rule applies only to joinder of claims by plaintiffs.

All the above cases are subject to rr. 1, 8, 9, of Order XVIII., which provide that if a plaintiff unites in the same action several causes of action which cannot be conveniently tried or disposed of together, a master or district registrar, on the application of the defendant, may order any of such causes of action to be excluded, and consequential amendments to be made.

Illustration.

The plaintiff was engaged by H. to act at a theatre, of which D. was lessee and manager. In an action brought by him against H. and D. in respect of an alleged slander spoken by one defendant on one occasion and by the other defendant on another occasion, and also in respect of an alleged conspiracy between them wrongfully to dismiss him from his employment : Held, that these claims could not be joined in one action.

> *Pope* v. *Hawtrey and another,* (1901) 85 L. T. 263 ; 17 Times L. R. 717.
> Overruling *Dessilla* v. *Schunok & Co.and Fels & Co.,* W. N. 1880, p. 96.

Jurisdiction.

The next question is, has the Court which the plaintiff wishes to select, jurisdiction over his cause of action. Want of jurisdiction may arise from two distinct causes. (i) The Court may have no power to try that class of action. (ii) The defendant may be outside the geographical area over which the Court can exercise its powers.

(i) *Choice of Court.*

The County Court has no jurisdiction in actions of libel or slander, except by consent of both parties (County Courts Act, 1888 (51 & 52 Vict. c. 43), ss. 56, 64) ; although an action commenced in the High Court may subsequently be remitted to the County Court under s. 66 of that Act. (See *post,* p. 618.)

Many inferior Courts of Record, such as the Mayor's Court, London, Liverpool Court of Passage, the Salford Hundred Court and the Tolzey Court of Bristol, can try actions of libel or slander. But in the absence of any express statutory provision to the contrary, it is necessary that the whole cause of action should arise within the limits of the territorial jurisdiction of such inferior Court. Hence, if the words be actionable *per se,* they must be published within the territorial jurisdiction; if they are not actionable without proof of special damage, both the publication and the accrual of special damage must take place within the limits of such jurisdiction. (*Littleboy* v. *Wright*, 1 Lev. 69; 1 Sid. 95.) A letter is deemed to be published both where it is posted and where it is received and opened. (*R.* v. *Burdett*, 4 B. & Ald. 95.)

The High Court of Justice has jurisdiction over all libels and slanders published within its territorial jurisdiction; and also over all libels and slanders published abroad, provided proceedings either civil or criminal can be taken for the publication of such words in the country in which they were published. (*Machado* v. *Fontes*, [1897] 2 Q. B. 231; 66 L. J. Q. B. 542; 45 W. R. 565; 76 L. T. 588; *Carr* v. *Fracis Times & Co.*, [1902] A. C. 176; 71 L. J. K. B. 361; 50 W. R. 257; 85 L. T. 144.) The writ should be issued in the King's Bench Division. Although the Chancery Division has jurisdiction to hear a case of libel or slander (*Lord Kinnaird* v. *Field*, [1905] 2 Ch. 361; 74 L. J. Ch. 692; 54 W. R. 85; 93 L. T. 190), such an action is rarely tried there, as no cases are tried in that Division with a jury. An injunction can be obtained as readily in one Division as the other.

If the defendant be an undergraduate resident within the University of Oxford or Cambridge, he must be sued in the University Court, although the plaintiff be in·no way connected with the University or resident within its limits, and although the libels complained of appeared in several London newspapers. (*Ginnett* v. *Whittingham*, 16 Q. B. D. 761; 55 L. J. Q. B. 409; 34 W. R. 565.)

(ii) *Service of Writ out of Jurisdiction.*

In actions in the High Court there remains the further question, Is the proposed defendant within jurisdiction so that he can be served with the process of the Court? If he is, it does not matter whether he is a British subject or an alien. But if he is not, leave must be obtained from a judge of the High Court to serve the writ or notice of it, out of jurisdiction. Such leave must be applied for before the writ is issued; and it will only be granted in the cases specified under Order XI., which forms a complete and exhaustive code upon this subject. (*In re Eager, Eager* v. *Johnstone*, 22 Ch. D. 86; 52 L. J. Ch. 56; 31 W. R. 33; 47 L. T. 685.)

This Order greatly limits the powers formerly possessed by the Court; it practically prevents any action being brought here for damages for any libel or slander published abroad, and also for any libel or slander published here by a person ordinarily resident abroad, unless he happens to come to England, so that personal service can be effected. And if the words be spoken out of jurisdiction, the fact that they incidentally affect property within jurisdiction is not sufficient to bring the case within Order XI. (*Casey* v. *Arnott,* 2 C. P. D. 24 ; 46 L. J. C. P. 3 ; 25 W. R. 46 ; 35 L. T. 424.)

If two or more persons carry on business together in partnership within the jurisdiction under a firm name, they may, by virtue of Order XLVIIIA. r. 1, be sued here under that firm name without leave, although all the partners reside out of jurisdiction. (*Worcester Banking Co.* v. *Firbank, Pauling & Co.,* [1894] 1 Q. B. 784 ; 63 L. J. Q. B. 542 ; *MacIver* v. *Burns,* [1895] 2 Ch. 630 ; 64 L. J. Ch. 681.) But if one man carries on business within jurisdiction, whether in his own name or under any other style or firm, he cannot be sued here if he reside abroad. (*Field* v. *Bennett,* 56 L. J. Q. B. 89 ; *De Bernales* v. *New York Herald,* [1893] 2 Q. B. 97, n. ; 62 L. J. Q. B. 385 ; 41 W. R. 481 ; 68 L. T. 658 ; *De Bernales* v. *Bennett,* (1894) 10 Times L. R. 419.) A foreign company may be sued here if it carries on business so as to be resident within the jurisdiction (*La Bourgogne,* [1899] A. C. 431 ; 68 L. J. P. 104 ; 80 L. T. 845 ; 8 Asp. M. C. 550) ; but the mere fact that it has a branch office in this country will not entitle a plaintiff to serve a writ at the branch office. (*Jones* v. *Scottish Accident Insurance Co., Limited,* 17 Q. B. D. 421 ; 55 L. J. Q. B. 415 ; 55 L. T. 218 ; *O'Connor* v. *Star Newspaper Co., Limited,* 30 L. R. Ir. 1.) And there can be no substituted service of a writ in an action in which there cannot in law be personal service. (*Field* v. *Bennett,* 56 L. J. Q. B. 89 ; *Wilding* v. *Bean,* [1891] 1 Q. B. 100 ; 60 L. J. Q. B. 10 ; 39 W. R. 40 ; 64 L. T. 41 ; *Jay* v. *Budd,* [1898] 1 Q. B. 12 ; 66 L. J. Q. B. 863 ; 46 W. R. 34 ; 77 L. T. 335.)

In actions of libel or slander leave will only be granted under Order XI. if the case falls within one or other of clauses (c), (f), (g), of r. 1 of that Order. The plaintiff may obtain leave under Order XI. r. 1 (f) if he adds a claim for an injunction on his writ. (*Tozier and wife* v. *Hawkins,* 15 Q. B. D. 650, 680 ; 55 L. J. Q. B. 152 ; 34 W. R. 223.) If the plaintiff has claimed an injunction on his writ, he may obtain leave to serve it out of jurisdiction under clause (f) ; but the judge has a discretion in the matter, and must at least be satisfied that the claim for an injunction is made in good faith, and that there is a reasonable probability that an injunction will be granted. (*Watson & Sons* v. *Daily Record (Glasgow) Limited,* [1907] 1 K. B. 853 ; 76 L. J. K. B. 448 ; 96 L. T. 485.) It has been held that it is not necessary that he should ask for an injunction only ; he may claim other relief as well. (*Lisbon-Berlyn Gold Fields, Limited* v. *Heddle*, 52 L. T. 796.) But the judge at chambers, when granting leave to serve the writ out of jurisdiction, may, if he think fit, limit the plaintiff to that portion of his claim in respect of which it shall appear at the trial that the writ could have been properly served out of jurisdiction. (*Thomas* v. *Duchess Dowager of Hamilton*, 17 Q. B. D. 592 ; 55 L. J. Q. B. 555 ; 35 W. R. 22 ; 55 L. T. 219, 385.) As to clause (g), where the writ has already been duly served on a defendant within jurisdiction, leave will be given in a proper case to serve another defendant who is outside jurisdiction, provided he be a necessary and proper party to the action. (*Croft* v. *King*, [1893] 1 Q. B. 419 ; 62 L. J. Q. B. 242 ; 41 W. R. 394 ; 68 L. T. 296 ; *Williams* v. *Cartwright and others*, [1895] 1 Q. B. 142 ; 64 L. J. Q. B. 92 ; 43 W. R. 145 ; 71 L. T. 834 ; *Chance* v. *Beveridge and Freeman's Journal*, (1895) 11 Times L. R. 528 ; *Joynt* v. *M'Crum*, [1899] 1 Ir. R. 217.) The Court will, in a proper case, give leave for the issue of a concurrent writ for service out of jurisdiction, although the original writ was issued for service within jurisdiction. (*Smalpage* v. *Tonge*, 17 Q. B. D. 644 ; 55 L. J. Q. B. 518 ; 34 W. R. 768 ; 55 L. T. 44.)

Statutes of Limitation.

It is seldom that a plaintiff in an action of defamation allows his remedy to be barred by lapse of time. He is generally too eager to commence proceedings, and will not wait till his special damage has fully accrued. (See *Ingram* v. *Lawson*, 6 Bing. N. C. 212 ; 8 Scott, 471 ; 9 C. & P. 326 ; 4 Jur. 151 ; *Goslin* v. *Corry*, 7 M. & Gr. 342 ; 8 Scott, N. R. 21.) Still, the Duke of Brunswick waited nearly eighteen years ; it may be as well, therefore, to state that an action of slander for words actionable *per se* must be brought " within two years next after the words spoken, and not after " (21 Jac. I. c. 16, s. 3), and that an action for libel must be brought " within six years next after the cause of such action," *i.e.*, from the date of publication. Whenever the words are actionable only by reason of special damage, the time does not begin to run till the damage has actually been sustained. (*Saunders* v. *Edwards*, 1 Sid. 95 ; 1 Keble, 389 ; Sir Thos. Raym. 61 ; *Littleboy* v. *Wright*, 1 Lev. 69 ; 1 Sid. 95 ; cf. *Darley Main Colliery Co.* v. *Mitchell*, 11 App. Cas. 127 ; 55 L. J. Q. B. 529 ; 54 L. T. 882 ; *West Leigh Colliery Company, Ltd.* v. *Tunnicliffe and Hampson, Ltd.*, [1908] A. C. 27.) And then the plaintiff has six years within which to sue and not merely *two*, for as the case is taken

out of the clause " within two years next after the words spoken,"
it must fall within the general clause as to actions on the case.
(*Saunders* v. *Edwards, suprà.*) In all other cases time runs from the
date of publication ; unless the plaintiff be then an infant or a
lunatic or the defendant be beyond the seas, when time begins to run
from the infant coming of age, or the lunatic becoming of sane
memory, or the defendant returning from beyond the seas. (21 Jac. I.
c. 16, s. 7 ; 4 & 5 Anne, c. 3 (al. c. 16), s. 19 ; 3 & 4 Will. IV. c. 42,
s. 7 ; 19 & 20 Vict. c. 97, ss. 10, 12.) But if once such disability be
removed and the time begin to run, nothing afterwards can stop it.

A still shorter period of limitation exists in cases to which the
Public Authorities Protection Act, 1893 (56 & 57 Vict. c. 61), applies.
If an action be brought against " any person " for any defamatory
words published " in pursuance or execution or intended execution
of any Act of Parliament, or of any public duty or authority," the
action must be commenced " within six months next after the act
complained of, or in case of a continuance of injury or damage,
within six months next after the ceasing thereof." (See *Reid* v.
Blisland School Board, (1901) 17 Times L. R. 626 ; *Carey* v. *Metropolitan Borough of Bermondsey,* (1903) 20 Times L. R. 2.) But it
would seem that an individual member of a public authority has no
such protection if an action be brought against him in respect of
words spoken in the intended execution of his duty. (*Royal
Aquarium* v. *Parkinson,* [1892] 1 Q. B. 431 ; 61 L. J. Q. B. 409 ; 40
W. R. 450 ; 66 L. T. 513.)

But the publication relied on to oust the statute need not be the
original or substantial publication. Thus, if any agent of the plaintiff can induce the defendant to sell him an old copy of the libel,
published many years ago, such second publication, although contrived by the plaintiff for the very purpose, will be sufficient to
disprove the plea of the Statute of Limitations. And that plea
being once ousted, the jury will not be confined, it is said, to that
single publication within the six years but may take all the circumstances into their consideration. (*Duke of Brunswick* v. *Harmer,*
14 Q. B. 185 ; 19 L. J. Q. B. 20 ; 14 Jur. 110 ; 3 C. & K. 10.)

Former Proceedings.

Where the words are actionable *per se,* the fact that a previous
action has already been brought and judgment recovered is a bar to
any subsequent action against the same defendant based on the
same publication even although fresh damage has since arisen

therefrom. For the jury in the former action must be taken to have assessed the damages once for all; and the probability or possibility that this subsequent damage would follow should have been submitted to their consideration then.

It was formerly thought that this was also the law when the words were not actionable *per se*. But in the closely analogous case of successive subsidences of the surface caused by underground workings which were not in themselves actionable, the contrary rule has now been clearly laid down. " Those who are so interfered with may bring actions as often as a fresh subsidence takes place and their enjoyment of their property is so interfered with . . . . An owner can bring a fresh action for the damage caused by each fresh subsidence, but he cannot recover anything for the risk of future damage." (Per Lord Ashbourne in *West Leigh Colliery Co., Ltd.* v. *Tunnicliffe and Hampson, Ltd.*, [1908] A. C. at pp. 31, 32.) It is submitted, therefore, that, where the words are not actionable *per se*, a fresh action can be brought whenever fresh special damage results from the publication of the words. Should the first action be still pending when the fresh damage accrues, the plaintiff can issue a second writ and apply, if he thinks fit, to have the two actions consolidated as was done in *Martin* v. *Martin & Co.*, [1897] 1 Q. B. 429; 66 L. J. Q. B. 241; 45 W. R. 260; 76 L. T. 44, see *post*, p. 620.

Judgment in a former action will be no bar to a subsequent action, unless it is clear that the cause of action is the same in both cases. Where in the first action the plaintiff sued for words imputing a felony, and in the second for words spoken of the plaintiff in the way of his trade, the Court held that recovery in the first action was no bar to the second. (*Wadsworth* v. *Bentley*, 23 L. J. Q. B. 3; 17 Jur. 1077; L. & M. 203.) But where a plaintiff brought an action on certain passages in a pamphlet which he alleged to contain libellous charges against himself, and failed, he was not allowed to bring a second action against the same defendants for other passages in the same pamphlet which expressed the same charges in other language. (*MacDougall* v. *Knight*, 25 Q. B. D. 1; 59 L. J. Q. B. 517; 38 W. R. 553; 63 L. T. 43. And see *Montgomery* v. *Russell*, (1894) 11 Times L. R. 112; *Le Mesurier* v. *Ferguson and another*, (1903) 20 Times L. R. 32.) And where a defendant admitted in one action publication and that the words were defamatory, and in a second action based on another publication of the same words pleaded that they were fair comment on a matter of public interest and privileged, it was held he was not estopped from setting up these defences. (*Mangena* v. *Wright* [1909] 2 K. B. at p. 975.)

So, too, a previous recovery against another person may be a bar
to the present action, if the former defendant was jointly concerned
with the present defendant in the very publication now sued on.
Thus, if A. and B. be in partnership, either as printers or
publishers of a newspaper, a previous judgment recovered against
A. will be a bar to any action against B. for the same libel, even
though the judgment in the prior action has been fruitless.*
(*Brown* v. *Wootton*, Cro. Jac. 73 ; Yelv. 67 ; Moo. 762 ;
King v. *Hoare*, 13 M. & W. 494, 504 ; *Duke of Brunswick* v. *Pepper*, 2 C. & K. 683 ; *Brinsmead* v. *Harrison*, L. R. 7
C. P. 547 ; 41 L. J. C. P. 190 ; 20 W. R. 784 ; 27 L. T.
99 ; *Munster* v. *Cox*, 10 App. Cas. 680 ; 53 L. T. 474.) For both
ought to have been sued jointly in the first action. But where two are
severally liable, judgment against one is no bar to an action against
the other. Thus, a previous judgment against the proprietor of a
newspaper, even though satisfied, is no bar to an action for the
same libel against the author. (*Frescoe* v. *May*, 2 F. & F. 123.)
À fortiori, the fact that damages have been recovered against one
newspaper is no bar to an action against another newspaper which
has published the same libel ; although the defendant may give
evidence of such previous recovery in mitigation of damages, by
virtue of sect. 6 of the Law of Libel Amendment Act, 1888, *ante*,
p. 397.

That criminal proceedings have already been taken by way of
indictment for the same libel is no bar to an action, whether the
prisoner was acquitted or convicted (*Peacock* v. *Reynal*, 2 Brownlow
& Goldesborough, 151 ; 16 M. & W. 825, n.) ; but it is inadvisable
to bring such an action in either case, except under very special
circumstances. If the former criminal proceedings were taken
by way of criminal information, then if the rule *nisi* has been made
absolute, clearly no civil action can be brought (*R.* v. *Sparrow*,
2 T. R. 198) ; and probably not if the rule was discharged on
showing cause, all the old Courts at Westminster being now merged
in the High Court of Justice (*Wakley* v. *Cooke and another*, 16
M. & W. 822 ; 16 L. J. Ex. 225) ; unless the Court thought a
civil action the more appropriate remedy, and discharged the rule
in order that civil proceedings might be taken. (*Ex parte Hoare*,
23 L. T. 83.)

---

* In America, it seems, no judgment against another will be a bar, unless
it be satisfied. (*Lovejoy* v. *Murray*, 3 Wallace (Supr. Ct.) 1 ; *Thomas*
v. *Rumsey*, 6 Johns. (N. Y.) 26 ; *Brown* v. *Hirley*, 5 Upper Canada Q. B.
Rep. (Old S.) 734 ; *Breslin* v. *Peck*, 38 Hun (45 N. Y. Supr. Ct.), 623.)

Letter before Action.

In the absence of any special Act of Parliament, it is not necessary for a plaintiff to serve any intended defendant with a formal notice of action. (See the Public Authorities Protection Act, 1893 (56 & 57 Vict. c. 61), s. 2, and *Royal Aquarium* v. *Parkinson,* [1892] 1 Q. B. 431; 61 L. J. Q. B. 409; 40 W. R. 450; 66 L. T. 513.) But in all cases, before actually issuing a writ, the plaintiff's solicitor should write to the defendant, demanding an apology and threatening proceedings if no apology be forthcoming. Nothing should be said in this letter about costs. If the charge was made publicly, a public apology should be demanded, to be advertised in a newspaper. If only a few heard it, the plaintiff should be content with a letter of apology, fully retracting the charge, which can be shown to everyone who heard what the defendant said.

Indorsement on Writ.

In actions of defamation the writ is always generally indorsed. In actions of slander it is enough to say " The plaintiff's claim is for damages for slander." But in an action of libel more details must now be given on the writ.

A rule made in 1903 requires that "in actions for libel the indorsement on the writ shall state sufficient particulars to identify the publications in respect of which the action is brought." (Order III. r. 9.) And a form of indorsement is given in Appendix A. Part III. sect. iv. of the R. S. C.: " The plaintiff's claim is for damages for libel contained in [*state sufficient particulars to identify the publications*]." If the plaintiff also desires to claim an injunction, the words "and for an injunction " should be added. As to an application for an *interim* injunction, see *ante,* p. 426.

Matters to be considered by the Defendant.

At the first hint of legal proceedings, the defendant should consider the advisability of apologising. If he is in the wrong, he ought to admit it at once. In the case of a newspaper, it is particularly desirable that this question should be dealt with at the earliest moment, in order that the apology, if any, may be published in the next issue of the paper.

A prompt apology will often put an end to the action. It is very difficult for the plaintiff to disregard it; if he does, the sympathies of judge and jury will probably be with the defendant, and it may assist to reduce materially the amount of damages. But such apology must be frank and full. A guarded, half-hearted apology will only injure the defendant's position. It is no use to publish a paragraph expressing astonishment at the receipt of a lawyer's letter and attempting to explain away or minimise an imputation clearly made. It is still worse to assert, as is sometimes done, that the defendant has done the plaintiff a kindness in making a false charge against him, as it "has afforded him an opportunity of publicly denying it." (See the remark of Mellor, J., L. R. 1 Q. B. 701.) A mere correction is not an apology. A so-called apology is not an apology at all, unless it unreservedly withdraws all imputations and expresses regret for having made any. If defendant apologises at all, he should do so freely and handsomely, as well as promptly.

Whether he has apologised or not, defendant should enter an appearance to the writ. He should not allow judgment to go by default, unless he is utterly and hopelessly in the wrong, and at the same time there is no hope of a compromise. If he has no defence, he should apologise and pay money into Court as amends. This he can do at any stage of the action; and the earlier it is done, the better for the defendant. He can give the plaintiff the notice in Form No. 3, Appendix B., referred to in Order XXII. r. 4. In most cases it is idle to pay into Court a contemptuous sum, such as a farthing or a shilling; it should be at least 40s.

If, however, the action is one that should be fought, the defendant should consider whether the plaintiff has properly shaped his claim. It may be that too many plaintiffs or defendants have been added (see *ante*, pp. 599, 601); or necessary parties may have been omitted. If in the same action claims by the plaintiffs jointly be combined with claims by them or any of them separately, the defendant may apply to have them severed, on the ground that they cannot be conveniently disposed of in the same action. (Order XVIII. rr. 1, 7, 8, 9.) That the plaintiff is an outlaw is ground for staying proceedings. (See *R.* v. *Lowe and Clements*, 8 Exch. 697; 22 L. J. Ex. 262; *Somers* v. *Holt*, 3 Dowl. 506; and 42 & 43 Vict. c. 59, s. 3.) Or if two or more actions be brought by the same plaintiff for the same libel, the defendants may apply to have them consolidated. (See *post*, p. 620.)

Writ of Inquiry.

If the defendant fails to appear to the writ, the plaintiff must file an affidavit of due service (Order XIII. r. 2), and he will then be entitled to sign interlocutory judgment, and a writ of inquiry will issue to the sheriff bidding him summon a jury to assess the damages, unless some other method of assessment be ordered by the Master. (*Ib.*, r. 5.) As there is no Statement of Claim, the plaintiff should give the defendant formal notice a reasonable time before the hearing that he intends to offer before the under-sheriff evidence of such and such special damage. Or under the amended rule 5 of 1902 the Master may now order a Statement of Claim or particulars to be filed before any assessment of damages, although the defendant has not appeared. Similarly, a writ of inquiry will issue if defendant does not deliver any Defence. (Order XXVII. r. 4.) The inquiry is conducted in the same way as a trial at Nisi Prius: the only difference is that the plaintiff *must* recover some damages, though as a rule he does not recover such heavy damages from a sheriff's jury as after a full trial at Nisi Prius. Rules 14, 15, 19, 34, 35, 36 and 37 of Order XXXVI. apply to an inquiry. The plaintiff need not adduce any evidence at all, but merely put in the libel. And the jury will not in such a case be bound to give him nominal damages only. (*Tripp* v. *Thomas*, 3 B. & C. 427; 1 C. & P. 477.) As to costs, see *ante*, p. 452. If the defendant desires to have the damages reduced, he must move for a new trial within the prescribed time. (See *Chattell* v. *Daily Mail Publishing Co., Limited*, (1901) 18 Times L. R. 165.)

Summons for Directions.

The writ being generally indorsed and the defendant having appeared, it is now the duty of the plaintiff to take out a summons for directions under Order XXX. This he must do, as a rule, before taking any other step in the action; and he must do so within fourteen days after appearance; otherwise the defendant will be entitled to apply to have the action dismissed. If, as usually happens, the Master declines to dismiss the action, he may yet on this application by the defendant give directions for its further conduct, as if it were a summons for directions (r. 8).

On either of these summonses the Court or a judge (which phrase usually means a Master) may make such order as may be just with respect to all the proceedings in the action from appearance till trial. The following are the directions most usually given :—

(i) *Pleadings.*—In actions of libel and slander, the Master invariably orders Pleadings. The precise words are material. (Order XIX. r. 21.)

(ii) *Particulars.*—If any allegation in any pleading is couched in such general terms that it does not give the other party detailed information to which he is entitled, the Master will order particulars. (See *post*, p. 629.)

(iii) *Security for Costs.*—If the plaintiff ordinarily resides out of the jurisdiction, he may be ordered to give security for costs, though he may be temporarily within the jurisdiction. (Order LXV. r. 6, *a.*) But no such order will be made if the plaintiff resides in Scotland or Ireland, or is abroad in an official capacity in the public service, or has substantial property within the jurisdiction on which execution can be levied ; nor if there is a co-plaintiff who resides in England. The mere fact that the plaintiff is insolvent (*Le Mesurier* v. *Ferguson and another*, (1903) 20 Times L. R. 32), or is a married woman, is not sufficient ground for ordering security.

(iv) *Remitting the Action to the County Court.*—See *post*, p. 618.

(v) *Consolidation of Actions.*—See *post*, p. 619.

(vi) *Stay of Proceedings.*—The Master has power to stay all proceedings, if the action is frivolous and vexatious (see Order XXV. r. 4), or if the plaintiff's mode of conducting the action is oppressive and vexatious, or if he has not paid the costs of a previous action brought on the same cause of action. But the mere fact that a plaintiff has not paid costs which he was ordered to pay upon an interlocutory application in the present action, is not a ground for staying proceedings in the action, if the plaintiff really is unable to pay them. (*Graham* v. *Sutton, Carden & Co.* (No. 2), [1897] 2 Ch. 367 ; 66 L. J. Ch. 666 ; 77 L. T. 35.) If the alleged libel was published by order of either House of Parliament, all proceedings will be stayed at once on production of a certificate to that effect by the Clerk of the House, with an affidavit verifying such certificate. (3 & 4 Vict. c. 9.)

(vii) *Evidence.*—It is on this summons, too, that the Master allows interrogatories (see *post*, p. 654) or grants discovery of documents (*post*, p. 649). He may in a proper case order that the evidence of some person abroad be taken under letters of request or on commission (*post*, p. 670), or that a witness who is dangerously ill or about to go abroad, be examined here before the trial under Order XXXVII. r. 5 ; or that a copy of an entry in a banker's book be supplied under the Bankers' Books Evidence Act, 1879 (*post*, p. 669).

(viii) *Place of Trial.*—The place of trial is now fixed by the

Master on the summons for directions. (Order XXXVI. r. 1.) He will fix it in the place which he deems least expensive and most convenient for both parties, and the majority of the witnesses on both sides. The plaintiff has no longer a preponderating voice in the matter; he has no *primâ facie* right to have the trial fixed in the place that best suits himself and his witnesses. Where the cause of action arose has now but little to do with the question. Where the defendant resides is equally immaterial. But if either party can satisfy the Master that he will not have a fair trial in the place which seems naturally most convenient (*e.g.*, because his opponent is especially popular or powerful in that neighbourhood), the Master will fix on some other place where he is sure the jury will be impartial.

(ix) *Time of Trial.*—The Master cannot compel a defendant, who is not in default and is not asking for any indulgence himself, to take short notice of trial. (*Laskier* v. *Tekeian*, (1892) 67 L. T. 121.) But if an action is to be tried at the Assizes he may direct that it shall not be tried before the third, fourth, or fifth day of the Assizes, and order the defendant to accept ten days' notice of trial for the day so fixed. (*Baxter* v. *Holdsworth*, [1899] 1 Q. B. 266; 68 L. J. Q. B. 154; 47 W. R. 179; 79 L. T. 434.)

(x) *Mode of Trial.*—In actions of libel or slander, the Master almost invariably orders trial by a judge with a jury. It is always best to have a jury in such actions, and, as a rule, both parties desire one. " Libel or no libel, since Fox's Act, is of all questions peculiarly one for a jury." (Per Lord Coleridge, C.J., in *Saxby* v. *Easterbrook*, 3 C. P. D. at p. 342.) It is true that Fox's Act applies in terms only to criminal proceedings. But it laid down no new principle; the procedure which it rendered imperative in criminal cases was already, before that enactment, the invariable rule in all civil cases, and has remained so ever since: it had, in earlier days, been the rule in criminal cases also. As Littledale, J., says in *Baylis* v. *Lawrence* (11 A. & E. at p. 925), " Although that Act applied more particularly to criminal cases, yet I know no distinction between the law in criminal cases and that in civil, in this respect. Therefore that which has been declared to be law in criminal cases is the law in civil cases." " Fox's Act was only declaratory of the common law." (Per Brett, L.J., in *Capital and Counties Bank* v. *Henty*, 5 C. P. D. at p. 539.) And see *Parmiter* v. *Coupland*, 6 M. & W. at p. 108.

Either party may obtain a special jury. But the application must be made in good time. (See *post*, p. 670.)

Remitting the Action to the County Court.

By virtue of sect. 66 of the County Courts Act, 1888 (51 & 52 Vict. c. 43), any person against whom an action of tort is brought in the High Court may make an affidavit that the plaintiff has no visible means of paying the costs of the defendant should a verdict be not found for the plaintiff; and thereupon a Master of the Supreme Court, if he is satisfied that the plaintiff has no visible means, may make an order that, unless the plaintiff shall, within a time to be therein mentioned, give full security for the defendant's costs to the satisfaction of a Master, or satisfy a Master that he has a cause of action fit to be prosecuted in the High Court, all proceedings in the action shall be stayed, or that the action be remitted for trial to a County Court to be named in the order.

This section applies, although the action be one which could not be commenced in the County Court. (*Stokes* v. *Stokes*, 19 Q. B. D. 62, 419; 56 L. J. Q. B. 494; 36 W. R. 28.) The application can be made at any stage of the action, but only by the defendant; it is usually made before any Defence is delivered. He must make an affidavit, showing that the plaintiff has no visible means, and that there will be a saving of costs and greater convenience in trying in the County Court. The plaintiff must show that the action is more fit to be tried in the High Court than in the County Court. (*Farrer* v. *Lowe*, (1889) 53 J. P. 183; 5 Times L. R. 234; *Banks* v. *Hollingsworth*, [1893] 1 Q. B. 442; 62 L. J. Q. B. 239; 41 W. R. 225; 68 L. T. 477.) No order under the section will be made where grave imputations have been cast on the plaintiff's moral character (*Critchley* v. *Brown*, (1886) 2 Times L. R. 238; *Williams* v. *Morris*, (1894) 10 Times L. R. 603), especially if the defendant has justified his words (*Farrer* v. *Lowe*, *suprà*). Again, no order will be made if the plaintiff can prove that he has visible means of paying costs. By the term "visible means" is intended such means as can be fairly ascertained by a reasonable person in the position of the defendant; not necessarily tangible property such as the defendant could reach in the event of his obtaining judgment for his costs. (*Lea* v. *Parker*, 13 Q. B. D. 835; 54 L. J. Q. B. 38; 33 W. R. 101.) An order will in a proper case be made under this section against a plaintiff who is a married woman, although she cannot be ordered to give security for costs. (*Ante*, p. 569; *Critchley* v. *Brown*, *suprà*.)

If an order be made remitting the action, its effect is practically to transform the action into a County Court cause. As to the further conduct of the action, see *post*, p. 711. It is practically useless for a defendant to appeal from the Master's order. (*Palmer* v. *Roberts*, 22 W. R. 577, n.; 29 L. T. 408.) The plaintiff may appeal, if the order is obviously wrong. (*Jennings and wife* v. *London General Omnibus Co.*, 30 L. T. 266; *Owens* v. *Woosman*, L. R. 3 Q. B. 469; 9 B. & S. 243; 37 L. J. Q. B. 159; *Holmes* v. *Mountstephen*, L. R. 10 C. P. 474; 33 L. T. 351.)

There is a similar provision in the Liverpool Court of Passage Act, 1893, enabling a judge of the High Court in certain cases to remit for trial in the Court of Passage any action of tort which might have been brought in the Court of Passage, but has been brought in the High Court. (56 & 57 Vict. c. 37, s. 4.)

Consolidation of Actions.

" Consolidation is much more rarely applicable than is generally supposed, because the expression is used in cases where the word is really not appropriate at all, as in cases where the trial of one action is stayed pending the hearing of another action. In a case like that the Court will not allow its process to be abused. That is often called ' consolidation,' but it is not really consolidation." (Per Moulton, L.J., in *Lee* v. *Arthur*, (1908) 100 L. T. at p. 62.) There are three distinct cases to be considered :—

(*a*) Where the same persons are plaintiffs and the same persons defendants in all the actions sought to be consolidated.

(*b*) Where the same person is defendant, but there is a different plaintiff in each of the actions sought to be consolidated.

(*c*) Where the same person is plaintiff, but there are different defendants in the various actions.

(*a*) At common law there was always power, at the request of the defendant, to consolidate two or more actions which had been brought by the same plaintiff against the same defendant, either alone or with others for the same words, or for separate publications of similar words, or for two distinct libels or slanders, or for a libel and a slander all arising out of the same transaction and intimately connected with each other. (*Whiteley* v. *Adams*, 15 C. B. N. S. 392; *Jones* v. *Pritchard*, 18 L. J. Q. B. 104; 6 D. & L. 529.) And this practice continues since the Judicature Act and applies in all the Divisions of the High Court. (Order XLIX. r. 8.) An application for consolidation can be made at any time after service of the writs, and without any consent on the plaintiff's part. (*Hollingsworth* v. *Brodrick*, 4 A. & E. 646; 6 N. & M. 240; 1 H. & W. 691.) Before the

Judicature Act, such an order could be obtained only by the defendant; but now a plaintiff may also apply for consolidation; such an application is made under the Summons for Directions. (*Martin* v. *Martin & Co.*, [1897] 1 Q. B. 429; 66 L. J. Q. B. 241; 45 W. R. 260; 76 L. T. 44.)

(*b*) The Court in former days would not consolidate actions brought by several different plaintiffs against the same defendant even for the same libel, as the damage to each plaintiff was not the same. (Cf. *Nicholls* v. *Lefevre*, 3 Dowl. 135; *Westbrook* v. *Australian Mail Co.*, 23 L. J. C. P. 42.) The Judicature Act gave the Court no greater power of consolidating actions than it formerly possessed. (Order XLIX. r. 8.) The cases in which two or more plaintiffs can now join their separate causes of action against the same defendant on one writ have been already discussed (*ante*, p. 600); but it is submitted that even in such cases the Court has no power to order the actions to be consolidated.*

(*c*) Again, until 1888 the Court had no power to intervene where the same plaintiff sued several different defendants for publishing the same libel. Hence, when an error made by one newspaper was copied into many others, the plaintiff was entitled to sue each paper separately, and recover damages and costs in each action. (See *Tucker* v. *Lawson*, (1886) 2 Times L. R. 593.) Where a plaintiff who had already recovered 3,100*l.* damages in actions against three newspapers, brought seventeen more actions against other newspapers who had copied the same libel, the Court refused to make any order for consolidation, the publications being distinct and the circumstances attending each being different. The Court did, however, stay sixteen out of the seventeen actions, on certain terms, till after the trial of the seventeenth. (*Colledge* v. *Pike*, 56 L. T. 124.) Hence it was thought desirable to provide by sect. 5 of the Law of Libel Amendment Act, 1888, that when two or more actions in respect to the same, or substantially the same, libel are brought by one and the same person, the defendants may apply for and in a proper case obtain an order for the consolidation of such actions, so that they shall be tried together. (See the section, *post*, p. 844.) It will be observed that the section is not limited to libels contained in a newspaper; it applies to all libels, though not to slanders. An order may be made under this section although no Defences have yet been delivered (*Stone* v. *Press*

---

* So decided by A. T. Lawrence, J., in Chambers, in *Grice* v. *Allnatt* and *Bailey* v. *Allnatt*, 14th January, 1910.

Association, Limited, [1897] 2 Q. B. 159 ; 66 L. J. Q. B. 662 ; 45 W. R. 641 ; 77 L. T. 41), or although the Defences delivered in the various actions are different : *e.g.*, where the defendant in the first action has justified, and the defendant in the second action has apologised and paid money into Court. (*Eddison* v. *Dalziel,* (1893) 9 Times L. R. 334.) It is sufficient if the libels be substantially the same : *i.e.*, if they in fact contain the same imputation on the plaintiff, though the language used be different. Thus, where one libel was in verse and the other in prose, a Divisional Court, being satisfied that the charges made in each were identical, confirmed an order made by the judge at Chambers consolidating the two actions. (Mathew and Collins, JJ., in *Todd* v. *Scott ;* and *Todd* v. *Johnson & Co., Limited,* February 6th, 1894.) But an order under this section can only be made on the application of the defendants. Where a *plaintiff* seeks to consolidate two or more actions brought by him against different defendants, no order for consolidation will be made without the consent of all parties, even though the issues in all the actions are similar. (*Lee* v. *Arthur,* (1908) 100 L. T. 61.)

After an order has been made for consolidation, only one set of pleadings is necessary, and the consolidated actions proceed as if they were one action. (See Precedent No. 10, *post,* p. 755.)

CHAPTER XXIII.

THE PLEADINGS.

The pleadings in an action of libel or slander are more important, perhaps, than in any other class of actions usually brought in the King's Bench Division. In his Statement of Claim the plaintiff must set out the precise words of which he complains : if the words be not obviously defamatory he must state the meaning which he ascribes to them ; and he must give details of any special damage which he has sustained. The defendant also must state clearly in his Defence the case which he will set up at the trial. He must make up his mind whether or no he is in a position to prove that the words are true and can therefore venture to plead a justification. At the same time he must consider what other defences he may be able to establish at the trial and be careful to raise them properly and sufficiently in his pleading.

A Reply is rarely needed in an action of libel or slander unless the defendant has pleaded a counterclaim.

Statement of Claim.

The very words complained of must be set out by the plaintiff in his Statement of Claim, " in order that the Court may judge whether they constitute a ground of action " (per Abbott, C.J., in *Wright* v. *Clements*, 3 B. & Ald. at p. 506), and also because " the defendant is entitled to know the precise charge against him, and cannot shape his case until he knows." (Per Lord Coleridge, in *Harris* v. *Warre*, 4 C. P. D. 128 ; 48 L. J. C. P. 310 ; 27 W. R. 461 ; 40 L. T. 429.) It is not sufficient to give the substance or purport of the libel or slander with innuendoes. (*Newton* v. *Stubbs*, 3 Mod. 71 ; *Cook* v. *Cox*, 3 M. & S. 110 ; *Wood* v. *Brown*, 6 Taunt. 169 ; *Saunders* v. *Bate*, 1 H. & N. 402 ; *Solomon* v. *Lawson*, 8 Q. B. 823 ; 15 L. J. Q. B. 253 ; 10 Jur. 796.) The precise words are material. (See Order XIX. r. 21.) So, too, in cases of slander of title the words must be set out *verbatim*. (*Gutsole* v. *Mathers*, 1 M. & W. 495 ; 5 Dowl. 69.) The defendant may be interrogated as to the exact words he uttered, if the plaintiff cannot otherwise discover them (*Atkinson* v. *Fosbroke*, L. R. 1 Q. B. 628; 35 L. J. Q. B. 182; 14 W. R. 832; 14 L. T. 553); but not before he delivers his Statement of Claim, except in very special circumstances. (*Strange* v. *Dowdney*, 38 J. P. 724, 756.) If the plaintiff does not know the exact words uttered, and cannot obtain leave to interrogate before Statement of Claim, he must draft his pleading as best he can and subsequently apply for leave to administer interrogatories, and after obtaining Answers amend his Statement of Claim, if necessary. If the words are in a foreign language, they should be set out *verbatim* in such language. (*Zenobio* v. *Axtell*, 6 T. R. 162; and see *R.* v. *Manasseh Goldstein*, 3 Brod. & B. 201; 7 Moore, 1; 10 Price, 88.) And an exact translation should be added. Care should be taken not to translate actionable words into non-actionable, as was done in *Ross* v. *Lawrence*, (1651) Style, 263. It was formerly necessary to aver expressly in the case of foreign words that those present understood them. (*Jones* v. *Davers*, Cro. Eliz. 496; *Price* v. *Jenkings*, Cro. Eliz. 865; and per Williams, J., in *Amann* v. *Damm*, 8 C. B. N. S. 597; 29 L. J. C. P. 313; 8 W. R. 470.) No such averment is now essential; though the fact must of course still be proved at the trial. (*Ante*, p. 125; and see Precedent No. 2.)

If the slander was contained in a question, it must be set out as a question, and not as a fact affirmed. (*Barnes* v. *Holloway*, 8 T. R. 150.) So, if the slander consists in the answer to a question, and the answer alone is unintelligible, both question and answer should be set out exactly as they were spoken. (See *Bromage* v. *Prosser*, 4 B. & C. 247.) Again, if the words were: "A. says B. is bankrupt," they must be so set out; if the declaration alleged that the defendant had said merely, "B. is bankrupt," the variance would formerly have been fatal (*M'Pherson* v. *Daniels*, 10 B. & C. at p. 274; *Bell* v. *Byrne*, 13 East, 554; *Pearce* v. *Rogers*, 2 F. & F. 137); but now such a variance would be amended on payment of the costs, if any, thereby occasioned. (*Smith* v. *Knowelden*, 2 M. & Gr. 561; see *post*, p. 681.) If the libel consists of two letters published in successive issues of a newspaper, neither of which is a complete libel without the other, both must be set out *verbatim*. (*Solomon* v. *Lawson*, 8 Q. B. 823; 15 L. J. Q. B. 253; 10 Jur. 796.) But in other cases it is not necessary to set out the whole of an article or review containing libellous passages; it is sufficient to set out the libellous passages only, provided that nothing be omitted which qualifies or alters their sense. If, however, the meaning of the libellous passages taken singly is not clear, or if the rest of the article would in any substantial degree vary the meaning of the words complained of, the whole must be set out. (*Cartwright* v. *Wright*, 5 B. & Ald. 615 ; *Buckingham* v. *Murray*, 2 C. & P. 47 ; *Rutherford* v. *Evans*, 6 Bing. 451 ; 4 C. & P. 74 ; *Rainy* v. *Bravo*, L. R. 4 P. C. 287 ; 20 W. R. 873.) Where detached portions of a book or article are pleaded it should appear on the Statement of Claim that they are detached portions (see Precedent No. 7) ; they should not be printed as though they ran on continuously. (Per Lord Ellenborough, in *Tabart* v. *Tipper*, 1 Camp. 353.)

It should be alleged that the defendant " spoke and published " or " wrote and published " the words. It is essential in cases of libel to add the words " and published," or their equivalent, as writing a libel which is never published is no tort. It is not absolutely necessary to use the very word " published ; " in *Baldwin* v. *Elphinston* (2 W. Bl. 1037) the phrase " printed and caused to be printed " was held sufficient. Further, it must always be alleged that the words were spoken or written " of and concerning the plaintiff." Then it should be averred that the defendant spoke or wrote and published the words " falsely and maliciously." This is a time-honoured phrase which appears in every Statement of Claim ; and it would be foolish to idly raise a point of law by omitting it, though in the present day its omission would probably not be a fatal defect. For, by rule 25 of Order XIX., " neither party need in any pleading allege any matter of fact which the law presumes in his favour, or as to which the burden of proof lies upon the other side." As long ago as 1652, Rolle, C.J., held these words unnecessary in a declaration. (*Anon.*, Style, 392, and again in 1654 in *Lamplew* v. *Hewson*, Style, 435.) In 1813 Lord Ellenborough held the absence of the word " falsely " immaterial, " unlawfully and maliciously " being present. (*Rowe* v. *Roach*, 1 M. & S. 309.) So, too, in 1586 it was decided that if " falsely " was inserted, " maliciously " might be omitted. (*Mercer* v. *Sparks*, Owen, 51 ; Noy, 35 ; *Anon.*, (1596) Moo. 459. See per Bayley, J., in *Bromage* v. *Prosser*, 4 B. & C. at p. 255, and per Brett, L.J., in *Clark* v. *Molyneux*, 3 Q. B. D. 247, *ante*, p. 342. And see *R.* v. *Munslow*, [1895] 1 Q. B. 758 ; 64 L. J. M. C. 138 ; 43 W. R. 495 ; 72 L. T. 301 ; *post*, p. 722.) There is, however, a practical convenience in alleging malice in the Statement of Claim, viz., if the defendant pleads privilege, no special reply is then necessary ; the formal averment in the Statement of Claim takes a new meaning, and becomes an allegation of express malice. And in all actions on the case for words causing damage, the Statement of Claim must contain an allegation that the words were published " maliciously " or " without just cause or excuse," or some equivalent phrase (see Chapter IV., *ante*, p. 77). But it is never necessary, or indeed permissible, to set out the evidence by which the plaintiff hopes to establish malice at the trial. (*Glossop* v. *Spindler*, (1885) 29 Sol. J. 556 ; Order XIX. r. 22.)

The part of the Statement of Claim which requires most care in drafting is the innuendo. As to its office, see *ante*, pp. 115—119. Where the words are clearly actionable on the face of them, no innuendo is necessary, though even here one is frequently inserted. But whenever the words are actionable only in some secondary sense, or by reason of some surrounding circumstances, an innuendo is essential to the plaintiff's success ; and such innuendo must place upon the words an actionable meaning. (*Jacobs* v. *Schmaltz*, 62 L. T. 121.) If the words are capable of two meanings, both defamatory, alternative innuendos may be pleaded (as in Precedent No. 14, *post*, p. 758. And see *Simmons* v. *Mitchell*, 6 App. Cas. 156 ; 50 L. J. P. C. 11). Whenever the plaintiff is not named in the libel, an innuendo must be inserted, " meaning thereby the plaintiff," &c. ; and it is sometimes desirable, though it is never essential, to state facts which make it clear that the plaintiff is the person referred to. (See *ante*, p. 149, and *Lawrence* v. *Newberry*, 39 W. R. 605 ; 64 L. T. 797.)

The plaintiff must give in his Statement of Claim " full particulars, with dates and items if necessary," of every material allegation. (Order XIX. r. 6.) Thus, in alleging publication of a libel, he must identify the newspaper or other document containing the libel, and give the date of each publication on which he relies as a cause of action. In the case of a letter or other private document, he must state the names of the persons to whom the publication was made and the date of each publication. (*Davey* v. *Bentinck*, [1893] 1 Q. B. at p. 188 ; *British Legal and United Provident Assurance Co.* v. *Sheffield*, [1911] 1 Ir. R. 69.) In cases of slander he must give the date of each slander, the names of the persons to whom, and the places where, each slander was uttered.* (*Roselle* v. *Buchanan*, 16 Q. B. D. 656 ; 55 L. J. Q. B. 376 ; 34 W. R. 488 ; *Bradbury* v. *Cooper*, 12 Q. B. D. 94 ; 53 L. J. Q. B. 558 ; 32 W. R. 32 ; *Glegg* v. *Bromley* (A. T. Lawrence, J.), reported in the Annual Practice for 1911 at p. 283.) A plaintiff may, however, allege publication to one or more persons named,

---

* The law is apparently otherwise in Ireland ; see *Keogh* v. *Incorporated Dental Hospital of Ireland*, [1910] 2 Ir. R. 166 (C. A.).

and then add that he will rely at the trial on every additional publication that may be ascertained on discovery; if he so pleads he cannot be compelled to give further or better particulars until after discovery. (*Russell* v. *Stubbs*, (1908) 52 Sol. J. 580 (H. L.).)

Where the words are actionable only by reason of being spoken of the plaintiff in the way of his office, profession, or trade, the Statement of Claim must always contain an averment that the plaintiff held the office or carried on the profession or trade at the time when the words were spoken. (*Gallwey* v. *Marshall*, 9 Exch. 300; 23 L. J. Ex. 78; 2 C. L. R. 399; *Ayre* v. *Craven*, 2 A. & E. 2; *James* v. *Brook*, 9 Q. B. 7; 16 L. J. Q. B. 17.) And there should also be an averment that the words were spoken of him in the way of such office, profession, or trade. But if the former allegation appear, the omission of the latter is not fatal, as the judge would in a proper case amend the Statement of Claim by inserting an allegation to that effect. (*Ramsdale* v. *Greenacre*, 1 F. & F. 61.) In no other case now is any introductory averment essential. (C. L. P. Act, 1852, s. 61.) But it is often desirable to plead some introductory averment which, though not strictly necessary, will help to make the case clear, by explaining what is to follow (see Precedents Nos. 4, 5, 8, 13, 14, 15). Remember, however, that the presence of such introductory averments will not cure the omission of a proper innuendo. (*Simmons* v. *Mitchell*, 6 App. Cas. 156; 50 L. J. P. C. 11; 29 W. R. 401; 43 L. T. 710; 45 J. P. 237.)

Also, where words not in themselves defamatory are spoken ironically, it must be averred that they were so spoken, or the Statement of Claim will disclose no cause of action. (*Ante*, p. 133.)

As to the claim for damages. Where the words are clearly actionable *per se*, it is only necessary to make a general claim for unliquidated damages. But any special damage that has accrued must in every case be specifically stated, and with sufficient particularity to enable the defendant to know precisely what case he has to meet; otherwise such evidence will be rejected at the trial. (*Bluck* v. *Lovering*, (1885) 1 Times L. R. 497.) If the special damage alleged be the loss of particular customers as distinct from a general diminution of income, the customers' names must be given, unless it is clear from the circumstances that plaintiff would not know their names. (*Evans* v. *Harries*, 26 L. J. Ex. 32; *Ratcliffe* v. *Evans*, [1892] 2 Q. B. 524; 61 L. J. Q. B. 535; 40 W. R. 578; 66 L. T. 794; *ante*, p. 382.) Where a falling off of income is alleged figures must be given showing the nature and extent of such diminution of income. So, if loss of marriage be alleged, the gentleman or lady must be named. (See Precedents Nos. 5, 9, 14, 16, 17, 18, 20, 21.) If such names and other details of the alleged loss be not given in the pleading, a Master at Chambers will, on the application of the defendant, order particulars to be delivered, or, in default, that the allegations be struck out of the Statement of Claim. (*Dimsdale* v. *Goodlake,* (1876) 40 J. P. 792.) As to what constitutes special damage, see *ante,* pp. 377—389. A plaintiff who succeeds in recovering general damages may yet be ordered to pay the costs occasioned by a claim for special damage which he has failed to substantiate. (*Forster* v. *Farquhar,* [1893] 1 Q. B. 564 ; 62 L. J. Q. B. 296 ; 41 W. R. 425 ; 68 L. T. 308.) As the damages are necessarily unliquidated it is not necessary to insert in the claim of damages at the end of the Statement of Claim any specific figure as the precise amount claimed (per Vaughan Williams, L.J., in *London and Northern Bank, Limited* v. *George Newnes, Limited,* (1900) 16 Times L. R. at p. 484), nor is it advisable for the plaintiff to do so. But if he does so he should be sure to claim enough ; for although the plaintiff may recover less than the amount specified, he cannot recover more, unless the judge at the trial will consent after verdict to amend the Statement of Claim under Order XXVIII. r. 1. (*Chattell* v. *Daily Mail Publishing Co., Limited,* (1901) 18 Times L. R. 165.)

An injunction may also be claimed, if there is any reason to apprehend any further publication of the defamatory words : *e.g.,* " An injunction to restrain the defendant from publishing the said pamphlet or any similar libels or slanders affecting the plaintiff in his profession and office," or more briefly : " An injunction to restrain the defendant from similar publications in future." (And see 15 Q. B. D. 650 ; and Precedents Nos. 7 and 15.)

Instructions for Defence.

On receiving the Statement of Claim, the defendant should carefully consider his position, and decide on his course of action. Often it would be well for him to apologise at once, and pay money into Court. In some few cases he should declare war to the knife, and justify. But it is no use for him to send his counsel merely a copy of the Statement of Claim with instructions consisting solely of the words " Counsel will please draw the necessary pleas." The Defence in an action of libel or slander is a most important document, and should not be drafted hurriedly or on insufficient materials. Before settling it, counsel should be put in possession of all the facts. If there is any thought of a justification, the evidence by which it is proposed to support that plea should be submitted to counsel in full detail, and his opinion taken as to its sufficiency. Counsel should also be informed of all facts which might support a plea of privilege.

Amendment.

The defendant's counsel, on receiving the Statement of Claim, should first consider if it discloses any cause of action. If the words are not actionable *per se*, and no special damage is alleged, he should apply under Order XXV. r. 4, to have the action dismissed as being frivolous and vexatious. (*Hubbuck & Sons* v. *Wilkinson, Heywood & Clark*, [1899] 1 Q. B. 86 ; 68 L. J. Q. B. 34; 79 L. T. 429.) So, if the words set out are not defamatory in their ordinary signification, and there is no innuendo, or if the innuendo alleges a meaning which it is clear that the words cannot bear. Again, if it appear on the Statement of Claim that the words were uttered on an occasion which is clearly absolutely privileged, the Statement of Claim will be struck out as disclosing no reasonable cause of action (*Gompas* v. *White*, (1889) 6 Times L. R. 20 ; *Law* v. *Llewellyn*, [1906] 1 K. B. 487) ; or the action will, on the defendant making the necessary application, be dismissed as frivolous and vexatious. (*Bottomley* v. *Brougham*, [1908] 1 K. B. 584 ; *Burr* v. *Smith*, [1909] 2 K. B. 306.) Where the words complained of are not set out *verbatim*, an application should be made under Order XIX. r. 27. But in other cases, unless the defect is seriously embarrassing, it is better policy to leave it unamended; it is no part of the defendant's duty to reform the plaintiff's pleading. And be careful in drawing the Defence not to aid the defect in the claim in any way; the less said about that part of the pleading, the better; do not admit it; if need be, traverse it in so many words; but after such denial, avoid the whole topic if possible; leaving the plaintiff's counsel to explain it to the judge at the trial, if he can.

Particulars before Defence.

But the more usual application at this stage is for particulars. (See Order XIX. rr. 7, 8.) If no particulars be given of a material allegation, the plaintiff will be entitled at the trial to give evidence as to any fact which tends to support the allegation. (*Hewson* v. *Cleeve*, [1904] 2 Ir. R. 536.) The defendant therefore should try to bind the plaintiff down to some particular state of facts of which alone evidence may be offered at the trial. If details to which the defendant is entitled (and as to this, see *ante*, p. 626) are not given in the Statement of Claim, an application for particulars should be promptly made. (*Gouraud* v. *Fitzgerald*, 37 W. R. 265 ; 5 Times L. R. 80.)

It is no objection that the defendant must know already the facts for which he asks by way of particulars ; he is entitled to know the case that is going to be made against him.* So, too, it is no objection to an order being made for such particulars that the plaintiff may be thus indirectly compelled to disclose the names of his witnesses. " If the particulars are those that he ought to give, he cannot refuse to do so merely on the ground that his answer will disclose the names of the witnesses he proposes to call." (Per Lord Esher, M.R., in *Zierenberg* v. *Labouchere*, [1893] 2 Q. B. at p. 187 ; and see *Humphries & Co.* v. *Taylor Drug Co.*, 39 Ch. D. 693 ; 37 W. R. 192 ; 59 L. T. 177 ; *Bishop* v. *Bishop*, [1901] P. 325 ; 70 L. J. P. 93 ; 85 L. T. 173.) And there is no distinction between actions of libel and of slander in this respect. But of course, the plaintiff cannot be compelled to give the names of the persons passing in the street at the time the alleged slander was uttered. (*Wingard* v. *Cox*, W. N. 1876, p. 106.) Nor can a person libelled in a newspaper be expected to give the names of all who take the paper. Where the words were uttered in a public room, the plaintiff was ordered to give the best particulars he could of the names of the persons present at the time. (*Williams* v. *Ramsdale*, 36 W. R. 125.) So in an action for slander of title the plaintiff was ordered to give particulars of the occasions when the words were spoken and of the persons present on such occasions. (*Roche* v. *Meyler*, [1896] 2 Ir. R. 35.)

So, too, whenever any special damage is claimed, but not with sufficient detail, particulars will be ordered of the alleged damage. Thus, the plaintiff can be compelled to state the names of the customers who he alleges have ceased to deal with him, or of the friends who have ceased to show him hospitality, in consequence of the defendant's words. This is a very useful order ; as, if the plaintiff cannot give the names, he will not be allowed at the trial to give any evidence in support of the allegation. (See *Dimsdale* v. *Goodlake*, (1876) 40 J. P. 792 ; and Precedents Nos. 16, 17, 23.) Particulars of general damage will never be ordered.

But no order will be made where the defendant does not really

---

* The law is otherwise in Ireland, *Keogh* v. *Incorporated Dental Hospital of Ireland* (*No.* 1), [1910] 2 Ir. R. 166 (C. A.).

need the information to enable him to prepare his case for trial, or where such an order would be oppressive. (See *Duke* v. *Wisden*, (1897) 77 L. T. 67; 13 Times L. R. 481; *London and Northern Bank, Limited* v. *George Newnes, Limited*, (1900) 16 Times L. R. 433.) Particulars will not be ordered of the general allegation in the Statement of Claim that the words are published maliciously (Order XIX. r. 22), nor of the meaning in which the defendant intended to use the words complained of. (*Heaton* v. *Goldney*, [1910] 1 K. B. at p. 757.)

Defence.

The defendant in his Defence may traverse every material allegation in the Statement of Claim, so as to put the plaintiff to proof of his case. He may at the same time set up some affirmative case in answer to the claim, the burden of proving which will lie on himself. He may also object to the sufficiency of the claim in law. The defendant may also set up a counterclaim. All the defences to which we have referred, or any number of them, may be pleaded together in the same action without leave, although they appear inconsistent. Thus, in *Restell and wife* v. *Steward*, W. N. 1875, pp. 231, 232, Quain, J., held that a denial of publication and a justification could be pleaded together. In *Stainbank* v. *Beckett*, W. N. 1879, p. 203, the defendant pleaded that the alleged libel did not relate to the plaintiff, that it was a fair comment upon a matter of public interest, and also that it was true in fact; and the Court of Appeal held that the Defence was not embarrassing. A defendant may "raise by his Statement of Defence without leave as many distinct and separate, and therefore inconsistent, defences, as he may think proper." (Per Thesiger, L.J., in *Berdan* v. *Greenwood*, 3 Ex. D. 255; 47 L. J. Ex. 628; 26 W. R. 902; 39 L. T. 223.) There is only one exception to this rule: the defendant in an action of libel or slander may not pay money into Court, if he has placed on the record any plea which denies liability to the plaintiff. (Order XXII. r. 1.)

1. *Traverses.*

The defendant must deal specifically with each allegation in the Statement of Claim which he does not admit to be true. (Order XIX. r. 17.) Sometimes it is advisable for the defendant to traverse an allegation in the Statement of Claim so as to compel the plaintiff to call a particular witness. But as a rule he should admit every statement of fact which he does not intend seriously to dispute at the trial. At the same time, he must be careful how he admits even the introductory paragraphs, which may appear immaterial; they were not inserted without some purpose. Every allegation of fact not denied specifically will be taken to be admitted. (Order XIX. r. 13.)

The following are the most usual traverses :—

(i) "The defendant never spoke or published any of the words set out in paragraph 2 of the Statement of Claim." The words "either falsely or maliciously" must not be added. (*Belt* v. *Lawes*, 51 L. J. Q. B. 359.) For the plea, as it stands without them, is a denial of the publication in fact; if the plaintiff prove publication, the law will presume it to have been false and malicious until the defendant proves either privilege or a justification; and both privilege and justification must be specially pleaded, not merely suggested by the addition of four words to a plea which really raises quite a different defence.

(ii) "The said words do not mean what is alleged in paragraph 2 of the Statement of Claim." This is a traverse of the innuendo. The plaintiff is sure to put the blackest construction on the words: hence the innuendo, if there be one, should always be traversed (except perhaps where the defendant pays money into court).

(iii) "The plaintiff did not, at the date of the publication, if any, of the said words, carry on the business of a butcher as alleged in paragraph 1 of the Statement of Claim"; or "The plaintiff was not at the date, &c., vicar of —— as alleged," or "was not then a partner in the firm of A., B. & Co. as alleged." This is a traverse of the special character in which the plaintiff sues; and must always be specially pleaded. (Rules of Trinity Term, 1853, r. 16; Order XXI. r. 5.) If the defendant also wishes to raise at the trial the defence that the plaintiff's trade is illegal, this also must now be specially pleaded. (*Manning* v. *Clement*, 7 Bing. 362; 5 M. & P. 211, is no longer law on this point.)

(iv) "The words did not refer to the plaintiff." (See R. S. C. App. E., s. 3, No. 2.) Or, if it be alleged that the words were spoken of the plaintiff in the way of his trade, office or profession, the traverse would run: "The defendant denies that he spoke or published any of the said words, with reference to the plaintiff in the way of his said trade (*or* office or profession of ——) or at all."

(v) No denial or defence is necessary "as to damages claimed or their amount; but they shall be deemed to be put in issue in all cases, unless expressly admitted." (Order XXI. r. 4. And see Order XIX. r. 17.)

2. *Objections in Point of Law.*

The defendant may raise in his Defence any objection in point of law to the Statement of Claim. But he is not bound to do so; he may urge at the trial any point of law he likes, whether raised on the pleadings or not. It is only when the defendant desires to have any point of law set down for hearing, and disposed of before the trial under the latter part of rule 2 of Order XXV., that he *must* raise it in his pleading by an objection in point of law. And it is clearly worth his while so to raise it whenever the objection may substantially dispose of the whole action, or of any distinct cause of action therein; as in that case the Court may dismiss the action under rule 3 of the same Order (as was done in *Mayor, &c., of Manchester* v. *Williams*, [1891] 1 Q. B. 94; 60 L. J. Q. B. 23; 39 W. R. 302; 63 L. T. 805), and so save the parties the expense of fighting unnecessary issues of fact.

A specimen of such an objection is given in the Rules of 1883, Appendix E., s. 3, No. 2 :—" The defendant will object that the special damage stated is not sufficient in point of law to sustain this action." Similarly, if no special damage be alleged, the defendant may object "that the said words are not actionable without proof of special damage, and that none is alleged." Again, if the defendant desires to contend that the words *cannot* possibly be construed into a libel or slander, such a contention may rightly be stated as a point of law; for, if it be well founded the judge should withdraw the case from the jury. If words which are not defamatory are set out in the Statement of Claim and accompanied by an innuendo which purports to give them an actionable meaning, the defendant should first traverse the innuendo and may then proceed to object " that the said words are incapable of the alleged or of any other actionable meaning."

3. *No Libel.*

" The said words are no libel." This was held a good plea in Ireland before the Judicature Act, on the ground that it raised a question of fact for the jury, not a point of law for the judge. (*Nixon* v. *Harvey*, 8 Ir. C. L. Rep. 446.) And since then such a plea has been freely used in Ireland. (See *Maguire* v. *Knox*, Ir. R. 5 C. L. 408; *Stannus* v. *Finlay*, Ir. R. 8 C. L. 264; *Cosgrave* v. *Trade Auxiliary Co.*, Ir. R. 8 C. L. 349; *M'Loughlin* v. *Dwyer* (1), Ir. R. 9 C. L. 170.) It is now in common use in England. But it is not a sufficient plea on which to found a defence of fair comment.

If the plaintiff has pleaded an innuendo which the defendant has traversed, the plea would run : " The said words without the said alleged meaning are no libel."

4. *Fair Comment.*

This is a defence that frequently arises, and in actions against newspapers is more commonly pleaded than any other. The earliest case in which such a defence is reported as being raised is, we believe, *Dibdin* v. *Swan and Bostock*, (1793) 1 Esp. 28, in which Lord Kenyon, C.J., " stated the law on this subject to be—That the editor of a public newspaper may fairly and candidly comment on any place or species of public entertainment, but it must be done fairly and without malice or view to injure or prejudice the proprietor in the eyes of the public. That if so done, however severe the censure, the justice of it screens the editor from legal animadversion ; but if it can be proved that the comment is unjust, is malevolent or exceeding the bounds of fair opinion, that such is a libel, and therefore actionable." The defence could formerly be raised by simply pleading the general issue (*Sir John Carr* v. *Hood*, (1808) 1 Camp. 355, n.; *Earl of Lucan* v. *Smith*, (1856) 1 H. & N. 481 ; 26 L. J. Ex. 94) ; but after the passing of the Common Law Procedure Act, 1852, it became common to plead a special plea in addition to the plea of " Not Guilty." Under the present rules Fair Comment must always be specially pleaded. The form of plea now in general use is that set out in Precedent No. 26, *post*, p. 768, which was sanctioned by the Divisional Court in *Lord Penrhyn* v. *Licensed Victuallers' Mirror*, (1890) 7 Times L. R. 1. As we have already pointed out (*ante*, p. 202) a plea in this form is a justification of all the statements of fact made by the defendant, and of such statements only ; it does not justify any statement made merely by way of comment.*

This form of plea, however, is indefinite and therefore embarrassing, unless particulars be given showing precisely what

---

* Some confusion on this point has been caused by the language used by the Lords Justices in *Digby* v. *Financial News, Ltd.*, [1907] 1 K. B. 502. But that was a very special case decided on peculiar facts. The basis of the comment made by the defendants was the plaintiff's own statements, and the decision merely amounts to this—that in such a case the Court will not regard such a plea as putting in issue the truth of the plaintiff's own statements. The word " justification " as used by Collins, M.R., in this case, means a justification of the whole of the imputation conveyed by the words complained of.

allegations in the libel the defendant is justifying. (*Fleming* v. *Dollar*, (1889) 23 Q. B. D. 388; and see the remarks of Vaughan Williams, L.J., in *Peter Walker & Son, Ltd.* v. *Hodgson*, [1909] 1 K. B. at p. 247.) Such particulars ought to be set out in the plea. But, if they are not, particulars will be ordered of the facts relied upon by the defendant in support of his plea. (*Digby* v. *The Financial News, Ltd.*, [1907] 1 K. B. 502; *Lyons* v. *Financial News, Ltd.*, (1909) 53 Sol. Jo. 671 (C. A.).)

The defendant should be ordered to give particulars showing which portions of the libel he will allege at the trial to be statements of fact, unless it is clear from the terms of the libel itself which are statements of fact and which are comment. "The Court cannot decompose this mass; but the party who requires the separation to be made for his own defence ought to have taken upon himself the burthen of doing it, in order that the Court might see with certainty what parts he meant to justify. . . . If they cannot be separated by the industry of the pleader, how can they be so by general reference?" (Per Lord Ellenborough, C.J., in *Stiles* v. *Nokes*, (1806) 7 East, 493.)

Further, a defendant who uses this form of plea will be ordered to give particulars of the facts on which he will rely to prove the truth of his statements of fact (*Yorkshire Provident Assurance Co.* v. *Gilbert*, [1895] 1 Q. B. 148), or in a special case of the materials on which the comment was based (*Peter Walker & Son, Ltd.* v. *Hodgson*, [1909] 1 K. B. 239). Where the basis of comment is statements of fact made by the plaintiff and accepted as true by the defendant the Court will not order particulars to be given beyond those necessary to show that such is the basis of comment. (*Digby* v. *Financial News, Ltd.*, [1907] 1 K. B. 502.)

It is not always necessary, however, for the defendant to justify the statements of fact contained in the libel. It may be that they are privileged as being a fair and accurate report of a judicial or Parliamentary proceeding, or extracts from a Parliamentary or other official paper. (See *ante*, p. 336.) In such a case it will be a good plea if the defendant sets out the facts which create the privilege on which he relies, and pleads that the rest of the alleged libel is fair comment on such privileged statements. (*Mangena* v. *Wright*, [1909] 2 K. B. 958.) No particulars will be ordered of facts relied on as showing that the subject of comment is a matter of public interest (*Lyons* v. *Financial News, Ltd.*, (1909) 53 Sol. J. 671); for this is a question of law for the judge.

The defence of fair comment in effect admits that the words are published of and concerning the plaintiff; for it is a plea in confession and avoidance. If it is in effect a colourable justification, it is bad. (*Earl of Lucan* v. *Smith*, (1856) 1 H. & N. 481; 26 L. J. Ex. 94.) If it seeks to show that the words are a fair comment on some matter entirely unconnected with the plaintiff it should be struck out. The proper way to raise such a defence is to traverse the allegation in the Statement of Claim that the words were published " of and concerning the plaintiff."

5. *Privilege.*

The defence of privilege must be specially pleaded, and facts and circumstances must also be stated showing why and how the occasion is privileged. (Order XIX. rr. 4, 15; *Elkington* v. *London Association for the Protection of Trade*, (1911) 27 Times L. R. 329.) "The question whether the occasion is privileged is a question of law; and therefore when this defence is pleaded, the facts necessary to show that the occasion is privileged must be stated." (*Per cur.* in *Simmonds* v. *Dunne*, Ir. R. 5 C. L. 358, at p. 362.) Several such pleas will be found collected on pp. 774—780.

When the occasion is not absolutely privileged, it is usual to aver that the defendant honestly believed his words to be true and published them *bonâ fide*, or without malice. But strictly this is unnecessary; for as soon as the judge rules that the occasion is privileged, it is for the plaintiff to prove malice. (*Jenoure* v. *Delmege*, [1891] A. C. 73; 60 L. J. P. C. 11.) The defendant should not allege that he had just and reasonable grounds for believing the charges against the plaintiff to be true; as, if he does, he may be ordered to state the grounds of such belief. (*Fitzgerald* v. *Campbell*, 18 Ir. Jur. 153; 15 L. T. 74; *contrà*, *Cave* v. *Torre*, 54 L. T. 515.) Such an allegation runs dangerously near to a justification, and the averment of *bona fides* covers and includes it.

6. *Justification.*

This is a most dangerous plea, and should never be placed on the record without careful consideration of the sufficiency of the evidence by which it is to be supported; for the strictest proof is required (see *Leyman* v. *Latimer*, 3 Ex. D. 15, 352; 47 L. J. Ex. 470); and, if it be not proved, the defendant's persistence in the charge is some evidence of malice, and will always tend to aggravate the damages given against him. The defence cannot be raised without a special plea; and counsel should never draw such a plea without express instructions, and even then should always caution the defendant as to the risk he runs.

When the libel consists of one precise and specific charge (*e.g.*, "He forged my name to this cheque"), it is sufficient to plead generally :—"The said words are true in substance and in fact;" and no particulars will be ordered. (*Gordon Cumming* v. *Green and others*, (1891) 7 Times L. R. 408.) But whenever a general charge is made, the very words alleged to have been uttered must be expressly justified, and also specific instances must be given in the Defence, so that the plaintiff may know on what facts the defendant intends to rely at the trial in support of his plea of justification. (*Hickinbotham* v. *Leach*, 10 M. & W. 361; *Zierenberg and wife* v. *Labouchere*, [1893] 2 Q. B. 183; 63 L. J. Q. B. 89; *Devereux* v. *Clarke*, [1891] 2 Q. B. 582; 60 L. J. Q. B. 773; *Arnold and Butler* v. *Bottomley and others*, [1908] 2 K. B. 151; 77 L. J. K. B. 584; 98 L. T. 777.) Where the words impute constant and habitual misconduct, it is not sufficient to allege and prove one solitary instance of such misconduct. (*Wakley* v. *Cooke and Healey*, 4 Exch. 511; 19 L. J. Ex. 91.) It is enough to cite three instances (*Moore* v. *Terrell and others*, 4 B. & Ad. 870; 1 N. & M. 559), and to clearly prove two. (*R. pros. Lambri* v. *Labouchere*, 14 Cox, C. C. 419.) But the defendant should set out in his pleading all the instances that he can prove. Such instances must be pleaded with sufficient particularity to inform the plaintiff precisely what are the facts to be tried. (See Precedent No. 34, *post*, p. 773.) These instances should be stated in the body of the plea. (*Honess and others* v. *Stubbs*, 7 C. B. N. S. 555; 29 L. J. C. P. 220; 6 Jur. N. S. 682; Order XIX. r. 6.) If they are not, the Master will order particulars to be given, and generally at the cost of the defendant.

If it appears from the words set out in the Statement of Claim that the defendant did not make a direct charge himself, but only repeated what A. said, then a general plea that the words are true will be insufficient (*Duncan* v. *Thwaites*, 3 B. & C. 556); for it will only amount to an assertion that A. said so; whereas the defendant must go further, and prove in addition that what A. said was true. (See *ante*, p. 186.)

The defendant must plead to the words set out in the Statement of Claim and not to some other words of his own. (*Rassam* v. *Budge*, [1893] 1 Q. B. 571; 62 L. J. Q. B. 312.) Nor may he put his own meaning on the words, and assert that in that sense they are true. (*Wood* v. *Earl of Durham*, (1888) 4 Times L. R. 556.) The precise charge must be justified; and the whole of the precise charge. (*Goodburne* v. *Bowman and others*, 9 Bing. 532; *Wernher, Beit & Co.* v. *Markham*, (1901) 18 Times L. R. 143; (1902) *ib.* 763. And see *ante*, p. 183.) " When a plea of justification is pleaded, it involves the justification of every injurious imputation which the jury may think is to be found in the alleged libel." (Per Collins, M.R., in *Digby* v. *Financial News, Ltd.*, [1907] 1 K. B. at p. 507.) Every fact stated must be proved true (*Weaver* v. *Lloyd*, 2 B. & C. 678; *Helsham* v. *Blackwood*, 11 C. B. 111; 20 L. J. C. P. 187; 15 Jur. 861), unless it is absolutely immaterial and trivial, and in no way alters the complexion of the affair. But not every comment on such facts need be justified. Thus, if the defendant states certain facts, and then calls the plaintiff a " scamp" and a " rascal," and such epithets would be deserved if the facts as stated are true, then it is sufficient to plead the truth of the facts; the epithets need not be expressly justified. (*Morrison* v. *Harmer*, 3 Bing. N. C. 767; 4 Scott, 533; *Tighe* v. *Cooper*, 7 E. & B. 639; 26 L. J. Q. B. 215.) But the defendant must state specific facts in support of his plea; and if he has said of the plaintiffs that they were " wrong 'uns," he must give particulars showing a foundation for such a charge. He will not be allowed to postpone the delivery of such particulars until after discovery. (*Arnold and Butler* v. *Bottomley and others*, [1908] 2 K. B. 151; 77 L. J. K. B. 584; 98 L. T. 777.) But if the comment introduces an independent fact, or substantially aggravates the main imputation, it must be expressly justified. Thus a libellous heading to a newspaper article must be justified as well as the facts stated in the article. (*Bishop* v. *Latimer*, 4 L. T. 775; *Clement* v. *Lewis and others*, 3 Br. & Bing. 297; 3 B. & Ald. 702. See *ante*, pp. 181—185.) As to giving particulars of facts on which the defendant says he has commented fairly, see *ante*, p. 634.

7. *Justifying Part of the Charge.*

The defendant may in mitigation of damages by a special plea (*Vessey* v. *Pike*, 3 C. & P. 512) justify a part of the libel, provided such part is distinct and severable from the rest. (See *Davis* v. *Billing*, (1891) 8 Times L. R. 58; and other cases cited *ante*, p. 188.) But the plea must distinctly identify the portion justified. (*Fleming* v. *Dollar*, 23 Q. B. D. 388; 58 L. J. Q. B. 548; 37 W. R. 684; 61 L. T. 230; and see Precedent No. 36.) If the defendant pleads a justification of the words without any qualification he must at the trial prove the words true in whatever sense the jury may put upon them. But if there is an innuendo in the Statement of Claim, the defendant may, if he thinks fit, qualify his justification by denying that such innuendo puts the true construction on the words, and asserting merely that in their natural and ordinary signification they are true. If he pleads in this way he will not be allowed at the trial to say that the words are true in the meaning ascribed to them by the innuendo; though he will be taken to have justified the words in any other defamatory sense that the jury may think fit to put upon them. If the jury come to the conclusion that the words bear the meaning ascribed to them by the innuendo the defendant will have no defence under this plea. (See note to Precedent No. 55, *post*, p. 783.) In every case the defendant must make it perfectly clear how much of the words he justifies, and in what sense he justifies them. (*Fleming* v. *Dollar, suprà.*) Any plea which wears a doubtful aspect, which may be either a justification, or a mere traverse, or a plea of privilege, will be struck out at Chambers as embarrassing. (*Carr* v. *Duckett*, 5 H. & N. 783; 29 L. J. Ex. 468; *Brembridge* v. *Latimer*, 12 W. R. 878; 10 L. T. 816; *O'Keefe* v. *Cardinal Cullen*, Ir. R. 7 C. L. 319.)

A defendant will not be allowed to amend his Defence and plead a justification at the last moment, *e.g.*, on the day before the trial. (*Kirby* v. *Simpson*, 3 Dowl. 791.)

8. *Other Special Defences.*

Statutes of Limitation (see *ante*, p. 609).—The objection that the action is brought too late must be raised by a special plea (Order XIX. r. 15), even though the defect is apparent on the face of the Statement of Claim. This was decided as long ago as 1636. (*Hawkings* v. *Billhead*, Cro. Car. 404.)

Previous Action.—That the plaintiff has previously sued the defendant for the same cause of action is a defence, whatever the result of the former action. (See *ante*, p. 610, and Precedent No. 52.) That judgment was recovered against one of several joint publishers is also a bar to any action against the others for the same publication. (See form of plea, 2 C. & K. 683, n.)

Accord and Satisfaction.—That the plaintiff agreed to accept certain apologies and that the defendant duly published them in accordance with such agreement was held a bar to the action in *Boosey* v. *Wood*, 3 H. & C. 484; 34 L. J. Ex. 65. (See also *Lane* v. *Applegate*, 1 Stark. 97; and *Marks* v. *Conservative Newspaper Co.*, (1886) 3 Times L. R. 244.) As to accord and satisfaction made by one jointly liable with the defendant, see *Bainbridge* v. *Lax*, 9 Q. B.

819 ; *Thurman* v. *Wild*, 11 A. & E. 453 ; *Hey* v. *Moorhouse*, 6 Bing. N. C. 52. An accord or satisfaction made by a third party on the defendant's behalf, and accepted by the plaintiff in discharge, will be a bar to the action. (*Jones* v. *Broadhurst*, 9 C. B. 173. See Precedent No. 53.)

Release.—A release must be specially pleaded. (Order XIX. r. 15.) In an American case (*Beach et ux.* v. *Beach*, (1842) 2 Hill (N. Y.), 260, *ante*, p. 572), a release by the plaintiff's husband was pleaded to an action for slander of the wife.

Husband and Wife.—By virtue of the Married Women's Property Act (1870), Amendment Act, 1874 (37 & 38 Vict. c. 50), s. 2, a husband when sued for a libel or slander published or uttered by his wife before her marriage may, if married between July 30th, 1874, and January 1st, 1883, in addition to any other pleas, plead that no property vested in him by reason of the marriage within the meaning of sect. 5, or if a certain amount of property did so vest in him, then that he is liable to that extent and no further. As to a husband married on or since January 1st, 1883, see *ante*, pp. 573—577.

9. *Payment into Court.*

Payment into Court is not strictly a defence ; it is rather an attempt at a compromise ; for it admits liability to the extent of such payment. In all other actions a defendant may pay money into Court, while at the same time he denies all liability. But this is not allowed in actions or counterclaims for libel or slander. (Order XXII. r. 1.) Here the defendant, if he pays money into Court at all, must do so "by way of satisfaction which shall be taken to admit the claim or cause of action in respect of which the payment is made" ; * and his Defence must not contain any plea which denies liability. Thus where a husband and wife were sued jointly, and the husband paid money into Court in satisfaction but the wife denied liability, the Court ordered that part of the Defence which was inconsistent with an admission of liability to be struck out. (*Beaumont* v. *Kaye and wife*, [1904] 1 K. B. 292 ; 73 L. J. K. B. 213 ; 52 W. R. 241 ; 90 L. T. 51 ; 20 Times L. R. 183.) Hence a defendant who has any defence on the merits should not pay money into Court.

---

* It follows that *Jones* v. *Mackie*, L. R. 3 Ex. 1 ; 37 L. J. Ex. 1 ; 16 W. R. 109 ; 17 L. T. 151 ; and *Hawkesley* v. *Bradshaw*, 5 Q. B. D. 302 ; 49 L. J. Q. B. 333 ; 28 W. R. 557 ; 42 L. T. 285, are no longer law since October 24th, 1883, when this rule was made.

Where, however, the words are defamatory in their natural and obvious meaning, and the plaintiff by his innuendo puts on them a more defamatory meaning, the defendant may traverse the innuendo and at the same time pay money into Court; provided it be made clear on the face of the plea that the money is paid into Court and liability admitted in respect of the words without the alleged meaning; as such a traverse is not in that case "a defence denying liability." (*Mackay* v. *Manchester Press Co.,* (1889) 54 J. P. 22; 6 Times L. R. 16.) But it is not always wise to adopt this course; see Precedent No. 55, and the note thereto (*post,* p. 783).

Where money has been paid into Court without any denial of liability (as it always must be in actions of libel or slander), the plaintiff has three courses open to him:—

(i) He may leave the money in Court, in which case it will be subject to any future order of the Court or a judge;

(ii) He may take the money out in satisfaction of his cause of action and proceed to tax his costs. (*Marriage* v. *Wilson,* (1889) 53 J. P. 120.)

(iii) He may take the money out of Court not in satisfaction and proceed for damages *ultra, i.e.,* continue the action in the hope of recovering a larger amount. (Order XXII. r. 5 (*b*).)

Money paid into Court with an admission of liability does not become the property of the plaintiff, and the Court has power, subject to the Rules, to say what shall be done with it. When the defendant dies before trial, the Court will order the money to be paid out to the plaintiff; but if the action is dismissed for want of prosecution, an order will be made in favour of the defendant. (*Brown* v. *Feeney,* [1906] 1 K. B. 563; 75 L. J. K. B. 494; 54 W. R. 445; 94 L. T. 460.) Where the party in favour of whom the order would be made is dead, the Court will order payment out to his executor. (*Maxwell* v. *Viscount Wolseley,* [1907] 1 K. B. 274; 76 L. J. K. B. 163; 96 L. T. 4.) As to payment out after trial of money paid into Court, see *post,* p. 700.

Neither the fact that money has been paid into Court nor the amount paid in can be mentioned to the jury. (Order XXII. r. 22.) This rule applies to actions of libel and slander, notwithstanding the observations of Lord Russell, L.C.J., in *Klamborowski* v. *Cooke,* (1897) 14 Times L. R. 88. (See *Veale* v. *Reid,* (1904) 117 L. T. Journal, 292.) If the defendant decides to pay money into Court, he should pay in a substantial sum —at least twice as much as he himself thinks the plaintiff is entitled to. It is seldom worth while to pay a farthing or a shilling into Court; though in some cases it may be good policy to pay in forty shillings.

Where an order has been made consolidating two or more actions under the Law of Libel Amendment Act, 1888, the defendants may, it seems, pay one lump sum into Court if they think fit. (*Stone* v. *Press Association, Limited*, [1897] 2 Q. B. 159 ; 66 L. J. Q. B. 662 ; 45 W. R. 641 ; 77 L. T. 41.)

As to questions of costs arising on payment into Court, see *ante*, p. 449, and *post*, p. 700.

10. *Payment into Court under Lord Campbell's Act.*

At common law the defendant in an action of libel or slander had no power to pay money into Court. Power to pay money into Court was for the first time given to a defendant by sect. 2 of Lord Campbell's Libel Act (6 & 7 Vict. c. 96), which enacted that in an action for a libel contained in a public newspaper or other periodical publication, the defendant might plead that the libel was published without gross negligence and without any malice towards the plaintiff, and that he had published a full apology. It also gave him liberty to pay money into Court " by way of amends." (See *post*, p. 829.) Two years later the payment of money into Court was rendered compulsory by the statute 8 & 9 Vict. c. 75, s. 2 which provided that it should not be competent for any defendant in such an action to file a plea under the earlier Act "without at the same time making a payment of money into Court by way of amends *as provided by the said Act*." (See *post*, p. 832.) From this time till 1875 money could not be paid into Court in an action of libel except under this Act. The Judicature Act permitted any defendant in any action to pay money into Court. Hence from 1875 to 1879 money could be paid into Court in an action brought for a libel in a newspaper or other periodical publication in two ways, either under Lord Campbell's Act, or under the Judicature Act. But in 1879 that portion of sect. 2 of Lord Campbell's Libel Act which enabled the defendant to pay money into Court, and also the words of the later Act (8 & 9 Vict. c. 75), " as provided by the said Act," were repealed, " as to the Supreme Court of Judicature in England," by the Civil Procedure Acts Repeal Act, 1879 (42 & 43 Vict. c. 59, Part II. of the Schedule), and later as to all Courts in England by sect. 4 of the Statute Law Revision and Civil Procedure Act, 1883 (46 & 47 Vict. c. 49) ; and again the words " as provided by the said

Act," were repealed for the whole United Kingdom by the Statute Law Revision - Act, 1891 (54 & 55 Vict. c. 67 s. 1). The two statutes 42 & 43 Vict. c. 59, and 46 & 47 Vict. c. 49, contain, it is true, words which provide that such repeal shall not affect any "principle or rule of law or equity established or confirmed, or right or privilege acquired, or duty or liability imposed or incurred"; but it is submitted that these words have no reference to a mode of payment into Court, especially as these Acts do not contain the words "form or course of pleading, practice, or procedure," which are found in the Statute Law Revision Act, 1891.

Hence although it is still open to a defendant to *plead* in the form allowed by Lord Campbell's Act, the payment into Court, which is a necessary concomitant of such a plea, can only be made under the Judicature Act. (*Veale* v. *Reid*, (1904) 117 L. T. Journal, 292.) Two results follow : (i) that such a payment into Court, operates as an admission of liability to the extent of the money paid in; (ii) that no plea denying liability can be pleaded therewith. In other words, a plea under Lord Campbell's Act is now, it is submitted, merely a plea in mitigation of damages. (But see the judgments in *Oxley* v. *Wilkes*, [1898] 2 Q. B. 56.)

Pleading in the form under Lord Campbell's Act does, however, expose the defendant to one grave risk, which he would avoid if he merely pleaded payment into Court in the usual form with an apology. That risk is that he may have to pay costs, even though the jury award the plaintiff as damages an amount less than the sum paid into Court. It has been held that if there be a plea under Lord Campbell's Act and the jury find that there was malice or gross negligence or that the apology was insufficient, judgment must be entered for the plaintiff with costs although he has recovered a sum not greater than the amount paid into Court. (*Oxley* v. *Wilkes*, [1898] 2 Q. B. 56 ; 67 L. J. Q. B. 678 ; 78 L. T. 728 ; *Sley* v. *Tillotson & Son*, (1898) 62 J. P. 505 ; 14 Times L. R. 545.) Hence in the present state of the authorities the defendant should not have recourse to a plea under Lord Campbell's Act, but should apologise and pay money into Court in the ordinary way.

As to payment of the money out of Court, see *post*, p. 700.

In Ireland, too, a distinction is still preserved between a payment into Court under Lord Campbell's Act and all other payments into Court. (See *Harris* v. *Arnott and others*, (No. 1) 24 L. R. Ir. 404 ; *Coughlan* v. *Morris*, 6 L. R. Ir. 405.)

11. *Pleading an Apology.*

The above section of Lord Campbell's Act applies only to public periodical publications; but sect. 1 of the same Act empowers *any* defendant to give in evidence, in mitigation of damages in any action, whether of slander or libel, that he made or offered an apology to the plaintiff before action, or at the earliest opportunity afterwards, if he had no opportunity before action. This section distinctly does not empower a defendant to plead an apology; for it requires him *with his plea* to give notice in writing to the plaintiff of his intention to give such apology in evidence. But there can be no objection now to the defendant making such written notice part of his Defence; indeed, that he made such an apology is a material fact on which he relies, within the meaning of Order XIX. r. 4. It is, we think, now open to a defendant, if he think fit, to state in his pleading facts which are no defence, but which tend to mitigate the damages. It can scarcely be said that such a method of pleading embarrasses the plaintiff, for it gives him notice what will be the defendant's case at the trial. Indeed, the decisions in *Scott* v. *Sampson,* 8 Q. B. D. 491; 51 L. J. Q. B. 380; 30 W. R. 541; 46 L. T. 412; 46 J. P. 408; and *Millington* v. *Loring,* 6 Q. B. D. 190; 50 L. J. Q. B. 214; 29 W. R. 207; 43 L. T. 657; 45 J. P. 268, if taken literally, imply that a defendant *must* always plead such facts in his Defence. But this is not the practice, and it may be inferred from Order XXXVI. r. 37, that a defendant is not *bound* to set out in his pleading the facts on which he proposes to rely in mitigation of damages. (See *Wood* v. *Earl of Durham,* 21 Q. B. D. 501; 57 L. J. Q. B. 547; 37 W. R. 222; 59 L. T. 142; and *Wood* v. *Cox,* (1888) 4 Times L. R. 550.)

But it is quite another matter for the defendant in his Defence to apologise for the first time, when he had previous opportunities of doing so, of which he did not avail himself. Still, this is often done when money is paid into Court. It is certainly strange pleading; but it is difficult to see how the plaintiff can effectually raise objection to it. (See Precedents Nos. 54, 56, 57.) It certainly cannot embarrass a plaintiff to have placed upon the record a full retractation of the charge accompanied by an expression of regret; and it should conduce to an amicable settlement. In cases within Order XXXVI. r. 37, the defendant should deliver particulars as therein required. (See Precedent No. 63.)

12. *Counterclaim.*

It is not often that there is a counterclaim in an action for libel or slander, and it would clearly be prejudicial to the fair trial of the action to permit a defendant to raise incongruous issues. Libels or slanders on the defendant published by the plaintiff may be made matter of counterclaim, and the fact that they arise out of a different transaction will be no ground for excluding them (*Quin* v. *Hession,* 40 L. T. 70; 4 L. R. (Ir.) 35), if they can be "conveniently disposed of in the pending action." But where the defendant counterclaims against the plaintiff and a third person, he must show on his counterclaim that he is seeking thereby "relief relating to or connected with the original subject of the cause or matter." (Judicature Act, 1873, s. 24, sub-s. 3; *S. F. Edge, Ltd.* v. *Weigel,* (1907) 97 L. T. 447.) In *Nicholson* v. *Jackson,* W. N. 1876, p. 38, where an action had been brought by a director of a company for libel, a counterclaim set up by the defendant for damages for loss sustained in respect of shares bought on false representations was struck out by Lindley, J. So, in *Lee* v. *Colyer,* W. N. 1876, p. 8, Quain, J., struck out a counterclaim for not repairing a house, the action being for assault and slander. And where the writ was specially indorsed for two quarters' rent, the defendant was not allowed to set up a counterclaim for libel and slander not connected with the claim for rent. (*Rotheram* v. *Priest,* 49 L. J. C. P. 104; 28 W. R. 277; 41 L. T. 558.) But in *Dobede* v. *Fisher,* at the Cambridge Summer Assizes, 1880, Lord Chief Baron Kelly had to try an action of slander, in which there was a counterclaim about a right of shooting over the land occupied by the defendant. (*Times* for July 29th, 1880.) In *South African Republic* v. *La Compagnie Franco-Belge, &c.,* [1897] 2 Ch. 487; 66 L. J. Ch. 747; 46 W. R. 67; 77 L. T. 241), it was held that a counterclaim for damages for libel could not be conveniently tried in an action for appointing a new trustee and protecting a trust fund, and that the fact that the company could not bring a separate action for libel against the Republic was no ground for allowing the counterclaim for libel to stand. But where in a Chancery action the defendant brought a counterclaim for libel, the Court refused to order that the action be transferred to the King's Bench Division as the plaintiff raised no objection to trial by a judge alone. (*Lord Kinnaird* v. *Field,* [1905] 2 Ch. 361; 74 L. J. Ch. 692; 54 W. R. 85; 93 L. T. 190.)

Amendment.

The plaintiff on receiving the Defence should first consider whether any portions of it require amendment. If, for instance, money has been paid into Court with a defence denying liability, in violation of Order XXII. r. 1, or if no money has been paid into Court with a plea under sect. 2 of Lord Campbell's Act, it may be worth while for the plaintiff to apply at Chambers for an order to strike out the paragraphs improperly inserted in the Defence. Or the whole Defence may be struck out under Order XXV. r. 4, where it is clearly frivolous and vexatious. (*Salomons* v. *Knight*, (1892) 8 Times L. R. 472.) But in other cases it is not always wise to apply to have your opponent's pleading struck out or amended, even where you are strictly entitled so to do. (See *ante*, p. 629.) It is often better policy to leave a flagrantly bad specimen of pleading unamended, and not kindly to strengthen your adversary's position. No party may dictate to the other how he shall plead; he must satisfy the Master at Chambers or district registrar that the passage to which he objects is either scandalous (that is, both offensive and at the same time irrelevant), or that it tends to prejudice, embarrass, or delay the fair trial of the action. Then, it may be that the plaintiff's own Statement of Claim may require amendment. But a plaintiff will not be allowed to amend by setting up fresh claims in respect of causes of action which since the issue of the writ have become barred by the Statute of Limitations. (*Weldon* v. *Neal*, 19 Q. B. D. 394; 56 L. J. Q. B. 621; 35 W. R. 820.) Where the action has been brought on a substantial publication, to which a good defence is pleaded, the plaintiff will not be allowed to amend his claim by including in it, for the first time, a trivial and merely technical publication which such defence may not cover. (*Dillon* v. *Balfour*, 20 L. R. Ir. 600.) In some cases the plaintiff may amend by adding a new defendant. (*Edward* v. *Lowther*, 45 L. J. C. P. 417; 24 W. R. 434; 34 L. T. 255; *Montgomery* v. *Foy, Morgan & Co.*, [1895] 2 Q. B. 321; 43 W. R. 691; 73 L. T. 12.)

Particulars after Defence.

Next, even if the defendant's pleading requires no amendment, as being bad in law, it may still have set up defences of which particulars may be demanded. If in any plea details which should be given under the Rules be omitted, the plaintiff should apply to the Master for particulars; else the plaintiff will be deemed to have waived his right to obtain particulars, and there will be no restriction on the evidence which the defendant will be entitled to give at the trial in support of his plea. (*Hewson* v. *Cleeve*, [1904] 2 Ir. R. 536.) If no facts be stated in a plea of justification, the plaintiff should apply for particulars of the facts upon which the defendant intends to rely at the trial in support of his plea (*Foster* v. *Perryman*, (1891) 8 Times L. R. 115), unless the charge itself be specific and precise. (See *ante*, p. 190.) Thus, where the libel imputed that the plaintiffs had infringed defendant's patents, the defendant was ordered to deliver particulars to the plaintiffs, showing in what respects he alleged that the plaintiffs had infringed his patents, and giving references to line and page of his own specifications. (*Wren and another* v. *Weild*, 38 L. J. Q. B. 88; *Union Electrical Power Co.* v. *Electrical Power Storage Co.*, 38 Ch. D. 325; 36 W. R. 913; 59 L. T. 427; *Arnold and Butler* v. *Bottomley*, [1908] 2 K. B. 151; 98 L. T. 777.) And it is no objection to an order being made for such particulars that the defendant may thereby be indirectly compelled to disclose the names of his witnesses. (Per Lord Esher, M.R., in *Zierenberg* v. *Labouchere*, [1893] 2 Q. B. at p. 187; *Humphries & Co.* v. *Taylor Drug Co.*, 39 Ch. D. 693; 37 W. R. 192; 59 L. T. 177.) And to the particulars so given the defendant will be strictly limited; he may not deliver further particulars without leave. (*Yorkshire Provident Co.* v. *Gilbert*, [1895] 2 Q. B. 148; 64 L. J. Q. B. 578; 72 L. T. 445; *Emden* v. *Burns*, (1894) 10 Times L. R. 400.) So, too, particulars may be obtained if a plea of privilege does not state the circumstances which render the occasion privileged, and on obtaining such particulars the plaintiff may object, as a matter of law, that they disclose no privilege. (See *ante*, p. 636.) Similarly, where fair comment is pleaded, the plaintiff is entitled to particulars showing what is alleged as the basis of the comment. (See *ante*, p. 634.)

Reply.

No Reply can now be delivered without the leave of a Master. If the plaintiff's only object in delivering a Reply is to deny what the defendant has stated in his Defence, the Master will not give leave; because for that purpose no Reply is necessary. If no Reply be delivered, all material statements of fact in the Defence will "be deemed to have been denied and put in issue" at the end of the period of ten days (Order XXVII. r. 13) ; and then the plaintiff can give notice of trial at once. (Order XXXVI. r. 11.) But if a Counterclaim has been pleaded, the Master will give leave to deliver a Reply and Defence to Counterclaim.

To a plea of absolute privilege no reply other than a joinder of issue is possible. (See *Scott* v. *Stansfield,* L. R. 3 Ex. 220 ; 37 L. J. Ex. 155 ; 16 W. R. 911 ; 18 L. T. 572 ; *Dawkins* v. *Lord Paulet,* L. R. 5 Q. B. 94 ; 39 L. J. Q. B. 53 ; 18 W. R. 336 ; 21 L. T. 584.) To a plea of qualified privilege a special reply is unnecessary, if malice be alleged in the Statement of Claim or negatived in the Defence ; the formal averment in the Statement of Claim that the words were spoken maliciously becomes an allegation of express malice. The defendant is not entitled to particulars of express malice. (Order XIX. r. 22. See *ante,* p. 626.) To a justification setting out a conviction, or to a plea of a previous action, the plaintiff must reply specially that there is no such record ; if such be the fact, or if the conviction be erroneously stated in the Defence (as in *Alexander* v. *N. E. Ry. Co.,* 34 L. J. Q. B. 152 ; 6 B. & S. 340), the plaintiff may set it out correctly in his Reply. Or to such a conviction the plaintiff may reply a pardon (*Cuddington* v. *Wilkins,* Hob. 67, 81 ; 2 Hawk. P. C. c. 37, s. 48), or that he had undergone his sentence, which will have the same effect (Precedent No. 61 ; *Leyman* v. *Latimer and others,* 3 Ex. D. 15, 352 ; 37 L. T. 360, 819 ; 14 Cox, C. C. 51) ; though neither reply would be an answer if the words complained of were that the plaintiff " was convicted of " a crime. To a plea of payment into Court it is unnecessary to reply specially that the sum paid in is insufficient.

CHAPTER XXIV.

PREPARING FOR TRIAL.

THE parties have now ascertained by interchange of pleadings what are the matters in issue in the action; the next step is to prepare the evidence which they will adduce at the trial on each issue. Each party probably has in his possession material documents which his opponent will desire to inspect, and of which he may wish to take copies. Each party may also desire to obtain from the other disclosure of certain facts. This is especially desirable when it is known that there will be a conflict of evidence at the trial; it will save trouble, delay, and expense if the parties can ascertain before the hearing what are the exact points on which there will be such conflict. So there may be a difficulty in proving some material fact, which the other party, if interrogated, would have to admit. The Court therefore in a proper case allows one party to administer Interrogatories to the other, and compels that other to answer them on oath before the trial, subject to certain restrictions. As a rule, it is prudent, if there be time, to obtain discovery of documents before administering interrogatories. Inspection of the documents disclosed may render unnecessary some of the proposed interrogatories. On this ground the Master will often postpone an application for leave to administer interrogatories until after discovery of documents. Moreover, discovery of documents may suggest fresh matter for interrogatories to the party inspecting.

Order for Discovery of Documents.

There are three distinct cases in which a party can obtain disclosure of documents.

(i) If either party has in his pleadings, particulars, or affidavits referred to some particular document (*e.g.*, the original libel), his opponent is entitled, without filing any affidavit or making any payment into Court, at once to give notice under Order XXXI. r. 15, that he will call and inspect that document, and take a copy of it, if he deems it sufficiently important. And the party who has referred to the document must produce it for inspection, if he has it in his possession at the time named in the notice, and permit the party who gave the notice or his solicitor to take a copy of it if he wishes so to do. (*Ormerod, Grierson & Co.* v. *St. George's Ironworks Ltd.*, [1905] 1 Ch. 505; 74 L. J. Ch. 373; 53 W. R. 502; 92 L. T. 541.) If he does not produce it, he cannot himself put it in evidence at the trial, unless he can satisfy the judge that he had some sufficient reason for not producing it. (See rules 16, 17, 18, and *Webster* v. *Whehall*, 15 Ch. D. 120; 49 L. J. Ch. 704; 28 W. R. 951; 42 L. T. 868; *Quilter* v. *Heatly*, 23 Ch. D. 49; 31 W. R. 331; 48 L. T. 373.)

(ii) Again, if one party knows or thinks he knows, that the other has certain material documents in his possession, though they are not referred to in any pleading, particular, or affidavit, he may, in such a case, file an affidavit stating his belief, and the grounds of his belief, specifying the particular documents, and showing that they are material. (*White* v. *Spafford*, [1901] 2 K. B. 241; 70 L. J. K. B. 658; 84 L. T. 574.) Upon this the Master will order his opponent to state on affidavit whether he has or ever had any of those documents in his possession or power, and, if he ever had one of them and has not now, when he parted with it, and what has become of it. (Order XXXI. r. 19A (3).) If in this affidavit he admits that he has any of the documents specified, and that such document is material, it becomes at once a document referred to in an affidavit within the preceding paragraph, and rule 15 of Order XXXI. applies to it.

(iii) If, however, either party desires a detailed list of all the material documents in his opponent's possession he may, without filing any affidavit or naming any particular document, apply to a Master for an order directing any opponent in the action to disclose on oath all documents which are, or have been, in his possession or power, relating to any matter in question in the action. But the party making the application must pay into Court to the " Security for Costs Account," to abide further order a sum of money to be fixed by the Master, usually 5*l*. (Rule 26.) But this payment does not *entitle* him to an order for general discovery. The Master now has full discretion in the matter. He will order discovery only when and only so far as he deems it necessary " either for disposing fairly of the cause or matter or for saving costs." (Order XXXI. r. 12.) If he is satisfied that discovery is not necessary he will refuse the application. If he is satisfied that discovery is not necessary at that stage of the action, he will adjourn the application. (Rule 20.) In other cases he will order discovery limited to certain classes of documents (*e.g.*, those relevant to some particular issue) or general discovery, as he thinks fit.

General discovery, at all events, will never be ordered before the Defence has been delivered : for till then the issues are not clear. (*British and Foreign Contract Co.* v. *Wright*, 32 W. R. 413.) Discovery, and inspection too, will be strictly limited to the matters in issue in the action. As to matters of which particulars have been given, *e.g.*, justification, discovery will be limited to the issues as narrowed by the particulars. (*Yorkshire Provident Co.* v. *Gilbert*, [1895] 2 Q. B. 148 ; 64 L. J. Q. B. 578 ; 72 L. T. 445 ; *Arnold and Butler* v. *Bottomley*, [1908] 2 K. B. 151 ; 77 L. J. K. B. 584; 98 L. T. 777.) And for this reason, among others, general discovery will not, as a rule, be ordered till after full particulars of the justification have been delivered. In *Vernon* v. *Battiscombe* the Court of Appeal made an order for discovery limited to the matters referred to in one paragraph of the defendant's Notice in mitigation of damages. (*Daily Telegraph*, January 19th, 1904.)

Documents Privileged from Production.

A party against whom an order for discovery has been made must thereupon make an affidavit in compliance with the terms of the order, stating what documents are in his possession or under his control. But he is not necessarily bound to produce all the documents set out in his affidavit; some of them may be privileged from inspection. If he claims any such privilege, he must state in his affidavit which documents he refuses to produce and the ground of such refusal.

That letters were written on a privileged occasion in the special sense in which that term is used in actions of defamation (*i.e.*, that the occasion renders them not actionable, unless the plaintiff can prove malice) is no ground for refusing to produce them : they are not privileged from inspection. (*Webb* v. *East*, 5 Ex. D. 23, 108; 49 L. J. Ex. 250 ; 28 W. R. 229, 336 ; 41 L. T. 715.) Communications passing between a solicitor and his client are privileged from production provided they are of a confidential character, and made for the purpose of obtaining legal advice. (*Gardner* v. *Irvin*, 4 Ex. D. 53 ; 48 L. J. Ex. 223 ; 27 W. R. 442 ; 40 L. T. 357 ; *O'Shea* v. *Wood*, [1891] P. 286 ; 60 L. J. P. 83; 65 L. T. 30.) It is not necessary that they should have been written in contemplation of litigation. (*Wheeler* v. *Le Marchant,* 17 Ch. D. 682 ; 50 L. J. Ch. 793 ; 30 W. R. 235 ; 44 L. T. 632.)

Any document which was prepared by the deponent in order that his solicitor might submit it to counsel for the purpose of obtaining his advice, is privileged from production, although it is alleged to contain a libel on the plaintiff (*Lowden* v. *Blakey,* 23 Q. B. D. 332 ; 58 L. J. Q. B. 617 ; 38 W. R. 64 ; 61 L. T. 251), and although it was prepared before the present or any litigation was contemplated. (*Minet* v. *Morgan,* L. R. 8 Ch. 361 ; 42 L. J. Ch. 627 ; 21 W. R. 467 ; 28 L. T. 573.) So, too, a solicitor, who is a party to an action may refuse to produce documents of which he is in possession solely as solicitor for a client. (*Procter* v. *Smiles,* (1886) 2 Times L. R. 474 ; *Ward* v. *Marshall,* (1887) 3 Times L. R. 578.) Letters passing between co-defendants with reference to the litigation are not necessarily privileged. (*Rochefoucauld* v. *Boustead,* [1897] 1 Ch. 196 ; 66 L. J. Ch. 74 ; 45 W. R. 272 ; 75 L. T. 502.) Moreover the privilege which attaches to communications between client and solicitor does not extend to communications made to third parties who have to decide whether or not legal proceedings shall be taken. (*Jones* v. *Great Central Railway,* [1910] A. C. 4 ; 79 L. J. K. B. 191 ; 100 L. T. 710.)

Sometimes, also, production is refused on the ground of public policy and convenience. This can only be where one party to the suit is officially in possession of State documents of importance. If the defendant be a subordinate officer of a public department sued in his official capacity, he cannot on his own authority claim privilege on the ground of public policy ; production can only be refused on that ground by the head of a department. (*Beatson* v. *Skene,* 5 H. & N. 838 ; 29 L. J. Ex. 430 ; 6 Jur. N. S. 780 ; 2 L. T. 378, *post,* p. 678). But it is not necessary that the head of the department should himself make an affidavit ; so long as it is made clear to the Court that the mind of the responsible person has been brought to bear upon the question, the objection will be upheld. (*Kain* v. *Farrer,* 37 L. T. 469 ; W. N. 1877, p. 266 ; *H.M.S. Bellerophon,* 44 L. J. Ad. 5 ; *Hennessy* v. *Wright* (No. 1), 21 Q. B. D. 509 ; 57 L. J. Q. B. 530 ; 59 L. T. 323 ; 53 J. P. 52 ; *Ford* v. *Blest,* (1890) 6 Times L. R. 295.)

It is also a ground of privilege that the documents, if produced, would tend to criminate the party producing them ; though this is not a ground on which the Court will refuse to order discovery. (*National Association of Co-operative Plasterers* v. *Smithies,* [1906] A. C. 434 ; 75 L. J. K. B. 861 ; 95 L. T. 71.) The objection can only be taken by the party himself; it must be taken on oath (*Webb* v. *East, suprà,* overruling *Hill* v. *Campbell,* L. R. 10 C. P. 222 ; 44 L. J. C. P. 97 ; 23 W. R. 336 ; 32 L. T. 59), and in clear and positive terms. His affidavit must show that he believes the production of the document will tend to criminate him. (*Kelly* v. *Colhoun,* [1899] 2 Ir. R. 199 ; and see under Interrogatories, *post,* p. 665.)

Illustrations.

Where the defendant was in possession of certain documents, but objected to produce them because, as he said in his affidavit, "the production may, to the best of my information and belief, tend to criminate me," the Court ordered their production.

> *Roe* v. *New York Press and another,* (1883) 75 L. T. Journal, 31.

The proprietor of a newspaper, even where he admits publication of an exact copy of the libel, cannot, when an order for production has been made, refuse to produce the manuscript of the libel, either on the ground of privilege or on the ground that its production might tend to incriminate him, if the Court comes to the conclusion that he does not honestly believe that its production will have that effect.

> *Kelly* v. *Colhoun,* [1899] 2 Ir. R. 199.
> But see *Hope* v. *Brash,* [1897] 2 Q. B. 188 ; 66 L. J. Q. B. 653 ; 45 W. R. 659 ; 76 L. T. 823.

He may, however, be entitled to cover up the name and address of the writer.

> *Blanc* v. *Burrows,* (1896) 12 Times L. R. 521.

Production and Inspection.

A Master at Chambers may at any stage of the action order any party to produce on oath any material document in his possession or power, and may deal with such documents when produced in such manner as shall appear just. (Order XXXI. r. 14.) Under rule 18 of the same Order, the Master may make an order for the inspection of any document in such place and in such manner as he may think fit, provided such inspection be necessary for disposing fairly of the action, or will save costs.

No such application is necessary in the case of documents for which no privilege is claimed ; these the other party is entitled to inspect at once. As to documents for which privilege has been claimed, the only question, as a rule, on such an application is, whether the deponent has in his affidavit said enough about the document to entitle him to refuse production. The Court will not go behind the oath of the deponent, unless there is ground for thinking that he has misconceived or misrepresented the effect of a document for which he has claimed privilege. (*Roberts* v. *Oppenheim*, 26 Ch. D. 724; 53 L. J. Ch. 1148; 32 W. R. 654; 50 L. T. 729.) The Master may himself in every case inspect the document if he thinks fit. (Order XXXI. r. 19A (2); *Ehrmann* v. *Ehrmann*, [1896] 2 Ch. 826; 65 L. J. Ch. 889; 75 L. T. 243.)

On production of any book or document the party producing may seal or cover up any part which he can swear is not material to any issue in the action. (*Graham* v. *Sutton, Carden & Co.*, [1897] 1 Ch. 761; 66 L. J. Ch. 320; 76 L. T. 369.) Thus a defendant who had been ordered to produce the original letter containing the information, which induced him to write the libel sued on, was allowed to cover up the address and signature of such letter when he produced it for inspection. (*Blanc* v. *Burrows*, (1896) 12 Times L. R. 521.) It is not a legitimate ground for seeking discovery that the party applying wishes to get at the name of the originator of the charge contained in the libel. (*Ib.*)

In a proper case (*e.g.*, where one party denies that he wrote the libel sued on), the Master will order the plaintiff to permit his opponent to take photographic or facsimile copies of it, of course at his own expense. (*Davey* v. *Pemberton*, 11 C. B. N. S. 628; *Lewis* v. *Earl of Londesborough*, [1893] 2 Q. B. 191; 62 L. J. Q. B. 452; 69 L. T. 353.)

Illustrations.

" The general practice of the judges of the Common Law Courts has been for a long series of years not to order inspection " of the manuscript of a libel which has been printed in a newspaper, " or to force the defendant to disclose who gave the information on which the libel was published." Hence, save in exceptional circumstances, the Court will not order the proprietor or editor of the newspaper to produce the original manuscript.

> *Hope* v. *Brash*, [1897] 2 Q. B. 188; 66 L. J. Q. B. 653; 45 W. R. 659; 76 L. T. 823.

If an order for production is made the name and address of the informant may be covered up.

> *Blanc* v. *Burrows*, (1896) 12 Times L. R. 521.

Interrogatories.

On any summons for directions either party may apply to the Master for leave to deliver interrogatories to his opponent, and for an order that the opponent answer them within ten days, or within such other time as the Master may think fit to name. (Order XXXI. rr. 1, 8.) Except by consent or in very special circumstances, such leave will not be given before the Defence is delivered. The particular interrogatories proposed to be delivered must be submitted to the Master, who will allow such of them only as he considers " necessary either for disposing fairly of the cause or matter or for saving costs." (Order XXXI. r. 2.) He will " take into account any offer, which may be made by the party sought to be interrogated, to deliver particulars, or to make admissions, or to produce documents relating to the matter in question." (*Ib. ;* and see *Cochrane* v. *Smith and others*, (1895) 12 Times L. R. 78.) Moreover, the party interrogating may be ordered, before delivering the interrogatories to his opponent, to pay into the " Security for Costs Account," to abide further order, a sum of money fixed by the Master, usually not less than 5*l*.

The function of interrogatories is to obtain admissions that will support the case of the party interrogating, or destroy the case of his opponent. They are directed to proof of the matters in issue, which matters have been defined by the particulars of the various allegations made in the pleadings, but they are not confined to the facts alleged. Interrogatories must be directed to prove facts which can fairly be said to be material to enable the party interrogating " either to maintain his own case or to destroy the case of his adversary." (Per Lord Esher, M.R., in *Hennessy* v. *Wright* (No. 2), 24 Q. B. D. at p. 447, n.)

Interrogatories must be relevant to the matters in issue. If publication is not admitted a plaintiff may always interrogate a defendant as to whether he did not speak the words set out in the Statement of Claim, " or words to that effect." (*Dalgleish* v. *Lowther*, [1899] 2 Q. B. 590; 68 L. J. Q. B. 956; 48 W. R. 37; 81 L. T. 161 ; and see Precedent No. 64.) Interrogatories will not be allowed which are directed to establishing a defence not raised on the pleadings. (*Hindlip* v. *Mudford*, (1890) 6 Times L. R. 367.) If particulars under any plea have been delivered the interrogatories must be confined to the matters stated in such particulars. (*Yorkshire Provident Co.* v. *Gilbert*, [1895] 2 Q. B. 148 ; 64 L. J. Q. B. 578 ; 72 L. T. 445 ; *Arnold and Butler* v. *Bottomley and others*, [1908] 2 K. B. 151 ; 77 L. J. K. B. 584 ; 98 L. T. 777.)

Illustrations.

Where a defendant has pleaded justification he may interrogate as to facts necessary to support his plea.

> *Marriott* v. *Chamberlain,* (1886) 17 Q. B. D. 154 ; 55 L. J. Q. B. 448 ; 34 W. R. 783 ; 54 L. T. 714.

And where a defendant has pleaded in the form of Precedent No. 26 he may interrogate as to the truth of the facts on which his comment is based with a view to proving that the comment is fair.

> *Peter Walker & Son, Ltd.* v. *Hodgson,* [1909] 1 K. B. 239 ; 78 L. J. K. B. 193 ; 99 L. T. 902.

A plaintiff may interrogate a defendant, who has set up a plea of privilege, as to facts relied on as creating privilege.

> *Barratt* v. *Kearns,* [1905] 1 K. B. 504 ; 74 L. J. K. B. 318 ; 53 W. R. 356 ; 92 L. T. 255 ; 21 Times L. R. 212.

Or as to facts from which an inference of malice may be drawn.

> *Martin and wife* v. *Trustees of British Museum and Thompson,* (1894) 10 Times L. R. 215.

Thus, in an action for slander where privilege is pleaded, the defendant may be asked what information he had which induced him to believe that the words were true, or what steps he had taken, before speaking the words, to ascertain whether they were true or not.

> *Elliott* v. *Garrett,* [1902] 1 K. B. 870 ; 71 L. J. K. B. 415 ; 50 W. R. 504 ; 86 L. T. 441.

And if the words were not published in a newspaper he may ask from whom such information was obtained.

> *White & Co.* v. *Credit Reform Association, &c., Ltd.,* [1905] 1 K. B. 653 ; 74 L. J. K. B. 419 ; 53 W. R. 369 ; 92 L. T. 817 ; 21 Times L. R. 337.
>
> *Saunderson* v. *Baron von Radeck,* (1905) 119 L. T. Jo. 33 (H. L.).

But if such interrogatory is not put *bonâ fide* for the purposes of the action but to enable another action to be started against the person who gave the information, it will be disallowed.

> *Edmondson* v. *Birch & Co., Limited,* [1905] 2 K. B. 523 ; 74 L. J. K. B. 777 ; 93 L. T. 462 ; 21 Times L. R. 657.

Where a defence of fair comment is pleaded interrogatories to prove malice are admissible as where the defence is ordinary privilege, but a newspaper in the absence of special circumstances will not be compelled to disclose the name of its informant.

> *Plymouth Mutual Co-operative and Industrial Society, Limited* v. *Traders' Publishing Association, Ltd.,* [1906] 1 K. B. 403 ; 75 L. J. K. B. 259 ; 94 L. T. 258 ; 22 Times L. R. 266.
>
> *Lever Brothers* v. *Associated Newspapers,* [1907] 2 K. B. 626 ; 76 L. J. K. B. 1141 ; 97 L. T. 530 ; 23 Times L. R. 652 ; *post,* p. 661.

But where in an action for a libel in a newspaper a defence of fair comment was pleaded, and the plaintiff sought to ask the defendants whether the words complained of were based on information obtained from the same source as an earlier and laudatory notice of the plaintiff, which had appeared in the same newspaper, and whether they had made any inquiries as to the truth of the statements in such notice, the interrogatories were disallowed as being irrelevant to the issue of malice, the earlier notice being neither defamatory nor malicious.

> *Caryll* v. *Daily Mail Publishing Co., Limited,* (1904) 90 L. T. 307.

"Interrogatories which do not relate to any matters in question in the cause or matter shall be deemed irrelevant, notwithstanding that they might be admissible on the oral cross-examination of a witness." (Order XXXI. r. 1.) Questions merely to credit cannot be administered as interrogatories. (*Allhusen* v. *Labouchere,* 3 Q. B. D. 654; 47 L. J. Ch. 819; 27 W. R. 12; 39 L. T. 207.) "We have never allowed interrogatories merely as to the credibility of a party as a witness." (Per Cockburn, C.J., in *Labouchere* v. *Shaw,* 41 J. P. 788.)

Again, no interrogatory need be answered which is not put *bonâ fide* for the purposes of the present action, but with a view to future litigation. (*Blanc* v. *Burrows,* (1896) 12 Times L. R. 521; *Edmondson* v. *Birch & Co., Ltd.,* [1905] 2 K. B. 523; 74 L. J. K. B. 777; 54 W. R. 52; 93 L. T. 462.) Such an interrogatory would be oppressive. (*White & Co.* v. *Credit Reform Association, &c., Ltd.,* [1905] 1 K. B. at p. 659); and so is any interrogatory which puts an undue burden on the party interrogated. (*Heaton* v. *Goldney,* [1910] 1 K. B. 754.)

Illustrations.

A defendant cannot be interrogated as to statements made on an occasion absolutely privileged.

> *Barratt* v. *Kearns,* [1905] 1 K. B. at p. 511.

Where a plaintiff put on the defendant's words a defamatory innuendo he was not allowed to interrogate the defendant as to whether he intended to make the imputations alleged in the innuendo.

> *Heaton* v. *Goldney,* [1910] 1 K. B. 754; 79 L. J. K. B. 541; 102 L. T. 451; 26 Times L. R. 383.

Interrogatories asking plaintiff whether similar charges had not been made against him previously in a newspaper, and whether he had contradicted them or taken any notice of them on that occasion, are clearly irrelevant.

> *Pankhurst* v. *Hamilton,* (1886) 2 Times L. R. 682.

The publisher of a newspaper must answer the interrogatory : "Was not the passage set out in paragraph 3 of the Statement of Claim intended to apply to the plaintiff?" But he need not answer the further question, "if not, say to whom?"; as, if the passage did not apply to the plaintiff, it is immaterial to whom it referred, so far as the present action is concerned.

> *Wilton* v. *Brignell,* W. N. 1875, 239.

So a defendant cannot be asked, "If you did not print the libel, did M'C. & Co., or some other and what firm print it ? "

> Pankhurst v. Wighton & Co., (1886) 2 Times L. R. 745.

If the proprietor of a newspaper accepts liability for a libel published in his paper, he cannot be interrogated as to the name of the writer of the libel, or as to the sources of his information, unless the identity of such writer or informant is a fact material to some issue raised in the case.

> Parnell v. Walter and another, (1890) 24 Q. B. D. 441 ; 59 L. J. Q. B. 125 ; 38 W. R. 270 ; 62 L. T. 75.
>
> Hennessy v. Wright (No. 2), (1888) 24 Q. B. D. 445, n. ; 36 W. R. 879.
>
> Gibson v. Evans, (1889) 23 Q. B. D. 384 ; 58 L. J. Q. B. 612 ; 61 L. T. 388.
>
> Caryll v. Daily Mail Publishing Co., Limited, (1904) 90 L. T. 307.
>
> M'Colla v. Jones, (1887) 4 Times L. R. 12.
>
> Mackenzie v. Steinkopff, (1890) 54 J. P. 327 ; 6 Times L. R. 141.
>
> Plymouth Mutual, &c. Society, Ltd. v. Traders' Publishing Association, Ltd., [1906] 1 K. B. 403 ; 75 L. J. K. B. 259 ; 54 W. R. 319 ; 94 L. T. 258 ; 22 Times L. R. 266.

But interrogatories are not, like pleadings, confined to the material facts on which a party relies for his claim or defence ; they may be directed to the facts which will be proved at the trial as evidence of those material facts.   Either party may interrogate as to any link in the chain of proof necessary to substantiate his case ; the question must be relevant as leading up to a matter in issue in the action. Thus, if the defendant has denied that he wrote the libel, he may be asked whether other documents produced to him are not in his handwriting, though such other documents have nothing to do with the case, but will only be used for comparison with the libel.   (Jones v. Richards, 15 Q. B. D. 439.)   So, too, a defendant who has justified may interrogate as to any fact which will help him to prove his particulars of justification.   (Marriott v. Chamberlain, 17 Q. B. D. 154 ; 55 L. J. Q. B. 448 ; 34 W. R. 783 ; 54 L. T. 714 ; and see ante, p. 651.)

Interrogatories addressed to matters which are relevant only in aggravation or diminution of damages are not encouraged. (Heaton v. Goldney, [1910] 1 K. B. 754 ; 79 L. J. K. B. 541 ; 102 L. T. 451.) But in some cases such interrogatories are clearly admissible. Thus, where the defendant has delivered a notice in mitigation of damages under Order XXXVI. r. 37, he is entitled to administer interrogatories to the plaintiff as to the matters referred to therein (Scaife v. Kemp & Co., [1892] 2 Q. B. 319 ; 61 L. J. Q. B. 515 ; 66 L. T. 589) ;

and we presume that the plaintiff may also interrogate the defendant
on such matters, though not perhaps with the same minuteness.
Again, since sect. 6 of the Law of Libel Amendment Act, 1888 (*ante,*
p. 397), it is material on the question of the amount of damages to
inquire whether the plaintiff has brought other actions for the same
libel. Hence, it is submitted, that interrogatories as to such other
actions are now admissible.

Illustrations.

A plaintiff is entitled to obtain an approximate statement in round numbers of the circulation of an obscure newspaper in which a libel has
appeared. But in the case of *The Times,* or any other leading London
newspaper, such an interrogatory would be deemed unnecessary and vexatious. In the case of any well-known and substantial newspaper, whether
in London or the provinces, an answer that "a considerable number of
copies" of the particular issue containing the libel were printed and published will be held sufficient.

> *Whittaker* v. *Scarborough Post,* [1896] 2 Q. B. 148 ; 65 L. J.
> Q. B. 564 ; 44 W. R. 657 ; 74 L. T. 753.
> *James and others* v. *Carr and others,* (1890) 7 Times L. R. 4.
> *Rumney* v. *Walter,* (1891) 61 L. J. Q. B. 149 ; 40 W. R. 174 ;
> 65 L. T. 757 ; 8 Times L. R. 96.
> Overruling on this point, *Parnell* v. *Walter,* (1890) 24 Q. B. D.
> 441 ; 59 L. J. Q. B. 125 ; 38 W. R. 270 ; 62 L. T. 75.

Prior to the passing of the Law of Libel Amendment Act, 1888, interrogatories were disallowed which asked the plaintiff for particulars of
sums already recovered by him in other actions in respect of other publications of the same libel. But now such interrogatories would, it is submitted, be admissible under sect. 6 of that Act.

> *Tucker* v. *Lawson,* (1886) 2 Times L. R. 593.

The party interrogating may put his whole case to his opponent
if he thinks fit, though it is not always wise to do so ; he may also
interrogate in full detail as to matters common to the case of both
parties ; but he is not entitled to obtain more than an outline of his
opponent's case. He cannot compel his adversary to disclose the
evidence by which he proposes to prove the facts on which he
intends to rely at the trial. (*Lever Brothers* v. *Associated Newspapers,* [1907] 2 K. B. 626 ; 76 L. J. K. B. 1141 ; 97 L. T. 530.)
He cannot claim to " see his opponent's brief," or ask him to name
the witnesses whom he means to call at the trial. The party
interrogating may ask anything to make out his own case or answer
his opponent's case, but he is not entitled to discover in what way
his opponent intends to prove his case. (*Ridgway* v. *Smith & Son,*
(1890) 6 Times L. R. 275.) Though if he is in other respects

entitled to certain information, he will not be debarred from it merely because supplying it will necessarily disclose the names of persons whom the party interrogated may hereafter wish to call as his witnesses, or otherwise give some clue to his evidence. (*Marriott* v. *Chamberlain*, 17 Q. B. D. 154; 55 L. J. Q. B. 448; 34 W. R. 783; 54 L. T. 714; *Birch* v. *Mather*, 22 Ch. D. 629; 52 L. J. Ch. 292; 31 W. R. 362; *M'Colla* v. *Jones*, (1887) 4 Times L. R. 12; *Ashworth* v. *Roberts*, 45 Ch. D. 623; 60 L. J. Ch. 27; 39 W. R. 170; 63 L. T. 160.)

Illustrations.

In an action of slander, where the defence consisted of a denial of publication, the plaintiff was allowed to ask the defendant whether he did not speak the words, or words to that effect, and whether they were not spoken in the presence of persons named in the plaintiff's particulars and others, or any and which of them.

> *Dalgleish* v. *Lowther*, [1899] 2 Q. B. 590; 68 L. J. Q. B. 956; 48 W. R. 37; 81 L. T. 161.
>
> *Russell* v. *Stubbs*, (1908) 52 Sol. Jo. 580.

Where the defendant was sued for publishing an anonymous letter to P. of which publication was denied, the plaintiff was allowed to ask the defendant whether he did not on or about the date alleged, or at some other and what date, write and send, or cause to be sent to P., a letter of which a copy, in the terms alleged, was annexed to the interrogatory.

> *Jones* v. *Richards*, (1885) 15 Q. B. D. 439; 1 Times L. R. 660.

A party cannot be asked to give the names of those who were present when any material act was done. This would be asking him to name his witnesses.

> *Eade* v. *Jacobs*, (1877) 3 Ex. D. 335; 47 L. J. Ex. 74; 26 W. R. 159; 37 L. T. 621.
>
> *Johns* v. *James*, (1879) 13 Ch. D. 370.
>
> *Ashley* v. *Taylor*, (1877) 37 L. T. 522; (C. A.) (1878) 38 L. T. 44.
>
> *White & Co.* v. *Credit Reform Association, &c., Ltd.*, [1905] 1 K. B. 653; 74 L. J. K. B. 419; 53 W. R. 369; 92 L. T. 817; 21 Times L. R. 337.

Where the defendant is entitled to certain information because it is material to his case upon a plea of justification, the plaintiff will be ordered to give such information in answer to interrogatories although he will thus be compelled to disclose the names of persons whom he intends to call as witnesses.

> *Marriott* v. *Chamberlain*, (1886) 17 Q. B. D. 154; 55 L. J. Q. B. 448; 34 W. R. 783; 54 L. T. 714.
>
> And see *Birch* v. *Mather*, (1883) 22 Ch. D. 629; 52 L. J. Ch. 292; 31 W. R. 362.
>
> *M'Colla* v. *Jones*, (1887) 4 Times L. R. 12.
>
> *Ashworth* v. *Roberts*, (1890) 45 Ch. D. 623; 60 L. J. Ch. 27; 39 W. R. 170; 63 L. T. 160.

But where a defendant has pleaded fair comment and the plaintiff has joined issue thereon, the defendant will not be allowed to administer to the plaintiff an interrogatory in the following form : Do you intend to set up that the defendant, in publishing the words complained of, was actuated by express malice towards the plaintiff ? If yea, state generally the facts and circumstances on which the plaintiff relies as showing actual malice.

> *Lever Brothers* v. *Associated Newspapers*, [1907] 2 K. B. 626 ;
> 76 L. J. K. B. 1141 ; 97 L. T. 530 ; 23 Times L. R. 652.
> Overruling *Cooper* v. *Blackmore*, (1886) 2 Times L. R. 746.

But even in interrogating as to his own case, the questions asked must not be "fishing," that is, they must refer to some definite and existing state of circumstances, not be put merely in the hope of discovering something which may help the party interrogating to make out *some* case.   They must be confined to matters which there is good ground for believing to have occurred.   "The moment it appears that questions are asked and answers insisted upon in order to enable the party to see if he can find a case, either of complaint or defence, of which at present he knows nothing, and which will be a different case from that which he now makes, the rule against 'fishing' interrogatories applies."   (Per Lord Esher, M.R., in *Hennessy* v. *Wright* (No. 2), 24 Q. B. D. at p. 448, n.; and see *Dalgleish* v. *Lowther*, [1899] 2 Q. B. 590; 68 L. J. Q. B. 956; 48 W. R. 37; 81 L. T. 161.)   "Fishing" interrogatories are especially objectionable when their object is to get at something or other to support a plea of justification.   (*Gourley* v. *Plimsoll*, L. R. 8 C. P. 362; 42 L. J. C. P. 121; 21 W. R. 683; 28 L. T. 598; *Buchanan* v. *Taylor*, W. N. 1876, p. 73.)

Illustrations.

Where the plaintiff was charged with having used certain blasphemous phrases interrogatories were disallowed as "fishing," the object of which was to show that if plaintiff had not said what he was charged with saying, still he had on other occasions said something very much like it.

> *Pankhurst* v. *Hamilton*, (1886) 2 Times L. R. 682.

A defendant who has justified without giving sufficient particulars will not be allowed to use discovery as a means of fishing out materials in support of his plea.

> *Arnold and Butler* v. *Bottomley*, [1908] 2 K. B. 151 ; 77 L. J.
> K. B. 584 ; 98 L. T. 777 ; 24 Times L. R. 365.

Interrogatories are not allowed as to the contents of written documents, unless it is first proved or admitted that such documents have been lost or destroyed. (*Stein* v. *Tabor*, 31 L. T. 444; *Fitz-*

gibbon v. *Greer*, Ir. R. 9 C. L. 294 ; *Dalrymple* v. *Leslie*, 8 Q. B. D. 5 ; 51 L. J. Q. B. 61 ; 30 W. R. 105 ; 45 L. T. 478.) Nor can either party as a rule be asked as to his having received or parted with a particular document; as he can always be called on to make an affidavit of documents. (*Hall* v. *Truman*, 29 Ch. D. 307 ; 54 L. J. Ch. 717 ; 52 L. T. 586 ; *Morris* v. *Edwards*, 15 App. Cas. 309 ; 60 L. J. Q. B. 292 ; 63 L. T. 26.) But an application can be made on affidavit to the Master for an order requiring the "other party to state by affidavit whether any one or more specific documents, to be specified in the application, is or are, or has or have at any time been, in his possession or power, and, if not then in his possession, when he parted with the same, and what has become thereof." (Order XXXI. r. 19ᴀ (3) ; see *ante*, p. 649.)

Illustrations.

A party who has made an affidavit of documents cannot be interrogated as to documents alleged to be in his possession unless either upon the face of the affidavit itself, or of the documents referred to in it, or in his pleading, there is something which affords a presumption that he has in his possession other relevant documents besides those whose possession he has admitted.

> *Hall* v. *Truman,* (1885) 29 Ch. D. 307 ; 54 L. J. Ch. 717 ; 52 L. T. 586.

And if in an affidavit of documents privilege has been claimed, the party making such affidavit cannot be interrogated as to any of the privileged documents.

> *Morris* v. *Edwards,* (1890) 15 App. Cas. 309 ; 60 L. J. Q. B. 292 ; 63 L. T. 26.

Questions which tend to criminate may certainly be asked, unless they are either irrelevant or "fishing," though the party interrogated is not bound to answer them. (*Post*, p. 665.) That the interrogatories will tend to criminate others is no objection, if they be put *bonâ fide* for the purposes of the present action. (*M'Corquodale* v. *Bell and another*, W. N. 1876, p. 39.) That to answer them would expose the party interrogated, or third persons, to civil actions, was never an objection. (*Tetley* v. *Easton*, 25 L. J. C. P. 293.)

Answers to Interrogatories.

The answers must be carefully drawn. The party interrogated may answer guardedly, and make qualified admissions only, so long as both the admission and the qualification are clear and definite. (*Malone* v. *Fitzgerald*, 18 L. R. Ir. 187.) He may answer "Yes"

or " No " simply, so long as it is clear how much he thus admits
or denies. It is generally wise to answer the interrogatory by
following the exact words and denying or admitting each part of it
specifically, as in this way the party interrogating is prevented from
applying for further and better answers. It is quite admissible to
say, " I do not know," where the matter is clearly not within the
deponent's own knowledge or that of his servants. He is not bound
to procure information, for the purpose of answering, from others
who are not his servants or agents. (Per Brett, J., in *Phillips* v.
Routh, L. R. 7 C. P. 287; *Field* v. *Bennett*, (1885) 2 Times L. R. 91,
122.) The following answer was held sufficient in *Dalrymple* v.
Leslie (8 Q. B. D. 5; 51 L. J. Q. B. 61; 30 W. R. 105; 45 L. T.
478) : " I kept no copy and have no copy of the said letter, and I
am unable to recollect with exactness what the statements contained
therein were." If, however, the interrogatories are addressed to
matters which are within the knowledge of his agents or servants,
and such knowledge was acquired by them in the ordinary course of
their employment as his agents or servants, then " their knowledge
is his knowledge and he is bound to answer in respect of that."
(*Bolckow, Vaughan & Co.* v. *Fisher and others*, 10 Q. B. D. 161; 52
L. J. Q. B. 12; 31 W. R. 235; 47 L. T. 724; *Rasbotham* v. *Shrop-
shire Union Rail. and Canal Co.*, 24 Ch. D. 110; 53 L. J. Ch. 327;
32 W. R. 117; 48 L. T. 902; *Hall* v. *L. & N. W. Rail. Co.*, 35 L. T.
848.) And if he is answering as the proper officer of a corporation
he must make all necessary inquiries of the servants or agents of
the corporation, but he is not bound to disclose information acquired
by himself or by such servants or agents otherwise than in the
capacity of agents of the corporation. (*Welsbach, &c.* v. *New Sun-
light Co.*, [1900] 2 Ch. 1; 69 L. J. Ch. 546; 48 W. R. 595; 83 L. T.
58.) " Agents " includes bankers or solicitors. (*Alliott* v. *Smith*,
[1895] 2 Ch. 111; 64 L. J. Ch. 684; 43 W. R. 597; 72 L. T. 789.)

Any objection to answering an interrogatory can be taken in the
affidavit in answer. (Order XXXI. r. 6.) Thus, either party may
object that a question is irrelevant or " fishing," or not put *bonâ fide*
for the purposes of this action. He may also object to name his
witnesses or set out the evidence by which he hopes to prove his
case. (But see *ante*, p. 659, and cases there cited.) Or he may
decline to state the contents of a written document, the document
when produced being the best evidence of its own contents. In
some cases professional privilege can be claimed as a ground for
refusing to answer. Thus, if the person interrogated be a solicitor,
it is sufficient for him to state " I have no personal knowledge of

the matters referred to in this interrogatory, and the only information and belief that I have received or have respecting any of such matters has been derived from and is founded on information of a confidential character procured by me as solicitor of the said C., and not otherwise, for the purpose of litigation between the plaintiff and the said C., either pending or threatened by the plaintiff. I claim to be privileged from answering this interrogatory further." (*Proctor* v. *Smiles*, 55 L. J. Q. B. 467, 527.) Similarly, a client may refuse to disclose information which he only obtained from his solicitor since action and which was the result of inquiries instituted by the solicitor for the purposes of the litigation (*Procter* v. *Raikes and another*, (1886) 3 Times L. R. 229; *Lyell* v. *Kennedy* (No. 2), 9 App. Cas. 81; 53 L. J. Ch. 449; 32 W. R. 497; 50 L. T. 277); unless such information could not possibly be the subject of a confidential communication between solicitor and client. (*Foakes* v. *Webb*, 28 Ch. D. 287; 54 L. J. Ch. 262; 33 W. R. 249; 51 L. T. 624; *Williams* v. *Quebrada, &c., Co.*, [1895] 2 Ch. 751; 44 W. R. 76; 73 L. T. 397.) A defendant when interrogated as to publication on a privileged occasion may object to answer on the ground that the occasion is absolutely privileged, but not on the ground that he did not publish the words. (*Barratt* v. *Kearns*, [1905] 1 K. B. 504; 74 L. J. K. B. 318; 53 W. R. 356; 92 L. T. 255.)

Again, the party interrogated may object to all or any of a set of interrogatories on the ground that they have been exhibited unreasonably or vexatiously, or that they are prolix, oppressive, unnecessary, or scandalous. But both the phrases "unreasonable or vexatious" and "scandalous" have special meanings. Masters at Chambers, following the *dictum* of Pollock, B., in *Gay* v. *Labouchere* (4 Q. B. D. 207), construe "unreasonable or vexatious" as referring to the time or stage in the cause at which they are exhibited; in short, that they are "premature." (See *Mercier* v. *Cotton*, 1 Q. B. D. 442; 46 L. J. Q. B. 184; 24 W. R. 566; 35 L. T. 79.) A "scandalous" interrogatory may be defined as an insulting or degrading question, which is irrelevant or impertinent to the matters in issue. "Certainly nothing can be scandalous which is relevant." (Per Cotton, L.J., in *Fisher* v. *Owen*, 8 Ch. D. 653.) "The mere fact that these matters state a scandalous fact does not make them scandalous." (Per Brett, L.J., in *Millington* v. *Loring*, 6 Q. B. D. at p. 196.) Questions which tend to criminate are not scandalous, unless they are also either irrelevant or "fishing." (*Allhusen* v. *Labouchere*, 3 Q. B. D. 654; 47 L. J. Ch. 819; 27 W. R. 12; 39 L. T. 207.)

Another objection that may be taken is that to answer the interrogatory would tend to criminate the deponent. This objection *must* be taken on oath in the answer. (*Fisher* v. *Owen*, 8 Ch. D. 645; 47 L. J. Ch. 477, 681; 26 W. R. 417, 581; 38 L. T. 252, 577; *Allhusen* v. *Labouchere, supra; National Association of Operative Plasterers* v. *Smithies*, [1906] A. C. 434; 75 L. J. K. B. 861; 95 L. T. 71.) The only case to the contrary since the Judicature Act came into operation (*Atherley* v. *Harvey*, 2 Q. B. D. 524; 46 L. J. Q. B. 518; 25 W. R. 727; 36 L. T. 551) was decided under a misapprehension of the previous practice in Equity, as has been frequently pointed out by learned judges, and is admittedly bad law. (See the remarks of Cotton, L.J., 8 Ch. D. at p. 654.) And the objection must be stated in clear and unequivocal language. In *Lamb* v. *Munster* (10 Q. B. D. 110; 52 L. J. Q. B. 46; 31 W. R. 117; 47 L. T. 442), it was held sufficient for the defendant to state on oath, "I decline to answer all the interrogatories upon the ground that my answer to them might tend to criminate me." And see *Jones* v. *Richards*, 15 Q. B. D. 439; *R.* v. *Slaney*, 5 C. & P. 213, and the cases cited under "Discovery of Documents," *ante*, p. 652.

To publish a libel is a crime. Hence, to ask whether the defendant had any share in writing, printing, or composing the alleged libel, or was the editor of the newspaper at the date of publication, has a direct tendency to criminate him; and he may therefore refuse to answer such questions, although there is not the faintest prospect in reality of any criminal proceedings being taken against him. And this answer (except in one case) is conclusive; it is idle for the party interrogating to argue that he does not see how the question can possibly criminate the deponent, if the deponent swears positively that it will.

But by statute an exception has been created. Sect. 19 of the 6 & 7 Will. IV. c. 76, was re-enacted by the 32 & 33 Vict. c. 24, sched. 2, while other sections were repealed by sched. 1. It therefore remains in force, though subsequently the whole original Act was repealed by the 33 & 34 Vict. c. 99. It runs as follows: "If any person shall file any bill in any Court for the discovery of the name of any person concerned as printer, publisher, or proprietor of any newspaper, or of any matters relative to the printing or publishing of any newspaper, in order the more effectually to bring or carry on any suit or action for damages alleged to have been sustained by reason of any slanderous or libellous matter contained in any such newspaper respecting such person, it shall not be lawful for the defendant to plead or demur to such bill, but such defendant shall be compellable to make the discovery required; provided always, that such discovery shall not be made use of as evidence or otherwise in any proceeding against the defendant, save only in that proceeding for which the discovery is made." Before the Judicature Act it was held that this section was confined to a bill for discovery in Equity, and was not incorporated by the C. L. P. Act, 1854, so as to apply to interrogatories at Common Law. It followed that if the defendant answered such interrogatories his answers could have been used against him in a criminal proceeding. The Court therefore refused to order the defendant to give the required information, he having objected on oath to answer the interrogatories, and this although by going into Equity the plaintiff could have compelled the defendant to answer. (*Bowden* v. *Allen,* 39 L. J. C. P. 217; 18 W. R. 695; 22 L. T. 342.)

Hence, till 1875, a plaintiff was compelled to file a bill for discovery in Equity to obtain this information, a cumbrous and expensive proceeding. There is only one instance reported in which a plaintiff availed himself of the privilege. (*Dixon* v. *Enoch,* L. R. 13 Eq. 394; 41 L. J. Ch. 231; 20 W. R. 359; 26 L. T. 127.) But directly the Judicature Act came into operation every Division of the High Court of Justice was empowered to grant all equitable remedies, and to exercise all powers formerly possessed by the Court of Chancery, with the especial object of avoiding all circuity and multiplicity of legal proceedings. Hence, as early as November 7th, 1875, Lush, J., in *Ramsden* v. *Brearley* (33 L. T. 322; W. N. 1875, p. 199), decided that the following interrogatory was allowable and must be answered: "Were you, on the 22nd of November, 1874, the printer or publisher, or both, of the *Standard* newspaper?" And his lordship decided that the protection accorded by the concluding proviso of sect. 19 of 6 & 7 Will. IV. c. 76, would attach to the defendant's answers, so that they could not be used against him in any other proceeding. To answer such an interrogatory cannot therefore tend to criminate the defendant. This decision was followed by Archibald, J., in *Carter* v. *Leeds Daily News Co. and Jackson,* W. N. 1876, p. 11.

So, too, in *Lefroy* v. *Burnside* (4 L. R. Ir. 340; 41 L. T. 199; 14 Cox, C. C. 260), the defendant in an action for libel, the alleged proprietor of a newspaper, was served with interrogatories by the plaintiff inquiring, *inter alia,* whether he was not such proprietor. This interrogatory the defendant in his answer declined to answer, on the ground that it might tend to criminate him in certain criminal proceedings which had been commenced against him by the same plaintiff and were then actually pending. On summons by the plaintiff to compel further answer to this interrogatory, the Exchequer Division in Ireland held that it must be answered; inasmuch as sect. 19 of the 6 & 7 Will. IV. c. 76, was still in force, and was by sect. 24, sub-sect. 7, of the Judicature Act, 1873, made enforceable by interrogatories in every action. (See *post*, p. 788.)

But it must be remembered that sect. 19 of 6 & 7 Will. IV. c. 76, applies only to the "printer, publisher, or proprietor" of a newspaper. A defendant may therefore object, on the ground of criminality, to answer any interrogatory asking whether he is the editor of the paper (*Carter* v. *Leeds Daily News Co. and Jackson, suprà*), or whether he is the author of the alleged libel. (*Wilton* v. *Brignell*, W. N. 1875, p. 239. And see *M'Loughlin* v. *Dwyer* (1), Ir. R. 9 C. L. 170.)

This point is still one of practical importance; for though the Newspaper Libel and Registration Act, 1881, compels the printer of every newspaper to make an annual return (*post*, p. 839), still it is possible that since the last return the defendant may have transferred all his interest in the paper to someone else before the libel appeared; and this it is open to him to prove at the trial, and if proved it will be a good defence. It is not therefore safe to rely wholly on a certificate under that Act where the defendant denies on the pleadings that he was proprietor of the paper at the date of the libel. (See *post*, p. 676.)

Where the plaintiff, who had sued the publisher of a newspaper, administered interrogatories and thereby ascertained, for the first time, after issue joined, the name of the proprietor of the paper, he was allowed to join the latter as a co-defendant with the publisher under Order XVI. r. 4. (*Edward* v. *Lowther*, 45 L. J. C. P. 417; 24 W. R. 484; 34 L. T. 255.)

The party interrogated, if a plaintiff, may avoid answering the interrogatories by discontinuing the action, but if leave to discontinue be necessary, it may be made a term of the order that he shall not bring a second action in respect of that cause of action. (*Hess* v. *Labouchere*, (1898) 14 Times L. R. 350.)

Advice on Evidence.

As soon as notice of trial is given, or in urgent cases even sooner the papers should be laid before counsel for his advice on evidence. This should always be done by both sides, even in cases apparently simple ; else the action may be lost for want of some certificate or other formal piece of proof, as in *Collins* v. *Carnegie,* 1 A. & E. 695. Every document in the case should be sent to counsel, especially the affidavits of documents, the answers to interrogatories, and the draft notices to produce and to inspect and admit. Also some statement as to the oral evidence proposed to be given.

Counsel should, in the first place, satisfy himself that all preliminary steps have been taken, and that everything is in order to enable him properly to present his client's case at the trial. Is any amendment of the pleadings necessary ? Are any particulars required ? Are interrogatories necessary, or if interrogatories have been administered, have they been sufficiently answered ? Have all material documents been disclosed or produced ? He must then proceed to write the Advice on Evidence, and the best and clearest mode of doing this is first to set out briefly what are the issues in the action and whether the burden of proving each issue lies on the plaintiff or on the defendant, and then to state *seriatim* how each is to be proved or rebutted.

The *onus* lies on the plaintiff to prove that the defendant published or uttered the defamatory words, that they were understood in the sense alleged in the innuendo, and that they referred to the plaintiff. If any special damage has been sustained, this also should be proved by the plaintiff, whether it is essential to the cause of action or not. It may further be necessary to prove that the plaintiff at the date of publication held some office or was engaged in some profession or trade, and that the words were spoken of him in the way of such office, profession, or trade. If a defence of " fair comment " has been pleaded, the *onus* is on the plaintiff to show that the comment is unfair. (*McQuire* v. *Western Morning News Co.,* [1903] 2 K. B. 100 ; 72 L. J. K. B. 612 ; 51 W. R. 689 ; 88 L. T. 757.) If the occasion be one of qualified privilege, it lies on the plaintiff to show that the words were published maliciously. If a Statute of Limitation has been pleaded, the *onus* lies on the plaintiff of proving that the cause of action arose within the prescribed period. (*Wilby* v. *Henman,* 2 Cr. & M. 658 ; and see *ante,* p. 609.)

On the defendant, on the other hand, lies the *onus* of proving privilege, justification, or an accord and satisfaction. If he has pleaded a plea under Lord Campbell's Act, the *onus* lies on the defendant to prove that the libel was inserted without malice or gross negligence, and that a full apology was inserted in proper type before action brought, or as soon as possible afterwards.

Each party should be prepared with evidence not only to prove the issues which lie upon him, but also to rebut his adversary's case. The plaintiff may also bring evidence in aggravation, the defendant in mitigation, of damages. (See *ante*, pp. 389, 393.) And defendant's counsel must consider the advisability of giving a notice under Order XXXVI., r. 37, *post*, p. 696. As to the effect and meaning of this rule, see *ante*, p. 402. For the form of such a notice, see Precedent No. 63, *post*, p. 787.

Having thus determined what facts his client has to prove at the trial, counsel should proceed to state how each is to be proved. In the first place, what witnesses must be called. It may be necessary to apply to postpone the trial in order to secure the attendance of witnesses who are ill or absent abroad (*Turner* v. *Meryweather*, 7 C. B. 251 ; 18 L. J. C. P. 155 ; *Brown* v. *Murray*, 4 D. & R. 830 ; *M'Cauley* v. *Thorpe*, 1 Chit. 685 ; 5 Madd. 19), or on other grounds. (See *Parnell* v. *Walter and another*, (1889) 5 Times L. R. 577.) In other cases it may be necessary to apply for letters of request or a commission abroad, or for the examination before trial of a witness who is dangerously ill or about to leave the country. (Order XXXVII. r. 5 ; *Procter* v. *Tyler*, (1887) 3 Times L. R. 282; *Ross* v. *Woodford*, [1894] 1 Ch. 38 ; 63 L. J. Ch. 191 ; 42 W. R. 188 ; 70 L. T. 22 ; see *post*, p. 670.) In some cases the necessity of calling evidence to prove a particular fact may be obviated by giving a Notice to Admit Facts under Order XXXII. r. 4.

Counsel must next consider what documents will be required to prove his client's case, and also what documents will be needed for the cross-examination of the witnesses called by the other side. On this several questions arise : Are such documents still in existence ? In whose handwriting are they ? Are they within jurisdiction ? If the originals cannot be produced, can copies be procured or any other secondary evidence of their contents ? If so, are the copies admissible ? How can they be proved to be correct copies ? Need the person who made such copies be called as a witness ? Counsel should go carefully through the notice to inspect and admit, and the notice to produce, and advise on their sufficiency. Several statutes have been passed which make copies of registers and other public and official documents admissible in evidence, if duly authenticated. Counsel must be careful to advise the solicitor to obtain the proper kind of copy which is made admissible by the particular Act. Where the defendant justified a libel which imputed insolvency to the plaintiff, he was not allowed to obtain a copy of the plaintiff's banking account under the Bankers' Books Evidence Act, 1879 (42

Vict. c. 11, s. 7). (*Emmott* v. *Star Newspaper Co.*, (1892) 9 Times L. R. 111.)

Counsel is often at this stage of the proceedings consulted as to the advisability of securing a special jury, or of applying to change the venue.

Mode and place of trial are usually dealt with by the Master on the Summons for Directions. If no order has been made in respect of these matters, or if either party desires that the order made be varied, a special application should be made by notice under Order XXX. r. 5. An action of libel or slander is almost invariably tried by a jury, though it can be tried by a judge alone; trial by a jury will always be ordered if the defendant wishes it. (*Lord Kinnaird* v. *Field*, [1905] 2 Ch. 361.) If the trial is to be by jury either party can obtain a special jury if he gives notice within the time mentioned in Order XXXVI. r. 7 (*b*) and (*c*); if he allows this period to elapse, he cannot demand a special jury as of right; but there is generally no difficulty in securing one, unless the application is made with the object of delaying the trial. There is practically only one ground now on which either party can at this stage of the proceedings ask the Master to change the venue, and that is " local prejudice." The Master will alter the place of trial if he is satisfied that there is no probability of a fair trial in the place originally fixed, *e.g.*, if a local newspaper of extensive circulation has recently published unfair attacks on either party with reference to the subject-. matter of the action. (*Thorogood* v. *Newman*, (1907) 23 Times L. R. 97.) Such extraneous facts must be proved by affidavit.

Letters of Request, or Commission Abroad.

Several foreign Governments object to commissions being issued, and to examiners administering oaths to witnesses within their dominions. Hence, now the Foreign Office, at the request of the Lord Chancellor or the Lord Chief Justice, frequently sends through diplomatic channels a letter of request addressed to the tribunal of such other country asking the judges of that tribunal to order the required evidence to be taken and remitted to the English Court. This plan is found to be cheaper than the writ of commission, which, however, is still employed for the examination of witnesses in the United States of America, and occasionally in our Colonies.

A defendant will obtain letters of request or a commission more readily than a plaintiff who has chosen his own *forum*. (*Ross* v.

Woodford, [1894] 1 Ch. 38; 63 L. J. Ch. 191; 42 W. R. 188; 70 L. T. 22.) The affidavit filed in support of such an application must state the name of at least one witness whom it is desired to examine. (*Howard* v. *Dulau & Co.*, (1895) 11 Times L. R. 451.) And the general nature of the evidence which such witness is expected to give should also be stated. (*Barry* v. *Barclay*, 15 C. B. N. S. 849.) If such evidence is not directly material to some issue in the cause, but only incidentally useful in corroboration of other evidence, the application will not be granted. (*Ehrmann* v. *Ehrmann*, [1896] 2 Ch. 611; 65 L. J. Ch. 745; 45 W. R. 149 ; 75 L. T. 37.) The plaintiff himself will not, as a rule, be allowed to give his evidence abroad on commission ; it should be given before the jury here. (*Keeley* v. *Wakley*, (1893) 9 Times L. R. 571.) But a defendant, if resident abroad, will be allowed this indulgence. (*New* v. *Burns*, 64 L. J. Q. B. 104; 43 W. R. 182; 71 L. T. 681.) The application is not usually made till after Defence; but it may be made earlier, if there be special reasons for such urgency. The application will fail if it can be shown that the witnesses could be brought to England without much greater expense, or that witnesses now in England could give the same evidence. (*The M. Moxham*, 1 P. D. 107, 115; 24 W. R. 597; *Spiller* v. *Paris Skating Rink Co.*, W. N. 1880, 228.) Sometimes the mere delay, which will thus necessarily be caused, is a sufficient reason for refusing the application. (*Steuart* v. *Gladstone*, 7 Ch. D. 394; 47 L. J. Ch. 154; 26 W. R. 277; 37 L. T. 575 ; but see *Milissich* v. *Lloyd's*, W. N. 1875, 200.) The costs of the commission must be borne by the party who applied for it, unless the judge at the trial makes any order in respect of them. (*In re Imperial Land Co. of Marseilles*, 37 L. T. 588 ; W. N. 1877, 244.)

CHAPTER XXV.

TRIAL.

As soon as Notice of Trial has been given the cause must be entered for trial in accordance with rules 11—20 of Order XXXVI.: the case will eventually make its appearance in the day's cause list. When once the case has been called on in Court, and the jury have been sworn, the trial must proceed. The plaintiff cannot discontinue. (*Fox* v. *Star Newspaper Co.*, [1900] A. C. 19; 69 L. J. Q. B. 117; 48 W. R. 321; 81 L. T. 562.)

At the trial of any action of libel or slander the plaintiff is always entitled to begin, even where the burden of proof lies on the defendant: for the damages are unliquidated. (*Carter* v. *Jones*, 6 C. & P. 64; 1 M. & R. 281; *Mercer* v. *Whall*, 5 Q. B. 447, 462, 463; 14 L. J. Q. B. 267, 272.) The plaintiff's counsel generally begins by proving the plaintiff's special character, if any, and the publication of the words complained of.

Proof of the Plaintiff's special Character.

Where the words are actionable only by reason of the plaintiff's holding an office or exercising a profession or trade, the plaintiff must prove that he held such office or exercised such profession or trade at the date of publication, and that the words complained of were spoken of him in that capacity. Sometimes the words themselves admit the plaintiff's special character, or it may be admitted on the pleadings; if so, it is, of course, unnecessary to give any evidence on the point. (*Yrisarri* v. *Clement*, 3 Bing. 432; 4 L. J. C. P. (Old S.) 128; 11 Moore, 308; 2 C. & P. 223.)

Strict proof of the plaintiff's special character is not, as a rule, required. Thus, to prove that a person holds a public office, it is not necessary to produce his written or sealed appointment thereto. (*Berryman* v. *Wise*, 4 T. R. 366; *Cannell* v. *Curtis*, 2 Bing. N. C. 228; 2 Scott, 379.) It is sufficient to show that he acted in that office, and it will be presumed that he acted legally. So, where the libel imputes to the plaintiff misconduct in his practice as a physician, surgeon, or solicitor, and does not call in question or deny his qualification to practice, he need only prove that he was acting in the particular professional capacity imputed to him at the time of the publication of the libel. (*Smith* v. *Taylor*, 1 B. & P. N. R. 196, 204; *Rutherford* v. *Evans*, 6 Bing. 451; 8 L. J. C. P. (Old S.) 86.) It is, as a rule, sufficient to call the plaintiff to say, "I am an M.R.C.S.," or "I am a solicitor." But when the libel or slander imputes to a medical or legal practitioner that he is not properly qualified, and the professional qualification is again denied on the pleadings, the plaintiff should always be prepared to prove it strictly, by producing his diploma or certificate, duly sealed or signed, and stamped, where a stamp is requisite. At Common Law there was no other way. (*Moises* v. *Thornton*, 8 T. R. 303; *Collins* v. *Carnegie*, 1 A. & E. 695; 3 N. & M. 703; *Sparling* v. *Haddon*, 9 Bing. 11; 2 Moo. & Scott, 14.)

But now the "Law List" is by the 23 & 24 Vict. c. 127, s. 22, made *primâ facie* evidence that any one whose name appears therein as a solicitor is a solicitor duly certificated for the current year; and similarly, by the 21 & 22 Vict. c. 90, s. 27, the "Medical Register" is *primâ facie* evidence that the persons specified therein are duly registered medical practitioners. But if it is known the plaintiff's qualification will be seriously challenged at the trial, it is safer not to rely solely on such *primâ facie* proof, but to produce all diplomas and certificates. If the plaintiff sues as a solicitor, and his name does not appear in the "Law List," that may be only because he has not taken out his certificate for the present year; in which case he may still sue for a libel on him as solicitor. (*Jones* v. *Stevens*, (1822) 11 Price, 235.) So, too, a medical man can sue for a libel on him professionally, although his name does not appear in the "Medical Register," if he can show by a certificate under the hand of the registrar, or in any other way, that he is duly qualified and entitled to be registered.

Proof of Publication.

The plaintiff must next prove that the defendant published the libel or spoke the slanderous words to some third person. As to what is a sufficient publication in law, see *ante*, Chapter VI., pp. 157—180. As to constructive publication by a servant or agent, see *ante*, pp. 583—591. As to publication by telegram, see *Williamson* v. *Freer*, L. R. 9 C. P. 393; 43 L. J. C. P. 161; 22 W. R. 878; 30 L. T. 332; *Chattell* v. *Turner*, (1896) 12 Times L. R. 360; by postcard, *Robinson* v. *Jones*, 4 L. R. Ir. 391; *Sadgrove* v. *Hole*, [1901] 2

K. B. 1; 70 L. J. K. B. 455; 49 W. R. 473; 84 L. T. 647. The
sale of each copy is a distinct publication. (*R.* v. *Carlisle,*
1 Chitty, 451; *Duke of Brunswick* v. *Harmer,* 14 Q. B. 185; *R.* v.
Stanger, L. R. 6 Q. B. 352; 40 L. J. Q. B. 96; 19 W. R. 640.)
Causing a libel to be printed may be a *primâ facie* publication.
(*Baldwin* v. *Elphinston,* 2 W. Bl. 1037.) The fact that the libellous
document has printed on it the words "A. B., printer," is in itself
no proof that A. B. printed it. (*R.* v. *Williams and Romney,* 2
L. J. K. B. (Old S.) 30.)

If the defendant wrote a libel, which is in some way subsequently
published, this is, *primâ facie* at all events, a publication by the
defendant. (Per Holt, C.J., in *R.* v. *Beere,* 12 Mod. 221; 1 Ld. Raym.
414.) A letter is published as soon as it is posted, provided it ever
reaches the party to whom it is addressed, and this will be presumed if there be no evidence to the contrary. Thus, if a letter in
the handwriting of the defendant be produced in Court with the
seal broken, and the proper postmarks outside, that is sufficient
primâ facie evidence of publication. (*Warren* v. *Warren,* 1 C. M. &
R. 250; 4 Tyr. 850; *Ward* v. *Smith,* 6 Bing. 749; 4 M. & P. 595;
4 C. & P. 302; *Shipley* v. *Todhunter,* 7 C. & P. 680.) So, where a
libel has appeared in print, and the manuscript from which it was
printed is proved to be in the defendant's handwriting, this is
primâ facie a publication by the defendant. It is not necessary to
prove expressly that he directed or authorised the printing. (Per
Lord Erskine in *Burdett* v. *Abbot,* 5 Dow, H. L. at p. 201; *Bond* v.
Douglas, 7 C. & P. 626; *Tarpley* v. *Blabey,* 2 Bing. N. C. 437; 7
C. & P. 395; *R.* v. *Lovett,* 9 C. & P. 462; *Adams* v. *Kelly,* Ry. & M. 157.)

Any one who has ever seen the defendant write (even though
once only, *Garrells* v. *Alexander,* 4 Esp. 37) can be called to prove
his handwriting. So can any one who has corresponded with the
defendant, or seen letters which have arrived in answer to letters
addressed to the defendant. Thus, a clerk in a merchant's office
who has corresponded with the defendant on his master's behalf,
may be called to prove the handwriting. (*R.* v. *Slaney,* 5 C. & P.
213.) The usual course is for the plaintiff's counsel merely to ask
the witness, "Are you acquainted with the defendant's handwriting?" leaving it to the defendant's counsel to cross-examine as
to the extent of his acquaintance. Such cross-examination will only
weaken the force of his evidence, not destroy its admissibility.
(*Eagleton* v. *Kingston,* 8 Ves. 473; *Doe* d. *Mudd* v. *Suckermore,* 5
A. & E. 730.) By sect. 27 of the C. L. P. Act, 1854, "comparison
of a disputed writing with any writing proved to the satisfaction of

the judge to be genuine, shall be permitted to be made by the witnesses; and such writings, and the evidence of witnesses respecting the same, may be submitted to the Court and jury as evidence of the genuineness or otherwise of the writing in dispute." (See *Jones* v. *Richards*, 15 Q. B. D. 439.) But the evidence of experts must be received with caution. If the defendant be present in Court, he may, it seems, be then and there required to write something which the Court and jury may compare with the document in dispute. (*Doe* d. *Devine* v. *Wilson*, 10 Moore, P. C. C. at p. 530.) So, too, letters not otherwise evidence in the cause, written by the defendant, and in which the plaintiff's name was spelt in a peculiar manner, were held admissible as evidence that the libel which contained the plaintiff's name spelt with the same peculiarity was written by the defendant. (*Brookes* v. *Tichborne*, 5 Exch. 929; 20 L. J. Ex. 69; 14 Jur. 1122.)

In the last resort the plaintiff may call the defendant as his witness, show him the libel, and ask if he wrote it. But the defendant may object to answer this question on the ground that he might thereby incriminate himself. And it seems that he may on the same ground object to state whether he wrote any other document which the plaintiff intends to use for comparison of handwriting. (Per Lawrance, J., in *Chattell* v. *Turner*, (1896) 12 Times L. R. at p. 361.)

The Newspaper Libel and Registration Act, 1881, was passed to facilitate proof of the publication of a libel contained in a newspaper. It established a " register of newspaper proprietors " to be kept at Somerset House, and to be open to the inspection of the public. Every printer and publisher of a newspaper is bound to make a return each July, giving the names and addresses of all the proprietors of the paper. And a certified copy of any entry in this register is made " sufficient *primâ facie* evidence of all matters and things thereby appearing " (sect. 15, *post*, p. 842), that is, that the person named therein is the proprietor of the newspaper, and, as such, liable for any libel that has appeared therein.

It is still, however, open to the defendant, though registered as the proprietor of the paper, to prove at the trial that since the last return, and before the publication of the libel, he transferred all his interest in the paper to some one else. Sect. 11, which deals with transfers, *permits*, but unfortunately does not *require*, registration in the event of a change in the proprietorship of a newspaper. The transferee may register his name and address or not as he pleases. Hence, a plaintiff or prosecutor can never be quite certain that the registered proprietor is the person liable for the publication of which he complains. In a civil case this difficulty may be overcome by administering interrogatories. (See *ante*, pp. 654—659.) Or, if no satisfactory admission be thus obtained, the plaintiff must prove that the newspaper was purchased of the defendant, or at any house, shop, or office belonging to or occupied by the defendant or by his servants or workmen, or where he usually carries on the business of printing or publishing such newspaper, or where it is usually sold. But it would have been better if the legislature had made the "return according to Schedule B." compulsory on every transfer, and had further enacted that, till such return was registered, the former proprietor should remain liable for everything published in the newspaper.

Publication may also be proved by the evidence of any one who took any part in it (*R.* v. *Haswell and Bate*, 1 Dougl. 387 ; *R.* v. *Steward*, 2 B. & Ad. 12), or by the defendant's own admission. (*R.* v. *Hall*, 1 Str. 416.) But such admission will not be extended beyond its exact terms. Thus, an admission that the defendant wrote the libel is no admission that he also published it. (*The Seven Bishops' Case*, 4 St. Tr. 300.) In *Macleod* v. *Wakley*, 3 C. & P. 311, it was held that an admission that defendant was the editor of a periodical at a certain date was no evidence that he was editor at a later date, so as to connect him with a libel subsequently published in the same periodical. (*Sed quære.*) But where the defendant admitted that he was the author of the book containing the libel, " errors of the press and some small variations excepted," it was held that this was sufficient to entitle the prosecutor to put in the book, and that it lay upon the defendant to show that there were material variations. (*R.* v. *Hall*, 1 Str. 416.) A witness may be asked if he knows who wrote the libel; but if he answers " yes," he cannot be compelled to name the person, because it may be himself. (*R.* v. *Slaney*, 5 C. & P. 213.) The plaintiff may even call the defendant as a witness, and counsel for the defendant cannot object that no relevant question can be asked him that will not tend to criminate him. The defendant must go into the box and take the objection himself, when the question is asked. No one can take it for him. He must state on oath in open Court that in his opinion to answer the question would tend to criminate him. (*Boyle* v. *Wiseman*, 10 Exch. 647; 24 L. J. Ex. 160 ; 24 L. T. (Old S.) 274.)

Where the facts are in dispute it will be for the jury to decide whether the defendant wrote the libel, whether it was ever published to a third person other than the plaintiff, whether the shop or bookstall at which the libel was purchased was the defendant's or not, &c. When the facts are found, it is for the judge to decide whether there has been a publication in law by the defendant.

Proof of the Libel.

The libel itself must be produced at the trial; the jury are entitled in all cases to see it. (*Wright* v. *Woodgate*, 2 C. M. & R. 573; *Gilpin* v. *Fowler*, 9 Exch. 615; 23 L. J. Ex. 156.) The defendant is entitled to have the whole of it read. (*Cooke* v. *Hughes*, R. & M. 112.) The original must be carefully traced, where it has passed through many hands. (*Fryer* v. *Gathercole*, 4 Exch. 262; 18 L. J. Ex. 389; *Adams* v. *Kelly*, Ry. & Moo. 157.) But where a large number of copies are printed from the same type, or lithographed at the same time by the same process, none of them are copies in the legal sense of the word. They are all counterpart originals, and each is primary evidence of the contents of the rest. (*R.* v. *Watson*, 2 Stark. 129; *Johnson* v. *Hudson and Morgan*, 7 A. & E. 233, n.)

Where the libel is contained in a letter or memorial sent to a Secretary of State, or to some Government department, an objection is often raised to its production on grounds of public policy. This objection must be taken by the head of the public department of State, who is alone able to judge whether the production of the document will or will not be injurious to the public service. It is not for the judge at the trial to decide that question. (*Hughes* v. *Vargas*, (1893) 9 Times L. R. 551; 9 R. 661; *Beatson* v. *Skene*, 5 H. & N. 838; 29 L. J. Ex. 430; *Swann* v. *Vines*, cited 37 L. T. 469; *M'Elveney* v. *Connellan*, 17 Ir. C. L. R. 55.) The rule on the point is that " the Court is entitled to have the pledge and security of the head officer of State to give the reason for the non-production of those documents which it is objected to produce, and to demand that he shall come into the witness-box, and there say that he is the head of the department, and objects to such and such documents being produced, specifying them, on the ground of public policy." (Per Grove, J. in *Kain* v. *Farrer*, 37 L. T. 470.) The judge, however, will not as a rule trouble the head of the department to attend in person provided his representative attends and satisfies the judge that the mind of the responsible person has been brought to bear on the question, and that he has decided that the production of the document would be injurious to the public service. (*In re*

Joseph Hargreaves, Limited, [1900] 1 Ch. 347 ; 69 L. J. Ch. 183 ; 48 W. R. 241 ; 82 L. T. 132.) On this the judge will exclude all evidence of the contents of such document. But a letter written by a private individual to the Chief Secretary of the Postmaster-General, complaining of the conduct of the guard of the Exeter mail, though it may be a privileged communication in the sense that the plaintiff must prove actual malice, is not a document privileged from production on the ground of public policy. (*Blake* v. *Pilfold*, 1 Moo. & Rob. 198.)

If the original libel has been lost or destroyed, secondary evidence may of course be given of it (*Rainy* v. *Bravo*, L. R. 4 P. C. 287 ; 20 W. R. 873 ; *Gathercole* v. *Miall*, 15 M. & W. 319), except where the libel is contained in an official document, which is privileged from production on the ground of public policy, in which case the same public policy requires that no secondary evidence of its contents shall be given. (*Home* v. *Bentinck*, 2 Brod. & B. 130 ; *Anderson* v. *Hamilton, Ib.* 156, n. ; *Stace* v. *Griffith*, L. R. 2 P. C. 428 ; 6 Moore, P. C. C. (N. S.) 18 ; 20 L. T. 197 ; *Dawkins* v. *Lord Rokeby*, (Ex. Ch.) L. R. 8 Q. B. 255.) Where the libel is written or placarded on a wall, so that it cannot conveniently be brought into Court, secondary evidence may be given of its contents. (Per Lord Abinger, in *Mortimer* v. *M'Callan*, 6 M. & W. at p. 68 ; *Bruce* v. *Nicolopulo*, 11 Exch. at p. 133 ; 24 L. J. Ex. at p. 324.) Where, however, the document is still in existence and capable of being brought into Court, the party desiring to give secondary evidence of its contents must in the first place prove that he has done all in his power to obtain the original document. Thus, the plaintiff is entitled to give secondary evidence of the contents of the libel, if the original is in the defendant's possession and is not produced when called for, provided due notice to produce it was served on the defendant's solicitor a reasonable time before the trial (*R.* v. *Boucher*, 1 F. & F. 486) ; and also if the libel is in the possession of someone beyond the jurisdiction of the Court, who refuses to produce it, on request, although informed of the purpose for which it is required. (*Boyle* v. *Wiseman*, 10 Exch. 647 ; 24 L. J. Ex. 160 ; *R.* v. *Llanfaethly*, 2 E. & B. 940 ; 23 L. J. M. C. 33 ; *R.* v. *Aickles*, 1 Leach, 330.) If it be in the possession of a third person within jurisdiction, but a stranger to the cause, who refuses to produce it, although duly served with a *subpœna duces tecum* for the purpose, then the right to give secondary evidence of its contents appears to depend on whether such refusal be rightful or wrongful. If it be a *wrongful* refusal, then, it is said, the remedy of the party is against the

witness only. (*Sed quære*.) If it be a *rightful* refusal, then secondary
evidence is as a rule admitted : as the party has done all in his
power to produce primary proof. Even here, however, the privilege
arising from considerations of public policy may prevent *any* evidence being given of the contents of the document. But where
the privilege is only of a private character, secondary evidence may
be given of the contents of documents privileged from production,
e.g., of a document entrusted to a solicitor by his client. (*Mills
v. Oddy*, (1834) 6 C. & P. 728 ; *Doe* d. *Gilbert* v. *Ross*, (1840) 7
M. & W. 102 ; *Doe* d. *Loscombe* v. *Clifford*, (1847) 2 C. & K. 448 ;
Newton v. *Chaplin*, (1850) 10 C. B. 356 ; *Paris* v. *Levy*, (1860) 2 F.
& F. 73 ; *Calcraft* v. *Guest*, [1898] 1 Q. B. 759 ; 67 L. J. Q. B. 505 ;
46 W. R. 420 ; 78 L. T. 283.) All questions as to the admissibility
of secondary evidence are for the judge, and should be decided by
him then and there. (*Boyle* v. *Wiseman*, 11 Exch. 360 ; 24 L. J. Ex.
284 ; 25 L. T. (Old S.) 203.)

If the words proved differ materially from those set out in the
Statement of Claim, this is "a variance" which would formerly
have been fatal. (*Bell* v. *Byrne*, 13 East, 554 ; *Tabart* v. *Tipper*,
1 Camp. 350 ; *Cartwright* v. *Wright*, 1 D. & Ry. 230 ; *Cook* v. *Stokes
and wife*, 1 Moo. & R. 237 ; *Rainy* v. *Bravo*, L. R. 4 P. C. 287 ; 20
W. R. 873.) Now, however, the judge has ample power to amend
the record, if in his discretion he considers such amendment can be
made without prejudice to the defendant. (Order XXVIII. rr. 1, 6.)
But no amendment will be made, the result of which will be to
substitute a totally different cause of action for the former one
(*C—— v. Lindsell*, 11 J. P. 352), or to render the Statement of
Claim demurrable. (*Martyn* v. *Williams*, 1 H. & N. 817 ; 26 L. J.
Ex. 117 ; *Caulfield* v. *Whitworth*, 16 W. R. 936 ; 18 L. T. 527.)
The defendant is entitled to an adjournment if he really desires to
justify any words newly inserted in the Statement of Claim by such
amendment. (*Saunders* v. *Bate*, 1 H. & N. 402. And see *Foster* v.
Pointer, 9 C. & P. 718 ; *May* v. *Brown*, 3 B. & C. 113 ; *Lord
Churchill* v. *Hunt*, 2 B. & Ald. 685.)

Proof of the Speaking of the Slander.

In cases of slander, practically the only way to prove publication
is by calling those who heard the defendant speak the words. It is
not, in strictness, sufficient to prove that the defendant spoke words
equivalent to those set out in the Statement of Claim. (*Armitage
v. Dunster*, (1785) 4 Dougl. 291 ; *Maitland and others* v. *Goldney
and another*, (1802) 2 East, 426.) Thus, where the plaintiff alleged

that the defendant stated as a fact that "A. could not pay his labourers," and the evidence was that he had asked a question, "Have you heard A. cannot pay his labourers?" the plaintiff was nonsuited. (*Barnes* v. *Holloway*, (1799) 8 T. R. 150.) And so where the words alleged in the Declaration were : " This is my umbrella, and he stole it from my back-door," and the words proved by the witnesses were : "*It* is my umbrella, and he stole it from my back-door," Garrow, B., nonsuited the plaintiff, and the full Court of King's Bench upheld the nonsuit. (*Walters* v. *Mace*, (1819) 2 B. & Ald. 756.) But now, if the words proved convey practically the same meaning as the words laid, the variance will be held immaterial, or else the judge will amend. (*Dancaster* v. *Hewson*, (1828) 2 Man. & Ry. 176 ; *Sydenham* v. *Man*, (1617) Cro. Jac. 407 ; *Orpwood* v. *Barkes*, vel *Parkes*, (1827) 4 Bing. 261 ; 12 Moore, 492 ; *Smith* v. *Knowelden*, (1841) 2 M. & Gr. 561 ; *Ecklin* v. *Little*, (1890) 6 Times L. R. 366.)

It was never necessary, however, to prove all the words set out in the Statement of Claim, provided such of them as are proved are intelligible and actionable by themselves. (Per Lawrence, J., 2 East, 434.) So it is not necessary that all the words set out should be actionable; so long as any of the words proved will maintain the action " the damages may be given entirely ; for it shall be intended that the damages were given for the words which are actionable, and that the others were inserted only for aggravation." (2 Wms. Saunders, 171, c. ; *Chadwick* v. *Trower*, 6 Bing. N. C. at p. 7.)

If the witness committed the words to writing shortly after the defendant uttered them, he may refer to such writing to refresh his memory ; but it must be the original memorandum that is referred to, not a fair copy. (*Burton* v. *Plummer*, 2 A. & E. 343.) And so where the action is for procuring a libel to be published by making a verbal statement to the reporter of a newspaper, who took it down in writing ; the original writing taken down by the reporter and handed by him to the editor should be produced in Court. (*Adams* v. *Kelly*, Ry. & Moo. 157.)

Where the governor of a British colony spoke to the Attorney-General in his official capacity words defamatory of the plaintiff, and the Attorney-General was called as a witness in an action against the governor, it was held that he was not bound to disclose what the governor had said to him. (*Wyatt* v. *Gore*, Holt, N. P. 299.) So the Lord Chamberlain cannot be compelled to disclose in evidence communications made to him in his official capacity. (*West* v. *West*, (1911) 27 Times L. R. 189.)

If the words spoken be in a foreign language, someone must be called to prove their meaning; and it must be further shown that those who heard them understood that language; else there is no publication. But publication will be presumed where the words are spoken in the vernacular of the locality. (*Ante*, p. 125.)

Evidence as to the Innuendo.

A Statement of Claim which contains an innuendo is equivalent to a declaration under the old system with two counts, one with an innuendo, and one without. (Per Blackburn, J., in *Watkin* v. *Hall*, L. R. 3 Q. B. 402; 37 L. J. Q. B. 125.) Hence, if the plaintiff fails to prove his innuendo, he may fall back on the other count, and succeed on that, if the words in their natural signification are actionable. (*Fisher* v. *Nation Newspaper Co.*, [1901] 2 Ir. R. 465.) But if the words in their natural meaning are not actionable, then the plaintiff is bound by his innuendo. He must prove that or fail. He cannot now discard the innuendo stated in his pleading and set up a new innuendo which does not appear on the record. (*Hunter* v. *Sharpe*, 4 F. & F. 983; 15 L. T. 421; *Ruel* v. *Tatnell*, 29 W. R. 172; 43 L. T. 507.) If the words are not actionable even with the meaning ascribed to them by the innuendo (as in *Jacobs* v. *Schmaltz*, 62 L. T. 121; 6 Times L. R. 155), or if the words are not reasonably capable of that meaning, the judge will stop the case.

If, however, the words are reasonably capable of the meaning ascribed to them by the innuendo, and in that sense are actionable, still it may be necessary for the plaintiff to call evidence to support his innuendo and to satisfy the jury that the words were in fact understood in that sense. For instance, there may have been facts, known both to the writer and the person to whom he wrote, which could reasonably induce the latter to understand the words in the sense ascribed to them by the innuendo. If so, evidence of such facts is admissible. (*Capital and Counties Bank* v. *Henty & Sons*, (C. A.) 5 C. P. D. 514; 49 L. J. C. P. 830; (H. L.) 7 App. Cas. 741; 52 L. J. Q. B. 232.) But evidence is not admissible of any fact not known to the persons addressed and to which the defendant does not at the time expressly refer. (*Martin* v. *Loeï*, 2 F. & F. 654.)

The plaintiff need not prove the whole of his innuendo. (*Prudhomme* v. *Fraser*, 2 A. & E. 645.) It is sufficient if he satisfy the jury that the words bear any actionable meaning alleged in the innuendo, and refer to himself. Whenever the words used are not well-known and perfectly intelligible English, but are foreign, local, technical, provincial, or obsolete expressions, parol evidence is admissible to explain their meaning, provided such meaning has been properly alleged in the Statement of Claim by an innuendo. The rule is the same where words which have a meaning in ordinary English are yet, in the particular instance before the Court, clearly used not in that ordinary meaning, but in some peculiar sense; as in the case of many slang expressions. But where the words are well-known and perfectly intelligible English, evidence cannot be given to explain that meaning away, unless it is first in some way shown that that meaning is for once inapplicable. This may appear from the words themselves; to give them their ordinary English meaning may make nonsense of them. But if with their ordinary meaning the words are perfectly good sense as they stand, facts must be given in evidence to show that they may have conveyed a special meaning on this particular occasion. After that has been done, a bystander may be asked, " What did you understand by the expression used? " But without such a foundation being laid, the question is not admissible. (*Daines* v. *Hartley*, 3 Exch. 200 ; 18 L. J. Ex. 81 ; 12 Jur. 1093 ; *Barnett* v. *Allen*, 3 H. & N. 376 ; 27 L. J. Ex. 415 ; *Humphreys* v. *Miller*, 4 C. & P. 7 ; *Duke of Brunswick* v. *Harmer*, 3 C. & K. 10 ; *Gallagher* v. *Murton*, (1888) 4 Times L. R. 304.) And if it be put and answered, the answer is not evidence; the jury must not act on it. (*Simmons* v. *Mitchell*, 6 App. Cas. 156 ; 50 L. J. P. C. 11 ; 29 W. R. 401 ; 43 L. T. 710.) And this is so, whether the word can be found in the last edition of the English dictionary or not. (*Homer* v. *Taunton*, 5 H. & N. 661.) Figurative or allegorical terms of a defamatory character, if of well-known import, need no evidence to explain their meaning ; *e.g.*, words imputing to a person the qualities of the " frozen snake " in the fable. (*Hoare* v. *Silverlock*, 12 Q. B. 624 ; 17 L. J. Q. B. 306.) Nor do historical allusions or comparisons to odious, notorious, or disreputable persons : where the conduct of the plaintiff, who was an attorney, was compared to that of " Messrs. Quirk, Gammon and Snap," the novel " Ten Thousand a Year " was put in and taken as read. (*Woodgate* v. *Ridout*, 4 F. & F. 202.)

Wherever the words sued on are capable of being reasonably understood both in a harmless and in an injurious sense, it will be a question for the jury to decide which meaning was in fact conveyed to the hearers or readers at the time of publication. (*Ritchie & Co.* v. *Sexton*, 64 L. T. 210 ; 55 J. P. 389.) It will be of no avail for the defendant to urge (except, perhaps, in mitigation of damages) that he intended the words to convey the innocent meaning, if the jury are satisfied that ordinary bystanders or readers would certainly have understood them in the other sense. (*Fisher* v. *Clement*, 10 B. & C. 472.) Every man must be taken to have intended the natural and probable consequences of his act. The plaintiff may give evidence of surrounding circumstances from which a defamatory meaning can be inferred; he may call witnesses to state how they understood the libel; though the jury are not bound to adopt the opinions of such witnesses. (*Broome* v. *Gosden*, 1 C. B. 732.)

Evidence may also be given to explain and point the charge. Thus it may be shown that the defendant subsequently used the same words or others of the same import with reference to the plaintiff. (*Pearce* v. *Ornsby*, 1 M. & Rob. 455; *Pearson* v. *Lemaitre*, 5 M. & Gr. 700.)

Proof that the Words refer to the Plaintiff.

If the libel does not name the plaintiff, there may be need of some evidence to show who was meant. The plaintiff may give evidence of all "surrounding circumstances"; *i.e.*, the cause and occasion of publication, later statements made by the defendant, and other extraneous facts which will explain and point the allusion. The plaintiff may also call at the trial his friends or others acquainted with the circumstances, to state that on reading the libel they at once concluded that it was aimed at the plaintiff. (*Broome* v. *Gosden*, 1 C. B. 728; *R.* v. *Barnard, Ex parte Lord R. Gower*, 43 J. P. 127; *Hulton & Co.* v. *Jones*, [1909] 2 K. B. 444; [1910] A. C. 20; *ante*, p. 150.) It is not necessary that all the world should understand the libel; it is sufficient if those who know the plaintiff can make out that he is the person meant. (*Bourke* v. *Warren*, 2 C. & P. 310.) Evidence that the plaintiff was jeered at at a public meeting shortly after the publication is admissible to show that his neighbours understood the libel as referring to him. (*Cook* v. *Ward*, 4 M. & P. 99; 6 Bing. 412.) So, in *Du Bost* v. *Beresford* (2 Camp. 511), Lord Ellenborough held that the declarations made by spectators, while they were looking at a libellous caricature, were admissible in evidence to show whom the figures were intended to represent.

But if the libel does not on the face of it refer to the plaintiff, and there is nothing to connect the plaintiff with it, judgment will be entered for the defendant. (*Fournet* v. *Pearson, Limited*, (1897) 14 Times L. R. 82.)

Proof that the Words were spoken of the Plaintiff in the way of his Office, Profession, or Trade.

It is not enough for the plaintiff to prove his special character, and that the words refer to himself; he must further prove that the words refer to himself in that special character, if they be not otherwise actionable. Whether the words were spoken of the plaintiff in the way of his office, profession, or trade, is a question for the jury. It is by no means necessary that the defendant should expressly name the plaintiff's office or trade at the time he spoke, if his words must necessarily affect the plaintiff's credit and reputation therein. (*Jones* v. *Littler*, 7 M. & W. 423; 10 L. J. Ex. 171. See *ante*, p. 53.) But often words may be spoken of a professional man which, though defamatory, in no way affect him in his profession, *e.g.*, an imputation that an attorney had been horsewhipped (*Doyley* v. *Roberts*, 3 Bing. N. C. 835), or that a physician had committed adultery. (*Ayre* v. *Craven*, 2 A. & E. 2; *ante*, p. 63.) But any imputation on the solvency of a trader, any suggestion that he had been bankrupt years ago, is clearly a reflection on him in the way of his trade. (*Ante*, pp. 32, 65.)

Evidence of Malice.

The judge must decide whether the occasion is or is not privileged, and also whether such privilege is absolute or qualified. If he decide that the occasion was one of absolute privilege, the defendant is entitled to judgment, however maliciously and treacherously he may have acted. If, however, the privilege was only qualified, the *onus* lies on the plaintiff of proving actual malice. This he may do either by *extrinsic* evidence of personal ill-feeling (*ante*, pp. 348—352), or by *intrinsic* evidence, such as the exaggerated language of the libel, the mode and extent of publication, and other matters in excess of the privilege. (*Ante*, pp. 352—360.) Any other words written or spoken by the defendant of the plaintiff, and indeed all previous transactions or communications between the parties, are evidence on this issue. Even if both parties were to blame in such previous transactions, still if they left in the defendant's mind a feeling of resentment or injured innocence, this may be used by the plaintiff as some evidence of malice. The defendant should therefore be careful how far he cross-examines to such matters with a view to showing provocation.

Placing a plea of justification on the record is no evidence of malice. (*Wilson* v. *Robinson* 7 Q. B. 68; 14 L. J. Q. B. 196; 9

Jur. 726; *Caulfield* v. *Whitworth*, 16 W. R. 936; 18 L. T. 527.)
But groundlessly persisting in it may be. (*Warwick* v. *Foulkes*, 12
M. & W. 508.) Care must be taken in citing *Simpson* v. *Robinson*
(12 Q. B. 511), to refer to the judgments of the Court; as the headnote is declared by Willes, J., in *Caulfield* v. *Whitworth*, to be
misleading. That the words are, in fact, untrue is no evidence of
malice (*ante*, p. 346); the falsity of the words is indeed always
presumed in the plaintiff's favour. Proof that the defendant at
the time of publication knew that what he was saying or writing
was false, is proof positive of malice. Hence the plaintiff cannot, as
a rule, give any evidence of his own good character. But where the
parties have been living in the same house for a long time, as master
and servant, and the master must have known the true character of
his servant, and yet has given a false one, there the plaintiff is
allowed to give general evidence of his good character, and to call
other servants of the defendant to show that no complaints of misconduct were made against the plaintiff whilst he was in defendant's
service; for such evidence tends to show that the defendant, at the
time he gave plaintiff a bad character, knew that what he was
writing was untrue. (*Fountain* v. *Boodle*, 3 Q. B. 5; 2 G. & D.
455; *Rogers* v. *Sir Gervas Clifton*, 3 B. & P. 587, *ante*, p. 363.) But
in any other case, if no justification be pleaded, and yet the plaintiff's
counsel gives evidence of the falsity of the libel, this will, in strictness,
let in evidence on the other side of the truth of the statement. (Per
Lord Ellenborough in *Brown* v. *Croome*, 2 Stark. 298, 299.)

Rebutting Justification.

The plaintiff may object at the trial that a plea of justification
is insufficient, or that the particulars delivered under it do not
justify the charge made, whether such objection has been taken on
the pleadings or no. The plaintiff's counsel may, if he chooses, in
the first instance rebut the justification; or he may leave such proof
till the reply, when he will know the strength of defendant's case.
(See *Maclaren & Sons* v. *Davis and another*, (1890) 6 Times L. R.
373.) But he cannot, in the absence of special circumstances, call
some evidence to rebut the justification in the first instance, and
more afterwards, thus dividing his proof. (*Browne* v. *Murray*,
R. & M. 254.)

Evidence of Damage.

The plaintiff need give no evidence of any actual damage where
the words are actionable *per se*; he can nevertheless recover

substantial damages. (*Tripp* v. *Thomas*, 3 B. & C. 427; 1 C. & P.
477; *Ingram* v. *Lawson*, 6 Bing. N. C. 212.) But if the plaintiff has
suffered any special damage, this should be pleaded and proved. It
cannot be proved unless it has been pleaded. (*Bluck* v. *Lovering*,
(1885) 1 Times L. R. 497.) As to what constitutes special damage,
see *ante*, pp. 377—384. As to what damage is too remote, see *ante*,
pp. 406—419.

Where the plaintiff relies on the loss of particular customers, or
on loss of hospitality, as special damage, he must call the individual
customers and friends to state why they have ceased to deal at his
shop, or to entertain him. (*Ante*, p. 383.) It is true that in *Skinner &
Co.* v. *Shew & Co.*, [1894] 2 Ch. 581; 63 L. J. Ch. 826, North, J.,
accepted a letter from the solicitor of the intending customer as
evidence of the reasons why the negotiations were broken off. But
there were special circumstances in that case. (See [1894] 2 Ch.
pp. 595, 596.) In an ordinary action at Nisi Prius, no such letter
would be received. (See *Clarke* v. *Morgan*, 38 L. T. at p. 355.) Such
witnesses cannot, however, be called unless their names have been
set out in the Statement of Claim or the particulars. It must also
be proved that they heard of the charge against the plaintiff from the
defendant's own lips. It will not be sufficient to prove that they
heard a rumour, and that the defendant set such a rumour afloat.
(See *ante*, p. 407; *Dixon* v. *Smith*, 5 H. & N. 450; 29 L. J. Ex.
125; *Bateman* v. *Lyall*, 7 C. B. N. S. 638.)

The plaintiff may also call evidence in aggravation of damages.
The matter most commonly urged in aggravation of damages is that
the defendant was actuated by malice. (See *ante*, pp. 389—393.)
Where an action is brought against one defendant only, evidence of
malice in some third person, who might have been joined as a
defendant, is not admissible against the person sued. (*Ante*, p. 344.)
It has been contended, therefore, that where two or more persons
are joined as defendants in respect of a joint publication, the
plaintiff may not give evidence of malice in one to aggravate the
damages against all. There can only be one judgment in such an
action, a judgment for the same amount against all the defendants.
(*Dawson* v. *M'Clelland*, [1899] 2 Ir. R. 486.) Each defendant is,
no doubt, liable for all the damage which the plaintiff has actually
sustained in consequence of the joint publication. But should
evidence of malicious acts committed by A., to which B. and C. were
not parties, be given in an action brought against A., B. and C. as
joint tort-feasors? Andrews, J., in *Dawson* v. *M'Clelland* (*ib.* at
p. 490) seems to have been of opinion that such evidence was

inadmissible. (And see Mayne on *Damages*, 8th ed. 562.) But such is not at present the practice in England.

If the defendant has paid money into Court this fact should not be mentioned in the hearing of the jury before verdict. (Order XXII. r. 22 ; and see *ante*, p. 641.)

Provinces of Judge and Jury.

In actions of libel and slander it is most important to distinguish the respective provinces of judge and jury. In some circumstances it is the right, and indeed the duty, of the judge (*Turner* v. *Bowley & Son*, (1896) 12 Times L. R. 402) to withdraw the case from the jury and to direct judgment to be entered for the defendant.* This should be done in the following cases :—

   (i) If there is no evidence that the defendant published the words.

  (ii) If there is no evidence that the words refer to the plaintiff. (*Fournet* v. *Pearson, Limited*, (1897) 14 Times L. R. 82.)

 (iii) If the words proved are not actionable *per se*, and either there is no evidence of any special damage, or the special damage is in law too remote. (*Speake* v. *Hughes*, [1904] 1 K. B. 138 ; 73 L. J. K. B. 172; 89 L. T. 576.)

  (iv) If the plaintiff's claim is barred by a Statute of Limitation, which the defendant has pleaded. (See *ante*, p. 609.)

   (v) If the words are actionable by reason only of being spoken of the plaintiff in the way of his office, profession, or trade, and there is no evidence that the words were so spoken, or that the plaintiff held such office or carried on such profession or trade at the time of publication. (See *ante*, p. 673.)

  (vi) If the words are not actionable in their natural and primary signification, and there is no innuendo ; or if the innuendo puts upon the words a meaning which they cannot possibly bear or which is not actionable. (*Cooney* v. *Edeveain*, (1897) 14 Times L. R. 34 ; *Dauncey* v. *Holloway*, [1901] 2 K. B. 441 ; 70 L. J. K. B. 695 ; 49 W. R. 546 ; 84 L. T. 649 ;

---

* There is no longer such a thing as a common law nonsuit (*Fox* v. *Star Newspaper Co.*, [1900] A. C. 19 ; 69 L. J. Q. B. 117 ; 48 W. R. 321 ; 81 L. T. 562) ; but the term "nonsuit" is still sometimes used by learned judges to denote the action of the judge, when he withdraws the case from the jury or directs judgment to be entered for the defendant in spite of their verdict.

Beswick **v.** *Smith*, (1908) 24 Times L. R. 169); and see *ante*, p. 134.

(vii) If the occasion of publication was one of absolute privilege.

(viii) If the occasion is clearly or admittedly one of qualified privilege, and there is no evidence, or not more than a *scintilla* of evidence, of malice to go to the jury. (*Cooke* v. *Wildes*, 5 E. & B. 328; 24 L. J. Q. B. 367, *ante*, p. 346; *Turner* v. *Bowley & Son*, (1896) 12 Times L. R. 402.)

(ix) Where the words are clearly or admittedly a comment on a matter of public interest and are not reasonably capable of being interpreted as an unfair comment. (*McQuire* v. *Western Morning News Co.*, [1903] 2 K. B. 100; 72 L. J. K. B. 612; 51 W. R. 689; 88 L. T. 757; *Dakhyl* v. *Labouchere*, [1908] 2 K. B. 325, n.; 77 L. J. K. B. 728; 96 L. T. 399.)

The judge cannot withdraw the case from the jury upon the opening statement of facts made by the plaintiff's counsel without the consent of such counsel (*Fletcher* v. *L. & . W. Ry. Co.*, [1892] 1 Q. B. 122; 61 L. J. Q. B. 24; 65 L. T. 605), except, perhaps, where no evidence that the plaintiff intends to call would cure the defect in the plaintiff's case as so opened. (See *Speake* v. *Hughes*, [1904] 1 K. B. 138; 73 L. J. K. B. 172; 89 L. T. 576.)

The jury has no right to interpose and stop the case by finding in favour of one party until they have heard all the evidence tendered by the other party and the speech of his counsel.

The proper time for the defendant's counsel to submit that there is no case to go to the jury is at the close of the plaintiff's case. Some judges, however, decline to allow the question to be argued at this stage of the action, unless the defendant's counsel at once announces that he intends to call no witnesses. Where the facts, to which the law has to be applied, are in dispute, it is generally best to discuss the law of the case after all the evidence on both sides has been given. (*Hope* v. *I'Anson and Weatherby*, (1901) 18 Times L. R. 201.) Moreover, the judge has power to call and examine a witness who has not been called by either party, but only with the consent of both parties. (See *In re Enoch, &c., Bock & Co.*, [1910] 1 K. B. at p. 333.) If he does so, neither party has a right to cross-examine that witness without the leave of the judge, but such leave will always be granted if the evidence of the witness called by the judge is adverse to either party. (*Coulson* v. *Disborough*, [1894] 2 Q. B. 316; 42 W. R. 449; 70 L. T. 617.)

The question whether the words complained of are capable of a defamatory meaning is for the judge. Whether the words in fact conveyed a defamatory meaning is a question for the jury. (See Chapter V., *ante*, p. 109.) "Libel or no libel is, of all questions, peculiarly one for a jury." (Per Lord Coleridge, C.J., in *Saxby* v. *Easterbrook*, 3 C. P. D. at p. 342.) If the words are reasonably susceptible of two constructions, the one an innocent, the other a libellous construction, it is a question for the jury which is the proper one. (*Jenner and another* v. *A'Beckett*, L. R. 7 Q. B. 11 ; 41 L. J. Q. B. 14 ; 20 W. R. 181 ; 25 L. T. 464.) If the words are capable of being either a defamatory libel on a person or merely a disparagement of goods, it is a question for the jury in which sense the words were understood. (*Linotype Co., Limited* v. *British Empire, &c., Co.*, (1899) 81 L. T. 331 ; 15 Times L. R. 524.)

If the words, though primarily not actionable, are yet reasonably susceptible of a defamatory meaning, which is set out in an innuendo in the Statement of Claim, the judge should not stop the case ; if he does so, the Court of Appeal will order a new trial. (*Hart and another* v. *Wall*, 2 C. P. D. 146 ; 46 L. J. C. P. 227 ; 25 W. R. 373 ; *Ritchie & Co.* v. *Sexton*, 64 L. T. 210 ; *Beamish* v. *Dairy Supply Co., Limited*, (1897) 13 Times L. R. 484.) "It is only when the judge is satisfied that the publication cannot be a libel, and that, if it is found by the jury to be such, their verdict will be set aside, that he is justified in withdrawing the question from their cognisance." (Per Kelly, C.B., in *Cox* v. *Lee*, L. R. 4 Ex. at p. 288 ; per Field, J., in *O'Brien* v. *Marquis of Salisbury*, (1889) 6 Times L. R. at pp. 136, 137.) "If the document was capable of being a libel, no judge in the kingdom could nonsuit the plaintiff." (Per A. L. Smith, L.J., in *Cooney* v. *Edeveain*, (1897) 14 Times L. R. 34.) But where the words on the face of them are not actionable in themselves, and also are not reasonably capable of the defamatory meaning alleged in the innuendo, there the judge should direct judgment to be entered for the defendant (*Hunt* v. *Goodlake*, 43 L. J. C. P. 54 ; 29 L. T. 472 ; *Mulligan* v. *Cole and others*, L. R. 10 Q. B. 549 ; 44 L. J. Q. B. 153 ; *Frost* v. *London Joint Stock Bank*, (1906) 22 Times L. R. 760) ; unless, indeed, it be alleged that there are some facts, known both to the defendant and to those whom he addressed, which would lead the latter to put upon the words the secondary meaning ascribed to them by the innuendo. If this be alleged, the learned judge must first consider whether it is reasonably conceivable that the existence of the facts alleged would induce those addressed to put that meaning on the words ; if it is not reasonably conceivable, he should stop the case. Next, he should consider whether there is any evidence to go to the jury of such facts. If there is no such evidence, he should stop the case. But if it be reasonably conceivable that the facts alleged would induce those who heard or read the words to put that meaning on them, and there is evidence to go to the jury of such facts, then the judge must leave the question to the jury, and they must decide in what meaning the words were in fact understood. (*Capital and Counties Bank* v. *Henty & Sons*, (C. A.) 5 C. P. D. 514 ; 49 L. J. C. P. 830 ; (H. L.) 7 App. Cas. 741 ; 52 L. J. Q. B. 232.)

If privilege has been pleaded, the facts on which the claim of privilege is based must be proved before the judge can rule whether the occasion is privilegéd or not. If at the conclusion of the plaintiff's case facts sufficient to support the plea of privilege have been clearly established and no evidence of malice has been given, the judge should enter judgment for the defendant and not let the case go to the jury. (*Turner* v. *Bowley & Son*, (1896) 12 Times L. R. 402.) Where, however, the question of privilege involves matters of fact which are disputed, it will be for the jury to find the facts, and for the judge subsequently to decide whether on the facts so found the occasion is privileged. (*Beatson* v. *Skene*, 5 H. & N. 838 ; 29 L. J. Ex. 430 ; 6 Jur. N. S. 780 ; 2 L. T. 378 ; *Stace* v. *Griffith*, L. R. 2 P. C. 420 ; 6 Moore, P. C. C. (N. S.) 18 ; 20 L. T. 197 ; *Hope* v. *I'Anson and Weatherby*, (1901) 18 Times L. R. 201.) For the judge is not bound to rule whether the occasion is privileged or not till after the defendant has called all his witnesses. (Per Cockburn, C.J., in *Hancock* v. *Case*, 2 F. & F. at p. 715.)

The question of malice or no malice is always one for the jury, but it is for the judge to say whether there is any evidence of malice to go to the jury. If there is not any such evidence, or not more than a *scintilla* of such evidence, the judge should direct judgment to be entered for the defendant. If the evidence adduced to prove malice is equally consistent with either the existence or the non-existence of malice, the judge should stop the case ; for there is nothing to rebut the presumption which the privileged occasion has raised in the defendant's favour. (*Somerville* v. *Hawkins*, 10 C. B. 583 ; 20 L. J. C. P. 131 ; 15 Jur. 450 ; *Harris* v. *Thompson*, 13 C. B. 333 ; *Taylor* v. *Hawkins*, 16 Q. B. 308 ; 20 L. J. Q. B. 313 ; 15 Jur. 746. See *ante*, Chapter XII., p. 341.)

If the defendant relies on the defence of fair comment, the judge must decide whether the matters commented on are matters of public interest. (*Dakhyl* v. *Labouchere, Times*, July 29th, 1904.) It will then be for the jury to find whether the words are a fair comment. (See Chapter VIII., *ante*, p. 193.)

The judge at the trial has full power to amend any defect or error in any pleading or proceeding on such terms as may seem just (Order XXVIII. rr. 1, 6, 12), and to add, or strike out, or substitute, a plaintiff or defendant. (Order XVI. r. 12.)

Evidence for the Defendant.

When the plaintiff's case has been closed, if the defendant elects to call no evidence, and has put in no documents, the plaintiff's counsel must proceed at once to sum up his case and the defendant's counsel has the last word to the jury. But if the defendant intends to call evidence he must open his case at once, call his witnesses, and then sum up, and the plaintiff's counsel will have the general reply. If there are two defendants, of whom one calls evidence material to the defence of both, and the other calls no evidence at all, the latter has apparently a right of reply after the plaintiff's counsel has addressed the jury. (*Ryland* v. *Jackson and Brodie*, (1902) 18 Times L. R. 574.)

The defendant, as we have seen, is entitled to have the whole libel read, or the whole of the conversation in which the slander was uttered, detailed in evidence. If the alleged libel refers to any other document, the defendant is also entitled to have that other document read, as part of the plaintiff's case. (*Weaver* v. *Lloyd*, 1 C. & P. 296 ; *Thornton* v. *Stephen*, 2 M. & Rob. 45 ; *Hedley* v. *Barlow and another*, 4 F. & F. 227.) So where the action is brought for a criticism on the plaintiff's book, no imputation being cast on him personally, it was held that the plaintiff ought to put in the book criticised as part of his own case. (*Strauss* v. *Francis*, 4 F. & F. 939, 1107.) This may save the defendant from the necessity of giving any evidence. But where a paragraph in a subsequent number of a newspaper is given in evidence by the plaintiff to show malice, the rest of the newspaper is no part of plaintiff's case, unless it refers to the special paragraph put in. The defendant is, therefore, not entitled to have other passages in that newspaper read. (*Darby* v. *Ouseley*, 1 H. & N. 1 ; 25 L. J. Ex. 227.)

When the defendant's counsel prefers not to call any witnesses, so as to secure the last word with the jury, he must rely on the cross-examination of the plaintiff's witnesses. These may be cross-examined not only as to the facts of the case, but also to " credit ; "

that is, as to matters not material to the issue, with a view of shaking their whole testimony. But in order to prevent the case from thus branching out into all manner of irrelevant issues, it is wisely provided that on such matters the defendant must take the witness's answer : he cannot call any evidence to contradict it. There is one exception. By sect. 24 of the Common Law Procedure Act, 1854, if a witness in any cause be questioned as to whether he has been convicted of any felony or misdemeanour, and if he either denies the fact, or refuses to answer, the opposite party may prove such conviction, however irrelevant the fact of such conviction may be to the matter in issue in the cause. (*Ward* v. *Sinfield*, 49 L. J. C. P. 696 ; 43 L. T. 253.) The right method of proving a conviction for felony or misdemeanour at the Assizes or Quarter Sessions, either for this purpose or as evidence under a plea of justification, is by a certificate under sect. 25 of the Common Law Procedure Act, 1854. A conviction at Petty Sessions must be proved by a certificate under sect. 18 of the Prevention of Crimes Act, 1871 (34 & 35 Vict. c. 112).

The defendant must be careful, however, not to increase, by such cross-examination, the amount of damages that may be given against him. Thus, where the libel consisted of comments in a newspaper on a criminal trial, in which the plaintiff was acquitted, and the defendant's counsel, although no justification had been pleaded, put to the plaintiff a series of questions tending to show that he really had been guilty of the crime with which he was charged, such a course of cross-examination was held a serious aggravation of the libel. (*Risk Allah Bey* v. *Whitehurst*, 18 L. T. 615.) Note, however, that Order XXXVI. r. 37, in no way restricts cross-examination ; it is confined to evidence called by the defendant in chief.

Where the words are actionable only because they were spoken of the plaintiff in the way of his trade, the defendant may show that such trade is illegal (*Hunt* v. *Bell*, 1 Bing. 1), if he has pleaded such defence ; and it is no objection to such evidence that it also indirectly proves the truth of the defendant's words. (*Manning* v. *Clement*, 7 Bing. 362, 368 ; 5 M. & P. 211.)

The defendant may also give evidence of antecedent conversations and transactions or other circumstances well known to the bystanders, which show that the words were not used in their ordinary signification. Thus, they may have been uttered in joke ; or the preceding part of the conversation may limit or qualify the words sued on. But the defendant cannot give in evidence some particular transaction which he says he had in his mind at the time he spoke, but to which he did not expressly refer, and which was unknown to the person addressed. (*Hankinson* v. *Bilby*, 16 M. & W. 442; 2 C. & K. 440; *Martin* v. *Loeï*, 2 F. & F. 654; *ante*, pp. 109—111.) For the question which the jury have to determine is not, " What did the defendant intend ?" but " What would a reasonable person have inferred from the language used ? " So, too, where a libel is unambiguous in itself, and does not refer to any other document, the defendant cannot use any other document for the purpose of explaining away the natural meaning of the libel.

The defendant's counsel may also urge that the occasion of publication was privileged. If the facts necessary to raise this defence are not already in evidence, he must call witnesses to prove them. Thus, it is often necessary to put the defendant himself in the box to state the facts as they were presented to him at the date of publication, the information which he received and on which he acted, and all surrounding circumstances. He will also state that he acted *bonâ fide*, and under a sense of duty. But there is danger in calling the defendant in such a case : he will be severely cross-examined, and may let slip some observation which will be seized upon as evidence of malice. It is better, if possible, by denying the fact of publication, to compel the plaintiff to call those to whom the defendant wrote or spoke, and to elicit from them, in cross-examination, circumstances which show that the occasion was privileged. Statements made to the defendant behind the plaintiff's back, and acts to which the plaintiff was no party, are admissible in evidence on this issue to show the state of the defendant's mind at the moment when he spoke or wrote the words. (*Cockayne* v. *Hodgkisson*, 5 C. & P. 543.)

So where the defence is that the libel complained of is a *bonâ fide* comment on certain facts, the defendant must prove those facts, unless the plaintiff will admit them, or unless they are well known historical facts of which the Court will take judicial notice. The judge must then decide whether such facts are matters of public interest ; if he holds that they are, it will be for the plaintiff to show that the comment on them is unfair. (*Dakhyl* v. *Labouchere*, [1908] 2 K. B. 325, n. ; 77 L. J. K. B. 728 ; 96 L. T. 399.)

The defendant may also prove a justification. The attempt, if unsuccessful, will aggravate the damages. Strict proof must be given that the whole charge made is true in every particular. Books are no evidence of the facts stated in them. (*Darby* v. *Ouseley*,

1 H. & N. 1; 25 L. J. Ex. 227; 2 Jur. N. S. 497; *Collier* v. *Simpson*, 5 C. & P. 73.) Sometimes a libel contains two or more distinct and severable charges against the plaintiff; if so, it will tend in mitigation, if the defendant can prove any one of such charges true (see *ante*, p. 393); but all of them must be proved true to entitle him to a verdict. Where, however, a libel conveys a general charge, and several specific instances are given (as they must be) in the plea or in the particulars as evidence of such general charge, then it is enough for the defendant to prove any two or three of these specific instances which will justify the libel; he is not bound to prove the whole of his particulars. (Per Cockburn, C.J., in *R. pros. Lambri* v. *Labouchere*, 14 Cox, C. C. 419.) If the charge made against the plaintiff is that he was *convicted* of an offence, then such conviction may be proved in the manner stated, *ante*, p. 693. (See *Alexander* v. *N. E. Ry. Co.*, 6 B. & S. 340; 34 L. J. Q. B. 152; 13 W. R. 651; *Gwynn* v. *S. E. Ry. Co.*, 18 L. T. 738.) If, however, the imputation is that the plaintiff has *committed* a crime, then the charge must be proved as strictly as on an indictment for the same offence. And here, the fact that the plaintiff had been previously tried and acquitted, or convicted, is irrelevant; and the record of the criminal trial is not admissible in evidence either way, for the parties are not the same. (*Justice* v. *Gosling and others*, 12 C. B. 39; 21 L. J. C. P. 94; *England* v. *Bourke*, 3 Esp. 80.)

Where no justification is pleaded, the defendant can give no evidence of the truth of his words, not even in mitigation of damages. (*Smith* v. *Richardson*, Willes, 20.) But evidence admissible and pertinent under another issue cannot be excluded merely because it happens incidentally to prove the truth of the libel. (*Manning* v. *Clement*, 7 Bing. 362, 368; 5 M. & P. 211.) Thus, if the defendant has pleaded privilege, he may show that he reasonably and *bonâ fide* believed in the truth of the charge he made, and it is no objection that the grounds of his belief are so forcible as to convince every reasonable man of the plaintiff's guilt. (*Huson* v. *Dale*, 19 Mich. 17.) Where the plaintiff, in order to prove malice, has given in evidence other words of the defendant not set out on the record, the defendant may prove the truth of such other words, for he had no opportunity of pleading a justification. (*Stuart* v. *Lovell*, 2 Stark. 93; *Warne* v. *Chadwell*, 2 Stark. 457; *Collison* v. *Loder*, Buller's N. P. 10.)

If the present defendant is liable, the fact that someone else is also liable is, of course, no defence. The plaintiff may at his option sue one or all in the same or in different actions. Evidence to show that other actions have been brought for the same or similar libels or slanders was formerly inadmissible for every purpose. (*Ante,* p. 397.) But now, in an action against a newspaper, such evidence is admissible in reduction of damages by virtue of sect. 6 of the Law of Libel Amendment Act, 1888 (51 & 52 Vict. c. 64), which enacts that " at the trial of an action for a libel contained in any newspaper the defendant shall be at liberty to give in evidence in mitigation of damages that the plaintiff has already recovered (or has brought actions for) damages, or has received or agreed to receive compensation in respect of a libel or libels to the same purport or effect as the libel for which such action has been brought." That others have previously published the same charges against the plaintiff, and have *not* been sued, is not in any way admissible. It is no justification for the defendant's republication ; still less is it any evidence of the truth of such charges. (*R.* v. *Newman,* 1 E. & B. 268 ; 22 L. J. Q. B. 156 ; 3 C. & K. 252 ; 17 Jur. 617.) It is wholly immaterial that plaintiff omitted to contradict or complain of such previous publications. (*R.* v. *Holt,* 5 T. R. 436 ; *Pankhurst* v. *Hamilton,* (1886) 2 Times L. R. 682 ; and per Maule, J., in *Ingram* v. *Lawson,* 9 C. & P. 333.) If, however, the libel purports on the face of it to be derived from a certain newspaper, the defendant may prove in mitigation of damages that a paragraph to the same effect had appeared in that newspaper. (*Wyatt* v. *Gore,* Holt, N. P. 303 ; see also *ante,* p. 394.) The defendant may not give evidence that there was a rumour current to the same effect as the words he spoke. (*Ante,* p. 393.) If the defendant relies on sect. 2 of Lord Campbell's Act, he must, as a rule, give some evidence to show affirmatively that there was no gross negligence. (Per Wills, J., in *Peters and another* v. *Edwards and another,* (1887) 3 Times L. R. 423 ; and see *ante,* p. 643.) General evidence of the plaintiff's bad character is only admissible in reduction of damages : it is not an answer to the action. (*Wood* v. *Earl of Durham,* 21 Q. B. D. 501 ; 57 L. J. Q. B. 547.) As to other evidence in mitigation of damages, see *ante,* pp. 403—406. " In actions for libel or slander, in which the defendant does not by his Defence assert the truth of the statement complained of, the defendant shall not be entitled on the trial to give evidence in chief, with a view to mitigation of damages, as to the circumstances under which the libel or slander was published, or as to the character of the plaintiff, without the leave of the judge, unless seven days at least before the trial he furnishes particulars to the plaintiff of the matters as to which he intends to give evidence." (Order XXXVI. r. 37.) As to the effect and meaning of this rule, see *ante*, p. 402. It in no way alters the law laid down in *Scott v. Sampson* (8 Q. B. D. 491; 51 L. J. Q. B. 380), save only that it relieves the defendant from the necessity of pleading such matters in his Defence.

Any point of law which either party desires to raise must be taken before verdict ; otherwise he will be deemed to have waived it. (*Graham & Sons* v. *Mayor, &c., of Huddersfield*, (1895) 12 Times L. R. 36.)

Withdrawing a Juror.

Actions of defamation are often compromised before the judge comes to sum up the evidence. A juror is often withdrawn, sometimes at the suggestion of the judge. This means that neither party cares for the case to proceed. If no special terms are agreed on, the effect of withdrawing a juror is that the action is at an end, that no fresh action can be brought on the same libel or slander, and that each party pays his own costs. (See *Strauss v. Francis*, 4 F. & F. 939, 1107; 15 L. T. 674; *Moscati* v. *Lawson*, 7 C. & P. 35, n.; *Norburn* v. *Hilliam*, L. R. 5 C. P. 129; 39 L. J. C. P. 183; 18 W. R. 602; 22 L. T. 67.) If any other terms be agreed on, they should be indorsed on counsel's briefs, and each indorsement signed by the leading counsel on both sides. Counsel has full authority to make such a compromise, unless expressly forbidden to do so by the client at the time (*Strauss* v. *Francis*, L. R. 1 Q. B. 379; 35 L. J. Q. B. 133; 14 W. R. 634; 14 L. T. 326; *Matthews* v. *Munster*, 20 Q. B. D. 141; 57 L. J. Q. B. 49; 36 W. R. 178; 57 L. T. 922; *Neale* v. *Gordon-Lennox*, [1902] A. C. 465; 71 L. J. K. B. 939; 51 W. R. 140; 87 L. T. 341), provided the compromise does not include or affect matters outside the scope of the action. (*Kempshall* v. *Holland*, (1895) 14 R. 336.) The terms of such a compromise will be strictly enforced, if necessary, by an order of the Court. (*Tardrew* v. *Brook*, 5 B. & Ad. 880; *Riley* v. *Byrne, Ib.* 882, n. But see *Lewis's* v. *Lewis*, 45 Ch. D. 281; 59 L. J. Ch. 712; 39 W. R. 75; 63 L. T. 84.) If after such a compromise the defendant reiterates the libel, the judge may give leave for the action to proceed. (*Thomas* v. *Exeter Flying Post Co.*, 18 Q. B. D. 822; 56 L. J. Q. B. 313; 35 W. R. 594; 56 L. T. 361.)

Summing-up.

The judge, when all the evidence has been placed before the Court and counsel on both sides have addressed the jury, sums up the facts of the case to the jury, and directs them as to the law. (See sect. 22 of Judicature Act, 1875.) He must always leave to the jury the question whether the words are or are not a libel, except, of course, where it is already admitted on the pleadings that they are. (*Maclaren & Sons* v. *Davis and another*, (1890) 6 Times L. R. 372.) He may tell the jury his own view of the matter (*Darby* v. *Ouseley*, 1 H. & N. at p. 13); but he must not direct them, as a matter of law, that the publication complained of is or is not a libel (*Baylis* v. *Lawrence*, 11 A. & E. 920; *Hearne* v. *Stowell*, 12 A. & E. 719; 11 L. J. Q. B. 25; 4 P. & D. 696); or that they must take from him what is the proper meaning to be put on the words complained of. (*Dakhyl* v. *Labouchere*, [1908] 2 K. B. 325, n.; 77 L. J. K. B. 728; 96 L. T. 399.) The proper course is for him to define what is a libel in point of law and to leave it to the jury, as men of ordinary intelligence, to say whether the publication in question falls within that definition. (*Parmiter* v. *Coupland and another*, 6 M. & W. 105; approved in *Cox* v. *Lee*, L. R. 4 Ex. 284; 38 L. J. Ex. 219; *Grant* v. *Yates*, (1886) 2 Times L. R. 368.) The jury are bound to take the judge's definition of a libel, and find in accordance therewith (*Levi* v. *Milne*, 4 Bing. 195; 12 Moore, 418); though the question for them, " Libel or no libel ? " is not precisely the same as " What is the legal definition of an actionable libel ? " (Per Barry, J., in *Stannus* v. *Finlay*, Ir. R. 8 C. L. 264.) In a proper case the jury should also be reminded that the question for them is not, " Did the defendant intend to injure the plaintiff ? " but, " Has he in fact injured the plaintiff's reputation ? "

If the judge decides that the occasion is privileged, then on the issue of " malice " or " no malice," he should leave to the jury the question whether the defendant *honestly* believed his words to be true, not whether he *reasonably* believed them to be true. (*Clark* v. *Molyneux*, 3 Q. B. D. 237; 47 L. J. Q. B. 230; 26 W. R. 104; 37 L. T. 694; *Collins* v. *Cooper*, (1902) 19 Times L. R. 118.)

Where other libels, &c., have been given in evidence to prove malice, the judge should caution the jury not to give any damages in respect of them. (*Pearson* v. *Lemaitre*, 5 M. & Gr. 700.) But the omission of the judge to give such caution is not a misdirection. (*Darby* v. *Ouseley*, 1 H. & N. 1; 25 L. J. Ex. 229.)

Verdict and Judgment.

Last of all, the jury consider their verdict. They must first decide whether the words are a libel (unless this has been admitted, *Maclaren* v. *Davis*, (1890) 6 Times L. R. 372). They should look at the whole of the publication to see whether it is calculated to injure the plaintiff's character, not study detached and isolated sentences. The conclusion may modify the commencement, and if so, "the bane and antidote must be taken together." (Per Alderson, B., in *Chalmers* v. *Payne*, 2 C. M. & R. 159; see also *Hunt* v. *Algar and others*, 6 C. & P. 245; *R.* v. *Lambert and Perry*, 2 Camp. 398.) And see *ante*, p. 24.

Where the words are actionable *per se*, the amount of damages is entirely a matter for the jury. They are not confined to the pecuniary loss actually sustained by the plaintiff. (*Ante*, p. 372.) They may consider the libel itself, the mode and extent of publication, and the malice evinced by the defendant. Also, in an action against a newspaper, they may have regard to the gross negligence shown by the editor in allowing the libel to appear in print. (*Smith* v. *Harrison*, 1 F. & F. 565.) The jury must assess the damages once for all, as no fresh action can be brought for any subsequent damage. (See *ante*, p. 375.) And in assessing the damages, the jury should not regard at all the question of costs. (*Poole* v. *Whitcomb*, 12 C. B. N. S. 770; *Levi* v. *Milne*, 4 Bing. 195; 12 Moore, 418; *Best* v. *Osborne, Garrett & Co.*, (1896) 12 Times L. R. 419.) They must not be told that any money has been paid into Court. (Order XXII. r. 22; and see *ante*, p. 641.) But they cannot find a verdict for the plaintiff without awarding him some damages. (Per Lord Coleridge, C.J., in *Wisdom* v. *Brown*, (1885) 1 Times L. R. 412.)

"The judge shall at or after trial direct judgment to be entered as he shall think right." (Order XXXVI. r. 39.) He cannot direct judgment to be entered for an amount larger than that claimed on the Statement of Claim, unless he give leave to amend. (*Chattell* v. *Daily Mail Publishing Co., Limited*, (1901) 18 Times L. R. 165.) Order XXVIII. r. 1, gives the judge full power to amend, even at this stage of the proceedings. (*Wyatt* v. *Rosherville Gardens Co.*, (1886) 2 Times L. R. 282.) Where distinct issues are separately left to the jury, the judge may accept their verdict on those issues on which they agree, and discharge them on others on which they cannot agree. (*Marsh* v. *Isaacs*, 45 L. J. C. P. 505; and see *Nevill* v. *Fine Arts Insurance Co.*, [1895] 2 Q. B. at p. 158.)

If an action is brought against joint wrong-doers for damages for the joint wrong, there can only be one verdict and one judgment against all the defendants. Thus, where the proprietor and editor of a newspaper are sued for the libel which has been published in the paper and the editor persists in a plea of justification which he cannot prove, whilst the proprietor apologises and pays money into Court, the judge will direct the jury to find one verdict against both defendants, and there will be one judgment entered against them both. (*Hopton* v. *Licensed Victuallers' Gazette and others, Times,* November 1st and 2nd, 1900; *Damiens* v. *Modern Society (Ltd.) and another,* (1911) 27 Times L. R. 164.) Where the libel is a joint one and the defendants are sued jointly, the jury has no power, even with the permission of the judge, to sever the damages, and if they do so and return separate verdicts against the different defendants, a new trial will be ordered. (*Dawson* v. *M'Clelland,* [1899] 2 Ir. R. 486.) Where, however, two or more plaintiffs join in one action under Order XVI. r. 1, though strictly the jury should assess the damages in favour of each plaintiff separately yet if neither party insists on this at the trial, and the jury consequently award the damages generally in one lump sum, the Court will not grant a new trial. (*Booth and others* v. *Briscoe,* 2 Q. B. D. 496 ; 25 W. R. 838.)

Application for Costs and Payment out of Court.

If an action of libel or slander be tried by a jury, there is no longer any need to ask for the general costs of the action. The successful party gets such costs as of right, unless the judge for good cause makes an order depriving him of his costs. (Order LXV. r. 1.) As to what is good cause, see *ante,* p. 441. Hence, if there be a verdict for the plaintiff for contemptuous damages only, his counsel should say nothing about costs; it is the duty of the defendant's counsel to ask the judge to interfere.

To this rule there are two exceptions * :—

(i) Special costs such as costs of a special jury, of a commission to take evidence abroad, of photographic copies of the libel, or any costs reserved to be dealt with by the judge at the trial (*British Provident Association* v. *Bywater,* [1897] 2 Ch. 531; 66 L. J. Ch. 787 ; 46 W. R. 28 ; 77 L. T. 22), must be asked for now. The party, who has incurred these costs, will have to pay them unless he obtain, before judgment is entered, an order for their allowance on taxation. (*Ante,* p. 447.)

(ii) If any woman or girl brings an action for spoken words, which are not actionable at common law, but were made

---

* The provisions of the Public Authorities Protection Act, 1893, which entitle the defendants in certain events to costs as between solicitor and client, do not restrict the power of the judge for good cause to deprive the successful party of his costs. (*Bostock* v. *Ramsey U. D. C.,* [1900] 2 Q. B. 616; 69 L. J. Q. B. 945; 48 W. R. 254; 83 L. T. 358.)

actionable by the Slander of Women Act, 1891 (54 & 55 Vict. c. 51), her counsel must apply to the judge for a certificate that there was reasonable ground for bringing the action: as without such a certificate she will recover no more for her costs than the amount of the damages awarded by the jury.

If by any chance an action of libel or slander be tried by a judge alone, the costs are wholly in his discretion. As to the general law of costs, see Chapter XV., *ante*, p. 439.

If money has been paid into Court but the jury assess the damages at a larger amount, the plaintiff is entitled to judgment and to the whole costs of the action. And the judge will order the amount in Court to be paid out to the plaintiff. If, however, the jury assess the damages at an amount not greater than the sum paid into Court, the defendant is entitled to judgment and *primâ facie* to the whole costs of the action. And the Court will order the balance, if any, of the sum paid into Court, to be paid out to the defendant. (*Gray* v. *Bartholomew*, [1895] 1 Q. B. 209; 64 L. J. Q. B. 125; 43 W. R. 177; 71 L. T. 867; *Veale* v. *Reid*, (1904) 117 L. T. Journal, 292, overruling *Dunn* v. *Devon and Exeter Constitutional Newspaper Co.*, [1895] 1 Q. B. 211, n.; 63 L. J. Q. B. 342; 70 L. T. 593.) The plaintiff's counsel, however, should in such a case apply to the judge to order that the plaintiff shall have his costs up to the time of payment into Court. (See *ante*, p. 449.) The defendant's counsel, on the other hand, should apply to the judge to direct that a portion of the money in Court, equal to the amount of the verdict, shall remain in Court as security for the costs payable by the plaintiff, and that the balance be paid out to the defendant. (*Best* v. *Osborne, Garrett & Co.*, (1896) 12 Times L. R. 419.)

A different practice as to costs prevails if the money has been paid into Court with a plea under Lord Campbell's Libel Act, and the jury award the plaintiff a less amount than the sum paid in. This is discussed, *ante*, p. 642. Should the jury in such a case deem the apology insufficient, or find that there was malice, or gross negligence on the part of the defendant, and yet assess the damages at an amount less than the sum paid into Court, the plaintiff is entitled to judgment and costs; and, it is submitted, he is also entitled to have the amount of the damages paid to him out of the money in Court, the balance of that money to remain in Court during taxation, and then to be applied in satisfaction of the costs which the defendant has to pay him.

Now is the time for the plaintiff's counsel to apply to the judge for an injunction, provided he can show that there is any probability that the defendant will repeat the publication.

If there is any thought of further proceedings, the unsuccessful party should ask the judge to stay execution. This the judge will do if he thinks there is any ground for such an application. The usual order is, that execution be stayed for eight days, and if within that time notice of motion be served and £ —— brought into Court execution be further stayed till the appeal is disposed of.

CHAPTER XXVI.

PROCEEDINGS AFTER TRIAL.

WHENEVER an action has been tried by a jury, any motion for judgment must be heard and determined by the judge before whom the trial took place; but any motion for a new trial, or to set aside a verdict, finding, or judgment must be heard and determined by the Court of Appeal. (53 & 54 Vict. c. 44, ss. 1 and 2; and see Order XL. rr. 3, 4 and 5; Order XXIX. r. 1.)

Upon the hearing of a motion to set aside a judgment, the Court of Appeal can, if it think fit, order that the verdict and judgment shall be set aside, and that a new trial shall be had. (Order LVIII. r. 5.) So, on a motion for a new trial, the Court of Appeal has power, in a proper case, to direct judgment to be entered for either of the parties instead of ordering a new trial. (*Allcock* v. *Hall*, [1891] 1 Q. B. 444; 60 L. J. Q. B. 416; 39 W. R. 443; 64 L. T. 309.) So, too, where the trial is by a judge without a jury, the Court of Appeal may either grant a new trial or order judgment to be entered for the appellant, as justice may require, whatever the terms of the notice of motion may be. (Order XXXIX. r. 1, a; *Jones* v. *Hough*, 5 Ex. D. 115, 125; 49 L. J. C. P. 211; 42 L. T. 108; *Waddell* v. *Blockey*, 10 Ch. D. 416; 27 W. R. 233; 40 L. T. 286.) The Court of Appeal has full power to make any amendment and to receive further evidence upon questions of fact. (Order LVIII. r. 4; and see *Ecklin* v. *Little* (1890) 6 Times L. R. 366.)

MOTION FOR NEW TRIAL.

An application for a new trial may be made on the ground that the verdict is against the weight of evidence, that the judge wrongly received or rejected evidence, that the jury misbehaved, that the damages are excessive or inadequate, on the ground of misdirection or surprise, &c. The notice of motion must state the grounds of the application. (Order XXXIX. r. 3.) See Precedent No. 65, *post*, p. 792. It is not enough to state simply "misdirection"; the notice must state how and in what matter the jury were misdirected.

(*Pfeiffer* v. *Midland Ry. Co.*, 18 Q. B. D. 243 ; 35 W. R. 335 ; *Murfett* v. *Smith*, 12 P. D. 116 ; 57 L. T. 498.)

Misdirection.

A new trial will not be granted on the ground of misdirection if the respondent can satisfy the Court that no substantial wrong or miscarriage has been thereby occasioned. (Order XXXIX. r. 6 ; *Anthony* v. *Halstead*, 37 L. T. 433 ; *Faund* v. *Wallace*, 35 L. T. 361 ; *Floyd* v. *Gibson*, (1909) 100 L. T. 761 ; *Tait* v. *Beggs*, [1905] 2 Ir. R. 525) If an important and serious topic has been practically withdrawn from the jury, that is a substantial wrong to the party in whose favour it might have told, and a new trial will be ordered ; the Court will not speculate as to what might have been the result had the judge rightly directed the jury. (*Bray* v. *Ford*, [1896] A. C. 44 ; 65 L. J. Q. B. 213 ; 73 L. T. 609.) If the judge has so directed the jury as to the meaning of the words that there must be a verdict for the plaintiff if that direction is followed, the Court will order a new trial. (*Dakhyl* v. *Labouchere* [1908] 2 K. B. 325, n. ; 96 L. T. 399 ; 23 Times L. R. 364 ; and see *Hunt* v. *Star Newspaper Co. Ltd.*, *ib.* at p. 318 ; 77 L. J. K. B. 732 ; 98 L. T. 629.) It is only where the Court can clearly see that the jury, if rightly directed, would still have returned the same verdict, that it will decline to interfere. (Per Lord Esher, M.R., in *Merivale* v. *Carson*, 20 Q. B. D. at p. 281.) And where any miscarriage is proved, the Court may grant a new trial as to so much of the matter only as the miscarriage affects, without interfering with the decision upon any other question. (Order XXXIX. r. 7 ; *Marsh* v. *Isaacs*, 45 L. J. C. P. 505.) So, too, the Court may grant a new trial as against one defendant without granting it as to all ; though notice of motion must be served on all. (*Price* v. *Harris*, 10 Bing. 331 ; *Purnell* v. *G. W. Ry. Co. and Harris*, 1 Q. B. D. 636 ; 45 L. J. Q. B. 687 ; 24 W. R. 720, 909 ; 35 L. T. 605.)

Verdict against Weight of Evidence.

In the absence of any misdirection, the Court will rarely interfere to set aside a verdict or grant a new trial on the ground that the verdict was against the weight of evidence ; they will not do so unless the verdict was one which reasonable men could not properly find. (*Australian Newspaper Co., Limited* v. *Bennett*, [1894] A. C.

284; 63 L. J. P. C. 105; 70 L. T. 597; 6 R. 484; *Webster* v. *Friede-berg*, 17 Q. B. D. 786; 55 L. J. Q. B. 403; *Phillips* v. *Martin*, 15 App. Cas. 193.) " The verdict ought not to be disturbed unless it was one which a jury, viewing the whole of the evidence reasonably, could not properly find." (Per Lord Herschell, L.C., in *Metropolitan Ry. Co.* v. *Wright*, 11 App. Cas. at p. 154.) " If reasonable men *might* find the verdict which has been found, I think no Court has jurisdiction to disturb a decision of fact which the law has confided to juries, not to judges." (Per Lord Halsbury, 11 App. Cas. at p. 156.) Where on any issue there is evidence both ways properly submitted to the jury, their verdict on that issue once found must stand. (*Commissioner for Railways* v. *Brown*, 13 App. Cas. 133; 57 L. J. P. C. 72; 57 L. T. 895.)

If the words are capable of being a libel, and the question of "libel or no libel" has been properly left to the jury, the Court will not set aside their verdict. (*Cooney* v. *Edeveain*, (1897) 14 Times L. R. 34.) Where the words are fairly susceptible both of an innocent and of an actionable meaning, the finding of the jury is final; whichever construction they may have placed upon the words will be upheld. (*Burgess* v. *Bracher*, (1724) 8 Mod. 240; 2 Ld. Raym. 1366; *Walter* v. *Beaver* and *Naden* v. *Micocke*, (1684) 3 Lev. 166; 2 Ventr. 172; *Grant* v. *Yates*, (1886) 2 Times L. R. 368.) So, whenever the words are ambiguous, allegorical, or in any way equivocal, and the jury have found that they were meant and used in a defamatory sense, the Court will not set aside their verdict, unless it can be clearly shown that, on reading the whole passage, there is no possible ground for the construction put upon it by the jury. (*Hoare* v. *Silverlock*, 12 Q. B. 624; 17 L. J. Q. B. 306; *Fray* v. *Fray*, 17 C. B. N. S. 603; 34 L. J. C. P. 45; 10 Jur. N. S. 1153.)

A new trial will, however, be granted when the matter complained of is clearly libellous, and there is no question as to the fact of publication, or as to its application to the plaintiff, and yet the jury have perversely found a verdict for the defendant in spite of the summing-up of the learned judge. (*Levi* v. *Milne*, 4 Bing. 195, *ante*, p. 152; *Hakewell* v. *Ingram*, 2 C. L. R. 1397.) The reluctance of a Court to set aside the verdict of a jury is very natural: and the rule is that it will not do so, unless the Court can say with certainty that there has been a miscarriage of justice. (Per Tindal, C.J., in *Broome* v. *Gosden*, 1 C. B. 731; per Field, J., in *O'Brien* v. *Marquis of Salisbury*, (1889) 6 Times L. R. at p. 137; 54 J. P. 215.) " But it seems to me to be a condition of any such rule that the question which had to be determined should have been so left to the jury that one is satisfied that it was before their minds, that their minds were applied to it, and that they did really on the determination of that question give their verdict." (Per Lord Herschell, in *Jones* v. *Spencer*, (1897) 77 L. T. at p. 538.)

It was formerly the custom that the Court would not grant a new trial on the ground that the verdict was against the weight of evidence where the damages did not exceed 20*l.* But it was doubtful whether this custom applied in actions of libel or slander (*Booth and others* v. *Briscoe*, (1877) 2 Q. B. D. 496 ; *Joyce* v. *Metropolitan Board of Works*, (1881) 44 L. T. 811); and it is now no longer observed.

Irregularities at the Trial.

A new trial will not be granted on the ground that the jury expressed an opinion during the judge's summing-up inconsistent with their subsequent verdict (*Napier* v. *Daniel and another*, 3 Bing. N. C. 77 ; 3 Scott, 417); nor on the ground that either judge or jury prematurely expressed a strong opinion as to the case either way. (*Lloyd* v. *Jones*, 7 B. & S. 475 ; *Fox* v. *Evening News, Limited*, (1898) 14 Times L. R. 280.) It would be otherwise if a juror before being sworn had expressed a determination to give a verdict in favour of the plaintiff. (*Ramadge* v. *Ryan*, 9 Bing. 333 ; 2 Moo. & Sc. 421.)

It is, however, ground for a new trial that the counsel for either party in his speech made suggestions which misled the jury as to the amount of the verdict which they should give (*Praed* v. *Graham*, 24 Q. B. D. at p. 55 ; *Chattell* v. *Daily Mail Publishing Co., Limited*, (1901) 18 Times L. R. 165); or read letters written without prejudice (even unwittingly) or cross-examined the plaintiff in a most insulting and offensive manner for which there was no justification. (*Watt* v. *Watt*, [1905] A. C. at pp. 117, 118.)

Fresh Evidence.

In some cases the Court will grant a new trial on the ground that fresh evidence has come to light since the first trial : but this will only be done where the applicant can show that the new evidence will entirely change the aspect of the case, and further that it could not by reasonable diligence have been obtained before the trial. (*Phosphate Sewage Co.* v. *Molleson*, (1879) 4 App. Cas. 801 ; *Young* v. *Kershaw*, (1899) 81 L. T. 531 ; 16 Times L. R. 52 ; *Turnbull & Co.* v. *Duval*, [1902] A. C. 429 ; 71 L. J. P. C. 84 ; 87 L. T. 154.)

If it is desirable to bring fresh evidence before the Court of Appeal (Order LVIII. r. 4), then if such evidence be documentary, the party wishing to adduce it must give notice to the other side of his intention to apply at the hearing of the appeal for leave to adduce such evidence. (*Hastie* v. *Hastie*, 1 Ch. D. 562; *Justice* v. *Mersey Steel and Iron Co.*, 24 W. R. 199; *In re Chennell*, 8 Ch. D. at p. 505.) But if a party wishes to call fresh witnesses, he must apply for leave by motion previous to the hearing of the appeal, after giving notice to the other side. (*Dicks* v. *Brooks*, 13 Ch. D. 652.)

Verdict not Assented to by the whole of the Jury.

It is no ground for a new trial that a juryman has since the trial declared that he did not assent to a verdict, against which he did not protest when the foreman gave it in Court. And if a juryman has made an affidavit stating that the verdict as announced was never assented to by him, the Court will not allow such affidavit to be read in evidence on a motion for a new trial. (*Nesbitt* v. *Parrett and another*, (1902) 18 Times L. R. 510.)

Excessive Damages.

In actions of defamation the Court seldom grants a new trial on the ground that the damages are either too small or too great. " The assessment of damages is peculiarly the province of the jury in an action of libel. The damages in such an action are not limited to the amount of pecuniary loss which the plaintiff is able to prove." (*Davis & Sons* v. *Shepstone*, 11 App. Cas. at p. 191; 55 L. J. P. C. 51; 34 W. R. 722; 55 L. T. 1.) The Court will not grant a new trial on the ground of excessive damages, unless they think that, having regard to all the circumstances of the case, the damages are so large that no jury could reasonably have given them. (*Praed* v. *Graham*, 24 Q. B. D. 53; 59 L. J. Q. B. 230; 38 W. R. 103; *Magrath* v. *Bourne*, Ir. R. 10 C. L. 160; *Harris* v. *Arnott and others*, 26 L. R. Ir. at p. 68.) Nor will they do so where the publication of other libels has been proved in aggravation of damages and the judge at the trial has omitted to direct the jury not to give damages for these as for separate causes of action. (*Anderson* v. *Calvert*, (1908) 24 Times L. R. 399.) In *Lord Townshend* v. *Dr. Hughes* (2 Mod. 150), the Court refused to order a new trial which was asked for on the ground that the damages (4,000*l.*) were excessive; a similar application was refused in *Highmore* v. *Earl and Countess of Harrington* (3 C. B. N. S. 142), where 750*l.* damages was awarded. The Court of Appeal on an application for a new trial has no power, without the consent of both parties, to alter the amount of damages awarded by the jury. It cannot make an order that there shall be a new trial unless the plaintiff consents to accept a reduced amount of damages. (*Watt* v. *Watt*, [1905] A. C. 115 ; overruling *Belt* v. *Lawes*, 12 Q. B. D. 356 ; *Gatty* v. *Farquharson*, (1893) 9 Times L. R. 593 ; and *Farquhar, North & Co.* v. *Edward Lloyd, Ltd.*, (1901) 17 Times L. R. 568.)

Smallness of Damages.

So, too, there is no inexorable rule of practice which precludes the Court from granting a new trial on account of the smallness of damages. In *Kelly* v. *Sherlock* (L. R. 1 Q. B. 686, 697 ; 35 L. J. Q. B. 209), a rule *nisi* was granted on that ground, though it was discharged on the argument. There seems to be no case reported in which a new trial has been granted on this ground in an action of libel ; but in an action of slander a new trial was granted where the smallness of the amount recovered ($\frac{1}{4}d$.) showed, in the special circumstances of that case, that the jury had made an improper compromise, and had not really tried the issues submitted to them. (*Falvey* v. *Stanford*, L. R. 10 Q. B. 54 ; 44 L. J. Q. B. 7.) See, however, *Forsdike and wife* v. *Stone* (L. R. 3 C. P. 607 ; 37 L. J. C. P. 301), and *Rendall* v. *Hayward* (5 Bing. N. C. 424), which cases lay down the rule that where there has been no misconduct on the part of the jury, no error in the calculation of figures, and no mistake in law on the part of the judge, a new trial will not be granted. That the jury intended their verdict to carry costs, but have returned an amount insufficient in law to do so, never was a ground for granting a new trial. (*Mears* v. *Griffin*, 1 M. & Gr. 796 ; 2 Scott, N. R. 15 ; *Kilmore* v. *Abdoolah*, 27 L. J. Ex. 307 ; *Forsdike and wife* v. *Stone, supra*.) There is no necessary inconsistency in a jury finding that a libel was written maliciously, and yet awarding only a farthing damages ; and such a verdict will not be set aside. (*Cooke* v. *Brogden & Co.*, (1885) 1 Times L. R. 497.) But a new trial will perhaps be granted if it can be shown that the jury wholly omitted to take into consideration some substantial element of damage. (*Phillips* v. *L. & S. W. Ry. Co.*, 5 Q. B. D. 78 ; 49 L. J. Q. B. 233 ; 28 W. R. 10 ; 41 L. T. 121.)

Surprise.

The plaintiff may not during the trial set up a third construction of the words different both from their *primâ facie* meaning and from that alleged by the innuendo ; if he win a verdict in that way, the Court will grant a new trial on the ground of surprise. (*Hunter* v. *Sharpe*, 4 F. & F. 983 ; 15 L. T. 421 ; *Ruel* v. *Tatnell*, 29 W. R. 172 ; 43 L. T. 507.) Whenever a new trial is moved for on the ground of surprise, the absence of a material witness at the trial, &c., there must be an affidavit setting out the facts. "Surprise is a matter extrinsic to the record and the judge's notes, and consequently can only be made to appear by affidavit ; and here we have no affidavit of surprise, in the sense required by the practice of the Court." (Per Maule, J., in *Hoare* v. *Silverlock* (No. 2), (1850) 9 C. B. 22.)

Judge's Note.

The judge's note is decisive as to the evidence taken in the Court below ; but either party may read a shorthand writer's note, to supplement, though not to overrule, the judge's note. (*Laming* v. *Gee*, 28 W. R. 217.) If either party at the trial deliberately elects to fight one question only, on which he is beaten, he cannot afterwards on appeal raise another question, although that question was at the trial open to him on the pleadings and on the evidence. (*Martin* v. *G. N. Ry. Co.*, 16 C. B. 179, approved in *Browne* v. *Dunn*, (H. L.) (1893) 6 R. 67. And see *Eyre* v. *New Forest Highway Board*, (1892) 8 Times L. R. 648 ; *Page* v. *Bowdler*, (1894) 10 Times L. R. 423 ; *Graham & Sons* v. *Mayor, &c., of Huddersfield*, (1895) 12 Times L. R. 36.)

Costs.

If a new trial be ordered on the ground of misdirection, the Court will, as a general rule, order the costs of the first trial to abide the event of the new trial. If no special order be made by the Court of Appeal, they become costs of the action, and the judge at the second trial has the same power over them as he has over the costs of the second trial. (See *ante*, p. 452.) The costs of a successful application for a new trial will, as a rule, be given to the applicant. (*Hamilton* v. *Seal*, [1904] 2 K. B. 262 ; 73 L. J. K. B. 560 ; 52 W. R. 581 ; 90 L. T. 592, in which case the former decisions in *Bray* v. *Ford*, [1896] A. C. at p. 56, and *Jones* v. *Richards*, (1899) 15 Times L. R. 398, were treated as exceptional and not followed.) Where an appeal to the House of Lords is contemplated no special order as to costs will be made except in an extreme case. (*Griffiths* v. *Benn*, (1911) 27 Times L. R. 346.)

It is only in exceptional cases that the House of Lords will entertain an application asking them to revise a discretionary order of the Court of Appeal confirming the opinion of the judge of first instance. (*Kent Coal Concessions* v. *Duguid*, [1910] A. C. 452 ; 79 L. J. K. B. 872 ; 103 L. T. 89).

CHAPTER XXVII.

CIVIL PROCEEDINGS IN INFERIOR COURTS.

County Court Proceedings.

No action of libel or slander can be commenced in the County Court, except by consent. (See sects. 56 and 64 of the County Courts Act, 1888 (51 & 52 Vict. c. 43).) Whether the word " slander " includes " slander of title " may be doubted. In cases of a trifling nature, it may be desirable that both parties should consent to such a course, especially if all the witnesses reside in a town where a County Court is held. The parties or their respective solicitors must in that case sign a memorandum of consent, which must be filed ; and thereupon a plaint will be entered and a summons issued, and all further proceedings will be taken as in an ordinary County Court case. (County Court Order V. r. 2.)

But an action of libel or slander commenced in the High Court of Justice, whatever may be the amount of damages claimed, may be transferred to the County Court, under sect. 66 of the County Courts Act, 1888. (*Ante*, p. 618.) When such a transfer is ordered, the plaintiff must lodge the writ and other proceedings, and the order remitting the action, with the registrar of the County Court. Until this is done, the action remains in the Superior Court, which consequently has jurisdiction to vary the order. (*Welply* v. *Buhl*, 3 Q. B. D. 80, 253 ; 47 L. J. Q. B. 151 ; *D'Errico* v. *Samuel*, [1896] 1 Q. B. 163 ; 65 L. J. Q. B. 197.) If the plaintiff omit to lodge the order of transfer within a reasonable time after it is made, the defendant can apply at Chambers for an order dismissing the action for want of prosecution. As soon as the necessary documents are filed, the action becomes a County Court cause. (*Moody* v. *Steward*, L. R. 6 Ex. 35 ; 40 L. J. Ex. 25.) The County Court judge is bound to assume jurisdiction; he cannot inquire into the circumstances under which the order was made. (*Blades* v. *Lawrence*, L. R. 9 Q. B. 374 ; 43 L. J. Q. B. 133.)

The plaintiff is required by County Court Order XXXIII. r. 1, to lodge with the registrar the writ and the order remitting the action or a duplicate thereof, and a copy or copies of any affidavit or affidavits on which the order was made, and a statement of the names and addresses of the several parties to the action, and their solicitors, if any, and also a concise statement of the particulars of claim, signed by the plaintiff or his solicitor, such as would be required upon entering a plaint in the County Court. The registrar must thereupon enter the action for trial, and give notice to the parties of the day appointed for such trial, by post or otherwise, ten clear days before such day ; and must annex to the notice to the defendant a copy of the particulars. Such statement of the plaintiff's particulars should be in the form given in Precedent No. 67. The registrar must forthwith indorse on the order or duplicate thereof the date on which the same was lodged, and file the same ; and the action will proceed in all things as if it were an ordinary action in the County Court. (County Court Order XXXIII. r. 2.)

The defendant upon being served with such a notice of trial must proceed in all things in the same way as if the action had been brought in the County Court, and the notice so served upon him was an ordinary summons. (County Court Order XXXIII. r. 3.)

Thus he may, five clear days at least before the day named in such notice of trial, pay money into Court, either generally or under Lord Campbell's Act, paying a Court fee proportionate to the amount paid in. (County Court Order IX. r. 12.) Or he may set up a counterclaim (County Court Order X. rr. 2, 11), or plead the Statute of Limitations (*Ib.* r. 14, a), or any other special defence. This he does by sending in to the registrar five clear days at least before the day named for trial a concise statement of the grounds of such special defence. (See Precedent No. 68.) If the defendant omit to send such statement, he will not be allowed to avail himself of the defence, unless the plaintiff consents thereto ; but the judge will in a proper case adjourn the trial of the action to enable the defendant to give such notice. (County Court Order X. r. 10.) So, too, if the defendant intends to avail himself of the provisions of sects. 1 and 2 of Lord Campbell's Libel Act (6 & 7 Vict. c. 96), he must give to the registrar five clear days before the day appointed for the trial notice in writing of such intention, signed by himself or his solicitor. (County Court Order XXXIII. r. 4.) Such notice should be in form (ii) of Precedent No. 68, if under sect. 1 of Lord Campbell's Libel Act; in form (iii) of the same Precedent, if under sect. 2. And see County Court Order IX. r. 12, as to the necessary payment into Court. If the plaintiff claims more than £50, apparently County Court Order XXIIa. applies and the defendant must take any of the above steps at least ten days before trial.

Where in any action of libel or slander the defendant relies as a defence upon the fact that the libel or slander is true, he must in his statement set forth that the libel or slander complained of is true in substance (County Court Order X. r. 16), unless he has already done so in a Defence delivered in the High Court. Such statement should be in form (i) of Precedent No. 68. Where in any action of libel or slander the defendant does not rely as a defence upon the fact that the libel or slander is true, but relies in mitigation of damages on the circumstances under which the libel or slander was published, or the character of the plaintiff, he must in his statement give particulars of the matters relating thereto as to which he intends to give evidence. (*Ib.* r. 17.)

Interrogatories may be administered in the County Court by leave of the judge or registrar. (County Court Order XVI. r. 1.) Any objection to answer must be taken in the affidavit in answer. Discovery and inspection of documents may also be obtained as in the High Court.

If either party desires to have the action tried by a jury, he must proceed in the manner indicated by sects. 101 and 102 of the County Courts Act, 1888, and County Court Order XXII. r. 1. And where no demand for a jury has been so made, but at the trial both parties desire one, the judge may adjourn the trial upon terms in order that notice for a jury may be given. (County Court Order XXII. r. 2.) It is generally desirable to have a jury in an action of libel or slander.

The trial takes place in all respects as in an ordinary County Court cause; save that if any pleadings were delivered in the action in the High Court before the order was made remitting it to the County Court, the judge must not disregard them. Thus, if a plaintiff has shaped his action differently on his Statement of Claim and on his writ, the judge must look rather to the Statement of Claim than to the writ. (*Johnson* v. *Palmer,* 4 C. P. D. 258; 27 W. R. 941; *Large* v. *Large,* W. N. 1877, p. 198.) Care should be taken to ask the judge before delivering judgment to make a note of any point of law on which either party relies. (*Rhodes* v. *Liverpool Investment Co.,* 4 C. P. D. 425; *Pierpoint* v. *Cartwright,* 5 C. P. D. 139; 28 W. R. 583; 42 L. T. 295; *Seymour* v. *Coulson,* 28 W. R. 664.)

Judgment is entered and all subsequent proceedings taken as in an ordinary County Court action. Any motion for a new trial must be made to the judge in the County Court (County Court Order XXXI.); any appeal must be had in accordance with the provisions of the Rules of the Supreme Court, Order LIX. rr. 9—18. (County Court Order XXXII.) The costs will follow the event unless the judge at the trial make any order to the contrary ; he has full power to make any order as to costs which he " shall think just." (County Courts Act, 1888, s. 118.)   In taxing the costs incurred in the High Court of Justice, previous to the transmission of the action to the County Court, the registrar must tax the same according to the scale of costs in use in the High Court ; the costs subsequent to the order remitting the action will be taxed according to the scale in use in the County Courts.   (County Courts Act, 1888, s. 66.) The High Court has no jurisdiction to make any order as to the costs of a remitted action.   (*Moody* v. *Steward*, L. R. 6 Ex. 35 ; 40 L. J. Ex. 25 ; 19 W. R. 161 ; 23 L. T. 465.)

Other Inferior Courts.

There are many inferior Courts in which actions of libel and slander can be brought, such as the Mayor's Court, London, the Tolzey Court of Bristol, the Salford Hundred Court of Record, the Court of Passage, Liverpool, &c.   As to the jurisdiction of such Courts generally, see *ante*, p. 606.   The Mayor's Court, London, has jurisdiction to try actions of libel or slander, and can award costs, even though the verdict be for less than 5*l.* (*Hall* v. *Launspach,*,[1898] 1 Q. B. 513 ; 67 L. J. Q. B. 372 ; 78 L. T. 243.)   The Salford Hundred Court has power to hear all cases of libel or slander arising within the jurisdiction of the Court, provided the damages claimed do not exceed 50*l.*   If they exceed 50*l.*, it appears that the Court has no jurisdiction, even by consent.   (9 & 10 Vict. c. cxxvi. ; *Farrow* v. *Hague*, 3 H. & C. 101 ; 33 L. J. Ex. 258.)   The costs will follow the event, both in the Salford Hundred Court (*Turner* v. *Heyland*, 4 C. P. D. 432 ; 48 L. J. C. P. 535 ; 41 L. T. 556), and in the Liverpool Court of Passage (*King and another* v. *Hawkesworth*, 4 Q. B. D. 371 ; 48 L. J. Q. B. 484 ; 27 W. R. 660 ; 41 L. T. 411), and indeed wherever the case is tried by a jury ; subject, however, to the power reserved to a judge by Order LXV. r. 1, to deprive a successful plaintiff of his costs on good cause shown.

Under clause 12 of the schedule to the Borough and Local Courts of Record Act, 1872 (which was applied to the Mayor's Court by Order in Council), if an action be commenced in an inferior Court the judge of a superior Court may at any time before judgment order the action to be removed into the superior Court if he be satisfied that it is more fit to be tried there.   (*Banks* v. *Hollingsworth and another*, [1893] 1 Q. B. 442 ; 62 L. J. Q. B. 239 ; 41 W. R. 225 ; 68 L. T. 477.)

PART III.
PRACTICE AND EVIDENCE IN CRIMINAL CASES.

———•———

CHAPTER XXVIII.

PROCEEDINGS BY WAY OF INDICTMENT.

Preliminary Application to the Judge at Chambers.

By sect. 8 of the Law of Libel Amendment Act, 1888, no criminal prosecution can be commenced " against any proprietor, publisher, editor, or any person responsible for the publication of a newspaper, for any libel published therein, without the order of a judge at Chambers being first had and obtained." This section does not apply to any criminal information, whether *ex officio* or otherwise. (*Yates* v. *The Queen,* 14 Q. B. D. 648 ; 54 L. J. Q. B. 258 ; 33 W. R. 482 ; 52 L. T. 305 ; 49 J. P. 436 ; 15 Cox, C. C. 686.) The application to the judge at Chambers for an order under this section must be made " on notice to the person accused, who shall have an opportunity of being heard against such application." The intending prosecutor generally files affidavits, verifying a copy of the libel, proving its publication by the intended defendant, swearing to the falsity of the imputation made, and also showing reasons why it is necessary to have recourse to criminal proceedings, *e.g.,* that the intended defendant is insolvent and cannot pay damages. The learned judge will not order a prosecution if he considers that a civil action will meet all the requirements of the case. The person whom it is proposed to prosecute must be named in the order; he must not be merely referred to in general terms as " the editor " or " the publisher " of a certain paper. (*R.* v. *Allison, Judd and others,* 37 W. R. 143 ; 59 L. T. 933 ; 53 J. P. 215 ; 16 Cox, C. C. 559.) No appeal can be brought from the decision of a judge at Chambers under this section, allowing a criminal prosecution to be commenced. (*Ex parte Pulbrook,* [1892] 1 Q. B. 86 ; 61 L. J. M. C. 91 ; 40 W. R.

175 ; 66 L. T. 159 ; 56 J. P. 293 ; 17 Cox, C. C. 464.) And it would seem to follow from the judgments in this case that no appeal would lie in the converse case also, where leave to prosecute has been refused. (See also a decision under the former Act, *Ex parte Hubert, Hurter & Son,* 47 J. P. 724 ; 15 Cox, C. C. 166.)

It is only where the libel has appeared in a newspaper that any application need be made under this section. Nor does the section apply where criminal proceedings are about to be taken against the actual author of the libel, even though the words which he wrote be afterwards printed in a newspaper, unless the author be the proprietor, publisher, editor, or other person responsible for the publication of a newspaper. It is submitted that the printer is included in this phrase, but not the writer and composer of the libel, even though he be a reporter on the staff of the paper.

Proceedings before Magistrates.

By sect. 6 of the Newspaper Libel and Registration Act, 1881, " every libel or alleged libel " is included in the Vexatious Indictments Act (22 & 23 Vict. c. 17) ; and this section applies to all libels, whether published in a newspaper or not. Hence, in every criminal proceeding for libel the accused must be summoned before a police or stipendiary magistrate, or before two justices of the peace. The magistrate may, indeed, if he think fit, on good cause shown and information sworn, issue a warrant for his apprehension in the first instance without any previous summons (*Butt* v. *Conant,* 1 Brod. & B. 548; 4 Moore, 195 ; Gow, 84; 11 & 12 Vict. c. 42, ss. 1, 8); but such a step will seldom be taken on a charge of libel. If the accused does not appear in answer to the summons, the magistrate may, on proof of due service, go into the case in his absence, but he more usually issues a warrant for his apprehension. (11 & 12 Vict. c. 42, ss. 1, 9.)

When the accused comes before the magistrate the prosecutor has merely to prove publication, unless it is not clear that the libel refers to the prosecutor, in which case it may be necessary to call someone acquainted with the circumstances to state that on reading the libel he understood it to refer to the prosecutor. The magistrate must decide for himself whether the written matter before him is in law capable of being a libel. Unless it is clearly no libel, he will, after proof of publication by the defendant, or some agent or servant on his behalf (see *ante,* pp. 583—589), commit the defendant for trial. He may not adjourn the case merely because civil proceedings are pending between other parties for a similar libel. (*R.* v. *Evans and others,* 62 L. T. 570 ; 6 Times L. R. 248.) But, before the defendant is committed for trial, he must be asked whether he desires to call any witnesses. (30 & 31 Vict. c. 35, s. 3, Russell Gurney's Act.) The defendant may then call witnesses to prove that he did not publish the libel, that it does not refer to prosecutor, that it is on the face of it a fair and *bonâ fide* comment on certain well-known or admitted facts of public interest, &c.

Upon the hearing of a charge against a proprietor, publisher, or editor, or any person responsible for the publication of a newspaper, for a libel published therein, a different procedure may be adopted. The Court may, by virtue of sect. 4 of the Newspaper Libel and Registration Act, 1881, "receive evidence as to the publication being for the public benefit, and as to the matters charged in the libel being true, and as to the report being fair and accurate and published without malice, and as to any matter which under this or any other Act or otherwise might be given in evidence by way of defence by the person charged on his trial or indictment ; and the Court, if of opinion after hearing such evidence that there is a strong or probable presumption that the jury on the trial would acquit the person charged, may dismiss the case." This section only applies to the proprietor, publisher, editor, and possibly the printer of a newspaper ; hence, the actual composer of every libel, and all persons concerned in the publication of any libel which has not appeared in a newspaper, are still bound by the former procedure. Moreover, the section only enables a magistrate to receive and record such evidence as would be admissible, if proper pleas be filed, on the trial of an indictment for the same libel. It does not make evidence admissible to prove the truth of a blasphemous, obscene, or seditious libel. Thus, upon an application to a magistrate to commit the proprietor of a newspaper for trial for a seditious libel, the defendant cannot give evidence either of the truth of the libel, or that its publication was for the public benefit. (*Ex parte O'Brien,* 12 L. R. Ir. 29 ; 15 Cox, C. C. 180.)

When the case does not come within this section, the accused may not give any evidence before the magistrate of the truth of the matters charged in the libel, unless the information charges him with an offence under sect. 4 of Lord Campbell's Act. "The duty and province of the magistrate before whom a person is brought, with a view to his being committed for trial or held to bail, is to determine, on hearing the evidence for the prosecution and that for the defence, if there be any, whether the case is one in which the accused ought to be put upon his trial. It is no part of his province to try the case. That being so, in my opinion, unless there is some further statutory duty imposed on the magistrate, the evidence before him must be confined to the question whether the case is such as ought to be sent for trial, and if he exceeds the limits of that inquiry, he transcends the bounds of his jurisdiction. This case was one of a charge of libel, and the magistrate had to inquire, first, whether the matter complained of was libellous, and, secondly, whether the publication of it was brought home to the accused, so far as that there ought to be a committal. Independently of statute, the magistrate could not receive evidence of the truth of the libel. The question then arises whether Lord Campbell's Act enables him to do so. In my opinion it does not, because by the provisions of the Act the defence founded upon the truth of the libel does not arise at that stage, and cannot be put forward before the magistrate. Suppose the defendant had succeeded fully and entirely in showing the truth of the libel. What then would have been the duty of the magistrate ? He would nevertheless have been bound to send the case for trial, because by the statute the truth of the libel does not constitute a defence until the statutory conditions are complied with, and they cannot be complied with at that stage of the inquiry." (Per Cockburn, C.J., in *R.* v. *Sir Robert Carden* (*Labouchere's Case*), 5 Q. B. D. 6, 7 ; 49 L. J. M. C. 1 ; 28 W. R. 133 ; 41 L. T. 504 ; 14 Cox, C. C. 359.) And this decision was followed in *R.* v. *Flowers* (44 J. P. 377) ; there the defence was that the libel was a fair criticism on a public entertainment, and the magistrate excluded evidence of the facts commented on, and disallowed all cross-examination thereon ; and it was held that he was right in so doing. But when the defendant is charged before the magistrate with an offence under the 4th section of Lord Campbell's Act, that is, with maliciously publishing a defamatory libel *knowing the same to be false*, then it is open to the defendant to call evidence of the truth of the libel, so as, if possible, to reduce the charge to the minor offence. (*Ex parte Ellissen* (not reported), approved by Lush, J., in *R.* v. *Carden*, 5 Q. B. D. 11, 13.)

The defendant may himself in every case make a statement before the magistrate. And by sect. 9 of the Law of Libel Amendment Act, 1888, and again by the Criminal Evidence Act, 1898, the defendant and his or her wife or husband may go into the box and give evidence. This right is especially valuable where the defendant himself has seen or heard something justifying the libel.

Cases of libel were never disposed of summarily by the magistrate or justices in Petty Sessions. It is true that there is authority for holding that in some cases of libel, if there is any danger of a breach of the peace, the justices have the power to demand sureties of good behaviour from the libeller, instead of committing him for trial; and may themselves, in default of such sureties, commit him to gaol. (*Haylock* v. *Sparke*, 1 E. & B. 471; 22 L. J. M. C. 67; 16 J. P. 308, 359; 17 J. P. 262, overruling the *dictum* of Lord Camden in *R.* v. *Wilkes*, 2 Wils. 160; and see *R.* v. *Summers*, 1 Lev. 139, and *R.* v. *Shuckburgh*, 1 Wils. 29.) Such power, if any, was never exercised; it was regarded as a violation of the principle of Fox's Libel Act, that libel or no libel is a question for the jury. But now, by sect. 5 of the Newspaper Libel and Registration Act, 1881, " If a Court of summary jurisdiction upon the hearing of a charge against a proprietor, publisher, editor, or any person responsible for the publication of a newspaper for a libel published therein is of opinion that though the person charged is shown to have been guilty the libel was of a trivial character, and that the offence may be adequately punished by virtue of the powers of this section, the Court shall cause the charge to be reduced into writing and read to the person charged, and then address a question to him to the following effect :— ' Do you desire to be tried by a jury, or do you consent to the case being dealt with summarily ?' and, if such person assents to the case being dealt with summarily, the Court may summarily convict him and adjudge him to pay a fine not exceeding fifty pounds. Sect. 27 of the Summary Jurisdiction Act, 1879, shall, so far as is consistent with the tenor thereof, apply to every such proceeding." But this procedure can only be adopted where the defendant is the proprietor, publisher, editor, or perhaps the printer of a newspaper within the meaning of the Act. The writer of the libel must be committed for trial in the usual way.

If the magistrate decide to dismiss the case, the prosecutor may still, under sect. 2 of the Vexatious Indictments Act (22 & 23 Vict. c. 17), which, by sect. 6 of the Act of 1881, is made applicable to *every* libel, require the magistrate to bind him over to prosecute and the magistrate thereupon must take the prosecutor's recognisance and forward the depositions to the Court in which the indictment will be preferred. But in that case the prosecutor, if unsuccessful, will have to pay all the defendant's costs. (See 30 & 31 Vict. c. 35, s. 2.)

If the magistrate decide to send the case for trial, the defendant is entitled to be bailed. Reasonable, but not excessive, bail should be demanded, and it is for the justices to determine whether the sureties offered are sufficient. If no sufficient bail can be found, the accused must be committed to prison; but if sufficient sureties come forward the magistrates have no discretion but to allow the defendant to be at large on bail.

In the case of an obscene libel the prisoner may be committed for trial to the Quarter Sessions; in every other case he must be sent to the Assizes or Central Criminal Court. (5 & 6 Vict. c. 38, s. 1.) As to Ireland, see *In re Armstrong*, 9 Cox, C. C. 342. By the ordinary practice, which has been approved in the Courts, the incriminating document is put before the magistrates and is annexed to the depositions, and forms part of them. It is then in the legal custody of the magistrates' clerk and is sent by him to the clerk of assize or clerk of the peace, in whose custody it remains. It is then at the disposal of the judge and may be seen by the grand jury and counsel. Annexed to the bill of indictment are particulars showing what part of the incriminating document are relied upon as being obscene libels. (*R.* v. *Barraclough*, [1906] 1 K. B. 201; 75 L. J. K. B. 77; 54 W. R. 147; 94 L. T. 111.)

As to the powers of magistrates, &c., in the case of obscene books and prints, see *ante*, p. 507. In the case of a seditious libel there is no power to issue a search warrant to seize the author's papers. (*Leach's Case*, 11 St. Tr. 307; 19 Howell's St. Tr. 1002; *Entick* v. *Carrington and others*, 11 St. Tr. 317; 19 Howell's St. Tr. 1029.)

Indictment.

Counsel should next be instructed to draft the indictment. This requires care, as the old rules of pleading apply in all their strictness. The words must be set out *verbatim*, however great their length. (*Bradlaugh and Besant* v. *The Queen*, 3 Q. B. D. 607; 48 L. J. M. C. 5; 26 W. R. 410; 38 L. T. 118.) Any material variation between the words as laid in the indictment and the words proved at the trial will still be fatal, in spite of the powers of amendment given by the 14 & 15 Vict. c. 100, s. 1. (See *In re Crowe*, 3 Cox, C. C. 123; *R.* v. *Fussell*, 3 Cox, C. C. 291.) In the one case, however, of an obscene libel, it is no longer necessary to set out in the indictment the obscene passages in full. It is "sufficient to deposit the book, newspaper, or other documents containing the alleged libel with the indictment or other judicial proceeding, together with particulars showing precisely, by reference to pages, columns, and lines, in what part of the book, newspaper, or other document the alleged libel is to be found, and such particulars shall be deemed to form part of the record." (Law of Libel Amendment Act, 1888, s. 7.) The decision in

Bradlaugh and Besant v. *The Queen* is so far overruled. It is unfortunate that the section does not extend to blasphemous as well as to obscene libels.

If the words are in a foreign language, they must be set out in the original, and a correct translation added. (*Zenobio* v. *Axtell,* 6 T. R. 162; *R.* v. *Goldstein,* 3 Brod. & B. 201; 7 Moore, 1; 10 Price, 88; R. & R. C. C. 473.) The indictment must expressly charge the defendant with "publishing"; as merely writing a libel is no crime. (*R.* v. *Burdett,* 4 B. & Ald. 95.) It must also declare that the libel was written and published "of and concerning the prosecutor." The omission of those words was held fatal in *R.* v. *Marsden,* 4 M. & S. 164; Russ. on Crimes, 7th ed. 1028; and in *R.* v. *Sully,* 12 J. P. 536. But if it sufficiently appears from other allegations in the indictment to whom the libel refers, it will be held good. (*Gregory* v. *The Queen,* 15 Q. B. 957; 15 Jur. 74; 5 Cox, C. C. 247.) The indictment must also aver all facts necessary to explain the meaning of the libel and to connect it with the person defamed; for sect. 61, of the Common Law Procedure Act, 1852, applies only to pleadings in civil cases, so that in an indictment an innuendo still requires a prefatory averment to support it. Hence there is still considerable technicality in criminal pleading; although modern judges will never be quite so strict as their predecessors. (See *ante,* pp. 136, 138.) The innuendo can only explain and point the defamatory meaning of the words; it must not introduce new matter. The judgment of De Grey, C.J., in *R.* v. *Horne* ((1777) Cowp. 682; 11 St. Tr. 264; 20 How. St. Tr. 651), "has universally been considered the best and most perfect exposition of the law on this subject." (Per Abbott, C.J., in *R.* v. *Burdett,* 4 B. & Ald. 316.) Extrinsic facts must be averred where without such averments, the libel would appear innocent or unmeaning. (*R.* v. *Yates,* 12 Cox, C. C. 233.) But where the writing on the face of it imports a libel, no innuendo is necessary, nor any introductory averments. (*R.* v. *Tutchin,* (1704) 14 How. St. Tr. 1095; 5 St. Tr. 527; 2 Lord Raym. 1061; 1 Salk. 50; 6 Mod. 268; Holt, 424.) See further as to the office of the innuendo, *ante,* p. 115.

In 1652, Rolle, C.J., laid it down that "in an indictment a thing must be expressed to be done *falso et malitiose,* because that is the usual form." (*Anon.,* Style, 392.) But in *R.* v. *Burks* (7 T. R. 4), the Court of King's Bench decided that in an information, at all events, it is unnecessary to allege that the libellous matter is false. And the Court for Crown Cases Reserved has decided that if an indictment under sect. 5 of Lord Campbell's Act charges the defendant with having published a libel " unlawfully," the omission of the word " maliciously " is immaterial. (*R. v. Munslow*, [1895] 1 Q. B. 758; 64 L. J. M. C. 138; 43 W. R. 495; 72 L. T. 301.) Still, it is always safer to aver that the defendant published the libellous words " falsely and maliciously; " if for no other reason, " because that is the usual form."

In some few cases it is necessary to aver a special intent. Thus, Abbott, J., held in *R. v. Wegener* (2 Stark. 245), that where a letter is sent direct to the prosecutor, and published to no one else, an intention to provoke the prosecutor and to excite him to a breach of the peace must be alleged, and that an allegation that it was sent with intent to injure, prejudice, and aggrieve him in his profession and reputation could not, in such a case, be supported. But the Recorder of London held the contrary in *R. v. Brooke* (7 Cox, C. C. 251); and in *R. v. Price*, tried at the Swansea Assizes on August 9th, 1881, Baggallay, L.J., after consulting Pollock, B., decided that the averment of an intention to provoke the prosecutor to a breach of the peace was not essential, the indictment ending as usual with the words " against the peace of our lady the Queen." Still, it will always be safer to insert the words which Abbott, J., thought necessary. Where a letter containing a libel on a married man is sent to his wife, " it ought to be alleged as sent with intent to disturb the domestic harmony of the parties." (2 Stark. 245; see also *R. v. Benfield*, 2 Burr. 980.) So in the case of a libel on a person deceased, an intent should be alleged to bring contempt and scandal on his family and relations, and so provoke them to a breach of the peace. (*R. v. Topham*, 4 T. R. 126, *ante*, p. 457; but now see *R. v. Ensor*, (1887) 3 Times L. R. 366; and Precedent No. 78, *post*, p. 804.)

An information for seditious libel is not bad because the words " seditious " and " seditiously " are not used, if it clearly appear on the face of the information that the publication was made with seditious intent. (*R. v. M'Hugh*, [1901] 2 Ir. R. 569.) And the same rule would no doubt be held to apply to an indictment. Where an indictment alleges that a defendant " unlawfully " published an " obscene " libel, it is not necessary (though it is safer) to allege that he did so to the corruption of public morals. (*R. v. Barraclough*, [1906] 1 K. B. 201; 75 L. J. K. B. 77; 54 W. R. 147; 94 L. T. 111.)

There is no objection to joining several counts, each for a separate libel, in the same indictment (per Lord Ellenborough, in

R. v. *Jones*, 2 Camp. 132); and the grand jury may of course ignore one count, and find a true bill on any other. Or a count for libel may be joined in the same indictment with a count for any other misdemeanour, though this will not be found convenient in practice, as the judge may call on the prosecutor to elect on which he will proceed (*R.* v. *Murphy*, 8 C. & P. 297); although he will not do so where the counts are all for libel, and for libels appearing at different dates in the same periodical. (15 Cox, C. C. 220.) But counts may not be added for any libels in respect of which the prisoner was not committed for trial, unless the express leave of the judge be obtained under 30 & 31 Vict. c. 35, s. 1, before the bill is presented to the grand jury. The obtaining of such leave is not a mere formality, but must conform to the spirit and intention of that Act; and the additional counts will be quashed, if leave was granted on insufficient materials. (*R. pros. Tyler* v. *Bradlaugh and others*, 31 W. R. 229; 47 L. T. 477; 47 J. P. 71; 15 Cox, C. C. 156.) And now since the Newspaper Libel and Registration Act, 1881, s. 6, it is no longer in the power of the prosecutor, when the magistrate has only committed the defendant under sect. 5 for the common law offence, to add a count under sect. 4 of Lord Campbell's Act (as it was formerly; see 5 Q. B. D. p. 12; *Boaler* v. *Holder*, 54 L. T. 298). The count for the graver offence will now be quashed or amended so as to make the indictment correspond with the committal. (*R.* v. *Felbermann and Wilkinson*, 51 J. P. 168; *Boaler* v. *Holder*, (1887) 3 Times L. R. 546; 51 J. P. 277.) But where the defendant has been committed for trial and indicted under sect. 4 for publishing a libel, "knowing the same to be false," he may nevertheless, be convicted of merely publishing a defamatory libel under sect. 5. (*Boaler* v. *The Queen*, 21 Q. B. D. 284; 57 L. J. M. C. 85; 37 W. R. 29; 59 L. T. 554; 52 J. P. 791; 16 Cox, C. C. 488.)

All who are in any way concerned in the composition or publication of a libel may be joined in the same indictment. For by the 24 & 25 Vict. c. 94, s. 8, " whosoever shall aid, abet, counsel or procure the commission of any misdemeanour, whether indictable at common law or by virtue of any statute, may be tried, indicted, and punished as a principal offender." But if one defendant denies that he is in any way connected with the libel, and desires to call his co-defendants as witnesses in support of his case, the judge will order him to be tried separately from the others, unless such separate trial would embarrass the prosecution more than a joint trial would prejudice the defendant. It is a question of the balance of convenience. (Per Lord Coleridge, C.J., in *R.* v. *Bradlaugh and others*, 15 Cox, C. C. 217, 220.)

Pleading to the Indictment.

When a true bill has been found by the grand jury, the defendant is arraigned, the substance of the indictment is read over to him, and he is then called on to plead.   At common law he might—

(1) Demur to the indictment ;

(2) Plead to the jurisdiction of the Court;

(3) Plead specially in bar—

    (*a*) Autrefois acquit;

    (*b*) Autrefois convict;

    (*c*) Pardon ;

(4) Plead guilty; or

(5) Plead the general issue—Not Guilty.

    If the prisoner stands mute of malice, or does not answer directly to the charge, a plea of Not Guilty shall be entered for him, and the trial shall proceed as though he had actually pleaded the same.   (7 & 8 Geo. IV. c. 28, s. 2.)

By virtue of 6 & 7 Vict. c. 96, s. 6, he may now also—

(6) Plead a justification that the words are true and that it was for the public benefit that they should be published. (See *ante*, p. 473.)   This plea may be pleaded with Not Guilty; it must be in writing and must be entered and filed at the Crown Office or with the clerk of assize, and a copy delivered to the prosecutor.

There is now but little use in demurring to an indictment except where the words are clearly not libellous in themselves, and are not reasonably susceptible of the meaning ascribed to them by the innuendo.   In such a case it might be well to put an end to the case as quickly as possible.   But if the demurrer be for a mere formal defect, the Court has power to amend, after the demurrer, either an information (*R.* v. *Wilkes*, 4 Burr. 2568 ; *R.* v. *Holland*, 4 T. R. 457), or even an indictment.   (14 & 15 Vict. c. 100, ss. 1, 2, 3, 25.)   If, on the other hand, the defect is one of substance, it will not be waived by pleading over, nor will it be cured by verdict ; but the defendant may still bring error, or move in arrest of judgment after conviction. (See 14 & 15 Vict. c. 100, s. 25.)   Moreover, there is this danger in demurring, that the defendant may not demur and plead Not Guilty at the same time (*R.* v. *Odgers*, 2 Moo. & Rob. 479) ; hence, in strict law, if he fail on his demurrer, final judgment may be entered for the Crown on the whole case.   (*R.* v. *Taylor*,

3 B. & C. 509, 515; 5 D. & R. 422.) But the Court has power to permit the defendant afterwards to plead over, and in these more merciful days will generally exercise that power. (*R.* v. *Mitchell*, 3 Cox, C. C. 93; *R.* v. *Birmingham and Gloucester Ry. Co.*, 3 Q. B. 223, 233; 10 L. J. M. C. 136.)

The plea of Not Guilty puts the prosecutor to proof of every material allegation in the indictment. The defendant may show under this plea that the occasion of publication was privileged, and may indeed raise every other defence permitted him by law, except that the words or any part of them are true. As to the defence of fair and *bonâ fide* comment on a matter of public interest, if the libel contains no allegation of fact, but is merely comment, this defence can be raised under the plea of Not Guilty. But if the libel contains allegations of fact, as distinct from comment, every such allegation of fact, if not otherwise protected, must be justified by a plea under Lord Campbell's Act; else the defence of fair comment under the plea of not guilty will fail. (See *ante*, p. 197); also Precedents Nos. 26 and 70; and *Penrhyn* v. *The Licensed Victuallers' Mirror*, (1890) 7 Times L. R. 1.)

It is only in the case of a defamatory libel on a private individual that the defendant may justify under Lord Campbell's Act. (*Ante*, p. 473.) And he does so at his peril; for placing such a plea on the record will be deemed an aggravation of his offence, should he fail to prove it. By the express words of Lord Campbell's Act, a plea of justification under sect. 6 shall be pleaded " in the manner now required in pleading a justification to an action for defamation." But in spite of these words there is no power in any Court to order particulars of such a plea to an indictment or information, or to strike it out. (*In re Rea*, 9 Cox, C. C. 401.) If sufficient details be not given in the plea, the only course is for the prosecutor to demur. (*R.* v. *Hoggan*, *Times*, November 4th, 1880.) To such a plea the prosecutor may reply generally, denying the whole thereof. If he does not reply, judgment will be given for the defendant. (*R.* v. *De la Porte*, 59 J. P. 617.) See Precedents of such plea and reply, Nos. 70, 71, 83 and 84. The other pleas mentioned above are now of rare occurrence. (See *post*, p. 808.)

Certiorari.

An application is frequently made to the King's Bench Division for a writ of *certiorari* to bring up an indictment for libel from another Court that it may be tried in the High Court. The application is usually made before the indictment is found by the grand jury, the Court being asked to remove "any indictment which may be found." Where the indictment is found at the Assizes, no *certiorari* is necessary to bring the case into the High Court of Justice. A simple order of the King's Bench Division, that the record be brought into Court by the officer of the Circuit and filed in the High Court of Justice, is sufficient. (*R.* v. *Dudley and Stephens*, 14 Q. B. D. 273, 560.) In no other ways can the Court change the venue in a criminal case. (*R.* v. *Casey*, 13 Cox, C. C. 614 ; *R.* v. *Hon. F. Cavendish*, 2 Cox, C. C. 175.) One of the advantages obtained by the removal is that in the King's Bench Division a special jury can be secured.

Where the application is made by the Attorney-General officially, the writ issues as a matter of course. (*R.* v. *Thomas*, 4 M. & S. 442.) But where a private individual applies for the writ, whether prosecutor or defendant, he will have to file affidavits showing some special ground for the removal within the provisions of rule 13 of the Crown Office Rules, 1906, and he must also enter into recognisances to pay all costs incurred subsequent to the removal, if he be ultimately unsuccessful. (16 & 17 Vict. c. 30, ss. 4, 5.) The application may in vacation be made to a judge at Chambers. (5 & 6 Will. & Mary, c. 11, s. 3 ; Crown Office Rules, 1906, r. 19.)

One of several defendants may obtain the writ ; if he does, this will remove the indictment as to all. (*R.* v. *Boxall*, 4 A. & E. 513.) But the judge who grants the *certiorari* will require the defendant who applies for it to give security for the costs of the prosecution occasioned by the removal, in the event of any one of the defendants being convicted. (*R.* v. *Jewell*, 7 E. & B. 140; 26 L. J. Q. B. 177 ; *R.* v. *Foulkes*, 1 L. M. & P. 720; 20 L. J. M. C. 196.)

The affidavits should be entitled "in the King's Bench Division " simply. The mere fact that the defendant desires a special jury is not alone a sufficient ground for removal. (*R.* v. *Morton*, 1 Dowl. N. S. 543.) Nor is it enough to show on affidavit that difficult questions of law may arise (*R.* v. *Joule*, 5 A. & E. 539), especially if the indictment be in the Central Criminal Court. (*R.* v. *Templar*, 1 Nev. & P. 91.) But if it can be proved that a fair and impartial trial of the case cannot be had in the Court below, the application will be readily granted. (*R.* v. *Hunt and others*, 3 B. & Ald. 444; *R.* v. *Palmer*, 5 E. & B. 1024.) No appeal lies to the Court of Appeal from the refusal of the King's Bench Division to grant a *certiorari*. (*R.* v. *Rudge*, 16 Q. B. D. 459 ; 55 L. J. M. C. 112 ; 34 W. R. 207 ; 53 L. T. 851 ; 50 J. P. 755.)

Formerly in cases of misdemeanour the Court made the order absolute in the first instance. (*R.* v. *Spencer*, 8 Dowl. 127; *R.* v. *Chipping Sodbury*, 3 N. & M. 104.) But now in all cases an order *nisi* only is granted, unless there be great urgency. (See Crown Office Rules, 1906, r. 12.) If an order *nisi* for such a writ be obtained, the Court below will, as of course, order the trial to stand over till the argument. If the order be made absolute, either prosecutor or defendant can apply for a special jury. (6 Geo. IV. c. 50, s. 30.) After the removal the defendant must appear in the King's Bench Division, and plead or demur to the indictment within four days, if not immediately; but the Court will grant him further time on good cause shown. (60 Geo. III. & 1 Geo. IV. c. 4, ss. 1, 2.)

The trial may take place, either at bar in the King's Bench Division at the Royal Courts of Justice, or at the Assizes on the civil side, or at the Central Criminal Court. (19 & 20 Vict. c. 16, s. 1.) A successful prosecutor will be entitled to his costs, whether he be "the party grieved or injured" by the defendant's words or not. (*R.* v. *Oastler*, L. R. 9 Q. B. 132; 43 L. J. Q. B. 42; 22 W. R. 490; 29 L. T. 830; overruling *R.* v. *Dewhurst*, 5 B. & Ad. 405.) The costs will be taxed under a side-bar rule; and if they are not paid within ten days the recognisance will be estreated, and the sureties compelled to pay. (16 & 17 Vict. c. 30, s. 6.) The sureties may then sue the defendant and recover the amount for which they became bail in an action for money paid at the defendant's request. (*Jones* v. *Orchard*, 16 C. B. 614; 24 L. J. C. P. 229; 3 W. R. 554.)

A writ of *certiorari* may also be applied for to bring up an indictment in order that its validity may be considered and determined, and that it may be quashed, if proved invalid. Such an application must be made after the bill is found and before judgment has been given thereon; for after judgment has been given no writ of *certiorari* can issue. (*R.* v. *Seton*, 7 T. R. 373; *In re Pratt*, 7 A. & E. 27; *R.* v. *Unwin*, 7 Dowl. 578; *R.* v. *Christian*, 12 L. J. M. C. 26; *R.* v. *Wilson*, 14 L. J. M. C. 3; *R.* v. *Boaler*, 67 L. T. 854; 56 J. P. 792.) The Court below has full power to hear a motion in arrest of judgment.

Evidence for the Prosecution.

When the case comes on for trial the *onus* lies on the prosecutor to prove—

(1) That the defendant published the defamatory words. As to

what is a sufficient publication in law, see *ante*, Chapter VI., pp. 157—180. As to constructive publication by the act of the defendant's servant or agent, see *ante*, pp. 583—589. The proof of publication in criminal cases is the same as in civil cases, save that it is not essential to prove a publication to a third person, where the indictment alleges an intent to provoke a breach of the peace. (*R. v. Wegener,* 2 Stark. 245 ; *Phillips* v. *Jansen,* 2 Esp. 624 ; *Clutterbuck* v. *Chaffers,* 1 Stark. 471.) Sect. 15 of the Newspaper Libel and Registration Act, 1881, which facilitates the proof of the ownership of a newspaper, applies to criminal as well as to civil proceedings. (See *ante,* p. 676.) Sect. 27 of the Common Law Procedure Act, 1854 (*ante,* p. 675), as to comparison of handwriting, though originally confined to civil proceedings (sect. 103), now applies to criminal trials as well. (28 Vict. c. 18, s. 8. See also *R. v. Beere,* 1 Lord Raym. 414 ; 12 Mod. 221 ; 2 Salk. 417 ; Carth. 409 ; Holt, 422 ; *R. v. Slaney,* 5 C. & P. 213.) Whoever requests or procures another to write or publish a libel will be held equally guilty with the actual publisher. (*R. v. Cooper,* 8 Q. B. 533 ; 15 L. J. Q. B. 206.) If the manuscript from which a libel has been printed be produced and proved to be in the handwriting of the defendant, this is *primâ facie* proof that he authorised or directed the printing and publishing, though the defendant may give evidence to rebut it. (*R. v. Lovett,* 9 C. & P. 462. And see the remarks of Lord Erskine, 5 Dow, H. L. at p. 201.)

(2) It is, however, necessary in a criminal case to prove further that the prisoner published the libel in the county in which the venue is laid. However, if the defendant write a libellous letter and cause it to be posted, that letter is published both in the county where it is posted, and in the county to which it is addressed, if it be opened there. (*R. v. Burdett,* 4 B. & Ald. 95 ; *R. v. Girdwood,* 1 Leach, 169 ; East, P. C. 1120, 1125 ; *R. v. Holmes,* 12 Q. B. D. 23 ; 49 L. T. 540.) If the person to whom it is addressed be not then at the address given on the envelope, and the letter be forwarded unopened to him in another county and there opened, then this is a publication by the defendant in that other county. (*R. v. Watson,* 1 Camp. 215.) The post-mark is sufficient *primâ facie* evidence that the letter was in the post-office named on the date of the mark. (*R. v. Plumer,* Russ. & Ry. 264 ; *R. v. Canning,* 19 St. Tr. 370 ; *R. v. Hon. Robert Johnson,* 7 East, 65 ; 3 Smith, 94 ; 29 How. St. Tr. 103 ; *Stocken* v. *Collin,* 7 M. & W. 515 ; 10 L. J. Ex. 227.) These cases must be taken to overrule the *dictum* of Lord Ellenborough in *R. v. Watson,* 1 Camp. 215. An

admission by the defendant that he wrote the libel is no admission that he published it, still less that he published it in any particular county. (*The Seven Bishops' Case*, 4 St. Tr. 304 ; *R. v. Burdett*, 4 B. & Ald. 95.)

(3) The prosecutor must now put in the libel and have it read to the jury. The libel itself must, if possible, be produced at the trial. If it be in the possession of the defendant, and notice has been given to him to produce it, and he refuses so to do, secondary evidence may be given of its contents. (*Attorney-General* v. *Le Merchant*, 2 T. R. 201, n. ; *R. v. Boucher*, 1 F. & F. 486.) But proof that the document was last seen in the possession of a servant of the defendant does not of itself entitle the prosecutor to give parol evidence of its contents. (*R. v. Pearce*, Peake, 75.) Notice to produce must be given a reasonable time before the trial. No general rule can be laid down as to what is a reasonable time ; each case must be governed by its particular circumstances ; but if it appear that since the notice was given there was an opportunity of fetching the document, the notice will be held sufficient. (Per Bramwell, B., in *R. v. Barker*, 1 F. & F. 326.) Any other documents which explain the libel, and are referred to in it, may also be put in and read. (*R.* v. *Slaney*, 5 C. & P. 213.)

Any variance between the words as proved and the words as laid will be fatal, if it in any way affects the sense. But a variance which is immaterial to the merits of the case may be amended by the judge at the trial, at any time before verdict, if he thinks that such amendment cannot prejudice the defendant in his defence on the merits. (7 Geo. IV. c. 64, s. 20 ; 14 & 15 Vict. c. 100, ss. 1, 24, 25.) But once such amendment has been made, there is no power of amending the amendment, or of reverting to the indictment as it originally stood ; but the case must be decided upon the indictment in its amended form.

The prosecution must further prove the innuendoes and all explanatory averments of extrinsic facts, whenever such proof is necessary to bring out the libellous nature of the publication, or to point its application to the person defamed. That asterisks or blanks are left where the name of the person defamed should appear is no defence, if those who knew the circumstances understood the libel to refer to the prosecutor. Any declarations of the defendant as to what he meant are admissible in evidence against him. (*R.* v. *Tucker*, Ry. & Moo. 134.) Strict proof must be given of all material and necessary allegations in the indictment, which the libel itself does not admit to be true. (*R.* v. *Sutton*, 4 M. & S. 548 ; *R.* v. *Holt*,

5 T. R. 436; *R. v. Martin*, 2 Camp. 100; *R. v. Budd*, 5 Esp. 230.)

It will then be for the jury, after considering this evidence, to say whether the publication, when taken as a whole, is or is not a libel.

(4) In a few cases the prosecution must also prove a special intent stated in the indictment. (*Ante*, pp. 456, 722.) Whether such special intent existed or no is a question for the jury. An averment of intention is divisible; so that where a libel is alleged to have been published with intent to defame certain magistrates, and also to bring the administration of justice into contempt, it is sufficient to prove a publication with either of these intentions. (*R. v. Evans*, 3 Stark. 35.) Malice need never be proved, unless the occasion be privileged.

(5) If the indictment be framed under sect. 4 of Lord Campbell's Act, the prosecutor must give some evidence that the defendant *knew* that the words were false. But in no other case need the prosecutor give any evidence to show that the libel is false.

(6) On an indictment for publishing an obscene libel, evidence to prove the publication of other indecent works may be given to prove the intent. (*R. v. Thomson*, (1900) 64 J. P. 456; *R. v. Barraclough*, [1906] 1 K. B. at p. 212.)

Evidence for the Defence.

The defendant may call evidence rebutting the case for the prosecution. By sect. 9 of the Law of Libel Amendment Act, 1888, and again by the Criminal Evidence Act, 1898, s. 1, the defendant in every proceeding for libel may now give evidence at every stage of the proceeding, if he or she think fit; and so may his wife or her husband. Such witnesses, though competent, are not compellable to give evidence. But if the defendant elects to go into the box he may be cross-examined with a view of proving him guilty of the offence with which he stands charged. (Criminal Evidence Act, 1898, s. 1, sub-s. (e).) So, too, in any proceeding for an illegal practice under the Corrupt and Illegal Practices Prevention Act, 1895, the person charged, and the husband or wife of such person, are competent to give evidence in answer to the charge. (58 & 59 Vict. c. 40, s. 2.) The defendant may dispute the fact of publication, or negative the innuendo, or show that the libel referred to someone else, not the prosecutor. He may give in evidence any facts which put a different complexion on the libel, *e.g.*, other passages contained in the same publication, fairly connected with the same subject. (*R. v.*

Lambert and Perry, 2 Camp. 398 ; 31 How. St. Tr. 340.) So, too, the defendant may give evidence of any collateral facts which show that the libel complained of is a fair and *bonâ fide* comment on a matter of public interest, or is privileged by reason of the occasion on which it was published. Unless such privilege be absolute, the prosecutor may rebut the defence of privilege by evidence of malice, precisely as in civil cases.

The defendant may also cross-examine the plaintiff's witnesses as to any previous statements made by them on the subject-matter of the indictment, and if such statements were reduced into writing, such writing may be produced to contradict them. (28 Vict. c. 18, ss. 4, 5.) As to proving a previous conviction of a witness, see *ante*, p. 698.

The defendant may call evidence to show that though he published the libel with his own hand he was not at the time conscious of its contents. The *onus* of proving this lies on the defendant ; the bare delivery of the letter, though sealed, has been held to be *primâ facie* evidence of a knowledge of its contents. (*R.* v. *Girdwood*, 1 Leach, 169 ; East, P. C. 1120, 1125.) But if the defendant can prove that he cannot read, or that he never had any opportunity of reading the libel, but delivered it pursuant to orders, having no reason to suppose its contents illegal, this will be a defence. (See *ante*, p. 469.)

Again, where evidence has been given which has established a *primâ facie* case of publication against the defendant by the act of some other person acting by his authority, the defendant may prove that such publication was made without his authority, consent, or knowledge, and arose from no want of due care or caution on his part. (6 & 7 Vict. c. 96, s. 7.) The leading case on this section is *R.* v. *Holbrook and others*, 3 Q. B. D. 60 ; 47 L. J. Q. B. 35 ; 4 Q. B. D. 42 ; 48 L. J. Q. B. 113. (*Ante*, p. 589.) Mr. Bradlaugh succeeded in establishing a defence under this section in *R.* v. *Bradlaugh and others*, 15 Cox, C. C. 217. (*Ante*, p. 472.)

Also, if the defendant has pleaded a plea under sect. 6 of Lord Campbell's Act, but not otherwise, he may give evidence of the truth of the libel. But the truth alone is no defence in a criminal case ; the defendant must also show that it was for the public benefit that the matters charged should be published. In *R.* v. *Warnsborough* ((1888) 4 Times L. R. 520), Baron Huddleston is reported to have ruled that, while the issue of truth was for the jury, it was for the judge to decide whether the publication was or was not for the public benefit. (*Sed quære ;* see the judgment of the same learned judge in *Pankhurst* v. *Sowler*, (1886) 3 Times L. R. 193.) No such plea under Lord Campbell's Act can be pleaded in the case of a blasphemous, obscene, or seditious libel. (*R.* v. *Duffy*, 9 Ir. L. R. 329 ; 2 Cox, C. C. 45 ; *Ex parte O'Brien*, 12 L. R. Ir. 29 ; 15 Cox, C. C. 180 ; *R.* v. *M'Hugh*, [1901] 2 Ir. R. 569.) If a general charge be made in the libel, specific instances must be set out in the plea. It will be sufficient, however, if at the trial two or three distinct instances are proved to the satisfaction of the jury. (*R. pros. Lambri* v. *Labouchere*, 14 Cox, C. C. 419 ; *ante*, p. 185.)

Evidence that the identical charges contained in the libel which is the subject of the indictment had, before the time of composing and publishing such libel, appeared in another publication which was brought to the prosecutor's knowledge, and against the publisher of which he took no legal proceedings, is not admissible either at common law or under this section. (*R.* v. *Holt*, 5 T. R. 436 ; *R.* v. *Newman*, Dears. C. C. 85 ; 3 C. & K. 252 ; 1 E. & B. 268 ; 22 L. J. Q. B. 156 ; 17 Jur. 617 ; *Pankhurst* v. *Hamilton*, (1886) 2 Times L. R. 682.) That rumours to the same effect had previously been circulated in other newspapers is no justification for the defendant's repeating the statement in his own paper, if he purports to speak " from authority." (*R.* v. *Harvey and Chapman*, 2 B. & C. 257.) So, too, it is no defence to a charge of publishing a seditious libel, that it is an extract from an American paper, reprinted as foreign news, especially if such seditious extracts be habitually published by the defendant at a time of great political excitement, without one word of warning or one note of disapproval. (*R.* v. *Pigott*, 11 Cox, C. C. 46.) Where the libel contains several charges the defendant must prove the truth of them all ; otherwise the jury will be bound to find a verdict for the Crown ; and the Court, in giving judgment, will consider whether the guilt of the defendant is aggravated or mitigated by the plea, and by the evidence given to prove or disprove it, and form its own conclusion on the whole case. (*R.* v. *Newman*, 1 E. & B. 558 ; 22 L. J. Q. B. 156.)

If no such plea has been placed on the record, no evidence can be given of the truth of the defendant's words. But if evidence be admissible on other issues in the case, it will not be excluded merely because it tends to show the truth of the libel. (*R.* v. *Grant and others*, 5 B. & Ad. 1081 ; 3 N. & M. 106.)

The defendant may also, as in other criminal cases, call witnesses to his good character ; but such evidence will be of very little use, except perhaps in cases of mistaken identity ; and there are dangers attending an attempt to establish the good character of the defendant (see Criminal Evidence Act, 1898, s. 1, sub-s. (f) (ii.)).

Evidence of good character may also be given after verdict in mitigation of punishment. Where several prisoners are indicted jointly and some of them call witnesses, while others do not, the counsel for the prisoners who have called witnesses must address the jury first; then the counsel for the Crown; and last, the counsel for the prisoners who called no witnesses. (*R.* v. *Burns and others*, 16 Cox, C. C. 195.) The fact that the defendant has been called as a witness shall not of itself confer on the prosecution the right of reply. (Criminal Evidence Act, 1898, s. 3.)

Summing-up and Verdict.

The judge at the conclusion of the case sums up the evidence to the jury, and directs them as to the law. Before Fox's Libel Act it had come to be the rule that in a criminal case the judge, and not the jury, should decide whether or no the publication was a libel. On proof of publication, of the innuendoes, and of the other necessary averments, the judge would direct the jury to find the defendant guilty. (See *R.* v. *Woodfall*, 5 Burr. 2661; *R.* v. *Shipley* (*Dean of St. Asaph*), 21 St. Tr. 1043; 3 T. R. 428, n.; 4 Dougl. 73; *R.* v. *Withers*, 3 T. R. 428.) But that Act (32 Geo. III., c. 60, s. 1), declares and enacts that on the trial of an indictment or information for libel the jury may give a general verdict of Guilty or Not Guilty upon the whole matter put in issue before them. Or the jury may in their discretion find a special verdict as in other criminal cases. (Sect 3.) The judge of course may still direct the jury on any point of law, stating his own opinion thereon if he think fit; but the question, libel or no libel, must ultimately be decided by the jury. Fitzgerald, J., thus addressed the jury in a case of seditious libel :—" You are the sole judges of the guilt or innocence of the defendant. The judges are here to give any help they can, but the jury are the judges of law and fact, and on them rests the whole responsibility. In this sense the jury are the true guardians of the liberty of the press." (*R.* v. *Sullivan*, 11 Cox, C. C. 52.) The jury should of course pay attention to and accept the judge's statement of the law, and then take the alleged libel into their hands and consider it carefully; not dwelling too much on isolated passages, but judging it fairly as a whole. If the libel be contained in a book they may look at the rest of the book. (Per Lord Kenyon in *R.* v. *Reeves*, Peake's Ad. Cas. 84.) So if it be contained in a newspaper, the jury may read other parts of the same paper referring to the same topic as the libel, though locally disjoined from it.

(Per Lord Ellenborough, in *R.* v. *Lambert and Perry*, 2 Camp. 399. See also *Cooke* v. *Hughes*, R. & M. 112, and *ante*, pp. 114, 398.) And on the trial of Horne Tooke for treason the matter was carried much further; for in that case the prisoner was allowed to read in his defence various extracts from other works published by him at a former period of his life; and the jury were permitted to carry these along with them when they retired to consider their verdict. Lord Ellenborough, however, expressed grave doubts as to the propriety of this course. (2 Camp. at p. 400.)

If the defendant be indicted under sect. 4 of Lord Campbell's Act, and the jury find that he published the libel, but did not know at the time that the same was false, he may be convicted on that indictment and sentenced under sect. 5. (*Boaler* v. *The Queen*, 21 Q. B. D. 284; 57 L. J. M. C. 85; 37 W. R. 29; 59 L. T. 554; 52 J. P. 791; 16 Cox, C. C. 488.)

Proceedings after Verdict.

If at the trial the defendant is acquitted, no further proceedings can be taken; the verdict of the jury is conclusive in favour of the defendant. (*R.* v. *Cohen and Jacob*, 1 Stark. 516; *R.* v. *Mann*, 4 M. & S. 337.) If the jury cannot agree, they must be discharged and the prisoner tried again, unless a *nolle prosequi* be entered, for which the leave of the Attorney-General is necessary. The prisoner is apparently not entitled to be admitted to bail in the interval between the two trials. (*R.* v. *Foote*, 10 Q. B. D. 378; 48 L. T. 394; 48 J. P. 36; 15 Cox, C. C. 240.)

If, however, the defendant is convicted, then, if the judge before whom the trial took place has reserved any point of law arising thereat for the consideration of the Court above, he may still, if he thinks fit, state a case in the manner pointed out by the 11 & 12 Vict. c. 78, s. 2. This case will be argued before the Court of Criminal Appeal when the conviction will be either quashed or affirmed. (Criminal Appeal Act, 1907, s. 20, sub-s. 4.)

If no point of law has been thus reserved, then the prisoner may move in arrest of judgment, as in a civil case under the old procedure, on the ground that the words as laid do not sufficiently appear to be libellous, or on some other ground appearing on the face of the record. Power to make this motion is expressly reserved by Fox's Libel Act. (32 Geo. III. c. 60, s. 4.) Such a motion must be made after verdict and before judgment to the judge at the trial. The absence of any essential introductory averment or innuendo will be a good ground for arresting judgment. (*R.* v. *Shipley* (*Dean of St. Asaph*), 21 St. Tr. 1043 ; 3 T. R. 428, n. ; 4 Dougl. 73 ; *R.* v. *Topham*, 4 T. R. 126.) But mere formal defects cannot now be taken advantage of in such a motion. (14 & 15 Vict. c. 100, s. 25.) And " it is a general rule of pleading at common law, that where an averment which is necessary for the support of the pleading is imperfectly stated, and the verdict on an issue involving that averment is found, if it appears to the Court, after verdict, that the verdict could not have been found on this issue without proof of this averment, then, after verdict, the defective averment which might have been bad on demurrer is cured by the verdict." (Per Blackburn, J., in *Heymann* v. *The Queen*, L. R. 8 Q. B. 105, 106 ; 21 W. R. 357 ; 28 L. T. 162 ; per Brett, L.J., in *R.* v. *Aspinall*, 2 Q. B. D. 57, 58 ; 46 L. J. M. C. 145 ; 25 W. R. 283 ; 36 L. T. 297. See also Serjeant Williams' note (1) to *Stennel* v. *Hogg*, 1 Wms. Saund. 228 ; *R.* v. *Goldsmith*, L. R. 2 C. C. R. 79 ; 42 L. J. M. C. 94 ; 21 W. R. 791 ; 28 L. T. 881 ; *R.* v. *Munslow*, [1895] 1 Q. B. 758 ; 64 L. J. M. C. 138 ; 43 W. R. 495 ; 72 L. T. 301). In all other cases, however, every objection which could have been taken by demurrer before the jury were sworn may still be taken upon motion in arrest of judgment. (Per Cockburn, C.J., 2 Q. B. D. 572 ; and per Bramwell, L.J., 3 Q. B. D. 624 ; *R.* v. *Larkin*, Dears. C. C. 365 ; 23 L. J. M. C. 125.) For instance, if the indictment does not set out the words of the libel *verbatim*, this defect is not cured by a verdict convicting the defendant, nor is it waived by the defendant's omitting to demur. (*Bradlaugh and Besant* v. *The Queen*, 3 Q. B. D. 607 ; 48 L. J. M. C. 5 ; 26 W. R. 410 ; 38 L. T. 118 ; 14 Cox, C. C. 68.) But now as to the case of an obscene libel, see sect. 7 of the Law of Libel Amendment Act, 1888. (*Ante*, p. 720.) Where, however, an indictment or information contains several counts, if any one of them be found good, the judgment will stand. (*R.* v. *Benfield and others*, 2 Burr. 985.)

On a motion in arrest of judgment the Court has no power to amend the record. (*R.* v. *Larkin*, Dears. C. C. 365 ; 23 L. J. M. C. 125.) If the judgment be arrested, all the proceedings are set aside and judgment of acquittal is given ; but this will be no bar to a fresh indictment, for the defendant was never really in jeopardy under the defective indictment. (*Vaux's Case*, 4 Rep. 45 a.) Proceedings by way of writ of error are now abolished. (Criminal Appeal Act, 1907, s. 20, sub-s. 1.)

But now the usual course is for a convicted person to appeal to the Court of Criminal Appeal, which came into existence on

April 19th, 1908.   This Court may either affirm the sentence passed at the trial, or pass such sentence in substitution as it thinks proper, or quash the conviction and direct a judgment and verdict of acquittal to be entered.   (Criminal Appeal Act, 1907, ss. 4 and 5.) But neither the Court of Criminal Appeal nor the King's Bench Division can grant a new trial in a criminal case.

Sentence.

Sentence is generally passed directly the verdict of guilty is given; but not always, especially in the King's Bench Division. If sentence be deferred the defendant, unless the case be exceptional, is allowed out on the same bail as before. In the interval, the defendant may file affidavits in mitigation of punishment, which the prosecutor may, answer. Such affidavits may show that the defendant reasonably and *bonâ fide* believed in the truth of the charges made in the libel, but not that the libel is in fact true. (*R. v. Burdett*, 4 B. & Ald. 314; *R. v. Halpin*, 9 B. & C. 65; 4 M. & R. 8; *R. v. Newman*, 17 J. P. 84.)   Or they may contain general evidence of good character, or disclaim any personal malice against the prosecutor (*R. v. Tanfield*, 42 J. P. 423), or show that the defendant voluntarily stopped the sale of the book complained of as soon as proceedings were commenced (*R. v. Williams*, Lofft, 759), or any other circumstance showing provocation by the prosecutor or an absence of malice in the defendant. But the defendant should be careful not to attack the character of the prosecutor or his witnesses, or impugn the justice of the verdict, lest he thereby aggravate his original offence. Blackburn, J., in *R. v. Shimmens*, 34 J. P. 308, refused to receive a memorial in favour of the defendant, which was not on affidavit.

If, in the interval since the verdict, the defendant has republished the libel, or continued its sale, or been guilty of other misconduct, the prosecutor may file affidavits in aggravation of punishment. (See *R. v. Withers*, 3 T. R. 428.)   As to the procedure when the defendant is brought up for judgment, see *R. v. Bunts*, 2 T. R. 683. The defendant must be personally present, if his state of health will permit.   (*R. v. Ryder-Burton*, 38 J. P. 758; *R. v. Kinglake*, W. N. 1870, p. 130.)   If he has absconded, judgment apparently cannot be pronounced; all the Court can do is to estreat the recognisances. (*R. v. Chichester*, 17 Q. B. 504, n.; *R. v. Elizabeth Williams*, W. N. 1870, p. 120.)   The judge in passing sentence will consider whether the guilt of the defendant is aggravated or mitigated by any plea of justification which he may have placed on the record, and by the evidence given to prove or to disprove the same. (6 & 7 Vict. c. 96, s. 6; *R.* v. *Newman,* 17 J. P. 84.)

Where judgment has been suffered by default, both parties should state their case on affidavit. If there is any matter in the prosecutor's affidavit which the defendant could not be expected to have come prepared to answer, he will be allowed an opportunity of answering it on a future day. (*R.* v. *Archer,* 2 T. R. 203, n.; *R.* v. *Wilson,* 4 T. R. 487.)

As to the sentence that may be passed in the case of a defamatory libel at common law, see *ante,* p. 459; under the various statutes, pp. 459—462; in the case of a blasphemous libel, p. 477; an obscene libel, p. 505; a seditious libel, p. 516. If the prisoner be found guilty of publishing a blasphemous or seditious libel, all copies found in his possession may be seized and destroyed by an order of the Court under 60 Geo. III. & 1 Geo. IV. c. 8, ss. 1, 2.

Costs.

In the case of an indictment or information by a private prosecutor for the publication of a defamatory libel, if judgment shall be given for the defendant, he shall be entitled to recover his costs from the prosecutor. (6 & 7 Vict. c. 96, s. 8.) Such costs must first be taxed by the proper officer of the Court before which the indictment or information is tried; and this should be done before the next commission of assize issues, if the case was tried at the Assizes, else the clerk of assize will be *functus officio.* His taxation cannot be reviewed by the King's Bench Division (*R.* v. *Newhouse,* 1 L. & M. 129; 22 L. J. Q. B. 127; 17 J. P. 57); such at least was the practice before the Judicature Act, 1873; and it does not appear to be affected by sect. 16 of that Act, which makes Courts of Oyer and Terminer and Gaol Delivery part of the High Court. (See *R.* v. *Dudley and Stephens,* 14 Q. B. D. at pp. 280, 560.) No special order to tax is necessary. (*R.* v. *Sully,* 12 J. P. 536.) In the case of an information, the record being in the King's Bench Division, execution may issue on taxation in the ordinary way. (*R.* v. *Latimer,* 15 Q. B. 1077; 20 L. J. Q. B. 129; 15 Jur. 314.) But in the case of an indictment not in the King's Bench Division, there is no way of issuing execution for such costs; they must be recovered therefore by an ordinary action at law. (*Richardson* v. *Willis,* L. R. 8 Ex. 69; 42 L. J. Ex. 15, 68; 27 L. T. 828; 12 Cox, C. C. 298, 351.) If the grand jury throw out the bill, the Court has, unfortunately, no power to give the defendant his costs; this is a *casus omissus* in drafting sect. 8. (*R.* v. *Murry,* 57 J. P. 136.)

So if a defendant pleads a justification and the issue be found for the prosecutor, the prosecutor may recover from the defendant the costs which he has sustained by reason of such plea, whatever be the result of any other issue. (6 & 7 Vict. c. 96, s. 8.)

But this section does not apply to Crown prosecutions, or to any proceedings for blasphemous, obscene, or seditious libels. And there is no provision enabling a prosecutor to recover the general costs of the prosecution. If, however, a fine be imposed on the defendant as part of his sentence, the prosecutor may sometimes, by memorialising the Treasury, obtain a portion of the fine towards the payment of his costs.

Where an indictment is removed by *certiorari* into the King's Bench Division, the party applying for the writ (not being the Attorney-General) must give security for all subsequent costs.

Where a municipal corporation has directed a prosecution for a libel on one of its officers, the costs cannot be paid out of any borough fund. (*R.* v. *Mayor, &c., of Liverpool,* 41 L. J. Q. B. 175; 20 W. R. 389; 26 L. T. 101.) Where the directors of a company have instituted a prosecution for a libel on themselves, the costs should not be paid out of the assets of the company, though the directors will not, as a rule, be ordered to repay any costs already so paid. (*Pickering* v. *Stephenson,* L. R. 14 Eq. 322; 41 L. J. Ch. 493; 20 W. R. 654; 26 L. T. 608.) But where the libel is an attack upon the company itself, and calculated to injure its credit or diminish its business, the costs of a prosecution may rightly be paid out of the funds of the company. (*Studdert* v. *Grosvenor,* 33 Ch. D. 528; 55 L. J. Ch. 689; 34 W. R. 754; 55 L. T. 171; 50 J. P. 710; and see *Breay* v. *Royal British Nurses' Association,* [1897] 2 Ch. 272; 66 L. J. Ch. 587; 46 W. R. 86; 76 L. T. 735; *ante,* p. 454.)

CHAPTER XXIX.

PROCEEDINGS BY WAY OF CRIMINAL INFORMATION.

Motion for the Order Nisi.

AN *ex officio* information is filed by the Attorney-General of his own motion. All other criminal informations are filed by the King's coroner and attorney, formerly called the Clerk of the Crown; he may not file any information without an express order of the King's Bench Division granted in open Court. (4 Will. & Mary, c. 18, s. 1, Crown Office Rules, 1906, r. 35.) Counsel must move the Court upon proper affidavits for an order *nisi* calling upon the defendant to show cause why an information should not be granted. The motion must be made within a reasonable time after the offence complained of. (*Ib.* r. 37.) The former rule was that the application must be made within two terms after the publication, or at all events within two terms after the libel came to the knowledge of the prosecutor. The prosecutor, too, must come to the Court in the first instance, and must not have attempted to obtain redress in other ways. (*R.* v. *Marshall,* 4 E. & B. 475; *Ex parte Pollard,* (1901) 17 Times L. R. 773; *ante,* p. 467.) He must submit himself to the Court, and consent to waive his civil remedy by action, if need be, and must be prepared to go through with the criminal proceedings to conviction. It is not necessary to obtain the order of a judge at chambers before moving the Court; sect. 3 of the Newspaper Libel and Registration Act, 1881 (now repealed), did not apply to any application for a criminal information whether *ex officio* or otherwise (*Yates* v. *The Queen,* 14 Q. B. D. 648; 54 L. J. Q. B. 258; 33 W. R. 482; 52 L. T. 305; 49 J. P. 436; 15 Cox, C. C. 686); and the same practice prevails under the provision which was substituted for it, sect. 8 of the Law of Libel Amendment Act, 1888.

The affidavits on which the application is based should be carefully drawn up; as no second application may be made on amended or additional affidavits. (*R.* v. *Franceys,* 2 A. & E. 49.) They should in the first place prove the publication by the defendant. Mere *primâ facie* evidence of this will not be sufficient. (*R.* v. *Baldwin,* 8 A. & E. 168; *R.* v. *Willett,* 6 T. R. 294.) There must be before

3 B 2

the Court legal evidence sufficient to justify a grand jury in returning a true bill for the same offence. Thus, in *R.* v. *Stanger*, L. R. 6 Q. B. 352 ; 40 L, J. Q. B. 96 ; 19 W. R. 640 ; 24 L. T. 266, the affidavits merely showed that the annexed copy of the *Newcastle Daily Chronicle*, the newspaper containing the libel, had been purchased from a salesman in the office of that paper, and that in a footnote at the end of that copy the defendant was stated to be the printer and publisher of the newspaper, and that the relator believed him so to be ; it was held that this was no legal evidence of publication, and the rule was discharged. Similarly it was held that the mere fact that the libel has printed on it the words : " Romney, printer " is in itself no proof that Romney was the printer. (*R.* v. *Williams and Romney*, 2 L. J. K. B. (Old S.) 30.) If the defendant keeps an office or shop at which copies of the paper can be purchased, then an affidavit by a person who purchased a copy of the libel at such office or shop will be the best evidence of a publication by the defendant, and also that most easily obtainable. That the purchase was made expressly for the purpose of enabling such affidavit to be sworn is no objection. (*Duke of Brunswick* v. *Harmer*, 14 Q. B. 189 ; 19 L. J. Q. B. 20 ; 14 Jur. 110 ; 3 C. & K. 10.)

It is a doubtful point whether the omission of such strict proof of publication can subsequently be supplied by the admissions, if any, in the defendant's affidavits filed to show cause against the order being made absolute. The Courts have generally refused to look at defendant's affidavits to supply a defect in those of the prosecutor. (*R.* v. *Baldwin*, 8 A. & E. 169.) For the rule is that the prosecutor cannot on the argument refer to any document which does not appear on the face of the order itself to have been read at the first application. (*R.* v. *Woolmer and another*, 12 A. & E. 422.) But Lord Kenyon, in *R.* v. *Mein*, 3 T. R. 597, and Blackburn, J., in *R.* v. *Stanger*, L. R. 6 Q. B. 355 ; 40 L. J. Q. B. 96 ; 19 W. R. 640 ; 24 L. T. 266, expressed an opinion that the Court might look at any evidence lawfully before them for any purpose they pleased.

The prosecutor must also swear to his innocence in all particulars of the charge contained in the libel. (*R.* v. *Webster*, 3 T. R. 388.) For although at the trial of the information when granted truth will be no defence, except under Lord Campbell's Act, still it is " sufficient cause to prevent the interposition of the Court in this extraordinary manner " ; the Court will leave the prosecutor to proceed by way of indictment in the ordinary course. (*R.* v. *Bickerton*, 1 Stra. 498 ; *R.* v. *Draper*, 3 Smith, 390.)

If there is no specific charge in the libel, no such affidavit is necessary (*R.* v. *Williams*, 5 B. & Ald. 595), and it has also been dispensed with in other special circumstances. But as a rule there must be a specific denial on oath of the particular charges, even where it is a duke that is aspersed. (*R.* v. *Haswell and Bate*, 1 Dougl. 387.) If a general charge be made and a specific instance alleged, the affidavit must expressly negative not only the general charge, but also the specific instance. (*R.* v. *Aunger*, 37 J. P. 645; 12 Cox, C. C. 407.)

The affidavits should be sworn with *no* heading or title. They should not contain irrelevant or improper matter; if the prosecutor abuses the alleged libeller or shows an *animus* against him, the Court will very probably reject the application. (*R.* v. *Burn*, 7 A. & E. 190.)

The order *nisi*, if granted, should be drawn up " Upon reading " the alleged libel and the affidavits and all other documents to which it is desired to refer on the argument. It should be personally served on the defendant.

Argument.

The defendant now shows cause. He generally files affidavits in reply. It is open to him to maintain that the libel is true. (*R.* **v.** *Eve and Parlby*, 5 A. & E. 780; 1 N. & P. 229.) (See *ante*, p. 191.) He may also contend that the libel complained of does not apply to the relator. (*R.* **v.** *Barnard, Ex parte Lord R. Gower*, 43 J. P. 127.) This decision is perhaps to be regretted; as it opens a door by which a libeller may escape punishment, provided he is careful not to expressly name his victim. The writer of a libel may richly deserve punishment, although it may not be clear to whom he intended the libel to apply; and the Court in granting a criminal information regards the interests of public morality and order rather than those of the individual prosecutor. (See *R.* v. *Jenour*, 7 Mod. 400, and *In re The Evening News*, (1886) 3 Times L. R. 255.)

If the order be discharged on the merits, the Court generally gives the defendant his costs. And no second application may be made to the Court, even upon additional affidavits (*R.* v. *Smithson*, 4 B. & Ad. 862; *Ex parte Munster*, (1869) 20 L. T. 612), except in very peculiar circumstances, as where the only person who had made an affidavit on behalf of the defendant on the argument of the first order has since been convicted of perjury in respect of such affidavit. (*R.* v. *Eve and Parlby*, 5 A. & E. 780; 1 N. & P.

229.) But though the prosecutor cannot apply a second time for a criminal information, he can still prefer an indictment in the ordinary way. (Per Lord Denman, in *R.* v. *Cockshaw*, 2 N. & Man. 378.)

Compromise.

Frequently, however, the defendant files exculpatory affidavits, apologising to the prosecutor, withdrawing all imputations upon him, and entreating the mercy of the Court. When this happens, the prosecutor is generally quite satisfied; he has obtained all he desired : and by no means courts the expense and notoriety of a prolonged criminal trial. But the Court is not disposed on that account merely to allow the proceedings to drop, even at the request of the prosecutor. The rule may still be made absolute, although the defendant has withdrawn all imputations, and apologised. (*R.* v. *Leng*, (1870) 34 J. P. 309.) And in more than one case the King's Bench Division has compelled a reluctant prosecutor to take a rule in the interest of the public. Having invoked the aid of the criminal law, it is his duty not to abandon the proceedings merely because his own private purpose is attained. (See *R.* v. *" The World,"* (1876) 13 Cox, C. C. 305 ; *R.* v. *Newton*, (1903) 19 Times L. R. 627 ; 67 J. P. 453.)

Trial and Costs.

If the order be made absolute, the prosecutor must enter into a recognizance to effectually prosecute the information and to abide by and observe the order of the Court. The amount of the recognizance is fixed by r. 35 of the Crown Office Rules, 1906, at 50*l.* (But see 4 Will. & Mary, c. 18, s. 1, and *R.* v. *Brooke*, 2 T. R. 190.)

The information must set out the libel, &c., with all the certainty and precision of an indictment. (See *ante*, p. 720 ; and Precedents No. 69, 72.) As soon as it is filed, a copy must be served on the defendant. The defendant must appear thereto within the times specified in rr. 72—87 of the Crown Office Rules, 1906 ; and see r. 33. If he does not, he may be attached under a judge's warrant (48 Geo. III. c. 58, s. 1). After appearance the defendant has ten days within which to plead or demur. (Crown Office Rules, 1906, r. 120.) His plea is duly entered on the record, which is then made up and sent down for trial to the county in which the libel was published, unless a trial at bar be demanded. The record may be amended by a judge at chambers after plea and before trial. (*R.* v.

Wilkes, 1764—1770, 4 Burr. 2568 ; 2 Wils. 151.) The trial of an information for libel in all respects resembles the trial of an indictment ; save that in *ex officio* informations the counsel for the Crown (whether the Attorney-General himself or any one appearing for him) has the right to reply, although the defendant calls no witness. (*R.* v. *Horne*, 20 How. St. Tr. 660 ; 11 St. Tr. 264 ; Cowp. 672.) The trial must take place within one year after issue joined ; and if not, or if the prosecutor enters a *nolle prosequi*, the Court, on motion for the same, may award the defendant his costs to the amount of the recognizance entered into by the prosecutor on filing the information. (Crown Office Rules, 1906, r. 38.)

Every criminal information is a proceeding in the King's Bench Division, but the Rules of the Supreme Court (Order LXVIII. r. 1) do not apply to criminal proceedings on the Crown side of that Division ; nor does the Judicature Act, 1890 (see s. 4). Hence the former practice remains unchanged, subject only to the Crown Office Rules of 1906. If on any information by a private prosecutor for the publication of any defamatory libel, judgment be given for the defendant, he will be entitled to recover from the prosecutor the costs which he has sustained by reason of such information. (*Ib.* r. 39.) And the judge at the trial cannot in this case deprive the successful defendant of his costs by certifying that there was reasonable cause for the information. (*R.* v. *Latimer*, 15 Q. B. 1077 ; 20 L. J. Q. B. 129 ; 15 Jur. 314.) The Master of the Crown Office taxes the costs under a side-bar rule ; and he may allow costs incurred by the defendant previously to the filing of the information. There is no appeal from the King's Bench Division to the Court of Appeal as to such costs, or indeed on any matter relating to a criminal information. (*R.* v. *Steel and others*, 1 Q. B. D. 482 ; 45 L. J. Q. B. 391 ; 13 Cox, C. C. 159 ; (C. A.) 2 Q. B. D. 37 ; 46 L. J. M. C. 1.) On such taxation execution issues in the ordinary way. (*R.* v. *Latimer, suprà.*) There is no power, however, to condemn the defendant to pay the costs of the prosecution, if he be convicted or plead guilty, unless indeed he files a special plea of justification under Lord Campbell's Act, in which case he will have to pay the costs incurred by reason of that plea. (See 6 & 7 Vict. c. 96, s. 8, *post*, p. 831 ; and r. 39 of Crown Office Rules, 1906.)

An appeal lies to the Court of Criminal Appeal from a conviction on a criminal information as in the case of a conviction on indictment. (Criminal Appeal Act, 1907, s. 20, sub-s. (2).)

APPENDIX A.

———◆———

PRECEDENTS OF PLEADINGS.

CONTENTS.

I. Pleadings, &c., in Actions in The High Court.

Statements of Claim.

Defences and Replies.

29. No Publication.   (No Slander.)
30. No Conscious Publication.
31. Innocent Publication of a Libellous Novel.
32. No Conscious Publication.   (Madness.)
33. Words spoken in Jest.
34. Justification.
35. Justification of the Words without the alleged meaning.
36. Justification of a portion of a Libel.
37. Justification and Privilege.
38. Absolute Privilege.   (Litigant in person.)
39. Absolute Privilege.   (Witness.)
40. Absolute Privilege.   (Military Duty.)   ·
41. Qualified Privilege : Character of Servant.
42. Qualified Privilege : Common Interest.
43. Qualified Privilege : Master and Servant.
44. Qualified Privilege : Communication volunteered.
45. Particulars under Plea of Qualified Privilege : Self-Defence.
46. Particulars under Plea of Qualified Privilege : Common Interest. (Church Members.)
47. Particulars under Plea of Qualified Privilege : Offer of Reward for Discovery of Offender.
48. Particulars under Plea of Qualified Privilege : Complaint to Persons in Authority.
49. Privileged Report : Published as a Pamphlet.
50. Privileged Report : Report of a Public Meeting.
51. Defence to Slander of Title to Goods.
52. Defence of Previous Action : Res Judicata.
53. Accord and Satisfaction.
54. Payment into Court : Pleading Matters in Mitigation of Damages.
55. Payment into Court, with an Admission of the Innuendoes.
56. Apologising in a Defence.
57. Consolidated Actions : Payment into Court denying the Innuendo, with Apology.
58. Pleading an Apology previously published.
59. Notice under s. 1 of Lord Campbell's Act.
60. Plea under s. 2 of Lord Campbell's Act.
61. Reply : Pardon.
62. Reply : Refusal to publish Contradiction.
63. Particulars under Order XXXVI. r. 37.

INTERROGATORIES, &c.

64. Interrogatories.   As to Publication.
                As to Conscious Publication.
                As to " Gross Negligence."
                As to Privilege.
                As to Malice.
                As to Damages.
                In an Action against a Newspaper.

I. PRECEDENTS OF PLEADINGS IN ACTIONS OF LIBEL AND SLANDER.

STATEMENTS OF CLAIM.

No. 1.

Character of a Servant.

1903—J.—1986.

In the High Court of Justice.
    King's Bench Division.
        Writ issued Dec. 13th, 1903.
    Between Sarah Johnston (Spinster) .   . *Plaintiff*,
                and
        Henry Robertson
        and Alice his wife   .   .   . *Defendants.*

STATEMENT OF CLAIM.

1. The male defendant is a gentleman residing at —— Hall, near Evesham in the county of Worcester, and the female defendant is his wife. The plaintiff is a domestic servant, and was from June 4th, 1902, to August 31st, 1903, in the service of the defendants in that capacity.

2. On September 15th, 1903, the female defendant falsely and maliciously wrote and published of the plaintiff and of her as a domestic servant, in a letter of that date sent by the defendants to Mrs. M., of 19, Newhall Street, Birmingham, the following words: "While she (meaning the plaintiff) was with us, she stole a quantity of house-linen, and pawned it in the High Street." *

The plaintiff claims damages.

[Signed] ——

Delivered, etc.

* No innuendo is necessary.

No. 2.

Words in a Foreign Language.

1. The plaintiff is a farmer, residing at —— in the county of Glamorgan.

2. On March 20th, 1895, the defendant falsely and maliciously printed and published of the plaintiff in the Welsh language in a newspaper called the *Welsh Journal* the following words :—[*Here set out the libel verbatim in Welsh.*]

[*If no innuendo is necessary*]

3. The said words mean in English, and were understood by those to whom they were published to mean :—[*Here set out the translation.*]

[*Or, if an innuendo is necessary*]

3. The following is a literal translation of the said words :— " He is a devil of a shaved pig." The said words mean and were understood by those who read them to mean that the plaintiff was insolvent and had been stripped of his last penny and was unable to pay his just debts and was a person of no credit and unworthy of trust or confidence.

4. The plaintiff has thereby suffered damage and has been greatly injured in his credit and reputation.

The plaintiff claims damages.

No. 3.

Libel contained in a Placard.

1. The plaintiff is, &c.

2. The defendant on or about January 10th, 1895, falsely and maliciously caused to be printed and published of the plaintiff the words following :—[*Here set out the words with innuendo if one is necessary.*]

PARTICULARS.

The best particulars which the plaintiff can at this stage give are as follows :—(*a*) The said words were contained in placards one of which was posted up opposite the plaintiff's shop in the High Street, —— ; (*b*) Others were posted up in the neighbourhood of his shop [*state exactly where if possible*]. The said words were also by some persons unknown to the plaintiff widely distributed to the public in the town of —— in the form of handbills.

3. The plaintiff has in consequence suffered much annoyance, and has been injured in his credit and good name, and has incurred public odium, ridicule and contempt.

The plaintiff claims damages.

No 4.

Action for Reading a Libel aloud.

M. AND WIFE *v.* N. AND WIFE.

1. The plaintiff Henry is the husband of the plaintiff Mary. They reside in Dover and have one child, a little girl, eight years old.

2. On November 8th, 1894, the following anonymous letter appeared in the *Dover Express* :—

[*The letter described a brutal assault on a child by a tipsy woman, who was not in any way identified.*]

3. On the same day the female defendant read the said letter aloud to Mrs. M., the mother of the plaintiff Henry, and then falsely and maliciously spoke and published to her of the plaintiff Mary the following words :—" The woman referred to in that letter is Henry's wife "; meaning thereby that the plaintiff Mary was a drunken and violent woman, and had cruelly and brutally assaulted and ill-treated her own child, and that she had been drunk in one of the public streets of Dover.

4. Alternatively, the female defendant on November 8th, 1894, falsely and maliciously published of the plaintiff Mary the libellous words set out in paragraph 2 above, by showing them to the said Mrs. M. and reading them aloud to her, and verbally representing to her that the woman therein referred to was the plaintiff Mary and thereby conveyed the meanings in the last paragraph alleged.

The plaintiffs claim damages.

No. 5.

Showing an Anonymous Letter—Special Damage.

1. The plaintiff carries on business as a merchant at —— Street, in the City of London. The defendant is the general manager of the London and Yorkshire Bank (Limited).

2. Prior to the publication hereinafter complained of one J. H., also a merchant, by a letter dated the 20th May, 1902, offered to take the plaintiff into his employment as manager of the business of the said J. H. at a salary of £1,000 a year.

3. On the 31st May, 1902, the said J. H. called upon the defendant, and the defendant then falsely and maliciously

published to the said J. H. the following letter concerning the plaintiff:—

[*Here copy letter.*]

4. In consequence of such publication the said J. H., by a letter to the plaintiff dated the 2nd June, 1902, refused to take the plaintiff into his employment as he would otherwise have done, and the plaintiff has lost the benefit of such employment and the said salary, and has been much injured in his credit and reputation.

The plaintiff claims damages.

[See *Robshaw* v. *Smith*, (1878) 38 L. T. 423 ; *ante*, pp. 256, 257.]

No. 6.

Libel on a Town Clerk.

1. The plaintiff has been for thirty-three years town clerk of the parliamentary and municipal borough of —— in the county of ——, and has for many years practised as a solicitor within the said borough, and held various appointments therein.

2. The defendant is a member of the town council of the said borough.

3. The —— *Gazette* is a weekly newspaper which has a large circulation in the said borough.

4. The defendant falsely and maliciously wrote and caused to be printed and published in the issue of the said newspaper of the 12th October, 1904, of the plaintiff in respect of his said office of town clerk the following words :—[*Here set out the libel verbatim*] ; meaning thereby that the plaintiff had been guilty of gross misconduct in the discharge of his official duties, and had acted as such town clerk in a manner which was unjustifiable and discreditable to him, and had not been neutral, impartial, and without respect of person or party in the discharge of his said duties, but had been actuated by improper, partial, and corrupt motives therein, and had forfeited and deserved to forfeit the respect, confidence, and esteem of his fellow-townsmen.

The plaintiff claims damages.

No. 7.

Action by a Solicitor—Injunction.

1. The plaintiff is a solicitor and the senior partner in the firm of W., G. and T., which carries on an extensive practice as solicitors in the county of ——. He is also election agent for the Conservative

party in the Southern Division of the said county, and acted as such election agent at the general election of 1910.

2. The defendant was the Liberal candidate at the said election, and was defeated at the poll by a large majority.

3. The defendant, on January 9th, 1911, in a speech delivered at a public meeting held in the Town Hall at —— in the said county, falsely and maliciously spoke and published of the plaintiff as such solicitor and election agent the following words :—

[*Here set out the alleged slander, adding any innuendoes which may be necessary.*]

4. Subsequently, in the month of January, 1911, the defendant falsely and maliciously, and with intent still further to wound and annoy the plaintiff, and to injure him in his said profession, caused a report of the speech, set out in paragraph 3, to be reprinted from a newspaper called —— and to be published of the plaintiff, and with the meaning aforesaid, in the shape of a leaflet or sheet for distribution. This report was (omitting for the sake of brevity certain words appearing in the original at the places marked with asterisks) as follows :—

" Those gentlemen " (meaning the plaintiff amongst others) " had worked against him " (meaning the defendant), " most unfairly. * * * It was his fervent hope and prayer that their villany might soon be made manifest to all the electors. * * * The Tory agent " (meaning the plaintiff) " was the ringleader. He never hesitated, &c."

5. The defendant caused the said leaflet to be widely circulated throughout the said county on January 21st and 22nd, 1911, and is still circulating and intends to continue to circulate and distribute the same.

6. The plaintiff has thereby been much injured in his credit and reputation, and in his said profession and office, and has been brought into public odium and contempt.

And the plaintiff claims :—

(1) Damages.

(2) An injunction to restrain the defendant and his agents from further circulating, distributing, or otherwise publishing, the said leaflet, or any other reprint of the said speech, or any similar libels affecting the plaintiff in his said profession and office.*

---

* As to the precise form of the injunction, see *Hill* v. *Hart Davies,* 21 Ch. D. at p. 802 ; *Hermann Loog* v. *Bean,* 26 Ch. D. at p. 307 ; *Liverpool Household Stores* v. *Smith,* 37 Ch. D. at p. 182 ; *ante,* p. 429.

No. 8.

Libel on Architects in the way of their Profession.

BOTTERILL AND ANOTHER *v.* WHYTEHEAD, (1879) 41 L. T. 588.

1. The plaintiffs are brothers carrying on in partnership at ―― the profession and business of architects.

2. At or about the time of the writing and publishing of the libels hereinafter complained of, the plaintiffs were, as the defendant well knew, employed by a committee formed for the restoration of a church at South Skirlaugh, near Hull, to superintend and carry out the restoration of the said church, and were appointed by the said committee as architects for that purpose.

3. On the 8th April, 1878, after the appointment of the plaintiffs as such architects as aforesaid, the defendant, in a letter written and sent to Mr. Bethel, a member of the said committee, falsely and maliciously wrote and published of the plaintiffs, in relation to their profession and business of architects, and the carrying on and conducting thereof by them, the following words :—

"I see in the *Hull News* of Saturday that the restoration of Skirlaugh Church has fallen into the hands of an architect who is a Wesleyan, and can show no experience in church work. Can you not do something to avert the irreparable loss which must be caused if any of the masonry of this ancient gem of art be ignorantly tampered with ? Your great influence would surely have much weight in the matter."

Meaning thereby that the plaintiffs were incompetent to superintend and carry out the restoration of the said church, and that, if the restoration were left in the hands of the plaintiffs, the old masonry of the church would be ignorantly tampered with and would not be treated with proper spirit and feeling, and would suffer from their incompetence and want of skill.

4. On or about the 16th April, 1878, and after the appointment of the plaintiffs as such architects as aforesaid, the defendant, in a letter addressed to Mr. Barnes, the incumbent of Skirlaugh Church, falsely and maliciously wrote and published of the plaintiffs, in relation to their profession and business of architects, and the carrying on and conducting thereof by them, the following words :—

"I am annoyed to see that you and your committee have engaged Messrs. B. as architects for the restoration of your church. Are you aware that they are Wesleyans, and cannot have any religious acquaintance with such work ? "

Meaning thereby that the plaintiffs were incompetent to undertake and superintend the restoration of the said church, and were unable to carry it out with adequate spirit and feeling.

5. By reason of the publication of the said libels the plaintiffs have been and are injured in their said profession and business and have suffered in their credit and reputation as architects.

The plaintiffs claim, &c.

No. 9.

Libel on Professional Singers: Slander of Title.

1. The plaintiffs were at all times material hereto and are vocalists and music-hall artistes.

2. By an agreement in writing made the 10th of December, 1895, the plaintiffs were engaged by E. L., the proprietor of the —— Music-hall, to appear and sing at the said music-hall twice in every evening on week-days from the 1st of January to the 30th of June, 1896, at a salary at the rate of £50 per week.

3. On the 16th of January, 1896, the plaintiffs advertised in the *Era* newspaper to the following effect :—

" The sisters H. have great pleasure in thanking Messrs. C. & Co., Messrs. M. & Co., and others, for their kind unhesitating permission to sing any *morceaux* from their musical publications."

4. On or about the 18th of January, 1896, the defendant falsely and maliciously wrote and published of the plaintiffs and of them in the way of their profession, in a letter of that date addressed to the said E. L., the words following :—

" That you may not be misled, I beg to state, that with reference to an advertisement in the last *Era*, where the Misses H. (meaning the plaintiffs) give notice that they have received unhesitating permission to publish any *morceaux* from any publications of certain publishers therein mentioned, it would be as well for you to know that, if two of the firms really had pretended to give such unqualified sanction, I hold powers of attorney over certain publications issued by them as to the sole liberty of public performance, which right they never possessed. But Messrs. C. & Co.'s representative to-day informed me that they only granted permission for two songs in particular (which were named). Moreover, the representative of Messrs. M. & Co. stated to me yesterday that they had granted no permission whatever, but had informed the ladies (meaning the plaintiffs) that their charge for such permission would be 7s. per night."

5. By the said words the defendant meant and was understood

to mean that the plaintiffs had no right or title to sing any of the songs referred to in their said advertisement; that the plaintiffs had fraudulently and dishonestly advertised that they had received permission to sing songs which they knew they had no right to sing, and thereby fraudulently had induced the said E. L. and were attempting to induce other music-hall managers to engage them to sing; that their conduct had made the said E. L. and would make other persons who engaged them to sing, liable to pay penalties under the Copyright Acts; and that the plaintiffs could not safely be employed as professional singers.

6. By reason of the premises the plaintiffs have been greatly injured in their reputation and credit and in their profession, and have suffered much loss and damage.

PARTICULARS OF SPECIAL DAMAGE.

On the 18th of January, 1896, the said E. L., by a letter of that date addressed to the plaintiffs, dismissed the plaintiffs from his service, and refused to allow them to sing at his said music-hall, whereby the plaintiffs have lost the salary payable to them under the said contract of the 10th of December, 1895.

The plaintiffs claim damages.

[See *Hart* v. *Wall*, (1877) 2 C. P. D. 146; and Precedent No. 23.]

No. 10.

Dramatic Criticism.

Similar but not Identical Libels in Different Newspapers.

(Consolidated Actions.)

1903.—T.—No. 746.

1903.—T.—No. 768.

In the High Court of Justice,
King's Bench Division.

(Writ issued the 26th September, 1903)

Between **Henry Thompson** . . . *Plaintiff,*

and

The West of England Printing
Company, Limited . . . *Defendants.*

and

(Writ issued the 3rd October, 1903)

Between Henry Thompson . . . *Plaintiff,*

and

The —— *Gazette* Company,
Limited . . . . . *Defendants.*

(Consolidated by order dated the 10th October, 1903.)

STATEMENT OF CLAIM.

1. The plaintiff is a theatrical playwright and the author of a play known as " A Modern Dido."

2. The defendants, the West of England Printing Company, Limited, are the printers and publishers and registered proprietors of a newspaper called the —— *County Herald.* The defendants the —— *Gazette* Company, Limited, are the printers and publishers of a newspaper called the —— *Gazette.* Each of the said newspapers has a large circulation.

3. On or about the 10th September, 1903, the defendants, the West of England Printing Company, Limited, falsely and maliciously printed and published and caused to be printed and published of the plaintiff and of him in the way of his profession in the issue of the —— *County Herald* of that date the words following :—

[Here set out the libel.]

4. On or about the 13th September, 1903, the defendants, the —— *Gazette* Company, Limited, falsely and maliciously printed and published and caused to be printed and published of the plaintiff and of him in the way of his profession in the issue of the —— *Gazette* of that date the following words :—

[Here set out the libel.]

5. By the said words the defendants and each of them meant and were understood to mean that the plaintiff's said play was written in bad taste and was vulgar and indecent; and that the plaintiff had plagiarised the plot and the chief characters from a low-class French novel, and was a person of no literary or dramatic skill or ability.

[If the libels convey different imputations each should be followed by its appropriate innuendo.]

6. By reason of the premises the plaintiff has been greatly injured in his reputation and in his said profession, and has been brought into public odium, ridicule, and contempt.

The plaintiff claims damages.

No. 11.

Slander Imputing a Crime.

On May 4th, 1895, the defendant falsely and maliciously spoke and published of the plaintiff to Frederick Norton and David Griggs the following words:—" He is a regular smasher"; meaning thereby that the plaintiff had uttered, and was in the habit of uttering, counterfeit coin, well knowing it to be counterfeit, and had been guilty of an indictable offence.

The plaintiff claims damages.

No. 12.

Slander Imputing a Contagious Disorder—Special Damage.

1. The plaintiff is a married man, residing at —— with his wife.

2. On March 3rd, 1903, the defendant falsely and maliciously spoke and published of the plaintiff to one Frederick Hatton the following words: " I " (meaning the defendant) " hear L." (meaning the plaintiff) "has, &c."; thereby meaning that the plaintiff was suffering from a loathsome contagious disorder, and had communicated the same to his wife, and was unfit by reason of such disorder to be admitted into society.

3. By reason of the premises the plaintiff was injured in his credit and reputation and brought into disgrace among his neighbours and friends, *and has been deprived of, and ceased to receive their hospitality.**

The plaintiff claims damages.

* The plaintiff was ordered to give particulars of the names of the neighbours and friends whose hospitality he alleged he had lost, referred to in paragraph 3, but was unable to do so : thereupon the words in italics were struck out of his Statement of Claim, and the plaintiff ordered to pay the costs of the application and the amendment in any event. Such particulars should have been given in the Statement of Claim ; the allegations struck out should not have been inserted if the plaintiff knew that he could not give the particulars.

No. 13.

Slander of a Clergyman.

1. The plaintiff is and at all times hereinafter mentioned was a clergyman of the Church of England, a doctor of divinity and vicar of the parish of ——.

2. It was the custom and the duty of the plaintiff as such vicar as aforesaid constantly to visit the parochial school in his said parish and to superintend the management thereof. Miss E. B. was at the time of the publication hereinafter complained of and is the mistress of the said school.

3. The defendant on the 25th day of April, 1880, falsely and maliciously spoke and published to one C. D. of the plaintiff in relation to his profession as a clergyman of the Church of England, and to his office as such vicar as aforesaid the following words:— " Miss E. B." (meaning thereby the said schoolmistress), " &c. . . ." Meaning thereby that the plaintiff had been guilty of undue familiarity with the said Miss E. B., and had habitually been guilty of conduct unbecoming a clergyman of the Church of England, and had misconducted himself in his office as such vicar as aforesaid, and was unfit to continue in the same, or to hold any other preferment.

4. The plaintiff has thereby been greatly injured in his credit and reputation, and in his said profession as a clergyman of the Church of England and in his office as such vicar as aforesaid, and brought into public scandal, ridicule, and contempt.

The plaintiff claims damages.

No. 14.

Slander of a Medical Man.

1. The plaintiff is a duly qualified surgeon and general medical practitioner, and carries on his profession in the city of —— and its neighbourhood.

2. On January 9th, 1895, the plaintiff was called in by the defendant to attend his infant daughter, who was then lying dangerously ill. On January 14th, the said daughter died.

3. On January 17th, 1895, the defendant falsely and maliciously spoke and published to one C. D., of the plaintiff in relation to his said profession and his conduct therein, the following words:— " Mr. E. (meaning the plaintiff) killed my child."

4. The said words mean, and were understood to mean, that the plaintiff had been guilty of feloniously killing the defendant's daughter by treating her negligently and improperly and with gross ignorance and culpable want of caution and skill, and thus causing or accelerating her death.

5. In the alternative, the plaintiff says that the said words mean, and were understood to mean, that the plaintiff had been guilty of misconduct and negligence in his said profession, and had acted in his said profession negligently and improperly, and had not done his duty by his patient, and was unfit to be employed as a medical man.

6. The plaintiff has been much prejudiced by the defendant's words, and has been injured in his credit and reputation, and in his said profession of surgeon and general medical practitioner. [*Here set out particulars of special damage if any. See Precedents Nos. 9, 16 and 17.*]

The plaintiff claims damages.

[See *Edsall* v. *Russell*, (1843) 4 M. & Gr. 1090 ; 12 L. J. C. P. 4.]

No. 15.

Slander of a Solicitor—Injunction.

1. The plaintiff is a solicitor carrying on business at ——. In the months of April and May, 1902, the plaintiff acted as solicitor for the defendant in an action brought by him against one X. Y. in the Blackburn County Court.

2. On June 1st, 1902, the defendant falsely and maliciously spoke and published the following words to Messrs. C. D. and E. F., of the plaintiff in the way of his profession as a solicitor :— . . .; meaning thereby that the plaintiff had been guilty of dishonourable and unprofessional conduct in his practice as a solicitor, and that the said action had been lost through the culpable negligence or fraudulent malpractice of the plaintiff, and that the plaintiff had cheated and defrauded his client, the defendant, and would similarly cheat and defraud other clients.

3. The plaintiff has thereby been greatly injured in his credit and reputation, and in his profession as a solicitor.

And the plaintiff claims :—

(1.) Damages.
(2.) An injunction to restrain the defendant from repeating the said slander, and from publishing any similar slander injuriously affecting the plaintiff in his profession as a solicitor.*

* See note, *ante*, p. 752, as to form of injunction.

No. 16.

Slander of a Trader in the way of his Trade—Special Damage.

1. The plaintiff is a baker, carrying on business at ——, in the county of ——.

2. On March 19th, 1903, the defendant falsely and maliciously spoke and published of the plaintiff in the way of his trade as a baker, the following words to Messrs. X., Y. and Z. :—[*Here set out the slander verbatim*] ; meaning thereby that the plaintiff cheated or was guilty of fraudulent, corrupt and dishonest practices in his said trade.

3. In consequence of the said words the plaintiff was injured in his credit and reputation as a baker and in his said business, and the said X., Y. and Z., who had previously dealt with the plaintiff, ceased to deal with him.

PARTICULARS OF SPECIAL DAMAGE.

Name of Customer.	Average Annual Value of Custom.	Date of ceasing to deal with Plaintiff.
X.	£30	March 23rd, 1903.
Y.	£27	April 6th, 1903.
Z.	£48	April 10th, 1903.

The plaintiff claims damages.

No. 17.

Repeated Slanders imputing Insolvency to a Trader—
Special Damage.

1. The plaintiff is an auctioneer and estate agent, carrying on business at Shrewsbury, in the county of Salop. The defendant is a solicitor.

2. On the 13th of January, 1897, the defendant falsely and maliciously spoke and published to A. B. of the plaintiff in the way of his business, the words following :—" Mr. X." (meaning the plaintiff) " is insolvent. He owes money right and left. He cannot face his creditors."

3. On the 31st of January, 1897, the defendant falsely and maliciously spoke and published to C. D. of the plaintiff in the way of his business, the words following :—" He " (meaning the plaintiff) " is leaving the town deeply in debt. Does he owe you any money ? You must look sharp after it. He cannot pay. You had better let me issue a writ against him for the amount."

4. On various dates between the 13th of January, 1897, and the 31st of January, 1897, not more precisely known to the plaintiff, the defendant falsely and maliciously repeated of the plaintiff in the

way of his business the words set out in paragraph 2 to E. F. and G. H. and to divers other persons whose names the plaintiff is unable to give at this stage of the action.*

5. By reason of the premises the plaintiff has suffered damage and has been injured in his credit and reputation, and has been pressed for payment of debts that he would not otherwise have been pressed to pay and has suffered a general loss of business.

(*a*) In consequence of what the defendant said to him A. B. pressed the plaintiff for payment of the sum of £100 before the agreed period of credit had expired, and on the 10th of March, 1897, issued a writ against the plaintiff for that amount, which he would not otherwise have done.†

(*b*) C. D. was induced by what the defendant said to him to call in by a letter dated the 11th of February, 1897, the sum of £350 secured to him by an indenture of mortgage dated the 18th of July, 1894, and made between him and the plaintiff, and by letters dated the 11th and 16th February, 1897, to threaten in default of payment to exercise the power of sale contained in the said indenture, which he otherwise would not have done.†

(*c*) In consequence of what the defendant said to E. F. and G. H. they verbally on the 20th of February, 1897, applied to the plaintiff for the sum of £250 for which he was a surety to them for one R. S., and required the immediate payment thereof, which they would not otherwise have done.†

PARTICULARS OF LOSS OF BUSINESS.

Period.	Total Receipts.	Average per month.		
	£	£	s.	d.
Year ending 31st Dec., 1892	5,340	445	0	0
,, ,, ,, ,, 1893	5,521	460	1	8
,, ,, ,, ,, 1894	5,608	467	6	8
,, ,, ,, ,, 1895	5,603	466	18	4
,, ,, ,, ,, 1896	5,712	476	0	0
Three months ending 31st Mar., 1897	630	210	0	0

The plaintiff claims damages.

* If such an allegation is put on the record, the Master will probably order that at a reasonable time, say three weeks, before the trial the plaintiff give particulars of the other persons to whom the slanders were uttered, and of the dates of publication, or that in default he be precluded from giving evidence thereof at the trial.

† It may be doubted whether these are allegations of special damage ; nevertheless, as the words alleged are actionable *per se,* they may be pleaded in aggravation.

No. 18.

Action by Husband and Wife for a Slander of the Wife, actionable
per se, and causing Special Damage to the Husband.

1. The plaintiff George is a licensed victualler, and keeps the
" White Horse " Inn at ——— ; the plaintiff Elizabeth is his wife,
and assists him in the business of the said inn.

2. On January 15th, 1885, the plaintiff Elizabeth was, in the
absence of her husband, managing and superintending the said
business at the said inn, when the defendant came into the said
inn and asked her to serve him with a drink, which she refused to
do on the ground that he had already had enough.

3. Thereupon the defendant falsely and maliciously spoke and
published of the plaintiff Elizabeth and of her as manager of the
said business of the plaintiff George, and in the hearing of A. B.
and C. D. and of several customers of the said inn whose names are
unknown to the plaintiffs, the following words :—[*Set them out
verbatim*] ; meaning thereby that the plaintiff Elizabeth was an
immoral character, and was living in adultery, and was unfit to
have the management and superintendence of the said business,
and that the plaintiff George allowed his business to be conducted
by an immoral and disreputable person.

4. By reason of the premises the plaintiff George was injured in
his said business, and the plaintiff Elizabeth was injured in her
character and reputation.

[*Particulars of special damage suffered by the plaintiff George. See
Precedents Nos. 16 and 17.*]

The plaintiffs and each of them claim damages.

No. 19.

Conspiracy to Libel and Slander the Plaintiff.

1. The plaintiff is a married man, and resides and carries on
business as a joiner at ———, near ———, in the county of ———.
The defendant C. D. is a butcher at ——— aforesaid. The defendant E. D. is the wife, and the defendant F. D. is the daughter, of
the defendant C. D.

2. In the month of February, 1895, the defendants C. and E. D.
discovered that their daughter F. was with child.

3. Thereupon the defendants wrongfully conspired together to
falsely and maliciously assert and declare and to cause it to be

believed that the plaintiff was the father of such child, with intent to extort money from him.

4. In pursuance of the said conspiracy the defendants severally spoke, wrote, and published, and widely circulated the words following :—

(*a*) On February 27th, 1895, the defendant C. D. said to L. M., &c.

(*b*) On March 3rd, 1895, the defendant E. D. said to Mrs. N., &c.

(*c*) On March 21st, 1895, the defendant F. D. wrote to R. S., &c.

5. The plaintiff has thereby been much injured in his reputation, credit, and good name, and has been brought into public hatred and contempt.

And the plaintiff claims damages.

No. 20.

Slander of Title to Goods.

1. The plaintiff, at all the times hereinafter mentioned, was a stone-mason and contractor carrying on business at ——, in the county of ——.

2. On January 10th, 1895, the plaintiff in the ordinary course of his business advertised in the newspaper known as the *Peterborough Gazette* that on Friday and Saturday, January 25th and 26th, 1895, the following goods would be sold by auction at the Auction Mart, Peterborough :—

PARTICULARS OF GOODS.

[*Here specify goods to be sold.*]

3. The plaintiff was the owner of the said goods.

4. Thereupon the defendant falsely and maliciously caused to be printed and published of the plaintiff and in relation to the said intended sale the following "Notice" :—[*Here set out the words verbatim*]. The said notice was inserted as an advertisement in the issue of the *Peterborough Gazette* for January 21st, 1895.

5. The defendant thereby meant, and was understood to mean, that the goods named in the plaintiff's advertisement were the property of the defendant and not of the plaintiff, and that no person could safely purchase any goods to be exposed for sale at the said advertised sale.

6. By reason of such publication the plaintiff has suffered damage and was and is and will be prevented from selling the said goods.

PARTICULARS OF SPECIAL DAMAGE.

X., Y. and Z., all of ——, in the said county, who were desirous of purchasing the said goods or some of them, and who would otherwise have attended at the said sale, and would have bidden for and purchased the said goods or the greater part of them, were prevented from attending at the time and place appointed for the sale, and were deterred from bidding at such sale, and declined to purchase the said goods or any part thereof. The said goods were put up for auction by M. N., acting as auctioneer and agent of the plaintiff, on the day and at the time advertised, but the said M. N. was unable to procure a fair and reasonable price for the same, and the said intended sale failed altogether; and the expenses incurred by the plaintiff in advertising and otherwise preparing for the said intended sale were thrown away. [*Particulars of expenses thrown away should be inserted here.*]

The plaintiff claims, &c.

[See *Carr* v. *Duckett*, (1860) 5 H. & N. 783; 29 L. J. Ex. 468.]

No. 21.

Slander of Title to a Patent.

1. The plaintiff was the first inventor of [*Here describe the invention*], and on October 18th, 1894, obtained letters patent for such invention No. ——, of the year —— [*State the number and year.*] In the months of June and July, 1895, the plaintiff was negotiating with the —— company for the purchase by it of the said letters patent at a price of £3,200.

[*Here set out particulars of the negotiations.*]

2. On July 15th, 1895, the defendants falsely and maliciously wrote and published of the plaintiff in a letter to the manager of the said company the following words :—[*Here set out the words.*]

3. The defendant by the said words meant and was understood to mean that the plaintiff had fraudulently pretended that he was the inventor of the said invention, that he was not such inventor, but had in fact pirated or stolen the same from one A. B., and that the plaintiff had proposed fraudulently to sell for a considerable sum of money the said letters patent for the invention so pirated or stolen.

4. By reason of the publication of the said libel the plaintiff has suffered damage. He was unable to sell the said letters patent to

the said company. Grave doubts were cast upon the validity of the said letters patent, and the plaintiff was ultimately compelled to dispose of the same at the price of £2,200, which was the best offer he could obtain after the publication of the said words.

The plaintiff claims £1,000 damages.

No. 22.
Action on the case for Words disparaging Goods.

1. The plaintiffs carry on business as manufacturers and sellers of artificial manures at Plymouth.

2. In the month of February, 1873, the defendants, contriving and intending to injure the plaintiffs in their said business, falsely and maliciously printed and published and widely circulated of them as such manufacturers and sellers of artificial manures, and of them in the way of their said business, the following words :—
[*For the words of the libel, see the report of the case.*]
[*Here insert particulars of publication.*]

3. The said words meant, and were understood to mean, that the said artificial manure manufactured and sold by the plaintiffs was largely composed of coprolites and other improper ingredients, and was a worthless and useless compound and unfit for the purposes for which it was advertised for sale.*

4. The said artificial manures so manufactured and sold by the plaintiffs were not in fact largely or at all composed of coprolites or other or any improper ingredients, and were not a worthless or useless compound or unfit for the purposes or any of them for which it was advertised for sale.

5. In consequence of such publication many customers of the plaintiffs have ceased to deal with them, and other persons who would have bought the said artificial manures of the plaintiffs were induced to refrain from buying the same, and the plaintiffs have been injured in their trade and have lost profits which they otherwise would have made.

PARTICULARS.
[*See Precedents Nos. 16 and 17.*]

And the plaintiff claims £2,000.

[See *Western Counties Manure Co.* v. *Lawes Chemical Manure Co.*, (1874) L. R. 9 Ex. 218; 43 L. J. Ex. 171; 23 W. R. 5.]

* If the words would support the innuendo that the plaintiffs were knowingly selling goods useless for the purposes for which they were advertised, the words would be actionable *per se*. See *ante*, p. 34.

No. 23.

Attack on Goods : Libel—Slander of Title.

1. The plaintiffs are a firm of wine merchants, and carry on the business of importing foreign wines, and in particular champagne, at —— Street, in the city of London. The defendants are a French firm of wine-growers and wine-shippers carrying on business in France and in England.

2. The plaintiffs have from time to time extensively advertised that they are sellers of a brand of champagne known in the trade and to the public as " Monte Cristo Champagne;" and have sold large quantities of such champagne to various customers, and are known in the trade and to the public as sellers of such champagne, and have acquired the right to the exclusive use of the name " Monte Cristo Champagne." Particulars of such advertisements are as follows :—

[*Here insert particulars of advertisements. Particulars of customers to whom sales were made need not be given. See Duke v. Wisden, (1897) 77 L. T. 67 ; 13 Times L. R. 481.*]

3. The defendants have falsely and maliciously published of the plaintiffs and of them in the way of their trade, the words following :—" Caution.—Monte Cristo Champagne. Messrs. X. & Co. (meaning the defendants) finding that wine stated to be Monte Cristo Champagne is being advertised for sale in Great Britain, hereby give notice that such wine cannot be the wine that it is represented to be, as no champagne shipped under that name can be genuine unless it has their names on the labels."

Particulars.

The said words were published in a circular distributed by the defendants among members of the wine trade in the months of May and June, 1903, and were inserted in the following newspapers on the dates set opposite their names :—

May 22nd, 1903, the *Times, Financial News, Daily Telegraph.*
May 24th, 1903, the *Times, Wine Merchants' Gazette*, &c., &c.

4. By the said words the defendants meant and were understood to mean that the plaintiffs had fraudulently advertised for sale wines which were not what the plaintiffs represented them to be, but of a much inferior quality ; and that they had falsely and fraudulently advertised and knowingly sold such inferior wines as and for the defendants' wines and under a trade name to which the defendants had the exclusive right, and had thereby cheated the public and

were dishonest and dishonourable persons and traders ; and that the plaintiffs had no right or title to use the trade name "Monte Cristo Champagne" or to advertise or sell any wines bearing that name.

5. By reason of the premises the plaintiffs have suffered much loss and damage and have been injured in their credit and good name and in their said business.

PARTICULARS OF SPECIAL DAMAGE.

Loss of Business.

[*Here insert particulars. See Precedent No.* 17.]

Loss of Customers.

[*Here insert particulars. See Precedent No.* 16.]
The plaintiff claims damages.
[See *Hatchard* v. *Mège*, (1887) 18 Q. B. D. 771 ; 56 L. J. Q. B. 397 ; 35 W. R. 576 ; 56 L. T. 662. *Also Precedent No.* 9.]

DEFENCES.

No. 24.

Defence in an Action of Libel.

1. The defendants never wrote or published any of the words set out in paragraph 2 of the Statement of Claim.*

2. The said words do not mean what is alleged in the said paragraph. They are incapable of the said alleged meaning or any other defamatory meaning.

3. The said words without the said alleged meaning are no libel.

4. The said words are part of a fair and accurate report of a judicial proceeding, viz., an action tried before Mr. Justice —— on March 14th, 1893, in which A. B. was plaintiff and C. D. defendant, and were published by the defendants *bonâ fide* for the information of the public, and in the usual course of their business as public journalists, and without any malice towards the plaintiff.

* The words "falsely and maliciously" must not be traversed, unless pleas of justification and privilege follow ; and even then such a traverse is superfluous. (*Belt* v. *Lawes*, (1882) 51 L. J. Q. B. 359.)

No. 25.

DEFENCE IN AN ACTION OF SLANDER.

Objection in Point of Law.

1. The plaintiff did not at the date of the alleged publication carry on the said trade of a ——, as alleged in paragraph 1 of the Statement of Claim.

2. The defendant never spoke or published any of the words set out in paragraph 2 of the Statement of Claim.*

3. The defendant never spoke or published any of the said words of the plaintiff either in relation to his said trade, &c. [*Follow the exact words of the Statement of Claim.*]

4. The said words do not mean what is alleged in the said paragraph. They are incapable of the said meaning or of any other defamatory or actionable meaning.

5. The defendant will object that the said words are not actionable without proof of special damage, and that none is alleged [*or, that the special damage alleged is too remote, and is not sufficient in law to sustain the action†*].

* The words "falsely and maliciously" must not be traversed, unless pleas of justification and privilege follow ; and even then such a traverse is superfluous. (*Belt* v. *Lawes*, (1882) 51 L. J. Q. B. 359.)

† See Precedent No. 2 in Section III. of Appendix E. of the Rules of the Supreme Court.

No. 26.

· No LIBEL.

Bonâ fide Comment on Matters of Public Interest.

1. The defendant is the proprietor of a weekly newspaper called the —— *Gazette*, in which the words set out in paragraph 2 of the Statement of Claim appeared.

2. The said words do not mean what is alleged in that paragraph. They are incapable of any such meanings, or of any defamatory meaning.

3. In so far as the said words consist of allegations of fact, they are true in substance and in fact ; in so far as they consist of expressions of opinion they are fair comments made in good faith and without malice upon the said facts, which are matters of public interest.*

* This form of pleading was approved by the Divisional Court in *Penrhyn* v. *The Licensed Victualler's Mirror*, (1890) 7 Times L. R. 1 (Mathew and Grantham, JJ.), in which case the Court ordered particulars to be given of paragraph 3. See further as to this plea, *ante*, pp. 202, 634.

No. 27.

Fair and Accurate Report and Fair Comment thereon.

1. The defendant is, and at the time of the alleged grievances was, the proprietor of the *Times* newspaper.

2. On the evening of the 12th of February, 1867, the plaintiff had presented to the House of Lords a petition, making a serious charge against one of Her Majesty's judges; a debate ensued on the presentation of the said petition, and the said charge was utterly refuted.

3. The words set out in paragraph 3 of the Statement of Claim are a portion of the Parliamentary Report, published in the *Times* of the 13th of February, 1867. They are a fair and accurate report of the proceedings in the House of Lords on the preceding evening, and were published by the defendant *bonâ fide*, and without any malice towards the plaintiff.*

4. The said petition, the charge it contained, and the said debate, were all matters of general public interest and concern.

5. The words set out in paragraph 5 of the Statement of Claim are a portion of a leading article which appeared in the *Times* for the 13th of February, 1867. The said article was a fair and honest comment on the matters above referred to, and was published by the defendant *bonâ fide* for the benefit of the public and without any malice towards the plaintiff.

[See *Wason* v. *Walter*, (1868) L. R. 4 Q. B. 73; 8 B. & S. 671; 38 L. J. Q. B. 34; 17 W. R. 169; 19 L. T. 409.]

* *If the report and the comment thereon all form part of the same article the plea might run thus :—*"The said words, in so far as they consist of statements of fact, are a fair and accurate report of Parliamentary proceedings published *bonâ fide* and without malice, and in so far as they consist of expressions of opinion they are a fair and honest comment on a matter of public interest."

[Particulars should be given identifying the Parliamentary proceedings.]

No. 28.

No Libel—Fair Comment.

1. The defendants admit that on May 3rd, 1895, they printed and published the words set out in the Statement of Claim. Such words formed part of a leading article which appeared in the defendants' newspaper the *Daily Post* for that day. The defendants

refer to the whole of such leading article, which was as follows:—
[*Here set out the whole article verbatim.*]

2. The said words do not mean what the plaintiff in his Statement of Claim alleges them to mean. They are incapable of the said meanings, or of any other defamatory meaning.

3. The said words are no libel.

4. The plaintiff was tried on May 2nd, 1895, at the ——— Assizes, before Mr. Justice ——— on a charge of manslaughter. A full report of the said trial appeared in the same issue of the defendants' paper as the words complained of. And the said article (including the said words) was published by the defendants in the ordinary course of their business as public journalists, and without any malice towards the plaintiff, and was a fair and *bonâ fide* comment on the trial of the plaintiff, and the evidence given thereat, which were then matters of public interest in ——— and the neighbourhood.

No SUFFICIENT PUBLICATION.

No. 29.

No Publication.—No Slander.

DEFENCE TO CLAIM No. 15.

1. The defendant denies that the plaintiff was or had at any time been retained or employed by him to act as his solicitor.

2. The defendant denies that he spoke or published the words alleged or any of them.

3. The defendant denies that he spoke the said words of or concerning the plaintiff in the way of his profession, or that the said words bear or were understood to bear the meaning alleged.

4. If the defendant did speak the said words (which he denies), he says that no person other than the plaintiff was present or heard the same.

5. The defendant will contend that the words which he spoke, if any, were, and were understood as, vulgar abuse, and did not amount to defamatory matter.

No. 30.

No Conscious Publication.

The defendants are booksellers and newsvendors carrying on such business on a very extensive scale at 186, Strand, in the city of Westminster, and at branches at Birmingham, Liverpool, and Manchester, and at upwards of 500 railway stations in the United Kingdom. Their servants in the course of their employment in the defendants' said business received the newspaper mentioned in the second paragraph of the Statement of Claim from the publisher thereof, and the said newspaper was thereupon sold by the defendants' servants in the ordinary course of the defendants' said business and not otherwise, and without any knowledge of its contents, which is the alleged publication. Neither of the defendants nor their servants knew at the time they sold it that the said newspaper contained any libel on the plaintiff; it was not by negligence on the part of the defendants or their servants that they did not know that there was any libel in the said newspaper; and the defendants did not know that the said newspaper was of such a character that it was likely to contain libellous matter, nor ought they to have known so; wherefore the defendants say that they never published the alleged libel.

[See *Emmens* v. *Pottle & Son*, (1885) 16 Q. B. D. 354; 55 L. J. Q. B. 51; 34 W. R. 116; 53 L. T. 808.]

No. 31.

Innocent Publication of a Libellous Novel.

The defendants admit that they printed and published the book or novel in the Statement of Claim mentioned, but deny that they did so maliciously or with any reference to the plaintiff. The defendants printed and published the said book or novel for the writer thereof, reasonably and *bonâ fide* believing the same to be a work of pure fiction. The defendants were not then aware and do not now admit that the said book or novel alluded to the plaintiff or to any other living person.

[See *Harrison* v. *Smith*, (1869) 20 L. T. at p. 715; *R.* v. *Knell*, (1728) 1 Barnard. 305; *Smith* v. *Ashley*, (1846) 52 Mass. (11 Met.) 367. And see *ante*, pp. 150—155.]

No. 32.

No Conscious Publication—Madness.

1. The defendant does not admit that he ever spoke or published any of the words complained of in paragraphs 3 and 4 of the Statement of Claim.

2. Throughout the month of April and the early part of May, 1879, the defendant was suffering from acute mania, brought on by overwork; he has no recollection of having spoken any such words as alleged either then or at any other time. If, however, the defendant did in fact utter any such words (which he does not admit), they were not spoken intentionally or maliciously, but solely in consequence, and under the influence, of the said mania; as all who heard the said words then well knew. There is and was no foundation whatever for any such charge; and the defendant unreservedly withdraws all imputations on the plaintiff's character, and exceedingly regrets that he ever spoke the said words (if in fact he did speak them, which he does not admit).

[It may be doubted whether this is a good defence, or only a pleading in mitigation of damages. A somewhat similar plea of drunkenness will be found, *post*, No. 54. See *ante*, p. 578.]

WORDS SPOKEN IN JEST.

No. 33.

DEFENCE TO CLAIM No. 11.

1. The defendant admits that he spoke and published the words set out in the Statement of Claim, but denies that he spoke them with the meaning therein alleged, or with any other actionable meaning.

2. The defendant is, and at all times hereinafter mentioned was, clerk to Mr. N., a wholesale baker. The plaintiff is one of Mr. N.'s retail customers. It is and was one of the duties of the defendant as such clerk to call on Mr. N.'s retail customers every Saturday morning and receive the money due for the bread delivered to them in the course of the week.

3. On the morning of Saturday, March the 23rd, 1895, the defendant called on the plaintiff and took the money for the bread delivered to him during the week. Amongst the change then given by the plaintiff to the defendant was a counterfeit florin. Neither the plaintiff nor the defendant knew or observed at the time that the florin was counterfeit.

4. Later in the day, when the defendant was paying the money over at the office, his employer, Mr. N., discovered that the said florin was counterfeit. The defendant thereupon took the said florin back to the plaintiff's shop, and the plaintiff gave him without demur two good shillings in exchange therefor.

5. On the morning of Saturday, May the 4th, 1895, when the defendant called on the plaintiff as usual, the plaintiff again gave the defendant a counterfeit florin amongst the money for the bread. And again neither the plaintiff nor the defendant knew or observed at the time that the florin was counterfeit.

6. Again, when the defendant was paying the money over to his employer at the office, Mr. N. discovered that the florin was counterfeit. Thereupon the defendant, recollecting the similar occurrence mentioned in paragraphs 3 and 4 above, exclaimed : " Why, that's the second bad florin Mr. H. has passed to me within the last six weeks. He's a regular ' smasher ' ! "

7. The defendant spoke these words as a joke, and never intended seriously to impute to the plaintiff any criminal offence.

8. The only persons who were present at the time or who heard the said words were the defendant's employer, Mr. N., and a fellow-clerk of his, one David Griggs. Both Mr. N. and David Griggs were aware of the circumstances detailed above, and knew to what the defendant was referring, and understood that he spoke in jest, and did not intend to make any charge against the plaintiff.

JUSTIFICATION.

No. 34.

ANOTHER DEFENCE TO CLAIM No. 11.

1. The defendant does not admit that he spoke or published the words set out in the Statement of Claim.

2. The said words are true in substance and in fact. On March 23rd, 1895, the plaintiff uttered and passed to the defendant a counterfeit florin, well knowing the same to be counterfeit. On May 4th, 1895, the plaintiff uttered and passed to the defendant another counterfeit florin, well knowing the same to be counterfeit. [*State any other instances in which the plaintiff passed bad coin to the defendant and others.*]

No. 35.

Justification of the Words without the alleged Meaning.

1. The defendant denies that he spoke or published any of the words set out in paragraph 5 of the Statement of Claim. The said words do not mean what is in that paragraph alleged.

2. The defendant denies that he spoke or published any of the said words of the plaintiff in the way of his trade or at all.

3. The said words were not spoken or understood in the alleged or any defamatory sense; they are incapable of the alleged meaning.

4. The said words, without the said meaning, and according to their natural and ordinary signification, are true in substance and in fact.

PARTICULARS.

[*Here set out particulars of justification. See ante, pp.* 181 *and* 636.]

No. 36.

Justification of a Portion of a Libel.

DEFENCE.

1. The defendants do not admit that the plaintiff is the proprietor and editor of the *Dartmouth Advertiser* newspaper.

2. As to such portion of the said words as alleges that the plaintiff is a felon editor, the defendants say that the same is true in substance and in fact. The plaintiff was on the —— of —— convicted of larceny at the Quarter Sessions for the county of Cornwall, and was on the same day sentenced to twelve months' hard labour for stealing feathers.

3. As to the residue of the said words the defendants say that the same were parts of certain articles printed and published in the defendants' said newspaper, each of which was a fair and *bonâ fide* comment upon a matter of public interest, viz., the conduct of the plaintiff in his public character as the nominal editor of the *Dartmouth Advertiser*, a public newspaper.

[See *Leyman* v. *Latimer and others*, (1878) 3 Ex. D. 15, 352; 47 L. J. Ex. 470; 25 W. R. 751; 26 W. R. 305; 37 L. T. 360, 819.]

No. 37.

Justification and Privilege—Moral or Social Duty.

DEFENCE TO CLAIM No. 1.

1. The defendants admit that the defendant Alice wrote and published the words set out in paragraph 2 of the Statement of Claim.

2. The said words are true in substance and in fact. While the plaintiff was in the service of the defendants, to wit, on the 18th of August, 1903, she stole two pairs of sheets and one counterpane, of the goods and chattels of the defendant Henry, and on the

same day pawned them at the shop of John Smith, No. 28, High Street, Evesham; wherefore the defendants, as they lawfully might, discharged the plaintiff from their service on the 31st of August, 1903.

3. The said words were published on a privileged occasion and without malice.

PARTICULARS.

In the month of September, 1903, the plaintiff was desirous of entering into the service of Mrs. M., of 19, Newhall Street, Birmingham, and Mrs. M., on the 14th of September, 1903, wrote a letter to the defendant Alice inquiring as to the plaintiff's character, and asking especially why she left the defendants' service. Thereupon it became the duty of the defendant Alice to write, and she did write on the 15th of September, 1903, to Mrs. M., a letter telling her what she knew as to the plaintiff's character, and stating the reason of her dismissal. This letter contained the words complained of. The said words were written in answer to Mrs. M.'s said inquiries, and under a sense of duty and without any malice towards the plaintiff and in the honest belief that the charge therein made was true.

PRIVILEGE.

No. 38.

Absolute Privilege—Litigant in Person.

The said words were published on an occasion which was absolutely privileged. Before the alleged slander was spoken the plaintiff had on the 1st of November, 1895, issued a writ against the defendant claiming an account, and had taken out a summons in the said action for an account, which on the 12th of November, 1895, came on for hearing before Mr. E. A., the District Registrar for ——. The defendant, who is a solicitor, appeared in person before the said Registrar to oppose the said summons, and the said words were spoken, if at all, to the said Registrar in the course of argument during the hearing of the said summons.

No. 39.

Absolute Privilege—Witness.

The said words were spoken by the defendant on an occasion which was absolutely privileged, viz., during his examination on oath as a witness in the course of the hearing of a charge of forgery against X. Y., on May 10th, 1874, before an alderman lawfully exercising jurisdiction in that behalf at the Guildhall, in the city of London.

[See *Seaman* v. *Netherclift*, (1876) 2 C. P. D. 53 ; 46 L. J. C. P. 128 ; 25 W. R. 159 ; 35 L. T. 784.]

No. 40.

Absolute Privilege—Military Duty.

The plaintiff was a colonel in the —— Regiment, and the defendant was the general commanding the district in which the said regiment was stationed. On the 4th of May, 1904, the plaintiff forwarded to the defendant as his superior officer a letter addressed to the Commander-in-chief making a complaint against a brother officer in the same regiment, Major ——. It thereupon became, and was under Article —— of the "Regulations for the Army" then in force, the duty of the defendant as such superior officer to forward the plaintiff's said letter and also to make a written report thereon to the Commander-in-chief. The defendant therefore, in accordance with his said duty, on the 6th of May, 1904, forwarded the plaintiff's said letter to the Commander-in-chief, and accompanied the same by a report in writing, which is the alleged libel. Such report was published by the defendant in discharge of his said duty to the Commander-in-chief, and not otherwise.

[*Dawkins* v. *Lord Paulet*, (1869) L. R. 5 Q. B. 94 ; 39 L. J. Q. B. 53 ; 18 W. R. 336 ; 21 L. T. 584.]

No. 41.

Qualified Privilege—Character of a Servant.

See *ante*, Precedent No. 37.

No. 42.

Qualified Privilege—Common Interest.

DEFENCE TO CLAIM No. 5.

The publication of the said letter to J. H., if made, was made *bonâ fide* and without malice and on a privileged occasion.

PARTICULARS.

The defendant's bank had on the 2nd February, 1902, advanced to J. H., in response to a request contained in a letter from J. H. to the defendant dated the 26th January, 1902, the sum of £1,000 to assist J. H. in his business and in carrying out the contracts referred to in the said letter. On the 31st May, 1902, J. H. called upon the defendant and verbally inquired of the defendant whether he considered the plaintiff would be a suitable man to act as manager of his business. It was in answer to the said inquiry that the said words were published.

No. 43.

Qualified Privilege—Master and Servant.

The defendant is head gardener to one Sir John M., of ——. The plaintiff and others at the time mentioned in the Statement of Claim were employed as labourers by Sir John M., and the defendant was verbally requested by him on the 10th day of March 1904, to see that the said labourers did their work in a proper and diligent manner. On the 31st day of March, 1904, Sir John M. verbally inquired of the defendant whether the said labourers were sober and honest and attentive to their work. It thereupon became and was the duty of the defendant to state such facts as were within his knowledge to Sir John M. Such statements are the alleged slanders; but they were made *bonâ fide* in the discharge of the said duty, and in answer to the said inquiry, and in the honest belief that the facts so stated were true, and without any malice towards the plaintiff. The occasion was therefore privileged.

No. 44.

Qualified Privilege—Communication Volunteered—Confidential Relation—Common Interest.

The said words were published by the defendant on a privileged occasion *bonâ fide* and without malice.

PARTICULARS.

The defendant is the eldest son of the Mrs. Hawkins mentioned in paragraph 3 of the Statement of Claim. She is a widow.

On the 4th day of June, 1903, Mrs. Hawkins told the defendant confidentially that she was about to marry the plaintiff. Thereupon the defendant spoke the said words to the said Mrs. Hawkins confidentially and in the honest desire to protect her interests and his own. The defendant at the time *bonâ fide* believed in the truth of what he said. This is the only publication by the defendant of the said words.

[*Todd* v. *Hawkins*, (1837) 8 C. & P. 88 ; 2 Moo. & Rob. 20.]

Particulars under a Plea of Qualified Privilege.

No. 45.

Communication published in Self-defence.

" The plaintiff in May, 1896, published and caused to be published a pamphlet entitled ' The Case of Salem Chapel, ——,' which was sold by all the booksellers in the said town of ——. This pamphlet contained serious charges against the defendant, both personally and as secretary and one of the deacons of the said chapel. The defendant published the words set out in paragraph 5 of the Statement of Claim in reply to the said pamphlet published by the plaintiff, and *bonâ fide* for the purpose of vindicating his character against the plaintiff's attack, and in order to prevent the plaintiff's said charges from operating to his prejudice, and in reasonable and necessary self-defence, and without any malice towards the plaintiff."

No. 46.

Common Interest — Church Members.

The words set out in paragraph 2 of the Statement of Claim were part of a requisition summoning a meeting of the members of the English Baptist Church at ——, which was signed by 122 of such members, and addressed to the deacons of such chapel. The defendant published the said requisition solely to members of the said church, who had a common interest with him in all the matters therein referred to and without any malice toward the plaintiff.

No. 47.

Offer of Reward for Discovery of Offender.

DEFENCE TO CLAIM No. 3.

The defendant published the placard referred to in paragraph 2 of the Statement of Claim solely for the purpose of endeavouring to discover the person who committed the assault referred to therein, and with the *bonâ fide* object and intention of bringing such person to justice and of prosecuting him to conviction.

No. 48.

Complaint to Persons in Authority.

The plaintiff and defendant are both members of the " —— Poultry Club," and were competitors at the Annual Show of the club which was held on the 12th October, 1895. During the show exhibitors named A. B., C. D., and E. F. verbally complained to the defendant of the plaintiff's conduct as such competitor that [*Here particulars of the complaints must be set out*]. Thereupon the defendant drew up a written protest against the plaintiff being allowed to compete, and on the same day lodged the same with the committee whose duty it was by the rules of the club to investigate such a complaint. This protest is the alleged libel. It was written by the defendant, without any malice towards the plaintiff, with the sole object of ensuring a fair competition at the show, and in the honest belief that every statement therein contained was true. It was a communication made *bonâ fide* on a matter in which the defendant had an interest, and was published only to the said committee, who had a corresponding interest and duty in that behalf.

PRIVILEGED REPORT.

No. 49.

Report of a Judgment published as a Pamphlet.

MACDOUGALL *v.* KNIGHT & SON, (1886) 17 Q. B. D. 636 ; 55 L. J. Q. B. 464 ; 34 W. R. 727 ; 55 L. T. 274.

" 1. The defendants admit that they published of the plaintiff a pamphlet which is a *verbatim* report of the judgment of the Honourable Mr. Justice North, given on the 30th day of June, 1884, in the action of *MacDougall* v. *Knight & Son,* and which really gives all the information necessary to be known by anyone feeling an interest in the matter. But the defendants deny that they did so maliciously, or that they distributed the said pamphlet broadcast in the city of Bath, or the counties of Somerset and Gloucester, or elsewhere, or at all.

" 2. The said pamphlet contained the words set out in paragraph 2 of the Statement of Claim. The said words were in fact spoken by the Honourable Mr. Justice North in delivering judgment in the said action ; but the defendants do not admit that he or they published the said words with the meanings alleged in the said paragraph.

" 3. The defendants are auctioneers and upholsterers carrying on business at Bath, and having a large number of customers resident in Bath and the neighbourhood. The plaintiff brought the said action against the defendants in the Chancery Division of the High Court of Justice charging the defendants with breach of contract, misrepresentation, and breach of faith. The said action was assigned for trial to the Honourable Mr. Justice North, who after a trial which lasted five days gave judgment in favour of the defendants. The said pamphlet is a fair, accurate, and honest report of the said judgment of the Honourable Mr. Justice North, and was published by the defendants *bonâ fide* and with the honest intention of making known the true facts of the case, and in order to protect their reputation and their said business, and in reasonable self-defence, and without any malice towards the plaintiff."

No. 50.

Report privileged by virtue of Section 4 of the Law of Libel Amendment Act, 1888.

The words set out in paragraph 2 of the Statement of Claim were published in the defendant's said newspaper on the date alleged and formed part of a fair and accurate report of the proceedings of a public meeting (*or,* of a meeting of the town council of the borough of S——, in the county of L——), which was held at the Guildhall, S——, on the —— day of ——, 1895. The matter published was of public concern, and its publication was for the public benefit.

No. 51.

DEFENCE TO CLAIM No. 20.

Slander of Title to Goods.

1. The defendant admits that the plaintiff caused the goods referred to in paragraph 2 of the Statement of Claim to be advertised for sale.

2. Of the goods so advertised for sale those numbered 19 to 28, both inclusive, in the plaintiff's particulars were the property of the defendant, and not of the plaintiff, but had been unlawfully seized and carried away by the plaintiff on the —— day of ——, and the same were in the plaintiff's possession at the date of the said advertisement.

3. The defendant admits that he caused to be printed and published the " Notice " set out in paragraph 4 of the Statement of Claim, but denies that he did so falsely or maliciously. He published the said words in the honest belief that the plaintiff was seeking to sell the defendant's said goods and for the purpose of warning all persons from purchasing the said goods of the defendant, and in the *bonâ fide* belief that such warning was necessary for the protection of the defendant's own property, and without any malice towards the plaintiff.

[See *Carr* v. *Duckett*, (1860) 5 H. & N. 783; 29 L. J. Ex. 468.]

No. 52.

Defence of Previous Action—Res Judicata.

The plaintiff on the 13th March, 1892, sued the defendant, in an action of which the short title is " 1892.—R.—No. 645 " in the King's Bench Division of this Honourable Court, for the same cause of action as is alleged in the Statement of Claim herein; and in that action the plaintiff on the 15th July, 1892, recovered judgment against the defendant for £——, and his costs; which judgment still remains in force.

A plea that in a former action judgment was given against the plaintiff, is really a plea in estoppel. Commence as above:

And in that action it was adjudged that the plaintiff should recover nothing against the defendant, and that the defendant should recover against the plaintiff £—— for his costs of defence. The said judgment was signed on the —— day of ——, 1893, and still remains in force. [The proceedings are entered on roll, No. ——.] Wherefore the defendant says that the plaintiff is estopped, and ought not to be admitted to bring the present action against the defendant.

No. 53.

Defence of Accord and Satisfaction.

The plaintiff was the proprietor and publisher of a certain weekly journal called the *Musical Review;* and the defendant was the proprietor and publisher of another weekly journal called the *Orchestra.* And after the publication, if any, of the said words, the plaintiff and defendant by letters interchanged between the parties on the 29th March, 1864, agreed together to accept mutual apologies, to be published by the plaintiff and defendant respectively in their said weekly journals, in full satisfaction and discharge of the cause of action set out in the Statement of Claim, and of all damages and costs sustained by the plaintiff in respect thereof. And thereupon, in pursuance of the said agreement, the defendant on the 14th May, 1864, printed and published his part of the said mutual apologies in the form agreed on in his weekly journal the *Orchestra,* of which the plaintiff had notice. And the plaintiff on the same day printed and published his part of the said apologies in the form agreed on in his said weekly journal, the *Musical Review.* And such apologies so published as aforesaid the plaintiff accepted and received in full satisfaction and discharge of the causes of action set out in the Statement of Claim.

[See *Boosey* v. *Wood,* (1865) 3 H. & C. 484 ; 34 L. J. Ex. 65.]

No. 54.

Payment into Court—Pleading Matters in Mitigation of Damages.

" 1. The defendant brings into Court the sum of £5, and says that the same is sufficient to satisfy the plaintiffs' claim in this action.

" 2. The defendant proposes to give evidence at the trial of the following matters, with a view to mitigation of damages :—

The defendant was a total stranger to both plaintiffs, and bore no malice to either. He was drunk when he uttered the said words, and the fact that he was drunk was obvious to all who heard them. He has no recollection of having ever uttered any such words, but does not dispute that he did so. Everyone who heard what the defendant said was fully aware that he was not peaking deliberately, and that he did not seriously mean to make any charge against either plaintiff, but was talking wildly in consequence of drink. The said words are wholly untrue. There is and was no foundation whatever for any such statement. The defendant exceedingly regrets that he should ever have uttered any such words; he unreservedly withdraws all imputation on the plaintiffs' character, and apologizes for the abusive language which he uttered without any reason while under the influence of liquor."

No. 55.

Payment into Court with an Admission of the Innuendoes.

1. The defendants admit that they sold and circulated the book called " ——," and that such book contained the words set out in paragraph 3 of the Statement of Claim. They admit that the said words are capable of the meanings alleged in the innuendoes contained in the said paragraph, and that they refer to the plaintiff.

2. The defendants bring into Court the sum of £——, and say that the same is sufficient to satisfy the plaintiff's claim.

[N.B.—When the words are libellous in their natural and ordinary meaning, and the plaintiff has alleged an innuendo, the defendant may deny the innuendo and yet pay money into Court, provided it is made clear that the money is paid into Court in respect of the words without the innuendo, which is denied. (*Mackay* v. *Manchester Press Co.*, (1889) 54 J. P. 22; 6 Times L. R. 16.) The proper course in such a case is to plead that the libel does not bear the meaning imputed to it by the plaintiff, and to plead that as it is nevertheless a libel, although not bearing that meaning, the defendant pays money into Court in respect of it. (Per Lord Esher, M.R., in *Davis* v. *Billing*, (1891) 8 Times L. R. 58.) See Precedent No. 57. But it is not wise to adopt this course, unless the innuendo is extravagant. For if the jury should find that the innuendo places on the words their true meaning, the payment into Court will strictly speaking be of no avail to the defendant. The money in such a case is paid into Court to the count for the words without the innuendo (see *ante*, p. 116), and the plaintiff has succeeded on the other count (viz., that comprising the innuendo), in respect of which no payment has been made; and it would probably be held that the plaintiff was entitled not merely to the costs of that issue but to the general costs of the action, even though he recovered less than the amount paid into Court. (See also *ante*, pp. 447, 638, 640.)]

No. 56.

Apologizing in a Defence.

1. The defendants admit that they wrote the words set out in

paragraph 2 of the Statement of Claim, and published the same to Messrs. A. and B., the plaintiffs' solicitors.

2. They now apologize to the plaintiffs for the said words, and express their sincere regret that they ever wrote them. They unreservedly withdraw all imputations on the plaintiffs. They bring into Court the sum of forty shillings, and say that that sum, together with this apology and withdrawal, is sufficient to satisfy the plaintiffs' claim in this action.

[As to a pleading of this kind, see *ante*, p. 644.]

No. 57.

Consolidated Actions—Denial of the Innuendoes—Payment into Court with Apology.

Defence to Claim No. 10.

[*Heading similar to that in Precedent No. 10.*]

1. The defendants, the West of England Printing Company, Limited, admit that they printed and published the words set out in paragraph 3 of the Statement of Claim and that the same are libellous, but deny that the said words bore or are capable of the meaning alleged in the Statement of Claim.

2. The defendants, the —— *Gazette* Company, Limited, admit that they printed and published the words set out in paragraph 4 of the Statement of Claim and that the same are libellous, but deny that the said words bore or are capable of the meaning alleged in the Statement of Claim.

3. On the 17th September, 1903, the defendants, the West of England Printing Company, Limited, published in the issue of the —— *County Herald* of that date the following apology:—[*Here insert the apology*].

4. On the 21st September, 1903, the defendants, the —— *Gazette* Company, Limited, published in the issue of the —— *Gazette* of that date the following apology:—[*Here insert the apology*].

5. The defendants now repeat their respective apologies and bring the sum of £50 into Court, and say that such sum, together with the said apologies, is sufficient to satisfy the plaintiff's claim in this action in respect of the said words without the said alleged meanings, which are denied.

No. 58.

Pleading an Apology previously Published. *

" 1. The defendant has paid into Court the sum of fifty guineas, and says that that sum is sufficient to satisfy the plaintiff's claim in this action.

" 2. At the earliest opportunity after the commencement of this action the defendant made and offered an apology to the plaintiff for the said words by means of a letter written by the defendant's solicitors to the plaintiff's solicitor in the following words :—

[*Here set out letter, with date.*]

" 3. On the 31st day of October, 1882, the defendant caused to be printed in the —— *Journal* the following apology to the plaintiff for the said words :—

APOLOGY.

I, ——, of ——, desire to express my sincere regret that I incautiously repeated a statement made to me by one of my father's clerks concerning Mr. K., of ——. Such statement now proves to have been wholly unfounded, and I beg to withdraw and contradict the same, and to apologize to Mr. K. for having made it.

An action having been commenced against me by Mr. K. for slander, I have this day paid into Court the sum of £52 10*s.*, and I trust that Mr. K. will accept that sum, together with this apology, as the best amends it is in my power to make for the injury or annoyance which I have inadvertently caused him.

Dated this 25th day of October, 1882.

(Signed)
[*Defendant.*]

Witness,
  A. B.,
    Solicitor.

" This apology also appeared in the issue of the said journal for November 7th, and will appear in the next four consecutive issues thereof.

" 4. Take notice, that the defendant intends on the trial of this action to give in evidence in mitigation of damages the matters alleged in paragraphs 2 and 3 above."

---

* We doubt whether such a Defence as this is strictly permissible ; but it is not embarrassing ; and we do not see that it is otherwise objection-

No. 59.

Notice under Section 1 of Lord Campbell's Act.

1904.—B.—No. 732.

In the High Court of Justice.
King's Bench Division.

Between A. B.   .   .   Plaintiff,

and

E. F.   .   .   Defendant.

Take notice, that the defendant intends on the trial of this action to give in evidence in mitigation of damages, if any shall be found to be due, that on the —— day of ——, he made [*or* offered] an apology to the plaintiff for the defamation complained of in the Statement of Claim herein, before the commencement of this action [*or* as soon after the commencement of this action as there was an opportunity of making or offering such apology, the action having been commenced before there was an opportunity of making or offering such apology]. Such apology was published by the defendant in the —— *News* for October 3rd, 1904.

Dated, &c.

Yours, &c.,
G. H.,
Defendant's solicitor [*or* agent].

To Mr. C. D., plaintiff's
solicitor or agent.

No. 60.

Plea under Section 2 of Lord Campbell's Act.

The alleged libel was contained in a public daily newspaper called the —— *Daily Press*, and was inserted in such newspaper without actual malice and without gross negligence. Before [*or* at the earliest opportunity after] the commencement of this action the defendant inserted in the said newspaper a full apology for the said libel [*or* offered to publish a full apology for the said libel in any newspaper selected by the plaintiff] according to the statute in such case made and provided. The defendant has paid into Court the

able. It may be urged that the fact that the defendant has apologized since action is neither matter of defence nor a topic within the scope of Order XXXVI. r. 37 ; it is only ground for a notice under section 1 of Lord Campbell's Act. But the above pleading passed muster, and the jury, at the trial, found the apology sufficient.

sum of forty shillings by way of amends for the injury sustained by the plaintiff through the publication of the said libel, and says that the said sum is enough to satisfy the plaintiff's claim in this action.

[As to dangers attending the use of this plea, see *ante*, p. 642.]

No. 61.

Reply to Defence No. 36.

1. The plaintiff joins issue upon the 1st and 3rd paragraphs of the Defence.

2. The plaintiff admits that he was convicted of felony as alleged in paragraph 2 of the Defence, but does not admit that he in fact committed the said felony. The Court by which the plaintiff was so convicted sentenced the plaintiff as his punishment for the said felony to be imprisoned and kept to hard labour for twelve calendar months. The plaintiff, as the defendants well knew, duly endured the said punishment, and was released from the said imprisonment as having served his sentence on the —— day of ——, and thereby became, and is, in the same situation as if a pardon under the Great Seal had been granted to him for the said felony.

No. 62.

Reply to Defence No. 50.

1. The plaintiff joins issue with the defendant on his Defence.

2. The plaintiff by a letter dated May 22nd, 1895, requested the defendant to insert in the newspaper in which the words complained of appeared, a reasonable letter or statement by way of contradiction or explanation. But the defendant refused (*or*, neglected) to insert the same.

No. 63.

Particulars

Delivered pursuant to Order XXXVI. r. 37.

TAKE NOTICE, that at the trial of this action the defendant intends to give the following matters in evidence with a view to mitigation of damages :—

1. On August 10th, 1895, before the publication of the letter set out in paragraph 4 of the Statement of Claim, the plaintiff wrote and caused to be printed and published in the —— *County Gazette* an anonymous letter with regard to the matters mentioned in paragraph 2 of the Statement of Claim, in which he commended his own conduct, and then referred to the defendant in the following words:—[*Set out so much of the anonymous letter as attacked the defendant.*]

2. It was in reply to the attack made on the defendant by this anonymous letter that the defendant spoke [*or* wrote] the words set out in paragraph 3 of the Statement of Claim.

3. Thereupon the plaintiff on August 24th, 1895, wrote and caused to be printed and published in the —— *County Gazette* the libellous letter set out in paragraph 5 of the defendant's Counterclaim. This letter the defendant was entitled, and indeed compelled, to answer. And in reply thereto, he wrote the words set out in paragraph 4 of the Statement of Claim which the plaintiff alleges to be a libel upon him.

4. The plaintiff has brought an action against the —— newspaper for damages in respect of a libel to the same purport or effect as the libel for which this action is brought, viz., in respect of the words set out in paragraph 4 of the Statement of Claim.

Dated the —— day of ——, 1895.

Yours, &c.,

A. B., of ——,

Defendant's solicitor.

To the plaintiff,

and Messrs. C. and D.,

his solicitors or agents.

[N.B.—There is nothing to prevent such particulars being printed on the same piece of paper as the Defence, if the defendant wishes it. In that case, they should not be printed as part of the pleading, but should follow the signature of counsel. If, however, the Defence contains pleas in bar to the whole action, it is better to deliver such particulars separately and subsequently.]

No. 64.

INTERROGATORIES.

As to Publication.

Is it not the fact that in the issue of the —— *Gazette* of the 6th July, 1878, an article appeared containing the words set out in paragraph 6 of the Statement of Claim, or some and which of them or other and what words to the same effect ?

Were not you, the defendant William Burnside, upon and before the said 6th day of July, 1878, or some other and what date, the proprietor $\frac{\text{and}}{\text{or}}$ publisher, either alone or jointly with some other and what person or persons, of the said newspaper ?

(*Lefroy* v. *Burnside*, (1879) 4 L. R. Ir. 340 ; 41 L. T. 199 ; 14 Cox, C. C. 260 ; *ante*, p. 666.)

Did you write or cause to be written the letter to the editor dated 23rd November, 1881, published in the *Hereford Times* of 26th November, 1881, under the heading of " The distraint for rent case at Leominster," and signed by your name T. A. Colt ?

Do not the words in the said letter [*Here set out the words*] refer to the plaintiff ?

By your allegation in that letter that one of the holders of the bill of sale mentioned in your letter had affirmed sometime since in a Court of law that he did not possess a 5*l.* note, did you not intend to refer to the plaintiff ?

Did you, on or about the 16th of February, 1885, or at some other and what date, write and send or cause to be sent to Colonel Pryse, of, &c., a letter, of which a copy is annexed hereto, marked A., of which the original will, if you require it, be shown to you before swearing your affidavit in answer to these interrogatories on your giving reasonable notice in that behalf ?*

Did you, on or about the 26th of January, 1885, or at some other and what date, write and send or cause to be sent a letter, of which a copy is annexed, marked B. [the letter containing the alleged libel], of which the original will, if you require it, be shown to you before swearing your affidavit in answer to these interrogatories on your giving reasonable notice in that behalf ?

(*Jones* v. *Richards*, (1885) 15 Q. B. D. 439.)

Did you, on or about the —— of —— speak the following words of the plaintiff [*Here insert words*] or words to that effect ?

Were the said words spoken in the presence of [*Here insert names from Particulars in Statement of Claim*] or some and which of them ?

(*Dalgleish* v. *Lowther*, [1899] 2 Q. B. 590.)

---

* The document referred to in this interrogatory was not the libel sued on but a document on which the plaintiff intended to rely as proof that the libel was in the defendant's handwriting.

As to Conscious Publication.

[*Book in Library of British Museum.*]

How did the trustees become possessed of the said book? Was it not bought or otherwise and how acquired by them or with their authority and when and from whom?

Were any and what steps taken by the trustees or the librarian or any other and what servant of theirs to ascertain the character of the said book before it was so bought or acquired, or after it was so bought and acquired, or when first?

What care did the defendants take, as alleged by them in their Defence, with reference to the said book and on what occasions to ascertain its contents and whether it contained libellous matter or to prevent its being read?

(*Martin* v. *Trustees of the British Museum*, (1894) 10 Times L. R. 215.)

As to Gross Negligence under Lord Campbell's Act where a Newspaper had Published a Letter signed " A Ratepayer."

When and from and through whom and how did you receive the letter set out in the Statement of Claim?

Are there any and what circumstances known to you or any and which of your servants or agents which led you to suspect or from which it might be inferred who was the writer or sender of the said letter?

Did you ever receive any and what request to publish the said letter? If yea, when and from whom was such request received? If verbal, give the substance thereof, and if in writing identify the document.

Had you or any and which of your servants or agents any and what means of knowing or ascertaining when and by whom the said letter was written or sent to you?

Did you before you published the said letter make any, and what, inquiries as to whether the writer thereof was a ratepayer of St. Saviour's parish, or as to who the writer was? If yea, when, and how, and of whom did you make it and what was the nature and result of each such inquiry?

Did you, before you published the said letter, take any and what precautions, or make any, and what, inquiries as to the truth of the statements contained in it, or make any, and what, inquiry at all with respect to the said letter? Have you ever made any such, and what, inquiries, and when? And what was the result of each such inquiry?

Was the letter received by you altered in any and what respects before insertion in the —— *Gazette?*

As to Privilege.

How and when do you say that the plaintiff invited you to speak the words set out in the Statement of Claim? If you allege that such invitation was in writing, identify the documents.

(*Barratt* v. *Kearns*, [1905] 1 K. B. 504.)

As to malice.

What information, if any, had you that induced you to believe that the said words were true, or what steps, if any, had you taken before speaking the words to ascertain whether they were true or not?

(*Elliott* v. *Garrett*, [1902] 1 K. B. 870.)
(*Saunderson* v. *Baron von Radeck*, (1905) 119 L. T. Jo. 33 (H. L.).)
(*Edmondson* v. *Birch & Co., Ltd.*, [1905] 2 K. B. 523.)
(*Plymouth Mutual, &c., Ltd.* v. *Plymouth Traders Association, Ltd.*, [1906] 1 K. B. 403.)

From whom did you obtain such information?

(*White & Co.* v. *Credit Reform Association, &c., Ltd.*, [1905] 1 K. B. 653.)

As to Damages.

What number of copies of the —— *Gazette* for the 26th March, and for the 2nd of April, were printed and published respectively? How many copies of the issue of the 26th of March circulated in St. Saviour's parish? Was not that a larger number than usual? (See *ante*, p. 658.)

At what date was the pamphlet entitled " Parnellism and Crime " first issued in that form as a separate publication? At what date (if any) was the public circulation of the said pamphlet stopped? How many editions of the said pamphlet and how many copies of each such edition were issued and circulated by sale or otherwise between the said dates?

(*Parnell* v. *Walter*, (1890) 24 Q. B. D. 441.)

[*For Objections to answer particular interrogatories, see ante,* pp. 663, 667.]

No. 65.

Notice of Motion on Appeal.

In the Court of Appeal.

Between A. B.   .   .   . Plaintiff,
and
C. & D.   .   . Defendants.

TAKE NOTICE, that this honourable Court will be moved on ——, the —— day of ——, 1895, or so soon thereafter as counsel can be heard, by [Mr. ——, of] counsel for the above-named defendants, that the verdict and judgment obtained in this action by the plaintiff at the —— Assizes before the Hon. Mr. Justice —— and a special jury on the —— day of ——, 1895, be set aside, and that judgment be entered for the defendants; or that a new trial may be had between the parties on the grounds :—

1. That there was no evidence to go to the jury of [*or,* that ——].

2. That the learned Judge misdirected the jury by telling them that :—

[*Here state the direction to which exception is taken.*]

3. That the verdict was against the weight of the evidence.

And that the costs of this appeal and in the Court below may be paid by the plaintiff to the defendants.

Dated this —— day of ——, 1895.

Yours, &c.,

E. & F.,
Defendants' solicitors.

To the above-named plaintiff,
   and to Messrs. G. & H., his
   solicitors or agents.

No. 66.

*Notice of Motion to Commit for Contempt of Court and for an
Injunction.*

TAKE NOTICE, that this honourable Court will be moved before the Divisional Court, sitting at the Royal Courts of Justice, Strand, London, on ——, the —— day of ——, 1896, or so soon thereafter as counsel can be heard, by counsel on behalf of the above-named plaintiff, for an order that E. F., of ——, the printer and publisher, and G. H., of ——, the proprietor of the —— newspaper, may be committed to —— Prison for a contempt of this honourable Court in printing and publishing, in the issue of the said newspaper for January 21st, 1896, certain comments and statements relating to the above action now awaiting trial in this honourable Court, and for printing and publishing, in the issue of the said newspaper for January 23rd, 1896, a letter relating to the said action, purporting to be from C. D., one of the above-named defendants.

And that the said E. F. and G. H., their servants or agents, may be restrained from printing or publishing in the said newspaper any comments or correspondence calculated to prejudice or interfere with the fair trial of the said action.

And that the said E. F. and G. H. may be ordered to pay the costs of this motion.

And for such further or other relief as the nature of the case may require.

Dated this —— day of ——, 1896.

K. L.

[*Address*],

To E. F.,   Plaintiff's solicitor.

    Printer and publisher of the —— newspaper,
    And to G. H., the proprietor thereof.

TAKE NOTICE, that in support of the above motion the under-mentioned affidavits will be read, copies whereof are served herewith, viz. :—

Affidavit of A. B., filed ——, 1896.
Affidavit of J. S., filed ——, 1896.

II. FORMS OF PLEADINGS, ETC., IN THE COUNTY COURT.

No. 67.

(County Court Rules, 1903—Appendix, Form 282.)

Statement of Plaintiff's Cause of Action in Actions of Libel or Slander Remitted for Trial in a County Court.

In the County Court of ——, holden at ——.

Between A. B.   .   . Plaintiff,

[*Address and description*],

and

C. D.   .   . Defendant,

[*Address and description*].

Being an action of libel [*or* slander] commenced in the High Court of Justice, and remitted by order of a Judge [*or* Master *or*

District Registrar] thereof under section 66 of the County Courts Act, 1888, to be tried before this Court.

Libel.

The defendant falsely and maliciously wrote and published of and concerning the plaintiff the words following :—"*He is a liar, a blackguard, and a scoundrel ;*" and the plaintiff claims 200*l.* damages.

Libel of the Plaintiff in the Way of his Trade.

The defendant falsely and maliciously caused to be printed and published of and concerning the plaintiff in the way of his trade as a grocer the words following :—"*Mr. A. B. sands his sugar, and dusts his pepper,*" whereby the plaintiff was injured in his trade, and lost the custom of several persons, particularly X., Y. and Z., who had before dealt at the plaintiff's shop ; and the plaintiff claims 50*l.* damages.

Slander.

The defendant falsely and maliciously spoke and published of and concerning the plaintiff the words following :—"*A. B. is a thief, and stole Mr. Brown's ducks ;*" and the plaintiff claims 30*l.* damages.

Slander of Plaintiff in the Way of his Calling.

The defendant falsely and maliciously spoke and published of and concerning the plaintiff, in the way of his business and calling as a ratcatcher, the words following :—"*A. B. is a great rogue, and instead of doing his best to kill the rats, he encourages the breed, so that he may have more employment from the farmers,*" whereby the plaintiff was injured in his business, and several farmers, particularly X., Y. and Z., who had usually employed him to kill the rats on their farms, ceased to do so ; and the plaintiff claims 20*l.* damages.

Above is the statement of the plaintiff's cause of action.

Dated this —— day of ——, 19—.

A. B., plaintiff,

or,

E. F., plaintiff's solicitor.

To the Registrar of the Court,
   and to the defendant.

[*N.B.—The above Forms are only given as examples : and the statement of the plaintiff's cause of action must in all cases be according to the facts, and be as concise as possible.*]

No. 68.

(County Court Rules, 1903—Appendix, Forms 85, 86, and 87.)

Notice of Special Defences, &c.

[Heading as in Form No. 67.]

TAKE NOTICE, that the defendant intends at the hearing of this action to give in evidence and rely upon the following ground of defence :—

Dated this —— day of ——, 19—.

       Defendant [*or* defendant's solicitor.]

To the Registrar of the Court,
 and to the plaintiff.

(i) *Justification.*

That the libel [*or* slander] complained of is true in substance and in fact.

(ii) *Under section 1 of Lord Campbell's Act.*

TAKE NOTICE, that the defendant on the trial of this action will give in evidence in mitigation of damages that he made [*or* offered] an apology to the plaintiff for the libel [*or* slander] complained of before the commencement of the action [*or* as soon after the commencement of the action as he had an opportunity of so doing].

(iii) *Under section 2 of Lord Campbell's Act.*

TAKE NOTICE, that the defendant on the trial of this action will give in evidence and rely upon the following ground of defence ; (that is to say,)

That the libel was inserted in the newspaper called or known by the name of —— without actual malice and without gross negligence, and that before the commencement of the action [*or* as soon after the commencement of the action as he had an opportunity of doing so] the defendant inserted in the said newspaper [*or* offered to publish in any newspaper or periodical publication to be selected by the plaintiff] a full apology for the said libel, and that the defendant has paid into Court £—— by way of amends for the injury sustained by the plaintiff by the publication of the said libel.

[*N.B.—If the libel was published in any periodical publication other than a newspaper, alter the notice accordingly.*]

III. PRECEDENTS OF CRIMINAL PLEADINGS.

No. 69.

Information for a Libel on a Private Individual.

R. v. *Newman* ((1852) 1 E. & B. 268, 558 ; 22 L. J. Q. B. 156 ; 17 Jur. 617 ; 3 C. & K. 252 ; Dears. C. C. 85).

" In the Queen's Bench.

" Michaelmas Term, 15 Vict., A.D. 1851.

" Middlesex to wit.

" Be it remembered, that C. F. Robinson, Esq., coroner and attorney of our Lady the Queen in the Court of Queen's Bench, who prosecutes for our said Lady the Queen in this behalf, comes here into the said Court at Westminster, the 21st day of November, in the fifteenth year of the reign of our said Lady, and gives the Court to understand and be informed that John Henry Newman, Doctor of Divinity, late of the parish of Aston, in the county of Warwick, contriving and wickedly and maliciously intending to injure and vilify one Giovanni Giacinto Achilli, and to bring him into great contempt, scandal, infamy, and disgrace, on the 1st of October, A.D. 1851, did falsely and maliciously compose and publish a certain false, scandalous, malicious and defamatory libel, containing divers false, scandalous, malicious, and defamatory matters, concerning the said Giovanni Giacinto Achilli, that is to say :—
[*Here follows the libel, set out verbatim, with the necessary innuendoes*].
Which said false, scandalous, malicious, and defamatory libel, the said John Henry Newman did then publish to the great damage, scandal, and disgrace of the said Giovanni Giacinto Achilli, in contempt of our said Lady the Queen, to the evil and pernicious example of all others in like case offending and against the peace of our said Lady the Queen, her crown and dignity. Whereupon the said coroner and attorney of our said Lady the Queen, who for our said Lady the Queen in this behalf prosecuteth, prayeth the consideration of the Court here in the premises, and that due process of law may be awarded against the said John Henry Newman in this behalf to make him answer to our said Lady the Queen touching and concerning the premises aforesaid."

[See Crown Office Rules, 1906, Form, No. 30.]

For a precedent of an information for a libel on a body or class of persons, see *R.* v. *Gathercole*, (1838) 2 Lewin, C. C. pp. 238—253.

No. 70.

*Pleas to the above Information.**

" In the Queen's Bench.

" Michaelmas Term, 15 Vict., A.D. 1851.

" 1. And the said John Henry Newman appears here in Court by Henry Lewin, his attorney, and the said information is read to him, which being by him heard and understood, he complains to have been grievously vexed and molested under colour of the premises, and the less justly because he saith that he is Not Guilty of the said supposed offences in the said information alleged, &c.

" 2. And for a further plea, the said John Henry Newman saith that before the composing and publishing of the said alleged libel to wit, on the 1st of January, 1830, &c. :— [*Here follow facts showing the truth of the matters charged.*] And so the said John Henry Newman says that the said alleged libel consists of allegations true in substance and in fact, and of fair and reasonable comments thereon.†

" And the said John Henry Newman further saith, that at the time of publishing the said alleged libel, it was for the public benefit that the matters therein contained should be published, because, he says, that great excitement prevailed and numerous public discussions had been held in divers places in England on divers matters of controversy between the Churches of England and Rome, with respect to which it was important the truth should be known ; and inasmuch as the said G. G. Achilli took a prominent part in such discussions, and his opinion and testimony were by many persons appealed to and relied on as of a person of character and respectability, with reference to the matters in controversy, it was necessary for the purpose of more effectually examining and ascertaining the truth, that the matters in the said alleged libel should be publicly known, in order that it might more fully appear that the opinion and testimony of the said G. G. Achilli were not deserving of credit or consideration by reason of his previous misconduct :—[*Here follow other facts showing that it was for the public benefit that the said matters charged should be published.*] And so the said John Henry Newman says he published the said alleged libel as he lawfully might for the causes aforesaid, and this the said John Henry Newman is ready to verify. Wherefore he prays judgment, &c."

[See Crown Office Rules, 1906, Form, No. 81.]

* The pleas originally filed were demurred to, and amended ; the amended pleas were again demurred to, as being too general in their statements, and were then altered to the above form.

† As to the form of this plea, see *ante,* pp. 724, 725.

No. 71.

Replication.

"Hilary Term, 16 Vict., 1852.

"The said C. F. Robinson, Esq., coroner and attorney of our said Lady the Queen, in the Court of Queen's Bench, who prosecutes for our Lady the Queen as to the plea first pleaded, puts himself upon the country, and as to the plea secondly pleaded, saith that the said J. H. Newman of his own wrong and without the cause in his said plea alleged, composed, and published the said libel as in the said information alleged, &c."

Issue joined, Hilary Term, 16 Vict. 1852.

[See Crown Office Rules, 1906, Form, No. 83.]

No. 72.

Information ex officio *for a Seditious Libel.*

R. v. *John Horne*, clerk (afterwards *John Horne Tooke*) ((1777) Cowp. 672; 11 St. Tr. 264; 20 How. St. Tr. 651).

Michaelmas Term, 17 Geo. III., A.D. 1776.

"London, to wit.

"Be it remembered that Edward Thurlow, Esq., Attorney-General of our present sovereign Lord the King, who for our said present sovereign Lord the King prosecutes in this behalf, in his proper person comes into the Court of our said present sovereign Lord the King before the King himself, at Westminster in the county of Middlesex, on Thursday next after fifteen days from the day of St. Martin in this same term, and for our said Lord the King giveth the Court here to understand and be informed, that John Horne, late of London, clerk, being a wicked, malicious, seditious, and ill-disposed person, and being greatly disaffected to our said present sovereign Lord the King, and to his administration of the government of this kingdom, and the dominions thereunto belonging, and wickedly, maliciously, and seditiously intending, devising, and contriving to stir up and excite discontents and seditions among His Majesty's subjects, and to alienate and withdraw the affection, fidelity, and allegiance of His said Majesty's subjects from His said Majesty, and to insinuate and cause it to be believed that divers of His Majesty's innocent and deserving subjects had been inhumanly murdered by His said Majesty's troops in the province, colony, or plantation of the Massachusetts-Bay, in New England, in America, belonging to the crown of Great Britain, and unlawfully and wickedly to seduce and encourage His said Majesty's subjects in the said province, colony, or plantation, to resist and oppose His Majesty's government, on the 8th day of June, in the 15th year of the reign of our present sovereign Lord George the Third, &c., with force and arms at London aforesaid, in the parish of St. Mary-le-Bow, in the ward of Cheap, wickedly, maliciously, and seditiously, did write and publish, and cause and procure to be written and published, a certain false, wicked, malicious, scandalous and seditious libel, of and concerning His said Majesty's government, and the employment of his troops, according to the tenor and effect following: ' *King's Arms Tavern, Cornhill, June 7th,* 1775. At a special meeting this day of several members of the Constitutional Society, during an adjournment, a gentleman proposed, that a subscription should be immediately entered into (by such of the members present who might approve the purpose), for raising the sum of 100*l.*—to be applied to the relief of the widows, orphans, and aged parents of our beloved American fellow subjects, who, faithful to the character of Englishmen, preferring death to slavery, were, for that reason only, inhumanly murdered by the King's (meaning His said Majesty's) troops, at or near Lexington and Concord, in the province of Massachusetts (meaning the said province, colony, or plantation of the Massachusetts-Bay, in New England, in America) on the 19th of last April; which sum being immediately collected, it was thereupon resolved, that Mr. Horne (meaning himself the said John Horne) do pay to-morrow into the hands of Messieurs Brownes and Collison, on the account of Dr. Franklin, the said sum of 100*l.*, and that Dr. Franklin be requested to apply the same to the above-mentioned purpose,—John Horne ' (meaning himself the said John Horne), in contempt of our said Lord the King, in open violation of the laws of this kingdom, to the evil and pernicious example of all others in the like case offending, and also against the peace of our said present sovereign Lord the King, his crown and dignity. [*Then follow several counts for the several publications of the same libel in the various newspapers.*]

" And the said Attorney-General of our said Lord the King for our said Lord the King further gives the Court here to understand and be informed that the said John Horne, being such person as aforesaid, and again unlawfully, wickedly, maliciously, and seditiously intending, devising, and contriving as aforesaid, afterwards, to wit, on the 14th day of July, in the 15th year aforesaid, with force and arms at London aforesaid, in the parish and ward aforesaid, wickedly, maliciously and seditiously did write and publish, and cause and procure to be written and published, a certain false, wicked, malicious, scandalous, and seditious libel, of and concerning His said Majesty's government, and the employment of his troops, according to the tenor and effect following :—'I (meaning himself the said John Horne) think it proper to give the unknown contributor this notice that I (again meaning himself the said John Horne) did yesterday pay to Messieurs Brownes and Collison, on the account of Dr. Franklin, the sum of 50*l.* and that I (again meaning himself the said John Horne) will write to Dr. Franklin, requesting him to apply the same to the relief of the widows, orphans, and aged parents of our beloved American fellow subjects, who, faithful to the character of Englishmen, preferring death to slavery, were (for that reason only) inhumanly murdered by the King's (meaning His said Majesty's) troops, at or near Lexington and Concord, in the province of Massachusetts (meaning the said province, colony, or plantation of the Massachusetts-Bay in New England in America) on the 19th of April last,—John Horne' (again meaning himself the said John Horne) in contempt of our said Lord the King, in open violation of the laws of this kingdom, to the evil and pernicious example of all others in the like case offending, and also against the peace of our said present sovereign Lord the King, his crown, and dignity. [*Then follow other counts for other publications of the same libel.*] Whereupon the said Attorney-General of our said Lord the King, who for our said present sovereign Lord the King prosecutes in this behalf, prays the consideration of the Court here in the premises, and that due process of law may be awarded against him, the said John Horne, in this behalf, to make him answer to our said present sovereign Lord the King touching and concerning the said premises aforesaid, &c.

" E. Thurlow."

[See Crown Office Rules, 1906, Form, No. 31.]

No. 73.

Indictment for a Blasphemous Libel.

———, to wit.

The jurors for our Lord the King upon their oath present that A. B., being a wicked and evil-disposed person, and disregarding the laws and religion of the realm, and wickedly and profanely devising and intending to bring the Holy Scriptures and the Christian religion into disbelief and contempt among the people of this kingdom, on the —— day of ——, A.D. ——, unlawfully and wickedly did compose, print, and publish, and cause and procure to be composed, printed, and published, a certain scandalous, impious, blasphemous and profane libel, of and concerning the Holy Scriptures and the Christian religion, in one part of which said libel there were and are contained, amongst other things, certain scandalous, impious, blasphemous and profane matters and things, of and concerning the Holy Scriptures and the Christian religion, according to the tenor and effect following, that is to say :— [*Here set out the first blasphemous passage*], and in another part thereof there were and are contained, amongst other things, certain other scandalous, impious, blasphemous, and profane matters and things, of and concerning the said Holy Scriptures and the Christian religion, according to the tenor and effect following, that is to say :— [*Here set out other blasphemous passages*] : to the high displeasure of Almighty God, to the great scandal and reproach of the Christian religion, to the evil example of all others in the like case offending, and against the peace of our said Lord the King, his crown and dignity.

[See another Precedent in *R.* v. *Ramsey and Foote*, (1883) 1 C. & E. pp. 126—131.]

No. 74.

Indictment for Publishing and Selling an Obscene Picture.

——, to wit.

The jurors for our Lord the King upon their oath present that A. B., being a wicked and evil-disposed person, and unlawfully devising, contriving and intending to debauch and corrupt the morals of the young and of divers other liege subjects of our said Lord the King, on the —— day of ——, A.D. ——, in a certain open and public shop of him, the said A. B., situate and being at number —— High Street, in the parish of ——, in the town of ——, in the county aforesaid, unlawfully, wickedly, designedly, and maliciously did publish and sell, and cause and procure to be published and sold, to one C. D., a certain lewd, scandalous and obscene picture [print, photograph, *or* engraving], intituled —— and representing —— [*Here give such a detailed description of the picture as will manifestly show its indecency*], to the manifest corruption of the morals of the young, and of other liege subjects of our said Lord the King, in contempt of our said Lord the King and his laws, to the evil example of all others in the like case offending, and against the peace of our said Lord the King, his crown and dignity.

[See another Precedent, 1 Cox, C. C. 229; and also sect. 7 of the Law of Libel Amendment Act, 1888, *post*, p. 844.]

No. 75.

Indictment for Seditious Words.

——, to wit.

The jurors for our Lord the King upon their oath present that A. B., being a wicked, malicious, seditious, and evil-disposed person, and wickedly, maliciously, and seditiously contriving and intending the peace of our Lord the King and of this realm to disquiet and disturb, and the liege subjects of our said Lord the King to incite and move to hatred and dislike of the person of our said Lord the King and of the government established by law within this realm, and to incite, move, and persuade great numbers of the liege subjects of our said Lord the King, to insurrections, riots, tumults, and breaches of the peace, and to prevent by force and arms the execution of the laws of this realm and the preservation of the public peace, on the —— day of ——, A.D. ——, in the presence and hearing of divers, to wit, —— of the liege subjects of our said Lord the King then assembled together, in a certain speech and discourse by him the said A. B. then addressed to the said liege subjects so then assembled together, as aforesaid, unlawfully, wickedly, maliciously, and seditiously did publish, utter, pronounce, and declare with a loud voice of and concerning the government established by law within this realm, and of and concerning our said Lord the King, and the crown of this realm, and of and concerning the liege subjects of our said Lord the King, committing and being engaged in divers insurrections, riots, and breaches of the public peace, amongst other words and matter, the false, wicked, seditious and inflammatory words and matter following, that is to say :—[*Here set out the seditious words verbatim*] : in contempt of our said Lord the King in open violation of the laws of this realm, to the evil and pernicious example of all others in the like case offending, and against the peace of our said Lord the King, his crown and dignity.

No. 76.

Indictment for Defamatory Words spoken to a Magistrate in the execution of his Duty.

Middlesex, to wit.

The jurors for our Lord the King upon their oath, present, that heretofore, to wit, on the —— day of ——, in the year of our Lord ——, one A. B. was brought before C. D., Esquire, then and yet being one of the justices of our said Lord the King, assigned to keep the peace of our said Lord the King in and for the county of Middlesex, and also to hear and determine divers felonies, trespasses, and other misdeeds committed in the said county; and the said A. B. was then charged before the said C. D., upon the oath of one E. F., that he, the said A. B., had then lately before feloniously taken, stolen, and taken away divers goods and chattels of the said E. F. And the jurors aforesaid, upon their oath aforesaid, do further present, that the said A. B., being a scandalous and ill-disposed person, and wickedly and maliciously intending and contriving to scandalize and vilify the said C. D. as such justice as aforesaid, and to bring the administration of justice in this kingdom into contempt, afterwards, and whilst the said C. D., as such justice as aforesaid, was examining and taking the depositions of divers witnesses against him the said A. B., in that behalf, to wit, on the day and year aforesaid, wickedly and maliciously, in the presence and hearing of divers good and liege subjects of our said Lord the King, did publish, utter, pronounce, declare, and say with a loud voice to the said C. D., and whilst he the said C. D. was so acting as such justice as aforesaid, the false, wicked, malicious, and seditious words and matter following, that is to say :— [*Here set out the seditious words verbatim*]; to the great scandal and reproach of the administration of justice in this kingdom, to the great scandal and damage of the said C. D., in contempt of our said Lord the King and his laws, to the evil example of all others in the like case offending, and against the peace of our said Lord the King, his crown and dignity.

No. 77.

Indictment for a Libel on a Private Individual at Common Law.

——, to wit.

The jurors for our Lord the King, upon their oath, present that [before and at the time of the committing of the offence hereinafter mentioned, one C. D. was, and still is, a solicitor of the Supreme Court, and exercised and carried on the profession or business of such solicitor at ——, in the county of ——; and that] A. B. being a person of an evil and wicked mind, and wickedly, maliciously, and unlawfully contriving and intending to injure, vilify, and prejudice the said C. D., and to bring him into public contempt, scandal, infamy, and disgrace, and to deprive him of his good name, fame, credit, and reputation [in his said profession and business, and otherwise to injure and aggrieve him therein], on the —— day of ——, in the year of our Lord ——, wickedly, maliciously, and unlawfully did write and publish, and cause and procure to be written and published, [in the form of a letter directed to one E. F.,] of and concerning the said C. D. [and of and concerning him in his said profession and business, and of and concerning his conduct and behaviour therein], the false, scandalous, malicious, and defamatory words following, that is to say :— [*Here set out the libel verbatim, with all necessary innuendoes*], to the great damage, scandal, and disgrace of the said C. D. [in his said profession and business], to the evil example of all others in the like case offending, and against the peace of our said Lord the King, his crown and dignity.

[See another Precedent, 2 Cox, C. C. App. xxix.]

No. 78.

Indictment for a Libel on a Dead Man.

——, to wit.

The jurors for our Lord the King, upon their oath, present that before the committing of the offence hereinafter mentioned to wit, on the —— day of —— John Batchelor, of Penarth, in the county of Glamorgan, died, and that Thomas Henry Ensor, being a person of an evil and wicked mind, wickedly, maliciously and unlawfully designing and intending to injure and defame the character, reputation and memory of the said John Batchelor, and to vilify and to throw scandal upon his family and posterity, and to bring them into public contempt and infamy, and to stir up the hatred and ill-will of the subjects of our Lord the King against them, and to deprive them of their good name, fame, and reputation, and to provoke them to a breach of the peace, on the —— day of ——, wilfully, maliciously and unlawfully did write and

publish, and cause and procure to be printed and published*
of and concerning the said John Batchelor, his family and posterity,
the false, scandalous, malicious and defamatory words following,
that is to say :—" Suggested epitaph for the Batchelor statue "
[*Here copy the libel verbatim*], to the scandal and reproach of the
name and memory of the said John Batchelor, to the great damage
and disgrace of his family and posterity, to the evil example of all
others in the like case offending, and against the peace of our said
Lord the King, his crown and dignity.

* In the case of *R.* v. *Ensor,* (1887) 3 Times L. R. 366, four of the counts
ran thus :—" A false, scandalous, and defamatory libel, having a tendency
to cause a breach of the peace, and which on the 27th day of July, 1886,
did cause a certain breach of the peace, to wit, an assault by one Cyril
Batchelor and one Llewellyn Batchelor upon one Henry Lascelles Carr at
Cardiff, in the county of Glamorgan, in the form of a letter or newspaper
paragraph delivered and read by the said T. H. Ensor to John Henry
Taylor, James Harris, Henry Lascelles Carr, and divers other persons at
Cardiff aforesaid, according to the tenor and effect following, that is to
say." These words were inserted because in that case an assault had actually
followed the libel ; but they are not essential to an indictment for such
an offence. Where there has been no assault the defendant is still criminally
liable if there be other evidence of a criminal intent.

No. 79.

Indictment under Sect. 4 of Lord Campbell's Act.

[*Commence as in precedent No.* 77 ; *then set out the libel with all
necessary innuendoes, and conclude as follows*]:—he, the said A. B.,
then well knowing the said defamatory libel to be false; to the
great damage, scandal, and disgrace of the said C. D., to the evil
example of all others in the like case offending, against the form
of the statute in such case made and provided, and against the
peace of our Lord the King, his crown and dignity.

No. 80.

Indictment under Sect. 5 of Lord Campbell's Act.

[*This will precisely follow the preceding form, merely omitting the
words :*—" he, the said A. B., then well knowing the said defamatory
libel to be false."]

For a precedent of indictment for sending a threatening letter, see 1 Cox, C. C. App. xi.

No. 81.

Demurrer to an Indictment or Information.

And the said A. B., in his own proper person, cometh into Court here, and, having heard the said indictment [*or* information] read, saith, that the said indictment [*or* information] and the matters therein contained, in manner and form as the same are above stated and set forth, are not sufficient in law, and that he the said A. B. is not bound by the law of the land to answer the same ; and this he is ready to verify : wherefore, for want of a sufficient indictment [*or* information] in this behalf, the said A. B. prays judgment, and that by the Court he may be dismissed and discharged from the said premises in the said indictment [*or* information] specified.

[See Crown Office Rules, 1906, Form No. 80.]

No. 82.

Joinder in Demurrer.

And J. N., who prosecutes for our said Lord the King in this behalf, saith, that the said indictment [*or* information] and the matters therein contained, in manner and form as the same are above stated and set forth, are sufficient in law to compel the said A. B. to answer the same; and the said J. N., who prosecutes as aforesaid, is ready to verify and prove the same, as the Court here shall direct and award : wherefore, inasmuch as the said A. B. hath not answered to the said indictment [*or* information], nor hitherto in any manner denied the same, the said J. N., for our said Lord the King, prays judgment, and that the said A. B. may be convicted of the premises in the said indictment [*or* information] specified.

No. 83.

Pleas to an Indictment.

R. *v.* NIBLETT.

" At the assizes and general delivery of the Queen's gaol for the county of Berkshire, holden in and for the said county on the fourth day of May in the year of our Lord 1886, cometh into Court the said E. N., in her own proper person, and having heard the said indictment read, saith she is not guilty of the said premises in the said indictment above specified and charged upon her, and of this she the said E. N. puts herself upon the country, &c.

" And for a further plea in this behalf, the said E. N. says that our Lady the Queen ought not further to prosecute the said indictment against her, because she says that it is true that the Reverend A. B. is the man who slept at her house on the fourth day of June last with the said X. Y. [*and so on, stating facts showing the truth of every matter charged in the alleged libel*] ; and so the said E. N. says that the said alleged libel is true in substance and in fact. And the said E. N. further saith that before and at the time of publishing the said alleged libel, it was for the public benefit that the matters contained therein should be published to the extent that they were published by her, because the Reverend A. B. then was and still is a clergyman of the Church of England, in charge of the parish of ——, in the said county, and the said X. Y. had been a servant of the said Reverend A. B. in the said parish, and because it was notorious in the said parish that the said X. Y. was a woman of immoral character, and because scandal and evil report existed in the said parish to the effect that she had had improper connection with the said Reverend A. B. whilst she was in his service, and also that he had since cohabited with her at —— in the county of Middlesex, where she passed under the name of Mrs. B., and at other places and under other names to such parishioners unknown, and because these reports created great scandal to the church, and greatly disquieted the parishioners of the said parish, and because it was of the greatest consequence to such parishioners to know whether these reports were true or false, and to obtain evidence which might be laid before the bishop of the diocese in which such parish was situated, in order that proceedings might be taken to inquire into the truth or falsity of such reports : wherefore the said E. N. being aware of the premises and being herself a member of the said Church of England, and believing it to be her duty to acquaint the said parishioners with the facts above mentioned as to the conduct of the said Reverend A. B., such facts being within her own knowledge, published the said alleged libel to the churchwarden of the said parish, and to the parish clerk, and to six of the parishioners of the said parish, all of whom were churchmen and interested therein, in order that the said alleged libel, or a copy thereof, should be forwarded to the said bishop, and a copy thereof was forwarded to the said bishop, who thereupon at once began to inquire into the truth or falsity of the said report; and the said E. N. in no way published the said alleged libel save to the said bishop, churchwarden, parish clerk, and parishioners aforesaid. Wherefore the said E. N. says it was for the public benefit that the matters charged in the said alleged libel, and all and every of them, should be so published by her as aforesaid. And this she is ready to verify, wherefore she prays judgment, and that by the Court here she may be dismissed and discharged from the said premises in the said indictment above specified."

[See another precedent, 2 Cox, C. C. App. xxxii.; and Crown Office Rules, 1906, Form No. 81.]

For a plea in abatement to an indictment for libel, see *R.* v. *Gavan Duffy*, 1 Cox, C. C. 282, and *R.* v. *J. Mitchell*, 11 L. T. (Old S.) 112.

For a plea in abatement on the ground that other proceedings for the same libel were still pending, see *R.* v. *J. Mitchell*, (1848) 3 Cox, C. C. 94, 106; with demurrer thereto and joinder in demurrer (*ib.* 96), and replication (*ib.* 107).

For a plea to the jurisdiction of the Court in a criminal case of libel, and a demurrer thereto, see *R.* v. *Hon. Robert Johnson*, (1805) 6 East, 583; 2 Smith, 591; 29 How. St. Tr. 103.

No. 84.

Replication to the above Pleas.

And thereupon J. N. [*the clerk of arraigns, &c.*] who prosecutes for our said Lady the Queen in this behalf, as to the plea of the said E. N. by her firstly above pleaded, and whereof the said E. N. hath put herself upon the country, doth the like, &c. And as to the plea of the said E. N. by her secondly above pleaded, the said J. N., who prosecutes as aforesaid, says that our said Lady the Queen ought not by reason of anything in the said second plea alleged to be barred or precluded from prosecuting the said indictment against the said E. N., because he says that he denies the said several matters in the said second plea alleged, and saith that the same are not, nor are nor is any or either of them, true; but that the said E. N. of her own wrong, and without the cause and matter of defence in her said second plea alleged and set forth, committed the offence and published the said libel in manner and form as in the said indictment is mentioned. And this he, the said J. N., prays may be inquired of by the country, &c. And the said A. B. doth the like.

[See another Precedent 2 Cox, C. C., App. xxxiv., and Crown Office Rules, 1906, Form No. 83.]

No. 85.

Demurrer to a Plea.

And J. N., who prosecutes for our said Lady the Queen in this behalf, as to the said plea of the said E. N. by her above pleaded, saith that the same, and the matters therein contained, in manner and form as the same are above pleaded and set forth, are not sufficient in law to bar or preclude our said Lady the Queen from prosecuting the said indictment against her the said E. N., and that our said Lady the Queen is not bound by the law of the land to answer the same; and this he, the said J. N., who prosecutes as aforesaid, is ready to verify: wherefore, for want of a sufficient plea in this behalf, he the said J. N. for our said Lady the Queen, prays judgment, and that the said E. N. may be convicted of the premises in the said indictment specified.

[See Crown Office Rules, 1906, Form No. 84.]

No. 86.

Joinder in Demurrer.

And the said E. N. saith, that her said plea, by her above pleaded, and the matters therein contained, in manner and form as the same are above pleaded and set forth, are sufficient in law to bar and preclude our said Lady the Queen from prosecuting the said indictment against her the said E. N., and the said E. N. is ready to verify and prove the same, as the said Court here shall direct and award: wherefore, inasmuch as the said J. N., for our said Lady the Queen, hath not answered the said plea, nor hitherto in any manner denied the same, the said E. N. prays judgment, and that by the Court here she may be dismissed and discharged from the said premises in the said indictment specified.

[See Crown Office Rules, 1906, Form No. 85.]

No. 87.

Election Petition under the Corrupt and Illegal Practices Prevention Act, 1895.

In the High Court of Justice.
King's Bench Division.

The Parliamentary Elections Act, 1868,
and
The Corrupt and Illegal Practices Prevention Acts, 1883 and 1895.

Election for the Borough of S——, holden on July 15th, 1904.
The Petition of A., of——, whose name is subscribed.

1. Your petitioner is a person who was a candidate at the above election.

2. The said election was holden on July 15th, 1904, when B., C., and your petitioner were candidates; and the returning officer has returned the said B. and C. as being duly elected.

3. And your petitioner says that during the said election the said B. by himself and his election agent and by other persons on his behalf made and published false statements of fact in relation to the personal character and conduct of your petitioner for the purpose of affecting the return of your petitioner at the said election.

[Here insert particulars.]

4. And as to such of the said illegal practices as were committed by an agent of the said B. other than his election agent, your petitioner further says that B. or his election agent authorised or consented to the committing thereof by such other agent, or paid for circulation of the false statement constituting such illegal practice, and that the election of the said B. was procured or materially assisted in consequence of the making and publishing of such false statements.

[Here insert particulars.]

5. By reason of the matters hereinbefore set out the said B. was and is incapacitated from serving in the present Parliament for the said Borough of S——, and the said election and return of the said B. were and are wholly null and void.

Wherefore your petitioner prays that it may be determined that the said B. was not duly elected or returned, and that his election and return were and are wholly null and void.

Dated the 2nd day of September, 1904.

(Signed)   A.

APPENDIX B.

———◆———

LEGISLATION AS TO LIBELS IN NEWSPAPERS, &c.

SINCE the first edition of this book appeared, two important statutes have been passed modifying the law of libel in some material particulars, especially with regard to libels published in newspapers. In this Appendix, we propose to trace the history of this legislation, showing the causes which led to the introduction of the measures, and the extent to which the grievances complained of have been thereby remedied.

In former days, newspaper proprietors had undoubtedly good reason to complain of the severity of the common law. The contents of a newspaper largely consist of reports of the proceedings of public meetings, or of meetings of various public bodies, such as town councils, vestries, boards of guardians and others. To reports of such meetings no privilege attached at common law. Reports of judicial or parliamentary proceedings were alone privileged. (*Davison* v. *Duncan*, (1857) 7 E. & B. 229; 26 L. J. Q. B. 104; *Popham* v. *Pickburn*, (1862) 7 H. & N. 891; 31 L. J. Ex. 133.) Hence, if a report containing any defamatory statement of fact was printed in a newspaper, the proprietor had no defence to an action for damages, unless he could prove the statement to be literally true. In the absence of any privilege, the fact that the report was fair and accurate would not avail him.

In such an action the defendant no doubt could always give evidence to show that the report was correct, that the speaker had in fact uttered the words attributed to him in the paper. But such evidence only went in mitigation of damages; it was no defence to the action. On the other hand, the counsel for the plaintiff would not fail to impress upon the jury that it was the republication of the defamatory words in the newspaper which had really injured the reputation of the plaintiff. In one case of this kind the late Baron Huddleston in summing-up to the jury quoted with approval the following passage from page 382 of the 2nd edition of this work: "The consequence of publishing in the papers calumnies uttered at some political or parish meeting may be most injurious to the person calumniated. The original slander may not be actionable *per se*, or the communication may be privileged, so that no action lies against the speaker; moreover, the meeting may have been thinly attended, and the audience may have known that the speaker was not worthy of credit. But it would be a terrible thing for the person defamed if such words could therefore be printed and published to all the world and remain in a permanent form recorded against him, without any remedy being permitted him for the injury caused by their extended circulation." (*Kelly* v. *O'Malley and others*, (1889) 6 Times L. R. at p. 64; and see *ante*, pp. 330, 375.)

This being the state of the law, public attention was forcibly called to the matter by the case of *Purcell* v. *Sowler*, which was decided in the Court of Appeal in February, 1877. There the defendant was the proprietor of the *Manchester Courier*, and he had published a report, which was admitted to be accurate, of the proceedings at a meeting of the board of guardians for the Altrincham Poor Law Union. At that meeting serious charges were made against the plaintiff, who was the medical officer of the union workhouse at Knutsford, of neglecting his duties, and refusing to attend pauper patients who needed his services. These charges proved to be utterly unfounded, and they were made in the absence of the plaintiff, and without any notice having been given him. Mr. Sowler's defence was that the matter was one of public interest, and that it was his duty to report what had actually occurred at that meeting for the information of the ratepayers. The jury, however, found a verdict for the plaintiff for forty shillings, which carried costs. Mr. Sowler appealed to the Divisional Court, but they upheld the verdict on the ground that the matter was not one of public interest at all. (See (1876) 1 C. P. D. 781.) Mr. Sowler appealed to the Court of Appeal, which differed from the Divisional Court on this point, and held that the administration of the poor law and the treatment of the paupers, in each union district, was clearly a matter of public interest in that locality. But the Court of Appeal held that as the plaintiff was absent, and had had no notice of the charges made against him, the board of guardians ought not to have discussed the matter at that meeting, or at all events not while reporters were present in the room; and that, though reporters had been permitted to remain during the discussion, still the editor when reading over the report ought to have exercised his discretion, and struck this portion out of the report; for it was obviously unfair to the plaintiff that such *ex parte* statements should be published in the local papers; and so the verdict was again upheld. ((1877) 2 C. P. D. 215.)

This case created considerable consternation in the newspaper world; and to it we mainly owe the Newspaper Libel Act of 1881. Here was a report, which was admitted to be accurate, of a discussion that had taken place on a matter of public interest at a meeting of a public body, and yet the proprietor of the newspaper must pay damages because the editor had not cut out certain passages which in the opinion of the Court should not have been published. Proprietors of newspapers always contend, as Mr. Sowler did in this very case, that in the hurry of setting up the type for a daily paper it is practically impossible for the editor to read through the copy and weigh each word it contains; that he cannot be expected to edit the report of a public meeting and cut out passages which relate to matters of public interest, so as to make the report incomplete; that so long as the meeting is one that ought to be reported, and the report printed is fairly accurate, nothing more can be required. But this is a view which the Legislature and the law courts have, so far, steadily refused to adopt; and the editor of a paper must edit the whole paper or his employers must take the consequences.

The public had their grievance too. There were formerly in force many statutes which facilitated the proof of the publication of any libel contained in a newspaper, and enabled the person libelled readily to discover the name and address of the person liable to him therefor. Such were the 10 Anne, c. 19; the 38 Geo. III. cc. 71 and 78; the 6 & 7 Will. IV. c. 76, &c. But these were all repealed: the last of them in 1870 by the 33 & 34 Vict. c. 99. And an instance occurred in which a father and two sons owned a paper in turns, and whichever one was sued was always able to prove that he had ceased to be owner and had transferred the paper to one of the others just before the libel in question had appeared; so that he was not liable. There was no objection on the part of the Press as a body to a simple method of registration such as the public required, to prevent such a subterfuge.

Accordingly, in 1879, Mr. Hutchinson moved for the appointment of a Select Committee of the House of Commons to inquire into the law of newspaper libel. The Committee was appointed, but had not time to report before the close of the session. It consisted of the then Attorney-General (Sir John Holker), Sir Henry James, Mr. Courtney, Mr. Staveley Hill, Mr. Alexander Sullivan, Baron

Henry de Worms, Mr. Edward Leatham, Mr. Gregory, Mr. Blenner-
hassett, Mr. Floyer, Dr. Cameron, Mr. Richard Paget, Mr. Errington,
Mr. Master, and Mr. Hutchinson.   They were reappointed in 1880,
and reported as follows on July 14, 1880 :—

"Your Committee have not thought it necessary to call witnesses upon
the matters referred to them. They have had the advantage of the evidence
taken by the Select Committee of 1879, who, owing to the short time at their
disposal, were unable to report, and your Committee are of opinion that,
through the labours of the former Committee, sufficient information has
been accumulated for the purposes of their inquiry.

"Your Committee have confined themselves to an examination of the
state of the law affecting civil actions and criminal prosecutions for newspaper libel, and to the changes which, in their judgment, should be made
therein.

"It appears to your Committee that one of the most important points
of the subject referred to them is the question of extension of privilege to
newspaper reports of the proceedings of public meetings.

"Your Committee, after careful consideration, have come to the conclusion that the balance of convenience requires that further protection
should be given to such reports.

"Your Committee accordingly recommend that any report published in
any newspaper of the proceedings of a public meeting should be privileged,
if such meeting was lawfully convened for a lawful purpose, and was open
to the public, and if such report was fair and accurate, and published
without malice, and if the publication of the matter complained of was
for the public benefit. But your Committee are of opinion that such protection should not be available as a defence in any proceeding if the plaintiff
or prosecutor can show that the defendant has refused to insert a reasonable letter, or statement of explanation or contradiction by or on behalf
of such plaintiff or prosecutor.

"Your Committee recommend that no criminal prosecution shall be commenced against the proprietor, publisher, editor, or anyone responsible for
the publication of a newspaper, for any libel published therein, without
the *fiat* of the Attorney-General being first obtained.

"Your Committee are also of opinion that the name of every proprietor
of a newspaper, or in the case of several persons engaged as partners in
such proprietorship, the names of all such persons should be registered at
the office of the Registrar of Joint Stock Companies, with full particulars
of the addresses and occupation of all such persons, or of any change
therein."

In the following year (1881) a Bill was accordingly introduced
embodying the recommendations contained in the above report: it
passed hurriedly through both Houses, without any adequate discussion in either ; it received the Royal Assent on August 27th,
1881, and so became the Newspaper Libel and Registration Act,
1881, which is printed in full in the next Appendix, pp. 835—842.

Baron Pollock has described this Act as " a sort of settlement between the public on the one hand and newspaper proprietors on the other. On the one hand, proprietors of newspapers are to be registered; and on the other hand, they are protected by the Act from what the Legislature deemed to be not necessarily trivial, but improper or unnecessary prosecutions for libel." (*Ex parte Hubert, Hurter & Son,* (1883) 47 J. P. 724; 15 Cox, C. C. 166.) We think, however, the public got the best of the bargain. The public obtained a very valuable system of registration, by which anyone can find out for a shilling who is responsible to him for any libel that has been printed in a paper. There are two defects, however, in the system at present. One is that when a newspaper changes hands, there is no provision compelling the transferee to register himself as proprietor till the following July; the other, that where a newspaper is published by a limited company the Act does not apply, and there is no entry at Somerset House to assist the person libelled. (See note to sections 11 and 18, *post,* pp. 840, 842.) On the other hand, the newspaper proprietors procured some valuable amendments of the criminal law in their favour, and overruled the case of *R.* v. *Sir Robert Carden,* (1879) 5 Q. B. D. 1; but they signally failed to attain their chief object. The law relating to reports of public meetings remained practically unaltered. It is true that by sect. 2 of the Act such reports were declared privileged; but this privilege was very cautiously guarded by all manner of limitations. Still, it was something to have secured an admission of the principle that such reports under proper restrictions are privileged; it has proved to be "the thin end of the wedge," and some restrictions have already been removed. The section ran as follows: "Any report published in any newspaper of the proceedings of a public meeting shall be privileged, if such meeting was lawfully convened for a lawful purpose and open to the public, and if such report was fair and accurate, and published without malice, and if the publication of the matter complained of was for the public benefit; provided always that the protection intended to be afforded by this section shall not be available as a defence in any proceeding, if the plaintiff or prosecutor can show that the defendant had refused to insert, in the newspaper in which the report containing the matter complained of appeared, a reasonable letter or statement of explanation or contradiction by or on behalf of such plaintiff or prosecutor."

Hence, in order to bring himself within the protection afforded by this enactment, the defendant had to prove—

(i.) That the meeting was a public meeting,

(ii.) Lawfully convened

(iii.) For a lawful purpose,

(iv.) And open to the public ;

 (v.) That the report was fair and accurate

(vi.) And published without malice,

(vii.) And that the publication of the matter complained of was for the public benefit ;

(viii.) And, after proving all these facts, the defendant lost his privilege, if the plaintiff or prosecutor could show that the defendant had refused, when asked, to insert a reasonable letter of explanation or contradiction.

It was the seventh proviso, that the publication of the matter complained of must be for the public benefit, which rendered this provision practically nugatory. It was not enough for the defendant to prove that the meeting was of such a kind that its proceedings ought to be reported ; the defendant had to satisfy the jury that it was for the public benefit that the libellous words complained of should have appeared in that report. If the jury thought that the report would have been as beneficial to the public without the libellous words as with them, all privilege was lost. The *Manchester Courier* was again to the fore. It reported a speech made at a public election meeting held at Manchester in October, 1885, in the course of which a speaker made a most serious charge against a Manchester gentleman who was then a candidate, *not* for any division of Manchester, but for a constituency 200 miles away. The editor, in spite of the decision in *Purcell* v. *Sowler*, allowed a full report of this speech to appear the next morning, though the gentleman libelled was not present at the meeting, and had had no notice of the attack that was going to be made upon him. The Court held, on December 11th, 1886, that the defendant could claim no privilege, unless the jury found as a fact that it was for the public benefit that the actual libel complained of should be published broadcast. (*Pankhurst* v. *Sowler*, (1886) 3 Times L. R. 193.)

This decision gave great dissatisfaction to the Press ; for it again asserted the principle that it was absolutely necessary for the editor to edit a report of a public meeting just as he would a letter from a private correspondent. It made it clear that the editor must not rely on the known accuracy of his reporter ; he must read through the report and exercise his discretion as before. For it clearly is not for the public benefit that every word uttered at every public meeting should be printed and widely disseminated. For instance, if anything seditious, blasphemous or obscene be uttered there, that must be omitted from the report. Similarly, if anything defamatory be said of a private citizen, not a public man, the passage must be excised from the report before publication. So, too, if an unfair attack be made on a public man. And the editor must decide for himself, before going to press, whether any such attack is fair or unfair.

This, no doubt, imposes on the editor an arduous task, and subjects the proprietor of the paper to serious risk. So Mr. Sowler and his friends again approached the Legislature. On February 10th, 1888, Sir Algernon Borthwick, the Chairman of the Newspaper Press Fund (later Lord Glenesk), brought in a Bill in the House of Commons, which was backed by Sir Albert Rollit, Mr. Lawson, Mr. Jennings, Dr. Cameron, Mr. John Morley, and Mr. E. Dwyer W. Gray. This Bill was very thoroughly discussed in both Houses of Parliament, and also in the columns of the *Times*, and very important amendments and additions were made; till in the end it became a Bill materially different from that introduced by its promoters; still it is a valuable and workable measure. In the form in which it ultimately became law, it will be found in the next Appendix (pp. 843—845). It will, we think, be convenient to set out here the Bill as originally introduced :—

A BILL TO AMEND THE LAW OF LIBEL.

Whereas it is expedient to amend the law of libel :

Be it therefore enacted by the Queen's most Excellent Majesty, by and with the advice and consent of the Lords Spiritual and Temporal, and Commons, in this present parliament assembled, and by the authority of the same, as follows :

1. In the construction of this Act the word "newspaper" shall have the same meaning as in the Newspaper Libel and Registration Act, 1881.

2. Section two of the Newspaper Libel and Registration Act, 1881, is hereby repealed.

3. A fair and accurate report published in any newspaper of proceedings of and in any Court exercising judicial authority shall be absolutely privileged.

4. A fair and accurate report published in any newspaper of the proceedings of a public meeting, or of any meeting of a vestry, town council, school board, board of guardians, board or local authority formed or constituted under the provisions of the Public Health Act, 1875, or of any Act amending the same, or of any committee appointed by any of the abovementioned bodies, or of any meeting of any commissioners authorised to act by letters patent, Act of Parliament, warrant under the Royal Sign Manual, or other lawful warrant or authority, select committees of either House of Parliament, justices of the peace in quarter sessions assembled

for administrative or deliberative purposes, or of any other duly and legally constituted body of persons acting in a public capacity and for public purposes, and the publication by any newspaper of any notice or report issued for the information of the public by or by order of any Government office or department, officer of state, commissioner of police or chief constable, or by any of the bodies or authorities hereinbefore mentioned, or of any other matter of public interest which is a fair subject of newspaper report, shall be privileged, unless it shall be proved by the plaintiff or prosecutor, as the case may be, that such report or publication was published or made with actual malice. Provided always, that the protection intended to be afforded by this section shall not be available as a defence in any proceedings if the plaintiff or prosecutor can show that the defendant has been requested by such plaintiff or prosecutor, or by some other person acting on his behalf or by his authority, to insert in the newspaper in which the report or other publication complained of appeared a reasonable letter or statement by way of contradiction or explanation of such report or other publication, and has refused or neglected to insert the same : Provided, further, that nothing in this section contained shall be deemed or construed to limit or abridge any privilege now by law existing.

5. In an action for a libel contained in any newspaper it shall be lawful for the defendant to raise by his defence a plea under the second section of the Act of the session of the six and seventh years of the reign of her present Majesty, chapter ninety-six, intituled "An Act to amend the Law respecting Defamatory Words and Libel," without making any payment into Court, and where such a plea has been raised (either with or without payment into Court), if it shall appear at the trial that such libel was published without actual malice and without gross negligence, and that the defendant has inserted an apology, as by the said Act provided, the plaintiff shall not be entitled to recover any damages except such special damages as he can prove that he has sustained by the publication of such libel.

Section two of the Act of the session of the eighth and ninth years of the reign of her present Majesty, chapter seventy-five, intituled "An Act to amend an Act passed in the Session of Parliament held in the sixth and seventh years of the reign of her present Majesty, intituled 'An Act to amend the Laws respecting Defamatory Words and Libel,'" is hereby repealed.

6. At the trial of an action for a libel contained in any newspaper, the defendant shall be at liberty to give in evidence, in mitigation of damages, that the plaintiff has already recovered (or has brought actions for) damages or has received or agreed to receive compensation in respect of a libel or libels to the same purport or effect as the libel for which such action has been brought.

7. In any action for libel, if the defendant can show by affidavit or other evidence to the satisfaction of a judge of the division of the High Court of Justice in which such action is brought, that the plaintiff has been adjudicated bankrupt, or has no visible means of paying the costs of the defendant should not a verdict be found for the plaintiff, the judge, unless just cause to the contrary be shown, shall make an order that the plaintiff shall, within a time therein mentioned, give full security for the defendant's costs to the satisfaction of one of the masters of such Court, and

that until such security be given all proceedings in the action shall be stayed.

8. No person shall be found guilty upon the trial of any indictment or information for the publication of a libel unless it be proved by affirmative evidence on behalf of the prosecution that such person was party or privy to the publication of the libel charged in such indictment or information.

9. Every person charged with the offence of libel before any Court of criminal jurisdiction, and the husband or wife of the person so charged, shall be competent, but not compellable, witnesses on every hearing at every stage of such charge.

10. This Act shall not apply to Scotland.

11. This Act may be cited as "The Law of Libel Amendment Act, 1888."

If this Bill be compared with the Act (*post*, p. 843), it will be seen at once that three clauses contained in it never became law.

Clause 5 was thrown out on the third reading in the House of Commons, and Lord Campbell's Act thus remains law. It could hardly be supposed that the House would consent in any case to limit the damages which a jury might award to such special damage as the plaintiff could prove. It is very difficult to prove special damage, even where it is clear that the plaintiff's reputation has been seriously impaired. A married woman, as a rule, cannot suffer any special damage, unless she is employed in some situation. A gentleman of independent means can very rarely sustain any special damage in the legal meaning of that term. Hence the clause was rightly rejected.

Clause 7, enabling the defendant in certain cases to obtain security for costs from a plaintiff, was thrown out in Committee; it introduced a new and dangerous precedent; and the necessity of the case was already met by section 10 of the County Courts Act of 1867, which has now been re-enacted by section 66 of the County Courts Act of 1888.

Clause 8 passed the House of Commons, after considerable amendment, and reached the House of Lords in the following form : " No person shall be found guilty upon the trial of any indictment or information for the publication of a libel, if it be proved on behalf of the defence that such person was not party or privy to the publication of the libel charged in such indictment or information, and that the said publication did not arise from want of due care or caution on his part." In Committee in the House of Lords this clause was withdrawn by Lord Monkswell, who had charge of the Bill, in deference to the late Lord Coleridge, who pointed out that the section, as amended, closely resembled section 7 of Lord Campbell's Act, and that it was undesirable to have two provisions to the same effect expressed in different words in two different statutes.

On the other hand, the Act contains three sections which were not in the original Bill.

The present section 5, which allows actions against different defendants for the same libel to be consolidated, was inserted in the House of Commons. There had recently been two cases in which an error made by one newspaper was copied into many others, and the plaintiff sued each paper separately and recovered large amounts; thus making a living out of the injury to his reputation. (See *Tucker* v. *Lawson*, (1886) 2 Times L. R. 593; and *Colledge* v. *Pike*, (1886) 56 L. T. 124; 3 Times L. R. 126.) In the latter case, the Court held that as the publications were distinct, and the liabilities of the various defendants different, the actions could not be consolidated. (See *ante*, p. 619.) Hence the necessity for this section.

Section 7 deals with prosecutions for obscene libels. It dispenses with the necessity for setting out the obscene passages *verbatim* in the indictment. This section was introduced and carried by Mr. Samuel Smith on the third reading of the Bill in the House of Commons. It overrules the decision in *Bradlaugh and Besant* v. *The Queen*, (1878) 3 Q. B. D. 607; 48 L. J. M. C. 5; 26 W. R. 410; 38 L. T. 118; 14 Cox, C. C. 68. It is unfortunate that this beneficial provision was not extended so as to apply to blasphemous as well as to obscene libels.

Section 8, which substitutes the order of a judge at chambers for the *fiat* of the Public Prosecutor required by section 3 of the Act of 1881, was introduced in the House of Lords by the late Lord Coleridge, L.C.J. It is found in practice more difficult to obtain an order from a judge at chambers under this section than it was in former days to obtain the *fiat* of the Public Prosecutor; a result which Lord Coleridge probably contemplated. There is, however, one curious result from this provision. If criminal proceedings be taken for a libel contained in a newspaper, the case must now be gone into *four* times—once, by the judge at chambers; next, before the magistrate, where evidence on both sides will probably be taken (see sections 4 and 6 of the Act of 1881); then before the grand jury; and, lastly, in open Court, before the petty jury. Would it not have been simpler and better to have abolished the remedy by indictment altogether, leaving the person defamed his civil remedy only, except in those cases where the libel is of so serious a character as to call for a criminal information?

The Bill, as we have already said, was carefully and thoroughly discussed in both Houses. One of the earliest amendments made in the Commons was the omission of the word "absolutely" in section 3. Reports of judicial proceedings are privileged at common law; but such privilege is destroyed by proof of actual malice. If, for instance, one of the parties to the action or his solicitor sent such report to the papers, the party or his solicitor (*not* the newspaper) would be liable to pay damages, if the jury thought this was done maliciously. (*Stevens* v. *Sampson*, (1879) 5 Ex. D. 53.) So again, if a newspaper published every day during an election a fair and accurate report of a trial that had taken place, say ten years ago, in which one of the candidates cut a disgraceful figure, here, too, it would be open to the jury to find malice, and in that case the proprietor would have to pay damages. But it is very seldom that the proprietor or editor of any newspaper acts maliciously, and when he does, it is right that he should pay damages to the person whom he has defamed. Hence there was no sufficient reason for creating any absolute privilege. But the battle raged chiefly over section 4, which relates to reports of public meetings.

In the House of Commons some of the safeguards formerly provided by the Act of 1881 were again inserted in this clause, *e.g.*, that the meeting must be "lawfully convened and held for a lawful purpose." How the editor reading the report of a meeting is to know who convened it and whether they convened it lawfully, we do not know! Again, the Committee of the Commons added a proviso that nothing in the section should "protect the publication of any matter not of public interest and the publication of which is not for the public benefit," thus restoring the law as laid down in the cases of *Purcell* v. *Sowler* and *Pankhurst* v. *Sowler*, cited above. But the Lords abridged the proviso, omitting the words "lawfully convened," and introduced a new phrase into the law of libel, "any matter of public concern," instead of the time-honoured phrase, "a matter of public interest." When the Bill returned to the Commons, Mr. Kelly succeeded in adding the words, "and the publication of which is not for the public benefit," after the words "of public concern." A point of law has been raised as to the exact meaning of this proviso: some lawyers contending that the "and" must be taken to mean "or." But the section as it stands is clear and sensible, and affords a satisfactory solution of the difficulty which it was framed to meet. It is unquestionably an extension of the privileges afforded by the former Act. It removes the doubts attendant on the phrase "a public meeting and open to the public;"

it embraces the publication of police notices and other official announcements; but it still leaves it the duty of the editor to edit all reports of public meetings and excise all matter that is "not of public concern and the publication of which is not for the public benefit." And he must remember that while there are many matters which concern the public in which they take no interest, they take great interest in many other matters with which they have no concern.

On the third reading of the Bill in the House of Lords, the Marquis of Waterford proposed and carried a provision which might have been of great practical importance, providing that the man who utters defamatory words at a public meeting which are consequently reported in a newspaper, shall be held answerable for their publication in the paper, just as though he had directed the reporter so to print and publish them. The clause as introduced by the noble Marquis was as follows: "Where any person makes a speech to a meeting, and a report containing libellous words, purporting to be a report of such speech, is published in any newspaper, then on proof that the words so published, or words of like import, were uttered by the person making such speech, that person shall, in the event of any civil proceedings being instituted against him for libel in respect of such words, be deemed for the purposes of such proceedings to have himself written and published the libellous words attributed to him in such report, or words of like import. The report so published shall be *primâ facie* evidence of the words therein attributed to the speaker having been spoken, but it shall be competent to him to prove any inaccuracy in the report of any matter explaining the words attributed to him. Such proceedings, if taken, shall be in substitution for, and not in addition to, any proceedings, whether civil or criminal, that may be instituted against him." The Marquis of Salisbury moved to insert the following proviso: "Provided also, that no proceeding under the section shall be taken more than two months after the words were uttered," which was agreed to; and Lord Monkswell then moved the following addition: "Provided also that the speaker shall be entitled to any defence of privilege arising from the occasion on which the words were spoken which he would have had in case the spoken words had been of themselves actionable," which was also carried. But in the end the House of Commons (which contains so many speakers whose words are always reported) rejected the whole section. It was no doubt intended as a corollary to section 4, which renders the newspaper report privileged in certain circumstances.

It is right that the speaker who first utters the words complained of should be held responsible for all damages which are the natural and probable consequences of his act; but we think the section should have been limited to cases where the speaker either knew or ought to have known that reporters were present, and would take down his words.

Four clauses of the Bill passed through both Houses without any amendment—the two formal sections 1 and 2, and sections 6 and 9, which are both of obvious value. Section 9 allows the defendant and his wife to give evidence in prosecutions for libel. Section 6 enables the defendant to prove at the trial of a civil action that the plaintiff has already recovered damages or brought actions for substantially the same libel—a fact which always tends to mitigate the damages. Under the law as it previously existed, the defendant could cross-examine the plaintiff if he went into the box about other actions; but he was bound by plaintiff's answer, and could not call any evidence to contradict it, as such evidence would have been irrelevant to any issue in the case. For the same reason interrogatories as to such other actions were disallowed in *Tucker* v. *Lawson*, (1886) 2 Times L. R. 593. But that decision is now no longer law, so far as newspapers are concerned. It is, in our opinion, a great pity that the beneficial provisions of section 6 should be limited to libels contained in a newspaper. Precisely the same considerations apply to booksellers and circulating libraries, and they ought to be protected in the same way. Instances have occurred in which a plaintiff has recovered heavy damages, first from the publishers of a book, then from Messrs. Mudie and Messrs. Smith & Son, and has then proceeded to attack various small booksellers up and down the country, who had sold some two or three copies in the ordinary way of their business without the least suspicion that the book contained a word libelling any one. We should like to see the words "contained in a newspaper" struck out of this section; so that, like sections 5 and 9, it might apply to all libels.

But, in spite of the trifling defects which we have thus ventured to point out, there is no doubt that the Law of Libel Amendment Act, 1888, is a useful and practical measure, for which its framer, the late Lord Glenesk, earned the thanks of all journalists.

APPENDIX C.

STATUTES.

Contents.

1.

MR. FOX'S LIBEL ACT.*

32 Geo. III. c. 60.

An Act to remove Doubts respecting the Functions of Juries in Cases of Libel. [A. D. 1792]

WHEREAS doubts have arisen whether on the trial of an indictment or information for the making or publishing any libel, where an issue or issues are joined between the king and the defendant or defendants, on the plea of not guilty pleaded, it be competent to the jury empanelled to try the same to give their verdict upon the whole matter in issue : Be it therefore declared and enacted by the King's most excellent Majesty, by and with the advice and consent of the

* This Act is "only declaratory of the common law." Per Brett, L.J., 5 C. P. D. at p. 539 ; see *ante*, p. 617.

lords spiritual and temporal, and commons, in this present Parliament assembled, and by the authority of the same, that on every such trial the jury sworn to try the issue may give a general verdict of guilty or not guilty upon the whole matter put in issue upon such indictment or information, and shall not be required or directed by the Court or judge before whom such indictment or information shall be tried to find the defendant or defendants guilty merely on the proof of the publication by such defendant or defendants of the paper charged to be a libel, and of the sense ascribed to the same in such indictment or information.

2. Provided always, that on every such trial the Court or judge before whom such indictment or information shall be tried shall, according to their or his direction, give their or his opinion and directions to the jury on the matter in issue between the King and the defendant or defendants, in like manner as in other criminal cases.

3. Provided also, that nothing herein contained shall extend or be construed to extend to prevent the jury from finding a special verdict, in their discretion, as in other criminal cases.

4. Provided also, that in case the jury shall find the defendant or defendants guilty it shall and may be lawful for the said defendant or defendants to move in arrest of judgment, on such ground and in such manner as by law he or they might have done before the passing of this Act, anything herein contained to the contrary notwithstanding.

See *ante*, pp. 110, 617, 733.

2.

3 & 4 VICT. c. 9.

An Act to give summary Protection to Persons employed in the Publication of Parliamentary Papers.   [14th *April*, 1840.]

WHEREAS it is essential to the due and effectual exercise and discharge of the functions and duties of Parliament, and to the promotion of wise legislation, that no obstructions or impediments should exist to the publication of such of the reports, papers, votes, or proceedings of either House of Parliament as such House of Parliament may deem fit or necessary to be published: And whereas objections or impediments to such publication have arisen, and hereafter may arise, by means of civil or criminal proceedings being taken against persons employed by or acting under the authority of the Houses of Parliament, or one of them, in the publication of such reports, papers, votes, or proceedings ; by reason and for remedy whereof it is expedient that more speedy protection should be afforded to all persons acting under the authority aforesaid, and that all such civil or criminal proceedings should be summarily put an end to and determined in manner herein-after mentioned : Be it therefore enacted by the Queen's most excellent Majesty, by and with the advice and consent of the lords spiritual and temporal, and commons, in this present Parliament assembled, and by the authority of the same, that it shall and may be lawful for any person or persons who now is or are, or hereafter shall be, a defendant or defendants in any civil or criminal proceeding commenced or prosecuted in any manner soever, for or on account or in respect of the publication of any such report, paper, votes, or proceedings by such person or persons, or by his, her, or their servant or servants, by or under the authority of either House of Parliament, to bring before the Court in which such proceeding shall have been or shall be so commenced or prosecuted, or before any judge of the same (if one of the superior Courts at Westminster), first giving twenty-four hours notice of his intention so to do to the prosecutor or plaintiff in such proceeding, a certificate under the hand of the Lord High Chancellor of Great Britain, or the Lord Keeper of the Great Seal, or of the Speaker of the House of Lords, for the time being, or of the Clerk of the Parliaments, or of the Speaker of the House of Commons, or of the Clerk of the same House, stating that the report, paper, votes, or proceedings, as the case may be, in respect whereof such civil or criminal proceeding shall have been commenced or prosecuted, was published by such person or persons, or by his, her, or their servant or servants, by order or under the authority of the House of Lords or of the House of Commons, as the case may be, together with an affidavit verifying such certificate ; and such Court or judge shall thereupon immediately stay such civil or criminal proceeding, and the same, and every writ or process issued therein, shall be and shall be deemed and taken to be finally put an end to, determined, and superseded by virtue of this Act.

2. And be it enacted, that in case of any civil or criminal proceeding hereafter to be commenced or prosecuted for or on account or in respect of the publication of any copy of such report, paper, votes, or proceedings, it shall be lawful for the defendant or defendants at any stage of the proceedings to lay before the Court or judge such report, paper, votes, or proceedings, and such copy, with an affidavit verifying such report, paper, votes, or proceedings,

and the correctness of such copy, and the Court or judge shall immediately stay such civil or criminal proceeding, and the same, and every writ or process issued therein, shall be and shall be deemed and taken to be finally put an end to, determined, and superseded by virtue of this Act.

3. And be it enacted, that it shall be lawful in any civil or criminal proceeding to be commenced or prosecuted for printing any extract from or abstract of such report, paper, votes, or proceedings, to give in evidence under the general issue such report, paper, votes, or proceedings, and to show that such extract or abstract was published *bonâ fide*, and without malice; and if such shall be the opinion of the jury, a verdict of not guilty shall be entered for the defendant or defendants.

4. Provided always, and it is hereby expressly declared and enacted, that nothing herein contained shall be deemed or taken, or held or construed, directly or indirectly, by implication or otherwise, to affect the privileges of Parliament in any manner whatsoever.

3.

LORD CAMPBELL'S LIBEL ACT.

6 & 7 Vict. c. 96.

An Act to amend the Law respecting Defamatory Words and Libel. [*24th August,* 1843.]

In any action for defamation it shall be lawful for the defendant (after notice in writing of his intention so to do, duly given to the plaintiff at the time of filing or delivering the plea in such action) to give in evidence, in mitigation of damages, that he made or offered an apology to the plaintiff for such defamation before the commencement of the action, or as soon afterwards as he had an opportunity of doing so, in case the action shall have been commenced before there was an opportunity of making or offering such apology.

See *ante,* pp. 404, 644, 786.

2. In an action for a libel contained in any public newspaper or other periodical publication it shall be competent to the defendant to plead that such libel was inserted in such newspaper or other periodical publication without actual malice, and without gross negligence, and that before the commencement of the action, or at the earliest opportunity afterwards, he inserted in such newspaper or

other periodical publication a full apology for the said libel, or, if the newspaper or periodical publication in which the said libel appeared should be ordinarily published at intervals exceeding one week, had offered to publish the said apology in any newspaper or periodical publication to be selected by the plaintiff in such action, *and that every such defendant shall, upon filing such plea, be at liberty to pay into Court a sum of money by way of amends for the injury sustained by the publication of such libel, and such payment into Court shall be of the same effect and be available in the same manner and to the same extent, and be subject to the same rules and regulations as to payment of costs and the form of pleading, except so far as regards the pleading of the additional facts hereinbefore required to be pleaded by such defendant, as if actions for libel had not been excepted from the personal actions in which it is lawful to pay money into Court under an Act passed in the session of Parliament held in the fourth year of his late Majesty, intituled "An Act for the further amendment of the law, and the better advancement of justice,"* and that to such plea to such action it shall be competent to the plaintiff to reply generally denying the whole of such plea.

See *ante,* pp. 404, 642, 646, 696, 786.

3. If any person shall publish or threaten to publish any libel upon any other person, or shall directly or indirectly threaten to print or publish or shall directly or indirectly propose to abstain from printing or publishing, or shall directly or indirectly offer to prevent the printing or publishing, of any matter or thing touching any other person, with intent to extort any money or security for money, or any valuable thing from such or any other person, or with intent to induce any person to confer or procure for any person any appointment or office of profit or trust, every such offender, on being convicted thereof, shall be liable to be imprisoned, with or without hard labour, in the common gaol or house of correction, for any term not exceeding three years: Provided always, that nothing herein contained shall in any manner alter or affect any law now in force in respect of the sending or delivery of threatening letters or writings.

See *ante,* p. 459.

4. If any person shall maliciously publish any defamatory libel, knowing the same to be false, every such person, being convicted thereof, shall be liable to be imprisoned in the common gaol or house

---

* As to the words in italics see note on *post,* p. 831, and *ante,* p. 642.

of correction for any term not exceeding two years, and to pay such fine as the Court shall award.

See *ante,* pp. 460, 717, 730, 805.

5. If any person shall maliciously publish any defamatory libel, every such person, being convicted thereof, shall be liable to fine or imprisonment, or both, as the Court may award, such imprisonment not to exceed the term of one year.

See *ante,* pp. 460, 475, 805.

6. On the trial of any indictment or information for a defamatory libel, the defendant having pleaded such plea as hereinafter mentioned, the truth of the matters charged may be inquired into, but shall not amount to a defence, unless it was for the public benefit that the said matters charged should be published, and that to entitle the defendant to give evidence of the truth of such matters charged as a defence to such indictment or information, it shall be necessary for the defendant, in pleading to the said indictment or information, to allege the truth of the said matters charged in the manner now required in pleading a justification to an action for defamation, and further to allege that it was for the public benefit that the said matters charged should be published, and the particular fact or facts by reason whereof it was for the public benefit that the said matters charged should be published, to which plea the prosecutor shall be at liberty to reply generally, denying the whole thereof ; and that if after such plea the defendant shall be convicted on such indictment or information, it shall be competent to the Court, in pronouncing sentence, to consider whether the guilt of the defendant is aggravated or mitigated by the said plea, and by the evidence given to prove or to disprove the same : Provided always, that the truth of the matters charged in the alleged libel complained of by such indictment or information shall in no case be inquired into without such plea of justification : Provided also, that in addition to such plea it shall be competent to the defendant to plead a plea of not guilty : Provided also, that nothing in this Act contained shall take away or prejudice any defence under the plea of not guilty, which it is now competent to the defendant to make under such plea to any action or indictment, or information, for defamatory words or libel.

See *ante,* pp. 473, 474, 724, 737.

7. Whensoever, upon the trial of any indictment or information for the publication of a libel, under the plea of not guilty, evidence

shall have been given which shall establish a presumptive case of publication against the defendant by the act of any other person by his authority, it shall be competent to such defendant to prove that such publication was made without his authority, consent, or knowledge, and that the said publication did not arise from want of due care or caution on his part.

See *ante,* pp. 470—472, 587—589, 731.

8. In the case of any indictment or information by a private prosecutor for the publication of any defamatory libel, if judgment shall be given for the defendant, he shall be entitled to recover from the prosecutor the costs sustained by the said defendant by reason of such indictment or information; and that upon a special plea of justification to such indictment or information, if the issue be found for the prosecutor, he shall be entitled to recover from the defendant the costs sustained by the prosecutor by reason of such plea, such costs so to be recovered by the defendant or prosecutor respectively to be taxed by the proper officer of the Court before which the said indictment or information is tried.

See *ante,* pp. 738, 743.

9. Wherever throughout this Act, in describing the plaintiff or the defendant, or the party affected or intended to be affected by the offence, words are used importing the singular number or the masculine gender only, yet they shall be understood to include several persons as well as one person, and females as well as males, unless when the nature of the provision or the context of the Act shall exclude such construction.

10. . . . nothing in this Act contained shall extend to Scotland.

[N.B.—The words in italics in section 2 were repealed by the Civil Procedure Acts Repeal Act, 1879 (42 & 43 Vict. c. 59), Schedule, Part II., as to the Supreme Court of Judicature in England; and generally throughout England by the 46 & 47 Vict. c. 49, s. 4. And now they are again repealed by the 55 & 56 Vict. c. 19, s. 1. See *ante,* p. 642.]

4.

8 & 9 Vict. c. 75.

An Act to amend an Act passed in the Session of Parliament held in the Sixth and Seventh years of the Reign of her present Majesty, intituled " An Act to amend the Law respecting Defamatory Words and Libel." [*31st July,* 1845.]

2. It shall not be competent to any defendant in such action, whether in England or in Ireland, to file any such plea, without at the same time making a payment of money into Court by way of amends *as provided by the said Act,* but every such plea so filed without payment of money into Court shall be deemed a nullity, and may be treated as such by the plaintiff in the action.

[N.B.—The words in italics in section 2 were repealed by the Civil Procedure Acts Repeal Act, 1879 (42 & 43 Vict. c. 59), Schedule, Part II. as to the Supreme Court of Judicature in England ; and generally throughout England by the 46 & 47 Vict. c. 49, s. 4. They were again repealed by 54 & 55 Vict. c. 67, s. 1. Section 1 of this Act is wholly repealed by 55 & 56 Vict. c. 19, s. 1.]

5.

COMMON LAW PROCEDURE ACT.

15 & 16 Vict. c. 76.

[*June 30th,* 1852.]

Section 61. *In actions of libel and slander the plaintiff shall be at liberty to aver that the words or matter complained of were used in a defamatory sense, specifying such defamatory sense without any prefatory averment to show how such words or matter were used in that sense ; and such averment shall be put in issue by the denial of the alleged libel or slander ; and where the words or matter set forth, with or without the alleged meaning, show a cause of action, the declaration shall be sufficient.*

[Repealed by statute 46 & 47 Vict. c. 49 ; but the rule established by it still remains in full force (section 5 (*b*)). See *ante,* pp. 116, 119, 138, 627.]

6.

20 & 21 VICT. c. 83.

An Act for more effectually preventing the Sale of Obscene Books,
Pictures, Prints, and other Articles.

[*25th August,* 1857.]

1. It shall be lawful for any metropolitan police magistrate or other stipendiary magistrate, or for any two justices of the peace, upon complaint made before him or them upon oath that the complainant has reason to believe, and does believe, that any obscene books, papers, writings, prints, pictures, drawings, or other representations are kept in any house, shop, room, or other place within the limits of the jurisdiction of any such magistrate or justices, for the purpose of sale or distribution, exhibition for purposes of gain, lending upon hire, or being otherwise published for purposes of gain, which complainant shall also state upon oath that one or more articles of the like character have been sold, distributed, exhibited, lent, or otherwise published as aforesaid, at or in connexion with such place, so as to satisfy such magistrate or justices that the belief of the said complainant is well founded, and upon such magistrate or justices being also satisfied that any of such articles so kept for any of the purposes aforesaid are of such a character and description that the publication of them would be a misdemeanour, and proper to be prosecuted as such, to give authority by special warrant to any constable or police officer into such house, shop, room, or other place, with such assistance as may be necessary, to enter in the daytime, and, if necessary, to use force, by breaking open doors or otherwise, and to search for and seize all such books, papers, writings, prints, pictures, drawings, or other representations as aforesaid found in such house, shop, room, or other place, and to carry all the articles so seized before the magistrate or justices issuing the said warrant, or some other magistrate or justices exercising the same jurisdiction ; and such magistrate or justices shall thereupon issue a summons calling upon the occupier of the house or other place which may have been so entered by virtue of the said warrant to appear within seven days before such police or stipendiary magistrate or any two justices in petty sessions for the district, to show cause why the articles so seized should not be destroyed ; and if such occupier or some other person claiming to be the owner of the said articles shall not appear within the time aforesaid, or shall appear, and

such magistrate or justices shall be satisfied that such articles or any of them are of the character stated in the warrant, and that such or any of them have been kept for any of the purposes aforesaid, it shall be lawful for the said magistrate or justices, and he or they are hereby required, to order the articles so seized, except such of them as he or they may consider necessary to be preserved as evidence in some further proceeding, to be destroyed at the expiration of the time hereinafter allowed for lodging an appeal, unless notice of appeal as hereinafter mentioned be given, and such articles shall be in the meantime impounded ; and if such magistrate or justices shall be satisfied that the articles seized are not of the character stated in the warrant, or have not been kept for any of the purposes aforesaid, he or they shall forthwith direct them to be restored to the occupier of the house or other place in which they were seized.

2. No plaintiff shall recover in any action for any irregularity, trespass, or other wrongful proceeding made or committed in the execution of this Act, or in, under, or by virtue of any authority hereby given, if tender of sufficient amends shall have been made by or on behalf of the party who shall have committed such irregularity, trespass, or other wrongful proceeding, before such action brought ; and in case no tender shall have been made, it shall be lawful for the defendant in any such action, by leave of the Court, where such action shall depend, at any time before issue joined, to pay into Court such sum of money as he shall think fit ; whereupon such proceeding, order, and adjudication shall be had and made in and by such Court as in other actions where defendants are allowed to pay money into Court.

3. *No action, suit, or information, or any other proceeding, of what nature soever, shall be brought against any person for anything done or omitted to be done in pursuance of this Act, or in the execution of the authorities under this Act, unless notice in writing shall be given by the party intending to prosecute such action, suit, information, or other proceeding, to the intended defendant, one calendar month at least before prosecuting the same, nor unless such action, suit, information, or other proceeding shall be brought or commenced within three calendar months next after the act or omission complained of, or, in case there shall be a continuation of damage, then within three calendar months next after the doing such damage shall have ceased.* [Repealed by 56 & 57 Vict. c. 61, s. 2.]

4. Any person aggrieved by any act or determination of such magistrate or justices in or concerning the execution of this Act,

may appeal to the next general or quarter sessions for the county, riding, division, city, borough, or place in and for which such magistrate or justices shall have so acted, giving to the magistrate or justices of the peace, whose act or determination shall be appealed against, notice in writing of such appeal and of the grounds thereof, within seven days after such act or determination and before the next general or quarter sessions, and entering within such seven days into a recognizance, with sufficient surety, before a justice of the peace for the county, city, borough, or place in which such act or determination shall have taken place, personally to appear and prosecute such appeal, and to abide the order of and pay such costs as shall be awarded by such Court of quarter sessions or any adjournment thereof; and the Court at such general or quarter sessions shall hear and determine the matter of such appeal, and shall make such order therein as shall to the said Court seem meet; and such Court, upon hearing and finally determining such appeal, shall and may, according to their discretion, award such costs to the party appealing or appealed against as they shall think proper; and if such appeal be dismissed or decided against the appellant or be not prosecuted, such Court may order the articles seized forthwith to be destroyed: Provided always, that it shall not be lawful for the appellant on the hearing of any such appeal to go into or give evidence of any other grounds of appeal against any such order, act, or determination, than those set forth in such notice of appeal.

5. This Act shall not extend to Scotland.

See *ante,* p. 507.

7.

THE NEWSPAPER LIBEL AND REGISTRATION ACT, 1881.

44 & 45 Vict. c. 60.

An Act to Amend the Law of Newspaper Libel and to provide for the Registration of Newspaper Proprietors. [*27th August,* 1881.]

1. In the construction of this Act, unless there is anything in the subject or context repugnant thereto, the several words and phrases hereinafter mentioned shall have and include the meanings following; (that is to say,)

The word "registrar" shall mean in England the registrar for the time being of joint stock companies, or such person as the Board of Trade may for the time being authorise in that behalf, and in Ireland the assistant registrar for the time being of joint

3 H 2

stock companies for Ireland, or such person as the Board of Trade may for the time being authorise in that behalf.

The phrase "registry office" shall mean the principal office for the time being of the registrar in England or Ireland, as the case may be, or such other office as the Board of Trade may from time to time appoint.

The word "newspaper" shall mean any paper containing public news, intelligence, or occurrences, or any remarks or observations therein [*sic; an obvious misprint for* "thereon"] printed for sale, and published in England or Ireland periodically, or in parts or numbers at intervals not exceeding twenty-six days between the publication of any two such papers, parts, or numbers.

Also any paper printed in order to be dispersed, and made public weekly or oftener, or at intervals not exceeding twenty-six days, containing only or principally advertisements.

The word "occupation" when applied to any person shall mean his trade or following [*qu.* calling], and if none, then his rank or usual title, as esquire, gentleman.

The phrase "place of residence" shall include the street, square, or place where the person to whom it refers shall reside, and the number (if any) or other designation of the house in which he shall so reside.

The word "proprietor" shall mean and include as well the sole proprietor of any newspaper, as also in the case of a divided proprietorship the persons who, as partners or otherwise, represent and are responsible for any share or interest in the newspaper as between themselves and the persons in like manner representing or responsible for the other shares or interests therein, and no other person.

(And see stat. 52 & 53 Vict. c. 63.)

The above definition of a "newspaper" is also adopted in the subsequent Law of Libel Amendment Act, 1888, see *post*, p. 843. It is taken almost *verbatim* from Schedule (A) of the 6 & 7 Will. IV. c. 76, which was repealed by the 33 & 34 Vict. c. 99. It was held that a paper or pamphlet, though printed for sale, and containing public news, was not a "newspaper" within the former Act, if published periodically at intervals exceeding twenty-six days. (*Att.-Gen.* v. *Bradbury and Evans,* (1851) 7 Exch. 97 ; 21 L. J. Ex. 12 ; 16 Jur. 130.)

This definition is entirely different from that contained in the Post Office Act, 1870, which requires newspapers to be registered at the Post Office. It may well be, therefore, that a publication which is a "newspaper" within this Act and that of 1888, will not be a "newspaper" within the Act of 1870. If a newspaper be duly registered at Somerset House it by no means follows that it will go through the post as a newspaper : it must first be registered over again at the Post Office. And there must be a third registration for copyright purposes ; see *Cate* v. *Devon and Exeter Constitutional Newspaper Co.*, (1889) 40 Ch. D. 500. It would have been far better to have only one definition of a " newspaper " and only one registration.

2. *Any report published in any newspaper of the proceedings of a public meeting shall be privileged, if such meeting was lawfully convened for a lawful purpose and open to the public, and if such report was fair and accurate and published without malice, and if the publication of the matter complained of was for the public benefit ; provided always, that the protection intended to be afforded by this section shall not be available as a defence in any proceeding, if the plaintiff or prosecutor can show that the defendant has refused to insert in the newspaper in which the report containing the matter complained of appeared a reasonable letter or statement of explanation or contradiction by or on behalf of such plaintiff or prosecutor.*

This section is repealed by section 2 of the Law of Libel Amendment Act, 1888, and section 4 thereof substituted. See *post*, p. 843.

3. *No criminal prosecution shall be commenced against any proprietor, publisher, editor, or any person responsible for the publication of a newspaper for any libel published therein, without the written fiat or allowance of the Director of Public Prosecutions in England or Her Majesty's Attorney-General in Ireland being first had and obtained.*

This section is now repealed, and section 8 of the Law of Libel Amendment Act, 1888, substituted therefor ; see *post*, p. 845.

4. A Court of summary jurisdiction, upon the hearing of a charge against a proprietor, publisher, or editor, or any person responsible for the publication of a newspaper, for a libel published therein, may receive evidence as to the publication being for the public benefit, and as to the matters charged in the libel being true, and as to the report being fair and accurate, and published without malice, and as to any matter which under this or any other Act, or otherwise, might be given in evidence by way of defence by the person charged on his trial on indictment, and the Court, if of opinion after hearing such evidence that there is a strong or probable presumption that the jury on the trial would acquit the person charged, may dismiss the case.

This section was passed in consequence of the decision in *R.* v. *Sir Robert Carden*, 5 Q. B. D. 1 ; 49 L. J. M. C. 1 ; 28 W. R. 133 ; 41 L. T. 504 ; 44 J. P. 119 ; 14 Cox, C. C. 359, where it was held that a magistrate before whom a writer is charged with an offence against section 5 of the 6 & 7 Vict. c. 96, had no jurisdiction to receive and record evidence of the truth of the libel; as such a defence could only be raised at the trial upon a special plea framed in accordance with the Act. See *ante,* p. 475.

5. If a Court of summary jurisdiction upon the hearing of a charge against a proprietor, publisher, editor, or any person responsible for the publication of a newspaper for a libel published therein is of opinion that though the person charged is shown to have been guilty the libel was of a trivial character, and that the offence may be adequately punished by virtue of the powers of this section, the Court shall cause the charge to be reduced into writing and read to the person charged, and then address a question to him to the following effect: " Do you desire to be tried by a jury or do you consent to the case being dealt with summarily ? " and, if such person assents to the case being dealt with summarily, the Court may summarily convict him and adjudge him to pay a fine not exceeding fifty pounds.

Section 27 of the Summary Jurisdiction Act, 1879 (42 & 43 Vict. c. 49), shall, so far as is consistent with the tenor thereof, apply to every such proceeding as if it were herein enacted and extended to Ireland, and as if the Summary Jurisdiction Acts were therein referred to instead of the Summary Jurisdiction Act, 1848.

6. Every libel or alleged libel, and every offence under this Act, shall be deemed to be an offence within and subject to the provisions of the Act of the session of the twenty-second and twenty-third years of the reign of her present Majesty, chapter seventeen, intituled " An Act to prevent vexatious indictments for certain misdemeanours."

This section, it will be observed, applies to all libels, whether published in a newspaper or not.

7. Where, in the opinion of the Board of Trade, inconvenience would arise or be caused in any case from the registry of the names of all the proprietors of the newspaper (either owing to minority, coverture, absence from the United Kingdom, minute subdivision of shares, or other special circumstances), it shall be lawful for the Board of Trade to authorise the registration of such newspaper in the name or names of some one or more responsible " representative proprietors."

This section is out of place. It should have come after section 10.

Where it is desired to make a return of " representative proprietors " under this section, a statement should be sent to the registrar, setting forth the circumstances which render it inconvenient to register the names of all the proprietors, and giving such information as will show that the proposed representatives are well able to meet any claims that may arise for libel or otherwise in connection with the management of the paper.

The Board of Trade very properly require to be satisfied that the person put forward as the " representative proprietor " is " responsible " in every sense of the word.

8. A register of the proprietors of newspapers as defined by this Act shall be established under the superintendence of the registrar.

See the interpretation clause, section 1.

9. It shall be the duty of the printers and publishers for the time being of every newspaper to make or cause to be made to the registry office *on or before the thirty-first of July one thousand eight hundred and eighty-one, and thereafter annually* in the month of July in every year, a return of the following particulars according to the Schedule A. hereunto annexed ; that is to say,

(*a*) The title of a newspaper :

(*b*) The names of all the proprietors of such newspaper together with their respective occupations, places of business (if any), and places of residence.

The words in italics are repealed by 57 & 58 Vict. c. 56, s. 1. Schedule A. is as follows :—

SCHEDULE A.

Return made pursuant to the Newspaper Libel and Registration Act, 1881.

Title of Newspaper.	Names of the Proprietors.	Occupations of the Proprietors.	Places of business (if any) of the Proprietors.	Places of Residence of the Proprietors.

The prescribed forms on which the returns are to be made will be sent, either stamped with the requisite fee stamps or unstamped, on application to the Registrar, Companies' Registration Office, Somerset House, London, W.C. No charge is made for the forms ; but when stamped forms are required a Postal Order for the amount of the fee must accompany the application.

A separate return will be required for each paper, though the same proprietor may own more than one. The person presenting the return for registration is required to sign his name and address on the front of it, probably with a view to section 12. The printers are required to make the return because their name must be on the paper by the 2 & 3 Vict. c. 12, s. 2.

10. If within the further period of one month after the time hereinbefore appointed for the making of any return as to any newspaper such return be not made, then each printer and publisher of such newspaper shall, on conviction thereof, be liable to a penalty

not exceeding twenty-five pounds, and also to be directed by a summary order to make a return within a specified time.

Such an order can be enforced in the manner provided by section 34 of the Summary Jurisdiction Act, 1879, that is, by ordering the person in default to pay a sum not exceeding 1*l.* for every day during which he is in default, or to be imprisoned until he make a return.

11. Any party to a transfer or transmission of or dealing with any share of or interest in any newspaper whereby any person ceases to be a proprietor or any new proprietor is introduced may at any time make or cause to be made to the registry office a return according to the Schedule B. hereunto annexed and containing the particulars therein set forth.

Schedule B. is as follows :—

SCHEDULE B.

Return made pursuant to the Newspaper Libel and Registration Act, 1881.

Title of Newspaper.	Names of Persons who cease to be Proprietors.	Names of Persons who become Proprietors.	Occupation of new Proprietors.	Places of business (if any) of new Proprietors.	Places of Residence of new Proprietors.

It will be observed that this section is permissive merely. The transferee may register his name and address, or not, as he pleases. Hence a plaintiff or prosecutor can never be certain that the registered proprietor is the person liable for the publication complained of. No doubt the presumption would be that the person who was proprietor in July last was proprietor still ; but it will be open to him to prove at the trial, after all the costs have been incurred, that since July last he transferred his interest in the paper to some one else. (See *post,* section 15.) In a civil case this difficulty may be overcome by administering interrogatories. (See *ante,* pp. 654—662, 677.) But it would have been better if the Legislature had made the " return according to Schedule B." compulsory on every transfer, and had further enacted that, till such return was registered, the former proprietor should remain liable for everything published in the newspaper.

12. If any person shall knowingly and wilfully make or cause to be made any return by this Act required or permitted to be made in which shall be inserted or set forth the name of any person as a proprietor of a newspaper who shall not be a proprietor thereof, or in which there shall be any misrepresentation, or from which there shall be any omission in respect of any of the particulars by this Act required to be contained therein whereby such return shall

be misleading, or if any proprietor of a newspaper shall knowingly and wilfully permit any such return to be made which shall be misleading as to any of the particulars with reference to his own name, occupation, place of business (if any), or place of residence, then and in every such case every such offender being convicted thereof shall be liable to a penalty not exceeding one hundred pounds.

13. It shall be the duty of the registrar and he is hereby required forthwith to register every return made in conformity with the provisions of this Act in a book to be kept for that purpose at the registry office and called "the register of newspaper proprietors," and all persons shall be at liberty to search and inspect the said book from time to time during the hours of business at the registry office, and any person may require a copy of any entry in or an extract from the book to be certified by the registrar or his deputy for the time being or under the official seal of the registrar.

On payment of one shilling, any one may inspect both the returns for the present year and also the back returns, at Room No. 7, Somerset House.

14. There shall be paid in respect of the receipt and entry of returns made in conformity with the provisions of this Act, and for the inspection of the register of newspaper proprietors, and for certified copies of any entry therein, and in respect of any other services to be performed by the registrar, such fees (if any) as the Board of Trade with the approval of the Treasury may direct and as they shall deem requisite to defray as well the additional expenses of the registry office caused by the provisions of this Act, as also the further remunerations and salaries (if any) of the registrar, and of any other persons employed under him in the execution of this Act, and such fees shall be dealt with as the Treasury may direct.

The fees which the Board of Trade have, with the approval of the Treasury, directed to be paid are as follows :—

	£	s.	d.
For the registration for the first time of any " representative proprietor " (section 7)	1	0	0
On registration in other cases	0	10	0
On the rendering of subsequent returns	0	5	0
For inspection	0	1	0
For a copy of a return	0	1	0

and a further fee of fourpence per folio to be charged if the copy exceeds three folios.

For a certificate, a further fee of one shilling is charged for the stamp required by the Inland Revenue Commissioners.

15. Every copy of an entry in or extract from the register of newspaper proprietors, purporting to be certified by the registrar or his deputy for the time being, or under the official seal of the registrar, shall be received as conclusive evidence of the contents of the said register of newspaper proprietors, so far as the same appear in such copy or extract without proof of the signature thereto or of the seal of office affixed thereto, and every such certified copy or extract shall in all proceedings, civil or criminal, be accepted as sufficient *primâ facie* evidence of all the matters and things thereby appearing, unless and until the contrary thereof be shown.

16. All penalties under this Act may be recovered before a Court of summary jurisdiction, in manner provided by the Summary Jurisdiction Acts.

Summary orders under this Act may be made by a Court of summary jurisdiction, and enforced in manner provided by section thirty-four of the Summary Jurisdiction Act, 1879 ; and, for the purposes of this Act, that section shall be deemed to apply to Ireland in the same manner, as if it were re-enacted in this Act.

17. [*This section is repealed by* 57 *&* 58 *Vict. c.* 56, *s.* 1.]

18. The provisions as to the registration of newspaper proprietors contained in this Act shall not apply to the case of any newspaper which belongs to a joint stock company duly incorporated under and subject to the provisions of the Companies Acts, 1862 to 1879.

This is a mistaken and mischievous provision. Many newspapers now are published by limited liability companies, with names that suggest no connection between the company and the paper. For instance, the *Graphic* is the property of " H. R. Baines & Co., Limited." Assuming that it were possible that a libel should appear in the *Graphic,* how could the person libelled discover whom to make defendant ? Owing to this section there would be no entry at all at Somerset House to assist him.

19. This Act shall not extend to Scotland.

20. This Act may for all purposes be cited as the Newspaper Libel and Registration Act, 1881.

8.

LAW OF LIBEL AMENDMENT ACT, 1888.

51 & 52 VICT. c. 64.

An Act to Amend the Law of Libel.   [*24th December*, 1888.]

1. In the construction of this Act the word " newspaper " shall have the same meaning as in the Newspaper Libel and Registration Act, 1881. (*Ante*, p. 836.)

2. Section 2 of the Newspaper Libel and Registration Act, 1881, is hereby repealed.

3. A fair and accurate report in any newspaper of proceedings publicly heard before any Court exercising judicial authority shall, if published contemporaneously with such proceedings, be privileged ; provided that nothing in this section shall authorise the publication of any blasphemous or indecent matter.

As to this section, see ante, p. 324.

4. A fair and accurate report published in any newspaper of the proceedings of a public meeting or (except where neither the public nor any newspaper reporter is admitted) of any meeting of a vestry, town council, school board, board of guardians, board or local authority formed or constituted under the provisions of any Act of Parliament, or of any committee appointed by any of the above-mentioned bodies, or of any meeting of any commissioners authorised to act by letters patent, Act of Parliament, warrant under the Royal Sign Manual, or other lawful warrant or authority, select committees of either House of Parliament, justices of the peace in quarter sessions assembled for administrative or deliberative purposes, and the publication at the request of any Government office or department, officer of state, commissioner of police or chief constable, of any notice or report issued by them for the information of the public, shall be privileged, unless it shall be proved that such report or publication was published or made maliciously : Provided that nothing in this section shall authorise the publication of any blasphemous or indecent matter : Provided also, that the protection intended to be afforded by this section shall not be available as a defence in any proceedings if it shall be proved that the defendant has been requested to insert in the newspaper in which the report or other publication complained of appeared a reasonable letter or statement by way of contradiction or explanation of such report or other publication, and has refused or neglected to insert the same : Provided further, that nothing in this section contained shall be deemed or construed to limit or abridge

any privilege now by law existing, or to protect the publication of any matter not of any public concern, and the publication of which is not for the public benefit. For the purposes of this section, " public meeting " shall mean any meeting *bonâ fide* and lawfully held for a lawful purpose, and for the furtherance or discussion of any matter of public concern, whether the admission thereto be general or restricted.

For a detailed examination of the provisions of this section, see *ante,* pp. 328—336.

5. It shall be competent for a judge or the Court, upon an application by or on behalf of two or more defendants in actions in respect to the same, or substantially the same, libel brought by one and the same person, to make an order for the consolidation of such actions, so that they shall be tried together ; and after such order has been made, and before the trial of the said actions, the defendants in any new actions instituted in respect to the same, or substantially the same, libel shall also be entitled to be joined in a common action upon a joint application being made by such new defendants and the defendants in the action already consolidated.

In a consolidated action under this section the jury shall assess the whole amount of the damages (if any) in one sum, but a separate verdict shall be taken for or against each defendant in the same way as if the actions consolidated had been tried separately ; and if the jury shall have found a verdict against the defendant or defendants in more than one of the actions so consolidated, they shall proceed to apportion the amount of damages which they shall have so found between and against the said last-mentioned defendants ; and the judge at the trial, if he awards to the plaintiff the costs of the action, shall thereupon make such order as he shall deem just for the apportionment of such costs between and against such defendants.

As to this new practice, see *ante,* pp. 619—621. And note that the section applies to all libel actions ; it is not confined to libels contained in a newspaper.

6. At the trial of an action for a libel contained in any newspaper the defendant shall be at liberty to give in evidence in mitigation of damages that the plaintiff has already recovered (or has brought actions for) damages or has received or agreed to receive compensation in respect of a libel or libels to the same purport or effect as the libel for which such action has been brought.

See *ante,* pp. 172, 397, 696.

7. It shall not be necessary to set out in any indictment or other judicial proceeding instituted against the publisher of any obscene

libel the obscene passages, but it shall be sufficient to deposit the book, newspaper or other documents containing the alleged libel with the indictment or other judicial proceeding, together with particulars showing precisely by reference to pages, columns, and lines in what part of the book, newspaper, or other document the alleged libel is to be found, and such particulars shall be deemed to form part of the record, and all proceedings may be taken thereon as though the passages complained of had been set out in the indictment or judicial proceeding.

This section applies to all obscene libels, whether printed in a newspaper or not, and see *ante,* p. 505.

8. Section three of the forty-fourth and forty-fifth Victoria, chapter sixty, is hereby repealed, and instead thereof be it enacted that no criminal prosecution shall be commenced against any proprietor, publisher, editor, or any person responsible for the publication of a newspaper for any libel published therein without the order of a judge at Chambers being first had and obtained.

Such application shall be made on notice to the person accused who shall have an opportunity of being heard against such application.

See *ante,* pp. 715, 820.

9. Every person charged with the offence of libel before any Court of criminal jurisdiction, and the husband or wife of the person so charged, shall be competent, but not compellable, witnesses on every hearing at every stage of such charge.

This section applies to all libels, whether published in a newspaper or not.

10. This Act shall not apply to Scotland.

11. This Act may be cited as the Law of Libel Amendment Act, 1888.

9.

INDECENT ADVERTISEMENTS ACT, 1889.

52 & 53 Vict. c. 18.

An Act to suppress Indecent Advertisements.   [*26th July,* 1889.]

1. This Act may be cited as the Indecent Advertisements Act, 1889.

2. This Act shall come into operation on the 1st day of January, one thousand eight hundred and ninety.

3. Whoever affixes to or inscribes on any house, building, wall,

hoarding, gate, fence, pillar, post, board, tree or any other thing whatsoever so as to be visible to a person being in or passing along any street, public highway, or footpath, and whoever affixes to or inscribes on any public urinal, or delivers or attempts to deliver, or exhibits, to any inhabitant or to any person being in or passing along any street, public highway, or footpath, or throws down the area of any house, or exhibits to public view in the window of any house or shop, any picture or printed or written matter which is of an indecent or obscene nature, shall, on summary conviction in manner provided by the Summary Jurisdiction Acts, be liable to a penalty not exceeding forty shillings, or, in the discretion of the Court, to imprisonment for any term not exceeding one month, with or without hard labour.

4. Whoever gives or delivers to any other person any such pictures, or printed or written matter mentioned in section three of this Act with the intent that the same, or some one or more thereof, should be affixed, inscribed, delivered, or exhibited as therein mentioned, shall, on conviction in manner provided by the Summary Jurisdiction Acts, be liable to a penalty not exceeding five pounds, or, in the discretion of the Court, to imprisonment for any term not exceeding three months, with or without hard labour.

5. Any advertisement relating to syphilis, gonorrhœa, nervous debility, or other complaint or infirmity arising from or relating to sexual intercourse, shall be deemed to be printed or written matter of an indecent nature within the meaning of section three of this Act, if such advertisement is affixed to or inscribed on any house, building, wall, hoarding, gate, fence, pillar, post, board, tree, or other thing whatsoever, so as to be visible to a person being in or passing along any street, public highway, or footpath, or is affixed to or inscribed on any public urinal, or is delivered or attempted to be delivered to any person being in or passing along any street, public highway, or footpath.

6. Any constable or other peace officer may arrest without warrant any person whom he shall find committing any offence against this Act.

7. In this Act the expression "Summary Jurisdiction Acts"—

In England means the Summary Jurisdiction (English) Acts within the meaning of the Summary Jurisdiction Act, 1879;

In Scotland means the Summary Jurisdiction (Scotland) Acts, 1864 and 1881, and any Acts amending the same; and

In Ireland means within the police district of Dublin metropolis the Acts regulating the powers and duties of justices of the peace for such district or of the police of such district, and elsewhere in Ireland the Petty Sessions (Ireland) Act, 1851, and any Act amending the same.

10.

SLANDER OF WOMEN ACT, 1891.

54 & 55 VICT. c. 51.

An Act to amend the Law relating to the Slander of Women.

[*5th August,* 1891.]

1. Words spoken and published after the passing of this Act, which impute unchastity or adultery to any woman or girl, shall not require special damage to render them actionable.

Provided always, that in any action for words spoken and made actionable by this Act, a plaintiff shall not recover more costs than damages, unless the judge shall certify that there was reasonable ground for bringing the action.

2. This Act may be cited as the Slander of Women Act, 1891, and shall not apply to Scotland.

See *ante,* pp. 69—71.

11.

THE CORRUPT AND ILLEGAL PRACTICES PREVENTION ACT, 1895.

58 & 59 VICT. c. 40.

An Act to amend the Corrupt and Illegal Practices Prevention Act, 1883.   [*6th July,* 1895.]

1. Any person who, or the directors of any body or association corporate which, before or during any parliamentary election, shall, for the purpose of affecting the return of any candidate at such election, make or publish any false statement of fact in relation to the personal character or conduct of such candidate shall be guilty of an illegal practice within the meaning of the provisions of the Corrupt and Illegal Practices Prevention Act, 1883 (46 & 47 Vict. c. 51), and shall be subject to all the penalties for and consequences of committing an illegal practice in the said Act mentioned, and

the said Act shall be taken to be amended as if the illegal practice defined by this Act had been contained therein.

2. No person shall be deemed to be guilty of such illegal practice if he can show that he had reasonable grounds for believing, and did believe, the statement made by him to be true.

Any person charged with an offence under this Act, and the husband or wife of such person, as the case may be, shall be competent to give evidence in answer to such charge.

3. Any person who shall make or publish any false statement of fact as aforesaid may be restrained by interim or perpetual injunction by the High Court of Justice from any repetition of such false statement or any false statement of a similar character in relation to such candidate, and for the purpose of granting an interim injunction *primâ facie* proof of the falsity of the statement shall be sufficient.

4. A candidate shall not be liable, nor shall be subject to any incapacity, nor shall his election be avoided, for any illegal practice under this Act committed by his agent other than his election agent, unless it can be shown that the candidate or his election agent has authorised or consented to the committing of such illegal practice by such other agent, or has paid for the circulation of the false statement constituting the illegal practice, or unless upon the hearing of an election petition the election court shall find and report that the election of such candidate was procured or materially assisted in consequence of the making or publishing of such false statements.

5. This Act may be cited as the Corrupt and Illegal Practices Prevention Act, 1895, and shall be construed as one with the Corrupt and Illegal Practices Prevention Act, 1883, and that Act and this Act may be cited together as the Corrupt and Illegal Practices Prevention Acts, 1883 and 1895.

See *ante,* pp. 437, 461, 810.

12.

THE PATENTS AND DESIGNS ACT, 1907.

7 EDW. VII. c. 29.

[28*th August,* 1907.]

36. Where any person claiming to be the patentee of an invention, by circulars, advertisements, or otherwise, threatens any

other person with any legal proceedings or liability in respect of any alleged infringement of the patent, any person aggrieved thereby may bring an action against him, and may obtain an injunction against the continuance of such threats, and may recover such damage (if any) as he has sustained thereby, if the alleged infringement to which the threats related was not in fact an infringement of any legal rights of the person making such threats: Provided that this section shall not apply if the person making such threats with due diligence commences and prosecutes an action for infringement of his patent.

See *ante,* pp. 97—105, 435—437.

GENERAL INDEX.

----◆----

A.

ANNUAL PROFITS,
    diminution of, 378, 382, 388.
    how proved, 382, 383.

ANONYMOUS LETTER,
    shown confidentially, 256, 257, 750.
    opinion as to handwriting of, when privileged, 283.

ANSWERS
    to interrogatories, 662—667.

APOLOGY, 404—406, 644.
    should be demanded before action, 613.
    what is a sufficient, 614.
    jury to judge of sufficiency of, 406, 785.
    should be frank and full, 406, 614.
    notice of intention to give evidence of, 644, 795.
    absence or inadequacy of, may aggravate the damages, 373.
    publication of, 405, 406.
    form of plea of, 404, 644, 783—787.

APOSTACY, 485.

APOTHECARY,
    words concerning, 63.

APPEAL,
    proceedings in the Court of, 703, 704.
    to Court of Criminal Appeal, 735, 736, 743.
    from County Court, 713.
    as to costs, 445—447.
    notice of motion on, 792.

APPEARANCE, 614.

APPOINTMENT,
    to Government office is matter of public concern, 207, 208.
    proof of, 673.

APPORTIONMENT
    of costs of issues, 440, 447, 448.

ARBITRATOR
    cannot commit for contempt, 559.

ARCHBISHOP,
    language concerning, 27.

ARCHITECT,
    criticisms on the works of, 31, 184, 215.
    words concerning, 269, 753, 754.

ARREST OF JUDGMENT,
    motion for, in criminal cases, 727, 734, 735.

ARSON,
    charge of, 130, 141, 145, 151.

ARTICLES OF THE PEACE,
    absolutely privileged, 243.

CHAPLAIN,
    words concerning, 58—60.
    loss of post, special damage, 379.

CHARACTER,
    proof of plaintiff's special, 673, 674.
    bonâ fide communications as to, 252—280.
    of servant, *primâ facie* privileged, 228, 252, 253, 270—272, 361—363, 748, 774.
            master not bound to give, 253.
            maliciously giving bad, 253, 361—363.
            retracting former good, 271.
    evidence of good, not receivable unless impeached, 391, 686.
    evidence of plaintiff's bad, 401—403.
    evidence for defendant as to, on trial of indictment, 732, 733.
    of witnesses, evidence to impeach, 692, 693.
    attack on private, actionable, 195, 199.

CHARGE
    of crime must be precise, 138—143.
    of attempt to commit a crime, 41, 44, 143.
    of an impossible crime, 50.
    of being a felon, 39—42, 183.
    of being a returned convict, 45, 191, 365, 695.
    to a constable in his character as such, 273—276.
    irrelevant, 305, 367.

CHARGE-SHEET
    of police court is not part of the record of the court, 242, 313, 318, 319.

CHARITABLE INSTITUTION,
    criticism on officers of, 131, 212, 286, 287.
    trustees of, words concerning, 26, 601.
    report by officer of, privileged, 270.

CHASTITY,
    charge of want of, formerly not actionable, 69—72.
            actionable if in writing, 20.
    of a girl, soliciting in writing is a libel, 468.
    Slander of Women Act, 1891...69, 847.

" CHEAT," 49, 57, 61, 65, 68, 74.

CHEATING,
    charge of, libellous, 20.
            in way of trade, actionable, 67, 68.
    at cards, charge of, actionable, 42, 126, 185.

CHEMIST,
    libel on, 199.

CHEQUE,
    action for dishonouring, 13, 132.
    refusal to receive, of a particular bank, 22, 132, 283.

"CLIPPER," 126.

CLUB,
　　"black-balled," 19, 416.
　　notice posted in, 21.
　　charge of misconduct in, 73, 380.

COINING,
　　charge of, 45, 757, 772.

COLLEGE, MANAGEMENT OF,
　　a matter of public interest, 211.

COLLIERY,
　　libel on proprietor of, 32.
　　sanitary condition of property of, is a matter of public interest, 212.

COLLOQUIUM,
　　or application of the slander, 121, 136, 627.
　　provisions of C. L. P. Act as to, 138.

COLONIAL COURT,
　　power of, to commit for contempt, 559, 560.

COLONIAL LEGISLATIVE ASSEMBLY,
　　power of, to commit for contempt, 527.

COMMAND,
　　of master, no defence to servant, 584.

COMMENT, 193—225, 634—636.
　　on matters of public interest, what is, 205—218.
　　on matters of local interest, 211—213.
　　allegation of fact, not a, 197—205, 438.
　　every citizen has a right to make, 193, 195, 206, 207, 219.
　　not privileged in the strict sense of that term, 194.
　　differs from a report, 200, 201, 320.
　　bad motives must not be recklessly imputed, 221.
　　must be fair and honest, 196, 218—224, 370.
　　must not be published maliciously, 224, 225, 370.
　　honest belief in truth of, not alone sufficient, 199, 224, 225.
　　justification, when necessary, 182, 202, 203.
　　to what extent "no libel," 194.
　　limits on, 195—197.
　　immaterial errors excused, 199.
　　affairs of State, 206—209, 769.
　　trials in law Courts, 209—211.
　　public institutions and local authorities, 211—213.
　　parochial charity, 212.
　　ecclesiastical affairs, 213.
　　books and pictures, 213—215.
　　architecture, 184, 215.
　　theatres and concerts, 215, 216.
　　public entertainments, 216.
　　appeals to the public notice, 216—218.
　　advertisements and circulars, 216, 217, 221.

COMPROMISE

    in civil case, 697.

    not generally allowed in criminal cases, 742.

    not allowed on motion to commit for contempt, 543.

CONCERTS

    may be criticised, 215, 216.

CONDUCT

    of defendant may aggravate damages, 389—393.

    of plaintiff may affect damages, 401—403.

CONFESSION

    of publication, 677.

CONFIDENTIAL COMMUNICATIONS, 252—272.

    in answer to inquiries, privileged, 227, 252—257, 363.

    volunteered, 257—259.

    in discharge of a duty arising from relationship, 259—263.

    volunteered where no confidential relationship, 263—270.

    charge that plaintiff had disclosed, libellous, 28.

CONFIDENTIAL RELATION

    defined, 259, 260.

CONSOLIDATION OF ACTIONS,

    at common law, 619—621.

    under the Act of 1888...620, 820, 844, 845.

    statement of claim, 755, 756.

    defence, 784.

    payment into court, 642, 784.

CONSORTIUM,

    loss of, 71, 108, 380, 418.

CONSPIRACY,

    charge of, actionable, 42, 148.

    to boycott a trader, 107.

    to induce persons to break contracts, 15.

    to prevent persons from entering into contracts, 15.

CONSTABLES,

    words concerning, 236, 262, 284, 417.

    words spoken on giving plaintiff in charge of, are privileged, 273—276.

CONSTITUTION,

    libels against the, 522—524.

CONSTRUCTION, 109—156.

    what meaning the speaker intended to convey is immaterial, 109, 119, 694.

    libel or no libel is a question for the jury, 24, 110, 682, 683, 698.

    duty of the judge, 110, 697, 698.

    words not to be construed *in mitiori sensu*, 111—113.

    jury to consider the words as a whole, 24, 114, 519, 699, 733.

    evidence of other defamatory publications, 114, 345.

    office of the innuendo, 115—135.

    words obviously defamatory, 119—121.

3 K 2

GRAND JURY,
  defamatory presentment by, privileged, 240.

GUARDIANS OF THE POOR,
  words concerning, 26.

GUNSMITH,
  libel on, 35.

H.

HABEAS CORPUS,
  Speaker's warrant an answer to, 526.

HABITUAL DRUNKENNESS,
  words imputing, actionable, 59.

HANDBILL
  of tradesman, may be criticised, 216, 221.

HANDWRITING,
  proof of, 675, 789.
  comparison of, 675, 676, 728.

HAUNTED HOUSE, 92, 106, 107, 408, 409.

HEAD-LINES,
  of paragraph may be libellous, 28, 114, 181, 184.
    must be justified, 184.
    may be a contempt of Court, 549.

" HEALER OF FELONS," 130.

HEARSAY,
  sufficient ground for *bonâ fide* belief, 353.

HEIR,
  slander of title of, 85, 86.

HERALD,
  words concerning, 57.

HERESY, 486—489.
  distinct from blasphemy, 486.
  no crime at common law, 486.
  statutory provisions as to, 487, 488.
  jurisdiction of Ecclesiastical Courts, 487—489.
  Nonconformity, 488, 489.
  Unitarianism, 488, 499—501.

" HERMAPHRODITE," 65.

HIEROGLYPHICS,
  may be a libel, 23, 113.

HISTORY,
  libel contained in a, 6, 200.
  matters of, may be discussed, 522—524.
  need not be strictly proved, 694.

" HOCUSSED," 117.

HOMŒOPATHIST,
  charge of meeting, in consultation, 27.

"HONEST LAWYER," 19, 133.

HONORARY OFFICE,
    words of one in, 25, 52—56.

HOSPITALITY,
    loss of, is special damage, 378—381, 418.

HOUSE OF COMMONS,
    member of, privileged, 231.
                may be committed for contempt of Court, 566.
    words defamatory of. 525.
    contempt of, 524—526.
    breach of privilege, 525.
    Speaker's warrant, an answer to *habeas corpus*, 526.
    committee of, evidence given before, privileged, 232.
    petition to, privileged, 232.
    report of proceedings in, privileged; 326.

HOUSE OF LORDS,
    contempts of, 12, 525.

HUSBAND AND WIFE, 567—577.
    costs, 453, 568, 569.
    proceedings by wife against husband, 50, 51, 570, 571.
    action for loss of *consortium,* 72, 108, 380, 418.
    liability of husband, 573—577.
    effect of judicial separation before judgment, 573.
    special damage, 380—382, 418, 419; 569.
    claim by husband for words defamatory of wife, 24, 155, 418, 419,
        568, 762.
    married woman defendant, 573—577.
    repetition by wife to husband of charge affecting herself, 178, 179,
            412, 415.
                by husband to wife of a charge affecting others, 159, 360.
    communication to wife of charge against husband, 159.
    communications between, privileged, 159, 260.
    husband or wife of defendant may give evidence, 730, 846.

"HYPOCRITE," 18, 133.

I.

IGNORANCE,
    words imputing, 26, 52, 53.

ILLEGAL TRADE,
    action for slander in respect of, not maintainable, 69.
    must be specially pleaded, 632.

ILLEGITIMATE CHILD,
    charge that plaintiff is an, libellous, 20.
    charge of having had an, libellous, 20.
                        when actionable, if spoken, 46, 65, 71, 72,
                        155, 416.

ILLNESS
    arising from slander is not special damage, 378—382, 408.

INTOLERANCE,
religious, charge of, libellous, 19.

INTRODUCTORY AVERMENTS,
to support innuendo, formerly essential, 116—118.
still sometimes useful, 627, 630, 685, 730.
should be traversed, 632.
costs of, 449.

IRONICAL WORDS,
may be actionable, 19, 23, 113, 133.
must be alleged to have been so spoken, 133, 627.

ISSUES, SEVERAL,
costs of, 445, 447.

ITCH,
charge of having, actionable, if written, 18.
not actionable, if merely spoken, 51.

J.

" JACOBITE," 56, 140.

JEST,
publication in, no defence, 5, 6, 109.
unless so understood by all, 121, 122, 124, 693, 772.

JOCKEY CLUB,
privilege as to publication of reports made to, 238, 289

JOINDER
of causes of action, 604—606.
of parties, 599—604.
in demurrer, 806, 809.

JOINT
plaintiffs, 26, 33, 600, 604.
defendants, 601, 612.
tort-feasors, 9, 171, 172.

JOINT PUBLICATION
of written language, 168—172, 469, 61

JOINT STOCK COMPANY,
actions by and against, 591—593.
costs of directors of, 453, 454, 738.

JOKE,
words intended as a, 5, 6, 108, 121, 122, 124, 693, 772.

JOURNALIST,
privileges of, 193—225, 811—823.
defamation of, 30, 774.

" JUDAS," 120.

JUDGE,
criticism of public action of, no libel, 205, 206, 529.
of superior Court, words concerning, 528—530, 542—560.
of inferior Court, words concerning, 530—533, 560—566.

LIBEL—*continued*.

  on a class, 147—150, 456, 463.

  proof of the, 678—680, 729.

  photographic copy of, 654, 700.

  contract for printing, cannot be enforced, 8.

  blasphemous, 477—504.

  obscene, 505—511.

  seditious, 513—533.

  publication of, 157—180, 467—472.

  charge of publishing a, actionable, 30, 42.

  in jest, 5, 6, 109, 121, 122, 124, 693, 772.

  lunatic may be sued for, 6.

  on things, 14, 15, 34—38, 77—108, 155, 156.

  County Court jurisdiction in, 439, 711.

  innocent dissemination of, 166—168, 471, 770.

  merely being in possession of, no crime, 469.

  corporation may sue and be sued for, 6, 34, 591—593.

  trade unions may be sued for, 594, 595.

  injunctions to restrain, 421—438, 752, 759.

  proving truth of, 181—192, 694, 695.

  PRECEDENTS OF PLEADINGS in actions for, 745—795.

                in criminal proceedings for, 796—810.

LIBEL ACTS,

  32 Geo. III. c. 60 (Mr. Fox's), 13, 110, 733, 825, 826.

  3 & 4 Vict. c. 9 (Protection for publication of parliamentary papers),
    231, 232, 337, 338, 826—828.

  6 & 7 Vict. c. 96 (Lord Campbell's), 828—831.

        s. 1...404, 644, 786, 795, 828.

        s. 2...404, 405, 642, 643, 696, 786, 795, 828, 831, n.

        s. 3...459, 460, 829.

        s. 4...460, 717, 723, 805, 829.

        s. 5...460, 475, 723, 805, 830.

        s. 6...473, 474, 737, 830.

        s. 7...470—472, 587—589, 731, 830.

        s. 8...737, 743, 831.

  Newspaper Libel and Registration Act, 1881...329, 811—817, 835—
  842.

  Law of Libel Amendment Act, 1888...324, 328, 506, 620, 715, 718,
  817—823, 843—846.

" LIBELLER,"

  charge of being, 42.

" LIBELLOUS JOURNALIST," 30, 146, 183.

LIBELLOUS WORKS,

  no copyright in, 8.

  printer cannot recover for printing, 8.

  no action lies for price of, 8.

LIBERTY,

  of the press, 10, 307—340, 521, 523.

          history of growth of, 10—13.

"MAINSWORN," 127.

MAINTENANCE,

    loss of, by wife, as special damage, 419.

MALICE, 341—370.

    means in this book "actual" or "express" malice, 5, 342, 343.

    not essential to the action, 5, 109, 341.

                                               unless occasion privileged, 5, 342, 635.

    destroys privilege of report, 323—326, 333, 369, 837, 844.

    is an answer to a plea of fair comment, 224, 225, 370.

    onus of proving, lies on the plaintiff, 77, 78, 324, 344, 636, 685.

    must be malice of the defendant himself or of his agent, 344, 369.

    in another, irrelevant, 344, 391.

    in the agent of a corporation, 6, 344, 592, 593.

    proof of actual, 348—370, 389—393, 472, 473, 635.

        I. Extrinsic evidence of, 345, 348—352.

            former publications by defendant of plaintiff, 349, 350, 635.

            former quarrels, 348, 685.

            acts of defendant subsequent to publication, 349.

            that the words are false is alone no evidence of, 685, 686.

            that defendant knew the words were false, is evidence of, 343, 346, 354, 686.

            plea of justification, when, 181, 350, 636—638, 685, 686.

        II. Evidence of, derived from the mode and extent of publication, the terms employed, &c., 352—354.

            (i.) Where the expressions employed are exaggerated and unwarrantable, 354—357.

            (ii.) Where the mode and extent of publication is excessive, 166, 167, 358—361, 367, 390.

    may be proved in aggravation of damages, 390, 391.

    absence of, tends to mitigate damages, 4, 342, 395, 398—401.

    in actions on the case, 80, 84, 87, 93, 94.

    in actions of slander of title, 75, 84—88.

    or no malice, is for the jury, 323, 324, 346, 349, 352.

    mere mistake cannot be evidence of, 345.

    matters which are not evidence of, 345, 346.

    particulars need not be given, 625, 626, 648.

    interrogatories as to, 656, 661, 791.

"MAN FRIDAY,"

    charge of being, not actionable, 21, 130.

    judicial notice of the meaning of the term, 21.

"MAN OF STRAW,"

    libellous, 18.

MANSLAUGHTER,

    charge of, actionable, 41.

MANUSCRIPT,

    parting with possession of, is publication, 162—165.

MARRIAGE,

    loss of, is special damage, 378, 384.

    communication warning against, when privileged, 260, 261, 777, 778.

MITIGATION OF DAMAGES—*continued.*
 particulars, when to be given, 696.
    under Order XXXVI. r. 37...400.
    form of notice of, 787, 788.
 damages previously recovered, 397, 696.

MITIORI SENSU,
 construction in, 112—114.

MONEY,
 charge of obtaining, by false pretences, 320.
 attempt to extort, by threatening letter, 460.
 unfit to be trusted with, charge of being, actionable, 18.
 charge of owing, not actionable, 22, 67, 132, 133, 135.
 paid into Court, 449, 640—643, 700, 701.

MOTION,
 in arrest of judgment, 111, 112, 136, 701, 703, 727, 734, 735.
 for a new trial, in a civil case, 703—709.
 for a rule for a criminal information, 739, 740.
 FORM OF NOTICE OF, ON APPEAL, 792.
      TO COMMIT FOR CONTEMPT, 792, 793.

MOTIVE,
 immaterial, unless occasion privileged, 4, 5, 341—343, 398.
 in criminal cases, 456, 464, 465.
 wicked, imputation of, libellous, 25.

"MOUNTEBANK," 28, 62.

"MULATTO," 47.

MURDER,
 charge of, actionable, 19, 41, 140.
 what is a sufficient charge of, 140.
 what insufficient, 140.
 charge of, explained away by context, 123.

MUSICAL PERFORMANCES,
 may be criticised, 215, 216.

N.

NAME,
 unauthorised use of, 27, 422.

NATURAL MEANING,
 words must be taken to bear, 112, 113, 688.
 secondary meaning may be shown, 119, 128—133, 693, 694.
 justification in, without innuendo, 189, 638, 639.

NAVAL AND MILITARY AFFAIRS,
 acts of State, 245—247, 776.

NAVAL AND MILITARY OFFICERS,
 reports by, privileged, 245—247, 256, 365.
 have a common interest, 284.

NEGLIGENCE,
 gross, of newspaper proprietor will enhance damages, 392, 404, 405.
 without gross, plea of, 771.

NEGRO.

charge of being, not libellous in England, 21.

NEUTRAL WORDS, 125—128.

NEW TRIAL,

when granted, 119, 703—709.
application for, to what Court, 703.
misdirection, 704.
finding which reasonable men could not honestly find, 111, 373, 705.
verdict against weight of evidence, 704—706.
for excessive damages, 707.
for insufficient damages, 708.
on the ground of surprise, 708, 709.
for irregularities at trial, 706.
to hear fresh evidence, 706, 707.
against one defendant, 704.
form of notice of motion for, 792.
in County Court, 713.
cost of former trial, 709.

NEWS,

false, fabrication of, 459, 519.

NEWSPAPER,

definition of a, 330, 836.
proprietors, liability of, 5, 6, 30, 170, 171, 328—336, 586—589, 769.
criminal liability of, 6, 469, 587—589.
libels on, 30, 36, 37, 223.
cannot sue editor for contribution, 172.
register of, 13, 838—842.
editor, liability of, 170, 171.
libels on, 30, 120, 183.
contempt of Court by, 548.
printer of, 10—13, 170, 171, 469.
must preserve one copy for six months, 13.
contempt of Court by, 548.
publisher of, 469.
contempt of Court by, 550.
reporter, duty of, 314—320.
letters written to, may be answered, 217.
how much may be read in evidence, 692, 730.
not justified in publishing story told by plaintiff against himself, 5, 6, 21.
proof of publication of, 676, 842.
interrogatories as to publication of libel in, 656—659.
latitude allowed to writers in, 193, 194, 210, 519, 523.
actionable language concerning, 30, 120.
imputation that it has a small circulation, may be libellous, 30, 31, 92.
advertisement in, when privileged, 290.
statutory provisions relating to, 13, 676, 811—823, 835—845.
statutory plea of apology for libel in, 404, 642—644, 786.
extent of circulation of libel in, increases damage, 32, 375.

3 N 2

PRODUCTION OF DOCUMENTS,
    order for, 649—651.
    privilege, 651—653.
    inspection, 653, 654.

PROFANE LIBELS, 477—504.

PROFESSION,
    words injuring the plaintiff in the way of his, 2, 17, 25—31, 39, 52—
        65, 685, 753—758.

PROFITS,
    loss of, is special damage, 373, 378, 382, 383, 388.

PROMISE
    to indemnify against consequences of publishing libel, 9.
    to abstain from publishing libel, 9.

PROOF
    of plaintiff's special character, 54, 673.
    of publication, 674.
    of the libel, 678.
    of the speaking of the slander, 680.
    that the words refer to the plaintiff, 684.
    that the words were spoken of the plaintiff in the way of his office,
        profession or trade, 685.

PROPRIETOR
    of newspaper liable for all libels contained therein, 5, 6, 163, 170,
        171, 587.
        not liable for malice of reporter, 369.
        liable for accidental slips of printer, 587.
        civilly, 6, 30, 170, 171, 328—336, 586—588, 769.
        criminally, 469, 587—589.
        register of, 13, 838—842.
        "representative," 838.

PROSECUTION,
    for libel, 455—475.
    procedure on, 715—743.
    when leave of judge required for, 715.

PROSPECTIVE DAMAGES, 376.

PROSTITUTE,
    verbal charge of being, now actionable by statute, 69—72, 847.
    charge of having, under protection, libellous, 20, 120.

PROSTITUTION,
    words imputing to a woman or girl, now actionable, 69—72, 416, 847.
            to the shopwoman of a trader, 66, 73.
            to a married woman, 69—72, 419.

PROVOCATION
    by libel to a breach of the peace, 455.
    by plaintiff's conduct, 291—298, 399, 462.
    by previous libels, when evidence in mitigation, 399.

RELIGIOUS INTOLERANCE,
    charge of, libellous, 19.
RELIGIOUS SECTS AND SOCIETIES,
    libels upon, 458, 463.
    expulsion from, 47, 71, 379.
    members have a common interest, 287—289.
                    a domestic tribunal, 289.
REMITTING ACTION,
    to the County Court, 451, 618, 619.
    proceedings in County Court, 711—714.
    costs of action remitted, 714.
REMOTENESS OF DAMAGES, 406—419.
    damage must be direct result of defendant's own words, 177, 409,
        410.
    damage must have accrued to the plaintiff, 418, 419.
    damage resulting to the husband of the female plaintiff, 407, 408.
    damage caused by the act of a third party, 409.
    not essential that such third person should believe the charge, 410.
    originator of a slander not liable for damage caused by its repetition,
        177, 413, 414.
    exceptions to this rule, 178, 179, 413—417.
REPETITION
    of slander heard from another, 146, 172—176, 394—396, 413—417.
                    by wife to husband, 159, 412.
    naming informant now no avail, 173—176, 395, 811, 812.
        formerly a defence, 173.
    every, of slander a separate cause of action, 172, 173, 300.
    bonâ fide repetition to person calumniated, 177, 294—298.
    libellous articles reproduced from other newspapers, 172, 395, 396,
        732.
    of words may be evidence of malice, 349—352.
        especially if exaggerated, 354, 355.
    damage caused by, 413, 414.
REPLICATION
    in criminal cases, 725, 798, 808.
REPLY
    as to pleading, 647, 648.
    of pardon to a plea charging felony, 45, 648, 724.
    to plea under Lord Campbell's Act, 405, 725.
    precedents of, 787, 788.
REPORTER,
    duty of, 209, 210, 315—322, 369.
REPORTS
    differ from comments, 320.
    of imaginary facts, 200, 201.
    (i.) Reports of judicial proceedings, 307, 308—326, 777, 821.
        of ex parte proceedings, 309.
        of a part of the proceedings, 309.
        of matters coram non judice, 309.
        must be fair and accurate, 315—326.
        in newspapers, not specially privileged, 316.

BRADBURY, AGNEW, & CO. LD., PRINTERS, LONDON AND TONBRIDGE.

PUBLICATIONS OF 1911.

Addison's Treatise on the Law of Contracts.—Eleventh Edition. By WILLIAM E. GORDON and J. RITCHIE, Barristers-at-Law. Price £2 2s. cloth.

Caporn's Selected Cases Illustrating the Law of Contracts. —By ARTHUR C. CAPORN and FRANCIS M. CAPORN. Price 12s. 6d. cloth.

Fry's Treatise on the Specific Performance of Contracts. —By the Rt. Hon. Sir EDWARD FRY, G.C.B. Fifth Edition. By W. D. RAWLINS, K.C. Price £1 16s. cloth.

Greenwood's Law Relating to Trade Unions.—By JOHN H. GREENWOOD, Barrister-at-Law. Price 10s. cloth.

Harris' Hints on Advocacy.—Conduct of Cases, Civil and Criminal. Classes of Witnesses and Suggestions for Cross-examining them, &c. Fourteenth Edition. By RICHARD HARRIS, K.C. Price 7s. 6d. cloth.

Heywood and Massey's Lunacy Practice.—Fourth Edition. By N. ARTHUR HEYWOOD and ARNOLD S. MASSEY, Solicitors, and RALPH C. ROMER, Esq., First Class Clerk in the Office of the Masters in Lunacy. Price £1 10s. cloth.

Highmore's Stamp Laws.—Third Edition. By Sir NATHANIEL J. HIGHMORE, Barrister-at-Law, Solicitor for His Majesty's Customs, and late Assistant Solicitor of Inland Revenue. Price 10s. cloth.

Innes' Digest of the Law of Easements.—Eighth Edition. By N. L. GODDARD, Barrister-at-Law. Price 7s. 6d. cloth.

Knowles' Electricity and Electric Traction.—The Law relating to the Generation, Distribution and use of Electricity, including Electric Traction. In two Parts: Part I. Electric Lighting and Power; Part II. Electric Traction. By C. M. KNOWLES, Barrister-at-Law. Price £2 2s. cloth.

₊ *The parts may be had separately, each 25s.*

Leake's Principles of the Law of Contracts.—Sixth Edition. By A. E. RANDALL, Barrister-at-Law. Price £1 12s. cloth.

Mannooch's Analysis of Pollock's Law of Torts.—For Students. By J. K. MANNOOCH. Price 5s. cloth.

Palmer's Company Law.—A Practical Handbook for Lawyers and Business Men. With an Appendix containing the Companies (Consolidation) Act, 1908, and other Acts and Rules. Ninth Edition. By Sir FRANCIS BEAUFORT PALMER, Bencher of the Inner Temple. Price 12s. 6d. cloth.

Pollock's Principles of Contract.—Eighth Edition. By Sir FREDERICK POLLOCK, Bart., Barrister-at-Law. Price £1 8s. cloth.

Prideaux's Forms and Precedents in Conveyancing.—Twentieth Edition. By BENJAMIN L. CHERRY and REGINALD BEDDINGTON, Barristers-at-Law. 2 vols. Price £3 10s. cloth.

Roscoe's Growth of English Law.—Being Studies in the Evolution of Law and Procedure in England. By EDWARD STANLEY ROSCOE, Barrister-at-Law, Admiralty Registrar. Price 7s. 6d. cloth.

Sebastian's Law of Trade Marks and their Registration.— Fifth Edition. By LEWIS BOYD SEBASTIAN, HARRY BAIRD HEMMING, and RAYMOND SEBASTIAN, Barristers-at-Law. Price £1 12s. cloth.

Wharton's Law Lexicon.—Forming an Epitome of the Law of England as existing in Statute Law and Decided Cases. Eleventh Edition. By W. HANBURY AGGS, Barrister-at-Law. Price £1 18s. cloth.

Williamson's Law of Licensing.—Fourth Edition. By JOHN BRUCE WILLIAMSON, Barrister-at-Law. Price £1 cloth.

STEVENS & SONS, Ltd., 119 & 120, Chancery Lane, London.

THE
Law Quarterly Review

EDITED BY

The Right Hon.
Sir FREDERICK POLLOCK, Bart., M.A., LL.D.,

Corpus Professor of Jurisprudence in the University of Oxford,
late Professor of Common Law in the Inns of Court.

**Vols. I. to XXVI. ; with GENERAL INDICES to Vols. I.
to XXV. Royal 8vo. 1885—1910. Price, each, 12s.,
cloth lettered.**

*** **Annual Subscription, net 12s. 6d., postage
free.**

Single numbers, 5s. each.

The objects of the Review include—

The discussion of current decisions of importance in the Courts of this country, and (so far as practicable) of the Colonies, the United States, British India, and other British Possessions where the Common Law is administered.

The consideration of topics of proposed legislation before Parliament.

The treatment of questions of immediate political and social interest in their legal aspect.

Inquiries into the history and antiquities of our own and other systems of law and legal institutions.

Endeavour is also made to take account of the legal science and legislation of Continental States in so far as they bear on general jurisprudence, or may throw light by comparison upon problems of English or American legislation.

The current legal literature of our own country receives careful attention ; and works of serious importance, both English and foreign, are occasionally discussed at length.

"The 'Law Quarterly' is well packed with learned dissertations as well as with Notes and Reviews which may be considered the lighter side of the issue. Legal experts may always count on finding some article on their special subject."—*Saturday Review.*

STEVENS & SONS, Ltd., 119 & 120, Chancery Lane, London.